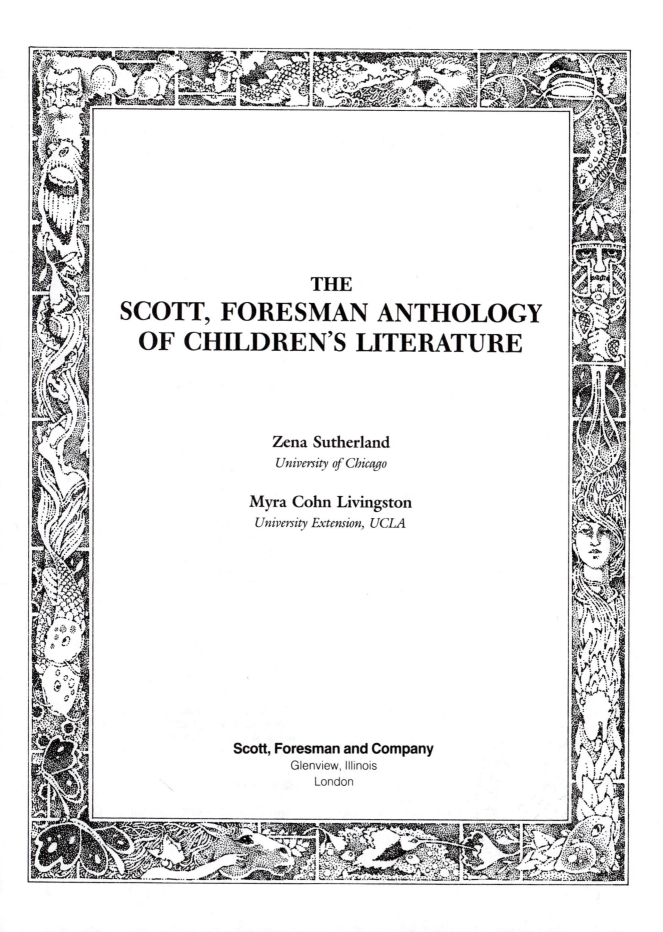

THE
SCOTT, FORESMAN ANTHOLOGY
OF CHILDREN'S LITERATURE

Zena Sutherland
University of Chicago

Myra Cohn Livingston
University Extension, UCLA

Scott, Foresman and Company
Glenview, Illinois
London

Cover art by Dick Martin

Illustrators

Part One   Jean Helmer
Part Two   Dick Martin
Part Three   Margaret Briody

Milestones in Children's Literature courtesy of Margaret E. Hill

Library of Congress Cataloging in Publication Data
Main entry under title:

The Scott, Foresman anthology of children's literature.

Bibliography: p. 879
Includes index.
Summary: An anthology of nursery rhymes, poetry, folk literature, fantasy, realistic fiction, historical fiction, biography, and nonfiction. Also includes a list of major books, a list of highlights in the history and development of children's literature, and essays for adults working with children.

1. Children's literature. [1. Literature—Collections] I. Sutherland, Zena. II. Livingston, Myra Cohn. III. Scott, Foresman and Company.
PZ5.S425   1984   808.8'99282   83-17194

ISBN 0-673-15527-7

Preface

In recent years there have been many changes in the field of children's book publishing, changes that mirror developments in our society. These changes have fostered a growing understanding of the role literature can play in children's lives and the techniques that adults can use in bringing children and books together. *The Scott Foresman Anthology of Children's Literature* has been designed to reflect some of these changes by introducing the work of fine authors, new and old, as well as introducing the broad spectrum of contemporary and traditional literature. The variety in style, subject, and genre is designed to appeal to children of all ages, reading alone or in groups, or hearing selections read aloud. The critical essays offer new insights to adults working with children; the original art is instrumental in making the book visually appealing both to children and to students in classes in children's literature, for whom the book serves as a source of material that is balanced in treatment and selective in quality.

This material is divided into three main parts: *An Invitation to Poetry, An Invitation to Folklore and Fantasy,* and *An Invitation to Fiction and Fact.* Part Four, *An Invitation to Children's Literature,* includes useful ancillary material in addition to three critical essays.

Part One, *An Invitation to Poetry,* ranges from the familiar Mother Goose rhymes and favorites of the past to the most contemporary poetry, with emphasis on the broad scope of concerns that characterize poets writing for a diverse audience of children today. This is paralleled by a wide spectrum of form, from the more traditional to free verse, that appeals to a variety of tastes, as well as a variety of rhythmic patterns. The poems are grouped in sections that reflect the growth of children from concern with self and home to their growing consciousness of reality and limitless boundaries of thought and imagination. Because of the nature of poetry itself, this arrangement is not meant to be absolute but to serve as a means of ready access to the subject matter.

Part Two, *An Invitation to Folklore and Fantasy,* is a selection of folk literature from many countries: folk tales, myths, fables, epics and hero tales, and modern fantasy. In the selection of fantasy there are some short stories and some excerpts from longer works; although many selections contain elements of different types of stories (i.e., an animal story may also be a humorous tale), they are divided into groups by type: Animals and Toys, Stories of Enchantment, Humorous Tales, and Science Fiction. Here, as in other parts of the anthology, there is a representation of new authors as well as old favorites.

Part Three, *An Invitation to Fiction and Fact,* comprises realistic fiction, historical fiction, biography, and informational books. In the first section, an effort has been made to reflect, in some of the selections, contemporary life-styles and concerns. Many of today's books show the growing awareness, in the children's book field, of the ethnic, social, and economic diversity of the children for whom the books are written. In the biographical selections, there is the same reflection of the new candor in children's literature. Selections have been arranged in order of reading difficulty to facilitate use of the book by or for children of different ages, although the compilers are well aware that there are no narrow restrictions on the ages of readers to whom an excerpt may appeal. Indeed, given the diversity of styles and subjects, as well as the fine quality of the books from which excerpts have been chosen, all selections should appeal to some readers.

The introductions to the main parts of the anthology and to the several sections are designed to provide helpful information to those adults who would like background information about the broad range of children's books and their authors and illustrators. This should help those who are working with children to choose selections, understand the literary form, and establish evaluative criteria.

Part Four, *An Invitation to Children's Literature,* begins with "Milestones in Children's Literature," a list that includes major books and highlights in the history and development of children's literature. It serves not only as a chronological guide but also gives information that points to new developments and trends in the field.

The three essays that constitute the major portion of Part Four are intended to provide useful information for adults working with children. In "What Literature Can Do for Children," Rebecca Lukens discusses the types of literature and the contributions each makes to children's needs and enjoyment, and describes such literary elements as style, plot, and characterization. She discusses ways of bringing children and books together, emphasizing the importance of reading aloud, and stressing the teacher's responsibility in developing children's reading interests.

"Children's Literature in the Classroom," by Sue Peterson, is a practical and explicit overview of the ways in which teachers can choose and use books with children. The essay includes ways of involving children in literature, such as reading aloud, storytelling, and setting apart a time for silent reading, with specific suggestions for goals and techniques. It also considers ways of extending literature by using it in the curriculum, and in this section gives advice on such activities as children's theater, puppetry, and creative writing. This

section concludes with a commentary on the importance of using literature throughout the school curriculum.

In "Illustrations in Children's Books," Patricia Cianciolo addresses those aspects of illustration by which a book may be evaluated, focusing on the need for integration of text and pictures, and describing artistic styles and techniques. She concludes by describing contemporary trends in book illustration after having explored the subjects of children's preferences and aesthetic responses to visual aspects of their books. A bibliography of the many books cited in the essay is provided.

The last section of Part Four includes a listing of children's book awards, citing the prizewinning books, authors, and illustrators and giving information about the establishment of the awards. There is an extensive annotated bibliography in three parts: a list of books that give background information and provide reference sources for adults; a list of sources of audiovisual materials; and a list of books for children, organized to correspond with the genre divisions of Parts One, Two, and Three.

Appended material includes a subject index that provides analytical access by bringing together selections on the same subject that may occur in various literary genres, a general index of authors, titles, and illustrators, and a pronunciation guide.

Line drawings for each of the three major sections are the work of Jean Helmer, Dick Martin, and Margaret Briody. In addition to the eight-page color section, and the black-and-white illustrations complementing "Illustrations in Children's Books," the section on historical milestones in children's literature includes work by major artists.

The authors would like to express their appreciation of the contributions of the essayists and illustrators mentioned in this preface, their gratitude for the assistance of researchers Cheryl Jones and Judy Zuckerman, and their thanks to Christopher Jennison, Anita Portugal, and Paula Meyers of Scott, Foresman. Special thanks to the advisors whose suggestions on content were so useful and thoughtful: Catherine Bowles, Francelia Butler, James Duggins, Elbert Hill, Eric Kimmel, Margaret Kimmel, Shirley Lukenbill, Rebecca Lukens, Marilyn Miller, Hughes Moir, Dianne Monson, Alleen Nilsen, and Nancy Roser.

The authors hope that the book will be used for reading aloud as well as by independent readers, that it will serve to stimulate discussion, and above all that it will stimulate users to read more of the work of the many fine authors represented on its pages.

Zena Sutherland

Myra Cohn Livingston

Overview

One
An Invitation to Poetry

Two
An Invitation to Folklore and Fantasy

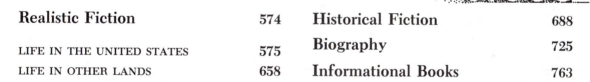

Three
An Invitation to Fiction and Fact

Four
An Invitation to Children's Literature

Contents

One
An Invitation to Poetry

Small Creatures, Insects, and Rodents
"little things"   49

Dogs and Cats
"little wiggly warmness"   55

Animals
"I think I could turn and live with animals"   63

Nonsense People
"And yet you incessantly stand on your head" 112

The Seasons
"green whisper of the year" 123

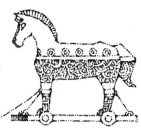

Two
An Invitation to Folklore and Fantasy

Three
An Invitation to Fiction and Fact

Four
An Invitation to Children's Literature

The titles within the text that appear in brackets were supplied by the compilers for untitled chapters or excerpts.

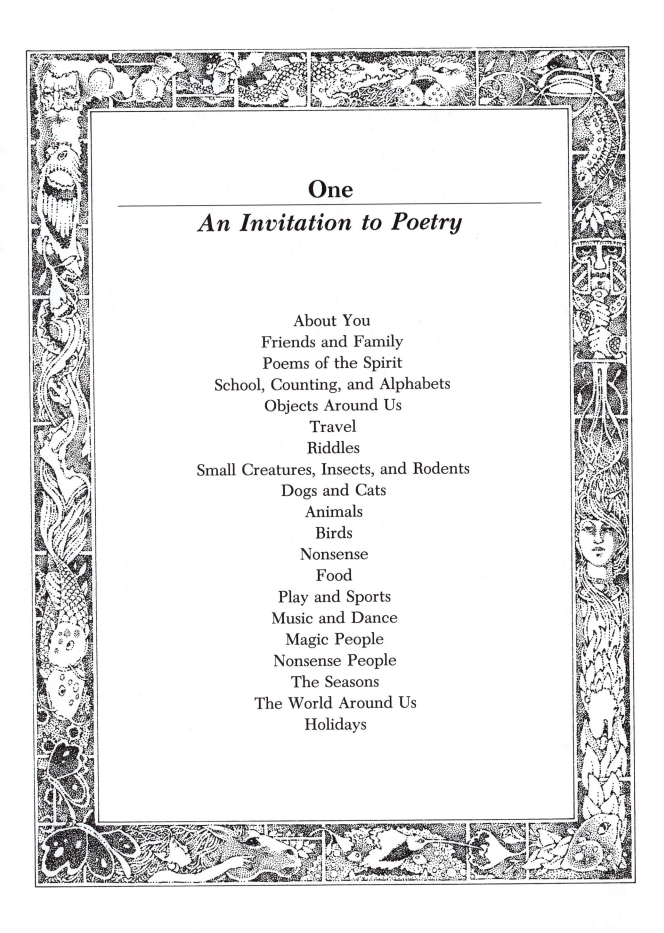

One

An Invitation to Poetry

About You
Friends and Family
Poems of the Spirit
School, Counting, and Alphabets
Objects Around Us
Travel
Riddles
Small Creatures, Insects, and Rodents
Dogs and Cats
Animals
Birds
Nonsense
Food
Play and Sports
Music and Dance
Magic People
Nonsense People
The Seasons
The World Around Us
Holidays

Poetry: An Invitation

I

An invitation may come in a variety of forms, from the briefest of messages to the most elaborate of letters. It may be written in a traditional manner or be far more casual. It may come over the telephone or through conversation. Whatever its form, our curiosity is aroused.

We wonder who will be there and what will happen. Will we meet old friends or new? Will there be music and dancing? Will we stay late or leave early? Will it be exciting?

An invitation, of course, involves *us* and *our* responses. If we are pleased, we accept; if the occasion holds no promise of pleasure, we decline.

Poetry too is an invitation!

I'm going out to clean the pasture spring;
I'll only stop to rake the leaves away
(And wait to watch the water clear, I may):
I sha'n't be gone long. —You come too.

I'm going out to fetch the little calf
That's standing by the mother. It's so young
It totters when she licks it with her tongue.
I sha'n't be gone long. —You come too.

Robert Frost's invitation—*you come too*—is addressed to an unseen person within his poem "The Pasture." But beyond that he has extended an invitation to us, as readers and listeners, to take time out of our busy, chore-filled lives to observe the wonders about us. The phrase "You come too" repeated twice makes this an obvious invitation. Most invitations within poems are not so direct, yet they exist. And because we are excited by the prospect of being asked, poetry can become more enticing if we make this metaphoric leap. For poets, through their words, themes, rhythms, extend invitations to attend the subject of their choice, to join in a moment of observation or flight of the imagination, to be where they have been, to see and hear what they have experienced or dreamed.

Their invitations often come to us as unexpected surprises!

"The Pasture" from THE POETRY OF ROBERT FROST edited by Edward Connery Lathem. Copyright 1916, 1923, 1939, © 1967, 1969 by Holt, Rinehart and Winston. Copyright 1942, 1944, 1951 by Robert Frost. Copyright © 1970 by Lesley Frost Ballantine. Reprinted by permission of Holt, Rinehart and Winston, Publishers, and the Estate of Robert Frost.

II

Much has been said about the importance of poetry; many exhortations have been invoked to awaken us to its pleasures and possibilities. Beauty, we are told, is inherent in its words and rhythms, wisdom and truth in its very being. Many seek to define it, to alert us to what we should admire, and to direct our response. Some texts and teachers' guides analyze it, compare it, point out strengths and weaknesses, discuss its rhythms and link it to the inner life of the poet. What more can be attempted, we wonder, to present poetry in a way that will allay our fears about a genre of literature that eludes definition, that remains, in the end, a body of work that we may—or may not—choose to offer ourselves and young people?

Some adults love poetry, read and share it with children. Others eschew it because of various unpleasant associations in the past; memorization, analyzation, sentimental thoughts in a stilted diction. Still others dread it as an incomprehensible, difficult form without relevance to their lives.

Frost's observation that "poetry begins in delight and ends in wisdom" has too often been interpreted to mean that poetry is the repository of wisdom. Such a viewpoint is certain to keep us—and children—at arm's length, for it makes of poetry a lesson and a drudgery. Most of us shun invitations that purport to instill us with beauty, truth, and wisdom; we prefer to seek pleasure in a subject or event that invites us to participate and allows us a certain suspension of disbelief.

If we can think of poetry as an invitation, we are given the choice to read or listen with a certain apprehension. We are relieved of the burden of comprehension, free to explore further if we so wish. For the poem that may affect and awaken some of us may not appeal to others. What attracts the individual is that combination of voice, words, rhythm, form, and idea that does not say "What does a poem mean?" but rather, in the words of John Ciardi, "How does a poem mean?"

Children need this freedom even more. They must *apprehend*, respond with immediate intuitive perception, before they can *comprehend*, understand fully and completely. They must know delight before they can begin to explore the beauty or approach the wisdom. "What the heart knows today," James Stephens wrote in *The Crock of Gold*, "the head will understand tomorrow."

If we wish to share poetry with children, let us extend the invitation with our hearts!

III

Invitations to the youngest children lie in nursery rhymes, succinct stories that engage because of their brevity, amusement, rhythms, and rhyme. These may serve as introductions to a variety of people and situations, the familiar as well as the unusual. They make the child aware of joy with their invocations of "Hey diddle diddle" or "Hickory dickory dock." They challenge children to discern the differences between what they know to be sensible and nonsensical.

A man in the wilderness asked me,
How many strawberries grow in the sea?
I answered him, as I thought good,
As many as red herrings grow in the wood.

"Of course," thinks the child, "strawberries do not grow in the sea, nor herrings in a wood. I know better than that."

In addition, nursery rhymes offer children the chance to participate in the fun of counting ("One, two/Buckle my shoe"), naming the days of the week, and answering riddles.

Beyond these first encounters with verse there are poems that tell longer stories. Edward Lear's "The Owl and the Pussy Cat" beckons the child to sail off "to the land where the Bong tree grows." "The Table and the Chair" is another sort of invitation to overcome the impossible. If the Chair knows that he cannot walk, the Table answers "It can do no harm to try." And here begins an invitation to children to go beyond the immediacy of here and now in search of adventure.

For older readers there are ballads that characterize our earliest forms of communication about real events, with rhyming patterns that please the ear and often invite memorization. "John Henry," "The Streets of Laredo," and "Buffalo Gals" are but a few American folk pieces that invite the young to see history in a new way. And there are literary ballads, "The Pied Piper of Hamelin," "The Ballad of the Harp Weaver," "The Highwayman," and others that combine story and imagination, taking children beyond the real into the mystical and imaginary.

Invitations that encourage children to look into themselves and their own feelings have found their way into poetry chiefly within the last few decades. Robert Louis Stevenson and Walter de la Mare dominated this lyrical approach to poetry for many years. But the work of a number of contemporary poets invites children to explore their emotions and reactions more fully in today's world where lamplighters and coaches have vanished.

Every time I climb a tree
Every time I climb a tree
Every time I climb a tree
I scrape a leg
Or skin a knee
And every time I climb a tree
I find some ants
Or dodge a bee
And get the ants
All over me . . .

This is David McCord's invitation to children to remember what has happened to them when climbing a tree, what they have seen or what might be found. For a child who has never climbed a tree, it holds the promise of a new experience.

Similarly they may compare the events in their own lives to those of Nikki Giovanni's child who at "Ten Years Old" tells how

i paid my 30¢ and rode by the bus
window all the way down . . .

Reading about the reactions of others is an invitation to children to look and think in new ways about the happenings in their own lives.

Beyond actual experiences there is an invitation that bids children wonder:

I never saw a Moor,
I never saw the Sea;
Yet know I how the Heather looks,
And what a Wave must be.

While Emily Dickinson speaks of moor, sea, and heather, today's child may think of space, submarines, and plastic flowers, but inherent in poetry is an invitation to go beyond the specifics of the poet's circumscribed world.

In light verse and nonsense children are invited to laughter. It is levity which removes the burden—awe and trepidation—from poetry. Whether it is simply the mixed-up words of Laura Richard's "Eletelephony"

Once there was an elephant,
Who tried to use the telephant—

"Every Time I Climb a Tree" from ONE AT A TIME by David McCord (British title: MR. BIDERY'S SPIDERY GARDEN). Copyright 1952 by David McCord. Reprinted by permission of Little, Brown and Company and George G. Harrap Ltd.

"Ten Years Old" from SPIN A SOFT BLACK SONG by Nikki Giovanni. Copyright © 1971 by Nikki Giovanni. Reprinted by permission of Farrar, Straus & Giroux, Inc.

"I never saw a moor." Reprinted by permission of the publishers and the Trustees of Amherst College from THE POEMS OF EMILY DICKINSON, edited by Thomas H. Johnson, Cambridge, Mass.: The Belknap Press of Harvard University Press. Copyright 1951, © 1955, 1979 by the President and Fellows of Harvard College.

"Eletelephony" from TIRRA LIRRA: RHYMES OLD AND NEW by Laura E. Richards. Copyright 1932 by Laura E. Richards; © renewed 1960 by Hamilton Richards. Reprinted by permission of Little, Brown and Company.

or Lewis Carroll's "Father William"

*"You are old, Father William," the young
man said,
"And your hair has become very white;
And yet you incessantly stand on your
head—
Do you think, at your age, it is right?"*

or N. M. Bodecker's concept of a cherry marrying a pea, the enticement is delight. And there is no invitation more important than that which involves the leap of imagination for both child and adult.

All poetry invites children to participate in the delights of bounding rhythm, to clap their hands, tap their feet, move their bodies if they wish to do so. Some may respond more physically than others. Many children are moved by the sound of the words, whether humorous or serious.

IV

An anthology is an invitation in itself to explore the work of many poets. Anthologies are usually built around a theme; they focus on one specific area of interest or span a given time or culture. The purpose of this anthology is to invite those who work with the young to become aware of the great variety of invitations extended by poets past and present who speak to the emotions and interests of today's child.

The inclusion of nursery rhymes presupposes that the day has passed when children learned these in the home or early grades. Many a fourth- or fifth-grader is unacquainted with Humpty Dumpty, Little Boy Blue, or Jack and Jill. The rhymes, therefore, are to be found throughout the various sections and may be used, or omitted, dependent not so much upon the age of children as their exposure to Mother Goose. For those

children who know some of the rhymes, there will be the added pleasure of recognizing the familiar, a chance to become reacquainted with old friends!

In addition to nursery rhymes there are other well-known selections which seem as fresh today as when they were written. They have not lost their charm in spite of the changes in the world; they speak of the eternals with which all ages and people are confronted. It would be a comfort to some readers to read an anthology of only the familiar, but there is so much new being written for children that it must also be offered. Certainly no period in history has enjoyed such an outpouring of verse and poetry written with children in mind as the present. The time is gone when anthologists had to rely on work produced by a few poets in England and America. Here the choice has been made to retain the best of earlier poets and introduce many new voices from a broader range of cultural and ethnic backgrounds.

Certainly an anthology might be compiled based on poetry that is popular. Light and humorous verse instantly appeals to adult and child alike and it is found throughout this book. But a preponderance of laughter would not do justice to those who look to poetry as a way of expressing other moods. Delight and apprehension certainly! But beyond that, poetry of a more serious nature is an invitation to approach other facets of life, an opportunity for the listener and reader to know that wonder, sorrow, disappointment also lie within the province of the poet. More than a catalog of raw emotion, good poetry points toward humanism.

New voices in poetry also invite us to discover new ways of writing. Although most poets in the children's field choose traditional forms for expression—the couplet, quatrain, limerick, ballad, and rhyming patterns, others have experimented with free verse and open

"You are old, Father William . . ." from ALICE'S ADVENTURES IN WONDERLAND by Lewis Carroll.

forms. It is for each of us to decide which sort of invitation is most meaningful.

The beliefs of Dr. Isaac Watts and his followers that children be given didactic verse in rhyme, in order that it be remembered, have given way to an understanding that didacticism stifles and turns children away from poetry. Yet rhyme enlivens and serves as a mode of aural pleasure. A trace of didacticism still may be found in some light verse, often artfully concealed. Admonitions to proper behavior or cautionary verses, and avoidance of pleasure, dreaming, and play, as offered by Watts and the Taylor sisters have recurred throughout the centuries. Mother Goose is rewritten with a purpose in mind, even to this day. Such verse is not the province of this anthology.

But invitations are not confined to those who write poetry especially for children. There are many poems addressed to adults which, because of their keen sensitivity to a child's way of looking and feeling, can be enjoyed by the young. Such a poet is Langston Hughes, whose eloquent simplicity and sensitivity speaks to all ages.

I loved my friend.
He went away from me.
There's nothing more to say.
The poem ends,
Soft as it began—
I loved my friend.

The poetry in this anthology, therefore, avoids the didactic and sentimental which characterize some children's verse. The emphasis is placed, rather, on presenting poetry and verse that comes from poets who respect the child and the child's viewpoint.

V

The categories of subject matter in this book suggest the growth pattern of children. This pattern begins with concepts of self and family and moves out into the world of school, the realities of the universe as well as the realm of the imagination and spirit. The arrangement is neither arbitrary nor absolute; some poems defy classification but demand inclusion.

Nonsense and humorous verse appear not only in the sections bearing their names. Funny poems may be found in most sections. For example, Ted Hughes' poem about "My Sister Jane" appears in the *Friends and Family* classification. Likewise, John Ciardi's verse "Mummy Slept Late and Daddy Fixed Breakfast" will be found in the *Nonsense* section. Onitsura's haiku, "It is nice to read" is as much about friendship as it is about the spring rain.

Beginning with *About You,* children are invited to become aware of themselves and their first relationships with others. Love for others in *Friends and Family* plays an important role. *School, Counting, and Alphabets* extends the world in which children move to early learning experiences followed by *Riddles,* another form of inquiry and answer. *Objects Around Us* focuses on further observations of both the familiar and unfamiliar.

The next group of sections, *Food, Play and Sports, Music and Dance,* and *Holidays,* covers a broad range of objects and ideas which elicit immediate response. *Poems of the Spirit* arouse wonder and suggest a level of deeper thought.

Travel offers another way of expanding consciousness and hints at journeys into worlds of magic and nonsense beyond the mundane. Here are *Magic People, Nonsense,* and *Nonsense People.*

Children's interest in other living creatures is addressed in sections on *Small Creatures, Insects, and Rodents, Dogs and Cats, Birds,* and *Animals.* And as the cycle of a human life is caught up in a larger life, the young look to the eternals of nature, *The World Around Us* and *The Seasons.*

For us, as for the individual child, the order might be changed. These are broad classifications, meant only to serve as guidelines for adults, inviting children to grow and expand.

Henry Adams once said that if he was able to reach one student in a class of four hundred, he would feel that his teaching was successful. Perhaps then if there are one or two selections in this anthology that touch us or the children with whom we are in contact, the book will serve its purpose. In a single poem we may find a voice that our children may wish to hear again. From there to the index of authors to the bibliography is but a short way. Beyond that lie more invitations!

About You

"no one but me"

The Lamb

The Lamb just says, I AM!
He frisks and whisks, *He* can.
He jumps all over. Who
Are *you?* You're jumping too!

Theodore Roethke

Solitude

I have a house where I go
   When there's too many people,
I have a house where I go
   Where no one can be;
I have a house where I go,
Where nobody ever says "No";
Where no one says anything—so
   There is no one but me.

A. A. Milne

Who Am I?

The trees ask me,
And the sky,
And the sea asks me
   Who am I?

The grass asks me,
And the sand,
And the rocks ask me
   Who I am.

The wind tells me
At nightfall,
And the rain tells me
   Someone small.

   Someone small
   Someone small
   But a piece
      of
      it
      all.

Felice Holman

I'm Nobody! Who are you?
Are you—Nobody—too?
Then there's a pair of us?
Don't tell! they'd banish us—you know!

How dreary—to be—Somebody!
How public—like a Frog—
To tell one's name—the livelong June—
To an admiring Bog!

Emily Dickinson

"The Lamb" from THE COLLECTED POEMS OF THEODORE ROETHKE. Reprinted by permission of Doubleday & Company, Inc. and Faber and Faber Ltd.

"Solitude" from NOW WE ARE SIX by A. A. Milne. Copyright 1927 by E. P. Dutton & Co., Inc. Renewal copyright 1955 by A. A. Milne. Reprinted by permission of the publisher, E. P. Dutton, The Canadian Publishers, McClelland and Stewart Limited, Toronto, and Methuen Children's Books.

"Who Am I?" from AT THE TOP OF MY VOICE AND OTHER POEMS by Felice Holman. Copyright © 1970 by Felice Holman (New York: Charles Scribner's Sons, 1970). Reprinted with the permission of Charles Scribner's Sons.

"I'm nobody! Who are you?" Reprinted by permission of the publishers and the Trustees of Amherst College from THE POEMS OF EMILY DICKINSON, edited by Thomas H. Johnson, Cambridge, Mass.: The Belknap Press of Harvard University Press. Copyright 1951, © 1955, 1979 by the President and Fellows of Harvard College.

My Voice

Sing, sing, voice of mine,
While there is something
You have not yet said.
You have said nothing at all.

Juan Ramón Jiménez
Translated by *H. R. Hayes*

Busy

I think I am a Muffin Man. I haven't got a bell,
I haven't got the muffin things that muffin
    people sell.
Perhaps I am a Postman. No, I think I am a
    Tram.
I'm feeling rather funny and I don't know
    what I am—
            BUT
    Round about
    And *round* about
    And *round* about I go—
    All around the table,
    The table in the nursery—
    Round about
    And *round* about
    And *round* about I go;

I think I am a Traveller escaping from a Bear;
I think I am an Elephant,
Behind another Elephant
Behind *another* Elephant who isn't really
    there. . . .
            SO
    Round about
    And *round* about
    And *round* about and *round* about
    And *round* about
    And *round* about I go.

"My Voice" from THE SELECTED WRITINGS OF JUAN RAMÒN JIMÈNEZ, translated by H. R. Hayes. Copyright © 1957 by Juan Ramón Jiménez. Reprinted by permission of Farrar, Straus & Giroux, Inc.
    "Busy" from NOW WE ARE SIX by A. A. Milne. Copyright 1927 by E. P. Dutton & Co., Inc. Renewal copyright 1955 by A. A. Milne. Reprinted by permission of the publisher, E. P. Dutton, The Canadian Publishers, McClelland and Stewart Limited, Toronto, and Methuen Children's Books.
    "Phizzog" from GOOD MORNING, AMERICA by Carl Sandburg. Copyright 1928, 1956 by Carl Sandburg. Reprinted by permission of Harcourt Brace Jovanovich, Inc.

I think I am a Ticket Man who's selling
    tickets—please,
I think I am a Doctor who is visiting a Sneeze;
Perhaps I'm just a Nanny who is walking with
    a pram
I'm feeling rather funny and I don't know
    what I am—
            BUT
    Round about
    And *round* about
    And *round* about I go—
    All around the table,
    The table in the nursery—
    Round about
    And *round* about
    And *round* about I go:

I think I am a Puppy, so I'm hanging out my
    tongue;
I think I am a Camel who
Is looking for a Camel who
Is looking for a Camel who is looking for its
    Young. . . .
            SO
    Round about
    And *round* about
    And *round* about and *round* about
    And *round* about
    And *round* about I go.

A. A. Milne

Phizzog

This face you got,
This here phizzog you carry around,
You never picked it out for yourself, at all, at
    all—did you?
This here phizzog—somebody handed it to
    you—am I right?
Somebody said, "Here's yours, now go see
    what you can do with it."
Somebody slipped it to you and it was like a
    package marked:
"No goods exchanged after being taken
    away"—
This face you got.

Carl Sandburg

I Woke Up This Morning

I woke up this morning
At quarter past seven.
I kicked up the covers
And stuck out my toe.
And ever since then
(That's a quarter past seven)
They haven't said anything
Other than "no."
They haven't said anything
Other than "Please, dear,
Don't do what you're doing,"
Or "Lower your voice."
Whatever I've done
And however I've chosen,
I've done the wrong thing
And I've made the wrong choice.
I didn't wash well
And I didn't say thank you.
I didn't shake hands
And I didn't say please.
I didn't say sorry
When passing the candy
I banged the box into
Miss Witelson's knees.
I didn't say sorry.
I didn't stand straighter.
I didn't speak louder
When asked what I'd said.
Well, I said
That tomorrow
At quarter past seven
They can
Come in and get me.
I'm Staying In Bed.

Karla Kuskin

A Song of Greatness

When I hear the old men
Telling of heroes,
Telling of great deeds
Of ancient days,
When I hear that telling
Then I think within me
I too am one of these.

When I hear the people
Praising great ones,
Then I know that I too
Shall be esteemed,
I too when my time comes
Shall do mightily.

Mary Austin

Sunbake

Sometimes I pretend
I'm a loaf of bread,
baking on my green towel
in the sun.
Waves are breaking.
Breezes are blowing.
My brother is digging

                    a
                hole
                    in
                        the
                            sand.

But I am just baking—
rising,
rising,
RISING
to the sun.

Bobbi Katz

My Shadow

I have a little shadow that goes in and out
    with me,
And what can be the use of him is more than
    I can see.
He is very, very like me from the heels up to
    the head;
And I see him jump before me, when I jump
    into my bed.

The funniest thing about him is the way he
    likes to grow—
Not at all like proper children, which is al-
    ways very slow;
For he sometimes shoots up taller like an
    India-rubber ball,
And he sometimes gets so little that there's
    none of him at all.

He hasn't got a notion of how children ought
    to play,
And can only make a fool of me in every sort
    of way.
He stays so close beside me, he's a coward
    you can see;
I'd think shame to stick to nursie as that
    shadow sticks to me!

One morning, very early, before the sun was
    up,
I rose and found the shining dew on every
    butter-cup;
But my lazy little shadow, like an arrant
    sleepy-head,
Had stayed at home behind me and was fast
    asleep in bed.

Robert Louis Stevenson

Thumbprint

In the heel of my thumb
are whorls, whirls, wheels
in a unique design:
mine alone.
What a treasure to own!
My own flesh, my own feelings.
No other, however grand or base,
can ever contain the same.
My signature,
thumbing the pages of my time.
My universe key,
my singularity.
Impress, implant,
I am myself,
of all my atom parts I am the sum.
And out of my blood and my brain
I make my own interior weather,
my own sun and rain.
Imprint my mark upon the world,
whatever I shall become.

Eve Merriam

It is Grey Out

It is grey out.
It is grey in.
In me
It is as grey as the day is grey.
The trees look sad
And I,
Not knowing why I do,
Cry.

Karla Kuskin

ten years old

i paid my 30¢ and rode by the bus
window all the way down

i felt a little funny with no hair
on my head
but my knees were shiny 'cause
aunty mai belle cleaned me up
and i got off on time and walked
past the lions and the guard straight
up to the desk and said
      "dr. doolittle steroscope please"
and this really old woman said
      "Do You Have A Library Card?"
and i said
      "i live here up the street"
and she said
      "Do You Have a LIBRARY Card?"
and i said
      "this is the only place i can use the
        steroscope for
      dr. dooolittle miss washington brought us
        here this spring
      to see it"
and another lady said
"GIVE THE BOY WHAT HE WANT. HE
      WANT TO LEAD THE RACE"
and i said
      "no ma'am i want to see dr. dooolitttle"
and she said "same thang son same thang"

Nikki Giovanni

Boys' Names

What splendid names for boys there are!
There's Carol like a rolling car,
And Martin like a flying bird,
And Adam like the Lord's First Word,
And Raymond like the Harvest Moon,
And Peter like a piper's tune,
And Alan like the flowing on
Of water. And there's John, like John.

Eleanor Farjeon

Girls' Names

What lovely names for girls there are!
There's Stella like the Evening Star,
And Sylvia like a rustling tree,
And Lola like a melody,
And Flora like a flowery morn,
And Sheila like a field of corn,
And Melusina like the moan
Of water. And there's Joan, like Joan.

Eleanor Farjeon

the drum

daddy says the world is
a drum tight and hard
and i told him
i'm gonna beat
out my own rhythm

Nikki Giovanni

poem for rodney

people always ask what
am i going to be
when i grow
up and i always
just think
i'd like to grow
up

Nikki Giovanni

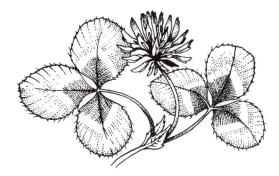

The Centaur

The summer that I was ten—
Can it be there was only one
summer that I was ten? It must

have been a long one then—
each day I'd go out to choose
a fresh horse from my stable

which was a willow grove
down by the old canal.
I'd go on my two bare feet.

But when, with my brother's jack-knife,
I had cut me a long limber horse
with a good thick knob for a head,

and peeled him slick and clean
except a few leaves for the tail,
and cinched my brother's belt

around his head for a rein,
I'd straddle and canter him fast
up the grass bank to the path,

trot along in the lovely dust
that talcumed over his hoofs,
hiding my toes, and turning

his feet to swift half-moons.
The willow knob with the strap
jouncing between my thighs

was the pommel and yet the poll
of my nickering pony's head.
My head and my neck were mine,

yet they were shaped like a horse.
My hair flopped to the side
like the mane of a horse in the wind.

My forelock swung in my eyes,
my neck arched and I snorted.
I shied and skittered and reared,

stopped and raised my knees,
pawed at the ground and quivered.
My teeth bared as we wheeled

and swished through the dust again.
I was the horse and the rider,
and the leather I slapped to his rump

spanked my own behind.
Doubled, my two hoofs beat
a gallop along the bank,

the wind twanged in my mane,
my mouth squared to the bit.
And yet I sat on my steed

quiet, negligent riding,
my toes standing the stirrups,
my thighs hugging his ribs.

At a walk we drew up to the porch.
I tethered him to a paling.
Dismounting, I smoothed my skirt

and entered the dusky hall.
My feet on the clean linoleum
left ghostly toes in the hall.

Where have you been? said my mother.
Been riding, I said from the sink,
and filled me a glass of water.

What's that in your pocket? she said.
Just my knife. It weighted my pocket
and stretched my dress awry.

Go tie back your hair, said my mother,
and *Why is your mouth all green?*
*Rob Roy, he pulled some clover
as we crossed the field,* I told her.

May Swenson

Mean Song

Snickles and podes,
Ribble and grodes:
That's what I wish you.

A nox in the groot,
A root in the stoot
And a gock in the forbeshaw, too.

Keep out of sight
For fear that I might
Glom you a gravely snave.

Don't show your face
Around any place
Or you'll get one flack snack in the bave.

Eve Merriam

The Forbidden Play

I'll tell you the truth, Father, though your
    heart bleed:
    To the Play I went,
With sixpence for a near seat, money's worth
    indeed,
    The best ever spent.

You forbade me, you threatened me, but
    here's the story
    Of my splendid night:
It was colour, drums, music, a tragic glory,
    Fear with delight.

Hamlet, Prince of Denmark, title of the tale:
    He of that name,
A tall, glum fellow, velvet cloaked, with a
    shirt of mail,
    Two eyes like flame.

All the furies of Hell circled round that man,
    Maddening his heart,
There was old murder done before play
    began,
    Aye, the ghost took part.

There were grave-diggers delving, they
    brought up bones,
    And with rage and grief
All the players shouted in full, kingly tones,
    Grand, passing belief.

Ah, there were ladies there radiant as day,
    And changing scenes:
Fabulous words were tossed about like hay
    By kings and queens.

I puzzled on the sense of it in vain,
    Yet for pain I cried,
As one and all they faded, poisoned or slain,
    In great agony died.

Drive me out, Father, never to return,
    Though I am your son,
And penniless! But that glory for which I
    burn
    Shall be soon begun:

I shall wear great boots, shall strut and shout,
    Keep my locks curled;
The fame of my name shall go ringing about
    Over half the world.

Robert Graves

A Small Discovery

Father,
Where do giants go to cry?

To the hills
Behind the thunder?
Or to the waterfall?
I wonder.

(Giants cry.
I know they do.
Do they wait
Till nighttime too?)

James A. Emanuel

Dinky

O what's the weather in a Beard?
It's windy there, and rather weird,
And when you think the sky has cleared
  —Why, there is Dirty Dinky.

Suppose you walk out in a Storm,
With nothing on to keep you warm,
And then step barefoot on a Worm
  —Of course, it's Dirty Dinky.

As I was crossing a hot hot Plain,
I saw a sight that caused me pain,
You asked me before, I'll tell you again:
  —It *looked* like Dirty Dinky.

Last night you lay a-sleeping? No!
The room was thirty-five below;

The sheets and blankets turned to snow.
  —He'd got in: Dirty Dinky.

You'd better watch the things you do.
You'd better watch the things you do.
You're part of him; he's part of you
  —*You* may be Dirty Dinky.

Theodore Roethke

They're Calling

They're calling, "Nan,
Come at once."
But I don't answer.
      It's not that I don't hear,
      I'm very sharp of ear,
But I'm not Nan,
I'm a dancer.

They're calling, "Nan,
Go and wash."
But I don't go yet.
      Their voices are quite
      clear,
      I'm humming but I hear,
But I'm not Nan,
I'm a poet.

They're calling, "Nan,
Come to dinner!"
And I stop humming.
      I seem to hear them
      clearer,
      Now that dinner's
      nearer.
Well, just for now I'm Nan,
And I say, "Coming."

Felice Holman

A Sick Child

The postman comes when I am still in bed.
"Postman, what do you have for me today?"
I say to him. (But really I'm in bed.)
Then he says—what shall I have him say?

"This letter says that you are president
Of—this word here; it's a republic."
Tell them I can't answer right away.
"It's your duty." No, I'd rather just be sick.

Then he tells me there are letters saying
      everything
That I can think of that I want for them to
      say.
I say, "Well, thank you very much.
      Good-bye."
He is ashamed, and turns and walks away.

If I can think of it, it isn't what I want.
I want . . . I want a ship from some near star
To land in the yard, and beings to come out
And think to me: "So this is where you are!

Come." Except that they won't do,
I thought of them. . . . And yet somewhere
      there must be
Something that's different from everything.
All that I've never thought of—think of me!

Randall Jarrell

Friends and Family
"you always come back to my thoughts"

Rock-a-bye, baby,
  Thy cradle is green,
Father's a nobleman,
  Mother's a queen;
And Betty's a lady,
  And wears a gold ring;
And Johnny's a drummer,
  And drums for the king.

(Mother Goose)

The Mocking Bird

Hush up, baby,
Don't say a word,
Papa's going to buy you
A mocking bird.

If it can't whistle
And it can't sing,
Papa's going to buy you
A diamond ring.

If that diamond ring
Turns to brass,
Papa's going to buy you
A looking-glass.

If that looking-glass
Gets broke,
Papa's going to buy you
A Billy-goat.

If that Billy-goat
Runs away,
Papa's going to buy you
Another today.

If that Billy-goat
Won't pull,
Papa's going to buy you
A cart and bull.

If that cart and bull
Turn over,
Papa's going to buy you
A dog named Rover.

If that dog named Rover
Won't bark,
Papa's going to buy you
A horse and cart.

If that horse and cart
Fall down,
You'll still be the sweetest little
Baby in town.

(American Folk)

"The Mocking Bird" from ENGLISH FOLK SONGS FROM THE SOUTHERN APPALACHIANS collected by Cecil Sharp. Reprinted by permission of Oxford University Press.

Mother to Son

Well, son, I'll tell you:
Life for me ain't been no crystal stair.
It's had tacks in it,
And splinters,
And boards torn up,
And places with no carpet on the floor—
Bare.
But all the time
I'se been a-climbin' on,
And reachin' landin's,
And turnin' corners,
And sometimes goin' in the dark
Where there ain't been no light.
So, boy, don't you turn back.
Don't you set down on the steps
'Cause you finds it kinder hard.
Don't you fall now—
For I'se still goin', honey,
I'se still climbin',
And life for me ain't been no crystal stair.

Langston Hughes

Do not weep, little one,
Your mother will fetch you,
Mother is coming for you
As soon as she has finished
Her new kamiks.

Do not weep, little one,
Your father will fetch you,
Father is coming as soon as he has made
His new harpoon head,
Do not weep, little one,
    Do not weep!

(Eskimo)

Mama Is a Sunrise

When she comes slip-footing through the
    door,
    she kindles us
    like lump coal lighted,
    and we wake up glowing.
She puts a spark even in Papa's eyes
and turns out all our darkness.

When she comes sweet-talking in the room,
    she warms us
    like grits and gravy,
    and we rise up shining.
Even at night-time Mama is a sunrise
that promises tomorrow and tomorrow.

Evelyn Tooley Hunt

Taught Me Purple

My mother taught me purple
    Although she never wore it.
Wash-grey was her circle,
    The tenement her orbit.

My mother taught me golden
    And held me up to see it,
Above the broken molding,
    Beyond the filthy street.

My mother reached for beauty
    And for its lack she died,
Who knew so much of duty
    She could not teach me pride.

Evelyn Tooley Hunt

Aunt Roberta

What do people think about
When they sit and dream
All wrapped up in quiet
    and old sweaters
And don't even hear me 'til I
Slam the door?

Eloise Greenfield

My Name

I wrote my name on the sidewalk
But the rain washed it away.

I wrote my name on my hand
But the soap washed it away.

I wrote my name on the birthday card
I gave to Mother today

And there it will stay
For mother never throws

       ANYTHING

of mine away!

Lee Bennett Hopkins

My Sister Jane

And I say nothing—no, not a word
About our Jane. Haven't you heard?
She's a bird, a bird, a bird, a bird.
Oh it never would do to let folks know
My sister's nothing but a great big crow.

Each day (we daren't send her to school)
She pulls on stockings of thick blue wool
To make her pin crow legs look right,
Then fits a wig of curls on tight,
And dark spectacles—a huge pair
To cover her very crowy stare.
Oh it never would do to let folks know
My sister's nothing but a great big crow.

When visitors come she sits upright
(With her wings and her tail tucked out of
    sight).
They think her queer but extremely polite.
Then when the visitors have gone
She whips out her wings and with her wig on
Whirls through the house at the height of
    your head—

Duck, duck, or she'll knock you dead.
Oh it never would do to let folks know
My sister's nothing but a great big crow.

At meals whatever she sees she'll stab it—
Because she's a crow and that's a crow habit.
My mother says "Jane! Your manners!
    Please!"
Then she'll sit quietly on the cheese,
Or play the piano nicely by dancing on the
    keys—
Oh it never would do to let folks know
My sister's nothing but a great big crow.

Ted Hughes

My Uncle Dan

My Uncle Dan's an inventor, you may think
    that's very fine.
You may wish he was your Uncle instead of
    being mine—
If he wanted he could make a watch that
    bounces when it drops
He could make a helicopter out of string and
    bottle tops
Or any really useful thing you can't get in the
    shops.
    But Uncle Dan has other ideas:
    The bottomless glass for ginger beers,
    The toothless saw that's safe for the tree,
    A special word for a spelling bee
    (Like Lionocerangoutangadder),
    Or the roll-uppable rubber ladder,
    The mystery pie that bites when it's bit—
    My Uncle Dan invented it.
My Uncle Dan sits in his den inventing night
    and day.
His eyes peer from his hair and beard like
    mice from a load of hay.
And does he make the shoes that will go
    walks without your feet?
A shrinker to shrink instantly the elephants
    you meet?
A carver that just carves from the air steaks
    cooked and ready to eat?
    No, no, he has other intentions—
    Only perfectly useless inventions:

"My Name" from KIM'S PLACE AND OTHER POEMS by Lee Bennett Hopkins. Copyright © 1974 by Lee Bennett Hopkins. Reprinted by permission of Curtis Brown Ltd.

"My Sister Jane" and "My Uncle Dan" from MEET MY FOLKS by Ted Hughes. Copyright © 1961, 1973 by Ted Hughes. Used with permission of the publisher, The Bobbs-Merrill Company, Inc., and Faber and Faber Ltd.

Glassless windows (they never break),
A medicine to cure the earthquake,
The unspillable screwed-down cup,
The stairs that go neither down nor up,
The door you simply paint on a wall—
Uncle Dan invented them all.

Ted Hughes

Portrait by a Neighbor

Before she has her floor swept
    Or her dishes done,
Any day you'll find her
    A-sunning in the sun!

It's long after midnight
    Her key's in the lock,
And you never see her chimney smoke
    Till past ten o'clock!

She digs in her garden
    With a shovel and a spoon,
She weeds her lazy lettuce
    By the light of the moon.

She walks up the walk
    Like a woman in a dream,
She forgets she borrowed butter
    And pays you back cream!

Her lawn looks like a meadow,
    And if she mows the place
She leaves the clover standing
    And the Queen Anne's lace!

Edna St. Vincent Millay

I Cannot Forget You

No matter how hard I try to forget you, you
    always come back to my thoughts.
When you hear me singing I am really crying
    for you.

(Makah)

A Red, Red Rose

O my Luve's like a red, red rose
    That's newly sprung in June:
O my Luve's like the melodie
    That's sweetly play'd in tune!

As fair art thou, my bonnie lass,
    So deep in luve am I:
And I will luve thee still, my dear,
    Till a' the seas gang dry:

Till a' the seas gang dry, my dear,
    And the rocks melt wi' the sun;
I will luve thee still, my dear,
    While the sands o' life shall run.

And fare thee weel, my only Luve
    And fare thee weel awhile!
And I will come again, my Luve,
    Tho' it were ten thousand mile.

Robert Burns

The Pasture

I'm going out to clean the pasture spring;
I'll only stop to rake the leaves away
(And wait to watch the water clear, I may):
I sha'n't be gone long.—You come too.

I'm going out to fetch the little calf
That's standing by the mother. It's so young
It totters when she licks it with her tongue.
I sha'n't be gone long.—You come too.

Robert Frost

"Portrait by a Neighbor" from COLLECTED POEMS by Edna St. Vincent Millay (Harper & Row, 1922). Copyright 1922, 1923, 1950, 1951 by Edna St. Vincent Millay and Norma Millay Ellis. Reprinted by permission of Norma Millay Ellis.

"I Cannot Forget You" from IN THE TRAIL OF THE WIND by John Bierhorst. Copyright © 1971 by John Bierhorst. Reprinted by permission of Farrar, Straus & Giroux, Inc.

"A Red, Red Rose" by Robert Burns.

"The Pasture" from THE POETRY OF ROBERT FROST edited by Edward Connery Lathem. Copyright 1916, 1923, 1939, © 1967, 1969 by Holt, Rinehart and Winston. Copyright 1942, 1944, 1951 by Robert Frost. Copyright © 1970 by Lesley Frost Ballantine. Reprinted by permission of Holt, Rinehart and Winston, Publishers, and the Estate of Robert Frost.

First Love

I remember sadness
And I remember gay
And I remember a small boy
With turtles in the May,
With turtles in his two hands
And turtles at his feet
And out among the lily pads,
Turtles, fast asleep.
I remember sadness
And I remember gay
And I remember a small girl
Early in the May;
I remember a small girl
With flowers in her hair
Looking at the lily pads
To see the turtles there.

Patricia Hubbell

Poem

I loved my friend.
He went away from me.
There's nothing more to say.
The poem ends,
Soft as it began—
I loved my friend.

Langston Hughes

Little Bush

A Song

A little bush
At the picnic place,
A little bush could talk to me.

I ran away
And hid myself,
And I found a bush that could talk to me,
A smooth little bush said a word to me.

Elizabeth Madox Roberts

Always Room for One More

1

There was a wee house in the heather—
  'Twas a bit o' a but and a ben—
And in it there lived all together
    Lachie MacLachlan
      And his good wife,
        And his bairns to the number of ten.
"There's a fire on the hearthstone to warm me,
  And porridge to spare in the pot,"
Said Lachie. "The weather is stormy,
  So me and my wife
    And our ten bairns,
      Will be sharing whatever we've got."

So he hailed every traveler that passed by his door.
  Said Lachie MacLachlan, "There's room galore.

Och, come awa' in! There's room for one
   more,
      Always room for one more!"

A tinker came first, then a tailor,
   And a sailor with line and lead;
A gallowglass and a fishing lass,
   With a creel o' fish on her head;
A merry auld wife full o' banter,
   Four peat-cutters up from the bog,
Piping Rury the Ranter,
      And a shepherd laddie
         Down from the brae,
            With his canny wee shepherd dog.

He hailed them all in as he stood at the door.
   Said Lachie MacLachlan, "There's room
   galore.
   Och, come awa' in! There's room for one
   more,
      Always room for one more!"

2

Rury's pipes set the rafters a-ringing
   Till the clock danced a reel on the shelf,
And they all fell to dancing and singing,
   And the little dog danced by himself.
Och, the walls they bulged out and bulged in
   then,
      The walls they bulged in and out.
There will never be heard such a din, then,
   As came from the folks
      In the wee little house
         While they rollicked and frolicked
         about.

They filled all the house up from door to
   door,
   But Lachie cried out, "There's room galore.
   'Twould be a tight fit, but there's room for
   one more,
      Always room for one more!"

Then the rafters they clappit like thunder,
   And folks in the nearby town
Stood stock-still to listen and wonder,
   When the wee little house
      With its but and its ben
         And its walls and its roof DINGED
DOWN!

Then the tinker and the tailor,
   And the sailor with line and lead;
The gallowglass, and the fishing lass,
   With the creel o' fish on her head;
The auld wife full o' banter,
   The four peat-cutters up from the bog,

3

Piping Rury the Ranter,
   And the shepherd laddie down from the
   brae,
With his canny wee shepherd dog,
      AND
         Lachie MacLachlan,
            His good wife,
               And his bairns to the
               number of ten,
                  They all tumbled
                  out again!

And they gowked at the place where the
   house stood before.
   "Och, Lachie," they cried, "there was
   room galore,
   But worry and woe, there's no room no
   more,
      Never no room no more!"

They wailed for a while in the heather,
   As glum as a grumpetie grouse,
Then they shouted, "Have done with this
   blether!
   For Lachie MacLachlan,
      His wife and bairns,
         We'll raise up a bonny new house."
The house that they raised from the auld one
   Was double as wide and as high.
Should an army come by it could hauld one,
   With Lachie MacLachlan,
      His wife and bairns,
         And whoever else happened by.

And then the whole lot of them stood at the
   door,
   And merrily shouted, "There's room galore!
   Now there will always be room for one
   more,
      Always room for one more!"

Sorche Nic Leodhas

The Streets of Laredo

As I walked out in the streets of Laredo,
As I walked out in Laredo one day,
I spied a poor cowboy wrapped up in white
    linen,
Wrapped in white linen as cold as the clay.

Oh, beat the drums slowly, and play the fife
    lowly,
Play the dead march as you carry me along,
Take me to the green valley, there lay the
    sod o'er me,
For I'm a young cowboy, and I know I've
    done wrong.

Let sixteen gamblers come handle my coffin,
Let sixteen cowboys come sing me a song,
Take me to the graveyard, and lay the sod
    o'er me,
For I'm a poor cowboy, and I know I've done
    wrong.

It was once in the saddle I used to go dashing,
It was once in the saddle I used to go gay,

First to the dram house, and then to the card
    house,
Got shot in the breast, and I'm dying today.

Get six jolly cowboys to carry my coffin,
Get six pretty maidens to bear up my pall,
Put bunches of roses all over my coffin,
Put roses to deaden the sods as they fall.

Oh, bury me beside my knife and my six-
    shooter,
My spurs on my heel, my rifle by my side,
And over my coffin put a bottle of brandy,
That's the cowboy's drink, and carry me
    along.

We beat the drums slowly and played the fife
    lowly,
And bitterly wept as we bore him along,
For we all loved our comrade, so brave,
    young, and handsome,
We all loved our comrade, although he'd
    done wrong.

(American Folk)

"The Streets of Laredo" from AMERICAN FOLK PO-
ETRY.

Poems of the Spirit
"Who makes much of a miracle?"

The Creation

And God stepped out on space,
And he looked around and said:
I'm lonely—
I'll make me a world.

And as far as the eye of God could see
Darkness covered everything,
Blacker than a hundred midnights
Down in a cypress swamp.

Then God smiled,
And the light broke,
And the darkness rolled up on one side,
And the light stood shining on the other,
And God said: That's good!

Then God reached out and took the light in
    his hands,
And God rolled the light in his hands
Until he made the sun;
And he set that sun a-blazing in the heavens.
And the light that was left from making the
    sun
God gathered it up in a shining ball
And flung it against the darkness,
Spangling the night with the moon and stars.
Then down between
The darkness and the light
He hurled the world;
And God said: That's good!

Then God himself stepped down—
And the sun was on his right hand,

And the moon was on his left;
The stars were clustered about his head,
And the earth was under his feet.
And God walked, and where he trod
His footsteps hollowed the valleys out
And bulged the mountains up.

Then he stopped and saw
That the earth was hot and barren.
So God stepped over to the edge of the world
And he spat out the seven seas—
He batted his eyes, and the lightnings
    flashed—
He clapped his hands, and the thunders
    rolled—
And the waters above the earth came down,
The cooling waters came down.

Then the green grass sprouted,
And the little red flowers blossomed,
The pine tree pointed his finger to the sky,
And the oak spread out his arms,
The lakes cuddled down in the hollows of the
    ground,
And the rivers ran down to the sea;
And God smiled again,
And the rainbow appeared,
And curled itself around his shoulder.

Then God raised his arm and waved his
    hand,
Over the sea and over the land,
And he said: Bring forth! Bring forth!
And quicker than God could drop his hand,
Fishes and fowls
And beasts and birds
Swam the rivers and the seas,
Roamed the forests and the woods,
And split the air with their wings.
And God said: That's good!

Then God walked around,
And God looked around

On all that he had made.
He looked at his sun,
And he looked at his moon,
And he looked at his little stars;
He looked on his world
With all its living things,
And God said: I'm lonely still.

Then God sat down—
On the side of a hill where he could think;
By a deep, wide river he sat down;
With his head in his hands,
God thought and thought,
Till he thought: I'll make me a man!

Up from the bed of the river
God scooped the clay;
And by the bank of the river
He kneeled him down;
And there the great God Almighty
Who lit the sun and fixed it in the sky,
Who flung the stars to the most far corner of
    the night,
Who rounded the earth in the middle of his
    hand;
This great God,
Like a mammy bending over her baby,
Kneeled down in the dust
Toiling over a lump of clay
Till he shaped it in his own image;

Then into it he blew the breath of life,
And man became a living soul.
Amen. Amen.

James Weldon Johnson

Miracles

Why, who makes much of a miracle?
As to me I know of nothing else but miracles,
Whether I walk the streets of Manhattan,
Or dart my sight over the roofs of houses
    toward the sky,
Or wade with naked feet along the beach just
    in the edge of the water,

Or stand under trees in the woods,
Or talk by day with any one I love, or sleep
    in the bed at night with any one I love,
Or sit at table at dinner with the rest,
Or look at strangers opposite me riding in the
    car,
Or watch honey-bees busy around the hive of
    a summer forenoon,
Or animals feeding in the fields,
Or birds, or the wonderfulness of insects in
    the air,
Or the wonderfulness of the sundown, or of
    stars shining so quiet and bright,
Or the exquisite delicate thin curve of the
    new moon in spring;
These with the rest, one and all, are to me
    miracles,
The whole referring, yet each distinct and in
    its place.

To me every hour of the light and dark is a
    miracle,
Every cubic inch of space is a miracle,
Every square yard of the surface of the earth
    is spread with the same,
Every foot of the interior swarms with the
    same.

To me the sea is a continual miracle,
The fishes that swim—the rocks—the motion
    of the waves—the ships with men in
    them,
What stranger miracles are there?

Walt Whitman

The Dream

One night I dreamed
I was lost in a cave,
A cave that was empty
And dark and cool,
And down into nothing
I dropped a stone
And it fell like a star
Far and alone,
And a sigh arose
The sigh of a wave
Rippling the heart
Of a sunless pool.

And after a while
In my dream I dreamed
I climbed a sky
That was high and steep
And still as a mountain
Without a cave,
As still as water
Without a wave,
And on that hill
Of the sun it seemed
That all sad sounds
In the world fell asleep.

Harry Behn

Dreams

Hold fast to dreams
For if dreams die
Life is a broken-winged bird
That cannot fly.

Hold fast to dreams
For when dreams go
Life is a barren field
Frozen with snow.

Langston Hughes

Dust of Snow

The way a crow
Shook down on me
The dust of snow
From a hemlock tree

Has given my heart
A change of mood
And saved some part
Of a day I had rued.

Robert Frost

The Lord is my shepherd; I shall not want.
He maketh me to lie down in green pastures:
He leadeth me beside the still waters.
He restoreth my soul:
He leadeth me in the paths of righteousness
    for his name's sake.
Yea, though I walk through the valley of the
    shadow of death,

I will fear no evil: for thou art with me;
Thy rod and thy staff they comfort me.
Thou preparest a table before me in the
    presence of mine enemies:
Thou anointest my head with oil; my cup
    runneth over.
Surely goodness and mercy shall follow me
    all the days of my life:
And I will dwell in the house of the Lord for
    ever.

(Psalm 23)

The earth *is* the Lord's, and the fulness
    thereof;
The world, and they that dwell therein.
For he hath founded it upon the seas.
And established it upon the floods.
Who shall ascend into the hill of the Lord?
Or who shall stand in his holy place?
He that hath clean hands, and a pure heart;
Who hath not lifted up his soul unto vanity,
Nor sworn deceitfully.
He shall receive the blessing from the Lord,
And righteousness from the God of his
    salvation.
This is the generation of them that seek him,
That seek thy face, O Jacob.
Lift up your heads, O ye gates;
And be ye lifted up, ye everlasting doors;
And the King of glory shall come in.
Who is this King of glory?
The Lord strong and mighty,
The Lord mighty in battle.
Lift up your heads, O ye gates;
Even lift them up, ye everlasting doors;
And the King of glory shall come in.
Who is this King of glory?
The Lord of hosts,
He *is* the King of glory.

(Psalm 24)

Bless the Lord, O my soul:
And all that is within me, bless his holy name.
Bless the Lord, O my soul,
And forget not all his benefits:
Who forgiveth all thine iniquities;
Who healeth all thy diseases;
Who redeemeth thy life from destruction;
Who crowneth thee with loving-kindness
    and tender mercies;
Who satisfieth thy mouth with good things;
So that thy youth is renewed like the eagle's.
Bless the Lord, O my soul:
And all that is within me, bless his holy name.

(Psalm 103)

Night

Stars over snow,
   And in the west a planet
Swinging below a star—
   Look for a lovely thing and you will find it,
It is not far—
   It never will be far.

Sara Teasdale

The Black Fern

Here is the fossil
Preserving in anthracite
Its shining pattern   its still shape

Which in green silence
Was a fern uncurling
Beneath birdsong   under the trees

Its tender fronds were
Softer than fingers
In that young world   in the beginning

But the wind is dead
That shook its softness
And time has pressed it   in layers of years

Time has buried it
In heaviest darkness
And the living fern is   in this black rock

Touch with your fingers
The leafy fossil
The delicate statue   the coal-black fern

Leslie Norris

Swift things are beautiful:
Swallows and deer,
And lightning that falls
Bright-veined and clear,
Rivers and meteors,
Wind in the wheat,
The strong-withered horse,
The runner's sure feet.

And slow things are beautiful:
The closing of day,
The pause of the wave
That curves downward to spray,
The ember that crumbles,
The opening flower,
And the ox that moves on
In the quiet of power.

Elizabeth Coatsworth

Francis Jammes: A Prayer to Go to Paradise with the Donkeys

When I must come to you, O my God, I pray
It be some dusty-roaded holiday,
And even as in my travels here below,
I beg to choose by what road I shall go
To Paradise, where the clear stars shine by
    day.

I'll take my walking-stick and go my way,
And to my friends the donkeys I shall say,
"I am Francis Jammes, and I'm going to
    Paradise,
For there is no hell in the land of the loving
    God."
And I'll say to them: "Come, sweet friends of
    the blue skies,
Poor creatures who with a flap of the ears or
    a nod
Of the head shake off the buffets, the bees,
    the flies . . ."
Let me come with these donkeys, Lord, into
    your land,
These beasts who bow their heads so gently,
    and stand
With their small feet joined together in a
    fashion
Utterly gentle, asking your compassion.
I shall arrive, followed by their thousands of
    ears,
Followed by those with baskets at their
    flanks,
By those who lug the carts of mountebanks
Or loads of feather-dusters and kitchen-
    wares,
By those with humps of battered water-cans,
By bottle-shaped she-asses who halt and
    stumble,
By those tricked out in little pantaloons
To cover their wet, blue galls where flies
    assemble
In whirling swarms, making a drunken hum.
Dear God, let it be with these donkeys that
    I come,
And let it be that angels lead us in peace
To leafy streams where cherries tremble in
    air,
Sleek as the laughing flesh of girls; and there
In that haven of souls let it be that, leaning
    above
Your divine waters, I shall resemble these
    donkeys,
Whose humble and sweet poverty will
    appear
Clear in the clearness of your eternal love.

Richard Wilbur

The Secret Sits

We dance round in a ring and suppose,
But the Secret sits in the middle and knows.

Robert Frost

John Henry

When John Henry was a little babe,
    A-holding to his mama's hand,
Says, "If I live till I'm twenty-one,
    I'm going to make a steel-driving man, my
        babe,
    I'm going to make a steel-driving man."

When John Henry was a little boy,
    A-sitting on his father's knee,
Says, "The Big Bend Tunnel on the C. & O.
    Road
    Is going to be the death of me, my babe,
    Is going to be the death of me."

John he made a steel-driving man,
    They took him to the tunnel to drive;
He drove so hard he broke his heart,
    He laid down his hammer and he died, my
        babe,
    He laid down his hammer and he died.

O now John Henry is a steel-driving man,
    He belongs to the steel-driving crew,
And every time his hammer comes down,
    You can see that steel walking through, my
        babe,
    You can see that steel walking through.

The steam drill standing on the right-hand
    side,
    John Henry standing on the left;
He says, "I'll beat that steam drill down,
    Or I'll die with my hammer in my breast,
        my babe,
    Or I'll die with my hammer in my breast."

He placed his drill on the top of the rock,
    The steam drill standing close at hand;
He beat it down one inch and a half
    And laid down his hammer like a man, my
        babe,
    And laid down his hammer like a man.

Johnny looked up to his boss-man and said,
    "O boss-man, how can it be?
For the rock is so hard and the steel is so
        tough,
    I can feel my muscles giving way, my babe,
    I can feel my muscles giving way."

Johnny looked down to his turner and said,
    "O turner, how can it be?
The rock is so hard and the steel is so tough
    That everybody's turning after me, my
        babe,
    That everybody's turning after me."

They took poor Johnny to the steep hillside,
    He looked to his heavens above;
He says, "Take my hammer and wrap it in
        gold

And give it to the girl I love, my babe,
    And give it to the girl I love."

They took his hammer and wrapped it in
        gold
    And gave it to Julia Ann;
And the last word John Henry said to her
    Was, "Julia, do the best you can, my babe,"
    Was, "Julia, do the best you can."

"If I die a railroad man,
    Go bury me under the tie,
So I can hear old Number Four,
    As she goes rolling by, my babe,
    As she goes rolling by.

"If I die a railroad man,
    Go bury me under the sand,
With a pick and shovel at my head and feet,
    And a nine-pound hammer in my hand,
        my babe,
    And a nine-pound hammer in my hand."

(American Folk)

School, Counting, and Alphabets
"the way to my school"

A diller, a dollar, a ten o'clock scholar!
  What makes you come so soon?
You used to come at ten o'clock,
  But now you come at noon.

(Mother Goose)

Snow makes a new land.
One step, two steps. I explore
The way to my school.

Kazue Mizumura

September

I already know where Africa is
and I already know how to
count to ten and
I went to school every day last year,
why do I have to go again?

Lucille Clifton

The A B C Bunny

A for Apple, big and red
B for Bunny snug a-bed
C for Crash!
D for Dash!
E for Elsewhere in a flash

F for Frog—he's fat and funny
"Looks like rain," says he to Bunny
G for Gale!
H for Hail!
Hippy-hop goes Bunny's tail
I for Insects here and there
J for Jay with jaunty air
K for Kitten, catnip-crazy
L for Lizard—look how lazy
M for Mealtime—munch, munch, munch!
M-m-m these greens are good for lunch
N for Napping in a Nook
O for Owl with bookish look
P for prickly Porcupine
Pins and needles on his spine
Q for Quail
R for Rail
S for Squirrel Swishy-tail
T for Tripping back to Town
U for Up and Up-side-down
V for View
Valley too
W—"We welcome you!"
X for eXit—off, away!
That's enough for us today
Y for You, take one last look
Z for Zero—close the book!

Wanda Gág

1, 2, 3, 4, 5!
I caught a hare alive;
6, 7, 8, 9, 10!
I let her go again.

(Mother Goose)

Text of "Snow makes a new land" from FLOWER MOON SHOW: A BOOK OF HAIKU by Kazue Mizumura. Copyright © 1977 by Kazue Mizumura. Reprinted by permission of Thomas Y. Crowell, Publishers.

"September" from EVERETT ANDERSON'S YEAR by Lucille Clifton. Copyright © 1974 by Lucille Clifton. Reprinted by permission of Holt, Rinehart and Winston, Publishers, and Curtis Brown Ltd.

THE ABC BUNNY by Wanda Gág. Copyright 1933; renewed 1961 by Wanda Gág. Reprinted by permission of Coward, McCann & Geoghegan, Inc.

One, two,
Buckle my shoe;
Three, four,
Knock at the door;
Five, six,
Pick up sticks;
Seven, eight,
Lay them straight;
Nine, ten,
A good, fat hen;
Eleven, twelve,
Dig and delve;
Thirteen, fourteen,
Maids a-courting;
Fifteen, sixteen,
Maids in the kitchen;
Seventeen, eighteen,
Maids a-waiting;
Nineteen, twenty,
My plate's empty.

(Mother Goose)

Back to School

When summer smells like apples
and shadows feel cool
and falling leaves make dapples
of color on the pool
and wind is in the maples
and sweaters are the rule
and hazy days spell lazy ways,
it's hard to go to school.

But I go!

Aileen Fisher

One, one
Cinnamon bun

Two, two
Chicken stew

Three, three
Cakes & tea

Four, four
I want more

Five, five
Honey in a hive

Six, six
Pretzel sticks

Seven, seven
Straight from heaven

Eight, eight
Clean your plate

Nine, nine
Look at mine

Ten, ten
Start over again!

Clyde Watson

Numbers

When I can count the numbers far,
And know all the figures that there are,

Then I'll know everything, and I
Can know about the ground and sky,

And all the little bugs I see,
And I'll count the leaves on the silver-leaf
    tree,
And all the days that ever can be.

I'll know all the cows and sheep that pass,
And I'll know all the grass,

And all the places far away,
And I'll know everything some day.

Elizabeth Madox Roberts

"Back to School" from OUT IN THE DARK AND DAY-LIGHT by Aileen Fisher. Text Copyright © 1980 by Aileen Fisher. Reprinted by permission of Harper & Row, Publishers, Inc.

"One, One" from CATCH ME & KISS ME & SAY IT AGAIN by Clyde Watson. Copyright © 1978 by Clyde Watson. Reprinted by permission of Philomel Books, a Division of The Putnam Publishing Group and Collins Publishers.

"Numbers" from UNDER THE TREE by Elizabeth Madox Roberts. Copyright 1930 by The Viking Press, Inc. Copyright renewed 1958 by Ivor S. Roberts. Reprinted by permission of Viking Penguin Inc.

Arithmetic

Arithmetic is where numbers fly like pigeons
in and out of your head.
Arithmetic tells you how many you lose or
win if you know how many you had before you lost or won.
Arithmetic is seven eleven all good children
go to heaven—or five six bundle of sticks.
Arithmetic is numbers you squeeze from
your head to your hand to your pencil to
your paper till you get the answer.
Arithmetic is where the answer is right and
everything is nice and you can look out
of the window and see the blue sky—or
the answer is wrong and you have to
start all over and try again and see how
it comes out this time.
If you take a number and double it and double it again and then double it a few
more times, the number gets bigger and
bigger and goes higher and higher and
only arithmetic can tell you what the
number is when you decide to quit doubling.
Arithmetic is where you have to multiply—
and you carry the multiplication table in
your head and hope you won't lose it.
If you have two animal crackers, one good
and one bad, and you eat one and a
striped zebra with streaks all over him
eats the other, how many animal crackers will you have if somebody offers you
five six seven and you say No no no and
you say Nay nay nay and you say Nix nix
nix?
If you ask your mother for one fried egg for
breakfast and she gives you two fried
eggs and you eat both of them, who is
better in arithmetic, you or your
mother?

Carl Sandburg

Blum

Dog means dog,
And cat means cat;
And there are lots
Of words like that.

A cart's a cart
To pull or shove,
A plate's a plate,
To eat off of.

But there are other
Words I say
When I am left
Alone to play.

Blum is one.
Blum is a word
That very few
Have ever heard.

I like to say it,
"Blum, Blum, Blum"—
I do it loud
Or in a hum.

All by itself
It's nice to sing:
It does not mean
A single thing.

Dorothy Aldis

A Word

A word is dead
When it is said,
    Some say.
I say it just
Begins to live
    That day.

Emily Dickinson

School Buses

You'd think that by the end of June they'd
    take themselves
Away, get out of sight—but no, they don't;
    they
Don't at all. You see them waiting through
July in clumps of sumac near the railroad, or
Behind a service station, watching, always
    watching for a

Child who's let go of summer's hand and
    strayed. I have
Seen them hunting on the roads of August—
    empty buses
Scanning woods and ponds with rows of
    empty eyes. This morning
I saw five of them, parked like a week of
Schooldays, smiling slow in orange paint and
Smirking with their mirrors in the sun—
But summer isn't done! Not yet!

Russell Hoban

Objects Around Us
"made of metal and glass"

Brooklyn Bridge at Dawn

Out of the cleansing night of stars and tides,
Building itself anew in the slow dawn,
The long sea-city rises: night is gone,
Day is not yet; still merciful, she hides
Her summoning brow, and still the night-car
    glides
Empty of faces; the night-watchmen yawn
One to the other, and shiver and pass on,
Nor yet a soul over the great bridge rides.

Frail as a gossamer, a thing of air,
A bow of shadow o'er the river flung,
Its sleepy masts and lonely lapping flood;
Who, seeing thus the bridge a-slumber there,
Would dream such softness, like a picture
    hung,
Is wrought of human thunder, iron and
    blood?

Richard Le Gallienne

Circles

The things to draw with compasses
Are suns and moons and circleses
And rows of humptydumpasses
Or anything in circuses
Like hippopotamusseses
And hoops and camels' humpasses
And wheels on clownses busseses
And fat old elephumpasses.

Harry Behn

Flashlight

My flashlight tugs me
through the dark
like a hound
with a yellow eye,

sniffs
at the edges
of steep places,

paws
at moles'
and rabbits'
holes,

points its nose
where sharp things
lie asleep—

and then it bounds
ahead of me
on home ground.

Judith Thurman

Skyscratcher

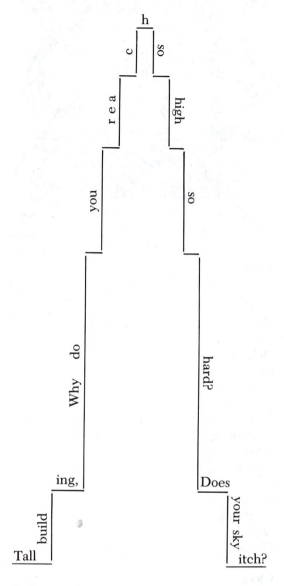

Robert Froman

Hose

The hose
Can squeeze
Water to
A silver rod
That digs
Hard holes
In the mud,

Or, muzzled
Tighter by
The nozzle,
Can rain
Chill diamond
Chains
Across the yard,

Or, fanned
Out fine,
Can hang
A silk
Rainbow
Halo
Over soft fog.

Valerie Worth

House Blessing

May it be delightful my house;
From my head may it be delightful;
To my feet may it be delightful;
Where I lie may it be delightful;
All above me may it be delightful;
All around me may it be delightful.

(Navajo)

Oil Slick

There, by the curb,
a leaky truck
has drooled
a grease-pool,

a black, pearly
slick
which rainbows
when the sun
strikes it.

"Skyscratcher" from STREET POEMS by Robert Froman. Copyright © 1971 by Robert Froman. Reprinted by permission of the publisher, E. P. Dutton, Inc. and Curtis Brown Ltd.

"Hose" from MORE SMALL POEMS by Valerie Worth. Copyright © 1976 by Valerie Worth. Reprinted by permission of Farrar, Straus & Giroux, Inc. and Curtis Brown Ltd.

"House Blessing" from IN THE TRAIL OF THE WIND by John Bierhorst. Copyright © 1971 by John Bierhorst. Reprinted by permission of Farrar, Straus & Giroux, Inc.

Judith Thurman, "Oil Slick," in FLASHLIGHT AND OTHER POEMS. Copyright © 1976 by Judith Thurman (New York: Atheneum, 1976). Reprinted with the permission of Atheneum Publishers.

I could spend
all day
marbling
its flashy colors
with a stick.

Judith Thurman

from Five Chants

3

The pickety fence
The pickety fence
Give it a lick it's
The pickety fence
Give it a lick it's
A clickety fence
Give it a lick it's
A lickety fence
Give it a lick
Give it a lick
Give it a lick
With a rickety stick
Pickety
Pickety
Pickety
Pick

David McCord

Safety Pin

Closed, it sleeps
On its side
Quietly,
The silver
Image
Of some
Small fish;

Opened, it snaps
Its tail out
Like a thin
Shrimp, and looks
At the sharp
Point with a
Surprised eye.

Valerie Worth

Clock

This clock
Has stopped,
Some gear
Or spring
Gone wrong—
Too tight,
Or cracked,
Or choked
With dust;
A year
Has passed
Since last
It said
Ting ting
Or tick
Or tock.
Poor
Clock.

Valerie Worth

Taxis

Ho, for taxis green or blue,
  Hi, for taxis red,
They roll along the Avenue
  Like spools of colored thread!

Jack-o'-Lantern yellow,
Orange as the moon,
Greener than the greenest grass
Ever grew in June.
Gayly striped or checked in squares,
Wheels that twinkle bright,
Don't you think that taxis make
A very pleasant sight?
Taxis shiny in the rain,
Scudding through the snow,
Taxis flashing back the sun
Waiting in a row.

Ho, for taxis red and green,
  Hi, for taxis blue,
I wouldn't be a private car
  In sober black, would you?

Rachel Field

City Traffic

Green as a seedling the one lane shines,
Red ripened blooms for the opposite lines;
Emerald shoot,
Vermilion fruit.

Now amber, now champagne, now honey:
  go slow:
Shift, settle, then gather and sow.

Eve Merriam

Queens of the River

STAR NADINE, GOLDEN SPEAR,
  GYPSUM KING
floating along
majestically—

CHROMALLOY, MANISTEE
loaded with crates,
with oil,
ships of industry—

NORTHERN EAGLE OF MONROVIA,
  DAPHNE
colors flat, plain,
black and white,
faded green,

but on the bows the beautiful names—

NEPCO COURAGEOUS, GOLDEN
  ENDEAVOR
to let the world know
that only they are
        kings of the sea
        queens of the river.

Claudia Lewis

The Toaster

A silver-scaled Dragon with jaws flaming red
Sits at my elbow and toasts my bread.
I hand him fat slices, and then, one by one,
He hands them back when he sees they are
  done.

William Jay Smith

Reflections

On this street
of windowed stores
see,
in the glass
shadow people meet
and pass
and glide to
secret places.

Ghostly mothers
hold
the hands of dim gray children,
scold
them silently
and melt away.

And
now and then,
before
the window mirror
of a store,
phantom faces
stop
and window shop.

Lilian Moore

Our Washing Machine

Our washing machine went whisity whirr
Whisity whisity whisity whirr
One day at noon it went whisity click
Whisity whisity whisity click
click grr click grr click grr click
   Call the repairman
   Fix it . . . Quick!

Patricia Hubbell

Composed Upon
Westminster Bridge

Earth has not anything to show more fair:
Dull would he be of soul who could pass by
A sight so touching in its majesty:
This City now doth like a garment wear
The beauty of the morning; silent, bare,
Ships, towers, domes, theaters, and temples
   lie
Open unto the fields, and to the sky;
All bright and glittering in the smokeless air.
Never did sun more beautifully steep
In his first splendor valley, rock, or hill;
Ne'er saw I, never felt, a calm so deep!
The river glideth at his own sweet will:
Dear God! the very houses seem asleep;
And all that mighty heart is lying still!

William Wordsworth

Southbound on the Freeway

A tourist came in from Orbitville,
parked in the air, and said:

The creatures of this star
are made of metal and glass.

Through the transparent parts
you can see their guts.

Their feet are round and roll
on diagrams or long

measuring tapes, dark
with white lines.

They have four eyes.
The two in back are red.

Sometimes you can see a five-eyed
one, with a red eye turning

on the top of his head.
He must be special—

the others respect him
and go slow

when he passes, winding
among them from behind.

They all hiss as they glide,
like inches, down the marked

tapes. Those soft shapes,
shadowy inside

the hard bodies—are they
their guts or their brains?

May Swenson

   Patricia Hubbell, "Our Washing Machine" in THE APPLE
VENDOR'S FAIR. Copyright © 1963 by Patricia Hubbell (New
York: Atheneum, 1963). Reprinted with the permission of
Atheneum Publishers.
   "Composed Upon Westminster Bridge" by William Words-
worth.
   "Southbound on the Freeway" from NEW & SELECTED
THINGS TAKING PLACE by May Swenson. Poem copyright
© 1963 by May Swenson. First appeared in *The New Yorker.*
Reprinted by permission of Little, Brown and Company in asso-
ciation with the Atlantic Monthly Press.

Air on an Escalator

Gallop up the instant stair
running is as good as flying
past the ads for underwear
things you'd never dream of buying
what's that echo of despair?
that's the escalator sighing

past the ads for underwear
things you'd never dream of buying
diving belles with floating hair
take us with you! sadly crying
what's that echo of despair?
that's the escalator sighing

diving belles with floating hair
take us with you! sadly crying
no we couldn't, wouldn't dare
sorry dears, it's no use trying
what's that echo of despair?
that's the escalator sighing

no we couldn't, wouldn't dare
sorry dears, it's no use trying
gallop up the instant stair
running is as good as flying
what's that echo of despair?
that's the escalator sighing

Joan Aiken

Travel
"far, far will I go"

Ride away, ride away,
  Johnny shall ride,
And he shall have pussy-cat
  Tied to one side;
And he shall have little dog
  Tied to the other,
And Johnny shall ride
  To see his grandmother.

(Mother Goose)

There was an old woman tossed up in a
    basket,
Seventeen times as high as the moon;
Where she was going I couldn't but ask it,
For in her hand she carried a broom.
Old woman, old woman, old woman, quoth I,
Where are you going to up so high?
To brush the cobwebs off the sky!
May I go with you?
Aye, by-and-by.

(Mother Goose)

How many miles to Babylon?
Three score miles and ten.
Can I get there by candle-light?
Yes, and back again.
If your heels are nimble and light,
You may get there by candle-light.

(Mother Goose)

Ride a cock horse
To Banbury Cross
To see a fair lady upon a white horse;
With rings on her fingers,
And bells on her toes,
She shall have music wherever she goes.

(Mother Goose)

I never saw a Moor—
I never saw the Sea—
Yet know I how the Heather looks
And what a Wave must be.

I never spoke with God
Nor visited in Heaven—
Yet certain am I of the spot
As if the Chart were given—

Emily Dickinson

There was an Old Man of the Hague,
Whose ideas were excessively vague;
    He built a balloon
    To examine the moon,
That deluded Old Man of the Hague.

Edward Lear

"I never saw a moor." Reprinted by permission of the publishers and the Trustees of Amherst College from THE POEMS OF EMILY DICKINSON, edited by Thomas H. Johnson, Cambridge, Mass.: The Belknap Press of Harvard University Press. Copyright 1951, © 1955, 1979 by the President and Fellows of Harvard College.

"There was an old man of the Hague" from THE COMPLETE NONSENSE BOOK by Edward Lear.

No Man On Any Moon

Go, go
You rocket men
To Mars
And to the moon
And to the stars—

In all of space
You'll never see
A man's face.

Explore
A million worlds
Or more

You'll never meet a boy
Or girl
On any shore.

No man
On any moon
Late or soon—
No man.

For we alone
Are breath and bone.

Yet—
Minds you'll find,
Powers unlike ours,
Symmetries
Unnamed,
Unknown.

O who can guess
Where,
How far—

Or know
If they sight our world
Among the moons
And wonder
Who we are?

Claudia Lewis

Three Skies

Three skies
Above our world—

Grey sky when clouds are high.

Break through the clouds
And it's blue where the planes fly.

Break through the blue on a rocket flight
And the skies are black, day and night.

Break through the black—
       Who knows
       To what fourth sky,
       On what flight?

Claudia Lewis

I saw a ship a-sailing,
A-sailing on the sea;
And, oh! it was all laden
With pretty things for thee!

There were comfits in the cabin,
And apples in the hold;
The sails were made of silk,
And the masts were made of gold.

The four-and-twenty sailors
That stood between the decks,
Were four-and-twenty white mice
With chains about their necks.

The captain was a duck,
With a packet on his back;
And when the ship began to move,
The captain said, "Quack! Quack!"

(Mother Goose)

Tunnel

Tunnel coming!
I'm not afraid—
I plunge
through its
dark hoop,

feel-hear
its walls
rumble and hum,
as if I were
inside a drum.

Light!
I can see sun
piercing
the tight
drumskin.

I wish
I could keep
daybreak
in sight
that way—
all through
the night.

Judith Thurman

Message from a Mouse, Ascending in a Rocket

Attention, architect!
Attention, engineer!
A message from mouse,
Coming clear:

"Suggesting installing
Spike or sprocket
Easily turned by
A mouse in a rocket;
An ejection gadget
Simple to handle
To free mouse quickly
From this space-age ramble.
Suggest packing
For the next moon trip
A mouse-sized parachute
Somewhere in the ship,
So I can descend
(When my fear comes strong)
Back to earth where I was born.
Back to the cheerful world of cheese
      And small mice playing,
      And my wife waiting."

Patricia Hubbell

Footprints

Where did they start? those well-marked
      white
Cloud-footprints, two by two,
Moving at leisured pace across
The skylight's square of blue?

I ran outside: the trails traversed
From skyscape's rim to rim;
Abominable Skymen? Or
Two strolling Seraphim?

A smaller trail, of dogprints, turned
Meandering through the air
Diverging (on some sky-hunt?) from
The heedless, strolling pair.

Who were those strollers? Where their home?
What quarter of the sky?
Why were their footprints seen by none,
No single soul but I?

Joan Aiken

ORBITER 5 SHOWS
HOW EARTH LOOKS FROM THE MOON

There's a woman in the earth, sitting on
her heels. You see her from the back, in three-
quarter profile. She has a flowing pigtail. She's
holding something in her right hand—some holy jug. Her left arm is thinner,
in a gesture like a dancer. She's the Indian Ocean. Asia is
light swirling up out of her vessel. Her pigtail points to Europe
and her dancer's arm is the Suez Canal. She is a woman
in a square kimono, bare feet tucked beneath the tip of Africa. Her tail of long hair is
the Arabian Peninsula.

A woman in the earth.

A man in the moon.

May Swenson

Note: A telephoto of the earth, taken from above the moon
by Lunar Orbiter 5 (printed in *The New York Times* August 14,
1967) appeared to show the shadow-image of "a woman in a
square Kimono" between the shapes of the continents. The title
is the headline over the photo.

Recuerdo

We were very tired, we were very merry—
We had gone back and forth all night on the
ferry.
It was bare and bright, and smelled like a
stable—
But we looked into a fire, we leaned across a
table,
We lay on the hill-top underneath the moon;
And the whistles kept blowing, and the dawn
came soon.

We were very tired, we were very merry—
We had gone back and forth all night
on the ferry;

And you ate an apple, and I ate a pear,
From a dozen of each we had bought somewhere;
And the sky went wan, and the wind came
cold,
And the sun rose dripping, a bucketful of
gold.

We were very tired, we were very merry—
We had gone back and forth all night
on the ferry.
We hailed, "Good morrow, mother!" to a
shawl-covered head,
And bought a morning paper, which neither
of us read;
And she wept, "God bless you!" for the apples and the pears,
And we gave her all our money but our subway fares.

Edna St. Vincent Millay

The Hiker

Backpacking Max,
past racks of shacks,
past all trail tracks,
bushwhacks,
thwacks,
with an ax
hacks.

Mosquito attacks,
bites through his slacks;

Max,
lax,
too late the bug smacks—

cracks open
his rucksack's
stack of Snackpacks.

Eve Merriam

Far, far will I go,
Far away beyond the high hills,
Where the birds live,
Far away over yonder, far away over yonder.

Two pieces of rock barred the way,
Two mighty rocks,
That opened and closed
Like a pair of jaws.
There was no way past,
One must go in between them
To reach the land beyond and away,
Beyond the high hills,
The birds' land.

Two land bears barred the way,
Two land bears fighting
And barring the way.
There was no road,
And yet I would gladly pass on and away
To the farther side of the high hills,
To the birds' land.

(Eskimo)

One Saturday night as we set sail,
Not being far from shore,
'Twas then that I spied a pretty fair maid
With a glass and a comb in her hand, her
    hand,
With a glass and a comb in her hand.
    The stormy wind did blow,
    And the raging sea did roll,
    And we poor sailors came leaping to the
    top
    While the landsmen lay down below,
    below, below,
    While the landsmen lay down below.

Then up came a boy of our gallant ship
And a noble-spoken boy was he,
Saying, "I've a mother in distant York town
This night is a-weeping for me."

Then up came a lad of our gallant ship
And a beautiful lad was he,
Saying, "I've a sweetheart in distant York
    town
This night is a-looking for me."

Then up came the clerk of our gallant ship
And a noble-spoken man was he,
Saying, "I've a wife in distant York town
This night a widow will be."

Then up came the captain of our gallant
    ship—
There is no braver man than he—
Saying, "For the want of a yawl-boat we'll be
    drowned
And we'll sink to the bottom of the sea."

Then three times round our gallant ship
    turned,
Three times round turned she;
Three times round our gallant ship turned,
Then she sank to the bottom of the sea.

(American Folk)

I Ride an Old Paint

I ride an old Paint and I lead an old Dan,
I'm going to Montan' for to throw the
  hoolihan,
They feed in the coolees, they water in the
  draw,
Tails are all matted, their backs are all raw.

  Ride around, little dogies, ride around
    them slow,
  The fiery and the snuffy are raring to go.

I've worked in the town and I've worked on
  the farm,
And all I got to show is just this muscle in my
  arm;
Got a blister on my foot, got a callus on my
  hand,
But I'll be a cowpuncher long as I can.

  Ride around, little dogies, ride around
    them slow,
  The fiery and the snuffy are raring to go.

Old Bill Jones had two daughters and a song,
One daughter went to Denver and the other
  went wrong,
His wife she died in a poolroom fight,
But still old Bill sings from morning to night.

  Ride around, little dogies, ride around
    them slow,
  The fiery and the snuffy are raring to go.

When I die, take my saddle from the wall
And lead my old pony out of his stall;
Tie my bones to his saddle, turn our faces
  toward the west,
We'll ride the prairies that we love the best.

  Ride around, little dogies, ride around
    them slow,
  The fiery and the snuffy are raring to go.

(American Folk)

The Lake Isle of Innisfree

I will arise and go now, and go to Innisfree,
And a small cabin build there, of clay and
  wattles made;
Nine bean rows will I have there, a hive for
  the honey-bee,
And live alone in the bee-loud glade.

And I shall have some peace there, for peace
  comes dropping slow,
Dropping from the veils of the morning to
  where the cricket sings;
There midnight's all a glimmer, and noon a
  purple glow,
And evening full of the linnet's wings.

I will arise and go now, for always night and
  day
I hear lake water lapping with low sounds by
  the shore;
While I stand on the roadway, or on the pave-
  ments gray,
I hear it in the deep heart's core.

William Butler Yeats

"One Saturday night as we set sail" and "I ride an old paint" from AMERICAN FOLK POETRY.

"The Lake Isle of Innisfree" from COLLECTED POEMS by William Butler Yeats. Copyright 1919 by Macmillan Publishing Co., Inc., renewed 1947 by Bertha Georgie Yeats. Reprinted by permission of Macmillan Publishing Co., Inc. and A. P. Watt Ltd.

Riddles

"a riddle, a riddle"

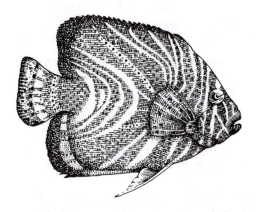

Thirty white horses upon a red hill,
Now they tramp, now they champ,
    Now they stand still.
                    (*The Teeth and Gums*)

(Mother Goose)

Runs all day and never walks,
Often murmurs, never talks.
It has a bed but never sleeps,
It has a mouth, but never eats.
                    (*A River*)

(Mother Goose)

Old Mother Twitchett has but one eye,
And a long tail which she can let fly,
And every time she goes over a gap,
She leaves a bit of her tail in a trap.
                    (*A Needle*)

(Mother Goose)

    Lives in winter,
    Dies in summer,
And grows with its roots upward!
                    (*An Icicle*)

(Mother Goose)

Little Nanny Etticoat
In a white petticoat,
    And a red nose;
The longer she stands
The shorter she grows.
                    (*A Candle*)

(Mother Goose)

I have a little sister they call her "Peep-
    peep,"
    She wades in the ocean deep, deep, deep.
She climbs up the mountain high, high, high,
    The poor little thing hasn't got but one
    eye.   (*A Star*)

(Mother Goose)

    Higher than a house,
    Higher than a tree,
Oh! whatever can that be?
                    (*A Star*)

(Mother Goose)

Hick-a-more, Hack-a-more,
On the King's kitchen door;
All the King's horses,
And all the King's men,
Couldn't drive Hick-a-more,
    Hack-a-more,
Off the King's kitchen door.
                    (*Sunshine*)

(Mother Goose)

As round as an apple, as deep as a cup,
And all the king's horses can't fill it up.
                    (*A Well*)

(Mother Goose)

Puzzle

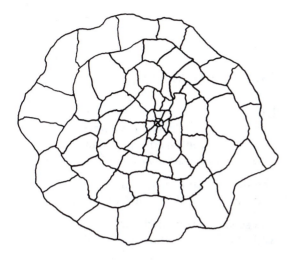

Map of a city with streets meeting at center?

Net to catch people jumping from a burning
    building?

Spider's web?

Burner on an electric stove?

Fingerprint?

No.

Frozen puddle after a hit by a rock.

Robert Froman

Answers

What weighs the littlest
you can think?
What hardly weighs at all?

"An aspen leaf," says Jennifer,
"that flickers down in fall."

"A milkweed seed," says Christopher.

"A thistledown," says Clive.

"A butterfly," says Mary Ann,
"and it's alive . . . *alive.*"

Aileen Fisher

A riddle, a riddle, as I suppose,
A hundred eyes and never a nose!

(*A Sieve*)

(Mother Goose)

A hill full, a hole full,
Yet you cannot catch a bowl full.

(*The Mist*)

(Mother Goose)

I come more softly than a bird,
And lovely as a flower;
I sometimes last from year to year
And sometimes but an hour.

I stop the swiftest railroad train
Or break the stoutest tree.
And yet I am afraid of fire
And children play with me.

(*Snow*)

Mary Austin

First I am frosted,
Second, I am beaten,
Third, I am roasted,
Fourth, I am eaten.

(*Chestnut*)

Mary Austin

I never speak a word
But when my voice is heard
Even the mountains shake,
No hands I have
And yet great rocks I break.
(*Thunder and Lightning*)

Mary Austin

This thing all things devours:
Birds, beasts, trees, flowers;
Gnaws iron, bites steel;
Grinds hard stones to meal;
Slays king, ruins town,
And beats high mountain down.
(*Time*)

J. R. R. Tolkien

Alive without breath,
As cold as death;
Never thirsty, ever drinking,
All in mail never clinking.
(*Fish*)

J. R. R. Tolkien

Voiceless it cries,
Wingless flutters,
Toothless bites,
Mouthless mutters.
(*Wind*)

J. R. R. Tolkien

It cannot be seen, cannot be felt,
Cannot be heard, cannot be smelt.
It lies behind stars and under hills,
    And empty holes it fills.
It comes first and follows after,
    Ends life, kills laughter.
(*Dark*)

J. R. R. Tolkien

A box without hinges, key, or lid,
Yet golden treasure inside is hid,
(*Egg*)

J. R. R. Tolkien

The Riddling Knight

There were three sisters fair and bright,
    Jennifer, Gentle and Rosemary,
And they three loved one valiant knight—
    As the dow flies over the mulberry-tree.

The eldest sister let him in,
And barr'd the door with a silver pin.

The second sister made his bed,
And placed soft pillows under his head.

The youngest sister that same night
Was resolved for to wed wi' this valiant
    knight.

"And if you can answer questions three,
O then, fair maid, I'll marry wi' thee.

"O what is louder nor a horn,
Or what is sharper nor a thorn?

"Or what is heavier nor the lead,
Or what is better nor the bread?

"Or what is longer nor the way,
Or what is deeper nor the sea?"—

"O shame is louder nor a horn,
And hunger is sharper nor a thorn.

"O sin is heavier nor the lead,
The blessing's better nor the bread.

"O the wind is longer nor the way
And love is deeper nor the sea."

"You have answer'd aright my questions
    three,
    Jennifer, Gentle and Rosemary;
And now, fair maid, I'll marry wi' thee,
    As the dow flies over the mulberry-tree."

(Anonymous)

Small Creatures, Insects, and Rodents
"little things"

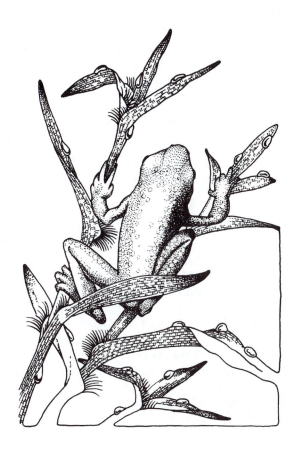

There was an Old Man in a tree,
Who was horribly bored by a Bee;
    When they said, "Does it buzz?"
    He replied, "Yes, it does!
It's a regular brute of a Bee."

Edward Lear

"There was an old man in a tree" from THE COMPLETE NONSENSE BOOK by Edward Lear.

"Little Things" from COLLECTED POEMS by James Stephens. Poem copyright 1926 by Macmillan Publishing Co., Inc., renewed 1954 by Cynthia Stephens. Reprinted by permission of Macmillan Publishing Co., Inc., and The Society of Authors on behalf of the copyright owner, Mrs. Iris Wise.

"The Bat" copyright 1938 by Theodore Roethke from the book THE COLLECTED POEMS OF THEODORE ROETHKE. Reprinted by permission of Doubleday & Company, Inc. and Faber and Faber Ltd.

"Tea party" from WINDY MORNING by Harry Behn. Copyright 1953 by Harry Behn. Reprinted by permission of Harcourt Brace Jovanovich, Inc.

Little Things

Little things, that run, and quail,
And die, in silence and despair!

Little things, that fight, and fail,
And fall, on sea, and earth, and air!

All trapped and frightened little things,
The mouse, the coney, hear our prayer!

As we forgive those done to us,
—The lamb, the linnet, and the hare—

Forgive us all our trespasses,
Little creatures, everywhere!

James Stephens

The Bat

By day the bat is cousin to the mouse.
He likes the attic of an aging house.

His fingers make a hat about his head.
His pulse beat is so slow we think him dead.

He loops in crazy figures half the night
Among the trees that face the corner light.

But when he brushes up against a screen,
We are afraid of what our eyes have seen:

For something is amiss or out of place
When mice with wings can wear a human
    face.

Theodore Roethke

Tea Party

Mister Beedle Baddlebug,
Don't bandle up in your boodlebag
Or numble in your jimblejug,
Now eat your nummy tiffletag
Or I will never invite you
To tea again with me. Shoo!

Harry Behn

Brown and furry
Caterpillar in a hurry
Take your walk
To the shady leaf, or stalk,
Or what not,
Which may be the chosen spot.
No toad spy you,
Hovering bird of prey pass by you;
Spin and die,
To live again a butterfly.

Christina Rossetti

Message From a Caterpillar

Don't shake this
bough.
Don't try
to wake me
now.

In this cocoon
I've work to
do.
Inside this silk
I'm changing
things.

I'm worm-like now
but in this
dark
I'm growing
wings.

Lilian Moore

Crickets

all busy punching tickets,
clicking their little punches.
The tickets come in bunches,
good for a brief excursion,
good for a cricket's version
of travel (before it snows) to
the places a cricket goes to.
Alas! the crickets sing alas
in the dry September grass.
Alas, alas, in every acre,
every one a ticket-taker.

David McCord

Firefly

A little light is going by,
Is going up to see the sky,
A little light with wings.

I never could have thought of it,
To have a little bug all lit
And made to go on wings.

Elizabeth Madox Roberts

An old silent pond . . .
A frog jumps into the pond,
    splash! Silence again.

Basho

The Frog

Be kind and tender to the Frog,
    And do not call him names,
As 'Slimy skin,' or 'Polly-wog,'
    Or likewise 'Ugly James,'
Or 'Gap-a-grin,' or 'Toad-gone-wrong,'
    Or 'Bill Bandy-knees':
The Frog is justly sensitive
    To epithets like these.
No animal will more repay
    A treatment kind and fair;
At least
            so lonely people say
Who keep a frog (and, by the way,
They are extremely rare).

Hilaire Belloc

Small Frogs

We climbed to the pond,
I and my cousin,
And frogs by the swarm
And bundle and dozen

Came bustling down
The coal-dark hill.
So many frogs
We both stood still.

Each black frog
Was spider-small,
Small as clover,
As a fingernail.

Small as raindrops
They hurried through the grass
As we stood watching
The baby frogs pass.

And two little frogs
From the pilgrimage
I put in prison
In my fingers' cage.

They were so light,
Their skin so cool,
I could not feel them
There at all

But watched them sitting
On my hand,
Two alive creatures
Of water and land,

Their legs no longer
Than a drawing-pin,
Their wide mouths drinking
The warm air in,

Their skin like paper,
Their tiny paws,

The brilliant particles
Of their eyes,

And put them down
And watched them go,
All knowing something
We can't know.

They'd lived in water!
They'd grown four legs!
What a world we live in
For boys and frogs.

Leslie Norris

A narrow Fellow in the Grass
Occasionally rides—
You may have met Him—did you not
His notice sudden is—

The Grass divides as with a Comb—
A spotted shaft is seen—
And then it closes at your feet
And opens further on—

He likes a Boggy Acre
A Floor too cool for Corn—
Yet when a Boy, and Barefoot—
I more than once at Noon
Have passed, I thought, a Whip lash
Unbraiding in the Sun
When stooping to secure it
It wrinkled, and was gone—

Several of Nature's People
I know, and they know me—
I feel for them a transport
Of cordiality—

But never met this Fellow
Attended, or alone
Without a tighter breathing
And Zero at the Bone—

Emily Dickinson

Well! Hello down there,
friend snail! When did you arrive
in such a hurry?

Issa

The Grasshopper

Down
a
deep
well
a
grasshopper
fell.
By kicking about
He thought to get out.
He might have known better,
For that got him wetter.
To kick round and round
Is the way to get drowned,
And drowning is what
I should tell you he got.
But
the
well
had
a
rope
that
dangled
some
hope.
And sure as molasses
On one of his passes
He found the rope handy
And up he went, *and he*
it
up
and
it
up
and
it
up
and
it
up
went
And hopped away proper
As any grasshopper.

David McCord

The Mosquito

A mosquito tried to provoke
and bite an old fox one day.
The fox just flicked it away
and treated it as a joke.
The mosquito managed to cloak
its body but not its buzz.
The wily old fox, which was
hardly taken by surprise,
asked growling, "Why all the disguise
when I recognize your buzz?"

Translated by *Cheli Durán*

Un mosquito

Un mosquito impertinente
picar a un zorro quería,
pero éste se defendía
y lo burlaba altamente.
Sin usar voz diferente
se disfraza en el vestido;
el zorro lo ha conocido
y le dice con ultraje:
—¿Qué importa mudes de traje
si no mudas el zumbido?

(Anonymous)

The Meadow Mouse

1

In a shoe box stuffed in an old nylon stocking
Sleeps the baby mouse I found in the
    meadow,
Where he trembled and shook beneath a
    stick

"The Grasshopper" from ONE AT A TIME by David McCord (British title: MR. BIDERY'S SPIDERY GARDEN). Copyright 1952 by David McCord. Reprinted by permission of Little, Brown and Company and George G. Harrap Ltd.

"The Mosquito" from THE YELLOW CANARY WHOSE EYE IS SO BLACK edited and translated by Cheli Durán. Copyright © 1977 by Cheli Durán Ryan. Reprinted by permission of Macmillan Publishing Co., Inc.

"The Meadow Mouse" copyright © 1963 by Beatrice Roethke as Administratrix to the Estate of Theodore Roethke from THE COLLECTED POEMS OF THEODORE ROETHKE. Reprinted by permission of Doubleday & Company, Inc. and Faber and Faber Ltd.

Till I caught him up by the tail and brought
    him in,
Cradled in my hand,
A little quaker, the whole body of him trem-
    bling,
His absurd whiskers sticking out like a car-
    toon-mouse,
His feet like small leaves,
Little lizard-feet,
Whitish and spread wide when he tried to
    struggle away,
Wriggling like a miniscule puppy.

Now he's eaten his three kinds of cheese and
    drunk from his bottle-cap watering-
    trough—
So much he just lies in one corner,
His tail curled under him, his belly big
As his head; his bat-like ears
Twitching, tilting toward the least sound.

Do I imagine he no longer trembles
When I come close to him?
He seems no longer to tremble.

2

But this morning the shoe-box house on the
    back porch is empty.
Where has he gone, my meadow mouse,
My thumb of a child that nuzzled in my
    palm?—
To run under the hawk's wing,
Under the eye of the great owl watching
    from the elm-tree,
To live by courtesy of the shrike, the snake,
    the tom-cat.

I think of the nestling fallen into the deep
    grass,
The turtle gasping in the dusty rubble of the
    highway,

The paralytic stunned in the tub, and the
    water rising,—
All things innocent, hapless, forsaken.

Theodore Roethke

Mice

I think mice
Are rather nice.

    Their tails are long,
    Their faces small,
    They haven't any
    Chins at all.

    Their ears are pink,
    Their teeth are white,
    They run about
    The house at night.
    They nibble things
    They shouldn't touch
    And no one seems
    To like them much.

But *I* think mice
Are nice.

Rose Fyleman

The Little Turtle

There was a little turtle.
He lived in a box.
He swam in a puddle.
He climbed on the rocks.

He snapped at a mosquito.
He snapped at a flea.
He snapped at a minnow.
And he snapped at me.

He caught the mosquito.
He caught the flea.
He caught the minnow.
But he didn't catch me.

Vachel Lindsay

Little Snail

I saw a little snail
Come down the garden walk.
He wagged his head this way . . .
     that way . . .
Like a clown in a circus.
He looked from side to side
As though he were from a different country.
I have always said he carries his house on his
     back . . .
To-day in the rain
I saw that it was his umbrella!

Hilda Conkling

*Meditations
of a Tortoise
Dozing under a Rosetree
near a Beehive
at Noon
while
a Dog
scampers about
and a Cuckoo calls
from a
Distant Wood*

So far as I can see,
There is no one like me.

E. V. Rieu

Dogs and Cats
"little wiggly warmness"

Bow, wow, wow!
Whose dog art thou?
Little Tommy Tinker's dog.
   Bow, wow, wow!

(Mother Goose)

The Animal Store

If I had a hundred dollars to spend,
   Or maybe a little more,
I'd hurry as fast as my legs would go
   Straight to the animal store.

I wouldn't say, "How much for this
      or that?"—
   "What kind of a dog is he?"
I'd buy as many as rolled an eye,
   Or wagged a tail at me!

I'd take the hound with the drooping ears
   That sits by himself alone;
Cockers and Cairns and wobbly pups
   For to be my very own.

I might buy a parrot all red and green,
   And the monkey I saw before,
If I had a hundred dollars to spend,
   Or maybe a little more.

Rachel Field

Ding, dong, bell!
Pussy's in the well!
   Who put her in?
Little Johnny Green.
   Who pulled her out?
Little Johnny Stout.

(Mother Goose)

At Night

When night is dark
my cat is wise
to light the lanterns
in his eyes.

Aileen Fisher

Concrete Cat

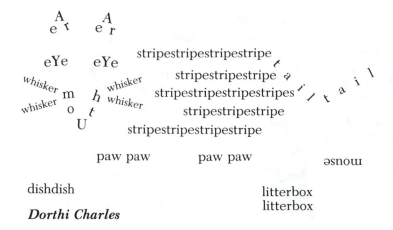

Dorthi Charles

Cat

The black cat yawns,
Opens her jaws,
Stretches her legs,
And shows her claws.

Then she gets up
And stands on four
Long stiff legs
And yawns some more.

She shows her sharp teeth,
She stretches her lip,
Her slice of a tongue
Turns up at the tip.

Lifting herself
On her delicate toes,
She arches her back
As high as it goes.

She lets herself down
With particular care,
And pads away
With her tail in the air.

Mary Britton Miller

The Mysterious Cat

I saw a proud, mysterious cat,
I saw a proud, mysterious cat
Too proud to catch a mouse or rat—
Mew, mew, mew.

But catnip she would eat, and purr,
But catnip she would eat, and purr.
And goldfish she did much prefer—
Mew, mew, mew.

I saw a cat—'twas but a dream,
I saw a cat—'twas but a dream,
Who scorned the slave that brought her
     cream—
Mew, mew, mew.

Unless the slave were dressed in style,
Unless the slave were dressed in style
And knelt before her all the while—
Mew, mew, mew.

Did you ever hear of a thing like that?
Did you ever hear of a thing like that?
Did you ever hear of a thing like that?
Oh, what a proud mysterious cat.
Oh, what a proud mysterious cat.
Oh, what a proud mysterious cat.
Mew . . . Mew . . . Mew.

Vachel Lindsay

The Lost Cat

She took a last and simple meal when there
      were none to see her steal—
   A jug of cream upon the shelf, a fish pre-
      pared for dinner;
And now she walks a distant street with deli-
      cately sandalled feet,
   And no one gives her much to eat or weeps
      to see her thinner.

O my belovèd, come again, come back in joy,
      come back in pain,
   To end our searching with a mew, or with
      a purr our grieving;
And you shall have for lunch or tea whatever
      fish swim in the sea
   And all the cream that's meant for me—
      and not a word of thieving!

E. V. Rieu

Moon

I have a white cat whose name is Moon;
He eats catfish from a wooden spoon,
And sleeps till five each afternoon.

Moon goes out when the moon is bright
And sycamore trees are spotted white
To sit and stare in the dead of night.

Beyond still water cries a loon,
Through mulberry leaves peers a wild
      baboon,
And in Moon's eyes I see the moon.

William Jay Smith

The Prayer of the Cat

Lord,
I am the cat.
It is not, exactly, that I have something to ask
   of You!
No—
I ask nothing of anyone—
but,
if You have by some chance, in some celestial
      barn,
a little white mouse,
or a saucer of milk,
I know someone who would relish them.
Wouldn't You like someday
to put a curse on the whole race of dogs?
If so I should say,
                                    Amen

Carmen Bernos de Gasztold
Translated by *Rumer Godden*

Vern

When walking in a tiny rain
Across the vacant lot,
A pup's a good companion—
If a pup you've got.

And when you've had a scold,
And no one loves you very,
And you cannot be merry,
A pup will let you look at him,
And even let you hold
His little wiggly warmness—

And let you snuggle down beside.
Nor mock the tears you have to hide.

Gwendolyn Brooks

Buying a Puppy

"Bring an old towel," said Pa,
"And a scrap of meat from the pantry.
We're going out in the car, you and I,
Into the country."

I did as he said, although
I couldn't see why he wanted
A scrap of meat and an old towel.
Into the sun we pointed

Our Ford, over the green hills.
Pa sang. Larks bubbled in the sky.
I took with me all my cards—
It was my seventh birthday.

We turned down a happy lane,
Half sunlight, half shadow,
And saw at the end a white house
In a yellow meadow.

Mrs. Garner lived there. She was tall.
She gave me a glass of milk
And showed me her black spaniel.
"Her name is Silk,"

Mrs. Garner said. "She's got
Three puppies, two black, one golden.
Come and see them." Oh,
To have one, one of my own!

"You can choose one," said Pa.
I looked at him. He wasn't joking.

I could scarcely say thank you,
I was almost choking.

It was the golden one. He slept
On my knee in the old towel
All the way home. He was tiny,
But he didn't whimper or howl,

Not once. That was a year ago,
And now I'm eight.
When I get home from school
He'll be waiting behind the gate,

Listening, listening hard,
Head raised, eyes warm and kind;
He came to me as a gift
And grew into a friend.

Leslie Norris

Sunning

Old Dog lay in the summer sun
Much too lazy to rise and run.
He flapped an ear
At a buzzing fly.
He winked a half opened
Sleepy eye.
He scratched himself
On an itching spot,
As he dozed on the porch
Where the sun was hot.
He whimpered a bit
From force of habit
While he lazily dreamed
Of chasing a rabbit.
But Old Dog happily lay in the sun
Much too lazy to rise and run.

James S. Tippett

The Old Dog's Song

What does the old dog say?
Well, here's another day
To sit in the sun.
And when my master's up
I'll skip around like a pup
And we'll go for a run.
But now I'll lift my head
Out of my warm bed
To greet the dawn,
Sigh gently, and slowly turn,
Slowly lie down again,
And gently yawn.

All night I've kept an eye
Open protectingly
In case of danger.
If anything had gone wrong,
I would have raised my strong
Voice in anger.
But all was safe and still.
The sun's come over the hill,
No need for warning.
When he comes down the stair
I shall be waiting there
To say Good Morning.

Leslie Norris

Lone Dog

I'm a lean dog, a keen dog, a wild dog, and
    lone;
I'm a rough dog, a tough dog, hunting on my
    own;
I'm a bad dog, a mad dog, teasing silly sheep;
I love to sit and bay the moon, to keep fat
    souls from sleep.

I'll never be a lap dog, licking dirty feet,
A sleek dog, a meek dog, cringing for my
    meat,
Not for me the fireside, the well-filled plate,
But shut door, and sharp stone, and cuff, and
    kick, and hate.
Not for me the other dogs, running by my
    side,
Some have run a short while, but none of
    them would bide.
O mine is still the lone trail, the hard trail,
    the best,
Wide wind, and wild stars, and hunger of the
    quest!

Irene Rutherford McLeod

Meditatio

When I carefully consider the curious habits
    of dogs
I am compelled to conclude
That man is the superior animal.

When I consider the curious habits of man
I confess, my friend, I am puzzled.

Ezra Pound

The Naming of Cats

The Naming of Cats is a difficult matter,
    It isn't just one of your holiday games;
You may think at first I'm as mad as a hatter
When I tell you, a cat must have THREE
    DIFFERENT NAMES.
First of all, there's the name that the family
    use daily,
    Such as Peter, Augustus, Alonzo or James,
Such as Victor or Jonathan, George or
    Bill Bailey—
    All of them sensible everyday names.
There are fancier names if you think they
    sound sweeter,
    Some for the gentlemen, some for the
    dames:
Such as Plato, Admetus, Electra, Demeter—
    But all of them sensible everyday names.

But I tell you, a cat needs a name that's
    particular,
    A name that's peculiar, and more
    dignified,
Else how can he keep up his tail perpen-
    dicular,
    Or spread out his whiskers, or cherish his
    pride?
Of names of this kind, I can give you a
    quorum,
    Such as Munkustrap, Quaxo, or Coricopat,
Such as Bombalurina, or else Jellylorum—
    Names that never belong to more than
    one cat.
But above and beyond there's still one name
    left over,
    And that is the name that you never will
    guess;
The name that no human research can
    discover—
    But THE CAT HIMSELF KNOWS, and will
    never confess.
When you notice a cat in profound medita-
    tion,
    The reason, I tell you, is always the same:
His mind is engaged in a rapt contemplation
    Of the thought, of the thought, of the
    thought of his name:
        His ineffable effable
        Effanineffable
Deep and inscrutable singular Name.

T. S. Eliot

Macavity: The Mystery Cat

Macavity's a Mystery Cat: he's called the
    Hidden Paw—
For he's the master criminal who can defy
    the Law.
He's the bafflement of Scotland Yard, the
    Flying Squad's despair:
For when they reach the scene of crime—
    Macavity's not there!

Macavity, Macavity, there's no one like
    Macavity,
He's broken every human law, he breaks the
    law of gravity.

His powers of levitation would make a fakir
    stare,
And when you reach the scene of crime—
    Macavity's not there!
You may seek him in the basement, you may
    look up in the air—
But I tell you once and once again,
    Macavity's not there!

Macavity's a ginger cat, he's very tall and
    thin;
You would know him if you saw him, for his
    eyes are sunken in.
His brow is deeply lined with thought, his
    head is highly domed;
His coat is dusty from neglect, his whiskers
    are uncombed.
He sways his head from side to side, with
    movements like a snake;
And when you think he's half asleep, he's
    always wide awake.

Macavity, Macavity; there's no one like
    Macavity,
For he's a fiend in feline shape, a monster of
    depravity.
You may meet him in a by-street, you may
    see him in the square—
But when a crime's discovered, then
    Macavity's not there!

He's outwardly respectable. (They say he
    cheats at cards.)
And his footprints are not found in any file of
    Scotland Yard's.
And when the larder's looted, or the jewel-
    case is rifled,
Or when the milk is missing, or another
    Peke's been stifled,
Or the greenhouse glass is broken, and the
    trellis past repair—
Ay, there's the wonder of the thing!
    Macavity's not there!

And when the Foreign Office find a Treaty's
    gone astray,
Or the Admiralty lose some plans and draw-
    ings by the way,
There may be a scrap of paper in the hall or
    on the stair—
But it's useless to investigate—*Macavity's
    not there!*

And when the loss has been disclosed, the
   Secret Service say:
"It *must* have been Macavity!"—but he's a
   mile away.
You'll be sure to find him resting, or a-licking
   of his thumbs,
Or engaged in doing complicated long divi-
   sion sums.

Macavity, Macavity, there's no one like
   Macavity,
There never was a Cat of such deceitfulness
   and suavity.
He always has an alibi, and one or two to
   spare:
At whatever time the deed took place—
   MACAVITY WASN'T THERE!
And they say that all the Cats whose wicked
   deeds are widely known,
(I might mention Mungojerrie, I might men-
   tion Griddlebone)
Are nothing more than agents for the Cat
   who all the time
Just controls their operations: the Napoleon
   of Crime!

T. S. Eliot

The Cat and the Moon

The cat went here and there
And the moon spun round like a top,
And the nearest kin of the moon,
The creeping cat, looked up.
Black Minnaloushe stared at the moon,
For, wander and wail as he would,
The pure cold light in the sky
Troubled his animal blood.
Minnaloushe runs in the grass
Lifting his delicate feet.
Do you dance, Minnaloushe, do you dance?
When two close kindred meet,
What better than call a dance?

Maybe the moon may learn,
Tired of that courtly fashion,
A new dance turn.
Minnaloushe creeps through the grass
From moonlit place to place,
The sacred moon overhead
Has taken a new phase.
Does Minnaloushe know that his pupils
Will pass from change to change,
And that from round to crescent,
From crescent to round they range?
Minnaloushe creeps through the grass
Alone, important and wise,
And lifts to the changing moon
His changing eyes.

William Butler Yeats

Fiddle-I-Fee

Had me a cat, the cat pleased me,
I fed my cat in yonders tree,
Cat went fiddle-i-fee.

Had me a hen, and the hen pleased me,
I fed my hen in yonders tree,
Hen went kaa-kaa-kaa,
And the cat went fiddle-i-fee.

Had me a pig and the pig pleased me,
And I fed my pig on yonders tree,
Pig went krucy-krucy,
The hen went kaa-kaa-kaa,
And the cat went fiddle-i-fee.

Had me a dog and the dog pleased me,
And I fed my dog in yonders tree,
Dog went boo-boo-boo,
The pig went krucy-krucy,
The hen went kaa-kaa-kaa,
And the cat went fiddle-i-fee.

Had me a sheep, the sheep pleased me,
I fed my sheep in yonders tree,
Sheep went baa-baa-baa,
The dog went boo-boo-boo,
The pig went krucy-krucy,
The hen went kaa-kaa-kaa,
And the cat went fiddle-i-fee.

(American Folk)

Diamond Cut Diamond

Two cats
One up a tree
One under the tree
The cat up a tree is he
The cat under the tree is she
The tree is witch elm, just incidentally.
He takes no notice of she, she takes no notice of he.
He stares at the woolly clouds passing, she stares at the tree.
There's been a lot written about cats, by Old Possum, Yeats and Company
But not Alfred de Musset or Lord Tennyson or Poe or anybody
Wrote about one cat under, and one cat up, a tree.
God knows why this should be left for me
Except I like cats as cats be
Especially one cat up
And one cat under
A witch elm
Tree.

Ewart Milne

"Diamond Cut Diamond" by Ewart Milne from DIAMOND
CUT DIAMOND. Reprinted by permission of the author.

Animals
"I think I could turn and live with animals"

Baa, baa, black sheep,
  Have you any wool?
Yes, marry, have I,
  Three bags full;

One for my master,
  One for my dame,
But none for the little boy
  Who cries in the lane.

(Mother Goose)

I think I could turn and live with animals,
    they are so placid and self-contain'd,
I stand and look at them long and long.

They do not sweat and whine about their
    condition,
They do not lie awake in the dark and weep
    for their sins,
They do not make me sick discussing their
    duty to God,

Not one is dissatisfied, not one is demented
    with the mania of owning things,
Not one kneels to another, nor to his kind
    that lived thousands of years ago,
Not one is respectable or unhappy over the
    whole earth.

Walt Whitman

Dinosaurs

Dinosaurs
Do not count,
Because
They are all
Dead:

None of us
Saw them, dogs
Do not even
Know that
They were there—

But they
Still walk
About heavily
In everybody's
Head.

Valerie Worth

When Dinosaurs Ruled the Earth

Brontosaurus, diplodocus, gentle trachodon,
Dabbled in the muds of time,
Once upon, upon.

Tyrannosaurus raised his head
And rolled his evil eye,
Bared his long and yellow teeth
And bid his neighbors 'bye.
His pygmy brain was slow to grasp
The happenings of the day,
And so he roamed and slew his friends
And ate without delay.

Brontosaurus, diplodocus, gentle trachodon,
Dabbled in the muds of time,
Once upon, upon.

  Allosaurus awed his foe,
  He awed his friends who passed,
  His teeth were made for tearing flesh,
  His teeth were made to gnash.
  Taller than a building now,
  Taller than a tree,
  He roamed about the swamp-filled world
  And ate his company.

Brontosaurus, diplodocus, gentle trachodon,
Dabbled in the muds of time,
Once upon, upon.

  Eaters of their friends and foe
  Or dabblers in the slime,
  Their pygmy brains were slow to grasp,
  Once upon a time.

Patricia Hubbell

Dinosaur Din

Did stegosaurus bellow
Like a longhorn steer from Texas?
Could a bird's sweet tweet
Conceivably beat
Tyrannosaurus rex's?

Did pterodactyl cackle?
Did brachiosaurus bray?
Did monoclonius toot
Through his horny snoot
Ta ra ra boom de ay?

Did little lambeosauruses baa
Or bay like hounds in chorus?
Did the ankles clank
Like an army tank
Upon ankylosaurus?

Today, cars, planes and subway trains
Make a hubbubish hullabaloo
But the rumble and roar
Of a dinosaur
I never have heard. Have you?

X. J. Kennedy

Grizzly Bear

If you ever, ever, ever meet a grizzly bear,
You must never, never, never ask him *where*
He is going,
Or *what* he is doing;
For if you ever, ever, dare
To stop a grizzly bear,
You will never meet *another* grizzly bear.

Mary Austin

The Polar Bear

The Polar Bear is unaware
    Of cold that cuts me through:
For why? He has a coat of hair.
    I wish I had one too!

Hilaire Belloc

Buffalo Dusk

The buffaloes are gone.
And those who saw the buffaloes are gone.
Those who saw the buffaloes by thousands and
    how they pawed the prairie sod into dust
    with their hoofs, their great heads down
    pawing on in a great pageant of dusk,
Those who saw the buffaloes are gone.
And the buffaloes are gone.

Carl Sandburg

    X. J. Kennedy, "Dinosaur Din," in THE PHANTOM ICE CREAM MAN: MORE NONSENSE VERSE. Copyright © 1979 by X. J. Kennedy. A Margaret K. McElderry book (New York: Atheneum, 1979). Reprinted with the permission of Atheneum Publishers and Curtis Brown Ltd.

    "Grizzly Bear" from THE CHILDREN SING IN THE FAR WEST by Mary Austin. Copyright 1928 by Mary Austin. Copyright renewed 1956 by Kenneth M. Chapman and March C. Wheelwright. Reprinted by permission of Houghton Mifflin Company.

    "The Polar Bear" from CAUTIONARY VERSES by Hilaire Belloc (British title: COMPLETE VERSE). Published 1941 by Alfred A. Knopf, Inc. Reprinted by permission of Alfred A. Knopf, Inc. and Gerald Duckworth & Co. Ltd.

    "Buffalo Dusk" from SMOKE AND STEEL by Carl Sandburg. Copyright 1920 by Harcourt Brace Jovanovich, Inc.; copyright 1948 by Carl Sandburg. Reprinted by permission of the publisher.

Speaking of Cows

Speaking of cows
(Which no one was doing)
Why are they always
Staring and chewing?
Staring at people,
Chewing at clover,
Doing the same things
Over and over?

Once in a while,
You see a cow mooing,
Swishing her tail
At a fly that needs shooing.
Most of the time, though,
What's a cow doing?
Munching and looking,
Staring and chewing.

Eyes never blinking,
Jaws always moving,
What are cows thinking?
What are they *proving?*

Cows mustn't care for
New ways of doing.
That's what they stare for;
That's why they're chewing.

Kaye Starbird

Whoopee Ti Yi Yo, Git Along Little Dogies

As I walked out one morning for pleasure,
I spied a cow-puncher all riding alone;
His hat was thrown back and his spurs was
    a-jingling,
And he approached me a-singin' this song,

Whoopee ti yi yo, git along little dogies,
It's your misfortune, and none of my own.
Whoopee ti yi yo, git along little dogies,
For you know Wyoming will be your new
    home.

"Speaking of Cows" from SPEAKING OF COWS AND
OTHER POEMS by Kaye Starbird. Reprinted by permission of
Paul R. Reynolds, Inc., 12 East 41st Street, New York, NY 10017.

"Whoopee Ti Yi Yo, Git Along Little Dogies" from COW-
BOY SONGS, compiled by J. A. Lomax.

"How doth the little crocodile" from ALICE'S ADVEN-
TURES IN WONDERLAND by Lewis Carroll.

Early in the spring we round up the dogies,
Mark and brand and bob off their tails;
Round up our horses, load up the chuck-
    wagon,
Then throw the dogies upon the trail.

It's whooping and yelling and driving the
    dogies;
Oh how I wish you would go on;
It's whooping and punching and go on little
    dogies,
For you know Wyoming will be your new
    home.

Some boys goes up the trail for pleasure,
But that's where you get it most awfully
    wrong:
For you haven't any idea the trouble they
    give us
While we go driving them along.

When the night comes on and we hold them
    on the bedground,
These little dogies that roll on so slow;
Roll up the herd and cut out the strays,
And roll the little dogies that never rolled
    before.

Your mother she was raised way down in
    Texas,
Where the jimson weed and sand-burrs
    grow;
Now we'll fill you up on prickly pear and
    cholla
Till you are ready for the trail to Idaho.

Oh, you'll be soup for Uncle Sam's Injuns;
"It's beef, heap beef," I hear them cry.
Git along, git along, git along little dogies,
You're going to be beef steers by and by.

(Unknown)

How doth the little crocodile
    Improve his shining tail,
And pour the waters of the Nile
    On every golden scale!

How cheerfully he seems to grin,
    How neatly spreads his claws,
And welcomes little fishes in,
    With gently smiling jaws!

Lewis Carroll

Don't Ever Cross a Crocodile

Don't ever cross a crocodile,
However few his faults.
Don't ever dare
A dancing bear
To teach you how to waltz.

Don't ever poke a rattlesnake
Who's sleeping in the sun
And say the poke
Was just a joke
And really all in fun.

Don't ever lure a lion close
With gifts of steak and suet.
Though lion-looks
Are nice in books,
Don't ever, ever do it.

Kaye Starbird

The Octopus

Tell me, O Octopus, I begs,
Is those things arms, or is they legs?
I marvel at thee, Octopus;
If I were thou, I'd call me Us.

Ogden Nash

The Elephant

When people call this beast to mind,
　They marvel more and more
At such a *little* tail behind,
　So LARGE a trunk before.

Hilaire Belloc

Oliphaunt

Grey as a mouse,
Big as a house,
Nose like a snake,
I make the earth shake,
As I tramp through the grass;
Trees crack as I pass.

With horns in my mouth
I walk in the South,
Flapping big ears.
Beyond count of years
I stump round and round,
Never lie on the ground,
Not even to die.
Oliphaunt am I,
Biggest of all,
Huge, old, and tall.
If ever you'd met me,
You wouldn't forget me.
If you never do,
You won't think I'm true;
But old Oliphaunt am I,
And I never lie.

J. R. R. Tolkien

Foal

Come trotting up
Beside your mother,
Little skinny.

Lay your neck across
Her back, and whinny,
Little foal.

You think you're a horse
Because you can trot—
But you're not.

Your eyes are so wild,
And each leg is as tall
As a pole;

And you're only a skittish
Child, after all,
Little foal.

Mary Britton Miller

The Runaway

Once, when the snow of the year was begin-
ning to fall,
We stopped by a mountain pasture to say,
"Whose colt?"
A little Morgan had one forefoot on the wall,
The other curled at his breast. He dipped his
head
And snorted to us. And then he had to bolt.
We heard the miniature thunder where he
fled
And we saw him or thought we saw him dim
and gray,
Like a shadow against the curtain of falling
flakes.
"I think the little fellow's afraid of the snow.
He isn't winter-broken. It isn't play
With the little fellow at all. He's running
away.
I doubt if even his mother could tell him,
'Sakes,
It's only weather.' He'd think she didn't
know!
Where is his mother? He can't be out alone."
And now he comes again with a clatter of
stone,
And mounts the wall again with whited eyes
And all his tail that isn't hair up straight.

"The Runaway" from THE POETRY OF ROBERT FROST edited by Edward Connery Lathem. Copyright 1916, 1923, 1939, © 1967, 1969 by Holt, Rinehart and Winston. Copyright 1942, 1944, 1951 by Robert Frost. Copyright © 1970 by Lesley Frost Ballantine. Reprinted by permission of Holt, Rinehart and Winston, Publishers and the Estate of Robert Frost.

"Giraffes" from THE RAUCOUS AUK by Mary Ann Hoberman. Text Copyright © 1973 by Mary Ann Hoberman. Reprinted by permission of Viking Penguin Inc.

"The Horse" from THE YELLOW CANARY WHOSE EYE IS SO BLACK edited and translated by Cheli Durán. Copyright © 1977 by Cheli Durán Ryan. Reprinted by permission of Macmillan Publishing Co., Inc.

He shudders his coat as if to throw off flies.
"Whoever it is that leaves him out so late,
When other creatures have gone to stall and
bin,
Ought to be told to come and take him in."

Robert Frost

Giraffes

I like them.
Ask me why.
    Because they hold their heads so high.
    Because their necks stretch to the sky.
    Because they're quiet, calm, and shy.
    Because they run so fast they fly.
    Because their eyes are velvet brown.
    Because their coats are spotted tan.
    Because they eat the tops of trees.
    Because their legs have knobby knees.
    Because
    Because
    Because. That's why
I like giraffes.

Mary Ann Hoberman

The Horse

Under pared moons
it walks around,
a horse once killed
on a battleground.

Its ghostly hoofs . . .
it shudders, slips,
and darkly neighs
to distant whips.

At the leaden bend
of the barricade,
with hollow eyes
it stops, afraid.

And later its slow
step retreats
through ruined squares,
desolate streets.

Translated by *Cheli Durán*

El caballo

Viene por las calles,
a la luna parva,
un caballo muerto
en antigua batalla.

Sus cascos sombríos . . .
trepida, resbala;
da un hosco relincho
con sus voces lejanas.

En la plúmbea esquina
de la barricada,
con ojos vacíos
y con horror, se para.

Más tarde se escuchan
sus lentas pisadas,
por vías desiertas,
y por ruinosas plazas.

José Maria Eguren

The Lamb

  Little Lamb, who made thee?
  Dost thou know who made thee?
Gave thee life, and bid thee feed,
By the stream and o'er the mead;
Gave thee clothing of delight,
Softest clothing, woolly, bright;
Gave thee such a tender voice,
Making all the vales rejoice?
  Little Lamb, who made thee?
  Dost thou know who made thee?

  Little Lamb, I'll tell thee,
  Little Lamb, I'll tell thee:
He is callèd by thy name,
For He calls Himself a Lamb.
He is meek, and He is mild;
He became a little child.
I a child, and thou a lamb,
We are callèd by His name.
  Little Lamb, God bless thee!
  Little Lamb, God bless thee!

William Blake

Saucy Little Ocelot

Saucy, little ocelot
    ocelot
        ocelot
You like to turn and toss a lot
    toss a lot
        ocelot
You often fret and fuss a lot
    fuss a lot
        ocelot
Speckled, spotted
    polka-dotted
Saucy little ocelot

Saucy little ocelot
    ocelot
        ocelot
You're often mean and cross a lot
    cross a lot
        ocelot
You want to be the boss a lot
    boss a lot
        ocelot
Bossy, brassy
    cross and sassy
Saucy little ocelot

Jack Prelutsky

White Season

In the winter the rabbits match their pelts to
        the earth.
With ears laid back, they go
Blown through the silver hollow, the silver
        thicket,
Like puffs of snow.

Frances M. Frost

The Prayer of the Little Pig

Lord,
their politeness makes me laugh!
Yes, I grunt!
Grunt and snuffle!
I grunt because I grunt
and snuffle
because I cannot do anything else!
All the same, I am not going to thank them
for fattening me up to make bacon.
Why did You make me so tender?
What a fate!
Lord,
teach me how to say

                                            Amen

Carmen Bernos de Gasztold
Translated by *Rumer Godden*

Rhinoceros

I often wonder whether
The rhinoceros's leather
Is as bumpy on the inside
As it is upon the skinside.

Mary Ann Hoberman

The Snare

I hear a sudden cry of pain!
There is a rabbit in a snare:
Now I hear the cry again,
But I cannot tell from where.

But I cannot tell from where
He is calling out for aid!
Crying on the frightened air,
Making everything afraid!

Making everything afraid!
Wrinkling up his little face!
As he cries again for aid;
—And I cannot find the place!

And I cannot find the place
Where his paw is in the snare!
Little One! Oh, Little One!
I am searching everywhere!

James Stephens

Seal

See how he dives
From the rocks with a zoom!
See how he darts
Through his watery room
Past crabs and eels
And green seaweed,
Past fluffs of sandy
Minnow feed!
See how he swims
With a swerve and a twist,
A flip of the flipper,
A flick of the wrist!
Quicksilver-quick,
Softer than spray,
Down he plunges
And sweeps away;
Before you can think,
Before you can utter
Words like "Dill pickle"
Or "Apple butter,"
Back up he swims
Past Sting Ray and Shark,
Out with a zoom,
A whoop, a bark;
Before you can say
Whatever you wish,
He plops at your side
With a mouthful of fish!

William Jay Smith

To a Squirrel at Kyle-Na-No

Come play with me;
Why should you run
Through the shaking tree
As though I'd a gun
To strike you dead?
When all I would do
Is to scratch your head
And let you go.

William Butler Yeats

The Tiger

Tiger! Tiger! burning bright
In the forests of the night,
What immortal hand or eye
Could frame thy fearful symmetry?

In what distant deeps or skies
Burnt the fire of thine eyes?
On what wings dare he aspire?
What the hand dare seize the fire?

And what shoulder, and what art,
Could twist the sinews of thy heart?
And when thy heart began to beat,
What dread hand? and what dread feet?

What the hammer? what the chain?
In what furnace was thy brain?
What the anvil? what dread grasp
Dare its deadly terrors clasp?

When the stars threw down their spears,
And watered heaven with their tears,
Did He smile His work to see?
Did He who made the Lamb make thee?

Tiger! Tiger! burning bright
In the forests of the night,
What immortal hand or eye
Dare frame thy fearful symmetry?

William Blake

The Yak

There was a most odious Yak
Who took only toads on his Back:
If you asked for a Ride,
He would act very Snide,
And go humping off, yicketty-yak.

Theodore Roethke

"To a Squirrel at Kyle-Na-No" from COLLECTED POEMS by William Butler Yeats. Copyright 1919 by Macmillan Publishing Co., Inc., renewed 1947 by Bertha Georgie Yeats. Reprinted by permission of Macmillan Publishing Co., Inc. and A. P. Watt Ltd.

"The Tiger" by William Blake.

"The Yak" copyright 1952 by Theodore Roethke from the book THE COLLECTED POEMS OF THEODORE ROETHKE. Reprinted by permission of Doubleday & Company, Inc. and Faber and Faber Ltd.

Birds
"be like the bird"

The north wind doth blow,
And we shall have snow,
And what will poor robin do then?
　　Poor thing.
He'll sit in a barn,
And keep himself warm,
And hide his head under his wing.
　　Poor thing.

(Mother Goose)

There was an Old Man with a beard,
Who said, "It is just as I feared!—
　　Two Owls and a Hen,
　　Four Larks and a Wren,
Have all built their nests in my beard."

Edward Lear

The Blackbird

In the far corner
close by the swings,
every morning
a blackbird sings.

His bill's so yellow,
his coat's so black,
that he makes a fellow
whistle back.

Ann, my daughter,
thinks that he
sings for us two
especially.

Humbert Wolfe

The Last Word of a Bluebird
(As Told to a Child)

As I went out a Crow
In a low voice said 'Oh,
I was looking for you.
How do you do?
I just came to tell you
To tell Lesley (will you?)
That her little Bluebird
Wanted me to bring word
That the north wind last night
That made the stars bright
And made ice on the trough
Almost made him cough
His tail feathers off.
He just had to fly!
But he sent her Good-by,
And said to be good,
And wear her red hood,
And look for skunk tracks
In the snow with an ax—
And do everything!
And perhaps in the spring
He would come back and sing.'

Robert Frost

The Crow

Flying loose and easy, where does he go
Swaggering in the sky, what does he know,
Why is he laughing, the carrion crow?
Why is he shouting, why won't he sing,
How did he steal them, whom will he bring
Loaves of blue heaven under each wing?

Russell Hoban

Ducks' Ditty

All along the backwater,
Through the rushes tall,
Ducks are a-dabbling,
Up tails all!

Ducks' tails, drakes' tails,
Yellow feet a-quiver,
Yellow bills all out of sight
Busy in the river!

Slushy green undergrowth
Where the roach swim—
Here we keep our larder,
Cool and full and dim.

Everyone for what he likes!
We like to be
Heads down, tails up,
Dabbling free!

High in the blue above
Swifts whirl and call—
We are down a-dabbling
Up tails all!

Kenneth Grahame

The Eagle

He clasps the crag with crooked hands;
Close to the sun in lonely lands,
Ringed with the azure world, he stands.

The wrinkled sea beneath him crawls;
He watches from his mountain walls,
And like a thunderbolt he falls.

Alfred, Lord Tennyson

Go Tell Aunt Rhody

Go tell Aunt Rhody,
Go tell Aunt Rhody,
Go tell Aunt Rhody
The old gray goose is dead.

The one she was saving,
The one she was saving,
The one she was saving
To make a feather bed.

The old gander is mourning,
The old gander is mourning,
The old gander is mourning
Because his wife is dead.

The little goslings are weeping,
The little goslings are weeping,
The little goslings are weeping
Because their mammy's dead.

The whole family's weeping,
The whole family's weeping,
The whole family's weeping
Because the mama's dead.

(American Folk)

Something Told the Wild Geese

Something told the wild geese
    It was time to go.
Though the fields lay golden
    Something whispered, "Snow."

"The Crow" from THE PEDALING MAN AND OTHER POEMS by Russell Hoban. Copyright © 1968 by Russell Hoban. Reprinted by permission of Grosset & Dunlap, Inc., and World's Work Ltd.

"Ducks' Ditty" from THE WIND IN THE WILLOWS by Kenneth Grahame. Copyright under the Berne Convention (New York: Charles Scribner's Sons, 1908). Reprinted by permission of Charles Scribner's Sons and Methuen Children's Books.

"The Eagle" by Alfred, Lord Tennyson.

"Go Tell Aunt Rhody" from AMERICAN FOLK POETRY.

"Something Told the Wild Geese" from BRANCHES GREEN by Rachel Field. Copyright 1934 by Macmillan Publishing Co., Inc., renewed 1962 by Arthur S. Pederson. Reprinted by permission of Macmillan Publishing Co., Inc.

Leaves were green and stirring,
    Berries, luster-glossed,
But beneath warm feathers
    Something cautioned, "Frost."
All the sagging orchards
    Steamed with amber spice,
But each wild breast stiffened
    At remembered ice.
Something told the wild geese
    It was time to fly—
Summer sun was on their wings,
    Winter in their cry.

Rachel Field

The Hens

The night was coming very fast;
It reached the gate as I ran past.

The pigeons had gone to the tower of
    the church
And all the hens were on their perch,

Up in the barn, and I thought I heard
A piece of a little purring word.

I stopped inside, waiting and staying,
To try to hear what the hens were saying.

They were asking something, that was plain,
Asking it over and over again.

One of them moved and turned around,
Her feathers made a ruffled sound,

A ruffled sound, like a bushful of birds,
And she said her little asking words.

She pushed her head close into her wing,
But nothing answered anything.

Elizabeth Madox Roberts

    When my canary
flew away, that was the end
of spring in my house.

Shiki

The Mockingbird

Look one way and the sun is going down,
Look the other and the moon is rising.
The sparrow's shadow's longer than the
    lawn.
The bats squeak: "Night is here," the birds
    cheep: "Day is gone."
On the willow's highest branch, monopoliz-
    ing
Day and night, cheeping, squeaking, soaring,
The mockingbird is imitating life.

All day the mockingbird has owned the yard.
As light first woke the world, the sparrows
    trooped
Onto the seedy lawn: the mockingbird
Chased them off shrieking. Hour by hour,
    fighting hard
To make the world his own, he swooped
On thrushes, thrashers, jays, and
    chickadees—
At noon he drove away a big black cat.

"The Hens" from UNDER THE TREE by Elizabeth Madox Roberts. Copyright 1930 by The Viking Press, Inc. Copyright renewed 1958 by Ivor S. Roberts. Reprinted by permission of Viking Penguin Inc.

"When my canary" from CRICKET SONGS: JAPANESE HAIKU translated by Harry Behn. Copyright © 1964 by Harry Behn. Reprinted by permission of Harcourt Brace Jovanovich, Inc. and Curtis Brown Ltd.

"The Mockingbird" from THE BAT-POET by Randall Jarrell. Copyright © 1963, 1964 by Macmillan Publishing Co., Inc. This poem originally appeared in *The New Yorker*. Reprinted by permission of Macmillan Publishing Co., Inc., and Penguin Books Ltd.

Now, in the moonlight, he sits here and sings.
A thrush is singing, then a thrasher,
    then a jay—
Then, all at once, a cat begins meowing.
A mockingbird can sound like anything.
He imitates the world he drove away
So well that for a minute, in the moonlight,
Which one's the mockingbird? which one's
    the world?

Randall Jarrell

Mrs. Peck-Pigeon

Mrs. Peck-Pigeon
Is picking for bread,
Bob-bob-bob
Goes her little round head.
Tame as a pussy-cat
In the street,
Step-step-step
Go her little red feet.
With her little red feet
And her little round head,
Mrs. Peck-Pigeon
Goes picking for bread.

Eleanor Farjeon

The Sparrow Hawk

Wings like pistols flashing at his sides,
Masked, above the meadow runway rides,
Galloping, galloping with an easy rein.
Below, the fieldmouse, where the shadow
    glides,
Holds fast the small purse of his life, and
    hides.

Russell Hoban

There Once Was an Owl

There once was an Owl perched on a shed.
Fifty years later the Owl was dead.

Some say mice are in the corn.
Some say kittens are being born.

Some say a kitten becomes a cat.
Mice are likely to know about that.

Some cats are scratchy, some are not.
Corn grows best when it's damp and hot.

Fifty times fifty years go by.
Corn keeps best when it's cool and dry.

Fifty times fifty and one by one
Night begins when day is done.

Owl on the shed, cat in the clover,
Mice in the corn—it all starts over.

John Ciardi

The Bird of Night

A shadow is floating through the moonlight.
Its wings don't make a sound.
Its claws are long, its beak is bright.
Its eyes try all the corners of the night.

It calls and calls: all the air swells and heaves
And washes up and down like water.
The ear that listens to the owl believes
In death. The bat beneath the eaves,

The mouse beside the stone are still
    as death—
The owl's air washes them like water.
The owl goes back and forth inside the night,
And the night holds its breath.

Randall Jarrell

Song—The Owl

I

When cats run home and light is come,
    And dew is cold upon the ground,
And the far-off stream is dumb,
    And the whirring sail goes round,
    And the whirring sail goes round;
        Alone and warming his five wits,
        The white owl in the belfry sits.

II

When merry milkmaids click the latch,
    And rarely smells the new-mown hay,
And the cock hath sung beneath the thatch
    Twice or thrice his roundelay,
    Twice or thrice his roundelay;
        Alone and warming his five wits,
        The white owl in the belfry sits.

Alfred, Lord Tennyson

The Woodpecker

The woodpecker pecked out a little round
    hole
And made him a house in the telephone pole.

One day when I watched he poked out his
    head,
And he had on a hood and a collar of red.

When the streams of rain pour out of the sky,
And the sparkles of lightning go flashing by,

And the big, big wheels of thunder roll,
He can snuggle back in the telephone pole.

Elizabeth Madox Roberts

A lonely sparrow
Hops upon the snow and prints
Sets of maple leaves.

Kazue Mizumura

Be Like the Bird

Be like the bird, who
Halting in his flight
On limb too slight
Feels it give way beneath him,
Yet sings
Knowing he hath wings.

Victor Hugo

Nonsense

"I never saw a purple cow"

How much wood would a wood-chuck
  chuck
If a wood-chuck could chuck wood?
He would chuck as much wood as a wood-
  chuck would chuck,
If a wood-chuck could chuck wood.

(American Mother Goose)

The Purple Cow

I never saw a Purple Cow,
  I never hope to see one;
But I can tell you, anyhow,
  I'd rather see than be one.

Gelett Burgess

If a pig wore a wig,
  What could we say?
Treat him as a gentleman,
  And say 'Good day.'

If his tail chanced to fail,
  What could we do?—
Send him to the tailoress
  To get one new.

Christina Rossetti

I asked my mother for fifteen cents
To see the elephant jump the fence,
He jumped so high that he touched the sky
And never came back 'till the Fourth of July.

(American Mother Goose)

Eletelephony

Once there was an elephant,
Who tried to use the telephant—
No! no! I mean an elephone
Who tried to use the telephone—
(Dear me! I am not certain quite
That even now I've got it right.)
Howe'er it was, he got his trunk
Entangled in the telephunk;
The more he tried to get it free,
The louder buzzed the telephee—
(I fear I'd better drop the song
Of elephop and telephong!)

Laura E. Richards

"Let's Marry!" Said the Cherry

"Let's marry,"   " 'Cause you're sweet,"
said the cherry.   said the beet.

"Why me?"   "Say you will,"
said the pea.   said the dill.

"How Much Wood Would a Wood-Chuck Chuck" and "I Asked my Mother for Fifteen Cents" from THE AMERICAN MOTHER GOOSE, compiled by Roy Wood.

"The Purple Cow" by Gelett Burgess from THE BURGESS NONSENSE BOOK by Gelett Burgess. Published 1901 by the J. B. Lippincott Co.

"If a pig wore a wig" from SING-SONG by Christina Rossetti.

"Eletelephony" from TIRRA LIRRA: RHYMES OLD AND NEW by Laura E. Richards. Copyright 1932 by Laura E. Richards; © renewed 1960 by Hamilton Richards. Reprinted by permission of Little, Brown and Company.

N. M. Bodecker, "Let's Marry! Said the Cherry," in LET'S MARRY SAID THE CHERRY AND OTHER NONSENSE POEMS. Copyright © 1974 by N. M. Bodecker. A Margaret K. McElderry book (New York: Atheneum, 1974). Reprinted with the permission of Atheneum Publishers and Faber and Faber Ltd.

"Think it over,"
said the clover.

"Come, let's dine,"
said the vine.

"Don't rush,"
said the squash.

"Yeah—let's eat!"
said the wheat.

"Here's your dress,"
said the cress.

"And get stout,"
said the sprout.

"White and green,"
said the bean.

"Just wait,"
said the date.

"And your cape,"
said the grape.

"Who will chime?"
said the lime.

"Trimmed with fur,"
said the burr.

"I'll chime!"
said the thyme.

"Won't that tickle?"
said the pickle.

"Who will preach?"
said the peach.

"Who knows?"
said the rose.

"It's my turn!"
said the fern.

"Where's the chapel?"
said the apple.

"You would ramble,"
said the bramble.

"In Greenwich,"
said the spinach.

"Here they come!"
cried the plum.

"We'll be there!"
said the pear.

"Start the tune!"
cried the prune.

"Wearing what?"
said the nut.

"All together!"
cried the heather.

"Pants and coats,"
said the oats.

"Here we go!"
said the sloe.

"Shoes and socks,"
said the phlox.

"NOW—let's marry!"
said the cherry.

"Shirt and tie,"
said the rye.

"Why me?"
said the pea.

"We'll look jolly,"
said the holly.

"Oh, my gosh!"
said the squash.

"You'll look silly,"
said the lily.

"Start all over,"
said the clover.

"You're crazy,"
said the daisy.

"NO WAY!"
said the hay.

N. M. Bodecker

"The Owl and the Pussy-Cat" from THE OWL AND THE PUSSY-CAT by Edward Lear.

"The Table and the Chair" from THE COMPLETE NONSENSE BOOK by Edward Lear.

The Owl and the Pussy-Cat

The Owl and the Pussy-Cat went to sea
    In a beautiful pea-green boat,
They took some honey, and plenty of money
    Wrapped up in a five-pound note.
The Owl looked up to the stars above,
    And sang to a small guitar,
"O lovely Pussy, O Pussy, my love,
    What a beautiful Pussy you are,
            You are,
            You are!
    What a beautiful Pussy you are!"

Pussy said to the Owl, "You elegant fowl,
    How charmingly sweet you sing!
Oh! let us be married, too long we have
    tarried:
    But what shall we do for a ring?"
They sailed away, for a year and a day,
    To the land where the Bong-tree grows;
And there in a wood a Piggy-wig stood,
    With a ring at the end of his nose,
            His nose,
            His nose,
    With a ring at the end of his nose.

"Dear Pig, are you willing to sell for one
    shilling
    Your ring?" Said the Piggy, "I will."
So they took it away, and were married
    next day
    By the Turkey who lives on the hill.
They dined on mince and slices of quince,
    Which they ate with a runcible spoon;
And hand in hand, on the edge of the sand,
    They danced by the light of the moon,
            The moon,
            The moon,
    They danced by the light of the moon.

Edward Lear

The Table and the Chair

I

Said the Table to the Chair,
"You can hardly be aware
How I suffer from the heat
And from chilblains on my feet.

If we took a little walk,
We might have a little talk;
Pray let us take the air,"
Said the Table to the Chair.

II

Said the Chair unto the Table,
"Now, you *know* we are not able:
How foolishly you talk.
When you know we *cannot* walk!"
Said the Table with a sigh,
"It can do no harm to try.
I've as many legs as you:
Why can't we walk on two?"

III

So they both went slowly down,
And walked about the town
With a cheerful bumpy sound
As they toddled round and round;
And everybody cried,
As they hastened to their side,
"See! the Table and the Chair
Have come out to take the air!"

IV

But in going down an alley,
To a castle in a valley,
They completely lost their way,
And wandered all the day;
Till, to see them safely back,
They paid a Ducky-quack,
And a Beetle, and a Mouse,
Who took them to their house.

V

Then they whispered to each other,
"O delightful little brother,
What a lovely walk we've taken!
Let us dine on beans and bacon."
So the Ducky and the leetle
Browny-Mousy and the Beetle
Dined, and danced upon their heads
Till they toddled to their beds.

Edward Lear

Mr. 'Gator

Elevator operator
P. Cornelius Alligator,
when his passengers
were many,
never
ever
passed up
any:
when his passengers
were few,
always managed
to make do.
When they told him:
"Mister 'Gator!
quickly
in your elevator
take us
to the nineteenth floor!"
they were never
seen no more.

N. M. Bodecker

The Microbe

The Microbe is so very small
You cannot make him out at all,
But many sanguine people hope
To see him through a microscope.
His jointed tongue that lies beneath
A hundred curious rows of teeth;
His seven tufted tails with lots
Of lovely pink and purple spots,

On each of which a pattern stands,
Composed of forty separate bands;
His eyebrows of a tender green;
All these have never yet been seen—

N. M. Bodecker, "Mr. 'Gator," in LET'S MARRY SAID THE CHERRY AND OTHER NONSENSE POEMS. Copyright © 1974 by N. M. Bodecker. A Margaret K. McElderry book (New York: Atheneum, 1974). Reprinted with the permission of Atheneum Publishers and Faber and Faber Ltd.

"The Microbe" from CAUTIONARY VERSES by Hilaire Belloc (British title: COMPLETE VERSE). Published 1941 by Alfred A. Knopf, Inc. Reprinted by permission of Alfred A. Knopf, Inc. and Gerald Duckworth & Co. Ltd.

But Scientists, who ought to know,
Assure us that they must be so. . . .
Oh! let us never, never doubt
What nobody is sure about!

Hilaire Belloc

Exploding Gravy

My mother's big green gravy boat
Once thought he was a navy boat.

I poured him over my mashed potatoes
And out swam seven swift torpedoes.

Torpedoes whizzed and whirred, and—
WHAM!
One bumped smack into my hunk of ham

And blew up with an awful roar,
Flinging my carrots on the floor.

Exploding gravy! That's so silly!
Now all I ever eat is chili.

X. J. Kennedy

The Walrus and the Carpenter

The sun was shining on the sea,
  Shining with all his might:
He did his very best to make
  The billows smooth and bright—
And this was odd, because it was
  The middle of the night.

The moon was shining sulkily,
  Because she thought the sun
Had got no business to be there
  After the day was done—
"It's very rude of him," she said,
  "To come and spoil the fun!"

The sea was wet as wet could be,
  The sands were dry as dry.

"Exploding Gravy" from ONE WINTER NIGHT IN AU-
GUST AND OTHER NONSENSE JINGLES by X. J. Kennedy.
Copyright © 1975 by X. J. Kennedy. A Margaret K. McElderry
book (New York: Atheneum, 1975). Reprinted with the permis-
sion of Atheneum Publishers and Curtis Brown Ltd.
  "The Walrus and the Carpenter" by Lewis Carroll.

You could not see a cloud, because
  No cloud was in the sky:
No birds were flying overhead—
  There were no birds to fly.

The Walrus and the Carpenter
  Were walking close at hand:
They wept like anything to see
  Such quantities of sand:
"If this were only cleared away,"
  They said, "it would be grand!"

"If seven maids with seven mops
  Swept it for half a year,
Do you suppose," the Walrus said,
  "That they could get it clear?"
"I doubt it," said the Carpenter,
  And shed a bitter tear.

"O Oysters, come and walk with us!"
  The Walrus did beseech.
"A pleasant walk, a pleasant talk,
  Along the briny beach:
We cannot do with more than four,
  To give a hand to each."

The eldest Oyster looked at him,
  But never a word he said:
The eldest Oyster winked his eye,
  And shook his heavy head—
Meaning to say he did not choose
  To leave the oyster-bed.

But four young Oysters hurried up,
  All eager for the treat:
Their coats were brushed, their faces washed,
  Their shoes were clean and neat—
And this was odd, because, you know,
  They hadn't any feet.

Four other Oysters followed them,
  And yet another four;
And thick and fast they came at last,
  And more, and more, and more—
All hopping through the frothy waves,
  And scrambling to the shore.

The Walrus and the Carpenter
  Walked on a mile or so,
And then they rested on a rock
  Conveniently low:

And all the little Oysters stood
  And waited in a row.

"The time has come," the Walrus said,
  "To talk of many things:
Of shoes—and ships—and sealing wax—
  Of cabbages—and kings—
And why the sea is boiling hot—
  And whether pigs have wings."

"But wait a bit," the Oysters cried,
  "Before we have our chat;
For some of us are out of breath,
  And all of us are fat!"
"No hurry!" said the Carpenter.
  They thanked him much for that.

"A loaf of bread," the Walrus said,
  "Is what we chiefly need:
Pepper and vinegar besides
  Are very good indeed—
Now, if you're ready, Oysters dear,
  We can begin to feed."

"But not on us!" the Oysters cried,
  Turning a little blue.
"After such kindness, that would be
  A dismal thing to do!"
"The night is fine," the Walrus said,
  "Do you admire the view?"

"It was so kind of you to come!
  And you are very nice!"
The Carpenter said nothing but
  "Cut us another slice.
I wish you were not quite so deaf—
  I've had to ask you twice!"

"It seems a shame," the Walrus said,
  "To play them such a trick.
After we've brought them out so far,
  And made them trot so quick!"
The Carpenter said nothing but
  "The butter's spread too thick!"

"I weep for you," the Walrus said:
  "I deeply sympathize."
With sobs and tears he sorted out
  Those of the largest size,
Holding his pocket-handkerchief
  Before his streaming eyes.

"O Oysters," said the Carpenter,
  "You've had a pleasant run!

Shall we be trotting home again?"
  But answer came there none—
And this was scarcely odd, because
  They'd eaten every one.

Lewis Carroll

The Hen and the Carp

  Once, in a roostery
there lived a speckled hen, and whenever she laid an egg this hen
  ecstatically cried:
'O progeny miraculous, particular
  spectaculous,
  what a wonderful hen am I!'

  Down in a pond nearby
perchance a fat and broody carp
was basking, but her ears were sharp—
  she heard Dame Cackle cry:
'O progeny miraculous, particular
  spectaculous,
  what a wonderful hen am I!'

  'Ah, Cackle,' bubbled she,
'for your single egg, O silly one,
I lay at least a million;
  suppose for each I cried:
"O progeny miraculous, particular
  spectaculous!'
  what a hullaballoo there'd be!'

Ian Serraillier

The Six Badgers

As I was a-hoeing, a-hoeing my lands,
Six badgers walked up, with white wands in
  their hands.
They formed a ring round me and, bowing,
  they said:
'Hurry home, Farmer George, for the table
  is spread!
There's pie in the oven, there's beef on the
  plate:

Hurry home, Farmer George, if you would
  not be late!'

So homeward went I, but could not understand
Why six fine dog-badgers with white wands
  in hand
Should seek me out hoeing, and bow in a
  ring,
And all to inform me so common a thing!

Robert Graves

The Stone Troll

Troll sat alone on his seat of stone,
And munched and mumbled a bare old bone;
  For many a year he had gnawed it near,
    For meat was hard to come by.
      Done by! Gum by!
  In a cave in the hills he dwelt alone,
    And meat was hard to come by.

Up came Tom with his big boots on.
Said he to Troll: 'Pray, what is yon?
  For it looks like the shin o' my nuncle Tim,
    As should be a-lyin' in graveyard.
      Caveyard! Paveyard!
  This many a year has Tim been gone,
    And I thought he were lyin' in grave-
    yard.'

'My lad,' said Troll, 'this bone I stole.
But what be bones that lie in a hole?
  Thy nuncle was dead as a lump o' lead,
    Afore I found his shinbone.
      Tinbone! Thinbone!
  He can spare a share for a poor old troll;
    For he don't need his shinbone.'

"The Stone Troll" from THE ADVENTURES OF TOM
BOMBADIL by J. R. R. Tolkien. Copyright © 1962 by George
Allen & Unwin (Publishers) Ltd. Reprinted by permission of
Houghton Mifflin Company and George Allen & Unwin (Pub-
lishers) Ltd.

Said Tom: 'I don't see why the likes o' thee
Without axin' leave should go makin' free
  With the shank or the shin o' my father's
  kin;
    So hand the old bone over!
      Rover! Trover!
  Though dead he be, it belongs to he;
    So hand the old bone over!'

'For a couple o' pins,' says Troll, and grins,
'I'll eat thee too, and gnaw thy shins.
  A bit o' fresh meat will go down sweet!
    I'll try my teeth on thee now.
      Hee now! See now!
  I'm tired o' gnawing old bones and skins;
    I've a mind to dine on thee now.'

But just as he thought his dinner was caught,
He found his hands had hold of naught.
  Before he could mind, Tom slipped behind
    And gave him the boot to larn him.
      Warn him! Darn him!
  A bump o' the boot on the seat, Tom
  thought,
    Would be the way to larn him.

But harder than stone is the flesh and bone
Of a troll that sits in the hills alone.
  As well set your boot to the mountain's
  root,
    For the seat of a troll don't feel it.
      Peel it! Heal it!
  Old Troll laughed, when he heard Tom
  groan,
    And he knew his toes could feel it.

Tom's leg is game, since home he came,
And his bootless foot is lasting lame;
  But Troll don't care, and he's still there
    With the bone he boned from its owner.
      Doner! Boner!
  Troll's old seat is still the same,
    And the bone he boned from its owner!

J. R. R. Tolkien

Food

"packs of chocolate dreams"

from Eats

Sunny

    side

        up

    bull_s

    eye

    egg

    turn

    over

    easy

      and

    don_t bre_{ak}

    the

    yoke

Arnold Adoff

Alas, Alack!

Ann, Ann!
  Come! Quick as you can!
There's a fish that *talks*
  In the frying-pan.
Out of the fat,
  As clear as glass,
He put up his mouth
  And moaned "Alas!"
Oh, most mournful,
  "Alas, alack!"
Then turned to his sizzling,
  And sank him back.

Walter de la Mare

To market, to market, to buy a fat pig,
Home again, home again, jiggety jig.

To market, to market, to buy a fat hog,
Home again, home again, jiggety jog.

To market, to market, to buy a plum bun,
Home again, home again, market is done.

(Mother Goose)

What is the opposite of *nuts?*
It's *soup!* Let's have no ifs or buts.
In any suitable repast
The soup comes first, the nuts come last.
Or that is what *sane* folk advise;
You're nuts if you think otherwise.

Richard Wilbur

Pease porridge hot,
    Pease porridge cold,
Pease porridge in the pot,
    Nine days old.
Some like it hot,
    Some like it cold,
Some like it in the pot,
    Nine days old.

(Mother Goose)

My great corn plants,
Among them I walk.
I speak to them;
They hold out their hands to me.

My great squash vines,
Among them I walk.
I speak to them;
They hold out their hands to me.

(Navajo)

"My great corn plants" from FOUR CORNERS OF THE SKY by Theodore Clymer, illustrated by Marc Brown. Copyright © 1975 by Theodore Clymer. Reprinted by permission of Little, Brown and Company in association with the Atlantic Monthly Press.

"Spring Diet" from BLUEBERRIES LAVENDER by Nancy D. Watson. Copyright © 1977 by Nancy Dingman Watson. Reprinted by permission of Addison-Wesley Publishing Company, Reading, MA. All rights reserved.

"Mix a pancake" from SING-SONG by Christina Rossetti.

"My Aunt Kept Turnips in a Flock" from RANDALL JAR-RELL: THE COMPLETE POEMS. Copyright 1949 by The Nation. Copyright © 1967, 1969 by Mrs. Randall Jarrell. Copyright renewed © 1976 by Mrs. Randall Jarrell. Reprinted by permission of Farrar, Straus & Giroux, Inc. and Faber and Faber Ltd.

Miss T.

It's a very odd thing—
    As odd as can be—
That whatever Miss T. eats
    Turns into Miss T.;
Porridge and apples,
    Mince, muffins and mutton,
Jam, junket, jumbles—
    Not a rap, not a button
It matters; the moment
    They're out of her plate,
Though shared by Miss Butcher
    And sour Mr. Bate;
Tiny and cheerful,
    And neat as can be,
Whatever Miss T. eats
    Turns into Miss T.

Walter de la Mare

Spring Diet

Nibble on a fiddle fern
Chew a birch twig
Sip upon a honeysuckle
Then you'll grow big.

Nancy Dingman Watson

Mix a pancake,
Stir a pancake,
    Pop it in the pan;
Fry the pancake,
Toss the pancake,—
    Catch it if you can.

Christina Rossetti

My aunt kept turnips in a flock—
Did you ever hear of such strange stock?
They'd the funniest wool you ever did see;
It looked like turnip greens to me.

Turnip greens, oh turnip greens!
There's nothing I love like turnip greens!

Randall Jarrell

Millions of Strawberries

Marcia and I went over the curve,
Eating our way down
Jewels of strawberries we didn't deserve,
Eating our way down.
Till our hands were sticky, and our lips
    painted,
And over us the hot day fainted,
And we saw snakes,
And got scratched,
And a lust overcame us for the red
    unmatched
Small buds of berries,
Till we lay down—
Eating our way down—
And rolled in the berries like two little dogs,
Rolled
In the late gold.
And gnats hummed,
And it was cold,
And home we went, home without a berry,
Painted red and brown,
Eating our way down.

Genevieve Taggard

Little Miss Muffet
    Sat on a tuffet,
Eating her curds and whey;
    There came a big spider,
Who sat down beside her
    And frightened Miss Muffet away.

(Mother Goose)

Oh my goodness, oh my dear,
Sassafras & ginger beer,
Chocolate cake & apple punch:
I'm too full to eat my lunch.

Clyde Watson

Unusual Shoelaces

To lace my shoes
I use spaghetti.
Teacher and friends
All think I'm batty.

Let 'em laugh, the whole
Kit and kaboodle.
But I'll get by.
I use my noodle.

X. J. Kennedy

from Eats

Chocolate
Chocolate
                i
love
        you so
                i
want
        to
marry
        you
        and
live
    forever
                in the
                    flavor
of your
    brown

Arnold Adoff

"Millions of Strawberries" by Genevieve Taggard. Copyright 1929, © 1957 by Genevieve Taggard. Originally appeared in THE NEW YORKER. Reprinted by permission.

"Unusual Shoelaces" from ONE WINTER NIGHT IN AUGUST AND OTHER NONSENSE JINGLES by X. J. Kennedy. Copyright © 1975 by X. J. Kennedy. A Margaret K. McElderry book (New York: Atheneum, 1975). Reprinted with the permission of Atheneum Publishers and Curtis Brown Ltd.

"Oh my goodness, oh my dear" from FATHER FOX'S PENNYRHYMES by Clyde Watson. Text copyright © 1971 by Clyde Watson. Reprinted by permission of Thomas Y. Crowell, Publishers, and Curtis Brown Ltd.

"Supermarket" from AT THE TOP OF MY VOICE AND OTHER POEMS by Felice Holman. Copyright © 1970 by Felice Holman (New York: Charles Scribner's Sons, 1970). Reprinted with the permission of Charles Scribner's Sons.

Supermarket

I'm
lost
among a
maze of cans,
behind a pyramid
of jams, quite near
asparagus and rice,
close to the Oriental spice,
and just before sardines.
I hear my mother calling, "Joe.
Where are you, Joe? Where did you
Go?" And I reply in voice concealed among
the candied orange peel, and packs of Chocolate Dreams.

"I
hear
you, Mother
dear, I'm here—
quite near the ginger ale
and beer, and lost among a

                maze
              of cans
           behind a
        pyramid of jams,
      quite near asparagus
    and rice, close to the
Oriental spice, and just before sardines."

                        But
                        still
                  my mother
                calls me, "Joe!
            Where are you, Joe?
           Where did you go?"

"Somewhere
around asparagus
that's in a sort of
      broken glass,
          beside a kind of m-
                ess-
                    y jell
        that's near a tower of cans that f
                           e
                         l
                       l
       and squashed the Chocolate Dreams."

Felice Holman

Mummy Slept Late and Daddy Fixed Breakfast

Daddy fixed the breakfast.
He made us each a waffle.
It looked like gravel pudding.
It tasted something awful.

"Ha, ha," he said, "I'll try again.
This time I'll get it right."
But what *I* got was in between
Bituminous and anthracite.

"A little too well done? Oh well,
I'll have to start all over."
That time what landed on my plate
Looked like a manhole cover.

I tried to cut it with a fork:
The fork gave off a spark.
I tried a knife and twisted it
Into a question mark.

I tried it with a hack-saw.
I tried it with a torch.
It didn't even make a dent.
It didn't even scorch.

The next time Dad gets breakfast
When Mommy's sleeping late,
I think I'll skip the waffles.
I'd sooner eat the plate!

John Ciardi

Lazy Mary

Lazy Mary, will you get up,
Will you, will you, will you get up?
Lazy Mary, will you get up,
Will you get up today?

What will you give me for my breakfast,
For my breakfast, for my breakfast,
What will you give me for my breakfast
If I'll get up today?

(*spoken*) Butter and bread.

No, mother, I won't get up,
I won't get up, I won't get up,
No, mother, I won't get up,
I won't get up today.

Lazy Mary, will you get up,
Will you, will you, will you get up?
Lazy Mary, will you get up,
Will you get up today?

What will you give me for my dinner,
For my dinner, for my dinner,
What will you give me for my dinner
If I'll get up today?

(*spoken*) Peas and cornbread.

No, mother, I won't get up,
I won't get up, I won't get up,
No, mother, I won't get up,
I won't get up today.

Lazy Mary, will you get up,
Will you, will you, will you get up?
Lazy Mary, will you get up,
Will you get up today?

(American Folk)

Text of "Mummy Slept Late and Daddy Fixed Breakfast" from YOU READ TO ME, I'LL READ TO YOU by John Ciardi. Copyright © 1962 by John Ciardi. Reprinted by permission of J. B. Lippincott, Publishers.

"Lazy Mary" from THE FRANK C. BROWN COLLECTION OF NORTH CAROLINA FOLKLORE edited by Newman Ivey White. Reprinted by permission of Duke University Press.

Play and Sports

"Boys and girls come out to play"

Boys and girls come out to play,
The moon doth shine as bright as day.
Leave your supper and leave your sleep,
And join your playfellows in the street.
Come with a whoop and come with a call,
Come with a good will or not at all.
Up the ladder and down the wall,
A half-penny loaf will serve us all;
You find milk, and I'll find flour,
And we'll have a pudding in half an hour.

(Mother Goose)

Here am I, little jumping Joan,
    When nobody's with me
    I'm always alone.

(Mother Goose)

Hiding

I'm hiding, I'm hiding,
And no one knows where;
For all they can see is my
Toes and my hair.

"Hiding" from EVERYTHING & ANYTHING by Dorothy Aldis. Copyright 1925–27; renewed 1953–55 by Dorothy Aldis. Reprinted by permission of G. P. Putnam's Sons.
"Henry and Mary" from THE PENNY FIDDLE by Robert Graves. Reprinted by permission of Robert Graves.

And I just heard my father
Say to my mother—
"But, darling, he must be
Somewhere or other;

"Have you looked in the ink well?"
And Mother said, "Where?"
"In the INK WELL," said Father. But
I was not there.

Then "Wait!" cried my mother—
"I think that I see
Him under the carpet." But
It was not me.

"Inside the mirror's
A pretty good place,"
Said Father and looked, but saw
Only his face.

"We've hunted," sighed Mother,
"As hard as we could
And I AM so afraid that we've
Lost him for good."

Then I laughed out aloud
And I wiggled my toes
And Father said—"Look, dear,
I wonder if those

Toes could be Benny's.
There are ten of them. See?"
And they WERE so surprised to find
Out it was me!

Dorothy Aldis

Henry and Mary

Henry was a young king,
    Mary was his queen;
He gave her a snowdrop
    On a stalk of green.

Then all for his kindness
    And all for his care
She gave him a new-laid egg
    In the garden there.

'Love, can you sing?'
                    'I cannot sing.'
     'Or tell a tale?'
                    'Not one I know.'
'Then let us play at queen and king
     As down the garden walks we go.'

Robert Graves

Bike Ride

Look at us!

We ride a
road
the sun has paved with
shadows.

We glide
on leaf lace
across tree spires
over
shadow ropes
of droopy wires.

We roll
through a shade tunnel
into light.

Look!
Our bikes
spin
black-and-white
shadow
pinwheels.

Lilian Moore

The Kite

How bright on the blue
Is a kite when it's new!

With a dive and a dip
It snaps its tail

Then soars like a ship
With only a sail

As over tides
Of wind it rides,

Climbs to the crest
Of a gust and pulls,

Then seems to rest
As wind falls.

When string goes slack
You wind it back

And run until
A new breeze blows

And its wings fill
And up it goes!

How bright on the blue
Is a kite when it's new!

But a raggeder thing
You never will see

When it flaps on a string
In the top of a tree.

Harry Behn

Night Game

At first I thought it was the moon
gliding down with one
shining arm outstretched
carrying something dark.
Then I realized
it was the Statue of Liberty
arcing slowly through the sky
with a baseball glove on her
uplifted hand. She was saying,
"Umpire, you blind burglar,
You can't throw me out of the game."

Lillian Morrison

Rope Rhyme

Get set, ready now, jump right in
Bounce and kick and giggle and spin
Listen to the rope when it hits the ground
Listen to that clappedy-slappedy sound
Jump right up when it tells you to
Come back down, whatever you do
Count to a hundred, count by ten
Start to count all over again
That's what jumping is all about
Get set, ready now,
                    jump
                          right
                                out!

Eloise Greenfield

The Swing

How do you like to go up in a swing,
    Up in the air so blue?
Oh, I do think it the pleasantest thing
    Ever a child can do!

Up in the air and over the wall,
    Till I can see so wide,
Rivers and trees and cattle and all
    Over the countryside—

Till I look down on the garden green,
    Down on the roof so brown—
Up in the air I go flying again,
    Up in the air and down!

Robert Louis Stevenson

The Sidewalk Racer
or
On the Skateboard

Skimming
an asphalt sea
I swerve, I curve, I
sway; I speed to whirring
sound an inch above the
ground; I'm the sailor
and the sail, I'm the
driver and the wheel
I'm the one and only
single engine
human auto
mobile.

Lillian Morrison

The Rose on My Cake

I went to a party,
A party for Pearly,
With presents and ice cream,
With favors and games.
I stayed very late
And I got there quite early.
I met all the guests
And I know all their names.
We sang and we jumped.
We jumped and we jostled.
We jostled and rustled
At musical chairs.
We ate up the cake
And we folded the candy in baskets
In napkins
We folded in squares.

We blew up balloons
And we danced without shoes.
We danced on the floor
And the rug and the bed.
We tripped and we trotted
In trios and twos.
And I neatly balanced myself
On my head.

Pearly just smiled
As she blew out the candles.
I gave the rose from my cake
To a friend,
Millicent Moss,
In her black patent sandals.
The trouble with parties is
All of them end.

Karla Kuskin

74th Street

Hey, this little kid gets roller skates.
She puts them on.
She stands up and almost
flops over backwards.
She sticks out a foot like
she's going somewhere and
falls down and
smacks her hand. She
grabs hold of a step to get up and
sticks out the other foot and
slides about six inches and
falls and
skins her knee.

       And then, you know what?

She brushes off the dirt and the
blood and puts some
spit on it and then
sticks out the other foot

       again.

Myra Cohn Livingston

Forms of Praise

Basketball players
already tall
rise on springs
aspiring for the ball,
leap for the rebound
arms on high
in a dance
of hallelujahs.

Lillian Morrison

from **I Am the Running Girl**

i am the running girl

        there are walking girls
           and jogging
  girls
       in the streets

      girls who ride their
           bikes
    and hike along brown
    country roads with
          brothers
    and their friends
    and pull wild flowers
       for their hair
  but

i am the running girl
      there in the moving day
      and i cannot stop to
          say
  hello

Arnold Adoff

The Circus

Friday came and the circus was there,
And Mother said that the twins and I
And Charles and Clarence and all of us
Could go out and see the parade go by.

And there were wagons with pictures on,
And you never could guess what they had
   inside,
Nobody could guess, for the doors were shut,
And there was a dog that a monkey could
   ride.

A man on the top of a sort of cart
Was clapping his hands and making a talk.
And the elephant came—he can step pretty
        far—
It made us laugh to see him walk.

Three beautiful ladies came riding by,
And each one had on a golden dress,
And each one had a golden whip.
They were queens of Sheba, I guess.

A big wild man was in a cage,
And he had some snakes going over his feet
And somebody said "He eats them alive!"
But I didn't see him eat.

Elizabeth Madox Roberts

The Base Stealer

Poised between going on and back, pulled
Both ways taut like a tightrope-walker,

"The Base Stealer" from THE ORB WEAVER by Robert
Francis. Copyright 1948 by Robert Francis. Reprinted by per-
mission of Wesleyan University Press.
"The Women's 400 Meters" from THE SIDEWALK
RACER by Lillian Morrison. Poem copyright © 1968 by Lillian
Morrison. Reprinted by permission of Lothrop, Lee & Shepard
Books (A Division of William Morrow & Company).

Fingertips pointing the opposites,
Now bouncing tiptoe like a dropped ball
Or a kid skipping rope, come on, come on,
Running a scattering of steps sidewise,
How he teeters, skitters, tingles, teases,
Taunts them, hovers like an ecstatic bird,
He's only flirting, crowd him, crowd him,
Delicate, delicate, delicate, delicate—now!

Robert Francis

The Women's 400 Meters

Skittish,
they flex knees, drum heels and
shiver at the starting line

waiting the gun
to pour them over the stretch
like a breaking wave.

Bang! they're off
careening down the lanes,
each chased by her own bright tiger.

Lillian Morrison

Music and Dance
"way down inside the music"

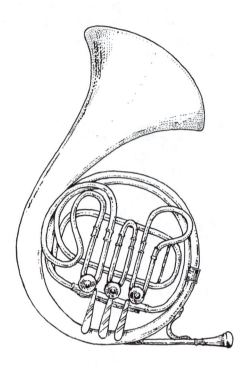

Knock! Knock! Anybody there?
I've feathers for your caps
And ribbons for your hair.
If you can't pay you can sing me a song,
But if you can't sing, I'll just run along.

Clyde Watson

Nicely while it is raining,
Corn plant, I am singing for you.
Nicely while the water is streaming,
Vine plant, I am singing for you.

(Acoma)

Tom he was a piper's son,
He learned to play when he was young,
But all the tunes that he could play,
Was "Over the hills and far away."

Now Tom with his pipe made such a noise,
That he pleased both girls and boys,
And they stopped to hear him play
"Over the hills and far away."

Tom with his pipe did play with such skill,
That those who heard him could never keep
    still;
Whenever they heard they began for to
    dance,
Even pigs on their hind legs would after him
    prance.

(Mother Goose)

Hey, diddle, diddle!
    The cat and the fiddle,
The cow jumped over the moon;
    The little dog laughed
    To see such sport,
And the dish ran away with the spoon.

(Mother Goose)

Dance to your daddy,
    My little babby,
Dance to your daddy, my little lamb;
    You shall have a fishy
    In a little dishy,
You shall have a fishy when the boat
    comes in.

(Mother Goose)

I Heard a Bird Sing

I heard a bird sing
  In the dark of December
A magical thing
  And sweet to remember.

"We are nearer to Spring
  Than we were in September,"
I heard a bird sing
  In the dark of December.

Oliver Herford

Piping down the valleys wild,
  Piping songs of pleasant glee,
On a cloud I saw a child,
  And he laughing said to me:

"Pipe a song about a Lamb!"
  So I piped with merry cheer.
"Piper, pipe that song again";
  So I piped; he wept to hear.

"Drop thy pipe, thy happy pipe;
  Sing thy songs of happy cheer!"
So I sang the same again,
  While he wept with joy to hear.

"Piper, sit thee down and write
  In a book, that all may read."
So he vanished from my sight;
  And I plucked a hollow reed,

And I made a rural pen,
  And I stained the water clear,
And I wrote my happy songs
  Every child may joy to hear.

William Blake

"Piping down the valleys wild" from SONGS OF INNO-
CENCE by William Blake.

"A Piper" by Seumas O'Sullivan from COLLECTED
POEMS (Orwell Press, 1940). Reprinted by permission of
Frances Sommerville for the Estate of E. Starkey.

"Gertrude" from BRONZEVILLE BOYS AND GIRLS by
Gwendolyn Brooks. Copyright © 1956 by Gwendolyn Brooks
Blakely. Reprinted by permission of Harper & Row, Publishers,
Inc.

A Piper

A piper in the streets to-day
Set up, and tuned, and started to play,
And away, away, away on the tide
Of his music we started; on every side
Doors and windows were opened wide,
And men left down their work and came,
And women with petticoats coloured like
    flame.
And little bare feet that were blue with cold,
Went dancing back to the age of gold,
And all the world went gay, went gay,
For half an hour in the street to-day.

Seumas O'Sullivan

Gertrude

When I hear Marian Anderson sing,
I am a STUFFless kind of thing.

Heart is like the flying air.
I cannot find it anywhere.

Fingers tingle. I am cold
And warm and young and very old.

But, most, I am a STUFFless thing
When I hear Marian Anderson sing.

Gwendolyn Brooks

Merry Are the Bells

Merry are the bells, and merry would they
  ring,
Merry was myself, and merry could I sing;
With a merry ding-dong, happy, gay, and
  free,
And a merry sing-song, happy let us be!

Merry have we met, and merry have we
  been;
Merry let us part, and merry meet again;
With our merry sing-song, happy, gay, and
  free,
With a merry ding-dong, happy let us be!

(Anonymous)

The Fiddler of Dooney

When I play on my fiddle in Dooney,
Folk dance like a wave of the sea;
My cousin is priest in Kilvarnet,
My brother in Moharabuiee.

I passed my brother and cousin:
They read in their books of prayer;
I read in my book of songs
I bought at the Sligo fair.

When we come at the end of time
To Peter sitting in state,
He will smile on the three old spirits,
But call me first through the gate;

For the good are always the merry,
Save by an evil chance,
And the merry love the fiddle
And the merry love to dance:

And when the folk there spy me,
They will all come up to me,
With 'Here is the fiddler of Dooney!'
And dance like a wave of the sea.

William Butler Yeats

I Hear America Singing

I hear America singing, the varied carols I
    hear,
Those of the mechanics, each singing his as it
    should be blithe and strong,
The carpenter singing his as he measures his
    plank or beam,
The mason singing his as he makes ready for
    work or leaves off work,
The boatman singing what belongs to him in
    his boat, the deck hand singing on the
    steamboat deck,
The shoemaker singing as he sits on his
    bench, the hatter singing as he stands,
The wood-cutter's song, the ploughboy's on
    his way in the morning, or at noon inter-
    mission or at sundown,
The delicious singing of the mother, or the
    young wife at work, or the girl sewing or
    washing,

Each sings what belongs to him or her and to
    none else,
The day what belongs to the day—at night
    the party of young fellows, robust,
    friendly,
Singing with open mouths their strong melo-
    dious songs.

Walt Whitman

dance poem

come Nataki dance with me
bring your pablum dance with me
pull your plait and whorl around
come Nataki dance with me

won't you Tony dance with me
stop your crying dance with me
feel the rhythm of my arms
don't lets cry now dance with me

Tommy stop your tearing up
don't you hear the music
don't you feel the happy beat
don't bite Tony dance with me
Mommy needs a partner

here comes Karma she will dance
pirouette and bugaloo
short pink dress and dancing shoes
Karma wants to dance with me
don't you Karma don't you

all you children gather round
we will dance and we will whorl
we will dance to our own song
we must spin to our own world
we must spin a soft Black song
all you children gather round
we will dance together

Nikki Giovanni

The Song of the Jellicles

Jellicle Cats come out tonight,
Jellicle Cats come one come all:
The Jellicle Moon is shining bright—
Jellicles come to the Jellicle Ball.

Jellicle Cats are black and white,
Jellicle Cats are rather small;
Jellicle Cats are merry and bright,
And pleasant to hear when they caterwaul.
Jellicle Cats have cheerful faces,
Jellicle Cats have bright black eyes;
They like to practise their airs and graces
And wait for the Jellicle Moon to rise.

Jellicle Cats develop slowly,
Jellicle Cats are not too big;
Jellicle Cats are roly-poly,
They know how to dance a gavotte and a jig.
Until the Jellicle Moon appears
They make their toilette and take their
    repose:
Jellicles wash behind their ears,
Jellicles dry between their toes.

Jellicle Cats are white and black,
Jellicle Cats are of moderate size;
Jellicles jump like a jumping-jack,
Jellicle Cats have moonlit eyes.
They're quiet enough in the morning hours,
They're quiet enough in the afternoon,
Reserving their terpsichorean powers
To dance by the light of the Jellicle Moon.

Jellicle Cats are black and white,
Jellicle Cats (as I said) are small;
If it happens to be a stormy night
They will practise a caper or two in the hall.
If it happens the sun is shining bright
You would say they had nothing to do at all:
They are resting and saving themselves to be
    right
For the Jellicle Moon and the Jellicle Ball.

T. S. Eliot

A Mermaid Song

She sits by the sea in the clear, shining air,
    And the sailors call her Moonlight,
        Moonlight;
They see her smoothing her wavy hair
    And they hear her singing, singing.
The sea-shells learn their tunes from her
And the big fish listen with never a stir
    To catch the voice of Moonlight,
        Moonlight,
And I would hark for a year and a year
    To hear her singing, singing.

James Reeves

Way Down in the Music

I get way down in the music
Down inside the music
I let it wake me
        take me
Spin me around and make me
Uh-get down

Inside the sound of the Jackson Five
Into the tune of Earth, Wind and Fire
Down in the bass where the beat comes from
Down in the horn and down in the drum
I get down
I get down

I get way down in the music
Down inside the music
I let it wake me
        take me
Spin me around and shake me
I get down, down
I get down

Eloise Greenfield

The Potatoes' Dance
(A Poem Game)

I

"Down cellar," said the cricket,
"Down cellar," said the cricket,
"Down cellar," said the cricket,
"I saw a ball last night,
In honor of a lady,
In honor of a lady,
In honor of a lady,
Whose wings were pearly white.
The breath of bitter weather,
The breath of bitter weather,
The breath of bitter weather,
Had smashed the cellar pane.
We entertained a drift of leaves,
We entertained a drift of leaves,
We entertained a drift of leaves,
And then of snow and rain.
But we were dressed for winter,
But we were dressed for winter,
But we were dressed for winter,

And loved to hear it blow
In honor of the lady,
In honor of the lady,
In honor of the lady,
Who makes potatoes grow,
Our guest the Irish lady,
The tiny Irish lady,
The airy Irish lady,
Who makes potatoes grow.

II

"Potatoes were the waiters,
Potatoes were the waiters,
Potatoes were the waiters,
Potatoes were the band,
Potatoes were the dancers
Kicking up the sand,
Kicking up the sand,
Kicking up the sand,
Potatoes were the dancers
Kicking up the sand.
Their legs were old burnt matches,
Their legs were old burnt matches,
Their legs were old burnt matches,
Their arms were just the same.
They jigged and whirled and scrambled,
Jigged and whirled and scrambled,
Jigged and whirled and scrambled,
In honor of the dame,
The noble Irish lady
Who makes potatoes dance,
The witty Irish lady,
The saucy Irish lady,
The laughing Irish lady
Who makes potatoes prance.

III

"There was just one sweet potato.
He was golden brown and slim.
The lady loved his dancing,
The lady loved his dancing,
The lady loved his dancing,

She danced all night with him,
She danced all night with him.
Alas, he wasn't Irish.
So when she flew away,
They threw him in the coal-bin,
And there he is today,
Where they cannot hear his sighs
And his weeping for the lady,
The glorious Irish lady,
The beauteous Irish lady,
Who
Gives
Potatoes
Eyes."

Vachel Lindsay

Skip to My Lou

I lost my pardner, what'll I do?
I lost my pardner, what'll I do?
I lost my pardner, what'll I do?
Skip to my Lou, my darling!

> Gone again, skip to my Lou!
> Gone again, skip to my Lou!
> Gone again, skip to my Lou!
> Skip to my Lou, my darling!

The cat's in the buttermilk, skip to my Lou,
Cat's in the buttermilk, skip to my Lou,
Cat's in the buttermilk, skip to my Lou,
Skip to my Lou, my darling!

Flies in the sugarbowl, skip to my Lou,

Mama churns the butter in Grandpa's boot,

Mice in the cream jar, what'll I do?

Chickens in the haystack, shoo, shoo, shoo,

Pigs in the 'tater patch, two by two,

Gone again, and I don't care,

I'll get another one better than you,

Rats in the bread-pan, chew, chew, chew,

Little red wagon painted blue,

Hair in the biscuit, two by two,

"Skip to My Lou," "Buffalo Girls," and "Mississippi Sounding Calls" from AMERICAN FOLK POETRY.

Pretty as a blackbird, and prettier too,

If I can't get a blackbird, a white bird'll do,

Gone again, what'll I do?

I'll get another one sweeter than you,

I'll get her back again, you bet you!

When I go courting, I take two,

My Ma says, I can have you,
My Ma says, I can have you,
My Ma says, I can have you,
Skip to my Lou, my darling!

> Gone again, skip to my Lou!
> Gone again, skip to my Lou!
> Gone again, skip to my Lou!
> Skip to my Lou, my darling!

(American Folk)

Buffalo Girls

Buffalo girls, ain't you coming out tonight,
Ain't you coming out tonight, ain't you
    coming out tonight,
Buffalo girls, ain't you coming out tonight,
To dance by the light of the moon?

> You bet your socks I'm a-coming out
>   tonight,
> I'm a-coming out tonight, I'm a-coming out
>   tonight,
> You bet your socks I'm a-coming out
>   tonight
> To dance by the light of the moon.

As I was a-walking down the street,
Down the street, down the street,
I passed my girl and she looked so neat
Under the light of the moon.

> You bet your socks I'm a-coming out
>   tonight,
> I'm a-coming out tonight, I'm a-coming out
>   tonight,
> You bet your socks I'm a-coming out
>   tonight
> To dance by the light of the moon.

(American Folk)

Blow, Bugle, Blow

The splendour falls on castle walls
    And snowy summits old in story:
The long light shakes across the lakes,
    And the wild cataract leaps in glory.
Blow, bugle, blow, set the wild echoes flying,
Blow, bugle; answer, echoes, dying, dying,
    dying.

O hark, O hear! how thin and clear,
    And thinner, clearer, farther going!
O sweet and far from cliff and scar
    The horns of Elfland faintly blowing!
Blow, let us hear the purple glens replying:
Blow, bugle; answer, echoes, dying, dying,
    dying.

O love, they die in yon rich sky,
    They faint on hill or field or river:
Our echoes roll from soul to soul,
    And grow for ever and for ever.
Blow, bugle, blow, set the wild echoes flying,
And answer, echoes, answer, dying, dying,
    dying.

Alfred, Lord Tennyson

Mississippi Sounding Calls

Samuel Clemens (Mark Twain) took his pseudonym from calls such as these.

I

No bottom,
Mark four,
Quarter less four,
Quarter less five,
Half twain,
Quarter twain.

II

Quarter less four,
Half twain,
Quarter twain,
Mark twain,
Quarter less twain,
Nine and a half feet,
Nine feet,
Eight and a half feet.

(American Folk)

"Blow, Bugle, Blow" from THE PRINCESS by Alfred, Lord Tennyson.

Magic People
"follow me and follow me"

Some One

Some one came knocking
   At my wee, small door;
Some one came knocking,
   I'm sure—sure—sure;
I listened, I opened,
   I looked to left and right,
But nought there was a-stirring
   In the still dark night;
Only the busy beetle
   Tap-tapping in the wall,
Only from the forest
   The screech-owl's call,
Only the cricket whistling
   While the dew drops fall,
So I know not who came knocking,
   At all, at all, at all.

Walter de la Mare

The Little Elfman

I met a little Elfman once,
   Down where the lilies blow.
I asked him why he was so small,
   And why he didn't grow.

He slightly frowned, and with his eye
   He looked me through and through—
"I'm just as big for me," said he,
   "As you are big for you!"

John Kendrick Bangs

I Did Not See a Mermaid?

I did not see a mermaid
The day I looked for one.
Perhaps the sun was in my eyes—
There was a lot of sun.

Just as the teardrops started down
My disappointed face,
I blinked my eyes to stop them
And I looked away in space;

I looked away in space and saw,
Almost far out at sea,
A porpoise and a Something—
And the porpoise winked at me!

Siddie Joe Johnson

"Some One" from COLLECTED POEMS 1901–1918 by Walter de la Mare. Copyright 1920 by Henry Holt and Company, Inc. Copyright 1948 by Walter de la Mare. Reprinted by permission of The Literary Trustees of Walter de la Mare and The Society of Authors as their representative.

"The Little Elfman" by John Kendrick Bangs. Copyright 1923, 1951 by Mary Gray Bangs for the Estate of John Kendrick Bangs. Reprinted by permission of Hawthorn Properties (Elsevier-Dutton Publishing Co., Inc.).

Siddie Joe Johnson, "I Did Not See a Mermaid" in FEATHER IN MY HAND. Copyright © 1967 by Siddie Joe Johnson (New York: Atheneum, 1967). Reprinted with the permission of Atheneum Publishers.

"What is the opposite of a prince?" from OPPOSITES by Richard Wilbur. Copyright © 1973 by Richard Wilbur. Reprinted by permission of Harcourt Brace Jovanovich, Inc.

What is the opposite of a *prince?*
A *frog* must be the answer, since,
As all good fairy stories tell,
When some witch says a magic spell,
Causing the prince to be disguised
So that he won't be recognized,
He always ends up green and sad
And sitting on a lily pad.

Richard Wilbur

Bobadil

Far from far
    Lives Bobadil
In a tall house
    On a tall hill.

Out from the high
    Top window-sill
On a clear night
    Leans Bobadil

To touch the moon,
    To catch a star,
To keep in her tall house
    Far from far.

James Reeves

For a Mocking Voice

Who   calls?   Who   calls?   Who?
Did you call?   Did you?—
I call!   I call!   I!
Follow where I fly.—
Where?   O where?   O where?
On Earth or in the Air?—
Where you come, I'm gone!
Where you fly, I've flown!—
Stay! ah, stay! ah, stay,
Pretty Elf, and play!
Tell me where you are—
Ha, ha, ha, ha, ha!

Eleanor Farjeon

Overheard on a Saltmarsh

Nymph, nymph, what are your beads?

Green glass, goblin. Why do you stare at
    them?

Give them me.

            No.

Give them me. Give them me.

                No.

Then I will howl all night in the reeds,
Lie in the mud and howl for them.

Goblin, why do you love them so?

They are better than stars or water,
Better than voices of winds that sing,
Better than any man's fair daughter,
Your green glass beads on a silver ring.

Hush, I stole them out of the moon.

Give me your beads, I desire them.

                No.

I will howl in a deep lagoon
For your green glass beads, I love them so.
Give them me. Give them.

                No.

Harold Monro

Behind the Waterfall

A little old woman
    In a thin white shawl,
Stepped straight through the column
    Of the silver waterfall,

"Bobadil" from THE BLACKBIRD IN THE LILAC by James Reeves (1952). Reprinted by permission of Oxford University Press.

"For a Mocking Voice" by Eleanor Farjeon from SILVER-SAND AND SNOW, published by Michael Joseph Ltd. Reprinted by permission of David Higham Associates, Ltd., Authors' Agents.

"Overheard on a Saltmarsh" from COLLECTED POEMS by Harold Monro. Reprinted by permission of Gerald Duckworth & Co. Ltd.

"Behind the Waterfall" from SKIPPING ALONG ALONE by Winifred Welles. Reprinted by permission of State National Bank of Connecticut, Agent for James Welles Shearer.

As if the fall of water
   Were not anything at all.
I saw her crook her finger,
   I heard her sweetly call.
Over stones all green and glossy
   I fled and did not fall;
I ran along the river
   And through the waterfall,
And that heavy curve of water
   Never hindered me at all.
The little old woman
   In the thin white shawl
Took my hand and laughed and led me
   Down a cool, still hall,
Between two rows of pillars
   That were glistening and tall.
At her finger's tap swung open
   A wide door in the wall,
And I saw the crystal city
   That's behind the waterfall.

Winifred Welles

Musetta of the Mountains

Musetta of the mountains
   She lives amongst the snow,
Coming and going softly
   On a white doe.
Her face is pale and smiling
   Her hair is of gold;
She wears a red mantle
   To keep her from the cold.

Musetta of the mountains,
   She rides in the night
On her swift-footed doe
   So gentle and light;
In the frosty starlight
   Sometimes you may hear
The bells on its bridle
   Far away but clear.

Sometimes from the far snows
   The winter wind brings
The thin voice of Musetta,
   And this is what she sings:
'Follow me and follow me
   And come to my mountains.
I will show you eagles' nests
   By the frozen fountains.

'Death-cold are the high peaks
   Of the mountains lone,
But a marvellous sight
   Is the snow-queen's throne.
Death-cold are the mountains
   And the winds sharp as spite,
But warm is the welcome
   In my cabin at night.'

Thus sings Musetta
   In the frosty air,
While the delicate snowflakes
   Light on her hair.
But there is none to follow her,
   No one to ride
Away with fair Musetta
   To the far mountain-side.

James Reeves

The Unicorn

While yet the Morning Star
Flamed in the sky
A Unicorn went mincing by,
Whiter by far than blossom of the thorn:
His silver horn
Glittered as he danced and pranced
Silver-pale in the silver-pale morn.

The folk that saw him, ran away.
Where he went, so gay, so fleet,
Star-like lilies at his feet
Flowered all day,
Lilies, lilies in a throng,
And the wind made for him a song:

But he dared not stay
Over-long!

Ella Young

"Musetta of the Mountains" from THE WANDERING MOON by James Reeves. Reprinted by permission of William Heinemann Ltd.

"The Unicorn" by Ella Young, reprinted from THE HORN BOOK MAGAZINE (March/April, 1939). Copyright 1939 by The Horn Book, Inc. Reprinted by permission.

hist   whist
little ghostthings
tip-toe
twinkle-toe

little twitchy
witches and tingling
goblins
hob-a-nob   hob-a-nob

little hoppy happy
toad in tweeds
tweeds
little itchy mousies

with scuttling
eyes   rustle and run   and
hidehidehide
whisk

whisk   look out for the old woman
with the wart on her nose
what she'll do to yer
nobody knows

for she knows the devil   ooch
the devil   ouch
the devil
ach   the great

green
dancing
devil
devil

devil
devil

            wheeEEE

e. e. cummings

The Kraken

Below the thunders of the upper deep;
Far, far beneath in the abysmal sea,
His ancient, dreamless, uninvaded sleep
The Kraken sleepeth: faintest sunlights flee
About his shadowy sides: above him swell
Huge sponges of millennial growth and
    height;

And far away into the sickly light,
From many a wondrous grot and secret cell
Unnumber'd and enormous polypi
Winnow with giant arms the slumbering
    green.
There hath he lain for ages and will lie
Battening upon huge seaworms in his sleep,
Until the latter fire shall heat the deep;
Then once by man and angels to be seen,
In roaring he shall rise and on the surface die.

Alfred, Lord Tennyson

Meg Merrilies

Old Meg she was a Gipsy,
    And liv'd upon the Moors:
Her bed it was the brown heath turf,
    And her house was out of doors.

Her apples were swart blackberries,
    Her currants pods o' broom;
Her wine was dew of the wild white rose,
    Her book a churchyard tomb.

Her Brothers were the craggy hills,
    Her Sisters larchen trees—
Alone with her great family
    She liv'd as she did please.

No breakfast had she many a morn,
    No dinner many a noon,
And 'stead of supper she would stare
    Full hard against the Moon.

But every morn of woodbine fresh
    She made her garlanding,
And every night the dark glen Yew
    She wove, and she would sing.

And with her fingers old and brown
    She plaited Mats o' Rushes,
And gave them to the Cottagers
    She met among the Bushes.

Old Meg was brave as Margaret Queen
   And tall as Amazon:
An old red blanket cloak she wore;
   A chip hat had she on.
God rest her aged bones somewhere—
   She died full long agone!

John Keats

The Magical Picture

Glinting on the roadway
A broken mirror lay;
Then what did the child say
   Who found it there?
He cried there was a goblin
Looking out as he looked in:
Wild eyes and speckled skin,
   Black, bristling hair!

He brought it to his father
Who, being a simple sailor,
Swore: 'This is a true wonder,
   Deny it who can!
Plain enough to me, for one,
'Tis a picture deftly done
Of Admiral Horatio Nelson
   When a young man.'

The sailor's wife perceiving
Her husband had some pretty thing
At which he was peering,
   Seized it from his hand.
Then tears started and ran free:
'Jack, you have deceived me,
I love you no more,' said she,
   'So understand!'

'But, Mary,' cries the sailor,
'This is a famous treasure;
Admiral Nelson's picture
   Taken in youth.'
'O cruel man,' she cries,
'To trick me with such lies,
Who is this lady with bold eyes?
   Tell me the truth!'

Up rides their parish priest
Mounted on a thin beast.
Grief and anger have not ceased
   Between those two;
Little Tom still weeps for fear:
He has seen Hobgoblin, near—
Ugly face and foul leer
   That pierced him through.

Now the old priest lifts his glove
Bidding all, for God's love,
To stand and not to move,
   Lest blood be shed.
'O, O!' cries the urchin,
'I saw the Devil grin,
He glared out as I looked in—
   Like a death's head!'

Mary weeps: 'Ah, Father,
My Jack loves another!
On some voyage he courted her
   In a land afar.'
This, with cursing, Jack denies:
'Father, use your own eyes—
It is Lord Nelson in the guise
   Of a young tar.'

When the priest took the glass,
Fresh marvels came to pass:
'A saint of glory, by the Mass!
   Where got you this?'
He signed him with the good sign;
Be sure the relic was divine,
He would fix it in a shrine
   For pilgrims to kiss.

Robert Graves

The Highwayman

The wind was a torrent of darkness among
   the gusty trees.
The moon was a ghostly galleon tossed upon
   cloudy seas.
The road was a ribbon of moonlight over the
   purple moor,
And the highwayman came riding—
   Riding—riding—
The highwayman came riding, up to the old
   inn-door.

"The Magical Picture" from THE PENNY FIDDLE by Robert Graves. Reprinted by permission of Robert Graves.

"The Highwayman" from COLLECTED POEMS by Alfred Noyes. Copyright 1906, 1934 by Alfred Noyes. Reprinted by permission of J. B. Lippincott, Publishers and Hugh Noyes.

He'd a French cocked-hat on his forehead, a
　　bunch of lace at his chin,
A coat of the claret velvet, and breeches of
　　brown doe-skin.
They fitted with never a wrinkle. His boots
　　were up to the thigh.
And he rode with a jewelled twinkle,
　　His pistol butts a-twinkle,
His rapier hilt a-twinkle, under the jewelled
　　sky.

Over the cobbles he clattered and clashed in
　　the dark inn-yard.
He tapped with his whip on the shutters, but
　　all was locked and barred.
He whistled a tune to the window, and who
　　should be waiting there
But the landlord's black-eyed daughter,
　　Bess, the landlord's daughter,
Plaiting a dark red love-knot into her long
　　black hair.

And dark in the dark old inn-yard a stable-
　　wicket creaked
Where Tim the ostler listened. His face was
　　white and peaked.
His eyes were hollows of madness, his hair
　　like mouldy hay,
But he loved the landlord's daughter,
　　The landlord's red-lipped daughter.
Dumb as a dog he listened, and he heard the
　　robber say—

"One kiss, my bonny sweetheart, I'm after a
　　prize to-night,
But I shall be back with the yellow gold be-
　　fore the morning light;
Yet, if they press me sharply, and harry me
　　through the day,
Then look for me by moonlight,
　　Watch for me by moonlight,
I'll come to thee by moonlight, though hell
　　should bar the way."

He rose upright in the stirrups. He scarce
　　could reach her hand,
But she loosened her hair in the casement.
　　His face burnt like a brand
As the black cascade of perfume came tum-
　　bling over his breast;
And he kissed its waves in the moonlight,
　　(O, sweet black waves in the moonlight!)

Then he tugged at his rein in the moonlight,
　　and galloped away to the west.

He did not come in the dawning. He did not
　　come at noon;
And out of the tawny sunset, before the rise
　　of the moon,
When the road was a gypsy's ribbon, looping
　　the purple moor,
A red-coat troop came marching—
　　Marching—marching—
King George's men came marching, up to
　　the old inn-door.

They said no word to the landlord. They
　　drank his ale instead.
But they gagged his daughter, and bound
　　her, to the foot of her narrow bed.
Two of them knelt at her casement, with
　　muskets at their side!
There was death at every window;
　　And hell at one dark window;
For Bess could see, through her casement,
　　the road that *he* would ride.

They had tied her up to attention, with many
　　a sniggering jest.
They had bound a musket beside her, with
　　the muzzle beneath her breast!
"Now, keep good watch!" and they kissed
　　her. She heard the doomed man say—
Look for me by moonlight;
　　Watch for me by moonlight;
I'll come to thee by moonlight, though hell
　　should bar the way!

She twisted her hands behind her; but all the
　　knots held good!
She writhed her hands till her fingers were
　　wet with sweat or blood!
They stretched and strained in the darkness,
　　and the hours crawled by like years,
Till, now, on the stroke of midnight,
　　Cold, on the stroke of midnight,
The tip of one finger touched it! The trigger
　　at least was hers!

The tip of one finger touched it. She strove
　　no more for the rest.
Up, she stood up to attention, with the
　　muzzle beneath her breast.
She would not risk their hearing; she would
　　not strive again;

For the road lay bare in the moonlight;
  Blank and bare in the moonlight;
And the blood of her veins, in the moonlight,
  throbbed to her love's refrain.

Tlot-tlot; tlot-tlot! Had they heard it? The
  horse-hoofs ringing clear;
Tlot-tlot, tlot-tlot, in the distance? Were they
  deaf that they did not hear?
Down the ribbon of moonlight, over the
  brow of the hill,
The highwayman came riding—
  Riding—riding—
The red-coats looked to their priming! She
  stood up, straight and still.

Tlot-tlot, in the frosty silence! *Tlot-tlot,* in
  the echoing night!
Nearer he came and nearer. Her face was
  like a light.
Her eyes grew wide for a moment; she drew
  one last deep breath,
Then her finger moved in the moonlight,
  Her musket shattered the moonlight,
Shattered her breast in the moonlight and
  warned him—with her death.

He turned. He spurred to the west; he did
  not know who stood
Bowed, with her head o'er the musket,
  drenched with her own blood!
Not till the dawn he heard it, and his face
  grew grey to hear
How Bess, the landlord's daughter,
  The landlord's black-eyed daughter,
Had watched for her love in the moonlight,
  and died in the darkness there.

Back, he spurred like a madman, shouting a
  curse to the sky,
With the white road smoking behind him
  and his rapier brandished high.
Blood-red were his spurs in the golden noon;
  wine-red was his velvet coat;
When they shot him down on the highway,
  Down like a dog on the highway,

And he lay in his blood on the highway, with
  a bunch of lace at his throat.

*And still of a winter's night, they say, when
  the wind is in the trees,*
*When the moon is a ghostly galleon tossed
  upon cloudy seas,*
*When the road is a ribbon of moonlight over
  the purple moor,*
*A highwayman comes riding—
  Riding—riding—*
*A highwayman comes riding, up to the old
  inn-door.*

*Over the cobbles he clatters and clangs in the
  dark inn-yard.*
*He taps with his whip on the shutters, but all
  is locked and barred.*
*He whistles a tune to the window, and who
  should be waiting there*
*But the landlord's black-eyed daughter,
  Bess, the landlord's daughter,*
*Plaiting a dark red love-knot into her long
  black hair.*

Alfred Noyes

Tell Me, Tell Me, Sarah Jane

Tell me, tell me, Sarah Jane,
  Tell me, dearest daughter,
Why are you holding in your hand
  A thimbleful of water?
Why do you hold it to your eye
  And gaze both late and soon
From early morning light until
  The rising of the moon?

*Mother, I hear the mermaids cry,
  I hear the mermen sing,
And I can see the sailing ships
  All made of sticks and string.
And I can see the jumping fish,
  The whales that fall and rise
And swim about the waterspout
  That swarms up to the skies.*

Tell me, tell me, Sarah Jane,
  Tell your darling mother,
Why do you walk beside the tide
  As though you loved none other?

Why do you listen to a shell
  And watch the waters curl,
And throw away your diamond ring
  And wear instead the pearl?

Mother, I hear the water
  Beneath the headland pinned,
And I can see the sea gull
  Sliding down the wind.
I taste the salt upon my tongue
  As sweet as sweet can be.

Tell me, my dear, whose voice you hear?

  It is the sea, the sea.

Charles Causley

The Ballad of the Harp-Weaver

"Son," said my mother,
  When I was knee-high,
"You've need of clothes to cover you,
  And not a rag have I.

"There's nothing in the house
  To make a boy breeches,
Nor shears to cut a cloth with
  Nor thread to take stitches.

"There's nothing in the house
  But a loaf-end of rye,
And a harp with a woman's head
  Nobody will buy,"
  And she began to cry.

That was in the early fall.
  When came the late fall,
"Son," she said, "the sight of you
  Makes your mother's blood crawl,—

"Little skinny shoulder-blades
  Sticking through your clothes!
And where you'll get a jacket from
  God above knows.

"It's lucky for me, lad,
  Your daddy's in the ground,
And can't see the way I let
  His son go around!"
  And she made a queer sound.

That was in the late fall.
  When the winter came,
I'd not a pair of breeches
  Nor a shirt to my name.

I couldn't go to school,
  Or out of doors to play.
And all the other little boys
  Passed our way.

"Son," said my mother,
  "Come, climb into my lap,
And I'll chafe your little bones
  While you take a nap."

And, oh, but we were silly
  For half an hour or more,
Me with my long legs
  Dragging on the floor,

A-rock-rock-rocking
  To a mother-goose rhyme!
Oh, but we were happy
  For half an hour's time!

But there was I, a great boy,
  And what would folks say
To hear my mother singing me
  To sleep all day,
  In such a daft way?

Men say the winter
  Was bad that year;
Fuel was scarce,
  And food was dear.

A wind with a wolf's head
  Howled about our door,
And we burned up the chairs
  And sat upon the floor.

All that was left us
  Was a chair we couldn't break,
And the harp with a woman's head
  Nobody would take,
  For song or pity's sake.

The night before Christmas
  I cried with the cold,

"The Ballad of the Harp-Weaver" from COLLECTED POEMS by Edna St. Vincent Millay (Harper & Row, 1922). Copyright 1922, 1923, 1950, 1951 by Edna St. Vincent Millay and Norma Millay Ellis. Reprinted by permission of Norma Millay Ellis.

I cried myself to sleep
　Like a two-year-old.

And in the deep night
　I felt my mother rise,
And stare down upon me
　With love in her eyes.

I saw my mother sitting
　On the one good chair,
A light falling on her
　From I couldn't tell where,

Looking nineteen,
　And not a day older,
And the harp with a woman's head
　Leaned against her shoulder.

Her thin fingers, moving
　In the thin, tall strings,
Were weav-weav-weaving
　Wonderful things.

Many bright threads,
　From where I couldn't see,
Were running through the harp-strings
　Rapidly,

And gold threads whistling
　Through my mother's hand.
I saw the web grow,
　And the pattern expand.

She wove a child's jacket,
　And when it was done
She laid it on the floor
　And wove another one.

She wove a red cloak
　So regal to see,
"She's made it for a king's son,"
　I said, "and not for me."
But I knew it was for me.

She wove a pair of breeches
　Quicker than that!
She wove a pair of boots
　And a little cocked hat.

She wove a pair of mittens,
　She wove a little blouse,

She wove all night
　In the still, cold house.

She sang as she worked,
　And the harp-strings spoke;
Her voice never faltered,
　And the thread never broke.
　And when I awoke,—

There sat my mother
　With the harp against her shoulder,
Looking nineteen
　And not a day older,

A smile about her lips,
　And a light about her head,
And her hands in the harp-strings
　Frozen dead.

And piled up beside her
　And toppling to the skies,
Were the clothes of a king's son,
　Just my size.

Edna St. Vincent Millay

The Pied Piper of Hamelin

　　Hamelin Town's in Brunswick
By famous Hanover city;
　The river Weser, deep and wide,
　Washes its wall on the southern side;
　A pleasanter spot you never spied;
But, when begins my ditty,
　Almost five hundred years ago,
　To see the townsfolk suffer so
　　From vermin was a pity.

　　　　　　　　　　　　　　　Rats!

They fought the dogs, and killed the cats,
　And bit the babies in the cradles,
And ate the cheeses out of the vats,
　And licked the soup from the cook's own
　　ladles,
Split open the kegs of salted sprats,
Made nests inside men's Sunday hats,
And even spoiled the women's chats,
　By drowning their speaking
　With shrieking and squeaking
In fifty different sharps and flats.

"The Pied Piper of Hamelin" by Robert Browning.

At last the people in a body
To the Town Hall came flocking:
" 'Tis clear," cried they, "our Mayor's a
     noddy;
And as for our Corporation—shocking
To think that we buy gowns lined with
     ermine
For dolts that can't or won't determine
What's best to rid us of our vermin!
You hope, because you're old and obese,
To find in the furry civic robe ease?
Rouse up, sirs! Give your brain a racking
To find the remedy we're lacking,
Or, sure as fate, we'll send you packing!"
At this the Mayor and Corporation
Quaked with a mighty consternation.

An hour they sat in council,
     At length the Mayor broke silence:
"For a guilder I'd my ermine gown sell;
     I wish I were a mile hence!
It's easy to bid one rack one's brain—
I'm sure my poor head aches again
I've scratched it so, and all in vain,
Oh for a trap, a trap, a trap!"
Just as he said this, what should hap
At the chamber door but a gentle tap?
     "Bless us," cried the Mayor, "what's that?"
(With the Corporation as he sat,
Looking little though wondrous fat;
Nor brighter was his eye, nor moister,
Than a too-long-opened oyster,
Save when at noon his paunch grew
     mutinous
For a plate of turtle green and glutinous),
"Only a scraping of shoes on the mat?
Anything like the sound of a rat
Makes my heart go pit-a-pat!"

"Come in!"—the Mayor cried, looking
     bigger:
And in did come the strangest figure.
His queer long coat from heel to head
Was half of yellow and half of red;
And he himself was tall and thin,
With sharp blue eyes, each like a pin,
And light loose hair, yet swarthy skin,
No tuft on cheek nor beard on chin,
But lips where smiles went out and in—
There was no guessing his kith and kin!

And nobody could enough admire
The tall man and his quaint attire.
Quoth one: "It's as my great grandsire,
Starting up at the Trump of Doom's tone,
Had walked this way from his painted
     tombstone."

He advanced to the council-table:
And, "Please, your honours," said he,
     "I'm able,
By means of a secret charm, to draw
All creatures living beneath the sun,
That creep, or swim, or fly, or run,
After me so as you never saw!
And I chiefly use my charm
On creatures that do people harm,
The mole, and toad, and newt, and viper;
And people call me the Pied Piper."
(And here they noticed round his neck
     A scarf of red and yellow stripe,
To match with his coat of the selfsame
     cheque;
     And at the scarf's end hung a pipe;
And his fingers, they noticed, were ever
     straying
As if impatient to be playing
Upon this pipe, as low it dangled
Over his vesture so old-fangled.)
     "Yet," said he, "poor piper as I am,
In Tartary I freed the Cham,
Last June, from his huge swarms of gnats;
I eased in Asia the Nizam
Of a monstrous brood of vampire bats:
And, as for what your brain bewilders,
If I can rid your town of rats
Will you give me a thousand guilders?"
"One? fifty thousand!"—was the exclama-
     tion
Of the astonished Mayor and Corporation.

Into the street the Piper stept,
     Smiling first a little smile,
As if he knew what magic slept
     In his quiet pipe the while;
Then, like a musical adept,
To blow the pipe his lips he wrinkled,
And green and blue his sharp eyes
     twinkled
Like a candle-flame where salt is sprinkled;
And ere three shrill notes the pipe uttered,

You heard as if an army muttered;
And the muttering grew to a grumbling;
And the grumbling grew to a mighty
    rumbling;
And out of the house the rats came
    tumbling.
Great rats, small rats, lean rats, brawny
    rats,
Brown rats, black rats, gray rats, tawny
    rats,
Grave old plodders, gay young friskers,
    Fathers, mothers, uncles, cousins,
Cocking tails and pricking whiskers,
    Families by tens and dozens,
Brothers, sisters, husbands, wives—
Followed the Piper for their lives.
From street to street he piped advancing,
And step by step they followed dancing,
Until they came to the river Weser
Wherein all plunged and perished
—Save one, who, stout as Julius Caesar,
Swam across and lived to carry
(As he the manuscript he cherished)
To Rat-land home his commentary,
Which was, "At the first shrill notes of the
    pipe,
I heard a sound as of scraping tripe,
And putting apples, wondrous ripe,
Into a cider press's gripe;
And a moving away of pickle-tub boards,
And a drawing the corks of train-oil flasks,
And a breaking the hoops of butter casks;
And it seemed as if a voice
(Sweeter far than by harp or by psaltery
Is breathed) called out, Oh, rats! rejoice!
The world is grown to one vast drysaltery!
To munch on, crunch on, take your
    nuncheon,
Breakfast, supper, dinner, luncheon!
And just as a bulky sugar puncheon,
All ready staved, like a great sun shone
Glorious scarce an inch before me,
Just as methought it said, come, bore me!
—I found the Weser rolling o'er me."

You should have heard the Hamelin people
Ringing the bells till they rocked the steeple.
    "Go," cried the Mayor, "and get long
        poles!

Poke out the nests and block up the holes!
Consult with carpenters and builders,
And leave in our town not even a trace
Of the rats!"—when suddenly up the face
Of the Piper perked in the market-place,
With a, "First, if you please, my thousand
    guilders!"

A thousand guilders! The mayor looked blue;
So did the Corporation too.
For council dinners made rare havoc
With Claret, Moselle, Vin-de-Grave, Hock;
And half the money would replenish
Their cellar's biggest butt with Rhenish.
To pay this sum to a wandering fellow
With a gipsy coat of red and yellow!
    "Beside," quoth the Mayor, with a
        knowing wink,
    "Our business was done at the river's
        brink;
    We saw with our eyes the vermin sink,
    And what's dead can't come to life, I think.
    So, friend, we're not the folks to shrink
    From the duty of giving you something to
        drink,
    And a matter of money to put in your poke,
    But, as for the guilders, what we spoke
    Of them, as you very well know, was in
        joke.
    Besides, our losses have made us thrifty;
    A thousand guilders! Come, take fifty!"

The piper's face fell, and he cried,
"No trifling! I can't wait, beside!
I've promised to visit by dinnertime
Bagdad, and accepted the prime
Of the Head Cook's pottage, all he's rich
    in,
For having left the Caliph's kitchen,
Of a nest of scorpions no survivor—
With him I proved no bargain-driver,
With you, don't think I'll bate a stiver!
And folks who put me in a passion
May find me pipe to another fashion."

"How?" cried the Mayor, "d'ye think I'll
    brook
Being worse treated than a Cook?
Insulted by a lazy ribald
With idle pipe and vesture piebald?

You threaten us, fellow? Do your worst,
Blow your pipe there till you burst!"

Once more he stept into the street;
   And to his lips again
Laid his long pipe of smooth straight cane;
   And ere he blew three notes (such sweet
Soft notes as yet musicians cunning
   Never gave the enraptured air),
There was a rustling, that seemed like a
   bustling
Of merry crowds justling, at pitching and
   hustling,
Small feet were pattering, wooden shoes
   clattering,
Little hands clapping, and little tongues
   chattering,
And, like fowls in a farmyard when barley is
   scattering,
Out came the children running.
All the little boys and girls,
With rosy cheeks and flaxen curls,
And sparkling eyes and teeth like pearls,
Tripping and skipping, ran merrily after
The wonderful music with shouting and
   laughter.

The Mayor was dumb, and the Council stood
As if they were changed into blocks of wood,
Unable to move a step, or cry
To the children merrily skipping by—
And could only follow with the eye
That joyous crowd at the Piper's back.
But how the Mayor was on the rack,
And the wretched Council's bosoms beat,
As the piper turned from the High Street
To where the Weser rolled its waters
Right in the way of their sons and daughters!
However, he turned from South to West,
And to Koppelberg Hill his steps addressed,
And after him the children pressed;
Great was the joy in every breast.
   "He never can cross that mighty top!
   He's forced to let the piping drop
   And we shall see our children stop!"
When lo! As they reached the mountain's
   side,
A wondrous portal opened wide,
As if a cavern was suddenly hollowed;
And the Piper advanced and the children
   followed,

And when all were in to the very last,
The door in the mountain-side shut fast.
Did I say all? No! one was lame,
And could not dance the whole of the way;
And in after years, if you would blame
His sadness, he was used to say:
   "It's dull in our town since my playmates
     left;
   I can't forget that I'm bereft
   Of all the pleasant sights they see,
   Which the Piper also promised me;
   For he led us, he said, to a joyous land,
   Joining the town and just at hand,
Where waters gushed and fruit trees grew,
And flowers put forth a fairer hue,
And everything was strange and new.
The sparrows were brighter than peacocks
   here,
And their dogs outran our fallow deer,
And honey-bees had lost their stings;
And horses were born with eagle's wings;
And just as I became assured
My lame foot would be speedily cured;
The music stopped, and I stood still,
   And found myself outside the Hill,
   Left alone against my will,
   To go now limping as before,
   And never hear of that country more!"

Alas, alas for Hamelin!
   There came into many a burger's pate
   A text which says, that Heaven's Gate
Opes to the Rich at as easy rate
As the needle's eye takes a camel in!
The Mayor sent East, West, North and
   South,
To offer the Piper by word of mouth,
   Wherever it was men's lot to find him,
Silver and gold to his heart's content,
If he'd only return the way he went,
   And bring the children all behind him.
But when they saw 'twas a lost endeavour,
And Piper and dancers were gone forever
They made a decree that lawyers never
   Should think their records dated duly
If, after the day of the month and year,
These words did not as well appear,
   "And so long after what happened here
   On the twenty-second of July,
   Thirteen hundred and seventy-six:"

And the better in memory to fix
The place of the Children's last retreat,
They called it, the Pied Piper's street—
Where anyone playing on pipe or tabor,
Was sure for the future to lose his labour.
Nor suffered they hostelry or tavern
To shock with mirth a street so solemn;
But opposite the place of the cavern
    They wrote the story on a column,
And on the great church window painted
The same, to make the world acquainted
How their children were stolen away;
And there it stands to this very day.
And I must not omit to say
That in Transylvania there's a tribe
Of alien people that ascribe
The outlandish ways and dress,
On which their neighbours lay such stress,
To their fathers and mothers having risen
Out of some subterraneous prison,
Into which they were trepanned
Long time ago in a mighty band
Out of Hamelin town in Brunswick land,
But how or why they don't understand.

Robert Browning

Kubla Khan

In Xanadu did Kubla Khan
A stately pleasure-dome decree:
Where Alph, the sacred river, ran
Through caverns measureless to man
    Down to a sunless sea.
So twice five miles of fertile ground
With walls and towers were girdled round:
And there were gardens bright with sinuous
    rills,
Where blossomed many an incense-bearing
    tree;
And here were forests ancient as the hills,
Enfolding sunny spots of greenery.

But oh! that deep romantic chasm which
    slanted
Down the green hill athwart a cedarn cover!

A savage place! as holy and enchanted
As e'er beneath a waning moon was haunted
By woman wailing for her demon-lover!
And from this chasm, with ceaseless turmoil
    seething,
As if this earth in fast thick pants were
    breathing,
A mighty fountain momently was forced:
Amid whose swift half-intermitted burst
Huge fragments vaulted like rebounding
    hail,
Or chaffy grain beneath the thresher's flail:
And 'mid these dancing rocks at once and
    ever
It flung up momently the sacred river.
Five miles meandering with a mazy motion
Through wood and dale the sacred river ran,
Then reached the caverns measureless to
    man,
And sank in tumult to a lifeless ocean:
And 'mid this tumult Kubla heard from far
Ancestral voices prophesying war!
    The shadow of the dome of pleasure
    Floated midway on the waves;
    Where was heard the mingled measure
    From the fountain and the caves,
It was a miracle of rare device,
A sunny pleasure-dome with caves of ice!

    A damsel with a dulcimer
    In a vision once I saw:
    It was an Abyssinian maid,
    And on her dulcimer she played,
    Singing of Mount Abora.
    Could I revive within me
    Her symphony and song,
    To such a deep delight 'twould win me,
That with music loud and long,
I would build that dome in air,
That sunny dome! those caves of ice!
And all who heard should see them there,
And all should cry, Beware! Beware!
His flashing eyes, his floating hair!
Weave a circle round him thrice,
And close your eyes with holy dread,
For he on honey-dew hath fed,
And drunk the milk of Paradise.

Samuel Taylor Coleridge

"Kubla Khan" from POEMS OF SAMUEL TAYLOR
COLERIDGE by Samuel Taylor Coleridge.

Nonsense People

"And yet you incessantly stand on your head"

Jack and Jill went up the hill
   To fetch a pail of water;
Jack fell down and broke his crown,
   And Jill came tumbling after.

Up Jack got, and home did trot,
   As fast as he could caper,
To old Dame Dob, who patched his nob
   With vinegar and brown paper.

(Mother Goose)

Little Boy Blue,
   Come blow your horn,
The sheep's in the meadow,
   The cow's in the corn;
But where is the boy
   Who looks after the sheep?
He's under a haycock,
   Fast asleep.
Will you wake him?
   No, not I,
For if I do,
   He's sure to cry.

(Mother Goose)

Simple Simon met a pieman,
   Going to the fair;
Says Simple Simon to the pieman,
   Let me taste your ware.

Says the pieman to Simple Simon,
   Show me first your penny;
Says Simple Simon to the pieman,
   Indeed I have not any.

Simple Simon went a-fishing,
   For to catch a whale;
All the water he had got
   Was in his mother's pail.

Simple Simon went to look
   If plums grew on a thistle;
He pricked his finger very much,
   Which made poor Simon whistle.

(Mother Goose)

A farmer went trotting upon his gray mare;
   Bumpety, bumpety, bump!
With his daughter behind him so rosy and
      fair;
   Lumpety, lumpety, lump!

A raven cried "Croak!" and they all tumbled
      down,
   Bumpety, bumpety, bump!
The mare broke her knees, and the farmer
      his crown,
   Lumpety, lumpety, lump!

The mischievous raven flew laughing away,
   Bumpety, bumpety, bump!
And vowed he would serve them the same
      the next day,
   Lumpety, lumpety, lump!

(Mother Goose)

There was an Old Man who said, "Well!
Will *nobody* answer this bell?
　　I have pulled day and night,
　　Till my hair has grown white.
But nobody answers this bell!"

Edward Lear

Diddle, diddle, dumpling, my son John,
　　Went to bed with his trousers on;
One shoe off, and one shoe on,
　　Diddle, diddle, dumpling, my son John.

(Mother Goose)

The grand Old Duke of York
　　He had ten thousand men,
He marched them up a very high hill
　　And he marched them down again.
And when he was up he was up
　　And when he was down he was down
And when he was only halfway up
　　He was neither up nor down.

(Mother Goose)

Bobbily Boo and Wollypotump

Bobbily Boo, the king so free,
He used to drink the Mango tea.
Mango tea and coffee, too,
He drank them both till his nose turned blue.

Wollypotump, the queen so high,
She used to eat the Gumbo pie.
Gumbo pie and Gumbo cake,
She ate them both till her teeth did break.

Bobbily Boo and Wollypotump,
Each called the other a greedy frump.
And when these terrible words were said,
They sat and cried till they both were dead.

Laura E. Richards

The King's Breakfast

The King asked
The Queen, and
The Queen asked
The Dairymaid:
"Could we have some butter for
The Royal slice of bread?"
The Queen asked
The Dairymaid,
The Dairymaid
Said, "Certainly,
I'll go and tell
The cow
Now
Before she goes to bed."

The Dairymaid
She curtsied,
And went and told
The Alderney:
"Don't forget the butter for
The Royal slice of bread."
The Alderney
Said sleepily:
"You'd better tell
His Majesty
That many people nowadays
Like marmalade
Instead."

The Dairymaid
Said, "Fancy!"
And went to
Her Majesty
She curtsied to the Queen, and
She turned a little red:

"There was an old man who said, 'Well!'" from THE COMPLETE NONSENSE BOOK by Edward Lear.

"Bobbily Boo and Wollypotump" from TIRRA LIRRA: RHYMES OLD AND NEW by Laura E. Richards. Copyright 1932 by Laura E. Richards; ⓒ renewed 1960 by Hamilton Richards. Reprinted by permission of Little, Brown and Company.

"The King's Breakfast" from WHEN WE WERE VERY YOUNG by A. A. Milne. Copyright 1924 by E. P. Dutton & Co., Inc. Renewal copyright 1952 by A. A. Milne. Reprinted by permission of the publisher, E. P. Dutton, Inc., The Canadian Publishers, McClelland and Stewart Limited, Toronto, and Methuen Children's Books.

"Excuse me,
Your Majesty,
For taking of
The liberty,
But marmalade is tasty, if
It's very
Thickly
Spread."

The Queen said
"Oh!"
And went to
His Majesty:
"Talking of the butter for
The Royal slice of bread,
Many people
Think that
Marmalade
Is nicer.
Would you like to try a little
Marmalade
Instead?"

The King said,
"Bother!"
And then he said,
"Oh, deary me!"
The King sobbed, "Oh, deary me!"
And went back to bed.
"Nobody,"
He whimpered,
"Could call me
A fussy man;
I *only* want
A little bit
Of butter for
My bread!"

The Queen said,
"There, there!"
And went to
The Dairymaid.
The Dairymaid
Said, "There, there!"
And went to the shed.
The cow said,
"There, there!
I didn't really
Mean it;
Here's milk for his porringer
And butter for his bread."

The Queen took
The butter
And brought it to
His Majesty;
The King said,
"Butter, eh?"
And bounced out of bed.
"Nobody," he said,
As he kissed her
Tenderly,
"Nobody," he said,
As he slid down
The banisters,
"Nobody,
My darling,
Could call me
A fussy man—

BUT

"I do like a little bit of butter to my bread!"

A. A. Milne

Little Dimity

Poor little pigeon-toed Dimity Drew,
The more she ate, the smaller she grew.
When some people eat, they get taller and
    taller;
When Dimity ate, she got smaller and
    smaller.
She went for a walk, and all you could see
Was a tam-o'-shanter the size of a pea,
An umbrella as big as the cross on a *t*,
And a wee pocketbook of butterfly blue.
She came to a crack one half an inch wide,
Tripped on a breadcrumb, fell inside,
And slowly disappeared from view.

William Jay Smith

Sarah Cynthia Sylvia Stout
Would Not Take
the Garbage Out

Sarah Cynthia Sylvia Stout
Would not take the garbage out!
She'd scour the pots and scrape the pans,
Candy the yams and spice the hams,
And though her daddy would scream and
    shout,
She simply would not take the garbage out.
And so it piled up to the ceilings:
Coffee grounds, potato peelings,
Brown bananas, rotten peas,
Chunks of sour cottage cheese.
It filled the can, it covered the floor,
It cracked the window and blocked the door
With bacon rinds and chicken bones,
Drippy ends of ice cream cones,
Prune pits, peach pits, orange peel,
Gloppy glumps of cold oatmeal,
Pizza crusts and withered greens,
Soggy beans and tangerines,
Crusts of black burned buttered toast,
Gristly bits of beefy roasts . . .
The garbage rolled on down the hall,
It raised the roof, it broke the wall . . .
Greasy napkins, cookie crumbs,
Globs of gooey bubble gum,
Cellophane from green baloney,
Rubbery blubbery macaroni,
Peanut butter, caked and dry,
Curdled milk and crusts of pie,
Moldy melons, dried-up mustard,
Eggshells mixed with lemon custard,
Cold french fries and rancid meat,
Yellow lumps of Cream of Wheat.
At last the garbage reached so high
That finally it touched the sky.
And all the neighbors moved away,
And none of her friends would come to play.

And finally Sarah Cynthia Stout said,
"OK, I'll take the garbage out!"
But then, of course, it was too late . . .
The garbage reached across the state,
From New York to the Golden Gate.
And there, in the garbage she did hate,
Poor Sarah met an awful fate,
That I cannot right now relate
Because the hour is much too late.
But children, remember Sarah Stout
And always take the garbage out!

Shel Silverstein

Adelaide

Adelaide was quite dismayed;
the more she ate, the less she weighed;
the less she weighed, the more she ate,
and addled Adelaide lost weight.

She stuffed herself with meat and cheese,
potatoes, pumpkins, pies and peas,
but standing on the scale she found
that she had shed at least a pound.

She gorged herself on breasts of veal,
on roasted fish, on pickled eel,
but on completion of this feast
her scale read—ten pounds less, at least.

Poor Adelaide, that foolish glutton,
filled herself with heaps of mutton,
but when this was finally done
the scale said—minus twenty-one.

She ate until her face turned blue—
she did not know what else to do—
but when she'd finished with her plate,
she'd lost a hundred pounds of weight.

Soon Adelaide, by all accounts,
was down to hardly half an ounce,
and yet what filled her with despair
was that her cupboard shelves were bare.

For Adelaide still wished to eat—
then spied a breadcrumb by her feet;
she swiftly plucked it off the floor,
and swallowed it, then was—no more!

Jack Prelutsky

Higgledy Piggledy

Higgledy piggledy
Wiggledy wump,
I met a man
Who caught a mump:
With his left cheek lumpy
And his right cheek bumpy—
Higgledy piggledy
Wiggledy wump.

Higgledy piggledy
Sniggledy sneezle,
I met a man
Who caught a measle:
With his chest all dots
And his face all spots—
Higgledy piggledy
Sniggledy sneezle.

Dennis Lee

Jimmy Jet and His TV Set

I'll tell you the story of Jimmy Jet—
And you know what I tell you is true.
He loved to watch his TV set
Almost as much as you.

He watched all day, he watched all night
Till he grew pale and lean,
From "The Early Show" to "The Late Late
    Show"
And all the shows between.

He watched till his eyes were frozen wide,
And his bottom grew into his chair.
And his chin turned into a tuning dial,
And antennae grew out of his hair.

And his brains turned into TV tubes,
And his face to a TV screen.
And two knobs saying "VERT." and "HORIZ."
Grew where his ears had been.

And he grew a plug that looked like a tail
So we plugged in little Jim.
And now instead of him watching TV
We all sit around and watch him.

Shel Silverstein

J. Prior, Esq.

Johnson Prior
(country squire)
kept a mixed
but earnest
choir:
seven pigs,
a mule
(or donkey)
fourteen parrots,
and a monkey,
sixteen cats,
a Mr. Ford,
(Mrs. Ford on harpsichord).
When they cried:
"Oh! Johnson Prior!
Your agglomeratious
choir
is an insult to the ear!"
Squire Prior
couldn't hear.

N. M. Bodecker

Eat-It-All Elaine

I went away last August
To summer camp in Maine,
And there I met a camper
Called Eat-it-all Elaine.
Although Elaine was quiet,
She liked to cause a stir
By acting out the nickname
Her camp-mates gave to her.

The day of our arrival
At Cabin Number Three
When girls kept coming over
To greet Elaine and me,
She took a piece of Kleenex
And calmly chewed it up,
Then strolled outside the cabin
And ate a buttercup.

Elaine, from that day forward,
Was always in command.
On hikes, she'd eat some birch-bark.
On swims, she'd eat some sand.
At meals, she'd swallow prune-pits
And never have a pain,
While everyone around her
Would giggle, "Oh Elaine!"

One morning, berry-picking,
A bug was in her pail,
And though we thought for certain
Her appetite would fail,
Elaine said, "Hmm, a stinkbug."
And while we murmured, "Ooh,"
She ate her pail of berries
And ate the stinkbug, too.

The night of Final Banquet
When counselors were handing
Awards to different children
Whom they believed outstanding,
To every *thinking* person
At summer camp in Maine
The Most Outstanding Camper
Was Eat-it-all Elaine.

Kaye Starbird

"Johnnie Crack and Flossie Snail" from UNDER MILK
WOOD by Dylan Thomas. Copyright 1954 by New Directions.
Reprinted by permission of New Directions Publishing Corpora-
tion and David Higham Associates Ltd.

Mr. Skinner

Orville Skinner
(kite-string spinner)
never stopped
to eat his dinner,
for he found it
too rewarding
and exciting
to go kiteing.
Flying kites,
he used to sing:
"I'm a spinner
on a string!"
When they warned him:
"Mister Skinner,
capable
but high-strung spinner,
it may take you
to Brazil,"
Skinner cried:
"I hope it will!"

N. M. Bodecker

from Under Milk Wood

Johnnie Crack and Flossie Snail
Kept their baby in a milking pail
Flossie Snail and Johnnie Crack
One would pull it out and one would put it
    back

O it's my turn now said Flossie Snail
To take the baby from the milking pail
And it's my turn now said Johnnie Crack
To smack it on the head and put it back

Johnnie Crack and Flossie Snail
Kept their baby in a milking pail
One would put it back and one would pull it
    out
And all it had to drink was ale and stout
For Johnnie Crack and Flossie Snail
Always used to say that stout and ale
Was *good* for a baby in a milking pail.

Dylan Thomas

Some Sound Advice from Singapore

There was a man from Singapore
Who dressed in everything he wore
And took a walk along the shore.

The shore was right beside the sea.
Mostly—or so it seems to me—
Because of nowhere else to be.

For the same reason as before
The sea was right beside the shore.
As for the man from Singapore.

His reason was: If you take care
To dress in everything you wear,
You won't get sunburned walking bare.

John Ciardi

Jim,
Who ran away from his Nurse, and was eaten by a Lion.

There was a Boy whose name was Jim;
His Friends were very good to him.
They gave him Tea, and Cakes, and Jam,
And slices of delicious Ham,
And Chocolate with pink inside,
And little Tricycles to ride,
And
   read him Stories through and through,
And even took him to the Zoo—
But there it was the dreadful Fate
Befell him, which I now relate.

You know—at least you *ought* to know,
For I have often told you so—
That Children never are allowed
To leave their Nurses in a Crowd;

Now this was Jim's especial Foible,
He ran away when he was able,
And on this inauspicious day
He slipped his hand and ran away!
He hadn't gone a yard when—
           Bang!

With open Jaws, a Lion sprang,
And hungrily began to eat
The Boy: beginning at his feet.

Now just imagine how it feels
When first your toes and then your heels,
And then by gradual degrees,
Your shins and ankles, calves and knees,
Are slowly eaten, bit by bit.

No wonder Jim detested it!
No wonder that he shouted "Hi!"
The Honest Keeper heard his cry,
Though very fat
           he almost ran
To help the little gentleman.
"Ponto!" he ordered as he came
(For Ponto was the Lion's name),
"Ponto!" he cried,
           with angry Frown.
"Let go, Sir! Down, Sir! Put it down!"

The Lion made a sudden Stop,
He let the Dainty Morsel drop,
And slunk reluctant to his Cage,
Snarling with Disappointed Rage
But when he bent him over Jim,
The Honest Keeper's
           Eyes were dim.
The Lion having reached his Head,
The Miserable Boy was dead!

When Nurse informed his Parents, they
Were more Concerned than I can say:—
His Mother, as She dried her eyes,
Said, "Well—it gives me no surprise,
He would not do as he was told!"
His Father, who was self-controlled,
Bade all the children round attend
To James' miserable end,
And always keep a-hold of Nurse
For fear of finding something worse

Hilaire Belloc

"Some Sound Advice from Singapore" from FAST AND SLOW by John Ciardi. Copyright © 1975 by John Ciardi. Reprinted by permission of Houghton Mifflin Company.

"Jim" from CAUTIONARY VERSES by Hilaire Belloc (British title: COMPLETE VERSE). Published 1941 by Alfred A. Knopf, Inc. Reprinted by permission of Alfred A. Knopf, Inc. and Gerald Duckworth & Co. Ltd.

Poor Old Penelope

Poor old Penelope,
great are her woes,
a pumpkin has started
to grow from her nose.
"My goodness," she warbles,
"this makes me so glum,
I'm perfectly certain
I planted a plum."

Poor old Penelope,
wet are her tears,
two pigeons are perched
on the lobes of her ears.
"How dreadful," she moans,
"I've such terrible luck.
I'd hoped for a goose
and a dear little duck."

Poor old Penelope,
sad is her tale,
this morning an elephant
reached her by mail.
"Oh bother," she mutters,
"I fear that I'm sunk
for all that I sent for
was one little trunk."

Jack Prelutsky

Minnie Morse

Of all the problems no one's solved
The worst is Minnie Morse's;
I mean why Minnie's so involved
With horses.

Since Minnie bought a horse this spring
(An animal named Mable)
She doesn't care to do a thing
But hang around the stable.

In school, she'll never ever pass.
She fills her notebook spaces
And messes up her books in class
By drawing horses' faces.

Last week our teacher, Miss McGrew,
Made Minnie stand—and said
She didn't mind a sketch or two
But now please write instead.
And Minnie sat again, and drew
Another horse's head.

"I said to *write,*" cried Miss McGrew.
"Does someone have to force you?"
At which point, Minnie stomped her shoe
As if she wore a horseshoe,
And tossing back her mane of hair
While all the class just waited,
She said that horses didn't *care*
If girls got educated.

Well, if a horse is what you've got,
It's fine to want to please one;
But what I brood about a lot
Is Minnie acts like *she's* one.

In fact, the way she is today,
You can't get far with Minnie
Unless you live on oats and hay—
And whinny.

Kaye Starbird

There was a young lady named Bright,
Who traveled much faster than light.
    She started one day
    In the relative way,
And returned on the previous night.

(Anonymous)

The Headless Gardener

A Gardener, Tobias Baird,
sent his head to be repaired;
he thought, as nothing much was wrong,
he wouldn't be without it long.

Ten years he's weeded path and plot,
a headless gardener, God wot,
always hoping (hope is vain)
to see his noddle back again.

"The Headless Gardener" by Ian Serraillier. Copyright 1951 by Ian Serraillier. Reprinted by permission of the author.

Don't pity him for his distress—
he never sent up his address.

Ian Serraillier

King Tut

King Tut
Crossed over the Nile
On stepping stones
Of crocodile.

King Tut!
His mother said,
Come here this minute!
You'll get wet feet.
King Tut is dead

And now King Tut
Tight as a nut
Keeps his big fat Mummy shut.

King Tut,
Tut, tut.

X. J. Kennedy

Jabberwocky

'Twas brillig, and the slithy toves
    Did gyre and gimble in the wabe:
All mimsy were the borogoves,
    And the mome raths outgrabe.

"Beware the Jabberwock, my son!
    The jaws that bite, the claws that catch!
Beware the Jubjub bird, and shun
    The frumious Bandersnatch!"

He took his vorpal sword in hand:
    Long time the manxome foe he sought—
So rested he by the Tumtum tree,
    And stood awhile in thought.

And, as in uffish thought he stood,
    The Jabberwock, with eyes of flame,
Came whiffling through the tulgey wood,
    And burbled as it came!

One, two! One, two! And through and
    through
The vorpal blade went snicker-snack!

He left it dead, and with its head
    He went galumphing back.

"And hast thou slain the Jabberwock?
    Come to my arms, my beamish boy!
O frabjous day! Callooh! Callay!"
    He chortled in his joy.

'Twas brillig, and the slithy toves
    Did gyre and gimble in the wabe:
All mimsy were the borogoves,
    And the mome raths outgrabe.

Lewis Carroll

Father William

"You are old, Father William," the young
    man said,
    "And your hair has become very white;
And yet you incessantly stand on
    your head—
    Do you think, at your age, it is right?"

"In my youth," Father William replied to
    his son,
    "I feared it might injure the brain;
But, now that I'm perfectly sure I have none,
    Why, I do it again and again."

"You are old," said the youth, "as I
    mentioned before.
    And have grown most uncommonly fat;
Yet you turned a back-somersault in at
    the door—
    Pray, what is the reason of that?"

"In my youth," said the sage, as he shook his
    grey locks,
    "I kept all my limbs very supple
By the use of this ointment—one shilling
    the box—
    Allow me to sell you a couple?"

"You are old," said the youth, "and your jaws
    are too weak

For anything tougher than suet;
Yet you finished the goose, with the bones
    and the beak—
Pray, how did you manage to do it?"

"In my youth," said his father, "I took to
    the law,
And argued each case with my wife;
And the muscular strength, which it gave
    to my jaw
Has lasted the rest of my life."

"You are old," said the youth, "one would
    hardly suppose
That your eye was as steady as ever;
Yet you balanced an eel on the end of
    your nose—
What made you so awfully clever?"

"I have answered three questions, and that
    is enough,"
    Said his father. "Don't give yourself airs!
Do you think I can listen all day to such stuff?
    Be off, or I'll kick you down-stairs!"

Lewis Carroll

The Ballad of Newington Green

There was a young lady of Newington Green
Had the luck to be loved by a sewing
    machine
Its foot was so slender, its eye was so bright
It sewed so obligingly, morning or night
On nylon or seersucker, silk or sateen
Her sturdy, reliable Singer machine!

It made her a shirt, and a shift, and a shawl
Pants, petticoat, poncho, pyjamas, and all
A jacket, a jerkin, a veil, and a vest
For every affair she was perfectly dressed
A coat and some curtains, a pink crinoline
Were made by her hard-working Singer
    machine.

It hemmed and it quilted, it ran and it felled
At tucks and at pleats and at darts it excelled
If she gave it some smocking or basting or
    shirring
It worked with a will and was often heard
    purring
How I love you! she cried, oh my darling
    machine
My shapely sweet Singer of Newington
    Green.

She went to a dance in the Holloway Road
In the pink crinoline that her Singer had
    sewed
Fell in love as she sipped on a Coke at the bar
With the fellow who played the electric
    guitar
Her love was returned; he exclaimed,
    My princess
We'll be married next week; all you need is
    a dress.

Come help me, my Singer, here's satin and
    lace
For I'm to be married in seven days' space
Come make me a wedding dress pleated and
    frilled
My swift shapely Singer, so sturdy and
    skilled.
The Singer obliged, but it sighed in between
Every stitch that it sewed, poor heartbroken
    machine.

The wedding was over, the couple were
    gone
The heartbroken Singer was left all alone
In grief and despair it stood sighing and
    sobbing
Tears ran down its needle and into its bobbin
Till rust had demolished that lovelorn
    machine
The sorrowful Singer of Newington Green.

Joan Aiken

Clementine

In a cavern in a canyon, excavating for a
    mine,
Dwelt a miner, forty-niner, and his daughter,
    Clementine.

"The Ballad of Newington Green" from THE SKIN SPIN-
NERS by Joan Aiken. Copyright © 1960, 1973, 1974, 1975, 1976
by Joan Aiken. Reprinted by permission of Viking Penguin Inc.
    "Clementine" from AMERICAN FOLK POETRY.

Oh, my darling, oh, my darling, oh, my
    darling Clementine,
You are lost and gone forever, dreadful
    sorry, Clementine.

Light she was and like a fairy, and her shoes
    were number nine,
Herring boxes without topses, sandals were
    for Clementine.

Drove her ducklings to the water, every
    morning just at nine,
Hit her foot against a splinter, fell into the
    foaming brine.

Ruby lips above the water, blowing bubbles
    soft and fine,
Alas, for me! I was no swimmer, so I lost my
    Clementine.

In a churchyard, near the canyon, where the
    myrtle doth entwine,
There grow roses and other posies fertilized
    by Clementine.

Then the miner, forty-niner, soon began to
    droop and pine,
Thought he ought to join his daughter, now
    he's with his Clementine.

In my dreams she still doth haunt me, robed
    in garments soaked in brine,
Though in life I used to kiss her, now she's
    dead, I draw the line.

(American Folk)

The Seasons

"green whisper of the year"

January brings the snow,
    Makes our feet and fingers glow.
February brings the rain,
    Thaws the frozen lake again.
March brings breezes loud and shrill,
    Stirs the dancing daffodil.

April brings the primrose sweet,
    Scatters daisies at our feet.
May brings flocks of pretty lambs,
    Skipping by their fleecy dams.
June brings tulips, lilies, roses,
    Fills the children's hands with posies.

Hot July brings cooling showers,
    Apricots and gillyflowers.
August brings the sheaves of corn,
    Then the harvest home is borne.
Warm September brings the fruit,
    Sportsmen then begin to shoot.

Fresh October brings the pheasant,
    Then to gather nuts is pleasant.
Dull November brings the blast,
    Then the leaves are whirling fast.
Chill December brings the sleet,
    Blazing fire and Christmas treat.

(Mother Goose)

It is nice to read
news that our spring rain also
    visited your town.

Onitsura

"It is nice to read" from CRICKET SONGS: JAPANESE HAIKU translated by Harry Behn. Copyright © 1964 by Harry Behn. Reprinted by permission of Harcourt Brace Jovanovich, Inc. and Curtis Brown Ltd.

Text of "Spring" from DOGS & DRAGONS, TREES & DREAMS: *A Collection of Poems by Karla Kuskin*. Poems copyright © 1958 by Karla Kuskin. Reprinted by permission of Harper & Row, Publishers, Inc.

Spring

I'm shouting
I'm singing
I'm swinging through trees
I'm winging sky-high
With the buzzing black bees.
I'm the sun
I'm the moon
I'm the dew on the rose.

I'm a rabbit
Whose habit
Is twitching his nose.
I'm lively
I'm lovely
I'm kicking my heels.
I'm crying "Come dance"
To the freshwater eels.
I'm racing through meadows
Without any coat
I'm a gamboling lamb
I'm a light leaping goat
I'm a bud
I'm a bloom
I'm a dove on the wing.
I'm running on rooftops
And welcoming spring!

Karla Kuskin

A Charm for Spring Flowers

Who sees the first marsh marigold
Shall count more wealth than hands
   can hold.

Who bends a knee where violets grow
A hundred secret things shall know.

Who finds hepatica's dim blue
Shall have his dearest wish come true.

Who spies on lady-slippers fair
Shall keep a heart as light as air.

But whosoever toucheth not
One petal, sets no root in pot,

He shall be blessed of earth and sky
Till under them he, too, shall lie.

Rachel Field

Who Calls?

"Listen, children, listen, won't you come into
   the night?
The stars have set their candle gleam, the
   moon her lanthorn light.
I'm piping little tunes for you to catch your
   dancing feet.

There's glory in the heavens, but there's
   magic in the street.
There's jesting here and carnival: the cost of
   a balloon
Is an ancient rhyme said backwards, and a
   wish upon the moon.
The city walls and city streets!—you shall
   make of these
As fair a thing as country roads and blossomy
   apple trees."

"What watchman calls us in the night, and
   plays a little tune
That turns our tongues to talking now of
   April, May and June?
Who bids us come with nimble feet and snap-
   ping finger tips?"
"I am the Spring, the Spring, the Spring with
   laughter on my lips."

Frances Clarke Sayers

April Rain Song

Let the rain kiss you.
Let the rain beat upon your head with silver
   liquid drops.
Let the rain sing you a lullaby.

The rain makes still pools on the sidewalk.
The rain makes running pools in the gutter.
The rain plays a little sleep-song on our roof
   at night—

And I love the rain.

Langston Hughes

Rain, rain, go away,
   Come again another day;
Little Johnny wants to play.

(Mother Goose)

"A Charm for Spring Flowers" from POEMS by Rachel
Field (New York: Macmillan, 1957). Reprinted by permission of
Macmillan Publishing Co., Inc.

"Who Calls?" by Frances Clarke Sayers. Reprinted by permission of the author.

"April Rain Song" from THE DREAM KEEPER AND
OTHER POEMS by Langston Hughes. Copyright 1932 by Al-
fred A. Knopf, Inc., and renewed 1960 by Langston Hughes.
Reprinted by permission of the publisher.

Spring

Sound the flute!
Now it's mute.
Birds delight
Day and night;
Nightingale
In the dale,
Lark in sky,
Merrily,
Merrily, merrily, to welcome in the year.
Little boy,
Full of joy;
Little girl,
Sweet and small;
Cock does crow,
So do you;
Merry voice,
Infant noise,
Merrily, merrily, to welcome in the year.
Little lamb,
Here I am;
Come and lick
My white neck;
Let me pull
Your soft wool;
Let me kiss
Your soft face:
Merrily, merrily, to welcome in the year.

William Blake

Who tossed those golden coins,
The dandelions glittering
On my lawn?

Kazue Mizumura

"Spring" from THE POETICAL WORKS OF WILLIAM BLAKE by William Blake.

Text of "Who tossed those golden coins" from FLOWER MOON SNOW: A BOOK OF HAIKU by Kazue Mizumura. Copyright © 1977 by Kazue Mizumura. Reprinted by permission of Thomas Y. Crowell, Publishers.

"Spring Grass" and "Summer Grass" (p. 126) from GOOD MORNING, AMERICA by Carl Sandburg. Copyright 1928, 1956 by Carl Sandburg. Reprinted by permission of Harcourt Brace Jovanovich, Inc.

"in Just . . ." from TULIPS & CHIMNEYS by E. E. Cummings. Copyright 1923, 1925 and renewed 1951, 1953 by E. E. Cummings. Copyright © 1973, 1976 by George James Firmage. Copyright © 1973, 1976 by Nancy T. Andrews. Reprinted by permission of Liveright Publishing Corporation and Granada Publishing Limited.

Spring Grass

Spring grass, there is a dance to be danced
    for you.
Come up, spring grass, if only for young feet.
Come up, spring grass, young feet ask you.

Smell of the young spring grass,
You're a mascot riding on the wind horses.
You came to my nose and spiffed me. This is
    your lucky year.

Young spring grass just after the winter,
Shoots of the big green whisper of the year,
Come up, if only for young feet.
Come up, young feet ask you.

Carl Sandburg

in Just-
spring   when the world is mud-
luscious the little
lame balloonman

whistles   far   and wee

and eddieandbill come
running from marbles and
piracies and it's
spring

when the world is puddle-wonderful

the queer
old balloonman whistles
far   and   wee
and bettyandisbel come dancing

from hop-scotch and jump-rope and
it's
spring
and
    the

        goat-footed

balloonMan   whistles
far
and
wee

e. e. cummings

Summer Grass

Summer grass aches and whispers.

It wants something; it calls and sings; it pours
    out wishes to the overhead stars.

The rain hears; the rain answers; the rain is
    slow coming; the rain wets the face
    of the grass.

Carl Sandburg

There is joy in
Feeling the warmth
Come to the great world
And seeing the sun
Follow its old footprints
In the summer night.

(Eskimo)

Earthy Anecdote

Every time the bucks went clattering
Over Oklahoma
A firecat bristled in the way.

Wherever they went,
They went clattering,
Until they swerved
In a swift, circular line
To the right,
Because of the firecat.

Or until they swerved
In a swift, circular line
To the left,
Because of the firecat.

The bucks clattered.
The firecat went leaping,
To the right, to the left,
And
Bristled in the way.

Later, the firecat closed his bright eyes
And slept.

Wallace Stevens

That Was Summer

Have you ever smelled summer?
Sure you have.
Remember that time
when you were tired of running
or doing nothing much
and you were hot
and you flopped right down on the ground?
Remember how the warm soil smelled
and the grass?
That was summer.

Remember that time
when you were trying to climb
higher in the tree
and you didn't know how
and your foot was hurting in the fork
but you were holding tight
to the branch?
Remember how the bark smelled then—
all dusty dry, but nice?
That was summer.

Remember that time
when the storm blew up quick
and you stood under a ledge
and watched the rain till it stopped
and when it stopped
you walked out again to the sidewalk,
the quiet sidewalk?
Remember how the pavement smelled—
all steamy warm and wet?
That was summer.

If you try very hard
can you remember that time
when you played outside all day
and you came home for dinner
and had to take a bath right away,
right away?

"There is joy in" from BEYOND THE HIGH HILLS translated by Knud Rasmussen. Copyright © 1961 by World Publishing Company. Reprinted by permission of Philomel Books, a division of The Putnam Publishing Group.

"Earthy Anecdote," copyright 1923 and renewed 1951 by Wallace Stevens. Reprinted from THE COLLECTED POEMS OF WALLACE STEVENS, by permission of Alfred A. Knopf, Inc. and Faber and Faber Ltd.

"That Was Summer" from THAT WAS SUMMER by Marci Ridlon. Copyright © 1969 by Marci Ridlon. Reprinted by permission of the author.

It took you a long time to pull
your shirt over your head.
Do you remember smelling the sunshine?
That was summer.

Marci Ridlon

Dandelion

O little soldier with the golden helmet,
What are you guarding on my lawn?
You with your green gun
And your yellow beard,
Why do you stand so stiff?
There is only the grass to fight!

Hilda Conkling

Upside Down

A field of clouds,
a wildflower sky;
upside down
goes Summer by.

My hammock rocks
a leafy lake;
I dive: the crystal
ceilings break.

A bird goes burrowing
down in the air;
an ant hangs high
in my tangled hair.

I'll skin-the-cat
and cartwheels turn
till proper Fall
rights earth again.

Rose Burgunder

Fog

The fog comes
on little cat feet.

It sits looking
over harbor and city
on silent haunches
and then moves on.

Carl Sandburg

I Will Go With My Father A-Ploughing

I will go with my Father a-ploughing
To the Green Field by the sea,
And the rooks and crows and seagulls
Will come flocking after me.
I will sing to the patient horses
With the lark in the shine of the air,
And my Father will sing the Plough-Song
That blesses the cleaving share.

I will go with my Father a-sowing
To the Red Field by the sea,
And blackbirds and robins and thrushes
Will come flocking after me.
I will sing to the striding sowers
With the finch on the flowering sloe,
And my Father will sing the Seed-Song
That only the wise men know.

I will go with my Father a-reaping
To the Brown Field by the sea,
And the geese and pigeons and sparrows
Will come flocking after me.
I will sing to the weary reapers
With the wren in the heat of the sun,
And my Father will sing the Scythe-Song
That joys for the harvest done.

Joseph Campbell

Dragon Smoke

Breathe and blow
white clouds
        with every puff.
It's cold today,
        cold enough
to see your breath.
Huff!
    Breathe dragon smoke
            today!

Lilian Moore

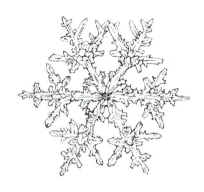

Once I Dreamt I Was the Snow

Once I dreamt I was the snow
that covered all the town
with a comforter on each roof,
a blanket on each lawn.
I let a white cat of snow
stretch on every branch,
each berry got a hat
as soft as wool,
and inside every silent room
bells were ringing WHITE,
WHITE, WHITE, WHITE.

Siv Cedering Fox

Cynthia in the Snow

It SUSHES.
It hushes
The loudness in the road.
It flitter-twitters,
And laughs away from me.
It laughs a lovely whiteness,
And whitely whirs away,
To be
Some otherwhere,
Still white as milk or shirts.
So beautiful it hurts.

Gwendolyn Brooks

The Snowflake

Before I melt,
Come, look at me!
This lovely icy filigree!
Of a great forest
In one night
I make a wilderness
Of white:

By skyey cold
Of crystals made,
All softly, on
Your finger laid,
I pause, that you
My beauty see:
Breathe, and I vanish
Instantly.

Walter de la Mare

Velvet Shoes

Let us walk in the white snow
  In a soundless space;
With footsteps quiet and slow,
  At a tranquil pace,
  Under veils of white lace.

I shall go shod in silk,
  And you in wool,
White as a white cow's milk,
  More beautiful
  Than the breast of a gull.

We shall walk through the still town
  In a windless peace;
We shall step upon white down,
  Upon silver fleece,
  Upon softer than these.

We shall walk in velvet shoes:
  Wherever we go
Silence will fall like dews
  On white silence below.
  We shall walk in the snow.

Elinor Wylie

Stopping by Woods on a Snowy Evening

Whose woods these are I think I know.
His house is in the village though;
He will not see me stopping here
To watch his woods fill up with snow.

My little horse must think it queer
To stop without a farmhouse near
Between the woods and frozen lake
The darkest evening of the year.

He gives his harness bells a shake
To ask if there is some mistake.
The only other sound's the sweep
Of easy wind and downy flake.

The woods are lovely, dark and deep.
But I have promises to keep,
And miles to go before I sleep,
And miles to go before I sleep.

Robert Frost

There is fear in
Feeling the cold
Come to the great world
And seeing the moon
—Now new moon, now full moon—
Follow its old footprints
In the winter night.

(Eskimo)

The World Around Us
"With the sun and the sea, the wind and the moon"

The Ballad of Mad Fortune

With the sun and the sea, the wind and the
  moon
I'm going to pile up a fortune soon.

With the sun I will mint me coins of gold,
Dark on one side, on the other side bright
To play games of toss-up coin as of old.

I'll bottle the water up out of the sea,
With pretty bright labels, with tags gayly,
I'll sell it with a glass-dropper to keep
For all who want to learn how to weep.

I'll kidnap the wind, then control its flight,
And in nights of quiet with breathlessness
  blent,
Sell its sighs to lovers for their delight,
And its songs to poets who are silent.

I will keep her a while,
As for the moon,
A kind of protection all of my own,
Safe in my heart's strong-box of stone.

With the sun and the sea, the wind and the
  moon,
What a mad fortune I'll pile up soon!

Translated by *Edna Worthley Underwood*

Balada de la loca fortuna

Con el sol, el mar, el viento y la luna
voy a amasar una loca fortuna.

Con el sol haré monedas de oro
(al reverso, manchas; al anverso, luz)
para jugarlas a cara o a cruz.

Cerraré en botellas las aguas del mar,
con lindos marbetes y expresivas notas,
y he de venderlas con un cuentagotas
a todo el que quiera llorar.

Robador del viento, domaré sus giros,
y en las noches calladas y quietas,
para los amantes venderé suspiros,
y bellas canciones para los poetas . . .

En cuanto a la luna,
la guardo, por una
sabia precaución,
en la caja fuerte de mi corazón . . .

Con el sol, la luna, el viento y el mar,
¡qué loca fortuna voy a improvisar!

Enrique González Martínez

That duck, bobbing up
from the green deeps of a pond,
  has seen something strange . . .

Jōsō

"The Ballad of Mad Fortune" by Enrique González Mar-
tínez, translated by Edna Worthley Underwood, SPANISH-
AMERICAN POETRY. Reprinted by permission of Harvey
House, Publishers.

"That duck, bobbing up" from CRICKET SONGS: JAPA-
NESE HAIKU translated by Harry Behn. Copyright © 1964 by
Harry Behn. Reprinted by permission of Harcourt Brace Jovano-
vich, Inc. and Curtis Brown Ltd.

Song of Creation

I have made the sun!
  I have made the sun!
Hurling it high
  In the four directions
To the east I threw it
  To run its appointed course.

I have made the moon!
  I have made the moon!
Hurling it high
  In the four directions
To the east I threw it
  To run its appointed course.

(Pima)

The Brave Man

The sun, that brave man,
Comes through boughs that lie in wait,
That brave man.

Green and gloomy eyes
In dark forms of the grass
Run away.

The good stars,
Pale helms and spiky spurs,
Run away.

Fears of my bed,
Fears of life and fears of death,
Run away.

That brave man comes up
From below and walks without meditation,
That brave man.

Wallace Stevens

Some say the sun is a golden earring,
the earring of a beautiful girl.
A white bird took it from her
when she walked in the fields one day.
But it caught on a spider web
that stretches between the homes of men
and the homes of the gods.

Natalia Belting

The great sea
Has sent me adrift
It moves me as the weed in a great river,
Earth and the great weather
Move me,
Have carried me away
And move my inward parts with joy.

(Eskimo)

Old Man Ocean

Old Man Ocean, how do you pound
Smooth glass rough, rough stones round?
  Time and the tide and the wild waves
    rolling,
  Night and the wind and the long gray
    dawn.

Old Man Ocean, what do you tell,
What do you sing in the empty shell?
  Fog and the storm and the long bell
    tolling,
  Bones in the deep and the brave men gone.

Russell Hoban

How Everything Happens
(Based on a Study of the Wave)

                                                             happen.
                                                          to
                                                       up
                                                 stacking
                                            is
                                     something
When nothing is happening

When it happens
                    something
                            pulls
                                back
                                    not
                                        to
                                          happen.

When   has happened.
        pulling back   stacking up
                  happens

        has happened   stacks up.
When it   something   nothing
                        pulls back while

Then nothing is happening.

                                    happens.
                                and
                          forward
                    pushes
                  up
            stacks
        something
Then

May Swenson

"How Everything Happens (Based on a Study of the Wave)" from NEW & SELECTED THINGS TAKING PLACE by May Swenson. Poem copyright © 1966 by May Swenson. First appeared in *The Southern Review.* Reprinted by permission of Little, Brown and Company in association with the Atlantic Monthly Press.

The River Is a Piece of Sky

From the top of a bridge
The river below
Is a piece of sky—
      Until you throw
      A penny in
      Or a cockleshell
      Or a pebble or two
      Or a bicycle bell
      Or a cobblestone
      Or a fat man's cane—
And then you can see
It's a river again.

The difference you'll see
When you drop your penny:
The river has splashes,
The sky hasn't any.

John Ciardi

The Negro Speaks of Rivers

I've known rivers:
I've known rivers ancient as the world and
    older than the flow of human blood in
    human veins.

My soul has grown deep like the rivers.

I bathed in the Euphrates when dawns were
    young.
I built my hut near the Congo and it lulled
    me to sleep.
I looked upon the Nile and raised the pyra-
    mids above it.
I heard the singing of the Mississippi when
    Abe Lincoln went down to New Or-
    leans, and I've seen its muddy bosom
    turn all golden in the sunset.

I've known rivers:
Ancient, dusky rivers.

My soul has grown deep like the rivers.

Langston Hughes

Sir Patrick Spence

The king sits in Dumferling town,
    Drinking the blood-red wine:
"O where will I get a good sailor,
    To sail this ship of mine?"

Up and spoke an elderly knight,
    (Sat at the king's right knee),
"Sir Patrick Spence is the best sailor
    That sails upon the sea."

The king has written a broad letter,
    And signed it with his hand,
And sent it to Sir Patrick Spence,
    Was walking on the sand.

The first line that Sir Patrick read,
    A loud laugh laughed he;
The next line that Sir Patrick read,
    A tear blinded his eye.

"O who is this has done this deed,
    This ill deed done to me,
To send me out this time of year,
    To sail upon the sea!

"Make haste, make haste, my merry men all,
    Our good ship sails the morn:"
"O say not so, my master dear,
    For I fear a deadly storm.

"Late late yestereven I saw the new moon
    With the old moon in her arm,
And I fear, I fear, my master dear,
    That we will come to harm."

O our Scotch nobles were right loathe
    To wet their cork-heeled shoes;
But long after the play was played
    Their hats floated into view.

O long, long may their ladies sit,
    With their fans within their hand,
Or ever they see Sir Patrick Spence
    Come sailing to the land.

O long, long may their ladies stand,
   With their gold combs in their hair,
Waiting for their own dear lords,
   For they'll see them never more.

Half o'er, half o'er to Aberdour,
   It's fifty fathoms deep,
And there lies good Sir Patrick Spence,
   With the Scotch lords at his feet.

(English Ballad)

Who has seen the wind?
   Neither I nor you:
But when the leaves hang trembling
   The wind is passing thro'.

Who has seen the wind?
   Neither you nor I:
But when the trees bow down their heads
   The wind is passing by.

Christina Rossetti

Windy Nights

Whenever the moon and stars are set,
   Whenever the wind is high,
All night long in the dark and wet,
   A man goes riding by.
Late in the night when the fires are out,
Why does he gallop and gallop about?

Whenever the trees are crying aloud,
   And ships are tossed at sea,
By, on the highway, low and loud,
   By at the gallop goes he:
By at the gallop he goes, and then
By he comes back at the gallop again.

Robert Louis Stevenson

I called to the wind,
"Who's there?". . . Whoever it was
   still knocks at my gate.

Kyorai

Wind Song

Wind now commences to sing;
   Wind now commences to sing.
The land stretches before me,
   Before me stretches away.

Wind's house now is thundering.
   Wind's house now is thundering.
I go roaring over the land,
   The land covered with thunder.

Over the windy mountains;
   Over the windy mountains,
Came the myriad-legged wind;
   The wind came running hither.

The black Snake Wind came to me;
   The Black Snake Wind came to me,
Came and wrapped itself about,
   Came here running with its songs.

(Pima)

The Wind

I saw you toss the kites on high
And blow the birds about the sky;
And all around I heard you pass,
Like ladies' skirts across the grass—
   O wind, a-blowing all day long,
   O wind, that sings so loud a song!

I saw the different things you did,
But always you yourself you hid.
I felt you push, I heard you call,
I could not see yourself at all—
   O wind, a-blowing all day long,
   O wind, that sings so loud a song!

"Who has seen the wind?" from SING-SONG by Christina Rossetti.

"Windy Nights" and "The Wind" from A CHILD'S GARDEN OF VERSES by Robert Louis Stevenson.

"I called to the wind" from MORE CRICKET SONGS: JAPANESE HAIKU, translated by Harry Behn. Copyright © 1971 by Harry Behn. Reprinted by permission of Harcourt Brace Jovanovich, Inc. and Curtis Brown Ltd.

"Wind Song" from IN THE TRAIL OF THE WIND by John Bierhorst. Copyright © 1971 by John Bierhorst. Reprinted by permission of Farrar, Straus & Giroux, Inc.

O you that are so strong and cold,
O blower, are you young or old?
Are you a beast of field and tree,
Or just a stronger child than me?
　　O wind, a-blowing all day long,
　　O wind, that sings so loud a song!

Robert Louis Stevenson

The Moon's the North Wind's Cooky

(What the Little Girl Said)

The Moon's the North Wind's cooky.
He bites it, day by day,
Until there's but a rim of scraps
That crumble all away.

The South Wind is a baker.
He kneads clouds in his den,
And bakes a crisp new moon *that . . . greedy*
North . . . Wind . . . eats . . . again!

Vachel Lindsay

Star-light, star-bright
First star I've seen tonight;
I wish I may, I wish I might
Get the wish I wish tonight.

(American Mother Goose)

O moon, why must you
inspire my neighbor to chirp
　　all night on a flute!

Koyo

The Star

Twinkle, twinkle, little star,
How I wonder what you are!
Up above the world so high,
Like a diamond in the sky.

Jane Taylor

The Falling Star

I saw a star slide down the sky,
Blinding the north as it went by,
Too burning and too quick to hold,
Too lovely to be bought or sold,
Good only to make wishes on
And then forever to be gone.

Sara Teasdale

The Star in the Pail

I took the pail for water when the sun
　　was high
And left it in the shadow of the barn nearby.

When evening slippered over like the
　　moth's brown wing,
I went to fetch the water from the cool
　　wellspring.

The night was clear and warm and wide,
　　and I alone
Was walking by the light of stars as thickly
　　sown

As wheat across the prairie, or the first
　　fall flakes,
Or spray upon the lawn—the kind the
　　sprinkler makes.

But every star was far away as far can be,
With all the starry silence sliding over me.

And every time I stopped I set the pail down
    slow,
For when I stooped to pick the handle up
    to go
Of all the stars in heaven there was one
    to spare,
And he silvered in the water and I left him
    there.

David McCord

Once, when the sky was very near the earth,
a woman hoeing in her garden took off her
    necklace
and hung it in the sky.
The stars are her silver necklace.

Natalia Belting

In a Starry Orchard

Lean your ladder light
against a tree by night.

Climbing, examine how
stars hang on every bough.

Wearing a gossamer glove
on your right hand, remove

the ripest fruit of all:
that star about to fall.

Norma Farber

When I Heard the Learn'd Astronomer

When I heard the learn'd astronomer,
When the proofs, the figures, were ranged in
    columns before me,
When I was shown the charts and diagrams,
    to add, divide, and measure them,
When I sitting heard the astronomer where
    he lectured with much applause in the
    lecture-room,
How soon unaccountable I became tired and
    sick,
Till rising and gliding out I wander'd off by
    myself,
In the mystical moist night-air, and from
    time to time,
Look'd up in perfect silence at the stars.

Walt Whitman

from Five Chants

1

Every time I climb a tree
Every time I climb a tree
Every time I climb a tree
I scrape a leg
Or skin a knee
And every time I climb a tree
I find some ants
Or dodge a bee
And get the ants
All over me

And every time I climb a tree
Where have you been?

They say to me
But don't they know that I am free
Every time I climb a tree?
I like it best
To spot a nest
That has an egg
Or maybe three

And then I skin
The other leg
But every time I climb a tree
I see a lot of things to see
Swallows rooftops and TV
And all the fields and farms there be
Every time I climb a tree
Though climbing may be good for ants
It isn't awfully good for pants
But still it's pretty good for me
Every time I climb a tree

David McCord

I had a little nut tree, nothing would it bear
    But a silver nutmeg and a golden pear;
    The king of Spain's daughter came to
        visit me,
And all for the sake of my little nut tree.
    I skipped over water, I danced over sea,
    And all the birds in the air couldn't
        catch me.

(Mother Goose)

Under the greenwood tree
Who loves to lie with me,
And turn his merry note
Unto the sweet bird's throat,
Come hither, come hither, come hither:
    Here shall he see
    No enemy
But winter and rough weather.

William Shakespeare

"Under the greenwood tree" from AS YOU LIKE IT, Act II,
Scene 5, by William Shakespeare.
    "The Tree in the Wood" from AMERICAN FOLK PO-
ETRY.

Spendthrift

Coins—coins—coins—
a bushel to a breeze—
are pouring from the pockets
of the elm in the square.
Gather up the money-heaps—
as many as you please.
So rich an old tree
doesn't count them or care.

Norma Farber

The Tree in the Wood

On the ground there was a tree,
The prettiest little tree you ever did see.
The tree's on the ground
And the green grass growing all around-
        round-round,
And the green grass growing all around.

On the tree there was a limb,
The prettiest little limb you ever did see.
The limb's on the tree
And the tree's on the ground
And the green grass growing all around-
        round-round,
And the green grass growing all around.

On that limb there was a nest,
The prettiest little nest you ever did see.
The nest's on the limb
The limb's on the tree
And the tree's on the ground
And the green grass growing all around-
        round-round,
And the green grass growing all around.

On that nest there was a bird,
The prettiest little bird you ever did see
The bird's on the nest
And the nest's on the limb
And the limb's on the tree
And the tree's on the ground
And the green grass growing all around-
        round-round,
And the green grass growing all around.

On that bird there was a wing,
The prettiest little wing you ever did see.
The wing's on the bird
And the bird's on the nest
And the nest's on the limb
And the limb's on the tree
And the tree's on the ground
And the green grass growing all around-
    round-round,
And the green grass growing all around.

On that wing there was a flea,
The prettiest little flea you ever did see.
The flea's on the wing
And the wing's on the bird
And the bird's on the nest
And the nest's on the limb
The limb's on the tree
The tree's on the ground

And the green grass growing all around-
    round-round,
And the green grass growing all around.

On that flea there was a mosqueetee,
The prettiest little mosqueetee you ever did
    see.
The mosqueetee's on the flea
And the flea's on the wing
And the wing's on the bird
And the bird's on the nest
And the nest's on the limb
And the limb's on the tree
And the tree's on the ground
And the green grass growing all around-
    round-round,
And the green grass growing all around.

(American Folk)

Holidays
"through all our history"

New Year's Water

Here we bring new water from the well so
    clear,
For to worship God with, this happy New
    Year.
Sing levy dew, sing levy dew, the water and
    the wine,

With seven bright gold wires, and bugles that
    do shine.
Since reign of fair maid, with gold upon her
    toe,
Open you the west door, and turn the Old
    Year go.
Sing reign of fair maid, with gold upon her
    chin,
Open you the east door, and let the New
    Year in.

(Traditional, Welsh)

Family Needs

You'll find whene'er the new year come,
The kitchen god will want a plum;
The girls will want some flowers new,
The boys will want some crackers, too;
A new felt cap will please papa,
And sugar-cake will please mama.

(Chinese)

Martin Luther King

Got me a special place
For Martin Luther King.
His picture on the wall
Makes me sing.

I look at it for a long time
And think of some
Real good ways
We will overcome.

Myra Cohn Livingston

Harriet Tubman

Harriet Tubman didn't take no stuff
Wasn't scared of nothing neither
Didn't come in this world to be no slave
And wasn't going to stay one either

"Farewell!" she sang to her friends one night
She was mighty sad to leave 'em
But she ran away that dark, hot night
Ran looking for her freedom

She ran to the woods and she ran through the
     woods
With the slave catchers right behind her
And she kept on going till she got to the
     North
Where those mean men couldn't find her

Nineteen times she went back South
To get three hundred others
She ran for her freedom nineteen times
To save Black sisters and brothers

Harriet Tubman didn't take no stuff
Wasn't scared of nothing neither
Didn't come in this world to be no slave
And didn't stay one either

          And didn't stay one either

Eloise Greenfield

from Hamlet, Act IV, Scene V

Tomorrow is Saint Valentine's day,
   All in the morning betime,
And I a maid at your window
   To be your Valentine.

William Shakespeare

Country Bumpkin
Pick a pumpkin
Put it in your cart:
For little Jenny
Half-a-penny
Valentine sweetheart.

Clyde Watson

Abraham Lincoln 1809–1865

Lincoln was a long man.
He liked out of doors.

He liked the wind blowing
And the talk in country stores.

He liked telling stories,
He liked telling jokes.
"Abe's quite a character,"
Said quite a lot of folks.

Lots of folks in Springfield
Saw him every day,
Walking down the street
In his gaunt, long way.

Shawl around his shoulders,
Letters in his hat.
"That's Abe Lincoln."
They thought no more than that.

Knew that he was honest,
Guessed that he was odd,
Knew he had a cross wife
Though she was a Todd.

Knew he had three little boys
Who liked to shout and play,
Knew he had a lot of debts
It took him years to pay.

Knew his clothes and knew his house.
"That's his office, here.
Blame good lawyer, on the whole,
Though he's sort of queer.

"Sure, he went to Congress, once,
But he didn't stay.
Can't expect us all to be
Smart as Henry Clay.

"Need a man for troubled times?
Well, I guess we do.
Wonder who we'll ever find?
Yes—I wonder who."

"Tomorrow is Saint Valentine's day" from HAMLET, Act IV, Scene 5 by William Shakespeare.

"Country Bumpkin" from FATHER FOX'S PENNY-RHYMES by Clyde Watson. Text copyright © 1971 by Clyde Watson. Reprinted by permission of Thomas Y. Crowell, Publishers and Curtis Brown Ltd.

"Abraham Lincoln" from A BOOK OF AMERICANS by Rosemary and Stephen Vincent Benét. Copyright 1933 by Rosemary and Stephen Vincent Benét. Copyright renewed © 1961 by Rosemary Carr Benét. Reprinted by permission of Brandt & Brandt Literary Agents, Inc.

That is how they met and talked,
Knowing and unknowing.
Lincoln was the green pine.
Lincoln kept on growing.

Rosemary Carr and
Stephen Vincent Benét

from To His Excellency George Washington

Proceed, great chief, with virtue on thy side,
Thy ev'ry action let the goddess guide.
A crown, a mansion, and a throne that shine,
With gold unfading. Washington! be thine.

Phillis Wheatley

Yankee Doodle

Father and I went down to camp
Along with Captain Goodwin,
And there we saw the men and boys
As thick as hasty pudding.

    Yankee Doodle, keep it up,
    Yankee Doodle dandy!
    Mind the music and the steps,
    And with the girls be handy!

There was Captain Washington
Upon a slapping stallion,
Giving orders to his men,
I guess there was a million.

And there they had a swamping gun
As big as a log of maple,
On a deuced little cart,
A load for father's cattle.

And every time they fired it off,
It took a horn of powder;
It made a noise like father's gun,
Only a nation louder.

And there I saw a little keg,
Its heads were made of leather—
They knocked upon it with little sticks
To call the folks together.

The troopers, too, would gallop up
And fire right in our faces,
It scared me almost half to death
To see them run such races.

But I can't tell you half I saw,
They kept up such a smother,
So I took off my hat, made a bow,
And scampered home to mother.

    Yankee Doodle, keep it up,
    Yankee Doodle dandy!
    Mind the music and the steps,
    And with the girls be handy!

(American Folk)

Easter

On Easter morn
Up the faint cloudy sky
I hear the Easter bell,
    Ding dong . . . ding dong . . .
Easter morning scatters lilies
On every doorstep;
Easter morning says a glad thing
Over and over.
Poor people, beggars, old women
Are hearing the Easter bell . . .
    Ding dong . . . ding dong . . .

Hilda Conkling

Oh Have You Heard

Oh have you heard it's time for vaccinations?
I think someone put salt into your tea.
They're giving us eleven-month vacations.
And Florida has sunk into the sea.

"Proceed, great chief" from TO HIS EXCELLENCY GEORGE WASHINGTON by Phillis Wheatley.

"Yankee Doodle" from AMERICAN FOLK POETRY.

"Easter" from POEMS BY A LITTLE GIRL by Hilda Conkling. Copyright 1920 by J. B. Lippincott Company. Reprinted by permission of the author.

"Oh Have You Heard" and "The Fourth" from WHERE THE SIDEWALK ENDS: The Poems and Drawings of Shel Silverstein. Copyright © 1974 by Shel Silverstein. Reprinted by permission of Harper & Row, Publishers, Inc.

Oh have you heard the President has
   measles?
The principal has just burned down the
   school.
Your hair is full of ants and purple weasels—

APRIL FOOL!

Shel Silverstein

The Fourth

Oh
CRASH!
my
BASH!
it's
BANG!
the
ZANG!
Fourth
WHOOSH!
of
BAROOOM!
July
WHEW!

Shel Silverstein

Fourth of July Night

Pinwheels whirling round
Spit sparks upon the ground,
And rockets shoot up high
And blossom in the sky—
Blue and yellow, green and red
Flowers falling on my head,
And I don't ever have to go
To bed, to bed, to bed!

Dorothy Aldis

12 October

From where I stand now
      the world is flat,
      flat out flat,
      no end to that.

Where my eyes go the land moves out.
How is it then
five hundred years ago (about)
Columbus found
that far beyond the flat on flat
the world was round?

Myra Cohn Livingston

from **A Cornish Litany**

From Ghoulies and Ghosties,
And long-leggity Beasties,
And all Things that go bump in the Night,
Good Lord deliver us.

(Traditional, English)

from **Macbeth**, Act IV, Scene 1

FIRST WITCH

Thrice the brinded cat hath mew'd.

SECOND WITCH

Thrice and once the hedge-pig whined.

THIRD WITCH

Harpier cries 'Tis time, 'tis time.'

FIRST WITCH

Round about the cauldron go:
In the poison'd entrails throw.
Toad, that under cold stone
Days and nights has thirty one
Swelter'd venom sleeping got,
Boil thou first i' the charmed pot.

ALL

Double, double toil and trouble;
Fire burn and cauldron bubble.

"Fourth of July Night" from HOP, SKIP AND JUMP by Dorothy Aldis. Copyright 1934; renewed © 1961 by Dorothy Aldis. Reprinted by permission of G. P. Putnam's Sons.

Myra Cohn Livingston, "12 October," in THE MALIBU AND OTHER POEMS. Copyright © 1972 by Myra Cohn Livingston, A Margaret K. McElderry Book (New York: Atheneum, 1972). Reprinted with the permission of Atheneum Publishers and Marian Reiner for the author.

From MACBETH, Act IV, Scene 1 by William Shakespeare.

SECOND WITCH

Fillet of a fenny snake,
In the cauldron boil and bake:
Eye of newt and toe of frog.
Wool of bat and tongue of dog,
Adder's fork and blind-worm's sting,
Lizard's leg and howlet's wing,
For a charm of powerful trouble,
Like a hell-broth boil and bubble.

ALL

Double, double toil and trouble;
Fire burn and cauldron bubble.

THIRD WITCH

Scale of dragon, tooth of wolf,
Witches' mummy, maw and gulf
Of the ravin'd salt-sea shark,
Root of hemlock digg'd i' the dark,
Liver of blaspheming Jew,
Gall of goat and slips of yew
Sliver'd in the moon's eclipse,
Nose of Turk and Tartar's lips,
Finger of birth-strangled babe
Ditch-deliver'd by a drab,
Make the gruel thick and slab:
Add thereto a tiger's chaudron,
For the ingredients of our cauldron.

ALL

Double, double toil and trouble;
Fire burn and cauldron bubble.

SECOND WITCH

Cool it with a baboon's blood,
Then the charm is firm and good.

William Shakespeare

Halloween Witches

Magical prognosticator,
Chanting, canting, calculator,
Exorcist and necromancer,
Venificial, sabbat dancer,
Striga, arted and capricious,
Conjurer and *maleficius.*
    Tonight, how many witches fly?
    How many brooms will sweep the sky?

Felice Holman

Make a joyful noise unto the Lord, all ye
    lands.
Serve the Lord with gladness:
Come before his presence with singing.
Know ye that the Lord he is God:
It is he that hath made us, and not we
    ourselves;
We are his people, and the sheep of his
    pasture.
Enter into his gates with thanksgiving,
And into his courts with praise:
Be thankful unto him, and bless his name.
For the Lord is good; his mercy is ever-
    lasting;
And his truth endureth to all generations.

(Psalm 100)

Christmas is coming, the geese are getting
    fat,
Please to put a penny in an old man's hat;
If you haven't got a penny a ha'penny will do,
If you haven't got a ha'penny, God bless you.

(Mother Goose)

In the Week When Christmas Comes

This is the week when Christmas comes.

Let every pudding burst with plums,
And every tree bear dolls and drums,
    In the week when Christmas comes.

"Halloween Witches" from AT THE TOP OF MY VOICE AND OTHER POEMS by Felice Holman. Copyright © 1970 by Felice Holman (New York: Charles Scribner's Sons, 1970). Reprinted with the permission of Charles Scribner's Sons.

"In the Week When Christmas Comes" by Eleanor Farjeon from ELEANOR FARJEON'S POEMS FOR CHILDREN. Poem copyright 1927, 1955 by Eleanor Farjeon. Reprinted by permission of J. B. Lippincott, Publishers and Harold Ober Associates Incorporated.

Let every hall have boughs of green,
With berries glowing in between,
   In the week when Christmas comes.

Let every doorstep have a song
Sounding the dark street along,
   In the week when Christmas comes.

Let every steeple ring a bell
With a joyful tale to tell,
   In the week when Christmas comes.

Let every night put forth a star
To show us where the heavens are,
   In the week when Christmas comes.

Let every stable have a lamb
Sleeping warm beside its dam,
   In the week when Christmas comes.

This is the week when Christmas comes.

Eleanor Farjeon

little tree
little silent Christmas tree
you are so little
you are more like a flower

who found you in the green forest
and were you very sorry to come away?
see   i will comfort you
because you smell so sweetly

i will kiss your cool bark
and hug you safe and tight
just as your mother would,
only don't be afraid

look   the spangles
that sleep all the year in a dark box
dreaming of being taken out and allowed to
   shine,
the balls the chains red and gold the fluffy
   threads,

put up your little arms
and i'll give them all to you to hold
every finger shall have its ring
and there won't be a single place dark or
   unhappy

then when you're quite dressed
you'll stand in the window for everyone to
   see

and how they'll stare!
oh but you'll be very proud

and my little sister and i will take hands
and looking up at our beautiful tree
we'll dance and sing
"Noel Noel"

e. e. cummings

Otto

It's Christmas Day. I did not get
The presents that I hoped for. Yet,
It is not nice to frown or fret.

To frown or fret would not be fair.
My Dad must never know I care
It's hard enough for him to bear.

Gwendolyn Brooks

A Visit from St. Nicholas

" 'Twas the night before Christmas, when all
   through the house
Not a creature was stirring, not even a
   mouse;
The stockings were hung by the chimney
   with care,
In hopes that St. Nicholas soon would be
   there;
The children were nestled all snug in their
   beds
While visions of sugar-plums danced in their
   heads;
And Mamma in her 'kerchief, and I in my
   cap,
Had just settled our brains for a long winter's
   nap,
When out on the lawn there arose such a
   clatter,

I sprang from my bed to see what was the
matter.
Away to the window I flew like a flash,
Tore open the shutters and threw up the
sash.
The moon on the breast of the new-fallen
snow
Gave a lustre of midday to objects below,
When, what to my wondering eyes did
appear,
But a miniature sleigh and eight tiny rein-
deer,
With a little old driver, so lively and quick,
I knew in a moment it must be St. Nick.
More rapid than eagles his coursers they
came,
And he whistled, and shouted, and called
them by name:
"Now, Dasher! now, Dancer! now, Prancer
and Vixen!
On, Comet! on, Cupid! on, Donder and
Blitzen!
To the top of the porch! to the top of the wall!
Now dash away! dash away! dash away, all!"
As dry leaves that before the wild hurricane
fly,
When they meet with an obstacle, mount to
the sky,
So up to the housetop the coursers they flew,
With the sleigh full of toys, and St. Nicholas
too.
And then, in a twinkling, I heard on the roof
The prancing and pawing of each little hoof.
As I drew in my head, and was turning
around,
Down the chimney St. Nicholas came with a
bound.
He was dressed all in fur, from his head to his
foot,
And his clothes were all tarnished with ashes
and soot;
A bundle of toys he had flung on his back,
And he looked like a peddler just opening his
pack.
His eyes—how they twinkled! his dimples,
how merry!

His cheeks were like roses, his nose like a
cherry!
His droll little mouth was drawn up like a
bow,
And the beard on his chin was as white as the
snow;
The stump of a pipe he held tight in his teeth,
And the smoke, it encircled his head like a
wreath;
He had a broad face and a little round belly
That shook, when he laughed, like a bowl full
of jelly.
He was chubby and plump, a right jolly old
elf,
And I laughed when I saw him, in spite of
myself;
A wink of his eye and a twist of his head,
Soon gave me to know I had nothing to
dread;
He spoke not a word, but went straight to his
work,
And filled all the stockings; then turned with
a jerk,
And laying his finger aside of his nose,
And giving a nod, up the chimney he rose.
He sprang to his sleigh, to his team gave a
whistle,
And away they all flew like the down of a
thistle.
But I heard him exclaim, ere he drove out of
sight,
"HAPPY CHRISTMAS TO ALL,
AND TO ALL A GOOD-NIGHT!"

Clement C. Moore

At Hannukah

1

Enough oil to last? *They cry,*
Never! There's barely enough for one dark
night.
And yet, no harm to try.

Our Temple won back, it seems only right
Once rededicated, the lamp should burn!
Surely others will seek the light;

Each man, each tribe has a will to earn
What is believed. Has not Judah Maccabee
Showed us the way to learn

That those who persist must know victory
However facts may seem to lie—
And how do you know this can be?

Two thousand years have passed; can you
    deny
The oil lasted. There was no harm to try.

2

For Judah Maccabee
I light the candles.

For the brave Maccabees
Following Judah,
I light the candles.

For this Feast of Lights,
For these eight days,
For this Festival
I light the candles.

For Judah of old,
For the Maccabees,
For the Temple,
For Hannukahs to come,
I light the candles.

Myra Cohn Livingston

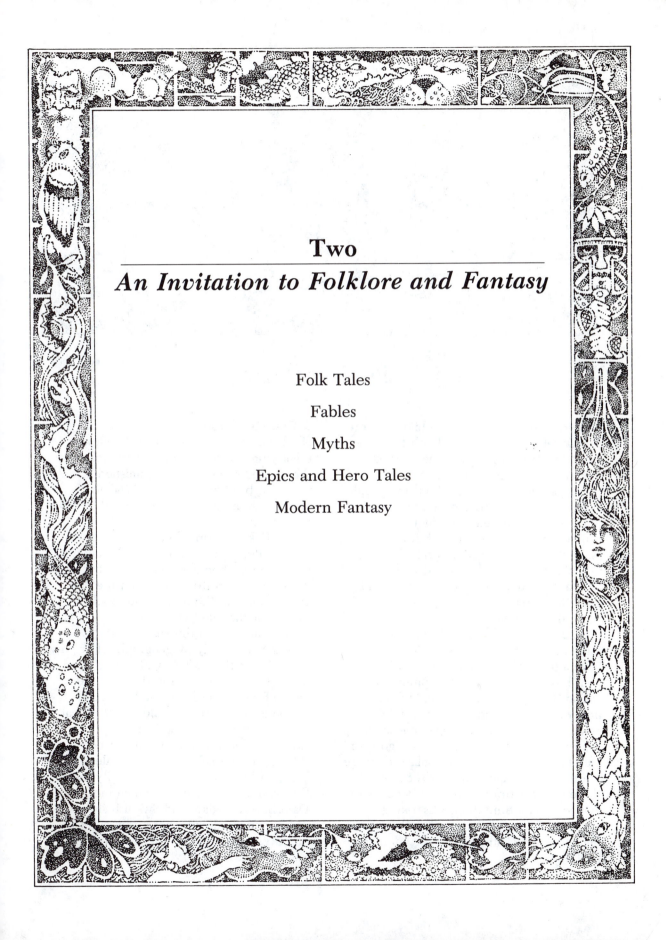

Two

An Invitation to Folklore and Fantasy

Folk Tales

Fables

Myths

Epics and Hero Tales

Modern Fantasy

Folk Tales

No part of the literature for children more clearly reflects the oral tradition than the folk tale. Used to preserve the records of the tribe before there was a written language, folk tales were meant for people of all ages; as time passed, the tales came to be used for teaching the mores of the tribe or village as well as its history. To make it a more appealing form of lesson, the folk tale was embroidered with dramatic incident, suspense, humor, and any other device that might make the pedantic more palatable.

Because of the fact that the stories were told long before they were written, they have a directness equaled by no other genre. It is in part this brisk plunge into action that appeals to children, who are now the major audience for folk tales. Seldom is there depth of characterization: the real or magical characters are good or bad, kind or cruel, wise or foolish; they are more symbols than individuals. Seldom is there any description: the tale begins with "Once upon a time there was a king . . ." or a poor farmer, or an orphaned servant maid, or a cruel stepmother, or an angry troll.

There is a strong sense of justice in children, and they delight in the almost unvarying cause-and-effect of the folk tale: the wicked stepsisters are punished, the youngest brother is rewarded for his kindness to a beggar, the greedy thief loses everything.

The folk tale can be enjoyed by an independent reader and it can be enjoyed by listeners when it is read aloud, but it is at its best when it is told, when the flow and cadence of the oral tradition add to the joy of the tale itself.

The folk tales in this section are arranged primarily by geographical origins, since that is the way they are most often used by teachers and librarians. As the table of contents shows, the five broad divisions are continents and geographical regions: Europe, Africa, Asia, Oceania and Australia, and North and South America. Where there is subdivision, the tales are grouped by geographical contiguity (as in the Scandinavian section, which includes Danish, Norwegian, and Swedish stories), or by individual countries, or by cultural identity, as in "North American Indian and Eskimo Tales."

Serious students of folklore today include psychologists, who are concerned with the inner meanings and archetypal emotions of the stories, and cultural historians, who are aware of the clues within the tales to the customs and attitudes of the past. The folklore specialists are interested in motifs, themes, and origins of the tales, in tracing cultural diffusion, and in comparing different versions of the same stories.

Teachers and librarians use folk tales with children to stimulate dramatic creativity, to learn about other cultures, and to illustrate elements of writing when working in a language arts program. Most of all, they use the tales to introduce children to the pleasures of the genre: the wit, humor, adventure, suspense, moral values, and romance of the folk tale.

Folk Tales of Europe

Great Britain

 We owe an incalculable debt to the great British collector of folk tales, Joseph Jacobs. Like the Brothers Grimm, he gathered his stories from storytellers, and he was particularly aware that by his time (1854–1916) the primary audience for folk tales had come to be children, so that his versions were most appropriate for a young audience. Among the British tales are some of the classics loved by young children, such as "The Story of the Three Bears." There is great variety in this group of folk tales, not only because they include such humorous tales as "Henny-Penny" or tales of magic like the Scottish "The Bride Who Out Talked the Water Kelpie" but also because there are distinct flavors to English, Cornish, Welsh, Scottish, and Northern Irish folklore. Among the British folk tales are many of the classics most familiar to children, and along with the beloved pranksters, giant-killers, little people, and animal heroes are some of the richest uses of language in our literary heritage.

The Story of the Three Bears
(England)

The story included here is the version in which Goldilocks visits the bears' home, which is best known by children. It is not the original version by Robert Southey, in which a little old woman encounters the bears.

Once upon a time there were three Bears, who lived together in a house of their own, in a wood. One of them was a Little Wee Bear, and one was a Middle-sized Bear, and the other was a Great Big Bear. They had each a bowl for their porridge; a little bowl for the Little Wee Bear; and a middle-sized bowl for the Middle-sized Bear; and a great bowl for the Great Big Bear. And they had each a chair to sit in; a little chair for the Little Wee Bear; and a middle-sized chair for the Middle-sized Bear; and a great chair for the Great Big Bear. And they had each a bed to sleep in; a little bed for the Little Wee Bear; and a middle-sized bed for the Middle-sized Bear; and a great bed for the Great Big Bear.

One day, after they had made the porridge for their breakfast, and poured it into their porridge-bowls, they walked out into the wood while the porridge was cooling, that they might not burn their mouths by beginning too soon, for they were polite, well-brought-up Bears. And while they were away a little girl called Goldilocks, who lived at the other side of the wood and had been sent on an errand by her mother, passed by the house, and looked in at the window. And then she peeped in at the keyhole, for she was not at all a well-brought-up little girl. Then seeing nobody in the house she lifted the latch. The door was not fastened, because the Bears were good Bears, who did nobody any harm, and never suspected that anybody would harm them. So Goldilocks opened the door and went in; and well pleased was she when she saw the porridge on the table. If she had been a well-brought-up little girl she would have waited till the Bears came home, and then, perhaps, they would have asked her to breakfast; for they were good Bears— a little rough or so, as the manner of Bears is, but for all that very good-natured and hospitable. But she was an impudent, rude little girl, and so she set about helping herself.

First she tasted the porridge of the Great Big Bear, and that was too hot for her. Next she tasted the porridge of the Middle-sized Bear, but that was too cold for her. And then she went to the porridge of the Little Wee Bear, and tasted it, and that was neither too hot nor too cold, but just right, and she liked it so well, that she ate it all up, every bit!

Then Goldilocks, who was tired, for she had been catching butterflies instead of running on her errand, sat down in the chair of the Great Big Bear, but that was too hard for her. And then she sat down in the chair of the Middle-sized Bear, and that was too soft for her. But when she sat down in the chair of the Little Wee Bear, that was neither too hard, nor too soft, but just right. So she seated herself in it, and there she sat till the bottom of the chair came out, and down she came, plump upon the ground; and that made her very cross, for she was a bad-tempered little girl.

Now, being determined to rest, Goldilocks went upstairs into the bedchamber in which the three Bears slept. And first she lay down upon the bed of the Great Big Bear, but that was too high at the head for her. And next she lay down upon the bed of the Middle-sized Bear, and that was too high at the foot for her. And then she lay down upon the bed of the Little Wee Bear, and that was neither too high at the head, nor at the foot, but just right. So she covered herself up comfortably, and lay there till she fell fast asleep.

By this time the Three Bears thought their porridge would be cool enough for them to eat it properly; so they came home to breakfast. Now careless Goldilocks had left the spoon of the Great Big Bear standing in his porridge.

"SOMEBODY HAS BEEN AT MY PORRIDGE!"

said the Great Big Bear in his great, rough, gruff voice.

Then the Middle-sized Bear looked at his porridge and saw the spoon was standing in it too.

"SOMEBODY HAS BEEN AT MY PORRIDGE!"

said the Middle-sized Bear in his middle-sized voice.

Then the Little Wee Bear looked at his, and there was the spoon in the porridge-bowl, but the porridge was all gone!

"SOMEBODY HAS BEEN AT MY PORRIDGE, AND HAS EATEN IT ALL UP!"

said the Little Wee Bear in his little wee voice.

Upon this the Three Bears, seeing that some one had entered their house, and eaten up the Little Wee Bear's breakfast, began to look about them. Now the careless Goldilocks had not put the hard cushion straight when she rose from the chair of the Great Big Bear.

"The Story of the Three Bears" from ENGLISH FAIRY TALES retold by Flora Annie Steel. New York: The Macmillan Company, 1918.

"SOMEBODY HAS BEEN SITTING IN MY
CHAIR!"

said the Great Big Bear in his great, rough,
gruff voice.

And the careless Goldilocks had squatted
down the soft cushion of the Middle-sized
Bear.

"SOMEBODY HAS BEEN SITTING IN MY CHAIR!"

said the Middle-sized Bear in his middle-
sized voice.

"SOMEBODY HAS BEEN SITTING IN MY CHAIR, AND
HAS SAT THE BOTTOM THROUGH!"

said the Little Wee Bear in his little wee
voice.

Then the Three Bears thought they had
better make further search in case it was a
burglar, so they went upstairs into their bedchamber. Now Goldilocks had pulled the pillow of the Great Big Bear out of its place.

"SOMEBODY HAS BEEN LYING IN MY BED!"

said the Great Big Bear in his great, rough,
gruff voice.

And Goldilocks had pulled the bolster of
the Middle-sized Bear out of its place.

"SOMEBODY HAS BEEN LYING IN MY BED!"

said the Middle-sized Bear in his middle-
sized voice.

But when the Little Wee Bear came to
look at his bed, there was the bolster in its
place!

And the pillow was in its place upon the
bolster!

And upon the pillow—?

There was Goldilocks' yellow head—which
was not in its place, for she had no business
there.

"SOMEBODY HAS BEEN LYING IN MY BED,—AND HERE
SHE IS STILL!"

said the Little Wee Bear in his little wee
voice.

Now Goldilocks had heard in her sleep the
great, rough, gruff voice of the Great Big
Bear; but she was so fast asleep that it was no
more to her than the roaring of wind, or the
rumbling of thunder. And she had heard the
middle-sized voice of the Middle-sized Bear,
but it was only as if she had heard some one
speaking in a dream. But when she heard the
little wee voice of the Little Wee Bear, it was
so sharp, and so shrill, that it awakened her
at once. Up she started, and when she saw
the Three Bears on one side of the bed, she
tumbled herself out at the other, and ran to
the window. Now the window was open, because the Bears, like good, tidy Bears, as they
were, always opened their bedchamber window when they got up in the morning. So
naughty, frightened little Goldilocks
jumped; and whether she broke her neck in
the fall, or ran into the wood and was lost
there, or found her way out of the wood and
got whipped for being a bad girl and playing
truant no one can say. But the Three Bears
never saw anything more of her.

Henny-Penny
(England)

*A perennial favorite of very young
children, this brisk and funny tale that
began in India is loved for its repetition
and humor.*

One day Henny-penny was picking up corn
in the cornyard when—whack!—something
hit her upon the head. "Goodness gracious
me!" said Henny-penny; "the sky's a-going to
fall: I must go and tell the king."

So she went along and she went along and
she went along till she met Cocky-locky.
"Where are you going, Henny-penny?" says
Cocky-locky. "Oh! I'm going to tell the king
the sky's a-falling," says Henny-penny. "May
I come with you?" says Cocky-locky. "Certainly," says Henny-penny. So Henny-penny
and Cocky-locky went to tell the king the sky
was falling.

They went along, and they went along,
and they went along, till they met Ducky-
daddles. "Where are you going to, Henny-
penny and Cocky-locky?" says Ducky-daddles. "Oh! we're going to tell the king the

sky's a-falling," said Henny-penny and Cocky-locky. "May I come with you?" says Ducky-daddles. "Certainly," said Henny-penny and Cocky-locky. So Henny-penny, Cocky-locky, and Ducky-daddles went to tell the king the sky was a-falling.

So they went along, and they went along, and they went along, till they met Goosey-poosey. "Where are you going to, Henny-penny, Cocky-locky, and Ducky-daddles?" said Goosey-poosey. "Oh! we're going to tell the king the sky's a-falling," said Henny-penny and Cocky-locky and Ducky-daddles. "May I come with you?" said Goosey-poosey. "Certainly," said Henny-penny, Cocky-locky, and Ducky-daddles. So Henny-penny, Cocky-locky, Ducky-daddles, and Goosey-poosey went to tell the king the sky was a-falling.

So they went along, and they went along, and they went along, till they met Turkey-lurkey. "Where are you going, Henny-penny, Cocky-locky, Ducky-daddles, and Goosey-poosey?" says Turkey-lurkey. "Oh! we're going to tell the king the sky's a-falling," said Henny-penny, Cocky-locky, Ducky-daddles, and Goosey-poosey. "May I come with you, Henny-penny, Cocky-locky, Ducky-daddles, and Goosey-poosey?" said Turkey-lurkey. "Oh, certainly, Turkey-lurkey," said Henny-penny, Cocky-locky, Ducky-daddles, and Goosey-poosey. So Henny-penny, Cocky-locky, Ducky-daddles, Goosey-poosey, and Turkey-lurkey all went to tell the king the sky was a-falling.

So they went along, and they went along, and they went along, till they met Foxy-woxy, and Foxy-woxy said to Henny-penny, Cocky-locky, Ducky-daddles, Goosey-poosey, and Turkey-lurkey: "Where are you going, Henny-penny, Cocky-locky, Ducky-daddles, Goosey-poosey, and Turkey-lurkey?" And Henny-penny, Cocky-locky, Ducky-daddles, Goosey-poosey, and Turkey-lurkey said to Foxy-woxy: "We're going to tell the king the sky's a-falling." "Oh! but this is not the way to the king, Henny-penny, Cocky-locky, Ducky-daddles, Goosey-poosey, and Turkey-lurkey," says Foxy-woxy; "I know the proper way; shall I show it you?"

"Oh, certainly, Foxy-woxy," said Henny-penny, Cocky-locky, Ducky-daddles, Goosey-poosey, and Turkey-lurkey. So Henny-penny, Cocky-locky, Ducky-daddles, Goosey-poosey, Turkey-lurkey, and Foxy-woxy all went to tell the king the sky was a-falling. So they went along, and they went along, and they went along, till they came to a narrow and dark hole. Now this was the door of Foxy-woxy's cave. But Foxy-woxy said to Henny-penny, Cocky-locky, Ducky-daddles, Goosey-poosey, and Turkey-lurkey: "This is the short way to the king's palace: you'll soon get there if you follow me. I will go first and you come after, Henny-penny, Cocky-locky, Ducky-daddles, Goosey-poosey, and Turkey-lurkey." "Why of course, certainly, without doubt, why not?" said Henny-penny, Cocky-locky, Ducky-daddles, Goosey-poosey, and Turkey-lurkey.

So Foxy-woxy went into his cave, and he didn't go very far, but turned round to wait for Henny-penny, Cocky-locky, Ducky-daddles, Goosey-poosey, and Turkey-lurkey. So at last at first Turkey-lurkey went through the dark hole into the cave. He hadn't got far when "Hrumph," Foxy-woxy snapped off Turkey-lurkey's head and threw his body over his left shoulder. Then Goosey-poosey went in, and "Hrumph," off went her head and Goosey-poosey was thrown beside Turkey-lurkey. Then Ducky-daddles waddled down, and "Hrumph," snapped Foxy-woxy, and Ducky-daddles' head was off and Ducky-daddles was thrown alongside Turkey-lurkey and Goosey-poosey. Then Cocky-locky strutted down into the cave, and he hadn't gone far when "Snap, Hrumph!" went Foxy-woxy and Cocky-locky was thrown alongside of Turkey-lurkey, Goosey-poosey, and Ducky-daddles.

But Foxy-woxy had made two bites at Cocky-locky, and when the first snap only hurt Cocky-locky, but didn't kill him, he called out to Henny-penny. But she turned tail and off she ran home, so she never told the king the sky was a-falling.

"Henny-Penny" from ENGLISH FAIRY TALES, collected by Joseph Jacobs, third edition, revised. London: David Nutt, 1907 (originally published 1892 by G. P. Putnam's Sons).

Tom Tit Tot
(England)

This is one of the many variants of the Rumpelstiltzkin story, in which the point of the story turns on the heroine remembering or guessing the name of someone who has helped her.

Once upon a time there was a woman, and she baked five pies. And when they came out of the oven, they were that overbaked the crusts were too hard to eat. So she says to her daughter:

"Darter," says she, "put you them there pies on the shelf, and leave 'em there a little, and they'll come again." She meant, you know, the crust would get soft.

But the girl, she says to herself, "Well, if they'll come again, I'll eat 'em now." And she set to work and ate 'em all, first and last.

Well, come supper time the woman said, "Go you, and get one o' them there pies. I dare say they've come again now."

The girl went and she looked, and there was nothing but the dishes. So back she came and says she, "Noo, they ain't come again."

"Not one of 'em?" says the mother.

"Not one of 'em," says she.

"Well, come again, or not come again," said the woman, "I'll have one for supper."

"But you can't, if they ain't come," said the girl.

"But I can," says she. "Go you, and bring the best of 'em."

"Best or worst," says the girl, "I've ate 'em all, and you can't have one till that's come again."

Well, the woman she was done, and she took her spinning to the door to spin, and as she span she sang:

"My darter ha' ate five, five pies to-day.
My darter ha' ate five, five pies to-day."

The king was coming down the street, and he heard her sing, but what she sang he couldn't hear, so he stopped and said:

"Tom Tit Tot" from ENGLISH FAIRY TALES, collected by Joseph Jacobs, third edition, revised. London: David Nutt, 1907 (originally published 1892 by G. P. Putnam's Sons).

"What was that you were singing, my good woman?"

The woman was ashamed to let him hear what her daughter had been doing, so she sang, instead of that:

"My darter ha' spun five, five skeins to-day.
My darter ha' spun five, five skeins to-day."

"Stars o' mine!" said the king, "I never heard tell of anyone that could do that."

Then he said: "Look you here, I want a wife, and I'll marry your daughter. But look you here," says he, "eleven months out of the year she shall have all she likes to eat, and all the gowns she likes to get, and all the company she likes to keep; but the last month of the year she'll have to spin five skeins every day, and if she don't I shall kill her."

"All right," says the woman, for she thought what a grand marriage that was. And as for the five skeins, when the time came, there'd be plenty of ways of getting out of it, and likeliest, he'd have forgotten all about it.

Well, so they were married. And for eleven months the girl had all she liked to eat, and all the gowns she liked to get, and all the company she liked to keep.

But when the time was getting over, she began to think about the skeins and to wonder if he had 'em in mind. But not one word did he say about 'em, and she thought he'd wholly forgotten 'em.

However, the last day of the last month he takes her to a room she'd never set eyes on before. There was nothing in it but a spinningwheel and a stool. And says he: "Now, my dear, here you'll be shut in tomorrow with some victuals and some flax, and if you haven't spun five skeins by the night, your head'll go off."

And away he went about his business.

Well, she was that frightened, she'd always been such a gatless girl that she didn't so much as know how to spin, and what was she to do tomorrow with no one to come nigh her to help her? She sat down on a stool in the kitchen, and law! how she did cry!

However, all of a sudden she heard a sort of a knocking low down on the door. She upped and oped it, and what should she see but a small little black thing with a long tail. That looked up at her right curious, and that said:

"What are you a-crying for?"

"What's that to you?" says she.

"Never you mind," that said, "but tell me what you're a-crying for."

"That won't do me no good if I do," says she.

"You don't know that," that said, and twirled that's tail round.

"Well," says she, "that won't do no harm, if that don't do no good," and she upped and told about the pies, and the skeins, and everything.

"This is what I'll do," says the little black thing, "I'll come to your window every morning and take the flax and bring it spun at night."

"What's your pay?" says she.

That looked out of the corner of that's eyes, and that said, "I'll give you three guesses every night to guess my name, and if you haven't guessed it before the month's up, you shall be mine."

Well, she thought she'd be sure to guess that's name before the month was up. "All right," says she, "I agree."

"All right," that says, and law! how that twirled that's tail.

Well, the next day, her husband took her into the room, and there was the flax and the day's food.

"Now there's the flax," says he, "and if that ain't spun up this night, off goes your head." And then he went out and locked the door.

He'd hardly gone, when there was a knocking against the window.

She upped and she oped it, and there sure enough was the little old thing sitting on the ledge.

"Where's the flax?" says he.

"Here it be," says she. And she gave it to him.

Well, come the evening a knocking came again to the window. She upped and she oped it, and there was the little old thing with five skeins of flax on his arm.

"Here it be," says he, and he gave it to her.

"Now, what's my name?" says he.

"What, is that Bill?" says she.

"Noo, that ain't," says he, and he twirled his tail.

"Is that Ned?" says she.

"Noo, that ain't," says he, and he twirled his tail.

"Well, is that Mark?" says she.

"Noo, that ain't," says he, and he twirled his tail harder, and away he flew.

Well, when her husband came in, there were the five skeins ready for him. "I see I shan't have to kill you tonight, my dear," says he. "You'll have your food and your flax in the morning," says he, and away he goes.

Well, every day the flax and the food were brought, and every day that there little black impet used to come mornings and evenings. And all the day the girl sat trying to think of names to say to it when it came at night. But she never hit on the right one. And as it got towards the end of the month, the impet began to look so maliceful, and that twirled that's tail faster and faster each time she gave a guess.

At last it came to the last day but one. The impet came at night along with the five skeins, and that said:

"What, ain't you got my name yet?"

"Is that Nicodemus?" says she.

"Noo, t'ain't," that says.

"Is that Sammle?" says she.

"Noo, t'ain't," that says.

"A-well, is that Methusalem?" says she.

"Noo, t'ain't that neither," that says.

Then that looks at her with that's eyes like a coal o'fire, and that says, "Woman, there's only tomorrow night, and then you'll be mine!" And away it flew.

Well, she felt that horrid. However, she heard the king coming along the passage. In he came, and when he sees the five skeins, he says, says he:

"Well, my dear," says he. "I don't see but what you'll have your skeins ready tomorrow night as well, and as I reckon I shan't have to kill you, I'll have supper in here tonight." So they brought supper, and another stool for him, and down the two sat.

Well, he hadn't eaten but a mouthful or so,

when he stops and begins to laugh.

"What is it?" says she.

"A-why," says he, "I was out a-hunting today, and I got away to a place in the wood I'd never seen before. And there was an old chalk-pit. And I heard a kind of a sort of a humming. So I got off my hobby, and I went right quiet to the pit, and I looked down. Well, what should there be but the funniest little black thing you ever set eyes on. And what was that doing, but that had a little spinning wheel, and that was spinning wonderful fast, and twirling that's tail. And as that span that sang:

> "Nimmy nimmy not
> My name's Tom Tit Tot."

Well, when the girl heard this, she felt as if she could have jumped out of her skin for joy, but she didn't say a word.

Next day that there little thing looked so maliceful when he came for the flax. And when night came, she heard that knocking against the window panes. She oped the window, and that come right in on the ledge. That was grinning from ear to ear, and Oo! that's tail was twirling round so fast.

"What's my name?" that says, as that gave her the skeins.

"Is that Solomon?" she says, pretending to be afeard.

"Noo, t'ain't," that says, and that came further into the room.

"Well, is that Zebedee?" says she again.

"Noo, 'tain't," says the impet. And then that laughed and twirled that's tail till you couldn't hardly see it.

"Take time, woman," that says; "next guess, and you're mine." And that stretched out that's black hands at her.

Well, she backed a step or two, and she looked at it, and then she laughed out, and says she, pointing her finger at it:

> "Nimmy nimmy not
> Your name's Tom Tit Tot."

Well, when that heard her, that gave an awful shriek and away that flew into the dark, and she never saw it any more.

Tattercoats
(England)

"Tattercoats" is one of the gentler versions of the Cinderella story.

In a great Palace by the sea there once dwelt a very rich old lord, who had neither wife nor children living, only one little granddaughter, whose face he had never seen in all her life. He hated her bitterly, because at her birth his favourite daughter died; and when the old nurse brought him the baby, he swore, that it might live or die as it liked, but he would never look on its face as long as it lived.

So he turned his back, and sat by his window looking out over the sea, and weeping great tears for his lost daughter, till his white hair and beard grew down over his shoulders and twined round his chair and crept into the chinks of the floor, and his tears, dropping on to the window-ledge, wore a channel through the stone, and ran away in a little river to the great sea. And, meanwhile, his granddaughter grew up with no one to care for her, or clothe her; only the old nurse, when no one was by, would sometimes give her a dish of scraps from the kitchen, or a torn petticoat from the rag-bag; while the other servants of the Palace would drive her from the house with blows and mocking words, calling her "Tattercoats," and pointing at her bare feet and shoulders, till she ran away crying, to hide among the bushes.

And so she grew up, with little to eat or wear, spending her days in the fields and lanes, with only the gooseherd for a companion, who would play to her so merrily on his little pipe, when she was hungry, or cold, or tired, that she forgot all her troubles, and fell to dancing, with his flock of noisy geese for partners.

But, one day, people told each other that the King was travelling through the land, and in the town near by was to give a great ball, to all the lords and ladies of the country, when the Prince, his only son, was to choose a wife.

One of the royal invitations was brought to the Palace by the sea, and the servants carried it up to the old lord who still sat by his window, wrapped in his long white hair and weeping into the little river that was fed by his tears.

But when he heard the King's command, he dried his eyes and bade them bring shears to cut him loose, for his hair had bound him a fast prisoner and he could not move. And then he sent them for rich clothes, and jewels, which he put on; and he ordered them to saddle the white horse, with gold and silk, that he might ride to meet the King.

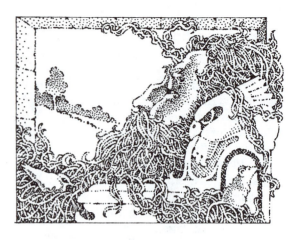

Meanwhile Tattercoats had heard of the great doings in the town, and she sat by the kitchen-door weeping because she could not go to see them. And when the old nurse heard her crying she went to the Lord of the Palace, and begged him to take his granddaughter with him to the King's ball.

But he only frowned and told her to be silent, while the servants laughed and said: "Tattercoats is happy in her rags, playing with the gooseherd, let her be—it is all she is fit for."

A second, and then a third time, the old nurse begged him to let the girl go with him, but she was answered only by black looks and fierce words, till she was driven from the room by the jeering servants, with blows and mocking words.

Weeping over her ill-success, the old nurse went to look for Tattercoats; but the girl had been turned from the door by the cook, and had run away to tell her friend the gooseherd, how unhappy she was because she could not go to the King's ball.

But when the gooseherd had listened to her story, he bade her cheer up, and proposed that they should go together into the town to see the King, and all the fine things; and when she looked sorrowfully down at her rags and bare feet, he played a note or two upon his pipe, so gay and merry, that she forgot all about her tears and her troubles, and before she well knew, the herdboy had taken her by the hand, and she, and he, and the geese before them, were dancing down the road towards the town.

Before they had gone very far, a handsome young man, splendidly dressed, rode up and stopped to ask the way to the castle where the King was staying; and when he found that they too were going thither, he got off his horse and walked beside them along the road.

The herdboy pulled out his pipe and played a low sweet tune, and the stranger looked again and again at Tattercoats' lovely face till he fell deeply in love with her, and begged her to marry him.

But she only laughed, and shook her golden head.

"You would be finely put to shame if you had a goosegirl for your wife!" said she; "go and ask one of the great ladies you will see to-night at the King's ball, and do not flout poor Tattercoats."

But the more she refused him the sweeter the pipe played, and the deeper the young man fell in love; till at last he begged her, as a proof of his sincerity, to come that night at twelve to the King's ball, just as she was, with the herdboy and his geese, and in her torn petticoat and bare feet, and he would dance with her before the King and the lords and ladies, and present her to them all, as his dear and honoured bride.

So when night came, and the hall in the castle was full of light and music, and the lords and ladies were dancing before the

"Tattercoats" from MORE ENGLISH FAIRY TALES, collected and edited by Joseph Jacobs. London: David Nutt, 1894.

King, just as the clock struck twelve, Tatter-coats and the herdboy, followed by his flock of noisy geese, entered at the great doors, and walked straight up the ball-room, while on either side the ladies whispered, the lords laughed, and the King seated at the far end stared in amazement.

But as they came in front of the throne, Tattercoats' lover rose from beside the King, and came to meet her. Taking her by the hand, he kissed her thrice before them all, and turned to the King.

"Father!" he said, for it was the Prince himself, "I have made my choice, and here is my bride, the loveliest girl in all the land, and the sweetest as well!"

Before he had finished speaking, the herd-boy put his pipe to his lips and played a few low notes that sounded like a bird singing far off in the woods; and as he played, Tatter-coats' rags were changed to shining robes sewn with glittering jewels, a golden crown lay upon her golden hair, and the flock of geese behind her, became a crowd of dainty pages, bearing her long train.

And as the King rose to greet her as his daughter, the trumpets sounded loudly in honour of the new Princess, and the people outside in the street said to each other:

"Ah! now the Prince has chosen for his wife the loveliest girl in all the land!"

But the gooseherd was never seen again, and no one knew what became of him; while the old lord went home once more to his Palace by the sea, for he could not stay at Court, when he had sworn never to look on his granddaughter's face.

So there he still sits by his window, if you could only see him, as you some day may, weeping more bitterly than ever, as he looks out over the sea.

Black Bull of Norroway
(England)

The magical potion of a witch-bride proves to be less strong than the power of true love.

In Norroway, long time ago, there lived a certain lady, and she had three daughters: The oldest of them said to her mother: "Mother, bake me a bannock, and roast me a collop, for I'm going away to seek my fortune." Her mother did so; and the daughter went away to an old witch washerwife and told her purpose. The old wife bade her stay that day, and look out of her back-door, and see what she could see. She saw nought the first day. The second day she did the same, and saw nought. On the third day she looked again, and saw a coach-and-six coming along the road. She ran in and told the old wife what she saw. "Well," quoth the old woman, "yon's for you." So they took her into the coach and galloped off.

The second daughter next says to her mother: "Mother, bake me a bannock, and roast me a collop, for I'm going away to seek my fortune." Her mother did so; and away she went to the old wife, as her sister had done. On the third day she looked out of the back-door, and saw a coach-and-four coming along the road. "Well," quoth the old woman, "yon's for you." So they took her in, and off they set.

The third daughter says to her mother: "Mother, bake me a bannock, and roast me a collop, for I'm going away to seek my fortune." Her mother did so; and away she went to the old witch. She bade her look out of her back-door, and see what she could see. She did so; and when she came back, said she saw nought. The second day she did the same, and saw nought. The third day she looked again, and on coming back said to the old wife she saw nought but a great Black Bull coming crooning along the road. "Well," quoth the old witch, "yon's for you." On hearing this she was next to distracted with grief and terror; but she was lifted up and set on his back, and away they went.

Aye they travelled, and on they travelled, till the lady grew faint with hunger. "Eat out of my right ear," says the Black Bull, "and drink out of my left ear, and set by your leaving." So she did as he said, and was wonderfully refreshed. And long they rode, and hard they rode, till they came in sight of a very big

and bonny castle. "Yonder we must be this night," quoth the Bull; "for my elder brother lives yonder"; and presently they were at the place. They lifted her off his back, and took her in, and sent him away to a park for the night. In the morning, when they brought the Bull home, they took the lady into a fine shining parlour, and gave her a beautiful apple, telling her not to break it till she was in the greatest strait ever mortal was in in the world, and that would bring her out of it. Again she was lifted on the Bull's back, and after she had ridden far, and farther than I can tell, they came in sight of a far bonnier castle, and far farther away than the last. Says the Bull to her: "Yonder we must be this night, for my second brother lives yonder"; and they were at the place directly. They lifted her down and took her in, and sent the Bull to the field for the night. In the morning they took the lady into a fine and rich room, and gave her the finest pear she had ever seen, bidding her not to break it till she was in the greatest strait ever mortal could be in, and that would get her out of it. Again she was lifted and set on his back, and away they went. And long they rode, and hard they rode, till they came in sight of the far biggest castle, and far farthest off, they had yet seen. "We must be yonder to-night," says the Bull, "for my young brother lives yonder"; and they were there directly. They lifted her down, took her in, and sent the Bull to the field for the night. In the morning they took her into a room, the finest of all, and gave her a plum, telling her not to break it till she was in the greatest strait mortal could be in, and that would get her out of it. Presently they

brought home the Bull, set the lady on his back, and away they went.

And aye they rode, and on they rode, till they came to a dark and ugsome glen, where they stopped, and the lady lighted down. Says the Bull to her: "Here you must stay till I go and fight the Old One. You must seat yourself on that stone, and move neither hand nor foot till I come back, else I'll never find you again. And if everything round about you turns blue, I have beaten the Old One; but should all things turn red, he'll have conquered me." She set herself down on the stone, and by-and-by all round her turned blue. Overcome with joy, she lifted one of her feet, and crossed it over the other, so glad was she that her companion was victorious. The Bull returned and sought for her, but never could find her.

Long she sat, and aye she wept, till she wearied. At last she rose and went away, she didn't know where. On she wandered, till she came to a great hill of glass, that she tried all she could to climb, but wasn't able. Round the bottom of the hill she went, sobbing and seeking a passage over, till at last she came to a smith's house; and the smith promised, if she would serve him seven years, he would make her iron shoon, wherewith she could climb over the glassy hill. At seven years' end she got her iron shoon, clomb the glassy hill, and chanced to come to the old washerwife's habitation. There she was told of a gallant young knight that had given in some clothes all over blood to wash, and whoever washed them was to be his wife. The old wife had washed till she was tired, and then she set her daughter at it, and both washed, and they washed, and they washed, in hopes of getting the young knight; but for all they could do they couldn't bring out a stain. At length they set the stranger damsel to work; and whenever she began, the stains came out pure and clean, and the old wife made the knight believe it was her daughter had washed the clothes. So the knight and the

"Black Bull of Norroway" from ENGLISH FAIRY TALES, collected and edited by Joseph Jacobs, third edition, revised. London: David Nutt, 1907 (originally published 1892 by G. P. Putnam's Sons).

eldest daughter were to be married, and the stranger damsel was distracted at the thought of it, for she was deeply in love with him. So she bethought her of her apple, and breaking it, found it filled with gold and precious jewellery, the richest she had ever seen. "All these," she said to the eldest daughter, "I will give you, on condition that you put off your marriage for one day, and allow me to go into his room alone at night." The lady consented; but meanwhile the old wife had prepared a sleeping drink, and given it to the knight, who drank it, and never wakened till next morning. The live-long night the damsel sobbed and sang:

"Seven long years I served for thee,
The glassy hill I clomb for thee,
Thy bloody clothes I wrang for thee;
And wilt thou not waken and turn to me?"

Next day she knew not what to do for grief. Then she broke the pear, and found it filled with jewellery far richer than the contents of the apple. With these jewels she bargained for permission to be a second night in the young knight's chamber; but the old wife gave him another sleeping drink, and again he slept till morning. All night she kept sighing and singing as before:

"Seven long years I served for thee,
The glassy hill I clomb for thee,
Thy bloody clothes I wrang for thee;
And wilt thou not waken and turn to me?"

Still he slept, and she nearly lost hope altogether. But that day, when he was out hunting, somebody asked him what noise and moaning was that they heard all last night in his bedchamber. He said: "I have heard no noise." But they assured him there was; and he resolved to keep waking that night to try what he could hear. That being the third night, and the damsel being between hope and despair, she broke her plum, and it held far the richest jewellery of the three. She bargained as before; and the old wife, as before, took in the sleeping drink to the young knight's chamber; but he told her he couldn't drink it that night without sweetening. And when she went away for some honey to sweeten it with, he poured out the drink, and

so made the old wife think he had drunk it. They all went to bed again, and the damsel began, as before, singing:

"Seven long years I served for thee,
The glassy hill I clomb for thee,
Thy bloody clothes I wrang for thee;
And wilt thou not waken and turn to me?"

He heard, and turned to her. And she told him all that had befallen her, and he told her all that had happened to him. And he caused the old washerwife and her daughter to be burnt. And they were married, and he and she are living happy to this day, for aught I know.

Molly Whuppie
(England)

One of the most daring heroines of folk literature outwits a giant, in a tale that uses a common device of the genre, the repeated bit of verse.

Once upon a time, there was an old woodcutter who had too many children. Work as hard as he might, he couldn't feed them all. So he took the three youngest of them, gave them a last slice of bread and treacle each, and abandoned them in the forest.

They ate the bread and treacle and walked and walked until they were worn out and utterly lost. Soon they would have lain down together like the babes in the wood, and that would have been the end of them if, just as it was beginning to get dark, they had not spied a small and beaming light between the trees. Now this light was chinkling out from a window. So the youngest of them, who was called Molly Whuppie and was by far the cleverest, went and knocked at the door. A woman came to the door and asked them what they wanted. Molly Whuppie said: "Something to eat."

"Eat!" said the woman. "Eat! Why, my husband's a giant, and soon as say knife, he'd eat *you.*"

But they were tired out and famished, and still Molly begged the woman to let them in.

So at last the woman took them in, sat them down by the fire on a billet of wood, and gave them some bread and milk. Hardly had they taken a sup of it when there came a thumping at the door. No mistaking that: it was the giant come home; and in he came.

"Hai!" he said, squinting at the children. "What have we here?"

"Three poor, cold, hungry, lost little lasses," said his wife. "You get to your supper, my man, and leave them to me."

The giant said nothing, sat down and ate up his supper; but between the bites he looked at the children.

Now the giant had three daughters of his own, and the giant's wife put the whole six of them into the same bed. For so she thought she would keep the strangers safe. But before he went to bed the giant, as if in play, hung three chains of gold round his daughters' necks, and three of golden straw round Molly's and her sisters' between the sheets.

Soon the other five were fast asleep in the great bed, but Molly lay awake listening. At last she rose up softly, and, creeping across, changed over one by one the necklaces of gold and of straw. So now it was Molly and her sisters who wore the chains of gold, and the giant's three daughters the chains of straw. Then she lay down again.

In the middle of the night the giant came tiptoeing into the room, and, groping cautiously with finger and thumb, he plucked up out of the bed the three children with the straw necklaces round their necks, carried them downstairs, and bolted them up in his great cellar.

"So, so, my pretty chickabiddies!" he smiled to himself as he bolted the door. "Now you're safe!"

As soon as all was quiet again, Molly Whuppie thought it high time she and her sisters were out of that house. So she woke them, whispering in their ears, and they slipped down the stairs together and out into the forest, and never stopped running till morning.

But daybreak came at last, and lo and behold, they came to another house. It stood beside a pool of water full of wild swans, and stone images there, and a thousand windows; and it was the house of the King. So Molly went in, and told her story to the King. The King listened, and when it was finished, said:

"Well, Molly, that's one thing done, and done well. But I could tell another thing, and that would be a better." This King, indeed, knew the giant of old; and he told Molly that if she would go back and steal for him the giant's sword that hung behind his bed, he would give her eldest sister his eldest son for a husband, and then Molly's sister would be a princess.

Molly looked at the eldest prince, for there they all sat at breakfast, and she smiled and said she would try.

So, that very evening, she muffled herself up, and made her way back through the forest to the house of the giant. First she listened at the window, and there she heard the giant eating his supper; so she crept into the house and hid herself under his bed.

In the middle of the night—and the shutters fairly shook with the giant's snoring—Molly climbed softly up on to the great bed and unhooked the giant's sword that was dangling from its nail in the wall. Lucky it was for Molly this was not the giant's great fighting sword, but only a little sword. It was heavy enough for all that, and when she came to the door, it rattled in its scabbard and woke up the giant.

Then Molly ran, and the giant ran, and they both ran, and at last they came to the Bridge of the One Hair, and Molly ran over. But not the giant; for run over he couldn't. Instead, he shook his fist at her across the great chasm in between, and shouted:

"Woe betide ye, Molly Whuppie,
If ye e'er come back again!"

But Molly only laughed and said:

"Maybe twice I'll come to see 'ee,
If so be I come to Spain."

Then Molly carried off the sword to the King; and her eldest sister married the King's eldest son.

"Well," said the King, when the wedding was over, "that was a better thing done, Molly, and done well. But I know another, and that's better still. Steal the purse that lies under the giant's pillow, and I'll marry your second sister to my second son."

Molly looked at the King's second son, and laughed, and said she would try.

So she muffled herself up in another-coloured hood, and stole off through the forest to the giant's house, and there he was, guzzling as usual at supper. This time she hid herself in his linen closet. A stuffy place that was.

About the middle of the night, she crept out of the linen closet, took a deep breath, and pushed in her fingers just a little bit betwixt his bolster and pillow. The giant stopped snoring and sighed, but soon began to snore again. Then Molly slid her fingers in a little bit further under his pillow. At this the giant called out in his sleep as if there were robbers near. And his wife said: "Lie easy, man! It's those bones you had for supper."

Then Molly pushed in her fingers even a little bit further, and then they felt the purse. But as she drew out the purse from under the pillow, a gold piece dropped out of it and clanked on to the floor, and at sound of it the giant woke.

Then Molly ran, and the giant ran, and they both ran. And they both ran and ran until they came to the Bridge of the One Hair. And Molly got over, but the giant stayed; for get over he couldn't. Then he cried out on her across the chasm:

"Woe betide ye, Molly Whuppie,
If ye e'er come back again!"

But Molly only laughed, and called back at him:

"Once again I'll come to see 'ee,
If so be I come to Spain."

So she took the purse to the King, and her second sister married his second son; and there were great rejoicings.

"Well, well," said the King to Molly, when the feasting was over, "that was yet a better thing done, Molly, and done for good. But I know a better yet, and that's the best of all. Steal the giant's ring for me from off his thumb, and you shall have my youngest son for yourself. And all solemn, Molly, you always were my favourite."

Molly laughed and looked at the King's youngest son, turned her head, frowned, then laughed again, and said she would try. This time, when she had stolen into the giant's house, she hid in the chimney niche.

At dead of night, when the giant was snoring, she stepped out of the chimney niche and crept towards the bed. By good chance the giant lay on his back, his head on his pillow, with his arm hanging down out over the bedside, and it was the arm that had the hand at the end of it on which was the great thumb that wore the ring. First Molly wetted the giant's thumb, then she tugged softly and softly at the ring. Little by little it slid down and down over the knuckle-bone; but just as Molly had slipped it off and pushed it into her pocket, the giant woke with a roar, clutched at her, gripped her, and lifted her clean up into the dark over his head.

"Ah-ha! Molly Whuppie!" says he. "Once too many is never again. Ay, and if *I'd* done the ill to you as the ill you have done's been done to me, what would I be getting for *my* pains?"

"Why," says Molly all in one breath, "I'd bundle you up into a sack, and I'd put the cat and dog inside with you, and a needle and thread and a great pair of shears, and I'd hang you up on the wall, be off to the wood, cut the thickest stick I could get, come home, take you down, and beat you to a jelly. *That's* what I'd do!"

"And that, Molly," says the giant, chuckling to himself with pleasure and pride at his cunning, "that's just what I will be doing with you." So he rose up out of his bed and fetched a sack, put Molly into the sack, and the cat and the dog besides, and a needle and thread and a stout pair of shears, and hung her up on the wall. Then away he went into the forest to cut a cudgel.

When he was well gone, Molly, stroking the dog with one hand and the cat with the other, sang out in a high, clear, jubilant voice: "Oh, if only everybody could see what I can see!"

" 'See,' Molly?" said the giant's wife. "What do you see?"

But Molly only said, "Oh, if only everybody could see what I see! Oh, if only they could see what *I* see!"

At last the giant's wife begged and entreated Molly to take her up into the sack so that she could see what Molly saw. Then Molly took the shears and cut a hole in the lowest corner of the sack, jumped out of the sack, helped the giant's wife up into it, and, as fast as she could, sewed up the hole with the needle and thread.

But it was pitch black in the sack, so the giant's wife saw nothing but stars, and they were inside of her, and she soon began to ask to be let out again. Molly never heeded or answered her, but hid herself far in at the back of the door. Home at last came the giant, with a quickwood cudgel in his hand and a knob on the end of it as big as a pumpkin. And he began to belabour the sack with the cudgel.

His wife cried: "Stay, man! It's me, man! Oh, man, it's me, man!" But the dog barked and the cat squalled, and at first he didn't hear her voice.

Then Molly crept softly out from behind the door. But the giant saw her. He gave a roar. And Molly ran, and the giant ran, and they both ran, and they ran and they ran and they ran—Molly and the giant—till they came to the Bridge of the One Hair. And Molly skipped along over it; but the giant stayed, for he couldn't. And he cried out after her in a dreadful voice across the chasm:

> "Woe betide ye, Molly Whuppie,
> If ye e'er come back again!"

But Molly waved her hand at the giant over the chasm, and flung back her head:

> "Never *again I'll come to see 'ee*,
> *Though so be I come to Spain.*"

Then Molly ran off with the ring in her pocket, and she was married to the King's youngest son; and there was a feast that was a finer feast than all the feasts that had ever been in the King's house before, and there were lights in all the windows.

Lights so bright that all the dark long the hosts of the wild swans swept circling in space under the stars. But though there were guests by the hundred from all parts of the country, the giant never so much as gnawed a bone!

The Bride Who Out Talked the Water Kelpie
(Scotland)

In a special tale for wedding celebrations, a bride outwits that malicious creature, the water kelpie.

A soldier there was once, and he was coming home from the foreign wars with his heart light and free, and his bagpipes under his arm. He was marching along at a good pace, for he had a far way to go, and a longing in his heart to get back to his home again. But as the sun lowered to its setting, he could plainly see that he'd not get there by that day's end so he began to be thinking about a place where he could bide for the night.

The road had come to the top of a hill and he looked down to see what lay at the foot of it. Down at the bottom was a village, and there was a drift of smoke rising from the chimneys where folks were getting their suppers, and lights were beginning to twinkle on here and there in the windows.

"There'll be an inn down there, to be sure," said the soldier, "and they'll have a bite of supper for me and a place for me to sleep."

"The Bride Who Out Talked the Water Kelpie" from THISTLE AND THYME by Sorche Nic Leodhas. Copyright © 1962 by Leclaire G. Alger. Reprinted by permission of Holt, Rinehart and Winston, Publishers, and McIntosh and Otis, Inc.

So down the hill he went at a fast trot with his kilt swinging, and the ribbons on his bagpipes fluttering in the wind of his going.

But when he got near the foot of the hill, he stopped short. There by the road was a cottage and by the door of the cottage was a bench and upon the bench sat a bonny lass with black hair and blue eyes, taking the air in the cool of the evening.

He looked at her and she looked at him, but neither of them said a word, one to the other. Then the soldier went on his way again, but he was thinking he'd ne'er seen a lass he fancied so much.

At the inn they told him that they could find him a place to sleep and he could have his supper too, if he'd not be minding the wait till they got it ready for him. That wouldn't trouble him at all, said he. So he went into the room and laid off his bagpipes and sat down to rest his legs from his day's journey.

While the innkeeper was laying the table, the soldier and he began talking about one thing or another. At last the soldier asked, "Who is the bonny lass with the hair like the wing of a blackbird and eyes like flax flowers who bides in the house at the foot of the hill?"

"Och, aye," said the innkeeper. "That would be the weaver's lass."

"I saw her as I passed by on the road," said the soldier, "and I ne'er saw a lass that suited me so fine."

The innkeeper gave the soldier a queer sort of look, but said naught.

"I'm minded to talk to her father," the soldier said, "and if she could fancy me as I do her, happen we could fix it up to wed."

"Happen you'd better not," said the innkeeper.

"Why not, then?" asked the soldier. "Is she promised to someone already?"

"Nay, 'tis not that," the innkeeper replied quickly. "Only . . . Och, well! You see she's not a lass to be talking o'ermuch."

"'Tis not a bad thing for a lass to be quiet," the soldier said. "I ne'er could abide a woman with a clackiting tongue."

The innkeeper said no more, so that was the end o' that.

When he'd had his supper, the soldier went out of the house and back up the road till he came to the cottage again. The bonny lass was still sitting on the bench by the door.

"I'll be having a word with your father, my lass," said the soldier. She rose from the bench and opened the door and stood aside to let him go in. When he had gone in, she shut the door and left him standing in the room on one side of the door and herself outside on the other. But not a word did she say the while.

The soldier looked about the room, and saw at the far side a man who was taking a web of cloth from the loom.

"Is it yourself that's the weaver?" asked the soldier.

"Who else would I be?" asked the man, starting to fold the cloth.

"Then I've come to ask about your daughter."

The man laid the cloth by, and came over to the soldier. "What would you be asking then?" he asked.

"'Tis this," the soldier said, coming to the point at once. "I like the looks of your lass and if you've naught to say against it, I'd like to wed with her."

The weaver looked at the soldier, but said nothing at all.

"You need not fear I could not fend for her," the soldier said. "She'd want for naught. I have a good wee croft waiting for me at home and a flock of sheep and some bits of gear of my own. None so great, of course, but it would do fine for the lass and me, if she'd have me."

"Sit ye down," said the weaver.

So the two of them sat down at either side of the fire.

"I doubt ye'll be at the inn?" the weaver asked.

"Where else would one from a far place stay?" asked the soldier.

"Och, aye. Well, happen the folks at the inn were telling you about my lass?"

"What could they say that I could not see

for myself?" the soldier said. "Except that she doesn't talk o'ermuch. They told me that."

"O'ermuch!" exclaimed the weaver. "She doesn't talk at all!"

"Not at all?" the soldier asked.

"Och, I'll tell you about it," said the weaver. "She went out to walk in the gloaming a year or two ago, and since she came home that night, not a word has come from her lips. Nobody can say why, but folks all say she's bewitched."

"Talk or no," said the soldier, "I'll have her if she'll take me." So they asked her and she took him.

Then they were married, and the soldier took the lass away with him to his own croft.

They settled in, she to keep the house and look after the hens and do the cooking and baking and spinning, and he to tend his sheep and keep the place outside up good and proper.

The lass and he were well pleased with each other and all went well for a while. Though she did not talk, she was good at listening and it took a time for the soldier to tell her all about himself. Then she had a light hand with the baking and a quick hand at the spinning, and she kept the house tidy and shining clean. And she had a ready smile that was sweet as a song. The soldier was off and away most of the day, tending his sheep or mending his walls or working about the croft. When he came home to the lass, the smile and the kiss he got from her were as good as words.

But when the year turned toward its end, and the days grew short and the nights long and dark, the sheep were penned in the fold and the soldier was penned in the house because of the winter weather outside. Then 'twas another story. The house was that quiet you'd be thinking you were alone in it. The soldier stopped talking, for the sound of his own voice going on and on all by itself fair gave him the creeps.

She was still his own dear lass and he loved her dearly, but there were times he felt he had to get out of the house and away from all that silence.

So he took to going out at night just to hear the wind blowing and the dead leaves rustling and a branch cracking in the frost or maybe a tyke barking at some croft over the hill. It was noisy outside compared to the way it was in the house.

One night he said to the lass, "The moonlight's bright this night. I'll be going down the road a piece to walk." So after he'd had his tea, he went out of the house and started down the road. He paid little heed to where he was going, and that's how it happened he nearly walked into the horse. The horse stopped with a jingle of harness and then the soldier saw that the horse was hitched to a cart, and the cart was filled with household gear—furniture and the like. There were two people on the seat of the cart, a man and a woman. The man called out to him, "Are we on the road to Auchinloch?"

"Och, nay!" the soldier said. "You're well off your way. If you keep on this way you'll land in Crieff—some forty miles on. And not much else but hills between here and there."

"Och, me!" said the woman. "We'll have to go back."

"Poor lass," the man said tenderly, "and you so weary already."

"I'm no wearier than yourself," the woman replied. "'Twas you I was thinking of."

Suddenly the soldier said, "You're far out of your way and you'll never get there this night. Why do you not bide the night with us and start out fresh in the morn? Your horse will have a rest and so will you, and you'll travel faster by light of day, and you'll not be so much out in the end."

But it was not so much for them, he asked it, as for himself, just to be hearing other voices than his own in the house.

They saw he really meant it, so they were soon persuaded. It wasn't long till he had them in his house, and their horse with a feed of oats in his barn. They were friendly, likeable folks, and it was easy to get them talking, which was just what the soldier wanted. They were, flitting because their old uncle had left them his croft, and they wouldn't have come at such an unseasonable time, if they hadn't wanted to settle in before the lambing began. Besides, they'd never had a place of their own, and they couldn't wait to get there. So they talked and the soldier talked, and the lass sat and smiled. But if they noticed she had naught to say, neither of them mentioned it.

The next morning they got ready to leave, and the soldier came out to the gate to tell them how to go. After he'd told them, the woman leaned over and said, "What's amiss with your wife? Does she not talk at all?"

"Nay," said the soldier. "She's spoken not a single word for two years past."

"Och, me!" the woman said. "She's not deaf, is she?"

"That she's not!" the soldier told her. "She hears all one says. The folks where she comes from say that she's bewitched."

"I thought it might be that," the woman said. "Well, I'll tell you what to do. Back where we dwelt there's a woman that has the second sight and she's wonderful for curing folks of things. She cured my own sister after the doctors gave her up. It was ten years ago and my sister's living yet. You take your wife over there and see what she can do." She told the soldier where to find the old body, and as they drove away, she said, "You needn't be afraid of her for she's as good as gold. She'll never take anything for helping anybody, and if she's a witch, nobody ever laid it against her. She's just a good old body that has the second sight."

The soldier went into the house and told his lass to get herself ready, for they were going visiting. He did not tell her why, in case it all came to naught, for he couldn't bear to have her disappointed if the old body couldn't help her at all.

He hitched his own wee horse to his cart, and he and the lass drove off to the place where the folks that were going to Auchinloch had dwelt.

They found the old body without any trouble right where the woman said she'd be. She was little and round and rosy and as merry and kind as she could be. The only thing strange about her was her eyes, for they were the sort that made you feel that nothing in the world could ever be unseen if she took

the trouble to look at it, no matter where it was hidden.

When she heard the soldier's story, she said at once that she'd be glad to help them if she could. Folks were probably right when they said the lass was bewitched, but what she'd have to find out was how it had happened. That might take time because the lass couldn't help her, since she couldn't talk.

Then the old woman told the soldier to take himself off for a walk and leave the lass with her and not to come back too soon for if he did, she'd just send him away again.

The soldier walked around and around, and at last he found the village that belonged to the place. There was a blacksmith shop and an old stone church and a post office and a pastry shop and a little shop with jars of sweeties in the windows, that sold everything the other shops didn't have. When he'd seen them all, he went and sat in the only other place there was, which was the tavern, and the time went very slow. But at last he thought it must be late enough for him to go back and fetch his lass. Maybe he'd been foolish to bring her to the old body after all. He'd not go back if the old woman sent him away again. He'd just pack up his lass in the cart and take her home and keep her the way she was. If he'd known what was going to happen, maybe that's what he'd have done.

They were waiting for him when he got back to the little old woman's cottage, and the old body told him at once she'd found where the trouble lay.

"'Tis plain enough," said she. "Your wife has offended the water kelpie. When she went to walk in the gloaming, she drank from the well where the water kelpie bides. And as she leaned over to drink, one of the combs from her hair dropped into the water and she never missed it. The comb fouled the water, and the kelpie can bide in the well no more till she takes it out again. So angry he was, that while she drank of it, he laid a spell on the water that took her speech away."

"But what shall we do now?" asked the soldier.

"All you need to do," said the old woman, "is take your lass back to the well and have her take the comb from the water."

"And she'll talk then?" the soldier asked.

"Och, aye! She'll talk. But watch out for the water kelpie, lest he do her more harm for he's a queer creature always full of wicked mischief and nobody knows what he may do."

The lass and the soldier were so full of joy that they hardly knew how to contain it. The soldier wanted to pay the old woman for what she'd done, but she said it was nothing at all, and in any case she never took pay for doing a kindly service. So the soldier thanked her kindly, and he and his lass went home.

When they had found somebody to look after the croft, they started off to take the spell off the lass's tongue. When they got to the place, the soldier and the lass went out to find the well in the woods. The lass bared her arm and reached down into the water and felt around till she found the comb. She put it back in her hair, and as soon as she did, she found she could talk again.

The first thing she said was, "Och, my love, I can talk to you now!" And the second thing she said was, "Och, I have so much to say!"

They went back to the weaver's house, and when he found that his daughter could talk, he was that pleased. He ran about the village telling everybody, "My lass has found her tongue again!" 'Twas a rare grand day for the weaver. And of course for the soldier, too.

The weaver and the soldier couldn't hear enough of her chatter. They took to following her about just to listen to her as if it were music they were hearing.

After a day or two, she began to grow restless, for she wanted to go home to their own wee croft. So off they set, and she chattered to him every mile of the way. The sound of her voice was the sweetest sound he'd ever heard.

So they came home. It was still winter, and the sheep were still penned in the fold and the soldier in the house, but there wasn't a bit of silence in the cottage. There was this that she had to tell him, and something else she must say. The soldier could hardly slip a word in edgewise, but he still thought it was wonderful to hear her.

After a month or two had gone by and the winter was wearing off toward spring, he began to notice something he had not noticed before. And that was that his bonny wee wife talked away from morn to night, and he wasn't too sure that she did not talk in her sleep. He found he had in his house what he'd told the innkeeper he never could abide—a lass with a clackiting tongue.

He would not have had her silent again; ne'er the less, a little quiet now and then would not have come amiss. But he still loved her dearly, and she was his own dear lass.

So one fine morn after the lambing was over and the sheep were out on the hillside with their dams, he went off to see the old woman who had the second sight to find out if she could do aught about it.

"Deary me!" said she. "I misdoubted the kelpie would find a way to turn things against you."

"That he did!" said the soldier, "or I'd not be here."

"Did she drink of the water again?" the old body asked.

"She did not," said the soldier. "Not even a drop."

"'Twas not that way he got at her then," said the old woman. "Well, tell me what she did do then?"

"She took the comb from the water and she stuck it in her hair," the soldier told her, "and that's all she did do."

"Did she wipe it off first?" the old body asked anxiously.

"Nay. She did not," said the soldier.

"I see it plain," the old body said. "The water that was on the comb was bewitched again. Och, there's not a fairy in the land so full of malice as the water kelpie."

So the old woman sat and thought and thought, and the soldier waited and waited. At last the old woman said, "A little is good, but too much is more than enough. We'll give the kelpie a taste of his own medicine. Take your lass back to the well. Set her beside it and bid her to talk down the well to the kelpie the livelong day. The kelpie must answer whoever speaks to him, so the one of them that tires first will be the loser."

"'Twill not be my lass," said the soldier. "I'll back her to win the day."

So he took his wife back to the well and sat her down beside it, and bade her call the kelpie and talk to him until he came back for her.

So she leaned over the well as he told her to and called to the kelpie. "Kelpie! Kelpie! I'm here!" cried she.

"I'm here!" answered the kelpie from the bottom of the well.

"We'll talk the whole of the day," the lass said happily into the well.

"The whole of the day," the kelpie agreed.

"I've such a lot to tell you," the lass went on.

"A lot to tell you," the kelpie said in return.

The soldier went away, leaving the lass by the well talking so fast that her words tripped over themselves, with the kelpie answering her back all the time.

He came back when the sun had set and the gloaming lay over the wood, to find the lass still sitting there, bending over the well. She was still talking, but very slow, and he could hardly hear the kelpie answer at all.

Well, now that the day was safely over, the soldier laid his hand on her shoulder. "Come away, lass," said he. She looked at him so weary-like that his heart turned over with pity. He'd just take her the way she was from now on, silent or clackiting, he told himself.

She looked up and smiled at him, and then she called down the well. "I bid you good day, kelpie. 'Tis time for me to go home."

There wasn't a sound from the well for a moment. Then in a great loud angry voice the kelpie shouted, "GO HOME!"

So the soldier gave his arm to the lass, and they started to walk back through the woods to her father's house. She said only two things on the way home.

The first thing she said was, "I'm awful thirsty," but she drank no water from the well. The soldier made sure of that!

And the second thing she said was, "I'm tired of talking."

Well, from that time on, she neither talked too little or too much but just enough. The soldier was content, for she was his own dear lass, and he loved her dearly.

Since the old body with the second sight would never let them pay her for the good she'd done them, they invited her to be godmother when their first bairn was born. That pleased her more than if they'd given her a sack of gold. But never again in all her days did the wife go out alone in the gloaming or drink from a fairy well.

Ireland

If it can be said that there is a nation of storytellers, it probably can be said of the Irish. Although Celtic folklore abounds in stories of tricksters and beasties, many of the stories are serious and intricate, more appropriate for older readers than for children. "The Peddler of Ballaghadereen" is a good example of one of the chief attractions of the Irish folk tale, the story in which the lilting quality of Irish speech makes it a joy to tell or to read aloud. That there is humor is evident in "Hudden, Dudden, and Donald O'Neary" with its quick-witted hero who plays on the greed of his neighbors; this is a typical tale of Celtic peasant acumen. The long, romantic tales of folk heroes are less appropriate for those children in the middle grades who are usually the most avid audience for folk tales, but they can be appreciated by young people as their literary tastes mature.

Hudden and Dudden and Donald O'Neary

Children's sense of justice is satisfied by this tale of greed that is foiled by peasant wit.

There was once upon a time two farmers, and their names were Hudden and Dudden. They had poultry in their yards, sheep on the uplands, and scores of cattle in the meadow-land alongside the river. But for all that they weren't happy. For just between their two farms there lived a poor man by the name of Donald O'Neary. He had a hovel over his head and a strip of grass that was barely enough to keep his one cow, Daisy, from starving, and, though she did her best, it was but seldom that Donald got a drink of milk or a roll of butter from Daisy. You would think there was little here to make Hudden and Dudden jealous, but so it is, the more one has the more one wants, and Donald's neighbours lay awake of nights scheming how they might get hold of his little strip of grass-land. Daisy, poor thing, they never thought of; she was just a bag of bones.

One day Hudden met Dudden, and they were soon grumbling as usual, and all to the tune of "If only we could get that vagabond Donald O'Neary out of the country."

"Let's kill Daisy," said Hudden at last; "if that doesn't make him clear out, nothing will."

No sooner said than agreed; and it wasn't dark before Hudden and Dudden crept up to the little shed where lay poor Daisy trying her best to chew the cud, though she hadn't had as much grass in the day as would cover your hand. And when Donald came to see if Daisy was all snug for the night, the poor beast had only time to lick his hand once before she died.

Well, Donald was a shrewd fellow, and downhearted though he was, began to think if he could get any good out of Daisy's death. He thought and he thought, and the next day you could have seen him trudging off early to the fair, Daisy's hide over his shoulder, every penny he had jingling in his pockets. Just before he got to the fair, he made several slits

"Hudden and Dudden and Donald O'Neary" from CELTIC FAIRY TALES, selected and edited by Joseph Jacobs. New York: G. P. Putnam's Sons, 1892.

in the hide, put a penny in each slit, walked into the best inn of the town as bold as if it belonged to him, and, hanging the hide up to a nail in the wall, sat down.

"Some of your best whisky," says he to the landlord. But the landlord didn't like his looks. "Is it fearing I won't pay you, you are?" says Donald; "why I have a hide here that gives me all the money I want." And with that he hit it a whack with his stick and out hopped a penny. The landlord opened his eyes, as you may fancy.

"What'll you take for that hide?"

"It's not for sale, my good man."

"Will you take a gold piece?"

"It's not for sale, I tell you. Hasn't it kept me and mine for years?" and with that Donald hit the hide another whack and out jumped a second penny.

Well, the long and the short of it was that Donald let the hide go, and, that very evening, who but he should walk up to Hudden's door?

"Good-evening, Hudden. Will you lend me your best pair of scales?"

Hudden stared and Hudden scratched his head, but he lent the scales.

When Donald was safe at home, he pulled out his pocketful of bright gold and began to weigh each piece in the scales. But Hudden had put a lump of butter at the bottom, and so the last piece of gold stuck fast to the scales when he took them back to Hudden.

If Hudden had stared before, he stared ten times more now, and no sooner was Donald's back turned, than he was off as hard as he could pelt to Dudden's.

"Good-evening, Dudden. That vagabond, bad luck to him—"

"You mean Donald O'Neary?"

"And who else should I mean? He's back here weighing out sackfuls of gold."

"How do you know that?"

"Here are my scales that he borrowed, and here's a gold piece still sticking to them."

Off they went together, and they came to Donald's door. Donald had finished making the last pile of ten gold pieces. And he couldn't finish because a piece had stuck to the scales.

In they walked without an "If you please" or "By your leave."

"Well, *I* never!" that was all *they* could say.

"Good-evening, Hudden; good-evening Dudden. Ah! you thought you had played me a fine trick, but you never did me a better turn in all your lives. When I found poor Daisy dead, I thought to myself, 'Well, her hide may fetch something'; and it did. Hides are worth their weight in gold in the market just now."

Hudden nudged Dudden, and Dudden winked at Hudden.

"Good-evening, Donald O'Neary."

"Good-evening, kind friends."

The next day there wasn't a cow or a calf that belonged to Hudden or Dudden but her hide was going to the fair in Hudden's biggest cart drawn by Dudden's strongest pair of horses.

When they came to the fair, each one took a hide over his arm, and there they were walking through the fair, bawling out at the top of their voices: "Hides to sell! hides to sell!"

Out came the tanner:

"How much for your hides, my good men?"

"Their weight in gold."

"It's early in the day to come out of the tavern." That was all the tanner said, and back he went to his yard.

"Hides to sell! Fine fresh hides to sell!"

Out came the cobbler:

"How much for your hides, my men?"

"Their weight in gold."

"Is it making game of me you are! Take that for your pains," and the cobbler dealt Hudden a blow that made him stagger.

Up the people came running from one end of the fair to the other. "What's the matter? What's the matter?" cried they.

"Here are a couple of vagabonds selling hides at their weight in gold," said the cobbler.

"Hold 'em fast; hold 'em fast!" bawled the innkeeper, who was the last to come up, he was so fat. "I'll wager it's one of the rogues who tricked me out of thirty gold pieces yesterday for a wretched hide."

It was more kicks than halfpence that Hudden and Dudden got before they were well on their way home again, and they didn't run the slower because all the dogs of the town were at their heels.

Well, as you may fancy, if they loved Donald little before, they loved him less now.

"What's the matter, friends?" said he, as he saw them tearing along, their hats knocked in, and their coats torn off, and their faces black and blue. "Is it fighting you've been? or mayhap you met the police, ill luck to them?"

"We'll police you, you vagabond. It's mighty smart you thought yourself, deluding us with your lying tales."

"Who deluded you? Didn't you see the gold with your own two eyes?"

But it was no use talking. Pay for it he must, and should. There was a meal-sack handy, and into it Hudden and Dudden popped Donald O'Neary, tied him up tight, ran a pole through the knot, and off they started for the Brown Lake of the Bog, each with a pole-end on his shoulder, and Donald O'Neary between.

But the Brown Lake was far, the road was dusty, Hudden and Dudden were sore and weary, and parched with thirst. There was an inn by the roadside.

"Let's go in," said Hudden; "I'm dead beat. It's heavy he is for the little he had to eat."

If Hudden was willing, so was Dudden. As for Donald, you may be sure his leave wasn't asked, but he was lumped down at the inn door for all the world as if he had been a sack of potatoes.

"Sit still, you vagabond," said Dudden; "if we don't mind waiting, you needn't."

Donald held his peace, but after a while he heard the glasses clink, and Hudden singing away at the top of his voice.

"I won't have her, I tell you; I won't have her!" said Donald. But nobody heeded what he said.

"I won't have her, I tell you; I won't have her!" said Donald; and this time he said it louder; but nobody heeded what he said.

"I won't have her, I tell you; I won't have her!" said Donald; and this time he said it as loud as he could.

"And who won't you have, may I be so bold as to ask?" said a farmer, who had just come up with a drove of cattle, and was turning in for a glass.

"It's the king's daughter. They are bothering the life out of me to marry her."

"You're the lucky fellow. I'd give something to be in your shoes."

"Do you see that now! Wouldn't it be a fine thing for a farmer to be marrying a princess, all dressed in gold and jewels?"

"Jewels, do you say? Ah, now, couldn't you take me with you?"

"Well, you're an honest fellow, and as I don't care for the king's daughter, though she's as beautiful as the day, and is covered with jewels from top to toe, you shall have her. Just undo the cord and let me out; they tied me up tight, as they knew I'd run away from her."

Out crawled Donald; in crept the farmer.

"Now lie still, and don't mind the shaking; it's only rumbling over the palace steps you'll be. And maybe they'll abuse you for a vagabond, who won't have the king's daughter; but you needn't mind that. Ah! it's a deal I'm giving up for you, sure as it is that I don't care for the princess."

"Take my cattle in exchange," said the farmer; and you may guess it wasn't long before Donald was at their tails driving them homewards.

Out came Hudden and Dudden, and the one took one end of the pole, and the other the other.

"I'm thinking he's heavier," said Hudden.

"Ah, never mind," said Dudden; "it's only a step now to the Brown Lake."

"I'll have her now! I'll have her now!" bawled the farmer, from inside the sack.

"By my faith and you shall though," said Hudden, and he laid his stick across the sack.

"I'll have her! I'll have her!" bawled the farmer, louder than ever.

"Well, here you are," said Dudden, for

they were now come to the Brown Lake, and, unslinging the sack, they pitched it plump into the lake.

"You'll not be playing your tricks on us any longer," said Hudden.

"True for you," said Dudden. "Ah, Donald, my boy, it was an ill day when you borrowed my scales."

Off they went, with a light step and an easy heart, but when they were near home, whom should they see but Donald O'Neary, and all around him the cows were grazing, and the calves were kicking up their heels and butting their heads together.

"Is it you, Donald?" said Dudden. "Faith you've been quicker then we have."

"True for you, Dudden, and let me thank you kindly; the turn was good, if the will was ill. You'll have heard, like me, that the Brown Lake leads to the Land of Promise. I always put it down as lies, but it is just as true as my word. Look at the cattle."

Hudden stared, and Dudden gaped; but they couldn't get over the cattle; fine fat cattle they were too.

"It's only the worst I could bring up with me," said Donald O'Neary; "the others were so fat, there was no driving them. Faith, too, it's little wonder they didn't care to leave, with grass as far as you could see, and as sweet and juicy as fresh butter."

"Ah, now, Donald, we haven't always been friends," said Dudden, "but, as I was just saying, you were ever a decent lad, and you'll show us the way, won't you?"

"I don't see that I'm called upon to do that; there is a power more cattle down there. Why shouldn't I have them all to myself?"

"Faith, they may well say, the richer you get, the harder the heart. You always were a neighbourly lad, Donald. You wouldn't wish to keep the luck all to yourself?"

"True for you, Hudden, though 'tis a bad example you set me. But I'll not be thinking of old times. There is plenty for all there, so come along with me."

Off they trudged, with a light heart and an eager step. When they came to the Brown Lake the sky was full of little white clouds, and, if the sky was full, the lake was as full.

"Ah! now, look, there they are," cried Donald, as he pointed to the clouds in the lake.

"Where? where?" cried Hudden, and "Don't be greedy!" cried Dudden, as he jumped his hardest to be up first with the fat cattle. But if he jumped first, Hudden wasn't long behind.

They never came back. Maybe they got too fat, like the cattle. As for Donald O'Neary, he had cattle and sheep all his days to his heart's content.

Munachar and Manachar

A fine example of the cumulative story has a surprise ending.

There once lived a Munachar and a Manachar, a long time ago, and it is a long time since it was, and if they were alive now they would not be alive then. They went out together to pick raspberries, and as many as Munachar used to pick Manachar used to eat. Munachar said he must go look for a rod to make a gad to hang Manachar, who ate his raspberries every one; and he came to the rod. "What news to-day?" said the rod. "It is my own news that I'm seeking. Going looking for a rod, a rod to make a gad, a gad to hang Manachar, who ate my raspberries every one."

"You will not get me," said the rod, "until you get an axe to cut me." He came to the axe. "What news to-day?" said the axe. "It's my own news I'm seeking. Going looking for an axe, an axe to cut a rod, a rod to make a gad, a gad to hang Manachar, who ate my raspberries every one."

"You will not get me," said the axe, "until you get a flag to edge me." He came to the flag. "What news to-day?" says the flag. "It's my own news I'm seeking. Going looking for a flag, flag to edge axe, axe to cut a rod, a rod to make a gad, a gad to hang Manachar, who ate my raspberries every one."

"You will not get me," says the flag, "till you get water to wet me." He came to the water. "What news to-day?" says the water. "It's my own news I'm seeking. Going looking for water, water to wet flag, flag to edge axe, axe to cut a rod, a rod to make a gad, a gad to hang Manachar, who ate my raspberries every one."

"You will not get me," said the water, "until you get a deer who will swim me." He came to the deer. "What news to-day?" says the deer. "It's my own news I'm seeking. Going looking for a deer, deer to swim water, water to wet flag, flag to edge axe, axe to cut a rod, a rod to make a gad, a gad to hang Manachar, who ate my raspberries every one."

"You will not get me," said the deer, "until you get a hound who will hunt me." He came to the hound. "What news to-day?" says the hound. "It's my own news I'm seeking. Going looking for a hound, hound to hunt deer, deer to swim water, water to wet flag, flag to edge axe, axe to cut a rod, a rod to make a gad, a gad to hang Manachar, who ate my raspberries every one."

"You will not get me," said the hound, "until you get a bit of butter to put in my claw." He came to the butter. "What news to-day?" says the butter. "It's my own news I'm seeking. Going looking for butter, butter to go in claw of hound, hound to hunt deer, deer to swim water, water to wet flag, flag to edge axe, axe to cut a rod, a rod to make a gad, a gad to hang Manachar, who ate my raspberries every one."

"You will not get me," said the butter, "until you get a cat who shall scrape me." He came to the cat. "What news to-day?" said the cat. "It's my own news I'm seeking. Going looking for a cat, cat to scrape butter, butter to go in claw of hound, hound to hunt deer, deer to swim water, water to wet flag, flag to edge axe, axe to cut a rod, a rod to make a gad, a gad to hang Manachar, who ate my raspberries every one."

"You will not get me," said the cat, "until you will get milk which you will give me." He came to the cow. "What news to-day?" said the cow. "It's my own news I'm seeking. Going looking for a cow, cow to give me milk, milk I will give to the cat, cat to scrape butter, butter to go in claw of hound, hound to hunt deer, deer to swim water, water to wet flag, flag to edge axe, axe to cut a rod, a rod to make a gad, a gad to hang Manachar, who ate my raspberries every one."

"You will not get any milk from me," said the cow, "until you bring me a whisp of straw from those threshers yonder." He came to the threshers. "What news to-day?" said the threshers. "It's my own news I'm seeking. Going looking for a whisp of straw from ye to give to the cow, the cow to give me milk, milk I will give to the cat, cat to scrape butter, butter to go in claw of hound, hound to hunt deer, deer to swim water, water to wet flag, flag to edge axe, axe to cut a rod, a rod to make a gad, a gad to hang Manachar, who ate my raspberries every one."

"You will not get any whisp of straw from us," said the threshers, "until you bring us the makings of a cake from the miller over yonder." He came to the miller. "What news to-day?" said the miller. "It's my own news I'm seeking. Going looking for the makings of a cake which I will give the threshers, the threshers to give me a whisp of straw, the whisp of straw I will give to the cow, the cow to give me milk, milk I will give to the cat, cat to scrape butter, butter to go in claw of hound, hound to hunt deer, deer to swim water, water to wet flag, flag to edge axe, axe to cut a rod, a rod to make a gad, a gad to hang Manachar, who ate my raspberries every one."

"You will not get any makings of a cake from me," said the miller, "till you bring me the full of that sieve of water from the river over there."

He took the sieve in his hand and went over to the river, but as often as ever he would stoop and fill it with water, the moment he raised it the water would run out of it again, and sure, if he had been there, from that day till this, he never could have filled it.

"Munachar and Manachar" from CELTIC FAIRY TALES, selected and edited by Joseph Jacobs. New York: G. P. Putnam's Sons, 1892.

A crow went flying by him, over his head, "Daub! daub!" said the crow. "My blessings on ye, then," said Munachar, "but it's the good advice you have," and he took the red clay and the daub that was by the brink, and he rubbed it to the bottom of the sieve, until all the holes were filled, and then the sieve held the water, and he brought the water to the miller, and the miller gave him the makings of a cake, and he gave the makings of the cake to the threshers, and the threshers gave him a whisp of straw, and he gave the whisp of straw to the cow, and the cow gave him milk, the milk he gave to the cat, the cat scraped the butter, the butter went into the claw of the hound, the hound hunted the deer, the deer swam the water, the water wet the flag, the flag sharpened the axe, the axe cut the rod, and the rod made a gad, and when he had it ready to hang Manachar he found that Manachar had BURST.

The Peddler of Ballaghadereen

The cadence of Irish speech is one of the attractions of a story in which a man finds his fortune through a dream—but only pursues it through the dream of another.

More years ago than you can tell me and twice as many as I can tell you, there lived a peddler in Ballaghadereen. He lived at the crossroads, by himself in a bit of a cabin with one room to it, and that so small that a man could stand in the middle of the floor and, without taking a step, he could lift the latch on the front door, he could lift the latch on the back door, and he could hang the kettle over the turf. That is how small and snug it was.

Outside the cabin the peddler had a bit of a garden. In it he planted carrots and cabbages, onions and potatoes. In the center grew a cherry tree—as brave and fine a tree as you would find anywhere in Ireland. Every spring it flowered, the white blossoms covering it like a fresh falling of snow. Every summer it bore cherries as red as heart's blood.

But every year, after the garden was planted the wee brown hares would come from the copse near by and nibble-nibble here, and nibble-nibble there, until there was not a thing left, barely, to grow into a full-sized vegetable that a man could harvest for his table. And every summer as the cherries began to ripen the blackbirds came in whirling flocks and ate the cherries as fast as they ripened.

The neighbors that lived thereabouts minded this and nodded their heads and said: "Master Peddler, you're a poor, simple man, entirely. You let the wild creatures thieve from you without lifting your hand to stop them."

And the peddler would always nod his head back at them and laugh and answer: "Nay, then, 'tis not thieving they are at all. They pay well for what they take. Look you—on yonder cherry tree the blackbirds sing sweeter nor they sing on any cherry tree in Ballaghadereen. And the brown hares make good company at dusk-hour for a lonely man."

In the country roundabout, every day when there was market, a wedding, or a fair, the peddler would be off at ring-o'-day, his pack strapped on his back, one foot ahead of the other, fetching him along the road. And when he reached the town diamond he would open his pack, spread it on the green turf, and, making a hollow of his two hands, he would call:

"Come buy a trinket—come buy a brooch—
Come buy a kerchief of scarlet or yellow!"

In no time at all there would be a great crowding of lads and lasses and children about him, searching his pack for what they might be wanting. And like as not, some barefooted lad would hold up a jack-knife and ask: "How much for this, Master Peddler?"

"The Peddler of Ballaghadereen" from THE WAY OF THE STORYTELLER by Ruth Sawyer. Copyright 1942, © 1962 by Ruth Sawyer. Copyright renewed 1970 by Ruth Sawyer. Used by permission of Viking Penguin Inc. and The Bodley Head.

And the peddler would answer: "Half a crown."

And the lad would put it back, shaking his head dolefully. "Faith, I haven't the half of that, nor likely ever to have it."

And the peddler would pull the lad over to him and whisper in his ear: "Take the knife —'twill rest a deal more easy in your pocket than in my pack."

Then, like as not, some lass would hold up a blue kerchief to her yellow curls and ask: "Master Peddler, what is the price of this?"

And the peddler would answer: "One shilling sixpence."

And the lass would put it back, the smile gone from her face, and she turning away.

And the peddler would catch up the kerchief again and tie it himself about her curls and laugh and say: "Faith, there it looks far prettier than ever it looks in my pack. Take it, with God's blessing."

So it would go—a brooch to this one and a top to that. There were days when the peddler took in little more than a few farthings. But after those days he would sing his way homeward; and the shrewd ones would watch him passing by and wag their fingers at him and say: "You're a poor, simple man, Master Peddler. You'll never be putting a penny by for your old age. You'll end your days like the blackbirds, whistling for crumbs at our back doors. Why, even the vagabond dogs know they can wheedle the half of the bread you are carrying in your pouch, you're that simple."

Which likewise was true. Every stray, hungry dog knew him the length and breadth of the county. Rarely did he follow a road without one tagging his heels, sure of a noonday sharing of bread and cheese.

There were days when he went abroad without his pack, when there was no market-day, no wedding or fair. These he spent with the children, who would have followed him about like the dogs, had their mothers let them. On these days he would sit himself down on some doorstep and when a crowd of children had gathered he would tell them tales—old tales of Ireland—tales of the good folk, of the heroes, of the saints. He knew

them all, and he knew how to tell them, the way the children would never be forgetting one of them, but carry them in their hearts until they were old.

And whenever he finished a tale he would say, like as not, laughing and pinching the cheek of some wee lass: "Mind well your manners, whether you are at home or abroad, for you can never be telling what good folk, or saint, or hero you may be fetching up with on the road—or who may come knocking at your doors. Aye, when Duirmuid, or Fionn or Oisin or Saint Patrick walked the earth they were poor and simple and plain men; it took death to put a grand memory on them. And the poor and the simple and the old today may be heroes tomorrow—you never can be telling. So keep a kind word for all, and a gentling hand."

Often an older would stop to listen to the scraps of words he was saying; and often as not he would go his way, wagging his finger and mumbling: "The poor, simple man. He's as foolish as the blackbirds."

Spring followed winter in Ireland, and summer followed close upon the heels of both. And winter came again and the peddler grew old. His pack grew lighter and lighter, until the neighbors could hear the trinkets jangling inside as he passed, so few things were left. They would nod their heads and say to one another: "Like as not his pockets are as empty as his pack. Time will come, with winter at hand, when he will be at our back doors begging crumbs, along with the blackbirds."

The time did come, as the neighbors had prophesied it would, smug and proper, when the peddler's pack was empty, when he had naught in his pockets and naught in his cupboard. That night he went hungry to bed.

Now it is more than likely that hungry men will dream; and the peddler of Ballaghadereen had a strange dream that night. He dreamed that there came a sound of knocking in the middle of the night. Then the latch on the front door lifted, the door opened without a creak or a cringe, and inside the cabin stepped Saint Patrick. Standing in the doorway the good man pointed a finger; and he spoke in a voice tuned as low as the wind over the bogs. "Peddler, peddler of Ballaghadereen, take the road to Dublin town. When you get to the bridge that spans the Liffey you will hear what you were meant to hear."

On the morrow the peddler awoke and remembered the dream. He rubbed his stomach and found it mortal empty; he stood on his legs and found them trembling in under him; and he said to himself: "Faith, an empty stomach and weak legs are the worst traveling companions a man can have, and Dublin is a long way. I'll bide where I am."

That night the peddler went hungrier to bed, and again came the dream. There came the knocking on the door, the lifting of the latch. The door opened and Saint Patrick stood there, pointing the road: "Peddler, peddler of Ballaghadereen, take the road that leads to Dublin Town. When you get to the bridge that spans the Liffey you will hear what you were meant to hear!"

The second day it was the same as the first. The peddler felt the hunger and the weakness stronger in him, and stayed where he was. But when he woke after the third night and the third coming of the dream, he rose and strapped his pack from long habit upon his back and took the road to Dublin. For three long weary days he traveled, barely staying his fast, and on the fourth day he came into the city.

Early in the day he found the bridge spanning the river and all the lee-long day he stood there, changing his weight from one foot to the other, shifting his pack to ease the drag of it, scanning the faces of all who passed by. But although a great tide of people swept this way, and a great tide swept that, no one stopped and spoke to him.

At the end of the day he said to himself: "I'll find me a blind alley, and like an old dog I'll lay me down in it and die." Slowly he moved off the bridge. As he passed by the Head Inn of Dublin, the door opened and out came the landlord.

To the peddler's astonishment he crossed the thoroughfare and hurried after him. He clapped a strong hand on his shoulder and cried: "Arra, man, hold a minute! All day I've been watching you. All day I have seen you standing on the bridge like an old rook with rent wings. And of all the people passing from the west to the east, and of all the people passing from the east to the west, not one crossing the bridge spoke aught with you. Now I am filled with a great curiosity entirely to know what fetched you here."

Seeing hunger and weariness on the peddler, he drew him toward the inn. "Come; in return for having my curiosity satisfied you shall have rest in the kitchen yonder, with bread and cheese and ale. Come."

So the peddler rested his bones by the kitchen hearth and he ate as he hadn't eaten in many days. He was satisfied at long last and the landlord repeated his question. "Peddler, what fetched you here?"

"For three nights running I had a dream—" began the peddler, but he got no further.

The landlord of the Head Inn threw back his head and laughed. How he laughed, rocking on his feet, shaking the whole length of him!

"A dream you had, by my soul, a dream!" He spoke when he could get his breath. "I could be telling you were the cut of a man to have dreams, and to listen to them, what's more. Rags on your back and hunger in your cheeks and age upon you, and I'll wager not a farthing in your pouch. Well, God's blessing on you and your dreams."

The peddler got to his feet, saddled his pack, and made for the door. He had one foot over the sill when the landlord hurried after him and again clapped a hand on his shoulder.

"Hold, Master Peddler," he said, "I too had a dream, three nights running." He burst into laughter again, remembering it. "I dreamed there came a knocking on this very door, and the latch lifted, and, standing in the doorway, as you are standing, I saw Saint Patrick. He pointed with one finger to the road running westward and he said: 'Landlord, Landlord of the Head Inn, take *that* road to Ballaghadereen. When you come to the crossroads you will find a wee cabin, and beside the cabin a wee garden, and in the center of the garden a cherry tree. Dig deep under the tree and you will find gold—much gold.' "

The landlord paused and drew his sleeve across his mouth to hush his laughter.

"Ballaghadereen! I never heard of the place. Gold under a cherry tree—whoever heard of gold under a cherry tree! There is only one dream that I hear, waking or sleeping, and it's the dream of gold, much gold, in my own pocket. Aye, listen, 'tis a good dream." And the landlord thrust a hand into his pouch and jangled the coins loudly in the peddler's ear.

Back to Ballaghadereen went the peddler, one foot ahead of the other. How he got there I cannot be telling you. He unslung his pack, took up a mattock lying near by, and dug under the cherry tree. He dug deep and felt at last the scraping of the mattock against something hard and smooth. It took him time to uncover it and he found it to be an old sea chest, of foreign pattern and workmanship, bound around with bands of brass. These he broke, and lifting the lid he found the chest full of gold, tarnished and clotted with mold; pieces-of-six and pieces-of-eight and Spanish doubloons.

I cannot begin to tell the half of the goodness that the peddler put into the spending of that gold. But this I know. He built a chapel at the crossroads—a resting-place for all weary travelers, journeying thither.

And after he had gone the neighbors had a statue made of him and placed it facing the crossroads. And there he stands to this day, a pack on his back and a dog at his heels.

King O'Toole and His Goose

This is an unusual combination of a humorous tale and a religious story, with a saint in disguise who rescues and tests a sportive ruler.

Och, I thought all the world, far and near, had heerd of King O'Toole—well, well but the darkness of mankind is untollable! Well, sir, you must know, as you didn't hear it afore, that there was a king, called King O'Toole, who was a fine old king in the old ancient times, long ago; and it was he that owned the churches in the early days. The king, you see, was the right sort; he was the real boy, and loved sport as he loved his life, and hunting in particular; and from the rising o' the sun, up he got, and away he went over the mountains after the deer; and fine times they were.

Well, it was all mighty good, as long as the king had his health; but, you see, in the course of time the king grew old, by raison he was stiff in his limbs, and when he got stricken in years, his heart failed him, and he was lost entirely for want o' diversion, because he couldn't go a-hunting no longer; and, by dad, the poor king was obliged at last to get a goose to divert him. Oh, you may laugh, if you like, but it's truth I'm telling you; and the way the goose diverted him was this-a-way: You see, the goose used to swim across the lake, and go diving for trout and catch fish on a Friday for the king, and flew every other day round about the lake, diverting the poor king. All went on mighty well until, by dad, the goose got stricken in years like her master, and couldn't divert him no longer, and then it was that the poor king was lost entirely. The king was walkin' one mornin' by the edge of the lake, lamentin' his cruel fate, and thinking of drowning himself, that could get no diversion in life, when all of a sudden, turning round the corner, whom should he meet but a mighty decent young man coming up to him.

"God save you," says the king to the young man.

"God save you kindly, King O'Toole," says the young man.

"True for you," says the king. "I am King O'Toole," says he, "prince and plennypennytinchery of these parts," says he; "but how came ye to know that?" says he.

"Oh, never mind," says St. Kavin.

"King O'Toole and His Goose" from CELTIC FAIRY TALES, selected and edited by Joseph Jacobs. New York: G. P. Putnam's Sons, 1892.

You see it was Saint Kavin, sure enough— the saint himself in disguise, and nobody else. "Oh, never mind," says he, "I know more than that. May I make bold to ask how is your goose, King O'Toole?" says he.

"Blur-an-agers, how came ye to know about my goose?" says the king.

"Oh, no matter; I was given to understand it," says Saint Kavin.

After some more talk the king says, "What are you?"

"I'm an honest man," says Saint Kavin.

"Well, honest man," says the king, "and how is it you make your money so aisy?"

"By makin' old things as good as new," says Saint Kavin.

"Is it a tinker you are?" says the king.

"No," says the saint; "I'm no tinker by trade, King O'Toole; I've a better trade than a tinker," says he—"what would you say," says he, "if I made your old goose as good as new?"

My dear, at the word of making his goose as good as new, you'd think the poor old king's eyes were ready to jump out of his head. With that the king whistled, and down came the poor goose, just like a hound, wad-dling up to the poor cripple, her master, and as like him as two peas. The minute the saint clapt his eyes on the goose, "I'll do the job for you," says he, "King O'Toole."

"By *Jaminee!*" says King O'Toole, "if you do, I'll say you're the cleverest fellow in the seven parishes."

"Oh, by dad," says St. Kavin, "you must say more nor that—my horn's not so soft all out,"

says he, "as to repair your old goose for noth-ing; what'll you gi' me if I do the job for you? —that's the chat," says St. Kavin.

"I'll give you whatever you ask," says the king; "isn't that fair?"

"Divil a fairer," says the saint, "that's the way to do business. Now," says he, "this is the bargain I'll make with you, King O'Toole: will you gi' me all the ground the goose flies over, the first offer, after I make her as good as new?"

"I will," says the king.

"You won't go back o' your word?" says St. Kavin.

"Honour bright!" says King O'Toole, hold-ing out his fist.

"Honour bright!" says St. Kavin, back again, "it's a bargain. Come here!" says he to the poor old goose—"come here, you unfor-tunate ould cripple, and it's I that'll make you the sporting bird." With that, my dear, he took up the goose by the two wings—"Criss o' my cross an you," says he, markin' her to grace with the blessed sign at the same min-ute—and throwing her up in the air, "whew," says he, jist givin' her a blast to help her; and with that, my jewel, she took to her heels, flyin' like one o' the eagles themselves, and cutting as many capers as a swallow be-fore a shower of rain.

Well, my dear, it was a beautiful sight to see the king standing with his mouth open, looking at his poor old goose flying as light as a lark, and better than ever she was; and when she lit at his feet, patted her on the head, and *"Ma vourneen,"* says he, "but you are the *darlint* o' the world."

"And what do you say to me," says Saint Kavin, "for making her the like?"

"By Jabers," says the king, "I say nothing beats the art o' man, barring the bees."

"And do you say no more nor that?" says Saint Kavin.

"And that I'm beholden to you," says the king.

"But will you gi'e me all the ground the goose flew over?" says Saint Kavin.

"I will," says King O'Toole, "and you're welcome to it," says he, "though it's the last acre I have to give."

"But you'll keep your word true," says the saint.

"As true as the sun," says the king.

"It's well for you, King O'Toole, that you said that word," says he; "for if you didn't say that word, the divil the bit o' your goose would ever fly again."

When the king was as good as his word, Saint Kavin was pleased with him, and then it was that he made himself known to the king. "And," says he, "King O'Toole, you're a decent man, for I only came here to try you. You don't know me," says he, "because I'm disguised."

"Musha! then," says the king, "who are you?"

"I'm Saint Kavin," said the saint, blessing himself.

"Oh, queen of heaven!" says the king, making the sign of the cross between his eyes, and falling down on his knees before the saint; "is it the great Saint Kavin," says he, "that I've been discoursing all this time with-out knowing it," says he, "all as one as if he was a lump of a *gossoon?*—and so you're a saint?" says the king.

"I am," says Saint Kavin.

"By Jabers, I thought I was only talking to a dacent boy," says the king.

"Well, you know the difference now," says the saint. "I'm Saint Kavin," says he, "the greatest of all the saints."

And so the king had his goose as good as new, to divert him as long as he lived; and the saint supported him after he came into his property, as I told you, until the day of his death—and that was soon after; for the poor goose thought he was catching a trout one Friday; but, my jewel, it was a mistake he made—and instead of a trout, it was a thieving horse-eel; and instead of the goose killing a trout for the king's supper—by dad, the eel killed the king's goose—and small blame to him; but he didn't ate her, because he darn't ate what Saint Kavin had laid his blessed hands on.

Germany

 It is primarily through the diligent gathering of folk tales by the Brothers Grimm that most of the folk literature of Germany became known. Most of the stories included here were, in fact, familiar to English-speaking children before they became acquainted with the tales told (but collected later than the Grimms' *Household Tales*) in Great Britain and passed on, with variants, in the United States and Canada. Many of the German folk tales are romantic; many have a great deal of violence, as is evident when one compares the German and French versions of "Cinderella." Probably no national folk literature has been so often adapted or so often presented in picture book form as the German stories that have become the heritage of children all over the world.

Hansel and Grettel

The dramatic quality of this story of abandoned children who triumph over a witch has made it a favorite in theater and opera as well as in books.

Once upon a time there dwelt on the outskirts of a large forest a poor woodcutter with his wife and two children; the boy was called Hansel and the girl Grettel. He had always little enough to live on, and once, when there was a great famine in the land, he couldn't even provide them with daily bread. One night, as he was tossing about in bed, full of cares and worry, he sighed and said to his wife: "What's to become of us? How are we to support our poor children, now that we have nothing more for ourselves?"

"I'll tell you what, husband," answered the woman, who was the children's step-mother. "Early tomorrow morning we'll take the children out into the thickest part of the wood; there we shall light a fire for them and give them each a piece of bread; then we'll go on to our work and leave them alone. They won't be able to find their way home, and we shall thus be rid of them."

"No, wife," said her husband, "that I won't do; how could I find it in my heart to leave my children alone in the wood? The wild beasts would soon come and tear them to pieces."

"Oh! you fool," said she, "then we must all four die of hunger, and you may just as well go and plane the boards for our coffins"; and she left him no peace till he consented.

"But I can't help feeling sorry for the poor children," added the husband.

The children, too, had not been able to sleep for hunger, and had heard what their stepmother had said to their father. Grettel wept bitterly and spoke to Hansel: "Now it's all up with us."

"No, no, Grettel," said Hansel, "don't fret yourself; I'll be able to find a way of escape, no fear." And when the old people had fallen asleep he got up, slipped on his little coat, opened the back door and stole out.

The moon was shining clearly, and the white pebbles which lay in front of the house glittered like bits of silver. Hansel bent down and filled his pocket with as many of them as he could cram in. Then he went back and said to Grettel, "Be comforted, my dear little sister, and go to sleep. God will not desert us"; and he lay down in bed again.

"Hansel and Grettel" from THE BLUE FAIRY BOOK, edited by Andrew Lang. London: Longmans, Green, and Co., 1889.

At daybreak, even before the sun was up, the woman came and woke the two children: "Get up, you lie-abeds, we're all going to the forest to fetch wood." She gave them each a bit of bread and spoke: "There's something for your luncheon, but don't eat it up before, for it's all you'll get."

Grettel took the bread under her apron, as Hansel had the stones in his pocket. Then they all set out together on the way to the forest. After they had walked for a little, Hansel stood still and looked back at the house, and this manœuvre he repeated again and again.

His father observed him, and spoke: "Hansel, what are you gazing at there, and why do you always remain behind? Take care, and don't lose your footing."

"Oh! Father," said Hansel, "I am looking back at my white kitten, which is sitting on the roof, waving me a farewell."

The woman exclaimed: "What a donkey you are! That isn't your kitten, that's the morning sun shining on the chimney." But Hansel had not looked back at his kitten, but had always dropped one of the white pebbles out of his pocket onto the path.

When they had reached the middle of the forest the father said: "Now, children, go and fetch a lot of wood, and I'll light a fire that you mayn't feel cold."

Hansel and Grettel heaped up brushwood till they had made a pile nearly the size of a small hill. The brushwood was set fire to, and when the flames leaped high the woman said: "Now lie down at the fire, children, and rest yourselves; we are going into the forest to cut down wood; when we've finished we'll come back and fetch you."

Hansel and Grettel sat down beside the fire, and at midday ate their little bits of bread. They heard the strokes of the axe, so they thought their father was quite near. But it was no axe they heard, but a bough he had tied onto a dead tree, and that was blown about by the wind. And when they had sat for a long time their eyes closed with fatigue, and they fell fast asleep. When they awoke at last, it was pitch dark.

Grettel began to cry, and said: "How are we ever to get out of the wood?"

But Hansel comforted her. "Wait a bit," he said, "till the moon is up, and then we'll find our way sure enough." And when the full moon had risen he took his sister by the hand and followed the pebbles, which shone like new threepenny bits, and showed them the path. They walked all through the night, and at daybreak reached their father's house again.

They knocked at the door, and when the woman opened it she exclaimed: "You naughty children, what a time you've slept in the wood! We thought you were never going to come back." But the father rejoiced, for his conscience had reproached him for leaving his children behind by themselves.

Not long afterwards there was again great dearth in the land, and the children heard their step-mother address their father thus in bed one night: "Everything is eaten up once more; we have only half a loaf in the house, and when that's done it's all up with us. The children must be got rid of; we'll lead them deeper into the wood this time, so that they won't be able to find their way out again. There is no other way of saving ourselves."

The man's heart smote him heavily, and he thought: "Surely it would be better to share the last bite with one's children!" But his wife wouldn't listen to his arguments, and did nothing but scold and reproach him. If a man yields once, he's done for, and so, because he had given in the first time, he was forced to do so the second.

But the children were awake, and had heard the conversation. When the old people were asleep Hansel got up, and wanted to go out and pick up pebbles again, as he had done the first time; but the woman had barred the door, and Hansel couldn't get out. But he consoled his little sister, and said: "Don't cry, Grettel, and sleep peacefully, for God is sure to help us."

At early dawn the woman came and made the children get up. They received their bit of bread, but it was even smaller than the time before. On the way to the wood Hansel crumbled it in his pocket, and every few minutes he stood still and dropped a crumb on the ground.

"Hansel, what are you stopping and looking about you for?" said the father.

"I'm looking back at my little pigeon, which is sitting on the roof waving me a farewell," answered Hansel.

"Fool!" said the wife. "That isn't your pigeon, it's the morning sun glittering on the chimney." But Hansel gradually threw all his crumbs onto the path. The woman led the children still deeper into the forest, farther than they had ever been in their lives before.

Then a big fire was lit again, and the stepmother said: "Just sit down there, children, and if you're tired you can sleep a bit; we're going into the forest to cut down wood, and in the evening when we're finished we'll come back to fetch you."

At midday Grettel divided her bread with Hansel, for he had strewed his all along their path. Then they fell asleep, and evening passed away, but nobody came to the poor children.

They didn't awake till it was pitch dark, and Hansel comforted his sister, saying: "Only wait, Grettel, till the moon rises, then we shall see the bread crumbs I scattered along the path; they will show us the way back to the house." When the moon appeared they got up, but they found no crumbs, for the thousands of birds that fly about the woods and fields had picked them all up.

"Never mind," said Hansel to Grettel. "You'll see, we'll still find a way out." But all the same they did not.

They wandered about the whole night, and the next day, from morning till evening, but they could not find a path out of the wood. They were very hungry, too, for they had nothing to eat but a few berries they found growing on the ground. And at last they were so tired that their legs refused to carry them any longer, so they lay down under a tree and fell fast asleep.

On the third morning after they had left their father's house they set about their wandering again, but only got deeper and deeper into the wood, and now they felt that if help did not come to them soon they must perish. At midday they saw a beautiful little snow-white bird sitting on a branch, which sang so sweetly that they stopped still and listened to it. And when its song was finished it flapped its wings and flew on in front of them. They followed it and came to a little house, on the roof of which it perched; and when they came quite near they saw that the cottage was made of bread and roofed with cakes, while the window was made of transparent sugar.

"Now we'll set to," said Hansel, "and have a regular blow-out. I'll eat a bit of the roof, and you, Grettel, can eat some of the window, which you'll find a sweet morsel."

Hansel stretched up his hand and broke off a little bit of the roof to see what it was like, and Grettel went to the casement and began to nibble at it. Thereupon a shrill voice called out from the room inside:

> "Nibble, nibble, little mouse,
> Who's nibbling my house?"

The children answered:

> "'Tis Heaven's own child,
> The tempest wild,"

and went on eating, without putting themselves about. Hansel, who thoroughly appreciated the roof, tore down a big bit of it, while Grettel pushed out a whole round window-pane, and sat down the better to enjoy it. Suddenly the door opened, and an ancient dame leaning on a staff hobbled out. Hansel and Grettel were so terrified that they let what they had in their hands fall.

But the old woman shook her head and said: "Oh, ho! you dear children, who led you here? Just come in and stay with me, no ill shall befall you." She took them both by the hand and led them into the house, and laid a most sumptuous dinner before them—milk and sugared pancakes, with apples and nuts.

After they had finished, two beautiful little white beds were prepared for them, and when Hansel and Grettel lay down in them they felt as if they had got into heaven.

The old woman had appeared to be most friendly, but she was really an old witch who had waylaid the children, and had only built the little bread house in order to lure them in. When anyone came into her power she killed, cooked, and ate him, and held a regular feast-day for the occasion. Now witches have red eyes, and cannot see far, but, like beasts, they have a keen sense of smell, and know when human beings pass by. When Hansel and Grettel fell into her hands she laughed maliciously, and said jeeringly: "I've got them now; they shan't escape me."

Early in the morning, before the children were awake, the old woman rose up, and when she saw them both sleeping so peacefully, with their round rosy cheeks, she muttered to herself, "That'll be a dainty bite."

Then she seized Hansel with her bony hand and carried him into a little stable, and barred the door on him. He might scream as much as he liked, it did him no good.

Then she went to Grettel, shook her till she awoke, and cried: "Get up, you lazy-bones, fetch water and cook something for your brother. When he's fat I'll eat him up." Grettel began to cry bitterly, but it was of no use: she had to do what the wicked witch bade her.

So the best food was cooked for poor Hansel, but Grettel got nothing but crab-shells. Every morning the old woman hobbled out to the stable and cried: "Hansel, put out your finger, that I may feel if you are getting fat." But Hansel always stretched out a bone, and the old dame, whose eyes were dim, couldn't see it, and thinking always it was Hansel's finger, wondered why he fattened so slowly. When four weeks passed and Hansel still remained thin, she lost patience and determined to wait no longer.

"Hi! Grettel," she called to the girl, "be quick and get some water. Hansel may be fat or thin, I'm going to kill him tomorrow and cook him." Oh! how the poor little sister sobbed as she carried the water, and how the tears rolled down her cheeks!

"Kind heaven help us now!" she cried. "If only the wild beasts in the wood had eaten us, then at least we should have died together."

"Just hold your peace," said the old hag. "Crying won't help you."

Early in the morning Grettel had to go out and hang up the kettle full of water, and light the fire. "First we'll bake," said the old dame. "I've heated the oven already and kneaded the dough." She pushed Grettel out to the oven, from which fiery flames were already issuing. "Creep in," said the witch, "and see if it's properly heated, so that we can shove in the bread." For when she had got Grettel in she meant to close the oven and let the girl bake, that she might eat her up too.

But Grettel perceived her intention, and spoke: "I don't know how I'm to do it; how do I get in?"

"You silly goose!" said the hag. "The opening is big enough. See, I could get in myself." And she crawled toward it, and poked her head into the oven. Then Grettel gave her a shove that sent her right in, shut the iron door, and drew the bolt. Gracious! how she yelled! it was quite horrible; but Grettel fled, and the wretched old woman was left to perish miserably.

Grettel flew straight to Hansel, opened the little stable-door, and cried: "Hansel, we are free; the old witch is dead."

Then Hansel sprang like a bird out of a cage when the door is opened. How they rejoiced, and fell on each other's necks, and jumped for joy, and kissed one another! And as they had no longer any cause for fear, they went into the old hag's house, and there they found, in every corner of the room, boxes with pearls and precious stones.

"These are even better than pebbles," said Hansel, and crammed his pockets full of them.

Grettel said: "I too will bring something home"; and she filled her apron full.

"But now," said Hansel, "let's go and get well away from the witches' wood."

When they had wandered about for some hours they came to a big lake. "We can't get over," said Hansel; "I see no bridge of any sort or kind."

"Yes, and there's no ferry-boat either," answered Grettel; "but look, there swims a white duck; if I ask her she'll help us over"; and she called out:

"Here are two children, mournful very,
Seeing neither bridge nor ferry;
Take us upon your white back,
And row us over, quack, quack!"

The duck swam toward them, and Hansel got on her back and bade his little sister sit beside him.

"No," answered Grettel, "we should be too heavy a load for the duck; she shall carry us across separately."

The good bird did this, and when they were landed safely on the other side and had gone on for a while, the wood became more and more familiar to them, and at length they saw their father's house in the distance. Then they set off to run and, bounding into the room, fell on their father's neck. The man had not passed a happy hour since he left them in the wood, but the woman had died. Grettel shook out her apron so that the pearls and precious stones rolled about the room, and Hansel threw down one handful after the other out of his pocket. Thus all their troubles were ended, and they all lived happily ever afterwards.

My story is done. See! there runs a little mouse. Anyone who catches it may make himself a large fur cap out of it.

Snow-White and the Seven Dwarfs

In part it is the plight of the gentle princess cast out by her stepmother, in part the cheery assemblage of dwarfs, that has made this a folktale classic.

It was in the middle of winter, when the broad flakes of snow were falling around, that a certain queen sat working at a window, the frame of which was made of fine black ebony; and as she was looking out upon the snow, she pricked her finger, and three drops of blood fell upon it. Then she gazed thoughtfully upon the red drops which sprinkled the white snow, and said, "Would that my little daughter may be as white as that snow, as red as the blood, and as black as the ebony window-frame!"

And so the little girl grew up. Her skin was as white as snow, her cheeks as rosy as blood, and her hair as black as ebony; and she was called Snow-White.

But this queen died; and the king soon married another wife, who was very beautiful, but so proud that she could not bear to think that any one could surpass her. She had a magical mirror, to which she used to go and gaze upon herself in it, and say,

"Mirror, Mirror on the wall
Who is fairest of us all?"

And the glass answered,

"Thou, queen, art fairest of them all."

But Snow-White grew more and more beautiful; and when she was seven years old, she was as bright as the day, and fairer than the queen herself. Then the glass one day answered the queen, when she went to consult it as usual,

"Queen, you are full fair, 'tis true,
But Snow-White fairer is than you."

When the queen heard this she turned pale with rage and envy; and called to one of her servants and said, "Take Snow-White away into the wide wood, that I may never see her more." Then the servant led Snow-White away; but his heart melted when she begged him to spare her life, and he said, "I will not hurt thee, thou pretty child." So he left her by herself, and though he thought it most likely that the wild beasts would tear her in pieces, he felt as if a great weight were taken off his heart when he had made up his mind not to kill her, but leave her to her fate.

"Snow-White and the Seven Dwarfs" from GRIMM'S POPULAR STORIES, translated by Edgar Taylor (slightly adapted).

Then poor Snow-White wandered along through the wood in great fear; and the wild beasts roared about her, but none did her any harm. In the evening she came to a little cottage, and went in there to rest herself, for her little feet would carry her no further. Everything was spruce and neat in the cottage. On the table was spread a white cloth, and there were seven little plates with seven little loaves, and seven little glasses, and knives and forks laid in order; and by the wall stood seven little beds. Then, as she was very hungry, she picked a little piece off each loaf, and drank a very little from each glass; and after that she thought she would lie down and rest. So she tried all the little beds; and one was too long, and another was too short, till at last the seventh suited her; and there she laid herself down, and went to sleep.

Presently in came the masters of the cottage, who were seven little dwarfs that lived among the mountains, and dug and searched about for gold. They lighted up their seven lamps, and saw directly that all was not right. The first said, "Who has been sitting on my stool?" The second, "Who has been eating off my plate?" The third, "Who has been picking my bread?" The fourth, "Who has been meddling with my spoon?" The fifth, "Who has been handling my fork?" The sixth, "Who has been cutting with my knife?" The seventh, "Who has been drinking from my glass?" Then the first looked round and said, "Who has been lying on my bed?" And the rest came running to him, and every one cried out that somebody had been upon his bed. But the seventh saw Snow-White, and called all his brethren to come and see her; and they cried out with wonder and astonishment, and brought their lamps to look at her, and said, "Oh, what a lovely child she is!" And they were delighted to see her, and took care not to wake her; and the seventh dwarf slept an hour with each of the other dwarfs in turn, till the night was gone.

In the morning Snow-White told them all her story; and they pitied her, and said if she would keep all things in order, and cook and wash, and knit and spin for them, she might stay where she was, and they would take good care of her. Then they went out all day long to their work, seeking for gold and silver in the mountains; and Snow-White remained at home; and they warned her, and said, "The queen will soon find out where you are, so take care and let no one in."

But the queen, now that she thought Snow-White was dead, believed that she was certainly the handsomest lady in the land; and she went to her mirror and said,

"Mirror, Mirror on the wall
Who is fairest of us all?"

And the mirror answered,

"Queen, thou art of beauty rare,
But Snow-White living in the glen
With the seven little men,
Is a thousand times more fair."

Then the queen was very much alarmed; for she knew that the glass always spoke the truth, and was sure that the servant had betrayed her. And she could not bear to think that any one lived who was more beautiful than she was; so she disguised herself as an old pedlar and went her way over the hills to the place where the dwarfs dwelt. Then she knocked at the door, and cried, "Fine wares to sell!" Snow-White looked out at the window, and said, "Good-day, good-woman; what have you to sell?" "Good wares, fine wares," said she; "laces and bobbins of all colors." "I will let the old lady in; she seems to be a very good sort of body," thought Snow-White; so she ran down, and unbolted the door. "Bless me!" said the old woman, "how badly your stays are laced! Let me lace them up with one of my nice new laces." Snow-White did not dream of any mischief; so she stood up before the old woman, who set to work so nimbly, and pulled the lace so tight, that Snow-White lost her breath, and fell down as if she were dead. "There's an end of all thy beauty," said the spiteful queen, and went away home.

In the evening the seven dwarfs returned; and I need not say how grieved they were to see their faithful Snow-White stretched upon the ground motionless, as if she were quite dead. However, they lifted her up, and when they found what was the matter, they cut the lace; and in a little time she began to breathe, and soon came to life again. Then they said, "The old woman was the queen herself; take care another time, and let no one in when we are away."

When the queen got home, she went straight to her glass, and spoke to it as usual; but to her great surprise it still said,

"Queen, thou art of beauty rare,
But Snow-White living in the glen
With the seven little men,
Is a thousand times more fair."

Then the blood ran cold in her heart with spite and malice to see that Snow-White still lived; and she dressed herself up again in a disguise, but very different from the one she wore before, and took with her a poisoned comb. When she reached the dwarfs' cottage, she knocked at the door, and cried, "Fine wares to sell!" But Snow-White said, "I dare not let any one in." Then the queen said, "Only look at my beautiful combs"; and gave her the poisoned one. And it looked so pretty that Snow-White took it up and put it into her hair to try it. But the moment it touched her head the poison was so powerful that she fell down senseless. "There you may lie," said the queen, and went her way. But by good luck the dwarfs returned very early that evening, and when they saw Snow-White lying on the ground, they guessed what had happened, and soon found the poisoned comb. When they took it away, she recovered, and told them all that had passed; and they warned her once more not to open the door to any one.

Meantime the queen went home to her glass, and trembled with rage when she received exactly the same answer as before; and she said, "Snow-White shall die, if it costs me my life." So she went secretly into a chamber, and prepared a poisoned apple. The outside looked very rosy and tempting, but whoever tasted it was sure to die. Then she dressed herself up as a peasant's wife, and travelled over the hills to the dwarfs' cottage, and knocked at the door; but Snow-White put her head out of the window and said, "I dare not let any one in, for the dwarfs have told me not." "Do as you please," said the old woman, "but at any rate take this pretty apple; I will make you a present of it." "No," said Snow-White, "I dare not take it." "You silly girl!" answered the other, "what are you afraid of? Do you think it is poisoned? Come! Do you eat one part, and I will eat the other." Now the apple was so prepared that one side was good, though the other side was poisoned. Then Snow-White was very much tempted to taste, for the apple looked exceedingly nice; and when she saw the old woman eat, she could refrain no longer. But she had scarcely put the piece into her mouth, when she fell down dead upon the ground. "This time nothing will save you," said the queen; and she went home to her glass and at last it said,

"Thou, queen, art the fairest of them all."

And then her envious heart was glad, and as happy as such a heart could be.

When evening came, and the dwarfs returned home, they found Snow-White lying on the ground. No breath passed her lips, and they were afraid that she was quite dead. They lifted her up, and combed her hair, and washed her face with water; but all was in vain, for the little girl seemed quite dead. So they laid her down upon a bier, and all seven watched and bewailed her three whole days; and then they proposed to bury her; but her cheeks were still rosy, and her face looked just as it did while she was alive; so they said, "We will never bury her in the cold ground." And they made a coffin of glass, so that they might still look at her, and wrote her name upon it, in golden letters, and that she was a king's daughter. And the coffin was placed upon the hill, and one of the dwarfs always sat by it and watched. And the birds of the air came too, and bemoaned Snow-White; first of all came an owl, and then a raven, but at last came a dove.

And thus Snow-White lay for a long, long time, and still looked as though she were only asleep; for she was even now as white as snow, and as red as blood, and as black as ebony. At last a prince came and called at the dwarfs' house; and he saw Snow-White, and read what was written in golden letters. Then he offered the dwarfs money, and earnestly prayed them to let him take her away; but they said, "We will not part with her for all the gold in the world." At last, however, they had pity on him, and gave him the coffin; but the moment he lifted it up to carry it home with him, the piece of apple fell from between her lips, and Snow-White awoke, and said, "Where am I?" And the prince answered, "Thou art safe with me." Then he told her all that had happened, and said, "I love you better than all the world. Come with me to my father's palace, and you shall be my wife." And Snow-White consented, and went home with the prince; and everything was prepared with great pomp and splendour for their wedding.

To the feast was invited, among the rest, Snow-White's old enemy, the queen; and as she was dressing herself in fine rich clothes, she looked in the glass, and said,

"Mirror, Mirror on the wall,
Who is fairest of us all?"

And the glass answered,

"O Queen, although you are of beauty rare
The young queen is a thousand times more fair."

When she heard this, she started with rage; but her envy and curiosity were so great, that she could not help setting out to see the bride. And when she arrived, and saw that it was no other than Snow-White, who, as she thought, had been dead a long while, she choked with passion, and fell ill and died. But Snow-White and the prince lived and reigned happily over that land many, many years.

Rumpelstiltzkin

Children enjoy comparing this to "Tom Tit Tot" and are especially delighted, whether they are acting the parts, reading the story, or hearing it read aloud, with the ending.

There was once upon a time a poor miller who had a very beautiful daughter. Now it happened one day that he had an audience with the King, and in order to appear a person of some importance he told him that he had a daughter who could spin straw into gold.

"Now that's a talent worth having," said the King to the miller. "If your daughter is as clever as you say, bring her to my palace to-morrow, and I'll put her to the test."

When the girl was brought to him he led her into a room full of straw, gave her a spinning-wheel and spindle, and said: "Now set to work and spin all night till early dawn, and if by that time you haven't spun the straw into gold you shall die." Then he closed the door behind him and left her alone inside.

So the poor miller's daughter sat down, and didn't know what in the world she was to do. She hadn't the least idea of how to spin straw into gold, and became at last so miserable that she began to cry.

Suddenly the door opened, and in stepped a tiny little man and said: "Good-evening, Miss Miller-maid; why are you crying so bitterly?"

"Oh!" answered the girl, "I have to spin straw into gold, and haven't a notion how it's done."

"What will you give me if I spin it for you?" asked the manikin.

"My necklace," replied the girl.

The little man took the necklace, sat himself down at the wheel, and whir, whir, whir, the wheel went round three times, and the bobbin was full. Then he put on another, and whir, whir, whir, the wheel went round three times, and the second too was full; and so it went on till the morning, when all the straw was spun away, and all the bobbins were full of gold.

As soon as the sun rose the King came, and when he perceived the gold he was astonished and delighted, but his heart only lusted more than ever after the precious metal. He had the miller's daughter put into another room full of straw, much bigger than the first, and bade her, if she valued her life, spin it all into gold before the following morning.

The girl didn't know what to do, and began to cry; then the door opened as before, and the tiny little man appeared and said: "What'll you give me if I spin the straw into gold for you?"

"The ring from my finger," answered the girl. The manikin took the ring, and whir! round went the spinning-wheel again, and when morning broke he had spun all the straw into glittering gold.

The King was pleased beyond measure at the sight, but his greed for gold was still not satisfied, and he had the miller's daughter brought into a yet bigger room full of straw, and said: "You must spin all this away in the night; but if you succeed this time you shall become my wife."

"She's only a miller's daughter, it's true," he thought; "but I couldn't find a richer wife if I were to search the whole world over."

When the girl was alone the little man appeared for the third time, and said: "What'll you give me if I spin the straw for you once again?"

"I've nothing more to give," answered the girl.

"Then promise me when you are Queen to give me your first child."

"Who knows what mayn't happen before that?" thought the miller's daughter; and besides, she saw no other way out of it, so she promised the manikin what he demanded, and he set to work once more and spun the straw into gold. When the King came in the morning, and found everything as he had

"Rumpelstiltzkin" from THE BLUE FAIRY BOOK, edited by Andrew Lang. London: Longmans, Green, and Co., 1889.

desired, he straightway made her his wife, and the miller's daughter became a queen.

When a year had passed a beautiful son was born to her, and she thought no more of the little man, till all of a sudden one day he stepped into her room and said, "Now give me what you promised." The Queen was in a great state, and offered the little man all the riches in her kingdom if he would only leave her the child.

But the manikin said: "No, a living creature is dearer to me than all the treasures in the world."

Then the Queen began to cry and sob so bitterly that the little man was sorry for her, and said: "I'll give you three days to guess my name, and if you find it out in that time you may keep your child."

Then the Queen pondered the whole night over all the names she had ever heard, and sent a messenger to scour the land and to pick up far and near any names he should come across. When the little man arrived on the following day she began with Kasper, Melchior, Belshazzar, and all the other names she knew, in a string, but at each one the manikin called out, "That's not my name."

The next day she sent to inquire the names of all the people in the neighborhood, and had a long list of the most uncommon and extraordinary for the little man when he made his appearance. "Is your name, perhaps, Sheepshanks, Cruickshanks, Spindleshanks?"

But he always replied, "That's not my name."

On the third day the messenger returned and announced: "I have not been able to find any new names, but as I came upon a high hill round the corner of the wood, where the foxes and hares bid each other good night, I saw a little house, and in front of the house burned a fire, and round the fire sprang the most grotesque little man, hopping on one leg and crying:

'To-morrow I brew, to-day I bake,
And then the child away I'll take;
For little deems my royal dame
That Rumpelstiltzkin is my name!' "

You may imagine the Queen's delight at hearing the name, and when the little man stepped in shortly afterwards and asked, "Now, my lady Queen, what's my name?" she asked first: "Is your name Conrad?"

"No."

"Is your name Harry?"

"No."

"Is your name, perhaps, Rumpelstiltzkin?"

"Some demon has told you that, some demon has told you that," screamed the little man, and in his rage drove his right foot so far into the ground that it sank in up to his waist. Then in a passion he seized the left foot with both hands and tore himself in two.

The Elves and the Shoemaker

A folk tale that stresses a familiar theme, being repaid for kindness to the Little People.

There was once a shoemaker who worked very hard and was very honest; but still he could not earn enough to live upon, and at last all he had in the world was gone, except just leather enough to make one pair of shoes.

Then he cut them all ready to make up the next day, meaning to get up early in the morning to work. His conscience was clear and his heart light amidst all his troubles; so he went peaceably to bed, left all his cares to heaven, and fell asleep.

In the morning, after he had said his prayers, he set himself down to his work, when to his great wonder, there stood the shoes, all ready made, upon the table. The good man knew not what to say or think of this strange event. He looked at the workmanship; there was not one false stitch in the whole job, and all was so neat and true that it was a complete masterpiece.

That same day a customer came in, and the shoes pleased him so well that he willingly paid a price higher than usual for them; and the poor shoemaker with the money bought leather enough to make two pairs more. In the evening he cut out the work, and went to bed early that he might get up and begin betimes next day. But he was saved all the trouble, for when he got up in the morning the work was finished ready to his hand.

Presently in came buyers, who paid him handsomely for his goods, so that he bought leather enough for four pairs more. He cut out the work again over night, and found it finished in the morning as before; and so it went on for some time; what was got ready in the evening was always done by daybreak, and the good man soon became thriving and prosperous again.

One evening about Christmas time, as he and his wife were sitting over the fire chatting together, he said to her, "I should like to sit up and watch to-night, that we may see who it is that comes and does my work for me." The wife liked the thought; so they left a light burning, and hid themselves in the corner of the room behind a curtain and watched to see what would happen.

As soon as it was midnight, there came two little naked dwarfs; and they sat themselves upon the shoemaker's bench, took up all the work that was cut out, and began to ply with their little fingers, stitching and rapping and tapping away at such a rate that the shoemaker was all amazement, and could not take his eyes off for a moment. And on they went till the job was quite finished, and the shoes stood ready for use upon the table. This was long before daybreak; and then they bustled away as quick as lightning.

The next day the wife said to the shoemaker, "These little wights have made us rich, and we ought to be thankful to them, and do them a good office in return. I am quite vexed to see them run about as they do; they have nothing upon their backs to keep off the cold. I'll tell you what, I will make each of them a shirt, and a coat and waistcoat, and a pair of pantaloons into the bargain; do you make each of them a little pair of shoes."

The thought pleased the good shoemaker very much; and one evening, when all the things were ready, they laid them on the table instead of the work that they used to cut out, and then went and hid themselves to watch what the little elves would do.

About midnight the elves came in and were going to sit down to their work as usual; but when they saw the clothes lying for them, they laughed and were greatly delighted. Then they dressed themselves in the twinkling of an eye, and danced and capered and sprang about as merry as could be, till at last they danced out at the door and over the green; and the shoemaker saw them no more; but everything went well with him from that time forward, as long as he lived.

The Bremen Town Musicians

The horrible din of the four animals who fancy themselves musicians drives away the robbers whose house then provides the cat, cock, dog, and donkey with a pleasant home.

A certain man had a Donkey, which had carried the corn sacks to the mill faithfully for many a long year. But his strength was going, and he was growing more and more unfit for work.

Then his master began to consider how he might best save his keep. But the Donkey, seeing that no good wind was blowing, ran away and set out on the road to Bremen.

There, he thought, I can surely be town musician.

When he had walked some distance, he found a Hound lying on the road, gasping like one who had run till he was tired.

"Why are you gasping so, you big fellow?" asked the Donkey.

"Ah," replied the Hound, "as I am old, and daily grow weaker and no longer can hunt, my master wants to kill me. So I have taken to flight. But now how am I to earn my bread?"

"I tell you what," said the Donkey, "I am going to Bremen, and shall be town musician there. Come with me and engage yourself also as a musician. I will play the lute, and you shall beat the kettledrum."

The Hound agreed, and on they went.

Before long, they came to a Cat sitting on the path, with a face like three rainy days!

"Now then, old shaver, what has gone askew with you?" asked the Donkey.

"Who can be merry when his neck is in danger?" answered the Cat. "Because I am now getting old, and my teeth are worn to stumps, and I prefer to sit by the fire and spin, rather than hunt about after mice, my mistress wants to drown me, so I have run away. But now good advice is scarce. Where am I to go?"

"Come with us to Bremen. You understand night music, so you can be a town musician."

The Cat thought well of it and went with them.

After this, the three fugitives came to a farmyard, where a Cock was sitting upon the gate, crowing with all his might.

"Your crow goes through and through one," said the Donkey. "What is the matter?"

"I have been foretelling fine weather, because it is the day on which Our Lady washes the Christ Child's little shirts and wants to dry them," said the Cock. "But guests are coming for Sunday, so the housewife has no pity and has told the cook that she intends to cook me in the soup tomorrow. This evening I am to have my head cut off. Now I am crowing at full pitch while I can."

"Ah, but Red Comb," said the Donkey, "you had better come away with us. We are going to Bremen. You can find something better than death everywhere. You have a good voice, and if we make music together, it must have some quality!"

The Cock agreed to this plan, and all four went on together.

They could not, however, reach the city of Bremen in one day. In the evening they came to a forest where they meant to pass the night. The Donkey and the Hound laid themselves down under a large tree. The Cat

and the Cock settled themselves in the branches; but the Cock flew right to the top, where he was most safe.

Before he went to sleep, he looked around on all the four sides and thought he saw in the distance a little spark burning. So he called out to his companions that there must be a house not far off, for he saw a light.

The Donkey said, "If so, we had better get up and go on, for the shelter here is bad."

The Hound thought that a few bones with some meat would do him good, too!

They made their way to the place where the light was, and soon saw it shine brighter and grow larger, until they came to a well-lighted robbers' house. The Donkey, as the biggest, went to the window and looked in.

"What do you see, my Gray Horse?" asked the Cock.

"What do I see?" answered the Donkey. "I see a table covered with good things to eat and drink and robbers sitting at it enjoying themselves."

"That would be the sort of thing for us," said the Cock.

"Yes, yes! Ah, how I wish we were there!" said the Donkey. Then the animals took counsel together as to how they could drive away the robbers, and at last they thought of a plan. The Donkey was to place himself with his forefeet upon the window ledge, the Hound was to jump on the Donkey's back, the Cat was to climb upon the Hound, and lastly the Cock was to fly up and perch upon the head of the Cat.

When this was done, at a given signal, they began to perform their music together. The Donkey brayed, the Hound barked, the Cat mewed, and the Cock crowed. Then they burst through the window into the room, so that the glass clattered!

At this horrible din, the robbers sprang up, thinking no otherwise than that a ghost had come in, and fled in a great fright out into the forest.

The four companions now sat down at the table, well content with what was left, and ate as if they were going to fast for a month.

As soon as the four minstrels had done, they put out the light, and each sought for himself a sleeping place according to his nature and to what suited him. The Donkey laid himself down upon some straw in the yard, the Hound behind the door, the Cat upon the hearth near the warm ashes, and the Cock perched himself upon a beam of the roof. Being tired with their long walk, they soon went to sleep.

When it was past midnight, the robbers saw from afar that the light was no longer burning in their house and all appeared quiet.

The captain said, "We ought not to have let ourselves be frightened out of our wits." He ordered one of them to go and examine the house.

The messenger finding all still, went into the kitchen to light a candle, and, taking the glistening fiery eyes of the Cat for live coals, he held a lucifer match to them to light it. But the Cat did not understand the joke and flew in his face, spitting and scratching.

He was dreadfully frightened and ran to the back door, but the Dog, who lay there, sprang up and bit his leg.

Then, as he ran across the yard by the straw heap, the Donkey gave him a smart kick with his hind foot. The Cock, too, who had been awakened by the noise and had become lively, cried down from the beam:

Kicker-ee-ricker-ee-ree!

Then the robber ran back as fast as he could to his captain, and said, "Ah, there is a horrible witch sitting in the house, who spat on me and scratched my face with her long claws. By the door stands a man with a knife, who stabbed me in the leg. In the yard there lies a black monster, who beat me with a wooden club. And above, upon the roof, sits the judge, who called out:

Bring the rogue here to me!

"So I got away as well as I could."

After this the robbers did not trust themselves in the house again. But it suited the four musicians of Bremen so well that they did not care to leave it anymore.

And the mouth of him who last told this story is still warm.

The Spirit in the Bottle

A poor boy uses his wits to recapture the evil spirit he had kindly set free.

There was once a poor woodcutter who toiled from early morning till late at night. When at last he had laid by some money, he said to his son, "You are my only child, and I will spend the money which I have earned with the sweat of my brow on your education. If you learn an honest trade, you can support me in my old age, when my limbs have grown stiff, and I am obliged to stay at home."

Then the boy went to a high school and learned diligently so that his masters praised him, and he remained there a long time. When he had worked through two classes, but was still not perfect in everything, the little pittance which the father had earned was all spent, and the boy was obliged to return home.

"Ah," said the father, sorrowfully, "I can give you no more. In these hard times, I cannot earn a farthing more than will suffice for our daily bread."

"Dear Father," answered the son, "don't trouble yourself about it, if it is God's will, it will turn to my advantage. I shall soon get accustomed to it."

When the father wanted to go into the forest to earn money by helping to cut and stack wood, the son said, "I will go with you and help you."

"Nay, my son," said the father, "that would be hard for you. You are not accustomed to rough work and will not be able to bear it. Besides, I have only one axe and no money left with which to buy another."

"Go to our neighbor," answered the son, "he will lend you his axe until I have earned one for myself."

The father then borrowed an axe from the neighbor, and next morning, at break of day,

"The Spirit in the Bottle" from GRIMM'S FAIRY TALES, based on the Frances Jenkins Olcott edition of the English translation by Margaret Hunt. Copyright © 1968 by Follett Publishing Company. Used by permission of Follett Publishing Company.

they went out into the forest together. The son helped his father and was quite merry and brisk about it.

When the sun was right over their heads, the father said, "We will rest and have our dinner, and then we shall work twice as well."

The son, however, took his bread in his hands, and said, "Just you rest, Father, I am not tired; I will walk up and down for a while in the forest and look for birds' nests."

"Oh, you fool," said the father, "why should you want to run about? Afterwards, you will be tired and no longer able to raise your arm. Stay here, and sit down beside me."

The son, nevertheless, went into the forest, ate his bread, was very merry, and peered in among the branches to see if he could discover a bird's nest. So he walked to and fro until at last he came to a great dangerous-looking oak, which must have been already many hundreds of years old, and which five men could not have spanned. He stood still and looked at it, and thought, many a bird must have built its nest in that. Then, all at once, it seemed to him that he heard a voice. He listened and became aware that someone was crying in a very smothered voice, "Let me out! Let me out!"

He looked around, but could discover nothing. Then he thought that the voice came out of the ground. So he cried, "Where are you?" The voice answered, "I am down here amongst the roots of the oak tree. Let me out! Let me out!"

The son began to loosen the earth under the tree, and to search among the roots, until at last he found a glass bottle in a small hollow. He lifted it up and held it against the light. Then he saw a creature shaped like a frog, springing up and down inside. It kept crying, "Let me out! Let me out!"

The young lad, thinking no evil, drew the cork out of the bottle. Immediately a spirit ascended from it and began to grow and grow. It grew so fast that in a very few moments, he stood before the boy—a terrible fellow as big as half the tree.

"Do you know," he cried in a terrible voice, "what your reward is for having let me out?"

"No," answered the boy fearlessly, "how should I know that?"

"Then I will tell you," cried the spirit. "I must strangle you."

"You should have told me that sooner," said the boy, "for then I should have left you in the bottle. But my head shall remain fast for all you can do; more persons than one must be consulted about that."

"More persons here, more persons there," said the spirit, "you shall have the reward you have earned. Do you think that I was shut up for such a long time as a favor? No, it was a punishment for me. I am the mighty Mercurius. Whoever releases me, he must I strangle."

"Slowly," answered the boy, "not so fast. I must first know that you really were shut up in that little bottle and that you are the right spirit. If, indeed, you can get in again, I will believe it. Then you may do as you will with me."

The spirit said haughtily, "That is a very trifling feat." He drew himself together, made himself as small and thin as he had been at first, so that he could creep through the same opening and right through the neck of the bottle again. Scarcely was he within, than the boy thrust the cork back into the bottle and threw it among the roots of the oak, into its old place, and the spirit was deceived.

Now the schoolboy was about to return to his father, but the spirit cried out very piteously, "Ah, do let me out! Ah, do let me out!"

"No," replied the boy, "not a second time! He who has once tried to take my life shall not be set free by me, now that I have caught him again."

"If you will set me free," said the spirit, "I will give you so much that you will have plenty all the days of your life."

"No," answered the boy, "you would cheat me as you did the first time."

"You are spurning your own good luck," said the spirit, "I will do you no harm, but will reward you richly."

I will venture it, the boy thought, perhaps he will keep his word, and anyhow he shall not get the better of me. Then he took out the cork, and the spirit rose up from the bottle as he had done before, stretched himself until he became as big as a giant. "Now you shall have your reward," said he, and handed the boy a little rag just like sticking plaster, and said, "If you spread one end of this over a wound, it will heal, and if you rub steel or iron with the other end, it will be changed into silver."

"I must try that now," said the boy, and went to a tree, tore off the bark with his axe, and rubbed it with one end of the plaster. Immediately it closed together and was healed. "Now it is all right," he told the spirit, "and we can part."

The spirit thanked him for his release, and the boy thanked the spirit for his present and went back to his father.

"Where have you been racing about?" said the father. "Why have you forgotten your work? I always said that you would never come to anything."

"Be easy, Father, I will make it up."

"Make it up, indeed," said the father angrily, "that's no use."

"Take care, Father, I will soon hew that tree over there so that it will split." Then he took his plaster, rubbed the axe with it, and dealt the tree a mighty blow. But as the iron had changed into silver, the edge bent. "Just look, Father, what a bad axe you've given me! It has become quite crooked."

The father was shocked, and said, "Ah, what have you done? Now I shall have to pay for that, and have not the wherewithal, and that is all the good I have got from your work."

"Don't get angry," said the son, "I will soon pay for the axe."

"Oh, you blockhead," cried the father, "with what will you pay for it? You have nothing but what I give you. These are students' tricks that are sticking in your head; you have no idea of woodcutting."

After a while, the boy said, "Father, I can really work no longer. We had better take a holiday."

"Eh, what!" answered the father, "do you think I will sit with my hands lying in my lap like you? I must go on working, but you may take yourself off home."

"Father, I am here in this wood for the first time; I don't know my way alone. Do come with me."

As his anger had now abated, the father at last let himself be persuaded and went home with him. Then he said to his son, "Go and sell your damaged axe, and see what you can get for it, and I must earn the difference, in order to pay our neighbor."

The son took the axe and carried it into town to a goldsmith, who tested it, laid it in the scales, and said, "It is worth four hundred talers, but I have not so much as that by me."

"Give me what you have," said the son, "I will lend you the rest." The goldsmith gave him three hundred talers and remained a hundred in his debt.

The son thereupon went home and said, "Father, I have the money, go and ask our neighbor what he wants for the axe."

"I know that already," answered the old man, "one taler, six groschen."

"Then give him two talers, twelve groschen, that is double and enough. Here, I have money in plenty," and he gave his father a hundred talers. "You shall never know want anymore, for now you can live as comfortably as you like."

"How have you come by these riches?" cried the father. Then the son told how all had come to pass, and how he, trusting in his luck, had bargained with the spirit in the bottle.

With the money that was left, he went back to the high school and went on learning more, and as he could heal all wounds with his plaster, he became the most famous doctor in the whole world.

The Turnip

A peasant whose greedy, jealous brother has tried to kill him escapes by using his wits.

There were once two brothers, both of whom were soldiers. One was rich and the other poor. The poor one, to escape from his poverty, removed his soldier's coat and worked like a peasant. He dug and hoed his bit of land, and sowed it with turnips. When the seed sprouted, one of the turnips grew to a great size, and it would never stop growing. It might have been called the Queen of Turnips, for never before, nor since, has there been so enormous a turnip.

The peasant did not know what to do with the turnip. Was a turnip of that size good fortune or bad? He thought to himself, If I eat this turnip myself, it will taste just like the small turnips, so that will be a waste. If I sell it, it will not bring me any special fame or fortune, but only a little money to be quickly used up like the rest. Perhaps the best thing to do is to give it to the King as a present.

So he put it in a cart. It was so huge that it filled the cart completely and needed two strong oxen to pull it along. Then he took it to the palace and gave it to the King.

"What strange thing is this?" marveled the King. "Many wonderful things have I seen in my life, but never so strange and wonderful a thing as this! What seed did it grow from? Perhaps it belongs to you because you are a child of good luck?"

"Oh, no," sighed the poor peasant. "I certainly am not lucky. I am just a poor peasant, and before that I was an even poorer soldier. But I could not support myself as a soldier, and can barely do it now. I have a brother who is rich and well known to you, my Lord King, but I have neither fame nor fortune, only poverty."

The King felt sorry for the poor man, and said, "You shall be poor no longer." Then he gave him much gold and silver and gems and land and flocks and made him immensely rich, so that he was even wealthier than his brother.

Now when the rich brother heard what the poor brother had gained for himself with a single turnip, he envied him. He racked his brain to think of what he could do to get a reward like that from the King. Gathering together gold and horses, he took them to the King, expecting that the King would certainly reward him with far handsomer gifts. For if his brother got so much for a turnip, what would he not get for his beautiful things!

The King accepted his gifts and thanked him. He told the rich brother that there was nothing on earth he could give him in return, nothing rarer or of greater value than the magnificent Queen of Turnips.

So the rich brother was obliged to put his brother's huge turnip in a cart and have it taken to his home. He was furious. He did not know on whom to expend his wrath. Evil thoughts ran through his head, and finally he decided to kill his brother.

He hired murderers to lie in wait for the poor man. Then he went to his brother and said, "Dear Brother, I know of a hidden treasure. Let us dig it up together and divide it between us."

The other agreed to this and went with him trustingly. But they had gone only a little way when the murderers fell upon him, tied him up, and prepared to hang him. But just as they were about to hang him, they heard loud singing and the sound of horses' feet in the distance. They were terrified of getting caught, so they pushed their intended victim into a big sack, hung it quickly on a branch of the tree, and ran away.

The man in the sack worked and struggled until he had made a hole in the sack through which he could put his head. Just then, he looked down and saw that the man who was singing so joyfully was just about to pass beneath him. He was a traveling student. The man in the tree saw this and his eyes lit up. He called out, "Good day! What a lucky chap you are!"

The student looked around him on every side, but could not see from where that voice came. At last, he said, "Who is calling me?"

From the treetops came the answer, "Raise up your eyes. I sit here aloft in the

"The Turnip" from GRIMM'S FAIRY TALES, based on the Frances Jenkins Olcott edition of the English translation by Margaret Hunt. Copyright © 1968 by Follett Publishing Company. Used by permission of Follett Publishing Company.

Sack of Wisdom. I have learned so much in a very short time, that the wisdom of all schools is as air compared to mine. Soon I shall have learned everything, and when I come down I shall be the wisest man in the world since the beginning of time! I understand the stars, and the signs of the heavens, and the blowing of the winds, the sands of the sea, the healing of illness, and the virtues of all herbs, birds, and stones. If you were once inside the Sack, you would know just what wonders flow from this Sack of Knowledge."

The student, when he heard all this, was amazed, and said, "How lucky that I have found you! I, too, want to enter the Sack of Wisdom!"

The man in the tree pretended to be reluctant, and said, "Perhaps if you show yourself to be wise and patient, I will let you get in for a little while. But you must wait for another hour at least because I still have one or two more things to learn."

After the student had waited a while he became impatient and begged to be allowed to enter the Sack immediately. His thirst for knowledge became more unbearable by the moment. So the man in the Sack pretended to give in, and said, "Well then, in order that I may get out of the Sack, you must let it down so you can get in."

So the student let the Sack down, untied it, and set the imprisoned one free. Then he insisted, "Please draw me up at once!" And he began to climb into the Sack.

"Wait!" said the man. "Not that way." And he took him by the head, put him upside down into the Sack, tied it up, and taking hold of the rope, pulled the eager student up to the top of the tree.

Then he called up to him and said, "How is it going up there, my dear fellow? You will soon feel wisdom entering into you, and this will be a very valuable experience for you. Keep perfectly quiet until you are wiser!"

Then he mounted the student's horse and galloped away. But within an hour, he sent someone back to let the poor student out of the Sack.

France

 Whether it was Charles Perrault or his son Pierre who collected and published *Contes de ma Mère l'Oye* in 1697 has never been definitely established, but the eight tales in the book, translated in English in 1729 as *Tales of Mother Goose,* were immediately popular. The first of the great national collections, the stories it contained ("Cinderella," "Puss in Boots," "Little Red Riding Hood," and others) have become a part of the classic tradition. Mme. de Beaumont's "Beauty and the Beast" has been adapted into play form and appeared in film; it is a story that is simple enough in its dramatic impact to enthrall children and complex enough in its complexity of meaning to fascinate adults. Although not every tale has a courtly setting, the romantic panache of French folk tales is one of their most distinctive qualities.

The Sleeping Beauty in the Wood

In an adaptation of one of Perrault's most romantic tales, some of the violence of the original has been omitted.

There were formerly a king and a queen, who were sorry they had no children; so sorry that it cannot be expressed. They went to all the waters in the world; vows, pilgrimages, all ways were tried, and all to no purpose.

At last, however, the queen had a daughter. There was a very fine christening; and the princess had for her godmothers all the fairies they could find in the whole kingdom —they found seven. By this means the princess had all the perfections imaginable.

After the christening, all the company returned to the king's palace, where was prepared a great feast for the fairies. There was placed before every one of them a magnificent cover with a case of massive gold, wherein were a spoon, knife and fork, all of pure gold set with diamonds and rubies. But as they were all sitting down at table they saw come into the hall a very old fairy, who had not been invited. It was above fifty years since she had been seen, and she was believed to be either dead or enchanted.

The king ordered her a cover, but could not furnish her with a case of gold because seven only had been made for the seven fairies. The old fairy fancied she was slighted and muttered some threats between her teeth. One of the young fairies, who sat by her, overheard how she grumbled. Judging that she might give the little princess some unlucky gift the young fairy went, as soon as they rose from table, and hid herself behind the hangings, that she might speak last and repair, as much as she could, any evil which the old fairy intended.

"The Sleeping Beauty in the Wood" from THE BLUE FAIRY BOOK, edited by Andrew Lang. London: Longmans, Green, and Co., 1889.

Meanwhile all the fairies began to give their gifts to the princess. The youngest for her gift said that the princess should be the most beautiful person in the world; the next, that she should have the wit of an angel; the third, that she should have wonderful grace in everything she did; the fourth, that she should dance perfectly; the fifth, that she should sing like a nightingale; and the sixth, that she should play all kinds of music to perfection.

The old fairy's turn coming next, with her head shaking more with spite than age, she said that the princess should have her hand pierced with a spindle and die of the wound. This terrible gift made the whole company tremble, and everybody fell a-crying.

At this very instant the young fairy came out from behind the hangings, and spoke these words aloud:

"Assure yourselves, O King and Queen, that your daughter shall not die. It is true, I have no power to undo entirely what my elder has done. The princess shall indeed pierce her hand with a spindle. But instead of dying, she shall only fall into a profound sleep, which shall last a hundred years. After a hundred years a king's son shall come and wake her."

The king, to avoid the misfortune, immediately forbade spinning with a distaff and spindle, or to have so much as a spindle in the house. About fifteen or sixteen years after, the king and queen being gone to one of their pleasure houses, the young princess was diverting herself by running up and down the palace. She came into a little room at the top of the tower, where a good old woman was spinning with her spindle. This good woman had never heard of the king's proclamation against spindles.

"What are you doing there, goody?" said the princess.

"I am spinning, my pretty child," said the old woman.

"Ha," said the princess, "this is very pretty. How do you do it? Give it to me so I may see."

She had no sooner taken the spindle than it ran into her hand, and she fell down in a swoon.

The good old woman cried out for help. People came and threw water upon the princess' face, unlaced her, struck her on the palms of her hands, and rubbed her temples with Hungary water. But nothing would bring her to herself.

And now the king, who came up at the noise, bethought himself of the prediction of the fairies and, judging very well that this must necessarily come to pass since the fairies had said it, caused the princess to be carried into the finest apartment in his palace and laid upon a bed all embroidered with gold and silver.

One would have taken her for a little angel, she was so very beautiful, for her swooning had not dimmed her complexion: her cheeks were carnation and her lips were coral. Indeed her eyes were shut, but she was heard to breathe softly, which satisfied those about her she was not dead. The king commanded them not to disturb her, but let her sleep quietly till her hour of awakening was come.

The good fairy, who had saved the life of the princess by condemning her to sleep a hundred years, was in the kingdom of Mataquin, twelve thousand leagues off, when this accident befell the princess. But she was instantly informed of it by a little dwarf, who had boots with which he could go seven leagues in one stride. The fairy came immediately, in a fiery chariot drawn by dragons.

The king handed her out of the chariot, and she approved everything he had done. But she touched with her wand everything in the palace—except the king and the queen—governesses, maids of honor, ladies of the bedchamber, gentlemen, officers, stewards, cooks, undercooks, scullions, guards with their beefeaters, pages, footmen. She likewise touched all the horses in the stables, the great dogs in the outward court and pretty little Mopsey too, the princess' little spaniel, which lay by her on the bed.

Immediately upon her touching them they all fell asleep that they might not awake before their mistress and might be ready to wait upon her when she wanted them. The very spits at the fire, as full as they could hold of partridges and pheasants, fell asleep also. All this was done in a moment. Fairies are not long in doing their magic.

And now the king and the queen, having kissed their dear child without waking her, went out of the palace, and in a quarter of an hour's time there grew up all round about the park such a vast number of trees, great and small, bushes and brambles, twining one within another, that neither man nor beast could pass through. Nothing could be seen but the very tops of the towers, and those only from a great distance.

When a hundred years were gone and passed the son of the king then reigning, who was of another family, being gone a-hunting, asked what those towers were which he saw in the middle of a great thick wood?

All answered according to the story they had heard. Some said it was a ruinous old castle, haunted by spirits; others, that all the sorcerers and witches of the country kept their night meetings there. The common opinion was that an ogre lived there, who carried thither all the little children he could catch.

The prince was at a loss, not knowing what to believe, when a very aged countryman spoke to him:

"May it please Your Royal Highness, it is now about fifty years since I heard from my father, who heard my grandfather say, there was in this castle a princess, the most beautiful ever seen, who must sleep there a hundred years, and should be awakened by a king's son."

The young prince was all on fire at these words. Believing in this rare adventure, and pushed on by love and honor, he resolved that moment to look into it. Scarce had he advanced toward the wood when all the great trees, the bushes and brambles gave way of themselves to let him pass. He walked up a long avenue to the castle. What surprised him a little was that he saw none of his people could follow him. The trees closed behind him again as soon as he had passed through. However, he did not cease from continuing his way; a young prince is always valiant.

He came into a spacious outward court, where everything he saw might have frozen the most fearless person with horror. There was a frightful silence, and there was nothing to be seen but stretched-out bodies of men and animals, all seeming to be dead. He knew, however, by the ruby faces of the beefeaters, that they were only asleep; and their goblets, wherein still remained some drops of wine, showed plainly that they fell asleep in their cups.

The prince then crossed a court paved with marble, went up the stairs, and came into the guard chamber, where guards were standing in their ranks, with their muskets upon their shoulders, and snoring as loud as they could. After that he went through several rooms full of gentlemen and ladies, all asleep, some standing, others sitting. At last he came into a chamber all gilded with gold, where he saw upon a bed, the curtains of which were open, the finest sight a young prince ever beheld—a princess, who appeared to be about fifteen or sixteen years of age, and whose bright and resplendent beauty had somewhat in it divine. He approached with trembling and admiration and fell down before her upon his knees.

And now, as the enchantment was at an end, the princess awoke, and looking on him with eyes more tender than the first view might seem to admit, "Is it you, my Prince?" said she. "I have waited a long while."

The prince, charmed with these words, and much more with the manner in which they were spoken, knew not how to show his joy and gratitude. He assured her he loved her better than he did himself. Their discourse was not well connected, they did weep more than talk—little eloquence, a great deal of love. He was more at a loss than she, and we need not wonder at it: she had time to think on what to say to him; for it is very probable—though history mentions nothing of it—that the good fairy, during so long a sleep, had given her very agreeable dreams. In short, they talked four hours together, and yet they said not half what they had to say.

Meanwhile all the palace awoke; everyone thought upon their particular business, and as all of them were not in love they were ready to die for hunger. The chief lady of honor, being as sharp set as other folks, grew very impatient and told the princess loudly that supper was served. The prince helped the princess to rise. She was dressed magnificently, but his royal highness took care not to tell her she was dressed like his great-grandmother and had a point band peeping over a high collar. She looked not a bit the less charming and beautiful for all that.

They went into the great hall of looking glasses, where they supped, and were served by the princess' officers. The violins and hautboys played old tunes, very excellent, even though it was now above a hundred years since they had been played. After supper, without losing any time, the lord almoner married them in the chapel of the castle, and the chief lady of honor drew the curtains. They had but very little sleep—the princess had no need of it. The prince left her next morning to return to the city, where his father must needs have been anxious about him. The prince told him that he had lost his way in the forest as he was hunting and had lain in the cottage of a charcoal burner, who gave him cheese and brown bread.

The king, his father, who was a good man, believed him; but his mother could not be persuaded it was true. As he went almost every day a-hunting and always had some excuse ready for so doing, she began to suspect he was married.

He lived with the princess above two whole years, and had by her two children, the eldest, a daughter, was named Morning, and the youngest, a son, they called Day, because he was a great deal handsomer and more beautiful than his sister.

The queen spoke several times to her son, to inform herself after what manner he passed his time, and that in this he ought in duty to satisfy her. But he never dared to trust her with his secret. He feared her, though he loved her, for she was of the race of the ogres, and the king would never have married her had it not been for her vast riches. It was even whispered about the court that she had ogreish inclinations and that, whenever she saw little children passing by, she had all the difficulty in the world to avoid falling upon them. And so the prince would never tell her one word.

But when the king was dead, which happened about two years afterward, and the prince saw himself lord and master, he openly declared his marriage and went with great ceremony to conduct his queen to the palace. They made a magnificient entry into the capital city, she riding between her two children.

Soon afterward, the king went to war with the Emperor Contalabutte, his neighbor. He left the government of the kingdom to the queen, his mother, earnestly recommending to her care his wife and children. He was obliged to continue his expedition all the summer, and as soon as he departed the queen-mother sent her daughter-in-law to a country house in the woods, that she might with the more ease gratify her horrible longing.

Some few days afterward she went thither herself, and said to her clerk of the kitchen, "I have a mind to eat little Morning for my dinner tomorrow."

"Ah, madam!" cried the clerk of the kitchen.

"I will have it so," replied the queen-mother—and she spoke in the tone of an ogress who had a strong desire to eat fresh meat—"and will eat her with a *sauce Robert.*"

The poor man, knowing very well he must not play tricks with ogresses, took his great knife and went up into little Morning's chamber. She was then four years old and came up to him jumping and laughing, to take him about the neck, and ask him for some candy. Upon which he began to weep. Then he went into the back yard, where he killed a little lamb and dressed it with such good

sauce that his mistress assured him she had never eaten anything so good in her life. He had in the meantime taken little Morning to his wife, to conceal her in the lodging he had at the bottom of the courtyard.

About eight days afterward the wicked queen-mother said to the clerk of the kitchen, "I will sup upon little Day."

He answered not a word, being resolved to cheat her as he had done before. He went out to find little Day, and saw him with a small foil in his hand, fencing with a great monkey, the child being then only three years of age. He took him up in his arms and carried him to his wife, to conceal him along with his sister, and in place of little Day cooked up a young kid, very tender, which the ogress found to be wonderfully good.

This was all very well; but one evening this wicked queen-mother said to her clerk of the kitchen, "I will eat the queen with the same sauce I had with her children."

Now the poor clerk of the kitchen despaired. How could he find a beast to cook in her stead was what puzzled him. He put himself into as great fury as he could possibly and came into the young queen's room with his dagger in hand. He would not, however, surprise her, but told her with a great deal of respect the orders he had received from the queen-mother.

"Do it! Do it!" said she, stretching out her neck. "Execute your orders, and then I shall see my children, my poor children, whom I so much and so tenderly loved." For she thought them dead ever since they had been taken away without her knowledge.

"No, no, madam!" cried the poor clerk of the kitchen, all in tears. "You shall not die, and yet you shall see your children again. You must go home with me to my lodgings, where I have concealed them, and I shall deceive the queen-mother once more, by giving her in your stead a young hind."

Upon this he conducted her to her children and then went and dressed a young hind, which the queen-mother had for her supper and devoured with great appetite. She was delighted with her cruelty and had invented a story to tell the king, at his return, how the mad wolves had eaten up his wife and her two children.

One evening, as the queen-mother was rambling about the courts and yards of the palace to see if she could smell fresh meat, she heard little Day crying, for his mother was going to spank him because he had been naughty, and she heard at the same time little Morning begging pardon for her brother.

The ogress commanded next morning, with a voice which made everybody tremble, that they should bring into the middle of the great court a large tub. This she caused to be filled with toads, vipers, snakes and all sorts of serpents. Then she ordered the queen and her children, the clerk of the kitchen, his wife and maid, brought thither, with their hands tied behind them, to be thrown into the tub.

They were brought out accordingly, and the executioners were just going to throw them into the tub, when the king, who was not so soon expected, entered the court on horseback. With the utmost astonishment he asked the meaning of the horrible spectacle.

No one dared to tell him, when the ogress, enraged to see what had happened, threw herself head foremost into the tub, and was instantly devoured by the ugly creatures. The king could not but be sorry, for she was his mother; but he soon comforted himself with his beautiful wife and pretty children.

Toads and Diamonds

The theme of kindness to a stranger is frequently met in folk literature; here the young kind daughter is repaid by having pearls and diamonds fall from her lips, while her haughty sister is punished by the stranger and has toads and snakes fall from her lips.

"Toads and Diamonds" from THE BLUE FAIRY BOOK, edited by Andrew Lang. London: Longmans, Green, and Co., 1889.

There was once upon a time a widow who had two daughters. The elder was so much like her in face and humor that whosoever looked upon the daughter saw the mother. They were both so disagreeable and so proud there was no living with them.

The younger, who was the very picture of her father for courtesy and sweetness of temper, was withal one of the most beautiful girls ever seen. As people naturally love their own likeness, this mother doted on her elder daughter, and at the same time had a horrible aversion for the younger. She made her eat in the kitchen and work continually.

Among the other things, this poor child was forced twice a day to draw water above a mile and a half from the house and bring home a pitcher full of it. One day, as she was at this fountain, there came to her a poor woman, who begged of her to let her drink.

"Oh, ay, with all my heart, Goody," said this pretty girl. And immediately rinsing the pitcher, she took up some water from the clearest place of the fountain, and gave it to her, holding up the pitcher all the while that she might drink the easier.

The good woman having drunk, said to her, "You are so very pretty, my dear, so good and so mannerly, I cannot help giving you a gift." For this was a fairy, who had taken the form of a poor countrywoman, to see how far the civility and good manners of this pretty girl would go. "I will give you for gift," continued the fairy, "that, at every word you speak, there shall come out of your mouth either a flower or a jewel."

When this pretty girl came home her mother scolded her for staying so long at the fountain.

"I beg your pardon, mamma," said the poor girl, "for not making more haste." And in speaking these words out of her mouth there came two roses, two pearls, and two diamonds.

"What is it I see there?" said her mother, astonished. "I think I see pearls and diamonds come out of the girl's mouth! How happens this, child?"

This was the first time she had ever called her child.

The poor girl told her frankly all that had happened, not without dropping infinite numbers of diamonds.

"In good faith," cried the mother, "I must send my elder child thither. Come, look what comes out of your sister's mouth when she speaks. Would you not be glad, my dear, to have the same gift given to you? You have nothing to do draw water out of the fountain, and when a certain poor woman asks you to let her drink, to give it her very civilly."

"It would be a very fine sight indeed," said this ill-bred minx, "to see me draw water."

"You shall go, hussy," said the mother, "and this minute."

So she went, but grumbling all the way, taking with her the best silver tankard in the house. She was no sooner at the fountain than she saw coming out of the wood a lady most gloriously dressed, who came up to her and asked to drink. This was the very fairy who appeared to her sister, but had now taken the air and dress of a princess, to see how far this girl's rudeness would go.

"Am I come hither," said the proud, saucy girl, "to serve you with water, pray? I suppose the silver tankard was brought for your ladyship? However, you may drink out of it, if you have a fancy."

"You are not over and above mannerly," answered the fairy, without putting herself in a passion. "Well, then, since you have so little breeding, and are so disobliging, I give you for gift that at every word you speak there shall come out of your mouth a snake or a toad."

So soon as her mother saw her coming she cried out, "Well, daughter?"

"Well, mother?" answered the pert hussy, throwing out of her mouth two vipers and two toads.

"Oh, mercy!" cried the mother. "What is it I see? Oh, it is that wretch your sister who has occasioned all this, but she shall pay for it." And immediately she ran to beat her.

The poor child fled away from her and went to hide herself in the forest, not far thence. The king's son, then on his return from hunting, met her, and seeing her so pretty, asked what she did there alone and why she cried.

"Alas, sir, my mother has turned me out of doors."

The king's son, who saw five or six pearls and as many diamonds come out of her mouth, desired her to tell him how that happened. She thereupon told him the whole story. The king's son fell in love with her, and considering with himself that such a gift was worth more than any marriage portion, conducted her to the palace of the king his father, and there married her.

As for the proud elder sister, she soon made herself so much hated that her own mother turned her off.

Cinderella or The Little Glass Slipper

Not as humorous as the Italian version or as punitive as the German, this is the variant by Perrault best known to most English-language readers.

Once there was a gentleman who married, for his second wife, the proudest and most haughty woman that was ever seen. She had, by a former husband, two daughters of her own humour, who were, indeed, exactly like her in all things. He had likewise, by another wife, a young daughter, but of unparalleled goodness and sweetness of temper, which she took from her mother, who was the best creature in the world.

No sooner were the ceremonies of the wedding over but the stepmother began to show herself in her true colours. She could not bear the good qualities of this pretty girl, and the less because they made her own daughters appear the more odious. She employed her in the meanest work of the house. The girl scoured the dishes, tables, etc., and scrubbed madam's chamber, and those of

"Cinderella or The Little Glass Slipper" from THE BLUE FAIRY BOOK, edited by Andrew Lang. London: Longmans, Green, and Co., 1889.

misses, her daughters; she lay up in a sorry garret, upon a wretched straw bed, while her sisters lay in fine rooms, with floors all inlaid, upon beds of the very newest fashion, and where they had looking-glasses so large that they might see themselves at their full length from head to foot.

The poor girl bore all patiently and dared not tell her father, who would have rattled her off; for his wife governed him entirely. When she had done her work, she used to go into the chimney-corner and sit down among cinders and ashes, which made her commonly be called *Cinderwench;* but the youngest, who was not so rude and uncivil as the eldest, called her Cinderella. However, Cinderella, notwithstanding her mean apparel, was a hundred times handsomer than her sisters, though they were always dressed very richly.

It happened that the King's son gave a ball, and invited all persons of fashion to it. Our young misses were also invited, for they cut a very grand figure among the quality. They were mightily delighted at this invitation, and wonderfully busy in choosing out such gowns, petticoats, and head-clothes as might become them. This was a new trouble to Cinderella; for it was she who ironed her sisters' linen, and plaited their ruffles; they talked all day long of nothing but how they should be dressed.

"For my part," said the eldest, "I will wear my red velvet suit with French trimming."

"And I," said the youngest, "shall have my usual petticoat; but then, to make amends for that, I will put on my gold-flowered manteau and my diamond stomacher, which is far from being the most ordinary one in the world."

They sent for the best tire-woman they could get to make up their head-dresses and adjust their double pinners, and they had their red brushes and patches from Mademoiselle de la Poche.

Cinderella was likewise called up to them to be consulted in all these matters, for she had excellent notions, and advised them always for the best, nay, and offered her services to dress their heads, which they were very willing she should do. As she was doing this, they said to her:

"Cinderella, would you not be glad to go to the ball?"

"Alas!" said she, "you only jeer me; it is not for such as I am to go thither."

"Thou art in the right of it," replied they; "it would make the people laugh to see a Cinderwench at a ball."

Anyone but Cinderella would have dressed their heads awry, but she was very good, and dressed them perfectly well. They were almost two days without eating, so much they were transported with joy. They broke above a dozen laces in trying to be laced up close, that they might have a fine slender shape, and they were continually at their looking-glass. At last the happy day came; they went to court, and Cinderella followed them with her eyes as long as she could, and when she had lost sight of them, she fell a-crying.

Her godmother, who saw her all in tears, asked her what was the matter.

"I wish I could—I wish I could—" she was not able to speak the rest, being interrupted by her tears and sobbing.

This godmother of hers, who was a fairy, said to her, "You wish you could go to the ball; is it not so?"

"Y—es," cried Cinderella, with a great sigh.

"Well," said her godmother, "be but a good girl, and I will contrive that you shall go." Then she took her into her chamber, and said to her, "Run into the garden, and bring me a pumpkin."

Cinderella went immediately to gather the finest she could get, and brought it to her godmother, not being able to imagine how this pumpkin could make her go to the ball. Her godmother scooped out all the inside of it, having left nothing but the rind; which done, she struck it with her wand, and the pumpkin was instantly turned into a fine coach, gilded all over with gold.

She then went to look into her mouse-trap, where she found six mice, all alive, and ordered Cinderella to lift up a little the trap-door, when, giving each mouse, as it went out, a little tap with her wand, the mouse was that moment turned into a fine horse, which altogether made a very fine set of six horses of a beautiful mouse-coloured dapple-grey. Being at a loss for a coachman, Cinderella said, "I will go and see if there is never a rat in the rat-trap—we may make a coachman of him."

"You are right," replied her godmother; "go and look."

Cinderella brought the trap to her, and in it there were three huge rats. The fairy made choice of one of the three which had the largest beard, and, having touched him with her wand, he was turned into a fat, jolly coachman, who had the smartest whiskers eyes ever beheld.

After that, she said to her: "Go again into the garden, and you will find six lizards behind the watering-pot. Bring them to me."

She had no sooner done so but her godmother turned them into six footmen, who skipped up immediately behind the coach, with their liveries all bedaubed with gold and silver, and clung as close behind each other as if they had done nothing else their whole lives. The fairy then said to Cinderella:

"Well, you see here an equipage fit to go to the ball with; are you not pleased with it?"

"Oh! yes," cried she; "but must I go thither as I am, in these nasty rags?"

Her godmother only just touched her with her wand, and, at the same instant, her clothes were turned into cloth of gold and silver, all beset with jewels. This done, she gave her a pair of glass slippers, the prettiest in the whole world. Being thus decked out, she got up into her coach; but her godmother, above all things, commanded her not to stay till after midnight, telling her, at the same time, that if she stayed one moment longer, the coach would be a pumpkin again, her horses mice, her coachman a rat, her footmen lizards, and her clothes become just as they were before.

She promised her godmother she would not fail of leaving the ball before midnight; and then away she drove, scarce able to contain herself for joy. The King's son, who was told that a great princess, whom nobody knew, was come, ran out to receive her; he gave her his hand as she alighted from the coach, and led her into the hall, among all the company. There was immediately a profound silence. The dancing stopped, and the violins ceased to play, so eager was everyone to contemplate the singular beauties of the unknown new-comer. Nothing was then heard but a confused noise of: "Ha! how handsome she is! Ha! how handsome she is!"

The King himself, old as he was, could not help watching her and telling the Queen softly that it was a long time since he had seen so beautiful and lovely a creature.

All the ladies were busied in considering her clothes and head-dress, that they might have some made next day after the same pattern, provided they could meet with such fine materials and as able hands to make them.

The King's son conducted her to the most honourable seat, and afterwards took her out to dance with him; she danced so very gracefully that they all more and more admired her. A fine collation was served up, whereof the young prince ate not a morsel, so intently was he busied in gazing on her.

She went and sat down by her sisters, showing them a thousand civilities, giving them part of the oranges and citrons which the Prince had presented her with, which very much surprised them, for they did not know her. While Cinderella was thus amusing her sisters, she heard the clock strike eleven and three-quarters, whereupon she immediately made a curtsy to the company and hastened away as fast as she could.

Upon arriving home, she ran to seek out her godmother, and, after having thanked her, she said she could not but heartily wish she might go next day to the ball, because the King's son had invited her.

As she was eagerly telling her godmother whatever had passed at the ball, her two sisters knocked at the door, which Cinderella ran and opened.

"How long you have stayed!" cried she, gaping, rubbing her eyes and stretching herself as if she had been just waked out of her sleep; she had not, of course, had any inclination to sleep since they went from home.

"If you had been at the ball," said one of her sisters, "you would not have been tired with it. There came thither the finest princess, the most beautiful ever was seen with mortal eyes; she showed us a thousand civilities, and gave us oranges and citrons."

Cinderella seemed very indifferent in the matter; indeed, she asked them the name of that princess; but they told her they did not know it, and that the King's son was very uneasy on her account and would give all the world to know who she was. At this Cinderella, smiling, replied:

"She must, then, be very beautiful indeed; how happy you have been! Could not I see her? Ah! dear Miss Charlotte, do lend me your yellow suit of clothes which you wear every day."

"Ay, to be sure!" cried Miss Charlotte; "lend my clothes to such a dirty Cinderwench as you! I should be a fool."

Cinderella, indeed, expected well such answer, and was very glad of the refusal; for she would have been sadly put to it if her sister had lent her what she asked for jestingly.

The next day the two sisters were at the ball, and so was Cinderella, but dressed more magnificently than before. The King's son was always by her, and never ceased his compliments and kind speeches to her; to whom all this was so far from being tiresome that she quite forgot what her godmother had recommended to her; so that she, at last, counted the clock striking twelve when she took it to be no more than eleven; she then rose up and fled, as nimble as a deer. The Prince followed, but could not overtake her. She left behind one of her glass slippers, which the Prince took up most carefully. She got home, but quite out of breath, and in her nasty old clothes, having nothing left her of all her finery but one of the little slippers, fellow to that she dropped.

The guards at the palace gate were asked if they had not seen a princess go out. They said they had seen nobody go out but a young girl, very meanly dressed, who had more the air of a poor country wench than a gentlewoman.

When the two sisters returned from the ball Cinderella asked them if they had been well diverted, and if the fine lady had been there. They told her that she had, but that she hurried away immediately when it struck twelve, and with so much haste that she dropped one of her little glass slippers, the prettiest in the world, which the King's son had taken up; that he had done nothing but look at her all the time at the ball, and that most certainly he was very much in love with the beautiful person who owned the glass slipper.

What they said was very true; for a few days after, the King's son caused it to be proclaimed, by sound of trumpet, that he would marry her whose foot this slipper would just fit. They whom he employed began to try it upon the princesses, then the duchesses and all the court, but in vain; it was brought to the two sisters, who did all they possibly could to thrust their foot into the slipper, but they could not effect it.

Cinderella, who saw all this, and knew her slipper, said to them, laughing: "Let me see if it will not fit me."

Her sisters burst out a-laughing, and began to banter her. The gentleman who was sent to try the slipper looked earnestly at Cinderella, and, finding her very handsome, said it was but just that she should try, and that he had orders to let everyone make trial.

He obliged Cinderella to sit down, and, putting the slipper to her foot, he found it went on very easily, and fitted her as if it had been made of wax. The astonishment of her two sisters was excessively great, but still abundantly greater when Cinderella pulled out of her pocket the other slipper and put it on her foot. Thereupon, in came her godmother, who, having touched with her wand Cinderella's clothes, made them richer and more magnificent than any of those she had before.

And now her two sisters found her to be that fine, beautiful lady whom they had seen at the ball. They threw themselves at her feet to beg pardon for all the ill-treatment they had made her undergo. Cinderella took them up, and, as she embraced them, cried that she forgave them with all her heart, and desired them always to love her.

She was conducted to the young Prince, dressed as she was; he thought her more charming than ever and, a few days after, married her. Cinderella, who was no less good than beautiful, gave her two sisters lodgings in the palace, and that very same day matched them with two great lords of the court.

The Master Cat or Puss in Boots

One of the favorite animal heroes of folklore, the clever cat makes both his owner's fortune and his own.

There was a miller who left no more estate to the three sons he had than his mill, his ass, and his cat. The partition was soon made. Neither the scrivener nor attorney was sent for. They would soon have eaten up all the poor patrimony. The eldest had the mill, the second the ass, and the youngest nothing but the cat.

The poor young fellow was quite comfortless at having so poor a lot. "My brothers," said he, "may get their living handsomely enough by joining their stocks together; but, for my part, when I have eaten up my cat, and made me a muff of his skin, I must die of hunger."

The cat, who heard all this, but made as if he did not, said to him with a grave and serious air: "Do not thus afflict yourself, my good master; you have nothing else to do but to give me a bag, and get a pair of boots made for me, that I may scamper through the dirt and the brambles, and you shall see that you have not so bad a portion of me as you imagine."

The cat's master did not build very much upon what he said; he had, however, often seen him play a great many cunning tricks to catch rats and mice; as when he used to hang by the heels, or hide himself in the meal, and make as if he were dead; so that he did not

altogether despair of his affording him some help in his miserable condition. When the cat had what he asked for, he booted himself very gallantly, and, putting his bag about his neck, he held the strings of it in his two forepaws, and went into a warren where was great abundance of rabbits. He put bran and sow-thistle into his bag, and, stretching out at length, as if he had been dead, he waited for some young rabbits, not yet acquainted with the deceits of the world, to come and rummage his bag for what he had put into it.

Scarce had he lain down but he had what he wanted: a rash and foolish young rabbit jumped into his bag, and Monsieur Puss, immediately drawing close the strings, took and killed him without pity. Proud of his prey, he went with it to the palace, and asked to speak with his majesty. He was shown upstairs into the king's apartment, and, making a low reverence, said to him:

"I have brought you, sir, a rabbit of the warren, which my noble Lord, the Master of Carabas"—for that was the title which Puss was pleased to give his master—"has commanded me to present to Your Majesty from him."

"Tell thy master," said the king, "that I thank him, and that he does me a great deal of pleasure."

Another time he went and hid himself among some standing corn, holding his bag open; and, when a brace of partridges ran into it, he drew the strings, and so caught them both. He went and made a present of these to the king, as he had done before with the rabbit which he took in the warren. The king, in like manner, received the partridges with great pleasure, and ordered some money to be given to Puss.

The cat continued for two or three months thus to carry his majesty, from time to time, game of his master's taking. One day in particular, when he knew for certain that he was to take the air along the river-side with his daughter, the most beautiful princess in the world, he said to his master:

"The Master Cat or Puss in Boots" from THE BLUE FAIRY BOOK, edited by Andrew Lang. London: Longmans, Green, and Co., 1889.

"If you will follow my advice your fortune is made. You have nothing else to do but go and wash yourself in the river, in that part I shall show you, and leave the rest to me."

The Marquis of Carabas did what the cat advised him to, without knowing why or wherefore. While he was washing, the king passed by, and the cat began to cry out: "Help! help! My Lord Marquis of Carabas is going to be drowned."

At this noise the king put his head out of the coach-window, and, finding it was the cat who had so often brought him such good game, he commanded his guards to run immediately to the assistance of his lordship the Marquis of Carabas. While they were drawing the poor marquis out of the river, the cat came up to the coach and told the king that, while his master was washing, there came by some rogues who went off with his clothes, though he had cried out: "Thieves! thieves!" several times, as loud as he could.

This cunning cat had hidden them under a great stone. The king immediately commanded the officers of his wardrobe to run and fetch one of his best suits for the Lord Marquis of Carabas.

The fine clothes the king had given him extremely set off his good mien (for he was well made and very handsome in his person), and the king's daughter took a secret inclination to him, and the Marquis of Carabas had no sooner cast two or three respectful and somewhat tender glances but she fell in love with him to distraction. The king would needs have him come into the coach and take part of the airing.

The cat, quite over-joyed to see his project begin to succeed, marched on before and, meeting with some countrymen who were mowing a meadow, he said to them: "Good people, you who are mowing, if you do not tell the king that the meadow you mow belongs to my Lord Marquis of Carabas, you shall be chopped as small as herbs for the pot."

The king did not fail asking of the mowers to whom the meadow they were mowing belonged.

"To my Lord Marquis of Carabas," answered they altogether, for the cat's threats had made them terribly afraid.

"You see, sir," said the marquis, "this is a meadow which never fails to yield a plentiful harvest every year."

The Master Cat, who went still on before, met with some reapers and said to them:

"Good people, you who are reaping, if you do not tell the king that all this corn belongs to the Marquis of Carabas, you shall be chopped as small as herbs for the pot."

The king, who passed by a moment after, would needs know to whom all that corn, which he then saw, did belong.

"To my Lord Marquis of Carabas," replied the reapers, and the king was very well pleased with it, as well as the marquis, whom he congratulated thereupon. The Master Cat, who went always before, said the same words to all he met, and the king was astonished at the vast estates of my Lord Marquis of Carabas.

Monsieur Puss came at last to a stately castle, the master of which was an ogre, the richest had ever been known; for all the lands which the king had then gone over belonged to this castle. The cat, who had taken care to inform himself who this ogre was and what he could do, asked to speak with him, saying he could not pass so near his castle without having the honour of paying his respects to him.

The ogre received him as civilly as an ogre could do, and made him sit down.

"I have been assured," said the cat, "that you have the gift of being able to change yourself into all sorts of creatures you have a mind to; you can, for example, transform yourself into a lion, or elephant, and the like."

"That is true," answered the ogre very briskly "and to convince you, you shall see me now become a lion."

Puss was so sadly terrified at the sight of a lion so near him that he immediately got into the gutter, not without abundance of trouble and danger, because of his boots, which were of no use at all to him in walking upon the roof tiles. Shortly after, when Puss saw that the ogre had resumed his natural form, he came down, and owned he had been very much frightened.

"I have been moreover informed," said the cat, "but I know not how to believe it, that you have also the power to take on you the shape of the smallest animals; for example, to change yourself into a rat or a mouse; but I must own to you I take this to be impossible."

"Impossible!" cried the ogre; "you shall see that presently."

And at the same time he changed himself into a mouse, and began to run about the floor. Puss no sooner perceived this but he fell upon him and ate him up.

Meanwhile the king, who saw, as he passed, this fine castle of the ogre's, had a mind to go into it. Puss, who heard the noise of his majesty's coach running over the drawbridge, ran out, and said to the king: "Your Majesty is welcome to this castle of my Lord Marquis of Carabas."

"What! my Lord Marquis," cried the king, "and does this castle also belong to you? There can be nothing finer than this court and all the stately buildings which surround it; let us go into it, if you please."

The marquis gave his hand to the princess, and followed the king, who went first. They passed into a spacious hall, where they found a magnificent collation, which the ogre had prepared for his friends, who were that very day to visit him, but dared not to enter, knowing the king was there. His majesty was perfectly charmed with the good qualities of my Lord Marquis of Carabas, as was his

daughter, who had fallen in love with him, and, seeing the vast estate he possessed, said to him: "It will be owing to yourself only, my Lord Marquis, if you are not my son-in-law."

The marquis, making several low bows, accepted the honour which his majesty conferred upon him, and forthwith, that very same day, married the princess.

Puss became a great lord, and never ran after mice any more but only for his diversion.

Beauty and the Beast

The compassion that grows to love and ends a wicked enchantment has made this touching story popular in verse, dramatic form, and film, as well as in prose.

Once upon a time, in a very far-off country, there lived a merchant who had been so fortunate in all his undertakings that he was enormously rich. As he had, however, six sons and six daughters, he found that his money was not too much to let them all have everything they fancied, as they were accustomed to do.

But one day a most unexpected misfortune befell them. Their house caught fire and was speedily burnt to the ground, with all the splendid furniture, the books, pictures, gold, silver, and precious goods it contained; and this was only the beginning of their troubles. Their father, who had until this moment prospered in all ways, suddenly lost every ship he had upon the sea, either by dint of pirates, shipwreck, or fire. Then he heard that his clerks in distant countries, whom he trusted entirely, had proved unfaithful; and at last from great wealth he fell into the direst poverty.

All that he had left was a little house in a desolate place at least a hundred leagues from the town in which he had lived, and to

"Beauty and the Beast" from THE BLUE FAIRY BOOK, edited by Andrew Lang. London: Longmans, Green, and Co., 1889.

this he was forced to retreat with his children, who were in despair at the idea of leading such a different life. Indeed, the daughters at first hoped that their friends, who had been so numerous while they were rich, would insist on their staying in their houses now they no longer possessed one. But they soon found that they were left alone. Their former friends even attributed their misfortunes to their own extravagance and showed no intention of offering any help. So nothing was left for them but to take their departure to the cottage, which stood in the midst of a dark forest and seemed to be the most dismal place upon the face of the earth. As they were too poor to have any servants, the girls had to work hard and the sons, for their part, cultivated the fields to earn their living. Roughly clothed and living in the simplest way, the girls regretted unceasingly the luxuries and amusements of their former life; only the youngest tried to be brave and cheerful. She had been as sad as anyone when misfortune first overtook her father, but, soon recovering her natural gaiety, she set to work to make the best of things, to amuse her father and brothers as well as she could, and to try to persuade her sisters to join her in dancing and singing. But they would do nothing of the sort, and because she was not as doleful as themselves, they declared that this miserable life was all she was fit for. But she was really far prettier and cleverer than they were; indeed, she was so lovely that she was always called Beauty. After two years, when they were all beginning to get used to their new life, something happened to disturb their tranquillity. Their father received the news that one of his ships, which he had believed to be lost, had come safely into port with a rich cargo. All the sons and daughters at once thought that their poverty was at an end and wanted to set out directly for the town; but their father, who was more prudent, begged them to wait a little, and, though it was harvest-time and he could ill be spared, determined to go himself first, to make inquiries. Only the youngest daughter had any doubt but that they

would soon again be as rich as they were before, or at least rich enough to live comfortably in some town where they would find amusement and gay companions once more. So they all loaded their father with commissions for jewels and dresses which it would have taken a fortune to buy; only Beauty, feeling sure that it was of no use, did not ask for anything. Her father, noticing her silence, said: "And what shall I bring for you, Beauty?"

"The only thing I wish for is to see you come home safely," she answered.

But this reply vexed her sisters, who fancied she was blaming them for having asked for such costly things. Her father, however, was pleased, but as he thought that at her age she certainly ought to like pretty presents, he told her to choose something.

"Well, dear Father," she said, "as you insist upon it, I beg that you will bring me a rose. I have not seen one since we came here, and I love them so much."

So the merchant set out and reached the town as quickly as possible, but only to find that his former companions, believing him to be dead, had divided between them the goods which the ship had brought; and after six months of trouble and expense he found himself as poor as when he started, having been able to recover only just enough to pay the cost of his journey. To make matters worse, he was obliged to leave the town in the most terrible weather, so that by the time he was within a few leagues of his home he was almost exhausted with cold and fatigue. Though he knew it would take some hours to get through the forest, he was so anxious to be at his journey's end that he resolved to go on; but night overtook him, and the deep snow and bitter frost made it impossible for his horse to carry him any further. Not a house was to be seen; the only shelter he could get was the hollow trunk of a great tree, and there he crouched all the night, which seemed to him the longest he had ever known. In spite of his weariness the howling of the wolves kept him awake, and even when at last the day broke he was not much better off, for the falling snow had covered up every path, and he did not know which way to turn.

At length he made out some sort of track, and though at the beginning it was so rough and slippery that he fell down more than once, it presently became easier, and led him into an avenue of trees which ended in a splendid castle. It seemed to the merchant very strange that no snow had fallen in the avenue, which was entirely composed of orange trees, covered with flowers and fruit. When he reached the first court of the castle he saw before him a flight of agate steps. He went up them and passed through several splendidly furnished rooms. The pleasant warmth of the air revived him, and he felt very hungry; but there seemed to be nobody in all this vast and splendid palace whom he could ask to give him something to eat. Deep silence reigned everywhere, and at last, tired of roaming through empty rooms and galleries, he stopped in a room smaller than the rest, where a clear fire was burning and a couch was drawn up cosily close to it. Thinking that this must be prepared for someone who was expected, he sat down to wait till he should come, and very soon fell into a sweet sleep.

When his extreme hunger wakened him after several hours, he was still alone; but a little table, upon which was a good dinner, had been drawn up close to him, and, as he had eaten nothing for twenty-four hours, he lost no time in beginning his meal, hoping that he might soon have an opportunity of thanking his considerate entertainer, whoever it might be. But no one appeared, and even after another long sleep, from which he awoke completely refreshed, there was no sign of anybody, though a fresh meal of dainty cakes and fruit was prepared upon the little table at his elbow. Since he was naturally timid, the silence began to terrify him, and he resolved to search once more through all the rooms; but it was of no use. Not even a servant was to been seen; there was no sign of life in the palace! He began to wonder what he should do and to amuse himself by pretending that all the treasures he saw were

his own and considering how he would divide them among his children. Then he went down into the garden, and though it was winter everywhere else, here the sun shone, the birds sang, the flowers bloomed, and the air was soft and sweet. The merchant, in ecstasies with all he saw and heard, said to himself:

"All this must be meant for me. I will go this minute and bring my children to share all these delights."

In spite of being so cold and weary when he reached the castle, he had taken his horse to the stable and fed it. Now he thought he would saddle it for his homeward journey, and he turned down the path which led to the stable. This path had a hedge of roses on each side of it, and the merchant thought he had never seen or smelt such exquisite flowers. They reminded him of his promise to Beauty, and he stopped and had just gathered one to take to her when he was startled by a strange noise behind him. Turning round, he saw a frightful Beast, which seemed to be very angry and said, in a terrible voice:

"Who told you that you might gather my roses? Was it not enough that I allowed you to be in my palace and was kind to you? This is the way you show your gratitude, by stealing my flowers! But your insolence shall not go unpunished." The merchant, terrified by these furious words, dropped the fatal rose, and, throwing himself on his knees, cried: "Pardon me, noble sir. I am truly grateful to you for your hospitality, which was so magnificent that I could not imagine that you would be offended by my taking such a little thing as a rose." But the Beast's anger was not lessened by this speech.

"You are very ready with excuses and flattery," he cried; "but that will not save you from the death you deserve."

"Alas!" thought the merchant, "if my daughter Beauty could only know what danger her rose has brought me into!"

And in despair he began to tell the Beast all his misfortunes, and the reason of his journey, not forgetting to mention Beauty's request.

"A king's ransom would hardly have procured all that my other daughters asked," he said; "but I thought that I might at least take Beauty her rose. I beg you to forgive me, for you see I meant no harm."

The Beast considered for a moment, and then he said, in a less furious tone:

"I will forgive you on one condition—that is, that you will give me one of your daughters."

"Ah!" cried the merchant, "if I were cruel enough to buy my own life at the expense of one of my children's, what excuse could I invent to bring her here?"

"No excuse would be necessary," answered the Beast. "If she comes at all she must come willingly. On no other condition will I have her. See if any one of them is courageous enough and loves you well enough to come and save your life. You seem to be an honest man, so I will trust you to go home. I give you a month to see if any of your daughters will come back with you and stay

here, to let you go free. If none of them is willing, you must come alone, after bidding them goodbye for ever, for then you will belong to me. And do not imagine that you can hide from me, for if you fail to keep your word I will come and fetch you!" added the Beast grimly.

The merchant accepted this proposal, though he did not really think any of his daughters would be persuaded to come. He promised to return at the time appointed, and then, anxious to escape from the presence of the Beast, he asked permission to set off at once. But the Beast answered that he could not go until the next day.

"Then you will find a horse ready for you," he said. "Now go and eat your supper, and await my orders."

The poor merchant, more dead than alive, went back to his room, where the most delicious supper was already served on the little table which was drawn up before a blazing fire. But he was too terrified to eat, and only tasted a few of the dishes, for fear the Beast should be angry if he did not obey his orders. When he had finished he heard a great noise in the next room, which he knew meant that the Beast was coming. As he could do nothing to escape his visit, the only thing that remained was to seem as little afraid as possible; so when the Beast appeared and asked roughly if he had supped well, the merchant answered humbly that he had, thanks to his host's kindness. Then the Beast warned him to remember their agreement and to prepare his daughter exactly for what she had to expect.

"Do not get up to-morrow," he added, "until you see the sun and hear a golden bell ring. Then you will find your breakfast waiting for you here, and the horse you are to ride will be ready in the courtyard. He will also bring you back again when you come with your daughter a month hence. Farewell. Take a rose to Beauty, and remember your promise!"

The merchant was only too glad when the Beast went away, and though he could not sleep for sadness, he lay down until the sun rose. Then, after a hasty breakfast, he went to gather Beauty's rose, and mounted his horse, which carried him off so swiftly that in an instant he had lost sight of the palace, and he was still wrapped in gloomy thoughts when it stopped before the door of the cottage.

His sons and daughters, who had been very uneasy at his long absence, rushed to meet him, eager to know the result of his journey, which, seeing him mounted upon a splendid horse and wrapped in a rich mantle, they supposed to be favourable. But he hid the truth from them at first, only saying sadly to Beauty as he gave her the rose:

"Here is what you asked me to bring you; you little know what it has cost."

But this excited their curiosity so greatly that presently he told them his adventures from beginning to end, and then they were all very unhappy. The girls lamented loudly over their lost hopes, and the sons declared that their father should not return to this terrible castle, and began to make plans for killing the Beast if it should come to fetch him. But he reminded them that he had promised to go back. Then the girls were very angry with Beauty, and said it was all her fault, and that if she had asked for something sensible this would never have happened, and complained bitterly that they should have to suffer for her folly.

Poor Beauty, much distressed, said to them:

"I have indeed caused this misfortune, but I assure you I did it innocently. Who could have guessed that to ask for a rose in the middle of summer would cause so much misery? But as I did the mischief it is only just that I should suffer for it. I will therefore go back with my father to keep his promise."

At first nobody would hear of this arrangement, and her father and brothers, who loved her dearly, declared that nothing should make them let her go; but Beauty was firm. As the time drew near she divided all her little possessions among her sisters, and said good-bye to everything she loved, and when the fatal day came she encouraged and cheered her father as they mounted together the horse which had brought him back. It seemed to fly rather than gallop, but so smoothly that Beauty was not frightened; indeed, she would have enjoyed the journey if she had not feared what might happen to her at the end of it. Her father still tried to persuade her to go back, but in vain. While they were talking the night fell, and then, to their great surprise, wonderful coloured lights began to shine in all directions, and splendid fireworks blazed out before them; all the forest was illuminated by them, and even felt pleasantly warm, though it had been bitterly cold before. This lasted until they reached the avenue of orange trees, where were statues holding flaming torches, and when they got nearer to the palace they saw that it was illuminated from the roof to the ground, and music sounded softly from the courtyard. "The Beast must be very hungry," said Beauty, trying to laugh, "if he makes all this rejoicing over the arrival of his prey."

But, in spite of her anxiety, she could not help admiring all the wonderful things she saw.

The horse stopped at the foot of the flight of steps leading to the terrace, and when they had dismounted her father led her to the little room he had been in before, where they found a splendid fire burning, and the table daintily spread with a delicious supper.

The merchant knew that this was meant for them, and Beauty, who was rather less frightened now that she had passed through so many rooms and seen nothing of the Beast, was quite willing to begin, for her long ride had made her very hungry. But they had hardly finished their meal when the noise of the Beast's footsteps was heard approaching, and Beauty clung to her father in terror, which became all the greater when she saw how frightened he was. But when the Beast really appeared, though she trembled at the sight of him, she made a great effort to hide her horror, and saluted him respectfully.

This evidently pleased the Beast. After looking at her he said, in a tone that might have struck terror into the boldest heart, though he did not seem to be angry: "Good-evening, old man. Good-evening, Beauty."

The merchant was too terrified to reply, but Beauty answered sweetly: "Good-evening, Beast."

"Have you come willingly?" asked the Beast. "Will you be content to stay here when your father goes away?"

Beauty answered bravely that she was quite prepared to stay.

"I am pleased with you," said the Beast. "As you have come of your own accord, you may stay. As for you, old man," he added, turning to the merchant, "at sunrise to-morrow you will take your departure. When the bell rings get up quickly and eat your breakfast, and you will find the same horse waiting to take you home; but remember that you must never expect to see my palace again."

Then turning to Beauty, he said:

"Take your father into the next room, and help him to choose everything you think your brothers and sisters would like to have. You will find two travelling-trunks there; fill them as full as you can. It is only just that you should send them something very precious as a remembrance of yourself."

Then he went away, after saying, "Good-bye, Beauty; good-bye, old man;" and though Beauty was beginning to think with great dismay of her father's departure, she was afraid to disobey the Beast's orders; and they went into the next room, which had shelves and cupboards all round it. They were greatly surprised at the riches it contained. There were splendid dresses fit for a queen, with all the ornaments that were to be worn with them; and when Beauty opened the cupboards she was quite dazzled by the gorgeous jewels that lay in heaps upon every shelf. After choosing a vast quantity, which she divided between her sisters—for she had made a heap of the wonderful dresses for each of them—she opened the last chest, which was full of gold.

"I think, Father," she said, "that as the gold will be more useful to you, we had better take out the other things again and fill the trunks with it." So they did this; but the more they put in, the more room there seemed to be, and at last they put back all the jewels and dresses they had taken out, and Beauty even added as many more of the jewels as she could carry at once; and then the trunks were not too full, but they were so heavy that an elephant could have not have carried them!

"The Beast was mocking us," cried the merchant; "he must have pretended to give us all these things, knowing that I could not carry them away."

"Let us wait and see," answered Beauty. "I cannot believe that he meant to deceive us. All we can do is to fasten them up and leave them ready."

So they did this and returned to the little room, where, to their astonishment, they found breakfast ready. The merchant ate his with a good appetite, as the Beast's generosity made him believe that he might perhaps venture to come back soon and see Beauty. But she felt sure that her father was leaving her forever, so she was very sad when the bell rang sharply for the second time, and warned them that the time was come for them to part. They went down into the courtyard, where two horses were waiting, one loaded with the two trunks, the other for him to ride. They were pawing the ground in their impatience to start, and the merchant was forced to bid Beauty a hasty farewell; and as soon as he was mounted he went off at such a pace that she lost sight of him in an instant. Then Beauty began to cry, and wandered sadly back to her own room. But she soon found that she was very sleepy, and as she had nothing better to do she lay down and instantly fell asleep. And then she dreamed that she was walking by a brook bordered with trees and lamenting her sad fate, when a young prince, handsomer than anyone she had ever seen and with a voice that went straight to her heart, came and said to her, "Ah, Beauty! you are not so unfortunate as you suppose. Here you will be rewarded for all you have suffered elsewhere. Your every wish shall be gratified. Only try to find me out, no matter how I may be disguised, as I love you dearly, and in making me happy you will find your own happiness.

Be as true-hearted as you are beautiful, and we shall have nothing left to wish for."

"What can I do, Prince, to make you happy?" said Beauty.

"Only be grateful," he answered, "and do not trust too much to your eyes. And, above all, do not desert me until you have saved me from my cruel misery."

After this she thought she found herself in a room with a stately and beautiful lady, who said to her:

"Dear Beauty, try not to regret all you have left behind you, for you are destined to a better fate. Only do not let yourself be deceived by appearances."

Beauty found her dreams so interesting that she was in no hurry to awake, but presently the clock roused her by calling her name softly twelve times, and then she got up and found her dressing-table set out with everything she could possibly want; and when her toilet was finished she found dinner was waiting in the room next to hers. But dinner does not take very long when you are all by yourself, and very soon she sat down cosily in the corner of a sofa, and began to think about the charming Prince she had seen in her dream.

"He said I could make him happy," said Beauty to herself.

"It seems, then, that this horrible Beast keeps him a prisoner. How can I set him free? I wonder why they both told me not to trust to appearances? I don't understand it. But, after all, it was only a dream, so why should I trouble myself about it? I had better go and find something to do to amuse myself."

So she got up and began to explore some of the many rooms of the palace.

The first she entered was lined with mirrors, and Beauty saw herself reflected on every side, and thought she had never seen such a charming room. Then a bracelet which was hanging from a chandelier caught her eye, and on taking it down she was greatly surprised to find that it held a portrait of her unknown admirer, just as she had seen him in her dream. With great delight she slipped the bracelet on her arm and went on into a gallery of pictures, where she soon found a portrait of the same handsome Prince, as large as life, and so well painted that as she studied it he seemed to smile kindly at her. Tearing herself away from the portrait at last, she passed through into a room which contained every musical instrument under the sun, and here she amused herself for a long while in trying some of them, and singing until she was tired. The next room was a library, and she saw everything she had ever wanted to read, as well as everything she had read, and it seemed to her that a whole lifetime would not be enough even to read the names of the books, there were so many. By this time it was growing dusk, and wax candles in diamond and ruby candlesticks were beginning to light themselves in every room.

Beauty found her supper served just at the time she preferred to have it, but she did not see anyone or hear a sound, and, though her father had warned her that she would be alone, she began to find it rather dull.

But presently she heard the Beast coming and wondered tremblingly if he meant to eat her up now.

However, as he did not seem at all ferocious, and only said gruffly, "Good-evening, Beauty," she answered cheerfully and managed to conceal her terror. Then the Beast asked her how she had been amusing herself, and she told him all the rooms she had seen.

Then he asked if she thought she could be happy in his palace; and Beauty answered that everything was so beautiful that she would be very hard to please if she could not be happy. And after about an hour's talk Beauty began to think that the Beast was not nearly so terrible as she had supposed at first. Then he got up to leave her, and said in his gruff voice:

"Do you love me, Beauty? Will you marry me?"

"Oh! what shall I say?" cried Beauty, for she was afraid to make the Beast angry by refusing.

"Say yes or no without fear," he replied.

"Oh! no, Beast," said Beauty hastily.

"Since you will not, good-night, Beauty," he said.

And she answered, "Good-night, Beast," very glad to find that her refusal had not provoked him. And after he was gone she was very soon in bed and asleep, and dreaming of her unknown Prince. She thought he came and said to her:

"Ah, Beauty! why are you so unkind to me? I fear I am fated to be unhappy for many a long day still."

And then her dreams changed, but the charming Prince figured in them all; and when morning came her first thought was to look at the portrait and see if it was really like him, and she found that it certainly was.

This morning she decided to amuse herself in the garden, for the sun shone, and all the fountains were playing; but she was astonished to find that every place was familiar to her, and presently she came to the brook where the myrtle trees were growing where she had first met the Prince in her dream, and that made her think more than ever that he must be kept a prisoner by the Beast. When she was tired she went back to the palace, and found a new room full of materials for every kind of work—ribbons to make into bows, and silks to work into flowers. Then there was an aviary full of rare birds, which were so tame that they flew to Beauty as soon as they saw her, and perched upon her shoulders and her head.

"Pretty little creatures," she said, "how I wish that your cage was nearer to my room, that I might often hear you sing!"

So saying she opened a door, and found to her delight that it led into her own room, though she had thought it was quite the other side of the palace.

There were more birds in a room farther on, parrots and cockatoos that could talk, and they greeted Beauty by name; indeed, she found them so entertaining that she took one or two back to her room, and they talked to her while she was at supper; after which the Beast paid her his usual visit, and asked the same questions as before, and then with a gruff "good-night" he took his departure, and Beauty went to bed to dream of her mysterious Prince. The days passed swiftly in different amusements, and after a while Beauty found out another strange thing in the palace, which often pleased her when she was tired of being alone. There was one room which she had not noticed particularly; it was empty, except that under each of the windows stood a very comfortable chair; and the first time she had looked out of the window it had seemed to her that a black curtain prevented her from seeing anything outside. But the second time she went into the room, happening to be tired, she sat down in one of the chairs, when instantly the curtain was rolled aside, and a most amusing pantomine was acted before her; there were dances, and coloured lights, and music, and pretty dresses, and it was all so gay that Beauty was in ecstasies. After that she tried the other seven windows in turn, and there was some new and surprising entertainment to be seen from each of them, so that Beauty never could feel lonely any more. Every evening after supper the Beast came to see her, and always before saying good-night asked her in his terrible voice:

"Beauty, will you marry me?"

And it seemed to Beauty, now she understood him better, that when she said, "No, Beast," he went away quite sad. But her happy dreams of the handsome young Prince soon made her forget the poor Beast, and the only thing that at all disturbed her was to be constantly told to distrust appearances, to let her heart guide her, and not her eyes, and many other equally perplexing things, which, consider as she would, she could not understand.

So everything went on for a long time, until at last, happy as she was, Beauty began to long for the sight of her father and her brothers and sisters; and one night, seeing her look very sad, the Beast asked her what was the matter. Beauty had quite ceased to be afraid of him. Now she knew that he was really gentle in spite of his ferocious looks and his dreadful voice. So she answered that she was longing to see her home once more. Upon hearing this the Beast seemed sadly distressed, and cried miserably:

"Ah! Beauty, have you the heart to desert an unhappy Beast like this? What more do you want to make you happy? Is it because you hate me that you want to escape?"

"No, dear Beast," answered Beauty softly, "I do not hate you, and I should be very sorry never to see you any more, but I long to see my father again. Only let me go for two months, and I promise to come back to you and stay for the rest of my life."

The Beast, who had been sighing dolefully while she spoke, now replied:

"I cannot refuse you anything you ask, even though it should cost me my life. Take the four boxes you will find in the room next to your own, and fill them with everything you wish to take with you. But remember your promise and come back when the two months are over, or you may have cause to repent it, for if you do not come in good time you will find your faithful Beast dead. You will not need any chariot to bring you back. Only say good-bye to all your brothers and sisters the night before you come away, and when you have gone to bed turn this ring round upon your finger and say firmly: 'I wish to go back to my palace and see my Beast again.' Good-night, Beauty. Fear nothing, sleep peacefully, and before long you shall see your father once more."

As soon as Beauty was alone she hastened to fill the boxes with all the rare and precious things she saw about her, and only when she was tired of heaping things into them did they seem to be full.

Then she went to bed, but could hardly sleep for joy. And when at last she did begin to dream of her beloved Prince she was grieved to see him stretched upon a grassy bank sad and weary, and hardly like himself.

"What is the matter?" she cried.

But he looked at her reproachfully, and said:

"How can you ask me, cruel one? Are you not leaving me to my death perhaps?"

"Ah! don't be so sorrowful," cried Beauty; "I am only going to assure my father that I am safe and happy. I have promised the Beast faithfully that I will come back, and he would die of grief if I did not keep my word!"

"What would that matter to you?" said the Prince. "Surely you would not care?"

"Indeed I should be ungrateful if I did not care for such a kind Beast," cried Beauty indignantly. "I would die to save him from pain. I assure you it is not his fault that he is so ugly."

Just then a strange sound woke her—someone was speaking not very far away; and opening her eyes she found herself in a room she had never seen before, which was certainly not nearly so splendid as those she was used to in the Beast's palace. Where could she be? She got up and dressed hastily, and then saw that the boxes she had packed the night before were all in the room. While she was wondering by what magic the Beast had transported them and herself to this strange place she suddenly heard her father's voice, and rushed out and greeted him joyfully. Her brothers and sisters were all astonished at her appearance, as they had never expected to see her again, and there was no end to the questions they asked her. She had also much to hear about what had happened to them while she was away, and of her father's journey home. But when they heard that she had only come to be with them for a short time, and then must go back to the Beast's palace forever, they lamented loudly. Then Beauty asked her father what he thought could be the meaning of her strange dreams, and why the Prince constantly begged her not to trust to appearances. After much consideration he answered: "You tell me yourself that the Beast, frightful as he is, loves you dearly, and deserves your love and gratitude for his gentleness and kindness; I think the Prince must mean you to understand that you ought to reward him by doing as he wishes you to, in spite of his ugliness."

Beauty could not help seeing that this seemed very probable; still, when she thought of her dear Prince who was so handsome, she did not feel at all inclined to marry the Beast. At any rate, for two months she need not decide, but could enjoy herself with her sisters. But though they were rich now, and lived in a town again, and had plenty of acquaintances, Beauty found that nothing amused her very much; and she often thought of the palace, where she was so happy, especially as at home she never once dreamed of her dear Prince, and she felt quite sad without him.

Then her sisters seemed to have got quite used to being without her, and even found her rather in the way, so she would not have been sorry when the two months were over but for her father and brothers, who begged her to stay and seemed so grieved at the thought of her departure that she had not the courage to say good-bye to them. Every day when she got up she meant to say it at night, and when night came she put it off again, until at last she had a dismal dream which helped her to make up her mind. She thought she was wandering in a lonely path in the palace gardens, when she heard groans which seemed to come from some bushes hiding the entrance of a cave, and running quickly to see what could be the matter, she found the Beast stretched out upon his side, apparently dying. He reproached her faintly with being the cause of his distress, and at the same moment a stately lady appeared, and said very gravely:

"Ah! Beauty, you are only just in time to save his life. See what happens when people do not keep their promises! If you had delayed one day more, you would have found him dead."

Beauty was so terrified by this dream that the next morning she announced her intention of going back at once, and that very night she said good-bye to her father and all her brothers and sisters, and as soon as she was in bed she turned her ring round upon her finger, and said firmly:

"I wish to go back to my palace and see my Beast again," as she had been told to do.

Then she fell asleep instantly, and only woke up to hear the clock saying, "Beauty, Beauty," twelve times in its musical voice, which told her at once that she was really in the palace once more. Everything was just as before, and her birds were so glad to see her! But Beauty thought she had never known such a long day, for she was so anxious to see the Beast again that she felt as if supper-time would never come.

But when it did come and no Beast appeared she was really frightened; so, after listening and waiting for a long time, she ran down into the garden to search for him. Up and down the paths and avenues ran poor Beauty, calling him in vain, for no one answered, and not a trace of him could she find; until at last, quite tired, she stopped for a minute's rest, and saw that she was standing opposite the shady path she had seen in her dream. She rushed down it, and, sure enough, there was the cave, and in it lay the Beast—asleep, as Beauty thought. Quite glad to have found him, she ran up and stroked his head, but to her horror he did not move or open his eyes.

"Oh! he is dead; and it is all my fault," said Beauty, crying bitterly.

But then, looking at him again, she fancied he still breathed, and, hastily fetching some water from the nearest fountain, she sprinkled it over his face, and to her great delight he began to revive.

"Oh! Beast, how you frightened me!" she cried. "I never knew how much I loved you until just now, when I feared I was too late to save your life."

"Can you really love such an ugly creature as I am?" said the Beast faintly. "Ah! Beauty, you only came just in time. I was dying because I thought you had forgotten your promise. But go back now and rest, I shall see you again by-and-by."

Beauty, who had half expected that he would be angry with her, was reassured by his gentle voice, and went back to the palace, where supper was awaiting her; and afterwards the Beast came in as usual, and talked about the time she had spent with her father, asking if she had enjoyed herself and if they had all been very glad to see her.

Beauty answered politely, and quite enjoyed telling him all that had happened to her. And when at last the time came for him to go, and he asked, as he had so often asked before:

"Beauty, will you marry me?" she answered softly:

"Yes, dear Beast."

As she spoke a blaze of light sprang up before the windows of the palace; fireworks crackled and guns banged, and across the avenue of orange trees, in letters all made of fire-flies, was written: "Long live the Prince and his Bride."

Turning to ask the Beast what it could all mean, Beauty found that he had disappeared, and in his place stood her long-loved Prince! At the same moment the wheels of a chariot were heard upon the terrace, and two ladies entered the room. One of them Beauty recognized as the stately lady she had seen in her dreams; the other was also so grand and queenly that Beauty hardly knew which to greet first.

But the one she already knew said to her companion:

"Well, Queen, this is Beauty, who has had the courage to rescue your son from the terrible enchantment. They love one another, and only your consent to their marriage is wanting to make them perfectly happy."

"I consent with all my heart," cried the Queen. "How can I ever thank you enough, charming girl, for having restored my dear son to his natural form?"

And then she tenderly embraced Beauty and the Prince, who had meanwhile been greeting the Fairy and receiving her congratulations.

"Now," said the Fairy to Beauty, "I suppose you would like me to send for all your brothers and sisters to dance at your wedding?"

And so she did, and the marriage was celebrated the very next day with the utmost splendour, and Beauty and the Prince lived happily ever after.

Scandinavia

 Although the traditions of the Norse tales can be found in the folk literature of many European countries, they emanate from the three countries of Scandinavia: Denmark, Norway, and Sweden. These tales were first collected early in the seventeenth century and many of them seem to reflect the solitude and starkness of the lands from which they come. There are, however, many tales of brisk common-sense and peasant wit, like the Norwegian story of "The Husband Who Was to Mind the House," or the beloved nursery tales, "The Three Billy-Goats Gruff" and "The Pancake." The major collectors of Scandinavian folk tales were Peter Christian Asbjörnsen and Jörgen Moe, and most published versions of the stories are based on the fluent, direct translations by Sir George Webbe Dasent of *Popular Tales from the Norse* and *Tales from the Field.* Dasent, in Stockholm on a diplomatic assignment in the mid-nineteenth century, had become interested in folk literature through his acquaintance with Jacob Grimm.

The Most Obedient Wife
(Denmark)

Although more simply structured, this has the same theme and humor as Shakespeare's The Taming of the Shrew.

Long ago there was a rich farmer who had three daughters, all grown up and marriageable, and all three very pretty. The eldest of them was the prettiest, and she was also the cleverest, but she was so quarrelsome and obstinate, that there was never any peace in the house. She constantly contradicted her father, who was a kind, peace-loving man, and she quarrelled with her sisters, although they were very good-natured girls.

Many wooers came to the farm, and one of them wished to marry the eldest daughter. The farmer said that he had no objection to him as a son-in-law, but at the same time he thought it his duty to tell the suitor the truth. Accordingly he warned him that his eldest daughter was so violent and strong-minded that no one could live in peace with her. As some compensation for these faults, she would receive three hundred pounds more in her dowry than would her two sisters. That was, of course, very attractive, but the young man thought over the matter and, after he had been visiting the house for some time, he altered his mind and asked for the hand of the second daughter. The daughter accepted him, and, as her father was willing, the two became man and wife and lived very happily together.

Then came another wooer, from another part of the country, and he also wanted to marry the eldest daughter. The father warned him, as he had cautioned the first wooer; telling him that she would receive three hundred pounds more than her youngest sister, but that he must be careful, for she was so stubborn and quarrelsome that nobody could live in peace with her. So the second wooer changed his mind and asked for the hand of the youngest daughter. They married shortly after and lived happily and peacefully together.

The eldest sister was now alone with her father, but she did not treat him any better than before, and grew even more ill-humoured because her two sisters had found favour in the eyes of the first two wooers. She was obstinate and quarrelsome, violent and bad-tempered, and she grew more so from day to day.

At last another wooer came, and he was neither from their own district nor even from their country, but from a distant land. He went to the farmer and asked for the hand of his eldest daughter. "I do not want her to marry at all," said the father. "It would be a shame to allow her to do so; she is so ill-tempered and violent that no human being could live in peace with her and I do not want to be the cause of such unhappiness." But the wooer remained firm; he wanted her, he said, whatever her faults might be. At length the father yielded, provided that his daughter were willing to marry the young man, for, after all, he would be glad to get rid of her, and as he had told the suitor the whole truth about her, his conscience was clear. Accordingly, the young man wooed the girl, and she did not hesitate long, but accepted the offer, for she was tired of sitting at home a despised and spurned spinster.

The wooer said that he had no time to remain with them just then, as he must return home at once, and, as soon as the wedding day was fixed, he rode away. He also told them not to wait for him at the farm on the day of the wedding, he would appear in good time at the church. When the day came the farmer drove with his daughter to the church, where a great company of wedding guests had assembled; the bride's sisters and brothers-in-law were there, and all the village people arrived in their Sunday clothes.

"The Most Obedient Wife" from DANISH FAIRY TALES by Svend Grundtvig, translated by Gustav Hein (Thomas Y. Crowell, Publishers). Reprinted by permission of Harper & Row, Publishers, Inc.

The bridegroom was there also, but in ordinary travelling garments; and so the couple walked up to the altar and were married.

As soon as the ceremony was over, the bridegroom took his young wife by the hand and led her out of the church. He sent a message to his father-in-law asking him to excuse their absence from the marriage feast, as they had no time to waste. He had not driven in a coach, as is the custom at weddings, but travelled on horseback, on a fine big grey horse, with an ordinary saddle, and a couple of pistols in the saddlebags. He had brought no friends or relations with him, only a big dog, that lay beside the horse during the ceremony. The bridegroom lifted his bride on to the pommel, as if she had been a feather, jumped into the saddle, put the spurs to his horse and rode off with the dog trotting behind. The marriage party standing at the church door looked after them, and shook their heads in amazement. Then they got into their carriages, drove back to the house, and partook of the marriage feast without bride or bridegroom.

The bride did not like this at all, but as she did not want to quarrel with her bridegroom so soon, she held her tongue for a time; but as he did not speak either, she at last broke the ice and said that it was a very fine horse they were riding. "Yes," he replied; "I have seven other horses at home in my stables, but this is my favourite; it is the most valuable of all, and I like it best." Then she remarked that she liked the beautiful dog also. "It is indeed a jewel of a dog," he said, "and has cost me a lot of money."

After a while they came to a forest, where the bridegroom sprang from his horse and cut a thin switch from a willow-tree. This he wound three times round his finger, then tied it with a thread and gave it to his bride, saying: "This is my wedding gift to you. Take good care of it, and carry it about with you always! You will not repent it." She thought it a strange wedding gift, but put it in her pocket, and they rode on again. Presently the bride dropped her glove, and the bridegroom said to the dog: "Pick it up, Fido!" But the dog took no notice, and left the glove on the ground. Then his master drew his pistol from the holster, shot the dog, and rode on, leaving it lying dead. "How could you be so cruel?" said his bride. "I never say a thing twice," was the reply, and they journeyed on in silence.

After some time they came to a running stream that they had to cross. There being only a ford, and no bridge, the man said to his horse: "Take good care! Not a drop must soil my bride's dress!" When they had crossed, however, the dress was badly soiled, and the husband lifted his bride from the horse, drew out the other pistol and shot the horse, so that it fell dead to the ground. "Oh, the poor horse!" cried the bride. "Yes, but I never say a thing twice," answered her husband. Then he took saddle, bridle, and cover from the horse; bridle and cover he carried himself, but the saddle he gave to his young wife, and said: "You can carry that; we shall soon be home." He walked on in silence, and the bride quickly put the saddle on her back and followed him; she had no desire to make him say it twice.

Soon they arrived at his dwelling place, a very fine farm. The menservants and maidservants rushed to the door and received them, and the husband said to them: "See, this is my wife and your mistress. Whatever she tells you, you are to do, just as if I had ordered it." Then he led her indoors and showed her everything—livingrooms and bedrooms, kitchen and cellar, brewhouse and dairy—and said to her: "You will look after everything indoors, I attend to everything out-of-doors," and then they sat down to supper, and soon after went to bed.

Days, weeks and months passed; the young wife attended to all household matters while her husband looked after the farm, and not a single angry word passed between them. The servants had been accustomed to obey their master implicitly, and now they obeyed their mistress likewise, and so six months passed without there having arisen any necessity for the husband to say the same thing twice to his wife. He was always kind and polite to her, and she was always gentle and obedient.

One day he said to her: "Would you not like to visit your relations?" "Yes, dear husband, I should like to do so very much, if it is convenient," she replied. "It is quite convenient," he said, "but you have never mentioned it. It shall be done at once; get ready, while I have the horses put to the carriage." He went to the stable and saw to everything, while his wife ran upstairs to dress as quickly as possible for the journey. The husband drove up, cracked his whip and asked: "Are you ready?" "Yes, dear," came the reply, and she came running out and entered the carriage. She had not quite finished dressing and carried some of her things in her hand, and these she put on in the carriage.

Then they started. When they had driven nearly half the distance, they saw a great flock of ravens flying across the road. "What beautiful white birds!" said the husband. "No, they are black, dear!" said his wife. "I think it is going to rain," he said, turned the horses, and drove home again. She understood perfectly why he had done so; it was the first time that she had contradicted him, but she showed no resentment, and the two conversed in quite a friendly fashion all the way home. The horses were put into the stable—and it did not rain.

When a month had passed, the husband said one morning: "I believe it is going to be fine to-day. Would you not like to visit your relations?" She wished to do so very much indeed, and she hastened a little more than the last time, so that when her husband drove up and cracked his whip, she was quite ready and mounted the carriage beside him. They had driven considerably more than half the distance, when they met a large flock of sheep and lambs. "What a fine pack of wolves!" said the husband. "You mean sheep, dear!" said the wife. "I think it will rain before evening," said the husband, looking up at the sky. "It will be better for us to drive

home again." With these words he turned the horses and drove back home. They conversed in a friendly manner until they reached home; but it did not rain.

When another month had passed, the husband said one morning to his wife: "We really must see whether we cannot manage to visit your relations. What do you say to our driving across today? It looks as though the day would be fine." His wife thought so too; she was ready very soon and they set out. They had not travelled far when they saw a great flock of swans flying along over their heads. "That was a fine flock of storks," said the husband. "Yes, so it was, dear," said his wife, and they drove on; there was no change in the weather that day, so that they reached her father's farm in due course. He received them joyfully and sent at once for his two other daughters and their husbands, and a very merry family meeting it was.

The three married sisters went into the kitchen together, because they could talk more freely there, and they had a great deal to tell each other; the two younger ones in particular had many questions to ask their elder sister, because they had not seen her for a very long time. Then they helped to prepare the dinner; it goes without saying that nothing was too good for this festive occasion.

The three brothers-in-law sat meanwhile with their father-in-law in the sitting-room and they, too, had much to tell and ask each other. Then said the old farmer: "This is the first time that you have all three been gathered together under my roof, and I should like to ask you frankly how you are pleased with your wives." The husbands who had married the two younger, good-tempered sisters said at once that they were perfectly satisfied and lived very happily. "But how do you get on with yours?" the father-in-law asked the husband of the eldest sister. "Nobody ever married a better wife than I did," was the reply. "Well, I should like to see which of you has the most obedient wife," said the father-in-law, and then he fetched a heavy silver jug and filled it to the top with gold and silver coins. This he placed in the middle of the table before the three men, and said that he would give it to him who had the most obedient wife.

They put the matter to the test at once. The husband who had married the youngest sister went to the kitchen door and called: "Will you come here a moment, Gerda, please; as quickly as possible!" "All right, I am coming," she answered, but it was some time before she came, because as she explained, she had first to talk about something with one of her sisters. "What do you want with me?" she asked. The husband made some excuse, and she went out again.

Now it was the turn of the man who had married the middle sister. "Please come here a moment, Margaret!" he called. She also answered: "Yes, I am coming at once," but it was a good while before she came; she had had something in her hands and was compelled to put it down first. The husband invented some excuse, and she went out again.

Then the third husband went to the kitchen door, opened it slightly and just said: "Christine!"—"Yes!" she answered, as she stood there with a large dish of food in her hands. "Take this from me!" she said quickly to her sisters, but they looked at her in amazement and did not take the dish. Bang! she dropped it right on the middle of the kitchen floor, rushed into the room and asked: "What do you wish, dear?"—"Oh, I only wanted to see you," he said, "but since you are here, you may as well take that jug standing on the table; it is yours, with all that is in it.—You might also show us what you got from me as a marriage gift on your wedding day."—"Yes, dear, here it is," she said, and drew the willow ring from her bosom, where she had kept it ever since. The husband handed it to his father-in-law and asked: "Can you put that ring straight?"—No, that was impossible without breaking it. "Well, you see now," said the husband, "if I had not bent the twig when it was green, I could not have made it into this shape."

After that they sat down to a merry meal, then the husband of the oldest sister returned home with her, and they lived for many years very happily together.

Graylegs
(Denmark)

Not as comic, but like the previous tale in that a haughty princess is humbled by a rejected prince. In disguise as a cowherd, the prince wins his bride before he wins her love.

There was once a king of England who had an only daughter, and a king of Denmark who had an only son. The prince was very handsome, and the princess equally fair, and so the prince fell in love with her and wished her for his bride. But she would have none of him, for she was a haughty young miss, and when he sent her a gift of six milk-white horses with shoes of gold and reins of silver, she cut off their manes and tails and spattered them with mud. And when he sent her a ship with decks of gold and sails of silk, she tore the sails and sank the ship.

"I'd never marry the prince of Denmark," she cried. "I'd sooner marry the first beggar that passed 'neath my window."

"Well," said the prince, " 'tis plain to be seen Her Royal Highness must learn a thing or two."

Then he took off his royal robes and dressed himself like a beggarman. He put on old gray trousers and wooden shoes, and he let his whiskers grow and smudged his face and hands. He looked like a real tramp indeed, and not a soul in the world could have guessed he was a prince.

When all was finished, he sailed over to England and went straight to the king's palace. He asked for work in the barnyard, calling himself Graylegs, but no one would hire him, for he looked too old and feeble to lift so much as a wisp of hay. The stable hands felt sorry for him, however, and so they gave him a bowl of milk and a bed of hay, and he drank the milk and went to bed and slept soundly.

Bright and early in the morning he was up and about, and he said to the chief cowherd, "Since you helped me last night, I will help you today. I'll drive all the cattle to pasture for you."

"Very well," said the cowherd. "But mind you drive softly 'neath the window of the princess. She has delicate ears but a very harsh tongue."

"Never fear," said Graylegs.

"And have a good switch handy," said the cowherd.

"That I have," said Graylegs, and from out his pack he took a golden spindle.

"What a beautiful spindle!" said the cowherd. "But how strange that a beggar should own it."

"Oh, a beggar finds many things in his travels," said Graylegs.

"It's really too fine for driving cows," said the cowherd.

"Not for the king's cows," said Graylegs, and off he went with the cattle.

Soon he came to the princess's window, and he flashed the golden spindle in the sunlight. It caught the eye of the princess who was sitting by the open casement, and she cried out with delight. She had never seen anything so beautiful in all the world.

"Stop, stop," she called, leaning from the window. "Let me see what you have there."

" 'Tis a spindle too good for any but a princess," said Graylegs.

"Then I must have it," replied the princess. "I will pay you well for it."

"But it is not for sale," said Graylegs.

"But I want it, and I will have it," cried the princess. Then she stamped her foot and ran to her father. "Dear parent, good parent," she cried, "do make that old beggar sell me the golden spindle."

"Alas, I cannot," said the king. "What belongs to the beggar is his alone."

Then the princess set up a great weeping and wailing.

"You may have the spindle on one condition," said Graylegs.

"What is that condition?" asked the princess.

"You must let me sit 'neath your window when the moon rises tonight."

"That's easily done," said the princess, and so Graylegs gave her the spindle, and while she dried her tears, he went on with the cows to the pasture.

That night at moonrise he sat beneath her window, and when the moon went down, he returned to the barn and had a bowl of milk and a bed of hay. In the morning he rose early and said to the cowherd, "I thank you for my bed and board, but I wish to repay you a little, and so I'll drive the cows to pasture again today."

"Very well," said the cowherd. "But mind you drive carefully 'neath the princess's window. She has dainty ears but a bold tongue."

"Have no fear," said Graylegs.

"And have a good switch handy," said the cowherd.

"That I have," said Graylegs, and from out his bag he took a long skein of golden silk.

"What beautiful silk!" exclaimed the cowherd. "But how strange that a beggar should own it."

"A beggar finds many things on his way in this world," replied Graylegs.

"It's much too fine for driving cows," said the cowherd.

" 'T will find good use, never fear," said Graylegs, and away he went with the cows.

When he came to the princess's window, he waved the silk in the air, and it gleamed like spun gold. The princess caught a glimpse of it, and never had she seen anything so beautiful.

"Stop, stop!" she cried, leaning from her window. "Let me see what you have there."

"It is silk too good for any but a princess," said Graylegs.

"Then I must have it," said the princess. "I will pay you well for it."

"It is not for sale," answered the beggarman.

Then the princess set up a dreadful to-do. "Dear Father, good Father," she cried, "do make the beggarman sell me the golden silk."

"Alas, I cannot," said the king. "I am king of the country, but I am not the beggarman's lord and master."

"I will give you the golden silk on one condition," said Graylegs.

"And what is that condition?" asked the princess.

"You must let me sit 'neath your window tonight at moonrise, and you must open your window wide and look down at me."

"That's easily done," said the princess. Then she received the skein of silk, and Graylegs went on with the cows to the pasture.

That night at moonrise, Graylegs came and sat beneath the princess's window, and she opened wide the casement and looked down at him. Then when the moon was low, he rose quietly and went back to the barn to a bowl of milk and a bed of hay.

The next morning he was up early and said to the cowherd, "I thank you for my bed and board, but I must repay you a bit, so I'll drive the cows to pasture once more."

"Very well," said the cowherd. "But mind you drive carefully past the princess's window. She has tender ears and a sharp tongue."

"Have no fear," said Graylegs.

"And have a good switch handy," said the cowherd.

"That I have," said Graylegs, and he drew out a golden shuttle.

"What a beautiful shuttle!" exclaimed the cowherd. "But how strange that a beggar should own it."

"A beggar goes here and there and picks up a thing or two," replied Graylegs.

"It's too fine for driving cows," said the cowherd.

" 'T will do its duty well, never fear," said Graylegs, and away he went with the cows.

When he came to the princess's window, he waved the shuttle in the sunlight, and it shone like fire. The princess sat near by with the spindle and the silk, and at sight of the glittering shuttle she cried, "Stop, stop, let me see what you have there."

"It is a shuttle too good for any but a princess," answered Graylegs.

"Then I must have it," said the princess. "I will pay you well for it."

"It is not for sale," said Graylegs.

Then the princess set up a dreadful hue and cry. "Dear Father, good Father," she cried to the king, "tell the beggarman he must sell me the golden shuttle. I have the spindle and thread, and now I must have the shuttle, too."

"Alas," said the king, "I can tell the beggarman nothing. I am the king, but I am not his lord and master."

"I will give you the shuttle on one condition," said Graylegs.

"What is your condition?" asked the princess.

"You must let me sit 'neath your window when the moon rises tonight."

"Oh, yes, indeed, that is easy enough."

"And you must open wide your window and look down at me."

"That is as simple as A B C."

"And then you must answer yes when I speak to you."

"That will be nothing at all," said the princess, and so Graylegs gave her the golden shuttle, and then away he went with the cows.

And that evening when the moon came up, there he sat beneath the princess's window, and she opened it and looked down at him. Her face was fair as milk, her hair shone like silver, and all in all, she was the prettiest princess ever seen in the world.

"Well," said Graylegs, "you're pretty as a picture, and prettier still, so now I'll take you for my bride."

"Oh, no," cried the princess.

"You have promised to say yes," said Graylegs.

"But you are only an old beggarman," said the princess.

"A promise is a promise," said Graylegs, and the king agreed with him, and so the princess had to marry him. And then they were shown the door. They could go wherever they wished, but of course they couldn't stay at the palace.

They started on their way, and when they came to the cow barn, Graylegs said, "You can't tramp over the countryside dressed like a princess in silks and satins. You must wear something suited to a beggar's wife." And so she had to trade clothes with the cowherd's wife and put on a coarse dress and wooden shoes, and no one would have guessed in a thousand years that she had once been a proud princess.

They walked for a day and a night till they came to the sea, and there they got on a boat and sailed over the water to Denmark, though the princess little knew or cared where they went. They landed near the palace, and Graylegs took the princess to live in a mean little hut not far away. The bed was covered with straw, the chairs were broken, and the open fire smoked badly.

Through the window could be seen the tall round spires of the king's palace, and at sight of them the princess cried, "Alas, I could have married the Prince of Denmark, but I would not."

"It's no use worrying over spilt milk," said the beggar. Then he brought out a ball of wool and an old spinning wheel. "Now," said he, "I must seek work and earn a penny or two. But you must not be idle while I am gone. You must spin this wool and make cloth for our clothes."

Then he went off to find work, and the princess sat down at the spinning wheel. But she got nowhere fast, for the spindle pricked her fingers, the wool twisted and broke, and her poor knees were sore from working the treadle.

"Oh, dear!" she cried. "Graylegs will certainly be angry when he sees me tonight, but it's no more than I deserve."

Then she sat and wept, and when Graylegs came home that night and saw her bleeding fingers and the broken yarn, he said, "Well, I see we'll go cold and naked if we must depend upon your spinning. Tomorrow I'll bring you some dishes, and you can sell them in the market place. That's easy work, and even a princess should be able to do it."

"I will try," the princess replied.

"Very well," said Graylegs. "And now let us have a bit to eat. Fortunately I earned a penny or two so we will not starve." Then he brought out a loaf of bread and a jug of milk, and they ate and drank, and then went to bed on their hard cots.

The next day Graylegs brought the princess a barrel of dishes and she set them up in the market place and tried to sell them. But she had little luck for the day was cold and she couldn't count pennies well. Then worse luck befell her for a handsome young fellow came riding by on a prancing horse, and he rode straight through the dishes and broke them into a thousand pieces.

"Oh, dear, oh, dear!" wailed the princess. "Graylegs will surely turn me out now and I'll have no home at all. I wouldn't take a prince and I'm no use to a poor man." And she went home and wept some more.

When Graylegs returned that evening, he said, "Well, did you have a good day at the market place? If we make a penny or two more, perhaps we can find better lodgings."

"The crockery is broken," cried the princess.

"That is terrible," said Graylegs. "I had not paid for it, and now I'll be thrown into jail."

"Oh, no!" moaned the princess. "You must not go to jail. I must do something to pay for the crockery."

"Well, perhaps I can get you a place in the palace kitchen," said Graylegs. "I have a place in the stable, and I have heard there is going to be a wedding and that extra help will be needed in the kitchen."

"I will do anything I can," said the princess.

"You should do very nicely as palace help," said Graylegs. "But tonight we must eat and drink," and he brought out a loaf of bread and a jug of milk. He shared it equally with the princess, and they ate and drank, and then went early to bed.

In the morning Graylegs found a place for her and she went to work in the palace kitchen. Everyone was bustling about making preparations for the wedding, and she worked all day scrubbing floors and washing dishes and fetching one thing and another for the cooks and bakers. She had the hardest tasks of all, for of course she was only a princess and hadn't been trained to do fine cooking or baking, or even to polish silver or dry fine glassware.

Toward evening, however, the head cook sent her to wait on the king's table. He gave her a pot of stew filled with dumplings and told her to mind it carefully for it was the king's favorite dish. Full of fear and trembling, she crept into the dining room holding the precious stew tight in both hands. But just as she reached the table, a handsome courtier bumped into her, and down went the stew all over the floor.

"What a clumsy servant," cried the courtier. "Be off with you at once or I'll turn you over to the king and have your head chopped off."

And out went the poor princess crying as though her heart would break. When she got home, she found her husband there ahead of her.

"Well, at last you've earned a penny or two," he said, "and now we can pay off our debts and have a sweet for supper."

But, alas, no, the princess was as poor as ever, and they'd have none of her in the palace kitchen. "You'd best turn me out, too," said the princess. "I'm no use to man or beast."

"I can't turn you out," said Graylegs. "I married you for better or worse. But we'll not fret about it. We'll have a bit of supper now, and tomorrow perhaps I can find something else for you to do." Then he brought out a loaf of bread and a jug of milk. He gave half to the princess and half to himself, and they ate and drank, and then went early to bed.

The next day Graylegs came home rejoicing. "I've found another place for you at the palace," he said. "The seamstresses are coming to finish the wedding gowns and try them on for size and fit. But the bride has not yet arrived from Sweden, and as you are the same size and fit, the gowns will be tried on you. You can do all this well, I am sure, for it is no more than what a princess usually does."

"But, alas, I am a princess no longer," the poor girl said sadly.

"Still you must earn a penny where you can," said Graylegs, and the princess agreed with him. So the next morning she returned to the palace. She put on all the fine clothes of the bride, the long satin gown, the veil that was filmy as butterfly wings, the dainty satin slippers, and the lovely golden crown. Everything fitted her just right, as if it had been especially made for her, and once again she looked like the princess she really was.

When the seamstresses were all finished, the princess prepared to take off the bridal finery, but the chief lady-in-waiting stopped her. "Now you must ride to the church and practice for the wedding," she said. "The bride will be very late arriving from Sweden."

The princess was then led to a carriage lined with velvet and covered with gold. It was drawn by six milk-white horses shod with silver and harnessed with gold, and following behind, in an equally splendid carriage, came the Prince of Denmark himself. He was dressed in his royal robes with a crown upon his head, and he looked as tall and handsome as the day is long.

The way led past the poor cottage where the princess and Graylegs lived. As the carriages neared it, the princess saw that the house was afire and soon would be burned to the ground.

"Oh, stop, stop," she cried, and she tried to jump out, but only succeeded in tangling her long train and veil, and dropping her crown.

The carriages stopped and the prince came running up. "What is the meaning of all this?" he cried. "You are ruining the bridal finery."

"I cannot help it," sobbed the poor princess. "That is my house you see burning, and my poor husband may be trapped in it. I must save him."

"But what do you care about an old tramp like that?" said the prince.

"I was little use to him, but he's been good to me," said the princess. "He shared what he had with me."

"Do you really wish to see Graylegs?" asked the king's son.

"Yes, with all my heart," said the princess.

"Very well," said the prince, "you shall have your wish," and he disappeared around the corner of the carriage.

In a moment up came Graylegs, gray trousers, old hat, wooden shoes, and all, and the princess threw her arms around him and kissed him. Then she saw that her Graylegs was none other than the prince himself, and she kissed him again and was so sorry for all the cruel things she had once said that she never spoke a mean or haughty word the rest of her life.

She became Princess of Denmark and later Queen, and though it all happened so long ago there's no one left who remembers seeing her, still it's quite true that she was the prettiest and kindest queen ever to sit on the throne of Denmark, excepting the one who sits there now, of course.

The Talking Pot
(Denmark)

A bouncy breezy tale that is fun to dramatize, this is the tale of a pot that skips away from others to return to the home of a poor man and ease his life.

Once upon a time there was a man so poor that he had nothing in the world but a wife, a house, and one lone cow. And after a time, he got even poorer than that, and so he had to take the cow to market and sell her.

On the way he met a fine-faced stranger. "Well, my good man," said the stranger, "whither away with that fat cow?"

"To market, and thank you," said the man, though the cow was far from fat.

"Then perhaps you will sell her to me," said the stranger.

Yes, the farmer would sell and gladly, provided the price were twenty dollars or more.

"The Talking Pot" from THIRTEEN DANISH TALES by Mary C. Hatch. Copyright 1947 by Harcourt Brace Jovanovich, Inc.; renewed 1975 by Edgun Wulff. Reprinted by permission of the publisher.

The stranger shook his head. "Money I cannot give you," he said. "But I have a wonderful pot that I will trade you," and he showed the farmer a three-legged iron pot with a handle that was tucked under his arm.

Now, truth to tell, there was nothing at all wonderful-looking about the pot, and it might have hung in any chimney in the country. Besides, the poor man had nothing to put in it, neither food nor drink, so he declined to make the trade. "Money I need, and money I must have," he said, "so you may keep your wonderful pot."

But hardly had he said these words than the pot began to speak. "Take me, take me," cried the pot, "and you'll never have cause to rue it." And so the man changed his mind and made the trade, for if the pot could talk, then surely it could do other things, too.

Home he now returned, and when he reached there, he hid the pot in the stable where the cow had always been kept, for he wanted to surprise his wife. Then he went inside. "Well, good wife," he said, "fetch me a bit to eat and a sup to drink, for I've walked a long mile and back today."

But his wife would do none of it till she heard about her husband's success at the market. "Did you make a fine bargain?" she asked.

"Fine as fine," said her husband.

"That is well," nodded the wife, "for we've a hundred places to use the money."

But it wasn't a money bargain. No indeed, exclaimed her husband.

Not a money bargain! Well, pray then, what had the good man gotten for the cow, cried the wife, and she would not rest till her husband had taken her to the barn and showed her the three-legged pot tied up to the stall.

And then the good wife *was* angry! Trading a fine, fat cow—though truth to tell it was neither fine nor fat—for a common black pot that might hang in anyone's chimney.

"You are stupid as a goose," cried the wife. "Now what will we do for food and drink? If you were not so tough, I do believe I would stew you!" And she started to shake her husband. But before she could do the poor man much damage, the pot began to speak again.

"Clean me, and shine me, and put me on the fire," said the pot, and at that the woman sang a different tune. "Well!" she said. "If you can talk, perhaps you can do other things, too." And she took the pot and scrubbed it and polished it, and then hung it over the fire.

"I will skip, I will skip," said the pot.

"How far will you skip?" asked the woman.

"Up the hill, and down the dale, and into the rich man's house," cried the little pot, and with that, it jumped down from the hook, and skipping across the room, went out the door, and up the road to the rich man's house. Here the rich man's wife was making fine cakes and puddings, and the pot jumped up on the table and settled there still as a statue.

"Well!" exclaimed the rich man's wife. "You are just what I need for my finest pudding." Then she stirred in sugar and spices, and raisins and nuts, a whole host of good things, and the pot took them all without a murmur. In a few minutes, the pudding was made, and the woman picked up the pot and put it on the fire. But down the pot jumped and skipped to the door.

"Dear me," exclaimed the woman. "What are you doing, and where are you going?"

"I'm bound for home to the poor man's house," cried the little pot, and away it went skipping up the road till it was back at the poor man's little cottage.

When the couple saw that the pot had brought them a fine pudding, the finest they had ever seen, they were very pleased, and the farmer said, "Now, my good wife, did I not make a good bargain when I traded our poor old cow for this wonderful pot?"

"Indeed you did," said his wife, and she fell to eating the pot's fine pudding.

The next morning, the pot again cried, "I will skip, I will skip!" And the wife said, "How far will you skip?"

"Up hill and down dale, and into the rich man's barn," the little pot replied, and out the house and up the road it went skipping, straight to the rich man's barn.

The rich man's servants were threshing grain, and the pot skipped to the center of the floor and stood there still as a statue.

"Well!" said one of the threshers. "Here is just the pot to hold a bushel of grain," and he poured in a sackful. But this took up no room at all, and so he poured in another and another till there was not a grain of anything left in the whole barn.

"A most peculiar pot!" exclaimed the men. "Though it looks as if it had hung in any number of chimneys." And then they tried to lift it, but it slid away from them and went skipping across the floor.

"Dear me," cried the men. "What are you doing, and where are you going?"

"I'm bound for home to the poor man's house," said the pot, and out the door it skipped, and though the men ran after it, they were left huffing and puffing far behind.

When the little pot reached home again, it poured out the wheat in the poor man's barn, and there was enough to make bread and cakes for years to come.

But that was not the end of its good deeds, for on the third morning it said again, "I will skip, I will skip!" And the old wife asked, "Where will you skip?" And it answered, "Up hill and down dale to the rich man's house," and out the house it ran at once.

Now the rich man was in his counting house counting out his money, and when the little pot arrived, up it jumped on the table, right in the midst of all the gold pieces.

"What a fine pot," cried the rich man. "Just the thing for my money." And into the pot he tossed handful after handful of money till not one piece was left loose on the table. Then he picked up his treasure to hide it in his money cupboard, but the pot slipped from his fingers and hopped to the door.

"Stop, stop," cried the rich man. "You have all my money."

"But not yours for long," said the pot. "I carry it home to the poor man's house," and out the room it skipped and back to the poor man's cottage. There it poured out the golden treasure, and the old couple cried aloud with delight.

"Now you have enough," said the pot, and indeed they did, enough and more, too, and so the wife washed the pot carefully and put it aside.

But in the morning, the pot was off again, straight for the rich man's house, and when the rich man saw it, he cried, "There is the wicked pot that stole my wife's pudding, and my wheat, and all my gold. But it shall bring everything back, every last farthing and more." Then he grabbed the pot, but bless my soul, if he didn't stick fast! And though he tugged and he pulled, he couldn't get free.

"I will skip, I will skip," said the pot.

"Well, skip to the North Pole," cried the man, still furiously trying to free himself, and at that, away went the pot and the man with

it. Up the hill they waltzed and down the hill, and never once did they stop, not even to say hello or goodbye at the old couple's cottage, for the pot was in a great hurry. The North Pole, you know, is far, far away, even for a fast-skipping pot.

The Three Billy-Goats Gruff
(Norway)

The quick action, repetition, and tight structure make this a fine tale for dramatization by young children.

Once on a time there were three billy-goats, who were to go up to the hill-side to make themselves fat, and the name of all three was "Gruff."

On the way up was a bridge over a burn they had to cross; and under the bridge lived a great ugly troll, with eyes as big as saucers, and a nose as long as a poker.

So first of all came the youngest billy-goat Gruff to cross the bridge.

"Trip, trap! trip, trap!" went the bridge.

"WHO'S THAT tripping over my bridge?" roared the troll.

"Oh, it is only I, the tiniest billy-goat Gruff; and I'm going up to the hill-side to make myself fat," said the billy-goat, with such a small voice.

"Now, I'm coming to gobble you up," said the troll.

"Oh, no! pray don't take me. I'm too little, that I am," said the billy-goat. "Wait a bit till the second billy-goat Gruff comes. He's much bigger."

"Well, be off with you;" said the troll.

A little while after came the second billy-goat Gruff to cross the bridge.

"TRIP, TRAP! TRIP, TRAP! TRIP, TRAP!" went the bridge.

"WHO'S THAT tripping over my bridge?" roared the troll.

"Oh, it's the second billy-goat Gruff, and I'm going up to the hill-side to make myself fat," said the billy-goat, who hadn't such a small voice.

"Now I'm coming to gobble you up," said the troll.

"Oh, no! don't take me. Wait a little till the big billy-goat Gruff comes. He's much bigger."

"Very well! be off with you," said the troll.

But just then up came the big billy-goat Gruff.

"TRIP, TRAP! TRIP, TRAP! TRIP, TRAP!" went the bridge, for the billy-goat was so heavy that the bridge creaked and groaned under him.

"WHO'S THAT tramping over my bridge?" roared the troll.

"IT'S I! THE BIG BILLY-GOAT GRUFF," said the billy-goat, who had an ugly hoarse voice of his own.

"Now I'm coming to gobble you up," roared the troll.

> "Well, come along! I've got two spears,
> And I'll poke your eyeballs out at your ears;
> I've got besides two curling-stones,
> And I'll crush you to bits, body and bones."

That was what the big billy-goat said; and so he flew at the troll, and poked his eyes out with his horns, and crushed him to bits, body and bones, and tossed him out into the burn, and after that he went up to the hill-side. There the billy-goats got so fat they were scarce able to walk home again; and if the fat hasn't fallen off them, why, they're still fat; and so—

> "Snip, snap, snout.
> This tale's told out."

The Pancake
(Norway)

The cumulation of the tale and the wiliness of the runaway pancake make this a favorite tale in any of its many versions.

Once on a time there was a goody who had seven hungry bairns, and she was frying a pancake for them. It was a sweet-milk pancake, and there it lay in the pan bubbling and frizzling so thick and good, it was a sight for sore eyes to look at. And the bairns stood round about, and the goodman sat by and looked on.

"Oh, give me a bit of pancake, mother, dear; I am so hungry," said one bairn.

"Oh, darling mother," said the second.

"Oh, darling good mother," said the third.

"Oh, darling, good, nice mother," said the fourth.

"Oh, darling, pretty, good, nice mother," said the fifth.

"Oh, darling, pretty, good, nice, clever mother," said the sixth.

"Oh, darling, pretty, good, nice, clever, sweet mother," said the seventh.

So they begged for the pancake all round, the one more prettily than the other; for they were so hungry and so good.

"Yes, yes, bairns, only bide a bit till it turns itself,"—she ought to have said "till I can get it turned,"—"and then you shall all have some—a lovely sweet-milk pancake; only look how fat and happy it lies there."

When the pancake heard that, it got afraid, and in a trice it turned itself all of itself, and tried to jump out of the pan; but it fell back into it again t'other side up, and so when it had been fried a little on the other side too, till it got firmer in its flesh, it sprang out on the floor and rolled off like a wheel through the door and down the hill.

"Holloa! Stop, pancake!" and away went the goody after it, with the frying-pan in one hand and the ladle in the other, as fast as she could, and her bairns behind her, while the goodman limped after them last of all.

"Hi! won't you stop? Seize it. Stop, pancake," they all screamed out, one after the other, and tried to catch it on the run and

"The Three Billy-Goats Gruff," from POPULAR TALES FROM THE NORSE, by Peter Christian Asbjørnsen and Jörgen Moe, translated by Sir George Webbe Dasent. Edinburgh: David Douglas, 1888.

"The Pancake," from TALES FROM THE FJELD, from the Norse of Peter Christian Asbjørnsen and Jörgen Moe, translated by Sir George Webbe Dasent. London: Chapman and Hall, 1874.

hold it; but the pancake rolled on and on, and in the twinkling of an eye it was so far ahead that they couldn't see it, for the pancake was faster on its feet than any of them.

So when it had rolled awhile it met a man.

"Good-day, pancake," said the man.

"God bless you, Manny Panny!" said the pancake.

"Dear pancake," said the man, "don't roll so fast; stop a little and let me eat you."

"When I have given the slip to Goody Poody, and the goodman, and seven squalling children, I may well slip through your fingers, Manny Panny," said the pancake, and rolled on and on till it met a hen.

"Good-day, pancake," said the hen.

"The same to you, Henny Penny," said the pancake.

"Pancake, dear, don't roll so fast; bide a bit and let me eat you up," said the hen.

"When I have given the slip to Goody Poody, and the goodman, and seven squalling children, and Manny Panny, I may well slip through your claws, Henny Penny," said the pancake, and so it rolled on like a wheel down the road.

Just then it met a cock.

"Good-day, pancake," said the cock.

"The same to you, Cocky Locky," said the pancake.

"Pancake, dear, don't roll so fast, but bide a bit and let me eat you up."

"When I have given the slip to Goody Poody, and the goodman, and seven squalling children, and to Manny Panny, and Henny Penny, I may well slip through your claws, Cocky Locky," said the pancake, and off it set rolling away as fast as it could; and when it had rolled a long way it met a duck.

"Good-day, pancake," said the duck.

"The same to you, Ducky Lucky."

"Pancake, dear, don't roll away so fast; bide a bit and let me eat you up."

"When I have given the slip to Goody Poody, and the goodman, and seven squalling children, and Manny Panny, and Henny Penny, and Cocky Locky, I may well slip through your fingers, Ducky Lucky," said the pancake, and with that it took to rolling and rolling faster than ever; and when it had rolled a long, long while, it met a goose.

"Good-day, pancake," said the goose.

"The same to you, Goosey Poosey."

"Pancake, dear, don't roll so fast; bide a bit and let me eat you up."

"When I have given the slip to Goody Poody, and the goodman, and seven squalling children, and Manny Panny, and Henny Penny, and Cocky Locky, and Ducky Lucky, I can well slip through your feet, Goosey Poosey," said the pancake, and off it rolled.

So when it had rolled a long, long way farther, it met a gander.

"Good-day, pancake," said the gander.

"The same to you, Gander Pander," said the pancake.

"Pancake, dear, don't roll so fast; bide a bit and let me eat you up."

"When I have given the slip to Goody Poody, and the goodman, and seven squalling children, and Manny Panny, and Henny Penny, and Cocky Locky, and Ducky Lucky, and Goosey Poosey, I may well slip through your feet, Gander Pander," said the pancake, which rolled off as fast as ever.

So when it had rolled a long, long time, it met a pig.

"Good-day, pancake," said the pig.

"The same to you, Piggy Wiggy," said the pancake, which, without a word more, began to roll and roll like mad.

"Nay, nay," said the pig, "you needn't be in such a hurry; we two can then go side by side and see one another over the wood; they say it is not too safe in there."

The pancake thought there might be something in that, and so they kept company. But when they had gone awhile, they came to a brook. As for piggy, he was so fat he swam safe across, it was nothing to him; but the poor pancake couldn't get over.

"Seat yourself on my snout," said the pig, "and I'll carry you over."

So the pancake did that.

"Ouf, ouf," said the pig, and swallowed the pancake at one gulp; and then, as the poor pancake could go no farther, why—this story can go no farther either.

Soria Moria Castle
(Norway)

Elements of "Jack and the Beanstalk" occur in this adventure story in which a boy leaves home, outwits a troll, makes his fortune, and wins the hand of a princess.

There was once upon a time a couple who had a son called Halvor. Ever since he had been a little boy he had been unwilling to do any work, and just sat raking about among the ashes. His parents sent him away to learn several trades, but Halvor stayed nowhere, for when he had been gone two or three days he always ran away from his master, hurried off home, and sat down in the chimney corner to grub among the ashes again.

One day, however, a sea captain came and asked Halvor if he hadn't a fancy to come with him and go to sea and behold foreign lands. Halvor had a fancy for that, so he was not long in getting ready.

How long they sailed no one knows, but after a long, long time there was a terrible storm. When it was over and all had become calm again, they knew not where they were, for they had been driven away to a strange coast of which none of them had any knowledge.

As there was no wind at all they lay becalmed, and Halvor asked the skipper to give him leave to go on shore and look about him. He at last got leave, but he was to come back at once if the wind began to rise.

So he went on shore, and it was a delightful country; whithersoever he went there were wide plains with fields and meadows, but as for people, there were none to be seen. The wind began to rise, but Halvor thought he had not seen enough yet and would walk about a little longer, to try if he could not meet somebody. So after a while he came to a great highway, which was so smooth that an egg might have been rolled along it without breaking.

Halvor followed this, and when evening drew near he saw a castle far away in the distance, and there were lights in it. As he had now been walking the whole day and had not brought anything to eat with him, he was very hungry. Nevertheless, the nearer he came to the castle the more afraid he was.

A fire was burning in the castle, and Halvor went into the kitchen, which was more magnificent than any he had ever beheld. There were vessels of gold and silver, but not one human being was to be seen. When Halvor had stood there for some time, and no one had come out, he opened a door, and inside a princess was sitting at her wheel spinning.

"Nay!" she cried. "Can Christian folk dare to come hither? The best thing you can do is to go away again, for if not the troll will devour you. A troll with three heads lives here."

"I should have been just as well pleased if he had four heads more, for I should have enjoyed seeing the fellow," said the youth, "and I won't go away, for I have done no harm. But you must give me something to eat, for I am frightfully hungry."

When Halvor had eaten his fill, the princess told him to try if he could wield the sword which was hanging on the wall. But he could not wield it, nor could he even lift it up.

"Well, then, you must take a drink out of that bottle which is hanging by its side, for that's what the troll does whenever he goes out and wants to use the sword," said the princess.

Halvor took a draught, and in a moment he was able to swing the sword about with perfect ease. And now he thought it was high time for the troll to make his appearance, and at that very moment he came, panting for breath.

Halvor stood behind the door.

"Hutetu!" said the troll as he put his head in at the door. "It smells just as if there were a Christian man's blood here!"

"Yes, you shall learn there is!" said Halvor, and cut off all the troll's heads.

The princess was so rejoiced to be free that she danced and sang, but then she remembered her sisters, and said, "If my sisters were but free too!"

"Soria Moria Castle" from THE RED FAIRY BOOK, edited by Andrew Lang. London: Longmans, Green, and Co., 1890.

"Where are they?" asked Halvor.

So she told him where they were. One of them had been taken away by a troll to his castle, which was six miles off, and the other had been carried off to a castle which was nine miles farther off still.

"But now," said she, "you must first help me get this dead troll away from here."

Halvor was so strong that he cleared everything away and made all clean and tidy very quickly. So then they ate and drank and were happy, and next morning he set off in the gray light of dawn. He gave himself no rest but walked or ran the livelong day. When he came in sight of the castle again he was just a little afraid. It was much more splendid than the other, but here too there was not a human being to be seen. Halvor went into the kitchen, and did not linger there either, but went straight on.

"Nay! Do Christian folk dare to come here?" cried the second princess. "I know not how long it is since I myself came, but during all that time I have never seen a Christian man. It will be better for you to depart at once, for a troll lives here who has six heads."

"No, I shall not go," said Halvor, "even if he had six more I would not."

"He will swallow you up alive," said the princess.

But she spoke to no purpose, for Halvor would not go. He was not afraid of the troll, but he wanted some meat and drink, for he was hungry after his journey. So she gave him as much as he would eat, and then once more she tried to make him go away.

"No," said Halvor, "I will not go, for I have not done anything wrong and I have no reason to be afraid."

"He won't ask any questions about that," said the princess, "for he will take you without leave or right. But as you will not go, try if you can wield that sword which the troll uses in battle."

He could not brandish the sword, so the princess said that he was to take a draught from the flask which hung by its side, and when he had done that he could wield the sword.

Soon afterward the troll came, and he was so large and stout that he was forced to go sideways to get through the door. When the troll had his first head in he cried, "Hutetu! It smells of a Christian man's blood here!"

With that Halvor cut off the first head, and so on with all the rest. The princess was now exceedingly delighted, but then she remembered her sisters, and wished they too were free. Halvor thought that might be managed, and wanted to set off immediately, but first he had to help the princess remove the troll's body, so it was not until morning that he set forth on his way.

It was a long way to the castle, and he both walked and ran to get there in time. Late in the evening he caught sight of it, and it was much more magnificent than either of the others. And this time he was not in the least afraid, but went into the kitchen, and then straight on inside the castle. There a princess was sitting, who was so beautiful that never was anyone equal to her. She too said what the others had said, that no Christian folk had ever been there since she had come, and entreated him to go away again, else the troll would swallow him alive. The troll had nine heads, she told him.

"Yes, and if he had nine added to the nine, and then nine more still, I would not go away," said Halvor and went and stood by the stove.

The princess begged him again to go lest the troll should devour him. But Halvor said, "Let him come when he will." So she gave him the troll's sword and bade him take a drink from the flask to enable him to wield it.

At that same moment the troll came, breathing hard, and he was ever so much bigger and stouter than either of the others, and he too was forced to go sideways to get in through the door.

"Hutetu! What a smell of Christian blood there is here!" said he.

Then Halvor cut off the first head, and after that the others, but the last was the toughest of them all, and it was the hardest work Halvor had ever done, but he knew he would have strength enough to do it.

And now all the princesses came to the

castle and were together again, and they were happier than they had ever been in their lives. They were delighted with Halvor, and he with them, and he was to choose the one he liked best; but of the three sisters the youngest loved him best.

But Halvor went about and was so strange and so mournful and quiet that the princesses asked what it was he longed for, and if he did not like to be with them. He said that he did like to be with them, for they had enough to live on, and he was very comfortable there; but he longed to go home, for his father and mother were alive and he had a great desire to see them again.

They thought that this might easily be done.

"You shall go and return in perfect safety if you will follow our advice," said the princesses. So he said that he would do nothing they did not wish.

Then they dressed him so splendidly he was like a king's son, and they put a ring on his finger, and it was one which would enable him to go home and back again by wishing. But they told him he must not throw it away, or name their names, for if he did, all his magnificence would be at an end, and he would never see them more.

"If I were but at home again, or if home were but here!" said Halvor, and no sooner had he wished this than it was granted. Halvor was standing outside his father's and mother's cottage before he knew what he was about. The darkness of night was coming on, and when the father and mother saw a splendid and stately stranger walk in, they were so startled they both began to bow and curtsy.

Halvor then inquired if he could stay there and have lodging for the night. No, that he certainly could not. "We can give you no such accommodation," they said, "for we have none of the things needful when a great lord like you is to be entertained. It will be better for you to go up to the farm. It is not far off, you can see the chimney pots from here, and there they have plenty of everything."

Halvor would not hear of that, he was absolutely determined to stay where he was. But the old folks stuck to what they had said, and told him he was to go to the farm, where he could get both meat and drink, whereas they themselves had not even a chair to offer him.

"No," said Halvor, "I will not go there till early tomorrow morning; let me stay here tonight. I can sit down on the hearth."

They could say nothing against that, so Halvor sat down on the hearth and began to rake about among the ashes just as he had done before, when he lay there idling away his time.

They chatted about many things, and told Halvor of this and of that, and at last he asked them if they had never had any child.

"Yes," they said, they had had a boy who was called Halvor, but they did not know where he had gone, and they could not even say whether he were dead or alive.

"Could I be he?" asked Halvor.

"I should know him well enough," said the old woman, rising. "Our Halvor was idle and slothful and he was so ragged that one hole ran into another all over his clothes. Such a fellow as he was could never turn into such a man as you are, sir."

In a short time the old woman went to stir the fire, and when the blaze lit up Halvor, as it used to do when he was at home raking up the ashes, she knew him again.

"Good Heavens! Is that you, Halvor?" said she, and such great gladness fell on the old parents there were no bounds to it. And now he had to relate everything that had befallen him, and the old woman was so delighted with him she would take him up to the farm at once to show him to the girls who had formerly looked down on him so. She went first and told them how Halvor had come home again, and now they should just see how magnificent he was. "He looks like a prince," she said.

"We shall see that he is just the same ragamuffin he was before," said the girls, tossing their heads.

At that same moment Halvor entered, and the girls were so astonished they left their kirtles lying in the chimney corner and ran away in nothing but their petticoats. When they came in again they were so shamefaced they hardly dared to look at Halvor, toward whom they had always been so proud and haughty before.

"Ay, ay! you have always thought that you were so pretty and dainty no one was equal to you," said Halvor. "But you should just see the eldest princess whom I set free. You look like herdswomen compared with her, and the second princess is also much prettier than you; but the youngest, who is my sweetheart, is more beautiful than either sun or moon. I wish to Heaven they were here, and then you would see them." And he named their names.

Scarcely had he said this before they were standing by his side, but then he was very sorrowful, for the words which they had said to him came to his mind.

At the farm a great feast was made ready for the princesses, and much respect paid to them, but they would not stay there.

"We want to go down to your parents," they said to Halvor; "we will go out and look about us."

He followed them out, and they came to a large pond outside the farmhouse. Very near the water there was a pretty green bank, and there the princesses said they would sit down and while away an hour, for they thought it would be pleasant to sit and look out over the water.

There they sat down, and after a short time the youngest princess said, "I may as well comb your hair a little, Halvor."

So Halvor laid his head down on her lap, and she combed it, and it was not long before he fell asleep. Then she took her ring from him and put another in its place, and then she said to her sisters:

"Hold me as I am holding you. I would that we were at Soria Moria Castle."

When Halvor awoke he knew that he had lost the princesses and began to weep and lament and was so unhappy he could not be comforted. In spite of all his father's and mother's entreaties he would not stay, but

bade them farewell, saying that he would never see them more, for if he did not find the princess again he did not think it worthwhile to live.

He had some money which he put into his pocket and went on his way. When he had walked some distance he met a man with a tolerably good horse. Halvor longed to buy it, and began to bargain with the man.

"Well, I have not exactly been thinking of selling him," said the man, "but if we could agree, perhaps—"

Halvor inquired how much he wanted for the horse.

"I did not give much for him, and he is not worth much. He is a capital horse to ride, but good for nothing at drawing; but he will always be able to carry your bag of provisions and you too, if you walk and ride by turns."

At last they agreed about the price, and Halvor laid his bag on the horse, and sometimes he walked and sometimes he rode. In the evening he came to a green field, where stood a great tree, under which he seated himself. Then he let the horse loose and lay down to sleep, but before he did that he took his bag off the horse. At daybreak he set off again, for he did not feel he could take any rest.

So he walked and rode the whole day, through a great wood where there were many green places which gleamed prettily among the trees. Often he did not know where he was or whither he was going, but he never lingered longer in any place than was enough to let his horse graze a little when they came to one of the green spots, while he himself took out his bag of provisions.

So he walked and he rode, and it seemed to him that the wood would never come to an end. But on the evening of the second day he saw a light shining through the trees. If only there were some people there I might warm myself and get something to eat, thought Halvor.

When he reached the place where the light had come from, he saw a wretched little cottage, and through a small pane of glass he saw a couple of old folks inside. They were very old, and as gray-headed as a pigeon, and the old woman had such a long nose that she sat in the chimney corner and used it to stir the fire.

"Good evening! Good evening!" said the old woman. "What errand have you that can bring you here? No Christian folk have been here for more than a hundred years."

So Halvor told her he wanted to go to Soria Moria Castle, and inquired if she knew the way thither.

"No," said the old woman, "that I do not, but the Moon will be here presently and I will ask her; she will know. She can easily see it, for she shines on all things."

So when the Moon stood clear and bright above the treetops the old woman went out. "Moon! Moon!" she cried. "Canst tell me the way to Soria Moria Castle?"

"No," said the Moon, "that I can't, for when I shone there, a cloud was before me."

"Wait a little longer," said the old woman to Halvor, "for the West Wind will presently be here, and he will know it, for he breathes gently or blows into every corner."

"What! Have you a horse too?" she said when she came in again. "Oh, let the poor creature loose in our bit of fenced-in pasture, and don't let it stand there starving at our very door. But won't you exchange him with me? We have a pair of old boots here with which you can go fifteen quarters of a mile at each step. You shall have them for the horse, and then you will be able to get sooner to Soria Moria Castle."

Halvor consented to this at once, and the old woman was so delighted with the horse that she was ready to dance. "For now I, too, shall be able to ride to church," she said. Halvor could take no rest and wanted to set off immediately, but the old woman said there was no need to hasten. "Lie down on the bench and sleep a little, for we have no bed to offer you," said she, "and I will watch for the coming of the West Wind."

Ere long came the West Wind, roaring so loud that the walls creaked. The old woman went out and cried:

"West Wind! West Wind! Canst tell me the way to Soria Moria Castle? Here is one who would go thither."

"Yes, I know it well," said the West Wind. "I am just on my way there to dry the clothes for the wedding which is to take place. If he is fleet of foot he can go with me."

Out ran Halvor.

"You will have to make haste if you mean to go with me," said the West Wind. And away it went over hill and dale, and moor and morass, and Halvor had enough to do to keep up with it.

"Well, now I have no time to stay with you any longer," said the West Wind, "for I must first go and tear down a bit of spruce fir before I go to the bleaching ground to dry the clothes. Just go along the side of the hill and you will come to some girls who are standing there washing clothes, and then you will not have to walk far before you are at Soria Moria Castle."

Shortly afterward Halvor came to the girls who were washing, and they asked him if he had seen anything of the West Wind, who was to come there to dry the clothes for the wedding.

"Yes," said Halvor, "he has only gone to break down a bit of spruce fir. It won't be long before he is here." And then he asked them the way to Soria Moria Castle.

They put him on the right way, and when he came in front of the castle it was so full of horses and people that it swarmed with them. But Halvor was so ragged and torn with following the West Wind through bushes and bogs that he kept on one side and would not go among the crowd until the last day, when the feast was to be held at noon.

So when, as was the usage and custom, all were to drink to the bride and the young girls who were present, the cupbearer filled the cup for each in turn, both bride and bridegroom, and knights and servants, and at last, after a very long time, he came to Halvor. He drank their health, and then slipped the ring, which the princess had put on his finger when they were sitting by the waterside, into the glass, and ordered the cupbearer to carry the glass to the bride from him and greet her.

Then the princess at once rose up from the

table, and said, "Who is most worthy to have one of us—he who has delivered us from the trolls or he who is sitting here as bridegroom?"

There could be but one opinion as to that, everyone thought, and when Halvor heard what they said he was not long in flinging off his beggar's rags and arraying himself as a bridegroom.

"Yes, he is the right one," cried the youngest princess when she caught sight of him. So she held her wedding with Halvor.

The Husband Who Was to Mind the House
(Norway)

When he and his wife change jobs for one day, a man learns how complex the life of the homemaker is.

Once on a time there was a man, so surly and cross, he never thought his wife did anything right in the house. So one evening, in haymaking time, he came home, scolding and swearing, and showing his teeth and making a dust.

"Dear love, don't be so angry; there's a good man," said his goody; "to-morrow let's change our work. I'll go out with the mowers and mow, and you shall mind the house at home."

Yes, the husband thought that would do very well. He was quite willing, he said.

So, early next morning, his goody took a scythe over her neck, and went out into the hayfield with the mowers and began to mow; but the man was to mind the house, and do the work at home.

First of all he wanted to churn the butter; but when he had churned a while, he got thirsty, and went down to the cellar to tap a barrel of ale. So, just when he had knocked in

"The Husband Who Was to Mind the House" from POPULAR TALES FROM THE NORSE, by Peter Christian Asbjörnsen and Jörgen Moe, translated by Sir George Webbe Dasent. Edinburgh: David Douglas, 1888.

the bung, and was putting the tap into the cask, he heard overhead the pig come into the kitchen. Then off he ran up the cellar steps, with the tap in his hand, as fast as he could, to look after the pig, lest it should upset the churn; but when he got up he saw that the pig had already knocked the churn over and was routing and grunting amongst the cream, which was running all over the floor. He got so wild with rage that he quite forgot the ale-barrel, and ran at the pig as hard as he could. He caught it, too, just as it ran out of doors, and gave it such a kick that piggy lay for dead on the spot. Then all at once he remembered he had the tap in his hand; but when he got down to the cellar, every drop of ale had run out of the cask.

Then he went into the dairy and found enough cream left to fill the churn again, and so he began to churn, for butter they must have at dinner. When he had churned a bit, he remembered that their milking cow was still shut up in the byre, and hadn't had a bit to eat or a drop to drink all the morning, though the sun was high. Then all at once he thought 'twas too far to take her down to the meadow, so he'd just get her up on the house-top—for the house, you must know, was thatched with sods, and a fine crop of grass was growing there. Now their house lay close up against a steep down, and he thought if he laid a plank across to the thatch at the back he'd easily get the cow up.

But still he couldn't leave the churn, for there was his little babe crawling about on the floor, and "if I leave it," he thought, "the child is safe to upset it." So he took the churn on his back, and went out with it; but then he thought he'd better first water the cow before he turned her out on the thatch; so he took up a bucket to draw water out of the well; but, as he stooped down at the well's brink, all the cream ran out of the churn over his shoulders, and so down into the well.

Now it was near dinner-time, and he hadn't even got the butter yet; so he thought he'd best boil the porridge. He filled the pot with water and hung it over the fire. When he had done that, he thought the cow might perhaps fall off the thatch and break her legs or her neck. So he got up on the house to tie her up. One end of the rope he made fast to the cow's neck, and the other he slipped down the chimney and tied round his own thigh; and he had to make haste, for the water now began to boil in the pot, and he had still to grind the oatmeal.

So he began to grind away; but while he was hard at it, down fell the cow off the house top after all, and as she fell, she dragged the man up the chimney by the rope. There he stuck fast; and as for the cow, she hung half-way down the wall, swinging between heaven and earth, for she could neither get down nor up.

And now the goody had waited seven lengths and seven breadths for her husband to come and call them home to dinner; but never a call they had. At last she thought she'd waited long enough, and went home. But when she got there and saw the cow hanging in such an ugly place, she ran up and cut the rope in two with her scythe. But as she did this, down came her husband out of the chimney; and so when his old dame came inside the kitchen, there she found him standing on his head in the porridge-pot.

East o' the Sun and West o' the Moon
(Norway)

Older readers will recognize some of the elements of "Beauty and the Beast" in this tale despite the presence of other, typically Norse, facets.

Once on a time there was a poor husband-man who had so many children that he hadn't much of either food or clothing to give them. Pretty children they all were, but the prettiest was the youngest daughter, who was so lovely there was no end to her loveliness.

So one day, 'twas on a Thursday evening late at the fall of the year, the weather was so wild and rough outside, and it was so cruelly dark, and rain fell and wind blew, till the walls of the cottage shook again. There they all sat round the fire busy with this thing and that. But just then, all at once something gave three taps on the window-pane. Then the father went out to see what was the matter; and, when he got out of doors, what should he see but a great big White Bear.

"Good evening to you," said the White Bear.

"The same to you," said the man.

"Will you give me your youngest daughter? If you will, I'll make you as rich as you are now poor," said the Bear.

Well, the man would not be at all sorry to be so rich; but still he thought he must have a bit of a talk with his daughter first; so he went in and told them how there was a great White Bear waiting outside, who had given his word to make them so rich if he could only have the youngest daughter.

The lassie said "No!" outright. Nothing could get her to say anything else; so the man went out and settled it with the White Bear, that he should come again the next Thursday evening and get an answer. Meantime he talked his daughter over, and kept on telling her of all the riches they would get, and how well off she would be herself; and so at last she thought better of it, and washed and mended her rags, made herself as smart as she could, and was ready to start. I can't say her packing gave her much trouble.

Next Thursday evening came the White Bear to fetch her, and she got upon his back with her bundle, and off they went. So, when they had gone a bit of the way, the White Bear said, "Are you afraid?"

No! she wasn't.

"Well! mind and hold tight by my shaggy coat, and then there's nothing to fear," said the Bear.

So she rode a long, long way, till they came to a great steep hill. There, on the face of it, the White Bear gave a knock, and a door opened, and they came into a castle, where there were many rooms all lit up; rooms gleaming with silver and gold; and there too

"East o' the Sun and West o' the Moon" from POPULAR TALES FROM THE NORSE, by Peter Christian Asbjörnsen and Jörgen Moe, translated by Sir George Webbe Dasent. Edinburgh: David Douglas, 1888.

was a table ready laid, and it was all as grand as grand could be. Then the White Bear gave her a silver bell; and when she wanted anything, she was only to ring it, and she would get it at once.

Well, after she had eaten and drunk, and evening wore on, she got sleepy after her journey, and thought she would like to go to bed, so she rang the bell; and she had scarce taken hold of it before she came into a chamber, where there was a bed made, as fair and white as any one would wish to sleep in, with silken pillows and curtains, and gold fringe. All that was in the room was gold or silver; but when she had gone to bed, and put out the light, she heard someone come into the next room. That was the White Bear, who threw off his beast shape at night; but she never saw him, for he always came after she had put out the light, and before the day dawned he was up and off again. So things went on happily for a while, but at last she began to get silent and sorrowful; for there she went about all day alone, and she longed to go home to see her father and mother and brothers and sisters. So one day, when the White Bear asked what it was that she lacked, she said it was so dull and lonely there that she longed to go home to see her father and mother and brothers and sisters, and that was why she was so sad and sorrowful, because she couldn't get to them.

"Well, well!" said the Bear, "perhaps there's a cure for all this; but you must promise me one thing, not to talk alone with your mother, but only when the rest are by to hear; for she'll take you by the hand and try to lead you into a room alone to talk; but you must mind and not do that, else you'll bring bad luck on both of us."

So one Sunday the White Bear came and said now they could set off to see her father and mother. Well, off they started, she sitting on his back; and they went far and long. At last they came to a grand house, and there her brothers and sisters were running about out of doors at play, and everything was so pretty, 'twas a joy to see.

"This is where your father and mother live now," said the White Bear; "but don't forget what I told you, else you'll make us both unlucky."

"No! bless me, I'll not forget." And when she had reached the house, the White Bear turned right about and left her.

Then when she went in to see her father and mother, there was such joy, there was no end to it. None of them thought they could thank her enough for all she had done for them. Now, they had everything they wished, as good as good could be, and they all wanted to know how she got on where she lived.

Well, she said, it was very good to live where she did; she had all she wished. What she said besides I don't know; but I don't think any of them had the right end of the stick, or that they got much out of her. But so in the afternoon, after they had done dinner, all happened as the White Bear had said. Her mother wanted to talk with her alone in her bed-room; but she minded what the White Bear had said, and wouldn't go up stairs.

"Oh, what we have to talk about will keep," she said, and put her mother off. But somehow or other, her mother got round her at last, and she had to tell her the whole story. So she said that every night, when she had gone to bed, someone came into the next room as soon as she had put out the light, and that she never saw him, because he was always up and away before the morning dawned; and how she went about woeful and sorrowing, for she thought she should so like to see him, and that all day long she walked about there alone, and that it was dull and dreary and lonesome.

"My!" said her mother; "it may well be a troll you heard! But now I'll teach you a lesson how to set eyes on him. I'll give you a bit of candle, which you can carry home in your bosom; just light that while he is asleep, but take care not to drop the tallow on him."

Yes! she took the candle, and hid it in her bosom, and as night drew on, the White Bear came and fetched her away.

But when they had gone a bit of the way, the White Bear asked if all hadn't happened as he had said.

Well, she couldn't say it hadn't.

"Now, mind," said he, "if you have listened to your mother's advice, you have brought bad luck on us both, and then, all that has passed between us will be as nothing."

"No," she said, "I didn't listen to my mother's advice."

So when she reached home, and had gone to bed, it was the old story over again. There came someone into the next room; but at dead of night, when she heard he slept, she got up and struck a light, lit the candle, went into the room, and let the light shine on him, and so she saw that he was the loveliest prince one ever set eyes on, and she fell so deep in love with him on the spot, that she thought she couldn't live if she didn't give him a kiss there and then. And so she did, but as she kissed him, she dropped three hot drops of tallow on his shirt, and he woke up.

"What have you done?" he cried; "now you have made us both unlucky, for had you held out only this one year, I had been freed. For I have a stepmother who has bewitched me, so that I am a white bear by day, and a man by night. But now all ties are snapt between us; now I must set off from you to her. She lives in a castle which stands EAST O' THE SUN AND WEST O' THE MOON, and there, too, is a princess, with a nose three ells long, and she's the wife I must have now."

She wept and took it ill, but there was no help for it; go he must.

Then she asked if she mightn't go with him.

No, she mightn't.

"Tell me the way, then," she said, "and I'll search you out; *that* surely I may get leave to do."

"Yes, you might do that," he said; "but there is no way to that place. It lies EAST O' THE SUN AND WEST O' THE MOON, and thither you'd never find your way."

So next morning, when she woke up, both prince and castle were gone, and then she lay on a little green patch, in the midst of the gloomy thick wood, and by her side lay the same bundle of rags she had brought with her from her old home.

So when she had rubbed the sleep out of her eyes, and wept till she was tired, she set out on her way, and walked many, many days, till she came to a lofty crag. Under it sat an old hag, who played with a gold apple which she tossed about. Her the lassie asked if she knew the way to the prince, who lived with his stepmother in the castle that lay EAST O' THE SUN AND WEST O' THE MOON, and who was to marry the princess with a nose three ells long.

"How did you come to know about him?" asked the old hag; "But maybe you are the lassie who ought to have had him?"

Yes, she was.

"So, so; it's you, is it?" said the old hag. "Well, all I know about him is that he lives in the castle that lies EAST O' THE SUN AND WEST O' THE MOON, and thither you'll come, late or never; but still you may have the loan of my horse, and on him you can ride to my next neighbour. Maybe she'll be able to tell you; and when you get there, just give the horse a switch under the left ear, and beg him to be off home; and, stay, this gold apple you may take with you."

So she got upon the horse, and rode a long, long time, till she came to another crag, under which sat another old hag, with a gold carding-comb. Her the lassie asked if she knew the way to the castle that lay EAST O' THE SUN AND WEST O' THE MOON, and she answered, like the first old hag, that she knew nothing about it, except it was east o' the sun and west o' the moon.

"And thither you'll come, late or never; but you shall have the loan of my horse to my next neighbour; maybe she'll tell you all about it; and when you get there, just switch the horse under the left ear, and beg him to be off home."

And this old hag gave her the golden carding-comb; it might be she'd find some use for it, she said. So the lassie got up on the horse, and rode a far, far way, and a weary time; and so at last she came to another great crag, under which sat another old hag, spinning with a golden spinningwheel. Her, too, she asked if she knew the way to the prince, and where the castle was that lay EAST O' THE SUN AND WEST O' THE MOON. So it was the same thing over again.

"Maybe it's you who ought to have had the prince?" said the old hag.

Yes, it was.

But she, too, didn't know the way a bit better than the other two. "East o' the sun and west o' the moon it was," she knew—that was all.

"And thither you'll come, late or never; but I'll lend you my horse, and then I think you'd best ride to the East Wind and ask him; maybe he knows those parts, and can blow you thither. But when you get to him, you need only give the horse a switch under the left ear, and he'll trot home of himself."

And so, too, she gave her the gold spinningwheel. "Maybe you'll find a use for it," said the old hag.

Then on she rode many, many days, a weary time, before she got to the East Wind's house, but at last she did reach it, and then she asked the East Wind if he could tell her the way to the prince who dwelt east o' the sun and west o' the moon. Yes, the East Wind had often heard tell of it, the prince, and the castle, but he couldn't tell the way, for he had never blown so far.

"But, if you will, I'll go with you to my brother the West Wind. Maybe he knows, for he's much stronger. So, if you will just get on my back, I'll carry you thither."

Yes, she got on his back, and I should just think they went briskly along.

So when they got there, they went into the West Wind's house, and the East Wind said the lassie he had brought was the one who ought to have had the prince who lived in the castle EAST O' THE SUN AND WEST O' THE MOON; and so she had set out to seek him, and how he had come with her, and would be glad to know if the West Wind knew how to get to the castle.

"Nay," said the West Wind, "so far I've never blown; but if you will, I'll go with you to our brother the South Wind, for he's much stronger than either of us, and he has flapped his wings far and wide. Maybe he'll tell you.

You can get on my back, and I'll carry you to him."

Yes! she got on his back, and so they travelled to the South Wind, and weren't so very long on the way, I should think.

When they got there, the West Wind asked him if he could tell her the way to the castle that lay EAST O' THE SUN AND WEST O' THE MOON, for it was she who ought to have had the prince who lived there.

"You don't say so! That's she, is it?" said the South Wind.

"Well, I have blustered about in most places in my time, but so far have I never blown; but if you will, I'll take you to my brother the North Wind; he is the oldest and strongest of the whole lot of us, and if he doesn't know where it is, you'll never find

any one in the world to tell you. You can get on my back, and I'll carry you thither."

Yes! she got on his back, and away he went from his house at a fine rate. And this time, too, she wasn't long on her way.

So when they got to the North Wind's house, he was so wild and cross, cold puffs came from him a long way off.

"BLAST YOU BOTH, WHAT DO YOU WANT?" he roared out to them ever so far off, so that it struck them with an icy shiver.

"Well," said the South Wind, "you needn't be so foul-mouthed, for here I am, your brother, the South Wind, and here is the lassie who ought to have had the prince who dwells in the castle that lies EAST O' THE SUN AND WEST O' THE MOON, and now she wants to ask you if you ever were there, and can tell her the way, for she would be so glad to find him again."

"YES, I KNOW WELL ENOUGH WHERE IT IS," said the North Wind. "Once in my life I blew an aspen-leaf thither, but I was so tired I couldn't blow a puff for ever so many days after. But if you really wish to go thither, and aren't afraid to come along with me, I'll take you on my back and see if I can blow you thither."

Yes! with all her heart; she must and would get thither if it were possible in any way; and as for fear, however madly he went, she wouldn't be at all afraid.

"Very well, then," said the North Wind, "but you must sleep here to-night, for we must have the whole day before us, if we're to get thither at all."

Early next morning the North Wind woke her, and puffed himself up, and blew himself out, and made himself so stout and big, 'twas gruesome to look at him; and so off they went high up through the air, as if they would never stop till they got to the world's end.

Down here below there was such a storm; it threw down long tracts of wood and many houses, and when it swept over the great sea, ships foundered by hundreds.

So they tore on and on—no one can believe how far they went—and all the while they still went over the sea, and the North Wind got more and more weary, and so out of breath he could scarce bring out a puff, and his wings drooped and drooped, till at last he sunk so low that the crests of the waves dashed over his heels.

"Are you afraid?" said the North Wind.

No, she wasn't.

But they weren't very far from land; and the North Wind had still so much strength left in him that he managed to throw her up on the shore under the windows of the castle which lay EAST O' THE SUN AND WEST O' THE MOON; but then he was so weak and worn out, he had to stay there and rest many days before he could get home again.

Next morning the lassie sat down under the castle window, and began to play with the gold apple; and the first person she saw was the long-nose who was to have the prince.

"What do you want for your gold apple, you lassie?" said the long-nose, and threw up the window.

"It's not for sale, for gold or money," said the lassie.

"If it's not for sale for gold or money, what is it that you will sell it for? You may name your own price," said the princess.

"Well! if I may get to the prince, who lives here, and be with him to-night, you shall have it," said the lassie whom the North Wind had brought.

Yes! she might; that could be done. So the princess got the gold apple; but when the lassie came up to the prince's bed-room at night he was fast asleep; she called him and shook him, and between whiles she wept sore; but all she could do she couldn't wake him up. Next morning as soon as day broke, came the princess with the long nose, and drove her out again.

So in the day-time she sat down under the castle windows and began to card with her golden carding-comb, and the same thing happened. The princess asked what she wanted for it; and she said it wasn't for sale for gold or money, but if she might get leave to go up to the prince and be with him that night, the princess should have it. But when she went up she found him fast asleep again, and all she called, and all she shook, and wept, and prayed, she couldn't get life into him; and as soon as the first gray peep of day came, then came the princess with the long nose and chased her out again.

So in the day-time the lassie sat down outside under the castle window, and began to spin with her golden spinning-wheel, and that, too, the princess with the long nose wanted to have. So she threw up the window and asked what she wanted for it. The lassie said, as she had said twice before, it wasn't for sale for gold or money; but if she might go up to the prince who was there, and be with him alone that night, she might have it.

Yes! she might do that and welcome. But now you must know there were some folk who had been carried off thither, and as they sat in their room, which was next the prince, they had heard how a woman had been in there, and wept and prayed, and called to him two nights running, and they told that to the prince.

That evening, when the princess came with her sleepy drink, the prince made as if he drank, but threw it over his shoulder, for he could guess it was a sleepy drink. So, when the lassie came in, she found the prince wide awake; and then she told him the whole story how she had come thither.

"Ah," said the Prince, "you've just come in the very nick of time, for to-morrow is to be our wedding-day; but now I won't have the long-nose, and you are the only woman in the world who can set me free. I'll say I want to see what my wife is fit for, and beg her to wash the shirt which has the three spots of tallow on it; she'll say yes, for she doesn't know 'tis you who put them there; but that's a work only for Christian folk, and not for such a pack of trolls, and so I'll say that I won't have any other for my bride than the woman who can wash them out, and ask you to do it."

Next day, when the wedding was to be, the prince said, "First of all, I'd like to see what my bride is fit for."

"Yes!" said the step-mother, with all her heart.

"Well," said the prince, "I've got a fine shirt which I'd like for my wedding shirt, but somehow or other it has got three spots of tallow on it, which I must have washed out; and I have sworn never to take any other bride than the woman who's able to do that. If she can't, she's not worth having."

Well, that was no great thing they said, so they agreed, and she with the long nose began to wash away as hard as she could, but the more she rubbed and scrubbed, the bigger the spots grew.

"Ah!" said the old hag, her mother, "you can't wash; let me try."

But she hadn't long taken the shirt in hand, before it got far worse than ever, and with all her rubbing and wringing and scrubbing, the spots grew bigger and blacker, and the darker and uglier was the shirt.

Then all the other trolls began to wash, but the longer it lasted, the blacker and uglier the shirt grew, till at last it was as black all over as if it had been up the chimney.

"Ah!" said the prince, "you're none of you worth a straw; you can't wash. Why there, outside, sits a beggar lassie. I'll be bound she knows how to wash better than the whole lot of you. COME IN, LASSIE!" he shouted.

Well, in she came.

"Can you wash this shirt clean, lassie, you?" said he.

"I don't know," she said, "but I think I can."

And almost before she had taken it and dipped it in the water, it was as white as driven snow, and whiter still.

"Yes; you are the lassie for me," said the prince.

At that the old hag flew into such a rage, she burst on the spot, and the princess with the long nose after her, and the whole pack of trolls after her—at least I've never heard a word about them since.

As for the prince and princess, they set free all the folk who had been carried off and shut up there; and they took with them all the silver and gold, and flitted away as far as they could from the castle that lay EAST O' THE SUN AND WEST O' THE MOON.

Linda-Gold and the Old King
(Sweden)

A small and loving child wins the love and trust of a king, in a story that is more realistic than most folk tales.

Long, long ago there lived an old king who was rather eccentric. People said he was odd because he had had many sorrows, poor old king. His queen and children had died, and he himself said his heart had been torn apart. Who had done that and how it had happened, he never told; but it was someone with claws, he said, and since then he imagined that everyone had claws on his hands.

No one was allowed to come nearer than two arms' lengths to the king. His valets were not allowed to touch him, and his dining-room steward had to place his food at the very edge of the table. The king had not shaken anyone's hand for many, many years. If people were careless enough not to remember about the two arms' lengths, and came an inch closer, the king had them put in irons for a week to refresh their memory.

In all other ways, the old king was a good king. He governed his subjects well and justly. Everyone was devoted to him, and the only thing his people regretted was that he had not found a new queen, or appointed anyone prince or princess to inherit the realm. When they asked him about this, however, he always said, "Show me someone who does not have claws, and I will let that person be my heir."

But no one ever appeared who, in the king's mind, did not have claws. The claws might be under the fingernails, or curled in the palm, but they were always there, he believed.

Now one day it happened that the old king was walking alone in the forest. He grew tired and sat down to rest on the moss and listen to the birds singing in the trees. Suddenly a small girl rushed up the path, her hair streaming behind. And when the king looked up, he saw in the trees a shaggy grey beast with flashing eyes and a grinning red mouth. It was a wolf, who wanted the little

girl for breakfast. The old king rose and drew his sword, and straightaway the wolf turned in fear and ran back into the forest.

When the wolf had gone, the little girl began to weep and tremble. "Now you must walk home with me, too," she said, "or else the wolf will chase me again."

"Must I?" asked the king, who was not accustomed to taking orders.

"Yes. And my mother will give you a loaf of white bread for your trouble. My name is Linda-Gold, and my father is the miller on the other side of the forest."

What she said was right, the king decided. He couldn't very well let her be killed by the wolf, and so he was obliged to accompany her.

"You go first," he said. "I will follow behind you."

But the little girl did not dare walk first. "May I hold your hand?" she asked, and moved closer to him.

The king started, and looked closely at the little hand raised to his. "No, I am sure you have claws, too, though you are so small," he said.

Linda-Gold's eyes filled with tears, and she hid her hands behind her back. "My father says that, when all I have done is forgotten to cut my nails." She felt ashamed and looked at the ground. But then she asked if she might at least take hold of his mantle, and the king agreed to that. He simply could not make himself tell her to keep two arms' lengths away, for she was only a small child who would not understand.

So she skipped along beside him and told him of her cottage and all her toys. She had so many beautiful things she wanted to show him. There was a cow made of pine cones, with match sticks for legs; a boat made from an old wooden shoe, with burdock leaves for a sail; and then best of all was a doll her mother had sewn for her from an old brown apron and stuffed with yarn. It had a skirt made from the sleeve of a red sweater, and

"Linda-Gold and the Old King" by Anna Wahlenberg from GREAT SWEDISH FAIRY TALES Translated by Holger Lundbergh. English Translation Copyright © 1973 by Dell Publishing Co., Inc. Reprinted by permission of Delacorte Press/Seymour Lawrence.

a blue ribbon at the neck, and her big brother had drawn a face on it with coal and put on a patch of leather for a nose.

It was odd, but the king listened patiently to all her chattering, and smiled. He was sure the little hand had claws, yet he let it pull and jerk at his mantle as much as it wished. But when Linda-Gold and the king came to the highway, and the mill was not far away, the king said good-bye. Now Linda-Gold could go home by herself.

But Linda-Gold was disappointed. She did not want to say good-bye so soon. She clung to his arm and tugged it, and begged him. How could he *not* want white bread, which was so good? It couldn't be true that he did not want to look at her fine toys! She would let him play with her doll all the evening, if only he would come home with her. She would give him a present—the boat with the burdock-leaf sails—because he had saved her from the wolf.

When none of this helped, she at last asked the king where he lived.

"In the castle," he said.

"And what is your name?"

"Old Man Greybeard."

"Good. Then I will come to visit you, Old Man Greybeard." And she took off her little blue checked scarf, and stood waving it as long as the king could see her—and he turned to look back quite often because he thought her the sweetest little girl he had met in a long time.

Even after he had returned to the castle, he still thought of Linda-Gold, wondering if she really would come to visit him. He was worried because she did not want to keep her little hands at a respectful distance, but he could not deny that he longed to see her.

The king was still thinking of Linda-Gold the next morning, and feeling sure that she would not dare venture out so far for fear of the wolf, when he heard a clear child's voice calling from the palace yard. He went to the balcony and saw Linda-Gold with a rag doll under her arm. She was arguing with the gatekeeper. She said she must speak to Old Man Greybeard about something very important.

But the gatekeeper just laughed at her and replied that no Old Man Greybeard lived there. Then Linda-Gold got angry. He mustn't say that, she insisted, for she herself knew very well Old Man Greybeard did live there. He had told her so himself.

Next she went up to a lady-in-waiting who had just come outside, and asked her advice. No, the lady-in-waiting had never heard of Old Man Greybeard, either, and she too laughed heartily.

But Linda-Gold did not give up. She asked the cook, she asked the steward of the household, and she asked all the courtiers, who had begun to gather in the courtyard to stare at her. She turned red in the face as they all laughed, and her lower lip began to tremble. Her eyes were full of tears, but she still maintained firmly in a clear voice, "He must be here, because he told me so himself."

The king called from his balcony, "Yes, here I am, Linda-Gold."

Linda-Gold looked up, gave a shout of joy, and jumped up and down in excitement. "Do you see, do you see!" she called in triumph. "I told you he was here."

The courtiers could do nothing but stare in surprise. The king had to command twice that Linda-Gold be brought to him before anyone obeyed. Then it was no less a person than the royal court's Master of Ceremonies who led her to the king's chamber. When the door opened, Linda-Gold ran straight to the king and set her rag doll on his knee.

"I will give you this instead of the boat," she said, "because I thought that since you saved me from the wolf you should have the best thing of all."

The rag doll was the ugliest, most clumsy little bundle imaginable, but the old king smiled as if he were quite delighted with it.

"Isn't she sweet?" asked Linda-Gold.

"Yes, very."

"Kiss her, then."

And so the king had to kiss the doll on its black, horrible mouth.

"Since you like her, you should thank me, don't you think?"

"Thank you," said the king, nodding in a friendly way.

"That wasn't right," said Linda-Gold.

"Not right? How should it be then?"

"When you say thank you, you must also pat my cheek," said Linda-Gold.

And so the king had to pat her on the cheek; but it was a warm, soft little cheek, and not at all unpleasant to pat.

"And now—" said Linda-Gold.

"Is there something more?" asked the king.

"Yes, I would like to pat your cheek, too."

Here the king hesitated. This was really too much for him.

"Because, you see," Linda-Gold went on, "I cut my fingernails," and she held up both her small chubby hands for the king to see. He had to look at them whether he liked it or not.

And truly, he could not see anything unusual on the pink fingertips. The nails were cut as close as a pair of scissors could do it, and there wasn't the trace of a claw.

"You can't say I have claws now, Greybeard," said Linda-Gold.

"No . . . hmm . . . well, pat me, then."

Linda-Gold flew up on his lap and stroked the old sunken cheeks and kissed them, and soon a couple of tears came rolling down. It was so long since the old king had known love.

Now he took Linda-Gold in his arms and carried her to the balcony. "Here you see the one you have always longed for," he called to those in the courtyard.

A loud cry of joy broke out among them. "Hurrah for our little princess. Hurrah! Hurrah!" they shouted.

Surprised and bewildered, Linda-Gold turned to the king and asked him what this meant.

"It means they like you because you have fine small hands which never scratch and have no claws," he said. Then he kissed the two little hands so that everyone could see, and from below the people shouted again, "Hurrah for our little princess!"

And that is how Linda-Gold became a princess and in the course of time inherited the realm of the old king.

The Boy Who Was Never Afraid
(Sweden)

Each of the terrible creatures who are obstacles in his path is surprised and touched by the innocence and kindness of Nisse, and help him rescue the family cow from the terrible trolls.

Once there lived a poor crofter with eight hungry children and only one cow, so it is easy to see why his children often had to make do with little.

Yet the cow, Lily White, was a great blessing to the crofter, for she was the best cow in the whole county. She gave as much milk as the finest manor-house cow, which was lucky, considering all those children. She was big and handsome, and clever, too. She understood everything the children chattered about, and they chattered night and day.

Words cannot tell how kind and devoted the children were to their cow as they petted and fussed over her. Lily White was just a cow on a croft, yet she was happy as a wasp in a jam jar. In summertime she grazed in a large pasture by the manor house, but when the sun went down she always managed to come home by herself, because she was so clever.

But one evening a sad thing happened. Lily White did not return as usual. The crofter spent half the night looking for her, then he came home alone and tired.

At daybreak the next morning, he and his wife and the elder children went to look for their cow in the pasture. They walked from one end to the other without finding her. At last, in a far corner of the field, they found Lily White's hoofprints in the soft earth. But beside them were others, made by big, clumsy feet. The crofter was frightened, for he realized at once whose footprints those were. It was none other than the big troll in Hulta Wood.

Now it was not difficult to guess where Lily White had gone. The troll had come down to the pasture from his caves in the granite mountain and led the cow away with him. The troll must have known that Lily White was the finest milk cow in the whole county.

No wonder, now, the crofter's little home was full of sorrow and dismay. The children cried, and their father and mother were so worried they scarcely said a word. It was out of the question to try to get the cow back, for up to now no one had ever dared enter the terrible mountain caves where the trolls lived.

There were not only trolls to be frightened of in the deep haunted forest; there were three other creatures, too, nearly as dangerous. One was the green-haired witch of Hulta Wood. Then there was the bellowing watchdog of the forest; and the third was a bear, the shaggy king of the forest.

Now it happened that among the crofter's children was one small red-cheeked boy named Nisse. There was no one like him in seven parishes. It was strange: he wasn't afraid of anything in the world, no matter how dangerous it was.

The reason Nisse was not afraid was that he was so goodhearted and friendly towards every living thing that not even the fiercest animal had reason to harm him. So he wasn't afraid of wolves or bears or witches, or the trolls in fearsome Hulta Wood.

As soon as Nisse learned what had happened to Lily White, he immediately decided to walk to the troll caves and bring her back. His mother and father let him go, for they knew that Nisse, who was so good to everyone, had nothing to fear.

He took a stick in his hand and put a slice of buttered bread in his pocket, and set out. Soon he arrived at the forest. It was not easy for him to cross the ravines and boulders, the fallen trees and brooks and marshes; but Nisse was small and thin and quick. He went through the brushwood and groves like an eel.

After a while he caught sight of a witch sitting on a ledge combing her tousled green hair. It was the quick-footed witch of Hulta Wood, and her hair fell all the way down to her hips.

"What are you doing here in my forest?" she called, as Nisse came walking along.

"I'm looking for our cow, dear lady. The trolls have stolen her," replied Nisse without stopping.

"Now wait a minute, you," the witch screamed, and she jumped down from the ledge to grab his collar.

But at that moment her long hair caught in the spreading branches of a fir tree, and she was left hanging, the tips of her toes just above the ground, and she could not get free.

She began to kick and twist and shout as loud as she could. Anyone else would have laughed and said it served her right, but Nisse was not like that.

"Tch, tch, little Mother," he said in a friendly voice. "I'll help you."

So he climbed up the tree, pulled and loosened the thick tufts of hair, and at last managed to free the witch from the heavy branches.

"You're an odd one, to help someone who wants to hurt you," said the witch, surprised. "I intended to give you a thrashing, but now I might help you instead."

"That would be good of you, little Mother," said Nisse.

"You'll never be able to get past all the dangerous animals in the forest unless you know their language," said the witch. "But I will give you a magic herb. If you put it in your ear, you will understand everything they say while you are in the forest."

Nisse thanked the witch, did as she told him, and walked on. After he had gone some way, he came to the great angry watchdog of the forest. It limped towards him on three legs, and made a fierce face.

"Poor little doggy," said Nisse, full of confidence and sympathy. "Have you hurt yourself? Can I help you?"

The dog had been ready to jump on the boy, but was so surprised by his kindness that it sat down on its hind legs just like a well-behaved dog. "You're not like other people, are you?" it said.

"Perhaps not," said the boy. "Let me see your paw, little Father."

The dog gave him its forepaw, and Nisse saw there was a big thorn in it. He pulled the thorn out, put a little wet moss on the wound, and tied it together neatly with grass.

"That feels better," said the watchdog, standing on all fours. "I had intended to bite your ears, but I don't want to now. Where are you going?"

"Our cow is lost," Nisse replied. "I am going to the troll caves to find her."

"My, my!" said the watchdog with a pitying look. "That is not an easy errand, for those trolls are not to be trifled with. But since you were kind enough to cure my foot, I'll go with you and show you the way. Perhaps I can help you."

The watchdog did as it had promised. It leapt ahead, and the boy scampered after it, and then they went deep, deep into the forest. They had run for several hours when they caught sight of the bear lumbering through a peat bog, sniffing for cranberries.

"You had better go round," said the watchdog, "for he attacks people and cattle."

"Well, I like the way he looks, even if he is big and shaggy," said the boy, and kept on walking.

Just then the bear saw him. It rose on its hind legs, let out a terrible growl, and padded towards him.

"My, what a great rough voice you have," said the boy, putting out his small hand in greeting. "You would make a fine bass in a church choir."

"Uff," grunted the bear, stepping closer.

"Yes, a very loud voice," continued the boy. "But you seem very friendly, anyway, holding up both paws to greet me."

The bear was just about to gobble Nisse up, when the green-haired witch jumped out from the trees. She had followed Nisse at a distance to see what was going to happen to him in the troll caves.

"Don't touch that boy," she cried to the bear. "He is not like other people."

"It's none of your business," roared the bear, and opened its jaws wider.

Then the witch of the wood picked up a knotted fir stump and flung it into the bear's wide-open mouth. The stump stuck between its jaws so that it could neither growl nor bite.

"Ugh," said the boy. "That was a mean thing to do to old Father here, who was so friendly and wanted to greet me with both his paws. But wait, let's see if I can't help you out of this."

He found a long wooden stick and began poking it into the bear's mouth. The bear sat still, panting, and after much picking and prodding, Nisse at last managed to loosen the stump.

"That was well done," grunted the bear contentedly. "I can see you are a boy with pluck and nerve. I was going to swallow you in one gulp, but now you are safe from me for the rest of your life. What are you doing here in the forest?"

"I am looking for our cow. The trolls stole her," Nisse replied.

"Humph, you are a daring boy to set out on an errand like *that*," said the bear. "If you can outwit the trolls in Hulta Wood, you are cleverer than you look. I think I'll follow you and perhaps I may be of help."

They all set off again. The dog padded first in line, the bear lumbered along at the back, and the green-haired witch of the wood went on ahead to see how the adventure would turn out for the boy.

They arrived at the trolls' mountain caves as the sky began to darken. The entrance was covered by mighty boulders, but there was a small opening just about big enough for a bird dog to squeeze through.

"Nisse can crawl in there," said the bear. And it added, "If the troll attacks you, just call 'Bear, come in,' and then the trolls will have a *real* fight on their hands, I can promise you."

"I don't think it will be necessary," said Nisse. "But thank you just the same."

And so he crawled through the narrow opening. He entered a cave as big as a barn. The old troll was sitting by a fire, munching on a bone. He looked awful, with an enormous nose, hairy arms, and yellow-green cat's eyes. And there in one corner of the cave was Lily White, chewing on some rough thistles the troll had picked for her in the forest.

"Why, look, a little urchin!" exclaimed the troll, and grabbing Nisse around the waist he lifted him to the table. "Where do you come from?"

"Dear friend troll," said Nisse politely. "I have come to fetch our cow, who seems to have wandered into your cave."

"Don't be so foolish," clucked the troll. "Oh, no, my little fellow. I needed milk, you see, and so did my old woman. And you yourself will make a fine little chop for our dinner. As soon as Mother returns, she'll put the pan on the fire."

"Oh, you're joking," said Nisse. "You wouldn't be so cruel to a little boy who never did you any harm."

"What nonsense!" cried the troll. "Of course I'll fry you. Aren't you frightened?"

"No, I'm not afraid of you," said Nisse boldly. "I know you're not as bad as you pretend."

"I've never seen the likes of you in my life," growled the troll. "Mother, Mother, come here quick and light the fire."

A troll woman rushed out of a grotto and started rubbing flint and steel together to make a fire.

"It's good of you, Little Mother, to make a fire to warm your old man," said Nisse happily. "But now I think it's time for Lily White and me to go home."

But then the old troll caught hold of Nisse and prepared to fling him into the frying pan.

Now most creatures, it is true, can be won over by friendliness, kindness, and generosity, but only force helps with a troll. Nisse realized this now, and so he called, "Bear, come in! Bear, come in!"

You should have seen what happened next. The bear tossed the boulders at the entrance, left and right, with its great paws. Sparks flew in the air. Then the bear rushed into the cave, and behind it came the witch of the woods and the watchdog.

The bear caught the troll firmly by the neck, and flung him on to the floor. The dog dug its teeth into the troll woman's leather jacket, until she fell down with a splash right into the waterpail by the fire. Meanwhile, the witch of the woods went over to Lily White and loosened the rope with which she was tied.

Nisse lost no time in climbing on Lily White's back. He held tight to her long horns and called, "Thank you all for helping me. Don't be too hard on the trolls." Then he urged Lily White on: "Hurry, dear Lily White! Hurry, dear cow!"

And with the boy on her back and her tail in the air, Lily White set off. Nisse waved his cap in the air and shouted, "Hurrah!" They galloped over tree trunks and stones, through forest and meadow, and were both safe and sound back at the croft by the time the sun came up.

The rejoicing was great at the croft. But back in the cave the trolls were so frightened by the fact that their own forest friends had helped Nisse—just because he was kind and trusting—that they never dared show their noses in the manor-house pasture again.

Finland

Although the folk tales of Finland are not as well known throughout the world as are those of its neighboring countries, there is a large body of folk literature. Best known is the great folk epic, the *Kalevala,* and the approach of Finnish folklorists, the method of research that combines historical and geographical components, has been followed throughout the world. Eero Salmelainen was the first collector of national tales, in *Fables and Tales of the Finnish Nation.* The stories included here are from *Tales from a Finnish Tupa,* a collection popular in the United States and based on the tales in Salmelainen's book and on Iivo Härkönen's *Fables of the Finnish Nation,* as well as on stories heard by the compilers, James Bowman and Margery Bianco.

The Pig-Headed Wife

This amusing story has the sort of punchline that comes at the end of a long, well-told joke, and it's one of the most popular of the Tales from a Finnish Tupa.

When Matti married Liisa, he thought she was the pleasantest woman in the world. But it wasn't long before Liisa began to show her real character. Headstrong as a goat she was, and as fair set on having her own way.

Matti had been brought up to know that a husband should be the head of his family, so he tried to make his wife obey. But this didn't work with Liisa. It just made her all the more stubborn and pigheaded. Every time that Matti asked her to do one thing, she was bound to do the opposite, and work as he would she generally got her own way in the end.

Matti was a patient sort of man, and he put up with her ways as best he could, though his friends were ready enough to make fun of him for being henpecked. And so they managed to jog along fairly well.

But one year as harvest time came round, Matti thought to himself:

"Here am I, a jolly good-hearted fellow, that likes a bit of company. If only I had a pleasant sort of wife, now, it would be a fine

thing to invite all our friends to the house, and have a nice dinner and drink and a good time. But it's no good thinking of it, for as sure as I propose a feast, Liisa will declare a fast."

And then a happy thought struck him.

"I'll see if I can't get the better of Liisa, all the same. I'll let on I want to be quiet, and then she'll be all for having the house full of guests." So a few days later he said:

"The harvest holidays will be here soon, but don't you go making any sweet cakes this year. We're too poor for that sort of thing."

"Poor! What are you talking about?" Liisa snapped. "We've never had more than we have this year. I'm certainly going to bake a cake, and a good big one, too."

"It works," thought Matti. "It works!" But all he said was:

"Well, if you make a cake, we won't need a pudding too. We mustn't be wasteful."

"Wasteful, indeed!" Liisa grumbled. "We shall have a pudding, and a big pudding!"

Matti pretended to sigh, and rolled his eyes.

"Pudding's bad enough, but if you take it in your head to serve stuffed pig again, we'll be ruined!"

"You'll kill our best pig," quoth Liisa, "and let's hear no more about it."

"But wine, Liisa," Matti went on. "Promise me you won't open a single bottle. We've barely enough to last us through the winter as it is."

Liisa stamped her foot.

"Are you crazy, man? Who ever heard of stuffed pig without wine! We'll not only have wine, but I'll buy coffee too. I'll teach you to call me extravagant by the time I'm through with you!"

"Oh dear, oh dear," Matti sighed. "If you're going to invite a lot of guests, on top of everything else, that'll be the end of it. We can't possibly have guests."

"And have all the food spoil with no one to eat it, I suppose?" jeered Liisa. "Guests we'll have, and what's more, you'll sit at the head of the table, whether you like it or not."

"Well, at any rate I'll drink no wine myself," said Matti, growing bolder. "If I don't drink the others won't, and I tell you we'll need that wine to pull us through the winter."

Liisa turned on him, furious.

"You'll drink with your guests as a host should, till every bottle is empty. There! Now will you be quiet?"

When the day arrived, the guests came, and great was the feasting. They shouted and sang round the table, and Matti himself made more noise than any of his friends. So much so, that long before the feast was over Liisa began to suspect he had played a trick on her. It made her furious to see him so jolly and carefree.

As time went on she grew more and more contrary, until there was no living with her. Now, it happened one day in the spring when all the streams were high, that Matti and Liisa were crossing the wooden bridge over the little river which separated two of their meadows. Matti crossed first, and noticing that the boards were badly rotted, he called out without thinking:

"Look where you step, Liisa! The plank is rotten there. Go lightly or you'll break through."

"Step lightly!" shouted Liisa. "I'll do as . . ."

But for once Liisa didn't finish what she had to say. She jumped with all her weight on the rotted timbers, and fell plop into the swollen stream.

Matti scratched his head for a moment: then he started running upstream as fast as he could go.

Two fishermen along the bank saw him, and called: "What's the matter, my man? Why are you running upstream so fast?"

"My wife fell in the river," Matti panted, "and I'm afraid she's drowned."

"You're crazy," said the fishermen. "Anyone in his right mind would search downstream, not up!"

"Ah," said Matti, "but you don't know my Liisa! All her life she's been so pig-headed that even when she's dead she'd be bound to go against the current!"

Timo and the Princess Vendla

A young shepherd challenges the king's poser and wins the Princess Vendla, proving that the greatest wisdom is understanding one's limitations.

There was once a proud King who had an only daughter named Vendla. He said:

"My daughter shall be different from any other woman in the world. I want her to be wiser than anyone else, in order that she will do me honor."

So he sent for all the most famous teachers, and told them to teach his daughter every language in the world. After Vendla had learned French and English and German and Spanish and Greek and Latin and Chinese and all the other languages as well, so that she could talk to the courtiers of the world each in his own tongue, the King called his heralds and said:

"Go forth throughout the whole kingdom, and say to the people: 'The King will give the

Princess Vendla in marriage to the man who can speak a new tongue that she does not understand. But let everyone beware, for any man who dares to woo the Princess without speaking a new tongue shall be flung into the Baltic Sea.'"

It happened that there dwelt in the kingdom a young shepherd lad named Timo. Timo was a dreamer who spent his time wandering about the deep wild forest talking to the birds and the beasts. And by talking to them he had learned to understand their language, and they his.

When Timo heard the King's proclamation he laughed.

"It shouldn't be so hard to win the Princess Vendla. There are many tongues in the world. Even the wisest men and women cannot understand them all."

So he started on his way to the King's castle. Before he had gone very far he met a sparrow.

"Where are you going with such a happy face, Timo?" the sparrow chirped.

"I am going to marry the Princess Vendla. Come with me and I'll give you a ride in my fine leather pouch."

"Surely I'll go with you," said the sparrow. And he hopped into the pouch, while Timo went his way.

Presently Timo met a squirrel that sat under his fluffy tail and nibbled at a hazelnut.

"Where are you going with such a happy face, Timo?" chattered the squirrel.

"I am going to marry the learned Princess Vendla."

"How wonderful!"

"Come with me and I'll give you a ride in my fine leather pouch."

The squirrel hopped into the pouch, and Timo strode gaily onward. Soon he met a crow, then a raven, then an owl. Each in turn asked him where he was going, and each in turn hopped into Timo's leather pouch to keep him company. On he strode, and before he knew it he came to the gates of the King's castle.

"Halt! Who are you?" boomed one of the King's soldiers.

"I am Timo, and I've come to woo the fair and learned Princess Vendla."

"Why, you're only a shepherd boy," cried the guard. "What's more, you're a fool as well."

"You must be in a hurry to taste the Baltic Sea!" laughed another of the soldiers.

"You can't even speak your own tongue properly, let alone others," cried a third soldier. "Where you come from, the people all talk as if they had a hot potato in their mouth!"

"You'd better run along back to your flocks while you've still got a chance," added the first soldier.

But Timo stood his ground.

"I come to woo the most beautiful and learned Princess Vendla," he said again. "Open the gates and let me in, for I can speak a dozen tongues that the Princess has never even heard."

"Well, remember we warned you," said the guard as he slowly opened the gates. "Next thing you know, we'll be giving you a ride to the Baltic Sea!"

Vendla was seated beside her father on a high golden throne. Her hair was decked with jewels and her face was so beautiful that when Timo saw her he fell on his knees.

"Is it true, most beautiful and learned Princess, that you will marry the man who can speak a language you do not understand?"

"This must be a brave man," thought the Princess as she looked at Timo standing there with his leather pouch across his shoulder.

"Yes," she said, "it is true."

"Do you know what will happen to you if you dare to woo the Princess, and fail to speak this unknown tongue you talk about?" thundered the King.

"I would swim a dozen seas bigger than

"Timo and the Princess Vendla" from TALES FROM A FINNISH TUPA by James Cloyd Bowman and Margery Bianco. Copyright 1936, 1964 by Albert Whitman and Company. Reprinted by permission.

the Baltic for such a Princess," cried Timo as he looked into Vendla's blue eyes.

"Then let us hear this fine language of yours," said the King.

Timo turned to the Princess.

"Listen, most beautiful Princess, and tell me if you understand."

As he spoke Timo thrust his hand into the leather pouch, and touched the sparrow softly. The bird woke up and chirped:

"Tshiu, tshiu, tshiu, tshiu! What do you want, Timo?"

"What tongue is that?" Timo asked.

"Truly," said the Princess, "it is a language I have never heard."

"So you don't understand all the tongues in the world!" Timo laughed. He touched the squirrel's tail.

"Rak-rak-rak! Rak-rak! Ka-ka-ka-ka-ka-ka! Leave me alone!" chattered the squirrel.

"Do you understand that?" Timo asked.

"I do not," said the Princess meekly.

Then Timo touched the crow.

"Vaak, vaak, vaak—ak-ak! Don't disturb me!" cawed the crow.

The Princess shook her head in amazement. Neither could she understand the *"thiuu, thiuu, thiuu"* of the woodpecker, nor the *"kronk, kronk, kronk"* of the raven.

"It is all most strange," said the Princess. "I cannot understand why my teachers never taught me these words!"

"You see, there are many languages that even the wisest men on earth do not know," said Timo, smiling.

"Vendla, I thought you the most learned woman in the world," cried the King furiously, "yet you let a country lad make fools of us both!"

"O King, this is not so," Timo pleaded. "Vendla is still the most learned lady in the land, for she has admitted her ignorance, and truly the greatest wisdom is to know that one does not know everything."

The Princess was pleased with Timo's honest eyes and his understanding words. She was glad that he had won her hand.

"O King," asked Timo, "will you now keep your bargain with me?"

"Take Vendla for your bride," answered the King. "You have won her, and with her I give you the half of my kingdom. May you always be as wise in the future as you have shown yourself today!"

Then the Princess climbed down from her high throne, and Timo took her in his arms and kissed her cheek.

The King proclaimed a glorious holiday with feasting throughout the land, and Timo and Vendla lived happily ever after.

Spain

 Padre Porko is the dominant figure in Spanish folk literature, an animal hero who is the equivalent of the wise owl who has an answer to other animals' problems. The two tales included here are not representative of the body of Spanish folk tales, but were chosen because they seem more appropriate for children than the more serious tales that are comprised in a large portion of the genre. Spanish folk literature has a larger component of religious tales than do the stories of most European countries, and this aspect of the body of tales is reflected in the stories of many of the Spanish language countries of the New World.

The Half-Chick

The story of the odd chick who had only one leg, wing, eye, etc., has a didactic message, but it's also a "why" story that explains what a weathervane is.

Once upon a time there was a handsome black Spanish hen, who had a large brood of chickens. They were all fine, plump little birds, except the youngest, who was quite unlike his brothers and sisters. Indeed, he was such a strange, queer-looking creature, that when he first chipped his shell his mother could scarcely believe her eyes, he was so different from the twelve other fluffy, downy, soft little chicks who nestled under her wings. This one looked just as if he had been cut in two. He had only one leg, and one wing, and one eye, and he had half a head and half a beak. His mother shook her head sadly as she looked at him and said:

"My youngest born is only a half-chick. He can never grow up a tall handsome cock like his brothers. They will go out into the world and rule over poultry yards of their own; but this poor little fellow will always have to stay at home with his mother." And she called him Medio Pollito, which is Spanish for half-chick.

Now though Medio Pollito was such an odd, helpless-looking little thing, his mother soon found that he was not at all willing to remain under her wing and protection. Indeed, in character he was as unlike his brothers and sisters as he was in appearance. They were good, obedient chickens, and when the old hen chicked after them, they chirped and ran back to her side. But Medio Pollito had a roving spirit in spite of his one leg, and when his mother called to him to return to the coop, he pretended that he could not hear, because he had only one ear.

When she took the whole family out for a walk in the fields, Medio Pollito would hop away by himself, and hide among the Indian corn. Many an anxious minute his brothers and sisters had looking for him, while his mother ran to and fro cackling in fear and dismay.

As he grew older he became more self-willed and disobedient, and his manner to his mother was often very rude, and his temper to the other chickens very disagreeable.

One day he had been out for a longer expedition than usual in the fields. On his return he strutted up to his mother with the peculiar little hop and kick which was his way of walking, and cocking his one eye at her in a very bold way he said:

"Mother, I am tired of this life in a dull farmyard, with nothing but a dreary maize field to look at. I'm off to Madrid to see the King."

"To Madrid, Medio Pollito!" exclaimed his mother; "why, you silly chick, it would be a long journey for a grown-up cock, and a poor little thing like you would be tired out before you had gone half the distance. No, no, stay at home with your mother, and some day, when you are bigger, we will go a little journey together."

But Medio Pollito had made up his mind, and he would not listen to his mother's advice, nor to the prayers and entreaties of his brothers and sisters.

"What is the use of our all crowding each other up in this poky little place?" he said. "When I have a fine courtyard of my own at the King's palace, I shall perhaps ask some of you to come and pay me a short visit," and scarcely waiting to say good-bye to his family, away he stumped down the high road that led to Madrid.

"Be sure that you are kind and civil to everyone you meet," called his mother, running after him; but he was in such a hurry to be off, that he did not wait to answer her, or even to look back.

A little later in the day, as he was taking a short cut through a field, he passed a stream. Now the stream was all choked up and overgrown with weeds and water-plants, so that its waters could not flow freely.

"Oh! Medio Pollito," it cried, as the half-chick hopped along its banks, "do come and help me by clearing away these weeds."

"The Half-Chick" from THE GREEN FAIRY BOOK, edited by Andrew Lang. London: Longmans, Green, and Co., 1892.

"Help you, indeed!" exclaimed Medio Pollito, tossing his head, and shaking the few feathers in his tail. "Do you think I have nothing to do but to waste my time on such trifles? Help yourself, and don't trouble busy travellers. I am off to Madrid to see the King," and hoppity-kick, hoppity-kick, away stumped Medio Pollito.

A little later he came to a fire that had been left by some gypsies in a wood. It was burning very low, and would soon be out.

"Oh! Medio Pollito," cried the fire, in a weak, wavering voice as the half-chick approached, "in a few minutes I shall go quite out, unless you put some sticks and dry leaves upon me. Do help me, or I shall die!"

"Help you, indeed!" answered Medio Pollito. "I have other things to do. Gather sticks for yourself, and don't trouble me. I am off to Madrid to see the King," and hoppity-kick, hoppity-kick, away stumped Medio Pollito.

The next morning, as he was getting near Madrid, he passed a large chestnut tree, in whose branches the wind was caught and entangled. "Oh! Medio Pollito," called the wind, "do hop up here, and help me to get free of these branches. I cannot come away, and it is so uncomfortable."

"It is your own fault for going there," answered Medio Pollito. "I can't waste all my morning stopping here to help you. Just shake yourself off, and don't hinder me, for I am off to Madrid to see the King," and hoppity-kick, hoppity-kick, away stumped Medio Pollito in great glee, for the towers and roofs of Madrid were now in sight.

When he entered the town he saw before him a great splendid house, with soldiers standing before the gates. This he knew must be the King's palace, and he determined to hop up to the front gate and wait there until the King came out. But as he was hopping past one of the back windows the King's cook saw him:

"Here is the very thing I want," he exclaimed, "for the King has just sent a message to say that he must have chicken broth for his dinner," and opening the window he stretched out his arm, caught Medio Pollito, and popped him into the broth-pot that was standing near the fire. Oh! how wet and clammy the water felt as it went over Medio Pollito's head, making his feathers cling to his side.

"Water, water!" he cried in his despair, "do have pity upon me and do not wet me like this."

"Ah! Medio Pollito," replied the water, "you would not help me when I was a little stream away on the fields; now you must be punished."

Then the fire began to burn and scald Medio Pollito, and he danced and hopped from one side of the pot to the other, trying to get away from the heat, and crying out in pain:

"Fire, fire! do not scorch me like this; you can't think how it hurts."

"Ah! Medio Pollito," answered the fire, "you would not help me when I was dying away in the wood. You are being punished."

At last, just when the pain was so great that Medio Pollito thought he must die, the cook lifted up the lid of the pot to see if the broth was ready for the King's dinner.

"Look here!" he cried in horror, "this chicken is quite useless. It is burnt to a cinder. I can't send it up to the royal table." And opening the window he threw Medio Pollito out into the street. But the wind caught him up, and whirled him through the air so quickly that Medio Pollito could scarcely breathe, and his heart beat against his side till he thought it would break.

"Oh, wind!" at last he gasped out, "if you hurry me along like this you will kill me. Do let me rest a moment, or—" but he was so breathless that he could not finish his sentence.

"Ah! Medio Pollito," replied the wind, "when I was caught in the branches of the chestnut tree you would not help me; now you are punished." And he swirled Medio Pollito over the roofs of the houses till they reached the highest church in the town, and there he left him fastened to the top of the steeple.

And there stands Medio Pollito to this day. And if you go to Madrid, and walk through the streets till you come to the highest church, you will see Medio Pollito perched on his one leg on the steeple, with his one wing drooping at his side, and gazing sadly out of his one eye over the town.

The Jokes of Single-Toe

A squirrel who is a prankster learns a lesson from Spain's great animal hero, Padre Porko.

"Chestnuts are ripening and falling on the other side of the canal," said the black-headed sparrow, teetering on the edge of the table.

"Oh, but it's too early for chestnuts," observed the Padre. "It takes two or three frosty nights to open the prickles."

"Well, if you can't believe me," said the sparrow, ruffling his collar, "ask the squirrel. He keeps track of the nuts."

So the Padre asked Single-Toe (so named because he had only one on his left front foot). The squirrel put his paw beside his nose as though he were trying to think up an answer to a riddle. "I'll try to let you know in three days," he mumbled, "but don't do anything about chestnuts until you see me again." And he went off in such a rush that even the good Padre grew suspicious.

An hour later he laid down his pipe and beckoned to Mrs. Wren. "Do you mind having a little fly around the wood to see what the squirrel family is up to this morning?"

She came back twittering all over. "The squirrels, for miles around, are all in the grove across the canal, throwing down the chestnuts for dear life. Single-Toe is making them work all the harder, and giggling at something he seems to think very funny."

"Oh, the rascal," chuckled the Padre. "The sly little one-toed sinner! He will give me an answer in three days, will he? Yes, indeed, after he has gathered all the best nuts." He called to his housekeeper. "Mrs. Hedge-Hog, bring me three of the oatmeal sacks from the cupboard and some strong string." And folding the bags inside his belt, he trotted off, pushing his wheelbarrow.

Up among the leaves, busy pulling the polished nuts out of the burrs, Single-Toe and his relatives did not hear the Padre arrive. Patter, plop, plop, plop, patter—the brown nuts were falling on the grass.

"What a lark," beamed the Padre, stuffing four or five into his mouth at once. "And this year they are sweeter and juicier than they have been for a long time." He made little piles of the biggest ones, and began filling his sacks. Finally he had all the wheelbarrow would carry. Bouncing the last bag up and down so he could tie the string around the top, he called out in his silkiest voice, "Many thanks, Single-Toe. You will see that I have taken only the big ones. I do hope that the prickers haven't made your paws sore."

There was a sudden calm in the chestnut grove. The squirrels came leaping down to a low bough, from where they could send sour looks after the Padre, trundling his barrow along toward the bridge. He was singing,

> With chestnuts roasting in a row,
>   I love to hear them sizzle.
> I care not how the winds may blow,
>   Nor how the rain-drops drizzle.
> I welcome every Jack and Jill
>   Who knocks upon my door.
> We toast our toes and eat our fill,
>   For there are plenty more.

One day three or four weeks later the Padre was doing a little carpentering under the umbrella pine, when something behind him sniffed. He jumped, and dropped two nails out of his mouth. There, under the table, tears running down their noses, were Mrs. Single-Toe and the four children.

"Bless my blue-eyed buttons," exclaimed the Padre, spitting out the rest of the nails. "What can be as wrong as all that?"

"It's Papa," said the oldest boy. "He's been in a hole by the old oak for four days, and is almost starved."

"But why doesn't he come home?" said the Padre. "The oak isn't far away."

"The fox won't let him," sobbed Madame Single-Toe.

"And why not?"

"He's mad because of Papa's jokes," the youngest child explained.

The Padre's mouth opened in a wide grin. "More of the jokes that other people don't find funny, eh? Well, I'll take a stroll by the twisted oak and have a talk with the fox." As he started off, he called over his shoulder, "Mrs. Hedge-Hog, you might give these youngsters a couple of the pickled chestnuts we keep for company." He winked solemnly at Mrs. Single-Toe, who blushed.

The fox was lying with his muzzle just an inch from the hole. He did not budge, nor lift his eye when the Padre wished him good morning. "I've got him this time," he snarled. "Four days I've been watching this hole. My mother brings my meals and keeps guard while I eat. He'll not get away *this* time!"

"He is a nuisance with his jokes, I admit," said the Padre peaceably, "but he doesn't do any real harm. Don't you think a good scare would be enough for him?"

"No, I don't," snapped the fox. "And don't you mix in this business, Padre, with your talk about kindness. What I've suffered from that little pest you'd never believe. First he dropped a tomato on my nose—a tomato that was too ripe. And then he dribbled pitch all over my head and neck while I was asleep. So don't waste your time." The fox advanced his red tongue hungrily to the very edge of the hole.

The Padre walked away, deep in thought. His generous heart was very unhappy. What should he say to the near-orphans in his kitchen? There must be some way to save him. Suddenly he saw some crows gossiping in a dead pine. "Will one of you black boys do me a favor, in a great hurry?" he called.

"Certainly, Don Porko," they all cawed.

"Fly low through the woods, and tell every rabbit you see that I want their road commissioner to come to my house for dinner. Say that I'm going to have celery root and cabbage, chopped in parsley."

The Padre's guest was promptness itself. He used a turnip leaf as a napkin, and when he had wiped his whiskers, ate the napkin.

"It makes less for Ma'am Hedge-Hog to clear up," he explained.

"Now for serious business," said the Padre, leading the way to the garden, when they had finished their second glass of dandelion wine. "I have invited you here as an expert. We will draw a map." He made a cross in the soft earth with a stick. "Here is the oak that the lightning split. And here in front of it, so, is a rabbit hole that was begun, but never finished. Do you follow me?"

The road commissioner nodded. "I know it perfectly. The workman was caught by an owl when he came up with some dirt."

"Now," continued the Padre, "how far is the bottom of this unfinished hole from one of your regular tunnels, and how long would it take to dig up to it?"

"About half a jump," replied the road commissioner. "The 'Alley to the Ivy Rock' runs very close to that unfinished hole. A good digger can do a medium-sized jump of tunnel in half a day. I should say it would take two hours to dig upwards from 'Ivy Rock Alley' and join the hole."

The Padre beckoned the road commissioner to follow him to the cellar. Scraping away the sand, he laid bare ten carrots, each as smooth and straight as an orange-colored candle. "These are yours, Mr. Commissioner, if you will do this little job of digging for me."

The bargain was soon struck. "One thing more," said the Padre, as the commissioner was lolloping away. "You will find a friend of mine in the unfinished hole. Don't let him make a noise, but bring him here the moment you can get him free. I'll be waiting."

Daylight was fading when the rabbit returned, covered with damp earth to his armpits. He was supporting a hoarse, hungry, and grimy red squirrel. The Padre welcomed them, pointing to the cupboard. "Sh-h-h-sh, go and see what's inside, Single-Toe."

One might have thought a hundred squirrels were behind the cupboard door, such was the hugging and chattering, the rubbing of noses, and the scratching of ears. Single-Toe was invited to stay for a light lunch, even after the road commissioner had left for his burrow, the biggest carrot in his mouth.

Safe, fed, and warmed, the red squirrel became his own gay self again. He began to chuckle, then to shake with merriment. "Ha, ha, ha! That silly old fox is still there, watching an empty hole! Won't it be a priceless joke, if I climb the oak and drop a rotten egg on his nose?"

At the word "joke," Mrs. Single-Toe, the four little squirrels, and the good Padre, all stiffened.

"Don't you ever say that word again," said his wife. "Do you hear, no more jokes, never, never."

Single-Toe wilted. "Yes," he confessed, not daring to meet the Padre's eye, "jokes aren't always so terribly funny, are they? Not even for the joker."

Italy

 While there are older collections of Italian folk tales than Italo Calvino's *Italian Folktales,* few are more impressive in size or style; his retelling of "And Seven!" illustrates to perfection the robust humor and candor that are one of the distinctive features of Italian folk literature, the other typical feature being the story based on a religious or local legend. Tales from the oral tradition were recorded in Italy long before similar compilations were made in most European countries, one of the most notable examples being that of Giambattista Basile's collection, *Pentameron, or Entertainment for the Little Ones,* published in the Neapolitan dialect in the seventeenth century. An excellent source for storytellers is *The Priceless Cats and Other Italian Stories,* compiled by the indefatigable compiler Moritz Jagendorf, whose books represent the folk tales of many countries.

The Magic Box

A young farmer learns to mend his profligate ways, in a highly moral tale.

In one of the fertile valleys of the Apennines —north in Emilia—long ago there lived a rich farmer. He had much land. His vineyards were the best pruned and yielded the best vintage; his olive grove was watched over with the utmost care and never suffered a frost. His fields of grain harvested more than his neighbors'; his cattle were sleeker and his sheep gave more wool at the spring shearings. Yes, everything prospered with him. On market- and fair-days his neighbors would wag their thumbs at him and say:

"There goes Gino Tomba. His sons will be very rich men one of these days."

He had two sons. The older was a daredevil who handled a rapier better than a pruning-knife and could swing a broadsword with steadier aim than a mattock. Tonio, the younger, was an easy-going, pleasure-loving rascal who knew more about fiddling than he did about winnowing grain. "If I had a third son, he might have been a farmer," old Tomba used to say when he came bringing his skins of wine to the inn to sell. "But we

"The Magic Box" from THE WAY OF THE STORY-TELLER by Ruth Sawyer. Copyright 1942 by Ruth Sawyer. Reprinted by permission of Viking Penguin Inc.

must make the most of what the good Virgin provides," and so he let his older son march off to the wars and set about making Tonio ready to look after his lands when he had gone.

"Hearken to me, boy; I am leaving you as fine an inheritance as any here in the north. See that you keep a sharp eye on it and render it back with increase to your brother. Some day he will grow tired of fighting Spain and the French and come marching home."

In less than a twelvemonth old Tomba was dead. Tonio came from the burying, turned himself once about the farm to make sure it was all there, and settled down to easy living. He made what you call good company. It was, Tonio, come to the fair; and Tonio, stay longer at the inn; and Tonio, drink with this one; and Tonio, dance with that. He could step the tarantella as well as any man in the north, and he could fiddle as he danced. So it was here and there and anywhere that a feast was spread or a saint's day kept; and Tonio, the younger son of old Tomba, danced late and drank deep and was the last to stop when the dawn broke. Often he slept until the sun was already throwing late shadows on the foothills.

The time came when his thrifty neighbors took him soundly to task for idling away his days and wasting what his father had saved. Then he would laugh, braggadocio: "Am I a sheep to graze in the pasture or a grain of wheat to get myself planted and stay in my fields all day and every day? The lands have grown rich for my father for fifty years; let them grow rich for me for fifty more. That is all I ask—that, and for my neighbors to prune their tongues when next they prune their vineyards."

But Tonio had asked too much. A place with a master is one thing, but without a master it is quite different. The *banditti* came down from the mountains and stole his cattle while the herdsmen slept; wolves ravaged his sheep; the bad little oil-fly came in swarms and spoiled the olives as they ripened; the grapes hung too long, and the wine turned thin and sour. And so it went—a little here,

a little there, each year. The laborers took to small thieving—a few lambs from the spring dropping before they were driven in from the pastures for counting, a measure of wheat, a skin of wine, that would never be missed. The barns were not fresh-thatched in time, and the fall rains mildewed much of the harvest; the rats got in and ate their share. So, after years of adding one misfortune to another misfortune, there was a mountain of misfortune—large enough for even Tonio to see.

Over one night he became like a crazy man, for over one night he had remembered his brother. Any day he might be returning. At the inn the day before there had been two soldiers fresh from the wars, drinking and bragging of their adventures. Another night and who might not come? Once home, the older brother would be master. First, he would ask for an accounting. And what then? As master he could have him, Tonio, flogged or flung into prison. More final than that, he could run him through with his clever rapier, and no one would question his right to do it. The more Tonio thought about it, the more his terror grew. He began running about the country like a man with fever in his brain. First he ran to the inn and asked the landlord what he should do, and the landlord laughed aloud. "Sit down, Tonio, and drink some of my good Chianti. Why worry about your brother now, when he may be lying in a strange country, stuck through the ribs like a pig?"

He ran to a neighbor, who laughed louder than the landlord. "Take up your fiddle and see if you cannot play your cattle back into the pasture and the good wine into its skins."

He ran on to his favorite, Lisetta. She cocked her pretty head at him like a saucy macaw. "Let me see," she laughed, "you have forgotten your brother for ten years, yes? Then come to the inn tonight and dance the tarantella with me, and I will make you forget him for another ten years."

After that he ran to the priest, and found him finishing mass. He did not laugh, the priest. Instead he shook his head sorrowfully

and told him to burn candles for nine days before the shrine of Saint Anthony of Padua and pray for wisdom. On the way to the shrine he met the half-witted herdboy, Zeppo, who laughed foolishly when he saw his master's face and tapped his own forehead knowingly. "Master, you are so frightened it has made you quite mad, like me." Then he put his lips to Tonio's ear. "Hearken, I will tell you what to do. Go to the old tsigane woman of the grotto. She has much wisdom and she makes magic of all kinds—black and white. Go to her, master."

In the end it was the advice of the mad herdboy that Tonio took. He climbed the first spur of the mountain to a deep grotto that time or magic had hollowed out of the rock, and there he found the tsigane woman. She was ages old and withered as a dried fig. She listened to all Tonio had to tell, and left him without a word to go deeper into the grotto, where she was swallowed up altogether in blackness. When she came back at last, she was carrying something in her hand—a small casket bound strongly with bands of brass, and in the top a hole so small it could hardly be seen in the pattern of the carving. She put the box into Tonio's hand and fixed him with eyes, that were piercing as two rapier points. When she spoke, it was as if her voice rumbled out, not from her, but from deep in the rocks.

"Every morning, while the dew still lies heaviest, shake one grain of dust from the box in every corner of your lands—barns, pastures, and vineyards. See to it that no spot is left forgotten. Do this, and you will prosper

as your father prospered. But never let one morning pass, and never till the day you die break the bands or look inside. If you do, the magic will be gone."

That night Tonio did not fiddle or dance with Lisetta at the inn. He went to bed when the fowls went to roost, and was up at the crowing of the first cock. With the magic box under his arm, he went first to his barns to sprinkle the precious grains; but he found the men still asleep and the cattle unfed. Out of their beds he drove them with angry words. And, still lashing them with his tongue, he watched while they stumbled sleepily about, beginning the day's work. From the barns he went to the fields, and found the grain half cut and none of it stacked. The scythes were left rusting on the ground and the men still asleep in their huts. Tonio scattered more dust, and then drove the reapers to their work.

And so it was in the olive grove, the vineyards, and the pastures. Everywhere he found men sleeping and the work half done. "Holy Mother, defend us!" the men said among themselves after Tonio had gone. "The master is up early and looking about for himself, even as the old master did. We shall have to keep a sharper watch out on things or he will be packing us off to starve."

After that, every morning Tonio was abroad before the sun, shaking the dust from his magic box into every corner of his lands. And every morning he was seeing something new that was needing care. In a little time the inn and the market-place knew him no more; and Lisetta had to find a new dancing partner. A twelvemonth passed, and the farm of old Gino Tomba was prospering again. When Tonio came to the market-place to sell his grain and wine, his neighbors would wag their thumbs at him as they had wagged them at his father and they would say: "There goes Tonio Tomba. His sons—when he marries and they are born—will be very rich men."

And in the end what happened? The older brother never came home to claim his inheritance. He must have been killed in the wars; at any rate, all the lands were Tonio's for the keeping. He married the daughter of his richest neighbor, and had two sons of his own, even as his father had had. And when the time came for him to die he called them both to his side and commanded young Gino to bring him the casket and break the bands, his hands being too weak for the breaking. Raising the lid he looked in, eager, for all his dying, to discover the magic that the box had held all those years.

What did he find? Under the lid were written these words: "Look you—the master's eye is needed over all." In the bottom were a few grains of sand left, the common kind that any wayfarer can gather up for himself from the road that climbs to the Apennines.

King Clothes

A peasant lad scorns his neighbors for thinking that clothes make the man.

It is told that years ago there lived in Sicily, the largest island in all the Mediterranean, a young fellow named Giufa, who was so silly that, as the saying goes, he wasn't sure of the weather when it was raining in buckets. That is what folks said, but I'm not sure they were right. For people lived in Sicily before they lived anywhere in Italy, and there must have been silly fellows before him.

Giufa wore rags for clothes and never had shoes, so the dust on the road jumped between his toes. And who looks at a fellow who is dressed in rags? Nobody. Doors were closed in his face, and sometimes people wouldn't ever talk to him. He was never asked to a wedding or a feast. Life was not too pleasant for Giufa.

One sunny day his mother sent him to take something to the farm that was next to theirs.

Giufa went off whistling, kicking the dust on the road. Sometimes he stopped to speak to a bird or a butterfly. Soon he came to the farmhouse. At the gate stood the wife of the farmer.

"Good day, mistress," Giufa said politely. "My mother sent me to give you this," and he held out a basket to her.

The woman took one look at his ragged clothes and dusty face and feet.

"Drop it right there," she cried, "and go quickly. You look like a scarecrow, and the dogs will be after you."

Giufa did not say anything. What could he say? Besides, it was dinnertime just then, and his stomach was empty and growling. So he turned sadly toward home.

Though kith and kin said he was a noodle-head, he had sense enough to think that the farmwoman could have been a little nicer and could have asked him in to have a piece of bread and cheese.

When he reached home he told his mother how he had been treated, adding: "I could smell the bean soup out at the gate. They could have been good Christians and asked me to have a plate. They talk to me like that because I don't wear fine breeches and a velvet coat."

Giufa's mother worried about this, and a few weeks later she once again had to send her son with something to that same farm. Not wanting to put the boy to shame, she dressed him in a fine white shirt, good breeches, a nice blue coat, and good shoes.

You should have seen Giufa! He looked like a different fellow. He almost could not recognize himself.

Off he went, whistling gaily and joking with bird and beast until he came to the farmer's house. There stood both the farmer and his wife, and neither one recognized Giufa in his fine clean clothes.

"I have something for you," he cried.

It was noon then, and so they greeted him pleasantly and invited him into the farmhouse. They asked him to sit down to hot steaming minestrone soup that was filled with fresh vegetables and good sharp cheese. With it came crisp fresh bread and rich red wine.

Giufa ate and joked and had the best time of his life. At the end of the meal, the farmer sat back and asked the boy to tell him about this and that. But instead of doing so, Giufa stood up and put some of the cheese and bread in the pockets of his coat and breeches and into his hat. The farmer and his wife laughed because they thought this was so funny. Then Giufa bowed low and, looking down at his bulging pockets and over at his hat, said:

"Here is food for you, my good clothes and fine hat, and I want to thank you from the bottom of my heart, for it is you who were treated like a king, and it is because of you, my good clothes and fine hat, that I had a fine meal. When I came here the last time without you, fine clothes, I was treated like a crazy dog."

Then he turned around and walked out. You can guess what the farmer and his wife thought and said! Maybe they remembered the saying: "Dress up a stick and folks'll think it's a nobleman."

And Seven!

In an ebullient version of the Rumpelstiltzkin story, a girl must remember names rather than guess them.

A woman had a daughter who was big and fat and so gluttonous that when her mother brought the soup to the table she would eat one bowl, then a second, then a third, and keep on calling for more. Her mother filled her bowl, saying, "That makes three! And four! And five!" When the daughter asked for a seventh bowl of soup, her mother, instead of filling the bowl, whacked her over the head, shouting, "And seven!"

A well-dressed young man was passing by just then and saw the mother through the window hitting the girl and crying, "And seven!"

As the big fat young lady captured his fancy immediately, he went in and asked, "Seven of what?"

Ashamed of her daughter's gluttony, the mother replied, "Seven spindles of hemp! I have a daughter so crazy about work that she'd even spin the wool on the sheep's back!

Can you imagine that she's already spun seven spindles of hemp this morning and still wants to spin? To make her stop, I have to beat her."

"If she's that hard-working, give her to me," said the young man. "I'll try her out to see if you're telling the truth and then I'll marry her."

He took her to his house and shut her up in a room full of hemp waiting to be spun. "I'm a sea captain, and I'm leaving on a voyage," he said. "If you've spun all this hemp by the time I return, I'll marry you."

The room also contained exquisite clothes and jewels, for the captain happened to be very rich. "When you become my wife," he explained, "these things will all be yours." Then he left her.

The girl spent her days trying on dresses and jewels and admiring herself in the mirror. She also devoted much time to planning meals, which the household servants prepared for her. None of the hemp was spun yet, and in one more day the captain would be back. The girl gave up all hope of ever marrying him and burst into tears. She was still crying when through the window flew a bundle of rags and came to rest on its feet: it was an old woman with long eyelashes. "Don't be afraid," she told the girl. "I've come to help you. I'll spin while you make the skein."

You never saw anyone spin with the speed of that old woman. In just a quarter of an hour she had spun every bit of hemp. And the more she spun, the longer her lashes became; longer than her nose, longer than her chin, they came down more than a foot; and her eyelids also grew much longer.

When the work was finished, the girl said, "How can I repay you, my good lady?"

"I don't want to be repaid. Just invite me to your wedding banquet when you marry the captain."

"How do I go about inviting you?"

"Just call 'Columbina' and I'll come. But

heaven help you if you forget my name. It would be as though I'd never helped you, and you'd be undone."

The next day the captain arrived and found the hemp all spun. "Excellent!" he said. "I believe you're just the bride I was seeking. Here are the clothes and jewels I bought for you. But now I have to go on another voyage. Let's have a second test. Here's twice the amount of hemp I gave you before. If you spin it all by the time I return, I'll marry you."

As she had done before, the girl spent her time trying on gowns and jewels, eating soup and lasagna, and got to the last day with all the hemp still waiting to be spun. She was weeping over it when, lo and behold, something dropped down the chimney, and into the room rolled a bundle of rags. It came to rest on its feet, and there stood an old woman with sagging lips. This one too promised to help, began spinning, and worked even faster than the other old woman. The more she spun, the more her lips sagged. When the hemp was all spun in a half-hour, the old woman asked only to be invited to the wedding banquet. "Just call 'Columbara.' But don't forget my name, or my help will have been in vain and you will suffer."

The captain returned and asked before he even got into the house, "Did you spin it all?"

"I just now finished!"

"Take these clothes and jewels. Now, if I come back from my third voyage and find you've spun this third load of hemp, which is much bigger than the other two, I promise we'll get married at once."

As usual, the girl waited until the last day without touching the hemp. Down from the roof's gutter fell a bundle of rags, and out came an old woman with buckteeth. She began spinning, spinning ever faster, and the more she spun, the longer grew her teeth.

"To invite me to your wedding banquet," said the old woman, "you must call 'Columbun.' But if you forget my name, it would be better if you'd never seen me."

When the captain came home and found the hemp all spun, he was completely satisfied. "Fine," he said, "now you will be my wife." He ordered preparations made for the wedding, to which he invited all the nobility in town.

Caught up in the preparations, the bride thought no more of the old women. On the morning of the wedding she remembered that she was supposed to invite them, but when she went to pronounce their names, she found they had slipped her mind. She cudgeled her brains but, for the life of her, couldn't recall a single name.

From the cheerful girl she was, she sank into a state of bottomless gloom. The captain noticed it and asked her what the matter was, but she would say nothing. Unable to account for her sadness, the bridegroom thought, this is perhaps not the right day. He therefore postponed the wedding until the day after. But the next day was still worse, and the day following we won't even mention. With every day that passed, the bride became gloomier and quieter, with her brows knit in concentration. He told her jokes and stories in an effort to make her laugh, but nothing he said or did affected her.

Since he couldn't cheer her up, he decided to go hunting and cheer himself up. Right in the heart of the woods he was caught in a storm and took refuge in a hovel. He was in there in the dark, when he heard voices:

"O Columbina!"

"O Columbara!"

"O Columbun!"

"Put on the pot to make polenta! That confounded bride won't be inviting us to her banquet after all!"

The captain wheeled around and saw three crones. One had eyelashes that dragged on the ground, another lips that hung down to her feet, and the third teeth that grazed her knees.

Well, well, he thought to himself. Now I can tell her something that will make her laugh. If she doesn't laugh over what I've just seen, she'll never laugh at anything!

He went home and said to his bride, "Just listen to this. Today I was in the woods and went into a hovel to get out of the rain. I go in and what should I see but three crones: one with eyelashes that dragged on the ground, another with lips that hung down to her feet, and the third with teeth that grazed her knees. And they called each other: 'O Columbina,' 'O Columbara,' 'O Columbun!' "

The bride's face brightened instantly, and she burst out laughing, and laughed and laughed. "Order the wedding banquet right away. But I'm asking one favor of you: since those three crones made me laugh so hard, let me invite them to the banquet."

Invite them she did. For the three old women a separate round table was set up, but so small that what with the eyelashes of one, the lips of the other, and the teeth of the third, you no longer knew what was what.

When dinner was over, the bridegroom asked Columbina, "Tell me, good lady, why are your lashes so long?"

"That's from straining my eyes to spin fine thread!" said Columbina.

"And you, why are your lips so thick?"

"That comes from always rubbing my finger on them to wet the thread!" said Columbara.

"And you, how on earth did your teeth get so long?"

"That's from biting the knot of the thread!" said Columbun.

"I see," said the bridegroom, and he turned to his wife. "Go get the spindle." When she brought it to him, he threw it into the fire. "You'll spin no more for the rest of your life!"

So the big, fat bride lived happily ever after.

Poland

As is true of other European countries that have been governed or occupied by other peoples, Poland and Polish folk literature show the influences of both native peoples and invaders; there are Slavic and German elements in the literature, as well as evidence of indigenous strains. Many of the Polish tales in the compilation by Lucia Borski and Kate Miller, *The Jolly Tailor and Other Fairy Tales Translated from the Polish*, show this variety, reflect the deep piety of the Polish people, and evince the cheerful common sense that is an appealing aspect of "King Bartek."

King Bartek

Disguised as a page, the young king wins one of two sisters, while the other snobbish sister loses her chance, in a tale both moralistic and romantic.

On the outskirts of a village, in a hut fallen almost to ruins, there lived a very poor widow with her two daughters, Bialka and Spiewna. Both of them were so beautiful that their fame spread over seven mountains, over seven seas. Even at the King's palace the rumors were heard. Many of the knights wished to go at once and woo the girls.

The King disliked to lose his knights, as he had planned a great war, and besides he did not have much faith in the rumors. Instead of granting permission to the knights to go, he sent some of his faithful messengers to see the maidens and bring back pictures of Bialka and Spiewna.

The rumors were true. The pictures brought back by the messengers exceeded

"King Bartek" from THE JOLLY TAILOR AND OTHER FAIRY TALES, translated from the Polish by Lucia Merecka Borski and Kate B. Miller. Copyright 1928, 1956 by Lucia Merecka Borski and John F. Miller. Reprinted by permission of Lucia Merecka Borski.

everybody's expectations. Spiewna was a true sister to the lily; Bialka, to the red rose. The first had azure eyes, the other, eyes dark as the Black Sea; one was proud of her long, golden braids, the other of her raven black braids. The first one had the beauty of a sunny day in her face, the other, the charm of a May night. The knights became enamored of the maidens; no one could keep them from departing. Even the King himself, as he was young and thought of marriage, scratched himself behind the ear and looked at the pictures with great pleasure. The war was put off, the court was desolated, and only the King and his Jester, Pieś, who was old and ugly like the seven mortal sins, were left there.

For a long, long time the knights did not come back. They were enjoying themselves; or it might be the other way around, Bialka and Spiewna, sure of their beauty, might be taking their time picking and choosing, like sparrows in poppy seeds. The knights in love unwound entangled thread, killed partridges in the air, and sang serenades. Be it as it may, their long absence annoyed the King and he grew impatient and ill-tempered.

"Pieś," he once addressed the Jester, "do you know what I am thinking about?"

"I know, Your Lordship!"

"How?"

"Because our thoughts walk the same paths."

"I wonder!" laughed the King.

"Your Lordship wishes to go to the widow's daughters."

"You guessed!" cried the young King, rejoicing.

"Then we shall go together," said Pieś. "But we must change our places; I, a King; Your Lordship, a Jester."

"What an idea!" said the young ruler, shocked a bit.

"There won't be much of a difference," smiled the Jester.

"No, I shall not do it! You may, if you wish, become a King, but I shall put on a peasant's garb and call myself Bartek."

"As you please!" answered Pieś. "Something unpleasant may come of it though."

"Why?" asked the King, now Bartek.

"A King, be he as ugly and humpbacked as I am, will always have preference over Bartek. And then who knows? Your Highness may fall in love with either Spiewna or Bialka."

The youthful lord became alarmed.

"So much the better!" he said after a while, and added in a whisper, "The heart that loves will not fool itself."

They went on their journey.

In the meantime the widow's hut was as noisy as a beehive. One brought musicians, another singers. The hut changed into a music box adorned with garlands and flowers, as if in celebration of a holiday. The knights reveled, the girls danced, song followed song, and jokes, one after another. The mother's white bonnet swung on her white hair from one ear to the other from happiness.

Bialka liked Przegoń (Pshegon) more than all the others. Spiewna chose none as yet. Neither her mother's persuasion nor her sister's scoffs did any good. The girl's heart had not awakened yet, and without love she did not wish to marry even the richest of knights.

The betrothal of Przegoń to Bialka was announced. She had her wedding dress made, goods for which were brought by Przegoń. The jewelry, one could not describe, it could be gathered in measures.

Bialka was overwhelmed with joy, was triumphant with her success. She looked down on her sister with haughtiness and consoled her mother with scornful words.

"Do not worry, Mother! Spiewna awaits a prince. She will become wiser when she has to grow rue, and then I, Przegoń's wife, will try to get her an organist. Also I shall find a suitable nook for you, Mother."

Her mother's heart grieved, but what could she answer?

Then one day a golden carriage drove up before the door. All three of them ran quickly to the window, and Bialka shouted:

"The King has come!"

Sudden confusion possessed the hut. The old widow trotted to the kitchen to prepare some fowl for His Majesty, the King, while

Bialka snatched a hand-mirror and a comb and turning to her sister called in a commanding voice:

"Don't you dare to call the King's attention to yourself!"

Spiewna stopped in astonishment.

"Do you hear me?" shouted Bialka.

"I hear, but I don't understand."

"You don't understand—you don't understand!"

"For—how—" began Spiewna.

"Don't dare to call the King's attention to yourself!"

"What do you care about the King when you have Przegoń?"

"Have I or not, that is nothing to you!" grumbled Bialka. "And better take my advice, otherwise—you shall see!"

His Majesty, the King, was far from good looking. He was ugly, old, his right arm was higher than the left, and he was also limping. But all this was covered with the golden crown, was concealed by the purple cloak and was straightened by the long robe richly embroidered with pearls. Upon seeing the sisters, he at once laid his royal gifts at their feet, and loaded them with compliments. Spiewna refused all the gifts; she accepted only a white rose, which she pinned into her hair.

"How beautiful he is!" whispered Bialka.

"How ridiculous he is!" replied Spiewna.

Bialka looked at her with anger.

Among the King's numerous attendants, there was a young and handsome page, called Bartek. Spiewna's eyes met the youth's gaze. Bartek, dazzled with the girl's beauty, did not take his eyes off her, and when the King offered jewels to Bialka, he came near Spiewna and said:

"All my riches is this fife. It plays beautifully and the time will come when I shall present you with its song."

Spiewna, standing on the threshold, blushed like a rose, and Bialka seeing this, maliciously whispered in her ear:

"Just the kind of a husband for you. Keep away from the King!"

"And Przegoń?" questioned Spiewna.

"You may have him," threw out Bialka.

Przegoń did not see the King, but he learned of his arrival and of his gifts to Bialka. He wished to speak to Bialka, but she, busy with her guest, who exaggerated his compliments and promised golden mountains, did not care to see him. He stayed away from his unfaithful sweetheart and waited to see what time would bring forth.

One night, and 'twas a night with the full moon, a scented intoxicating night, under the window of the room where both sisters slept, there came sounds of a guitar accompanied by a song.

"The King!" murmured Bialka and she jumped to the window.

The King sang:

> Out of the mist thou shalt have palaces,
> For thy comfort and pleasures I will care
> And pay with gold for thy every smile.
> Attired, bejewelled like a peacock
> Thou shalt be Queen in the royal gardens.

"Do you hear, do you hear?" said Bialka to Spiewna. "Thus sings the King!"

Then later under the window fluted the country fife. Bialka looked out of the window and noticed Bartek. Seeing her sister moved by the sad and sweet tones of the fife, she roared with laughter.

The fife stopped playing and they heard this song:

> Do not come to me with pretense
> But with love in thy pure eyes
> That knows another's love.
> Be not touched with a royal gown
> That is worn by a fool's soul,
> A soul that knows not what is love.

"Thus sings Bartek!" called Spiewna.

"Ha-ha-ha!" rang out Bialka's venomous laughter. She leaned over the window and called aloud into the silent night:

"Drive away the fool, Your Majesty, who has the boldness to interrupt your song and insult your royal soul! Order him away, for he steals from us this beautiful night!"

"I will punish him more severely than you think," was the answer, "because to-morrow he will marry your sister."

"And when we?" asked Bialka.

"Even now. Come to me!"

Bialka jumped out of the window, and there she met face to face with Przegoń.

"What are you doing here?" she asked him haughtily.

"I came to wish you happiness with this— king's Jester," replied Przegoń pointing to Pies.

"What? What?" cried Bialka, looking with frightened eyes at the splendid dress, like a king's.

And in the room, where Spiewna remained, Bartek's fife rang out followed by a song:

'Tis hard to find true love
Under an alluring purple gown,
Infirmity shall remain in heart
With all the roses torn aside.
Ugly looks and lameness and a hump
May all be covered with a royal cloak.

The King wished for a true heart;
The fool desired fun and laughter;
And both are satisfied.
Therefore the fool dressed like a King;
The King put on the peasant's garb.
Now, maiden, cry for thy alluring loss
And understand these prophesying words:
That people are not judged by looks
But by their hearts and deeds.

The golden carriage came to the door, a thousand torches were lighted, a thousand knights with Przegoń at the head surrounded the royal carriage, into which Spiewna was led with her bridesmaids, and they all went to the King's palace to celebrate the wedding. The mother rejoiced at Spiewna's happiness, but she grieved over the neglected Bialka, who had to grow sixteen beds of rue before she married an old organist.

Hungary

 While Hungarian tales often appear in general or subject collections, as does "The Boy Who Could Keep a Secret," there are few collections available to English language readers that are devoted to the rich treasury of Hungarian or Magyar stories. *Once Upon a Time: Forty Hungarian Folk-Tales,* compiled by Gyula Illyes, is out of print, as is *The Glass Man and the Golden Bird: Hungarian Folk and Fairy Tales,* compiled by Ruth Manning-Sanders, although both can be found in libraries. Many of the Hungarian tales are richly embroidered stories of magic and adventure, and they are often available in such collections as Andrew Lang's *The Crimson Fairy Book* or in anthologies of tales from neighboring central European countries.

The Boy Who Could Keep a Secret

Only because he keeps his secret despite punishment, does a young lad find his dream come true by becoming King of Hungary, in this Magyar folk tale.

Once upon a time there lived a poor widow who had one little boy. At first sight you would not have thought that he was different from a thousand other little boys; but then you noticed that by his side hung the scabbard of a sword, and as the boy grew bigger the scabbard grew bigger too. The sword which belonged to the scabbard was found by the little boy sticking out of the ground in the garden, and every day he pulled it up to see if it would go into the scabbard. But though it was plainly becoming longer and longer, it was some time before the two would fit.

However, there came a day at last when it slipped in quite easily. The child was so delighted that he could hardly believe his eyes, so he tried it seven times, and each time it slipped in more easily than before. But pleased though the boy was, he determined not to tell anyone about it, particularly not his mother, who never could keep anything from her neighbours.

Still, in spite of his resolutions, he could not hide altogether that something had happened, and when he went in to breakfast his mother asked him what was the matter.

"Oh, mother, I had such a nice dream last night," said he; "but I can't tell it to anybody."

"You can tell it to me," she answered. "It must have been a nice dream, or you wouldn't look so happy."

"No, mother; I can't tell it to anybody," returned the boy, "till it comes true."

"I want to know what it was, and know it I will," cried she, "and I will beat you till you tell me."

But it was no use, neither words nor blows would get the secret out of the boy; and when her arm was quite tired and she had to leave off, the child, sore and aching, ran into the garden and knelt weeping beside his little sword. It was working round and round in its hole all by itself, and if anyone except the boy had tried to catch hold of it, he would have been badly cut. But the moment he stretched out his hand it stopped and slid quietly into the scabbard.

For a long time the child sat sobbing, and the noise was heard by the king as he was driving by. "Go and see who it is that is crying so," said he to one of his servants, and the man went. In a few minutes he returned saying: "Your Majesty, it is a little boy who is kneeling there sobbing because his mother has beaten him."

"Bring him to me at once," commanded the monarch, "and tell him that it is the king who sends for him, and that he has never cried in all his life and cannot bear anyone else to do so." On receiving this message the boy dried his tears and went with the servant to the royal carriage. "Will you be my son?" asked the king.

"Yes, if my mother will let me," answered the boy. And the king bade the servant go back to the mother and say that if she would give her boy to him, he should live in the palace and marry his prettiest daughter as soon as he was a man.

The widow's anger now turned into joy, and she came running to the splendid coach and kissed the king's hand. "I hope you will be more obedient to his Majesty than you were to me," she said; and the boy shrank away half-frightened. But when she had gone back to her cottage, he asked the king if he might fetch something that he had left in the garden, and when he was given permission, he pulled up his little sword, which he slid into the scabbard.

Then he climbed into the coach and was driven away.

After they had gone some distance the king said: "Why were you crying so bitterly in the garden just now?"

"Because my mother had been beating me," replied the boy.

"And what did she do that for?" asked the king again.

"Because I would not tell her my dream."

"And why wouldn't you tell it to her?"

"Because I will never tell it to anyone till it comes true," answered the boy.

"And won't you tell it to me either?" asked the king in surprise.

"No, not even to you, your Majesty," replied he.

"Oh, I am sure you will when we get home," said the king, smiling, and he talked to him about other things till they came to the palace.

"I have brought you such a nice present," he said to his daughters, and as the boy was very pretty they were delighted to have him and gave him all their best toys.

"You must not spoil him," observed the

"The Boy Who Could Keep a Secret" from THE CRIMSON FAIRY BOOK, edited by Andrew Lang. London: Longmans, Green and Company, 1903.

king one day, when he had been watching them playing together. "He has a secret which he won't tell to anyone."

"He will tell me," answered the eldest princess; but the boy only shook his head.

"He will tell me," said the second girl.

"Not I," replied the boy.

"He will tell me," cried the youngest, who was the prettiest too.

"I will tell nobody till it comes true," said the boy, as he had said before; "and I will beat anybody who asks me."

The king was very sorry when he heard this, for he loved the boy dearly; but he thought it would never do to keep anyone near him who would not do as he was bid. So he commanded his servants to take him away, and not to let him enter the palace again until he had come to his right senses.

The sword clanked loudly as the boy was led away, but the child said nothing, though he was very unhappy at being treated so badly when he had done nothing. However, the servants were very kind to him, and their children brought him fruit and all sorts of nice things, and he soon grew merry again, and lived amongst them for many years till his seventeenth birthday.

Meanwhile the two eldest princesses had become women, and had married two powerful kings who ruled over great countries across the sea. The youngest one was old enough to be married too, but she was very particular, and turned up her nose at all the young princes who had sought her hand.

One day she was sitting in the palace feeling rather dull and lonely, and suddenly she began to wonder what the servants were doing, and whether it was not more amusing down in their quarters. The king was at his council and the queen was ill in bed, so there was no one to stop the princess, and she hastily ran across the gardens to the houses where the servants lived. Outside she noticed a youth who was handsomer than any prince she had ever seen, and in a moment she knew him to be the little boy she had once played with.

"Tell me your secret and I will marry you," she said to him; but the boy only gave her the beating he had promised her long ago, when she asked him the same question. The girl was very angry, besides being hurt, and ran home to complain to her father.

"If he had a thousand souls, I would kill them all," swore the king.

That very day a gallows was built outside the town, and all the people crowded round to see the execution of the young man who had dared to beat the king's daughter. The prisoner, with his hands tied behind his back, was brought out by the hangman, and amidst dead silence his sentence was being read by the judge when suddenly the sword clanked against his side. Instantly a great noise was heard and a golden coach rumbled over the stones, with a white flag waving out of the window. It stopped underneath the gallows, and from it stepped the king of the Magyars, who begged that the life of the boy might be spared.

"Sir, he has beaten my daughter, who only asked him to tell her his secret. I cannot pardon that," answered the princess's father.

"Give him to me, I'm sure he will tell me the secret; or, if not, I have a daughter who is like the Morning Star, and he is sure to tell it to her."

The sword clanked for the third time, and the king said angrily: "Well, if you want him so much you can have him; only never let me see his face again." And he made a sign to the hangman. The bandage was removed from the young man's eyes, and the cords from his wrists, and he took his seat in the golden coach beside the king of the Magyars. Then the coachman whipped up his horses, and they set out for Buda.

The king talked very pleasantly for a few miles, and when he thought that his new companion was quite at ease with him, he asked him what was the secret which had brought him into such trouble. "That I cannot tell you," answered the youth, "until it comes true."

"You will tell my daughter," said the king, smiling.

"I will tell nobody," replied the youth, and as he spoke the sword clanked loudly. The king said no more, but trusted to his daughter's beauty to get the secret from him.

The journey to Buda was long, and it was several days before they arrived there. The beautiful princess happened to be picking roses in the garden, when her father's coach drove up.

"Oh, what a handsome youth! Have you brought him from fairyland?" cried she, when they all stood upon the marble steps in front of the castle.

"I have brought him from the gallows," answered the king; rather vexed at his daughter's words, as never before had she consented to speak to any man.

"I don't care where you brought him from," said the spoilt girl. "I will marry him and nobody else, and we will live together till we die."

"You will tell another tale," replied the king, "when you ask him his secret. After all he is no better than a servant."

"That is nothing to me," said the princess, "for I love him. He will tell his secret to me, and will find a place in the middle of my heart."

But the king shook his head, and gave orders that the lad was to be lodged in the summer-house.

One day, about a week later, the princess put on her finest dress, and went to pay him a visit. She looked so beautiful that, at the sight of her, the book dropped from his hand, and he stood up speechless. "Tell me," she said, coaxingly, "what is this wonderful secret? Just whisper it in my ear, and I will give you a kiss."

"My angel," he answered, "be wise, and ask no questions, if you wish to get safely back to your father's palace; I have kept my secret all these years, and do not mean to tell it now."

However, the girl would not listen, and went on pressing him, till at last he slapped her face so hard that her nose bled. She shrieked with pain and rage, and ran screaming back to the palace, where her father was waiting to hear if she had succeeded. "I will starve you to death, you son of a dragon," cried he, when he saw her dress streaming with blood; and he ordered all the masons and bricklayers in the town to come before him.

"Build me a tower as fast as you can," he said, "and see that there is room for a stool and a small table, and for nothing else. The men set to work, and in two hours the tower was built, and they proceeded to the palace to inform the king that his commands were fulfilled. On the way they met the princess, who began to talk to one of the masons, and when the rest were out of hearing she asked if he could manage to make a hole in the tower, which nobody could see, large enough for a bottle of wine and some food to pass through.

"To be sure I can," said the mason, turning back, and in a few minutes the hole was bored.

At sunset a large crowd assembled to watch the youth being led to the tower, and after his misdeeds had been proclaimed he was solemnly walled up. But every morning the princess passed him in food through the hole, and every third day the king sent his secretary to climb up a ladder and look down through a little window to see if he was dead. But the secretary always brought back the report that he was fat and rosy.

"There is some magic about this," said the king.

This state of affairs lasted some time, till one day a messenger arrived from the Sultan bearing a letter for the king, and also three canes. "My master bids me say," said the messenger, bowing low, "that if you cannot tell him which of these three canes grows nearest the root, which in the middle, and which at the top, he will declare war against you."

The king was very much frightened when he heard this, and though he took the canes and examined them closely, he could see no difference between them. He looked so sad that his daughter noticed it, and inquired the reason.

"Alas! my daughter," he answered, "how can I help being sad? The Sultan has sent me three canes, and says that if I cannot tell him which of them grows near the root, which in the middle, and which at the top, he will make war upon me. And you know that his army is far greater than mine."

"Oh, do not despair, my father," said she. "We shall be sure to find out the answer"; and she ran away to the tower, and told the young man what had occurred.

"Go to bed as usual," replied he, "and when you wake, tell your father that you have dreamed that the canes must be placed in warm water. After a little while one will sink to the bottom; that is the one that grows nearest the root. The one which neither sinks nor comes to the surface is the cane that is cut from the middle; and the one that floats is from the top."

So, the next morning, the princess told her father of her dream, and by her advice he cut notches in each of the canes when he took them out of the water, so that he might make no mistake when he handed them back to the messenger. The Sultan could not imagine how he had found out, but he did not declare war.

The following year the Sultan again wanted to pick a quarrel with the king of the Magyars, so he sent another messenger to him with three foals, begging him to say which of the animals was born in the morn-

ing, which at noon, and which in the evening. If an answer was not ready in three days, war would be declared at once. The king's heart sank when he read the letter. He could not expect his daughter to be lucky enough to dream rightly a second time, and as a plague had been raging through the country, and had carried off many of his soldiers, his army was even weaker than before. At this thought his face became so gloomy that his daughter noticed it, and inquired what was the matter.

"I have had another letter from the Sultan," replied the king, "and he says that if I cannot tell him which of three foals was born in the morning, which at noon, and which in the evening, he will declare war at once."

"Oh, don't be cast down," said she, "something is sure to happen"; and she ran down to the tower to consult the youth.

"Go home, idol of my heart, and when night comes, pretend to scream out in your sleep, so that your father hears you. Then tell him that you have dreamt that he was just being carried off by the Turks because he could not answer the question about the foals, when the lad whom he had shut up in the tower ran up and told them which was foaled in the morning, which at noon, and which in the evening."

So the princess did exactly as the youth had bidden her; and no sooner had she spoken than the king ordered the tower to be pulled down, and the prisoner brought before him.

"I did not think that you could have lived so long without food," said he, "and as you have had plenty of time to repent your wicked conduct, I will grant you pardon, on condition that you help me in a sore strait. Read this letter from the Sultan; you will see that if I fail to answer his question about the foals, a dreadful war will be the result."

The youth took the letter and read it through. "Yes, I can help you," replied he; "but first you must bring me three troughs, all exactly alike. Into one you must put oats, into another wheat, and into the third barley. The foal which eats the oats is that which was foaled in the morning; the foal which eats the wheat is that which was foaled at noon; and the foal which eats the barley is that which was foaled at night." The king followed the youth's directions, and, marking the foals, sent them back to Turkey, and there was no war that year.

Now the Sultan was very angry that both his plots to get possession of Hungary had been such total failures, and he sent for his aunt, who was a witch, to consult her as to what he should do next.

"It is not the king who has answered your questions," observed the aunt, when he had told his story. "He is far too stupid ever to have done that! The person who has found out the puzzle is the son of a poor woman, who, if he lives, will become King of Hungary. Therefore, if you want the crown yourself, you must get him here and kill him."

After this conversation another letter was written to the Court of Hungary, saying that if the youth, now in the palace, was not sent to Turkey within three days, a large army would cross the border. The king's heart was sorrowful as he read, for he was grateful to the lad for what he had done to help him; but the boy only laughed, and bade the king fear nothing, but to search the town instantly for two youths just like each other, and he would paint himself a mask that was just like them. And the sword at his side clanked loudly.

After a long search twin brothers were found, so exactly resembling each other that even their own mother could not tell the difference. The youth painted a mask that was the precise copy of them, and when he had put it on, no one would have known one boy from the other. They set out at once for the Sultan's palace, and when they reached it, they were taken straight into his presence. He made a sign for them to come near; they all bowed low in greeting. He asked them about their journey; they answered his questions all together, and in the same words. If one sat down to supper, the others sat down at the same instant. When one got up, the others got up too, as if there had been only one body between them. The Sultan could not detect any difference between them, and he told his aunt that he would not be so cruel as to kill all three.

"Well, you will see a difference to-morrow," replied the witch, "for one will have a cut on his sleeve. That is the youth you must kill." And one hour before midnight, when witches are invisible, she glided into the room where all three lads were sleeping in the same bed. She took out a pair of scissors and cut a small piece out of the boy's coat-sleeve which was hanging on the wall, and then crept silently from the room. But in the morning the youth saw the slit, and he marked the sleeves of his two companions in the same way, and all three went down to breakfast with the Sultan. The old witch was standing in the window and pretended not to see them; but all witches have eyes in the backs of their heads, and she knew at once that not one sleeve but three were cut, and they were all as alike as before. After breakfast, the Sultan, who was getting tired of the whole affair and wanted to be alone to invent some other plan, told them they might return home. So, bowing low with one accord, they went.

The princess welcomed the boy back joyfully, but the poor youth was not allowed to rest long in peace, for one day a fresh letter arrived from the Sultan, saying that he had discovered that the young man was a very dangerous person, and that he must be sent to Turkey at once, and alone. The girl burst into tears when the boy told her what was in the letter which her father had bade her to carry to him. "Do not weep, love of my heart," said the boy, "all will be well. I will start at sunrise to-morrow."

So next morning at sunrise the youth set forth, and in a few days he reached the Sultan's palace. The old witch was waiting for him at the gate, and whispered as he passed: "This is the last time you will ever enter it." But the sword clanked, and the lad did not even look at her. As he crossed the threshold fifteen armed Turks barred his way, with the Sultan at their head. Instantly the sword darted forth and cut off the heads of everyone but the Sultan, and then went quietly back to its scabbard. The witch, who was looking on, saw that as long as the youth had possession of the sword, all her schemes would be in vain, and tried to steal the sword in the night, but it only jumped out of its scabbard and sliced off her nose, which was of iron. And in the morning, when the Sultan brought a great army to capture the lad and deprive him of his sword, they were all cut to pieces, while he remained without a scratch.

Meanwhile the princess was in despair because the days slipped by, and the young man did not return, and she never rested until her father let her lead some troops against the Sultan. She rode proudly before them, dressed in uniform; but they had not left the town more than a mile behind them, when they met the lad and his little sword. When he told them what he had done they shouted for joy, and carried him back in triumph to the palace; and the king declared that as the youth had shown himself worthy to become his son-in-law, he should marry the princess and succeed to the throne at once, as he himself was getting old, and the cares of government were too much for him. But the young man said he must first go and see his mother, and the king sent him in state, with a troop of soldiers as his bodyguard.

The old woman was quite frightened at seeing such an array draw up before her little house, and still more surprised when a handsome young man, whom she did not know, dismounted and kissed her hand, saying: "Now, dear mother, you shall hear my secret at last! I dreamed that I should become King of Hungary, and my dream has come true. When I was a child, and you begged me to tell you, I had to keep silence, or the Magyar king would have killed me. And if you had not beaten me nothing would have happened that has happened, and I should not now be King of Hungary."

Czechoslovakia

 The folk tales of Czechoslovakia, like those of many other countries of central Europe, reflect both the lore of its several indigenous Slavic peoples and the acculturation engendered by either invaders or dominant neighbors. There are few collections of Czech stories, although many appear in folk tale anthologies with broad geographical representation. The retellings in Virginia Haviland's *Favorite Folk Tales Told in Czechoslovakia* are bland, suitable for younger readers; the two tales included here are from Parker Fillmore's *The Shepherd's Nosegay: Stories from Finland and Czechoslovakia;* and are crisp and polished, showing both the humor and the minatory purpose found in many Czech tales.

Budulinek

In a cautionary tale, a small boy learns to obey his elders and never open the door to strangers.

There was once a little boy named Budulinek. He lived with his old Granny in a cottage near a forest.

Granny went out to work every day. In the morning when she went away she always said:

"There, Budulinek, there's your dinner on the table and mind, you mustn't open the door no matter who knocks!"

One morning Granny said:

"Now, Budulinek, today I'm leaving you some soup for your dinner. Eat it when dinner time comes. And remember what I always say: don't open the door no matter who knocks."

She went away and pretty soon Lishka, the sly old mother fox, came and knocked on the door.

"Budulinek!" she called. "You know me! Open the door! Please!"

Budulinek called back:

"No, I mustn't open the door."

But Lishka, the sly old mother fox, kept on knocking.

"Listen, Budulinek," she said: "if you open the door, do you know what I'll do? I'll give you a ride on my tail!"

Now Budulinek thought to himself:

"Oh, that would be fun to ride on the tail of Lishka, the fox!"

So Budulinek forgot all about what Granny said to him every day and opened the door.

Lishka, the sly old thing, came into the room and what do you think she did? Do you think she gave Budulinek a ride on her tail? Well, she didn't. She just went over to the table and gobbled up the bowl of soup that Granny had put there for Budulinek's dinner and then she ran away.

When dinner time came Budulinek hadn't anything to eat.

In the evening when Granny came home, she said:

"Budulinek, did you open the door and let anyone in?"

Budulinek was crying because he was so hungry, and he said:

"Yes, I let in Lishka, the old mother fox, and she ate up all my dinner, too!"

Granny said:

"Now, Budulinek, you see what happens when you open the door and let some one in. Another time remember what Granny says and don't open the door."

The next morning Granny cooked some porridge for Budulinek's dinner and said:

"Now, Budulinek, here's some porridge for your dinner. Remember, while I'm gone you must not open the door no matter who knocks."

Granny was no sooner out of sight than Lishka came again and knocked on the door.

"Oh, Budulinek!" she called. "Open the door and let me in!"

But Budulinek said:

"No, I won't open the door!"

"Oh, now, Budulinek, please open the door!" Lishka begged. "You know me! Do you know what I'll do if you open the door? I'll give you a ride on my tail! Truly I will!"

Budulinek thought to himself:

"This time maybe she will give me a ride on her tail."

So he opened the door.

Lishka came into the room, gobbled up Budulinek's porridge, and ran away without giving him any ride at all.

When dinner time came Budulinek hadn't anything to eat.

In the evening when Granny came home she said:

"Budulinek, did you open the door and let anyone in?"

Budulinek was crying again because he was so hungry, and he said:

"Yes, I let in Lishka, the old mother fox, and she ate up all my porridge, too!"

"Budulinek, you're a bad boy!" Granny said. "If you open the door again, I'll have to spank you! Do you hear?"

The next morning before she went to work, Granny cooked some peas for Budulinek's dinner.

As soon as Granny was gone he began eating the peas, they were so good.

Presently Lishka, the fox, came and knocked on the door.

"Budulinek!" she called. "Open the door! I want to come in!"

But Budulinek wouldn't open the door. He took his bowl of peas and went to the window and ate them there where Lishka could see him.

"Oh, Budulinek!" Lishka begged. "You know me! Please open the door! This time I promise you I'll give you a ride on my tail! Truly I will!"

"Budulinek" from THE SHEPHERD'S NOSEGAY by Parker Fillmore, edited by Katherine Love. Copyright 1920 by Parker Fillmore; renewed 1948 by Louise Fillmore. Reprinted by permission of Harcourt Brace Jovanovich, Inc.

She just begged and begged until at last Budulinek opened the door. Then Lishka jumped into the room and do you know what she did? She put her nose right into the bowl of peas and gobbled them all up!

Then she said to Budulinek:

"Now get on my tail and I'll give you a ride!"

So Budulinek climbed on Lishka's tail and Lishka went running around the room faster and faster until Budulinek was dizzy and just had to hold on with all his might.

Then, before Budulinek knew what was happening, Lishka slipped out of the house and ran off swiftly into the forest, home to her hole, with Budulinek still on her tail! She hid Budulinek down in her hole with her own three children and she wouldn't let him out. He had to stay there with the three little foxes and they all teased him and bit him. And then wasn't he sorry he had disobeyed his Granny! And, oh, how he cried!

When Granny came home she found the door open and no little Budulinek anywhere. She looked high and low, but no, there was no little Budulinek. She asked everyone she met had they seen her little Budulinek, but nobody had. So poor Granny just cried and cried, she was so lonely and sad.

One day an organ-grinder with a wooden leg began playing in front of Granny's cottage. The music made her think of Budulinek.

"Organ-grinder," Granny said, "here's a penny for you. But, please, don't play any more. Your music makes me cry."

"Why does it make you cry?" the organ-grinder asked.

"Because it reminds me of Budulinek," Granny said, and she told the organ-grinder all about Budulinek and how somebody had stolen him away.

The organ-grinder said:

"Poor Granny! I tell you what I'll do: as I go around and play my organ I'll keep my eyes open for Budulinek. If I find him I'll bring him back to you."

"Will you?" Granny cried. "If you bring me back my little Budulinek I'll give you a measure of rye and a measure of millet and a measure of poppy seed and a measure of everything in the house!"

So the organ-grinder went off and everywhere he played his organ he looked for Budulinek. But he couldn't find him.

At last one day while he was walking through the forest he thought he heard a little boy crying. He looked around everywhere until he found a fox's hole.

"Oho!" he said to himself. "I believe that wicked old Lishka must have stolen Budulinek! She's probably keeping him here with her own three children! I'll soon find out."

So he put down his organ and began to play. And as he played he sang softly:

"One old fox
And two, three, four,
And Budulinek
He makes one more!"

Old Lishka heard the music playing and she said to her oldest child:

"Here, son, give the old man a penny and tell him to go away because my head aches."

So the oldest little fox climbed out of the hole and gave the organ-grinder a penny and said:

"My mother says, please will you go away because her head aches."

As the organ-grinder reached over to take the penny, he caught the oldest little fox and stuffed him into a sack. Then he went on playing and singing:

"One old fox
And two and three
And Budulinek
Makes four for me!"

Presently Lishka sent out her second child with a penny and the organ-grinder caught the second little fox in the same way and stuffed it also into the sack. Then he went on grinding his organ and softly singing:

"One old fox
And another for me,
And Budulinek
He makes the three."

"I wonder why that old man still plays his organ," Lishka said and sent out her third child with a penny.

So the organ-grinder caught the third little fox and stuffed it also into the sack. Then he kept on playing and singing softly:

"One old fox—
I'll soon get you!—
And Budulinek
He makes just two."

At last Lishka herself came out. So he caught her, too, and stuffed her in with her children. Then he sang:

"Four naughty foxes
Caught alive!
And Budulinek
He makes the five!"

The organ-grinder went to the hole and called down:

"Budulinek! Budulinek! Come out!"

As there were no foxes left to hold him back, Budulinek was able to crawl out.

When he saw the organ-grinder he cried and said:

"Oh, please, Mr. Organ-Grinder, I want to go home to my Granny!"

"I'll take you home to your Granny," the organ-grinder said, "but first I must punish these naughty foxes."

The organ-grinder cut a strong switch and gave the four foxes in the sack a terrible beating until they begged him to stop and promised that they would never again do anything to Budulinek.

Then the organ-grinder let them go and he took Budulinek home to Granny.

Granny was delighted to see her little Budulinek and she gave the organ-grinder a measure of rye and a measure of millet and a measure of poppy seed and a measure of everything else in the house.

And Budulinek never again opened the door!

Clever Manka

A farmer's wife is bested by a shepherd's daughter when the burgomaster poses a set of riddles to decide a court case. The burgomaster is so impressed that he marries clever Manka.

There was once a rich farmer who was as grasping and unscrupulous as he was rich. He was always driving a hard bargain and always getting the better of his poor neighbors. One of these neighbors was a humble shepherd who in return for service was to receive from the farmer a heifer. When the time of payment came the farmer refused to give the shepherd the heifer and the shepherd was forced to lay the matter before the burgomaster.

The burgomaster, who was a young man and as yet not very experienced, listened to both sides and when he had deliberated he said:

"Instead of deciding this case, I will put a riddle to you both and the man who makes the best answer shall have the heifer. Are you agreed?"

The farmer and the shepherd accepted this proposal and the burgomaster said:

"Well then, here is my riddle: What is the swiftest thing in the world? What is the sweetest thing? What is the richest? Think out your answers and bring them to me at this same hour tomorrow."

The farmer went home in a temper.

"What kind of a burgomaster is this young fellow!" he growled. "If he had let me keep the heifer I'd have sent him a bushel of pears. But now I'm in a fair way of losing the heifer for I can't think of any answer to his foolish riddle."

"What is the matter, husband?" his wife asked.

"It's that new burgomaster. The old one would have given me the heifer without any argument, but this young man thinks to decide the case by asking us riddles."

When he told his wife what the riddle was, she cheered him greatly by telling him that she knew the answers at once.

"Why, husband," said she, "our gray mare must be the swiftest thing in the world. You know yourself nothing ever passes us on the road. As for the sweetest, did you ever taste

"Clever Manka" from THE SHEPHERD'S NOSEGAY by Parker Fillmore, edited by Katherine Love. Copyright 1920 by Parker Fillmore; renewed 1948 by Louise Fillmore. Reprinted by permission of Harcourt Brace Jovanovich, Inc.

honey any sweeter than ours? And I'm sure there's nothing richer than our chest of golden ducats that we've been laying by these forty years."

The farmer was delighted.

"You're right, wife, you're right! That heifer remains ours!"

The shepherd when he got home was downcast and sad. He had a daughter, a clever girl named Manka, who met him at the door of his cottage and asked:

"What is it, father? What did the burgomaster say?"

The shepherd sighed.

"I'm afraid I've lost the heifer. The burgomaster set us a riddle and I know I shall never guess it."

"Perhaps I can help you," Manka said. "What is it?"

So the shepherd gave her the riddle and the next day as he was setting out for the burgomaster's, Manka told him what answers to make.

When he reached the burgomaster's house, the farmer was already there rubbing his hands and beaming with self-importance.

The burgomaster again propounded the riddle and then asked the farmer his answers.

The farmer cleared his throat and with a pompous air began:

"The swiftest thing in the world? Why, my dear sir, that's my gray mare, of course, for no other horse ever passes us on the road. The sweetest? Honey from my beehives, to be sure. The richest? What can be richer than my chest of golden ducats!"

And the farmer squared his shoulders and smiled triumphantly.

"H'm," said the young burgomaster, dryly. Then he asked:

"What answers does the shepherd make?"

The shepherd bowed politely and said:

"The swiftest thing in the world is thought for thought can run any distance in the twinkling of an eye. The sweetest thing of all is sleep for when a man is tired and sad what can be sweeter? The richest thing is the earth for out of the earth come all the riches of the world."

"Good!" the burgomaster cried. "Good! The heifer goes to the shepherd!"

Later the burgomaster said to the shepherd:

"Tell me, now, who gave you those answers? I'm sure they never came out of your own head."

At first the shepherd tried not to tell, but when the burgomaster pressed him he confessed that they came from his daughter, Manka. The burgomaster, who thought that he would like to make another test of Manka's cleverness, sent for ten eggs. He gave them to the shepherd and said:

"Take these eggs to Manka and tell her to have them hatched out by tomorrow and to bring me the chicks."

When the shepherd reached home and gave Manka the burgomaster's message, Manka laughed and said: "Take a handful of millet and go right back to the burgomaster. Say to him: 'My daughter sends you this millet. She says that if you plant, grow it, and have it harvested by tomorrow, she'll bring you the ten chicks and you can feed them the ripe grain.'"

When the burgomaster heard this, he laughed heartily.

"That's a clever girl of yours," he told the shepherd. "If she's as comely as she is clever, I think I'd like to marry her. Tell her to come to see me, but she must come neither by day nor by night, neither riding nor walking, neither dressed nor undressed."

When Manka received this message she waited until the next dawn when night was gone and day not yet arrived. Then she wrapped herself in a fishnet and, throwing one leg over a goat's back and keeping one foot on the ground, she went to the burgomaster's house.

Now I ask you: did she go dressed? No, she wasn't dressed. A fishnet isn't clothing. Did she go undressed? Of course not, for wasn't she covered with a fishnet? Did she walk to the burgomaster's? No, she didn't walk for she went with one leg thrown over a goat. Then did she ride? Of course she didn't ride for wasn't she walking on one foot?

When she reached the burgomaster's house she called out:

"Here I am, Mr. Burgomaster, and I've come neither by day nor by night, neither riding nor walking, neither dressed nor undressed."

The young burgomaster was so delighted with Manka's cleverness and so pleased with her comely looks that he proposed to her at once and in a short time married her.

"But understand, my dear Manka," he said, "you are not to use that cleverness of yours at my expense. I won't have you interfering in any of my cases. In fact if ever you give advice to any one who comes to me for judgment, I'll turn you out of my house at once and send you home to your father."

All went well for a time. Manka busied herself in her house-keeping and was careful not to interfere in any of the burgomaster's cases.

Then one day two farmers came to the burgomaster to have a dispute settled. One of the farmers owned a mare which had foaled in the marketplace. The colt had run under the wagon of the other farmer and thereupon the owner of the wagon claimed the colt as his property.

The burgomaster, who was thinking of something else while the case was being presented, said carelessly:

"The man who found the colt under his wagon is, of course, the owner of the colt."

As the owner of the mare was leaving the burgomaster's house, he met Manka and stopped to tell her about the case. Manka was ashamed of her husband for making so foolish a decision and she said to the farmer:

"Come back this afternoon with a fishing net and stretch it across the dusty road. When the burgomaster sees you he will come out and ask you what you are doing. Say to him that you're catching fish. When he asks you how you can expect to catch fish in a dusty road, tell him it's just as easy for you to catch fish in a dusty road as it is for a wagon to foal. Then he'll see the injustice of his decision and have the colt returned to you. But remember one thing: you mustn't let him find out that it was I who told you to do this."

That afternoon when the burgomaster chanced to look out the window he saw a man stretching a fishnet across the dusty road. He went out to him and asked: "What are you doing?"

"Fishing."

"Fishing in a dusty road? Are you daft?"

"Well," the man said, "it's just as easy for me to catch fish in a dusty road as it is for a wagon to foal."

Then the burgomaster recognized the man as the owner of the mare and he had to confess that what he said was true.

"Of course the colt belongs to your mare and must be returned to you. But tell me," he said, "who put you up to this? You didn't think of it yourself."

The farmer tried not to tell but the burgomaster questioned him until he found out that Manka was at the bottom of it. This made him very angry. He went into the house and called his wife.

"Manka," he said, "do you forget what I told you would happen if you went interfering in any of my cases? Home you go this very day. I don't care to hear any excuses. The matter is settled. You may take with you the one thing you like best in my house for I won't have people saying that I treated you shabbily."

Manka made no outcry.

"Very well, my dear husband, I shall do as you say: I shall go to my father's cottage and take with me the one thing I like best in your house. But don't make me go until after supper. We have been very happy together and I should like to eat one last meal with you. Let us have no more words but be kind to each other as we've always been and then part as friends."

The burgomaster agreed to this and Manka prepared a fine supper of all the dishes of which her husband was particularly fond. The burgomaster opened his choicest wine and pledged Manka's health. Then he set to, and the supper was so good that he ate and ate and ate. And the more he ate, the more he drank until at last he grew drowsy and fell sound asleep in his chair. Then without awakening him Manka had him carried out to the wagon that was waiting to take her home to her father.

The next morning when the burgomaster opened his eyes, he found himself lying in the shepherd's cottage.

"What does this mean?" he roared out.

"Nothing, dear husband, nothing!" Manka said. "You know you told me I might take with me the one thing I liked best in your house, so of course I took you! That's all."

For a moment the burgomaster rubbed his eyes in amazement. Then he laughed loud and heartily to think how Manka had outwitted him.

"Manka," he said, "you're too clever for me. Come on, my dear, let's go home."

So they climbed back into the wagon and drove home.

The burgomaster never again scolded his wife but thereafter whenever a very difficult case came up he always said:

"I think we had better consult my wife. You know she's a very clever woman."

Union of Soviet Socialist Republics

 Few countries have the quantity, diversity, and richness in their folk literature that can be found in the Soviet Union; while some of this range is due to the fact that so many bodies of national literature are included, all of these attributes can be found in Russian folklore alone. Most of the English language collections or single tales are based directly or indirectly on the work of the great collector Alexander Afanasiev, and the complete Afanasiev collection has been published by Pantheon. Some of the tales are too complex for younger children, some a bit grim; a small but choice selection is Arthur Ransome's *Old Peter's Russian Tales.* Of the many single-tale books, none are more striking than those retold by Alexander Pushkin and illustrated by I. Bilibin. Some of the richness, drama, and humor of this vast body of literature is shown in the tales included here.

The Foolish Man
(Armenia)

In this Armenian tale, the foolish man takes no advantage of the answers God has given to his questions, and comes to a very bad end.

Once there was and was not in ancient Armenia a poor man who worked and toiled hard from morn till night, but nevertheless remained poor.

Finally one day he became so discouraged that he decided to go in search of God in order to ask Him how long he must endure such poverty—and to beg of Him a favor.

On his way, the man met a wolf.

"Good day, brother man," asked the wolf. "Where are you bound in such a hurry?"

"I go in search of God," replied the man. "I have a complaint to lodge with Him."

"Well," said the wolf, "would you do me a kindness? When you find God, will you complain to Him for me, too? Tell Him you met a half-starved wolf who searches the woods and fields for food from morning till night—

and though he works hard and long, still finds nothing to eat. Ask God why He does not provide for wolves since He created them?"

"I will tell Him of your complaint," agreed the poor man, and continued on his way.

As he hurried over the hills and through the valleys, he chanced to meet a beautiful maid.

"Where do you go in such a hurry, my brother?" asked the maid.

"I go in search of God," replied the man.

"Oh, kind friend, when you find God, would you ask Him something for me? Tell Him you met a maid on your way. Tell Him she is young and fair and very rich—but very unhappy. Ask God why she cannot know happiness. What will become of her? Ask God why He will not help her to be happy."

"I will tell Him of your trouble," promised the poor man, and continued on his way.

Soon he met a tree which seemed all dried up and dying even though it grew by the side of a river.

"Where do you go in such a hurry, O traveler?" called the dry tree.

"I go in search of God," answered the man. "I have a complaint to lodge with Him."

"Wait a moment, O traveler," begged the tree, "I, too, have a question for God.

"Please ask Him why I am dry both in summer and winter. Though I live by this wet river, my leaves do not turn green. Ask God how long I must suffer. Ask Him that for me, good friend," said the tree.

The man listened to the tree's complaint, promised to tell God, and continued once again upon his way.

Finally, the poor man reached the end of his journey. He found God seated beneath the ledge of a cliff.

"Good day," said the man as he approached God.

"Welcome, traveler," God returned his greeting. "Why have you journeyed so far? What is your trouble?"

"Well, I want to know why there is injustice in the world. Is it fair that I toil and labor from morn till night—and yet never seem to earn enough for a full stomach, while many who do not work half as hard as I live and eat

as rich men do?"

"Go then," replied God. "I present you the Gift of Luck. Go find it and enjoy it to the end of your days."

"I have yet another complaint, my Lord," continued the man—and he proceeded to list the complaints and requests of the starved wolf, the beautiful maid, and the parched tree.

God gave appropriate answers to each of the three complaints, whereupon the poor man thanked Him and started on his way homeward.

Soon he came upon the dry, parched tree.

"What message did God have for me?" asked the tree.

"He said that beneath your trunk there lies a pot of gold which prevents the water from seeping up your trunk to your leaves. God said your branches will never turn green until the pot of gold is removed."

"Well, what are you waiting for, foolish man!" exclaimed the tree. "Dig up that pot of gold. It will make you rich—and permit me to turn green and live again!"

"Oh, no," protested the man. "I have no time to dig up a pot of gold. God has given me the Gift of Luck. I must hurry and search for it." And he hurried on his way.

Presently, he met the beautiful maid who was waiting for him. "Oh, kind friend, what message did God have for me?"

"God said that you will soon meet a kind man who will prove to be a good life's companion to you. No longer will you be lonely. Happiness and contentment will come to you," reported the poor man.

"In that case, what are you waiting for, foolish man?" exclaimed the maid. "Why don't you stay here and be my life's companion."

"Oh, no! I have no time to stay with you. God has given me the Gift of Luck. I must hurry and search for it." And the man hurried on his way.

Some distance away, the starving wolf impatiently awaited the man's coming, and hailed him with a shout.

"Well, what did God say? What message did He send to me?"

"Brother wolf, so many things have happened since I saw you last," said the man. "I hardly know where to begin. On my way to seek God, I met a beautiful maid who begged me to ask God the reason for her unhappiness. And I met a parched tree who wanted God to explain the dryness of its branches even though it stood by a wet river.

"I told God about these matters. He bade me tell the maid to seek a life's companion in order to find happiness. He bade me warn the tree about a pot of gold buried near its trunk which must be removed before the branches can receive nourishment from the earth.

"On my return, I brought God's answers to the maid and to the tree. The maid asked me to stay and be her life's companion, while the tree asked me to dig up the pot of gold.

"Of course, I had to refuse both since God gave me the Gift of Luck—and I must hurry along to search for it!"

"Ah-h-h, brother man, and what was God's reply to me?" asked the starving wolf.

"As for you," replied the man, "God said that you would remain hungry until you met a silly and foolish man whom you could eat up. Only then, said God, would your hunger be satisfied."

"Hmmmmmmm," mused the wolf, "where in the world will I find a man more silly and stupid than you?"

And he ate up the foolish man.

The Clever Thieves
(Armenia)

A brisk, brief, and comic tale that reverses the usual pattern, for the thieves outwit the hapless farmer.

Once there was and was not in ancient Armenia a hard-working peasant who had hitched his two mules to the plow and was working his field.

"The Clever Thieves" from THREE APPLES FELL FROM HEAVEN: ARMENIAN TALES, retold by Virginia A. Tashjian. Copyright © 1971 by Virginia A. Tashjian. Reprinted by permission of Little, Brown and Company.

Two thieves chanced to pass by and decided to steal one of the poor man's mules. The first thief hid behind a large rock at the edge of the field near where the peasant was working. The second thief walked to the far end of the field. He began to wave his arms about and mutter, "I can't believe it . . . I can't believe it . . ."

Of course, the peasant noticed the peculiar actions of the stranger. He left his plow and walked the length of the field toward the thief.

In the meantime, unseen by the peasant, the first thief crept out from behind the rock, released one mule from the plow, and made off with it.

"Ho there, stranger," said the peasant, upon reaching the far end of his field. "Why do you wave your arms thus? And why do you mutter, 'I can't believe it . . . I can't believe it . . .' What is it you cannot believe?"

"I can't believe that any intelligent farmer would work his field with only one mule hitched to a plow," replied the thief.

The farmer turned around. He looked at his plow and at the one mule hitched to it.

"I can't believe it . . . I can't believe it . . ." muttered the astonished peasant, rubbing his eyes and waving his arms in amazement.

"Well," said the thief. "Now tell me. Why are *you* shouting 'I can't believe it . . . I can't believe it . . .' What can't *you* believe?"

"Oh-h-h," said the witless peasant hopelessly. "I can't believe that my two poor mules have shrunk to one."

Three apples fell from heaven: one for the teller, one for the listener, and one for all the peoples of the world.

Master and Man
(Armenia)

It's the hired hand who wins the wager here, besting his master and returning home with a small fortune.

Once upon a time there were two brothers who lived together. They were very poor.

The elder brother decided to mend matters.

"I am going to hire myself out as a farm hand," he said to the younger brother. "You stay here and take care of things at home. When I have earned my wages I will bring them back with me, and we shall live well."

And so it was arranged. The younger brother stayed behind to look after their little house. The elder went off and hired himself out to a rich farmer.

It was agreed between him and his master that he should work until the following spring, then he should receive his wages and would be free to leave. But the master set one condition.

"If one of us should lose his temper before spring comes," said the master, "he must pay a fine. If you get angry, you pay me a thousand silver coins. If I get angry, I pay you a thousand."

"Where would a poor fellow like me get so much money?" asked the elder brother.

"Don't worry about that. You can earn it by working for me ten more years."

At first the elder brother wanted to refuse. But then he thought it over and decided to accept the condition. "No matter what happens," he said to himself, "I shall keep my temper. And if the master gets angry, why, then he will have to pay me a thousand silver coins. That is a fine sum! What couldn't my brother and I do with a thousand silver coins!" So he agreed, and the two shook hands on it.

Early next morning the rich farmer sent his new hired man out into the field.

"Go out with your scythe," he said, "and work as long as it is light."

The field hand worked hard the whole day. He was heartily glad when dusk fell and he could return to the farmhouse to rest. But when he got there the farmer asked him:

"Why have you come back?"

"And why not?" asked the field hand. "You told me to work as long as it was light. But now the sun has set."

"Oh, no, this won't do at all," said the farmer. "I did indeed tell you to work as long as there was light. But if the sun has set, his

sister, the moon, has risen. You must work by moonlight."

"Am I to have no rest at all?" asked the field hand, astonished.

"Are you getting angry?" the farmer wanted to know.

"Not at all," said the field hand quickly. "But I am very tired."

He was hardly able to move, but he remembered the agreement, and he went back to the field. He worked all night, until the moon set. But the moon had no sooner left the sky than the sun rose. The man could bear it no longer. He dropped to the ground, worn out.

"A curse on your field, your crops, and your money!" he gasped.

The words were barely out of his mouth when the farmer appeared, as if by magic.

"I see you have lost your temper," he said. "You remember our agreement. Either you pay me a thousand silver coins or you work for me ten more years."

The field hand did not know what to do. He had no money with which to pay the fine. But how could he undertake to work ten years for such a slave driver? At last he told the farmer that he would pay him the money as soon as he had earned it elsewhere. It was hard to make the farmer agree to this. But at last he let the poor man go to earn the sum by working in another place.

Tired, discouraged, empty-handed, the poor man returned home.

"How did you make out?" asked the younger brother.

The elder told him the whole story.

"What's to be done?" he asked, when he had finished. "Where shall I earn a thousand silver coins? And if I don't give the farmer the money soon, he will have me punished for not paying my debt."

"Don't take it to heart," said the younger brother. "You stay here and look after the house. I will go and hire myself out. I am

"Master and Man" from MORE TALES OF FARAWAY FOLK, chosen and retold by Babette Deutsch and Avrahm Yarmolinsky. Copyright © 1963 by Babette Deutsch and Avrahm Yarmolinsky. By permission of Harper & Row, Publishers, Inc.

young and strong. I can soon earn a good sum."

So the younger brother went off and hired himself out to the same rich farmer. The farmer wanted to set the same condition. If he lost his temper, he would pay the field hand a thousand silver coins and release him. If the field hand lost his temper, he would pay the farmer a thousand silver coins or work for ten years without wages.

"No," said the younger brother. "The sum is not large enough. If you get angry, you pay me two thousand silver coins. And the same holds for me, or I'll work twenty years without wages."

"That suits me capitally," said the rich, greedy farmer.

And so the younger brother entered his service.

When the sun rose early the next morning the young field hand was still asleep.

"Get up!" cried the farmer, prodding him. "It will be midday before you know it, and here you are still lying abed!"

"What's the matter?" asked the field hand, rubbing his eyes. "Are you angry at me?"

"Not at all," said the farmer hastily. "I only wanted to tell you that it's time to go out into the field and get in the crop."

"All right," drawled the field hand, yawning, and he got up, ever so slowly, and slowly began to draw on his clothes.

"Hurry, man, hurry! It's late!" cried the farmer.

"You're not angry, are you?" asked the field hand.

"No, no, I just want to remind you of the hour," said the farmer.

"That's all right, then. Only be sure to remember our agreement," said the field hand.

He dawdled so that it was nearly noon before he was ready to go out to the field.

"Is it worthwhile starting work now?" he asked the farmer. "You see, people are eating dinner at this hour. Let's sit down and have our dinner properly, too."

The farmer bit his lip with vexation, but he agreed, and they made a good meal. After dinner, as they were setting out for the field,

the hired man turned to the farmer with a yawn.

"We are working people," he said. "It is only right that we should take a nap after dinner. Then we'll have more strength with which to work."

With that he lay down under a shady tree, fell asleep, and slept till evening.

"This is too much!" cried the farmer. He strode over to the field hand and shook him by the arm. "In heaven's name, wake up! Here it is already dusk and not a stroke of work have you done!"

"You're really angry with me, eh?" said the field hand sleepily.

"No, no. I'm not at all angry," replied the farmer, remembering his agreement. "I just wanted to tell you that it's getting dark and it's time to go home."

"Very well," said the field hand pleasantly, and returned to the house with his master.

When they reached the farmhouse, the farmer found a guest waiting for him. So he sent the hired man out to butcher a sheep, that he might prepare a feast for his guest.

"Which sheep shall I butcher?" asked the hired man.

"Any that comes your way," answered the farmer hastily. He was happy to think that he was getting some work out of the man at last.

The hired man went off, and the farmer sat down with his guest for a good talk. Time passed, and the hired man did not return. The farmer began to grow uneasy. Suddenly he heard a clamor in the yard. It was crowded with neighbors; they were making a great to-do.

"Your hired man has lost his mind!" they cried. "He is butchering one sheep after another!"

The farmer rushed out to the sheep pen and saw that in truth the hired man had slaughtered the whole flock.

"What have you done, you good-for-nothing?" shouted the farmer. "Devil take you!"

"I only did what you ordered," answered the hired man quietly. "You told me to butcher any sheep that came my way. But you see, when one sheep came my way, all the rest followed. So I had to butcher them all. It's a pity, because now you are really angry."

"No, no!" insisted the farmer. "I'm not angry. I'm only sorry to see that you've done away with the whole flock."

"Oh, if you are not angry, I'll keep my part of the bargain and go on working for you until spring," said the hired man.

The farmer did not know whether to be glad or sorry about this. Indeed, during the next few months the hired man nearly drove him to despair. It was understood that they were to part in the spring as soon as they heard the first call of the cuckoo. But spring was still far off and the call of the cuckoo would not be heard for a long time. Finally the farmer thought up a scheme that would rid him of his unwanted helper.

He took his wife to the woods, had her climb a tree, and told her that as soon as she saw him again she should give the call of the cuckoo. Then he went home and told the hired man to fetch his gun: they were going hunting.

No sooner had they entered the woods than the farmer's wife saw them coming and began to call:

"Cuckoo, cuckoo, cuckoo!"

"Congratulations!" said the farmer. "The cuckoo is calling. That means your time is up."

But the hired man protested.

"Impossible!" he said. "A cuckoo calling in winter! I must fetch that bird down with a shot and see what sort it is."

He raised his rifle and took aim at the top of the tree where the farmer's wife was perched.

"Stop!" cried the farmer.

"I must shoot," insisted the man.

"Devil take you!" cried the farmer. "Will you never do what I want!"

"Ah, now you've lost your temper for fair," said the hired man.

"Temper or no temper, be off with you!" shouted the farmer.

"Gladly," answered the hired man. "But first you must give me the two thousand sil-ver coins you promised me if you got angry before my time was up."

"Take your two thousand and get out," said the farmer. "Now I understand the saying: 'Don't dig a pit for another, lest you fall into it yourself.'"

So the younger brother got the two thousand silver coins and took them home. What cheer there was then in the little house! The elder brother was able to pay his debt to the greedy farmer, and the brothers still had a thousand silver coins on which to live happily for many a long day.

The Old Traveler
(Estonia)

In a familiar pattern, one person is rewarded for kindness, and another tries unsuccessfully to win a similar reward.

Once upon a time, a poor old traveler was walking along the road. It was dusk, and night was fast approaching. The old man decided to seek shelter, as the darkness was kept company by a bone-chilling cold. He came upon a large house and knocked at the window.

The woman of the house, who happened to be very rich, came out. "Why do you rap upon my window, you dirty old tramp?" she exclaimed.

"Please, could you give me shelter for the night, good lady?" he asked quietly.

She began to scold and shout at him. "I'll let the dogs loose on you! Then you'll think twice about asking to stay the night! Get away from here!"

The old man walked wearily on into the darkening night. The wind was beginning to rise and a few flakes of snow touched his face. Soon he came to another house. This one was small and squat, but from inside came happy shouts, and the windows gave off a cheerful glow. Perhaps I might stay the night here, he thought, knocking at the door.

A woman opened it.

"Please, could you give me shelter for the night, good lady?" the old man asked.

"Come in, come in," the woman replied in friendly tones. "You are welcome here, though it's noisy and there is not much room."

The stranger entered and found himself in the midst of many children, all playing happily although their clothing was tattered and worn.

"Your children's clothing is in bad condition," said the traveler. "Why don't you make them new shirts?"

"Ah, but I cannot," the woman replied. "My husband has gone to his rest, and I must bring up my children alone. We have barely enough money for bread, to say nothing of clothing."

Soon the woman laid out supper on the table and invited the stranger to join in the meal, such as it was. But the old traveler refused. "No, thank you," he said, "I ate but a short while ago." Then, untying his sack, he took out all the food he possessed and treated the children to it.

Afterward he lay down and at once fell asleep. In the morning the old man arose, thanked the mistress of the house for her hospitality, and said in parting, "That which you do in the morning, you will do until evening."

The woman did not understand his words and soon forgot them. She saw him to the gate and then returned to the house. If even that poor old man says my children are ragamuffins, what do all the other folk say? she thought. I will make at least one shirt out of the last piece of cloth I have left in the house.

She went to the house of her neighbor, the rich woman, to borrow a yardstick to see if even that piece would be enough. Then she returned to her house and began measuring. As she measured, the cloth seemed to get longer and longer. The more she measured, the more there was. There seemed no end to it.

She spent the whole day measuring, and in the evening she found that there was enough cloth to make clothes for her family for the rest of their lives. At last she realized what the old traveler had meant by his parting words.

That night, when she returned the yardstick to her neighbor, she told her the whole story. The rich woman was beside herself with fury. What a fool I was, she thought. I could have fulfilled my every desire!

Calling a servant, she ordered him to harness a horse. "Quickly, ride after that old tramp and bring him back here! The poor man should be helped; I have always said so!"

The servant caught up with the traveler on the following day, but the old man refused to go back. The servant became very upset. "If I don't bring you back," said he, "my mistress will drive me away without my wages!"

"Then don't fret, my lad," the old man said. "I will return with you." And he climbed into the cart.

The rich woman stood impatiently at the gate as they arrived. She met the old man with bows and smiles and, leading him into the house, gave him food and drink and made up a soft bed for him. "Lie down, Father, and rest," she said with a simper.

The old man lived in the rich woman's house for a day, and then for another, and then for a third. He ate and drank and slept and smoked his pipe, all very comfortably because the rich woman treated him so kindly.

But inwardly she was fuming. When will this old good-for-nothing get out of here? she said to herself. But she dared not turn him out, for then all the trouble she had gone to on his account would be wasted. To her great joy, on the morning of the fourth day the old man began to pack his sack in preparation for leaving.

The rich woman went outside to see him off. The old traveler walked to the gate in silence, and in silence he passed through it. The rich woman could restrain herself no longer. "Tell me, tell me, what am I to do today?" she cried.

The old man looked at her for a long time. Finally he said, "That which you do in the morning, you will do until evening."

The rich woman rushed into the house, flew up the stairs, and opened her linen closet. She pulled all the cloth from the top shelf, raising a huge cloud of dust, and took out her money jar. She brought it down and sat on the floor with it. But just as she was about to begin counting, the dust she had raised tickled her nose, and she sneezed three times. When she sneezed she raised another cloud of dust, and she sneezed three times again, somewhat louder. Each time she sneezed, more dust was raised and she sneezed again.

A-tishoo! A-tishoo! A-tishoo! This time the chickens in the yard fluttered off in all directions, feathers flying.

A-tishoo! A-tishoo! A-tishoo! The cows and horses broke out of their stalls and scampered over the hill.

A-tishoo! A-tishoo! A-tishoo! The servants ran out of the house, their hands over their ears.

A-tishoo! A-tishoo! A-tishoo! The windows shattered out of their frames and cracks appeared in the plaster.

And so it went. *A-tishoo! A-tishoo! A-tishoo!* Until at the end of the day, when the sun had set, the rich woman sat alone in the dark hallway, her house tumbled in ruins about her ears.

The Magic Mill
(Latvia)

Like the preceding story, this shows how a greedy person can try in vain to win the same reward as another—but it is also a "why" story.

Once upon a time long ago there lived two brothers. One was rich, but the other was quite poor. The rich brother thought only of himself and hated the sight of his poor brother.

One day the poor brother, without even a penny in his pocket, ran out of bread. All his cupboards were bare and he was hungry. He went to his brother to ask for help. But the minute the rich brother saw him coming, he shouted gruffly, "Come to me, indeed!" He threw a moldy pork-bone out the window to him. "Here, take this pork-bone and run to hell. Sell it to the devil. Then you will get your pennies!"

The poor brother thanked him and ran off, in tears, to find the underworld. Soon a saintly man, as white as sunlight, walked beside him. "Why are you crying?" he asked.

"Because my brother sent me to hell to sell this pork-bone. But how will I ever find the way? And who down there would ever buy a bone?"

"Well, now," smiled the man, "why let such a simple thing discourage you? Nonsense! It will be easy to trade the bone, for the demons in the underworld are greedy for tidbits of pork. And to find the way, that is even easier. Look," he pointed, "simply follow down this path. It leads directly to the underworld. But remember one thing. Do not ask pennies for that pork-bone. Instead, ask for something worth having. Ask for the mill which lies cast aside in a corner."

The poor brother thanked him and went on his way. He walked and walked. Truly, it was a long way down to the world of the dead. Behind him were the sunny green fields and sweet, sparkling streams. The path became barren, hot, and dark.

At long last he reached the underworld, but a great, rusty, iron gate blocked his way. He knocked on the gate. Out came the devil's servant, a three-headed ogre.

"What do you want?" said the ogre gruffly.

"Look, I have this pork-bone to trade."

"A pork-bone, you say!" The three heads all shouted, "How splendid! What do you want for it?"

"Did you get the mill?" he asked.

"I did," said the brother. "But what am I ever to do with it? I have nothing to grind."

"Listen," said the man, "you will never say such things when you learn what the mill can do. It is a most wonderful mill! Simply ask it for anything you need, anything at all. Tell it what you wish, and at once it will spin with a roar and pour out all kinds of blessings. But its power is terrible, like fire or water, so be sure you use it well. I will teach you the words to stop its spinning, but this power must be yours alone. Tell no one else these holy words."

He taught the poor brother everything he needed to know to use the magic mill well. Then the man vanished.

Now happy days began for the poor brother. Every day the mill supplied him with the very best meals. It heaped up wealth and blessings of all kinds. And at last it ground him so much gold that he built a splendid, golden castle. He built it near the sea. It shone in the sun, and could be seen for miles around.

As soon as the rich brother saw the castle, he came running like mad to his brother. He was crazy with greed. There was nothing he would not do to get as much gold for himself.

"Gracious me!" he cried. "Where did you get your hands on so much gold? Why don't I have such a castle? Oh," he purred, "what a good and splendid brother you are! I simply can't tell you how fond I am of you. Tell me, where did you get the gold?"

So his brother told him about the magic mill.

"You say the mill did it?" asked the rich brother. "Can this really be true? Listen, dear little brother, sell me your mill. For heaven's sake, do sell it! I won't go until you do."

Well, his brother did not want money for the mill. And he was quite unselfish. So he said, "I will gladly give you the mill. I have enough wealth and blessings from the mill already. Now it is your turn."

The rich brother seized the mill and ran

"Not much. Let me have the mill that lies cast aside in the corner there. That will do."

"No no no! Not that! Ask for something else."

"I need nothing else," said the poor brother. "I will only trade for the mill."

"Not that! No no no!" The ogre shook his three heads stubbornly.

But the poor brother, seeing the three heads all lick their lips for the pork-bone, was determined not to give up.

At that, the ogre's three heads whispered to each other that no living man could keep the mill for long. Since men were no less greedy than demons, the sly heads whispered, the mill would soon come back to the underworld. So at last the ogre gave the poor brother the mill.

Wonderful! The greedy ogre ran back into hell with his precious pork-bone and locked the great gate from inside. And the poor brother hurried home with the mill. On the way he met the white man again.

home with it, huffing and grunting and puffing. He ran all the way and was out of breath when he got home, trembling and shouting for joy.

Since he ran so hard, his wife wondered what terrible misfortune had come to him. But he puffed and panted and showed her the mill and told her what it had done for his brother.

The next morning the rich brother got ready to take his workers to the fields. His wife, of course, wanted to stay at home to cook oatmeal for breakfast. "No such thing!" he told her. She would come along with the men to help in the fields, he insisted. And he, at breakfast time, would run home and grind oatmeal with the mill in a jiffy. So they both went to the fields.

At breakfast time, the rich brother dropped his scythe and ran home to make the oatmeal.

"Oatmeal!" he commanded. The mill spun with a roar and began to grind. It ground and ground oatmeal. Now all the pots were full of it.

"Enough!" he commanded. But the mill ground and ground. My, how it did grind!

"Enough!" he shouted. "Enough, enough!"

It was no use. The mill ground and ground. Already the whole room was full of oatmeal and still the mill ground. Now the oatmeal oozed out into his courtyard. Still the mill ground. My, how it did grind!

Terrified, the rich brother hauled the mill out behind the courtyard gate. More and more oatmeal poured out. It heaped higher and higher. It surged into the neighboring shops and houses, and soon the whole village was full of it. Oatmeal flooded over the meadow, turning sweet grass to mush. It made the streams a gummy mess.

"Devil take it!" he cried. "Look what a mess that infernal mill has gotten me into!"

Finally he seized the madly spinning mill and ran with it back to his brother.

"Here!" he said angrily. "You can do what you want with your mill!"

His brother only laughed when he saw the heaping oatmeal. Very quietly, he spoke the words to stop it. There was no more oatmeal.

For some while after, the poor brother received many more blessings from the magic mill.

Then one day a ship came in sight of his golden castle. This was a time, of course, when the sea was pure, sweet water. All the creatures of the Earth could drink from it.

On this bright, sunny day, the sailors saw the castle glittering. Wonder of wonders, they whispered among themselves, what sort of castle was this? They left their ship and came to inspect it. From its floors right up to its towering spires, they found it to be pure, solid gold. Truly, it must belong to a powerful lord.

"Whose castle is this?" they asked the poor brother.

"It is mine," he said.

"Where did you get such a noble castle?"

So he told them about the magic mill.

"You say the mill did it?" they asked, hardly believing their ears. "This simple little trifle of a mill?" They gazed about with looks of respectful wonder. But they were thorough scoundrels and cheats. That night they stole the mill.

In the morning the poor brother looked for his mill, growing angry and sad. But it was nowhere to be found. The sailors were far at sea.

In their greed, the sailors could not agree what to make the mill grind first. But while the others put their heads together and argued, one sailor—simply for a chicken-brained joke—shouted, "Hey mates! We've got no salt. We left it home. Let's see the mill grind salt first. Salt! We can't eat a thing without it!"

So be it. The mill spun with a roar. It began to grind salt. In a moment a dish was full.

"Enough!" said the sailors, but it was no use. The mill roared like crazy. Madly, it whirled. Nothing they did could stop it.

"What have we done?" they all shouted. They jumped on it, every man. They clutched it with their hands. But nothing, nothing could stop it.

In an instant the ship was full of salt.

It sank. Down, down to the bottom of the sea it sank with all of the sailors and the mill.

Yet under the sea the mill was grinding, grinding salt. It still grinds today.

And that, you see, is why sea water is now so very salty.

To Your Good Health
(Russia)

A canny shepherd refuses to wish for the king's health until he gets his way. He wears down the king's patience until he gets the princess, and gains the upper hand.

Long, long ago there lived a king who was such a mighty monarch that whenever he sneezed every one in the whole country had to say "To your good health!" Every one said it except the shepherd with the staring eyes, and he would not say it.

The king heard of this and was very angry, and sent for the shepherd to appear before him.

The shepherd came and stood before the throne, where the king sat looking very grand and powerful. But however grand or powerful he might be the shepherd did not feel a bit afraid of him.

"Say at once, 'To my good health!' " cried the king.

"To my good health!" replied the shepherd.

"To mine—to *mine,* you rascal, you vagabond!" stormed the king.

"To mine, to *mine,* your Majesty," was the answer.

"But to *mine*—to my own," roared the king, and beat on his breast in a rage.

"Well, yes; to mine, of course, to my own," cried the shepherd, and gently tapped his breast.

The king was beside himself with fury and did not know what to do, when the Lord Chamberlain interfered:

"To Your Good Health" from THE CRIMSON FAIRY BOOK, edited by Andrew Lang. London: Longmans, Green, and Company, 1903.

"Say at once—say this very moment: 'To your health, your Majesty'; for if you don't say it you'll lose your life," whispered he.

"No, I won't say it till I get the princess for my wife," was the shepherd's answer. Now the princess was sitting on a little throne beside the king, her father, and she looked as sweet and lovely as a little golden dove. When she heard what the shepherd said she could not help laughing, for there is no denying the fact that this young shepherd with the staring eyes pleased her very much; indeed he pleased her better than any king's son she had yet seen.

But the king was not as pleasant as his daughter, and he gave orders to throw the shepherd into the white bear's pit.

The guards led him away and thrust him into the pit with the white bear, who had had nothing to eat for two days and was very hungry. The door of the pit was hardly closed when the bear rushed at the shepherd; but when it saw his eyes it was so frightened that it was ready to eat itself. It shrank away into a corner and gazed at him from there, and, in spite of being so famished, did not dare to touch him, but sucked its own paws from sheer hunger. The shepherd felt that if he once removed his eyes off the beast he was a dead man, and in order to keep himself awake he made songs and sang them, and so the night went by.

Next morning the Lord Chamberlain came to see the shepherd's bones, and was amazed to find him alive and well. He led him to the king, who fell into a furious passion, and said: "Well, you have learned what it is to be very near death, and *now* will you say 'To my good health'?"

But the shepherd answered: "I am not afraid of ten deaths! I will only say it if I may have the princess for my wife."

"Then go to your death," cried the king; and ordered him to be thrown into the den with the wild boars. The wild boars had not been fed for a week, and when the shepherd was thrust into their den they rushed at him to tear him to pieces. But the shepherd took a little flute out of the sleeve of his jacket and began to play a merry tune, on which the wild boars first of all shrank shyly away, and then got up on their hind legs and danced gaily. The shepherd would have given anything to be able to laugh, they looked so funny; but he dared not stop playing, for he knew well enough that the moment he stopped they would fall upon him and tear him to pieces. His eyes were of no use to him here, for he could not have stared ten wild boars in the face at once; so he kept on playing, and the wild boars danced very slowly, as if in a minuet, then by degrees he played faster and faster till they could hardly twist and turn quickly enough, and ended by all falling over each other in a heap, quite exhausted and out of breath.

Then the shepherd ventured to laugh at last; and he laughed so long and so loud that when the Lord Chamberlain came early in the morning, expecting to find only his bones, the tears were still running down his cheeks from laughter.

As soon as the king was dressed the shepherd was again brought before him; but he was more angry than ever to think the wild boars had not torn the man to bits, and he said: "Well, you have learned what it feels to be near ten deaths, *now* say 'To my good health!' "

But the shepherd broke in with, "I do not fear a hundred deaths, and I will only say it if I may have the princess for my wife."

"Then go to a hundred deaths!" roared the king, and ordered the shepherd to be thrown down the deep vault of scythes.

The guards dragged him away to a dark dungeon, in the middle of which was a deep well with sharp scythes all round it. At the bottom of the well was a little light by which one could see if anyone was thrown in whether he had fallen to the bottom.

When the shepherd was dragged to the dungeons he begged the guards to leave him alone a little while that he might look down into the pit of scythes; perhaps he might after all make up his mind to say "To your good health" to the king. So the guards left him alone and he stuck up his long stick near the well, hung his cloak round the stick and put his hat on the top. He also hung his knapsack up inside the cloak so that it might seem to have some body within it. When this was done he called out to the guards and said that he had considered the matter but after all he could not make up his mind to say what the king wished. The guards came in, threw the hat and cloak, knapsack and stick all down the well together, watched to see how they put out the light at the bottom and came away, thinking that now there really was an end of the shepherd. But he had hidden in a dark corner and was laughing to himself all the time.

Quite early next morning came the Lord Chamberlain, carrying a lamp and he nearly fell backwards with surprise when he saw the shepherd alive and well. He brought him to the king, whose fury was greater than ever, but who cried:

"Well, now you have been near a hundred deaths; will you say: 'To your good health'?"

But the shepherd only gave the same answer:

"I won't say it till the princess is my wife."

"Perhaps after all you may do it for less," said the king, who saw that there was no chance of making away with the shepherd; and he ordered the state coach to be got ready, then he made the shepherd get in with him and sit beside him, and ordered the coachman to drive to the silver wood. When they reached it he said: "Do you see this silver wood? Well, if you will say, 'To your good health,' I will give it to you."

The shepherd turned hot and cold by turns, but he still persisted:

"I will not say it till the princess is my wife."

The king was much vexed; he drove further on till they came to a splendid castle, all of gold, and then he said:

"Do you see this golden castle? Well, I will give you that too, the silver wood and the golden castle, if only you will say that one thing to me: 'To your good health.' "

The shepherd gaped and wondered and was quite dazzled, but he still said:

"No; I will *not* say it till I have the princess for my wife."

This time the king was overwhelmed with

grief, and gave orders to drive on to the diamond pond, and there he tried once more.

"Do you see this diamond pond? I will give you that too, the silver wood and the golden castle and the diamond pond. You shall have them all—all—if you will but say: 'To your good health!' "

The shepherd had to shut his staring eyes tight not to be dazzled with the brilliant pond, but still he said:

"No, no; I will not say it till I have the princess for my wife."

Then the king saw that all his efforts were useless, and that he might as well give in, so he said:

"Well, well, it's all the same to me—I will give you my daughter to wife; but, then, you really and truly must say to me: 'To your good health.' "

"Of course I'll say it; why should I not say it? It stands to reason that I shall say it then."

At this the king was more delighted than anyone could have believed. He made it known all through the country that there were to be great rejoicings, as the princess was going to be married. And everyone rejoiced to think that the princess, who had refused so many royal suitors, should have ended by falling in love with the staring-eyed shepherd.

There was such a wedding as had never been seen. Everyone ate and drank and danced. Even the sick were feasted, and quite tiny new-born children had presents given them.

But the greatest merry-making was in the king's palace; there the best bands played and the best food was cooked; a crowd of people sat down to table, and all was fun and merry-making.

And when the groomsman, according to custom, brought in the great boar's head on a big dish and placed it before the king so that he might carve it and give everyone a share, the savoury smell was so strong that the king began to sneeze with all his might.

"To your very good health," cried the shepherd before anyone else, and the king was so delighted that he did not regret having given him his daughter.

In time, when the old king died, the shepherd succeeded him. He made a very good king and never expected his people to wish him well against their wills; but, all the same, everyone did wish him well, for they all loved him.

Vassilissa the Valiant
(Russia)

Posing as a messenger of the Khan, Vassilissa rescues her husband and thereby proves his boast that in a contest she can beat any man.

The Grand Duke Vladimir of Kiev was a proud man. He enjoyed inviting the princes of the land to feast in his castle, where he could show off his riches.

But one night, a young prince named Staver grew bored with Vladimir's boasting. Turning to Pavel, the prince next to him, Staver said, "Really, what the Duke owns is not so special. My own castle is so big that I ride horseback through its halls. I love the ringing sound of my horse's golden shoes on the floor." Staver drank some wine and plucked a loud chord on the strings of his gusla. "And my greatest treasure, by far, is Vassilissa, my beautiful and brave wife. She has eyes bright as an eagle's, and a face as smooth as snow. But her true beauty is her skill." Staver leaned over and whispered to Pavel, "In a contest, she can outdo any man."

Staver's words spread quickly around the Grand Duke's table. When Duke Vladimir heard what Staver had said, he rose and like a wild boar bellowed, "Enough! How dare this Staver brag in my castle. Put him in chains, drag him to the dungeon, and pile the sands high in front of his cell so he may never escape. Then go to his wretched castle and bring me this woman Vassilissa!" The Duke's men seized Staver roughly. The gusla slipped from his hands and clattered to the floor.

As Staver was being locked in chains, Pavel slipped quietly away. He hurried to Vassilissa and warned her that Duke Vladimir's men were coming to get her.

Quickly, Vassilissa dressed herself in men's clothing, tucked her hair under her hat, and pulled on riding boots of green morocco leather. She slung a quiver of arrows across her back, and grabbed her bow and Tartar sword. With twelve horsemen behind her dressed as Tartars, she rode off toward the castle of Duke Vladimir.

On the way, they came upon the Duke's men. "We're going to the castle of Staver," the Duke's men said, "to capture his wife Vassilissa. Who are you, young man?"

"I am the messenger of the Great Tartar Khan," said Vassilissa. "Your Grand Duke Vladimir owed the Khan twelve years' tribute in gold. The Khan is angry. He's tired of waiting for his gold, and we've come for it now."

The Duke's men were frightened. They knew the power of the Tartar Khan was far greater than Vladimir's.

Vassilissa continued. "As for this Vassilissa you seek, you've lost her. When we stopped there, seeking refreshment, her castle was deserted. She must be miles away by now."

The Duke's men galloped back to the castle of Vladimir to report the news.

"Vassilissa has escaped," they told him. "But far worse, the Tartar Khan has sent his men to collect twelve years of tribute in gold. They're almost at your gate."

When Vassilissa arrived with her twelve men, she saw the tables had been hurriedly set. She smiled to herself; how anxious Vladimir was to please the messenger of the Tartar Khan! She knew he could never come up with as much gold as she was demanding.

After greeting Vassilissa and bidding her welcome, Vladimir felt a tug on his sleeve. His wife Apraksiya pulled him aside. "That so-called messenger of the Khan is not a man at all," she said. "She glides across the courtyard with the grace of a ship on the waters. That's a woman, Vladimir."

"We'll soon see about that," said the Duke, raising his eyebrows. Perhaps his wife was right. In a hearty voice, Vladimir proposed a contest in wrestling.

Vassilissa bowed her head in agreement. She threw the first man to the ground so violently that he had to be carried away. She knocked a second off his feet before he knew what was happening. Vassilissa flipped a third man on his head and knocked him out cold.

Duke Vladimir scowled at his wife. "How could a woman beat three strong men! Don't make a fool of me."

But Apraksiya was not convinced. "Look again, my Duke. See the skin smooth as snow, and watch the way she moves. No man is quite so graceful, you must admit."

The Duke studied Vassilissa. Perhaps Apraksiya was right. The Duke then called for a contest in archery. "The bowmen must pierce that oak in the distance with their arrows," he said. One by one, his best archers took aim and struck the oak. Then Vassilissa took aim. Her arrow flew to the tree and hit it with such force that the oak shuddered and split wide open.

"There!" said Vladimir to Apraksiya. "Are you satisfied now? He is a man's man, indeed."

"Eyes sharp as an eagle's," said Apraksiya,

"Vassilissa the Valiant" from THE SKULL IN THE SNOW AND OTHER FOLKTALES by Toni McCarty. Copyright © 1981 by Toni McCarty. Reprinted by permission of Delacorte Press and Bill Berger Associates, Inc.

and walked away. The Duke would have given up, but his wife seemed so sure of herself he tried again.

This time the Duke challenged Vassilissa to a game of chess. She beat him three times in a row quite easily, then pushed the board aside.

"Enough playing games. I've come for the gold you owe the Tartar Khan. Let's not waste any more time."

Vladimir frowned and grumbled. "I'm a poor man, sir. I cannot pay the Khan in gold."

"Well, then, what *can* you give the Khan that might please him and make him forget what you owe?" asked Vassilissa.

"Look around my court," said Vladimir. "What would you choose for the Tartar Khan? You know what would please him better than I know."

"Nothing here would catch his fancy. You don't have many musicians. Good heavens! Not even *one* gusla player. The Khan is so fond of gusla music."

Vladimir's eyes brightened. "The gusla! We *do* have one young prince who plays the gusla beautifully. He sings, as well." The Duke leaped to his feet and ordered his men to fetch Staver immediately.

When Staver was brought from the dungeon to the banquet room, he looked bewildered. Vladimir shoved a gusla in his hands and ordered him to play.

Staver plucked the strings slowly and sadly, his eyes on the floor. Then he raised his head, and his eyes lit upon Vassilissa. He recognized her right away and his heart sang. His songs became so gay and lighthearted that all the people in the Duke's court began dancing.

At last Vassilissa said, "Enough. I suppose he will do. I'll take him to the Tartar Khan and you may pray that the Khan is satisfied."

Staver mounted his horse and galloped off with Vassilissa.

"How easily I got out of that one," said the Duke. "A gusla player! I was lucky to have had that Staver on hand just when I needed him."

But no one felt luckier than Staver himself as he rode away beside the gallant Vassilissa —she who could beat a man at any game.

Marietta's Choice
(Russia)

A clever woman teaches her husband that he's not always right, but at the same time she shows how much she loves him.

One day, a poor peasant found a gold mortar in the woods. "This bowl must have been used for grinding medicines," he thought, but he had no use for it.

"I'll take it to the palace and sell it to the prince," he told his daughter, Marietta, when he got home.

"Don't bother with him. He's so spoiled he'll think it's worthless because it doesn't have a pestle to grind with," she said. "Princes are often lacking in brains."

"But they aren't lacking in money," her father answered. So off he went to the palace.

When he offered to sell the prince the golden bowl, the prince took it and threw it against the wall. "It isn't worth anything, you fool. It hasn't got a pestle!" said the prince. The golden bowl lay dented at the peasant's feet.

"My daughter warned me that you have no brains," said the peasant, picking up his damaged goods.

"What?" shouted the prince. "Your daughter dares to speak so of the prince? Well! If she's so smart, tell her to make me a hundred yards of cloth out of four ounces of flax. If she can't do it, you both shall hang."

The peasant went home weeping and told Marietta about the prince's task. "Don't cry," she said. She handed her father four short cords of flax. "Take these. Tell him to make me a loom from these cords. If he can, I will use it to make him his cloth."

The father was afraid to go back, but Marietta insisted. When the father reported his daughter's request, the prince couldn't think of what to say.

Finally, the prince decided he would go and meet this clever young woman. He knocked at her door, but she refused to answer. The prince grew furious and broke the door down. Marietta looked at him coldly.

"How dare you refuse to open the door to the prince?" he asked.

"I don't open my door to strangers," she said.

The prince was impressed with her answer. "Then don't let me be a stranger," he said. "Marry me."

It pleased her to marry a young prince and become a princess. "I will," she said.

Things went well for the royal couple. Often the prince asked her advice on important matters. He always did as she suggested. But if she dared to express an idea without first being asked, he flew into a temper.

One day, an unusual case came before the prince to be judged. An old woman accused her young neighbor boy of stealing a basket of eggs. The boy said the eggs were his because his hen was found setting on them. "Well, she's a stupid hen," the old woman said to the prince. "Look—the eggs are hard-boiled!" She cracked and peeled one to prove it.

"A hen knows her own eggs," the prince said. "Give the boy the eggs and the basket, as well."

Now this old woman was a fighter at heart. She'd give up her eggs, perhaps, but not the basket she'd gotten for a wedding gift fifty years before. She'd heard about Marietta's good sense, so she went to her with the story.

"All right," said Marietta, "this afternoon, come to the garden behind the palace kitchen. Here's what I want you to do. . . ." She whispered the plan into the old woman's ear.

Later that day, Marietta invited her husband for a stroll around the palace grounds.

When they reached the kitchen gardens, the prince was surprised to see the old woman working there.

"What are you doing?" he asked.

The old woman bowed most politely. "I'm planting boiled beans," she explained.

"Boiled beans?" he said with a laugh. "Boiled beans will never grow!"

"Oh, surely they will, Your Highness," she said, "as surely as a hen can hatch hard-boiled eggs."

The prince was embarrassed. That same day he ordered the boy to give back the basket of eggs. But he guessed his wife was behind this, and he felt betrayed.

When he got home, he ordered her out of the palace. "Return to your hut. You can take with you whatever you care for the most, but be out of here tonight."

"All right, I'll go. But please, just have one last meal with me." He consented. Marietta ordered the cooks to fix the finest foods and to serve the best of the wine. Together they feasted, and the prince, rather sorry to lose his wife, drank more than usual. Finally, the food heavy in his stomach and the wine light in his head, he fell sound asleep at the table.

Marietta had the servants bundle him into her waiting carriage. She climbed in beside him and rode off through the falling snow to her old hut.

In the morning, the prince awoke in a cold bed. Snow sifted through the cracks in the wall onto his handsome face. He called for his servants, but the only voice that answered was Marietta's. "Whom are you ordering around? *I* command here," she said. "You sent me away, saying I could take whatever I liked best. So I brought *you,* my love!"

The prince laughed. He felt proud to be loved by such a wise woman. "Whatever you say," he said with a smile.

Marietta kissed his cheek. "Now let's go home," she said.

Turkey

While a large body of Turkish folk literature exists, little is available in English, in part because of the long tenure of the oral tradition as opposed to the recording of such material; in part because much of what is recorded is in Arabic. The classic tales about the quixotic scamp Nasr-ed-Din Hodja are known chiefly through Alice Kelsey's collection, *Once the Hodja*, and L. Juda's *Turkish Tales*, also about the Hodja.

Three Fridays

In a merry tale for older children, the rogue and folk-hero, Nasr-ed-Din Hodja, manages to get through three Fridays without preaching a sermon.

There was just one day of each week that worried Nasr-ed-Din Hodja. On six days he was as free as a butterfly. He could talk with his friends in the market place or ride his donkey to a nearby village. He could work in the vineyards or go hunting in the hills. He could lounge in the coffee house or sit in the sun in his own courtyard. There was nothing to hurry him to be at a certain place at a certain time to do a certain thing.

But Friday was different. It was much different. That was the day when all good Mohammedans went to their mosques. Because Nasr-ed-Din Hodja, years before, had attended the school for priests, he was expected each Friday to mount the pulpit of the mosque at a certain time and preach a sermon. That was all very well when he had something to say, but there were many Fridays when his mind was as empty as that of his own little gray donkey. It was one thing to swap stories with the men in the coffee house and quite another to stand alone in the high pulpit and talk to a mosque full of people. The men, each squatting on his own prayer rug on the floor, looked up at him with such solemn faces. Then there was the fluttering in the balcony behind the lattices, which told him that the women were waiting too. Of course, the chanting, which came before the sermon, was not hard because all the men joined in that, bowing till they touched their foreheads to the floor in the Nemaz. But the sermon—that was hard.

One Friday he walked more slowly than ever through the cobblestoned streets of Ak Shehir. He saw the veiled women slipping silently past him on their way to the latticed balcony of the mosque. He saw the men in their best clothes hurrying to the mosque to hear his sermon. But what sermon? He stopped at the mosque door to leave his shoes. He pattered with the other men across the soft thick rugs. But they could squat on the rugs, while he had to climb into the high pulpit.

Perhaps the beauty of the mosque would give him an idea. He looked up at the blues and reds and whites of the intricate tracery on the ceiling, but not a thought came. He looked at the rich yellows and reds of the mosaics on the walls, but there was no help there. He looked at the men's faces staring up at him. He heard the tittering in the latticed balcony where the veiled women sat. He must say something.

"Oh, people of Ak Shehir!" He leaned on the pulpit and eyed them squarely. "Do you know what I am about to say to you?"

"No!" boomed from the rugs where the men squatted.

"No!" floated down in soft whispers from the latticed balcony, whispers not meant for any ears beyond the balcony.

"You do not know?" said Nasr-ed-Din Hodja, shaking his head and looking from one face to another. "You are sure you do not know? Then what use would it be to talk to people who know nothing at all about this important subject. My words would be wasted on such ignorant people."

With that, the Hodja turned and climbed slowly down the pulpit steps. His eyes lowered, he walked with injured dignity through the crowds of men. He slipped on his shoes at the mosque door, and was out in the sunshine—free until next Friday.

That day came all too soon. The Hodja mingled with the crowds going to the mosque. His coarse, home-knit stockings pattered across the deep colorful rugs. He climbed the steps to the high pulpit. He looked down at the sea of solemn faces. He heard the rustling behind the lattices of the balcony. He had hoped that this week he could think of a sermon, but the carvings of the doorway did not help him, nor the embroidered hangings of the pulpit, nor the pigeons fluttering and cooing at the window. Still, he must say something.

"Oh, people of Ak Shehir!" intoned the Hodja, gesturing with both hands. "Do you know what I am about to say to you?"

"Yes," boomed the men who remembered what had happened when they said "No" last week.

"Yes," echoed in soft whispers from the balcony.

"You know what I am going to say?" said the Hodja, shrugging first one shoulder and then the other. "You are sure you know what I am going to say? Then I need not say it. It would be a useless waste of my golden words if I told you something that you already knew."

The Hodja turned and again climbed down the pulpit steps. He picked his way with unhurried dignity among the men. He scuffed into his shoes and escaped into the sunshine. Another free week was ahead of him.

But the best of weeks end. The third Friday found him once more climbing the pulpit steps, with not a word worth saying in that solemn mosque. The ancient Arabic writing on the bright ceiling had no help for him. The flickering candles in the large round chandelier winked at him but said nothing. Even the big Koran in front of him might have had blank pages instead of its fine Arabic words and its illuminated borders. Men's faces looked up at him expectantly. Bright eyes peered through the lattices of the women's balcony. The time had come again when he must speak.

"Oh, people of Ak Shehir!" declaimed the Hodja as he groped helplessly for an idea. "Do you know what I am about to say to you?"

"No," came from those who were thinking of the last Friday.

"Yes," came from those who were thinking of the Friday before that.

"Some of you know and some of you do not know!" The Hodja rubbed his hands together and beamed down at the men. "How very fine! Now let those who know tell those who do not know!"

The Hodja was humming to himself as he came down from the pulpit, two steps at a time. He nodded and smiled as he threaded his way through the men. Some thought he bowed and smiled toward the latticed balcony, but others said the good Hodja would not have made so bold. He picked his own worn shoes from the rows and rows by the mosque door. The sunshine was warm and friendly. The birds were singing and there was the fragrance of hawthorn blossoms in the air.

The Hodja had not a worry in the world—not till another Friday should come around.

A Tale from *Arabian Nights*

 The thousand-and-one tales of the *Arabian Nights* come from Arabic and non-Arabic sources; exchanged by travelers, adapted by storytellers, cherished by the Moslem peoples, the origins are uncertain. They had been recorded in Egypt, and it was from that source that Antoine Galland made his translation into French in 1704. Many of the tales are long and slow in pace, but some have remained favorites, like "Aladdin and the Wonderful Lamp," and illustrate the deft use of magic and the theatrical plot that are distinctive qualities of the collection.

Aladdin and the Wonderful Lamp

One of the most powerful and memorable stories of magic, this epitomizes the dream of acquiring wealth and status.

There once lived a poor tailor who had a son called Aladdin, a careless, idle boy who would do nothing but play all day long in the streets with little idle boys like himself. This so grieved the father that he died; yet, in spite of his mother's tears and prayers, Aladdin did not mend his ways. One day, when he was playing in the streets as usual, a stranger asked him his age, and if he were not the son of Mustapha the tailor.

"I am, sir," replied Aladdin; "but he died a long while ago."

On this the stranger, who was a famous African magician, fell on his neck and kissed him, saying, "I am your uncle and I knew you from your likeness to my brother. Go to your mother and tell her I am coming."

Aladdin ran home and told his mother of his newly found uncle.

"Indeed, child," she said, "your father had a brother, but I always thought he was dead."

However, she prepared supper and bade Aladdin seek his uncle, who came laden with wine and fruit. He presently knelt and kissed the place where Mustapha used to sit, bidding Aladdin's mother not to be surprised at not having seen him before, as he had been forty years out of the country.

He then turned to Aladdin and asked him his trade, at which the boy hung his head, while his mother burst into tears. On learning that Aladdin was idle and would learn no trade, he offered to take a shop for him and stock it with merchandise. Next day he bought Aladdin a fine suit of clothes and took him all over the city, showing him the sights, and brought him home at nightfall to his mother, who was overjoyed to see her son so fine.

Next day the magician led Aladdin into some beautiful gardens a long way outside the city gates. They sat down by a fountain, and the magician pulled a cake from his girdle, which he divided between them. They then journeyed onward till they almost reached the mountains. Aladdin was so tired that he begged to go back, but the magician beguiled him with pleasant stories and led him on in spite of himself.

At last they came to two mountains divided by a narrow valley. "We will go no farther," said the false uncle. "I will show you something wonderful; only do you gather up sticks while I kindle a fire."

"Aladdin and the Wonderful Lamp" from THE BLUE FAIRY BOOK, edited by Andrew Lang. London: Longmans, Green, and Company, 1889.

When the fire was lit the magician threw on it a powder he had with him, at the same time saying some magical words. The earth trembled a little and opened in front of them, disclosing a square flat stone with a brass ring in the middle to raise it by. Aladdin tried to run away, but the magician caught him and gave him a blow that knocked him down.

"What have I done, uncle?" he said piteously.

Whereupon the magician said more kindly, "Fear nothing, but obey me. Beneath this stone lies a treasure which is to be yours, and no one else may touch it, so you must do exactly as I tell you."

At the word treasure, Aladdin forgot his fears and grasped the ring as he was told, saying the names of his father and grandfather. The stone came up quite easily and some steps appeared.

"Go down," said the magician. "At the foot of those steps you will find an open door leading into three large halls. Tuck up your gown and go through them without touching anything, or you will die instantly. These halls lead into a garden of fine fruit trees. Walk on till you come to a niche in a terrace where stands a lighted lamp. Pour out the oil it contains and bring it to me." He drew a ring from his finger and gave it to Aladdin, bidding him prosper.

Aladdin found everything as the magician had said, gathered some fruit off the trees and, having got the lamp, arrived at the mouth of the cave.

The magician cried out in a great hurry, "Make haste and give me the lamp." This Aladdin refused to do until he was out of the cave. The magician flew into a terrible passion, and throwing some more powder on the fire, he said something, and the stone rolled back into its place.

The magician left Persia forever, which plainly showed that he was no uncle of Aladdin's, but a cunning sorcerer who had read in his magic books of a wonderful lamp which would make him the most powerful man in the world. Though he alone knew where to find it, he could only receive it from the hand of another. He had picked out the foolish Aladdin for this purpose, intending to get the lamp and kill him afterward.

For two days Aladdin remained in the dark, crying and lamenting. At last he clasped his hands in prayer, and in so doing rubbed the ring, which the magician had forgotten to take from him.

Immediately an enormous and frightful genie rose out of the earth, saying, "What wouldst thou with me? I am the slave of the ring and will obey thee in all things."

Aladdin fearlessly replied, "Deliver me from this place," whereupon the earth opened, and he found himself outside. As soon as his eyes could bear the light he went home, but fainted on the threshold. When he came to himself he told his mother what had passed, and showed her the lamp and the fruits he had gathered in the garden, which were in reality precious stones. He then asked for some food.

"Alas, child," she said, "I have nothing in the house, but I have spun a little cotton and will go and sell it."

Aladdin bade her keep her cotton, for he would sell the lamp instead. As it was very dirty she began to rub it, that it might fetch a higher price. Instantly a hideous genie appeared and asked what she would have.

She fainted away, but Aladdin, snatching the lamp, said boldly, "Fetch me something to eat!"

The genie returned with a silver bowl, twelve silver plates containing rich meats, two silver cups, and a bottle of wine.

Aladdin's mother, when she came to herself, said, "Whence comes this splendid feast?"

"Ask not, but eat," replied Aladdin.

So they sat at breakfast till it was dinner time, and Aladdin told his mother about the lamp. She begged him to sell it and have nothing to do with genii.

"No," said Aladdin, "since chance has made us aware of its virtues, we will use it and the ring likewise, which I shall always wear on my finger." When they had eaten all the genie had brought, Aladdin sold one of the silver plates, and so on till none were left.

He then had recourse to the genie, who gave him another set of plates, and thus they lived for many years.

One day Aladdin heard an order from the sultan proclaiming that everyone was to stay at home and close his shutters while the princess, his daughter, went to and from the bath. Aladdin was seized by a desire to see her face, which was very difficult as she always went veiled. He hid himself behind the door of the bath and peeped through a chink.

The princess lifted her veil as she went in, and looked so beautiful that Aladdin fell in love with her at first sight. He went home so changed that his mother was frightened. He told her he loved the princess so deeply he could not live without her and meant to ask her in marriage of her father. His mother, on hearing this, burst out laughing, but Aladdin at last prevailed upon her to go before the sultan and carry his request. She fetched a napkin and laid in it the magic fruits from the enchanted garden, which sparkled and shone like the most beautiful jewels. She took these with her to please the sultan and set out, trusting in the lamp. The grand vizir and the lords of council had just gone in as she entered the hall and placed herself in front of the sultan. He, however, took no notice of her. She went every day for a week and stood in the same place.

When the council broke up on the sixth day the sultan said to his vizir, "I see a certain woman in the audience chamber every day, carrying something in a napkin. Call her next time that I may find out what she wants."

Next day, at a sign from the vizir, she went up to the foot of the throne and remained kneeling till the sultan said to her, "Rise, good woman, and tell me what you want."

She hesitated, so the sultan sent away all but the vizir and bade her speak freely, promising to forgive her beforehand for anything she might say. She then told him of her son's violent love for the princess.

"I prayed him to forget her," she said, "but in vain; he threatened to do some desperate deed if I refused to go and ask Your Majesty for the hand of the princess. Now I pray you to forgive not me alone but my son Aladdin."

The sultan asked her kindly what she had in the napkin, whereupon she unfolded the jewels and presented them.

He was thunderstruck, and turning to the vizir, said, "What sayest thou? Ought I not to bestow the princess on one who values her at such a price?"

The vizir, who wanted her for his own son, begged the sultan to withhold her for three months, in the course of which he hoped his son would contrive to make him a richer present. The sultan granted this and told Aladdin's mother that, though he consented to the marriage, she must not appear before him again for three months.

Aladdin waited patiently for nearly three months, but after two had elapsed his mother, going into the city to buy oil, found everyone rejoicing and asked what was going on.

"Do you not know," was the answer, "that the son of the grand vizir is to marry the sultan's daughter tonight?"

Breathless, she ran and told Aladdin, who was overwhelmed at first, but presently bethought him of the lamp. He rubbed it, and the genie appeared, saying, "What is thy will?"

Aladdin replied, "The sultan, as thou knowest, has broken his promise to me, and the vizir's son is to have the princess. My command is that tonight you bring hither the bride and bridegroom."

"Master, I obey," said the genie.

Aladdin then went to his chamber where, sure enough at midnight, the genie transported the bed containing the vizir's son and the princess.

"Take this new-married man," Aladdin said, "and put him outside in the cold and return at daybreak."

Whereupon the genie took the vizir's son out of bed, leaving Aladdin with the princess.

"Fear nothing," Aladdin said to her; "you are my wife, promised to me by your unjust father, and no harm shall come to you."

The princess was too frightened to speak and passed the most miserable night of her life, while Aladdin lay down beside her and slept soundly. At the appointed hour the genie fetched in the shivering bridegroom, laid him in his place, and transported the bed back to the palace.

Presently the sultan came to wish his daughter good morning. The unhappy vizir's son jumped up and hid himself, while the princess would not say a word and was very sorrowful.

The sultan sent her mother to her, who said, "How comes it, child, that you will not speak to your father? What has happened?"

The princess sighed deeply, and at last told her mother how, during the night, the bed had been carried into some strange house, and what had passed there. Her mother did not believe her in the least but bade her rise and consider it an idle dream.

The following night exactly the same thing happened, and next morning, on the princess' refusing to speak, the sultan threatened to cut off her head. She then confessed all, bidding him ask the vizir's son if it were not so. The sultan told the vizir to ask his son, who owned the truth; adding that, dearly as he loved the princess, he had rather die than go through another such fearful night and that he wished to be separated from her. His wish was granted, and there was an end of feasting and rejoicing.

When the three months were over, Aladdin sent his mother to remind the sultan of his promise. She stood in the same place as before, and the sultan, who had forgotten Aladdin, at once remembered him and sent for her. On seeing her poverty the sultan felt less inclined than ever to keep his word and asked the vizir's advice, who counseled him to set so high a value on the princess that no man living could come up to it.

The sultan then turned to Aladdin's mother, saying, "Good woman, a sultan must remember his promises and I will remember mine, but your son must first send me forty basins of gold brimful of jewels, carried by forty black slaves, led by as many white ones, splendidly dressed. Tell him that I await his answer."

The mother of Aladdin bowed low and went home, thinking all was lost. She gave Aladdin the message, adding, "He may wait

long enough for your answer!"

"Not so long, mother, as you think," her son replied. "I would do a great deal more than that for the princess." He summoned the genie, and in a few moments the eighty slaves arrived and filled up the small house and garden.

Aladdin made them set out to the palace, two and two, followed by his mother. They were so richly dressed, with such splendid jewels in their girdles, that everyone crowded to see them and the basins of gold they carried on their heads.

They entered the palace and, after kneeling before the sultan, stood in a half-circle round the throne with their arms crossed, while Aladdin's mother presented them to the sultan.

He hesitated no longer but said, "Good woman, return and tell your son that I wait for him with open arms."

She lost no time in telling Aladdin, bidding him make haste. But Aladdin first called the genie.

"I want a scented bath," he said, "a richly embroidered habit, a horse surpassing the sultan's, and twenty slaves to attend me. Besides this I desire six slaves, beautifully dressed, to wait on my mother; and lastly, ten thousand pieces of gold in ten purses."

No sooner said than done. Aladdin mounted his horse and passed through the streets, the slaves strewing gold as they went. Those who had played with him in his childhood knew him not, he had grown so handsome.

When the sultan saw him, he came down from his throne, embraced him, and led him into a hall where a feast was spread, intending to marry him to the princess that very day. But Aladdin refused, saying, "I must build a palace fit for her," and took his leave.

Once home, he said to the genie, "Build me a palace of the finest marble, set with jasper, agate, and other precious stones. In the middle you shall build me a large hall with a dome, its four walls of massy gold and silver, each side having six windows whose lattices, all except one, which is to be left unfinished, must be set with diamonds and rubies. There must be stables and horses and grooms and slaves. Go and see about it!"

The palace was finished by next day, and the genie carried him there and showed him all his orders faithfully carried out, even to the laying of a velvet carpet from Aladdin's palace to the sultan's. Aladdin's mother then dressed herself carefully and walked to the palace with her slaves. The sultan sent musicians with trumpets and cymbals to meet them and the air resounded with music and cheers.

Aladdin's mother was taken to the princess, who saluted her and treated her with great honor. At night the princess said good-bye to her father and set out on the carpet for Aladdin's palace, with his mother at her side, and followed by the hundred slaves. She was charmed at the sight of Aladdin who ran to receive her.

"Princess," he said, "blame your beauty for my boldness if I have displeased you."

She told him that, having seen him, she willingly obeyed her father in this matter. After the wedding had taken place, Aladdin led her into the hall where a feast was spread, and she supped with him, after which they danced till midnight.

Next day Aladdin invited the sultan to see the palace. On entering the hall with the four-and-twenty windows, with their rubies, diamonds, and emeralds, he cried, "It is a world's wonder! There is only one thing that surprises me. Was it by accident that one window was left unfinished?"

"No, sir, by design," returned Aladdin. "I wished Your Majesty to have the glory of finishing this palace."

The sultan was pleased and sent for the best jewelers in the city. He showed them the unfinished window and bade them fit it up like the others.

"Sir," replied their spokesman, "we cannot find jewels enough."

The sultan had his own fetched, which they soon used, but to no purpose, for in a month's time the work was not half done. Aladdin, knowing that their task was vain, bade them undo their work and carry the jewels back, and the genie finished the window at his command. The sultan was surprised to receive his jewels again and visited Aladdin, who showed him the window finished. The sultan embraced him, the envious vizir meanwhile hinting that it was the work of enchantment.

Aladdin had won the hearts of the people by his gentle bearing. He was made captain of the sultan's armies and won several battles for him, but remained modest and courteous as before and lived thus in peace and content for several years.

But far away in Africa the magician remembered Aladdin, and by his magic arts discovered that Aladdin, instead of perishing miserably in the cave, had escaped and had married a princess, with whom he was living in great honor and wealth. He knew that the poor tailor's son could only have accomplished this by means of the lamp and traveled night and day till he reached the capital of China, bent on Aladdin's ruin. As he passed through the town he heard people talking everywhere about a marvelous palace.

"Forgive my ignorance," he asked, "what is this palace you speak of?"

"Have you not heard of Prince Aladdin's palace," was the reply, "the greatest wonder of the world? I will direct you if you have a mind to see it."

The magician thanked him who spoke and, having seen the palace, knew that it had been raised by the genie of the lamp and became half mad with rage. He determined to get hold of the lamp and again plunge Aladdin into the deepest poverty.

Unluckily, Aladdin had gone hunting for eight days, which gave the magician plenty of time. He bought a dozen copper lamps, put them into a basket, and went to the palace, crying, "New lamps for old!" followed by a jeering crowd.

The princess, sitting in the hall of four-and-twenty windows, sent a slave to find out what the noise was about. The slave came back laughing, so the princess scolded her.

"Madam," replied the slave, "who can help laughing to see an old fool offering to exchange fine new lamps for old ones?"

Another slave, hearing this, said, "There is an old one on the cornice there which he can have."

Now this was the magic lamp, which Aladdin had left there, as he could not take it out hunting with him. The princess, not knowing its value, laughingly bade the slave take it and make the exchange. She went and said to the magician, "Give me a new lamp for this."

He snatched it and bade the slave take her choice, amid the jeers of the crowd. Little he cared, but left off crying his lamps, and went out of the city gates to a lonely place, where he remained till nightfall, when he pulled out the lamp and rubbed it. The genie appeared and at the magician's command carried him, together with the palace and the princess in it, to a lonely place in Africa.

Next morning the sultan looked out of the window toward Aladdin's palace and rubbed his eyes, for it was gone. He sent for the vizir and asked what had become of the palace. The vizir looked out, too, and was lost in astonishment. He again put it down to enchantment and this time the sultan believed him and sent thirty men on horseback to fetch Aladdin in chains. They met him riding home, bound him, and forced him to go with them on foot.

The people, however, who loved him, followed, armed, to see that he came to no harm. He was carried before the sultan, who ordered the executioner to cut off his head. The executioner made Aladdin kneel down, bandaged his eyes, and raised his scimitar to strike. At that instant the vizir, who saw that the crowd had forced their way into the courtyard and were scaling the walls to rescue Aladdin, called to the executioner to stay his hand. The people, indeed, looked so threatening that the sultan gave way and ordered Aladdin to be unbound, and pardoned him in the sight of the crowd.

Aladdin now begged to know what he had done.

"False wretch!" said the sultan, "come hither," and showed him from the window the place where his palace had stood. Aladdin was so amazed that he could not say a word.

"Where is the palace and my daughter?" demanded the sultan. "For the first I am not so deeply concerned, but my daughter I must have and you must find her or lose your head."

Aladdin begged for forty days in which to find her, promising if he failed, to return and suffer death at the sultan's pleasure. His prayer was granted, and he went forth sadly from the sultan's presence. For three days he wandered about like a madman, asking everyone what had become of his palace, but they only laughed and pitied him.

He came to the banks of a river and knelt down to say his prayers before throwing himself in. In so doing he rubbed the magic ring he still wore. The genie he had seen in the cave appeared and asked his will.

"Save my life, genie," said Aladdin, "and bring my palace back."

"That is not in my power," said the genie. "I am only the slave of the ring, you must ask the slave of the lamp."

"Even so," said Aladdin, "but thou canst take me to the palace, and set me down under my dear wife's window." He at once found himself in Africa, under the window of the princess, where he fell asleep from sheer weariness.

He was awakened by the singing of the birds and his heart was lighter. He saw plainly that all his misfortunes were owing to the loss of the lamp and vainly wondered who had robbed him of it.

That morning the princess rose earlier than she had since she had been carried into Africa by the magician, whose company she was forced to endure once a day. She, however, treated him so harshly that he dared not live there altogether. As she was dressing, one of her women looked out and saw Aladdin. The princess ran and opened the window, and at the noise she made Aladdin looked up. She called him to come to her, and great was their joy at seeing each other again.

After he had kissed her Aladdin said, "I beg of you, Princess, before we speak of anything else, for your own sake and mine, tell me what has become of an old lamp I left on

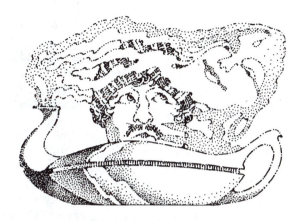

the cornice in the hall of four-and-twenty windows, when I went hunting."

"Alas," she said, "I am the innocent cause of our sorrows," and told him of the exchange of the lamp.

"Now I know," cried Aladdin, "that we have to thank the African magician for this! Where is the lamp?"

"He carries it about with him," said the princess, "I know, for he pulled it out of his robe to show me. He wishes me to break my faith with you and marry him, saying that you were beheaded by my father's command. He is forever speaking ill of you, but I only reply by my tears. If I persist, I doubt not that he will use violence."

Aladdin comforted her and left her for a while. He changed clothes with the first person he met in the town and, having bought a certain powder, returned to the princess, who let him in by a little side door.

"Put on your most beautiful dress," he said to her, "and receive the magician with smiles, leading him to believe that you have forgotten me. Invite him to sup with you and say you wish to taste the wine of his country. He will go for some and while he is gone I will tell you what to do."

She listened carefully to Aladdin and, when he left her, arrayed herself gaily for the first time since she left China. She put on a girdle and headdress of diamonds, and seeing in a glass that she looked more beautiful than ever, received the magician, saying to his great amazement, "I have made up my mind that Aladdin is dead and that all my tears will not bring him back to me, so I am resolved to mourn no more and therefore invite you to sup with me. But I am tired of the wines of China and would fain taste those of Africa."

The magician flew to his cellar and the princess put the powder Aladdin had given her in her cup. When he returned she asked him to drink her health in the wine of Africa, handing him her cup in exchange for his as a sign she was reconciled to him.

Before drinking, the magician made her a speech in praise of her beauty, but the princess cut him short, saying, "Let me drink first, and you shall say what you will afterward." She set her cup to her lips while the magician drained his to the dregs and fell back lifeless.

The princess then opened the door to Aladdin and flung her arms round his neck, but Aladdin put her away, bidding her to leave him, as he had more to do. He then went to the dead magician, took the lamp out of his vest, and bade the genie carry the palace and all in it back to China. This was done, and the princess in her chamber only felt two slight shocks and little thought she was at home again.

The sultan, who was sitting in his closet, mourning for his lost daughter, happened to look up and rubbed his eyes, for there stood the palace as before! He hastened thither, and Aladdin received him in the hall of the four-and-twenty windows, with the princess at his side. Aladdin told him what had happened and showed him the dead body of the magician, that he might believe. A ten days' feast was proclaimed, and it seemed as if Aladdin might now live the rest of his life in peace; but it was not to be.

The African magician had a younger brother, who was, if possible, more wicked and cunning than himself. He traveled to China to avenge his brother's death and went to visit a pious woman called Fatima, thinking she might be of use to him. He entered her cell and clapped a dagger to her breast, telling her to rise and do his bidding on pain of death. He changed clothes with her, colored his face like hers, put on her veil, and murdered her that she might tell no tales.

Then he went toward the palace of Aladdin, and all the people, thinking he was the holy woman, gathered round him, kissing his hands and begging his blessing. When he reached the palace there was such a noise round him that the princess bade her slave look out of the window and ask what was the matter. The slave said it was the holy woman, curing people of their ailments by her touch, whereupon the princess, who had long desired to see Fatima, sent for her.

On coming to the princess, the magician offered up a prayer for her health and prosperity. When he had done the princess made him sit by her and begged him to stay with her always. The false Fatima, who wished for nothing better, consented but kept his veil down for fear of discovery. The princess showed him the hall and asked him what he thought of it.

"It is truly beautiful," said the false Fatima. "In my mind it wants but one thing."

"And what is that?" said the princess.

"If only a roc's egg," replied he, "were hung up from the middle of this dome, it would be the wonder of the world."

After this the princess could think of nothing but a roc's egg, and when Aladdin returned from hunting he found her in a very ill humor. He begged to know what was amiss, but she told him that all her pleasure in the hall was spoilt for the want of a roc's egg hanging from the dome.

"If that is all," replied Aladdin, "you shall soon be happy."

He left her and rubbed the lamp, and when the genie appeared commanded him to bring a roc's egg. The genie gave such a loud and terrible shriek that the hall shook.

"Wretch," he cried, "is it not enough that I have done everything for you, but you must command me to bring my master and hang him up in the midst of this dome? You and your wife and your palace deserve to be burnt to ashes, but this request does not come from you but from the brother of the African magician whom you destroyed. He is now in your palace disguised as the holy woman—whom he murdered. He it was who put that wish into your wife's head. Take care of yourself, for he means to kill you." So saying the genie disappeared.

Aladdin went back to the princess, saying his head ached and requesting that the holy Fatima should be fetched to lay her hands on it. But when the magician came near, Aladdin, seizing his dagger, pierced him to the heart.

"What have you done?" cried the princess. "You have killed the holy woman!"

"Not so," replied Aladdin, "but a wicked magician," and told her of how she had been deceived.

After this Aladdin and his wife lived in peace. He succeeded the sultan when he died, and reigned for many years, leaving behind him a long line of kings.

Folk Tales of Africa

 Much of the African folk literature available in English has been collected and retold by writers in the United States; while some collections and single tales existed previously, most have been published late in the twentieth century. Many of the collections are regional: Eleanor Heady's *When the Stones Were Soft: East African Fireside Tales,* or Verna Aardema's *Tales for the Third Ear: from Equatorial Africa;* many are based on a tribal or language group, like Virginia Holladay's *Bantu Tales.* Varied as they are, African stories share certain qualities: a rollicking humor, a strong sense of justice, an emphasis on the natural world, and an emphasis on "why" stories and creation tales.

The Fire on the Mountain
(Ethiopia)

A young servant takes the advice of a wise man to prove to his master that he has earned his freedom.

People say that in the old days in the city of Addis Ababa there was a young man by the name of Arha. He had come as a boy from the country of Guragé, and in the city he became the servant of a rich merchant, Haptom Hasei.

Haptom Hasei was so rich that he owned everything that money could buy, and often he was very bored because he had tired of everything he knew, and there was nothing new for him to do.

One cold night, when the damp wind was blowing across the plateau, Haptom called to Arha to bring wood for the fire. When Arha was finished, Haptom began to talk.

"How much cold can a man stand?" he said, speaking at first to himself. "I wonder if it would be possible for a man to stand on the highest peak, Mount Sululta, where the coldest winds blow, through an entire night without blankets or clothing and yet not die?"

"I don't know," Arha said. "But wouldn't it be a foolish thing?"

"Perhaps, if he had nothing to gain by it, it would be a foolish thing to spend the night that way," Haptom said. "But I would be willing to bet that a man couldn't do it."

"I am sure a courageous man could stand naked on Mount Sululta throughout an entire night and not die of it," Arha said. "But as for me, it isn't my affair since I've nothing to bet."

"Well, I'll tell you what," Haptom said. "Since you are so sure it can be done, I'll make a bet with you anyway. If you can stand among the rocks on Mount Sululta for an entire night without food or water, or clothing or blankets or fire, and not die of it, then I

will give you ten acres of good farmland for your own, with a house and cattle."

Arha could hardly believe what he had heard.

"Do you really mean this?" he asked.

"I am a man of my word," Haptom replied.

"Then tomorrow night I will do it," Arha said, "and afterwards, for all the years to come, I shall till my own soil."

But he was very worried, because the wind swept bitterly across that peak. So in the morning Arha went to a wise old man from the Guragé tribe and told him of the bet he had made. The old man listened quietly and thoughtfully, and when Arha had finished he said:

"I will help you. Across the valley from Sululta is a high rock which can be seen in the daytime. Tomorrow night, as the sun goes down, I shall build a fire there, so that it can be seen from where you stand on the peak. All night long you must watch the light of my fire. Do not close your eyes or let the darkness creep upon you. As you watch my fire, think of its warmth, and think of me, your friend, sitting there tending it for you. If you do this you will survive, no matter how bitter the night wind."

Arha thanked the old man warmly and went back to Haptom's house with a light heart. He told Haptom he was ready, and in the afternoon Haptom sent him, under the watchful eyes of other servants, to the top of Mount Sululta. There, as night fell, Arha removed his clothes and stood in the damp cold wind that swept across the plateau with the setting sun. Across the valley, several miles away, Arha saw the light of his friend's fire, which shone like a star in the blackness.

The wind turned colder and seemed to pass through his flesh and chill the marrow in his bones. The rock on which he stood felt like ice. Each hour the cold numbed him more, until he thought he would never be warm again, but he kept his eyes upon the twinkling light across the valley, and remembered that his old friend sat there tending a fire for him. Sometimes wisps of fog blotted out the light, and then he strained to see until the fog passed. He sneezed and coughed and shivered, and began to feel ill. Yet all night through he stood there, and only when the dawn came did he put on his clothes and go down the mountain back to Addis Ababa.

Haptom was very surprised to see Arha, and he questioned his servants thoroughly.

"Did he stay all night without food or drink or blankets or clothing?"

"Yes," his servants said. "He did all of these things."

"Well, you are a strong fellow," Haptom said to Arha. "How did you manage to do it?"

"I simply watched the light of a fire on a distant hill," Arha said.

"What! You watched a fire? Then you lose the bet, and you are still my servant, and you own no land!"

"But this fire was not close enough to warm me, it was far across the valley!"

"I won't give you the land," Haptom said. "You didn't fulfill the conditions. It was only the fire that saved you."

Arha was very sad. He went again to his old friend of the Guragé tribe and told him what had happened.

"Take the matter to the judge," the old man advised him.

Arha went to the judge and complained, and the judge sent for Haptom. When Haptom told his story, and the servants said once more that Arha had watched a distant fire across the valley, the judge said:

"No, you have lost, for Haptom Hasei's condition was that you must be without fire."

Once more Arha went to his old friend with the sad news that he was doomed to the life of a servant, as though he had not gone through the ordeal on the mountaintop.

"Don't give up hope," the old man said. "More wisdom grows wild in the hills than in any city judge."

He got up from where he sat and went to find a man named Hailu, in whose house he had been a servant when he was young. He explained to the good man about the bet between Haptom and Arha, and asked if something couldn't be done.

"Don't worry about it," Hailu said after thinking for a while. "I will take care of it for you."

Some days later Hailu sent invitations to many people in the city to come to a feast at his house. Haptom was among them, and so was the judge who had ruled Arha had lost the bet.

When the day of the feast arrived, the guests came riding on mules with fine trappings, their servants strung out behind them on foot. Haptom came with twenty servants, one of whom held a silk umbrella over his head to shade him from the sun, and four drummers played music that signified the great Haptom was here.

The guests sat on soft rugs laid out for them and talked. From the kitchen came the odors of wonderful things to eat: roast goat, roast corn and durra, pancakes called injera, and many tantalizing sauces. The smell of the food only accentuated the hunger of the guests. Time passed. The food should have been served, but they didn't see it, only smelled vapors that drifted from the kitchen. The evening came, and still no food was served. The guests began to whisper among themselves. It was very curious that the honorable Hailu had not had the food brought out. Still the smells came from the kitchen. At last one of the guests spoke out for all the others:

"Hailu, why do you do this to us? Why do you invite us to a feast and then serve us nothing?"

"Why, can't you smell the food?" Hailu asked with surprise.

"Indeed we can, but smelling is not eating, there is no nourishment in it!"

"And is there warmth in a fire so distant that it can hardly be seen?" Hailu asked. "If Arha was warmed by the fire he watched while standing on Mount Sululta, then you have been fed by the smells coming from my kitchen."

The people agreed with him; the judge now saw his mistake, and Haptom was shamed. He thanked Hailu for his advice, and announced that Arha was then and there the owner of the land, the house, and the cattle.

Then Hailu ordered the food brought in, and the feast began.

Men of Different Colors
(East Africa)

The role of the storyteller as custodian of tribal lore is made evident in this story that explains why there are people of various skin colors.

There was great excitement in the village. A stranger had stopped that day. He carried large sheets of white paper. On these he drew pictures, mostly pictures of animals, but some of people and villages and even trees. This was strange, but the strangest thing of all was the man himself. He was different, a different color, a very light red, declared Kambo. But Karioki and Gachui said he was nearer white or maybe the color of cream. His hair was different, too. It didn't stay curled neatly to his scalp the way proper hair should do, but stuck up like dry grass straw, straight and spiky. It was nearly the color of straw, too.

At first the children were frightened of the stranger. They ran away and hid. Then, as they watched from their hiding places, they discovered that he was friendly despite his looks. He talked and smiled with the elders, then he gave the children sweets wrapped in paper. The children had eaten these before when the men had come back from trips to the duka, or shop, of Hamed, the Indian.

All day long the talk was of the stranger. Who was he? Where had he come from? Why was he so different?

When evening came and they gathered for their story, the talk was still of the stranger.

"Let's ask Mama Semamingi about him," said Wakai. "She knows everything."

"Yes, yes," agreed the others.

When the grandmother joined the circle, the children were still talking.

She smiled. "So you want to know about the stranger?"

"How did you know, Mama Semamingi?"

"I guessed," she said. "That is all anyone has been talking about today."

"Why is he so different?" asked one of the bigger boys.

"He was made that way, just as you were made as you are," answered the grandmother. "Did you know that people like Hamed, the Indian, are different, too?"

None of the children had been to the shop of Hamed. They had only heard of him. "No, is he red, too?" asked Kambo.

"He's not red, nor white, nor is he black. He is a brown man. My story tells about him, too."

"Tell us, please," said the children.

"Mzuri, good, here it is."

The great god Mungu lived in a white ice palace on the top of the high mountain, Kitingara. He became tired of his sparkling castle. He was lonely. *I must make a friend to live with me and to help with the thunder and lightning,* he thought. So the lonely mountain god set off downhill to look for some clay. He went down the mountain to the green forests below his palace.

In a little open place among the trees, he found a spring of bubbling water that sparkled off down the hillside in a little stream. On either side of this stream there was thick, dark clay, clay of a beautiful shiny blackness.

"Just the thing for my man," said Mungu. He knelt on the soft earth and began to work. For many hours he toiled. When at last he had finished, he arose, clapped his hands, and the still statue of a man opened his eyes, moved his head, and spoke to Mungu saying, "You are the great Mungu."

Mungu replied, "You shall be my helper and live with me in my white palace. I will call you Mutunyeusi, the black man."

For many weeks Mungu and Mutunyeusi, black like the clay from which he was made, lived in the ice palace. The man was cold at the top of the mountain. His clay became frozen so that he felt stiff and useless. He begged Mungu to allow him to go down below to the little streams and green valleys. "If you will only let me go down to the green forests then I shall really be able to help you.

"Men of Different Colors" from WHEN THE STONES WERE SOFT, EAST AFRICAN FIRESIDE TALES by Eleanor B. Heady. Copyright © 1968 by Eleanor B. Heady. Reprinted by permission of Curtis Brown Ltd.

I can care for the lower regions while you, oh master, guard the heavens."

Mungu granted the wish of Mutunyeusi. Down the black man went into the green valleys. He was happy there, hunting and living off wild berries and fruits, but he in his turn became lonely and returned to the top of Kitingara. "Please, oh great Mungu," he said. "Make another man for my companion, so that I shall not be lonely."

"That is easily done and quickly, too," replied Mungu. "Let us go at once to the stream with the black clay and make a friend for you."

They set off for the stream. When they arrived, Mutunyeusi helped his master make not one, but two, more men.

"Three will be less lonely than two," said Mungu. "And perhaps sometimes one of you can visit me on my lonely mountain top."

The great mountain god gazed into the distance, thinking. He was troubled. These three men were just alike. How could he tell them apart? He must devise some way to make them different. He returned to his mountain top, leaving the three men in the forest. There he thought and thought, trying to discover some way to make his men different.

One day when Mungu was out walking, he came upon a little pool of pure white water that stood in a hollow below the great river of ice on Kitingara. When he saw this water, he thought of a plan. He called his three black sons and said to them, "See that pool? I want each of you in turn to wash in it. Something wonderful will happen if you do."

"Very well, master," said Mutunyeusi, the first man. "Let my younger brothers wash before me." He pushed one black brother forward toward the water. In he went, the white liquid covering him completely; when he came out, wonder of wonders! He had lost his black color and was a shining, pinkish white!

"Oh, let *me* try!" cried the next brother, and ran into the shallow pool. Alas, there wasn't much water left and he was barely dampened. His color, when he came out, was

a light brown. At last came the turn of Mutunyeusi, but there was so little of the water left in the pool that all he could wet was the palms of his hands and the soles of his feet, which turned a pinkish color.

Mungu was very pleased. "Now I shall always know my children apart," he said. "You, Mutunyeusi, shall remain black and be the father of a family of black children. You shall live in the plains and forests surrounding my mountain. You shall be closest because you were my first son." Then, turning to the one who had bathed first, Mungu said, "You shall be known as Muzungu, the white man, and to you and your children I give all the lands to the north. Go to them and be happy." And to the second brother he said, "You will be the father of the brown people, Muhindi, and to you I give all the lands to the east. May your people prosper there."

Down from the mountain went the brothers, now each so different from the other. They went into the lands their father had given them. That is why to this very day you will find brown people in the eastern lands, white people to the north, and black people around the lonely mountain.

The Great Tug-of-War
(Nigeria)

Zomo the hare gets the better of his acquaintances in a story that will remind readers of Brer Rabbit, when he stirs up trouble and wisely disappears.

It happens one year that the rains come late and go early so the harvest is poor and food is scarce. Animals who usually reap a hundred baskets of corn find they have only fifty, and animals who usually reap fifty find they have only twenty-five. As for Zomo, who never reaps more than ten, even in the best of seasons, he is left with only five.

"The Great Tug-of-War" from ZOMO THE RABBIT, edited by Hugh Sturton. Copyright © 1966 by H. A. S. Johnston (New York: Atheneum, 1966). Reprinted with the permission of Atheneum Publishers and Hamish Hamilton Ltd.

"When are you going to fetch the rest of it?" asks his wife when he brings home his five baskets.

"There isn't any more," says Zomo.

"D'you mean to tell me," says his wife, "that this is all we have to eat for the next twelve months?"

"We shall have to manage as best we can," says Zomo.

The corn lasts through most of the dry season but by the time the hot weather comes round, it is nearly finished. First Zomo tries to borrow some more, but the other animals say they have none to lend. Then he tries to borrow money so that he can buy corn in the market, but they remember the last time they lent him money, and so they are sorry but they can't oblige.

When his wife tells him that they have food for only two more days, Zomo reckons that the time has come for him to have a good think. So he goes and sits under the *chediya* tree with his thinking cap on, and in the evening, when his wife calls him in to supper, he tells her that he is going to go and see Giwa the Elephant, who has more corn than he knows what to do with.

Next morning, Zomo puts on his best gown and goes and calls on Giwa. When he reaches the house, he says that he has a message for the master and he is taken into the audience chamber where Giwa is receiving those who come to pay their respects.

"God give you long life," cries Zomo in a loud voice, doing obeisance and looking very respectful.

"Amen, Zomo," says Giwa, who likes to be buttered up.

"I have a message for you," says Zomo. "It is from Dorina the Hippopotamus."

"We don't see much of him since he's taken to living in the river," says Giwa. "Tell me," he goes on, "does he still have that black stallion?"

"That is what the message is about," says Zomo.

"Well, you can tell him from me," says Giwa, "that if he still wants to swap the black for my chestnut, there is nothing doing; but

I will buy the black from him any time he likes."

"He is short of corn this year," says Zomo, "and he says that if you can let him have some, he will give you the black in exchange."

"Oho," says Giwa, "so that's how the land lies, is it? Well, how much does he want?"

"He says that he'll let him go for a hundred baskets," says Zomo, "so long as he can keep him until after the festival."

"Whatever does he want to do that for?" asks Giwa.

"He's his favorite mount," says Zomo, "and he likes to ride him in the procession."

"All right," says Giwa, "tell Dorina it's a bargain."

Without more ado, the elephant orders his wife and daughters to measure out a hundred baskets of corn.

"There you are, Zomo," he says when this is done. "If you lead the way, my boys will carry it for you. And tell Dorina," he goes on, "that he can keep the black until the festival, but no longer."

"I'll tell him that," says Zomo. So saying, he takes his leave and sets off with ten young elephants behind him who are each carrying ten baskets of corn.

"All right, put it down here, boys," says Zomo when they reach a place near his house. "You've done your share—I'll get those lazy young hippos to take it the rest of the way."

As soon as the young elephants have gone, Zomo calls to his wife and children and they carry the baskets into his house. When they have finished, his corn-stores are all full and running over.

"Where did you get all this?" asks Zomo's wife when they finish carting the corn.

"Giwa is my friend," says Zomo, "and when he hears that my corn is nearly finished, he insists on giving me some of his. 'Zomo,' he says, 'I won't have you going short.' Naturally I do not wish to offend him and so I accept."

When she hears this, Zomo's wife looks at him as if she doesn't believe a word he says, but she holds her tongue and says nothing.

Next morning, Zomo puts on his best gown again, and this time he makes for the river where Dorina the Hippopotamus has his house. Since Dorina lives in the water, the bad season does not hurt him and he has plenty of food.

When Zomo reaches Dorina's gate, he says that he has a message for him and is taken to the audience chamber.

"God give you victory," Zomo cries in a loud voice, doing obeisance and looking very respectful, just as he does with the elephant.

"Welcome, Zomo," says Dorina. "What brings you to these parts?"

"I have a message," says Zomo, "from Giwa the Elephant."

"Oh?" says Dorina. "What does Giwa want with me?"

"He wants to know," says Zomo, "whether you still want to buy his chestnut."

"Of course I do," says Dorina. "I even offer to swap my black for him, but Giwa will not have it."

"Well, he's changed his mind now," says Zomo, and tells Dorina the same tale that he already told Giwa, right down to the bit about Giwa wishing to keep the chestnut until the festival because it is the horse he likes to ride in the procession. Dorina is so pleased with the proposition that then and there he tells his wife and daughters to prepare a hundred baskets of dried fish.

When the fish is ready, Zomo takes his leave and sets off for dry land with twenty young hippos behind him, each carrying five baskets. By and by they reach a place near his house, and he tells them to put the stuff down and he will get the young elephants, who are fat and lazy he says, to carry it the rest of the way.

As soon as the young hippos have gone back to the river, Zomo fetches his wife and children and they carry the baskets home. Since the larder is already full of corn, the eight youngest rabbits have to give up their hut to make room for the fish, which fills it right up to the thatch and makes it bulge like a pumpkin.

Soon after this, the rains come and all through the rainy season Zomo keeps his wife and children busy plaiting a rope. It is the biggest rope you ever saw and so strong that you can tie Giwa the Elephant up with it and he won't get loose. His old woman is always asking Zomo what they want with such a rope, but Zomo won't say.

By and by, when the rains are nearly over, the festival comes round. All the animals ride in the procession, and the elephant sees that the hippo is mounted on the black, and the hippo sees that the elephant is mounted on the chestnut.

Next day, bright and early, Zomo takes one end of his rope and sets out for the river. When he comes to the bank, he finds a fig tree and passes the rope round the trunk. Then he goes on to the hippo's house.

"Ah, Zomo," says Dorina when he is ushered into his presence, "you are just the man I wish to see. Do you bring news about my horse?"

"God give you long life," says Zomo, "here is the end of his tethering rope, which Giwa the Elephant tells me to bring to you. When the sun rises tomorrow, he will take him down to the river by the fig tree, and he says when you see the leaves of the fig tree begin to shake, it will be the signal to pull him in on the rope."

"Very well," says Dorina. "We'll be ready."

"God give you victory," Zomo goes on, "Giwa also says to tell you that this chestnut of his is a mighty strong horse and that he can't answer for it if you let him get away."

"Never fear," says Dorina, "my boys will take care of him."

When Zomo leaves the hippo, he goes and gets the other end of the rope and takes it to the elephant's house. "God give you long life," he says to Giwa, and then he spins him the same yarn, right down to the bit about the black being a mighty strong horse and Dorina not answering for it if he lets him get away.

"Not to worry," says Giwa. "My boys will look after him all right."

When Zomo gets home that evening, he tells his wife that people may come asking for him next day, and that if they do, she is to say that he is gone to Gwanja.

"But," says she, "you aren't going to Gwanja, are you?"

"Not I," says Zomo, "but this is what you must say. And furthermore," he goes on, "if they ask how long I shall be away, you are to say six months if not eight."

Early next morning, before the sun rises, Giwa the Elephant lines up his ten sons outside his house. He tells them that the hippo's black is mighty strong and that when he gives the signal they must heave on the rope with all their might. On the river bank Dorina the Hippo is doing the same thing with his twenty sons.

By and by the sun rises, the breeze springs up, and the leaves of all the trees along the river bank begin to shake. But Giwa and Dorina do not notice the other trees because they are only watching the fig tree. As soon as they see its leaves shaking, they both shout, "Heave," and then all the young elephants and all the young hippos begin to pull on the rope as if their lives depend on it.

At first the hippos gain some ground. When the old elephant sees this, he thinks that his horse is getting away and so he becomes very agitated and dances up and down and shouts to his sons to pull harder. Then the elephants begin to gain ground and it is the turn of the old hippo at the other end to become agitated and dance up and down and shout.

While this goes on, Zomo slips out of his house and hides himself in the branches of the fig tree. He has to hold on tight because the elephants and the hippos are pulling it this way and that and at one time he thinks that the tree will come up by the roots. But he waits until the tree is steady because both sides strain so hard, and then he takes out his knife and reaches down and cuts the rope.

When Zomo cuts the rope, the young hippos, who are up on the bank of the river, go toppling back into the water and make such a mighty splash that it stuns all the fish for miles around and even gives old Kada the Crocodile a headache.

As for the young elephants at the other end, they are right in front of their father's house, and so when the rope parts, they all go tumbling backward and knock down the ornamental gateway, which Giwa made for himself the year before, and then go rolling on into the compound where they flatten two huts and a corn-store.

When the old elephant and the old hippo see the rope part, they both think they will lose their horse, and so they both dash out to the fig tree to catch it and there they run into one another. Now Giwa, besides being surprised, is by no means pleased to see Dorina just now. He scowls at him and says that the black broke his tethering rope and that unless Dorina catches him and brings him back he will have to ask for the return of all his corn.

Dorina doesn't care to be scowled at at the best of times, let alone just now when he thinks that his horse has got away, and so he scowls right back and says that he doesn't know about any corn, all he knows is that the chestnut has broken his rope and got away and that unless Giwa catches him and brings him back he will have to ask for the return of all his fish.

Giwa is not used to being spoken to like this, even by Zaki the Lion, and doesn't care for it any more than Dorina cares to be scowled at. "Dorina," he says, "you get above yourself. You may be a great man among the frogs and fishes, but here on land we don't consider you any great shakes."

This makes Dorina madder than ever because he doesn't like to be reminded that he now lives with frogs and fishes. "Giwa," he says, "the only reason I leave dry land and live in the water is that your belly rumbles so loud at night that it disturbs my children and they don't get their proper sleep."

At this, Giwa calls the hippo a baseborn, bandy-legged bog-trotter, and Dorina says that the elephant is a beady-eyed, swivel-nosed, loppy-lugged lounge-about. If the other animals don't come running up at this moment, they will certainly come to blows but as it is, they are just parted in time.

Later both of them send for Zomo, but they are told that Zomo is gone to Gwanja and won't be back for six months, if not eight. In fact it is much longer than this before Giwa and Dorina are on speaking terms again.

As for Zomo, he lies low and keeps out of everybody's sight. But his wife and children get so fat on Giwa's corn and Dorina's fish that the other animals think that Zomo must be working in Gwanja and sending money back to his family.

"That Zomo," they say to one another, "I do declare that he has turned over a new leaf at last."

Why Frog and Snake Never Play Together
(Nigeria)

Mama Frog and Mama Snake are equally horrified to learn that their children have become friends, and maternal instructions end the friendship forever in this lithely told "why" story.

Mama Frog had a son. Mama Snake also had a son. One morning both children went out to play.

Mama Snake called after her child:

"Watch out for big things with sharp claws and teeth that gnaw. Don't lose your way in the bush, baby, and be back to the burrow before dark."

"Clawsangnaws," sang Snake as he went looping through the grass. "Beware of the Clawsangnaws."

Mama Frog called after her son:

"Watch out for things that peck or bite. Don't go into the bush alone, dear. Don't fight, and get home before night."

"Peckorbite," sang Frog as he went hopping from stone to stone. "Beware of the Peckorbite!"

Snake was singing his Clawsangnaws song, and Frog was singing of Peckorbites when they met along the way. They had never met before.

"Who are you?" asked Frog. "Are you a Peckorbite?" and he prepared to spring out of reach.

"Oh no! I'm Snake, called by my Mama 'Snakeson': I'm slick, lithe and slithery. Who are you? Are you a Clawsangnaws?" and he got ready to move, just in case.

"No no! I'm Frog, called by my Mama 'Frogchild.' I'm hip, quick and hoppy."

They stood and stared at each other, then they said together:

"You don't look anything like me."

Their eyes brightened. They did not look alike, that's true, but some of their customs were alike. Both knew what to do when two say the same thing at the same time.

They clasped each other, closed their eyes and sang:

> "You wish a wish
> I'll wish a wish, too;
> May your wish and my wish
> Both come true."

Each made a wish then let go.

Just then a fly flew by, right past Frog's eyes. Flip! out went his tongue as he flicked in the fly.

A bug whizzed past Snake's nose. Flash! Snake flicked out his tongue and caught the bug.

They looked in admiration at each other and smiled. The two new friends now knew something of what each other could do. They felt at ease with each other, like old friends.

"Let's play!" said Frog.

"Hey!" said Snake, "that was my wish. Let's play in the bush."

"The bush! In the bush!" cried Frog. "That was my wish. If you go with me, it's all right 'cause Mama said I shouldn't go alone."

"Why Frog and Snake Never Play Together" from BEAT THE STORY-DRUM, PUM-PUM by Ashley Bryan. Copyright © 1980 by Ashley Bryan (New York: Atheneum, 1980). Reprinted with the permission of Atheneum Publishers.

Frog and Snake raced to the bush and started playing games.

"Watch this," said Frog. He crouched down and counted, "One a fly, two a fly, three a fly, four!"

He popped way up into the air, somersaulted and came down, whop!

"Can you do that, Snake?"

Snake bounded for a nearby mound to try the Frog-Hop. He got to the top of the slope, stood on the tip of his tail and tossed himself into the air. Down he came, flop! a tangle of coils. He laughed and tried again.

Sometimes Snake and Frog jumped together and bumped in midair. No matter how hard they hit, it didn't hurt. They had fun.

Then Snake said, "Watch this!" He stretched out at the top of the mound and counted, "One a bug, two a bug, three a bug, four!" Then swoosh! he slithered down the slope on his stomach.

"Try that, Frog. It's called the Snake-Slither."

Frog lay on his stomach and slipped down the hill. His arms and legs flailed about as he slithered. He turned over at the bottom of the slope, *blump!* and rolled up in a lump.

Frog and Snake slithered down together, entangling as they went. Their calls and laughter could be heard all over the bush. One game led to another. They were having such a good time that the day passed swiftly. By late afternoon there were not two better friends in all the bush.

The sun was going down when Snake remembered his promise to his mother.

"I promised to be home before dark," he said.

"Me too," said Frog. "Good-bye!"

They hugged. Snake was so happy that he'd found a real friend that he forgot himself and squeezed Frog very tightly. It felt good, very, very good.

"Ow! easy!" said Frog. "Not too tight."

"Oh, sorry," said Snake loosening his hug-hold. "My! but you sure feel good, good enough to eat."

At that they burst out laughing and hugged again, lightly this time.

"I like you," said Frog. "Bye, Snake."

"Bye, Frog. You're my best friend."

"Let's play again tomorrow," they said together.

Aha! they clasped and sang once again:

"You wish a wish
I'll wish a wish, too;
May your wish and my wish
Both come true."

Off they went, Snake hopping and Frog slithering all the way home.

When Frog reached home, he knocked his knock, and Mama Frog unlocked the rock door. She was startled to see her child come slithering in across the floor.

"Now what is this, eh?" she said. "Look at you, all covered with grass and dirt."

"It doesn't hurt," said Frog. "I had fun."

"Fun? Now what is this, eh? I can tell you haven't been playing in ponds or bogs with the good frogs. Where have you been all day? You look as if you've just come out of the bush."

"But I didn't go alone, Ma. I went with a good boy. He's my best friend."

"Best friend? Now what is this, eh?" said Mama Frog. "What good boy could that be, playing in the bush?"

"Look at this trick that he taught me, Ma," said Frogchild. He flopped on his stomach and wriggled across the floor, bungling up Mama Frog's neatly stitched lily-pad rug.

"That's no trick for a frog! Get up from there, child!" cried Mama Frog. "Now what is this, eh? Look how you've balled up my rug. Just you tell me, who was this playmate?"

"His name is Snakeson, Mama."

"Snake, son! Did you say Snake, son?"

"Yes. What's the matter, Mama?"

Mama Frog trembled and turned a pale green. She sat down to keep from fainting. When she had recovered herself, she said:

"Listen Frogchild, listen carefully to what I have to say." She pulled her son close.

"Snake comes from the Snake family. They are bad people. Keep away from them. You hear me, child?"

"Bad people?" asked Frog.

"Bad, too bad!" said Mama Frog. "Snakes are sneaks. They hide poison in their tongues, and they crush you in their coils."

Frogchild gulped.

"You be sure to hop out of Snake's reach if ever you meet again. And stop this slithering foolishness. Slithering's not for frogs."

Mama Frog set the table muttering to herself: "Playing with Snake! Now what is this, eh?" She rolled a steaming ball of gleaming cornmeal onto Frogchild's plate.

"Sit down and eat your funji, child," said Mama Frog. "And remember, I'm not fattening frogs for snakes, eh?"

Snake too reached home. He rustled the braided twig hatch-cover to his home. His mother knew his rustle and undid the vine latch. Snake toppled in.

"I'm hungry, Ma," he said, hopping all about.

"Eh, eh! Do good bless you! What a sight you are!" said Mama Snake. "Just look at you. And listen to your panting and wheezing. Where have you been all day?"

"In the bush, Mama, with my new friend. We played games. See what he taught me."

Snakeson jumped up on top of the table and leaped into the air. He came down on a stool, knocking it over and entangling himself in its legs.

"Eh, eh! Do good bless you. What a dangerous game that is," said Mama Snake. "Keep it up and see if you don't break every bone in your back. What new friend taught you that?"

She bent over and untangled her son from the stool.

"My frog friend taught me that. His name's Frogchild. It's the Frog-Hop, Mama. Try it. It's fun."

"Frog, child?" Mama Snake's jaws hung open showing her fangs. "Did you say Frog, child?"

"Yes," said Snakeson. "He's my best friend."

"You mean you played all day with a frog and you come home hungry?"

"He was hungry too, Mama, after playing the Snake Slither game that I taught him."

"Eh, eh! Well do good bless you! Come, curl up here son and listen carefully to what I have to tell you."

Snakeson curled up on the stool.

"Don't you know, son, that it is the custom of our house to eat frogs? Frogs are delicious people!"

Snakeson's small eyes widened.

"Ah, for true!" said Mama Snake. "Eating frogs is the custom of our house, a tradition in our family. Hopping isn't, so cut it out, you hear me?"

"Oh, Mama," cried Snakeson. "I can't eat frogs. Frog's a friend."

"Frog a friend! Do good bless you!" said Mama Snake. "That's not natural. Now you listen to me, baby. The next time you play with Frog, jump roll and romp all you like. But when you get hungry, his game is up. Catch him and eat him!"

The next morning Snakeson was up early. He pushed off his dry-leaf cover and stretched himself. He remembered his mother's words, and the delicious feel of his frog friend when they had hugged. He was ready to go.

Mama Snake fixed her son a light breakfast of spiced insects and goldfinch eggs. Snakeson was soon on his way.

"Now don't you forget my instructions about frogs, do good bless you," Mama Snake called out after him. "And don't let me have to tell you again to watch out for big things with sharp claws and teeth that gnaw."

"Clawsangnaw," sang Snakeson. "Clawsangnaw."

He reached the bush and waited for his friend. He looked forward to fun with Frog, and he looked forward to finishing the fun with a feast of his fine frog friend. He lolled about in the sun, laughing and singing:

"You wish a wish
I'll wish a wish, too;
Can your wish and my wish
Both come true?"

The sun rose higher and higher, but Frog did not come.

"What's taking Frogchild so long," said Snakeson. "Perhaps too much slithering has given him the bellyache. I'll go and look for him."

Snake found Frog's rock home by the pond. He rolled up a stone in his tail and knocked on the rock door.

"Anybody home?"

"Just me," answered Frogchild.

"May I come in?"

"Ah, it's you Snakeson. Sorry, my Mama's out, and she said not to open the door to anyone."

"Come on out then and let's play," said Snakeson. "I waited all morning for you in the bush."

"I can't," said Frog, "not now, anyway."

"Oh, that's too bad," said Snake. "My mother taught me a new game. I'd love to teach it to you."

"I'll bet you would," said Frog.

"You don't know what you're missing," said Snake.

"But I do know what you're missing," said Frog, and he burst out laughing.

"Aha!" said Snake. "I see that your mother has given you instructions. My mother has given me instructions too."

Snake sighed. There was nothing more to say or do, so he slithered away.

Frog and Snake never forgot that day when they played together as friends. Neither ever again had that much fun with anybody.

Today you will see them, quiet and alone in the sun, still as stone. They are deep in thought remembering that day of games in the bush, and both of them wonder:

"What if we had just kept on playing together, and no one had ever said anything?"

But from that day to this, Frog and Snake have never played together again.

> "You wish a wish
> I'll wish a wish, too;
> May your wish and my wish
> Both come true."

Anansi's Hat-Shaking Dance
(West Africa)

A trickster-hero, both man and spider, turns disaster into a temporary triumph, but his mendacity is exposed, in a tale that is a lesson about boasting.

If you look closely, you will see that Kwaku Anansi, the spider, has a bald head. It is said that in the old days he had hair, but that he lost it through vanity.

It happened that Anansi's mother-in-law died. When word came to Anansi's house, Aso, his wife, prepared to go at once to her own village for the funeral. But Anansi said to Aso: "You go ahead; I will follow."

When Aso had gone, Anansi said to himself: "When I go to my dead mother-in-law's house, I will have to show great grief over her death. I will have to refuse to eat. Therefore, I shall eat now." And so he sat in his own house and ate a huge meal. Then he put on his mourning clothes and went to Aso's village.

First there was the funeral. Afterwards there was a large feast. But Anansi refused to eat, out of respect for his wife's dead mother. He said: "What kind of man would I be to eat when I am mourning for my mother-in-law? I will eat only after the eighth day has passed."

Now this was not expected of him, because a man isn't required to starve himself simply because someone has died. But Anansi was the kind of person that when he ate, he ate twice as much as others, and when he danced, he danced more vigorously than others, and when he mourned, he had to mourn more loudly than anybody else. Whatever he did, he didn't want to be outdone by anyone else. And although he was very hungry, he couldn't bear to have people think he wasn't the greatest mourner at his own mother-in-law's funeral.

So he said: "Feed my friends, but as for me, I shall do without." So everyone ate—the porcupine, the rabbit, the snake, the guinea fowl, and the others. All except Anansi.

On the second day after the funeral they said to him again: "Eat, there is no need to starve."

But Anansi replied: "Oh no, not until the eighth day, when the mourning is over. What kind of man do you think I am?"

So the others ate. Anansi's stomach was empty, and he was unhappy.

On the third day they said again: "Eat, Kwaku Anansi, there is no need to go hungry."

But Anansi was stubborn. He said: "How can I eat when my wife's mother has been buried only three days?" And so the others ate, while Anansi smelled the food hungrily and suffered.

On the fourth day, Anansi was alone where a pot of beans was cooking over the fire. He smelled the beans and looked in the pot. At last he couldn't stand it any longer. He took a large spoon and dipped up a large portion of the beans, thinking to take it to a quiet place and eat it without anyone's knowing. But just then the dog, the guinea fowl, the rabbit, and the others returned to the place where the food was cooking.

To hide the beans, Anansi quickly poured them in his hat and put it on his head. The other people came to the pot and ate, saying again: "Anansi, you must eat."

He said: "No, what kind of man would I be?"

But the hot beans were burning his head. He jiggled his hat around with his hands. When he saw the others looking at him, he said: "Just at this very moment in my village the hat-shaking festival is taking place. I shake my hat in honor of the occasion."

The beans felt hotter than ever, and he jiggled his hat some more. He began to jump with pain, and he said: "Like this in my village they are doing the hat-shaking dance."

He danced about, jiggling his hat because of the heat. He yearned to take off his hat, but he could not because his friends would see the beans. So he shouted: "They are shaking and jiggling the hats in my village, like this! It is a great festival! I must go!"

They said to him: "Kwaku Anansi, eat something before you go."

But now Anansi was jumping and writhing with the heat of the beans on his head. He shouted: "Oh no, they are shaking hats, they are wriggling hats and jumping like this! I must go to my village! They need me!"

He rushed out of the house, jumping and pushing his hat back and forth. His friends followed after him saying: "Eat before you go on your journey!"

But Anansi shouted: "What kind of man do you think I am, with my mother-in-law just buried?"

Even though they all followed right after him, he couldn't wait any longer, because the pain was too much, and he tore the hat from his head. When the dog saw, and the guinea fowl saw, and the rabbit saw, and all the others saw what was in the hat, and saw the hot beans sticking to Anansi's head, they stopped chasing him. They began to laugh and jeer.

Anansi was overcome with shame. He leaped into the tall grass, saying: "Hide me." And the grass hid him.

That is why Anansi is often found in the tall grass, where he was driven by shame. And you will see that his head is bald, for the hot beans he put in his hat burned off his hair.

All this happened because he tried to impress people at his mother-in-law's funeral.

Unanana and the Elephant
(South Africa)

One enterprising woman rescues a group of people who have meekly accepted their fate.

Many, many years ago there was a woman called Unanana who had two beautiful children. They lived in a hut near the roadside and people passing by would often stop when they saw the children, exclaiming at the

"Anansi's Hat-Shaking Dance" from THE HAT-SHAKING DANCE AND OTHER ASHANTI TALES FROM GHANA by Harold Courlander. Copyright © 1957 by Harold Courlander. Reprinted by permission of Harcourt Brace Jovanovich, Inc.

"Unanana and the Elephant" from AFRICAN MYTHS AND LEGENDS retold by Kathleen Arnott. Copyright © 1962 by Kathleen Arnott. Reprinted by permission of Oxford University Press.

The children grew tired of their game, and taking a small gourd they dipped it in turn into the big pot full of water which stood at the door of their hut, and drank their fill.

A sharp bark made the cousin drop her gourd in fear when she looked up and saw the spotted body and treacherous eyes of a leopard, who had crept silently out of the bush.

"Whose children are those?" he demanded.

"They belong to Unanana," she replied in a shaky voice, slowly backing towards the door of the hut in case the leopard should spring at her. But he was not interested in a meal just then.

"Never have I seen such beautiful children before," he exclaimed, and with a flick of his tail he melted away into the bush.

The children were afraid of all these animals who kept asking questions and called loudly to Unanana to return, but instead of their mother, a huge elephant with only one tusk lumbered out of the bush and stood staring at the three children, who were too frightened to move.

"Whose children are those?" he bellowed at the little cousin, waving his trunk in the direction of the two beautiful children who were trying to hide behind a large stone.

"They . . . they belong to Una . . . Unanana," faltered the little girl.

The elephant took a step forward.

"Never have I seen such beautiful children before," he boomed. "I will take them away with me," and opening wide his mouth he swallowed both children at a gulp.

The little cousin screamed in terror and dashed into the hut, and from the gloom and safety inside it she heard the elephant's heavy footsteps growing fainter and fainter as he went back into the bush.

It was not until much later that Unanana returned, carrying a large bundle of wood on her head. The little girl rushed out of the house in a dreadful state and it was some time before Unanana could get the whole story from her.

"Alas! Alas!" said the mother. "Did he swallow them whole? Do you think they might still be alive inside the elephant's stomach?"

roundness of their limbs, the smoothness of their skin and the brightness of their eyes.

Early one morning Unanana went into the bush to collect firewood and left her two children playing with a little cousin who was living with them. The children shouted happily, seeing who could jump the furthest, and when they were tired they sat on the dusty ground outside the hut, playing a game with pebbles.

Suddenly they heard a rustle in the nearby grasses, and seated on a rock they saw a puzzled-looking baboon.

"Whose children are those?" he asked the little cousin.

"They belong to Unanana," she replied.

"Well, well, well!" exclaimed the baboon in his deep voice. "Never have I seen such beautiful children before."

Then he disappeared and the children went on with their game.

A little later they heard the faint crack of a twig and looking up they saw the big, brown eyes of a gazelle staring at them from beside a bush.

"Whose children are those?" she asked the cousin.

"They belong to Unanana," she replied.

"Well, well, well!" exclaimed the gazelle in her soft, smooth voice. "Never have I seen such beautiful children before," and with a graceful bound she disappeared into the bush.

"I cannot tell," said the child, and she began to cry even louder than before.

"Well," said Unanana sensibly, "there's only one thing to do. I must go into the bush and ask all the animals whether they have seen an elephant with only one tusk. But first of all I must make preparations."

She took a pot and cooked a lot of beans in it until they were soft and ready to eat. Then seizing her large knife and putting the pot of food on her head, she told her little niece to look after the hut until she returned, and set off into the bush to search for the elephant.

Unanana soon found the tracks of the huge beast and followed them for some distance, but the elephant himself was nowhere to be seen. Presently, as she passed through some tall, shady trees, she met the baboon.

"O baboon! Do help me!" she begged. "Have you seen an elephant with only one tusk? He has eaten both my children and I must find him."

"Go straight along this track until you come to a place where there are high trees and white stones. There you will find the elephant," said the baboon.

So the woman went on along the dusty track for a very long time but she saw no sign of the elephant.

Suddenly she noticed a gazelle leaping across her path.

"O gazelle! Do help me! Have you seen an elephant with only one tusk?" she asked. "He has eaten both my children and I must find him."

"Go straight along this track until you come to a place where there are high trees and white stones. There you will find the elephant," said the gazelle, as she bounded away.

"O dear!" sighed Unanana. "It seems a very long way and I am so tired and hungry."

But she did not eat the food she carried, since that was for her children when she found them.

On and on she went, until rounding a bend in the track she saw a leopard sitting outside his cave-home, washing himself with his tongue.

"O leopard!" she exclaimed in a tired voice. "Do help me! Have you seen an elephant with only one tusk? He has eaten both my children and I must find him."

"Go straight along this track until you come to a place where there are high trees and white stones. There you will find the elephant," replied the leopard, as he bent his head and continued his toilet.

"Alas!" gasped Unanana to herself. "If I do not find this place soon, my legs will carry me no further."

She staggered on a little further until suddenly, ahead of her, she saw some high trees with large white stones spread about on the ground below them.

"At last!" she exclaimed, and hurrying forward she found a huge elephant lying contentedly in the shade of the trees. One glance was enough to show her that he had only one tusk, so going up as close as she dared, she shouted angrily:

"Elephant! Elephant! Are you the one that has eaten my children?"

"O no!" he replied lazily. "Go straight along this track until you come to a place where there are high trees and white stones. There you will find the elephant."

But the woman was sure this was the elephant she sought, and stamping her foot, she screamed at him again:

"Elephant! Elephant! Are you the one that has eaten my children?"

"O no! Go straight along this track—" began the elephant again, but he was cut short by Unanana who rushed up to him waving her knife and yelling:

"Where are my children? Where are they?"

Then the elephant opened his mouth and without even troubling to stand up, he swallowed Unanana with the cooking-pot and her knife at one gulp. And this was just what Unanana had hoped for.

Down, down, down she went in the darkness, until she reached the elephant's stomach. What a sight met her eyes! The walls of the elephant's stomach were like a range of hills, and camped among these hills were little groups of people, many dogs and goats and cows, and her own two beautiful children.

"Mother! Mother!" they cried when they saw her. "How did you get here? Oh, we are so hungry."

Unanana took the cooking-pot off her head and began to feed her children with the beans, which they ate ravenously. All the other people crowded round, begging for just a small portion of the food, so Unanana said to them scornfully:

"Why do you not roast meat for yourselves, seeing that you are surrounded by it?"

She took her knife and cut large pieces of flesh from the elephant and roasted them over a fire she built in the middle of the elephant's stomach, and soon everyone, including the dogs and goats and cattle, was feasting on elephant-meat very happily.

But the groans of the poor elephant could be heard all over the bush, and he said to those animals who came along to find out the cause of his unhappiness:

"I don't know why it is, but ever since I swallowed that woman called Unanana, I have felt most uncomfortable and unsettled inside."

The pain got worse and worse, until with a final grunt the elephant dropped dead. Then Unanana seized her knife again and hacked a doorway between the elephant's ribs through which soon streamed a line of dogs, goats, cows, men, women and children, all blinking their eyes in the strong sunlight and shouting for joy at being free once more.

The animals barked, bleated or mooed their thanks, while the human beings gave Unanana all kinds of presents in gratitude to her for setting them free, so that when Unanana and her two children reached home, they were no longer poor.

The little cousin was delighted to see them, for she had thought they were all dead, and that night they had a feast. Can you guess what they ate? Yes, roasted elephant-meat.

The Sloogeh Dog and the Stolen Aroma
(Congo)

Poetic justice is meted out by a wise judge when a wealthy man complains that a hungry dog is stealing the smell of his food.

There was once a greedy African who through shrewd and sometimes dishonest dealings had become very rich. He was so rich in ivory that he had a fence of tusks all around his compound. He was so rich in sheep that he dared not count them, lest the evil spirits become jealous and destroy them.

He had so many wives that it took him from sunup to sundown just to walk past the doors of their huts. And he had so many daughters of marriageable age that he kept them in a herd guarded day and night by old women.

The favorite pastime of this rich man was eating. But no guest ever dipped the finger in the pot with him at mealtime. No pet sat near him waiting to pick up fallen crumbs.

He ate alone in the shade of a big tree near the ivory gate of his compound. He ate much food and he became very fat.

One day as he sat on his eating stool, a procession of wives filed over to him from the cookhouse. Each carried on her head a basket or platter or bowl of food.

Each put her offering before him and backed away to sit on her heels and watch him eat. This day among the delicacies were baked elephant's foot, fried locusts, and rice balls with peanut gravy.

A wonderful aroma came from the steaming food. It flooded the compound and seeped through and over the ivory fence.

Now it happened that, at the very moment the smell of the food was spreading through the jungle, the Sloogeh Dog was coming down a path near the rich man's gate. In his wanderings he had foolishly crossed the hot, barren "hungry country" and he was truly on the verge of starvation.

When the smell of the rich man's food met him, his head jerked up and saliva gathered at the corners of his mouth. New strength came into his long lean body. He trotted, following the scent, straight to the rich man's gate.

The Sloogeh Dog pushed on the gate. It was tied fast, so he peered between the ivory posts. Seeing the man eating meat off a big bone, he made polite little begging sounds deep in his throat.

Saliva made two long threads from the corners of his mouth to the ground.

The sight of the hungry creature at his very gate spoiled the rich man's enjoyment of his food. He threw a vex and bellowed, "Go away from my face, beggar!"

The Sloogeh Dog was outside the fence where anyone was free to be. He knew he didn't have to go away. But he had another idea. He trotted all the way around the compound searching for the pile of rich scraps which he was sure would be somewhere near the fence. He found not so much as a peanut shuck.

However, he didn't forget the wonderful smell of that food. Each day, at mealtime, he would come to sniff and drool at the rich man's gate. Each day the man would drive him away. And every day his anger grew until one day he left his food and went straight to the Council of Old Men.

He told his story. Then he said, "I want you to arrest that beggar of a dog!"

"On what grounds?" asked one of the old men.

"For stealing the aroma of my food!" said the rich man.

So the dog was arrested, a judge was appointed, and a day was set for the trial.

On the day of the trial, the whole village gathered about the Tree of Justice. From the start, the sympathy of the people was all with the Sloogeh Dog, for there was scarcely one of them who had not been swindled by the rich man.

But the judge was a just man. "I agree that the aroma was part of the food and so belonged to the accuser," he said. "And since the dog came every day to enjoy the smell of the food, one must conclude that it was intentional."

Murmurs of pity came from the crowd.

The Sloogeh Dog yawned nervously.

The judge continued, "If he had stolen only once, the usual punishment would be to cut off his paws!"

The Sloogeh Dog's legs gave way under him and he slithered on his belly to a hiding place back of the Tree of Justice.

"However," cried the judge, "since the crime was a daily habit, I must think about it overnight before I decide on a suitable punishment."

At sunup the next morning the people gathered to hear the sentence. They became very curious when the judge came leading a horse. He dropped the reins to the ground and left the animal standing where the trail enters the village.

Was the horse part of the punishment? Was the judge taking a trip later? He only shrugged when the people questioned him.

The judge called the rich man and the Sloogeh Dog to come before him. Handing a kiboko to the rich man, he said, "The accused will be beaten to death by the accuser!"

The rich man took off his gold-embroidered robe. He made a practice swing through the air with the whip.

The judge held up his hand. "Wait!" he commanded.

Then he turned to the people. "Do the people agree that it was the invisible part of the food, and therefore its spirit, that was stolen?"

"Ee, ee!" cried the people.

The judge held up his hand again. "Do the people agree that the spirit of the dog is his shadow?"

"Ee, ee!" they said.

"Then," boomed the judge, "since the crime was against the spirit of the food, *only* the spirit of the dog shall be punished!"

The people howled with laughter. Their feet drummed on the hard-packed earth. They slapped each other's backs and shouted, "Esu! Esu!"

The Sloogeh Dog leaped up and licked the judge's nose.

The judge turned to the rich man and, when he could be heard, he said, "The shadow is big now, but you must beat it until the sun is straight up in the sky. When there is nothing left of the shadow, we shall agree that it is dead."

The rich man threw down the whip, picked up his garment, and said, "I withdraw the charges."

The judge shook his head. "You caused the arrest," he said. "You wanted the trial. Now administer justice. And if the kiboko touches so much as a hair of the Sloogeh Dog, it will be turned upon you!"

There was nothing for the rich man to do but swing the whip hour after hour. The people watched and laughed as the dog leaped and howled, pretending to suffer with his shadow.

As the sun climbed higher and higher, the shadow became smaller and smaller—and much harder to hit. The whip became heavier in the man's flabby hands. He was dripping with sweat and covered with dust stirred up by the whip.

When the man could hardly bear the ordeal any longer, the dog lay down. That made it necessary for the man to get on his knees and put his arm between him and the dog to keep from touching a hair. When he brought down the whip, he hit his arm.

The people screamed with laughter.

The rich man bellowed and threw the kiboko. Then he leaped to the back of the judge's horse and rode headlong out of the village.

"He won't come back," said the oldest Old Man. "He would get *his* paws chopped off if he did. He stole the judge's horse!"

The Sloogeh Dog slunk off toward the rich man's house, his long nose sniffing for a whiff of something cooking beyond the ivory gate.

The Stepchild and the Fruit Trees
(Ibo)

By the magic of her song, Ijomah wins independence from the cruel stepmother who denies her any of the good things of life, in a tale that invites audience participation in the patterned chant.

Once upon a time there lived a family in a village where there were a lot of fruit trees. So many different kinds of fruit trees grew there that in every season, rainy or dry, there was always plenty of fruit in the market to sell. People came to the market from other villages and from the nearby town to buy the good fruit.

The father of the family in this fruit-tree village had four children, all of them girls. But one of the girls, Ijomah, was a stepchild. Her mother had died when Ijomah was twelve years old and her father had married again.

It was then that Ijomah's troubles began. Her stepmother, Nnekeh, never liked her. She only loved her own children and completely neglected Ijomah. Worse than that, she made the girl do all the hard work and did not even give her enough food.

Ijomah's father, Mazo, was too busy with his trade to know what was going on. Even on weekends he was out on business. The few times he was at home Ijomah complained to him in secret, but Mazo never wanted to offend his second wife. Instead of talking the matter over with Nnekeh, he always asked Ijomah to be patient, and once in a while he gave her some money to buy food.

Ijomah's mother had loved to plant flowers. After she died, Ijomah continued to tend the garden. Nnekeh often sent her own children to pick all the brightest and most beautiful flowers, but always once a month Ijomah took roses to her mother's grave. She would have taken the roses more often, but Nnekeh never gave her the chance. At times Ijomah cried over the loss of her mother and over her own sad state. But things never changed.

One day Nnekeh went to the market and bought some red juicy fruit called *odala.* Children love to eat the pink pulpy flesh of the *odala,* and they play games of marbles with the hard black seeds. Of course Nnekeh only gave the fruit to her own children, and Ijomah had none. Ijomah had to be content with the two scanty meals she was given that day. But after her half sisters had eaten their *odala,* Ijomah saw that they had thrown away the seeds. She collected the seeds and planted them in her garden.

When she woke up one day, she found little plants sprouting from the seeds. She was very happy and took great care to make the plants grow up strong and healthy. Early every morning, long before the others stirred from their beds, Ijomah would go to her garden to water the plants. As she watered them she sang this song:

"My *odala!* grow
Please
My *odala!* grow
Please
Grow, grow, grow
Please
My father's wife
Please
Bought *odala* from the market
Please
Ate, ate, ate
Please
Ate and did not give her stepdaughter
Please."

Each morning Ijomah sang her song and watered the *odala* plants she loved so much.

Soon the plants grew into trees, and one day Ijomah saw the first fruit beginning to grow. She was so happy she wanted to dance. She never stopped singing her song.

But when the fruit began to ripen, Nnekeh said the trees belonged to her children, not just to Ijomah. Ijomah was very unhappy. She told Nnekeh that the trees and fruit were hers, but Nnekeh said: "I bought the *odala* in the market, and without them you would have had no trees!"

As soon as the fruit were fully ripe, people came to Ijomah's garden to buy them. Very many people came because the *odala* were so big and sweet. Ijomah wanted to sell the fruit and have money to buy some of the beautiful things that her stepmother would never allow her to have.

Nnekeh was furiously angry. She raged at Ijomah and refused to let her sell the *odala.* She herself would be the one to sell them. Ijomah was so unhappy she could not sleep that night. Very, very early the following morning, just as the first rays of sunlight appeared, she crept to the garden, stood sadly by the *odala* trees, and started singing:

"My *odala!* die
Please
My *odala!* die
Please
Die, die, die
Please
My father's wife
Please
Bought *odala* from the market
Please
Ate, ate, ate
Please
Ate and did not give her stepdaughter
Please
My *odala!* die."

As she finished the song, the *odala* trees began to shrivel and shrivel until they were all withered up.

When daylight came, the people whom Nnekeh had told about the big juicy fruit went to the garden to buy some. But all that the people found were shriveled trees and withered fruit. Everyone was surprised and annoyed.

Nnekeh was so ashamed she wished the ground would open and swallow her up. She started shouting like an angry general in the army. She knew very well, she said, that her crafty stepdaughter had played a trick on her. Ijomah only laughed and told the villagers that the fruit trees were hers.

"But if Nnekeh wants to," Ijomah said, "she can bring the trees to life again. If the trees are hers, they will obey her! If they belong to me, they will obey me!"

"The Stepchild and the Fruit Trees" from SINGING TALES OF AFRICA by Adjai Robinson. Copyright © 1974 by Adjai Robinson (New York: Charles Scribner's Sons, 1974). Reprinted with the permission of Charles Scribner's Sons.

Nnekeh looked at the shriveled trees, but there was nothing she could do. She tried to pounce on Ijomah, but the people grabbed her and pulled her away. Then they asked Ijomah whether she could do anything to the trees.

Ijomah smiled and started singing:

"My *odala!* grow
Please
My *odala!* grow
Please. . . ."

While she sang, the trees began to grow! New green leaves sprouted from the withered branches, and soon the trees were loaded with fruit, larger and riper than ever. When the villagers saw that, they knew the stepmother was wrong. The fruit belonged to Ijomah, and Nnekeh had been trying to take them away from her.

So the villagers bought fruit from Ijomah. They bought and bought. They carried away basketloads of fruit and still there was more to buy. No one had ever seen so many *odala* or tasted fruit so fine and sweet. Soon Ijomah was the richest person in the village. She had money to buy all the things she wanted, and her stepmother never troubled her again.

Folk Tales of Asia

China

 While China has had a strong tradition of mythic and heroic folk and fairy tales for several thousand years, it is only in the twentieth century that these have become available to English-speaking people. Many of the old tales have been adapted to suit the contemporary culture, but they still illustrate the morally idealistic tone of ancient Chinese culture, and its emphasis on order, beauty, and obedience. The single-tale book is more often published in the United States, but there are some fine collections: Cyril Birch's *Chinese Myths and Fantasies,* Frances Carpenter's *Tales of a Chinese Grandmother,* and *The Magic Boat and Other Chinese Folk Stories,* by Moritz Jagendorf and Virginia Weng. One of the stories included here, "Two of Everything," is not a true folk tale but an original fairy tale that is especially popular with children.

The Chinese Red Riding Hoods

Although the wolf plays grandmother, this variant puts him at the mercy of three ingenious girls.

Many years ago in China there lived a young widow with her three children. On their grandmother's birthday, the mother went to visit her.

"Felice," she cautioned her oldest daughter before she left, "you must watch over your sisters Mayling and Jeanne while I am gone. Lock the door and don't let anyone inside. I shall be back tomorrow."

A wolf who was hiding near the house at the edge of the woods overheard the news.

When it was dark he disguised himself as an elderly woman and knocked at the door of the three girls' house.

"Who is it?" called Felice.

"Felice, Mayling, and Jeanne, my treasures, it is your Grammie," answered the wolf as sweetly as possible.

"Grammie," said Felice through the door, "Mummy just went to see you!"

"It is too bad I missed her. We must have taken different roads," replied the crafty wolf.

"Grammie," asked Mayling, "why is your voice so different tonight?"

"Your old Grammie caught cold and is hoarse. Please let me in quickly, for it is drafty out here and the night air is very bad for me."

The tenderhearted girls could not bear to keep their grandmother out in the cold, so they unlatched the door and shouted, "Grammie, Grammie!"

As soon as the wolf crossed the threshold, he blew out the candle, saying the light hurt his tired eyes. Felice pulled a chair forward for her grandmother. The wolf sat down hard on his tail hidden under the skirt.

"Ouch!" he exclaimed.

"Is something wrong, Grammie?" asked Felice.

"Nothing at all, my dear," said the wolf, bearing the pain silently.

Then Mayling and Jeanne wanted to sit on their Grammie's lap.

"What nice, plump children," said the wolf, holding Mayling on one knee and Jeanne on the other.

Soon the wolf said, "Grammie is tired and so are you children. Let's go to bed."

The children begged as usual to be allowed to sleep in the huge double bed with their Grammie.

Soon Jeanne felt the wolf's tail against her toes. "Grammie, what's that furry thing?" she asked.

"Oh, that's just a brush I always have by me to keep away mosquitoes and flies," answered the wolf.

Then Mayling felt the sharp claws of the wolf. "Grammie, what are these sharp things?"

"Go to sleep, dear, they are just Grammie's nails."

Then Felice lit the candle and caught a glimpse of the wolf's hairy face before he could blow out the light. Felice was frightened. She quickly grabbed hold of Jeanne and said, "Grammie, Jeanne is thirsty. She needs to get up to get a glass of water."

"Oh, for goodness sake," said the wolf, losing patience, "tell her to wait until later."

Felice pinched Jeanne so that she started to cry.

"All right, all right," said the wolf, "Jeanne may get up."

Felice thought quickly and said, "Mayling, hurry and help Jeanne get a glass of water!"

When the two younger ones had left the bedroom, Felice said, "Grammie, have you ever tasted our luscious gingko nuts?"

"What is a gingko nut?" asked the wolf.

"The meat of the gingko nut is softer and more tender than a firm baby and tastes like a delicious fairy food," replied Felice.

"Where can you get some?" asked the wolf, drooling.

"Those nuts grow on trees outside our house."

"Well, your Grammie is too old to climb trees now," laughed the wolf.

"Grammie, dear, I can pick some for you," said Felice sweetly.

"Will you, angel?" pleaded the wolf.

"Of course, I'll do it right now!" said Felice, leaping out of bed.

"Come back quickly," called the wolf after her.

Felice found Mayling and Jeanne in the other room. She told them about the wolf, and the three girls quickly decided to climb up the tallest gingko tree around their cottage.

The wolf waited and waited, but no one came back. Then he got up and went outside and shouted, "Felice, Mayling, Jeanne, where are you?"

"We're up in the tree, eating gingko nuts," called Felice.

"Throw some down for me," yelled the wolf.

"Ah, Grammie, we just remember Mummy telling us that gingkos are fairy nuts. They change when they leave the tree. You'll just have to climb up and eat these mouth-watering nuts here."

The wolf was raging as he paced back and forth under the tree.

Then Felice said, "Grammie, I just had an idea. There is a clothesbasket by the door with a long clothesline inside. Tie one end to the handle and throw the end of the rope up to me. We shall pull you up here."

The wolf happily went to get the clothesbasket.

Felice pulled hard on the rope. When the basket was halfway up, she let go, and the wolf fell to the ground badly bruised.

"Boo hoo, hoo!" cried Felice, pretending to be very sorry. "I did not have enough strength to pull poor Grammie up!"

"Don't cry, Sister," said Mayling, "I'll help you pull Grammie up!"

The greedy wolf got into the basket again.

Felice and Mayling pulled with all their might. The wolf was two thirds up the tree before they let go of the rope. Down he fell with a crash. He began to scold.

"Grammie, Grammie, please don't get so upset," begged Jeanne. "I'll help my sisters to pull you all the way up this time."

"All right, but mind you be very careful or I'll bite your heads off!" screeched the wolf.

The three children pulled with all their strength.

"Heave ho, heave ho!" they sang in rhythm as they hauled the wolf up slowly till he was thirty feet high. He was just beyond reach of a branch when Felice coughed, and everyone let go of the rope. As the basket spun down, the wolf let out his last howl.

When the children were unable to get any answer to their calls of "Grammie," they slid down the tree and ran into the house, latched the door and soon went to sleep.

Two of Everything

Children enjoy the inventive turn this story, which begins like many a magic-pot story, takes, and it's easy to dramatize.

Mr. and Mrs. Hak-Tak were rather old and rather poor. They had a small house in a village among the mountains and a tiny patch of green land on the mountain side. Here they grew the vegetables which were all they had to live on, and when it was a good season and they did not need to eat up everything as soon as it was grown, Mr. Hak-Tak took what they could spare in a basket to the next village which was a little larger than theirs and sold it for as much as he could get and bought some oil for their lamp, and fresh seeds, and every now and then, but not often, a piece of cotton stuff to make new coats and trousers for himself and his wife. You can imagine they did not often get the chance to eat meat.

Now, one day it happened that when Mr. Hak-Tak was digging in his precious patch, he unearthed a big brass pot. He thought it strange that it should have been there for so long without his having come across it before, and he was disappointed to find that it was empty; still, he thought they would find some use for it, so when he was ready to go back to the house in the evening he decided to take it with him. It was very big and heavy, and in his struggles to get his arms round it and raise it to a good position for carrying, his purse, which he always took with him in his belt, fell to the ground, and, to be quite sure he had it safe, he put it inside the pot and so staggered home with his load.

As soon as he got into the house Mrs. Hak-Tak hurried from the inner room to meet him.

"My dear husband," she said, "whatever have you got there?"

"For a cooking-pot it is too big; for a bath a little too small," said Mr. Hak-Tak. "I found it buried in our vegetable patch and so far it has been useful in carrying my purse home for me."

"Alas," said Mrs. Hak-Tak, "something smaller would have done as well to hold any money we have or are likely to have," and she stooped over the pot and looked into its dark inside.

As she stooped, her hairpin—for poor Mrs. Hak-Tak had only one hairpin for all her hair and it was made of carved bone—fell into the pot. She put in her hand to get it out again, and then she gave a loud cry which brought her husband running to her side.

"What is it?" he asked. "Is there a viper in the pot?"

"Oh, my dear husband," she cried. "What can be the meaning of this? I put my hand into the pot to fetch out my hairpin and your purse, and look, I have brought out two hairpins and two purses, both exactly alike."

"Open the purse. Open both purses," said Mr. Hak-Tak. "One of them will certainly be empty."

But not a bit of it. The new purse contained exactly the same number of coins as the old one—for that matter, no one could have said which was the new and which the old—and it meant, of course, that the Hak-Taks had exactly twice as much money in the evening as they had had in the morning.

"And two hairpins instead of one!" cried Mrs. Hak-Tak, forgetting in her excitement to do up her hair which was streaming over her shoulders. "There is something quite unusual about this pot."

"Let us put in the sack of lentils and see what happens," said Mr. Hak-Tak, also becoming excited.

They heaved in the bag of lentils and when they pulled it out again—it was so big it almost filled the pot—they saw another bag of exactly the same size waiting to be pulled out in its turn. So now they had two bags of lentils instead of one.

"Put in the blanket," said Mr. Hak-Tak. "We need another blanket for the cold weather." And, sure enough, when the blanket came out, there lay another behind it.

"Put my wadded coat in," said Mr. Hak-Tak, "and then when the cold weather comes there will be one for you as well as for me. Let us put in everything we have in turn. What a pity we have no meat or tobacco, for it seems that the pot cannot make anything without a pattern."

Then Mrs. Hak-Tak, who was a woman of great intelligence, said, "My dear husband, let us put the purse in again and again and again. If we take two purses out each time we put one in, we shall have enough money by tomorrow evening to buy everything we lack."

"I am afraid we may lose it this time," said Mr. Hak-Tak, but in the end he agreed, and they dropped in the purse and pulled out

"Two of Everything" from THE TREASURE OF LI-PO by Alice Ritchie. Copyright 1949 by Harcourt Brace Jovanovich, Inc.; renewed 1977 by M. T. Ritchie. Reprinted by permission of the publisher and Chatto and Windus Ltd.

two, then they added the new money to the old and dropped it in again and pulled out the larger amount twice over. After a while the floor was covered with old leather purses and they decided just to throw the money in by itself. It worked quite as well and saved trouble; every time, twice as much money came out as went in, and every time they added the new coins to the old and threw them all in together. It took them some hours to tire of this game, but at last Mrs. Hak-Tak said, "My dear husband, there is no need for us to work so hard. We shall see to it that the pot does not run away, and we can always make more money as we want it. Let us tie up what we have."

It made a huge bundle in the extra blanket and the Hak-Taks lay and looked at it for a long time before they slept, and talked of all the things they would buy and the improvements they would make in the cottage.

The next morning they rose early and Mr. Hak-Tak filled a wallet with money from the bundle and set off for the big village to buy more things in one morning than he had bought in a whole fifty years.

Mrs. Hak-Tak saw him off and then she tidied up the cottage and put the rice on to boil and had another look at the bundle of money, and made herself a whole set of new hairpins from the pot, and about twenty candles instead of the one which was all they had possessed up to now. After that she slept for a while, having been up so late the night before, but just before the time when her husband should be back, she awoke and went over to the pot. She dropped in a cabbage leaf to make sure it was still working properly, and when she took two leaves out she sat down on the floor and put her arms round it.

"I do not know how you came to us, my dear pot," she said, "but you are the best friend we ever had."

Then she knelt up to look inside it, and at that moment her husband came to the door, and, turning quickly to see all the wonderful things he had bought, she overbalanced and fell into the pot.

Mr. Hak-Tak put down his bundles and ran across and caught her by the ankles and pulled her out, but, oh, mercy, no sooner had he set her carefully on the floor than he saw the kicking legs of another Mrs. Hak-Tak in the pot! What was he to do? Well, he could not leave her there, so he caught her ankles and pulled, and another Mrs. Hak-Tak so exactly like the first that no one would have told one from the other, stood beside them.

"Here's an extraordinary thing," said Mr. Hak-Tak, looking helplessly from one to the other.

"I will not have a second Mrs. Hak-Tak in the house!" screamed the old Mrs. Hak-Tak.

All was confusion. The old Mrs. Hak-Tak shouted and wrung her hands and wept, Mr. Hak-Tak was scarcely calmer, and the new Mrs. Hak-Tak sat down on the floor as if she knew no more than they did what was to happen next.

"One wife is all *I* want," said Mr. Hak-Tak, "but how could I have left her in the pot?"

"Put her back in it again!" cried Mrs. Hak-Tak.

"What? And draw out two more?" said her husband. "If two wives are too many for me, what should I do with three? No! No!" He stepped back quickly as if he was stepping away from the three wives and, missing his footing, lo and behold, he fell into the pot!

Both Mrs. Hak-Taks ran and each caught an ankle and pulled him out and set him on the floor, and there, oh, mercy, was another pair of kicking legs in the pot! Again each caught hold of an ankle and pulled, and soon another Mr. Hak-Tak, so exactly like the first that no one could have told one from the other, stood beside them.

Now the old Mr. Hak-Tak liked the idea of his double no more than Mrs. Hak-Tak had liked the idea of hers. He stormed and raged and scolded his wife for pulling him out of the pot, while the new Mr. Hak-Tak sat down on the floor beside the new Mrs. Hak-Tak and looked as if, like her, he did not know what was going to happen next.

Then the old Mrs. Hak-Tak had a very good idea. "Listen, my dear husband," she said, "now, do stop scolding and listen, for it is really a good thing that there is a new one of you as well as a new one of me. It means that you and I can go on in our usual way, and these new people, who are ourselves and yet not ourselves, can set up house together next door to us."

And that is what they did. The old Hak-Taks built themselves a fine new house with money from the pot, and they built one just like it next door for the new couple, and they lived together in the greatest friendliness, because, as Mrs. Hak-Tak said, "The new Mrs. Hak-Tak is really more than a sister to me, and the new Mr. Hak-Tak is really more than a brother to you."

The neighbors were very much surprised, both at the sudden wealth of the Hak-Taks and at the new couple who resembled them so strongly that they must, they thought, be very close relations of whom they had never heard before. They said: "It looks as though the Hak-Taks, when they so unexpectedly became rich, decided to have two of everything, even of themselves, in order to enjoy their money more."

The Tale of the Golden Vase and the Bright Monkeys
(Tibet)

Justice is meted out in this Tibetan tale of a man who turns the tables when his friend cheats him.

A merry tale, a wise tale, a witty tale.

One that will bring you a pleasant smile as it did to ancient Tibetan folks and as it does to Chinese people everywhere.

Once upon a time in old China there lived in Tibet two friends, Dorje and Sonam, a little distance from each other. Just the same, they often worked together on their land.

One day they decided to go to the mountaintop to look for *jen-shen* fruits.

They searched and dug most of the day without much success, when suddenly Dorje's spade hit something hard. Both now dug eagerly and soon they took out a vase that gleamed in the setting sun.

"It is pure gold!" cried Sonam, brushing the earth from it.

"I am not so sure," said Dorje slyly. "I am not so sure. We must test it first."

"That's a good idea," said Sonam.

"Good," said Dorje. "I will take the vase to a friend of mine who is a goldsmith. He can tell us." But in his mind there were mean dishonest thoughts of how he could keep the golden vase for himself.

"If it is really gold, I will sell it to him and we will share the money."

Sonam, who trusted his friend, agreed, and the two friends parted, deciding to meet soon again, to divide the money if the vase was truly of gold, and then to go again to look for *jen-shen* fruits.

Dorje soon learned the vase was of gold, but he decided to keep it all for himself. So two days later, when his friend came again, he greeted him with a long, sad face.

"What is wrong, dear Dorje? You look so sad."

"Alas!" Dorje said, "I took the vase to show it to the goldsmith and accidentally put it near the fire. The vase was only cheap pewter and melted into a lump of worthless metal."

Sonam did not quite believe this, but he just said, "Never mind, we only found the vase by accident. If it is not worth anything, we have lost nothing."

Dorje was very happy that Sonam took the bad news well. He was so pleased that he asked his wife to prepare a fine meal to entertain his friend.

The next day when they were saying good-by to each other, Sonam said, "Dear friend Dorje, I want to thank you for your hospital-

"The Tale of the Golden Vase and the Bright Monkeys" from THE MAGIC BOAT AND OTHER CHINESE FOLK STORIES by Dr. M. A. Jagendorf and Virginia Weng. Copyright © 1980 by Dr. M. A. Jagendorf and Virginia Weng. Reprinted by permission of the publisher, Vanguard Press, Inc.

ity and all the trouble you took with the vase. In return I would like to invite your two dear children to my home. You have mountains here, but I have a pond as well as mountains, and many fruit trees. They can play with the rabbits and pigeons I keep, swim in the pond, and eat fruits to their hearts' desire. It would be a nice vacation for them. Why not send them to my home for a little time?"

The children shouted with joy when they heard this, and their father Dorje readily agreed.

Sonam held the children by the hand and started to lead them to his home. He was a kind man and loved children. He gave them sweetmeats to eat. On the way, they came to a mountain called "Monkey Hill," because many monkeys lived there.

Sonam said, "There are so many monkeys, we will catch some to play with."

The children shouted with pleasure and ran ahead of Sonam. They came to the woods where monkeys leaped from branch to branch, chattering and screaming.

The children were truly excited and ran around with the playful monkeys.

Sonam looked on for a while. Then he caught two very young animals and put them in a twig cage he had with him.

"We will play with those little fellows," Sonam said to the children. They went to his home gaily, happily shouting and running.

When they were at Sonam's home, he said, "I will give each little monkey the same name you have, and you must help me teach them each trick you know."

The young monkeys were good students, and the children and Sonam spent happy hours playing together. The young monkeys learned to imitate the children's walk and motions of their hands and head, and the children and Sonam laughed and laughed.

One day a friend of the family came to tell them that Dorje was coming the next day to take the children home. The next morning Sonam gave each of the children a large basket and said, "Go up the mountain to where the crickets are chirping in the woods. There you will find berries and all the fruits you like. Be sure to fill your baskets. Your father is coming for you and we will all have a nice feast before you go home."

When they were gone and Sonam heard Dorje coming, he sat down on the ground, holding a young monkey on each arm, and put on a long, sad face.

"What is wrong, friend?" cried Dorje.

"Woe!" moaned Sonam, "I am sorrowing for your two lovely children."

"What is wrong? What happened to them? Where are they?"

"They are here, friend Dorje. A weird thing happened to your two children. One day they suddenly turned into the little monkeys I am holding on my arms." He pulled each monkey's tail and, as they had been trained, at that signal they jumped off his arms and began to walk and dance as the children did. Then Sonam called them by the children's names and they came up just as they had been taught.

Dorje looked on, too surprised to talk. He sat silent for a few moments. Then he stuttered, "How did this happen? How could such a thing happen? How is this possible?"

"True, dear friend Dorje, it is a freak happening, but strange things happen all the time. Remember the strange affair of the golden vase turning into cheap pewter?"

For a moment Dorje seemed stunned. Then he looked at Sonam and an understanding smile came to his face.

"I understand, dear friend! Now, tell me where my children are, and I will give you half of the money I got for the gold vase. It was stupid of me to want to keep it all."

"They will soon be here, Dorje. They went to gather berries and fruits for us."

"Good," said Dorje. "That will give me time to bring half the money I owe you."

He ran and returned just as the children came with the baskets full of berries and fruits.

Everyone, even the two little monkeys, enjoyed a grand feast. And Dorje and Sonam remained understanding friends.

Japan

 Unlike other countries in the Far East, Japan has long had published versions of its folk tales; storytelling was in decline but is reviving as a performing art today, while folk literature was and is a strong influence on writers, painters, and the theater. Like other Oriental folk literature, the stories echo the courtesy and moderation of the traditional culture, and two of the stories included here show the vitality of the animal characters that appear in so many Japanese folk tales. Two outstanding anthologies are Helen and William McAlpine's *Japanese Tales and Legends* and Yoshiko Uchida's *The Dancing Kettle and Other Japanese Folk Tales.*

The Magic Kettle

There's a double moral here: honesty is indeed the best policy—and, as Jimmu learns—the wise man turns things to his own advantage.

Right in the middle of Japan, high up among the mountains, an old man lived in his little house. He was very proud of it, and never tired of admiring the whiteness of his straw mats, and the pretty papered walls, which in warm weather always slid back, so that the smell of the trees and flowers might come in.

One day he was standing looking at the mountain opposite, when he heard a kind of rumbling noise in the room behind him. He turned round, and in the corner he beheld a rusty old iron kettle, which could not have seen the light of day for many years. How the kettle got there the old man did not know, but he took it up and looked it over carefully, and when he found that it was quite whole he cleaned the dust off it and carried it into his kitchen.

"That was a piece of luck," he said, smiling to himself; "a good kettle costs money, and it is as well to have a second one at hand in case of need; mine is getting worn out, and the water is already beginning to come through its bottom."

Then he took the other kettle off the fire, filled the new one with water, and put it in its place.

No sooner was the water in the kettle getting warm than a strange thing happened, and the man, who was standing by, thought he must be dreaming. First the handle of the kettle gradually changed its shape and became a head, and the spout grew into a tail, while out of the body sprang four paws, and in a few minutes the man found himself watching, not a kettle, but a tanuki! The creature jumped off the fire, and bounded about the room like a kitten, running up the walls and over the ceiling, till the old man was in an agony lest his pretty room should be spoilt. He cried to a neighbour for help, and between them they managed to catch the tanuki, and shut him up safely in a wooden chest. Then, quite exhausted, they sat down on the mats, and consulted together what they should do with this troublesome beast. At length they decided to sell him, and bade a child who was passing send them a certain tradesman called Jimmu.

"The Magic Kettle" from THE CRIMSON FAIRY BOOK, edited by Andrew Lang. London: Longmans, Green, and Company, 1903.

When Jimmu arrived, the old man told him that he had something which he wished to get rid of, and lifted the lid of the wooden chest, where he had shut up the tanuki. But, to his surprise, no tanuki was there, nothing but the kettle he had found in the corner. It was certainly very odd, but the man remembered what had taken place on the fire, and did not want to keep the kettle any more, so after a little bargaining about the price, Jimmu went away carrying the kettle with him.

Now Jimmu had not gone very far before he felt that the kettle was getting heavier and heavier, and by the time he reached home he was so tired that he was thankful to put it down in the corner of his room, and then forgot all about it. In the middle of the night, however, he was awakened by a loud noise in the corner where the kettle stood, and raised himself up in bed to see what it was. But nothing was there except the kettle, which seemed quiet enough. He thought that he must have been dreaming, and fell asleep again, only to be roused a second time by the same disturbance. He jumped up and went to the corner, and by the light of the lamp that he always kept burning he saw that the kettle had become a tanuki, which was running round after his tail. After he grew weary of that, he ran on the balcony, where he turned several somersaults, from pure gladness of heart. The tradesman was much troubled as to what to do with the animal, and it was only towards morning that he managed to get any sleep; but when he opened his eyes again there was no tanuki, only the old kettle he had left there the night before.

As soon as he had tidied his house, Jimmu set off to tell his story to a friend next door. The man listened quietly, and did not appear so surprised as Jimmu expected, for he recollected having heard, in his youth, something about a wonder-working kettle. "Go and travel with it, and show it off," said he, "and you will become a rich man; but be careful first to ask the tanuki's leave, and also to perform some magic ceremonies to prevent him from running away at the sight of the people."

Jimmu thanked his friend for his counsel, which he followed exactly. The tanuki's consent was obtained, a booth was built, and a notice was hung up outside it inviting the people to come and witness the most wonderful transformation that ever was seen.

They came in crowds, and the kettle was passed from hand to hand, and they were allowed to examine it all over, and even to look inside. Then Jimmu took it back, and setting it on the platform, commanded it to become a tanuki. In an instant the handle began to change into a head, and the spout into a tail, while the four paws appeared at the sides. "Dance," said Jimmu, and the tanuki did his steps, and moved first on one side and then on the other, till the people could not stand still any longer, and began to dance too. Gracefully he led the fan dance, and glided without a pause into the shadow dance and the umbrella dance, and it seemed as if he might go on dancing for ever. And so very likely he would, if Jimmu had not declared he had danced enough, and that the booth must now be closed.

Day after day the booth was so full it was hardly possible to enter it, and what the neighbour foretold had come to pass, and Jimmu was a rich man. Yet he did not feel happy. He was an honest man, and he thought that he owed some of his wealth to the man from whom he had bought the kettle. So, one morning, he put a hundred gold pieces into it, and hanging the kettle once more on his arm, he returned to the seller of it. "I have no right to keep it any longer," he added when he had ended his tale, "so I have brought it back to you, and inside you will find a hundred gold pieces as the price of its hire."

The man thanked Jimmu, and said that few people would have been as honest as he. And the kettle brought them both luck, and everything went well with them till they died, which they did when they were very old, respected by everyone.

Momotaro: Boy-of-the-Peach

This story combines two folk tale themes: the miniature child who comes to a childless couple, and the reward for kindness, which in this popular Japanese tale helps Momotaro conquer the wicked ogre.

Once long, long ago, there lived a kind old man and a kind old woman in a small village in Japan.

One fine day, they set out from their little cottage together. The old man went toward the mountains to cut some firewood for their kitchen, and the old woman went toward the river to do her washing.

When the old woman reached the shore of the river, she knelt down beside her wooden tub and began to scrub her clothes on a round, flat stone. Suddenly she looked up and saw something very strange floating down the shallow river. It was a big, big peach; bigger than the round wooden tub that stood beside the old woman.

Rumbley-bump and a-bumpety-bump . . . Rumbley-bump and a-bumpety-bump. The big peach rolled closer and closer over the stones in the stream.

"My gracious me!" the old woman said to herself. "In all my long life I have never seen a peach of such great size and beauty. What a fine present it would make for the old man. I do think I will take it home with me."

Then the old woman stretched out her hand just as far as she could, but no matter how hard she stretched, she couldn't reach the big peach.

"If I could just find a long stick, I would be able to reach it," thought the old woman, looking around, but all she could see were pebbles and sand.

"Oh, dear, what shall I do?" she said to herself. Then suddenly she thought of a way to bring the beautiful big peach to her side. She began to sing out in a sweet, clear voice,

"The deep waters are salty!
The shallow waters are sweet!
Stay away from the salty water,
And come where the water is sweet."

She sang this over and over, clapping her hands in time to her song. Then, strangely enough, the big peach slowly began to bob along toward the shore where the water was shallow.

Rumbley-bump and a-bumpety-bump . . . Rumbley-bump and a-bumpety-bump. The big peach came closer and closer to the old woman and finally came to a stop at her feet.

The old woman was so happy, she picked the big peach up very carefully and quickly carried it home in her arms. Then she waited for the old man to return so she could show him her lovely present. Toward evening the old man came home with a big pack of wood on his back.

"Come quickly, come quickly," the old woman called to him from the house.

"What is it? What is the matter?" the old man asked as he hurried to the side of the old woman.

"Just look at the fine present I have for you," said the old woman happily as she showed him the big round peach.

"My goodness! What a great peach! Where in the world did you buy such a peach as this?" the old man asked.

The old woman smiled happily and told him how she had found the peach floating down the river.

"Well, well, this is a fine present indeed," said the old man, "for I have worked hard today and I am very hungry."

Then he got the biggest knife they had, so he could cut the big peach in half. Just as he was ready to thrust the sharp blade into the peach, he heard a tiny voice from inside.

"Wait, old man! Don't cut me!" it cried, and before the surprised old man and woman could say a word, the beautiful big peach broke in two, and a sweet little boy jumped out from inside. The old man and woman were so surprised, they could only raise their hands and cry out, "Oh, oh! My goodness!"

Now the old man and woman had always wanted a child of their own, so they were

"Momotaro: Boy-of-the-Peach" from THE DANCING KET-TLE AND OTHER JAPANESE FOLK TALES by Yoshiko Uchida. Copyright 1949, 1977 by Yoshiko Uchida. Reprinted by permission of Harcourt Brace Jovanovich, Inc.

very, very happy to find such a fine little boy and decided to call him "Momotaro," which means boy-of-the-peach. They took very good care of the little boy and grew to love him dearly, for he was a fine young lad. They spent many happy years together, and before long Momotaro was fifteen years old.

One day Momotaro came before the old man and said, "You have both been good and kind to me. I am very grateful for all you have done, and now I think I am old enough to do some good for others too. I have come to ask if I may leave you."

"You wish to leave us, my son? But why?" asked the old man in surprise.

"Oh, I shall be back in a very short time," said Momotaro. "I wish only to go to the Island of the Ogres, to rid the land of those harmful creatures. They have killed many good people, and have stolen and robbed throughout the country. I wish to kill the ogres so they can never harm our people again."

"That is a fine idea, my son, and I will not stop you from going," said the old man.

So that very day, Momotaro got ready to start out on his journey. The old woman prepared some millet cakes for him to take along on his trip, and soon Momotaro was ready to leave. The old man and woman were sad to see him go and called, "Be careful, Momotaro! Come back safely to us."

"Yes, yes, I shall be back soon," he answered. "Take care of yourselves while I am away," he added, and waved as he started down the path toward the forest.

He hurried along, for he was anxious to get to the Island of the Ogres. While he was walking through the cool forest where the grass grew long and high, he began to feel hungry. He sat down at the foot of a tall pine tree and carefully unwrapped the *furoshiki*[1] which held his little millet cakes. "My, they smell good," he thought. Suddenly he heard the tall grass rustle and saw something stalking through the grass toward him. Momotaro blinked hard when he saw what it was. It was a dog as big as a calf! But Momotaro was not

frightened, for the dog just said, "Momotaro-san, Momotaro-san, what is it you are eating that smells so good?"

"I'm eating a delicious millet cake which my good mother made for me this morning," he answered.

The dog licked his chops and looked at the cake with hungry eyes. "Please, Momotaro-san," he said, "just give me one of your millet cakes, and I will come along with you to the Island of the Ogres. I know why you are going there, and I can be of help to you."

"Very well, my friend," said Momotaro. "I will take you along with me," and he gave the dog one of his millet cakes to eat.

As they walked on, something suddenly leaped from the branches above and jumped in front of Momotaro. He stopped in surprise and found that it was a monkey who had jumped down from the trees.

"Greetings, Momotaro-san!" called the monkey happily. "I have heard that you are going to the Island of the Ogres to rid the land of these plundering creatures. Take me with you, for I wish to help you in your fight."

When the dog heard this he growled angrily. "Grruff," he said to the monkey. *"I am going to help Momotaro-san. We do not need the help of a monkey such as you! Out of our way! Grruff, grruff,"* he barked angrily.

"How dare you speak to me like that?" shrieked the monkey, and he leaped at the dog, scratching with his sharp claws. The dog and the monkey began to fight each other, biting, clawing, and growling. When Momotaro saw this he pushed them apart and cried, "Here, here, stop it, you two! There is no reason why you both cannot go with me to the Island of the Ogres. I shall have two helpers instead of one!" Then he took another millet cake from his *furoshiki* and gave it to the monkey.

Now there were three of them going down the path to the edge of the woods. The dog in front, Momotaro in the middle, and the monkey walking in the rear. Soon they came to a big field and just as they were about to cross it, a large pheasant hopped out in front of them. The dog jumped at it with a growl, but the pheasant fought back with such spirit that Momotaro ran over to stop the dog. "We could use a brave bird such as you to help us fight the ogres. We are on our way to their island this very day. How would you like to come along with us?"

"Oh, I would like that indeed, for I would like to help you rid the land of these evil and dangerous ogres," said the pheasant happily.

"Then here is a millet cake for you, too," said Momotaro, giving the pheasant a cake, just as he had to the monkey and the dog.

Now there were four of them going to the Island of the Ogres, and as they walked down the path together, they became very good friends.

Before long they came to the water's edge and Momotaro found a boat big enough for all of them. They climbed in and headed for the Island of the Ogres. Soon they saw the island in the distance wrapped in gray, foggy clouds. Dark stone walls rose up above towering cliffs and large iron gates stood ready to keep out any who tried to enter.

Momotaro thought for a moment, then turned to the pheasant and said, "You alone can wing your way over their high walls and gates. Fly into their stronghold now, and do what you can to frighten them. We will follow as soon as we can."

So the pheasant flew far above the iron gates and stone walls and down onto the roof of the ogres' castle. Then he called to the ogres, "Momotaro-san has come to rid the land of you and your many evil deeds. Give up your stolen treasures now, and perhaps he will spare your lives!"

When the ogres heard this, they laughed and shouted. "HO, HO, HO! We are not afraid of a little bird like you! We are not afraid of little Momotaro!"

The pheasant became very angry at this, and flew down, pecking at the heads of the ogres with his sharp, pointed beak. While the pheasant was fighting so bravely, the dog and monkey helped Momotaro to tear down the gates, and they soon came to the aid of the pheasant.

"Get away! Get away!" shouted the ogres, but the monkey clawed and scratched, the big dog growled and bit the ogres, and the

pheasant flew about, pecking at their heads and faces. So fierce were they that soon the ogres began to run away. Half of them tumbled over the cliffs as they ran and the others fell pell-mell into the sea. Soon only the Chief of the Ogres remained. He threw up his hands, and then bowed low to Momotaro. "Please spare me my life, and all our stolen treasures are yours. I promise never to rob or kill anyone again," he said.

Momotaro tied up the evil ogre, while the monkey, the dog and the pheasant carried many boxes filled with jewels and treasures down to their little boat. Soon it was laden with all the treasures it could hold, and they were ready to sail toward home.

When Momotaro returned, he went from one family to another, returning the many treasures which the ogres had stolen from the people of the land.

"You will never again be troubled by the Ogres of Ogre Island!" he said to them happily.

And they all answered, "You are a kind and brave lad, and we thank you for making our land safe once again."

Then Momotaro went back to the home of the old man and woman with his arms full of jewels and treasures from Ogre Island. My, but the old man and woman were glad to see him once again, and the three of them lived happily together for many, many years.

Urashima Taro and the Princess of the Sea

Readers who know the story of Rip Van Winkle will see the similarity between it and this tale of a lad who comes back from the bottom of the sea to find that he is a three-hundred-year-old legend.

Long, long ago, in a small village of Japan, there lived a fine young man named Urashima Taro. He lived with his mother and

"Urashima Taro and the Princess of the Sea" from THE DANCING KETTLE AND OTHER JAPANESE FOLK TALES by Yoshiko Uchida. Copyright 1949, 1977 by Yoshiko Uchida. Reprinted by permission of Harcourt Brace Jovanovich, Inc.

father in a thatched-roof house which over-looked the sea. Each morning he was up before the sun, and went out to sea in his little fishing boat. On days when his luck was good, he would bring back large baskets full of fish which he sold in the village market.

One day, as he was carrying home his load of fish, he saw a group of shouting children. They were gathered around something on the beach and were crying, "Hit him! Poke him!" Taro ran over to see what was the matter, and there on the sand he saw a big brown tortoise. The children were poking it with a long stick and throwing stones at its hard shell.

"Here, here," called Taro. "That's no way to treat him! Why don't you leave him alone, and let him go back to the sea?"

"But we found him," said one of the children. "He belongs to us!"

"Yes, yes, he is ours," cried all the children.

Now, because Urashima Taro was a fair and kindly young man, he said to them, "Suppose I give each of you something in return for the tortoise?" Then he took ten shiny coins out of a small bag of money and gave one to each child. "Now, isn't that a fair bargain?" he asked. "A coin for each of you, and the tortoise for me."

"Yes, yes. Thank you!" called the children, and away they ran to the village candy shop.

Taro watched the old tortoise crawl away slowly toward the sea and called, "You'd better stay at home in the sea from now on, old fellow!" Then, smiling happily because he had been able to save the tortoise, he turned to go home. There his mother and father were waiting for him with bowls of steaming rice and soup.

Several days passed, and Taro soon forgot all about the tortoise whom he had saved. One day he was sitting in his boat feeling very sad because he could catch no fish. Suddenly he heard a voice from the sea calling, "Urashima-san! Urashima-san!"

"Now who could be calling me here in the middle of the sea?" thought Urashima Taro. He looked high and low, but could see no one. Suddenly, from the crest of a big wave, out popped the head of the old tortoise.

"I came to thank you for saving me the other day," said the tortoise.

"Well, I'm glad you got away safely," said Taro.

"This time I would like to do something for you, Urashima-san," said the tortoise. "How would you like to visit the princess who lives in the Palace of the Sea?"

"The princess of the sea!" shouted Taro. "I have heard often of her beauty, and everyone says her palace is more lovely than any place on earth! But how can I go to the bottom of the sea, and how can I enter her palace?"

"Just leave everything to me," said the old tortoise. "Hop on my back and I will see that you get there safely. I will also take you into the palace, for I am one of the palace guards."

So Urashima Taro jumped onto the smooth round back of the tortoise, and away they went. Swish, swish . . . the waves seemed to part and make a path for them as the tortoise swam on. Soon Taro felt himself going down . . . down . . . down . . . into the sea, but he wasn't getting wet at all. He heard the waves lapping gently about his ears. "That's strange," thought Taro. "This is just like a dream—a nice happy dream."

Before long, they were at the bottom of the big blue sea. Taro could see bright-colored fish playing hide and seek among the long strands of swaying seaweed. He could see clams and other shellfish shyly peeking out at him from their shells. Soon Taro saw something big and shiny looming in the hazy blue water.

"Is that the palace?" he asked anxiously. "It looks very beautiful."

"Oh, no," answered the tortoise. "That is just the outer gate."

They came to a stop and Taro could see that the gateway was guarded by a fish in armor of silver. "Welcome home," the guard called to the tortoise, as he opened the gate for them to enter.

"See whom I have brought back with me," the tortoise answered happily. The guard in the armor of silver turned to Urashima Taro and bowed most politely. Taro just had time to return the bow when he looked up and saw another gate. This one was even larger than the first, and was made of silver stones and pillars of coral. A row of fish in armor of gold was guarding the second gate.

"Now, Urashima-san, if you will get off and wait here, I will tell the princess that you have come," said the tortoise, and he disappeared into the palace beyond the gate. Taro had never seen such a beautiful sight in all his life. The silver stones in the gate sparkled and glittered as though they were smiling at him. Taro had to blink hard.

Soon the tortoise was back at his side telling him that the princess was waiting to see him. He led Taro through the gate of coral and silver, and up a path of golden stones to the palace. There in front of the palace stood the beautiful princess of the sea with her ladies-in-waiting.

"Welcome to the Palace of the Sea, Urashima Taro," she said, and her voice sounded like the tinkling of little silver bells. "Won't you come with me?" she asked.

Taro opened his mouth to answer, but not a sound would come forth. He could only look at the beautiful princess and the sparkling emeralds and diamonds and rubies which glittered on the walls of the palace. The princess understood how Taro felt, so she just smiled kindly and led him down a hallway paved with smooth, white pearls. Soon they came to a large room, and in the center of the room was an enormous table and an enormous chair. Taro thought they might have been made for a great king.

"Sit down, Urashima-san," said the princess, and as he sat in the enormous chair, the ladies-in-waiting appeared from all sides. They placed on the table plate after plate of all the delicious things that Taro could think of. "Eat well, my friend," said the princess, "and while you dine, my maids will sing and dance for you." Soon there was music and singing and dancing. The room was filled with laughing voices. Taro felt like a king now! He thought surely this was all a dream, and that it would end soon. But no, after he had dined, the princess took him all through the beautiful palace. At the very last, she

brought him to a room that looked as though it were made of ice and snow. There were creamy pearls and sparkling diamonds everywhere.

"Now, how would you like to see all the seasons of the year?" whispered the princess.

"Oh, I would like that very much," answered Taro, and as he spoke, the east door of the room opened slowly and quietly. Taro could scarcely believe the sight before his eyes. He saw big clouds of pale pink cherry blossoms and tall green willow trees swaying in the breeze. He could hear bluebirds singing, and saw them fly happily into the sky.

"Ah, that is spring," murmured Taro. "What a lovely sunny day!" But before he could say more, the princess led him further on. As she opened the door to the south, Taro could see white lotus blossoms floating on a still green pond. It was a warm summer day, and he could hear crickets chirping lazily, somewhere in the distance. She opened the door to the west and he saw a hillside of maple trees. Their leaves of crimson and yellow were whirling and dancing down among golden chrysanthemums. He had seen such trees each fall in his own little village. When the princess opened the door to the north, Taro felt a blast of cold air. He shivered, and looked up to see snowflakes tumbling down from gray skies. They were putting white caps on all the fence posts and treetops.

"Now you have seen all the seasons of the year," said the princess.

"They were beautiful!" sighed Taro happily. "I have never seen such wonderful sights in all my life! I wish I could stay here always!"

Taro was having such a very good time that he forgot all about his home in the village. He feasted and danced and sang with his friends in the Palace of the Sea, and before he knew it, three long years had gone by. But to Taro they seemed to be just three short days.

At last Taro said to the princess, "Alas, I have been here much too long. I must go home to see my mother and father so they will not worry about me."

"But you will come back?" asked the princess.

"Oh, yes, yes. I will come back," answered Taro.

"Before you go I have something for you," said the princess, and she gave Taro a small jewel box studded with many precious stones.

"Oh, it is beautiful, Princess," said Taro. "How can I thank you for all you have done for me?"

But the princess went on, "There is just one thing about that box," she said. "You must never, never open it if you ever wish to return to the Palace of the Sea. Can you remember that, Urashima Taro?"

"I will never open it, no matter what happens," promised Taro. Then he said good-bye to all his friends in the palace. Once again he climbed on the back of the old tortoise and they sailed toward his village on the seacoast. The princess and her ladies-in-waiting stood at the coral gate and waved to Taro till he could no longer see them. The tortoise swam on and on, and one by one all the little bright-colored fish that had been following them began to turn back. Before long, Taro could see the seacoast where he used to go fishing, and soon they were back on the very beach where Taro had once saved the tortoise. Taro hopped off onto the smooth white sand. "Good-bye, old friend," he said. "You have been very good to me. Thank you for taking me to the most beautiful place I have ever seen."

"Farewell, Urashima-san," said the old tortoise. "I hope we may meet again some day." Then he turned and crawled slowly back into the sea.

Now that he was in his own village once more, Taro was most anxious to see his parents. He ran along the path which led to their house with his jewel box tucked securely under his arm. He looked up eagerly at each person whom he passed. He wanted to shout a greeting to them, but each face seemed strange and new. "How odd!" thought Taro. "I feel as though I were in some other village than my own. I don't seem to know anyone. Well, I'll soon see Mother and Father," he said, and hurried on. When he reached the spot where the house should have been, there was no house to be seen. There was just an empty lot full of tall green weeds. Taro couldn't believe his eyes. "Why, what has happened to my home? Where are my parents?" he cried. He looked up and down the dusty path and soon saw an old, old woman coming toward him. "I'll ask her what has happened to my home," thought Taro.

"Old woman, please, can you help me?" asked Taro.

The old woman straightened her bent back and cocked her gray head, "Eh, what did you say?" she asked.

"Can you tell me what happened to Urashima Taro's home? It used to be right here," said Taro.

"Never heard of him," said the old woman, shaking her head.

"But you must have," Taro replied. "He lived right here, on this very spot where you are standing."

"Now let me see," she sighed. "Urashima Taro. Yes, it seems I have heard of him. Oh, I remember now. There is a story that he went out to sea in his fishing boat one day and never came back again. I suppose he was drowned at sea. Well, anyway, that was over three hundred years ago. My great-great-grandfather used to tell me about Urashima Taro when I was just a little girl."

"Three hundred years!" exclaimed Taro. His eyes were like saucers now. "But I don't understand."

"Well, I don't understand what you want with a man who lived three hundred years ago," muttered the old woman, and she trudged on down the road.

"So three years in the Palace of the Sea has really been three hundred years here in my village," thought Taro. "No wonder all my friends are gone. No wonder I can't find my mother or father!" Taro had never felt so lonely or so sad as he did then. "What can I do? What can I do?" he murmured to himself.

Suddenly he remembered the little jewel box which the princess had given him. "Perhaps there is something in there that can help me," he thought, and forgetting the promise he had made to the princess, he quickly opened the box. Suddenly, there arose from it a cloud of white smoke which wrapped itself around Taro so that he could see nothing. When it disappeared, Urashima Taro peered into the empty box, but he could scarcely see. He looked at his hands and they were the hands of an old, old man. His face was wrinkled; his hair was as white as snow. In that short moment Urashima Taro had become three hundred years older. He remembered the promise he had made to the princess, but now it was too late and he knew that he could never visit the Palace of the Sea again. But who knows, perhaps one day the old tortoise came back to the beach once more to help his friend.

Korea

 The folk literature of Korea was recorded as early as the fifteenth century; two centuries later a student of folk literature, Im Bang, gathered and recorded a substantial number of additional tales, and these were translated into English in 1913 by James Gale in *Korean Folk Tales: Imps, Ghosts, and Fairies.* Many of these were used by Eleanor Jewett in *Which Was Witch?* the collection from which the title story was chosen for use here. The closeness of family life and the moral strength of its obligations are evident in many Korean tales; among the best collections are Frances Carpenter's *Tales of a Korean Grandmother* and *Korean Tales* by Horace Allen.

Which Was Witch?

Children respond to the wordplay at the close of a story that has an occult appeal and more suspense than most folk tales.

There was once a wise and learned man named Kim Su-ik. He lived just inside the south gate of Seoul but he might as well have lived anywhere for all the thought he gave the matter. His mind was entirely taken up with study and books, and one could say of him, as Im Bang said of another scholar, "He used to awake at first cockcrow, wash, dress, take up his book and never lay it aside. On his right were pictures, on his left were books, and he happy between. He rose to be a Prime Minister."

One night Kim Su-ik was absorbed in studying a Chinese classic when he suddenly felt hungry. He clapped his hands to summon a servant, and immediately the door of his room opened.

His wife stepped in.

"What does the master of the house desire?" said she.

"Food," he answered briefly, his attention already returned to the book in his lap.

"I have little in the house but a few roasted chestnuts. If that will suffice I will bring them to you myself. The servants have long since gone to their sleeping quarters."

Kim Su-ik grunted his approval and went on with his studies. In a very short time the door opened again and his wife came in bearing a brass bowl full of hot roasted chestnuts. He helped himself to one and was in the act of putting it into his mouth when once more the door opened and in stepped his wife with a brass bowl full of hot roasted chestnuts.

But his wife was already there, standing beside him with the bowl in her hands!

Kim Su-ik, his mouth still open and a chestnut half in it, looked in astonishment from one to the other of the identical women. They were as like as two pins—faces, features, figures, clothes, the way they stood, the way they used their fingers and moved their shoulders. Never were twins more completely alike. Kim Su-ik passed his hands before his eyes. He must have overdone his studying, he thought to himself, read too late and too steadily. His eyes were playing tricks on him, that was all. He was seeing double.

But when he looked again the two women were still there, and what was stranger still, they seemed not to be aware of each other, but stood quietly, gracefully, their eyes fastened on him as if waiting to know his pleasure.

The scholar leaped to his feet, choking back the cry of terror that rose in his throat. He knew, suddenly, without a doubt, what this meant. It was midnight, the moon was at the full, ghosts, evil spirits, witches and goblins would be abroad, filled with power. One of these two creatures standing before him was his wife, known and loved by him all his wedded life—and perhaps not quite fully appreciated, he hastily decided. The other must be a witch, able to change into any form she chose in the twinkling of an eye. But

which was which? How could he protect his wife and drive this evil double from beside her?

Being a quick thinker as well as a learned one, Kim Su-ik plunged into action. He seized the arm of one of the women with his right hand and before the other could realize what he was about, he had her arm fast in his left hand. They turned mildly reproachful eyes upon him but made no effort to free themselves.

"My dear," said one, "too much study has fevered your brain."

"My dear," said the other, "too much reading of books has affected your mind."

Kim Su-ik looked from one to the other. Not a particle of difference was there to give him a hint as to which was wife and which was witch. He shook them gently. They smiled indulgently as at a child. He shook harder. No resentment, no struggle to get free. He was tempted to relax his grip on the two arms, but he knew he must not for a moment do that, and hung on more firmly than ever.

Minutes went by, then hours, the dull slow moving hours between midnight and cockcrow. The three stood silent, motionless, in the same spot. Kim Su-ik grew weary beyond words. So, too, must his wife be weary, but neither of the two women he held so tightly by the arm said anything or showed by any movement or expression of the face that she was tired, puzzled or angry. His wife would have been tired and puzzled—angry, too, perhaps, but she would not have blustered or scolded. Any other woman would, were she witch or human. But surely his wife would say *something.* What in the world had got into her? Was she bewitched? Or walking in her sleep? Perhaps she was not either one of these two women. He wanted to rush into the other part of the house to see if she was there, thus proving that both of these were witches. But he did nothing, just hung on, grimly, silently.

At long last a cock crowed. Immediately the woman at his left tried to wrench her arm free. The other remained quiet. Kim

Su-ik dropped the unresisting one and threw all his strength into a struggle with the other. Like a wild thing the creature fought, biting, snarling, spitting, leaping back and forth. Still the scholar held on to her and would not let go. The arm in his hand shrank and grew hairy. The whole figure dwindled, the eyes grew round and green and blazed with fury.

Another cock crowed and another, and the first gray light of dawn melted the dark shadows out of doors. But Kim Su-ik had no thought or time to notice the coming of day. With a hideous shriek the creature changed before his very eyes into a powerful wildcat. In horror he loosed his hold, and she leaped through the window and was gone.

"I still think you are studying too much," said a quiet, familiar voice behind him, and there stood his wife, pale, trembling a little, but smiling confidently.

"Why didn't you let me know which was which?" demanded Kim Su-ik.

His wife laughed. "I don't know what you are talking about! You behaved very strangely, but then, one never knows what to expect of a scholar. Which was which what?"

"Witch!" said Kim Su-ik.

Vietnam

 Over the long history of Vietnam, there have been many invaders who have ruled the country: Chinese, French, and Japanese. With domination of political, educational, and cultural life as a barrier, the Vietnamese have clung to their religious beliefs and customs, and both of these are forcibly represented in those folk tales that have been published in English. The power of cultural diffusion is made evident by the fact that versions of the Cinderella and Rip Van Winkle stories exist in Vietnamese folk literature.

The Love Crystal

The style, subject, and language of this poignant tale indicate that it is most appropriate for older readers.

Long ago in the Serene Land, a beautiful maiden lived in a palace beside a tranquil river. Her father was a great Mandarin. So great was her beauty that it was forbidden anyone but the members of the Mandarin's household to look upon her. In order to keep the girl from the gaze of all others, the Mandarin had her put in the top of a tower which rose above the river. There she passed the lonely hours embroidering and reading, waiting for the man who was destined to come and make her his bride.

Often she would gaze out upon the river below and dream of all the places the river had been in its winding course. As she watched the river one day, she saw a poor fisherman sailing his small boat. She could not see him well from such a height, but he looked from afar to be young and strong. He played a flute, and its melody rose sweet and clear to the tower where the Mandarin's daughter looked down on him. She was struck with joy and wonder at the plaintive sound. It was somehow sad and tender, and as she listened she was deeply moved. The music spoke to her of faraway places she would never see. It spoke to her of feelings for which there are no words. It spoke to her of all the things which make the earth beautiful.

"The Love Crystal" from THE FISHERMAN AND THE GOBLET by Mark Taylor. Published in 1969 by Golden Gate Junior Books. Reprinted by permission of the author.

Day after day the fisherman played his flute as his small boat passed beneath the tower where the lonely girl listened in rapture. The pure tones of the flute wound upward like a silver thread of sound. Perhaps, she thought, he was some prince in disguise whom fate meant to be her husband. For the songs he played were like songs of love, especially one which he played over and over until the girl heard it repeated nightly in her dreams. Although she was too shy to send for him, she threw down flower petals to show him her delight.

The fisherman knew that a maiden dwelt high in the tower, and when the flower petals drifted down to the water beside his boat, he knew that she liked his songs. He thought she must be beautiful, even though he had never clearly seen her face.

And so a bond grew between them, a bond made of his songs and her pleasure in them. It was enough. As she listened to his flute and as he caught the softly falling petals, each fancied only the best about the other.

One day the fisherman did not appear. He had learned that it was the Mandarin's daughter who lived in the tower; he dared not return. The girl waited until the sun departed from the sky and would not leave the window until the cool evening breeze swept across the empty river.

When the fisherman did not appear the next day, the girl felt despair. She refused to turn away from the window either to eat or to sleep. All that night she kept vigil with the moon, praying that the fisherman and his flute songs would return. But when the day dawned and waned and the fisherman never came, the girl at last wept. As one day followed after the other, she sat by the window growing pale and thin. At first she wept often; then she became silent. Her loveliness began to pale as does a flower which slowly wilts and fades.

The doctors were summoned in vain to find the cause of her illness. The Mandarin and his wife were frantic. They were not bad people, they merely wanted to protect their beautiful daughter. Now all had somehow gone wrong and she was wasting away. Then the girl's maid could no longer be silent, and whether the Mandarin should be angry or not, she told him about the fisherman whose flute songs had charmed his daughter.

The Mandarin sent for the fisherman. He was brought to the palace. The poor fisherman was indeed young and strong as the girl had imagined, but his face was ugly.

"Although you are only a humble fisherman," said the Mandarin, "your songs hold the key to my daughter's well-being. Perhaps you are the man fate has destined to become her husband. Let us see if she will love you as she has loved your music."

The fisherman was distressed. "I do not want to have the power of life and death over your daughter," he said. "I only played my songs beneath the tower because she seemed to like them. I have never even gazed upon her face."

The fisherman was taken to the foot of the tower and bade to play his flute. When the girl heard the music, she was filled with joy. She rushed from the tower down the winding stairs to where the fisherman stood. Surely he would be as handsome as his songs were beautiful. Surely he was a prince in disguise. Alas, no! He was ugly. And as she tried to thank him for his music, the maiden turned away in dismay.

When the fisherman saw the Mandarin's daughter, he was struck with love for her. But when she turned from him, he knew such love was hopeless. Sadly he went away, and sadly the girl returned to the top of the tower. Although she was cured, something beautiful had gone from her life.

No more did the fisherman return in his boat. Never again did the girl hear his flute. In time she almost forgot him, except for the echo of his one most beautiful flute song in her dreams. A year passed, and still the girl lived in the tower, waiting for the prince who never came.

But long before the year had passed, the fisherman had died. For soon after he fell in love with the Mandarin's daughter, he died from the utter hopelessness of it. All his beauty was in his music and not in his face, and the girl wanted only his songs.

When the fisherman was to be buried, his family found beside him an exquisite crystal. Everyone realized that the crystal was made from his unanswered love. They put it in the prow of his boat as a remembrance of him whose flute would never be heard and enjoyed again. The flute they gave to the river.

One day, when the Mandarin was boating upon the river, he saw the fisherman's boat with the shining crystal fixed to its bow. When he learned how it came to be there, he was deeply moved and asked to buy it. A good price was paid for the crystal and the Mandarin had it taken to the turner and made into a teacup.

No cup more exquisite had ever been seen! But strange and wonderful to tell, when tea was poured into the cup an image would appear in it. It was the image of the dead fisherman in his boat. And as it sailed around the cup, one could faintly hear his flute.

Thinking to please his daughter, the Mandarin took her the crystal cup. When she saw the fisherman's image and heard the same flute song that haunted her dreams, she was overwhelmed with grief. Hiding her distress, however, she asked to be alone with the cup.

When all had left her, the girl poured tea in the cup and held it in her hands. As she gazed into it she saw the fisherman and heard—as clearly as though he were again on the river—his flute playing his song of love. Then she realized that a heart which can make music is more important than an ugly face. Our faces are given to us, but our hearts are fashioned by our own hands. She knew that the fisherman had loved her enough to die, and her indifference had brought him death.

Quietly the maiden wept, and as she did her tears fell into the cup. Slowly the crystal dissolved, for her tears were made of love and they at last brought peace to the fisherman's soul.

Later they found the girl sitting beside the window. Her soul had left her body, leaving her as still as stone. From the river they faintly heard the sound of someone unseen playing upon a flute. Then all knew that at last the Mandarin's beautiful daughter and the fisherman were together in happiness.

India

 Some scholars believe that India was the cradle of the folk tale; Joseph Jacobs, in his preface to *Indian Folk and Fairy Tales,* says, "So far as the children of Europe have their fairy stories in common, these—and they form more than a third of the whole—are derived from India." Many of the Jatakas, or Birth-stories of Buddha, have been used in part for adapted versions of Indian folk tales, and the student of folklore can recognize many of the themes and plots that are familiar in European folk tales, such as quests and talking beast stories. Among the better collections are *The Ivory City and Other Stories from India and Pakistan,* from which two stories are used here, the Jacobs book cited above, and John Gray's *India's Tales and Legends.*

The Hare That Ran Away

In this Jataka tale, it's the earth rather than the sky that is falling.

And it came to pass that the Buddha (to be) was born again as a Lion. Just as he had helped his fellow-men, he now began to help his fellow-animals, and there was a great deal to be done. For instance, there was a little nervous Hare who was always afraid that something dreadful was going to happen to her. She was always saying: "Suppose the Earth were to fall in, what would happen to me?" And she said this so often that at last she thought it really was about to happen. One day, when she had been saying over and over again, "Suppose the Earth were to fall in, what would happen to me?" she heard a slight noise: it really was only a heavy fruit which had fallen upon a rustling leaf, but the little Hare was so nervous she was ready to believe anything, and she said in a frightened tone: "The Earth *is* falling in." She ran away as fast as she could go, and presently she met an old brother Hare, who said: "Where are you running to, Mistress Hare?"

And the little Hare said: "I have no time to stop and tell you anything. The Earth is falling in, and I am running away."

"The Earth is falling in, is it?" said the old brother Hare, in a tone of much astonishment; and he repeated this to *his* brother hare, and *he* to *his* brother hare, and *he* to *his* brother hare, until at last there were a hundred thousand brother hares, all shouting: "The Earth is falling in." Now presently the bigger animals began to take the cry up. First the deer, and then the sheep, and then the wild boar, and then the buffalo, and then the camel, and then the tiger, and then the elephant.

Now the wise Lion heard all this noise and wondered at it. "There are no signs," he said, "of the Earth falling in. They must have heard something." And then he stopped them all short and said: "What is this you are saying?"

And the Elephant said: "I remarked that the Earth was falling in."

"How do you know this?" asked the Lion.

"Why, now I come to think of it, it was the Tiger that remarked it to me."

And the Tiger said: "*I* had it from the Camel," and the Camel said: "*I* had it from the Buffalo." And the buffalo from the wild boar, and the wild boar from the sheep, and the sheep from the deer, and the deer from the hares, and the Hares said: "Oh! *we* heard it from *that* little Hare."

And the Lion said: "Little Hare, *what* made you say that the Earth was falling in?"

And the little Hare said: "I *saw* it."

"You saw it?" said the Lion. "Where?"

"Yonder by the tree."

"Well," said the Lion, "come with me and I will show you how——"

"No, no," said the Hare, "I would not go near that tree for anything, I'm *so* nervous."

"But," said the Lion, "I am going to take you on my back." And he took her on his back, and begged the animals to stay where they were until they returned. Then he showed the little Hare how the fruit had fallen upon the leaf, making the noise that had frightened her, and she said: "Yes, I see —the Earth is *not* falling in." And the Lion said: "Shall we go back and tell the other animals?"

And they went back. The little Hare stood before the animals and said: "The Earth is *not* falling in." And all the animals began to repeat this to one another, and they dispersed gradually, and you heard the words more and more softly:

"The Earth is *not* falling in," etc., etc., etc., until the sound died away altogether.

The Tiger, the Brahman, and the Jackal

Often in folk literature the trickster like Anansi or Brer Rabbit is outwitted; here the jackal cleverly traps the tiger.

"The Hare That Ran Away" from EASTERN STORIES AND LEGENDS by Marie Shedlock. Copyright, 1920, by E. P. Dutton & Co., renewal, 1948, by Arthur C. Jennings. Reprinted by permission of the publisher, E. P. Dutton, Inc. and Routledge & Kegan Paul Ltd.

Once upon a time a tiger was caught in a trap. He tried in vain to get out through the bars, and rolled and bit with rage and grief when he failed.

By chance a poor Brahman came by. "Let me out of this cage, O pious one!" cried the tiger.

"Nay, my friend," replied the Brahman mildly, "you would probably eat me if I did."

"Not at all!" swore the tiger with many oaths; "on the contrary, I should be for ever grateful, and serve you as a slave!"

Now when the tiger sobbed and sighed and wept and swore, the pious Brahman's heart softened, and at last he consented to open the door of the cage. Out popped the tiger, and, seizing the poor man, cried, "What a fool you are! What is to prevent my eating you now, for after being cooped up so long I am just terribly hungry!"

In vain the Brahman pleaded for his life; the most he could gain was a promise to abide by the decision of the first three things he chose to question as to the justice of the tiger's action.

So the Brahman first asked a *pîpal* tree what it thought of the matter, but the *pîpal* tree replied coldly, "What have you to complain about? Don't I give shade and shelter to every one who passes by, and don't they in return tear down my branches to feed their cattle? Don't whimper—be a man!"

Then the Brahman, sad at heart, went farther afield till he saw a buffalo turning a well-wheel; but he fared no better from it, for it answered, "You are a fool to expect gratitude! Look at me! While I gave milk they fed me on cotton-seed and oil-cake, but now I am dry they yoke me here, and give me refuse as fodder!"

The Brahman, still more sad, asked the road to give him its opinion.

"My dear sir," said the road, "how foolish you are to expect anything else! Here am I, useful to everybody, yet all, rich and poor, great and small, trample on me as they go past, giving me nothing but the ashes of their pipes and the husks of their grain!"

On this the Brahman turned back sorrowfully, and on the way he met a jackal, who called out, "Why, what's the matter, Mr. Brahman? You look as miserable as a fish out of water!"

Then the Brahman told him all that had occurred. "How very confusing!" said the jackal, when the recital was ended; "would you mind telling me over again? for everything seems so mixed up!"

The Brahman told it all over again, but the jackal shook his head in a distracted sort of way, and still could not understand.

"It's very odd," said he sadly, "but it all seems to go in at one ear and out at the other! I will go to the place where it all happened, and then perhaps I shall be able to give a judgment."

So they returned to the cage, by which the tiger was waiting for the Brahman, and sharpening his teeth and claws.

"You've been away a long time!" growled the savage beast, "but now let us begin our dinner."

"*Our* dinner!" thought the wretched Brahman, as his knees knocked together with fright; "what a remarkably delicate way of putting it!"

"Give me five minutes, my lord!" he pleaded, "in order that I may explain matters to the jackal here, who is somewhat slow in his wits."

The tiger consented, and the Brahman

"The Tiger, the Brahman, and the Jackal" from TALES OF THE PUNJAB by Flora Annie Steel. New York: The Macmillan Company, 1933.

began the whole story over again, not missing a single detail, and spinning as long a yarn as possible.

"Oh, my poor brain! oh, my poor brain!" cried the jackal, wringing his paws. "Let me see! how did it all begin? You were in the cage, and the tiger came walking by—"

"Pooh!" interrupted the tiger, "what a fool you are! *I* was in the cage."

"Of course!" cried the jackal, pretending to tremble with fright; "yes! I was in the cage—no, I wasn't—dear! dear! where are my wits? Let me see—the tiger was in the Brahman, and the cage came walking by—no, that's not it either! Well, don't mind me, but begin your dinner, for I shall never understand!"

"Yes, you shall!" returned the tiger, in a rage at the jackal's stupidity; "I'll *make* you understand! Look here—I am the tiger—"

"Yes, my lord!"

"And that is the Brahman—"

"Yes, my lord!"

"And that is the cage—"

"Yes, my lord!"

"And I was in the cage—do you understand?"

"Yes—no—Please, my lord—"

"Well?" cried the tiger, impatiently.

"Please, my lord!—how did you get in?"

"How!—why, in the usual way, of course!"

"Oh dear me!—my head is beginning to whirl again! Please don't be angry, my lord, but what is the usual way?"

At this the tiger lost patience, and jumping into the cage, cried, "This way! Now do you understand how it was?"

"Perfectly!" grinned the jackal, as he dexterously shut the door; "and if you will permit me to say so, I think matters will remain as they were!"

Lambikin

This has elements of "The Pancake" as Lambikin rolls along, sure that he can outwit the jackal, a popular animal character in Indian folk literature.

One morning Lambikin set out to call on his Granny. He danced along on his long thin legs, jumping high in the air at the thought of all the good things she would give him to eat.

Very soon he met a jackal, who said: "Lambikin! Lambikin! I shall eat you."

Lambikin just gave a little frisk and said:

"Don't be so hasty.
I'll taste much more tasty
When I've gobbled Granny's pasty."

This made good sense to the jackal, and so he let Lambikin go on.

In a little while he came to a vulture in a tree, and the vulture looked down and said: "Lambikin! Lambikin! I will eat you."

Lambikin just gave a little frisk and said:

"Don't be so hasty.
I'll taste much more tasty
When I've gobbled Granny's pasty."

This made good sense to the vulture, and so he let Lambikin go on.

Now on his journey Lambikin met, one by one, a tiger and a wolf and a dog and an eagle, and each said, as he saw the fine juicy little lamb: "Lambikin! Lambikin! I shall eat you."

And to each of them Lambikin replied, giving a little frisk:

"Don't be so hasty.
I'll taste much more tasty
When I've gobbled Granny's pasty."

So at last he came to his Granny's house, and he said, all of a hurry: "Hello, Granny. I've promised to get fat. You have always said that I must keep my word, so just put me in the corn bin, if you please."

Granny thought that he was being very greedy, but she put him in the corn bin, and he stayed there for seven days, eating and eating and eating until he was so fat that he nearly filled the bin from side to side. Then his Granny said that he was fat enough for anything and must now go home. "I can't go home like this," said Lambikin. "I look so fat and tasty that some animal is sure to eat me up. This is what you must do," said the plump little lamb. "Take the skin of my poor little brother who died, and make it into a little drum. Then I can sit inside and roll along the road quite safely, because I'm tight like a drum myself."

So this is what Granny did. She made a little drumikin out of the sheepskin, with the wool inside, and Lambikin squeezed inside and curled up, just as snug as could be, then he set the drum rolling.

Soon he met the eagle, who said:

"Drumikin! Drumikin!
Have you seen Lambikin?"

Lambikin, curled up warm and safe, called out:

"Fell in the fire, and so will you.
Rub-a-dum! Rub-a-dum!"

"There goes my dinner," said the eagle, and Lambikin went rolling along the road, singing "Rub-a-dum! Rub-a-dum!"

On his way he met all the animals, one by one, and each one asked him:

"Drumikin! Drumikin!
Have you seen Lambikin?"

And to each of them the naughty Lambikin sang:

"Fell in the fire, and so will you.
Rub-a-dum! Rub-a-dum doo!"

And dog and wolf and tiger and vulture all went off hungry, missing their dinner of fat Lambikin.

At last, along came the jackal, all skin and bones and shabby coat, but cunning as cunning. He called out:

"Drumikin! Drumikin!
Have you seen Lambikin?"

And Lambikin sang, lying warm in his little bed and chirping like a cricket:

"Fell in the fire, and so will you.
Rub-a-dum! Rub . . ."

But the jackal knew his voice in a flash and interrupted him, saying: "Ahah! So you've turned yourself inside out, have you? I'll soon have you the right way round."

And he jumped on the drumikin, and with teeth and paws tore the inside out of it, and made himself a very good dinner.

Camel Gets His Own Back

This time the jackal loses, in a pithy story that makes a good encore for storytellers because of its brevity and its quick retribution.

You would never have thought that the camel and the jackal would get on well together, but there it was. They were the best of friends.

One morning the jackal said: "I'll tell you what we'll do today. Over the river I know where there is a very nice field of sugar-cane, just the kind of treat you would fancy. If you take me across the river I'll lead you there. While you are eating the cane, I will root about on the river-bank for crabs and fish-bones and I'll be sure to get a good dinner."

The camel agreed. He knelt down and let the jackal climb on his back. Then he waded into the river and swam across very easily. The camel settled down to enjoy his sugar-cane, while the jackal ran up and down the bank, finding plenty of fishy scraps to gobble.

His belly was much smaller than the camel's, and so he was satisfied quite soon while the camel was only just beginning his meal. No sooner had he finished eating than the jackal began racing around the field, yelping at the top of his loud voice.

"Hear that!" said the villagers. "There's a jackal in the sugar field. He will tear holes in the ground and ruin the plants." So they snatched up sticks and ran off to the field. When they got there, what they saw was not the jackal but the camel, calmly gnawing the canes and sucking out the sugar. They shouted and yelled and whacked the poor camel until he howled just as loudly. By the time they stopped he was half dead from his beating.

At last they gave up and went back to their work. "Come on," said the jackal; "we'd best go home."

The camel limped to the water, and knelt down. "Jump up," he said, and the jackal scrambled on his back again. The camel swam into midstream, then he trod water and said: "You're a fine friend to have, jackal. You made a good meal yourself and then spoilt mine. Why did you have to make such a din and draw the villagers down on me like a swarm of bees? Goodness knows, they stung like bees too!"

"Sorry!" said the jackal. "I just couldn't help it. It's my habit to sing a song or two after dinner."

So the camel swam on. He was in deep water now. He looked back at the jackal and said: "You know, it's a funny thing. I feel the most tremendous urge to roll."

"Don't do that!" said the jackal. "Whyever should you want to?"

"Oh, I don't know. It's just a habit I have. I always have a little roll after dinner."

Then the camel rolled once, twice, three times. The jackal was shaken off into the water and quickly disappeared. So the camel swam to land and went quietly to bed.

Folk Tales of Oceania and Australia

 While there is a vast storehouse of folk literature and a strong tradition of storytelling in Australia and among the islands of the South Pacific, little of this material has been published and made available to children. One of the few books that do exist is *The Sky-Eater and Other South Sea Tales*, from which "The Prisoner" is used here; the other selection included is from K. Langloh Parker's *Australian Legendary Tales*, a selection of Aborigine stories first published at the turn of the century. The stories illustrate the prevalence of "why" stories, the close relationships among people and animals, and the representation of the natural environment and cultural patterns.

Beereeun the Miragemaker
(Australia)

An intricate tale of Aborigine origin, this weaves together in colorful fashion an assortment of "why" stories.

Beereeun the lizard wanted to marry Bullai Bullai the green parrot sisters. But they did not want to marry him. They liked Weedah the mockingbird better. Their mother said they must marry Beereeun, for she had pledged them to him at their births, and Bee-

"Beereeun the Miragemaker" from AUSTRALIAN LEG-ENDARY TALES by K. Langloh Parker, selected and edited by H. Drake-Brockman. Originally published by The Viking Press, Inc. Reprinted by permission of The Viking Press, Inc. and Angus & Robertson Publishers, Sydney, Australia.

reeun was a great wirinun and would harm them if they did not keep her pledge.

When Weedah came back from hunting they told him what their mother had said, how they had been pledged to Beereeun, who now claimed them.

"Tomorrow," said Weedah, "old Beereeun goes to meet a tribe coming from the Springs country. While he is away we will go toward the Big River, and burn the track behind us. I will go out as if to hunt as usual in the morning. I will hide myself in the thick gidya scrub. You two must follow later and meet me there. We will then cross the big plain where the grass is now thick and dry. Bring with you a fire stick. We will throw it back into the plain, then no one can follow our tracks. On we will go to the Big River. There I have a friend who has a goombeelga, a bark canoe. Then shall we be safe from pursuit, for he will put us over the river. And we can travel on and on even to the country of the short-armed people if so we choose."

The next morning ere Goo-goor-gaga had ceased his laughter Weedah had started.

Some hours later, in the gidya scrub, the Bullai Bullai sisters joined him.

Having crossed the big plain they threw back a fire stick where the grass was thick and dry. The fire spread quickly through it, crackling and throwing up tongues of flame.

Through another scrub went the three, then across another plain, through another scrub and onto a plain again.

The day was hot, Yhi the sun was high in the sky. They became thirsty, but saw no water, and had brought none in their haste.

"We want water," the Bullai Bullai cried.

"Why did you not bring some?" said Weedah.

"We thought you had plenty, or would travel as the creeks run, or at least know of a goolagool, a water-holding tree."

"We shall soon reach water. Look even now ahead, there is water."

The Bullai Bullai looked eagerly toward where he pointed, and there in truth, on the far side of the plain, they saw a sheet of water. They quickened their steps, but the farther they went, the farther off seemed the water, but on they went ever hoping to reach it. Across the plain they went, only to find that on the other side of a belt of timber the water had gone.

The weary girls would have lain down, but Weedah said that they would surely reach water on the other side of the wood. Again they struggled on through the scrub to another plain.

"There it is! I told you so! There is the water."

And looking ahead they again saw a sheet of water.

Again their hopes were raised, and though the sun beat fiercely, on they marched, only to be again disappointed.

"Let us go back," they said. "This is the country of evil spirits. We see water, and when we come where we have seen it there is but dry earth. Let us go back."

"Back to Beereeun, who would kill you?"

"Better to die from the blow of a boondi in your own country than of thirst in a land of devils. We will go back."

"Not so. Not with a boondi would he kill you, but with a gooweera, a poison stick. Slow would be your death, and you would be always in pain until your shadow was wasted away. But why talk of returning? Did we not set fire to the big plain? Could you cross that? Waste not your breath, but follow me. See, there again is water!"

But the Bullai Bullai had lost hope. No longer would they even look up, though time after time Weedah called out, "Water ahead of us! Water ahead of us!" only to disappoint them again and again.

At last the Bullai Bullai became so angry with him that they seized him and beat him. But even as they beat him he cried all the time, "Water is there! Water is there!"

Then he implored them to let him go, and he would drag up the roots from some water trees and drain the water from them.

"Yonder I see a coolabah. From its roots I can drain enough to quench your thirst. Or here beside us is a bingawingul; full of water are its roots. Let me go. I will drain them for you."

But the Bullai Bullai had no faith in his promises, and they but beat him the harder until they were exhausted.

When they ceased to beat him and let him go, Weedah went on a little way, then lay down, feeling bruised all over, and thankful that the night had come and the fierce sun no longer scorched them.

One Bullai Bullai said to her sister, "Could we not sing the song our Bargi used to sing, and make the rain fall?"

"Let us try, if we can make a sound with our dry throats," said the other.

"We will sing to our cousin Dooloomai the thunder. He will hear us, and break a rain cloud for us."

So they sat down, rocking their bodies to and fro, and beating their knees, sang:

"Moogaray, Moogaray, May, May,
Eehu, Eehu, Doon-gara."

"Hailstones, hailstones, wind, wind,
Rain, rain, lightning."

Over and over again they sang these words as they had heard their Bargi, or mother's mother, do. Then for themselves they added:

"Eehu oonah wambaneah Dooloomai
Bullul goonung inderh gingnee
Eehu oonah wambaneah Dooloomai."

"Give us rain, Thunder, our cousin,
Thirsting for water are we,
Give us rain, Thunder, our cousin."

As long as their poor parched throats could make a sound they sang this. Then they lay down to die, weary and hopeless. One said faintly, "The rain will be too late, but surely it is coming, for strong is the smell of the gidya."

"Strong indeed," said the other.

But even this sure sign to their tribe that rain is near roused them not. It would come, they thought, too late for them. But even then away in the north a thundercloud was gathering. It rolled across the sky quickly, pealing out thunder calls as it came to tell of its coming. It stopped right over the plain in front of the Bullai Bullai. One more peal of thunder, which opened the cloud, then splashing down came the first big drops of rain. Slowly and few they came until just at the last, when a quick, heavy shower fell, emptying the thundercloud, and filling the gilguy holes on the plain.

The cool splashing of the rain on their hot, tired limbs gave new life to the Bullai Bullai and to Weedah. They all ran to the gilguy holes. Stooping their heads, they drank and quenched their thirst.

"I told you the water was here," said Weedah. "You see I was right."

"No water was here when you said so. If our cousin Dooloomai had not heard our song for his help, we should have died, and you too."

And they were angry. But Weedah dug them some roots, and when they ate they forgot their anger. When their meal was over they lay down to sleep.

The next morning on they went again. That day they again saw across the plains the same strange semblance of water that had lured them on before. They knew not what it could be, they knew only that it was not water.

Just at dusk they came to the Big River. There they saw Goolay-yali the pelican, with his canoe. Weedah asked him to put them over onto the other side. He said that he would do so one at a time, as the canoe was small. First he said he would take Weedah, that he might get ready a camp of the long grass in the bend of the river. He took Weedah over. Then back he came and, fastening his canoe, he went up to the Bullai Bullai, who were sitting beside the remains of his old fire.

"Now," said Goolay-yali, "you two will go with me to my camp, which is down in that bend. Weedah cannot get over again. You shall live with me. I shall catch fish to feed you. I have some even now in my camp cooking. There, too, have I wirrees of honey, and durri ready for the baking. Weedah has nothing to give you but the grass nunnoos he is but now making."

"Take us to Weedah," they said.

"Not so," said Goolay-yali, and he stepped forward as if to seize them.

The Bullai Bullai stooped and filled their hands with the white ashes of the burned-out fire, which they flung at him.

Handful after handful they threw at him until he stood before them white, all but his hands, which he spread out and shook, thus freeing them from the cloud of ashes enveloping him and obscuring his sight.

Having thus checked him, the Bullai Bullai ran to the bank of the river, meaning to get the canoe and cross over to Weedah.

But in the canoe, to their horror, was Bee-reeun! Beereeun, whom to escape they had sped across plain and through scrub.

Yet here he was, while between them and Weedah lay the wide river.

They had not known it, but Beereeun had been near them all the while. He it was who had made the mirage on each plain, thinking he would lure them on by this semblance of water until they perished of thirst. From that fate Dooloomai, their cousin the thunder, had saved them. But now the chance of Beereeun had come.

The Bullai Bullai looked across the wide river and saw the nunnoos, or grass shelters, Weedah had made. They saw him running in and out of them as if he were playing a game, not thinking of them at all. Strange nunnoos they were too, having both ends open.

Seeing where they were looking, Beereeun said, "Weedah is womba, deaf. I stole his Doowi while he slept and put in its place a mad spirit. He knows naught of you now. He cares naught for you. It is so with those who look too long at the mirage. He will trouble me no more, nor you. Why look at him?"

But the Bullai Bullai could not take their eyes from Weedah, so strangely he went on, unceasingly running in at one end of the grass nunnoo, through it and out of the other.

"He is womba," they said, but yet they could not understand it. They looked toward him and called him, though he heeded them not.

"I will send him far from you," said Beereeun, getting angry. He seized a spear, stood up in the canoe and sent it swiftly through the air into Weedah, who gave a great cry, screamed "Water is there! Water is there!" and fell back dead.

"Take us over! Take us over!" cried the Bullai Bullai. "We must go to him, we might yet save him."

"He is all right. He is in the sky. He is not there," said Beereeun. "If you want him you must follow him to the sky. Look, you can see him there now." And he pointed to a star that the Bullai Bullai had never seen before.

"There he is, Womba."

Across the grass nunnoo the Bullai Bullai looked, but no Weedah was there. Then they sat down and wailed a death song, for they knew well they should see Weedah no more. They plastered their heads with white ashes and water; they tied on their bodies green twigs; then, cutting themselves till the blood ran, they lit some smoke branches and smoked themselves, as widows.

Beereeun spoke to Goolay-yali the pelican, saying, "There is no brother of the dead man to marry these women. In this country they have no relation. You shall take one, and I the other. Tonight when they sleep we will each seize one."

"That which you say shall be," said Goolay-yali the pelican.

But the sisters heard what they said, though they gave no sign and mourned the dead Weedah without ceasing. And with their death song they mingled a cry to all of their tribe who were dead to help them, and save them from these men who would seize them while they were still mourning, before they had swallowed the smoke water, or their tribe had heard the voice of their dead.

As the night wore on, the wailing of the women ceased. The men thought that they were at length asleep, and crept up to their camp. But it was empty! Gone were the Bullai Bullai!

The men heaped fuel on their fire to light up the darkness, but yet saw no sign of the Bullai Bullai.

They heard a sound, a sound of mocking laughter. They looked around, but saw nothing.

Again they heard a sound of laughter. Whence came it? Again it echoed through the air.

It was from the sky. They looked up. It was the new star Womba, mocking them. Womba who once was Weedah, who laughed aloud to see that the Bullai Bullai had escaped their enemies, for even now they were stealing along the sky toward him, which the men on earth saw.

"We have lost them," said Beereeun. "I shall make a roadway to the skies and follow them. Thence shall I bring them back, or wreak my vengeance on them."

He went to the canoe where were his spears. Having grasped them, he took, too, the spears of Goolay-yali, which lay by the smoldering fire.

He chose a barbed one. With all his force he threw it up to the sky. The barb caught there, the spear hung down. Beereeun threw another, which caught on to the first, and yet another, and so on, each catching the one before it, until he could touch the lowest from the earth. This he clutched hold of, and climbed up, up, up, until he reached the sky. Then he started in pursuit of the Bullai Bullai. And he is still pursuing them.

Since then the tribe of Beereeun have always been able to swarm up sheer heights. Since then, too, his tribe, the little lizards of the plains, make eer-dher, or mirages, to lure on thirsty travelers, only to send them mad before they die of thirst. Since then Goolay-yali the pelican has been white, for ever did the ashes thrown by the Bullai Bullai cling to him; only where he had shaken them off from his hands are there a few black feathers. The tribe of Bullai Bullai are colored like the green of the leaves the sisters strung on themselves in which to mourn Weedah, with here and there a dash of whitish yellow and red, caused by the ashes and the blood of their mourning. And Womba the star, the mad star, still shines (our Canopus). And Weedah the mockingbird still builds grass nunnoos, open at both ends, in and out of which he runs, as if they were but playgrounds.

And the fire which Weedah and the Bullai Bullai made spread from one end of the country to the other, over ridges and across plains, burning the trees so that their trunks have been black ever since. Deenyi, the iron barks, smoldered the longest of all, and their trunks were so seared that the seams are deeply marked in their thick black bark still, making them show out grimly distinct on the ridges, to remind the Daens forever of Beereeun the miragemaker.

The Prisoner
(South Seas)

A large fish swallows the girl who refuses to marry him, and, in this Polynesian tale, makes her escape in a way that explains why fish have gills.

Once long ago, on the beautiful island of Rarotonga, there lived a girl named Rangi, who was very skillful in the making of tapa cloth from the wet bark of trees. She was especially good at cutting graceful designs with sharp shells on the tapa cloth she fashioned.

Her special place for working was on the open beach of the island, just by the shadow of some wild ginger plants that grew along the shore. Here, almost any day from early in the morning until sunset brought out the first stars, Rangi could be found working away at her tapa designs.

One day, while Rangi worked on the beach, a huge black grouper, a fish almost as big as a small whale, swam up to the edge of the reef from the deep sea. He peered over the reef at the shore, attracted by the splash of brightness made by the ginger blossoms. And when he looked over the reef at the ginger blossoms, he naturally couldn't help seeing Rangi near by, kneeling gracefully and wielding her tapa shells.

The great fish had never seen such a beautiful maiden as Rangi. He fell deeply in love with her in an instant, the way a beast or a fish can sometimes love a human being. And the grouper said to himself, "More than anything in the world, I would like to win that girl for my wife!"

So he set about wooing Rangi in the only way he knew: he swam over the reef into the lagoon on the next high tide, darted as fast as his sluggish body would go toward the beach where Rangi worked, and splashed at the water with his tail and his fins to draw the girl's attention to him.

Rangi looked up and saw him splashing there, near by. And since she was a very friendly girl, she said kindly, "Why, hello there. What a very large fish you are! And pretty, too. Do you mind if I copy some of your markings in my tapa cloth designs?"

"Not at all," returned the grouper, "if you will only consent to marry me."

"Marry you!" Rangi was quite surprised, needless to say. "I couldn't do that."

"Why not?"

"Because you're a fish and I'm a girl, that's why," said Rangi, laughing.

"Please," begged the fish. "I am madly in love with you!"

Rangi shook her head gently. "I'm sorry, fish," she said, "but I must refuse."

At these words, the grouper was very sad, and he slowly swam out toward the reef. Rangi thought he was swimming away forever and wouldn't bother her again, but she was wrong.

The fish swam only as far as the deep water under the reef. Then he went right down to the bottom and lay there, mourning in his heart for the beautiful girl who would not marry him. He decided that he could not give up Rangi as easily as that—he couldn't just swim away forever. So he determined to wait until the next high tide and try his luck again.

The second proposal of marriage, however, was no more successful than his first. Rangi smiled kindly at the grouper but steadfastly refused to consider marrying him. The fish pleaded and begged to no avail. Rangi could not be moved.

Still the fish would not give up. He *had* to have Rangi for his wife. Nothing else would satisfy him. So he decided on a bold plan.

When Rangi turned back to her work and was not looking at him, the fish stretched out a fin as big as a sail and gathered Rangi up in it. He flipped her from the beach into the sea in an instant. Before Rangi had time to do more than gasp and choke a little on the salt water she'd swallowed, the big grouper opened his enormous mouth wide and swallowed Rangi in one big swallow—tapa shells and all.

Rangi wasn't hurt. Not a bit. The fish loved her too much to hurt her. But he was determined to have Rangi for his own. He hoped to be able to talk her around to marrying him in the end. Once Rangi was safe and sound in his warm stomach, the fish swam rapidly through the pass into the open ocean and took her far, far from land.

"Let me out!" shouted Rangi angrily. "Let me out! You are a wicked fish to swallow me and steal me from my home."

"I love you," replied the fish, swimming faster than ever. "That's the only excuse I have. But I can't let you go."

"You must let me go," shouted Rangi up the fish's throat. "You must!"

"Oh, no," said the fish. "Not likely. Not until you agree to marry me."

Rangi, in despair, began to think about how she might escape from the fish's insides. She thought and thought for six days and nights without sleeping. And the only way she could think of to get out of the fish was to cut her way out. She still had with her the sharp cutting shells with which she patterned her tapa cloth. They were stuck into the girdle around her waist.

The first thing Rangi did was to examine very carefully the inside of her prison to find where the flesh was thinnest. She tapped around the walls of the fish's stomach, listening to the sound. She tapped the walls of the fish's throat. And at the upper end of his throat, not far below his enormous mouth, she found the thinnest part of the fish's body. So she began to cut there.

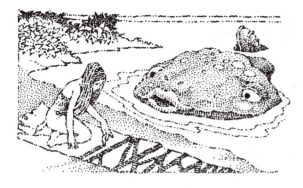

Hour after hour she toiled, drawing the sharp edges of her shells against the flesh of the fish's throat. She decided to make a cut on both sides of his throat, so that she would double her chances of escaping if she ever broke through. She worked very hard. *Cut, cut, cut, cut.*

At length the black grouper, feeling the pain in his throat, called out, "What are you doing in there, Rangi?"

"I'm cutting my way out of you, fish," reported Rangi honestly. "I'll stop if you'll let me out."

But the fish was stubborn. "Go ahead and cut me," he said. "I love you too much to let you out."

So Rangi cut some more.

On the fourth day of her work, she had cut so deeply into both sides of the fish's throat that she could see daylight through the gashes. Only a thin layer of skin now separated her from freedom.

She said to the fish, "You win, fish. I am weary to death of cutting. I shall never get out, I suppose, unless I agree to marry you. So take me to some near-by island where I can get ashore in safety, and I will reconsider marrying you."

"Do you mean it?" asked the grouper, overjoyed. "But how can I trust you?"

"I'm still your prisoner," Rangi reminded him. "How could I escape, even if I wanted to deceive you?"

"That's true," admitted the fish. He swam at once toward the nearest island. "I'm taking you to Mauke," said the fish. "Is that all right?"

"Perfect," said Rangi. "They have beautiful jasmine flowers on Mauke for my bridal bouquet. Let me know when we get there, will you, please?"

"Certainly," said the fish. "You have made me very happy." After an hour, he called out, "We are there, Rangi. Inside the reef at Mauke."

"Close to shore?" asked Rangi. She got her tapa shells ready to make the last cuts in the fish's throat.

"As close as I can get," said the fish.

"Then here I go!" cried Rangi, and slashed the final slash with her shells at each side of the fish's throat. The thin outer skin parted, and through the slits in the fish's gullet, Rangi could see blue sky and green water again. She looked out to see which of her windows in the fish's throat was nearest the shore and jumped quickly through it into the waters of the lagoon. Soon she rose to her feet in the shallow water and ran up on the shore, safely out of reach of her strange suitor.

As for the black grouper, once he became used to the water rushing in and out of his throat through Rangi's cuts, he found it rather a pleasant feeling. He sighed and swam slowly out to sea, vowing never to fall in love with a human girl again.

This story explains why *all* fish have gills in their throats today.

Folk Tales of North and South America

Canada

There is a rich accumulation of folk tales from the Indian and Eskimo cultures of Canada; these have been included in a later section of this section under the heading "North American Indian and Eskimo Tales," since many of the stories are found in the literature of both the United States and Canada. The third group of Canadian folk tales comes from a French Canadian heritage, particularly stories of the voyageurs. Both of the stories used here are from that heritage and reflect the rugged quality of the frontier experiences from which they emanate.

Little Nichet's Baby Sister

One of a series of traditional French-Canadian tales about inquisitive little Nichet is realistic rather than magical.

That little Nichet, Jean LeBlanc's youngest child, was one to keep his parents as busy as all the other thirteen tied together.

One day the little fellow had a new question for his wise father.

"Papa," said Nichet, "where did the Boulangers get their new baby?"

"That is an easy question," answered Jean LeBlanc. "The good Indians brought her, my little nest egg."

"Did the good Indians bring me to you?" asked Nichet.

"Of course," answered his father. "The good Indians bring all the babies."

Little Nichet thought about this for a while.

"Papa," he asked again, "will the good Indians bring us another baby? I would like to have a little sister like Marie Boulanger."

"*Tatata!*" exclaimed Jean LeBlanc. "Already the good Indians have brought us a houseful. Thirteen brothers and sisters are quite enough for such a little fellow as you. And if we had a new baby, you would no longer be our little nest egg."

But Nichet did not think that thirteen brothers and sisters were enough, especially when they were all older and bigger than he.

One afternoon little Nichet wanted to ask his father more about this. But his father and his mother had driven to town in the two-wheeled cart with his eight sisters squeezed together in back.

It was a lonely day for Nichet because his five brothers were out in the field working. And Grandmère kept falling asleep over the rug she was hooking.

So Nichet bravely decided to go to the Indian village himself and ask the Indians if they didn't have an extra baby for the LeBlancs.

Nichet started out on his own two short legs. He walked down the river road. He walked up the Indian trail.

At last he came to the Indian village with its houses scattered over the ground like half-melons.

The Indian village was deserted. The Indians must have gone to town too. Then Nichet saw a few squaws working among the corn sprouts on the hillside. He started toward them.

But he never got as far as the cornfields. For there, propped against a tree trunk, was exactly what Nichet wanted. It was a little papoose laced to its cradle board.

Nichet was so excited that he could scarcely unlace the baby from the board. He lifted it carefully in his arms. The baby did not cry like the Boulangers' new Marie. Nichet looked at its brown skin and its black eyes and its straight black hair. He tried to decide whether it looked more like his papa or his mamma.

The little baby waved its tiny brown arms at him.

"You are my little sister," said Nichet. "I think you look most like me. I will take you home to your papa and mamma."

Nichet LeBlanc carried the papoose down the trail to the river road. It was a long walk and Nichet was so tired he did not think he would ever get the baby to its home. But his sturdy legs carried them both there at last.

Papa and Mamma and the girls had not returned from town yet. The boys were still in the field. Nichet took the baby to show her to Grandmère, but the old lady was asleep with her mouth open and her glasses on the end of her nose.

So little Nichet carried the baby into his parents' bedroom. He carefully laid it in the middle of the bright quilt. Then he ran down the lane to wait for his mamma and papa. He wanted to be the first one to tell them the news that they had a new baby.

At first his papa and mamma thought that little Nichet had a fever. Then they thought that he had fallen asleep like Grandmère and had had a bad dream. But when they saw the brown baby with the black hair and black eyes lying on the bed, they knew that Nichet had told the truth.

"Where did this baby come from?" cried Mamma LeBlanc.

"The Indians brought her," said little Nichet. "That is, I went and got her myself so they wouldn't give her to someone else."

Then there was a great *tohu-bohu* of chattering among the LeBlancs.

"We will have to take it right back," said Jean LeBlanc. "If the Indians think we have stolen their baby, they might burn down our house."

Little Nichet was brokenhearted. He begged and begged his parents to keep his little brown sister with the black hair and black eyes who looked so much like him.

But back to the Indians went the little sister. Little Nichet held her in his arms all the way there in the two-wheeled cart.

There was another *tohu-bohu* of chattering going on at the Indian village.

"A bear has carried off one of the babies," a young brave explained to Jean LeBlanc.

"We have your baby here," said Jean. "It was carried off by a very little bear."

Nichet cried and cried at the loss of his Indian sister. He began feeling sorry for himself. He began thinking that if his papa and mamma had returned the baby to the Indians, they might do the same with him someday.

Little Nichet began feeling sorrier than ever for himself. He decided to return to the Indians of his own free will. How his parents would cry when they found he was gone! They would come galloping to the Indian village. They would take him home again—and his baby sister too.

He packed his nightshirt and his willow whistle and his lynx tail into a sack and set out for the Indian village once more. He walked all the way down the river road. He followed the trail to the houses that were like half-melons.

"I have come back to stay with my little sister," Nichet told one of the Indians.

Then the Indians were as worried as the LeBlancs had been.

"If we keep you here," said one of them, "your papa will think that we have stolen you. He will burn down our lodges."

Little Nichet refused to leave. "I want to stay here and be an Indian like my little sister," he said.

The Indians gathered together and talked their *micmac* talk, which Nichet could not understand. Then one of them turned to him.

"Can you shoot a bow and arrow?" he asked in Nichet's talk.

"No," said little Nichet.

"Can you skin a moose?"

"No," said little Nichet.

"Can you build a birch canoe?"

"No," said little Nichet.

"Then you cannot stay with us," said the brave. "An Indian must be able to do all those things."

So little Nichet sadly turned and started away. But another Indian came running to him with something furry in his hands.

"A gift for you," said the Indian. "A trade for the baby you returned to us."

He dropped a tiny baby animal into Nichet's arms. It had the head of a beaver, the body of a bear, and the tail of a rabbit.

"What is it?" asked Nichet.

"Your wise father will have a name for it," said the Indian, then he began talking his *micmac* talk that Nichet could not understand.

Nichet carried the baby animal home happily. All the way his busy mind wondered if it was a fox or a beaver or a mink or what.

All the LeBlancs were happy to see that Nichet was home again. For truth, they didn't even know he had gone away until they saw the furry little animal in his arms.

"It is a little whistler," said his wise father, Jean LeBlanc. "Some people call them woodchucks and some people call them groundhogs. But the people back in France call them marmots."

"What is it good for?" asked Grandmère. "Will it give milk or pull a cart or lay eggs?"

"It is good for a lonesome little boy who needs a companion smaller than himself," said Jean LeBlanc. He leaned over Nichet

and smiled at the new baby. "Across the ocean in France," he said, "chimney sweeps from the mountains keep whistlers for pets. They teach them to do a little dance like a bear's."

"Can I be a chimney sweep when I am bigger?" asked little Nichet.

"You may be a chimney sweep tomorrow," said Jean LeBlanc generously. "I am going to take down the stovepipe for your mamma and you may help me clean the soot out of it."

So little Nichet thought that he had made a very good trade with the Indians. The boy picked out the name of Pierrette for his tiny pet, and his father helped him to teach that whistler to dance.

Whenever Nichet whistled a special tune, Pierrette would sit up on her hindquarters and wave her forepaws from right to left as she did her dance of the bear. And from time to time she would make polite curtsies. You may be sure that Pierrette was as popular at the stay-awake parties as old Michel Meloche, the storyteller.

The Canoe in the Rapids

Friendship is tested in this tale of fur trappers that is almost a tall tale.

Once in another time, François Ecrette was an adventurer in the woods. Every winter he went north with Sylvain Gagnon. They trapped foxes, beavers, minks and any furred creature that would step into their traps.

When spring came and the ice in the river melted, the two men would load their furs into a canoe and paddle down the swift current to sell their winter's catch to the trader.

It was one such spring that François and Sylvain headed south with the finest catch that they had ever made. If only they could beat the other trappers to the trading post, they could make a fine bargain.

"A-ah, we will be rich men," said Sylvain, who already could hear the *tintin* of coins in his deep pockets.

"Yes," answered François, "if we get through the Devil's Jaws safely."

Nowhere on any of the rivers of Canada was there such a fearsome place. In the Devil's Jaws, there were waterfalls that roared and whirlpools that spun a boat about like a dry leaf. It was as if the river fell into a panic itself when squeezed into the Devil's Jaws and tried to run away in every direction.

"That's true," said Sylvain, "but you are lucky to have me for a partner. Nowhere in all Canada is there such a skillful boatman as Sylvain Gagnon."

Sylvain drew the cold air in through his nose and puffed out his chest with it.

So François Ecrette felt safe and happy, even though the worst ordeal of the long trip was ahead of them.

They loaded the canoe with their bundles of furs and their provisions. For days they paddled down the river, singing gay songs to pass away the long hours.

One late afternoon they beached their

boat on the bank and made for a clearing on the hill. They built a campfire, and François started to roast a young rabbit he had shot. He hung it over the coals by spearing it on a green willow branch.

"We must eat well," said Sylvain, "for we are close to the Devil's Jaws. We will need all our strength for that pull and push."

"But it will soon be dark," François reminded him. "Shouldn't we camp here all night so we can go through the rapids in daylight?"

"Pou, pou," laughed Sylvain, "what a scared rabbit you are! I can paddle at night as well as by day. I could shoot the Devil's Jaws with my eyes closed and a beaver riding on my paddle."

François rubbed his stubbly chin.

"My faith," he exclaimed, "I am the luckiest man in the world to have you for a partner, Sylvain Gagnon. I don't believe you have fear of anything."

As if to test the truth of this, an angry growl came from behind the bushes. Both men jumped to their feet, François seizing his rifle as he did so. The bushes broke open and a big brown bear came through them. He walked slowly on all fours, shuffling from this paw to that paw, and from that paw to this paw. Straight toward the two trappers he came.

François lifted his rifle to his shoulder and took careful aim. He pulled the trigger. Plink! Nothing happened. There was no bullet in the rifle because it had been used on the rabbit.

The bear gave another angry growl. He rose on his hind legs and walked toward François like a man, shuffling from this paw to that paw.

François dropped the gun and ran for his life. Already Sylvain Gagnon was far ahead of him, his fur coat making him look like a bear that ran too fast to shuffle from this paw to that paw. François made for a big tree, but he didn't have time to climb it as the bear was almost on him. So around the tree he ran. And behind him followed the bear. Round and round and round the tree ran François and the bear. Any little bird looking down from the treetop wouldn't have known whether the bear was chasing François Ecrette or François was chasing the bear. The trapper ran so fast that he was more behind the bear than in front of him. And as the bear ran around the tree, he clawed the air angrily. But his sharp claws only tore the bark from the tree. And if François had anything at all to be thankful for, it was that the ragged shreds flying through the air were bark from the tree and not skin from his back.

Around and around and around went the man and the beast. The bear got dizzy first. He ran slower and slower. Finally he broke away from the tree and went staggering away, first to this side and then to that side. And as he reeled and stumbled, he knocked his head into one tree trunk after another. Bump—bump—bump.

François lost no time in finding another tree to climb, for the tree they had been running around had been stripped of its bark as far up as a bear could reach. As he climbed, he could hear the bump, bump, bump of the bear's head as he stumbled into tree trunks.

Panting and dizzy himself, François settled into a crotch of the tree. Now where was that false friend, Sylvain Gagnon, who had left him to face the bear alone? He called and called but there was no answer. Perhaps the bear had eaten Sylvain. A-tout-tou, what bad luck that would be when there was still the Devil's Jaws ahead! How could he ever get through those treacherous waters without the skillful boatman Sylvain Gagnon?

And how could he get safely from the tree to the boat? Perhaps the bear was waiting for him among the bushes. The sleepy sun soon went to bed and it grew dark. It became colder than ever. François Ecrette's arms and legs were numb.

At last he jerkily lowered himself from the tree. He looked about in every direction, but it was too dark to see anything. He sniffed and sniffed like a bear, for if a bear can smell a man, maybe a man can smell a bear. But all François could smell was the sharp, icy air of early spring. Slowly he made his way down

the hill toward the place they had left the canoe.

Then great joy filled the heart of François Ecrette. Although the trees blackened the river, a faint moonlight glimmered through them. Its pale light fell upon a figure hunched in the bow of the canoe with the fur coat pulled up over its ears.

"Sylvain," cried François, "you are safe after all. Why didn't you come back to me?"

But Sylvain must have felt a deep shame, for he only put his head down between his arms and made a sad, apologetic sound.

"Believe me, my friend," said François, "I'm certainly glad you escaped, for we have a terrible ride ahead of us this night. Do you think we better try the rapids after all?"

But his companion resolutely straightened up and squared his shoulders in the fur coat. François pushed the boat into the stream, leaped aboard and grabbed a paddle. Silently they floated into the current; then the slender canoe headed for the dangers ahead.

"My faith, it is good to have you in this boat with me," cried François. "This current is like a bolt of lightning."

The boat raced faster and faster. Instead of paddling for speed, François had to spend his strength flattening the paddle like a brake. The trees made a dark tunnel of the river course so that François could barely see his companion's stout back.

On, on they went. The frail canoe sped in a zigzag flight like a swallow. François Ecrette's sharp ear caught the distant roar of the rapids.

"Brace yourself, Sylvain," he cried, "for the boat is now in your hands. I will help you as much as I can."

So he plied his paddle from this side to that side and from that side to this side. The river had become like an angry, writhing eel. He heard the waterfall ahead and began paddling like mad so the canoe would shoot straight and true. The least slant of the boat and the churning current would turn it over and over, and swallow them both.

François felt the icy wind and the cold

spray on his face as they plunged over the waterfall and bobbed in the whirlpool below. He fought the churning, frothing waters that he could hear more than see. His muscles tightened like iron and the air blew up his lungs.

"My faith, but it's a good thing to have such a boatman as Sylvain Gagnon guiding this canoe," rejoiced François. "In such a current as this, no other man could bring a boat through safely. I will forget the way he deserted me when that big brown bear attacked us."

All danger was not over yet, for the stern of the canoe was sucked into the outer rim of a whirlpool. The lurch of the boat wrenched François Ecrette's back like a blow from a giant hammer. The canoe spun around completely. For fully ten minutes, there was such a battle with the churning waters as François had never known before. Around and around, up and down rocked the canoe, with François fiercely wielding his paddle. If it hadn't been for the soothing figure in front of him, he would have given up in fright.

Finally the canoe straightened out and leaped straight ahead. The roar of the rapids grew fainter. François let his paddle drag and relaxed.

"My faith," he gasped. "I thought that was the last of us for sure. You have saved us both, Sylvain Gagnon. No boatman in all Canada but you could have gotten us out of that Devil's trap."

But his modest companion only shrugged his shoulders and humped lower into the bow.

Then because François was worn out from his paddling, he decided to take a little nap. With no other partner but Sylvain would he have dared doze off. But Sylvain had proved his mettle in getting them through the rapids, and the waters ahead were slow and peaceful. So François rested his paddle, closed his eyes and fell into a deep sleep.

When he awoke, it was morning. The sun had chased the shadows out from under the trees, and the river sparkled in the friendliest kind of way.

François rubbed the sleep out of his eyes. "Ah, Sylvain," he yawned, "what a night we had in the rapids. If it hadn't been for you —a-tou-tou-tou-tou!"

For François Ecrette's partner in the canoe was not Sylvain Gagnon, the great boatman, but the big brown bear of the clearing!

François jumped up and gave a bloodcurdling shriek. The bear slowly turned around and looked at him. He shook his great furry head as if to shake his brains back into their right place after they had been knocked apart by the tree trunks. He gave a low threatening growl.

François didn't wait any longer. He dived into the river and furiously swam through the icy water. After what seemed a sinner's lifetime, he reached the frosty shore. When he looked back at the river, he had a last glance of the canoe, full of furs, disappearing among the trees with the big brown bear standing in the bow.

Now this was a fine how-does-it-make of trouble. Here was François all alone in the wilderness without Sylvain, furs, provisions or even a dry match.

Luckily the trading post couldn't be too far away now. François gathered dry wood and started a fire in the Indian way, by rubbing two sticks together. Then he stood as close to the fire as he could, to dry out his clothes. He scorched and steamed like the uneaten rabbit back on the sharp stick in the clearing.

At last he was dry enough to brave the cold walk down the river bank. He set out slowly. The branches scratched his hands and face. His boots sloshed and squashed through the slush of early spring.

It was late afternoon by the time he reached the trader's village. Everyone seemed surprised to see him alive.

"Your canoe was found caught in a log jam below here, with bear tracks on the shore," said the trader. "We thought a bear had carried you off."

"But the furs," cried François. "What happened to them? Were they lost?"

"They are all safe," said the trader. "Your friend Sylvain Gagnon arrived only a little while ago. He helped me check through them."

Then a familiar face appeared in the crowd.

"François, my good friend," cried Sylvain. "I got a ride back with a party of Indians. But how did you ever get the canoe through the rapids all by yourself?"

"Sylvain, my false friend," retorted the trapper, "I was not alone. The big brown bear who chased me in the clearing was with me."

Then François Ecrette shivered and shook in a way that had nothing to do with the cold spring afternoon or his damp clothing.

So all turned out well for François Ecrette in the end. But he never went on any more trapping trips with Sylvain Gagnon. You see, my friends, one who turns into a big brown bear when you need him most is not a true friend.

United States: Variants of European Folk Tales

With the exception of the tall tale and an occasional humorous story in such collections as Moritz Jagendorf's *New England Bean-Pot,* most of the stories that are read and told in American variants are derived from European roots as are so many of our old ballads. Some of the variants have been changed by adaptation and are easily recognizable; some have taken on the color of the region (like the Appalachian tales) where they have been most popular. "Jack and the Robbers" is a good example of the latter, a tale in which the speech patterns mask the origin and the humor has the rough, robust quality of a pioneer society.

Jack and the Robbers

The Appalachian idiom gives freshness to this variant of "The Bremen Town Musicians."

This here's another tale about Jack when he was still a small-like boy. He was about twelve, I reckon, and his daddy started tryin' to make him help with the work around the place. But Jack he didn't like workin' much. He would piddle around a little and then he'd go on back to the house, till one day his daddy whipped him. He just tanned Jack good. Jack didn't cry none, but he didn't like

it a bit. So early the next mornin' he slipped off without tellin' his mother and struck out down the public road. Thought he'd go and try his fortune somewhere off from home.

He got down the road a few miles and there was an old ox standin' in a field by a rail fence, a-bellowin' like it was troubled over somethin'—

"Um-m-muh!
Um-m-m—muh-h-h!"

From THE JACK TALES by Richard Chase. Copyright 1943 and copyright © renewed 1971 by Richard Chase. Reprinted by permission of Houghton Mifflin Company.

"Hello!" says Jack. "What's the matter?"

"I'll just tell you," says the old ox. "I'm gettin' too old to plow and I heard the men talkin' about how they'd have to kill me tomorrow and get shet of me."

"Come on down here to the gap," says Jack, "and you can slip off with me."

So the old ox followed the fence to where the gap was at and Jack let the bars down and the old ox got out in front of Jack, and they went on down the public road.

Jack and the ox traveled on, and pretty soon they came where there was an old donkey standin' with his head hangin' down over the gate, a-goin'—

"Wahn-n-n-eh!
Wahn-n-n-eh!
Wahn-n-n-eh!"

"Hello," says Jack. "What's troublin' you?"

"Law me!" says the old donkey. "The boys took me out to haul in wood this mornin' and I'm gettin' so old and weak I couldn't do no good. I heard 'em say they were goin' to kill me tomorrow, get shet of me."

"Come on and go with us," says Jack.

So he let the old donkey out and they pulled on down the public road. The old donkey told Jack to get up on his back and ride.

They went on a piece, came to an old hound dog settin' in a man's yard. He would bark awhile and then howl awhile—

"A-woo! woo! woo!
A-oo-oo-oo!"

—sounded awful lonesome.

"Hello," says Jack. "What you a-howlin' so for?"

"Oh, law me!" says the old dog. "The boys took me coon-huntin' last night, cut a tree where the coon had got up in it. I got hold on the coon all right, but my teeth are all gone and hit got loose from me. They said they were goin' to kill me today, get shet of me."

"Come on, go with us," says Jack.

So the old dog scrouged under the gate.

The old donkey says to him, "Get up on my back and ride, if you want to."

Jack holp the old dog up behind him, and they went on down the public road.

Came to an old tomcat climbin' along the fence. Hit was a-squallin' and meowin', stop ever' now and then, sit down on the top rail—

"Meow-ow!
Meow-ow-ow!"

—sounded right pitiful.

"Hello!" says Jack. "What's the matter you squallin' so?"

"Oh, law!" says the old cat. "I caught a rat out in the barn this mornin', but my teeth are gettin' so old and bad I let him go. I heard 'em talkin' about killin' me to get shet of me, 'cause I ain't no good to catch rats no more."

"Come on and go with us," says Jack.

So the old cat jumped down off the fence.

The old donkey says, "Hop up there on my back and you can ride."

The old cat jumped up, got behind the dog, and they went on down the public road.

Came to where they saw an old rooster settin' on a fence post, crowin' like it was midnight, makin' the awfulest lonesome racket—

"Ur rook-a-roo!
"Ur-r-r rook-a-roo-oo-oo!"

"Hello!" says Jack. "What's troublin' you?"

"Law me!" says the old rooster. "Company's comin' today and I heard 'em say they were goin' to kill me, put me in a pie!"

"Come on with us," says Jack.

Old rooster flew on down, got behind the cat, says, "All right, boys. Let's go!"

So they went right on down the highway. That was about all could get on the old donkey's back. The old rooster was right on top its tail and a-havin' a sort of hard time stayin' on. They traveled on, traveled on, till hit got plumb dark.

"Well," says Jack, "we got to get off the road and find us a place to stay tonight."

Directly they came to a little path leadin' off in the woods, decided to take that, see could they find a stayin' place in there. Went on a right smart piece further, and 'way along up late in the night they came to a little house, didn't have no clearin' around it. Jack hollered hello at the fence but there didn't nobody answer.

"Come on," says the old donkey. "Let's go investigate that place."

Well, there wasn't nobody ever came to the door and there wasn't nobody around back of the house, so directly they went on in. Found a right smart lot of good somethin' to eat in there.

Jack says, "Now, who in the world do you reckon could be a-livin' out here in such a wilderness of a place as this?"

"Well," says the old donkey, "hit's my opinion that a gang of highway robbers lives out here."

So Jack says, "Then hit looks like to me we might as well take up and stay here. If they've done stole all these vittles, we got as much right to 'em as they have."

"Yes," says the old dog, "that's exactly what I think, too. But if we stay, I believe we better get fixed for a fight. I expect they'll be comin' back in here about midnight."

"That's just what I was goin' to say," says the old cat. "I bet it's pretty close to midnight right now."

"Hit lacks about a hour," says the old rooster.

"Come on, then," says Jack. "Let's all of us get set to fight 'em."

The ox said he'd stay out in the yard. The old donkey said he'd take up his stand on the porch just outside the door. The dog said he'd get in behind the door and fight from there. The old tomcat got down in the fireplace, and the old rooster flew up on the comb of the roof, says, "If you boys need any help now, just call on me, call on me-e-e!"

They all waited awhile. Heard somebody comin' directly; hit was seven highway robbers. They came on till they got pretty close to the house, then they told one of 'em to go on in and start up a fire so's they could have a light to see to get in and so they could divide out the money they'd stole that day.

One man went on in the house, the other six waited outside the gate.

That man went to the fireplace, got down on his knees to blow up the fire. The cat had his head right down on the hearth-rock and that man thought its eyes was coals of fire. Time he blowed in that old cat's eyes, it reached out its claws right quick and scratched him down both cheeks. The robber hollered and headed for the door. The dog ran out and bit him in the leg. He shook it off and ran on the porch and the old donkey raised up and kicked him on out in the yard. The ox caught him up on its horns and ran to the fence and threw him out in the bresh. About that time the old rooster settin' up there on top of the house started in to crowin' right big.

The other robbers, time they heard all that racket, they put out from there just as fast as they could run. The one they'd sent in the house finally got up and started runnin' like a streak, caught up with 'em in no time. They said to him, says, "What in the world was that in there?"

"Oh, I'm killed! I'm killed!" says the man. "I won't live over fifteen minutes!"

The other said, "Well, 'fore ye die, tell us what it was caused all that racket back yonder."

"Law me! That house is plumb full of men, and they've even got one on the roof. I went to blow up the fire and a man in the fireplace raked me all over the face with an awl. Started to run and a man behind the door took me in the leg with a butcher knife. Time I got out the door, a man out there hit me with a knot-maul, knocked me clean off the porch. A man standin' in the yard caught me on a pitchfork and threw me over the fence. And then that man up on the roof hollered out,

'Chunk him on up here!
Chunk him on up here.'

Ain't no use in us goin' back there with all of them men in the house. Let's leave here quick 'fore they come after us."

So them highway robbers ran for their life, and kept on runnin' till they were plumb out the country.

Jack and the ox and the old donkey and the dog and the cat and the rooster, they took possession of that house, and just had 'em a big time.

But the last time I was down that way, Jack had gone on back home to his folks. He was out in the yard a-cuttin' his mother a big pile of stovewood.

Young Melvin

There's a good portion of tall-tale braggadoccio in this tale with its familiar theme of the liar out-lied.

After his pappy passed on Young Melvin decided he wanted to travel. He'd always lived back at the forks of the creek and he hadn't ever at no time been farther from there than the crossroads.

So Young Melvin put out the fire and hid the ax and skillet and called up his hound named Bulger and he was on his way. He went over the hill and a good piece further and he come to the crossroads. He went straight to Old Man Bill Blowdy's house there. He knocked on the door.

Old Man Bill Blowdy come to the door and stuck his nose out the crack. "Who's there?" says he, not daring to come out for fear it was somebody he'd beat in some deal.

"It's me," says Young Melvin. "Just me and my hound dog Bulger."

Old Man Bill Blowdy opened the door then and gave Young Melvin a sly look. "Come in and rest and eat a bite," he says, faint-like.

He was a great big fat red man that was always grinning and easy talking, like butter wouldn't melt in his mouth. And he was just about the slickest, double-dealingest old cooter in the country or anywhere else at all. Nobody could beat him in a deal—never had, anyway—or when it come to a law-suit. Always

"Young Melvin" from GOD BLESS THE DEVIL!: LIARS' BENCH TALES by James R. Aswell and others of the Tennessee Writers' Project. Copyright 1940 The University of North Carolina Press. Reprinted by permission of the publisher.

lawing somebody, Old Man Bill Blowdy was.

"Why don't you come in, Young Melvin?" he says.

"Because I'm on my way, Mister Old Man Bill Blowdy. I'm a-going to town for sure. It's forty miles and across two counties but I aim to see that town. That's why I come to see you."

Old Man Bill Blowdy started shutting the door. "Now, now, Young Melvin," he says. "I'm hard up for money right now. I couldn't loan my sweet mother, now in heaven praise be, so much as a penny."

"I don't want no money," says Young Melvin. "I ain't the borrowing kind."

So Old Man Bill Blowdy poked his head out again. "What can I do for you then?"

"Well, it's like this. You're my twenty-third cousin, my only kin in this world. I got a favor for you to do for me."

Old Man Bill Blowdy started sliding that door shut. "No, no favors. I make it a rule to do no favors and don't expect none from nobody."

"It's a favor I'm aiming to pay for," says Young Melvin.

"Oh," says Old Man Bill Blowdy, opening the door once more, "that's different now. Come right in, Young Melvin."

"No sir, no need to come in, for I'd just be coming out again. What I want you to do is keep my fox hound Bulger while I'm off on my travels. I'll pay his keep, I'll pay what's right when I come back to get him."

Old Man Bill Blowdy grinned all over his face. He thought he saw a way to make himself something extry or get him a fox hound one. Everybody knew Young Melvin was simple. Honest as the day's long but simple.

"Why yes," says Old Man Bill Blowdy. "Why yes, I'll keep Bulger for you, Young Melvin, and glad to."

So Young Melvin gave his hound dog over and bid Old Man Bill Blowdy farewell. "I'll be back next week or month or sometime. I don't know how long it'll be, for it's forty miles and across two counties to town."

Well, one day the week or month or anyhow sometime after that, here come Young

Melvin down the pikeroad to the crossroads, limping and dusty and easy in mind. He went straight to Old Man Bill Blowdy's house and knocked his knuckles on the door.

Old Man Bill Blowdy stuck his nose out the crack and says, "Who's there?"

"It's me, it's Young Melvin."

"How are you, Young Melvin?"

"Fair to piddling. I walked to town and saw all the sights and then walked back here again. Forty miles and across two counties. Don't never want to roam no more. I'm satisfied now."

Old Man Bill Blowdy started shutting the door. "Glad to hear it, Young Melvin. Next time you come down to the crossroads, drop in and say hello. Any time, just any time, Young Melvin."

"Hold there! Wait a minute!" says Young Melvin.

"I'm busy," says the old man.

But Young Melvin got his foot in the door. "How about Bulger, Old Man Bill Blowdy? How about him?"

Old Man Bill Blowdy kept trying to shut the door and Young Melvin kept shoving his foot in.

"See here!" says Young Melvin. "I mean my fox hound."

"Oh him? Why, I declare to my soul I'd almost forgot that hound dog, Young Melvin. I sure almost had."

"Where is he at?" says Young Melvin, still trying to keep the old man from closing the door.

"I'll tell you," says Old Man Bill Blowdy, still trying to shut it, "I feel mighty bad about it, Young Melvin, but your Bulger is no more."

"How come? What do you mean?"

"Why, he's perished and gone, Young Melvin. The first night after you left I sort of locked him up in that little busted-down house over in the Old Ground. Well sir, Young Melvin, those last renters of mine that lived there was powerful dirty folks. They left the place just lousy with chinch bugs. Them bugs was mortal hungry by this time. So they just eat that Bulger of yours alive. Eat all but the poor thing's bones by morning—

and the bones was pretty well gnawed.

"It was my fault in one way. I ought to known better than put your dog in there, Young Melvin. But I done it. So I won't charge you a penny for his keep the night I had him. I aim to do the fair thing."

Well, Old Man Bill Blowdy stuck his sly eye to the crack of the door to see how Young Melvin was taking it. He knew the boy was simple. He figured he had him. Because Old Man Bill Blowdy had Bulger hid out and he aimed to swap him for something to a man he knew in the next county.

So Young Melvin stood there looking like the good Lord had shaken him off His Christian limb. Tears come in his eyes and he sleeved his nose. "That dog was folks to me," he says. "Them chinch bugs don't know what they done to me."

He pulled his foot out of the door and he backed down the steps. He started towards home.

Old Man Bill Blowdy eased out on the porch to watch him go.

About that time Young Melvin turned around. "Mister Old Man Bill Blowdy," he says, "my place is way over the hill and a good piece further. I'm beat out and tired. Wonder if you'd loan me your mule to ride on? I'll bring it back tomorrow."

The old man knew Young Melvin was honest as the livelong day. Besides, he was so tickled with how he'd got him a good hound to swap and it not costing anything that he just called across the way to the crossroads store and got a witness to the loan and let Young Melvin take the mule. It was a fine mule, too, with the three hind ribs showing, the best sort of sign in a mule—shows he's a hard worker.

Next morning Young Melvin never showed up and Old Man Bill Blowdy got worried. He got worrieder still in the middle of the day when no sign of Young Melvin did he see.

But along about afternoon he saw Young Melvin come walking over the hill and down towards the crossroads. He run out on his porch and yelled, "Hey, Young Melvin, where's my mule?"

Young Melvin kept walking. He just shook his head. "I feel mighty bad about that mule, Mister Old Man Bill Blowdy," he called. "I sure do."

"Hey! Wait there!"

But Young Melvin went on, heading for the store at the crossroads.

So Old Man Bill Blowdy was so mad he didn't wait to get his shoes. He just jumped off the porch and run across to Square Rogers, that good old man's house up the road a ways.

"Square," he says, "I want you to handle Young Melvin. He stole my mule."

The Square waked up his deputy and the deputy went down and brought in Young Melvin. Everybody at the crossroads come tagging along behind.

Square said, "Son, they tell me you stole a mule."

"No sir, Square Rogers, I never done it," says Young Melvin.

Old Man Bill Blowdy stomped his bare feet and shook his fists. "He's a bald-faced liar!"

"Curb yourself down, Old Man Bill Blowdy," says the Square, "and let the boy tell his side. Go ahead, Young Melvin."

So Young Melvin told his side, told how he borrowed the mule and started for home. "Well," he says, "you know I live over the hill and a good piece further. I rode that mule to the top of the hill. I was minding my own business and not giving nobody any trouble.

All on a sudden I see a turkey buzzard dropping down out of the sky. Here it come, dropping fast and crowing like a game rooster.

"First thing I knew that old buzzard just grabbed Old Man Bill Blowdy's mule by the tail and started heaving and the mule's hind legs lifted off the ground and I went flying over his head and hit a rock head-on. I failed in my senses a minute. When I could see straight I saw that buzzard sailing away with the mule, most a mile high and getting littler all the time.

"And that's how it happened. I sure am sorry, but there ain't much you can do with a thing like that, Square."

"Hold on there!" says Square Rogers, that good old man. "I've seen many a turkey buzzard in my time, Young Melvin, but never a one that could crow."

"Well," says Young Melvin, "it surprised me some too. But in a county where chinch bugs can eat up a full-grown fox hound in one night, why I just reckon a turkey buzzard has a right to crow and fly off with a mule if he wants to."

So it all come out and Square Rogers, that good old man, made Old Man Bill Blowdy fork up Bulger and then Young Melvin gave back the mule.

Old Man Bill Blowdy was mocked down to nothing. He just grieved and pined away and it wasn't no more than ten years before he taken sick and wasted away and died.

United States: Tall Tales

 It must be admitted that the tall tale is not truly a part of folk literature. It is included here because it is a subgenre, a folklike tale that incorporates many of the devices of the true folk tale, and because its protagonists are all folk heroes, but not of such stature (or believability) that they can be included among the proper hero tales. The United States is too young a country to have an oral tradition that preceded print, and the tall tale is our closest claim to that tradition. These tales combine the bragging prowess of the cracker-barrel competition with the occupations that reflect the frontier society—and all of it told with the bland contrapuntal tone of an event in a big-lie contest.

Mike Fink

Whether or not there was a Mike Fink, the legends of the riverboat men have produced this rambunctious hero.

Mike Fink was born just about the same time the country was. And, soon after, he was ready for anything that happened. A new, growing country needs strong, bold people, so it was a good thing Mike came along when he did.

Take, for instance, the *Mississippi River Trouble.*

The trouble with the Mississippi was that there was just too much bad weather. An ornery old alligator was stirring up the waters with a tail as long as a mountain is high. It could whip up a mighty fierce storm. Even the sturdiest pioneer hesitated to cross the river. Families in covered wagons came to a halt on the east bank of the Mississippi and would go no farther. The settling of the West came to a standstill. Things were in a fine mess—until Mike Fink took charge.

Mike wasn't afraid of *anything,* not even that ornery alligator. He jumped right into the stormy waters one day, tied up the alligator's tail with a heavy rope, and walked back to shore, dripping wet and boasting for all to hear.

"I'm the snapping turtle of the O-hi-o. My boat's the *Lightfoot,* and I can lick any man or any alligator on any river any time!"

After that, the weather calmed down on the Mississippi, and the pioneers were willing to cross. Thanks to Mike Fink, the West got settled after all. You can go out there and see for yourself.

Besides being an alligator tamer, Mike Fink was a fearless scout and a crack shot with a rifle. His aim was so good that he could flick mosquitoes off fence posts and drive nails into barn doors. Mike called his rifle "Bang-All." Everybody knew that Mike Fink and Bang-All couldn't be beat.

Mike grew up in Pennsylvania country. He'd never had much time for schooling, so people sometimes thought he talked funny. But he was the best shot anywheres about. He had the strongest muscles, the bushiest mustache, and the fanciest squirrel-tail cap. He could jump higher, swim faster, yell louder, and spit farther than anyone around. If you didn't believe it, you could just ask Mike.

At the time of the Mississippi Trouble, Mike was a riverboat man. This is how it happened.

The brand new United States of America was beginning to grow and stretch out all over. And rivers were the roads of the country. If farm people wanted flour for biscuits or cloth for a shirt or dress, it came to them on the riverboats. Wheat, corn, cider, and salt, planks, hogs, gunpowder, kegs of nails, and barrels of molasses were carried along the river from town to town on the riverboats—keelboats, flatboats, barges.

One day Mike got to talking with some riverboat men. They were loading cargo for a trip down the Ohio to New Orleans. Their muscles bulged as they worked. Knives glittered on their leather belts. They were strong, tough workers, and they didn't take second place to anybody, not even a fearless scout and crack rifle shot.

"Maybe scoutin' is risky work," one of the riverboat men said to Mike, "but the river's harder."

"Harder!" Mike tightened his muscles.

The riverboat man was sunburned and weatherbeaten and very tall. He looked at Mike a moment and then tossed a bundle of fur pelts into the cargo cabin as easy as a bundle of feathers.

"I can hold off sixty men at once," Mike shouted. "I can wrassle ten bears at a time. I'm half wildcat and half solid rock, and the rest of me's as hard as an iron skillet."

The boatmen went on loading their cargo as if they hadn't even heard all this wonderful news.

"We got lots to fight along the river, too,"

the captain said. "We got storms and whirl-pools and floodwaters. And gettin' back upriver is hard work every bit of the way."

"Not too hard for me!" Mike roared. "I'm ready for anything!"

"Get aboard then," the riverboat captain said. He was laughing to himself. But he didn't laugh long. Mike Fink was born to be a riverboat man.

When Mike joined up with the keelboat crew, he soon found out what hard work meant. Going downstream along the Ohio to the Mississippi was bad enough. There were sandbars and floating trees, uprooted by storms and blown into the river. The sandbars could hang up a boat, and the ragged ends of tree roots could tear a hole right through the hull.

But downstream, at least the boat was going with the flow of the river. It was after the men delivered their goods in New Orleans and started back up the Mississippi that Mike really saw some hard work.

Now the river was against them. The men rowed when the water was deep, and when it was shallow they poled the boat along. They stood on the boat deck and drove the ends of their long poles into the river bed, and *pushed*.

Each push sent the boat ahead a little. But it was a slow, hard haul every bit of the way. Tough men were needed, and Mike Fink was the toughest.

Mike took to riverboat life so fast that it wasn't long before he had his own boat. He built it all in one day and named it the *Lightfoot.* Then he hired his own crew.

Mike Fink needed only a crew of six instead of sixteen, because he was as strong as ten people all by himself. He rowed hard and he poled hard. And when he went ashore, he danced hard and fought hard and generally stirred things up a mite. Everybody knew when Mike Fink was in town.

"I'm a salt-river roarer!" Mike would yell when he hit town. "I'm half wild horse and half cockeyed alligator! And I'm ready for anything!"

Pecos Bill and His Bouncing Bride

It's partly the lure of the cowboy-ridden West, and partly the silliness of an English duke's daughter being named Slue-Foot Sue, that make the Pecos Bill story one that children relish.

There were two loves in the life of Pecos Bill. The first was his horse Widow-Maker, a beautiful creamy white mustang. The second, was a girl, a pretty, gay creature named Slue-Foot Sue.

Widow-Maker was the wildest pony in the West. He was the son of the White Mustang. Like his father he had a proud spirit which refused to be broken. For many years cowboys and *vaqueros* had tried to capture him. At last Pecos Bill succeeded. He had a terrible time of it. For a whole week he lay beside a water hole before he could lasso the white pony. For another week he had to ride across the prairies, in and out of canyons and briar patches, before he could bring the pony to a walk. It was a wild ride indeed. But after Bill's ride on the cyclone it was nothing.

At last the white stallion gave up the struggle. Pecos patted his neck gently and spoke to him in horse language. "I hope you will not be offended," he began as politely as possible, "but beauty such as yours is rare, even in this glorious state of Texas. I have no wish to break your proud spirit. I feel that together you and I would make a perfect team. Will you not be my partner at the I.X.L. Ranch?"

The horse neighed sadly. "It must be," he sighed. "I must give up my freedom. But since I must, I am glad that you are the man who has conquered me. Only Pecos Bill is worthy to fix a saddle upon the son of the great White Stallion, the Ghost King of the Prairie."

"I am deeply honored," said Pecos Bill, touched in his heart by the compliment.

"It is rather myself who am honored," replied the mustang, taking a brighter view of the situation.

The two of them went on for several hours saying nice things to each other. Before they were through, the pony was begging Pecos to be his master. Pecos was weeping and saying he was not fit to ride so magnificent a beast. In the end, however, Pecos Bill made two solemn promises. He would never place a bit in the pony's mouth. No other human would ever sit in his saddle.

When Bill rode back to I.X.L. with his new mount, the second promise was broken. Old Satan, the former bad man, had not completely recovered from his badness. He was jealous of Bill. When he saw the beautiful white stallion he turned green and almost burst with jealousy. One night he stole out to the corral. Quietly he slipped up beside the horse and jumped into the saddle.

Pegasus, as the horse was called, knew right away that his rider was not Pecos Bill. He lifted his four feet off the ground and bent his back into a perfect semicircle. Old Satan flew off like an arrow from a bow. He flew up into the air, above the moon, and came down with a thud on top of Pike's Peak. There he sat howling with pain and fright until the boys at I.X.L. spotted him.

Bill was angry. He knew, however, that Old Satan had had enough punishment. In his kind heart he could not allow the villain to suffer any more than he had to. So he twirled his lasso around his head, let it fly, and roped Old Satan back to the Texas ranch. The former desperado never tried to be bad again.

The cowhands were so impressed by the pony's bucking they decided to change his name. From that time on they dropped the name of Pegasus and called him Widow-Maker. It suited him better.

The story of Bill's other love, Slue-Foot Sue, is a long one. It began with the tale of the Perpetual Motion Ranch. Bill had bought a mountain from Paul Bunyan. It looked to him like a perfect mountain for a ranch. It was shaped like a cone, with smooth sides covered with grassy meadows. At the top it was always winter. At the bottom it was always summer. In between it was always spring and fall. The sun always shone on one side; the other was always in shade. The cattle could have any climate they wished.

Bill had to breed a special kind of steer for his ranch. These had two short legs on one side and two long legs on the other. By traveling in one direction around the mountain, they were able to stand up straight on the steep sides.

The novelty wore off, however, and at last Bill sold the Perpetual Motion Ranch to an English duke. The day that the I.X.L. boys moved out, the lord moved in. He brought with him trainload after trainload of fancy English things. He had featherbeds and fine china and oil paintings and real silver and linen tablecloths and silk rugs. The cowboys laughed themselves almost sick when they saw these dude things being brought to a cattle ranch.

Pecos Bill didn't laugh. He didn't even notice the fancy things. All he could see was the English duke's beautiful daughter. She was as pretty as the sun and moon combined. Her hair was silky and red. Her eyes were blue. She wore a sweeping taffeta dress and a little poke bonnet with feathers on it. She was the loveliest creature Pecos Bill had ever seen.

She was as lively and gay as she was pretty. Bill soon discovered that Slue-Foot Sue was a girl of talent. Before anyone could say "Jack Robinson," she changed into a cowboy suit and danced a jig to the tune of "Get Along, Little Dogies."

Bill soon lost all his interest in cowpunching. He spent his afternoons at the Perpetual Motion Ranch, teaching Sue to ride a broncho. Sue could ride as well as anyone, but she pretended to let him teach her. After several months of Bill's lessons, she put on a show. She jumped onto the back of a huge catfish in the Rio Grande River and rode all the way to the Gulf of Mexico, bareback. Bill was proud of her. He thought she had learned her tricks all from him.

Sue's mother was terribly upset by her daughter's behavior. She didn't care much for Bill. She was very proper. It was her fondest hope that Sue would stop being a tomboy and marry an earl or a member of Parliament.

As soon as she realized that her daughter was falling in love with a cowboy, she was nearly heart-broken. There was nothing she could do about it, however. Slue-Foot Sue was a headstrong girl who always had her own way.

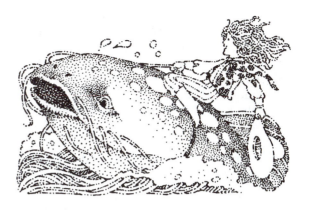

At last the duchess relented. She invited Bill to tea and began to lecture him on English manners. She taught him how to balance a teacup, how to bow from the waist, and how to eat scones and marmalade instead of beans and bacon. He learned quickly, and soon the duchess was pleased with him. She called him "Colonel."

When the boys from the I.X.L. Ranch saw what was going on they were disgusted. Here was their boss, their brave, big, cyclone-riding Pecos Bill, mooning around in love like a sick puppy. They laughed at his dude manners. They made fun of his dainty appetite. When he dressed up in his finery to call on his girl, they stood in the bunkhouse door. They simpered and raised their eyebrows and said to one another, "La-dee-da, dearie, ain't we fine today!"

But for all their kidding they were broken-hearted. None of them had anything against Sue. They admired the way she rode a horse and played a guitar and danced a jig. But the thought of losing Bill to a woman was too much. Even worse was the thought that Bill might get married and bring a woman home to live with them. That was awful.

In spite of their teasing and the duchess's lessons, Bill asked Slue-Foot Sue to marry him. She accepted before he could back out. Her father, the lord, had always liked Bill and was terribly pleased at the match.

On his wedding day Pecos Bill shone like the sun in his new clothes. His boys were dressed in their finest chaps and boots for the occasion. Half of them were going to be groomsmen. The other half were going to be bridesmen. At first Bill asked them to be bridesmaids, but they refused. They said that was going too far.

They rode to the Perpetual Motion Ranch in a fine procession, Bill at the head on Widow-Maker. The white horse pranced and danced with excitement.

At the ranch house waited the rest of the wedding party. The lord had sent back to England for a bishop to perform the ceremony. There stood His Eminence in his lace robes. On his one hand stood the duke in a cutaway coat. On his other hand stood the duchess in a stiff purple gown right from Paris.

Down the stairs came the bride. She was a vision of beauty. She wore a white satin dress cut in the latest fashion. It had a long lace train, but its chief glory was a bustle. A bustle was a wire contraption that fitted under the back of the dress. It made the skirt stand out and was considered very handsome in those days.

As Slue-Foot Sue danced down the steps even the cowhands forgot their sorrow. They jumped down from their horses and swept their sombreros from their heads. Pecos Bill lost his head. He leapt down from Widow-Maker and ran to meet her. "You are lovely," he murmured. "I promise to grant you every wish you make."

That was a mistake. A devilish gleam twinkled in Sue's eye. For months she had been begging Bill to let her ride Widow-Maker. Bill, of course, had always refused.

Now Sue saw her chance. Before she allowed the wedding to proceed, she demanded that Bill give her one ride on his white mustang.

"No, no!" cried Pecos Bill. Before he could stop her Sue dashed down the drive and placed her dainty foot into the stirrup. The duchess screamed. The bishop turned pale.

Widow-Maker gave an angry snort. This was the second time the promise to him had been broken. He lifted his four feet off the ground and arched his back. Up, up, up shot Slue-Foot Sue. She disappeared into the clouds.

"Catch her, catch her!" roared Bill at the boys. They spread themselves out into a wide circle. Then from the sky came a scream like a siren. Down, down, down fell Sue. She hit the earth with terrible force. She landed on her bustle. The wire acted as a spring. It bounced. Up again she flew.

Up and down, up and down between the earth and sky Sue bounced like a rubber ball. Every time she fell her bustle hit first. Back she bounced. This went on for a week. When at last she came back to earth to stay, she was completely changed. She no longer loved Pecos Bill.

The wedding was called off and the boys returned to the I.X.L. with their unhappy boss. For months he refused to eat. He lost interest in cowpunching. He was the unhappiest man Texas had ever seen.

At last he called his hands together and made a long speech. He told them that the days of real cowpunching were over. The prairie was being fenced off by farmers. These "nesters," as he called them, were ruining the land for the ranchers. He was going to sell his herd.

The I.X.L. had its last roundup. Bill gathered all the prime steers together and put them on the train for Kansas City. Then he divided the cows and calves among his boys. He himself mounted Widow-Maker and rode away.

The boys hated to see him go, but they knew how he felt. "Nesters" or no "nesters," the real reason for his going was his broken heart.

None of them ever saw him again. Some of them thought he had gone back to the coyotes. Others had an idea that Slue-Foot Sue had changed her mind and that she and Bill were setting up housekeeping in some private canyon. But they never knew.

Some years later an old cowhand claimed that Bill had died. The great cowpuncher had met a dude rancher at a rodeo. The dude was dressed up in an outfit he had bought from a movie cowboy. The dude's chaps were made of doeskin. His boots were painted with landscapes and had heels three inches high. The brim of his hat was broad enough to cover a small circus. Bill took a good look at him and died laughing.

The Boomer Fireman's Faster Sooner Hound

Almost every calling in a pioneer society had its hero, and here it's not only the intrepid fireman but his indefatigable dog who star.

In the days of the old railroad trains before diesel engines were ever thought of the fireman was an important man. A Boomer fireman could get him a job most anytime on most any railroad and was never long for any one road. Last year he might have worked for the Frisco, and this year he's heaving black diamonds for the Katy or the Wabash. He travelled light and travelled far and didn't let any grass grow under his feet when they got to itching for the greener pastures on the next road or the next division or maybe on the other side of the mountains. He didn't need furniture and he didn't need many clothes, and goodness knows he didn't need a family or a dog.

One day when one of these Boomer firemen pulled into the roadmaster's office looking for a job, there was that Sooner hound of his loping after him. That hound would sooner run than eat and he'd sooner eat than

"The Boomer Fireman's Faster Sooner Hound," by Jack Conroy. From A TREASURY OF AMERICAN FOLKLORE, edited by B. A. Botkin. Reprinted by permission of Jack Conroy.

fight or do something useful like catching a rabbit. Not that a rabbit would have any chance if the Sooner really wanted to nail him, but that crazy hound dog didn't like to do anything but run and he was the fastest thing on four legs.

"I might use you," said the roadmaster. "Can you get a boarding place for the dog?"

"Oh, he goes along with me," said the Boomer. "I raised him from a pup just like a mother or father and he ain't never spent a night or a day or even an hour far away from me. He'd cry like his poor heart would break and raise such a ruckus nobody couldn't sleep, eat or hear themselves think for miles about."

"Well, I don't see how that would work out," said the roadmaster. "It's against the rules of the road to allow a passenger in the cab, man or beast, or in the caboose and I aim to put you on a freight run so you can't ship him by express. Besides, he'd get the idea you wasn't nowhere about and pester folks out of their wits with his yipping and yowling. You look like a man that could keep a boiler popping off on an uphill grade, but I just don't see how we could work it if the hound won't listen to reason while you're on your runs."

"Why he ain't no trouble," said the Boomer. "He just runs alongside, and when I'm on a freight run he chases around a little in the fields to pass the time away. It's a little bit tiresome on him having to travel at such a slow gait, but that Sooner would do anything to stay close by me, he loves me that much."

"Oh, is that so? Well, don't try to tell that yarn around here," said the roadmaster.

"I'll lay my first paycheck against a fin[1] that he'll be fresh as a daisy and his tongue behind his teeth when we pull into the junction. He'll run around the station a hundred times or so to limber up."

"It's a bet," said the roadmaster.

On the first run the Sooner moved in what was a slow walk for him. He kept looking up

[1]Five dollar bill.
[2]Rule forbidding excessive overtime.

into the cab where the Boomer was shoveling in the coal.

"He looks worried," said the Boomer. "He thinks the hog law[2] is going to catch us, we're making such bad time."

The roadmaster was so sore at losing the bet that he transferred the Boomer to a local passenger run and doubled the stakes. The Sooner speeded up to a slow trot, but he had to kill a lot of time, at that, not to get too far ahead of the engine.

Then the roadmaster got mad enough to bite off a drawbar. People got to watching the Sooner trotting alongside the train and began thinking it must be a mighty slow road. Passengers might just as well walk; they'd get there just as fast. And if you shipped a yearling calf to market, it'd be a bologna bull before it reached the stockyards. Of course, the trains were keeping up their schedules the same as usual, but that's the way it looked to people who saw a no-good mangy Sooner hound beating all the trains without his tongue hanging out an inch or letting out the least little pant.

It was giving the road a black eye, all right. The roadmaster would have fired the Boomer and told him to hit the grit with his Sooner and never come back again, but he was stubborn from the word go and hated worse than anything to own up he was licked.

"I'll fix that Sooner," said the roadmaster. "I'll slap the Boomer into the cab of the Cannon Ball, and if anything on four legs can keep up with the fastest thing on wheels I'd admire to see it. That Sooner'll be left so far behind it'll take nine dollars to send him a post card."

The word got around that the Sooner was going to try to keep up with the Cannon Ball. Farmers left off plowing, hitched up, and drove to the right of way to see the sight. It was like a circus day or the county fair. The schools all dismissed the pupils, and not a factory could keep enough men to make a wheel turn.

The roadmaster got right in the cab so that the Boomer couldn't soldier on the job to let the Sooner keep up. A clear track for a hundred miles was ordered for the Cannon Ball, and all the switches were spiked down till after that streak of lightning had passed. It took three men to see the Cannon Ball on that run: one to say, "There she comes," one to say, "There she is," and another to say, "There she goes." You couldn't see a thing for steam, cinders and smoke, and the rails sang like a violin for a half hour after she'd passed into the next county.

Every valve was popping off and the wheels three feet in the air above the roadbed. The Boomer was so sure the Sooner would keep up that he didn't stint the elbow grease; he wore the hinges off the fire door and fifteen pounds of him melted and ran right down into his shoes. He had his shovel whetted to a nub.

The roadmaster stuck his head out of the cab window, and—whosh!—off went his hat and almost his head. The suction like to have jerked his arms from their sockets as he nailed a-hold of the window seat.

It was all he could do to see, and gravel pinged against his goggles like hailstones, but he let out a whoop of joy.

"THE SOONER! THE SOONER!" he yelled. "He's gone! He's gone for true! Ain't *nowhere* in sight!"

"I can't understand that," hollered the Boomer. "He ain't *never* laid down on me yet. It just ain't like him to lay down on me. Leave me take a peek."

He dropped his shovel and poked out his head. Sure enough, the Sooner was nowhere to be seen. The Boomer's wild and troubled gaze swept far and wide.

"Don't see him, do you?" the roadmaster demanded. "He's at least seventy-six miles behind."

The Boomer didn't answer. He just threw his head back into the cab and began to shovel coal. He shoveled without much spirit, shaking his head sadly. There was no need for hard work, anyhow, for the Cannon Ball was puffing into the station at the end of the run.

Before the wheels had stopped rolling, the roadmaster jumped nimbly to the ground. A mighty cheer was heard from a group of people nearby. The roadmaster beamed as he drew near them.

"Here I am!" he shouted. "Where are the cameras? Do you want to take my picture in the cab?"

"Go way back and sit down!" a man shouted as he turned briefly toward the railroad official. "You might as well scrap that Cannon Ball. The Sooner has been here a good half hour and time has been hanging heavy on his hands. Look at him!"

The Sooner was loping easily around a tree, barking at a cat which had taken refuge in the branches and was spitting angrily. The Sooner didn't look even a mite tired, and his tongue was behind his teeth.

"I'm through! Enough is enough, boys!" the roadmaster sputtered. "The rule about passengers in the cab is a dead duck from now on. Let the Sooner ride in the cab as often and as far as he wants to."

The Cannon Ball chugged out of the station with the Boomer waving his shovel in salute and the Sooner yelping proudly beside him. The people cheered until the train disappeared around a bend.

Mike Hooter and the Smart Bears in Mississippi

A Yazoo County tale of a stupid hunter and a clever bear.

There are bears and bears—smart bears and foolish bears. Folks in Mississippi used to say Mississippi bears are the smartest bears in all these United States.

That's what Mike Hooter, the great Bear-Hunter Preacher of the Magnolia State, used to say when he was alive, and he sure knew all anybody ever knew about bears. Fact is, he was the greatest bear hunter ever was in

"Mike Hooter and the Smart Bears in Mississippi" from FOLK STORIES OF THE SOUTH by M. A. Jagendorf. Copyright © 1972 by M. A. Jagendorf. Reprinted by permission of the publishers, Vanguard Press, Inc.

Mississippi. Ask any man in the state and he'll agree mighty quick.

Some folks called him Mike Shouter, for he was forever roaring louder than ten waterfalls when he got to preaching sermons or when he was arguing about the smartness of the Mississippi bears. If you tried to argue the point about bears, he'd come 'round quick with the tale of Ike Hamberlin and his funny bear hunt in the cane. It's a good tale worth telling.

One time Mike Hooter and Ike Hamberlin got to talking about bear hunting and they planned to go out together one day after the big game. But Ike was monstrous jealous of Mike, so he thought he'd steal a march on his friend and go out alone before him. He set out early in the morning, he and his dogs, without Mike.

But Mike had got wind of this, so he got up crack early himself that morning, took his two-shooter, and went off looking for Ike. But he didn't take his dogs along.

After a time he sighted Ike and just followed him right along a ways off.

Ike had gone pretty deep in the canes when his dogs started growling and barking. Their hairs began standing straight on their backs like tomcats in a fight. And there was another kind o' deep noise too, something a-tween a grunt and growl.

"Run, git 'm," Ike shouted to the dogs. But the dogs wouldn't. They just ran around Ike yapping and crying, as if they were scared to death, tails stuck a-tween the hind legs.

"Sic 'em! Sic 'em!" Ike kept on hollering to the dogs, but they minded him like birds in flight.

Mike was watching all the time, wondering what was coming next.

Ike was mad as a hornet, but he kept his temper, coaxing and coaxing the dogs to stir up the bear that was somewhere. Those dogs wasn't acting natural. Mike, watching, felt kind of sorry for Ike.

There was the man out hunting for bear! There was a bear for sure somewhere 'round the canebrake! There were bear-hunting dogs to stir the bear! And instead of doing their duty as good hunting dogs should, they just kept on whining, tail a-tween the legs. It sure was not right. You'd think a hant was on 'em.

Ike was mad fit to kill.

"I'll make you good-for-nothin' critters tend t' your business as you oughta," he shouted. Then he took his flintlock, leaned it against a tree, and ran to the creek and began picking up stones and throwing 'em at the dogs.

Well, when Ike Hamberlin got busy picking up stones and throwing them at the dogs that were howling t' heaven, there was suddenly heard an awful noise in the cane. A crackling and breaking and crashing like a hurricane, and out came the biggest and most powerful bear ever seen by Ike or Mike. He was a great giant standing on his hind legs. And what do you think that critter did! He just walked up to the tree where the gun was standing, picked it up with his front paws and looked at it, and then blowed into it with powerful breaths—blowing all the powder out!

Right then, Ike Hamberlin, his back to the bear, thought he'd thrown enough rocks at his cowardly or bewitched dogs and started out for his gun. When he turned around and saw the bear with it, he stood stock still. His hair stood up on his head, his mouth was wide open, and his eyes were ready to jump out of his head. And Mike, watching, was just as numb.

The bear looked at Ike with a bear grin, kind of plumb unconcerned, then he put the rifle back against the tree, turned around, and began easy loping off.

Ike rushed up to the gun, grabbed it, aimed straight at the bear, and snapped the lock! . . . Not a sound from the trusty old piece! But there was a sound of laughing afar off. Mike had seen what the bear had done and was laughing fit t' kill. The bear turned around and looked at the aiming Ike. His jaws opened wide in a bear laugh, one of his front paws went to his nose and—he thumbed his nose at good Ike, who was snapping and snapping. Then Ike turned the gun 'round and saw the powder was gone! His face looked like it'd been soaking in vinegar for six months. He shook his fist at the bear, shouted a few strong words, and turned 'round to go home. He'd had enough bear hunting for the day.

Mike turned home too, laughing till the tears ran out of his eyes.

He told the story for the rest of his life, just as I'm telling it to you. And it always brought a good laugh.

Now, wouldn't you say that Mississippi bears are mighty smart bears?

In Arkansas Stick to Bears; Don't Mess with Swampland Skeeters

The colorful language and exaggeration of the tall tale are augmented here by the humor of the concepts.

Back in the old days there lived a squatter in the Delta region not far from what is now the city of Helena. That squatter called himself Major Jones and he said he was slicker than a weasel, but his neighbors said he was a living bobcat that's dragged its tail through a briar patch. He wasn't a neighborly neighbor. He was forever complaining, but his biggest complaint was against Delta mosquitoes that were making life hard for man and beast.

They were as plentiful as ants at a picnic and big as wild turkeys. Some of them were nearly as big as deers in the woods.

One hot night the squatter set out to hunt bear. He was always bragging about his shooting strength. Truth to tell, he was lazy as pond water, so, instead of using his shooting piece on critters, he set bear traps deep in the swamps where he was sure bear were plentiful. After setting the contraptions he returned home. It was then nearly late candle-time, and it was mighty warm. Best time for mosquito-hunting. They were out thick as barn hay. They were zooming louder than frogs croaking. The squatter was hopping faster than a fox with a bumblebee in his tail, to steer clear of 'em. But those varmint mosquitoes smelled blood and they were hot after it. And I tell you when skeeters are on your trail, it's worse than snakes.

The man had come to his canoe, jumped in, and set down to paddle. But the crick skeeters were after him like a mighty army with banners, as it says in the Holy Book. Their zooming seemed like thunder in the springtime. The squatter fought them with paddle and gun to keep them off, but they were coming at him like a herd of buffalo. Major Jones was getting madder by the minute; he thought it was time to use powder and lead. He raised his hunting piece and began to fire. He brought down one or two of the zoomers and scared the rest, but only for a short time. Pretty soon they were at him again. By now he had come to where his cabin was. He leaped out of the canoe, ran to the door quicker than a jack rabbit, and put on the latch behind him, thanking the Lord for his safe escape.

The next morning early he went to the trap to see if it had caught a fat brown bear, for he was in need of meat and oil.

When he got there and saw what he saw, his face looked like soot on a stick.

That bear trap had caught . . . a skeeter the size of a young heifer.

Major Jones's face was fit to scare black cats at night. He held his teeth tight, threw a rope round the neck of the skeeter, tied a log to its borer, and hobbled its hind legs good. Then he got the varmint out of the trap and dragged it home slow-like. It wasn't easy, for that skeeter was bucking and rearing to beat running fire.

"Jest you keep on rearin' and buckin'! I'm gonna train you to be gentle as a lamb and I'm gonna train you to drill holes with that borer of yourn. Maybe I'll find oil."

In the end he got the varmint in the barn, but he put the boot on the wrong leg.

That critter began tearing and ripping around the barn like a bull with hornets all over. It was making such a racket with zooming, nobody could sleep. The third night the squatter couldn't stand it any longer.

"I'll teach that toad blister somethin'," he said to his wife. He took an old mule harness that was lying in the lot back of the cabin and went cautiously into the barn. With dodging and cross-running he got it on the skeeter, tied the skeeter to a post, and went to his cabin.

The mosquito didn't like the queer contraption one bit. So he began smashing it right and left and made enough noise to wake the dead. In the end Major Jones went to the door of the barn. Inside, the skeeter was banging and hitting away. Before Jones's hand touched the wooden latch, the door came down with a bang. The critter had broken the door and had got the harness off its neck.

Major Jones's eyes popped open big as goose eggs, for the next thing that happened no man in Arkansas had ever seen.

Before you could say Jehoshaphat that skeeter was up in the air flying in the moonlight. It was aiming straight for the pasture where the squatter's cow was mooing for the calf. Down went that critter in the pasture and, come gunpowder!, if it didn't get hold of that cow with its hind legs and begin lifting it off the grass.

Now, it is common knowledge in Arkansas that it needs two Bear State mosquitoes to carry off a fair-sized cow, and here just one skeeter was doing it! Major Jones was so flabbergasted that he didn't even run for his shooting piece. It wouldn't have done him any good anyway.

That skeeter with the cow in its hind legs was so high up by then, no lead could catch it.

"Wal!" Major Jones growled like a bobcat with a thorn in its leg, "wal, that'll teach me to stick to bears and not mess 'round skeeters in Arkansas swamplands."

From MR. YOWDER AND THE TRAIN ROBBERS by Glen Rounds. Copyright © 1981 by Glen Rounds. Reprinted by permission of Holiday House, Inc.

Mr. Yowder and the Train Robbers

Not strictly a folk tale, this is evidence that the tall-tale tradition lives on, combining outrageous nonsense and a bland, ingenuous style.

While the snakes were busy with their snacks, Mr. Yowder—being careful not to step on their tails—paced up and down the room, thinking.

When everyone was finished he told them all how much he appreciated their help in getting him out of the well.

The old rattlesnake said it wasn't anything, really. He'd simply happened to think of the square-knot trick and passed the word among his neighbors.

Then Mr. Yowder went on to say there most surely would be a large reward offered for the train robbers, and he'd figured out a way to capture them, if the snakes were willing to help him one more time.

After he had carefully explained his plan, the snakes talked it over among themselves, then said they'd be right pleased to help him out. It was years since anything exciting had happened in the neighborhood, and catching a band of robbers would make an even better story than their pulling Mr. Yowder out of the well. They'd probably even get their pictures in the paper.

Then a snake they called Joe spoke up and said that he'd purely like to help capture the

robbers, but he thought he'd strained his back that afternoon. Mr. Yowder said not to worry, the other snakes could handle the job without trouble, and for Joe to go along home and take it easy for a day or two.

By that time it was beginning to get dark, and they heard the robbers' horses outside. The snakes disappeared through holes in the floor, and Mr. Yowder hid himself in a little closet under the old stairs just as the robbers stomped in, dragging several heavy mail-bags, and an iron Wells Fargo chest.

They seemed to be in fine spirits, and from their loud talk, Mr. Yowder discovered that after they'd held up the train, they had robbed the passengers as well as the mail car.

The leader lit the lantern and emptied one of the sacks on the table. "We'll count the express car money later," he said. "But first let's see what we got off the passengers."

As soon as the robbers were busy sorting through the pile of loot, trying on diamond rings, selecting gold watches and watch chains and fancy stickpins, Mr. Yowder signaled the snakes by tapping twice, softly, on the floor with his boot heel.

The robbers were so busy with their loot they didn't notice the soft scaly rustlings as the rattlesnakes came up through the holes in the old floor and gathered in a circle around the table.

When they were all in their places, Mr. Yowder stepped quietly out of the closet and said, "Don't move, gents, until you've taken a good look at what's down by your feet."

They did as he said, and saw big rattlesnakes in the patches of lamplight while beady eyes and white fangs glittered in the shadows around their feet. And then, to add to their fright, the terrible buzzing of twenty-six sets of rattles suddenly filled the room.

One robber fainted but another caught him before he could fall down among the snakes.

Mr. Yowder told them that as long as they stood real still the snakes wouldn't bite them. So they stood REAL still while he gathered up all their guns and carried them out to the well and threw them in.

When he came back he pushed some broken chairs up to the table and told the robbers to make themselves comfortable. He said they could play cards if they wanted, providing they didn't make any quick moves to annoy the snakes, who buzzed and showed their fangs whenever a robber stirred.

None of them seemed to want to play cards. They just sat there glaring at one another all through the night, while Mr. Yowder dozed in his chair or thought about the fine reward he'd surely get for capturing the robber gang and returning all their loot.

When the sun came up, Mr. Yowder yawned and said, "Well, let's go to town and see the sheriff."

He told two of the unhappy robbers to each take a handle of the Wells Fargo chest while the others carried the heavy canvas bags. Then with rattlesnakes crawling in front, on either side, and behind them, they stumbled along the old road.

The robber leader complained that his feet hurt, and asked if they couldn't ride their horses. But Mr. Yowder told him that walking was fine exercise and, besides, they'd have no use for horses where they were going.

By the time they climbed the last rocky hill and came out onto the main road, the complaining robbers were footsore and out of breath, so Mr. Yowder let them stop for a little rest.

After making sure the circle of snakes was carefully guarding them, he looked towards the town and noticed a high, fast-moving cloud of dust rapidly moving his way. As it came closer he saw under it a big posse of mounted men riding at a gallop behind the sheriff, whose white hat and gold badge glittered in the sun.

Telling the rattlesnakes and the robbers to stay where they were, Mr. Yowder—with a big smile on his face—stepped out into the middle of the road and held up his hand.

But the posse neither slowed nor stopped. As they came nearer, the sound of the horses' hooves drowned out the fierce buzzing of the rattlesnakes, and at the last minute Mr. Yowder had to dive for the ditch to avoid being ridden down.

As he thundered past on his foam-flecked horse, the sheriff hollered, "Can't stop now. We're looking for the train robbers! THERE'S A BIG REWARD!"

After the posse had passed and the thick cloud of dust had finally settled, Mr. Yowder looked around and found himself alone.

To save themselves from being trampled by the horses, the rattlesnakes had scattered into the high grass, for which Mr. Yowder could not really blame them. And finding themselves unguarded, the train robbers had snatched up their loot and scuttled back into the thick brush at the bottom of the rocky slope.

There was no way Mr. Yowder could catch them again, so after a while he dusted himself off and walked on into town. When he got there the Denver train was just pulling in, so he bought himself a ticket and climbed aboard.

He often wondered, in years afterwards, if the robbers were ever caught, and if they were, who got the reward he so nearly collected.

And that is the TRUE STORY of Mr. Yowder's adventure with the train robber gang.

United States: Black Tales

 Most of the black folk tales that have been published come from three sources: animal stories and trickster tales (often combined) from African roots; stories told by slaves, some of which are humorous and some of which reflect the slaves' problems in relationships with their masters; and stories that have been reshaped from European roots. Undoubtedly the best-known are the Brer Rabbit tales collected by Joel Chandler Harris, although the dialect presents problems to many readers. Like most folk literature, the black tales have didactic elements, even in some of the amusing and vivacious animal tales. Among the best anthologies are Richard Dorson's *American Negro Folktales* and *The Book of Negro Folklore* by Langston Hughes and Arna Bontemps.

The Knee-High Man

This has both a moral: Don't want what you don't need, and a precept: Make the best of what you have.

Once upon a time there was a knee-high man. He was no taller than a person's knees. Because he was so short, he was very unhappy. He wanted to be big like everybody else.

One day he decided to ask the biggest animal he could find how he could get big. So he went to see Mr. Horse. "Mr. Horse, how can I get big like you?"

Mr. Horse said, "Well, eat a whole lot of corn. Then run around a lot. After a while you'll be as big as me."

The knee-high man did just that. He ate so much corn that his stomach hurt. Then he ran and ran and ran until his legs hurt. But he didn't get any bigger. So he decided that Mr. Horse had told him something wrong. He decided to go ask Mr. Bull.

"Mr. Bull? How can I get big like you?"

Mr. Bull said, "Eat a whole lot of grass. Then bellow and bellow as loud as you can. The first thing you know, you'll be as big as me."

So the knee-high man ate a whole field of grass. That made his stomach hurt. He bellowed and bellowed and bellowed all day and all night. That made his throat hurt. But he didn't get any bigger. So he decided that Mr. Bull was all wrong too.

Now he didn't know anyone else to ask. One night he heard Mr. Hoot Owl hooting, and he remembered that Mr. Owl knew everything. "Mr. Owl? How can I get big like Mr. Horse and Mr. Bull?"

"What do you want to be big for?" Mr. Hoot Owl asked.

"I want to be big so that when I get into a fight, I can whip everybody," the knee-high man said.

Mr. Hoot Owl hooted. "Anybody ever try to pick a fight with you?"

The knee-high man thought a minute. "Well, now that you mention it, nobody ever did try to start a fight with me."

Mr. Owl said, "Well, you don't have any reason to fight. Therefore, you don't have any reason to be bigger than you are."

"But, Mr. Owl," the knee-high man said, "I want to be big so I can see far into the distance."

Mr. Hoot Owl hooted. "If you climb a tall tree, you can see into the distance from the top."

The knee-high man was quiet for a minute. "Well, I hadn't thought of that."

Mr. Hoot Owl hooted again. "And that's what's wrong, Mr. Knee-High Man. You hadn't done any thinking at all. I'm smaller than you, and you don't see me worrying about being big. Mr. Knee-High Man, you wanted something that you didn't need."

Why the Waves Have Whitecaps

Children find the concept of this wistful "why" story appealing.

Long, long ago the wind and the water were the closest of friends. Every day Mrs. Wind would visit Mrs. Water, and they would spend the day talking. Mostly they enjoyed talking about their children. Especially Mrs. Wind. "Just look at my children," Mrs. Wind would say. "I have big children and little children. They can go anywhere in the world. They can stroke the grass softly, and they can knock down a tree. They can go fast or they can go slowly. Nobody has children like mine."

Every day Mrs. Wind would talk this way about her children. After a while Mrs. Water began to get very angry with Mrs. Wind for the way she always bragged about her children.

One day Mrs. Wind's children came to her. "Mother, we're thirsty. Can we get a cool drink of water?"

"Just run over to Mrs. Water and hurry right back," she told them.

The children went over to Mrs. Water. But when they got there, Mrs. Water grabbed them. "I'll teach Mrs. Wind to brag about her children all the time." And she drowned all of Mrs. Wind's children.

When her children did not come back, Mrs. Wind began to worry. She went down and asked Mrs. Water if she had seen them. "No," said Mrs. Water.

But Mrs. Wind knew her children had gone there, so she blew herself over the ocean, calling her children. Every time she called, little white feathers appeared on top of the water. And that's why there are whitecaps on the waves to this very day. They're Mrs. Wind's children trying to answer her. Whenever there is a storm on the water, it's Mrs. Wind and Mrs. Water fighting over the children. And the whitecaps on the waves are the children trying to tell their mother where they are.

The Wonderful Tar-Baby Story

Despite the barrier of the phonetic rendering of speech patterns, this remains a favorite tale about a trickster hero.

"Didn't the fox *never* catch the rabbit, Uncle Remus?" asked the little boy the next evening.

"He come mighty nigh it, honey, sho's you born—Brer Fox did. One day atter Brer Rabbit fool 'im wid dat calamus root, Brer Fox went ter wuk en got 'im some tar, en mix it wid some turkentime, en fix up a contrapshun wat he call a Tar-Baby, en he tuck dish yer Tar-Baby en he sot 'er in de big road, en den he lay off in de bushes fer to see what de news wuz gwineter be. En he didn't hatter wait long, nudder, kaze bimeby here come Brer Rabbit pacin' down de road—lippity-clippity, clippity-lippity—dez ez sassy ez a jay-bird. Brer Fox, he lay low. Brer Rabbit come prancin' 'long twel he spy de Tar-Baby, en den he fotch up on his behime legs like he wus 'stonished. De Tar-Baby, she sot dar, she did, en Brer Fox, he lay low.

" 'Mawnin'!' sez Brer Rabbit, sezee—'nice wedder dis mawnin',' sezee.

"Tar-Baby ain't sayin' nothin', en Brer Fox, he lay low.

" 'How duz yo' sym'tums seem ter segashuate?' sez Brer Rabbit, sezee.

"Brer Fox, he wink his eye slow, en lay low, en de Tar-Baby, she ain't sayin' nothin'.

" 'How you come on, den? Is you deaf?' sez Brer Rabbit, sezee. 'Kaze if you is, I kin holler louder,' sezee.

"Tar-Baby stay still, en Brer Fox, he lay low.

" 'Youer stuck up, dat's w'at you is,' says Brer Rabbit, sezee, 'en I'm gwineter kyore you, dat's w'at I'm a gwineter do,' sezee.

"Brer Fox, he sorter chuckle in his stummick, he did, but Tar-Baby ain't sayin' nothin'.

" 'I'm gwineter larn you howter talk ter 'specttubble fokes ef hit's de las' ack,' sez Brer Rabbit, sezee. 'Ef you don't take off dat hat en tell me howdy, I'm gwineter bus' you wide open,' sezee.

"Tar-Baby stay still, en Brer Fox, he lay low.

"Brer Rabbit keep on axin' 'im, en de Tar-Baby, she keep on sayin' nothin', twel present'y Brer Rabbit draw back wid his fis', he did, en blip he tuck 'er side er de head. Right dar's what he broke his merlasses jug. His fis' stuck, en he can't pull loose. De tar hilt 'im. But Tar-Baby, she stay still, en Brer Fox, he lay low.

" 'Ef you don't lemme loose, I'll knock you agin,' sez Brer Rabbit, sezee, en wid dat he

fotch 'er a wipe wid de udder han', en dat stuck. Tar-Baby, she ain't sayin' nothin', en Brer Fox, he lay low.

" 'Tu'n me loose, fo' I kick de natal stuffin' outen you,' sez Brer Rabbit, sezee, but de Tar-Baby, she ain't sayin' nothin'. She des hilt on, en den Brer Rabbit lose de use er his feet in de same way. Brer Fox, he lay low. Den Brer Rabbit squall out dat ef de Tar-Baby don't tu'n 'im loose he butt 'er cranksided. En den he butted, en his head got stuck. Den Brer Fox, he sa'ntered fort', lookin' des ez innercent ez one er yo' mammy's mockin'-birds.

" 'Howdy, Brer Rabbit,' sez Brer Fox, sezee. 'You look sorter stuck up dis mawnin',' sezee, en den he rolled on de groun', en laughed en laughed twel he couldn't laugh no mo'. 'I speck you'll take dinner wid me dis time, Brer Rabbit. I done laid in some calamus root, en I ain't gwineter take no skuse,' sez Brer Fox, sezee."

Here Uncle Remus paused, and drew a two-pound yam out of the ashes.

"Did the fox eat the rabbit?" asked the little boy to whom the story had been told.

"Dat's all de fur de tale goes," replied the old man. "He mout, en den again he moutent. Some say Jedge B'ar come long en loosed 'im—some say he didn't. I hear Miss Sally callin'. You better run 'long."

Master James' Nightmare
Charles Chesnutt

Based on slave stories collected by Charles Chesnutt, a black educator of the late nineteenth century, this speaks vividly of the relationships between the races.

Way back, there was this man, James McLean, and when his daddy died, he left the plantation to Master James, and he was a *hard* man. Was no use living if you had to live 'round Master James. His slaves had to work from daylight to dark, and they didn't get much to eat. And what they did get was least.

They couldn't sing, or dance, or play the banjo. He wouldn't let them marry, wouldn't even let them go courting. Said he wasn't in the business of raising slaves, he was in the cotton business.

Any time he saw signs of courting, he'd sell one of the two. Anybody complained, they'd get whipped. Well, they didn't complain, but they sure enough didn't like it. They hoped for a bit there that things would get better, because Master James was courting himself, and love can change a man. He was going over every day and every night to see Miss Libbie, that was Master Marlboro's oldest gal. But it appears that when Miss Libbie heard about the goings-on at Master James' plantation, she said she just never could trust a man like that. Why, he might be so used to abusing his slaves that he'd get to abusing a wife after she'd been around a while.

The slaves were mighty sorry when the match was bust up, 'cause Master James was worse than ever. All the time he'd spent courting, he put in now on abusing his slaves, and all his bad feeling about Miss Libbie he worked off on them.

Now while he'd been courting and too busy to notice, two of the slaves had got to setting a heap of store by one another. One was named Solomon, and the other—well, I forget, but it's not important in this tale. Anyway, when Miss Libbie throwed Master James over, he found out about Solomon and the gal monstrous quick. He gave Solomon a whipping and sent the gal off to another plantation, and then he told the others that if he ever caught them at any more such foolishness, he'd skin them alive and tan their hides before their very eyes.

Sometimes Master James would go down to his other plantation for a week or more, and his overseer would look after the work. He was a poor white man, Nick Johnson. The slaves called him Master Johnson to his face, but behind his back they called him Old Nick. And that name suited him to a T. They didn't like the way Master James used them,

"Master James' Nightmare" by Charles W. Chesnutt. Adapted by Zena Sutherland. Boston: Houghton Mifflin, 1899.

but he was master and had a right to do as he pleased. All the slaves despised Old Nick as much as they hated him, 'cause he didn't own anybody. Was no better than a slave himself, and in those days any respectable person would rather be a slave than a poor white man.

Now, after Solomon's gal had been sent away, he kept feeling more and more bad. Finally allowed that he was going to see if there couldn't be something done to get her back and to make Master James treat the slaves better. So he took a peck of corn out of the barn and went over to see Aunt Peggy, the free black conjure woman down by Wilmington Road.

Aunt Peggy, she listened to his tale and asked some questions, and then told him she'd work her roots and see what they said about it, and tomorrow night he should come back and fetch another peck of corn, and she'd have something for to tell him. So Solomon went back the next night, and sure enough, Aunt Peggy told him what to do. Gave him some stuff that looked like pounded-up roots and herbs.

"This here stuff," says she, "is a monstrous powerful kind of goopher. You take this home, give it to the cook if you can trust her, and tell her to put it in your master's soup the first cloudy day he has okra soup for dinner. Mind you follow the directions."

"Ain't going to poison him, is it?" asked Solomon, getting kind of scared; for he was a good man and didn't want to do nobody no real harm.

"Oh, no," says old Aunt Peggy, "it's going to do him good, but he'll have a monstrous bad dream first. A month from now you come down here and let me know how the goopher's working. For I ain't done much of this kind of conjuring of late, and I have to kind of keep track of it and see that it don't accomplish no more than I allow for it to do. And I have to be kind of careful about conjuring white folks; so you be sure and let me know, whatever you do, just what's going on around the plantation."

So Solomon said all right, and took the goo-

pher mixture up to the big house and gave it to the cook, and told her what to do. Happened the next day was a cloudy day, so the cook made okra soup for Master James' dinner, and put Solomon's powder in it. She made it real good, so Master James ate a whole lot of it and appeared to enjoy it.

Next morning, he told the overseer he was going away on business to his other plantation, and expected he'd be gone a month or so.

"But," he says, "I want you to run this here plantation for all it's worth. The slaves are getting monstrous trifling and lazy and careless. Can't depend on them. I want that to stop, and I want the expenses cut down while I'm away, and a heap more work done. Fact is, I want this plantation to make a record that'll show what kind of overseer you are."

Old Nick only said, "Yessir," but he grinned and showed his big yellow teeth, and he snapped the rawhide he carried around. Made cold chills run up and down the backbone of the slaves that heard Master James talking. And that night there was moaning and groaning down in the slave quarters, 'cause they all knew what was coming.

Well, next morning the trouble began, just as soon as Master James went away. Master Johnson, he started right off to see what he'd have to show Master James when he got back. He made the tasks bigger and the rations smaller, and when the slaves had worked the whole day, he'd find something for them to do to keep them busy until it was almost time for them to sleep.

About three or four days after Master James went away, young Master Duncan McSwayne rode up to the big house one day with a slave sitting behind him in the buggy, tied to the seat. Asked if Master James was home. Master Johnson, he said no.

"Well," says Master Duncan, "I fetched this slave over to Master McLean to pay a bet we made on a card game. I bet him a slave, and here's one I reckon will fill the bill. He was picked up t'other day for a stray slave; couldn't give an account of himself, and so he was sold at auction and I bought him. He's kind of brash, but I know your power, Master

Johnson, and I reckon if anybody can make him toe the mark, you're the man."

Master Johnson grinned one of them grins that showed all his snaggled teeth and make the slaves say he looks like the devil, and he says to Master Duncan, "I reckon you can trust me to tame any black man that was born. The slave don't live what I can't take down in about four days."

Well, Old Nick had his hands full longer than that with that new slave. The rest of them, they were sorry for him but they allowed he kept Master Johnson so busy that they got along better than they would have if the new slave had never come. The first thing that happened, Master Johnson said to this new man, "What's your name, Sambo?"

"My name ain't Sambo," answered the new slave.

"Did I ask what your name wasn't?" says Master Johnson. "You want to be particular how you talk to me. Now. What's your name and where did you come from?"

"I don't know my name and I don't know where I come from. My head is all kind of mixed up."

"Yes, I reckon I'll have to give you something to clear your head. At the same time, I'll learn you some manners, and after this maybe you'll say 'sir' when you speak to me."

Well, Master Johnson hauled off with his rawhide and hit the new slave once. New slave looked at Master Johnson as if he didn't know what to make of this here kind of learning. But when the overseer raised his whip to hit him again, the new slave just hauled off and made for Master Johnson. If some of the other slaves hadn't stopped him, it appears as if he might have made it warm for Old Nick there for a while. But the overseer made the other slaves help tie the new man up, gave him forty lashes with a dozen or so thrown in for good measure. Old Nick never was stingy with *that* kind of rations. New slave went on at a terrible rate, just like a wild man, but he had to take his medicine, 'cause he was tied up and couldn't help himself.

Master Johnson locked the new slave in the barn and gave him nothing to eat for a day or so, 'til he got him kind of quieted down, and

then he turned him loose and put him to work. New man said he wasn't used to working and wouldn't do it, so he got another forty lashes for impudence. Master Johnson let him fast a day or so more, then put him to work. The slave went to work, but he didn't appear to know how to handle a hoe. Took about half the overseer's time looking after him, and that poor slave got more lashing and cursing than any four others on the plantation. But he couldn't seem to get it through his mind that he was a slave and had to work and mind the white folks in spite of the fact that Old Nick gave him a lesson every day. Finally Master Johnson allowed he could do nothing with him; if it was *his* slave, he'd break his spirit or break his neck, one way or the other.

Of course, he'd only been sent over on trial, so Master Johnson could send him back before he killed him. So he did, he tied him up and sent him back to Master Duncan.

Now Master Duncan McSwayne was one of these easy-going people who didn't like to have trouble with slaves or anyone else, and he knew that if Master Old Nick couldn't get along with the slave nobody could, so he took the slave into town that day and sold him to a trader who was getting up a gang of slaves to ship off to New Orleans.

Next day after the new man had been sent away, Solomon was working in the cotton field and when he looked up at the end of the row, who should he see but Aunt Peggy, who beckoned to him—the overseer was down the other side of the field—and she said, "Why ain't you come and reported to me like I told you?"

"Aunt Peggy, there ain't nothing to report. Master James went away the day after we gave him the goopher mixture, we haven't seen hide nor hair of him since, and of course we don't know what effect it had."

"I don't care nothing about your Master James now, what I want to know is what's been going on among the slaves. Been getting along any better on the plantation?"

"No, Aunt Peggy, worse. Master Johnson is stricter than ever, the poor slaves hardly have time to draw a breath, and they allow they might as well be dead as alive."

"Uh huh," says Aunt Peggy. "I told you that was a monstrous powerful goopher and its work don't appear all at once."

"Long as we had the new slave, he kept Master Johnson busy most of the time, but now he's gone away, I suppose the rest of us'll catch it worse than ever."

"What's going on with the new slave?" asked Aunt Peggy quickly, batting her eyes and straightening up.

"Old Nick has sent him back to Master Duncan, and I hear he's sold him to a slave trader who's going to ship him off with a gang tomorrow."

Aunt Peggy appeared to get really stirred up when she heard this, and shook her stick at him.

"Why didn't you come and tell me about this new slave being sold away? Didn't you promise, if I gave you that goopher, that you' come and report to me everything that was going on at the plantation? By not doing it, I'm afraid you spoiled my conjuring. You come to my house tonight, and you do what I tell you or I'll put a spell on you that will make all your hair fall out, and your eyes drop out, and your ears grow up so you can't hear. When you're fooling around with a conjure woman like me, you mind your *P*s and *Q*s or there'll be trouble."

So of course Solomon went to Aunt Peggy's that night and she gave him a roasted sweet potato.

"You take this," says she, "I goophered it especially for the new slave—you better not eat it yourself or you'll wish you hadn't—you slip off to town and give it to him. He must eat it before morning if he doesn't want to be sold away to New Orleans."

"But suppose the patrollers catch me, Aunt Peggy, what am I going to do?" Solomon asked.

"The patrollers won't touch you, but if you don't find that slave, *I'm* going to get you, and you'll find I'm worse than the patrollers. I'll sprinkle some of this mixture on you so the patrollers can't see you, and you can rub your feet with the grease from this gourd so you can run fast. Rub some of it on your eyes

so you can see in the dark, and then find that slave and give him the potato or you'll have more trouble than you ever had before in your life or ever will have."

So Solomon took the potato, went up the road as fast as he could go, and before long reached the town. He went right by the patrollers and they didn't appear to notice him, and by and by he found out where the strange slave was kept. He walked right past the guard and found him. Solomon could see the slave, asleep, and he put the sweet potato right in front of the man's nose. Well, he reached up in his sleep and took it and ate it. Never woke up. Then Solomon went back and told Aunt Peggy, and he got back to his cabin along about two in the morning.

Next day was Sunday. Solomon was disturbed in his mind about his gal, and was wondering what Aunt Peggy had to do with the new slave. He sauntered into the woods to be by himself, when who should he see standing under a tree but a white man. Didn't know him at first, until the white man spoke up.

"Is that you, Solomon?" he says. Then Solomon recognized the voice.

"For the Lord's sake, Master James! Is that you?"

"Yes, Solomon," says his master, "this is me, or what's left of me."

No wonder Solomon hadn't known Master James at first, for he was dressed like a poor white man, and he was barefoot and looked kind of pale and peaked, as if he'd come through a hard spell of sickness.

"You look kind of poorly, Master James. Have you been sick, sir?"

"No, Solomon," says Master James, shaking his head slowly, "I haven't been sick, but I had a monstrous bad dream—in fact, a regular nightmare. But tell me how things have been going on at the plantation since I left."

So Solomon up and told him about the crops and the animals. And then when he started to tell about the new slave, Master James pricked up his ears, and every now and then he'd say, "Uh huh! Uh huh!" and nod his head. By and by, when he'd asked Solomon some questions, he says, "Now,

Solomon, I don't want you to say a word to nobody about meeting me here, but I want you to slip up to the house and fetch me some shoes and some clothes. I forgot to tell you that a man robbed me back yonder on the road and swapped clothes with me without asking whether or no—but you needn't say anything about that, either. Go fetch some clothes here, don't let anyone see you, keep your mouth shut, and I'll give you a dollar."

Solomon was so astonished he like to fell over in his tracks when Master James promised to give him a dollar. Certainly was a change come over Master James when he offered one of his slaves that much money. Solomon began to suspect that Aunt Peggy's conjuration had been working monstrous strong.

Solomon fetched Master James some clothes and shoes, and that same evening Master James appeared at the house and let on like he just got home from the other plantation. Master Johnson was all ready to talk to him, but Master James sent him word he wasn't feeling very well that night, and he'd see him tomorrow.

So next morning after breakfast, Master James sent for the overseer and asked him to give an account of his stewardship. Old Nick told Master James how much work had been done, and got the books and showed him how much money had been saved. Then Master James asked him how the slaves had been behaving, and Master Johnson said they had been behaving well, most of them, and them that didn't behave well at first changed their conduct after he got ahold of them a time or two.

"All," says he, "except the new slave Mr. Duncan brought over here and left on trial while you were gone."

"Oh, yes," answered Master James, "tell me all about that new slave. I heard a little about that queer new man last night and it was just ridiculous. Tell me all about him."

So, seeing Master James so good-natured about it, Master Johnson up and told him how he tied up the new hand the first day and gave him forty lashes because he wouldn't tell his name.

"Ha, ha, ha!" says Master James, laughing fit to kill, "But that's too funny for anything. Tell me more about the new slave."

So Master Johnson went on and told him how he had to starve the new slave before he could make him take hold of a hoe.

"That was the queerest notion for a slave," says Master James, "putting on airs just like he was a white man. And I reckon you didn't do nothing to him?"

"Oh, no sir," says the overseer, grinning like a Cheshire cat, "I didn't do nothing but take the hide off him."

Master James laughed and laughed, until it appeared like he was just going to bust. *Tell me some more about that new slave, oh, tell me some more. That new slave interests me, he does, and that's a fact."

Master Johnson didn't quite understand why Master James should make such a great admiration about the new slave, but of course he wanted to please the gentleman who hired him, so he explained all about how many times he'd had to cowhide the new slave, and how he made him do tasks twice as big as some of the other hands, and how he would chain him up in the barn at night and feed him on cornbread and water.

"Oh, but you're a monstrous good overseer; you're the best overseer in this country, Mr. Johnson," says Master James when the overseer got through with his tale, "and there ain't never been no slave breaker like you 'round here before. And you deserve great credit for sending that slave away before you spoilt him for the market. In fact, you're such a good overseer, and you got this plantation in such fine shape that I reckon I don't need you any more. You've got the slaves so well trained, I expect I can run them myself from this time on. But I wish you'd held on to that new slave until I got home, for I'd like to have seen him, I certainly should."

The overseer was so astonished he didn't hardly know what to say, but finally he asked Master James if he wouldn't give him a recommendation for another place.

"No sir," says Master James, "somehow or other I don't like your looks since I came back this time, and I'd much rather you wouldn't stay around here. Fact is, I'm afraid that if I met you alone in the woods sometime, I might want to harm you. But laying that aside, I've been over these here books of yours that you kept while I was away and for a year or so back, and there's some figures that just aren't clear to me. I haven't got time to talk about them now, but I expect before I settle with you for this last month, you'd better come up here tomorrow after I look over the books and accounts some more, and then we'll straighten our business all up."

Master James allowed afterward that he was just taking a shot in the dark when he said that about the books, but, howsoever, Master Nick Johnson left that neighborhood betwixt the next two suns, and nobody around there ever saw hide nor hair of him since. And all the slaves thanked the Lord and allowed it was good riddance to bad rubbish.

But all the things I done told you ain't nothing compared to the change that came over Master James from that time on. Aunt Peggy's goopher had made a new man of him entirely. Next day after he came back, he told the hands they need work only from sun to sun, and he cut their tasks down so nobody needed to stand over with a rawhide or a hickory. And he said if the slaves wanted to have a dance in the big barn any Saturday night, they could. And by and by, when Solomon saw how good Master James was, he asked him if he could please send down to the other plantation for his gal. Master James said certainly, and gave Solomon a pass and a note to the overseer on the other plantation, and sent him with a horse and buggy to fetch his gal back.

And Master James' own gal, Miss Libbie, heard about the new goings-on, and she changed her mind about Master James. And before long they had a fine wedding, and everyone on the plantation had a big feast, and there was fiddling and dancing and fun and frolic from sundown 'til morning.

North American Indian and Eskimo Tales

 The eminent folklorist Stith Thompson claimed that the North American Indians have the most extensive body of tales representative of any primitive people, and these tales have been diligently collected, as have Eskimo folk tales, by ethnologists and anthropologists as well as folklorists. Many of the Indian tales are long, complex, and associated with rituals; many are mythic hero tales, trickster tales, or "why" stories about nature or animals. While some of the Eskimo stories are humorous, many are devout or epic. Both groups of tales reflect the closeness to and respect for nature as well as the cultural patterns of the people from which they come.

Small Star and the Mud Pony
(Pawnee)

Few folk tales speak more clearly of the cultural patterns of a people than this touching tale of a small boy who became a great chief.

On the banks of a wide river that runs through the prairies of western Nebraska there was at one time a village called Fish-Hawk. None of the people in it was wealthy or famous; but their earth lodges were comfortable, corn grew in their fields, buffalo supplied meat, skin hides, cooking utensils, and household articles, and most of the families owned at least one horse.

During the long winters, stories were told around the fires; the women made moccasins, pouches, and shirts fringed, beaded, or decorated with porcupine quills dyed red, blue, yellow, and green. Often the people played with plum stones and baskets or darts. However, when spring and fall came, the women worked planting corn or harvesting it, drying meat and other foods. The men and boys enjoyed ring-and-stick contests or readied their weapons for the summer buffalo hunts. And there were many ceremonials to the great Tirawa, with dancing and feasting.

In one small lodge, however, where Small Star lived with his father and mother, there was little corn and little meat. Worst of all, there were no horses! This made Small Star very unhappy, for he loved horses more than anything. When the other boys took their horses to the river to water them, he sat apart and watched with envy.

One day Small Star decided to build a corral in a hollow across the river. He picked willow boughs and found some rocks, and he made a small gate. Then, when it was finished, he dug a great quantity of mud from the riverbank and brought it to the corral. He filled a buffalo bladder with water from the river and poured it over the mud, making it very sticky. Then, carefully, he began to mold two small ponies from the soft mud, taking great pains with the tails, the hooves and the ears. One little horse he left dun-colored; the other he made sorrel, by mixing in some red clay. He also smoothed some white clay across its face to make a blaze. It was dark when he had finished, and he was too tired to be hungry. When he arrived home, he immediately fell on his sleeping pad and went to sleep without telling his parents anything about his day's work.

Early the next morning he crept from the lodge, crossed the river, and unlatched the corral gate. There stood his two little ponies, their tails out and their heads lifted, almost as though they were breathing after a run. Small Star patted them with delight; then he gathered fresh grass and cottonwood shoots to feed them and spent the rest of the day talking to them as though they could understand his joy in their company. At night he closed the corral carefully, went home, and again told no one of his new ponies.

Every day after that he visited them, fed them, and brought them water to drink. But one morning he saw that the dun pony had dried out and lay crumbled to dust. The bald-faced sorrel still stood. Small Star cried and determined to take special care of the one that remained. After that he spent even more time in the corral, sleeping there at times.

One day a runner came into the village. "The buffalo are returning," he said. "They have been seen in great herds on the plains to the west. It is time to go out for the summer hunting." At once the tipis were brought out and packed, and food and equipment assembled for the hunt. Excitement was everywhere, with children running here and there, dogs barking, and horses trampling and neighing. Small Star's parents looked for him, as they packed their meager belongings, but they could not find him, for he was across the river in the corral with his mud pony. At last they left with the rest of the villagers, thinking he must be with the other children.

When Small Star returned to Fish-Hawk village, he saw only scattered possessions and empty earth lodges—no animals, no people, and no food remained. He felt very lonely and hungry, and he wondered what he should do. He had no idea where the villagers were going, and he knew they moved fast when they went on the summer buffalo hunt. He searched till he found some parched corn and jerky that had been left behind; then he lay down in his empty lodge, feeling lost and frightened. He slept fitfully and in his dreams seemed to be chasing his mud pony around.

"Small Star and the Mud Pony" retold by Dorothy de Wit in THE TALKING STONE: *An Anthology of Native American Tales and Legends* edited by Dorothy de Wit. Copyright © 1979 by Dorothy de Wit. Reprinted by permission of Greenwillow Books (A Division of William Morrow & Company).

Then, in his dream, a star rose in the western sky, brilliant and low-hanging, and he heard the voice of Great Tirawa speaking to him: "Small Star, I have seen your grief, and I know how you love your mud pony. I will help you. Go out to him tomorrow, and take care of him." The dream faded, and Small Star awoke; but only the night wind sighed around the lodge. A large star shone in the west, as in his dream, and Small Star slept again, with tears on his cheeks.

The following day he hunted through the village for more forgotten food, then ran to give his mud pony fresh grass. As he watered him, he kept thinking of the words of Tirawa and the dream, and he wondered what they meant. That night he slept beside his horse, and in his dreams the mud pony spoke to him: "Small Star, little master, do not be afraid, for I am of the earth, and you have fashioned me of the mud from the riverbank. Now Mother Earth has taken pity on you. If you will do as I say, all will go well for you, and someday you will become a great chief."

When morning came, Small Star looked for his mud pony. It was gone! But standing outside the corral and neighing softly was a sorrel horse with a white blaze across its face. The pony was pawing the ground and shaking its mane! Small Star leaped to his feet and ran to it. He felt its shining coat, nuzzled its velvety cheek. "Are you real, beautiful one? Are you indeed my mud pony come alive?

Ah, Tirawa, how great, how kind you are! Hear my thanks. I will remember your words and do as you wish!"

Small Star found a rope, put it around his pony's neck, and led him to the river to drink. The pony spoke to him: "I am truly your mud pony! Mother Earth has listened to your heart; you and I will travel to your people now. They are far away, but I know where to go. Lead me to the top of the bank; then mount, and do not direct me, for I know my way."

Small Star could hardly believe his ears, but he did as the pony told him. They traveled on and on, and when night fell, they came to the first site the villagers had used, and again the pony spoke: "Go forage for your food in the camp, for I shall find my own food." So Small Star picked up whatever he could find left behind. He slept the night with his head against the pony's warm flank. The next day, and the next, they did the same thing, each time moving farther out on the great plains, till at noon of the fourth day they found a campsite with coals still warm in the fire pit. Then Small Star knew they would soon catch up with the villagers. And indeed, at sunset they saw their tipis ahead.

Then the mud pony said, "Leave me here and go find your tipi. Waken your mother, for she has grieved for you. When the people break camp tomorrow, stay behind, and I shall be waiting for you to ride."

So Small Star went gladly and, after hunting for the smallest tipi, went in and threw some dried grass on the coals, which spurted up. He wakened his mother gently. "See, I am here! I have come back to you." At first his mother could not believe that he was real, but at last she hugged him and cried over him. Then she prepared food for him, and his parents rejoiced to find him alive and well. In the morning all the relatives and friends came to the tipi to share his parents' happiness. The next day Small Star rose early and went back to where the pony waited. Small Star mounted, and they followed the villagers at a distance.

For several days they continued on in this way. Then the pony spoke again: "My son, it is time for the people to see that you have a horse. The chief will send for it, and he will offer you four horses for me. Take them. I shall return to you!"

The boy rode his pony proudly into the camp, and everybody pressed around him. "What a fine little horse! How lively, how sturdy! He is just the color of Mother Earth!" They were happy and pleased for Small Star, for they knew how much he loved horses and how poor his parents were. Word reached the village chief, who came himself to see the pony. He examined it carefully and invited the boy to eat with him in his tipi that night —a great honor for anyone!

Small Star thought to himself, "It is just as the pony told me!" He went and ate in the great chief's tipi, and when the chief told him how pleased he was with the sorrel horse and offered four of his best mounts in exchange, Small Star accepted the offer.

The chief took the pony and set him out to graze, but the pony would not eat. Nevertheless, the chief was satisfied with his new horse and waited eagerly for the coming hunt to try him out. That night the boy was lonely and dreamed of his pony. In his dream the pony said, "Do not mourn, for I shall be back. But take a buffalo hide, and tan it carefully, my son. Be sure that you place it around me each night, to protect me." And so each night Small Star carefully covered the pony with the buffalo hide he had tanned.

Scouts appeared in the camp—a great herd of buffalo was approaching, and many hunters would be needed. At the head, and first into the herd, rode the chief on the sorrel pony. He was proud of the horse's speed and quick response to his leading and his skill in the hunt. When the chief was the first to bring down a buffalo, he was elated! It spurred him to try again and again, and he rode on and on—indeed, he would have taken many more, but suddenly the horse stumbled. Its hind foot was injured and hung disjointedly! The pony was ruined, and the chief was very angry! He returned to the encampment and demanded that Small Star return his four horses. Then, in disgust, he pushed the mud pony toward the boy. Small

Star appeared to be very upset, but secretly he was delighted! The chief exclaimed loudly, for all to hear, "Hah! A fine horse! Even though he could run well, he looks just like a mud pony!" From that time on, Small Star's name was changed, and he was called Mud-Pony-Boy.

He took his horse to the outskirts of the camp, and there he worked over him, using herbs and compresses. And before long the foot had healed. The chief wanted to have the pony back; but Mud-Pony-Boy would not agree, and no more was said.

The villagers of Fish-Hawk had moved on to try for more buffalo when suddenly an enemy force appeared on the horizon. The women and children ran to their tipis as the men rode out to war. The pony spoke to Mud-Pony-Boy: "My son, heed my words. Go and coat yourself with mud, the same color as mine. When the warriors shoot at you, their arrows will not pierce the earth covering. Therefore, do not be afraid. Be daring!" Mud-Pony-Boy covered himself with mud and rode out at full speed into the midst of the enemy braves. He unseated an enemy warrior, who turned and fled in fear!

Mud-Pony-Boy rode back to camp in triumph with the other men. They hailed him and said, "Mud-Pony-Boy has become a brave!"

Shortly thereafter the people of Fish-Hawk struck their summer camp and returned to their earth-lodge village on the bank of the great river, far to the east. They had plenty of food and other provisions for winter, and their corn stood waiting to be harvested.

But soon after they had returned, another enemy tribe invaded the village. There were many warriors, and among them was one whose spirit powers were those of Turtle. He was a very great warrior, and Mud-Pony-Boy watched him carefully and soon discovered that the warrior could not be hurt except in one place. Only under his arm could he be fatally wounded. Mud-Pony-Boy wheeled his pony around, and just as the warrior raised his arm to pull his bowstring, Mud-Pony-Boy thrust his sharp, long lance into Turtle Man's armpit and killed him. After that Mud-Pony-Boy took many horses and did many brave deeds. The enemy was routed, and peace returned to Fish-Hawk village. Each night, however, Mud-Pony-Boy was very careful to place the buffalo hide over his beloved pony.

Years passed, and the men met in council. "Mud-Pony-Boy has many times shown himself to be a brave and skillful leader. Our chief is old now. Let him choose Mud-Pony-Boy as his successor, to become chief when the time comes."

The months went by, and one day Mud-Pony-Boy found among his herd of horses a new colt, sorrel-colored with a white blaze on its face. It was the image of his mud pony! That night in his dream his beloved pony spoke to him again: "My son, you have done well. You have proved yourself a true brave and a wise man. You will become a great chief, and people will love you and trust your judgment. My task is finished. I must go back to Mother Earth. Raise the colt, and love it as you have loved me."

That night a storm arose, and when Mud-Pony-Boy took the buffalo hide to cover his horse, he could not find it. He grieved and could not sleep, and early the following morning he crossed the river and went to the corral he had built in his childhood. The sorrel pony lay on the ground, a mound of river mud, with only a dab of white clay where the blaze had once been.

He again heard the voice of his pony: "Do not weep. We were together over many years and have done all that was needed. I have gone back to Mother Earth. You will become a great chief, and your colt will become a great horse, as dear to you as I have been."

Mud-Pony-Boy returned to his village, and he did, indeed, become a great chief, and his colt, a great horse.

Gray Moss on Green Trees
(Choctaw)

A "why" story that explains the origin of the tree-moss of the South.

The Indians tell a tale down in Louisiana. Maybe it's the Choctaw Indians, maybe it's the Chitimacha Indians, who battled with the French for many years when they were not busy making fine baskets and bright copper things. It might even be another tribe that tells this tale, or it may be all the tribes.

There was an Indian mother working in the field along the river. Near her, her two children played with bows and arrows, and with blue and purple flowers.

Suddenly, cold Wind came racing in the air through the trees. Then Rain came on, sharp rain, running in all directions. Water in the river rose, high and cold.

The mother took the children by the hand and ran toward her hut of palmetto leaves. But she could not run as fast as the flying Wind, or as fast as the racing Water. Water was all around her, coming higher and higher, and held her feet down.

The mother climbed up a thick oak tree, holding the younger child in her arms. The older one followed her slowly. Soon they were high up, where Water could not reach them.

Wind kept on howling and Water kept on rising. Then Rain stopped, but cold Wind still ran wildly in the trees and around the three high up in the branches. The mother and the children were very cold and the children began to cry.

"Mother, I am cold, my feet are cold."

"Mother, my hands are cold and I can't hold on to the branches."

Moon came out over the black, flying clouds. Its white light was sharp and bright.

"Mother, I am cold," both the children cried.

The mother, too, was very cold.

"Man in the Sky," the mother prayed, "my children are very cold and will die. I am very cold and I can't keep them warm. I don't want my children to die from the cold. Take pity on them, they are very young. Take pity on them, they are very young. Take pity on me, so I can be with them. Be kind to us and don't let us die."

So the Indian mother prayed to Moon, while black and gray clouds flew all around the sky.

Moon spoke to Clouds, and to Wind. They listened. Moon shone strong on the mother and the children, and they fell asleep. Then Moon wove and wove and wove. . . .

Morning came. The sky was clear and warm. The Indian mother and her children awoke and were warm. They looked on the branches and saw what they had never seen before. All over the trees, in the branches and around them, was a thick green-gray blanket that had covered them. It was not made of cloth, but of grass, and Moon had woven it. The Indian mother looked and looked, and so did the children.

"Mother," cried the older boy, "it's a blanket all around us. It kept us warm all night. Moon heard you pray and tore up the clouds to make a blanket for us. Moon hung it on the tree to keep us warm."

"Yes, son, that's what Moon did for us. The sky is clear and the clouds are now on the tree."

They came down and went home.

The "Cloud-Cloth," folks call Spanish moss. It has been on the trees in Louisiana ever since and has spread to trees in other states.

Little Burnt-Face
(Micmac)

Both the Native American's tradition of closeness to nature and the personification of natural phenomena are seen in this story of the burnt desert.

Once upon a time, in a large Indian village on the border of a lake, there lived an old man who was a widower. He had three daughters. The eldest was jealous, cruel, and ugly; the second was vain; but the youngest of all was very gentle and lovely.

Now, when the father was out hunting in the forest, the eldest daughter used to beat the youngest girl, and burn her face with hot coals; yes, and even scar her pretty body. So the people called her "Little Burnt-Face."

When the father came home from hunting he would ask why she was so scarred, and the eldest would answer quickly: "She is a good-for-nothing! She was forbidden to go near the fire, and she disobeyed and fell in." Then the father would scold Little Burnt-Face and she would creep away crying to bed.

By the lake, at the end of the village, there was a beautiful wigwam. And in that wigwam lived a Great Chief and his sister. The Great Chief was invisible; no one had ever seen him but his sister. He brought her many deer and supplied her with good things to eat from the forest and lake, and with the finest blankets and garments. And when visitors came all they ever saw of the Chief were his moccasins; for when he took them off they became visible, and his sister hung them up.

Now, one Spring, his sister made known that her brother, the Great Chief, would marry any girl who could see him.

Then all the girls from the village—except Little Burnt-Face and her sisters—and all the girls for miles around hastened to the wigwam, and walked along the shore of the lake with his sister.

And his sister asked the girls, "Do you see my brother?"

And some of them said, "No"; but most of them answered, "Yes."

Then his sister asked, "Of what is his shoulder-strap made?"

And the girls said, "Of a strip of rawhide."

"And with what does he draw his sled?" asked his sister.

And they replied, "With a green withe."

Then she knew that they had not seen him at all, and said quietly, "Let us go to the wigwam."

So to the wigwam they went, and when they entered, his sister told them not to take the seat next the door, for that was where her brother sat.

Then they helped his sister to cook the supper, for they were very curious to see the Great Chief eat. When all was ready, the food disappeared, and the brother took off his moccasins, and his sister hung them up. But they never saw the Chief, though many of them stayed all night.

One day Little Burnt-Face's two sisters put on their finest blankets and brightest strings of beads, and plaited their hair beautifully, and slipped embroidered moccasins on their feet. Then they started out to see the Great Chief.

As soon as they were gone, Little Burnt-Face made herself a dress of white birch-bark, and a cap and leggings of the same. She threw off her ragged garments, and dressed herself in her birch-bark clothes. She put her father's moccasins on her bare feet; and the moccasins were so big that they came up to her knees. Then she, too, started out to visit the beautiful wigwam at the end of the village.

Poor Little Burnt-Face! She was a sorry sight! For her hair was singed off, and her little face was as full of burns and scars as a sieve is full of holes; and she shuffled along in her birch-bark clothes and big moccasins. And as she passed through the village the boys and girls hissed, yelled, and hooted.

And when she reached the lake, her sisters saw her coming, and they tried to shame her, and told her to go home. But the Great Chief's sister received her kindly, and bade her stay, for she saw how sweet and gentle Little Burnt-Face really was.

Then as evening was coming on, the Great Chief's sister took all three girls walking beside the lake, and the sky grew dark, and they knew the Great Chief had come.

And his sister asked the two elder girls,

"Do you see my brother?"

And they said, "Yes."

"Of what is his shoulder-strap made?" asked his sister.

"Of a strip of rawhide," they replied.

"And with what does he draw his sled?" asked she.

And they said, "With a green withe."

Then his sister turned to Little Burnt-Face and asked, "Do you see him?"

"I do! I do!" said Little Burnt-Face with awe. "And he is wonderful!"

"And of what is his sled-string made?" asked his sister gently.

"It is a beautiful Rainbow!" cried Little Burnt-Face.

"But, my sister," said the other, "of what is his bow-string made?"

"His bow-string," replied Little Burnt-Face, "is the Milky Way!"

Then the Great Chief's sister smiled with delight, and taking Little Burnt-Face by the hand, she said, "You have surely seen him."

She led the little girl to the wigwam, and bathed her with dew until the burns and scars all disappeared from her body and face. Her skin became soft and lovely again. Her hair grew long and dark like the Blackbird's wing. Her eyes were like stars. Then his sister brought from her treasures a wedding-garment, and she dressed Little Burnt-Face in it. And she was most beautiful to behold.

After all this was done, his sister led the little girl to the seat next the door, saying, "This is the Bride's seat," and made her sit down.

And then the Great Chief, no longer invisible, entered, terrible and beautiful. And when he saw Little Burnt-Face, he smiled and said gently, "So we have found each other!"

And she answered, "Yes."

Then Little Burnt-Face was married to the Great Chief, and the wedding-feast lasted for days, and to it came all the people of the village. As for the two bad sisters, they went back to their wigwam in disgrace, weeping with shame.

How the Little Owl's Name Was Changed
(Eskimo)

In a story about the owl that symbolizes the annual burgeoning of life that is the springtime, Little Owl steals light for his people.

Every spring in Alaska a little owl would come north with the other birds. It was a tiny owl and flew noiselessly over the tundra on its soft, downy wings. At first the Eskimos called him Anipausigak, which meant "the little owl." Later, after the Eskimos knew more about the bird, they called him Kerayule, which means in their language "the owl that makes no noise when he flies."

In the very early days, before the white men came to Alaska, the Eskimos had no matches and it was very difficult for them to have a fire. Also there was very little wood in the Eskimo country.

One spring there was one family living all by themselves that had a bit of fire, but there was no place where they could get any if this went out. In the middle of the igloo was a pit, or hole, in the floor. Here a tiny little fire was kept burning at all times. Always someone watched it and tended it. The smoke went curling out of the window in the top of the igloo.

In this igloo were a little boy and a little girl with their mother and father. All times of the day and night someone had to stay in the house and watch the tiny fire. One day when the little girl was all alone—her folks were out hunting seals—some bad people came to the igloo.

"Oh, so you are all alone, little girl," one of them said. "I suppose you are watching the fire so that it does not go out?"

"Yes," said the little girl. "It would be very bad if we lost our fire. We would be very cold and would have nothing to cook by. I must watch it carefully so that when my parents come home there will be a warm house here to greet them."

The bad man laughed. "You will not have to watch your fire any more, little girl, for we have no fire in our igloo and we are going to take yours with us."

How frightened the little girl was and how badly she felt to think she was going to lose the fire! She thought quickly. "Can't I make you some fire on another stick, Mr. Man?" she asked. "Then you can take it with you and I will still have some left for my mother and father and my little brother when they come home from hunting seals."

"I haven't time to wait for you to make new fire," the bad man said, "and, besides, I do not care if you are cold and hungry." With that he grabbed the fire and went away with it, leaving the poor little girl crying and all her fire gone.

When the mother and father and little brother came home they found the igloo cold, and the little girl told them what had happened. Hastily the father took his bow and arrow and set out to the igloo of the bad men to get his fire. When he got there, however, he found that they had two men who guarded the fire day and night. They were big men and had big spears, and bows and arrows too. So the poor man could not get his fire away from them. He begged them to let him have just a little of it to carry back to his wife and children, but they only laughed at him.

So for several days the good Eskimos had a terrible time. It was very cold and they could not make a fire with anything. At last, one night, the father Eskimo thought of a plan. He called for the little owl, Kerayule, who makes no noise when he flies.

"Please, little owl, will you help us?" the Eskimo man asked him. "You see we have no fire, and we are cold. Please will you get our fire back for us from the bad men who took it away?"

"How can I do that?" asked the little owl. "I would like to help you, but they have spears and bows and arrows. Besides, they are much stronger than I am. Just how do you think I could get the fire?"

"You make no noise when you fly," the Eskimo man replied. "They will not hear you coming in the night. Also you can see in the darkness, and you can go straight to their igloo. The window in the top of it will be open, and you can look in and see how you can get the fire for us."

"I never thought of that," said the little owl. "I think, maybe, I can get the fire for you. I *can* see in the darkness and I make no noise at all when I fly."

So the little owl set off through the dark night to the igloo where the bad men lived.

Carefully the owl flew over the igloo and he did not make a sound. He looked into the window in the top where the smoke came out. He saw the fire—just one small stick burning in the fire pit. Also he saw one of the bad men sitting by it. He seemed to be asleep. The little owl hovered lower and alighted without a sound on the edge of the window. Silently, like a great soft feather, the little owl fluttered down into the igloo.

Right by the fire pit, the little owl landed on the floor and the man did not see him. Maybe he was asleep, but the owl was not sure. Hopping softly across to the stick of fire, the little owl took the unburned end in his mouth and, with a great flutter, flew straight up through the open window in the top of the igloo. As he did, the man awakened. He grabbed his bow and arrow to shoot the little owl, but was too late. Out into the night sailed the little owl, through the black darkness. He flew straight to the igloo of the good Eskimos.

The children were watching for the little owl, and soon they saw the fire come flying through the black sky.

"Look!" shouted the little girl. "See the *sparkling fire* coming!"

And to this day the Eskimos at Hooper Bay call the little owl "sparkling fire owl," or Kennreirk in their language. Sometimes in the springtime, when the sparkling fire owl comes to Hooper Bay and hovers around the people, they will listen closely to see if they can hear him make any noise. Sometimes—very rarely—he makes a little snapping with his beak, or a flutter with his wings. If the people can hear him make any noise they are very glad, for that is the best of good omens. They say the little sparkling fire owl is sending them good luck. If they go hunting they are sure to get a seal, or an eider duck, or a fat fish.

The Eskimo people love the little sparkling fire owl because he brings them good luck and, too, when they see him they know the springtime has come to stay.

The West Indies

 When the black people of West Africa were conscripted and brought as workers to the Caribbean Islands, they brought with them a folk literature that became part of the heritage of the Caribs and Arawaks who were living on the islands. Thus the folk heroes of West Africa have become the folk heroes of the West Indies; tales of Anansi the Spider have been preserved, and new tales were added; and all of the stories are delightfully colored by the teasing humor and engaging cadence of West Indian speech patterns. A good example of the merging of African roots and West Indian culture is "Uncle Bouqui and Godfather Malice."

Tiger in the Forest, Anansi in the Web
(Jamaica)

The scamp Anansi tricks his friend Tiger and tries to put the blame on others in a story that explains why Tiger lives in the bush and the spider Anansi stays safely in his high web.

For a time Anansi and Tiger were friends. Anansi liked to be with Tiger, who was strong, while Tiger was amused by the tricks that clever Anansi played on all the animals, using his wits to avoid doing any work, yet always managing to persuade Monkey or Hen, Dog or Puss to share their meals with him. When everyone was hard at work, Anansi watched from the shade of a tree, yet his bag of food was always full, and his wife and children had enough to eat.

In the hot season Anansi and Tiger went every day to the river for a swim. One day Tiger took with him a delicious stew that his wife had made, with large dumplings, thick gravy, and tender pieces of meat of the gib-nut and accouri. This was Tiger's favourite dish and it was also a dish that Anansi could not resist. As the two friends strolled down to the river, Anansi kept his eyes on the large tin of stew. The smell made his mouth water so that he could hardly talk; and he began to think of ways of getting the stew for himself.

"Let's try a new place for our swim, Tiger," said Anansi; "up by the rocks where there is a deep hole, so deep that everybody calls it the Blue Hole."

"Very well," replied Tiger. "But do you think that you can swim there, Anansi? That is deep water."

"You swim so well that I won't worry," said Anansi. "If I get into trouble I know you will help me, Tiger, for we are good friends. We share everything."

"But I can't share my lunch with you today," replied Tiger. "This stew of accouri and gibnut is my favourite. My wife got the meat in the market and cooked it specially for me. You can smell how good it is, can't you, Anansi?"

"Yes, I can. Yes, I can. Yes, yes," said Anansi with that strange, soft lisp of his. He pronounced "s" like "sh," and spoke in a high-pitched voice. The smell of the stew was so tempting that he could not take his eyes off the tin.

At the Blue Hole, Anansi said, "Brother Tiger, you are a big man, you go in and try out the water first. I will come in after you."

Tiger replied, "Very well, Brother Anansi. I will put the tin of stew where no one can trouble it, on this stump of an old cotton-tree. There I can keep my eyes on it. Then I will dive in. But you must come in when I call you. I am not going to leave you with that stew for long."

"You go first, and try out the depth of the water," said Anansi, "and I will follow."

Tiger dived in. Anansi shouted, "Try out the deep deep parts, Tiger, where it looks blue-blue, yes, yes."

Tiger loved swimming and diving. He took a deep breath and dived, trying to reach the sandy bottom of the river, but the water was deeper than he expected. He came up to the surface, looked round quickly to make sure that his stew was safe, took a deep breath, and dived again. While Tiger was under the water Anansi emptied the tin of stew on to a large green plantain leaf, put the tin back on the stump, and sat in the shade where Tiger could not see him. There he quickly ate the stew, while Tiger dived and swam. At last Tiger called out:

"Come in, Anansi, come in." He could see the tin on the stump where he had left it. "Ah," he thought, "soon I will have my lunch." Then he shouted, "You are a lazy fellow, Anansi. I am coming to throw you into the water!"

"Tiger in the Forest, Anansi in the Web" from WEST IN-DIAN FOLK-TALES retold by Philip Sherlock. Copyright © 1966 by Philip Sherlock. Reprinted by permission of Oxford University Press.

Anansi was very frightened. What would Tiger do when he found that the tin was empty? He called out:

"No, Tiger, no; I am frightened. I don't want to be thrown into the water. I am going back home."

Anansi hurried to Big Monkey Town, which was only half a mile away. He said to Big Monkey, "Brother Monkey, I was down at the Blue Hole with Tiger and I heard them sing a song (he said "shing a shong") and this is how it went:

"This lunch-time I ate Tiger's stew,
This lunch-time I ate Tiger's stew,
This lunch-time I ate Tiger's stew
But Tiger didn't know."

Big Monkey shouted at Anansi, "What nonsense. Run away. Leave our town. We don't want to hear your silly song."

Anansi hurried on to Little Monkey Town near by, where all the little monkeys lived, the small brown monkey, the marmoset, and the capuchin monkey. He said to them:

"Brer Monkey, I heard a sweet, sweet song down by the river, and this is what it said:

"This lunch-time I ate Tiger's stew,
This lunch-time I ate Tiger's stew,
This lunch-time I ate Tiger's stew
But Tiger didn't know."

"That's a good dance-tune," cried Capuchin Monkey, who loved nothing better than dancing, "a very good dance-tune indeed. Let's learn it."

All the little monkeys began to learn the song. They said to Anansi, "Sing it slowly, so we can get the tune right." Anansi sang the song over and over again until the little monkeys had learnt it. Then they said:

"Anansi, we will have a big dance tonight, and you must come back to hear us sing this song."

That evening, when Anansi heard the little monkeys singing the song and dancing, he hurried off to Tiger, who was in a rage, questioning animal after animal about his lunch.

"Come with me, Tiger," said Anansi, "and you will find out what you want to know. Do you know what they are singing in Little Monkey Town? Listen."

The sound of singing and music came faintly on the night wind. Anansi began to pick up the words of the song as if they were new to him. "I can't get it all, Tiger, but it's something about eating Tiger's stew and Tiger didn't know."

Tiger and Anansi raced off to Little Monkey Town, Tiger bounding along with great strides so that Anansi could hardly keep up with him. Near the town, Anansi said:

"Hide in the bush, Tiger, for we must make sure first. Listen."

The little monkeys were playing and singing and dancing to the tune Anansi had taught them:

"This lunch-time I ate Tiger's stew
But Tiger didn't know."

"Hear that, Tiger?" asked Anansi. "Didn't I tell you? Do you hear? Listen again. There it is—

"This lunch-time I ate Tiger's stew
But Tiger didn't know."

"But I know now," roared Tiger, breaking through the bush into Little Monkey Town, with Anansi behind him. He leaped through an open window into the middle of the dance-hall and cried:

"So you ate my stew, did you?"

"What are you talking about?" asked one of the little monkeys. "We learnt that song from Anansi."

Tiger was too enraged to listen. "I am going to teach you all a lesson," he shouted, his teeth flashing in the light.

Capuchin Monkey, the fastest runner of all, made for Big Monkey Town at full speed to ask for help, while Tiger and Anansi began to attack the little monkeys, who were scattering in fright. Soon a troop of big monkeys arrived. At the sight of them Tiger took to the bush. He lives there to this day. Anansi, frightened almost out of his wits, climbed up into the top of the house. He lives there safe in his web, hiding from the monkeys.

Uncle Bouqui and Godfather Malice
(Haiti)

Comparing this with the German "Cat and Mouse Keep House" shows how much— and how delightfully—each culture shapes its variant of a widely dispersed tale.

One time Bouqui and Malice were farming together in the Red Mountains. Every day they went out to their fields with their hoes and machetes, and they worked until the middle of the afternoon when the sun was broiling hot.

Uncle Guinéda, who lived in the village, had chopped down a tree full of honey, and he gave Bouqui a big gourd full of it because Bouqui was godfather to Guinéda's youngest child. Bouqui was very proud and jealous of that gourd of honey, and he hung it up in the rafters of his house, intending to save it for a big holiday, such as Christmas or Dessaline's Day.

Now Ti Malice liked honey just about better than anything. His mouth watered at the sight of that gourd hanging there in the rafters. Four or five times he politely suggested that they sit down and have a glass of honey, but Bouqui shook his head and made an ugly face.

"I'm saving that honey for an occasion," Bouqui said.

"When two good friends get together that *is* an occasion," Malice said.

"Do you think I'm a rich man?" Bouqui said. "I can't eat honey every day."

One hot morning they were out in the field cultivating corn. The earth was dry, and the sun was hot, and Malice became thirstier and thirstier. He began to think of that cool gourd of honey hanging in the rafters of Bouqui's house. Two or three times he stood very still and closed his eyes, just so he could imagine the honey.

Finally he dropped his hoe on the ground.

"Wah!" he said. "Someone is calling me."

"I didn't hear anything but a lamb baaing," Bouqui said, "and it didn't sound like 'Malice.'"

"Wah! There it is again," Malice said. "I'll have to go to see who it is."

He picked up his hat and marched over the hill, and when he was out of Bouqui's sight he turned and headed for Bouqui's house. He went inside and climbed up into the rafters and took down the honey gourd. He poured some honey in a glass, mixed it with water, and drank it. Then he mixed some more and drank it. He kept mixing and drinking until he was so full he couldn't swallow another drop. Then he hung the gourd back in the rafters and went back to the field.

Bouqui was working away with his hoe, and he was mighty hot. He pushed out his lips and made an ugly face.

"You certainly were gone long enough! What happened to you?"

"Wah, Bouqui! Everyone wants me to be godfather to their children. Nobody leaves me alone. I had to go to a baptism."

"Woy, that's different!" Bouqui said, breaking into a smile. "Is it a boy or girl?"

"A girl, and a very nice one indeed," Malice said, licking the honey off his chin.

"Wonderful!" Bouqui said, beaming and resting his arms on the hoe handle. "I like babies. What's her name?"

"Her name?" Malice said. "Oh, yes. Well, I named her *Début.*" (Début means "beginning" in Creole.)

"*Début!*" Bouqui gasped. "Woy, what an elegant name! How did you ever think of it?"

"It just came to me," Ti Malice said modestly. And he picked up his hoe and went back to work.

The next day they were weeding the garden with their machetes, and the sun got hotter and hotter, and Malice got thirstier and thirstier. He tried to keep his mind on his work, but all he could think of was that honey gourd hanging in Uncle Bouqui's rafters. Suddenly he stood up straight and cocked his ear and said:

"Wah, Bouqui, did someone call me?"

"I don't think so," Bouqui answered. "I

heard a calf bawling on the next hill, but I don't think he mentioned your name."

"There!" Malice said. "There it is again! I'll have to go see who wants me." He stuck his machete into his belt and marched over the hill.

Bouqui shook his head and mumbled to himself. He rapped his right ear with his knuckles, and then he took hold of his left ear and tweaked it.

"My ears are asleep," he said. "I didn't hear a thing!"

As soon as he was out of sight, Malice turned and ran for Bouqui's house. He climbed up into the rafters and brought down the honey gourd and fixed himself a big drink. He fixed another, and another. He drank and drank and drank until he felt ready to burst. Then he hung the gourd in the rafters again and went down to the field where Bouqui was chopping away in the hot sun.

"Well, what happened?" Bouqui asked impatiently. "You were gone a tremendously long time!"

"Uncle Bouqui, my friends just won't leave me alone. They're always bothering me. It's always Malice-this and Malice-that. They needed me to come and baptise another baby."

"That's a different matter," Bouqui said with a grin. "Boy or girl?"

"A boy this time," Malice said, licking honey off his fingers.

"What's his name?" Bouqui said. "I certainly like babies."

"His name? Oh, well, I called this one *Dèmi,*" Malice said. (Dèmi means "halfway" in Creole.)

"*Dèmi!* What a fine name! You certainly have a wonderful imagination. *Dèmi!* It's mighty sweet."

"It certainly is," Malice answered. "There's probably just one more as sweet as that one." And they picked up their machetes and went back to work.

The next day they were out cultivating again. The sun got hotter and hotter. Malice started to sing to keep his mind off the honey, but it was no use. He threw his hoe down on the ground.

"Wah!" he said. "What an imposition!"

"What's the matter?"

"Didn't you hear?" Malice said.

"No, only some dogs barking."

"Someone's calling me again. What do you think they want?"

"People certainly are having babies!" Bouqui said. "Don't be gone long!" He twisted and jerked his ears. "They're half dead," he muttered. "I didn't hear anything but the dogs."

Malice headed over the hill, and then he scrambled for Uncle Bouqui's house. He took down the honey gourd and drank and drank. He drank until the gourd was empty. He stuck his tongue inside and licked it clean as far as he could reach. When he was through, the gourd was dry as an old cornstalk. He hung it up in the rafters and went back to where Uncle Bouqui was sweating and making dark faces in the hot sun.

"Well," Bouqui said, "what was it?"

"Another baby," Ti Malice said. "A girl. I think it's the last one."

"Wonderful!" Bouqui said. "What did you name it?"

"Name it? Oh. Well, I named this one *Sêche,*" Malice said. (Sêche means "dry" in Creole.)

"*Sêche!* What an unusual name!" Bouqui said. "Woy, you are just about the best baby-namer in Haiti."

When they went home after work that night Bouqui said, "You know, I think we should celebrate all those babies tonight. Why should I save the honey until Christmas? If we don't drink it the flies will."

He reached up in the rafters and took down the gourd. He stood there a long time looking into it. Then he carried it outside and looked again. He closed his eyes for a minute, then opened them. He turned the gourd upside-down, but nothing happened. He licked the edges, but they didn't even taste like honey. He smelled the gourd, but there wasn't even an odor left.

"Oh-oh!" he said at last. "It's gone!"

He turned around, but somehow Malice seemed to have disappeared too. Uncle Bouqui sat down to think. He thought, thought,

thought. He mumbled and argued with himself. He scratched his head first, and then he scratched his chin. He just couldn't make any sense out of it. Suddenly he began to tingle. For a moment he sat very still, tingling from head to toe. Then he leaped into the air and howled.

"Wah! The first one was named *Début!* And the second was named *Dèmi!* And the third was named *Sêche!* Beginning, Halfway, and Dry! Wah!" he wailed. "And all the time I was out there working! Beginning, Halfway, and Dry—*of my honey!*"

That night Uncle Bouqui waited until Ti Malice was asleep on his mat, and then he crawled into the house quietly on his hands and knees. "Beginning, Halfway, Dry," he kept saying over and over to himself. When he got to Malice's mat, Bouqui opened his mouth wide and—*pimme!* He clamped his teeth down hard on Malice's big toe. Malice let out a wild yowl and sprang into the air, but Bouqui hung on.

"Ouch!" Malice yelled. "Stop it, you're killing me!"

Bouqui let go with his teeth, and Malice's yelling died down to a moan.

"Uncle Bouqui!" he whimpered. "Uncle Bouqui! What do you call that, anyway?"

"I call that one *Début!*" Bouqui shouted. And he lunged forward, *pamme!* He caught Malice's other big toe right between his teeth.

Malice leaped and jerked and howled, but Bouqui held on. Malice hopped and crawled and jumped, but Uncle Bouqui wouldn't let go.

"Wah!" Malice screamed. "I'm hurt for life!"

Bouqui opened his mouth and made a ferocious face at Malice.

"Uncle Bouqui, Uncle Bouqui!" Malice groaned. "What do you call this business, anyway?"

"I call this one *Dèmi!*" Bouqui shouted. And he lunged forward to get another one of Malice's toes with his teeth.

But Ti Malice came to life. He sprang across the room as though he were running on hot coals. In no time at all he was outside, racing off into the hills.

"Wah!" he howled as he went through the gate. "Wah! There's one thing you'll never do, Bouqui! You'll never be godfather to *Sêche!* Not unless you catch me first!" And he disappeared into the darkness without another word.

Bouqui stood listening until the sound of Malice's feet slapping against the trail had died away. He got to thinking.

"*Sêche,*" he said. "It's a mighty unusual name, at that."

Who Rules the Roost?
(Dominican Republic)

Two men, arguing about whether men or women dominate their households, go to a judge who fails to practice what he preaches, in a realistic folk tale.

In a small town of the Dominican Republic there once lived two men who were good friends. Both were merchants. One, José, sold yucca and corn. The other, Francisco, sold yams. These two often talked together, about this, that, and the other.

One day José, the older of the two, said to his friend Francisco, "From the oldest days, from the days when the world began, from the first days Christopher Columbus saw our blessed Island of Hispaniola, and right on down to our day, woman has been the ruler of the house. She is not only queen of the house, but also king."

"Now, José," said Francisco, "I say you are wrong. True, I am not married, as you are, but I say man rules the house, and woman follows. The man heads his home, and his wife obeys him."

"Who Rules the Roost?" from THE KING OF THE MOUNTAINS: A TREASURY OF LATIN AMERICAN FOLK STORIES by M. A. Jagendorf and R. S. Boggs. Copyright © 1960 by M. A. Jagendorf and R. S. Boggs. Reprinted by permission of the publisher, Vanguard Press, Inc.

"My good friend Francisco! You are a thousand times wrong. Am I not married? I should know! Look around you, right here in our town, and on all the farms around the town. Look as far as you like, for that matter. You will always find that I am right, no matter where you look in this world. Woman rules the roost!"

"You are wrong, José, dead wrong. I tell you man is the rooster of the house, and woman just cackles."

And so they argued, but neither convinced the other he was right. It got so that every evening after their work was done they would look for each other and begin to argue the same question over and over.

One evening the argument became livelier than usual, and José said he would *prove* he was right.

"I'll tell you what we'll do, Francisco. You say that man rules the house, I say that woman rules the roost. We can argue this question until Judgment Day, and we'll get nowhere. Let us put the matter to a test. Whichever of us wins, the other must admit that he was wrong. Agreed?"

"I agree," said Francisco.

"Here's what we'll do. I'll take a dozen horses, and you take a dozen cows. We'll go from house to house and talk to people and find out whether the man of each house or his wife is master. If it's the woman, we'll give her a cow. If it's the man, we'll give him a horse. What do you say to that?"

"That's a good plan. I agree!" said Francisco.

Bright and early the next morning, José was at the meeting place with his dozen horses, and Francisco with his cows. They set out with the animals behind them. "Remember," said Francisco, "the first one who gives away all his animals loses."

When they came near the first house, they could hear before they ever reached the door who was master there. The woman was screaming at her husband for not having locked up the pigs the night before. The husband stood with head bowed and did not open his mouth.

"Give her a cow!" said José victoriously. And Francisco sadly did so without saying a word.

They went to the next house. While they were still out in the road they heard a woman shout, "Go and get the bread! Be quick about it, and don't argue with me!"

Francisco looked at José in despair and meekly gave that woman a cow.

And so they went from house to house, and quickly found out who was the head—the woman, of course! Poor Francisco had to give away cow after cow. Finally he had just one cow left, but José still had his twelve horses. Francisco's face had grown longer and longer, and José's smile had grown broader and broader.

At last they came to the house where the judge of the town lived. The judge was home, but his wife was out.

"Good morning, *buenos días, Señor Juez,*" they both said respectfully. "We are trying to find out who is the master of the house in the different homes of our community, the man or his wife."

"I say the woman always rules the house," said José with great certainty.

"And I said the man is master in his home," said Francisco sadly.

To his surprise, the judge said, "You are right, Francisco. Here in my house *I* am the head and master. Whatever I say goes. *My* wife does as I say."

"I'm glad to hear that, Señor Judge," said José.

"Yes, it's been that way from the day we were married," the judge said proudly.

"You're a lucky man, Señor Judge," said José. "The Lord has blessed you."

"It's really quite simple," continued the judge, encouraged by this respect and admiration. "All you have to do is to begin the very first hour you are married to show your wife that you are the head of the house."

"You are the first man we have found to say that," said Francisco, his spirits rising.

"In this house, my word is law," continued the judge.

"I'm delighted to hear that, indeed," said

José, "even though I lose a horse by it. You see, Señor Judge, we decided to give a horse to each man who is master of his house. You are the first to get one. I have a dozen horses here. Please come out and choose the one you like best."

"Do you really mean this?" asked the judge.

"Yes, I do," said José. "Come and take the one that pleases you most."

"This is my lucky day," said the judge joyfully. "You say there are twelve to choose from?"

"That's right!" said José. "See, here they are."

The judge came out and looked them over carefully. "Just look at that black one," he said. "He looks as if he could run a good race. But that brown one! He looks strong and healthy. And that spotted one! He is certainly a handsome horse. Well, well, well! It's really hard to choose. I tell you, José, just wait until my wife comes back. She's a fine judge of horses. Besides, I'd like to please her. It's funny, but she's right most of the time."

"Father in heaven!" cried José. "He's no better than the rest. Give him your last cow, Francisco. Unfortunately for us men, I win. You can easily see who rules the house here."

Francisco did not say one word. Sadly he handed over his last cow to the judge. Then he turned to José and said just two words: "You win!"

Now everyone knows who rules the roost in the Dominican Republic, just as in all the rest of the world: the woman!

The Three Fairies
(Puerto Rico)

Cultural diffusion may account for the similarity between this humorous story and the Italian tale, "And Seven!" although here the device of the forgotten name is absent.

There once was a widow who had a very pretty, kind and good daughter. Being sickly, the woman worried much about dying and leaving her daughter alone in the world. Every night she prayed that the girl would find a good husband who would care for and protect her.

The girl was indeed virtuous and industrious. But not flirtatious at all. Nor yet coy. Nor coquettish. So the young men of the town, being more jocund than judicious, avoided her.

There was in that place a wealthy *señor* who was looking for a girl to marry. A hard-working girl. A comely girl. A good girl. Well, you say, so there's the story. The *señor* married the widow's daughter, and that was that. Nooooo . . . there were complications, and that was *not* that. At least not right away.

True, the *señor* did come to visit the widow. True, he admired the daughter greatly—and said so. True, the widow was most encouraging, pointing out her daughter's attractions: her quietness, her diligence, her tenderness, her flawless complexion, her honey-hued hair, the beauty mark on her chin, and on and on.

"But," inquired the *señor,* who had been pondering, "can she spin? Can she sew? Can she embroider? For in my business there is much of cotton and silk."

"*Por supuesto,* naturally she can sew, spin and embroider to a fare-thee-well. There is nothing that girl cannot do. She spins a thread as fine as a spider's. Her stitches are smaller than the footprints of a fly. She can embroider a bird so you reach to stroke its feathers."

"In that case," announced the *señor,* "it is settled. If she is *that* good a spinner, a sewer, an embroiderer, I will marry her. I shall arrange at once for the wedding." And away he went.

The widow was overjoyed. You would have thought *she* was the one getting married. And what did the daughter have to say? (Though it was by now rather late for her to say anything, even about her own marriage.)

"The Three Fairies" from GREEDY MARIANI AND OTHER FOLKTALES OF THE ANTILLES edited by Dorothy Sharp Carter. Copyright © 1974 by Dorothy Sharp Carter. A Margaret K. McElderry Book (New York: Atheneum, 1974). Reprinted with the permission of Atheneum Publishers and Curtis Brown Ltd.

"Mama, I heard what you said. How could you be so foolish? I know little of sewing, nothing of embroidery, and less of spinning. What will that *señor* think of me when we are married?"

"You are the foolish one, daughter. Surely there is a solution to the problem. All you have to do is think of it. I did this for your good, you well know."

When she went to bed that night the poor girl wept a thousand or more tears thinking of the terrible lies her mother had told. Not to speak of what might befall *her* for having deceived the *señor*. She had just resolved to go to him early the next day and confess the truth about herself when she heard a slight noise. Sitting up, she saw three strangers. On top of everything else! The poor girl wept harder than ever.

However, the strangers assured her they were fairies and had come to help her. Their only condition, they said, would be an invitation to her wedding. The girl was only too happy to consent, saying they could come as her dearest relatives. They disappeared, and the girl fell asleep.

Days passed and preparations were made for the wedding. The girl informed her *novio* that she had invited a few of her cousins whom she loved very much to come to the wedding feast.

The day of the celebration arrived, passed and died away. That night all the wedding guests sat down at the table for dinner. Three chairs remained vacant.

"For whom are these reserved?" asked the groom.

At that moment came a knock at the door. It opened and three old horrors entered whom the girl introduced as her cousins.

Dinner was served, and the whole world was content and ate tremendously. When it was over the husband arose and went to speak to the girl's kin, who were now his cousins as well as his wife's.

He asked the first, "Hear me, cousin. Will you tell me why you are so humped and one-eyed?" (A blunt man, the bridegroom.)

"*Ay*, my son! From all the embroidery I did in my life."

The husband whispered to his wife, "From now on I forbid you to embroider. I can pay to have this done and I do not wish you to be so deformed as your unlucky cousin."

Then he asked the second, "And why is it your two arms are so unequal?"

"Because I have spent my whole life spinning."

The *señor* took his wife's hand. "Nevermore will you spin, my love."

And finally he questioned the third of the cousins. "What is the matter with your eyes, that they burst from your head as grapes from their skins?"

"Ah, so would yours if your life had been spent sewing and reviewing tiny stitches."

"This, my dear, shall not happen to you," said the *señor*, turning to his wife. "You are to do no more sewing. None at all."

The very next day the husband gathered up all his wife's sewing equipment and hurled it out the door, since he cared more for his wife's beauty than all the work she could do. The two lived most happily and the girl never had to grieve herself to explain away the lies her poor mother had told.

Latin America

 Like Canada and the United States, Latin America has had an influx of peoples from many other parts of the world, and the folk heritage they brought with them has mingled with that of the Indian peoples who were already living there. There are tales based on European lore, the widely traveled Anansi stories, tales of national heroes like "Pancho Villa and the Devil," and Indian stories like "The First Flute." While there are many collections of tales from individual countries, there are few comprehensive anthologies. One of the best general anthologies is *The King of the Mountains: A Treasury of Latin American Folk Stories* by Moritz Jagendorf and R. S. Boggs.

The King of the Mountains
(Bolivia)

Symbol of Bolivia, the condor is given that honor because he is the bird that flew closest to the sun when the birds of the earth decided to use that test to choose their king.

The sun, all gold in the sky, and the condor, the great and strong bird of the high mountains, are worshiped and loved in many parts of Andean South America. Beautiful temples were built to the sun, and large monuments were erected with the condor as the symbol of the land.

There are many stories about both the bird and the sun everywhere in that vast land, and here is one from Bolivia.

This happened long, long ago, soon after the earth first came into being. The birds in Bolivia wanted to have a king. But who would be king? There was so much chattering and arguing among them about this that the leaves got tired of listening. There was screaming and whistling and singing without end. Every bird wanted to be king.

Finally one wise old bird said, "Let Pachacámac, the great king of the earth, decide; or, better yet, let the one who comes nearest the sun, where Pachacámac has his golden palace, be king of the birds."

This made sense to all the birds, and they agreed, for no one was wiser than Pachacámac. The birds screamed their desire to Pachacámac, and the king of the earth spoke: "Yes, let the bird who flies highest and who comes nearest the sun and my palace be king. The bird who does this will have to be very brave."

Then, at a given signal, all the birds rose into the sky. They were like a great cloud of many colors, and there were so many of them that the sun could not be seen.

Up and up they went, streaking and circling about. Soon some dropped down. Others rose higher and higher. Then more dropped down.

The higher they went, the fewer there were. These few circled still higher. And still more dropped down until there were only three left in the great blue heaven with the gleaming sun. They were the eagle, the hawk, and the condor. Just these three, circling slowly, rising and rising, getting nearer and nearer to the sun.

Up they went, while all the birds below watched in silence. All the animals were watching, too, for it was a sight worth seeing, those three—the fearless eagle, the keen hawk, and the majestic condor—winging their way silently upward.

Soon those watching below saw one of the three becoming larger and larger, and the other two becoming smaller and smaller. It was the hawk who was coming down, while the eagle and condor kept going up.

"I am beaten by those who are stronger and more fearless than I. The heat was too strong for me," said the hawk.

The birds did not hear. They were watching the two left circling and soaring, soaring and circling, rising higher and higher. The birds and the animals on earth watched silently. Which one would win?

Sometimes the eagle looked at the condor; sometimes the condor looked at the eagle. The eagle looked more often. He was feeling hotter and hotter. His skin was burning dry, his eyes were burning hot. He had to shut them; he could no longer stand the golden fire of the sun, and he began to drop. The condor saw him falling. All the birds and the animals saw him coming down. A great stream of pride surged through the condor's body, and he did not feel the heat at all. He had won!

"I must get nearer the sun!" he cried. So he kept circling, circling, closer and closer to the great, shining sun. The feathers on his head were burned. He kept rising, rising, slowly. The feathers on his neck were burned. It was hard for him to breathe the fiery air, but he kept on rising! His eyes became red as fire! Still, he kept them open and kept on rising.

"I must rise to the sun! It matters not what pain I may feel."

Then, suddenly, there was a cool, sweet wind coming from the yellow, gleaming brightness. There was the Golden City of the Sun. And there, in the center, was Pachacámac, the father of all, sitting on his golden throne.

"Hail, great Mallcu, Condor, bird of the sun! Only you had the courage to come so high."

The condor was speechless before all that glory.

"No bird has ever come so close to my City of the Sun. For this you deserve to be king of the birds. You are the king, strong and fearless. Only the strong and fearless can stand the light of the sun that wounds the sight and burns the eyes. You are like me, so I shall take your form when I visit the earth or fly through the air. I am the great king of all that is on the earth, and you will be the great king of all the flying birds. My home is the City of the Sun. Yours will be the highest mountains that are nearest to the sun. Your palace of snow and ice will gleam like my palace of gold. And when you leave the earth, you will come here to me."

Since that time the people of Bolivia know, just as the birds know, that the condor is not only king of all the birds, but that he is sometimes even Pachacámac, king of the earth, flying in the form of the condor; and when they see Mallcu, the condor, they look upon him with love, respect, and worship.

To this day wonderful monuments are still built in Bolivia with the condor on top, wings spread wide, as if it were flying to the sun.

Oversmart Is Bad Luck
(Uruguay)

The theme of the animal that escapes its predator by guile is a common one in all countries, and this is a brisk variant.

Señor Rooster was a fine bird, and he lived in a village in Uruguay. He was smart, too, and he liked to take walks beyond the village to see the world.

One day he took a long walk and wandered deep into the forest. He came to a tall tree and decided to fly high up into the branches and look at the whole world from there. So he flew up into the tree, branch after branch, until he got high, high up.

Now Señor Fox came walking through the woods. As he passed under the tree he heard Señor Rooster flapping his wings in the branches, and he looked up. He saw the feathers of Señor Rooster and his fat body, and he thought what a fine dinner he would make. But Señor Fox had no wings and could not fly up into the tree. Nor could he climb. Well, he remembered that good words often pave good roads.

"My dear, dear friend, Señor Rooster!" he cried. "How are you today? I see you are all alone up there. It seems very strange for a famous gentleman like you to be all alone. I'm sure all the fine fat hens in the henhouse are worried about you, wondering where you have gone, and are anxious to see you."

"Good Señor Fox," replied Señor Rooster, "just let them wait. The longer they wait, the happier they will be to see me when I return."

"You're a smart gentleman, Señor Rooster, and very wise. But I wouldn't let the poor hens wait too long. Come down and we'll walk together to the henhouse. I'm going that way."

"Ha, ha, ha!" laughed the rooster. "What sweet and honeyed words you use to catch me! Do you really think I'll come down so you can make a good dinner of me? Sweet words catch fools."

"Don't say that, Señor Rooster. Maybe in my former days of sin I was guilty of such things, but no more . . . no more. . . . I've reformed completely. Besides, haven't you heard the news? Don't you know about the new decree now in force in our forest? No animal can eat another; all are to be friends. That's the new law. Anyone who breaks it will be punished severely. I'm surprised you haven't heard about it. Everyone knows it."

"Well, that's news to me, Señor Fox."

"I wouldn't dare to eat you now, even if I were starving to death, my good friend. Honestly. On my honor."

"Well, it must be so, when you talk like that."

"It's the absolute truth, Señor Rooster. So you see, you can come down now."

"Really!" said Señor Rooster, but still he did not come down. Instead, he looked around in all directions. Suddenly he saw a hunter approaching with his dogs. That gave him an idea. He began to count slowly: "One . . . two . . . three . . . four . . ."

"What are you counting, good friend Rooster?"

"Five . . . six . . ."

"What are you counting? Tell me, friend."

Señor Rooster pretended he hadn't heard, and said, "Six fine big hunting dogs running this way, and a man with a gun behind them!"

"Dogs! What dogs? Coming this way? With a hunter?"

"Yes, Señor Fox, all coming this way!"

"From which direction are they coming? Please tell me quickly! From where?"

"They're coming from over that way," and he pointed with his wing in exactly the opposite direction from which he saw them.

"I'd better run along now," cried Señor Fox. "I'm in a hurry." And off he ran, as fast as his legs would carry him.

"Señor Fox! Señor Fox!" called Señor Rooster. "Don't run away! Don't go! You can tell the dogs and the hunter about the new decree among the animals in the forest."

Señor Fox ran into the dogs, and Señor Rooster sat in the tree.

If you dig a pit to catch someone innocent, you often fall into it yourself. Oversmart is bad luck.

The First Flute
(Guatemala)

In a story of the ancient Mayans, a minstrel wins a princess by playing a flute given him by the god of the forest.

"Oversmart Is Bad Luck" from THE KING OF THE MOUNTAINS: A TREASURY OF LATIN AMERICAN FOLK STORIES by M. A. Jagendorf and R. S. Boggs. Copyright © 1960 by M. A. Jagendorf and R. S. Boggs. Reprinted by permission of the publisher, Vanguard Press, Inc.

"The First Flute" from THE ENCHANTED ORCHARD AND OTHER FOLKTALES OF CENTRAL AMERICA by Dorothy Sharp Carter. Copyright © 1973 by Dorothy Sharp Carter. Reprinted by permission of Harcourt Brace Jovanovich, Inc.

During the glory of the Mayan civilization, years before the coming of the Spanish, there lived a *cacique* who had a beautiful daughter, the Princess Nima-Cux, whom he loved dearly.

Not only was Nima-Cux beautiful, she was possessed of talents. She could plait grass into fine baskets. She could mold little animals out of clay—and you even knew exactly which animals they were supposed to be. The coati had a long ringed tail. The puma had an open mouth showing sharp teeth. The tapir's snout was definitely snoutish. The snake wound round and round and round—and if you unwound him, he reached from Nima-Cux's toes to her earplugs.

Above all, Nima-Cux could sing like a bird. Her voice tripped up and down the scale as easily as her feet tripped up and down the steps. The *cacique* sat back and counted his blessings. They all had to do with Nima-Cux, her beauty, her baskets, her clay work, and, especially, her voice.

As princesses should, Nima-Cux had everything she asked for—besides some things she hadn't thought of requesting. There were finely carved dolls, necklaces of rare shells, a cape of bright parrot feathers, an enormous garden filled with flowers and blossoming trees and singing birds and pet animals. No wonder Nima-Cux was happy.

Thus life flowed along, contentedly for everyone in the household until Nima-Cux neared her sixteenth birthday. Suddenly she became sad and melancholy. Nothing made her happy. Then again, nothing made her unhappy. She just *was,* for no reason at all, she said.

The *cacique* was greatly agitated. He strode up and down the garden, wondering, wondering what would please Nima-Cux. Another doll? A bright fish? A golden plate for her breast-of-pheasant? But to whatever he proposed, Nima-Cux would only murmur politely, "No. But thank you, Papa."

The cook sent boys scampering up the tallest palm trees to bring back heart of palm for Nima-Cux's dinner.

Hunters were ordered into the jungle to capture monkeys. "Mind you, *funny* monkeys to entertain the princess. Not a sad one in the crowd—or off comes your head."

Maidens roamed the royal gardens gathering orchids to ornament the princess' bedchamber.

What happened? Nima-Cux would peer at the rare *palmito* and moan softly, "I am not hungry."

She would stare at the monkeys cavorting on the branches while the royal household screamed in amusement and whisper, "Yes, yes, very comical," and sigh deeply. The household would hush its laughter and echo her sighs.

The orchids went unnoticed until they dropped to the floor with a dry rustle.

Herb doctors came. Witch doctors came. Old hunched crones said to know the secrets of life came. They all said, "But she seems quite well and normal. A bit pale. A trifle listless. Perhaps a good tonic . . ."

Nima-Cux was annoyed enough to argue about the tonic. "That smelly stuff? I won't even taste it."

Finally a sorcerer somewhat wiser than the others spoke to the *cacique.* "After all, the princess is practically sixteen. Other girls her age are married. Find a good husband for the Princess Nima-Cux—and she will again shine radiant as a star."

The *cacique* shook his head. A *husband?* How could a mere husband bring her happiness if her own father could not? A poor suggestion. What were sorcerers coming to?

He peeked once more at Nima-Cux's dismal face—and in desperation sent messengers throughout his kingdom. The young man skillful enough to impress the princess and coax a smile to her lips would become her husband. In a week the first tournament would be held.

During the next week the roads were worn into holes by the thousands of footsteps. Everyone in the kingdom hurried to the palace either to take part or to watch the take-parters (or is it takers-part?). Seats were constructed for the nobility. Those not so noble found a patch of thick grass, a loop of vine, or a high branch. The *cacique* and Nima-Cux sat on a canopied stand. The tournaments began.

The first contestant marched out proud and arrogant in his gold tunic, attended by a troop of warriors. A handsome youth he was. Maidens fainted with joy at the sight of him. The rest of the contestants growled and trembled.

But Nima-Cux frowned and asked, "What can he *do?* Besides prance and preen, worse than any *quetzal?*"

The *cacique* sighed and made a sign for the warrior to display his talents—if any. The soldiers stood before the young man and threw ears of corn into the air. With his bow and arrows the warrior shot kernels from the ears in regimental procession. One row, then the next and next until all the kernels were gone.

The spectators cheered and shouted with admiration. Such skill—and such elegance! Ayyyyyyy! The other contestants ground their teeth and sobbed.

Nima-Cux yawned and asked politely, "May we see the second match, Papa? The first has taken up *so* much time."

The *cacique* sighed again and motioned for the tournament to continue.

The second competitor strode out as confident and proud as the first. He walked alone, bearing a large basket. When he set it down, out slithered a tremendous snake of a poisonous variety, its eyes glaring with malevolence.

The spectators gasped with horror. Maidens fainted with fear. The remaining rivals watched with relish.

The youth engaged the angry snake in combat, artfully evading its deadly fangs. The spectators held their breaths.

"How boring!" muttered Nima-Cux, staring into the distance.

"Really? Really, daughter? You don't like it?" asked the *cacique* with regret. (He was enjoying the contests immensely.)

He motioned for more action. The youth complied by squeezing the life from the snake. Then he bowed to the applause of the crowd. Or most of the crowd. Nima-Cux was already on her way to the palace and her couch with a headache.

For days the tournaments continued. The most handsome and courageous of the Mayan youth competed with each other for the favor of Nima-Cux—favor that was nowhere to be seen. Certainly not on her lips, which remained clamped in a sulky line. Nor in her eyes, which gazed sadly at the competition without seeing it.

Finally the last contestant appeared, a merry boy wearing the tattered dress of a minstrel. The spectators smiled. The other contestants laughed scornfully. With a quick bow to the princess, the boy began to sing. He sang of the lakes, the forests, the hills of the highlands. He sang of the crystal stars flashing from the dark river of night. He sang of love.

Not bad, not bad, nodded the *cacique.* Not, of course, to compare with Nima-Cux's singing. He glanced at his daughter. What astonishment! Her eyes resembled the crystal of the song. Her lips were open and curving—upward. She was smiling! The *cacique* sat back and pondered the puzzle of life and love.

"I like him, Papa. We can sing together. I will marry him. Only first, he must learn the song of each bird of the forest. Then he can teach me."

The minstrel was happy to oblige. He had *meant* it when he sang of love. At once he disappeared into the jungle.

Day after day he practiced, imitating this bird, then that one. But Guatemala is home to hundreds, thousands of birds. Some whistle a complicated tune. The minstrel began to despair of his task.

The god of the forest, after listening for days to the young minstrel's efforts, took pity on him. Also on the birds and other wild inhabitants of the woods—not to mention himself. He appeared before the minstrel, wearing a kindly smile.

"Perhaps I can help you," he offered. "It is a difficult exercise you are engaged in."

Severing a small limb from a tree, the god removed the pith and cut a series of holes in the tube. "Now attend carefully," he said. And he instructed the young man exactly how to blow into one end while moving his fingers over the holes. The notes of the birds tumbled out, clear and sweet.

With a torrent of thanks, the minstrel flew on his way, carrying the *chirimia,* or flute. Just in time. Nima-Cux, anxious that the chore she had assigned her lover had been impossible, was on the point of another decline. She received the youth with joy. Enchanted she was with the flute and its airs . . . with the minstrel and his airs.

The two were married and lived long and happily in the palace of the *cacique.* And today the Indians of Guatemala will point to the *chirimia,* the most typical of native instruments, and tell you this is the way it came about.

The Sacred Drum of Tepozteco
(Mexico)

In a story taken from a cycle of Mexican tales of gods and heroes, a theme found in tales of other lands emerges: the wise man who teaches others not to base their respect on an outward show.

Long ago, in the valley of Tepoztlan, a valley in Mexico where there is much copper, Tepozteco was born. He was born to be different from other children, for he was destined to be a god.

In a short time he was a fully grown man, rich in wisdom and great in strength and speed. He could hunt better than other men, and he gave counsel that brought success.

So the people made him king. And as he grew in wisdom and understanding and strength, they worshiped him and made him a god.

He was known for his virtues even to the farthest corners of his kingdom, and he was loved and respected by all. The other kings feared him, although they never dared to say so.

One day the king of Ilayacapan asked Tepozteco to come to a great feast to be given in his honor. Other kings and nobles and men of strength were also invited.

The king told his cooks to prepare food such as had never been eaten before. He had new dishes painted in bright colors, and he ordered new blankets of lovely designs.

And the most beautiful blanket of all was to be for Tepozteco to sit upon. This was to be a feast of feasts.

On the appointed day, the kings and nobles arrived wearing their richest robes and jewels of jade and gold. It was a wonderful sight to see the great company seated on the many-colored mats, with the richly painted dishes before them. All around were beautiful servants ready to bring the fine food.

They sat and they sat. They were waiting for the great guest, Tepozteco.

They waited and they waited. After a long time they heard the *teponaztli,* the drum that always announced the coming of Tepozteco.

Soon he was seen, approaching with his followers. But he was not dressed for the feast. He was dressed in hunting clothes, with an ocelot skin thrown over his shoulders and weapons in his hands. His followers also were dressed in hunting clothes.

The king and his guests looked at them in silent surprise. Then the king spoke.

"Noble Tepozteco," he said, "you have put shame on me and my land and my guests. This feast was in your honor, and we came properly dressed to honor you, but you have come in your hunting clothes and not in your royal garments."

Tepozteco looked at the king and his company and did not say a word. For a long time he was silent. Then he spoke.

"Wait for me. I shall soon return in my royal clothes."

Then he and his followers vanished into the air like a cloud.

Again the company waited a long time, and finally the drum of Tepozteco was heard once again. Suddenly the whole company saw him.

He was alone, dressed more beautifully than anyone there. He was all covered with gold. From his shoulders hung a mantle in colors that gleamed more richly than birds in the sunlight. His headdress was of the most brilliant quetzal feathers ever seen. Gold bands bound his arms and jade beads encircled his neck. In his hand he held a shield studded with jewels and richly colored stones.

The king and his company were greatly pleased at the sight.

"Now you are dressed in a manner befitting this noble gathering in your honor. Let the food be served."

Tepozteco did not answer. He seated himself on a mat, and the food was served by beautiful maidens. Everyone ate except Tepozteco, who took the dishes and poured his food on his mantle.

Everyone stopped eating and looked at the guest of honor in surprise.

"Why do you do this?" asked the king.

"I am giving the food to my clothes, because it was they, not I, that you wanted at your feast. I was not welcome here in whatever clothes I chose to wear. Only when I came in these, my feast-day clothes, were you pleased. Therefore this feast is for them, not for me."

"Leave my palace," said the king sharply. Tepozteco rose and left.

When he had gone, a great cry of anger rose from all the guests.

"He is not fit to live among us," they cried. "We must destroy him!"

Everyone agreed to this, and the kings and nobles gathered a great army of warriors and marched on Tepoztlán.

Tepozteco knew he could not do battle against this great army, for his soldiers were too few. So he went up on the Montaña del Aire—the Mountain in the Air—where a vast temple had been built for him by his people.

There he stood, drawn up to his full height, almost reaching the sky. He raised his hands and waved them in all directions. The earth quaked and trembled and roared. Trees fell and rocks flew in every direction. Masses of earth rose into the air. Everything fell on the army that had come to destroy Tepozteco and his people, and the enemy was wiped out.

The temple of Tepozteco still stands on that mountain, and at night, when the wind screams through the canyons that the earthquake created along the Montaña del Aire, one can hear the sacred drum of Tepozteco, telling his people he is still there to guard and protect his city.

Pancho Villa and the Devil
(Mexico)

In this story about one of Mexico's greatest heroes, the humor and narrative style add zest to a good example of the way in which mythic qualities accrue to a national leader.

Do you want to hear a story about the Mexican people? Then I shall tell you one about a man who is *all* the Mexican people. He is a

"Pancho Villa and the Devil" from THE KING OF THE MOUNTAINS: A TREASURY OF LATIN AMERICAN FOLK STORIES by M. A. Jagendorf and R. S. Boggs. Copyright © 1960 by M. A. Jagendorf and R. S. Boggs. Reprinted by permission of the publisher, Vanguard Press, Inc.

great hero whom every Mexican loves: Pancho Villa.

He was stronger than any Mexican who ever lived—that is what people say. He knew everything—just ask any Mexican. He understood all things about men and animals, and he was not afraid of anything in the world. He was not even afraid of the Devil himself. Yes, that's right; not even of the Devil himself.

People say he sold himself to the Devil, and the Devil, in return, made him strong and brave. Maybe he did, but that was just to fool the Devil in the end, for that is exactly what Pancho Villa finally did. All his life he waited for the chance, and in the end he got it.

Pancho Villa had a horse with feet like dancing flames. Not only was this horse as swift as a tornado, but it was also as smart as a hare. It was a horse for a hero of Mexico—for Pancho Villa.

Villa's horse was always helping him. When he was hungry, the horse would lead him to a place where he could find something to eat. When he was thirsty, it would lead him to water. When he would lose contact with his soldiers, it would show him where they were.

To tell the truth, that horse actually *was* the Devil, waiting to carry off Pancho Villa to . . . you know where I mean.

Do you think Pancho Villa did not know who that horse really was? Of course he knew! And he was just waiting for the right time to show him which one of them was the smarter. He let the horse do everything for him. He gave it plenty of food. But he kept his eyes wide open, just the same.

Things went on that way for a long, long time, the horse doing everything for Pancho Villa, and the great hero accepting it but always watching, watching.

Now, you know they finally killed Pancho Villa. The fools! They did not know he was the greatest Mexican who ever lived. Ask any true Mexican, and he will tell you.

The only one who knew he was going to be killed was that horse, the Devil. It could talk, but it never said a word. It just kept waiting to carry him off to the Hill of Box, where the Devil lived, just north of San Juan del Río. It was there that Pancho Villa sold his soul, so he would become a great hero.

As soon as Pancho Villa was shot, the horse spoke.

He said, "Now, you come with me. I have kings and princes in my hill, but I don't have anyone there as fearless as you."

But that Devil-horse had forgotten one thing.

Said Pancho Villa, "You are right. I am fearless, and I am not afraid of anything, not even of *you*, Devil! I have gone to church ever since I gave up soldiering, and now you can't take me. I have a cross around my neck, so you can't touch me. You go back to your hill and I'll go the other way, where all good Mexicans go."

The Devil-horse couldn't answer that, so he galloped off, screaming and neighing, in the opposite direction. Fire and brimstone shot from his hoofs.

And Pancho Villa went off in the other direction, to heaven, where he really belongs.

Fables

Like the folk tale, the fable is a distinctive form of folklore. It is, with few exceptions, a brief story and one that points a moral; the moral is often used, as it is in the fables by Aesop, as a tag to underline the point of the story. In most fables the characters are animals, although their behavior is used to illustrate a point or teach a lesson about human behavior, and therefore the characters tend to have one dominant trait. Many of the precepts become familiar to children who have never read fables or even heard them read, since the moral tags have become so intrinsic a part of the cultural tradition that is passed on orally.

Although fables are seldom as popular with children as are folk tales, these pithy doses of advice are often appealing because they are so vivid and dramatic in their compression, and because they are so often humorous. Because they deal with abstractions and are usually symbolic or allegorical in form, they may need to be discussed in order to make sure that children understand and appreciate them; they are seldom appropriate, therefore, for young children. There are, however, some picture book versions in which the simplified treatment and the illustrations make the fables more easily comprehensible.

Aesop's Fables

There are many excellent editions of Aesop's fables. Although the stories included here are from *The Fables of Aesop*, by Joseph Jacobs, the edition illustrated by Heidi Holder or the compilation by Louis Untermeyer, illustrated by Alice and Martin Provensen, are also carefully retold and handsomely illustrated. The fables are easily put into dialogue and staged, and involving children in such dramatic presentations is enjoyable in itself and a good way to help them understand the message of the story.

The Hare with Many Friends

A hare was very popular with the other beasts who all claimed to be her friends. But one day she heard the hounds approaching and hoped to escape them by the aid of her many friends. So she went to the horse, and asked him to carry her away from the hounds on his back. But he declined, stating that he had important work to do for his master. He felt sure, he said, that all her other friends would come to her assistance. She then applied to the bull, and hoped that he would repel the hounds with his horns.

The bull replied: "I am very sorry, but I have an appointment with a lady; but I feel sure that our friend the goat will do what you want."

The goat, however, feared that his back might do her some harm if he took her upon it. The ram, he felt sure, was the proper friend to apply to. So she went to the ram and told him the case.

The ram replied: "Another time, my dear friend. I do not like to interfere on the present occasion, as hounds have been known to eat sheep as well as hares."

The hare then applied, as a last hope, to the calf, who regretted that he was unable to help her, as he did not like to take the responsibility upon himself, as so many older persons than himself had declined the task. By this time the hounds were quite near, and the hare took to her heels and luckily escaped.

He that has many friends, has no friends.

The Ant and the Grasshopper

In a field one summer's day a grasshopper was hopping about, chirping and singing to its heart's content. An ant passed by, bearing along with great toil an ear of corn he was taking to the nest.

"Why not come and chat with me," said the grasshopper, "instead of toiling and moiling in that way?"

"I am helping to lay up food for the winter," said the ant, "and recommend you to do the same."

"Why bother about winter?" said the grasshopper. "We have got plenty of food at present." But the ant went on its way and continued its toil. When the winter came the grasshopper had no food, and found itself dying of hunger, while it saw the ants distributing every day corn and grain from the stores they had collected in the summer. Then the grasshopper knew—

It is best to prepare for the days of necessity.

The Shepherd's Boy

There was once a young shepherd boy who tended his sheep at the foot of a mountain near a dark forest. It was rather lonely for him all day, so he thought upon a plan by which he could get a little company and some excitement. He rushed down towards the village calling out "Wolf, wolf," and the villagers came out to meet him, and some of them stopped with him for a considerable time. This pleased the boy so much that a few days afterwards he tried the same trick, and again the villagers came to his help. But shortly after this a wolf actually did come out from the forest, and began to worry the sheep, and the boy of course cried out "Wolf, wolf," still louder than before. But this time the villagers, who had been fooled twice before, thought the boy was again deceiving them, and nobody stirred to come to his help. So the wolf made a good meal off the boy's flock, and when the boy complained, the wise man of the village said:

"A liar will not be believed, even when he speaks the truth."

All the Aesop's Fables in this section are from THE FABLES OF AESOP, selected, told anew, and their history traced by Joseph Jacobs. London: Macmillan & Company, 1894.

The Lion and the Mouse

Once when a lion was asleep a little mouse began running up and down upon him; this soon wakened the lion, who placed his huge paw upon him, and opened his big jaws to swallow him. "Pardon, O King," cried the little mouse; "forgive me this time, I shall never forget it. Who knows but what I may be able to do you a turn some of these days?" The lion was so tickled at the idea of the mouse being able to help him, that he lifted up his paw and let him go. Some time after, the lion was caught in a trap, and the hunters, who desired to carry him alive to the king, tied him to a tree while they went in search of a wagon to carry him on. Just then the little mouse happened to pass by, and seeing the sad plight in which the lion was, went up to him and soon gnawed away the ropes that bound the king of the beasts. "Was I not right?" said the little mouse.

Little friends may prove great friends.

The Fox and the Crow

A fox once saw a crow fly off with a piece of cheese in its beak and settle on a branch of a tree. "That's for me, as I am a fox," said Master Renard, and he walked up to the foot of the tree. "Good-day, Mistress Crow," he cried. "How well you are looking to-day: how glossy your feathers; how bright your eye. I feel sure your voice must surpass that of other birds, just as your figure does; let me hear but one song from you that I may greet you as the Queen of Birds." The crow lifted up her head and began to caw her best, but the moment she opened her mouth the piece of cheese fell to the ground, only to be snapped up by Master Fox. "That will do," said he. "That was all I wanted. In exchange for your cheese I will give you a piece of advice for the future—do not trust flatterers."

The flatterer doth rob by stealth,
His victim, both of wit and wealth.

The Town Mouse and the Country Mouse

Now you must know that a town mouse once upon a time went on a visit to his cousin in the country. He was rough and ready, this cousin, but he loved his town friend and made him heartily welcome. Beans and bacon, cheese and bread, were all he had to offer, but he offered them freely. The town mouse rather turned up his long nose at this country fare, and said: "I cannot understand, Cousin, how you can put up with such poor food as this, but of course you cannot expect anything better in the country; come you with me and I will show you how to live. When you have been in town a week you will wonder how you could ever have stood a country life." No sooner said than done: the two mice set off for the town and arrived at the town mouse's residence late at night. "You will want some refreshment after our long journey," said the polite town mouse, and took his friend into the grand dining-room. There they found the remains of a fine feast, and soon the two mice were eating up jellies and cakes and all that was nice. Suddenly they heard growling and barking. "What is that?" said the country mouse. "It is only the dogs of the house," answered the other. "Only!" said the country mouse. "I do not like that music at my dinner." Just at that moment the door flew open, in came two huge mastiffs, and the two mice had to scamper down and run off. "Good-bye Cousin," said the country mouse. "What! going so soon?" said the other. "Yes," he replied:

"Better beans and bacon in peace than cakes and ale in fear."

The Dog in the Manger

A dog looking out for its afternoon nap jumped into the manger of an ox and lay there cosily upon the straw. But soon the ox, returning from its afternoon work, came up to the manger and wanted to eat some of the straw. The dog in a rage, being awakened from its slumber, stood up and barked at the ox, and whenever it came near attempted to bite it. At last the ox had to give up the hope of getting at the straw, and went away muttering:

"Ah, people often grudge others what they cannot enjoy themselves."

Belling the Cat

Long ago, the mice held a general council to consider what measures they could take to outwit their common enemy, the cat. Some said this, and some said that; but at last a young mouse got up and said he had a proposal to make, which he thought would meet the case. "You will all agree," said he, "that our chief danger consists in the sly and treacherous manner in which the enemy approaches us. Now, if we could receive some signal of her approach, we could easily escape from her. I venture, therefore, to propose that a small bell be procured, and attached by a ribbon round the neck of the cat. By this means we should always know when she was about, and could easily retire while she was in the neighborhood."

This proposal met with general applause, until an old mouse got up and said: "That is all very well, but who is to bell the cat?" The mice looked at one another and nobody spoke. Then the old mouse said:

"It is easy to propose impossible remedies."

The Wind and the Sun

The wind and the sun were disputing which was the stronger. Suddenly they saw a traveller coming down the road, and the sun said: "I see a way to decide our dispute. Whichever of us can cause that traveller to take off his cloak shall be regarded as the stronger. You begin." So the sun retired behind a cloud, and the wind began to blow as hard as it could upon the traveller. But the harder he blew the more closely did the traveller wrap his cloak round him, till at last the wind had to give up in despair. Then the sun came out and shone in all his glory upon the traveller, who soon found it too hot to walk with his cloak on.

Kindness effects more than Severity.

The Fox and the Grapes

One hot summer's day a fox was strolling through an orchard till he came to a bunch of grapes just ripening on a vine which had been trained over a lofty branch. "Just the thing to quench my thirst," quoth he. Drawing back a few paces, he took a run and a jump, and just missed the bunch. Turning round again with a one, two, three, he jumped up, but with no greater success. Again and again he tried after the tempting morsel, but at last had to give it up, and walked away with his nose in the air, saying: "I am sure they are sour."

It is easy to despise what you cannot get.

The Crow and the Pitcher

A crow, half-dead with thirst, came upon a pitcher which had once been full of water; but when the crow put its beak into the mouth of the pitcher he found that only very little water was left in it and that he could not reach far enough down to get at it. He tried, and he tried, but at last had to give up in despair. Then a thought came to him, and he took a pebble and dropped it into the pitcher. Then he took another pebble and dropped it into the pitcher. Then he took another pebble and dropped that into the pitcher. Then he took another pebble and dropped that into the pitcher. Then he took another pebble and dropped that into the pitcher. Then he took another pebble and dropped that into the pitcher. At last, at last, he saw the water mount up near him; and after casting in a few more pebbles he was able to quench his thirst and save his life.

Little by little does the trick.

The Hare and the Tortoise

The hare was once boasting of his speed before the other animals. "I have never yet been beaten," said he, "when I put forth my full speed. I challenge any one here to race with me."

The tortoise said quietly: "I accept your challenge."

"That is a good joke," said the hare; "I could dance round you all the way."

"Keep your boasting till you've beaten," answered the tortoise. "Shall we race?"

So a course was fixed and a start was made. The hare darted almost out of sight at once, but soon stopped and, to show his contempt for the tortoise, lay down to have a nap. The tortoise plodded on and plodded on, and when the hare awoke from his nap, he saw the tortoise just near the winning-post and could not run up in time to save the race. Then said the Tortoise:

"Plodding wins the race."

The Panchatantra

 Unlike the succession of comparatively terse stories that are attributed to Aesop, the tales from the *Panchatantra* are excerpted from within a larger work, a long treatise on conduct from India. *The Fables of Bidpai,* from which two of the tales below were taken, are the Arabic versions of the *Panchatantra,* which means "five books" and is the oldest collection of Indian fables.

The Partridge and the Crow

A Crow flying across a road saw a Partridge strutting along the ground.

"What a beautiful gait that Partridge has!" said the Crow. "I must try to see if I can walk like him."

She alighted behind the Partridge and tried for a long time to learn to strut. At last the Partridge turned around and asked the Crow what she was about.

"Do not be angry with me," replied the Crow. "I have never before seen a bird who walks as beautifully as you can, and I am trying to learn to walk like you."

"The Partridge and the Crow" from THE TORTOISE AND THE GEESE by Maude Barrows Dutton. Copyright 1900 by Maude Barrows Dutton. Copyright renewed 1935 by Maude Dutton Lynch. Reprinted by permission of Houghton Mifflin Company.

"Foolish bird!" responded the Partridge. "You are a Crow, and should walk like a Crow. You would look silly indeed if you were to strut like a partridge."

But the Crow went on trying to learn to strut, until finally she had forgotten her own gait, and she never learned that of the Partridge.

The Tyrant Who Became a Just Ruler

In olden times there lived a King who was so cruel and unjust towards his subjects that he was always called The Tyrant. So heartless was he that his people used to pray night and day that they might have a new king. One day, much to their surprise, he called his people together and said to them—

"My dear subjects, the days of my tyranny are over. Henceforth you shall live in peace and happiness, for I have decided to try to rule henceforth justly and well."

The King kept his word so well that soon he was known throughout the land as The Just King. By and by one of his favorites came to him and said—

"Your Majesty, I beg of you to tell me how it was that you had this change of heart towards your people?"

And the King replied—

"As I was galloping through my forests one afternoon, I caught sight of a hound chasing a fox. The fox escaped into his hole, but not until he had been bitten by the dog so badly that he would be lame for life. The hound, returning home, met a man who threw a stone at him, which broke his leg. The man had not gone far when a horse kicked him and broke his leg. And the horse, starting to

run, fell into a hole and broke his leg. Here I came to my senses, and resolved to change my rule. 'For surely,' I said to myself, 'he who doeth evil will sooner or later be overtaken by evil.'"

The Mice That Ate Iron

In a certain town lived a merchant named Naduk, who lost his money and determined to travel abroad. For

> The meanest of mankind is he
> Who, having lost his money, can
> Inhabit lands or towns where once
> He spent it like a gentleman.

And again:

> The neighbor gossips blame
> His poverty as shame
> Who long was wont to play
> Among them, proud and gay.

In his house was an iron balance-beam inherited from his ancestors, and it weighed a thousand *pals*. This he put in pawn with Merchant Lakshman before he departed for foreign countries.

Now after he had long traveled wherever business led him through foreign lands, he returned to his native city and said to Merchant Lakshman: "Friend Lakshman, return my deposit, the balance-beam." And Lakshman said: "Friend Naduk, your balance-beam has been eaten by mice."

To this Naduk replied: "Lakshman, you are in no way to blame, if it has been eaten by mice. Such is life. Nothing in the universe has any permanence. However, I am going to the river for a bath. Please send your boy Money-God with me, to carry my bathing things."

Since Lakshman was conscience-stricken at his own theft, he said to his son Money-God: "My dear boy, let me introduce Uncle Naduk, who is going to the river to bathe. You must go with him and carry his bathing things." Ah, there is too much truth in the saying:

> There is no purely loving deed
> Without a pinch of fear or greed
> Or service of a selfish need.

And again:

> Wherever there is fond attention
> That does not seek a service pension,
> Was there no timid apprehension?

So Lakshman's son took the bathing things and delightedly accompanied Naduk to the river. After Naduk had taken his bath, he thrust Lakshman's son Money-God into a mountain cave, blocked the entrance with a great rock, and returned to Lakshman's house. And when Lakshman said: "Friend Naduk, tell me what has become of my son Money-God who went with you," Naduk answered: "My good Lakshman, a hawk carried him off from the river-bank."

"Oh, Naduk!" cried Lakshman. "You liar! How could a hawk possibly carry off a big boy like Money-God?" "But, Lakshman," retorted Naduk, "the mice could eat a balance-beam made of iron. Give me my balance-beam, if you want your son."

Finally, they carried their dispute to the palace gate, where Lakshman cried in a piercing tone: "Help! Help! A ghastly deed! This Naduk person has carried off my son—his name is Money-God."

Thereupon the magistrates said to Naduk: "Sir, restore the boy to Lakshman." But Naduk pleaded: "What am I to do? Before my eyes a hawk carried him from the river-bank." "Come, Naduk!" said they, "you are not telling the truth. How can a hawk carry off a fifteen-year-old boy?" Then Naduk laughed outright and said: "Gentlemen, listen to my words.

> Where mice eat balance-beams of iron
> A thousand *pals* in weight,
> A hawk might steal an elephant;
> A boy is trifling freight."

"How was that?" they asked, and Naduk told them the story of the balance-beam. At this they laughed and caused the restoration of balance-beam and boy to the respective owners.

Arabian Fables

Although it is not printed separately, the last line of this serious fable gives the moral and is also reminiscent of our own saying that "Too many cooks spoil the broth." Both the language and the style of "The Owls and the Crows" indicate that it is most appropriate for older children.

The Owls and the Crows

The king said to the philosopher that now that he had heard the fable about brotherhood and how friends help one another, he would like to hear a story about an enemy one should never trust even though he appears to be friendly.

The philosopher answered that when a man trusts a cunning enemy, he is bound to have the same fate as what befell the owls at the mercy of the crows.

There was a certain forest with large trees and excellent pastures. One thousand crows and their king had built a rookery in the largest tree. Nearby was a hill where one thousand owls lived with their king. One night the owls attacked the crows without warn-

"The Owls and the Crows" from KALILA WA DIMNA: FABLES FROM A FOURTEENTH CENTURY ARABIC MANUSCRIPT by Esin Atil. Copyright © 1981 by Smithsonian Institution, Washington, D.C. Reprinted by permission of the Smithsonian Institution Press.

ing; they killed and wounded many crows and departed as suddenly as they had arrived.

After the owls retreated at dawn, the crows assembled around their king. When the king saw how many had been killed, badly wounded, or had a broken wing, he realized that the owls were much stronger and would attack again to finish them off. He asked five of his most learned ministers to find a solution and help him save the remaining population.

The first counselor said that since the enemy was too powerful, they should move far away. The second felt that they should prepare for battle and fight for their lives to the very end. The third disagreed and proposed that they find a mediator and make peace, even if they had to pay a yearly tribute. The fourth believed that they should surrender now, but secretly build up their arms and fight back when they were strong enough. The fifth considered the solutions given and found fault with each. He said that having more than one counselor was detrimental to rulers; a king should have only one advisor who was thoroughly devoted to the sovereign and to the good of the nation.

The king dismissed the group and called the fifth crow to his quarters to discuss the problem. The crow began by telling him the story of the hare and the elephant.

There was a region where many elephants lived. Their lake had dried up and the springs feeding it had disappeared. Suffering from thirst, the elephants gathered together and complained to their king. The king sent out his confidants and secretaries to explore the land and search for water. One of them came back with the news that he had found a lovely place with a clear and pleasant body of water, called the Lake of the Moon. The king moved his herd to this place and the elephants finally had plenty to eat and drink.

This region was inhabited by the king of the hares and his subjects. When the elephants arrived at night, they trampled a number of hares and killed them. The next morning the remaining hares gathered

around their king and asked him to devise a plan that would deliver them from the elephants, make them leave the pasture, and save the remaining hares. The king called upon his counselor, a wise and learned hare named Fairuz. Fairuz addressed the group and suggested that he go as a messenger to the elephants and talk to them.

Fairuz set out on a moonlit night to meet the elephants. Afraid that they might not see him and would step on him, he climbed on a rock overlooking the herd and called out to their king. He announced that he was the messenger of the moon. The moon had said that although the king of the elephants boasted of his strength and harmed the weak, his strength would cause his downfall; the king had disturbed the moon's lake and drunk its water wrongly; if he returned to the lake, the moon would blind him and his subjects; and if the king doubted these words, he should come to the lake and find out for himself.

The king of the elephants, curious to meet this powerful moon, set out to the lake with Fairuz. When they arrived, he saw the reflection of the moon in the water. Fairuz told him to pay homage to the moon by drinking the water and washing his face before speaking. The elephant went into the water and did as he was told. He hastily withdrew when he saw the reflection of the moon move; he thought that the moon was trembling in anger and quickly apologized for having entered the lake. He was overwhelmed by the power of the moon and gathered his herd and departed from the pasture, leaving it to the hares.

When the crow finished his story, the king asked him how they could be free from the enmity of the owls. The crow then told him other stories, which proved that a small but clever person could easily overpower a strong opponent with his intelligence. He explained his plan to trick the owls and asked that word be sent out saying that the king was angry with his confidant and counselor; then the crows were to beat him up and pluck his wings and cast him beside a tree; he also told the king to take his subjects and go into hiding.

They did as he requested and when the king of the owls came with his army that night, he found all the crows gone. The only one left was a badly beaten crow crawling on the ground. He questioned the crow, who told him that he had been beaten by his own kind and banished from their society since he had advised his king to surrender to the owls and make peace.

After hearing the crow's story, the king of the owls asked his advisors what they ought to do with him. The first said he should be killed since an enemy can never be trusted; the second advised that he should be treated with compassion; and the third suggested that he should be honored so that he might become loyal and help them later. The king agreed with the advice of the third counselor and ordered the crow fed and his wounds treated. The crow was given the best meats and his needs were attended to without delay. He soon recovered and began to gain the confidence of the owls. He learned their secrets and soon became acquainted with their habits.

When he had acquired sufficient information, he flew back to his companions. He told the king of the crows that the owls lived in a cave that had a small entrance. He asked all the crows to take a piece of dry wood and place it in front of the opening. One of them was to bring a flaming branch and set the dry wood afire. Then, they were to fly in front of the fire and fan the flames with their wings. If the owls came out, they would burn; if they remained inside the cave, they would die from the heat and smoke. The king ordered the crows to do as his counselor planned and the crows returned victorious, rejoicing in the death of their enemy.

After the enemy was eliminated, the king of the crows asked his counselor if he found the owls intelligent, skillful, and prudent. The counselor said that the only intelligent one among the lot was the owl who advised his king to kill the crow. This owl had warned him to beware the enemy and not to trust his friendship, even when he seemed weak and harmless. But the king was foolish and careless; he did not follow good advice and paid dearly for his mistake.

Fables of La Fontaine

 Jean de la Fontaine, a seventeenth-century French poet, used both Aesop and the *Bidpai* stories (in Latin versions) as well as the twelfth-century fabular versions of Marie de France as a basis for his own adaptations, which were in verse. In English, they are available in both verse and prose versions. They are witty, light, and often more humorous than the Aesop fables; they have a polished style and are more like the crisp, brief fables of Aesop than those of India.

The Fox and the Crow

Mister Crow sat on the limb of a tree with a big piece of cheese in his mouth.

Old Mister Fox smelled the cheese from a long way off. And he came to the foot of the tree and spoke to the crow.

> "Good morning, Mr. Coal Black Crow,
> How beautiful and shining your feathers grow,
> Black as the night and bright as the sun,
> If you sing as well, your fortune is won."

At these words Mr. Crow joyously opened his beak to sing his creaky old crow song.

And the cheese fell down to the ground. The fox snapped it up in his mouth.

As he ran away he called back over his bushy tail, "My dear Mr. Crow, learn from this how every flatterer lives at the expense of anybody who will listen to him. This lesson is well worth the loss of a cheese to you."

The Cricket and the Ant

All through the summer the cricket sang. He sang in the grass when they planted the seed. And he sang in the grass when the flowers bloomed. Why should a cricket work on a sunny day, when he could sing and dance and play? In the early fall when the seeds were blowing in the air the cricket chirped his song. But when winter came and the cold winds blew, the merry little cricket had nothing to eat and nowhere to go.

So he hopped to the house of his neighbor, the ant, who had worked all summer storing up her food for the winter. He knocked at the door and cried, "Oh, dear! Oh, dear! I am starving, hungry, starving! Kind ant, will you lend me some seeds to live on until spring? And I will give you five seeds in the spring for every seed that you give me today."

But the ant was practical—as ants are.

"What did you do in the summer when the days were warm and the flowers were going to seed?" asked the ant. "What did you do in the early fall when the seeds were blowing through the air?"

"Night and day I sang," said the cricket.

"You sang!" said the ant. "Then now you can dance to your own music. I will eat the seed I gathered and the house I have built will keep me warm. Maybe your dancing will keep you warm in the snow."

The Grasshopper and the Ant

> A grasshopper gay
> Sang the Summer away,
> And found herself poor
> By the winter's first roar.
> Of meat and of bread,
> Not a morsel she had!
> So a-begging she went,
> To her neighbour the ant,
>   For the loan of some wheat,
>   Which would serve her to eat,
> Till the season came round.
>   "I will pay you," she saith
>   "On an animal's faith,
> Double weight in the pound
> Ere the harvest be bound."
> The ant is a friend
>   (And here she might mend)
>   Little given to lend.
> "How spent you the summer?"
>   Quoth she, looking shame
>   At the borrowing dame.
> "Night and day to each comer
> I sang if you please."
>   "You sang! I'm at ease;
> For 'tis plain at a glance,
> Now, Ma'am, you must dance."

Myths

The mythic form of folklore is longer than the fable or folk tale, more complex, more often symbolic, and more often associated with the religious beliefs of the early cultures from which it evolved. They are imaginative explanations of major forces in life, unscientific but unquestioned truths to the primitive peoples who wove into them their fears and beliefs about natural phenomena, the origins of living things, and the powerful forces that shape human lives for good or ill. In the myths of all cultures we can see how these forces were personified, propitiated, and often deified. They assumed human forms, they became gods and goddesses, they stood for abstract virtues, and they not infrequently became parts of organized religions.

The myths that are most familiar to English-speaking children are those of the Greeks, Romans, and Norsemen; whether they are regarded as part of the literary heritage, as anthropological research, or as keys to the psychological needs and fears of human beings, they are deeply instilled in our culture. Many of the myths are long, intricate, and sophisticated. They are not loved by all children and many of them are not easily understood by younger children, but they are of interest today primarily to children or to scholars. Along with the epics and hero tales, they have a sweep, a scale, a grandeur that flavor the style and capture the imagination.

Greek and Roman Myths

Most of the Greek myths were collected and retold by the eighth-century poet Hesiod; although he wrote in verse of the gods, terrible and splendid, and of their dealings with men and women, our children read prose versions of these great events. Each of the gods had a special task or role or power, and through the stories about them the Greeks explained both the nature of the universe and the conflicts among its powerful forces. The tales that are known as Roman myths are actually versions of the Greek myths, for the Romans absorbed these as they did so much else in the culture of ancient Greece. Those children who enjoy mythology are often intrigued by learning the Roman equivalents of the Greek pantheon.

The Golden Fleece

This is both an explanation of one sign of the Zodiac, Aries the Ram, and an indication of the power of Zeus.

The palace of Zeus, king of gods and men, stands high on the peaks of Mount Olympos. A curtain of mist hides it from the eyes of mortal men. But Zeus looks down, and sees everything men do on earth.

One day Zeus looked down towards the temple at Delphi. What he saw made him frown with anger. A group of mortals was preparing a terrible sacrifice. On one side three priests held two terrified children, Phrixos and his sister Helle; on the other side stood a wicked king and his queen, the children's cruel stepmother. They were going to burn the children alive as a sacrifice to Zeus.

Zeus called to his pet ram. Instead of white wool, its fleece was made of curling yellow gold. "Hurry," he said. "Go down and rescue them."

Just as the priests lifted their knives to begin the sacrifice, there was a flash of lightning above their heads, and a golden cloud appeared before them. In the middle was the

"The Golden Fleece" from THE SHINING STARS by Ghislaine Vautier and Kenneth McLeish. Copyright © 1981 by Kenneth McLeish. Reprinted by permission of Cambridge University Press.

ram. "Climb on to my back," it said to the children. "Climb on. Hurry!"

Phrixos and Helle climbed up and took tight hold of the ram's soft golden fleece. The ram leapt into the sky, leaving the priests and the cruel king and queen far below.

For hours the ram soared across the sky. It passed over cloud-capped mountains, grey-blue seas, flat farmlands and villages with pencils of smoke rising from people's cooking fires below. Still holding tight, soothed by the soft breeze, Phrixos and Helle fell fast asleep.

At last, as the sun was setting, the ram came to earth with a little hop and bump. Phrixos woke up. "Where are we?" he asked sleepily.

"In Colchis, in a safe country," said the ram. "Here you'll grow up as the foster-son of King Aeëtes."

"Where's Helle?" said Phrixos in alarm. "She's fallen off! She's drowned!"

"No," said the ram. "Not drowned. While you were asleep, Poseidon lord of the sea took her to serve him in his palace under the sea."

Phrixos' eyes filled with tears. "Will I never see her again?"

"You must be brave and serve Zeus, just as she now serves Poseidon. Take your knife and sacrifice me. Then carry my golden fleece to your new father, King Aeëtes."

"But—"

"Do as Zeus commands!"

Tearfully Phrixos sacrificed the ram and gathered its fleece in his arms. Then he set off towards Aeëtes' palace. His heart was sad because Zeus had made him kill the ram which had saved his life.

Then he looked up at the starry sky, and understood. The ram's fleece was left on earth as a sign of Zeus' kindness to men. But the golden ram itself now gambolled in the sky, a constellation of bright stars that guided his steps as he went joyfully on his way.

Orion

The story of the birth and death of Orion introduces the sign of the scorpion and teaches a lesson in conservation.

This is how Orion was born. One day Zeus, Hermes, and Poseidon, feeling bored, decided to leave Olympos for a day and go for a walk on earth.

Disguised as mortal travellers, they walked all day in the woods and fields until they were footsore and hungry. They called at the house of a poor farmer, Hyrieus, and asked him to give them something to eat. Hyrieus was a kind and generous man. He made the travellers welcome, and because he had no other food in the house, he killed his only ox, a family pet, to make their evening meal.

After they'd eaten, the travellers revealed themselves as gods. "As a reward for your kindness," Zeus said to Hyrieus, "ask for any gift you like, and it will be yours."

"My lord," said Hyrieus, "the only gift I want in all the world is a son of my own. But how can that be? My wife has been dead and buried for many years."

"This is what you must do," said Zeus, "Take the ox-skin and bury it in your garden. After nine months it will turn into a handsome son." So saying, he touched the skin with his royal staff, and the three gods disappeared into the evening sky.

Hyrieus buried the ox-skin as he'd been told. For nine long months he waited impatiently—and then one day, standing on the spot where the skin had been, he found a newborn baby, and called him Orion.

Orion grew up strong and proud. He was a skilful hunter, and often used to go out into the countryside to look for game. When he was grown-up he left his father Hyrieus and set out to see the world. Wherever he went he was sure to go hunting in the local forests and mountain-sides, and his fame soon spread round all the world.

One day, while he was hunting on the island of Crete, he met Artemis the hunting-goddess herself. For days they hunted together, tracking the wild beasts of the hills and woods. Orion was so delighted with Artemis, and so proud of his own hunting skill that he decided to do something really unusual to surprise her. He went out alone one day, and that evening, when the goddess went to find him, he proudly showed her a huge heap of dead animals and birds. "There, Artemis!" he said. "In your honour, I've killed every living thing on Crete."

Unfortunately, Orion didn't know that Artemis, as well as being the goddess of hunting, was also the protector of all wild animals and birds. She looked at the pile of wasted bodies, and stamped her foot angrily on the ground. At once an enormous scorpion sprang up out of the earth. "Hunt *that*, Orion!" she said.

Orion lifted his bow. But he was too slow. The scorpion arched its venomous sting and killed him.

Artemis looked down at his body. "To hunt a few animals for sport is allowed," she said. "But to kill everything in sight is proud and foolish." And she set the scorpion among the stars, to remind men forever of the risks of pride.

"Orion" from THE SHINING STARS by Ghislaine Vautier and Kenneth McLeish. Copyright © 1981 by Kenneth McLeish. Reprinted by permission of Cambridge University Press.

Arachne

This is almost like a folk tale in the way it warns against vanity and greed and in its resemblance to a "why" story.

Not among mortals alone were there contests of skill, nor yet among the gods, like Pan and Apollo. Many sorrows befell men because they grew arrogant in their own devices and coveted divine honors. There was once a great hunter, Orion, who outvied the gods themselves, till they took him away from his hunting-grounds and set him in the heavens, with his sword and belt, and his hound at his heels. But at length jealousy invaded even the peaceful arts, and disaster came of spinning!

There was a certain maiden of Lydia, Arachne by name, renowned throughout the country for her skill as a weaver. She was as nimble with her fingers as Calypso, that nymph who kept Odysseus for seven years in her enchanted island. She was as untiring as Penelope, the hero's wife, who wove day after day while she watched for his return. Day in and day out, Arachne wove too. The very nymphs would gather about her loom, naiads from the water and dryads from the trees.

"Maiden," they would say, shaking the leaves or the foam from their hair, in wonder, "Pallas Athena must have taught you!"

But this did not please Arachne. She would not acknowledge herself a debtor, even to that goddess who protected all household arts, and by whose grace alone one had any skill in them.

"I learned not of Athena," said she. "If she can weave better, let her come and try."

The nymphs shivered at this, and an aged woman, who was looking on, turned to Arachne.

"Be more heedful of your words, my daughter," said she. "The goddess may pardon you if you ask forgiveness, but do not

"Arachne" from OLD GREEK FOLK STORIES TOLD ANEW by Josephine Preston. New York: Houghton Mifflin Company, 1897.

strive for honors with the immortals."

Arachne broke her thread, and the shuttle stopped humming.

"Keep your counsel," she said. "I fear not Athena; no, nor anyone else."

As she frowned at the old woman, she was amazed to see her change suddenly into one tall, majestic, beautiful—a maiden of gray eyes and golden hair, crowned with a golden helmet. It was Athena herself.

The bystanders shrank in fear and reverence; only Arachne was unawed and held to her foolish boast.

In silence the two began to weave, and the nymphs stole nearer, coaxed by the sound of the shuttles, that seemed to be humming with delight over the two webs—back and forth like bees.

They gazed upon the loom where the goddess stood plying her task, and they saw shapes and images come to bloom out of the wondrous colors, as sunset clouds grow to be living creatures when we watch them. And they saw that the goddess, still merciful, was spinning, as a warning for Arachne, the pictures of her own triumph over reckless gods and mortals.

In one corner of the web she made a story of her conquest over the sea-god Poseidon. For the first king of Athens had promised to dedicate the city to that god who should bestow upon it the most useful gift. Poseidon gave the horse. But Athena gave the olive—means of livelihood—symbol of peace and prosperity, and the city was called after her name. Again she pictured a vain woman of Troy, who had been turned into a crane for disputing the palm of beauty with a goddess. Other corners of the web held similar images, and the whole shone like a rainbow.

Meanwhile Arachne, whose head was quite turned with vanity, embroidered her web with stories against the gods, making light of Zeus himself and of Apollo, and portraying them as birds and beasts. But she wove with marvelous skill; the creatures seemed to breathe and speak, yet it was all as fine as the gossamer that you find on the grass before rain.

Athena herself was amazed. Not even her wrath at the girl's insolence could wholly overcome her wonder. For an instant she stood entranced; then she tore the web across, and three times she touched Arachne's forehead with her spindle.

"Live on, Arachne," she said. "And since it is your glory to weave, you and yours must weave forever." So saying, she sprinkled upon the maiden a certain magical potion.

Away went Arachne's beauty; then her very human form shrank to that of a spider, and so remained. As a spider she spent all her days weaving and weaving; and you may see something like her handiwork any day among the rafters.

Proserpine

This legend of the seasons, often entitled "Demeter and Persephone," is particularly appealing to children because of the pathos of the mother-child relationship.

When Jupiter and his brothers had defeated the Titans and banished them to Tartarus, a new enemy rose up against the gods. They were the giants Typhon, Briareus, Enceladus, and others. Some of them had a hundred arms, others breathed out fire. They were finally subdued and buried alive under Mount Ætna, where they still sometimes struggle to get loose, and shake the whole island with earthquakes. Their breath comes up through the mountain, and is what men call the eruption of the volcano.

The fall of these monsters shook the earth, so that Pluto was alarmed, and feared that his kingdom would be laid open to the light of day. Under this apprehension, he mounted his chariot, drawn by black horses, and took a circuit of inspection to satisfy himself of the extent of the damage.

While he was thus engaged, Venus, who was sitting on Mount Eryx playing with her boy Cupid, espied him, and said, "My son, take your darts with which you conquer all, even Jove himself, and send one into the breast of yonder dark monarch, who rules the realm of Tartarus. Why should he alone escape? Seize the opportunity to extend your empire and mine. Do you not see that even in heaven some despise our power? Minerva the wise, and Diana the huntress, defy us; and there is that daughter of Ceres, who threatens to follow their example. Now do you, if you have any regard for your own interest or mine, join these two in one."

The boy unbound his quiver, and selected his sharpest and truest arrow; then, straining the bow against his knee, he attached the string, and, having made ready, shot the arrow with its barbed point right into the heart of Pluto.

In the vale of Enna there is a lake embowered in woods, which screen it from the fervid rays of the sun, while the moist ground is covered with flowers, and Spring reigns perpetual. Here Proserpine was playing with her companions, gathering lilies and violets, and filling her basket and her apron with them, when Pluto saw her, loved her, and carried her off. She screamed for help to her mother and her companions; and when in her fright she dropped the corners of her apron and let the flowers fall, childlike she felt the loss of them as an addition to her grief. The ravisher urged on his steeds, calling them each by name, and throwing loose over their heads and necks his iron-colored reins. When he reached the River Cyane, and it opposed his passage, he struck the riverbank with his trident, and the earth opened and gave him a passage to Tartarus.

Ceres sought her daughter all the world over. Bright-haired Aurora, when she came forth in the morning, and Hesperus, when he led out the stars in the evening, found her still busy in the search. But it was all unavailing. At length weary and sad, she sat down upon a stone, and continued sitting nine days and nights, in the open air, under the sunlight and moonlight and falling showers. It was where now stands the city of Eleusis, then the home of an old man named Celeus.

"Proserpine" from THE AGE OF THE FABLE; OR BEAUTIES OF MYTHOLOGY by Thomas Bullfinch. Boston: J. E. Tilton and Company, 1863.

He was out in the field, gathering acorns and blackberries, and sticks for his fire. His little girl was driving home their two goats, and as she passed the goddess, who appeared in the guise of an old woman, she said to her, "Mother"—and the name was sweet to the ears of Ceres—"why do you sit here alone upon the rocks?"

The old man also stopped, though his load was heavy, and begged her to come into his cottage, such as it was. She declined, and he urged her.

"Go in peace," she replied, "and be happy in your daughter; I have lost mine." As she spoke, tears—or something like tears, for the gods never weep—fell down her cheeks upon her bosom.

The compassionate old man and his child wept with her. Then said he, "Come with us, and despise not our humble roof; so may your daughter be restored to you in safety."

"Lead on," said she, "I cannot resist that appeal!" So she rose from the stone and went with them.

As they walked he told her that his only son, a little boy, lay very sick, feverish and sleepless. She stooped and gathered some poppies. As they entered the cottage, they found all in great distress, for the boy seemed past hope of recovery. Metanira, his mother, received her kindly, and the goddess stooped and kissed the lips of the sick child. Instantly the paleness left his face, and healthy vigor returned to his body.

The whole family were delighted—that is, the father, mother, and little girl, for they were all; they had no servants. They spread the table, and put upon it curds and cream, apples, and honey in the comb. While they ate, Ceres mingled poppy juice in the milk of the boy. When night came and all was still, she arose, and taking the sleeping boy, moulded his limbs with her hands, and uttered over him three times a solemn charm, then went and laid him in the ashes. His mother, who had been watching what her guest was doing, sprang forward with a cry and snatched the child from the fire. Then Ceres assumed her own form, and a divine splendor shone all around.

While they were overcome with astonishment, she said, "Mother, you have been cruel in your fondness to your son. I would have made him immortal, but you have frustrated my attempt. Nevertheless, he shall be great and useful. He shall teach men the use of the plough, and the rewards which labor can win from the cultivated soil." So saying, she wrapped a cloud about her, and mounting her chariot rode away.

Ceres continued her search for her daughter, passing from land to land, and across seas and rivers, till at length she returned to Sicily, whence she at first set out, and stood by the banks of the River Cyane, where Pluto made himself a passage with his prize to his own dominions. The river nymph would have told the goddess all she had witnessed, but dared not, for fear of Pluto; so she only ventured to take up the girdle which Proserpine had dropped in her flight, and waft it to the feet of the mother. Ceres, seeing this, was no longer in doubt of her loss, but she did not yet know the cause, and laid the blame on the innocent land.

"Ungrateful soil," said she, "which I have endowed with fertility and clothed with herbage and nourishing grain, no more shall you enjoy my favors."

Then the cattle died, the plough broke in the furrow, the seed failed to come up; there was too much sun, there was too much rain; the birds stole the seeds—thistles and brambles were the only growth.

Seeing this, the fountain Arethusa interceded for the land. "Goddess," said she, "blame not the land; it opened unwillingly to yield a passage to your daughter. I can tell you of her fate, for I have seen her. . . . While I passed through the lower parts of the earth, I saw your Proserpine. She was sad, but no longer showing alarm in her countenance. Her look was such as became a queen—the queen of Erebus; the powerful bride of the monarch of the realms of the dead."

When Ceres heard this, she stood for a while like one stupefied; then turned her chariot towards heaven, and hastened to present herself before the throne of Jove. She told the story of her bereavement, and implored Jupiter to interfere to procure the restitution of her daughter. Jupiter consented on one condition, namely, that Proserpine should not during her stay in the lower world have taken any food; otherwise, the Fates forbade her release. Accordingly, Mercury was sent, accompanied by Spring, to demand Proserpine of Pluto. The wily monarch consented; but alas! the maiden had taken a pomegranate which Pluto offered her, and had sucked the sweet pulp from a few of the seeds. This was enough to prevent her complete release; but a compromise was made, by which she was to pass half the time with her mother, and the rest with her husband Pluto.

Ceres allowed herself to be pacified with this arrangement, and restored the earth to her favor. Now she remembered Celeus and his family, and her promise to his infant son Triptolemus. When the boy grew up, she taught him the use of the plough, and how to sow the seed. She took him in her chariot, drawn by winged dragons, through all the countries of the earth, imparting to mankind valuable grains, and the knowledge of agriculture. After his return, Triptolemus built a magnificent temple to Ceres in Eleusis, and established the worship of the goddess, under the name of the Eleusinian mysteries, which, in the splendor and solemnity of their observance, surpassed all other religious celebrations among the Greeks.

Theseus and the Minotaur

The drama of the encounter with a monster is exciting in a tale that lends itself to dramatization.

Among the heroes who took part in the Calydonian Hunt, one of the bravest was Theseus. His father was the king of Athens, the greatest of all Greek cities. Theseus had many adventures during his life, but it was his meeting with a deadly monster called the Minotaur that gained him everlasting fame.

The Minotaur was a huge, bloodthirsty creature, half human and half bull. It lived far underground, in a special cave known as the Labyrinth, on the distant island of Crete.

Years before, the Athenians—the people of Athens—had fought a war with the people of Crete. The Athenians had lost the war. Afterward, to keep their city from being destroyed, they were forced to make a horrible bargain. They agreed that every nine years they would send a number of their finest young men and women to Crete. There the unhappy victims would be taken to the Labyrinth, which was so full of twists and turns that no one ever had escaped from it. Sooner or later the Minotaur would find them, lost and wandering in the cave, and would kill and eat them, one by one.

This already had happened several times over the years. Finally Theseus, now grown to manhood, decided that he would go to Crete and fight the monster. He and the other young Athenians sailed to the island. When they arrived, they were paraded through the streets before being taken to the cave.

Luckily, a young woman named Ariadne, the king's daughter, saw the parade of victims. She fell in love with Theseus and decided to help him. Since Theseus thought Ariadne was very beautiful, he promised to marry her if he succeeded in killing the Minotaur, and with her help, managed to escape from the Labyrinth.

Ariadne gave the hero a ball of string and told him what to do. When he entered the cave, Theseus obeyed her instructions. Unnoticed by the guards, he tied the end of the string to the door of the Labyrinth. Then he unwound the string as he and the other victims were taken deeper into the cave. Finally he and the others were left in the Labyrinth, to face the Minotaur.

Instead of waiting for the monster to appear, Theseus boldly went in search of it. Un-

"Theseus and the Minotaur" from MONSTER MYTHS OF ANCIENT GREECE by William Wise. Copyright © 1981 by William Wise. Reprinted by permission of G. P. Putnam's Sons and Curtis Brown, Ltd.

winding still more of the string, he wandered for a long time through the vast cave, expecting to meet his deadly enemy at every turn. Just as he was beginning to wonder if he would ever find the monster, Theseus stumbled into his den. As it happened, the huge creature was asleep, and the hero had his chance. With all of his strength, Theseus flung himself upon the monster, and before it could awaken fully, struck it a terrific blow on the jaw. Then, since he had no weapon, Theseus pinned the struggling monster to the floor of the cave and strangled it with his bare hands.

After that Theseus returned to his companions and they followed the string back to the entrance and made their escape. Ariadne was waiting outside the cave, and together they found a ship and fled from Crete, sailing to an island north of Crete called Naxos.

On the journey Ariadne became seasick, and after their arrival in Naxos, Theseus put her ashore to rest. He and his men returned to their ship to make some repairs. But while they were working, a sudden storm came up and drove them far across the seas. Many days passed before they were able to return to Naxos. When they did, they learned that Ariadne had died. So Theseus was forced to return to Athens without her, a heartbroken hero who had slain the Minotaur but lost his future bride.

Icarus and Daedalus

A poignant way of saying that pride goeth before a fall.

Among all those mortals who grew so wise that they learned the secrets of the gods, none was more cunning than Daedalus.

He once built, for King Minos of Crete, a wonderful Labyrinth of winding ways so cunningly tangled up and twisted around that,

"Icarus and Daedalus" from OLD GREEK FOLK STORIES TOLD ANEW by Josephine Preston. New York: Houghton Mifflin Company, 1897.

once inside, you could never find your way out again without a magic clue. But the king's favor veered with the wind, and one day he had his master architect imprisoned in a tower. Daedalus managed to escape from his cell; but it seemed impossible to leave the island, since every ship that came or went was well guarded by order of the king.

At length, watching the sea-gulls in the air —the only creatures that were sure of liberty —he thought of a plan for himself and his young son Icarus, who was captive with him.

Little by little, he gathered a store of feathers great and small. He fastened these together with thread, moulded them in with wax, and so fashioned two great wings like those of a bird. When they were done, Daedalus fitted them to his own shoulders, and after one or two efforts, he found that by waving his arms he could winnow the air and cleave it, as a swimmer does the sea. He held himself aloft, wavered this way and that with the wind, and at last, like a great fledgling, he learned to fly.

Without delay, he fell to work on a pair of wings for the boy Icarus, and taught him carefully how to use them, bidding him beware of rash adventures among the stars. "Remember," said the father, "never to fly very low or very high, for the fogs about the earth would weigh you down, but the blaze of the sun will surely melt your feathers apart if you go too near."

For Icarus, these cautions went in at one ear and out by the other. Who could remember to be careful when he was to fly for the first time? Are birds careful? Not they! And not an idea remained in the boy's head but the one joy of escape.

The day came, and the fair wind that was to set them free. The father bird put on his wings, and, while the light urged them to be gone, he waited to see that all was well with Icarus, for the two could not fly hand in hand. Up they rose, the boy after his father. The hateful ground of Crete sank beneath them; and the country folk, who caught a glimpse of them when they were high above the treetops, took it for a vision of the gods—Apollo, perhaps, with Cupid after him.

At first there was a terror in the joy. The wide vacancy of the air dazed them—a glance downward made their brains reel. But when a great wind filled their wings, and Icarus felt himself sustained, like a halcyon-bird in the hollow of a wave, like a child uplifted by his mother, he forgot everything in the world but joy. He forgot Crete and the other islands that he had passed over: he saw but vaguely that winged thing in the distance before him that was his father Daedalus. He longed for one draught of flight to quench the thirst of his captivity: he stretched out his arms to the sky and made towards the highest heavens.

Alas for him! Warmer and warmer grew the air. Those arms, that had seemed to uphold him, relaxed. His wings wavered, drooped. He fluttered his young hands vainly —he was falling—and in that terror he remembered. The heat of the sun had melted the wax from his wings; the feathers were falling, one by one, like snowflakes; and there was none to help.

He fell like a leaf tossed down the wind, down, down, with one cry that overtook Daedalus far away. When he returned, and sought high and low for the poor boy, he saw nothing but the bird-like feathers afloat on the water, and he knew that Icarus was drowned.

The nearest island he named Icaria, in memory of the child; but he, in heavy grief, went to the temple of Apollo in Sicily, and there hung up his wings as an offering. Never again did he attempt to fly.

Atalanta's Race

Venus intervenes on behalf of a lover, in a myth more romantic than most.

Even if Prince Meleager had lived, it is doubtful if he could ever have won Atalanta to be his wife. The maiden was resolved to live unwed, and at last she devised a plan to be rid of all her suitors. She was known far and wide as the swiftest runner of her time; and so she said that she would only marry that man who could outstrip her in the race, but that all who dared to try and failed must be put to death.

This threat did not dishearten all of the suitors, however, and to her grief, for she was not cruel, they held her to her promise. On a certain day the few bold men who were to try their fortune made ready, and chose young Hippomenes as judge. He sat watching them before the word was given, and sadly wondered that any brave man should risk his life merely to win a bride. But when Atalanta stood ready for the contest, he was amazed by her beauty. She looked like Hebe, goddess of young health, who is a glad serving-maiden to the gods when they sit at feast.

The signal was given, and, as she and the suitors darted away, flight made her more enchanting than ever. Just as a wind brings sparkles to the water and laughter to the trees, haste fanned her loveliness to a glow.

Alas for the suitors! She ran as if Hermes had lent her his wingèd sandals. The young men, skilled as they were, grew heavy with weariness and despair. For all their efforts, they seemed to lag like ships in a calm, while Atalanta flew before them in some favoring breeze—and reached the goal!

To the sorrow of all on-lookers, the suitors were led away; but the judge himself, Hippomenes, rose and begged leave to try his fortune. As Atalanta listened, and looked at him, her heart was filled with pity, and she would willingly have let him win the race to save him from defeat and death; for he was comely and younger than the others. But her friends urged her to rest and make ready, and she consented, with an unwilling heart.

Meanwhile Hippomenes prayed within himself to Venus: "Goddess of Love, give ear, and send me good speed. Let me be swift to win as I have been swift to love her."

Now Venus, who was not far off—for she had already moved the heart of Hippomenes

"Atalanta's Race" from OLD GREEK FOLK STORIES TOLD ANEW by Josephine Preston. New York: Houghton Mifflin Company, 1897.

to love—came to his side invisibly, slipped into his hand three wondrous golden apples, and whispered a word of counsel in his ear.

The signal was given; youth and maiden started over the course. They went so like the wind that they left not a footprint. The people cheered on Hippomenes, eager that such valor should win. But the course was long, and soon fatigue seemed to clutch at his throat, the light shook before his eyes, and, even as he pressed on, the maiden passed him by.

At that instant Hippomenes tossed ahead one of the golden apples. The rolling bright thing caught Atalanta's eye, and full of wonder she stooped to pick it up. Hippomenes ran on. As he heard the flutter of her tunic close behind him, he flung aside another golden apple, and another moment was lost to the girl. Who could pass by such a marvel? The goal was near and Hippomenes was ahead, but once again Atalanta caught up with him, and they sped side by side like two dragon-flies. For an instant his heart failed him; then, with a last prayer to Venus, he flung down the last apple. The maiden glanced at it, wavered, and would have left it where it had fallen, had not Venus turned her head for a second and given her a sudden wish to possess it. Against her will she turned to pick up the golden apple, and Hippomenes touched the goal.

So he won that perilous maiden; and as for Atalanta, she was glad to marry such a valorous man. By this time she understood so well what it was like to be pursued, that she had lost a little of her pleasure in hunting.

The Trojan War

Most children remember this myth for the incident of the Trojan horse, but they enjoy the complexity and action of the longer narrative.

When Peleus, one of the heroes of the Argonautic Expedition, was married to Thetis, the loveliest of the Nereides, all the gods and goddesses were invited to the wedding feast with the exception of Eris, goddess of Discord. Enraged at the slight, she threw a golden apple among the guests, which bore the inscription: "For the fairest."

Juno, Venus and Minerva each claimed the apple, and soon were quarreling bitterly. Jupiter was not willing to decide in so delicate a matter, and he sent the goddesses to Mount Ida, where the beautiful shepherd Paris, the son of Priam, King of Troy, was tending his flocks. He asked Paris to make the decision. The goddesses gathered around him, extolling their own charms, and each one promised to reward him if he gave her the prize. Juno promised him power and riches; Minerva told him that she would see that he gained glory and renown; and Venus whispered that he should have the fairest woman in the world for his wife. Paris decided in favor of Venus and gave her the golden apple, thus making the two other goddesses his enemies.

Under the protection of Venus, Paris sailed for Greece, where he was hospitably received by Menelaus, king of Sparta. Now Helena, the wife of Menelaus, was the very woman whom Venus had destined for Paris. She was the most beautiful woman in the world, and had been sought as a bride by hundreds of suitors. The young men loved her so devotedly that they swore that no matter which of them she chose to wed, the others would defend her from harm all her life. She married Menelaus and was living with him happily when Paris became their guest.

Paris, aided by Venus, persuaded her to elope with him, and carried her to Troy. Overcome by grief, Menelaus called upon his brother chieftains of Greece to fulfill their pledges and join him in his efforts to recover his wife. Only one of them held back. His name was Ulysses, and he had married a woman named Penelope and was happy with his wife and child. He had no wish to embark on such a troublesome affair. Palamedes, one of his friends, was sent to beg him

to join the quest, and when he arrived at Ithaca where Ulysses lived, Ulysses pretended to be mad. Seeing Palamedes approaching, he hastily yoked an ass and an ox together to the plough and began to sow salt. Palamedes, suspecting a ruse, placed Ulysses' child before the plough, whereupon the father turned the plough aside, showing plainly that he was no madman. After that, he could no longer refuse to fulfill his promise.

Now, although Paris was the son of Priam, king of Troy, he had been brought up in obscurity, as the oracle had prophesied that he would one day be the ruin of the state. And with his entrance into Troy with Helena, these forebodings seemed likely to be realized. The army which was being assembled in Greece was the greatest that had ever been known. Agamemnon, brother of Menelaus, was chosen as commander-in-chief. Achilles was their most illustrious warrior. After him, ranked Ajax, who was gigantic in size and had great courage, though he was dull in intellect. Diomedes was enlisted, a man who had all the qualities of a hero. There was Ulysses, famous for his sagacity, and Nestor, the oldest of the Grecian chiefs.

Troy was no feeble enemy. Priam the king was now an old man, but he had been a wise ruler and had strengthened his state by good government at home and numerous alliances with his neighbors. The principal stay and support of his throne was his son Hector. He was a brave, noble young man, and he felt a presentiment of danger, when he realized the great wrong his brother Paris had done in bringing Helena back to Troy. He knew that he must fight for his family and country, yet he was sick with grief at the foolish circumstances that had set hero against hero. He was married to Andromache. The principal leaders on the side of the Trojans were, besides Hector, Aeneas, Deiphobus, Glaucus, and Sarpedon.

After two years of preparation, the Greek fleet and army assembled in the port of Aulis. Here they suffered more delays; pestilence broke out in the camps, and there was no wind to fill their sails. Eventually, they set out for the coast of Troy, and plunged at once into a battle with the Trojans. For nine years they fought, neither side winning over the other. The Greeks began to despair of ever conquering the city, and decided to resort to a trick. They pretended to be making ready to abandon the siege, and most of the ships set sail with many warriors on board. They did not head for home, but sailed to a nearby island where they hid in the friendly harbor. The Greeks who were left in the camp built a huge horse of wood, which they said was to be a peace offering to Minerva. They filled it with armed men, instead, and left it in their camp. The remaining Greeks then sailed away.

When the Trojans saw that the encampment had broken up and the fleet had gone, they threw open the gates to the city, and everyone rushed forth to look at the abandoned camp grounds. They found the immense horse and wondered what it could be. Some thought it should be carried back to the city and put on exhibition as a trophy of the war, but others, more cautious, were afraid of it. Laocoon, the priest of Neptune, tried to warn them against it. "What madness, citizens, is this?" he exclaimed. "Have you not learned enough of Grecian fraud to be on your guard against it? For my part, I fear the Greeks even when they offer gifts."

As he spoke, he threw his lance at the horse's side. It struck, and a hollow sound like a groan came forth from it. The people were almost ready to take his advice and destroy the horse, when a group appeared dragging a young man with them. He appeared to be a Greek prisoner, and he was brought before the Trojan chiefs. They promised him that they would spare his life on one condition; he was to answer truly the questions they asked him.

He told them that he was a Greek named Sinon, and that he had been abandoned by his countrymen, betrayed by Ulysses, for a trifling offense. He assured them that the wooden horse had been made as an offering to Minerva, and that the Greeks had made it so huge to prevent its being carried into the city. Sinon added that the Greeks had been told that if the Trojans took possession of the horse, the Greeks would lose the war.

Then the people began to think of how they could move the enormous horse into the city. And, suddenly, they saw two immense serpents advancing from the sea. They crawled up on the shore, and the crowd fled in all directions. The serpents slithered to the spot where Laocoon stood with his two sons. First they attacked the children, crushing their bodies and breathing their pestilential breath into the boys' faces. Laocoon tried to drag his children away, and the serpents wound their bodies around his. He struggled pitifully to free himself, but they soon strangled him and his two sons. In awe, the people crept back to the camp. Talking among themselves, they decided that the gods had taken revenge on Laocoon for talking against the wooden horse, which was a sacred object. And they began to move it into the city in triumph. All day, the Trojans feasted and sang around the horse which they had placed in the main square of Troy. At last, exhausted from the festivities, they went to their homes and fell into their beds.

When the city was quiet, the armed men who were hidden in the body of the horse, were let out by Sinon. They stole to the gates of the city which were closed for the night, and let in their friends who had returned under the cover of darkness. They set fire to the city, and the people, overcome with feasting and sleep, were ruthlessly killed. Troy had fallen.

King Priam was the last to be slain, and he fought bravely to the end.

Menelaus hastened to the palace and found his wife, Helena. And not even the powers of Venus could save Paris from the wrath of his enemies. He was killed, and Menelaus carried his wife safely back to Sparta.

Pegasus and the Chimæra

The eternal conflict between good and evil is evident in this myth of the monster and the winged horse.

When Perseus cut off Medusa's head, the blood sinking into the earth produced the winged horse Pegasus. Minerva caught and tamed him, and presented him to the Muses. The fountain Hippocrene, on the Muses' mountain Helicon, was opened by a kick from his hoof.

The Chimæra was a fearful monster, breathing fire. The fore part of its body was a compound of the lion and the goat, and the hind part a dragon's. It made great havoc in Lycia, so that the king Iobates sought for some hero to destroy it. At that time there arrived at his court a gallant young warrior, whose name was Bellerophon. He brought letters from Prœtus, the son-in-law of Iobates, recommending Bellerophon in the warmest terms as an unconquerable hero, but added at the close a request to his father-in-law to put him to death. The reason was that Prœtus was jealous of him, suspecting that his wife Antea looked with too much admiration on the young warrior. (From this instance of Bellerophon being unconsciously the bearer of his own death-warrant, the expression "Bellerophontic letters" arose, to describe any species of communication which a person is made the bearer of, containing matter prejudicial to himself.)

Iobates, on perusing the letters, was puzzled what to do, not willing to violate the claims of hospitality, yet wishing to oblige his son-in-law. A lucky thought occurred to him, to send Bellerophon to combat with the Chimæra. Bellerophon accepted the proposal, but before proceeding to the combat consulted the soothsayer Polyidus, who advised him to procure if possible the horse Pegasus for the conflict. For this purpose he directed him to pass the night in the temple of Minerva. He did so, and as he slept Minerva came to him and gave him a golden bridle. When he awoke the bridle remained in his hand. Minerva also showed him Pegasus drinking at the well of Pirene, and at sight of the bridle, the winged steed came willingly and suffered himself to be taken. Bellerophon mounted him, rose with him into the air, soon found the Chimæra, and gained an easy victory over the monster.

After the conquest of the Chimæra, Bellerophon was exposed to further trials and labors by his unfriendly host, but by the aid of Pegasus he triumphed in them all; till at length Iobates, seeing that the hero was a special favorite of the gods, gave him his daughter in marriage and made him his successor on the throne. At last Bellerophon by his pride and presumption drew upon himself the anger of the gods; it is said he even attempted to fly up into heaven on his winged steed; but Jupiter sent a gadfly which stung Pegasus and made him throw his rider, who became lame and blind in consequence. After this Bellerophon wandered lonely through the Aleian field, avoiding the paths of men, and died miserably.

The Golden Touch

The introduction of dialogue makes this version by Nathaniel Hawthorne of a favorite myth more vivid.

Once upon a time, there lived a very rich king whose name was Midas; and he had a little daughter, whom nobody but myself ever heard of, and whose name was Marygold.

This King Midas was fonder of gold than of anything else in the world. He valued his royal crown chiefly because it was composed of that precious metal. If he loved anything better, or half so well, it was the one little maiden who played so merrily around her father's footstool. But the more Midas loved his daughter, the more did he desire and seek for wealth. He thought, foolish man! that the best thing he could possibly do for this dear child would be to bequeath her the immensest pile of yellow, glistening coin, that had ever been heaped together since the world was made. Thus, he gave all his thoughts and all his time to this one purpose. If ever he happened to gaze for an instant at the gold-tinted clouds of sunset, he wished that they were real gold, and that they could be squeezed safely into his strong box. When little Marygold ran to meet him, with a bunch of buttercups and dandelions, he used to say, "Poh, poh, child! If these flowers were as golden as they look, they would be worth the plucking!"

And yet, in his earlier days, before he was so entirely possessed of this insane desire for riches, King Midas had shown a great taste for flowers. He had planted a garden, in which grew the biggest and beautifullest and sweetest roses that any mortal ever saw or smelt. These roses were still growing in the garden, as large, as lovely, and as fragrant, as when Midas used to pass whole hours in gazing at them, and inhaling their perfume. But now, if he looked at them at all, it was only to calculate how much the garden would be worth if each of the innumerable rose-petals were a thin plate of gold. And though he once was fond of music the only music for poor Midas, now, was the chink of one coin against another.

At length Midas had got to be so exceedingly unreasonable, that he could scarcely

"Pegasus and the Chimæra" from THE AGE OF FABLE; OR BEAUTIES OF MYTHOLOGY by Thomas Bullfinch. Boston: J. E. Tilton and Company, 1863.

"The Golden Touch" from A WONDER BOOK FOR GIRLS AND BOYS by Nathaniel Hawthorne.

bear to see or touch any object that was not gold. He made it his custom, therefore, to pass a large portion of every day in a dark and dreary apartment, under ground, at the basement of his palace. It was here that he kept his wealth. To this dismal hole—for it was little better than a dungeon—Midas betook himself, whenever he wanted to be particularly happy. Here, after carefully locking the door, he would take a bag of gold coin, or a gold cup as big as a washbowl, or a heavy golden bar, or a peck-measure of gold-dust, and bring them from the obscure corners of the room into the one bright and narrow sunbeam that fell from the dungeon-like window. He valued the sunbeam for no other reason but that his treasure would not shine without its help. And then would he reckon over the coins in the bag, toss up the bar, and catch it as it came down; sift the gold-dust through his fingers; look at the funny image of his own face, as reflected in the burnished circumference of the cup; and whisper to himself, "O Midas, rich King Midas, what a happy man art thou!"

Midas was enjoying himself in his treasure-room, one day, as usual, when he perceived a shadow fall over the heaps of gold; and, looking suddenly up, what should he behold but the figure of a stranger, standing in the bright and narrow sunbeam! It was a young man, with a cheerful and ruddy face. Whether it was that the imagination of King Midas threw a yellow tinge over everything, or whatever the cause might be, he could not help fancying that the smile with which the stranger regarded him had a kind of golden radiance in it. Certainly, although his figure intercepted the sunshine, there was now a brighter gleam upon all the piled-up treasure than before. Even the remotest corners had their share of it, and were lighted up, when the stranger smiled, as with tips of flame and sparkles of fire.

As Midas knew that he had carefully turned the key in the lock, and that no mortal strength could possibly break into his treasure-room, he, of course, concluded that his visitor must be something more than mortal. Midas had met such beings before now, and

was not sorry to meet one of them again.

The stranger gazed about the room; and when his lustrous smile had glistened upon all the golden objects that were there, he turned again to Midas.

"You are a wealthy man, friend Midas!" he observed. "I doubt whether any other four walls, on earth, contain so much gold as you have contrived to pile up in this room."

"I have done pretty well—pretty well," answered Midas, in a discontented tone. "But, after all, it is but a trifle, when you consider that it has taken me my whole life to get it together. If one could live a thousand years, he might have time to grow rich!"

"What!" exclaimed the stranger. "Then you are not satisfied?"

Midas shook his head.

"And pray what would satisfy you?" asked the stranger. "Merely for the curiosity of the thing, I should be glad to know."

Midas paused and meditated. He felt a presentiment that this stranger, with such a golden lustre in his good-humored smile, had come hither with both the power and the purpose of gratifying his utmost wishes. Now, therefore, was the fortunate moment, when he had but to speak, and obtain whatever possible, or seemingly impossible thing, it might come into his head to ask. So he thought, and thought, and thought, and heaped up one golden mountain upon another, in his imagination, without being able to imagine them big enough. At last, a bright idea occurred to King Midas. It seemed really as bright as the glistening metal which he loved so much.

Raising his head, he looked the lustrous stranger in the face.

"Well, Midas," observed his visitor, "I see that you have at length hit upon something that will satisfy you. Tell me your wish."

"It is only this," replied Midas. "I am weary of collecting my treasures with so much trouble, and beholding the heap so diminutive, after I have done my best. I wish everything that I touch be changed to gold!"

The stranger's smile grew so very broad, that it seemed to fill the room like an outburst of the sun, gleaming into a shadowy dell, where the yellow autumnal leaves—for so looked the lumps and particles of gold—lie strewn in the glow of light.

"The Golden Touch!" exclaimed he. "You certainly deserve credit, friend Midas, for striking out so brilliant a conception. But are you quite sure that this will satisfy you?"

"How could it fail?" said Midas.

"And will you never regret the possession of it?"

"What could induce me?" asked Midas. "I ask nothing else, to render me perfectly happy."

"Be it as you wish, then," replied the stranger, waving his hand in token of farewell. "Tomorrow, at sunrise, you will find yourself gifted with the Golden Touch."

The figure of the stranger then became exceedingly bright, and Midas involuntarily closed his eyes. On opening them again, he beheld only one yellow sunbeam in the room, and all around him, the glistening of the precious metal which he had spent his life in hoarding up.

Whether Midas slept as usual that night, the story does not say. At any rate, day had hardly peeped over the hills, when King Midas was broad awake, and stretching his arms out of bed, began to touch the objects that were within reach. He was anxious to prove whether the Golden Touch had really come, according to the stranger's promise. So he laid his finger on a chair by the bedside, and on various other things, but was grievously disappointed to perceive that they remained of exactly the same substance as before. Indeed, he felt very much afraid that he had only dreamed about the lustrous stranger, or else that the latter had been making game of him. And what a miserable affair would it be, if after all his hopes, Midas must content himself with what little gold he could scrape together by ordinary means, instead of creating it by a touch!

All this while, it was only the gray of the morning, with but a streak of brightness along the edge of the sky, where Midas could not see it. He lay in a very disconsolate mood, regretting the downfall of his hopes, and kept growing sadder and sadder, until the earliest sunbeam shone through the window, and gilded the ceiling over his head. It seemed to Midas that this bright yellow sunbeam was reflected in rather a singular way on the white covering of the bed. Looking more closely, what was his astonishment and delight, when he found that this linen fabric had been transmuted to what seemed a woven texture of the purest and brightest gold! The Golden Touch had come to him with the first sunbeam!

Midas started up, in a kind of joyful frenzy, and ran about the room, grasping at everything that happened to be in his way. He seized one of the bed-posts, and it became immediately a fluted golden pillar. He pulled aside a window-curtain, in order to admit a clear spectacle of the wonders which he was performing; and the tassel grew heavy in his hand,—a mass of gold. He took up a book from the table. At his first touch, it assumed the appearance of such a splendidly bound and gilt-edged volume as one often meets with, nowadays; but, on running his fingers through the leaves, behold! It was a bundle of thin golden plates, in which all the wisdom of the book had grown illegible. He hurriedly put on his clothes, and was enraptured to see himself in a magnificent suit of gold cloth, which retained its flexibility and softness, although it burdened him a little with its weight. He drew out his handkerchief, which little Marygold had hemmed for him. That was likewise gold, with the dear child's neat and pretty stitches running all along the border, in gold thread!

Somehow or other, this last transformation did not quite please King Midas. He would rather that his little daughter's handiwork should have remained just the same as when she climbed his knee and put it into his hand.

But it was not worth while to vex himself about a trifle. Midas now took his spectacles from his pocket, and put them on his nose, in order that he might see more distinctly what he was about. In those days, spectacles for common people had not been invented, but were already worn by kings; else, how could Midas have had any? To his great perplexity, however, excellent as the glasses were, he discovered that he could not possibly see through them. But this was the most natural thing in the world; for, on taking them off, the transparent crystals turned out to be plates of yellow metal, and, of course, were worthless as spectacles, though valuable as gold. It struck Midas as rather inconvenient that, with all his wealth, he could never again be rich enough to own a pair of serviceable spectacles.

"It is no great matter, nevertheless," said he to himself, very philosophically. "We cannot expect any great good, without its being accompanied with some small inconvenience. The Golden Touch is worth the sacrifice of a pair of spectacles, at least, if not of one's very eyesight. My own eyes will serve for ordinary purposes, and little Marygold will soon be old enough to read to me."

King Midas went down stairs, and smiled, on observing that the balustrade of the staircase became a bar of burnished gold, as his hand passed over it, in his descent. He lifted the door-latch (it was brass only a moment ago, but golden when his fingers quitted it), and emerged into the garden. Here, as it happened, he found a great number of beautiful roses in full bloom, and others in all the stages of lovely bud and blossom. Very delicious was their fragrance in the morning breeze. Their delicate blush was one of the fairest sights in the world; so gentle, so modest, and so full of sweet tranquillity, did these roses seem to be.

But Midas knew a way to make them far more precious, according to his way of thinking, than roses had ever been before. So he took great pains in going from bush to bush, and exercised his magic touch most indefatigably; until every individual flower and bud, and even the worms at the heart of some of them, were changed to gold. By the time this good work was completed, King Midas was summoned to breakfast; and as the morning air had given him an excellent appetite, he made haste back to the palace.

On this particular morning, the breakfast consisted of hot cakes, some nice little brooktrout, roasted potatoes, fresh boiled eggs, and coffee, for King Midas himself, and a bowl of bread and milk for his daughter Marygold.

Little Marygold had not yet made her appearance. Her father ordered her to be called, and, seating himself at table, awaited the child's coming, in order to begin his own breakfast. To do Midas justice, he really loved his daughter, and loved her so much the more this morning, on account of the good fortune which had befallen him. It was not a great while before he heard her coming along the passageway crying bitterly. This circumstance surprised him, because Marygold was one of the cheerfullest little people whom you would see in a summer's day, and hardly shed a thimbleful of tears in a twelvemonth. When Midas heard her sobs, he determined to put little Marygold in better spirits, by an agreeable surprise; so, leaning across the table, he touched his daughter's bowl (which was a China one, with pretty figures all around it), and transmuted it to gleaming gold.

Meanwhile, Marygold slowly and disconsolately opened the door, and showed herself with her apron at her eyes, still sobbing as if her heart would break.

"How now, my little lady!" cried Midas. "Pray what is the matter with you, this bright morning?"

Marygold, without taking the apron from her eyes, held out her hand, in which was one of the roses which Midas had so recently transmuted.

"Beautiful!" exclaimed her father. "And what is there in this magnificent golden rose to make you cry?"

"Ah, dear father!" answered the child, as well as her sobs would let her; "it is not beautiful, but the ugliest flower that ever grew! As soon as I was dressed I ran into the garden to gather some roses for you; because I know you like them. But, oh dear, dear me! What do you think has happened? Such a misfortune! All the beautiful roses, that smelled so sweetly and had so many lovely blushes, are blighted and spoilt! They are grown quite yellow, as you see this one, and have no longer any fragrance! What can have been the matter with them?"

"Poh, my dear little girl—pray don't cry about it!" said Midas, who was ashamed to confess that he himself had wrought the change which so greatly afflicted her. "Sit down and eat your bread and milk! You will find it easy enough to exchange a golden rose like that (which will last hundreds of years) for an ordinary one which would wither in a day."

"I don't care for such roses as this!" cried Marygold, tossing it contemptuously away. "It has no smell, and the hard petals prick my nose!"

The child now sat down to table, but was so occupied with her grief for the blighted roses that she did not even notice the wonderful transmutation of her China bowl. Perhaps this was all the better; for Marygold was accustomed to take pleasure in looking at the queer figures, and strange trees and houses, that were painted on the circumference of the bowl; and these ornaments were now entirely lost in the yellow hue of the metal.

Midas, meanwhile, had poured out a cup of coffee, and, as a matter of course, the coffee-pot, whatever metal it may have been when he took it up, was gold when he set it down. He thought to himself, that it was rather an extravagant style of splendor, in a king of his simple habits, to breakfast off a service of gold, and began to be puzzled with the difficulty of keeping his treasures safe. The cupboard and the kitchen would no longer be a secure place of deposit for articles so valuable as golden bowls and coffee-pots.

Amid these thoughts, he lifted a spoonful of coffee to his lips, and, sipping it, was astonished to perceive that, the instant his lips touched the liquid, it became molten gold, and, the next moment, hardened into a lump!

"Ha!" exclaimed Midas, rather aghast.

"What is the matter, father?" asked little Marygold, gazing at him, with the tears still standing in her eyes.

"Nothing, child, nothing!" said Midas. "Eat your milk, before it gets quite cold."

He took one of the nice little trouts on his plate, and, by way of experiment, touched its tail with his finger. To his horror, it was immediately transmuted from an admirably fried brook-trout into a gold-fish. A very

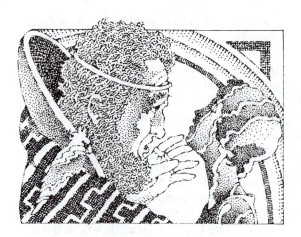

pretty piece of work, as you may suppose; only King Midas, just at that moment, would much rather have had a real trout in his dish than this elaborate and valuable imitation of one.

"I don't quite see," thought he to himself, "how I am to get any breakfast!"

He took one of the smoking-hot cakes, and had scarcely broken it, when, to his cruel mortification, though, a moment before, it had been of the whitest wheat, it assumed the yellow hue of Indian meal. Almost in despair, he helped himself to a boiled egg, which immediately underwent a change similar to those of the trout and the cake. The egg, indeed, might have been mistaken for one of those which the famous goose, in the story-book, was in the habit of laying; but King Midas was the only goose that had had anything to do with the matter.

"Well, this is a quandary!" thought he, leaning back in his chair, and looking quite enviously at little Marygold, who was now eating her bread and milk with great satisfaction. "Such a costly breakfast before me, and nothing that can be eaten."

Hoping that, by dint of great dispatch, he might avoid what he now felt to be a considerable inconvenience, King Midas next snatched a hot potato, and attempted to cram it into his mouth, and swallow it in a hurry. But the Golden Touch was too nimble for him. He found his mouth full, not of mealy potato, but of solid metal, which so burnt his tongue that he roared aloud, and, jumping up from the table, began to dance and stamp about the room, both with pain and affright.

"Father, dear father!" cried little Marygold, who was a very affectionate child, "pray what is the matter? Have you burnt your mouth?"

"Ah, dear child," groaned Midas, dolefully, "I don't know what is to become of your poor father!"

Already, at breakfast, Midas was excessively hungry. Would he be less so by dinnertime? And how ravenous would be his appetite for supper, which must undoubtedly consist of the same sort of indigestible dishes as those now before him.

These reflections so troubled wise King Midas, that he began to doubt whether, after all, riches are the one desirable thing in the world. But this was only a passing thought. So fascinated was Midas with the glitter of the yellow metal, that he would still have refused to give up the Golden Touch for so paltry a consideration as a breakfast.

Nevertheless, so great was his hunger, and the perplexity of his situation, that he again groaned aloud, and very grievously too. Our pretty Marygold could endure it no longer. She sat, a moment, gazing at her father, and trying, with all the might of her little wits, to find out what was the matter with him. Then, with a sweet and sorrowful impulse to comfort him, she started from her chair, and, running to Midas, threw her arms affectionately about his knees. He bent down and kissed her. He felt that his little daughter's love was worth a thousand times more than he had gained by the Golden Touch.

"My precious, precious Marygold!" cried he.

But Marygold made no answer.

Alas, what had he done? The moment the lips of Midas touched Marygold's forehead, a change had taken place. Her sweet, rosy face, so full of affection as it had been, assumed a glittering yellow color, with yellow tear-drops, congealing on her cheeks. Her beautiful brown ringlets took the same tint. Her soft and tender little form grew hard and inflexible within her father's encircling arms. Oh, terrible misfortune! The victim of his insatiable desire for wealth, little Marygold was a human child no longer, but a golden statue!

Yes, there she was, with the questioning look of love, grief, and pity, hardened into her face. It was the prettiest and most woeful sight that ever mortal saw. All the features and tokens of Marygold were there; even the beloved little dimple remained in her golden chin. But, the more perfect was the resemblance, the greater was the father's agony at beholding this golden image, which was all that was left him of a daughter. It had been a favorite phrase of Midas, whenever he felt particularly fond of the child, to say that she was worth her weight in gold. And now the phrase had become literally true. And now, at last, when it was too late, he felt how infinitely a warm and tender heart, that loved him, exceeded in value all the wealth that could be piled up betwixt the earth and sky!

Midas, in the fulness of all his gratified desires, began to wring his hands and bemoan himself; and now he could neither bear to look at Marygold, nor yet to look away from her. Except when his eyes were fixed on the image, he could not possibly believe that she was changed to gold. But, stealing another glance, there was the precious little figure, with a yellow tear-drop on its yellow cheek, and a look so piteous and tender, that it seemed as if that very expression must needs soften the gold, and make it flesh again. This, however, could not be.

While Midas was in this tumult of despair, he suddenly beheld a stranger standing near the door. Midas bent down his head, without speaking; for he recognized the same figure which had appeared to him, the day before, in the treasure-room, and had bestowed on him this disastrous faculty of the Golden Touch. The stranger's countenance still wore a smile, which seemed to shed a yellow lustre all about the room, and gleamed on little Marygold's image, and on the other objects that had been transmuted by the touch of Midas.

"Well, friend Midas," said the stranger, "pray how do you succeed with the Golden Touch?"

Midas shook his head.

"I am very miserable," said he.

"Very miserable, indeed!" exclaimed the stranger. "And how happens that? Have I not faithfully kept my promise with you? Have you not everything that your heart desired?"

"Gold is not everything," answered Midas. "And I have lost all that my heart really cared for."

"Ah! So you have made a discovery, since yesterday?" observed the stranger. "Let us see, then. Which of these two things do you think is really worth the most,—the gift of the Golden Touch, or one cup of clear cold water?"

"O blessed water!" exclaimed Midas. "It will never moisten my parched throat again!"

"The Golden Touch," continued the stranger, "or a crust of bread?"

"A piece of bread," answered Midas, "is worth all the gold on earth!"

"The Golden Touch," asked the stranger, "or your own little Marygold, warm, soft, and loving as she was an hour ago?"

"Oh, my child, my dear child!" cried poor Midas, wringing his hands. "I would not have given that one small dimple in her chin for the power of changing this whole big earth into a solid lump of gold!"

"You are wiser than you were, King Midas!" said the stranger, looking seriously at him. "Your own heart, I perceive, has not been entirely changed from flesh to gold. Were it so, your case would indeed be desperate. But you appear to be still capable of understanding that the commonest things, such as lie within everybody's grasp, are more valuable than the riches which so many mortals sigh and struggle after. Tell me, now, do you sincerely desire to rid yourself of this Golden Touch?"

"It is hateful to me!" replied Midas.

A fly settled on his nose, but immediately fell to the floor; for it, too, had become gold. Midas shuddered.

"Go, then," said the stranger, "and plunge into the river that glides past the bottom of your garden. Take likewise a vase of the same water, and sprinkle it over any object that you may desire to change back again from gold into its former substance. If you do this in earnestness and sincerity, it may possibly repair the mischief which your avarice has occasioned."

King Midas bowed low; and when he lifted his head, the lustrous stranger had vanished.

You will easily believe that Midas lost no time in snatching up a great earthen pitcher (but, alas me! it was no longer earthen after he touched it), and hastening to the riverside. As he scampered along, and forced his way through the shrubbery, it was positively marvellous to see how the foliage turned yellow behind him, as if the autumn had been there, and nowhere else. On reaching the river's brink, he plunged headlong in, without waiting so much as to pull off his shoes.

"Poof! poof! poof!" snorted King Midas, as his head emerged out of the water. "Well, this is really a refreshing bath, and I think it must have quite washed away the Golden Touch. And now for filling my pitcher!"

As he dipped the pitcher into the water, it gladdened his very heart to see it change from gold into the same good, honest earthen vessel which it had been before he touched it. He was conscious, also, of a change within himself. A cold, hard, and heavy weight seemed to have gone out of his bosom. Perceiving a violet, that grew on the bank of the river, Midas touched it with his finger, and was overjoyed to find that the delicate flower retained its purple hue, instead of undergoing a yellow blight. The curse of the Golden Touch had, therefore, really been removed from him.

King Midas hastened back to the palace; and, I suppose, the servants knew not what to make of it when they saw their royal master so carefully bringing home an earthen pitcher of water. But that water, which was to undo all the mischief that his folly had wrought, was more precious to Midas than an ocean of molten gold could have been. The first thing he did, as you need hardly be told, was to sprinkle it by handfuls over the golden figure of little Marygold.

No sooner did it fall on her than you would have laughed to see how the rosy color came back to the dear child's cheek! And how she began to sneeze and sputter!—and how astonished she was to find herself dripping wet, and her father still throwing more water over her!

"Pray do not, dear father!" cried she. "See how you have wet my nice frock, which I put on only this morning!"

For Marygold did not know that she had been a little golden statue; nor could she remember anything that had happened since the moment when she ran with outstretched arms to comfort poor King Midas.

Her father did not think it necessary to tell his beloved child how very foolish he had been, but contented himself with showing how much wiser he had now grown. For this purpose, he led little Marygold into the garden, where he sprinkled all the remainder of the water over the rosebushes, and with such good effect that above five thousand roses recovered their beautiful bloom. There were two circumstances, however, which as long as he lived, used to put King Midas in mind of the Golden Touch. One was, that the sands of the river sparkled like gold; the other, that little Marygold's hair had now a golden tinge, which he had never observed in it before she had been transmuted by the effect of his kiss.

When King Midas had grown quite an old man, and used to trot Marygold's children on his knee, he was fond of telling them this marvellous story, pretty much as I have now told it to you. And then would he stroke their glossy ringlets, and tell them that their hair, likewise, had a rich shade of gold, which they had inherited from their mother.

"And to tell you the truth, my precious little folks," quoth King Midas, diligently trotting the children all the while, "ever since that morning, I have hated the very sight of all other gold, save this!"

Norse Myths

 Like the cold and often harsh lands from which the Norse myths come, the stories of the Norse gods are often somber and foreboding when compared to the mythology of Greece and Rome, and more filled with death and darkness. They were preserved orally and first written down in Iceland, where an isolated people kept to the old language and revered the original tales, the *Prose Edda* and the *Poetic Edda* from which the tales we know in translation were taken. The *Prose Edda* was collected by an Icelander, Snorri Sturluson, in the thirteenth century, and it is from the first book in this collection, "The Beguiling of Gylfi," that the best-known Norse myths come.

Asgard and the Gods

Despite its intricacy, this is an excellent introduction to Norse mythology since it describes the beginnings of the world and the inhabitants of the land of the gods, Asgard.

"Asgard and the Gods" from A BOOK OF MYTHS retold by Roger Lancelyn Green. Children's Classics Series. Text copyright © 1965 by Roger Lancelyn Green. Reprinted by permission of J M Dent & Sons Ltd.

The world itself (so the Northmen believed) had been born out of the ice and rime. In the beginning there was no land, only Ginnungagap—the yawning gulf. Yet at the north of it was Nifelheim, the shadowland of absolute cold; and far to the south was Muspelheim, the region of fire, guarded by the fire-demon Surtur. Between the two Ginnungagap was filled with rolling vapour and frozen air which at last drew together and formed Ymir, the First Giant, whose children were the Hrimthursar, the Frost-giants. He was utterly wicked, as were all Giants after him.

As Ymir stood in Ginnungagap a second creature came into being, made also out of frozen vapour. This was the cow called Audhumla, whose milk made the great rivers of life which fed Ymir. Audhumla licked the stones which were covered with salt and hoar frost, and from them grew Bur who was the father of Bor who married a Giantess and so became the father of the gods Odin, Vili and Ve.

The three gods slew the Giant Ymir and dragged his body into the middle of Ginnungagap. From it they made Midgard, the world in which men dwell. His body formed the earth, his icy blood melted and became the sea; from his bones grew the mountains and from his flesh the fertile soil. The skull of Ymir was set over the earth to form the great dome of the sky with his brains floating about in it as the first clouds; and fire drawn from Muspelheim made the sun, the moon and the stars.

To hold all in place Odin caused the great ash tree Yggdrasill to grow. Its roots were in deepest Nifelheim; its trunk held up Midgard, the world of men, and its branches arched over the sky to support Asgard, the land of the gods.

Out of two chips of wood from Yggdrasill which were cast up on the shore in Midgard Odin formed the First Man and the First Woman, whose names were Ask and Embla. Odin breathed the breath of life into them, while Vili gave them the powers of thought and motion, and Ve caused them to see and hear and speak.

Now Odin became the all-father of gods and men, marrying Frigga, daughter of the mountains, who bore him the great gods Thor the thunderer, Tyr the war lord, Bragi the minstrel, Uller the archer, Heimdall the guardian of Bifrost—the rainbow bridge between Heaven and Earth—beautiful Baldur the shining god of the sunlight, and others of less renown.

There were also the three Vanir: the powers of peace who grew out of the summer air. Niord guarded all living creatures, his son Frey taught the arts of agriculture, and his daughter Freya was the goddess of love and beauty. Niord dwelt far from Asgard, by the sea-shore; but Frey and Freya came to join the Aesir—the gods of Asgard—and Freya married Odur, one of the sons of Odin.

The strangest inhabitant of Asgard was Loki, the Fire-god. He was one of the Giant race, but forswore their evil ways and became Odin's blood-brother, swearing most solemnly to use all his Giant skill in the service of Asgard. And for a long time he was faithful to the Aesir, showing his kinship with the Giants only by the tricks and pranks he would play, even on the highest gods. At first these were innocent enough, and caused much mirth in the halls of Asgard. But gradually Loki's Giant nature began to get the better of him and his tricks became crueller and more evil, until at last he became the secret enemy of the gods, the traitor in their midst fighting on the side of the Giants.

There was some excuse for Loki's first plot against Asgard. One day he accompanied Odin and Odin's brother Honir, the messenger to mankind, on a visit to Midgard. For Odin went frequently in disguise among men teaching them many things, and punishing those who did evil. And when he could not go himself he sent Honir to be teacher and guide.

On this occasion the three gods wandered far over the earth, and as night was falling found themselves in a lonely valley of the mountains where no house was to be seen. Presently they came upon a herd of cattle, and as they were very hungry Odin told Loki to kill one of them and roast it for supper.

Loki did as he was commanded, and soon an ox was cut up and roasting merrily on great spits over a roaring fire.

"That meat must be cooked by now," said Odin at last.

Loki went to look. What was his amazement to find the joints as red and raw as when he had cut them from the ox!

Loki stoked up the fire and they waited once more. At last he went to look at the meat again, and it was still as raw as ever.

"There is evil magic at work here," said Odin.

As he spoke there was a sound of harsh laughter above them, and looking up they saw a huge eagle perched on a rock.

"If you will give me my fair share of the meat I'll see to it that it roasts quickly!" screeched the eagle.

The gods agreed to this, and the eagle flew down and fanned the flames with his giant wings for a few minutes, while the meat sizzled merrily.

As soon as it was well cooked the eagle said: "I'll help myself first!" And with that he seized a shoulder in each claw and a leg in his hooked beak and prepared to fly off with them.

"You've taken too much!" cried Loki, who had a tremendous appetite; and in his anger he snatched up a heavy stick and struck the eagle on the back. At once the stick stuck to the eagle, and Loki found that he was stuck to the stick.

Off flew the huge bird, dragging Loki after it, and trailing him over the sharpest rocks and thorniest thickets it could find.

Loki shouted in vain for help, and begged the eagle to release him.

"That I will only do on my own terms," said the eagle. "I am Thiassi the Giant of the Winter, wearing my eagle-cloak with which I bring the storms. And I will drag you like this until you are torn to ribbons, unless you promise to give me Iduna and her magic Apples of Youth."

"How can I?" gasped Loki. "The gods of Asgard would never forgive me if I stole Iduna and her Apples. She was born out of the earth, bringing the magic fruit with her, and dwells always in Asgard, married to Bragi the minstrel. Each day the Aesir eat of the Apples and their youth returns to them; nor do the Apples ever grow fewer. How can I steal Iduna or the Apples?"

"Then you shall be torn to pieces!" screamed the eagle. "All I ask is for you to persuade Iduna to come down out of Asgard, bringing the Apples with her. Once she is on the soil of Midgard I can seize her and carry her off to my castle in Jotunheim, the frozen kingdom of the Giants. . . . That is all I ask. Choose life or death."

At last Loki swore solemnly to betray Iduna to Thiassi; and the eagle carried him back to his companions, released him from the stick, and flew away carrying his share of the feast.

Loki said nothing to Odin and Honir about his bargain, nor did he tell them that the eagle was really Thiassi. And although Odin suspected that the eagle was one of the evil powers in disguise, he thought that it had merely punished Loki cruelly for striking it.

Loki did not forget his oath to Thiassi. After much thought he went to Iduna and said:

"Beautiful goddess of youth, are there other apples such as those which you give each day to the Aesir and the Vanir who dwell here in Asgard?"

"I do not believe there are other apples such as mine," answered Iduna. "For kind Mother Earth gave them to me when I first came out into the light, bidding me guard them always and give them only to those who dwell in Asgard. Only those to whom I give them shall have eternal youth; and they must never be given to one of Giant race, nor to the Dwarfs who dwell under the earth—not even to Evaldi the Earth Dwarf, my father."

"Strange," mused Loki; "for there is a grove of apple trees not far from where the lower end of Bifrost Bridge rests on the earth. These apples are just such as those in your golden casket; and the men of Midgard have found them. Soon they will taste the wondrous fruit, and remain young for ever, even as the gods."

"That must not be!" exclaimed Iduna anxiously. "Lead me to this grove at once, for I must see whether the apples of which you speak are of the same growth as those in my casket."

So Loki led Iduna down over the rainbow bridge out of the safety of Asgard and on to

Midgard where Giants could roam unseen. And, in her eagerness, Iduna feared no evil but carried her magic Apples with her in their golden casket.

As soon as she was hidden among the trees, Thiassi in his eagle-robe swooped down and carried her and the Apples of Youth away to Thrymheim, his castle in the frozen land of Jotunheim where the Giants lived.

"Fair Iduna, be my bride and give me your Apples to eat!" cried Thiassi, throwing off his disguise as soon as she was safely shut in his highest tower.

"Never!" said Iduna bravely. "None but the gods of Asgard may eat of my Apples— and they lose all their power unless I give them freely."

"Then here you stay until you change your mind!" roared Thiassi; and swinging his eagle-cloak about him he flew out of the window and went rushing over the earth in a great storm of rage, bringing havoc and destruction wherever he passed.

In Asgard Iduna was sorely missed. Old age began to touch even the gods: Odin grew wrinkled, Thor's arm was not so strong, and strands of grey showed even in Baldur's golden hair.

No one knew what had become of Iduna. Bragi wept for his lost wife, singing only laments and dirges, and drawing melancholy notes from his harp. Odin sent out his swift messengers, the ravens of Hugin and Munin, who perched on his shoulders as he sat on his high throne looking out over the world; but for a long time they had nothing to report.

At last, however, they brought news that Iduna was held captive in the high tower of the castle of Thrymheim in the land of the Giants.

"That is Thiassi's castle," croaked Hugin.

"Thiassi flies wrathfully about the world in his eagle-cloak," croaked Munin.

"Just as he flew that day when the ox would not roast," croaked Hugin.

"The day when he dragged Loki over the sharp rocks," croaked Munin.

"Until Loki made his peace with Thiassi. . . ." croaked both ravens.

Now Odin began to suspect what had happened, and sent for Loki, who confessed all.

"I cannot blame you overmuch for buying your freedom from cruel pain," said Odin gravely. "But you must find a way of bringing back Iduna and the Apples of Youth to Asgard—and of punishing Thiassi, the Giant of the Winter."

"The Lady Freya has a magic cloak," said Loki. "Whoever wears it takes on any shape he chooses. If she will but give it to me, I'll fly as a falcon into Thrymheim and bring back Iduna."

Freya willingly handed her cloak to Loki, who set out at once in the shape of a falcon, and flew to Thiassi's high castle in Jotunheim. The Giant himself was out fishing, so Loki slipped safely in through the topmost window, where he found Iduna pale and troubled, but still refusing to part with her Apples.

When Loki flung off Freya's cloak and assumed his own form Iduna greeted him eagerly, and begged him to carry her back to Asgard.

So Loki turned her into a sparrow and himself back into a falcon. Then he seized her carefully in his claws and set out for Asgard.

It was not long, however, before Thiassi discovered what had happened. Wild with rage he donned his eagle-shape and flew off in a blast of wind so deadly that nothing remained standing on the earth beneath his flight.

Far away in Asgard the gods waited eagerly. Presently farsighted Heimdall cried:

"I see the falcon flying this way with a sparrow in its claws. But behind it comes a great eagle, and the earth grows black with the cruel cold beneath the beat of his wings!"

On the very rampart of Asgard the gods made haste to prepare a great heap of pine-chips soaked in resin, and stood ready with torches in their hands. With a last desperate effort Loki skimmed into Asgard and fell exhausted to the floor. The moment he had passed over the heap the gods cast their torches into it and a great flame shot fiercely up. Thiassi was close behind Loki, flying so fast that he could not stop or turn. The fierce flames set fire to his feathers so that he fell to the ground, and the gods slew him with their swords and axes on the very threshold of Asgard.

Then they turned, to find Iduna standing ready for them with the Apples of Youth in her hand. And when they had eaten, their youth returned to them, even as it returns to the world each spring when winter has been defeated and is dying in the beams of the summer sun.

Loki was forgiven now that Iduna and her Apples were safe in Asgard once more, nor did anyone yet suspect him of siding with the Giants. Yet already he was leaning more and more towards his own race; for even as he flew over Jotunheim to rescue Iduna his eyes fell on a young Giantess called Angurbodi, and he fell in love with her.

So he stole away from Asgard more and more often to visit his Giant bride in Jotunheim; and three terrible children had been born to them before Odin realized what Loki was up to. When he did, his wise heart was filled with trouble and foreboding, for his great wisdom, which he had purchased from the Giant Mimir in exchange for one of his eyes, told him that the three children of Loki would be among his deadliest enemies at Ragnarok.

As they were the children of his blood-brother, he could not slay them. But he sent Thor and Tyr to bring them to Asgard. The two gods set out in Thor's chariot drawn by goats, and the thunder roared and the lightning flashed as they sped across the sky by the roadway of the clouds.

When they returned, the gods gathered in horror round the three monsters whom they brought with them.

At once Odin took the second of these, a huge serpent, and flung him into the sea, where he grew so fast that at length he encircled the earth and could hold his tail in his mouth. Having disposed of Jormungand, the Midgard serpent, he turned to Loki's youngest child Hela, half of whose body was that of a woman and the other half that of a decay-

ing corpse, and sent her down to Nifelheim below the earth. There, at his command, she became queen of the dead, and a great wall was built round her realm, which was known as Helheim.

As for Loki's eldest child, the wolf Fenris, Odin thought at first to keep him in Asgard and train him to hunt and fight for the gods. But Fenris grew so fast and became so ferocious and cruel that at last it was decided to bind him in chains.

"Show us how strong you are!" cried Thor when the chain was ready. "I'll tie you up with this pretty toy, and we'll see how easily you can break it."

"Agreed!" smiled Fenris, looking scornfully at the chain. "That's a mere cobweb to me."

When Thor had bound him as firmly as he could, Fenris proved his words true. He yawned, he stretched—and the chain flew into small pieces all round him.

"You must make something stronger than that!" barked Fenris.

The gods tried again; but once more Fenris, putting out his vast strength, scattered the huge iron links all about him.

Then the gods took council; and Odin sent messengers to the Dark Elves who lived under the earth and who were skilled above all creatures both in smiths' work and in magic. It was they who had made Thor's great hammer Miolnir, which always returned to his hand however far he flung it at an enemy; and the spear Gungir for Odin, which never failed to hit its mark; and the gold ring Draupnir, from which eight rings of equal value fell on every ninth night. Now they forged the chain Gleipnir of thin shining steel, tempered in a magic brew made from the noise of a cat's footfall, the beards of women, the roots of stones, and the breath of fish—since when cats have made no noise, women have not grown beards, stones have lost their roots and fish no longer breathe.

When Fenris saw the chain Gleipnir he sniffed at it suspiciously, for it was as smooth and thin and soft as a thread of silk.

"There is magic in this," he said doubtfully.

"I do not trust any of you. . . . But I will let you bind me with Gleipnir if, as a pledge of good faith, one of you will put his right hand in my mouth while I am breaking the chain."

Now the gods hesitated, as well they might. But brave Tyr stepped forward and thrust his hand between the wolf's huge jaws. Then the rest bound Fenris with Gleipnir and drew the end of it through a rock. Struggle as he might, Fenris could not break the chain which bound him, and he was doomed to lie fettered in it at the world's end until the day of Ragnarok.

But Tyr lacked a hand ever afterwards.

It was after the binding of Fenris that Odin began to make ready for the day of the Last Great Battle. Up in Asgard he built a mighty hall called Valhalla, and decreed that all men who fell in battle should not go like other humans to the dark land of Helheim but come in triumph to feast in Valhalla and dwell there until the time came for them to form his army.

Now wars flourished in Midgard, and every man who could became a warrior and hoped to die in battle. And Odin sent out his daughters the Valkyries, the "Battle-choosers," to ride over the fields of war and choose all those who had died bravely. Then they rode back to Asgard carrying the chosen, and the feast was made ready in Valhalla for Odin's army, the Einheriar.

Every warrior who became one of the Einheriar found himself young and strong and healed of his wounds by the time he reached Valhalla. There the feast was spread each night, with roast pork in abundance and as much mead as they could drink. The Valkyries waited on them, having doffed their helmets and laid by their swords and shields; and no matter how much the Einheriar drank, they rose next morning fresh and clear-headed. All day long they rode and fought in the great meadow before Valhalla, hacking each other to pieces in glorious battle—yet appearing at the evening feast whole and unwounded. Each morning the cook Andhrimnir slew the great boar Saehrimnir and boiled his flesh in a huge kettle, and each morning he was alive and whole again, ready to be killed and eaten once more. Nor was there ever a shortage of meat, though Valhalla had five hundred and forty doors, by each of which eight hundred heroes might come in or out at once. Nor was there ever any lack of mead, which the goat Heidrun yielded instead of milk.

At night Odin would sit at the head of the banquet board in Valhalla, sipping his mead, but throwing his share of meat to his two wolves Geri and Freki—for the gods of Asgard did not need to eat, save only the Apples of Iduna; though when they went among men or giants they ate meat with the best, Thor and Loki being particularly famous for their appetites—which led them once into a contest with the Giant King of Jotunheim. In this they were defeated only because Loki was set to eat against the Fire Giant, and Thor to drink from a huge horn, the other end of which reached the sea—which ebbed for the first time, before Thor ceased from drinking and the tide came in again.

By day Odin went more often than ever in disguise to Midgard seeking fresh warriors to join the Einheriar in Valhalla, and training the sons of kings and the bravest of fighting men to become such great heroes as Sigurd the Volsung and Gunnar of Lithend and Grettir the Strong, whose deeds and deaths are told in the stirring words of the great Icelandic sagas. For the time was drawing nearer and nearer when the powers of evil would rise up to destroy the earth and invade Asgard, when Ragnarok, the day of the Last Great Battle, should dawn.

How Thor Found His Hammer

The constant struggle against the evil frost-giants reflects the source of Norse mythology, but few of the individual myths have the merry note that is found here.

'How Thor Found His Hammer" from NORSE STORIES by Hamilton Wright Mabie. Published by Dodd, Mead & Company.

The frost-giants were always trying to get into Asgard. For more than half the year they held the world in their grasp, locking up the streams in their rocky beds, hushing their music and the music of the birds as well, and leaving nothing but a wild waste of desolation under the cold sky. They hated the warm sunshine which stirred the wild flowers out of their sleep, and clothed the steep mountains with verdure, and set all the birds a-singing in the swaying tree-tops. They hated the beautiful god Balder, with whose presence summer came back to the ice-bound earth, and, above all, they hated Thor, whose flashing hammer drove them back into Jotunheim, and guarded the summer sky with its sudden gleamings of power. So long as Thor had his hammer Asgard was safe against the giants.

One morning Thor started up out of a long, deep sleep, and put out his hand for the hammer; but no hammer was there. Not a sign of it could be found anywhere, although Thor anxiously searched for it. Then a thought of the giants came suddenly in his mind; and his anger rose till his eyes flashed like great fires, and his red beard trembled with wrath.

"Look, now, Loke," he shouted, "they have stolen Mjolner by enchantment, and no one on earth or in heaven knows where they have hidden it."

"We will get Freyja's falcon-guise and search for it," answered Loke, who was always quick to get into trouble or to get out of it again. So they went quickly to Folkvang and found Freyja surrounded by her maidens and weeping tears of pure gold, as she had always done since her husband went on his long journey.

"The hammer has been stolen by enchantment," said Thor. "Will you lend me the falcon-guise that I may search for it?"

"If it were silver, or even gold, you should have it and welcome," answered Freyja, glad to help Thor find the wonderful hammer that kept them all safe from the hands of the frost-giants.

So the falcon-guise was brought, and Loke put it on and flew swiftly out of Asgard to the home of the giants. His great wings made broad shadows over the ripe fields as he swept along, and the reapers, looking up from their work, wondered what mighty bird was flying seaward. At last he reached Jotunheim, and no sooner had he touched ground and taken off the falcon-guise than he came upon the giant Thrym, sitting on a hill twisting golden collars for his dogs and stroking the long manes of his horses.

"Welcome, Loke," said the giant. "How fares it with the gods and the elves, and what has brought you to Jotunheim?"

"It fares ill with both gods and elves since you stole Thor's hammer," replied Loke, guessing quickly that Thrym was the thief; "and I have come to find where you have hidden it."

Thrym laughed as only a giant can when he knows he has made trouble for somebody.

"You won't find it," he said at last. "I have buried it eight miles under ground, and no one shall take it away unless he gets Freyja for me as my wife."

The giant looked as if he meant what he said, and Loke, seeing no other way of finding the hammer, put on his falcon-guise and flew back to Asgard. Thor was waiting to hear what news he brought, and both were soon at the great doors of Folkvang.

"Put on your bridal dress, Freyja," said Thor bluntly, after his fashion, "and we will ride swiftly to Jotunheim."

But Freyja had no idea of marrying a giant just to please Thor; and, in fact, that Thor should ask her to do such a thing threw her into such a rage that the floor shook under her angry tread, and her necklace snapped in pieces.

"Do you think I am a weak lovesick girl, to follow you to Jotunheim and marry Thrym?" she cried indignantly.

Finding they could do nothing with Freyja, Thor and Loke called all the gods together to talk over the matter and decide what should be done to get back the hammer. The gods were very much alarmed, because they knew the frost-giants would come upon Asgard as soon as they knew the hammer was gone. They said little, for they did not waste time with idle words, but they thought long and earnestly, and still they could find no way of getting hold of Mjolner once more. At last Heimdal, who had once been a Van, and could therefore look into the future, said: "We must have the hammer at once or Asgard will be in danger. If Freyja will not go, let Thor be dressed up and go in her place. Let keys jingle from his waist and a woman's dress fall about his feet. Put precious stones upon his breast, braid his hair like a woman's, hang the necklace around his neck, and bind the bridal veil around his head."

Thor frowned angrily. "If I dress like a woman," he said, "you will jeer at me."

"Don't talk of jeers," retorted Loke; "unless that hammer is brought back quickly, the giants will rule in our places."

Thor said no more, but allowed himself to be dressed like a bride, and soon drove off to Jotunheim with Loke beside him disguised as a servant-maid. There was never such a wedding journey before. They rode in Thor's chariot and the goats drew them, plunging swiftly along the way, thunder pealing through the mountains and the frightened earth blazing and smoking as they passed. When Thrym saw the bridal party coming he was filled with delight.

"Stand up, you giants," he shouted to his companions; "spread cushions upon the benches and bring in Freyja, my bride. My yards are full of golden-horned cows, black oxen please my gaze whichever way I look, great wealth and many treasures are mine, and Freyja is all I lack."

It was evening when the bride came driving into the giant's court in her blazing chariot. The feast was already spread against her coming, and with her veil modestly covering her face she was seated at the great table, Thrym fairly beside himself with delight. It wasn't every giant who could marry a goddess!

If the bridal journey had been so strange that any one but a foolish giant would have hesitated to marry a wife who came in such a turmoil of fire and storm, her conduct at the table ought certainly to have put Thrym on his guard; for never had a bride such an appetite before. The great tables groaned under the load of good things, but they were quickly relieved of their burden by the voracious bride. She ate a whole ox before the astonished giant had fairly begun to enjoy his meal. Then she devoured eight large salmon, one after the other, without stopping to take breath; and having eaten up the part of the feast specially prepared for the hungry men, she turned upon the delicacies which had been made for the women, and especially for her own fastidious appetite.

Thrym looked on with wondering eyes, and at last, when she had added to these solid foods three whole barrels of mead, his amazement was so great that, his astonishment getting the better of his politeness, he called out, "Did any one ever see such an appetite in a bride before, or know a maid who could drink so much mead?"

Then Loke, who was playing the part of a serving-maid, thinking that the giant might have some suspicions, whispered to him, "Freyja was so happy in the thought of coming here that she has eaten nothing for eight whole days."

Thrym was so pleased at this evidence of affection that he leaned forward and raised the veil as gently as a giant could, but he instantly dropped it and sprang back the whole length of the hall before the bride's terrible eyes.

"Why are Freyja's eyes so sharp?" he called to Loke. "They burn me like fire."

"Oh," said the cunning serving-maid, "she has not slept for a week, so anxious has she been to come here, and that is why her eyes are so fiery."

Everybody looked at the bride and nobody envied Thrym. They thought it was too much like marrying a thunder-storm.

The giant's sister came into the hall just then, and seeing the veiled form of the bride sitting there went up to her and asked for a bridal gift. "If you would have my love and friendship give me those rings of gold upon your fingers."

But the bride sat perfectly silent. No one had yet seen her face or heard her voice.

Thrym became very impatient. "Bring in the hammer," he shouted, "that the bride may be consecrated, and wed us in the name of Var."

If the giant could have seen the bride's eyes when she heard these words he would have sent her home as quickly as possible, and looked somewhere else for a wife.

The hammer was brought and placed in the bride's lap, and everybody looked to see the marriage ceremony; but the wedding was more strange and terrible than the bridal journey had been. No sooner did the bride's fingers close round the handle of Mjolner than the veil which covered her face was torn off and there stood Thor, the giant-queller, his terrible eyes blazing with wrath.

The giants shuddered and shrank away from those flaming eyes, the sight of which they dreaded more than anything else in all the worlds; but there was no chance of escape. Thor swung the hammer round his head and the great house rocked on its foundations. There was a vivid flash of lightning, an awful crash of thunder, and the burning roof and walls buried the whole company in one common ruin.

Thrym was punished for stealing the hammer, his wedding guests got crushing blows instead of bridal gifts, and Thor and Loke went back to Asgard, where the presence of Mjolner made the gods safe once more.

The Death of Balder

An interesting myth to compare to the story of Proserpine, as a tale symbolic of the seasons; here the focus on Balder, the sun, attests to the importance of summer in a northern land.

There was one shadow which always fell over Asgard. Sometimes in the long years the gods almost forgot it, it lay so far off, like a dim cloud in a clear sky; but Odin saw it deepen and widen as he looked out into the universe, and he knew that the last great battle would surely come, when the gods themselves would be destroyed and a long twilight would rest on all the worlds; and now the day was close at hand. Misfortunes never come singly to men, and they did not to the gods. Idun, the beautiful goddess of youth, whose apples were the joy of all Asgard, made a resting place for herself among the massive branches of Ygdrasil, and there every evening came Brage, and sang so sweetly that the birds stopped to listen, and even the Norns, those implacable sisters at the foot of the tree, were softened by the melody. But poetry cannot change the purposes of fate, and one evening no song was heard of Brage or birds, the leaves of the world-tree hung withered and lifeless on the branches, and the fountain from which they had daily been sprinkled was dry at last. Idun had fallen into the dark valley of death, and when Brage, Heimdal, and Loke went to question her about the future she could answer them only with tears. Brage would not leave his beautiful wife alone amid the dim shades that crowded the dreary valley, and so youth and genius vanished out of Asgard forever.

Balder was the most god-like of all the gods, because he was the purest and the best. Wherever he went his coming was like the coming of sunshine, and all the beauty of summer was but the shining of his face. When men's hearts were white like the light, and their lives clear as the day, it was because Balder was looking down upon them with those soft, clear eyes that were open windows to the soul of God. He had always lived in such a glow of brightness that no darkness had ever touched him; but one morning, after Idun and Brage had gone, Balder's face was sad and troubled. He walked slowly from room to room in his palace Breidablik, stainless as the sky when April showers have swept across it because no impure thing had ever crossed the threshold, and his eyes were heavy with sorrow. In the night terrible dreams had broken his sleep, and made it a long torture. The air seemed to be full of awful changes for him, and for all the gods. He knew in his soul that the shadow of the last great day was sweeping on; as he looked out and saw the worlds lying in light and beauty, the fields yellow with waving grain, the deep fiords flashing back the sunbeams from their clear depths, the verdure clothing the loftiest mountains, and knew that over all this darkness and desolation would come, with silence of reapers and birds, with fading of leaf and flower, a great sorrow fell on his heart.

Balder could bear the burden no longer. He went out, called all the gods together, and told them the terrible dreams of the night. Every face was heavy with care. The death of Balder would be like the going out of the sun, and after a long, sad council the gods resolved to protect him from harm by pledging all things to stand between him and any hurt. So Frigg, his mother, went forth and made everything promise, on a solemn oath, not to injure her son. Fire, iron, all kinds of metal, every sort of stone, trees, earth, diseases, birds, beasts, snakes, as the anxious mother went to them, solemnly pledged themselves that no harm should come near Balder. Everything had promised, and Frigg thought she had driven away the cloud; but fate was stronger than her love, and one little shrub had not sworn.

Odin was not satisfied even with these precautions, for whichever way he looked the shadow of a great sorrow spread over the worlds. He began to feel as if he were no longer the greatest of the gods, and he could almost hear the rough shouts of the frost-giants crowding the rainbow bridge on their way into Asgard. When trouble comes to men it is hard to bear, but to a god who had so many worlds to guide and rule it was a new and terrible thing. Odin thought and thought until he was weary, but no gleam of light could he find anywhere; it was thick darkness everywhere.

At last he could bear the suspense no longer, and saddling his horse he rode sadly out of Asgard to Niflheim, the home of Hel, whose face was as the face of death itself. As he drew near the gates, a monstrous dog came out and barked furiously, but Odin rode a little eastward of the shadowy gates to the grave of a wonderful prophetess. It was a cold, gloomy place, and the soul of the great god was pierced with a feeling of hopeless sorrow as he dismounted from Sleipner, and bending over the grave began to chant weird songs, and weave magical charms over it. When he had spoken those wonderful words which could waken the dead from their sleep, there was an awful silence for a moment, and then a faint ghost-like voice came from the grave.

"Who are thou?" it said. "Who breaketh the silence of death, and calleth the sleeper out of her long slumbers? Ages ago I was laid at rest here, snow and rain have fallen upon me through myriad years; why dost thou disturb me?"

"I am Vegtam," answered Odin, "and I come to ask why the couches of Hel are hung with gold and the benches strewn with shining rings?"

"It is done for Balder," answered the awful voice; "ask me no more."

Odin's heart sank when he heard these words; but he was determined to know the worst.

"I will ask thee until I know all. Who shall strike the fatal blow?"

"If I must, I must," moaned the prophetess. "Hoder shall smite his brother Balder and send him down to the dark home of Hel. The mead is already brewed for Balder, and the despair draweth near."

Then Odin, looking into the future across the open grave, saw all the days to come.

"The Death of Balder" from NORSE STORIES by Hamilton Wright Mabie. Published by Dodd, Mead & Company.

"Who is this," he said, seeing that which no mortal could have seen—"who is this that will not weep for Balder?"

Then the prophetess knew that it was none other than the greatest of the gods who had called her up.

"Thou art not Vegtam," she exclaimed, "thou art Odin himself, the king of men."

"And thou," answered Odin angrily, "art no prophetess, but the mother of three giants."

"Ride home, then, and exult in what thou has discovered," said the dead woman. "Never shall my slumbers be broken again until Loke shall burst his chains and the great battle come."

And Odin rode sadly homeward knowing that already Niflheim was making itself beautiful against the coming of Balder.

The other gods meanwhile had become merry again; for had not everything promised to protect their beloved Balder? They even made sport of that which troubled them, for when they found that nothing could hurt Balder, and that all things glanced aside from his shining form, they persuaded him to stand as a target for their weapons; hurling darts, spears, swords, and battle-axes at him, all of which went singing through the air and fell harmless at his feet. But Loke, when he saw these sports, was jealous of Balder, and went about thinking how he could destroy him.

It happened that as Frigg sat spinning in her house Fensal, the soft wind blowing in at the windows and bringing the merry shouts of the gods at play, an old woman entered and approached her.

"Do you know," asked the newcomer, "what they are doing in Asgard? They are throwing all manner of dangerous weapons at Balder. He stands there like the sun for brightness, and against his glory, spears and battle-axes fall powerless to the ground. Nothing can harm him."

"No," answered Frigg joyfully; "nothing can bring him any hurt, for I have made everything in heaven and earth swear to protect him."

"What!" said the old woman, "has everything sworn to guard Balder?"

"Yes," said Frigg, "everything has sworn except one little shrub which is called Mistletoe, and grows on the eastern side of Valhal. I did not take an oath from that because I thought it was too young and weak."

When the old woman heard this a strange light came into her eyes; she walked off much faster than she had come in, and no sooner had she passed beyond Frigg's sight than this same old feeble woman grew suddenly erect, shook off her woman's garments, and there stood Loke himself. In a moment he had reached the slope east of Valhal, and plucked a twig of the unsworn Mistletoe, and was back in the circle of the gods, who were still at their favorite pastime with Balder. Hoder was standing silent and alone outside the noisy throng, for he was blind. Loke touched him.

"Why do you not throw something at Balder?"

"Because I cannot see where Balder stands, and have nothing to throw if I could," replied Hoder.

"If that is all," said Loke, "come with me. I will give you something to throw, and direct your aim."

Hoder, thinking no evil, went with Loke and did as he was told.

The little sprig of Mistletoe shot through the air, pierced the heart of Balder, and in a moment the beautiful god lay dead upon the field. A shadow rose out of the deep beyond the worlds and spread itself over heaven and earth, for the light of the universe had gone out.

The gods could not speak for horror. They stood like statues for a moment, and then a hopeless wail burst from their lips. Tears fell like rain from eyes that had never wept before, for Balder, the joy of Asgard, had gone to Niflheim and left them desolate. But Odin was saddest of all, because he knew the future, and he knew that peace and light had fled from Asgard forever, and that the last day and the long night were hurrying on.

Frigg could not give up her beautiful son, and when her grief had spent itself a little, she asked who would go to Hel and offer her a rich ransom if she would permit Balder to return to Asgard.

"I will go," said Hermod; swift at the word of Odin, Sleipner was led forth, and in an instant Hermod was galloping furiously away.

Then the gods began with sorrowful hearts to make ready for Balder's funeral. When the once beautiful form had been arrayed in grave-clothes they carried it reverently down to the deep sea, which lay, calm as a summer afternoon, waiting for its precious burden. Close to the water's edge lay Balder's Ringhorn, the greatest of all the ships that sailed the seas, but when the gods tried to launch it they could not move it an inch. The great vessel creaked and groaned, but no one could push it down to the water. Odin walked about it with a sad face, and the gentle ripple of the little waves chasing each other over the rocks seemed a mocking laugh to him.

"Send to Jotunheim for Hyrroken," he said at last; and a messenger was soon flying for that mighty giantess.

In a little time, Hyrroken came riding swiftly on a wolf so large and fierce that he made the gods think of Fenrer. When the giantess had alighted, Odin ordered four Berserkers of mighty strength to hold the wolf, but he struggled so angrily that they had to throw him on the ground before they could control him. Then Hyrroken went to the prow of the ship and with one mighty effort sent it far into the sea, the rollers underneath bursting into flame, and the whole earth trembling with the shock. Thor was so angry at the uproar that he would have killed the giantess on the spot if he had not been held back by the other gods. The great ship floated on the sea as she had often done before, when Balder, full of life and beauty, set all her sails and was borne joyfully across the tossing seas. Slowly and solemnly the dead god was carried on board, and as Nanna, his faithful wife, saw her husband borne for the last time from the earth which he had made dear to her and beautiful to all men, her heart broke with sorrow, and they laid her beside Balder on the funeral pyre.

Since the world began no one had seen such a funeral. No bells tolled, no long procession of mourners moved across the hills, but all the worlds lay under a deep shadow, and from every quarter came those who had loved or feared Balder. There at the very water's edge stood Odin himself, the ravens flying about his head, and on his majestic face a gloom that no sun would ever lighten again; and there was Frigg, the desolate mother, whose son had already gone so far that he would never come back to her; there was Frey standing sad and stern in his chariot; there was Freyja, the goddess of love, from whose eyes fell a shining rain of tears; there, too, was Heimdal on his horse Goldtop; and around all these glorious ones from Asgard crowded the children of Jotunheim, grim mountain-giants seamed with scars from Thor's hammer, and frost-giants who saw in the death of Balder the coming of that long winter in which they should reign through all the worlds.

A deep hush fell on all created things, and every eye was fixed on the great ship riding near the shore, and on the funeral pyre rising from the deck crowned with the forms of Balder and Nanna. Suddenly a gleam of light flashed over the water; the pile had been kindled, and the flames, creeping slowly at first, climbed faster and faster until they met over the dead and rose skyward. A lurid light filled the heavens and shone on the sea, and in the brightness of it the gods looked pale and sad, and the circle of giants grew darker and more portentous. Thor struck the fast burning pyre with his consecrating hammer, and Odin cast into it the wonder ring Draupner. Higher and higher leaped the flames, more and more desolate grew the scene; at last they began to sink, the funeral pyre was consumed. Balder had vanished forever, the summer was ended, and winter waited at the doors.

Meanwhile Hermod was riding hard and fast on his gloomy errand. Nine days and nights he rode through valleys so deep and dark that he could not see his horse. Stillness and blackness and solitude were his only companions until he came to the golden bridge which crosses the river Gjol. The good horse Sleipner, who had carried Odin on so many strange journeys, had never travelled such a road before, and his hoofs rang drearily as he stopped short at the bridge, for in front of him stood its porter, the gigantic Modgud.

"Who are you?" she asked, fixing her piercing eyes on Hermod. "What is your name and parentage? Yesterday five bands of dead men rode across the bridge, and beneath them all it did not shake as under your single tread. There is no colour of death in your face. Why ride you hither, the living among the dead?"

"I come," said Hermod, "to seek for Balder. Have you seen him pass this way?"

"He has already crossed the bridge and taken his journey northward to Hel."

Then Hermod rode slowly across the bridge that spans the abyss between life and death, and found his way at last to the barred gates of Hel's dreadful home. There he sprang to the ground, tightened the girths, remounted, drove the spurs deep into the horse, and Sleipner, with a mighty leap, cleared the wall. Hermod rode straight to the gloomy palace, dismounted, entered, and in a moment was face to face with the terrible queen of the kingdom of the dead. Beside her, on a beautiful throne, sat Balder, pale and wan, crowned with a withered wreath of flowers, and close at hand was Nanna, pallid as her husband, for whom she had died. And all night long, while ghostly forms wandered restless and sleepless through Helheim, Hermod talked with Balder and Nanna. There is no record of what they said, but the talk was sad enough, doubtless, and ran like a still stream among the happy days in Asgard when Balder's smile was morning over the earth and the sight of his face the summer of the world.

When the morning came, faint and dim, through the dusky palace, Hermod sought Hel, who received him as cold and stern as fate.

"Your kingdom is full, O Hel!" he said, "and without Balder, Asgard is empty. Send him back to us once more, for there is sadness in every heart and tears are in every eye.

Through heaven and earth all things weep for him."

"If that is true," was the slow, icy answer, "if every created thing weeps for Balder, he shall return to Asgard; but if one eye is dry he remains henceforth in Helheim."

Then Hermod rode swiftly away, and the decree of Hel was soon told in Asgard. Through all the worlds the gods sent messengers to say that all who loved Balder should weep for his return, and everywhere tears fell like rain. There was weeping in Asgard, and in all the earth there was nothing that did not weep. Men and women and little children, missing the light that had once fallen into their hearts and homes, sobbed with bitter grief; the birds of the air, who had sung carols of joy at the gates of the morning since time began, were full of sorrow; the beasts of the fields crouched and moaned in their desolation; the great trees, that had put on their robes of green at Balder's command, sighed as the wind wailed through them; and the sweet flowers, that waited for Balder's footstep and sprang up in all the fields to greet him, hung their frail blossoms and wept bitterly for the love and the warmth and the light that had gone out. Throughout the whole earth there was nothing but weeping, and the sound of it was like the wailing of those storms in autumn that weep for the dead summer as its withered leaves drop one by one from the trees.

The messengers of the gods went gladly back to Asgard, for everything had wept for Balder; but as they journeyed they came upon a giantess, called Thok, and her eyes were dry.

"Weep for Balder," they said.

"With dry eyes only will I weep for Balder," she answered. "Dead or alive, he never gave me gladness. Let him stay in Helheim."

When she had spoken these words a terrible laugh broke from her lips, and the messengers looked at each other with pallid faces, for they knew it was the voice of Loke.

Balder never came back to Asgard, and the shadows deepened over all things, for the night of death was fast coming on.

Egyptian Myths

 The tale of Isis and Osiris is a good example of the complexity and dignity of the Egyptian pantheon, and it illustrates many of the customs of ancient Egypt and explains how they began. It is interesting to compare these stately and often violent myths with some of the related folk tales in Hasan El-Shamy's *Folktales of Egypt,* in which the ancient gods have been transformed into Muslim and Coptic saints of the contemporary culture.

Isis and Osiris

In the days before Ra had left the earth, before he had begun to grow old, his great wisdom told him that if the goddess Nut bore children, one of them would end his reign among men. So Ra laid a curse upon Nut—that she should not be able to bear any child upon any day in the year.

Full of sorrow, Nut went for help to Thoth, the thrice-great god of wisdom and magic and learning, Ra's son, who loved her. Thoth knew that the curse of Ra, once spoken, could never be recalled, but in his wisdom he found a way of escape. He went to Khonsu, the Moon-god, and challenged him to a contest at draughts. Game after game they played and always Thoth won. The stakes grew higher and higher, but Khonsu wagered the most, for it was some of his own light that he risked and lost.

At last Khonsu would play no more. Then Thoth the thrice-great in wisdom gathered up the light which he had won and made it into five extra days which forever after were set between the end of the old year and the beginning of the new. The year was of three hundred and sixty days before this, but the five days which were added, which were not days of any year, were ever afterwards held as days of festival in old Egypt.

But, since his match with Thoth, Khonsu the moon has not had enough light to shine throughout the month, but dwindles into darkness and then grows to his full glory again; for he had lost the light needed to make five whole days.

On the first of these days Osiris, the eldest son of Nut, was born, and the second day was set aside to be the birthday of Horus. On the third day the second son of Nut was born, dark Set, the lord of evil. On the fourth her daughter Isis first saw the light, and her second daughter Nephthys on the fifth. In this way the curse of Ra was both fulfilled and defeated: for the days on which the children of Nut were born belonged to no year.

When Osiris was born many signs and wonders were seen and heard throughout the world. Most notable was the voice which came from the holiest shrine in the temple at Thebes on the Nile, which today is called Karnak, speaking to a man called Pamyles bidding him proclaim to all men that Osiris, the good and mighty king, was born to bring joy to all the earth.

Pamyles did as he was bidden, and he also attended on the Divine Child and brought him up as a man among men.

When Osiris was grown up he married his sister Isis, a custom which the Pharaohs of Egypt followed ever after. And Set married Nephthys: for he too being a god could marry only a goddess.

After Isis by her craft had learned the Secret Name of Ra, Osiris became sole ruler of Egypt and reigned on earth as Ra had done. He found the people both savage and brutish, fighting among themselves and killing and eating one another. But Isis discovered the grain of both wheat and barley, which grew wild over the land with the other plants and was still unknown to man; and Osiris taught them how to plant the seeds when the Nile had risen in the yearly inundation and sunk again leaving fresh fertile mud over the fields; how to tend and water the crops; how to cut the corn when it was ripe, and how to thresh the grain on the threshing floors, dry it and grind it to flour and make it into bread. He showed them also how to plant vines and make the grapes into wine; and they knew already how to brew beer out of the barley.

When the people of Egypt had learned to make bread and eat only the flesh of such animals as he taught them were suitable, Osiris went on to teach them laws, and how to live peacefully and happily together, delighting themselves with music and poetry.

As soon as Egypt was filled with peace and plenty, Osiris set out over the world to bring his blessings upon other nations. While he was away he left Isis to rule over the land, which she did both wisely and well.

But Set the Evil One, their brother, envied Osiris and hated Isis. The more the people loved and praised Osiris, the more Set hated him; and the more good he did and the happier mankind became, the stronger grew Set's desire to kill his brother and rule in his place.

Isis, however, was so full of wisdom and so watchful that Set made no attempt to seize the throne while she was watching over the land of Egypt. And when Osiris returned from his travels Set was among the first to welcome him back and kneel in reverence before "the good god Pharaoh Osiris."

Yet he had made his plans, aided by seventy-two of his wicked friends and Aso the evil queen of Ethiopia. Secretly Set obtained the exact measurements of the body of Osiris, and caused a beautiful chest to be made that would fit only him. It was fashioned of the rarest and most costly woods: cedar brought from Lebanon, and ebony from Punt at the south end of the Red Sea—for no wood grows in Egypt except the soft and useless palm.

Then Set gave a great feast in honour of Osiris; but the other guests were the two-and-seventy conspirators. It was the greatest feast that had yet been seen in Egypt, and the foods were choicer, the wines stronger and the dancing girls more beautiful than ever before. When the heart of Osiris had been made glad with feasting and song, the chest was brought in, and all were amazed at its beauty.

Osiris marvelled at the rare cedar inlaid with ebony and ivory, with less rare gold and silver, and painted inside with figures of gods and birds and animals, and he desired it greatly.

"I will give this chest to whosoever fits it most exactly!" cried Set. And at once the conspirators began in turn to see if they could win it. But one was too tall and another too short; one was too fat and another too thin— and all tried in vain.

"Let me see if I will fit into this marvellous piece of work," said Osiris, and he laid himself down in the chest while all gathered round breathlessly.

"I fit exactly, and the chest is mine!" cried Osiris.

"It is yours indeed, and shall be so forever!" hissed Set as he banged down the lid. Then in desperate haste he and the conspirators nailed it shut and sealed every crack with molten lead, so that Osiris the man died in the chest and his spirit went west across the Nile into Duat the Place of Testing; but, beyond it to Amenti, where those live forever who have lived well on earth and passed the judgments of Duat, he could not pass as yet.

Set and his companions took the chest which held the body of Osiris and cast it into the Nile; and Hapi the Nile-god carried it out into the Great Green Sea where it was tossed for many days until it came to the shore of Phoenicia near the city of Byblos. Here the waves cast it into a tamarisk tree that grew on the shore; and the tree shot out branches and grew leaves and flowers to make a fit resting-place for the body of the good god Osiris—and very soon that tree became famous throughout the land.

Presently King Malcander heard of it, and he and his wife, Queen Astarte, came to the seashore to gaze at the tree. By now the branches had grown together and hidden the chest which held the body of Osiris in the trunk itself. King Malcander gave orders that the tree should be cut down and fashioned into a great pillar for his palace. This was done, and all wondered at its beauty and fragrance: but none knew that it held the body of a god.

Meanwhile in Egypt Isis was in great fear. She had always known that Set was filled with evil and jealousy, but kindly Osiris would not believe in his brother's wickedness. But Isis knew as soon as her husband was dead, though no one told her, and fled into the marshes of the delta carrying the baby Horus with her. She found shelter on a little island where the goddess Buto lived, and entrusted the divine child to her. And as a further safeguard against Set, Isis loosed the island from its foundations, and let it float so that no one could tell where to find it.

Then she went to seek for the body of Osiris. For, until he was buried with all the needful rites and charms, even his spirit could go no farther to the west than Duat, the Testing-place; and it could not come to Amenti.

Back and forth over the land of Egypt wandered Isis, but never a trace could she find of the chest in which lay the body of Osiris. She asked all whom she met, but no one had seen it—and in this matter her magic powers could not help her.

At last she questioned the children who were playing by the riverside, and at once they told her that just such a chest as she described had floated past them on the swift stream and out into the Great Green Sea.

Then Isis wandered on the shore, and again and again it was the children who had seen the chest floating by and told her which way it had gone. And because of this, Isis blessed the children and decreed that ever afterwards children should speak words of wisdom and sometimes tell of things to come.

At length Isis came to Byblos and sat down by the seashore. Presently the maidens who attended on Queen Astarte came down to bathe at that place; and when they returned out of the water Isis taught them how to plait their hair—which had never been done before. When they went up to the palace a strange and wonderful perfume seemed to cling to them; and Queen Astarte marvelled at it, and at their plaited hair, and asked them how it came to be so.

The maidens told her of the wonderful woman who sat by the seashore, and Queen Astarte sent for Isis, and asked her to serve in the palace and tend her children, the little Prince Maneros and the baby Dictys, who was ailing sorely. For she did not know that the strange woman who was wandering alone at Byblos was the greatest of all the goddesses of Egypt.

Isis agreed to this, and very soon the baby Dictys was strong and well, though she did no more than give him her finger to suck. But presently she became fond of the child, and thought to make him immortal, which she did by burning away his mortal parts while she flew round and round him in the form of a swallow. Astarte, however, had been watching her secretly; and when she saw that her baby seemed to be on fire she rushed into the room with a loud cry, and so broke the magic.

Then Isis took on her own form, and Astarte crouched down in terror when she saw the shining goddess and learned who she was.

Malcander and Astarte offered her gifts of all the richest treasures in Byblos, but Isis asked only for the great tamarisk pillar which held up the roof and for what it contained.

When it was given to her, she caused it to open and took out the chest of Set. But the pillar she gave back to Malcander and Astarte; and it remained the most sacred object in Byblos, since it had once held the body of a god.

When the chest which had become the coffin of Osiris was given to her, Isis flung herself down on it with so terrible a cry of sorrow that little Dictys died at the very sound. But Isis at length caused the chest to be placed on a ship which King Malcander provided for her, and set out for Egypt. With

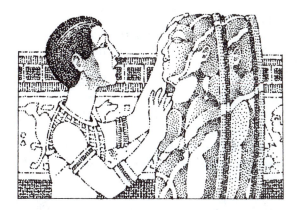

her went Maneros, the young prince of Byblos: but he did not remain with her for long, since his curiosity proved his undoing. For as soon as the ship had left the land Isis retired to where the chest of Set lay, and opened the lid. Maneros crept up behind her and peeped over her shoulder: but Isis knew he was there and, turning, gave him one glance of anger—and he fell backwards over the side of the ship into the sea.

Next morning, as the ship was passing the Phaedrus River, its strong current threatened to carry them out of sight of land. But Isis grew angry and placed a curse on the river, so that its stream dried up from that day.

She came safely to Egypt after this, and hid the chest in the marshes of the delta while she hastened to the floating island where Buto was guarding Horus.

But it chanced that Set came hunting wild boars with his dogs, hunting by night after his custom, since he loved the darkness in which evil things abound. By the light of the moon he saw the chest of cedar wood inlaid with ebony and ivory, with gold and silver, and recognized it.

At the sight hatred and anger came upon him in a red cloud, and he raged like a panther of the south. He tore open the chest, took the body of Osiris, and rent it into fourteen pieces which, by his divine strength, he scattered up and down the whole length of the Nile so that the crocodiles might eat them.

"It is not possible to destroy the body of a god!" cried Set. "Yet I have done it—for I have destroyed Osiris!" His laughter echoed through the land, and all who heard it trembled and hid.

Now Isis had to begin her search once more. This time she had helpers, for Nephthys left her wicked husband Set and came to join her sister. And Anubis, the son of Set and Nephthys, taking the form of a jackal, assisted in the search. When Isis travelled over the land she was accompanied and guarded by seven scorpions. But when she searched on the Nile and among the many streams of the delta she made her way in a boat made of papyrus: and the crocodiles, in their reverence for the goddess, touched neither the rent pieces of Osiris nor Isis herself. Indeed ever afterwards anyone who sailed the Nile in a boat made of papyrus was safe from them, for they thought that it was Isis still questing after the pieces of her husband's body.

Slowly, piece by piece, Isis recovered the fragments of Osiris. And wherever she did so, she formed by magic the likeness of his whole body and caused the priests to build a shrine and perform his funeral rites. And so there were thirteen places in Egypt which claimed to be the burial place of Osiris. In this way also she made it harder for Set to meddle further with the body of the dead god.

One piece only she did not recover, for it had been eaten by certain impious fishes; and their kind were accursed ever afterwards, and no Egyptian would touch or eat them.

Isis, however, did not bury any of the pieces in the places where the tombs and shrines of Osiris stood. She gathered the pieces together, rejoined them by magic, and by magic made a likeness of the missing member so that Osiris was complete. Then she caused the body to be embalmed and hidden away in a place of which she alone knew. And after this the spirit of Osiris passed into Amenti to rule over the dead until the last great battle, when Horus should slay Set and Osiris would return to earth once more.

But as Horus grew in this world the spirit of Osiris visited him often and taught him all that a great warrior should know—one who was to fight against Set both in the body and in the spirit.

One day Osiris said to the boy: "Tell me, what is the noblest thing that a man can do?"

And Horus answered: "To avenge his father and mother for the evil done to them."

This pleased Osiris, and he asked further: "And what animal is most useful for the avenger to take with him as he goes out to battle?"

"A horse," answered Horus promptly.

"Surely a lion would be better still?" suggested Osiris.

"A lion would indeed be the best for a man who needed help," replied Horus; "but a horse is best for pursuing a flying foe and cutting him off from escape."

When he heard this Osiris knew that the time had come for Horus to declare war on Set, and bade him gather together a great army and sail up the Nile to attack him in the deserts of the south.

Horus gathered his forces and prepared to begin the war. And Ra himself, the shining father of the gods, came to his aid in his own divine boat that sails across the heavens and through the dangers of the underworld.

Before they set sail Ra drew Horus aside so as to gaze into his blue eyes: for whoever looks into them, of gods or men, sees the future reflected there. But Set was watching; and he took upon himself the form of a black pig—black as the thunder-cloud, fierce to look at, with tusks to strike terror into the bravest heart.

Meanwhile Ra said to Horus: "Let me gaze into your eyes, and see what is to come of this war." He gazed into the eyes of Horus, and their colour was that of the Great Green Sea when the summer sky turns it to deepest blue.

While he gazed the black pig passed by and distracted his attention, so that he exclaimed: "Look at that! Never have I seen so huge and fierce a pig."

And Horus looked; and he did not know that it was Set, but thought it was a wild boar out of the thickets of the north, and he was not ready with a charm or a word of power to guard himself against the enemy.

Then Set aimed a blow of fire at the eyes of Horus; and Horus shouted with the pain and was in a great rage. He knew now that it was Set; but Set had gone on the instant and could not be trapped.

Ra caused Horus to be taken into a dark room, and it was long before his eyes could see again as clearly as before. When he was recovered Ra had returned to the sky; but Horus was filled with joy that he could see once more, and as he set out up the Nile at the head of his army, the country on either side shared his joy and blossomed into spring.

There were many battles in that war, but the last and greatest was at Edfu, where the great temple of Horus stands to this day in memory of it. The forces of Set and Horus drew near to one another among the islands and the rapids of the First Cataract of the Nile. Set, in the form of a red hippopotamus of gigantic size, sprang up on the island of Elephantinē and uttered a great curse against Horus and against Isis:

"Let there come a terrible raging tempest and a mighty flood against my enemies!" he cried, and his voice was like the thunder rolling across the heavens from the south to the north.

At once the storm broke over the boats of Horus and his army; the wind roared and the water was heaped into great waves. But Horus held on his way, his own boat gleaming through the darkness, its prow shining like a ray of the sun.

Opposite Edfu, Set turned and stood at bay, straddling the whole stream of the Nile, so huge a red hippopotamus was he. But Horus took upon himself the shape of a handsome young man, twelve feet in height. His hand held a harpoon thirty feet long with a blade six feet wide at its point of greatest width.

Set opened his mighty jaws to destroy Horus and his followers when the storm should wreck their boats. But Horus cast his harpoon, and it struck deep into the head of the red hippopotamus, deep into his brain.

And that one blow slew Set the great wicked one, the enemy of Osiris and the gods—and the red hippopotamus sank dead beside the Nile at Edfu.

The storm passed away, the flood sank and the sky was clear and blue once more. Then the people of Edfu came out to welcome Horus the avenger and lead him in triumph to the shrine over which the great temple now stands. And they sang the song of praise which the priests chanted ever afterwards when the yearly festival of Horus was held at Edfu:

"Rejoice, you who dwell in Edfu! Horus the great god, the lord of the sky, has slain the enemy of his father! Eat the flesh of the vanquished, drink the blood of the red hippopotamus, burn his bones with fire! Let him be cut in pieces, and the scraps be given to the cats, and the offal to the reptiles!

"Glory to Horus of the mighty blow, the brave one, the slayer, the wielder of the Harpoon, the only son of Osiris, Horus of Edfu, Horus the avenger!"

But when Horus passed from earth and reigned no more as the Pharaoh of Egypt, he appeared before the assembly of the gods, and Set came also in the spirit, and contended in words for the rule of the world. But not even Thoth the wise could give judgment. And so it comes about that Horus and Set still contend for the souls of men and for the rule of the world.

There were no more battles on the Nile or in the land of Egypt; and Osiris rested quietly in his grave, which (since Set could no longer disturb it) Isis admitted was on the island of Philae, the most sacred place of all, in the Nile a few miles upstream from Elephantinē.

But the Egyptians believed that the Last Battle was still to come—and that Horus would defeat Set in this also. And when Set was destroyed forever, Osiris would rise from the dead and return to earth, bringing with him all those who had been his own faithful followers. And for this reason the Egyptians embalmed their dead and set the bodies away beneath towering pyramids of stone and deep in the tomb chambers of western Thebes, so that the blessed souls returning from Amenti should find them ready to enter again, and in them to live forever on earth under the good god Osiris, Isis his queen, and their son Horus.

Epics and Hero Tales

Epics and hero tales, as well as sagas, are a part of mythology but are distinguished from the tales of the gods in two ways: they are tales of human heroes, and they comprise a cycle of tales rather than one story. Probably the most familiar to most children are the cycles of tales about Robin Hood or King Arthur, in which the heroes assume a larger-than-life status and about whom legends accrue; there are, however, in many epics and hero tales, magical elements or intervention by superhuman beings that affect the lives of the protagonists. Whether the heroes of these cycles of tales are as merry as Robin Hood, as patient as Odysseus, or as noble as Arthur, they embody those qualities and virtues that each society most prizes.

Oonagh and the Giants

In this humorous tale of two Irish legendary heroes, it is the clever wife of Finn McCoul who thinks of a way to help Finn outwit the ferocious Cucullin.

Oonagh's husband was a giant, a famous Irish giant, Finn McCoul. Big and strong as he was, there was another tougher than Finn: Cucullin. Yes, Cucullin was truly a *giant* of a giant, and even Finn was scared of him.

Finn was afraid with good reason, for when Cucullin stamped his foot, the ground shook for miles around. He was tall as a church tower. Once he had punched a bolt of light-ning down from the sky and pounded it flat as a pancake with his fist. He still carried that bolt of lightning in his pocket, flashing it with pride whenever he felt like boasting.

One day, Cucullin decided to fight with Finn. Finn heard he was coming and moaned. "What hope is there for me? Cucullin'll flatten me for sure if he catches me. And if I run, the green hills will laugh at me forever. Woe is me, poor Finn!"

"Now, hold on, husband," said his wife. "Leave it to Oonagh. Old Cucullin will never lay a finger on you."

"Don't even *speak* of his finger," Finn cried. "All of his strength lies in the middle finger of his right hand."

"And a nice fact that is to know," Oonagh answered. She reached in her work basket and picked out nine long strands of wool yarn, each a different color. She made three braids. One braid she tied around her right arm, the second around her right ankle, and the third and longest she tied over her heart.

When Finn saw this, he felt a bit of hope. Oonagh knew her share of the fairy wisdom and had her special way of doing things. This wouldn't be the first time she'd set things right.

"I'll be off to the neighbors," Oonagh said to her husband. "You just sit tight." She kissed him and left.

When she returned, she had all the iron griddles she could lay her hands on. She set to work making a pile of dough, then rolled it into flat, round cakes. Inside each cake, she hid a griddle. Only one cake did she bake in the proper way, with no pan inside it, and she set that cake apart from the rest.

"Now, Finn, put on this bonnet. Ah, it only sits on the top of your head, but it does look sweet, now, don't it! And wrap this lace around you like a baby's little gown—that's it —and climb into the cradle, dear."

Finn just stood there. "Our children are all grown up now, Oonagh. Must I play at being my own baby?"

But Oonagh was busy boiling up a sackful of cabbage and a side of bacon. "No time to argue," she called to him. Finn climbed into the cradle and kept quiet.

Suddenly there was a pounding on the door that shook the house. "Is that Finn McCoul there?" roared Cucullin.

Oonagh opened the door. "Finn's out and about, but come on in, mighty man."

Cucullin was twice as big as Finn, so he had to duck his head to get through the doorway. "I've come to fight Finn, I'll be telling you the truth."

"Well, sit yourself down if you wish. He's out looking for you, if Cucullin you be. What a terrible temper my Finn is in. I'm afraid he'll make a mess of you, poor wretched soul. A powerful giant is Finn McCoul!"

"Ha!" Cucullin laughed. "We'll see about that."

Oonagh began to cough. "Oh, dear. The smoke's coming down the chimney again. If Finn were home, he'd just turn the house around so's the wind couldn't blow down the chimney like that. But I don't suppose *you* could do it. . . ."

"Of course I can!" said Cucullin. Back outside he went, Oonagh following behind. She watched the giant pull on the middle finger of his right hand and heard it give three little cracks. Then Cucullin put his huge arms around the stone house, and puffing heavily, he turned it around.

In the house, Finn's cradle rocked wildly, and he shuddered.

"Now that you've been so kind," said Oonagh, "I'd like to fix your last meal for ye. It'll take awhile, I'm sorry to say, for I need to fetch water down the hill. Ah, yes, today Finn was going to tear open our mountain, out behind the house, so we'd not have so far to go for water. But then, 'tis a job only Finn himself could do. Don't be troubling yourself with thinking you should try."

"Try?" bellowed Cucullin. "Anything Cucullin tries he can do!" said the giant. But he was beginning to wonder about this Finn. Tearing apart a mountain made of solid rock was no small feat, even for Cucullin.

Once, twice, three times Cucullin pulled on his middle finger, cracking it nine times in all. Then he dug his big hands into the rock and pulled with all his might until—*Crack! Crumble!*—the mountain split wide open for a quarter of a mile, and the water ran free. The crack is still there; these days they call it Lumford's Glen.

When Cucullin came back in the house, he was beginning to worry about meeting up with Finn. These chores that Finn did around the house were almost too much for Cucullin himself.

"Now, sit yourself down and eat up," said Oonagh, dishing up a huge bowl of cabbage and piling up the griddle cakes in front of Cucullin.

The giant bit into one of the cakes and let out a yell. "What's wrong with this cake?"

"Why, that's just the way Finn loves them. But then, you take such dainty little bites. . . ."

At this, Cucullin opened his mouth wide and bit down on the cake as hard as he could. His giant tooth cracked, and he let out a yowl so ferocious that Finn in his cradle howled in fear.

Oonagh said, "There, now. You've awakened the baby with your hollering. Well, one of my griddle cakes will make him feel better." She picked up the cake without an iron pan. "Eat it, little one," she said to Finn.

Cucullin could hardly believe his eyes when he saw the size of the baby in the cradle. The baby gobbled the cake as if it were made of air.

"Is it special teeth this Finn family's got?" asked Cucullin.

"Come see for yourself," said Oonagh. "They're way back in his mouth, so best you feel with your longest finger." Oonagh grabbed Cucullin's middle finger and stuck it deep into Finn's mouth. Chomp! Finn bit down with all his strength, and off came Cucullin's magic finger.

Now Finn felt brave as could be. Up he jumped and chased Cucullin out of the house and down the mountainside, roaring like a bull all the way.

Oonagh watched him proudly as he ran. "And doesn't he look sweet in that bonnet!" she said.

Roland and Oliver

The use of folk literature in transmitting history is clearly seen in this classic French tale of the love and loyalty of two courtly warriors.

In the days of the Emperor Charlemagne, Charles the Great of the Franks, who ruled France and Germany and fought so mightily against the enemies of Christendom, there lived a count named Girard. Count Girard held the city and the castle of Vienne and the land that lay about it, but he was no friend to his Emperor, and with his vassals and his knights he rebelled and made war on him. Charlemagne, much angered, called together his army and marched against Vienne, whilst Girard and his followers retreated into the city, defending the walls bravely. For many months the advantage fell to neither side, and time passed until the siege had lasted for two whole years, and many there were among the besiegers, as well as among the besieged, who longed for the war to be over. Yet the city could not be taken, so well was it defended, and Charlemagne, glad though he would have been to be at peace with all his subjects, could not bring himself to withdraw his army, lest it should seem as though he acknowledged himself defeated by a rebel.

With the Emperor's army were those who were considered the great champions of France: Duke Naimes, his most trusted counsellor, Ganelon, who later brought such sorrow on France, Ogier the Dane, Yve and Yvoire, Gerin, Engelier the Gascon, Turpin the Archbishop of Rheims, who could wield a sword in defence of his faith as well as any knight, Duke Samson and brave Count Anseïs: ten champions famed throughout France.

There, too, with Charlemagne was his young nephew Roland, son of the Emperor's sister Berthe. Roland had but lately been knighted and he was anxious to prove himself, yet so long as the siege lasted it seemed as though he would have little chance of showing his worth. The days went slowly for him, and with the other young knights and the squires he often left the camp and hunted in the woods near Vienne, or jousted with his companions; and among them there was no one more skilled at feats of arms than he.

"Roland and Oliver" from FRENCH LEGENDS, TALES, AND FAIRY STORIES retold by Barbara Leonie Picard. Oxford University Press, 1955. Reprinted by permission.

Count Girard also had a nephew, Oliver, of an age with Roland; and one day, for an adventure, carrying plain arms, that he might be unknown, Oliver slipped unseen through the gates of Vienne and wandered into the Emperor's camp. Here in an open space he found Roland and his companions tilting together, and after watching for a while, he asked if he might join them. Though he was a stranger to them, they thought him one of the Emperor's men, and they lent him a horse and let him tilt with them. Soon it was apparent that Oliver surpassed them all. Not even Roland, who was accounted the best among them, was more skilled with lance and sword.

The youths were loud in admiration of the stranger and asked his name, but he only smiled and would not answer. Then someone whispered that he might be an enemy, since in two years no one of them had seen him before. And the murmur went round amongst them, so that their friendly smiles were changed to suspicious frowns, and they crowded about him, demanding his name. Rough hands were laid upon him, but he broke free, and leaping on a horse, rode for his life towards the walls of Vienne.

"After him!" cried Roland. "He must not escape. He is too good a prize to lose." And the young knights rode after him swiftly with Roland at their head. Steadily Roland gained on Oliver, until he was upon him, and close beneath the city walls, Oliver turned to face his pursuers, and Roland, in triumph, raised his sword to strike. But at that moment there came a cry of terror from the walls above, and Roland looked up and saw a maiden, the fairest he had ever seen, standing on the ramparts, her hands clasped in supplication and her face pale with fear. It was lovely Aude, the sister of Oliver. "Spare my brother Oliver," she pleaded. And Roland, staring at her, slowly lowered his sword and let Oliver ride on to the gates unharmed. "I could not bring grief to so fair a maiden," he said to himself.

During the days that followed, Roland thought much on Oliver and Aude, and wished that they had not been the Emperor's enemies. And for their part, they thought of Roland, and wished the war were at an end; and Oliver sought to persuade his uncle to peace.

After a time, his nephew's counsels prevailed, and Count Girard sent Oliver, well attended, to Charlemagne to ask that they might be accorded. "If you will withdraw your army, sire, my uncle the Count will come forth from Vienne and swear allegiance, and he will serve you faithfully for all his life," said Oliver.

But the Emperor, for all that he hated warring against his own vassals, could not find it in his heart to forgive Girard his rebellion so easily. "Let Count Girard humble himself before me, and I will consider pardoning him," he said.

"Sire," replied Oliver, "that would my uncle never do."

"Then the war goes on," said Charlemagne. But Duke Naimes spoke to him, counselling peace.

Oliver, standing before the Emperor, turned his head and looked at Roland and saw how he was watching him. He smiled and said impulsively, "You and I are of an age and well matched. How say you, if our uncles are willing, shall we settle this war in single combat?"

"Gladly," said Roland, and he begged the Emperor's permission. After thought, Charlemagne agreed. "Go back and tell Count Girard," he said to Oliver, "that if you are victorious in this contest I will depart from his lands with all my army, and leave him in peace for ever. But if my nephew Roland is the victor, then must Count Girard lose Vienne and all his lands to me."

"I shall tell him," said Oliver; and he returned to the city.

And so it was decided that the outcome of the war should be determined by single combat between the two young knights, and a day was named upon which they should meet on a little isle in a river that ran between the camp and the city walls.

On the appointed day, Roland, armed and carrying his sword Durendal, which no blade could withstand, went to the islet to await Oliver. Soon Count Girard's nephew came out through the city gates, wearing the armour and bearing the sword which had been given to him by a good Jew of Vienne on the day he had been made a knight.

Eagerly all those from the Emperor's camp crowded about Charlemagne and the champions of France upon the bank of the river to watch the fight, whilst Count Girard and his family, and Aude with them, stood upon the walls of Vienne with the defenders of the city.

The two young men greeted each other courteously, and at once the battle began. They were indeed well matched, giving blow for blow; and at any one of their strokes a lesser knight would have fallen. Soon their shields were dented and their armour battered, links from their chain mail falling about them as they hacked with their good swords. But at last with a great stroke from Durendal, the strongest sword in all France, Oliver's blade was broken and he fell to his knees with the force of the blow. A cry of fear went up from the watchers on the walls of Vienne, but from the Emperor's knights a shout of triumph rose. Oliver thought, "My last moment is come," and he braced himself to meet the stroke which would end his life. But Roland flung Durendal aside. "I cannot slay an unarmed man," he said.

Oliver rose, and he and Roland tore up two saplings to serve them as clubs, and with these they continued their fight until the green wood was broken all to splinters. And then the young knights wrestled together, each striving unsuccessfully to throw the other, until, at midday, both locked in each other's grip, they fell to the ground at the same time, so that neither could be said to have thrown the other. They stood up, breathless and exhausted. "The sun is high," said Roland. "It is too hot for fighting. Let us rest awhile."

They took off their helmets and smiled at one another. "I am happy," said Oliver, "that I am privileged to fight with so worthy an enemy." And the two young men embraced and sat down upon the grass and talked together as though they had been old friends. Wine was brought to them from the city, and another sword for Oliver; and when an hour or two had passed and the sun was lower in the sky, they helped each other to arm again, and once more began their fight.

As before, neither proved the better, and for long the battle raged, until suddenly, stepping aside to avoid a blow from Oliver, Roland lowered his sword and said, "Stay your hand awhile, for I feel a weakness come over me as though I had a fever, and I would rest."

With courtesy Oliver set aside his sword. "Rest for as long as you need, good Roland. I would not wish to be victor because you are unwell. Lie down and I will watch over you."

Roland, who was merely feigning sickness in order to test Oliver, took off his helmet and lay down upon the grass. Oliver placed his shield beneath his head to serve him as a pillow and fetched water for him from the river in his own helmet.

Watching, Charlemagne thought, "My nephew is vanquished and I have lost the day." While from the walls of Vienne fair Aude watched with pity; for though her brother's cause was hers, from her first sight of him she had felt a great admiration for Roland, an admiration which she knew could very easily turn to love.

But Roland sprang to his feet and laughed. "I did but try you, Oliver. And so courteously have you treated me that I wish we were brothers or friends, and not enemies."

"Brothers we could be," replied Oliver. "If we both live through this battle, I will give you my sister for your wife, since there is no other to whom I would rather see her wed. And as for friends, are we not friends already in our hearts?"

They fell once more to fighting, and again the advantage lay with neither, and still they fought as the sun went down the sky and sank from sight. Through the twilight they fought, while the watchers strained their eyes to see them and could not tell one from the other; and on into the darkness, so that only the sound of metal clashing upon metal told that the battle still went on.

And then at last from the darkness there was silence, as with one accord they ceased their strife. "Heaven does not mean that to either of us shall be the victory," they said. And they threw down their weapons and embraced, swearing friendship for ever. "Never again shall we take arms against each other," they vowed.

Each of them persuaded his uncle to be at peace, and for love of them Charlemagne and Count Girard were accorded, uniting against their common enemies, the Saracens, who held all Spain and were attacking France. And on a happy May morning Roland and Aude were betrothed, to their great joy and Oliver's.

From the day of their battle Roland and Oliver were comrades in arms, riding together against the Saracens and fighting side by side, winning such fame that they were accounted amongst the champions of France, the foremost of the twelve. Roland was ever brave, brave to the point of rashness, and very proud, and he hated the Saracens with all his heart and never trusted them. But Oliver, though no less brave, was gentle and cautious and never set his own glory before the good of France. Many adventures did the two young knights have in the years they were together, and until the day they died they were never parted.

"The Monster Humbaba" from GILGAMESH by Bernarda Bryson. Reprinted by permission of the author.

from Gilgamesh
Bernarda Bryson

Oldest of the recorded epics, the story of the Babylonian hero has elements that later appeared in the Old Testament and in Greek mythology. The Bryson version used here is as notable for its illustrations as its writing style.

The Monster Humbaba

Perfect was the friendship of Gilgamesh and Enkidu. The wild man asked only to be the servant of the King, but Gilgamesh called him "my younger brother," and Ninsun, the queen, looked upon him almost as a son. Everywhere, they went together and everywhere they were admired. They took part in feats of strength and daring, winning all prizes and all praise. And in all this Enkidu was content.

Not so, Gilgamesh. On one occasion he said to his friend, "Day and night I dream of a great enterprise. Whenever I close my eyes, voices come to me and say: 'Arouse yourself, Gilgamesh, there are great things to be done!' "

Enkidu's mind was full of foreboding.

"You and I, Enkidu, we will climb the mountain and destroy the monster Humbaba!"

Enkidu's eyes filled with tears and he turned away.

"Why should you cry, O Enkidu? Are you not the bravest of men? Are you no longer my friend and brother whom I admire more than anyone at all?"

Enkidu spoke: "I knew the presence of Humbaba even when I was a wild man on the steppes and in the forest. I could hear the sighing of his voice rise over the sound of thunder and high winds. I could hear the beating of his heart and feel the heat of his breath at a distance of five-hundred shar. I do not fear beast or mortal man, O Gilgamesh, but Humbaba is not mortal; he is the appointed servant of the gods, the guardian of the wild cows and the cedar forest. Whoever comes near him will grow weak. He will become paralyzed and will fail."

"The monster is an everlasting evil," said Gilgamesh. "It oppresses the people. Day and night it spreads fires and spews its ashes over the town. It is hated by great Shamash, constantly obscuring his face. O Enkidu, shall my life be as an empty wind? What am I, if I turn aside from the things I want to do? I am nothing, only someone waiting for death! But if I do this thing, O Enkidu, even though I should fail, then they will say, 'Gilgamesh died a hero's death! He died defending his people.' I will have made an everlasting name for myself and my life will not be as an empty wind!"

Still Enkidu turned away.

Gilgamesh then called in the armorers, the makers of spears and shields and axes. They cast for him swords of bronze inlaid with silver and gold. They made powerful long-bows and arrows tipped with stone, and most beautiful of all, a spear with a handle of lapis lazuli and gold inset with many glittering jewels.

Gilgamesh called Enkidu and laid the weapons before him, hoping to tempt him with their beauty. And still Enkidu said no.

Gilgamesh was downcast. "My brother has grown soft and timid. He no longer loves daring; he has forgotten adventure; I will go alone!"

The elders of Uruk, who had long ago forgotten their hatred of the King, now came to him: "O Gilgamesh, do not undertake this thing. You are young; your heart has carried you away. Settle down, O King; take a bride to yourself; let your life be tranquil!"

Gilgamesh laughed. "Save your wise counsel for my friend, Enkidu. He'll listen. You waste your words on me, good fathers!"

The elders came in secret to Enkidu. "If the King stubbornly insists on doing this thing, risking danger and defying the gods, then Enkidu you must accompany him!"

"Indeed, you must go ahead of him," a second elder said, "for it is known that whoever first enters the cedar gate will be the first killed."

"Besides, it is you who know the way, Enkidu. It is you who have trodden the road!"

"May Shamash stand beside you!"
"May he open the path for you!"

Enkidu went to Gilgamesh. "My head is bowed, O King. I am your brother and your servant; wherever you will go, I will go."

Tears came into the eyes of Gilgamesh; his faith in Enkidu was restored. "Now, my brother, we will go to Ninsun; we will tell our plan and ask her to petition the gods for our success!"

Pale as she was, Ninsun turned more pale. But since she could not dissuade her son, she merely kissed him, giving him her blessing. To Enkidu she said, "Even though you are not my son, O Enkidu, you are like a son to me, and I shall petition the gods for you as for Gilgamesh. But remember, please, that as a man protects his own person, so must he guard the life of his companion!"

The people of Uruk walked with the two friends through the streets admiring their weapons and praising their bold plan: "Praise be to Gilgamesh who dares everything! Praise be to Enkidu who will safeguard his companion!" But Harim the priestess mourned, "May your feet carry you back safely to the city, Enkidu!" And thus they set out.

Ninsun dressed herself in her finest garments. She attached the golden pendants to her ears and set the divine tiara upon her head. She anointed herself with perfumes and carried in her hand an incense that would carry its pleasant odors into the sky. Mounting with stately grace to the roof of her palace, she raised her voice to its highest pitch and called out, "O Shamash, listen to me!" Then waiting a little for her voice to reach the ears of the god, she went on: "O Shamash, why have you given my son Gilgamesh such a restless heart? Why have you made him so eager for adventure? Now he has gone up to fight with the indestructible monster Humbaba. Why have you sent him, O Shamash, to wipe out the evil that you abhor? It is all your plan! It is you who have planted the idea in his head! May you not sleep, O Shamash, until Gilgamesh and his friend Enkidu return to Uruk. If they fail, may you never sleep again!"

Ninsun extinguished the small blaze from under the incense and descended from the roof of the palace.

Gilgamesh and Enkidu walked toward the mountain of the cedar forest. At a distance of twenty double-hours they sat down beside the path and ate a small amount of food. At a distance of thirty double-hours, they lay down to sleep, covering themselves with their garments. On the following day they walked a distance of fifty double-hours. Within three days' time, they covered a distance that it would have taken ordinary men some fifteen days to cover. They reached the mountain and saw before them a towering and magnificent gate of cedar wood.

"Here," said Gilgamesh, "we must pour meal upon the earth, for that will gain us the goodwill of the gods; it will persuade them to reveal their purpose in our dreams!"

They poured meal on the ground and lay down to sleep. After some time Gilgamesh wakened his friend. "Enkidu, I have had a dream; it went like this: We were standing in a deep gorge beside a mountain. Compared to it, we were the size of flies! Before our very eyes the mountain collapsed; it fell in a heap!"

"The meaning of that seems very clear," said Enkidu. "It means that Humbaba is the mountain and that he will fall before us!"

They closed their eyes again and slept. After some time, Gilgamesh again awakened his friend. "I've had another dream, Enkidu. I saw the same mountain this time, and again it fell, but it fell on me. However, as I lay struggling, a beautiful personage appeared. He took me by my feet and dragged me out from under the mountain. Now I wonder what this means? Is it that you will rescue me from the monster, or will someone else come along?"

They pondered a little and went back to sleep. Next Enkidu wakened his brother, Gilgamesh. "Has a cold shower passed over us? Did the lightning strike fires, and was there a rain of ashes?"

"The earth is dry and clean," said Gilgamesh, "you must have dreamed!" But since neither of them could understand the meaning of this dream, they fell asleep again, and soon the day came.

They approached the magnificent gate. "Let's open it, Enkidu! Let's be on our way!"

For a last time, Enkidu tried to persuade his friend to turn back. But since the King would not listen, it was he who went first and placed his hand against the gate to push it open. Enkidu was thrown backward with such violence that he fell to the earth. He rose to his feet. "Gilgamesh, wait! My hand is paralyzed!"

"Put it on my arm, Enkidu! It will take strength from my arm because I am not afraid."

When the two friends threw their weight against the gate, however, it swung inward.

They walked up the mountainside through the sacred trees. And these became closer and thicker until the sky was blotted out. They could hear the giant heartbeat of Humbaba and smell the smoke from his lungs.

To show his daring, Gilgamesh cut one of the cedar trees. The blows of his axe rang out, and from afar the terrible Humbaba heard the sound.

With a crashing of timbers and a rolling of loose stones, Humbaba came down upon them. His face loomed among the treetops, creased and grooved like some ancient rock. The breath he breathed withered the boughs of cedar and set small fires everywhere.

Enkidu's fears now vanished and the two heroes stood side by side as the monster advanced. He loomed over them, his arms swinging out like the masts of a ship. He was almost upon them when suddenly the friends stepped apart. The giant demon lurched through the trees, stumbled, and fell flat. He rose to his feet bellowing like a bull and charged upon Enkidu. But the King brought down his axe on the toe of Humbaba so that he whirled about roaring with pain. He grasped Gilgamesh by his flowing hair, swung him round and round as if to hurl him through the treetops, but now Enkidu saw his giant ribs exposed and he thrust his sword into the monster's side. Liquid fire gushed from the wound and ran in small streams down the mountainside. Gilgamesh fell to the earth and lay still, trying to breathe. But meanwhile Humbaba grasped the horns of Enkidu and began to flail his body against a tree. Surely the wild man would have died, but now Gilgamesh roused himself. He lanced into the air his long spear with its handle of lapis lazuli and gold. The spear caught Humbaba in the throat and remained there poised and glittering among the fires that had ignited everywhere.

The giant loosened his hold on Enkidu; he cried out. The earth reverberated with the sound, and distant mountains shook.

Gilgamesh felt pity in his heart. He withdrew his sword and put down his axe, while the monster Humbaba crept toward him grovelling and wailing for help. Now Enkidu perceived that the monster drew in a long breath in order to spew forth his last weapon—the searing fire that would consume the King. He leaped on the demon and with many sword thrusts released the fire, so that it bubbled harmlessly among the stones.

Humbaba was dead; the two heroes, black with soot and dirt, were still alive. They hugged each other; they leaped about; and singing and shouting, they descended the mountainside. Gentle rains fell around them and the land was forever free from the curse of the giant Humbaba.

from The Merry Adventures of Robin Hood
Howard Pyle

The adventures of Robin's band of outlaws appeal both to children's sense of justice and to their love of action and humor. Pyle based much of his version on the early ballads that preceded the written account.

Little John and the Tanner of Blyth

It often comes about in this world that unlucky happenings fall upon one in such measure that it seems, as the saying is, that every cat that one strokes flies into one's face. Thus it was with Little John one bright day in the merry Maytime; so listen and you shall hear how Dame Luck so buffeted him that his bones were sore for many a day thereafter.

One fine day, not long after Little John had left abiding with the Sheriff and had come back, with his worship's cook, to the merry greenwood, as has just been told, Robin Hood and a few chosen fellows of his band lay upon the soft sward beneath the greenwood tree where they dwelt. The day was warm and sultry, so that whilst most of the band were scattered through the forest upon this mission and upon that, these few stout fellows lay lazily beneath the shade of the tree, in the soft afternoon, passing jests among themselves and telling merry stories, with laughter and mirth.

All the air was laden with the bitter fragrance of the May, and all the bosky shades of the woodlands beyond rang with the sweet song of birds,—the throstle-cock, the cuckoo, and the wood-pigeon,—and with the song of birds mingled the cool sound of the gurgling brook that leaped out of the forest shades, and ran fretting amid its rough, gray stones across the sunlit open glade before the trysting tree. And a fair sight was that halfscore of tall, stout yeomen, all clad in Lincoln green, lying beneath the broad-spreading branches of the great oak tree, amid the quivering leaves of which the sunlight shivered and fell in dancing patches upon the grass.

The good old times have gone by when such men grow as grew then; when sturdy quarterstaff and longbow toughened a man's thews till they were like leather. Around Robin Hood that day there lay the very flower of English yeomanrie. Here the great Little John, with limbs as tough as the gnarled oak,

"Little John and the Tanner of Blyth" from THE MERRY ADVENTURES OF ROBIN HOOD by Howard Pyle. New York: Scribner's, 1883.

yet grown somewhat soft from good living at the Sheriff's house in Nottingham Town; there Will Stutely, his face as brown as a berry from sun and wind, but, for all that, the comeliest yeoman in the mid-country, only excepting Allan a Dale the minstrel, of whom you shall hear anon. Beside these was Will Scathelock, as lank as a greyhound, yet as fleet of foot as a buck of three years' growth; young David of Doncaster, with great stout limbs only less than those of Little John in size, the tender beard of early youth now just feathering his chin, and others of great renown both far and near.

Suddenly Robin Hood smote his knee.

"By Saint Dunstan," quoth he, "I had nigh forgot that quarter-day cometh on apace, and yet no cloth of Lincoln green in all our store. It must be looked to, and that in quick season. Come, busk thee, Little John! stir those lazy bones of thine, for thou must get thee straightway to our good gossip, the draper, Hugh Longshanks of Ancaster. Bid him send us straightway twentyscore yards of fair cloth of Lincoln green; and mayhap the journey may take some of the fat from off thy bones, that thou hast gotten from lazy living at our dear Sheriff's."

"Nay," muttered Little John (for he had heard so much upon this score that he was sore upon the point), "nay, truly, mayhap I have more flesh upon my joints than I once had, yet, flesh or no flesh, I doubt not that I could still hold my place and footing upon a narrow bridge against e'er a yeoman in Sherwood, or Nottinghamshire, for the matter of that, even though he had no more fat about his bones than thou hast, good master."

At this reply a great shout of laughter went up, and all looked at Robin Hood, for each man knew that Little John spake of a certain fight that happened between their master and himself, through which they first became acquainted.

"Nay," quoth Robin Hood, laughing louder than all, "Heaven forbid that I should doubt thee, for I care for no taste of thy staff myself, Little John. I must needs own that there are those of my band can handle a seven-foot

staff more deftly than I; yet no man in all Nottinghamshire can draw gray-goose shaft with my fingers. Nevertheless, a journey to Ancaster may not be ill for thee; so go thou, as I bid, and thou hadst best go this very evening, for since thou hast abided at the Sheriff's many know thy face, and if thou goest in broad daylight, thou mayest get thyself into a coil with some of his worship's men-at-arms. Bide thou here till I bring thee money to pay our good Hugh. I warrant he hath no better customers in all Nottinghamshire than we." So saying, Robin left them and entered the forest.

Not far from the trysting tree was a great rock in which a chamber had been hewn, the entrance being barred by a massive oaken door two palms' breadth in thickness, studded about with spikes, and fastened with a great padlock. This was the treasure-house of the band, and thither Robin Hood went, and, unlocking the door, entered the chamber, from which he brought forth a bag of gold, which he gave to Little John, to pay Hugh Longshanks withal, for the cloth of Lincoln green.

Then up got Little John, and, taking the bag of gold, which he thrust into his bosom, he strapped a girdle about his loins, took a stout pikestaff full seven feet long in his hand, and set forth upon his journey.

So he strode whistling along the leafy forest path that led to Fosse Way, turning neither to the right hand nor the left, until at last he came to where the path branched, leading on the one hand onward to Fosse Way, and on the other, as well Little John knew, to the merry Blue Boar Inn. Here Little John suddenly ceased whistling, and stopped in the middle of the path. First he looked up and then he looked down, and then, tilting his cap over one eye, he slowly scratched the back part of his head. For thus it was: at the sight of these two roads, two voices began to alarum within him, the one crying, "There lies the road to the Blue Boar Inn, a can of brown October, and a merry night with sweet companions such as thou mayst find there"; the other, "There lies the way to Ancaster and the duty thou art sent upon." Now the first of these two voices was far the louder, for Little John had grown passing fond of good living through abiding at the Sheriff's house; so, presently, looking up into the blue sky, across which bright clouds were sailing like silver boats, and swallows skimming in circling flight, quoth he, "I fear me it will rain this evening, so I'll e'en stop at the Blue Boar till it passes by, for I know my good master would not have me wet to the skin." So, without more ado, off he strode down the path that lay the way of his likings. Now there was no sign of any foul weather, but when one wishes to do a thing, as Little John did, one finds no lack of reasons for the doing.

Four merry wags were at the Blue Boar Inn; a butcher, a beggar, and two barefoot friars. Little John heard them singing from afar, as he walked through the hush of the mellow twilight that was now falling over hill and dale. Right glad were they to welcome such a merry blade as Little John. Fresh cans of ale were brought, and with jest and song and merry tales the hours slipped away on fleeting wings. None thought of time or tide till the night was so far gone that Little John put by the thought of setting forth upon his journey again that night, and so bided at the Blue Boar Inn until the morrow.

Now it was an ill piece of luck for Little John that he left his duty for his pleasure, and he paid a great score for it, as we are all apt to do in the same case, as you shall see.

Up he rose at the dawn of the next day, and, taking his stout pikestaff in his hand, he set forth upon his journey once more, as though he would make up for lost time.

In the good town of Blyth there lived a stout tanner, celebrated far and near for feats of strength and many tough bouts at wrestling and the quarterstaff. For five years he had held the mid-country champion belt for wrestling, till the great Adam o' Lincoln cast him in the ring and broke one of his ribs; but at quarterstaff he had never yet met his match in all the country about. Beside all this, he dearly loved the longbow, and a sly jaunt in the forest when the moon was full and the dun deer in season; so that the King's rangers kept a shrewd eye upon him and his doings, for Arthur a Bland's house was apt to have a plenty of meat in it that was more like venison than the law allowed.

Now Arthur had been to Nottingham Town the day before Little John set forth on his errand, there to sell a halfscore of tanned cowhides. At the dawn of the same day that Little John left the Inn, he started from Nottingham, homeward for Blyth. His way led, all in the dewy morn, past the verge of Sherwood Forest, where the birds were welcoming the lovely day with a great and merry jubilee. Across the Tanner's shoulders was slung his stout quarterstaff, ever near enough to him to be gripped quickly, and on his head was a cap of double cowhide, so tough that it could hardly be cloven even by a broadsword.

"Now," quoth Arthur a Bland to himself, when he had come to that part of the road that cut through a corner of the forest, "no doubt at this time of year the dun deer are coming from the forest depths nigher to the open meadow lands. Mayhap I may chance to catch a sight of the dainty brown darlings thus early in the morn." For there was nothing he loved better than to look upon a tripping herd of deer, even when he could not tickle their ribs with a clothyard shaft. Accordingly, quitting the path, he went peeping this way and that through the underbrush, spying now here and now there, with all the wiles of a master woodcraft, and of one who had more than once donned a doublet of Lincoln green.

Now as Little John stepped blithely along, thinking of nothing but of such things as the sweetness of the hawthorn buds that bedecked the hedgerows, or the crab trees that stood here and there all covered with fair pink blossoms, or gazing upward at the lark, that, springing from the dewy grass, hung aloft on quivering wings in the yellow sunlight, pouring forth its song that fell like a falling star from the sky, his luck led him away from the highway, not far from the spot where Arthur a Bland was peeping this way and that through the leaves of the thickets. Hearing a rustling of the branches, Little

John stopped, and presently caught sight of the brown cowhide cap of the Tanner moving amongst the bushes.

"I do much wonder," quoth Little John to himself, "what yon knave is after, that he should go thus peeping and peering about. I verily believe that yon scurvy varlet is no better than a thief, and cometh here after our own and the good King's dun deer." For by much roving in the forest, Little John had come to look upon all the deer in Sherwood as belonging to Robin Hood and his band as much as to good King Harry. "Nay," quoth he again, after a time, "this matter must e'en be looked into." So, quitting the highroad, he also entered the thickets, and began spying around after stout Arthur a Bland.

So for a long time they both of them went hunting about, Little John after the Tanner, and the Tanner after the deer. At last Little John trod upon a stick, which snapped under his foot, whereupon, hearing the noise, the Tanner turned quickly and caught sight of the yeoman. Seeing that the Tanner had spied him out, Little John put a bold face upon the matter.

"Hilloa," quoth he, "what art thou doing here, thou naughty fellow? Who are thou that comest ranging Sherwood's paths? In very sooth thou hast an evil cast of countenance, and I do think, truly, that thou art no better than a thief, and comest after our good King's deer."

"Nay," quoth the Tanner boldly,—for, though taken by surprise, he was not a man to be frightened by big words,—"thou liest in thy teeth. I am no thief, but an honest craftsman. As for my countenance, it is what it is; and for the matter of that, thine own is none too pretty, thou saucy fellow."

"Ha!" quoth Little John, in a great loud voice, "wouldst thou give me backtalk? Now I have a great part of mind to crack thy pate for thee. I would have thee know, fellow, that I am, as it were, one of the King's foresters. Leastwise," muttered he to himself, "I and my friends do take good care of our good sovereign's deer."

"I care not who thou art," answered the bold Tanner, "and unless thou hast many more of thy kind by thee, thou canst never make Arthur a Bland cry 'A mercy.'"

"Is that so?" cried Little John in a rage. "Now, by my faith, thou saucy rogue, thy tongue hath led thee into a pit thou wilt have a sorry time getting out of; for I will give thee such a drubbing as ne'er hast thou had in all thy life before. Take thy staff in thy hand, fellow, for I will not smite an unarmed man."

"Marry come up with a murrain!" cried the Tanner, for he, too, had talked himself into a fume. "Big words ne'er killed so much as a mouse. Who art thou that talkest so freely of cracking the head of Arthur a Bland? If I do not tan thy hide this day as ne'er I tanned a calf's hide in all my life before, split my staff into skewers for lamb's flesh and call me no more brave man! Now look to thyself, fellow!"

"Stay!" said Little John; "let us first measure our cudgels. I do reckon my staff longer than thine, and I would not take vantage of thee by even so much as an inch."

"Nay, I pass not for length," answered the Tanner. "My staff is long enough to knock down a calf; so look to thyself, fellow, I say again."

So, without more ado, each gripped his staff in the middle, and, with fell and angry looks, they came slowly together.

Now news had been brought to Robin Hood how that Little John, instead of doing his bidding, had passed by duty for pleasure, and so had stopped over night with merry company at the Blue Boar Inn, instead of going straight to Ancaster. So, being vexed to his heart by this, he set forth at dawn of day to seek Little John at the Blue Boar, or at least to meet the yeoman on the way, and ease his heart of what he thought of the matter. As thus he strode along in anger, putting together the words he would use to chide Little John, he heard, of a sudden, loud and angry voices, as of men in a rage, passing fell words back and forth from one to the other. At this, Robin Hood stopped and listened. "Surely," quoth he to himself, "that is Little John's voice, and he is talking in anger also. Methinks the other is strange to my ears. Now Heaven forfend that my good trusty

Little John should have fallen into the hands of the King's rangers. I must see to this matter, and that quickly."

Thus spoke Robin Hood to himself, all his anger passing away like a breath from the window-pane, at the thought that perhaps his trusty right-hand man was in some danger of his life. So cautiously he made his way through the thickets whence the voices came, and, pushing aside the leaves, peeped into the little open space where the two men, staff in hand, were coming slowly together.

"Ha!" quoth Robin to himself, "here is merry sport afoot. Now I would give three golden angels from my own pocket if yon stout fellow would give Little John a right sound drubbing! It would please me to see him well thumped for having failed in my bidding. I fear me, though, there is but poor chance of my seeing such a pleasant sight." So saying, he stretched himself at length upon the ground, that he might not only see the sport the better, but that he might enjoy the merry sight at his ease.

As you may have seen two dogs that think to fight, walking slowly round and round each other, neither cur wishing to begin the combat, so those two stout yeomen moved slowly around, each watching for a chance to take the other unaware, and so get in the first blow. At last Little John struck like a flash, and, "rap," the Tanner met the blow and turned it aside, and then smote back at Little John, who also turned the blow; and so this mighty battle began. Then up and down and back and forth they trod, the blows falling so thick and fast that, at a distance, one would have thought that half a score of men were fighting. Thus they fought for nigh a half an hour, until the ground was all ploughed up with the digging of their heels, and their breathing grew labored like the ox in the furrow. But Little John suffered the most, for he had become unused to such stiff labor, and his joints were not as supple as they had been before he went to dwell with the Sheriff.

All this time Robin Hood lay beneath the bush, rejoicing at such a comely bout of quarterstaff. "By my faith!" quoth he to himself, "never had I thought to see Little John so evenly matched in all my life. Belike, though, he would have overcome yon stout fellow before this had he been in his former trim."

At last Little John saw his chance, and, throwing all the strength he felt going from him into one blow that might have felled an ox, he struck at the Tanner with might and main. And now did the Tanner's cowhide cap stand him in good stead, and but for it he might never have held staff in hand again. As it was, the blow he caught beside the head was so shrewd that it sent him staggering across the little glade, so that, if Little John had had the strength to follow up his vantage, it would have been ill for stout Arthur. But he regained himself quickly, and at arm's length, struck back a blow at Little John, and this time the stroke reached its mark, and down went Little John at full length, his cudgel flying from his hand as he fell. Then, raising his staff, stout Arthur dealt him another blow upon the ribs.

"Hold!" roared Little John. "Wouldst thou strike a man when he is down?"

"Ay, marry would I," quoth the Tanner, giving him another thwack with his staff.

"Stop!" roared Little John. "Help! hold, I say! I yield me! I yield me, I say, good fellow!"

"Hast thou had enough?" asked the Tanner, grimly, holding his staff aloft.

"Ay, marry, and more than enough."

"And thou dost own that I am the better man of the two?"

"Yea, truly, and a murrain seize thee!" said Little John, the first aloud and the last to his beard.

"Then thou mayst go thy ways; and thank thy patron saint that I am a merciful man," said the Tanner.

"A plague o' such mercy as thine!" said Little John, sitting up and feeling his ribs where the Tanner had cudgelled him. "I make my vow, my ribs feel as though every one of them were broken in twain. I tell thee, good fellow, I did think there was never a man in all Nottinghamshire could do to me what thou hast done this day."

"And so thought I, also," cried Robin Hood, bursting out of the thicket and shouting with laughter till the tears ran down his cheeks. "O man, man!" said he, as well as he could for his mirth, "'a didst go over like a bottle knocked from a wall. I did see the whole merry bout, and never did I think to see thee yield thyself so, hand and foot, to any man in all merry England. I was seeking thee, to chide thee for leaving my bidding undone; but thou hast been paid all I owed thee, full measure, pressed down and overflowing, by this good fellow. Marry, 'a did reach out his arm full length whilst thou stood gaping at him, and, with a pretty rap, tumbled thee over as never have I seen one tumbled before." So spoke bold Robin, and all the time Little John sat upon the ground, looking as though he had sour curds in his mouth. "What may be thy name, good fellow?" said Robin, next, turning to the Tanner.

"Men do call me Arthur a Bland," spoke up the Tanner, boldly; "and now what may be thy name?"

"Ha, Arthur a Bland!" quoth Robin, "I have heard thy name before, good fellow. Thou didst break the crown of a friend of mine at the fair at Ely last October. The folk there call him Jock o'Nottingham; we call him Will Scathelock. This poor fellow whom thou hast so belabored is counted the best hand at the quarterstaff in all merry England. His name is Little John, and mine Robin Hood."

"How!" cried the Tanner, "art thou indeed the great Robin Hood, and is this the famous Little John? Marry, had I known who thou art, I would never have been so bold as to lift my hand against thee. Let me help thee to thy feet, good Master Little John, and let me brush the dust from off thy coat."

"Nay," quoth Little John, testily, at the same time rising carefully, as though his bones had been made of glass, "I can help myself, good fellow, without thy aid; and, let me tell thee, had it not been for that vile cowskin cap of thine, it would have been ill for thee this day."

At this Robin laughed again, and, turning to the Tanner, he said, "Wilt thou join my band, good Arthur? for I make my vow thou art one of the stoutest men that ever mine eyes beheld."

"Will I join thy band?" cried the Tanner, joyfully; "ay, marry, will I! Hey for a merry life!" cried he, leaping aloft and snapping his fingers, "and hey for the life I love! Away with tanbark and filthy vats and foul cowhides! I will follow thee to the ends of the earth, good master, and not a herd of dun deer in all the forest but shall know the sound of the twang of my bowstring."

"As for thee, Little John," said Robin, turning to him and laughing, "thou wilt start once more for Ancaster, and we will go part way with thee, for I will not have thee turn again to either the right hand or the left till thou hast fairly gotten away from Sherwood. There are other inns that thou knowest yet, hereabouts." Thereupon, leaving the thickets, they took once more to the highway, and departed upon their business.

from **Glooskap's Country and Other Indian Tales**
Cyrus MacMillan

In this tale of the hero figure of Native American mythology, Glooskap uses his magic to lure Summer to his cold north to defeat the powerful giant who kept the land in frozen thrall.

How Summer Came to Canada

Once during Glooskap's lifetime and reign in Canada it grew very cold. Everywhere there was snow and ice, and in all the land there was not a flower nor a leaf left alive. The fires that the Indians built could not bring warmth. The food supply was slowly eaten up, and the people were unable to grow more corn because of the hard frozen ground. Great numbers of men and women and children died daily from cold and hunger, and it seemed as if the whole land must soon perish.

Over the extreme cold Glooskap had no power. He tried all his magic, but it was of no avail. For the cold was caused by a powerful giant who came into the land from the far north, bringing Famine and Death as his helpers. Even with his breath he could blight and wither the trees so that they brought forth no leaves nor fruit; and he could destroy the corn and kill man and beast. The giant's name was Winter. He was very old and very strong, and he had ruled in the far north long before the coming of man. Glooskap, being brave and wishing to help his people in their need, went alone to the giant's tent to try to coax or bribe or force him to go away. But even he, with all his magic power, at once fell in love with the giant's home; for in the sunlight it sparkled like crystal and was of many wonderful colours, but in the night under the moonlight it was spotlessly white. From the tent, when Glooskap looked out, the face of the earth was beautiful. The trees had a covering of snow that gave them strange fantastic shapes. The sky was filled by night with flashing quivering lights, and even the stars had a new brightness. The forest, too, was full of mysterious noises. Glooskap soon forgot his people amid his new surroundings. The giant told him tales of olden times when all the land was silent and white and beautiful like his sparkling tent. After a time the giant used his charm of slumber and inaction until Glooskap fell asleep, for the charm was the charm of the Frost. For six months he slept like a bear. Then he awoke, for he was very strong and Winter could not kill him even in his sleep. But when he arose he was hungry and very tired.

One day soon after he awoke, his talebearer, Tatler the Loon, brought him good news. He told of a wonderful Southland, far away, where it was always warm, and where lived a Queen who could easily overcome the giant; indeed, she was the only one on earth whose power the giant feared. Loon described carefully the road to the new country. Glooskap, to save his people from Winter and Famine and Death, decided to go to the Southland and find the Queen. So he went to the sea, miles away, and sang the magic song that the whales obeyed. His old friend Blob the Whale came quickly to his call and, getting on her back, he sailed away. Now the whale always had a strange law for travellers.

She said to Glooskap: "You must shut your eyes tight while I carry you; to open them is dangerous, for if you do, I will surely go aground on a reef or a sand-bar and cannot get off, and you may then be drowned." And Glooskap promised to keep his eyes shut.

Many days the whale swam, and each day the water grew warmer, and the air grew gentler and sweeter, for it came from spicy shores; and the smells were no longer those of the salt sea, but of fruits and flowers and pines. Soon they saw in the sky by night the Southern Cross. They found, too, that they were no longer in the deep sea, but in shallow water flowing warm over yellow sands, and that land lay not far ahead. Blob the Whale now swam more cautiously.

Down in the sand the clams were singing a song of warning, telling travellers in these strange waters of the treacherous sand-bar beneath. "Oh, big whale," they said, "keep out to sea, for the water here is shallow and you shall come to grief if you keep on to shore." But the whale did not understand the language of the little clams, and she said to Glooskap, who understood: "What do they sing?" But Glooskap, wishing to land at once, answered: "They tell you to hurry, for a storm is coming—to hurry along as fast as you can." Then the whale hurried until she was soon close to the land. Glooskap, wishing the whale to go aground so that he could more easily walk ashore, opened his left eye and peeped, which was contrary to the whale's laws. And at once the whale stuck hard and fast on the beach, so that Glooskap, springing from her head, walked ashore on dry land. The whale, thinking that she could never get off, was very angry, and sang a song of lament and blame. But Glooskap put one end of his strong bow against the whale's jaw and, taking the other end in his hands, he placed his feet against the high bank, and with a mighty push he sent Old Blob again into the deep water. Then, to keep the whale's friendship, he threw her an old pipe and a bag of Indian

HOW SUMMER CAME TO CANADA retold by William Toye. Retelling was freely based in part on the version in CANADIAN WONDER TALES by Cyrus MacMillan (The Bodley Head Limited). Copyright © 1969 by Oxford University Press Canada. Reprinted by permission.

tobacco leaves—for Glooskap was a great smoker—and the whale, greatly pleased with the gift, lighted the pipe and, smoking it, swam far out to sea. Glooskap watched her disappear from view until he could see only clouds of her smoke against the sky. And to this day the whale has Glooskap's old pipe, and sailors often see her rise to the surface to smoke it in peace and to blow rings of tobacco smoke into the air.

When the whale had gone, Glooskap walked with great strides far inland. Soon he found the way of which Loon had told him. It was the Rainbow Road that led to the Wilderness of Flowers. It lay through the land of the Sunrise, beautiful and fresh in the morning light. On each side were sweet magnolias and palms, and all kinds of trees and flowers. The grass was soft and velvety, for by night the dew was always on it; and snow and hail were unknown and winds never blew coldly, for here the charm of the frost had no power.

Glooskap went quickly along the flower-lined Rainbow Road until he came to an orange grove where the air was sweet with the scent of blossoms. Soon he heard sounds of music. He peered through the trees and saw that the sounds came from an open space not far ahead where the grass was soft and where tiny streams were flowing and making melody. It was lilac-time in the land, and around the open space all kinds of flowers in the world were blooming. On the trees numberless birds were singing—birds of wonderfully coloured feathers such as Glooskap had never heard or seen before. He knew that he had reached at last the Wilderness of Flowers of which old Tatler the Loon had spoken. He drew deep breaths of honeysuckle and heliotrope and countless other flowers until he soon grew strong again after his long voyage.

Then he crept close to the edge of the open space and looked in from behind the trees. On the flower-covered grass within, many fair maidens were singing and dancing, holding in their hands chains of blossoms like children in a Maypole game. In the centre of the group was one fairer than all the others—the most beautiful creature he ever seen, her long brown hair crowned with

flowers and her arms filled with blossoms. For some time Glooskap gazed in silence, for he was too surprised to move or to utter speech. Then he saw at his side an old woman —wrinkled and faded, but still beautiful— like himself watching the dance. He found his voice and asked: "Who are those maidens in the Wilderness of Flowers?" And the old woman answered: "The maiden in the centre of the group is the Fairy Queen; her name is Summer. She is the daughter of the rosy Dawn—the most beautiful ever born. The maidens dancing with her are her children, the Fairies of Light and Sunshine and Flowers."

Glooskap knew that here at last was the Queen who by her charms could melt old Winter's heart and force him to go away, for she was very beautiful and good. With his magic song he lured her from her children into the dark forest; there he seized her and held her fast by a crafty trick. Then, with her as a companion, he began his long return journey north by land. That he might know the way back to the Wilderness of Flowers, he cut a large moose hide, which he always carried, into a long slender cord, and as he ran north with Summer, he let the cord unwind behind him, for he had no time to mark the trail in the usual way. When they had gone, Summer's children mourned greatly for their Queen. For weeks the tears ran down their cheeks like rain on all the land, and for a long time, old Dawn, the Queen's mother, covered herself with dark mourning clouds and refused to be bright.

After many days, still holding Summer in his bosom—for she loved him because of his magic power—Glooskap reached the Northland. He found none of his people, for they were all asleep under the giant's power, and the whole country was cold and lonely. At last he came to the home of old Winter. The giant welcomed him and the beautiful girl, for he hoped to freeze them both and keep them with him always. For some time they talked together in the tent, but, although he tried hard, the giant was unable to put them to sleep. Soon old Winter felt that his power had vanished and that the charm of the Frost was broken. Large drops of sweat ran down his face; then his tent slowly disappeared and he was left homeless. Summer used her strange power until everything that Winter had put to sleep awoke again. Buds came again upon the trees; the snow ran down the rivers carrying away the dead leaves; and the grass and the corn sprang up with new life. And old Winter, being sorrowful, wept, for he knew that his reign was ended, and his tears were like cold rain.

Summer, the Queen, seeing him mourn and wishing to stop his tears, said: "I have proved that I am more powerful than you; I give you now all the country to the far north for your own, and there I shall never disturb you. You may come back to Glooskap's country six months of every year and reign as of old, but you will be less severe; during the other six months, I myself will come from the Southland and rule the land."

Old Winter could do nothing but accept this offer gracefully, for he feared that if he did not he would melt entirely away. So he built a new home farther north, and there he reigns without interruption. In the late autumn he comes back to Glooskap's country and reigns for six months, but his rule is softer than in olden times. And when he comes, Summer, following Glooskap's moosehide cord, runs home with her birds to the Wilderness of Flowers. But at the end of six months she always comes back to drive old Winter away to his own land, to awaken the northern world, and to bring it the joys that only she, the Queen, can give. And so in Glooskap's old country, Winter and Summer, the hoary old giant and the beautiful Fairy Queen, divide the rule of the land between them.

Walther of Aquitaine

Child hostages of the king of the Huns, Walther and Hildegund escape when they are older so that they can marry, and Walther defends his life when they are set upon by the King of Burgundy.

When he was young and eager for conquest, Etzel, the great king of the Huns, rode westwards with his men in search of plunder. From the small kingdoms of the west he took great treasure and much gold as the price of his friendship; and from those kings who asked for time to collect the gold, he took hostages, so that they should not forget to pay him all that they had promised.

From the king of the Franks he took his little daughter, Hildegund; while from the king of Aquitaine he took his young son, Walther. But Gibich, the king of Burgundy, had as yet no children, so he gave to Etzel the lad Hagen of Troneg, his kinsman and the most highly born of all his vassals.

Etzel and his men rode back into Hunland, their wagons and their packhorses laden with spoils, and satisfaction in their hearts at the thought of yet more to come. And with the wild, heathen Huns went Walther and Hildegund and Hagen.

The three children grew up in Etzel's court, where the two boys learnt to ride as only the Huns could ride; while Hildegund span and wove with Queen Helka's maidens. Walther and Hagen became firm friends and were together always; and, whenever she could, Hildegund would steal away from amongst the dark-haired, flat-faced Hunnish maidens and talk with Walther and Hagen, who reminded her of her own people and her home.

After a time, there came a day when King Gibich had sent into Hunland all the gold that he had promised, and Hagen was free to go home. King Etzel was sorry to lose him, for he always welcomed to his court brave warriors from other lands to serve him in his wars, and Hagen had grown into a strong and mighty warrior. But Hagen would not stay in Hunland, for all Etzel's wishes, and so Etzel gave him gifts and sent him on his way with all honour; and he returned home once more to Burgundy.

Walther and Hildegund, left in Hunland, sought each other's company more and more, and in time the two of them, so different from the black-eyed, sallow-skinned Huns they lived among, grew to love each other, and promised one another secretly that if ever they went safely home again they would persuade their fathers to allow their marriage.

But King Etzel, when he was merry with wine or in a jovial mood, would laugh and say to Walther, "The little boy I brought from Aquitaine has grown into a fine strong man and handsome besides. It is time you chose yourself a bride, young Walther. Is there one of our Hunnish maids who takes your fancy? You have only to ask, and she is yours. For though you are not of our people, we like you well."

But Walther would always answer, "I thank you, King Etzel, but there is time enough for that." Until he had answered thus so often that the Hunnish lords and warriors began to look askance at him, thinking he slighted them.

And one day Queen Helka said to Etzel, "Young Hildegund, with her yellow hair, is fairer by far than any of our Hunnish maids. She would be a prize for any man. Have you no kinsman or brave warrior whom you would wish to reward?" So Etzel chose a husband for Hildegund and would have married her to him right away but that she pleaded for a short delay.

"What shall we do?" she said to Walther. "For now, though you may go home when the time comes, I shall never leave Hunland again, if I am the wife of a Hunnish lord. And how can I ever be your wife, if I have to marry a Hun?" And she began to weep.

"There is only one thing for us to do," said Walther. "We must both leave Hunland, and soon. Just the two of us together. Will you be afraid?"

Hildegund dried her tears. "I will be afraid of nothing, so long as you are with me." She thought for a moment and then said eagerly, "I know where the keys are kept to Etzel's treasure house. When we leave, let us take with us some of the gold our fathers have

sent into Hunland, for it should have been ours by right."

One night soon after, while Etzel and his men were feasting and making merry, Walther and Hildegund, on one horse, rode away from King Etzel's house in the darkness, and with them they took two large bags of gold.

The ride out of Hunland was hard, for they had to ride fast, and they had little enough to eat and only the bare ground to sleep on, for they dared trust no one to ask food or shelter of him. But once out of Etzel's kingdom and into Christian lands again, they went slowly and rested often and accepted gratefully all shelter and hospitality which they were offered on their way, telling who they were and whence they had come to any who asked them. Thus it was that word of their escape from Hunland reached Worms in Burgundy while they were yet far from Aquitaine.

Hagen of Troneg smiled when he heard, and was glad, remembering his old comrade Walther; but he said nothing, for he was a man who spoke little, and then to the point.

But young Gunther, who was king in Burgundy, King Gibich being dead, said sullenly, "My father Gibich paid as much gold to Etzel as Aquitaine and the Frankish king. A third of that gold which Walther carries should be mine by right."

Hagen looked at him coldly. "That should it not, as you know full well."

But Gunther was young, indeed, little more than a boy, and he was wilful and used to having his own way. "I shall take all the gold from Walther, if I wish," he said. "A third, at the least, shall be mine." He sent for twelve of his best warriors and bade them make ready to go with him to find Walther. "And you shall come with us," he said to Hagen. And Hagen shrugged his shoulders and said nothing, but went with them, for Gunther was his king.

In a narrow mountain pass, Walther and Hildegund met with Gunther and his warriors. Gunther called out to Walther to give up the gold he carried. "For I am Gunther of Burgundy, and I demand it," he said.

"The gold belongs to me, King Gunther,

and to no man else," said Walther. "Yet will I give you as much as will lie on a shield, if you will let me pass in peace."

"Give me all the gold, and you may pass," said Gunther.

"Come and take it, if you dare," cried Walther. He dismounted, telling Hildegund to lead the horse away to a place of safety; then, with his sword in his hands, he waited.

Such was the narrowness of the path, that no more than one of the Burgundians could attack Walther at one time. As the first of the warriors fell upon him, Hildegund turned away in fear; but Gunther and his other eleven warriors looked on eagerly, calling out to encourage their comrade. Only Hagen was silent, standing a short way off, leaning on his sword, watching everything; for he alone of the Burgundians had no intention of fighting, since Walther was his former friend.

The combat was fierce, but soon over, and the first of the Burgundian warriors lay dead at Walther's feet.

"He fights well, this Walther," said Gunther, and sent the second of his men up the rocky path.

One after the other, Walther slew the Burgundian warriors, while Gunther ground his teeth in anger and Hagen still leant upon his sword, watching, with a grim little smile. He regretted the loss of so many good warriors, and in such a cause, but he was not sorry to see Walther acquit himself so well.

At last there came a time when the twelfth of Gunther's men lay dead beside the path, and Walther, looking down, saw only a young lad and his one-time comrade Hagen and, spent and bleeding from many wounds, he prayed that this might be the end and he might now be allowed to pass on his way in peace.

But Gunther, young though he was, was no coward, and with a cry of rage, he unslung the sword from about him and ran up the path against Walther. And Hagen straightened up a little, his hands tightening about the hilt of his own sword, and his eyes narrowed.

Walther was very weary, so his first blow fell wide, missing Gunther, and his sword rang against the ground, striking sparks from the rock. But before Gunther could take the advantage, Walther slashed upwards with his sword and cut deeply into Gunther's leg, so that he slipped and fell and could not rise again. "Hagen!" he cried. "Hagen, come to me!"

Walther placed one foot upon Gunther's body and took a fresh grip on his sword. "It is a pity, King Gunther," he said, "that you will die so young, and all for two bags of gold." He lifted up his sword slowly, for he had little strength left.

But Hagen had come running, before ever Gunther had called to him, and even as Walther would have brought down his sword upon Gunther's unprotected head, Hagen's sword flashed in the sunlight, all but severing one of Walther's arms from his body.

An arm hanging uselessly beside him, his blood streaming to the ground, half blinded by pain, Walther held tightly to his sword with his one hand and, in a last effort, raised the heavy weapon and struck wildly out at Hagen's head. The point of the sword caught Hagen high above the cheek bone, putting out an eye.

So ended a battle for gold that had cost the lives of twelve good warriors, and might have cost three lives more. And there, on the narrow pathway, while Hildegund tended them and bound up their wounds, Walther made peace with Gunther and Hagen and they swore friendship together; and that friendship they never broke.

from Hero Tales from the Age of Chivalry
Grant Uden

One of the few hero tales about a woman, this story is based on the Froissart Chronicles and is a smooth blend of history and legend.

The Adventure of the Countess Jeanne

Let us today take the case of the Countess Jeanne of Montfort, wife of Count John.

I hope that some day you will come to know the fair duchy of Brittany, far to the northwest from Chimay; a land of proud, sturdy, fierce men, always quick to fight beneath their ermine banner; a land of sunny streams and smiling villages on the one hand, and on the other, of battlefields and fortified towns. Chief among the towns is Rennes, where the black-a-vised young Bertrand of Brittany, only twenty years old, rode incognito in a great tournament and broke fifteen lances. Then his own father, not recognizing his son in his borrowed armor, rode against this presumptuous unknown knight, who pulled his horse aside and refused the challenge rather than lift weapon against his sire.

It was in the cathedral at Rennes, just before that tournament, that a great wedding took place between Countess Jeanne, niece of old Duke John of Brittany, and Charles, Count of Blois and nephew of King Philip of France. In the congregation that day, amid all the noblest blood of Brittany, was another Countess Jeanne, wife of the Count of Montfort, half brother to old Duke John.

A puzzle of names and relationships, is it not? But keep the two Jeannes and their husbands distinct in your mind, for, assuredly, they were very separate in life. Duke John died. And who should succeed to the throne of the duchy? The King of France, ever ready to get some grasp over the fair domain of Brittany, strongly supported his nephew Charles of Blois and his Breton bride. But, on the other hand, Count John of Montfort laid his claim, backed by his proud wife. And where should the lord of Montfort look for support? Where better than across the Channel to the ancient foe of the King of France, the King of England?

Edward III was ready enough to help any defiance of King Philip of France. So it came to war, with, ranged on one side, the King of France and Charles of Blois, and on the other the King of England and John of Montfort—

oh! and Countess Jeanne of Montfort. Let us never forget this Countess Jeanne, for, faith, she was not a lady to allow herself to be forgotten.

I will not weary you with all the struggle so far as John of Montfort is concerned. He was captured in Nantes by a great French army and carried off captive to Paris, where he was held for three years.

When this happened, the Countess of Montfort was in Rennes, where they brought her the news of her husband's defeat. Though she was sorrowful enough of heart, she did not waste time in useless pining, for she had the courage of a man and the heart of a lion. She immediately set about rallying her friends and all the soldiers she could muster, showing them her little son John, named after his father, and saying, "Sirs, do not be so cast down by the loss of my lord the Count. He is one man, and here is another, who shall restore his father and shall be sufficient leader to you all. I have money enough to pay all the soldiers and captains I need."

Having thus put good heart into those at Rennes, Countess Jeanne set out for all her other garrisons and fortresses in Brittany, taking with her always her young son, making the same plea, putting spirit into her followers, and paying them liberally into the bargain. Then she settled down for the winter in Hennebon, a fortress on the river Blavet near the coast, so that she could keep in touch with her ally the King of England across the water. And all through the winter she periodically sent to the other garrisons, paying them generous wages and keeping up their spirits for the next campaigning season.

With the coming of spring the armies stirred again and Charles of Blois came into Brittany with a great host, intent on subduing the duchy. The first place he tackled was Rennes which, you will remember, had been the city where he had been married in the cathedral; the place, too, where Countess Jeanne had begun her courageous tour of defiance. She had left there a strong Breton captain, Sir Walter Cadoudel, who held out with great valor and for a time inflicted much damage on the attackers.

"The Adventure of the Countess Jeanne" from HERO TALES FROM THE AGE OF CHIVALRY (British title: I, JOHN FROISSART) edited by Grant Uden. Copyright © 1968 by Grant Uden. Reprinted by permission of Philomel Books, a Division of The Putnam Publishing Group and Penguin Books Ltd.

Unfortunately, the citizens became so weary of the struggle and saw so little hope of relief that they implored Sir Walter to surrender, and when he would not consent, seized him and flung him into prison, after which they gave up the city to Charles of Blois on condition that all the Montfort followers could leave unharmed. This, Charles agreed to, and Sir Walter was able to make his way to Hennebon to continue his fight for Countess Jeanne who, immediately she knew of the invasion of Charles of Blois, had sent another of her knights, Sir Amery de Clisson, to England to beg the assistance of King Edward. He was very ready to give it and appointed Sir Walter Manny, one of the greatest English captains, to lead an army. Sir Walter embarked with a company of knights and some six thousand of the best archers in England. This was an encouraging start, but they ran into heavy gales and were at sea nearly six weeks before they could land in France.

Things had not begun well for my lady Jeanne. Sir Walter Manny hovered on the high seas, so near and yet so far, and Rennes had fallen. Moreover, Charles of Blois was sweeping triumphantly on to Hennebon, resolved to capture the Countess and bring the whole war to a quick end.

Inside Hennebon there was a great bustle. The alarm bell was rung and every man was ordered to arm and prepare for the defense of the town. When Charles of Blois arrived he encamped his forces, and some of the young bloods immediately tried a skirmish at the town barriers. They were dealt with sharply by the defenders and retired with little luck.

The third day a major attack was mounted, from early morning till noon. The first onslaught was repulsed with heavy losses to the attackers. Charles's captains, when they saw their men giving ground, were in a great rage and sent them in to try again more furiously than before.

Jeanne, Countess of Montfort, was everywhere at once. She put on armor, mounted a great warhorse, and rode from street to street, cheering on the citizens to the battle.

Neither did she confine her efforts to the men. Under her orders the girls and womenfolk cut their gowns short, loaded themselves with stones from the streets, and staggered with them to the walls so that they could be hurled down on the attackers. They also carried up pots full of lime to burn and choke any who tried to scale the walls.

All this would have been more than enough for most women. But not Countess Jeanne. She climbed the top of a tower to see how the French army was faring outside. As she looked out over the plain, with its press of steel-clad men storming to the attack, its shouting captains urging on the siege engines, she noticed one thing that interested her greatly. The camp was deserted. The long lines of tents and pavilions were emptied of soldiers. Only boys and camp servants were to be seen moving about. She came quickly down from the tower still in her armor, and called for her great courser again. She summoned three hundred mounted men and rode with them to one of the town gates that was free from attack. They flung it open, and at the head of her three hundred she dashed straight for the deserted enemy camp. There they slashed the tent ropes, demolished the fine lodgings of Charles of Blois and his lords, and set fire to the whole encampment.

The frightened camp servants scattered and fled.

Hearing the din, the French knights looked back from Hennebon to see the rising columns of smoke. Shouting "Treason! Treason!" they left the assault on the town and made their way back to what was left of their base.

The Countess Jeanne looked through the billowing smoke and saw the knights and men-at-arms crowding back. Her return to Hennebon was cut off! Rallying her force she turned her horse, skirted the town, and rode hard for the port of Brest some seventy miles away.

When the marshal of the French army saw the Countess and her company galloping away, he set off in pursuit with a great force and managed to cut off a few that were not

so well horsed as the rest. But most of them, riding hell-for-leather, got safely to Brest with the Countess Jeanne and were received by the garrison with great joy.

The disconsolate French, left with their camp and all their stores burned, wondered if they could make do with lodgings made of boughs and leaves from the trees outside Hennebon. Those inside the town, not knowing what had become of their valiant Countess, were desperately worried. For five days they heard nothing. Then at sunrise the watchers saw the distant light strike on bridle and armor. My lady Montfort came riding rapidly around the edge of the French army with five hundred men behind her. Leaving Brest at midnight, they had returned to the defense of Hennebon. With a great wave of cheering and a blare of trumpets, the defenders threw open the gates. The astonished French, who thought they had seen the last of this unusual captain, watched helplessly. By the time they had

recovered their wits, the gates were slammed and barred again.

The French army tried one more fierce assault on the town, struggling till noon, but with as little success as before. Then Charles of Blois called off the attack and held a council of war. In the end they decided to split forces. Count Charles marched off with half the host to besiege the castle of Aurai. The rest stayed on at Hennebon but made no further assaults. They sent to Rennes, however, for a dozen large siege engines they had left there, and with their aid kept up a bombardment of stones day and night. This harassed the defenders and was less expensive in lives than making direct attacks. Indeed, they made such good progress with their ceaseless battering that the courage of some of the defenders began to falter and a group of them talked of surrender on condition that they might keep their goods. This did not suit the lionhearted Countess Jeanne. She begged the Breton lords, for the love of God, not to give up, saying she was certain that before three days had passed relief would come.

But counsels against her were strong and made so deep an impression on the chief citizens that they were on the point of yielding up the town and had allowed the French to advance close to the walls for the purpose of taking it over.

Then came the final surprise of this surprising tale.

My lady Montfort, sick at heart that all her efforts should come to nothing, climbed a stair in the castle of Hennebon and, with little spirit left, stared out to sea. She could scarcely believe her eyes. For she saw a distant crowd of sail standing into harbor. Her joyful cries brought the townsfolk running. They crowded to the ramparts and saw for themselves the host of ships, great and small, making for hard-pressed Hennebon.

Sir Walter Manny and his storm-tossed fleet from England had at last arrived.

That is really the end of the story. If I wished, I could dwell on the reception the Countess gave to Sir Walter Manny when he landed with all his captains. I could tell of the feasting and jollity that made it difficult to remember the town was still under siege.

They did, however, receive a frequent reminder, for the French, furious at the collapse of the surrender negotiations, brought up their largest machine as near as possible to the walls and hurled great stones over them day and night.

In the end, Sir Walter Manny, that great knight who carried the golden lion on the black chevronels, had had enough of the unmannerly machine. He led out a company of archers and men-at-arms who shot down the men who were firing and then broke the siege engine in pieces. For good measure, before the laggard French host was properly astir, they set fire to the camp again! This was too much. The French commander struck camp and straggled off to rejoin Charles of Blois at Aurai.

The Countess Jeanne came down from the castle with a blithesome heart and in her excitement kissed Sir Walter Manny and his companions two or three times, one after the other. It must have been a formidable experience!

Modern Fantasy

Combining the appeal of magic, probable or improbable, of the folk tale and the structural and literary impositions of realistic fiction is modern fantasy, which differs from the folk tale in that the stories can be attributed to known authors. The best fantasy writing is firmly meshed with realistic details and meets the highest standards of depth in characterization, distinction in writing style, and logic in structure that are found in realistic writing. It also requires a consistency of the imaginary and a wholeness in conception of another world or magical power that make the impossible believable within the parameters of the author's fantasy world.

Because of the limitations of the experience of young children, the fantasy appropriate for them should be simply written and conceived; although there is no limit to the young child's imagination, there are limits of comprehension. Humor, so appealing an element in folk tales, is an important ingredient of many fanciful stories, as is true of action. Like any other aspect of writing, these must be used with restraint. A similar moderation should be observed in the use of strange place or personal names, especially in science fiction; this is often observed in the breach.

Not all children prefer, or even enjoy, fantasy, but they can be encouraged to appreciate it by hearing it read aloud. For such children it is wise to choose a story, or an episode from a story, that has a realistic base, is written with humor, or deals with a theme or subject that is of particular interest to the intended audience.

Animals and Toys

 For most children, the toys and stuffed animals they play with are the first objects of their imagination, and frequently these objects are so personified as to seem real to them. Children also feel a special affinity for real animals, and it is clear from studies of reading patterns and preferences that these interests influence a child's enjoyment in a book whether it is read aloud or read independently. There are other aspects of books that make them appealing to readers, such as humor and action, and all of them are present, in varying degrees, in the stories from which the excerpts included here were taken.

from **Paddington Abroad**
Michael Bond

Like all of the Paddington stories, written in episodic chapters and therefore a good choice for reading aloud, this is an adventure in which the small Peruvian bear gets into trouble and out again.

A Visit to the Bank

"Paddington looks unusually smart this morning," said Mrs. Bird.

"Oh, dear," said Mrs. Brown. "Does he? I hope he's not up to anything."

She joined Mrs. Bird at the window and followed the direction of her gaze up the road to where a small figure in a blue duffle coat was hurrying along the pavement.

Now that Mrs. Bird mentioned it Paddington did seem to have an air about him. Even from a distance his fur looked remarkably neat and freshly combed, and his old hat, instead of being pulled down over his ears, was set at a very rakish angle with the brim turned up, which was most unusual. Even his old suitcase looked as if it had had some kind of polish on it.

"He's not even going in his usual direction," said Mrs. Brown as Paddington, having reached the end of the road, looked carefully over his shoulder and then turned right and quickly disappeared from view. "He *always* turns left."

"If you ask me," said Mrs. Bird, "that young bear's got something on his mind. He was acting strangely at breakfast this morning. He didn't even have a second helping and he kept peering over Mr. Brown's shoulder at the paper with a very odd look on his face."

"I'm not surprised he had an odd look if it was Henry's paper," said Mrs. Brown. "I can never make head or tail of it myself."

Mr. Brown worked in the City of London and he always read a very important newspaper at breakfast time, full of news about stocks and shares and other money matters, which the rest of the Browns found very dull.

"All the same," she continued, as she led the way into the kitchen, "it's very strange. I do hope he hasn't got one of his ideas coming on. He spent most of yesterday evening doing his accounts and that's often a bad sign."

Mrs. Brown and Mrs. Bird were hard at work preparing for the coming holiday, and with only a few days left there were a thousand and one things to be done. If they hadn't been quite so busy they might well have put two and two together, but as it was the matter of Paddington's strange behavior was soon forgotten in the rush to get everything ready.

Unaware of the interest he had caused, Paddington made his way along a road not far from the Portobello market until he reached an imposing building which stood slightly apart from the rest. It had tall, bronze doors which were tightly shut, and over the entrance, in large gold letters, were the words FLOYDS BANK LIMITED.

After carefully making sure that no one was watching, Paddington withdrew a small cardboard-covered book from under his hat and then sat down on his suitcase outside the bank while he waited for the doors to open.

Like the building the book had the words FLOYDS BANK printed on the outside, and just inside the front cover it had P. BROWN ESQ., written in ink.

With the exception of the Browns and Mr. Gruber not many people knew about Paddington's banking account as it was a closely kept secret. It had all started some months before when Paddington came across an advertisement in one of Mr. Brown's old newspapers which he cut out and saved. In it a very fatherly-looking man smoking a pipe, who said he was a Mr. Floyd, explained how any money left with him would earn what he called "interest," and that the longer he kept it the more it would be worth.

Paddington had an eye for a bargain and having his money increase simply by leaving it somewhere had sounded like a very good bargain indeed.

The Browns had been so pleased at the idea that Mr. Brown had given him three shillings to add to his Christmas and birthday money, and after a great deal of thought Paddington had himself added another sixpence which he'd carefully saved from his weekly bun allowance. When all these sums were added together they made a grand total of one pound, three shillings and sixpence, and one day Mrs. Bird had taken him along to the bank in order to open an account.

For several days afterwards Paddington had hung about in a shop doorway opposite casting suspicious glances at anyone who went in or out. But after having been moved on by a passing policeman he'd had to let matters rest.

Since then, although he had carefully checked the amount in his book several times, Paddington had never actually been inside the bank. Secretly he was rather overawed by all the marble and thick polished wood, so he was pleased when at long last ten o'clock began to strike on a nearby church clock and he was still the only one outside.

As the last of the chimes died away there came the sound of bolts being withdrawn on the other side of the door, and Paddington hurried forward to peer eagerly through the letter-box.

" 'Ere, 'ere," exclaimed the porter, as he caught sight of Paddington's hat through the slit. "No hawkers 'ere, young feller-me-lad. This is a bank—not a workhouse. We don't want no hobbledehoys hanging around here."

"Hobbledehoys?" repeated Paddington, letting go of the letter-box flap in his surprise.

"That's what I said," grumbled the porter as he opened the door. "Breathing all over me knockers. I 'as to polish that brass, yer know."

"I'm not a hobbledehoy," exclaimed Paddington, looking most offended as he waved his bank book in the air. "I'm a bear and I've come to see Mr. Floyd about my savings."

"Ho, dear," said the porter, taking a closer look at Paddington. "Beggin' yer pardon, sir. When I saw your whiskers poking through me letter-box I mistook you for one of them bearded gentlemen of the road."

"That's all right," said Paddington sadly. "I often get mistaken." And as the man held the door open for him he raised his hat politely and hurried into the bank.

On several occasions in the past Mrs. Bird had impressed on Paddington how wise it was to have money in the bank in case of a rainy day and how he might be glad of it one day for a special occasion. Thinking things over in bed the night before, Paddington had decided that going abroad for a holiday was very much a special occasion, and after studying the advertisement once again he had thought up a very good idea for having the best of both worlds, but like many ideas he had at night under the bedclothes it didn't seem quite such a good one in the cold light of day.

Now that he was actually inside the bank, Paddington began to feel rather guilty and he wished he'd consulted Mr. Gruber on the matter, for he wasn't at all sure that Mrs. Bird would approve of his taking any money out without first asking her.

Hurrying across to one of the cubby-holes in the counter, Paddington climbed up on his suitcase and peered over the edge. The man on the other side looked rather startled when Paddington's hat appeared over the top and he reached nervously for a nearby ink-well.

"I'd like to take out all my savings for a special occasion, please," said Paddington importantly, as he handed the man his book.

Looking rather relieved, the man took Paddington's book from him and then raised one eyebrow as he held it up to the light. There were a number of calculations in red ink all over the cover, not to mention blots and one or two rather messy-looking marmalade stains.

"I'm afraid I had an accident with one of my jars under the bedclothes last night," explained Paddington hastily as he caught the man's eye.

"One of your *jars?*" repeated the man. "Under the *bedclothes?*"

"That's right," said Paddington. "I was working out my interest and I stepped back into it by mistake. It's a bit difficult under the bedclothes."

"It must be," said the man distastefully. "Marmalade stains indeed! And on a Floyds bank book!"

He hadn't been with the branch for very long, and although the manager had told him they sometimes had some very odd customers to deal with nothing had been mentioned about bears' banking accounts.

"What would you like me to do with it?" he asked doubtfully.

"I'd like to leave all my interest in, please," explained Paddington. "In case it rains."

"Well," said the man in a superior tone of voice as he made some calculations on a piece of paper. "I'm afraid you won't keep very dry on this. It only comes to three-pence."

"*What!*" exclaimed Paddington, hardly able to believe his ears. "*Threepence!* I don't think that's very interesting."

"Interest isn't the same thing as interesting," said the man. "Not the same thing at all."

He tried hard to think of some way of explaining matters for he wasn't used to dealing with bears and he had a feeling that Paddington was going to be one of his more difficult customers.

"It's . . . it's something we give you for letting us borrow your money," he said. "The longer you leave it in the more you get."

"Well, my money's been in since just after Christmas," exclaimed Paddington. "That's nearly six months."

"Threepence," said the man firmly.

Paddington watched in a daze as the man made an entry in his book and then pushed a one-pound note and some silver across the counter. "There you are," he said briskly. "One pound, three shillings and sixpence."

Paddington looked suspiciously at the note and then consulted a piece of paper he held in his paw. His eyes grew larger and larger as he compared the two.

"I think you must have made a mistake," he exclaimed. "This isn't my note."

"A mistake?" said the man stiffly. "We of Floyds never make mistakes."

"But it's got a different number," said Paddington hotly.

"A *different number?*" repeated the man.

"Yes," said Paddington. "And it said on mine that you promised to pay bear one pound on demand."

"Not *bear,*" said the assistant. "Bear*er.* It says that on all notes. Besides," he continued, "you don't get the same note back that you put in. I expect yours is miles away by now if it's anywhere at all. It might even have been burnt if it was an old one. They often burn old notes when they're worn out."

"*Burnt?*" repeated Paddington in a dazed voice. "*You've burnt my note?*"

"I didn't say it *had* been," said the man, looking more and more confused. "I only said it might have been."

Paddington took a deep breath and gave

more he saw of things the less he liked the look of them. Not only did his note have a different number but he had just caught sight of the dates on the coins and they were quite different to those on the ones he had left. Apart from that his own coins had been highly polished, whereas these were old and very dull.

Paddington climbed down off his suitcase and pushed his way through the crowd with a determined expression on his face. Although he was only small, Paddington was a bear with a strong sense of right and wrong, especially when it came to money matters, and he felt it was high time he took matters into his own paws.

After he had made his way out of the bank Paddington hurried down the road in the direction of a red kiosk. Locked away in the secret compartment of his suitcase there was a note with some special instructions Mrs. Bird had written out for him in case of an emergency, together with four pennies. Thinking things over as he went along, Paddington decided it was very much a matter of an emergency, in fact he had a job to remember when he'd had a bigger one, and he was glad when at long last the telephone kiosk came into view and he saw it was empty.

"I don't know what's going on at the bank this morning," said Mrs. Brown as she closed the front door. "There was an enormous crowd outside when I came past."

"Perhaps there's been a robbery," said Mrs. Bird. "You read of such nasty goings on these days."

"I don't think it was a robbery," said Mrs. Brown vaguely. "It was more like an emergency of some kind. The police were there and an ambulance *and* the fire-brigade."

"H'mm!" said Mrs. Bird. "Well, I hope for all our sakes it isn't anything serious. Paddington's got all his money there and if there has been a raid we shall never hear the last of it."

Mrs. Bird paused as she was speaking and a thoughtful expression came over her face. "Talking of Paddington, have you seen him since he went out?" she asked.

the assistant a hard stare. It was one of the extra special hard ones which his Aunt Lucy had taught him and which he kept for emergencies.

"I think I should like to see Mr. Floyd," he exclaimed.

"Mr. Floyd?" repeated the assistant. He mopped his brow nervously as he looked anxiously over Paddington's shoulder at the queue which was already beginning to form. There were some nasty murmurings going on at the back which he didn't like the sound of at all. "I'm afraid there isn't a Mr. Floyd," he said.

"We have a Mr. Trimble," he added hastily, as Paddington gave him an even harder stare. "He's the manager. I think perhaps I'd better fetch him—he'll know what to do."

Paddington stared indignantly after the retreating figure of the clerk as he made his way towards a door marked MANAGER. The

"No," said Mrs. Brown. "Good heavens!" she exclaimed. "You don't think . . ."

"I'll get my hat," said Mrs. Bird. "And if Paddington's not somewhere at the bottom of it all I'll eat it on the way home!"

It took Mrs. Brown and Mrs. Bird some while to force their way through the crowd into the bank, and when they at last got inside their worst suspicions were realised, for there, sitting on his suitcase in the middle of a large crowd of officials was the small figure of Paddington.

"What on earth's going on?" cried Mrs. Brown, as they pushed their way through to the front.

Paddington looked very thankful to see the others. Things had been going from bad to worse since he'd got back to the bank.

"I think my numbers have got mixed up by mistake, Mrs. Brown," he explained.

"Trying to do a young bear out of his life's savings, that's what's going on," cried someone at the back.

"Set fire to his notes, they did," cried someone else.

" 'Undreds of pounds gone up in smoke, so they say," called out a street trader who knew Paddington by sight and had come into the bank to see what all the fuss was about.

"Oh, dear," said Mrs. Brown nervously. "I'm sure there must be some mistake. I don't think Floyds would ever do a thing like that on purpose."

"Indeed not, madam," exclaimed the manager as he stepped forward.

"My name's Trimble," he continued. "Can you vouch for this young bear?"

"Vouch for him?" said Mrs. Bird. "Why, I brought him here myself in the first place. He's a most respectable member of the family and very law-abiding."

"Respectable he may be," said a large policeman, as he licked his pencil, "but I don't know so. much about being law-abiding. Dialling 999 he was without proper cause. Calling out the police, not to mention the fire-brigade and an ambulance. It'll all have to be gone into in the proper manner."

Everyone stopped talking and looked down at Paddington.

"I was only trying to ring Mrs. Bird," said Paddington.

"Trying to ring Mrs. Bird?" repeated the policeman slowly, as he wrote it down in his notebook.

"That's right," explained Paddington. "I'm afraid I got my paw stuck in number nine, and every time I tried to get it out someone asked me what I wanted so I shouted for help."

Mr. Trimble coughed. "I think perhaps we had better go into my office," he said. "It all sounds most complicated and it's much quieter in there."

With that everyone agreed wholeheartedly. And Paddington, as he picked up his suitcase and followed the others into the manager's office, agreed most of all. Having a banking account was quite the most complicated thing he had ever come across.

It was some while before Paddington finally got through his explanations, but when he had finished everyone looked most relieved that the matter wasn't more serious. Even the policeman seemed quite pleased.

"It's a pity there aren't more public-spirited bears about," he said, shaking Paddington by the paw. "If everyone called for help when they saw anything suspicious we'd have a lot less work to do in the long run."

After everyone else had left, Mr. Trimble took Mrs. Brown, Mrs. Bird and Paddington on a tour of the strong-room to show them where all the money was kept, and he even gave Paddington a book of instructions so that he would know exactly what to do the next time he paid the bank a visit.

"I do hope you *won't* close your account, Mr. Brown," he said. "We of Floyds never like to feel we're losing a valued customer. If you like to leave your three and sixpence with us for safe keeping I'll let you have a brand-new one-pound note to take away for your holidays."

Paddington thanked Mr. Trimble very much for all his trouble and then considered the matter. "If you don't mind," he said at last, "I think I'd like a used one instead."

Paddington wasn't the sort of bear who believed in taking any chances, and although the crisp new note in the manager's hand looked very tempting he decided he would much prefer to have one that had been properly tested.

from Charlotte's Web
E. B. White

A classic in its time, this is one of the great stories of friendship in children's literature, a book that is both funny and touching. White's polished style is evident in the chapter in which Charlotte the spider and Wilbur the pig first meet.

Charlotte

The night seemed long. Wilbur's stomach was empty and his mind was full. And when your stomach is empty and your mind is full, it's always hard to sleep.

A dozen times during the night Wilbur woke and stared into the blackness, listening to the sounds and trying to figure out what time it was. A barn is never perfectly quiet. Even at midnight there is usually something stirring.

The first time he woke, he heard Templeton gnawing a hole in the grain bin. Templeton's teeth scraped loudly against the wood and made quite a racket. "That crazy rat!" thought Wilbur. "Why does he have to stay up all night, grinding his clashers and destroying people's property? Why can't he go to sleep, like any decent animal?"

The second time Wilbur woke, he heard the goose turning on her nest and chuckling to herself.

"What time is it?" whispered Wilbur to the goose.

"Probably-obably-obably about half-past eleven," said the goose. "Why aren't you asleep, Wilbur?"

"Too many things on my mind," said Wilbur.

"Well," said the goose, "that's not *my* trouble. I have nothing at all on my mind, but I've too many things under my behind. Have you ever tried to sleep while sitting on eight eggs?"

"No," replied Wilbur. "I suppose it *is* uncomfortable. How long does it take a goose egg to hatch?"

"Approximately-oximately thirty days, all told," answered the goose. "But I cheat a little. On warm afternoons, I just pull a little straw over the eggs and go out for a walk."

Wilbur yawned and went back to sleep. In his dreams he heard again the voice saying, "I'll be a friend to you. Go to sleep—you'll see me in the morning."

About half an hour before dawn, Wilbur woke and listened. The barn was still dark. The sheep lay motionless. Even the goose was quiet. Overhead, on the main floor, nothing stirred: the cows were resting, the horses dozed. Templeton had quit work and gone off somewhere on an errand. The only sound was a slight scraping noise from the rooftop, where the weather-vane swung back and forth. Wilbur loved the barn when it was like this—calm and quiet, waiting for light.

"Day is almost here," he thought.

Through a small window, a faint gleam appeared. One by one the stars went out. Wilbur could see the goose a few feet away. She sat with head tucked under a wing. Then he could see the sheep and the lambs. The sky lightened.

"Oh, beautiful day, it is here at last! Today I shall find my friend."

Wilbur looked everywhere. He searched his pen thoroughly. He examined the window ledge, stared up at the ceiling. But he saw nothing new. Finally he decided he would have to speak up. He hated to break the lovely stillness of dawn by using his voice, but he couldn't think of any other way to locate the mysterious new friend who was nowhere to be seen. So Wilbur cleared his throat.

"Attention, please!" he said in a loud, firm voice. "Will the party who addressed me at bedtime last night kindly make himself or herself known by giving an appropriate sign or signal!"

Wilbur paused and listened. All the other animals lifted their heads and stared at him. Wilbur blushed. But he was determined to get in touch with his unknown friend.

"Attention, please!" he said. "I will repeat the message. Will the party who addressed me at bedtime last night kindly speak up. Please tell me where you are, if you are my friend!"

The sheep looked at each other in disgust.

"Stop your nonsense, Wilbur!" said the oldest sheep. "If you have a new friend here, you are probably disturbing his rest; and the quickest way to spoil a friendship is to wake somebody up in the morning before he is ready. How can you be sure your friend is an early riser?"

"I beg everyone's pardon," whispered Wilbur. "I didn't mean to be objectionable."

He lay down meekly in the manure, facing the door. He did not know it, but his friend was very near. And the old sheep was right —the friend was still asleep.

Soon Lurvy appeared with slops for breakfast. Wilbur rushed out, ate everything in a hurry, and licked the trough. The sheep moved off down the lane, the gander waddled along behind them, pulling grass. And then, just as Wilbur was settling down for his morning nap, he heard again the thin voice that had addressed him the night before.

"Salutations!" said the voice.

Wilbur jumped to his feet. "Salu-*what?*" he cried.

"Salutations!" repeated the voice.

"What are *they,* and where are *you?*" screamed Wilbur. "Please, *please,* tell me where you are. And what are salutations?"

"Salutations are greetings," said the voice. "When I say 'salutations,' it's just my fancy way of saying hello or good morning. Actually, it's a silly expression, and I am surprised that I used it at all. As for my whereabouts, that's easy. Look up here in the corner of the doorway! Here I am. Look, I'm waving!"

At last Wilbur saw the creature that had spoken to him in such a kindly way. Stretched across the upper part of the doorway was a big spiderweb, and hanging from the top of the web, head down, was a large grey spider. She was about the size of a gumdrop. She had eight legs, and she was waving one of them at Wilbur in friendly greeting. "See me now?" she asked.

"Oh, yes indeed," said Wilbur. "Yes indeed! How are you? Good morning! Salutations! Very pleased to meet you. What is your name, please? May I have your name?"

"My name," said the spider, "is Charlotte."

"Charlotte what?" asked Wilbur, eagerly.

"Charlotte A. Cavatica. But just call me Charlotte."

"I think you're beautiful," said Wilbur.

"Well, I *am* pretty," replied Charlotte. "There's no denying that. Almost all spiders are rather nice-looking. I'm not as flashy as some, but I'll do. I wish I could see you, Wilbur, as clearly as you can see me."

"Why can't you?" asked the pig. "I'm right here."

"Yes, but I'm near-sighted," replied Charlotte. "I've always been dreadfully near-sighted. It's good in some ways, not so good in others. Watch me wrap up this fly."

A fly that had been crawling along Wilbur's trough had flown up and blundered into the lower part of Charlotte's web and was tangled in the sticky threads. The fly was beating its wings furiously, trying to break loose and free itself.

"First," said Charlotte, "I dive at him." She plunged headfirst toward the fly. As she dropped, a tiny silken thread unwound from her rear end.

"Next, I wrap him up." She grabbed the fly, threw a few jets of silk around it, and rolled it over and over, wrapping it so that it couldn't move. Wilbur watched in horror. He could hardly believe what he was seeing, and although he detested flies, he was sorry for this one.

"There!" said Charlotte. "Now I knock him out, so he'll be more comfortable." She bit the fly. "He can't feel a thing now," she remarked. "He'll make a perfect breakfast for me."

"You mean you *eat* flies?" gasped Wilbur.

"Certainly. Flies, bugs, grasshoppers, choice beetles, moths, butterflies, tasty cockroaches, gnats, midges, daddy longlegs, centipedes, mosquitoes, crickets—anything that is careless enough to get caught in my web. I have to live, don't I?"

"Why, yes, of course," said Wilbur. "Do they taste good?"

"Delicious. Of course, I don't really eat them. I drink them—drink their blood. I love blood," said Charlotte, and her pleasant, thin voice grew even thinner and more pleasant.

"Don't say that!" groaned Wilbur. "Please don't say things like that!"

"Why not? It's true, and I have to say what is true. I am not entirely happy about my diet of flies and bugs, but it's the way I'm made. A spider has to pick up a living somehow or other, and I happen to be a trapper. I just naturally build a web and trap flies and other insects. My mother was a trapper before me. Her mother was a trapper before her. All our family have been trappers. Way back for thousands and thousands of years we spiders have been laying for flies and bugs."

"It's a miserable inheritance," said Wilbur, gloomily. He was sad because his new friend was so bloodthirsty.

"Yes, it is," agreed Charlotte. "But I can't help it. I don't know how the first spider in the early days of the world happened to think up this fancy idea of spinning a web, but she did, and it was clever of her, too. And since then, all of us spiders have had to work the same trick. It's not a bad pitch, on the whole."

"It's cruel," replied Wilbur, who did not intend to be argued out of his position.

"Well, *you* can't talk," said Charlotte. *"You* have your meals brought to you in a pail. Nobody feeds me. I have to get my own living. I live by my wits. I have to be sharp and clever, lest I go hungry. I have to think things out, catch what I can, take what comes. And it just so happens, my friend, that what comes is flies and insects and bugs. And *fur-**ther*more," said Charlotte, shaking one of her legs, "do you realize that if I didn't catch bugs and eat them, bugs would increase and multiply and get so numerous that they'd destroy the earth, wipe out everything?"

"Really?" said Wilbur. "I wouldn't want *that* to happen. Perhaps your web is a good thing after all."

The goose had been listening to this conversation and chuckling to herself. "There are a lot of things Wilbur doesn't know about life," she thought. "He's really a very innocent little pig. He doesn't even know what's going to happen to him around Christmastime; he has no idea that Mr. Zuckerman and Lurvy are plotting to kill him." And the goose raised herself a bit and poked her eggs a little further under her so that they would receive the full heat from her warm body and soft feathers.

Charlotte stood quietly over the fly, preparing to eat it. Wilbur lay down and closed his eyes. He was tired from his wakeful night and from the excitement of meeting someone for the first time. A breeze brought him the smell of clover—the sweet-smelling world beyond his fence. "Well," he thought, "I've got a new friend, all right. But what a gamble friendship is! Charlotte is fierce, brutal, scheming, bloodthirsty—everything I don't like. How can I learn to like her, even though she is pretty and, of course, clever?"

Wilbur was merely suffering the doubts and fears that often go with finding a new friend. In good time he was to discover that he was mistaken about Charlotte. Underneath her rather bold and cruel exterior, she had a kind heart, and she was to prove loyal and true to the very end.

from Just So Stories
Rudyard Kipling

No writer for children comes closer to the style of folk literature and to its "why" story structure than Kipling, and this tale is typical of the humor and wit of his writing.

The Elephant's Child

In the high and Far-Off times the Elephant, O Best Beloved, had no trunk. He had only a blackish, bulgy nose, as big as a boot, that he could wriggle about from side to side; but he couldn't pick up things with it. But there was one Elephant—a new Elephant—an Elephant's Child—who was full of 'satiable curtiosity, and that means he asked ever so many questions. *And* he lived in Africa, and he filled all Africa with his 'satiable curtiosities. He asked his tall aunt, the Ostrich, why her tail-feathers grew just so, and his tall aunt the Ostrich spanked him with her hard, hard claw. He asked his tall uncle, the Giraffe, what made his skin spotty, and his tall uncle, the Giraffe, spanked him with his hard, hard hoof. And still he was full of 'satiable curtiosity! He asked his broad aunt, the Hippopotamus, why her eyes were red, and his broad aunt, the Hippopotamus, spanked him with her broad, broad hoof; and he asked his hairy uncle, the Baboon, why melons tasted just so, and his hairy uncle, the Baboon, spanked him with his hairy, hairy paw. And *still* he was full of 'satiable curtiosity! He asked questions about everything that he saw, or heard, or felt, or smelt, or touched, and all his uncles and his aunts spanked him. And still he was full of 'satiable curtiosity!

One fine morning in the middle of the Precession of the Equinoxes this 'satiable Elephant's Child asked a new fine question that he had never asked before. He asked, "What does the Crocodile have for dinner?" Then everybody said, "Hush!" in a loud and dretful tone, and they spanked him immediately and directly, without stopping for a long time.

By and by, when that was finished, he came upon Kolokolo Bird sitting in the middle of a wait-a-bit thorn-bush, and he said, "My father has spanked me, and my mother has spanked me; all my aunts and uncles have spanked me for my 'satiable curtiosity; and *still* I want to know what the Crocodile has for dinner!"

Then Kolokolo Bird said, with a mournful cry, "Go to the banks of the great grey-green, greasy Limpopo River, all set about with fever-trees, and find out."

That very next morning, when there was nothing left of the Equinoxes, because the Precession had preceded according to precedent this 'satiable Elephant's Child took a hundred pounds of bananas (the little short red kind), and a hundred pounds of sugar-cane (the long purple kind), and seventeen melons (the greeny-crackly kind), and said to all his dear families, "Good-bye. I am going to the great grey-green, greasy Limpopo River, all set about with fever-trees, to find out what the Crocodile has for dinner." And they all spanked him once more for luck, though he asked them most politely to stop.

Then he went away, a little warm, but not at all astonished, eating melons, and throwing the rind about, because he could not pick it up.

He went from Graham's Town to Kimberley, and from Kimberley to Khama's Country, and from Khama's Country he went east by north, eating melons all the time, till he at last came to the banks of the great grey-green, greasy Limpopo River, all set about with fever-trees, precisely as Kolokolo Bird had said.

Now you must know and understand, O Best Beloved, that till that very week, and day, and hour, and minute, this 'satiable Elephant's Child had never seen a Crocodile, and did not know what one was like. It was all his 'satiable curtiosity.

The first thing that he found was a Bi-Coloured-Python-Rock-Snake curled round a rock.

" 'Scuse me," said the Elephant's Child most politely, "but have you seen such a thing as a Crocodile in these promiscuous parts?"

"*Have* I seen a Crocodile?" said the Bi-Coloured-Python-Rock-Snake, in a voice of dretful scorn. "What will you ask me next?"

" 'Scuse me," said the Elephant's Child, "but could you kindly tell me what he has for dinner?"

Then the Bi-Coloured-Python-Rock-Snake uncoiled himself very quickly from the rock, and spanked the Elephant's Child with his scalesome, flailsome tail.

"That is odd," said the Elephant's Child, "because my father and my mother, and my uncle and my aunt, not to mention my other

"The Elephant's Child" from JUST SO STORIES by Rudyard Kipling. Reprinted by permission of Doubleday & Company, Inc., The National Trust of Great Britain, and Macmillan London Limited.

aunt, the Hippopotamus, and my other uncle, the Baboon, have all spanked me for my 'satiable curtiosity—and I suppose this is the same thing."

So he said good-bye very politely to the Bi-Coloured-Python-Rock-Snake, and helped to coil him up on the rock again, and went on, a little warm, but not at all astonished, eating melons, and throwing the rind about because he could not pick it up, till he trod on what he thought was a log of wood at the very edge of the great grey-green, greasy Limpopo River, all set about with fever-trees.

But it was really the Crocodile, O Best Beloved, and the Crocodile winked one eye—like this!

" 'Scuse me," said the Elephant's Child most politely, "but do you happen to have seen a Crocodile in these promiscuous parts?"

Then the Crocodile winked the other eye, and lifted half his tail out of the mud; and the Elephant's Child stepped back most politely, because he did not wish to be spanked again.

"Come hither, Little One," said the Crocodile. "Why do you ask such things?"

" 'Scuse me," said the Elephant's Child most politely, "but my father has spanked me, my mother has spanked me, not to mention my tall aunt, the Ostrich, and my tall uncle, the Giraffe, who can kick ever so hard, as well as my broad aunt, the Hippopotamus, and my hairy uncle, the Baboon, *and* including the Bi-Coloured-Python-Rock-Snake, with the scalesome, flailsome tail, just up the bank, who spanks harder than any of them; and *so,* if it's quite all the same to you, I don't want to be spanked any more."

"Come hither, Little One," said the Crocodile, "for I am the Crocodile," and he wept crocodile-tears to show it was quite true.

Then the Elephant's Child grew all breathless, and panted, and kneeled down on the bank and said, "You are the very person I have been looking for all these long days. Will you please tell me what you have for dinner?"

"Come hither, Little One," said the Crocodile, "and I'll whisper."

Then the Elephant's Child put his head down close to the Crocodile's musky, tusky mouth, and the Crocodile caught him by his little nose, which up to that very week, day, hour, and minute, had been no bigger than a boot, though much more useful.

"I think," said the Crocodile—and he said it between his teeth, like this—"I think today I will begin with Elephant's Child!"

At this, O Best Beloved, the Elephant's Child was much annoyed, and he said, speaking through his nose, like this, "Led go! You are hurtig be!"

Then the Bi-Coloured-Python-Rock-Snake scuffled down from the bank and said, "My young friend, if you do not now, immediately and instantly, pull as hard as ever you can, it is my opinion that your acquaintance in the large-pattern leather ulster" (and by this he meant the Crocodile) "will jerk you into yonder limpid stream before you can say Jack Robinson."

This is the way Bi-Coloured-Python-Rock-Snakes always talk.

Then the Elephant's Child sat back on his little haunches, and pulled, and pulled, and pulled, and his nose began to stretch. And the Crocodile floundered into the water, making it all creamy with great sweeps of his tail, and *he* pulled, and pulled, and pulled.

And the Elephant's Child's nose kept on stretching; and the Elephant's Child spread all his little four legs and pulled, and pulled, and pulled, and his nose kept on stretching; and the Crocodile threshed his tail like an oar, and *he* pulled, and pulled, and pulled, and at each pull the Elephant's Child's nose grew longer and longer—and it hurt him hijjus!

Then the Elephant's Child felt his legs slipping, and he said through his nose, which was now nearly five feet long, "This is too butch for be!"

Then the Bi-Coloured-Python-Rock-Snake came down from the bank, and knotted himself in a double-clove-hitch round the Elephant's Child's hind legs, and said, "Rash and inexperienced traveller, we will now seriously devote ourselves to a little high tension, because if we do not, it is my impression that yonder self-propelling man-of-war with the armour-plated upper deck" (and by this, O Best Beloved, he meant the Crocodile), "will permanently vitiate your future career."

That is the way all Bi-Coloured-Python-Rock-Snakes always talk.

So he pulled, and the Elephant's Child pulled, and the Crocodile pulled; but the Elephant's Child and the Bi-Coloured-Python-Rock-Snake pulled hardest; and at last the Crocodile let go of the Elephant's Child's nose with a plop that you could hear all up and down the Limpopo.

Then the Elephant's Child sat down most hard and sudden; but first he was careful to say "Thank you" to the Bi-Coloured-Python-Rock-Snake; and next he was kind to his poor pulled nose, and wrapped it all up in cool banana leaves, and hung it in the great grey-green, greasy Limpopo to cool.

"What are you doing that for?" said the Bi-Coloured-Python-Rock-Snake.

" 'Scuse me," said the Elephant's Child, "but my nose is badly out of shape, and I am waiting for it to shrink."

"Then you will have to wait a long time," said the Bi-Coloured-Python-Rock-Snake. "Some people do not know what is good for them."

The Elephant's Child sat there for three days waiting for his nose to shrink. But it never grew any shorter, and besides, it made him squint. For, O Best Beloved, you will see and understand that the Crocodile had pulled it out into a really truly trunk same as all Elephants have today.

At the end of the third day a fly came and stung him on the shoulder, and before he knew what he was doing he lifted up his trunk and hit that fly dead with the end of it.

" 'Vantage number one!" said the Bi-Coloured-Python-Rock-Snake. "You couldn't have done that with a mere-smear nose. Try and eat a little now."

Before he thought what he was doing the Elephant's Child put out his trunk and plucked a large bundle of grass, dusted it clean against his forelegs, and stuffed it into his own mouth.

" 'Vantage number two!" said the Bi-Coloured-Python-Rock-Snake. "You couldn't have done that with a mere-smear nose. Don't you think the sun is very hot here?"

"It is," said the Elephant's Child, and before he thought what he was doing he schlooped up a schloop of mud from the banks of the great grey-green, greasy Limpopo, and slapped it on his head, where it made a cool schloopy-sloshy mud-cap all trickly behind his ears.

" 'Vantage number three!" said the Bi-Coloured-Python-Rock-Snake. "You couldn't have done that with a mere-smear nose. Now how do you feel about being spanked again?"

" 'Scuse me," said the Elephant's Child, "but I should not like it at all."

"How would you like to spank somebody?" said the Bi-Coloured-Python-Rock-Snake.

"I should like it very much indeed," said the Elephant's Child.

"Well," said the Bi-Coloured-Python-Rock-Snake, "you will find that new nose of yours very useful to spank people with."

"Thank you," said the Elephant's Child, "I'll remember that; and now I think I'll go home to all my dear families and try."

So the Elephant's Child went home across Africa frisking and whisking his trunk. When he wanted fruit to eat he pulled fruit down from a tree, instead of waiting for it to fall as he used to do. When he wanted grass he plucked grass up from the ground, instead of going on his knees as he used to do. When the flies bit him he broke off the branch of a tree and used it as a fly-whisk; and he made himself a new, cool, slushy-squshy mud-cap whenever the sun was hot. When he felt lonely walking through Africa he sang to himself down his trunk, and the noise was louder than several brass bands. He went especially out of his way to find a broad Hippopotamus (she was no relation of his), and he spanked her very hard, to make sure that the Bi-Coloured-Python-Rock-Snake had spoken the truth about his new trunk. The rest of the time he picked up the melon rinds that he had dropped on his way to the Limpopo—for he was a Tidy Pachyderm.

One dark evening he came back to all his dear families, and he coiled up his trunk and said, "How do you do?" They were very glad to see him, and immediately said, "Come here and be spanked for your 'satiable curtiosity."

"Pooh," said the Elephant's Child. "I don't think you peoples know anything about spanking; but *I* do, and I'll show you."

Then he uncurled his trunk and knocked two of his dear brothers head over heels.

"O Bananas!" said they, "where did you learn that trick, and what have you done to your nose?"

"I got a new one from the Crocodile on the banks of the great grey-green, greasy Limpopo River," said the Elephant's Child. "I asked him what he had for dinner, and he gave me this to keep."

"It looks very ugly," said his hairy uncle, the Baboon.

"It does," said the Elephant's Child. "But it's very useful," and he picked up his hairy uncle, the Baboon, by one hairy leg, and hove him into a hornet's nest.

Then that bad Elephant's Child spanked all his dear families for a long time, till they were very warm and greatly astonished. He pulled out his tall Ostrich aunt's tail-feathers; and he caught his tall uncle, the Giraffe, by the hind leg, and dragged him through a thorn-bush; and he shouted at his broad aunt, the Hippopotamus, and blew bubbles into her ear when she was sleeping in the water after meals; but he never let anyone touch Kolokolo Bird.

At last things grew so exciting that his dear families went off one by one in a hurry to the banks of the great grey-green, greasy Limpopo River, all set about with fever-trees, to borrow new noses from the Crocodile. When they came back nobody spanked anybody any more; and ever since that day, O Best Beloved, all the Elephants you will ever see, besides all those that you won't, have trunks precisely like the trunk of the 'satiable Elephant's Child.

from **Basil and the Pygmy Cats**
Eve Titus

The clever mouse-detective, Basil, is based on Sherlock Holmes, and while children may not appreciate the parody, they delight in the mystery element, the humor, and the word play as well as the concept of an animal sleuth.

The Clue of the Golden Goblet

Pygmy Cats! Breathes there, in all the world, a mouse who is not stirred by those two words?

Did the miniature monsters actually exist? Our leading mouse scientists were not certain, but they all believed the answer would be found in the Orient.

It was Basil of Baker Street, the Sherlock Holmes of the Mouse World, who solved the mystery. He used his skill as a scientific sleuth to bring to light secrets long hidden behind the curtains of the past, secrets no other mouse had been able to discover.

Professor Ratigan, leader of the mouse underworld, stalked him at every turn! Danger was Basil's constant companion. Ratigan's spies were at the border, in the jungle, on the ship, and—

But let me tell you how the adventure began. . . .

The year is 1894. The place is London, England, at Baker Street, Number 221,B, where live Mr. Sherlock Holmes and his friend, Dr. John H. Watson.

Mr. Holmes is the World's Greatest Human Detective. Basil is the World's Greatest Mouse Detective, and I, Dr. David Q. Dawson, am his friend.

We dwell in the cellar of 221,B, in the mouse town of Holmestead, which Basil named after his hero. My friend would often scurry up secret passageways to Mr. Holmes' rooms. There he would take notes in shortpaw as the human detective told Dr. Watson

exactly how he solved his difficult cases. One might say that Basil studied at the great man's feet.

Did Mr. Holmes ever see his small admirer, hidden in a corner? I believe he did, and that it pleased him to pass his methods on to a mouse.

And *such* a mouse! I am of average height, about five inches tall, but Basil towers a full inch above me.

My notebook is crammed with accounts of his cases. I am a busy doctor, but whenever possible, I take pen in paw to write of his achievements. Would that I had time to narrate them all!

There was the Mystery of the Bald-headed Mouse, a bank director. One foggy morning he stepped out of his office and vanished, along with a lot of the bank's money. Mouseland Yard detectives sought him with no success, but Basil studied the clues and found the bald banker in Edinburgh, wearing a wig and using another name. Most of the stolen funds were untouched, for spending large sums in Scotland would have drawn attention to the thief at once.

Then there was the Case of the Guinea-Pig Gang. The honest mice of London dared not venture out at night until Basil cleverly found the criminals' hideout and had them all jailed.

But of all his cases, Basil's own favorite is the Adventure of the Pygmy Cats. It put to use all his remarkable skill as a sleuth, plus his vast knowledge of the science of archeology.

Basil's hobby was archeology. He had discovered Rockhenge, the ancient mouse ruins near London.

Interviewed by newspapermice, Basil said, "The most exciting detective work in the world is archeology! As we dig, clues keep turning up. Arrowheads, old weapons, broken bowls—any or all may hold clues to the life and times of prehistoric mice. The calendar stone I found at Rockhenge, for example, proved that mice perfected a 365-day calendar long before mankind. Clearly, archeology is the highest form of detective work, for lessons we learn from the past help mice to build a better, brighter future!"

The clues concerning the pygmy cats were to take us halfway across the world, to the Far East.

Originally we had planned our trip to the Orient for a different reason—to restore the Maharajah of Bengistan to his rightful throne.

Cyril the Stoolpigeon had brought word that our enemy, Professor Ratigan, now ruled Bengistan, a mouse kingdom near India.

Too large to enter, the pigeon stood at our window to tell us what a little Oriental bird had told him.

In a surprise move the Professor and his gang had stormed and taken the palace. They guarded the border day and night. The Maharajah was unharmed, but kept prisoner in his private apartments in the palace. Ratigan taxed everything, even cheese! Mice too poor to pay the tax starved. And all the tax money went into Ratigan's pockets!

"Thank you, Cyril," said Basil. "You may pick up your reward at the back window. Mrs. Judson, our mousekeeper, baked blackberry tarts today."

Cyril, grinning happily, was off in a trice.

Basil's eyes blazed. "That rat Ratigan! Robbing our friend of his throne! I cannot stand idly by—we leave for the Orient at dawn. Can you arrange to have another doctor attend your patients?"

I could, and did, by nightfall. Then, having packed, we relaxed in easy chairs before the fire.

The doorbell jangled, and Mrs. Judson ushered in Dr. Edvard Hagerup, a Norwegian scientist from the British Mousmopolitan Museum.

After we all shook paws, he held up a golden goblet of ancient design.

Basil studied the goblet, and chuckled. "My word! Elotana, Goddess of Goodness! European mice worshipped her thousands of years ago. Look—kneeling before her are Oriental-looking pygmy cats scarcely the size of mice! Where was the goblet found?"

"In Turkey," said Hagerup. "It proves that pygmy cats existed. We of the Mousmopolitan know you are going to the Orient. We feel you are the only mouse who can solve this mystery. Will you try?"

Basil nodded. "Gladly, after I've captured Ratigan. A noted archeologist once said, 'One pits one's wits against the past!' How true! This will be the most challenging case of my career!"

Quickly Basil sketched the scene on the goblet, and the Norwegian departed with the original.

That night scores of midget cats marched through my slumbers, shaking with fright at sight of me. Seldom have I enjoyed more delightful dreams!

Off to the Orient!

At dawn London was blanketed by fog, and we could scarcely see our paws before our faces. By stealing rides, we reached Dover, then crossed the English Channel as stowaways on a steamer.

In France we boarded the boat-train for Paris, arriving in a downpour. Soaked to the fur, we called on Inspector Antoine Cherbou of the policemice.

Told of our mission, the Inspector arranged to join us, along with the famous General Garmize.

When the Simplon Express left Paris that night, four mice were aboard. Carrier pigeons had spread news of our plans, and as we sped across Europe on one crack express train after another, many well-known mice joined our party.

Our accommodations were often luxurious, but whenever people entered, we had to scamper off to the baggage car.

Lord Adrian, historian of the International Society of Mouse Mountaineers, boarded at Geneva. He was a famed hunter of sharks, those horrors of the deep. With him came Tillary Quinn, author and adventurer, Dr. Arthur Howard, a geologist, and Dr. Julian Wolff, a medical mouse. And so it went, until our party numbered twenty.

One night we reached Turkey. All were asleep but Basil and myself, and we stepped out for some air.

Waiting on the platform were Young Richard, an American scientist, and the archeologist Dr. Singh Lha. Two Turkish workmice stood behind them, bearing a large, bulky object. They unwrapped it to reveal a painted vase.

"A clue to the pygmy cats!" said Dr. Lha. "It was found on a site I am excavating, here in Turkey."

"Amazing! Astounding! Astonishing!" cried Basil. "Painted here are pygmy cats in Oriental robes and turbans, carrying bamboo chairs in which sit King Elyod and Queen Nairda, mouse rulers of ancient times. But Elyod and Nairda were Europeans, not Orientals—how strange!"

I, too, was mystified. Every schoolmouse knew of Elyod the Good. About two thousand years ago he had ruled Euphoria, a mouse kingdom near Athens, Greece. His court had been a center of learning, where all the great mouse minds of the time gathered.

Ancient Euphorians had also been explorers and traders, sailing far in their sturdy little ships.

One day Elyod set sail, seeking a short

route to India. Sixty mice embarked—the King's son, Semloh the Poet Prince, the Queen, and many nobles.

Cheering throngs lined the waterfront to wave farewell to their beloved rulers. Alas, the farewells were final—of all who sailed that fateful day, not one mouse returned!

Historians believed that a violent storm had wrecked the ship and drowned everyone aboard.

Basil's voice broke into my thoughts. "Can it be that the mice did not drown, but were cast ashore on an island in the Indian Ocean?"

He paced to and fro, thinking deeply.

"Suppose that pygmy cats lived on the island, cats who had never seen mice. Would they not have welcomed the castaways? As for King Elyod, an island paradise is every mouse's dream, and there was a challenge, too—could mice rule cats? Elyod took up that challenge. The painting on the vase proves it. But why was the vase discovered in Turkey, in the Near East, so far from the Far East?"

He gripped Singh Lha's paw. "Thanks for bringing the vase—I've memorized the painting. If I solve the mystery surrounding Elyod and the pygmy cats, cat and mouse history will be rewritten!"

The train moved slowly, then picked up speed.

Waving to Singh Lha, Basil, Young Richard, and I swung aboard.

from The Adventures of Pinocchio
Carlo Lorenzini

Writing under the pen name of Carlo Collodi, the author first published the story in a children's magazine. It became an immediate success, appeared in book form, and was translated into English in 1892. It is the story of a puppet who comes to life and becomes a boy.

Pinocchio's Ears Become Like Those of a Donkey

Every one, at one time or another, has found some surprise awaiting him. Of the kind which Pinocchio had on that eventful morning of his life, there are but few.

What was it? I will tell you, my dear little readers. On awakening, Pinocchio put his hand up to his head and there he found—

Guess!

He found that, during the night, his ears had grown at least ten full inches!

You must know that the Marionette, even from his birth, had very small ears, so small indeed that to the naked eye they could hardly be seen. Fancy how he felt when he noticed that overnight those two dainty organs had become as long as shoe brushes!

He went in search of a mirror, but not finding any, he just filled a basin with water and looked at himself. There he saw what he never could have wished to see. His manly figure was adorned and enriched by a beautiful pair of donkey's ears.

I leave you to think of the terrible grief, the shame, the despair of the poor Marionette.

He began to cry, to scream, to knock his head against the wall, but the more he shrieked, the longer and the more hairy grew his ears.

At those piercing shrieks, a Dormouse came into the room, a fat little Dormouse, who lived upstairs. Seeing Pinocchio so grief-stricken, she asked him anxiously:

"What is the matter, dear little neighbor?"

"I am sick, my little Dormouse, very, very sick—and from an illness which frightens me! Do you understand how to feel the pulse?"

"A little."

"Feel mine then and tell me if I have a fever."

The Dormouse took Pinocchio's wrist between her paws and, after a few minutes, looked up at him sorrowfully and said:

"Pinocchio's Ears Become Like Those of a Donkey" from THE ADVENTURES OF PINOCCHIO by C. Collodi, translated by Carol Della Chiesa. First published 1925; renewed 1969. Reprinted with permission of Macmillan Publishing Co., Inc.

"My friend, I am sorry, but I must give you some very sad news."

"What is it?"

"You have a very bad fever."

"But what fever is it?"

"The donkey fever."

"I don't know anything about that fever," answered the Marionette, beginning to understand even too well what was happening to him.

"Then I will tell you all about it," said the Dormouse. "Know then that, within two or three hours, you will no longer be a Marionette, nor a boy."

"What shall I be?"

"Within two or three hours you will become a real donkey, just like the ones that pull the fruit carts to market."

"Oh, what have I done? What have I done?" cried Pinocchio, grasping his two long ears in his hands and pulling and tugging at them angrily, just as if they belonged to another.

"My dear boy," answered the Dormouse to cheer him up a bit, "why worry now? What is done cannot be undone, you know. Fate has decreed that all lazy boys who come to hate books and schools and teachers and spend all their days with toys and games must sooner or later turn into donkeys."

"But is it really so?" asked the Marionette, sobbing bitterly.

"I am sorry to say it is. And tears now are useless. You should have thought of all this before."

"But the fault is not mine. Believe me, little Dormouse, the fault is all Lamp-Wick's."

"And who is this Lamp-Wick?"

"A classmate of mine. I wanted to return home. I wanted to be obedient. I wanted to study and to succeed in school, but Lamp-Wick said to me, 'Why do you want to waste your time studying? Why do you want to go to school? Come with me to the Land of Toys. There we'll never study again. There we can enjoy ourselves and be happy from morn till night.'"

"And why did you follow the advice of that false friend?"

"Why? Because, my dear little Dormouse, I am a heedless Marionette—heedless and heartless. Oh! If I had only had a bit of heart, I should never have abandoned that good Fairy, who loved me so well and who has been so kind to me! And by this time, I should no longer be a Marionette. I should have become a real boy, like all these friends of mine! Oh, if I meet Lamp-Wick I am going to tell him what I think of him—and more too!"

After this long speech, Pinocchio walked to the door of the room. But when he reached it, remembering his donkey ears, he felt ashamed to show them to the public and turned back. He took a large cotton bag from a shelf, put it on his head, and pulled it far down to his very nose.

Thus adorned, he went out. He looked for Lamp-Wick everywhere, along the streets, in the squares, inside the theaters, everywhere; but he was not to be found. He asked every one whom he met about him, but no one had seen him.

In desperation, he returned home and knocked at the door.

"Who is it?" asked Lamp-Wick from within.

"It is I!" answered the Marionette.

"Wait a minute."

After a full half hour the door opened. Another surprise awaited Pinocchio! There in the room stood his friend, with a large cotton bag on his head, pulled far down to his very nose.

At the sight of that bag, Pinocchio felt slightly happier and thought to himself:

"My friend must be suffering from the same sickness that I am! I wonder if he, too, has donkey fever?"

But pretending he had seen nothing, he asked with a smile:

"How are you, my dear Lamp-Wick?"

"Very well. Like a mouse in a Parmesan cheese."

"Is that really true?"

"Why should I lie to you?"

"I beg your pardon, my friend, but why then are you wearing that cotton bag over your ears?"

"The doctor has ordered it because one of my knees hurts. And you, dear Marionette, why are you wearing that cotton bag down to your nose?"

"The doctor has ordered it, because I have bruised my foot."

"Oh, my poor Pinocchio!"

"Oh, my poor Lamp-Wick!"

An embarrassingly long silence followed these words, during which time the two friends looked at each other in a mocking way.

Finally the Marionette, in a voice sweet as honey and soft as a flute, said to his companion:

"Tell me, Lamp-Wick, dear friend, have you ever suffered from an earache?"

"Never! And you?"

"Never! Still, since this morning my ear has been torturing me."

"So has mine."

"Yours, too? And which ear is it?"

"Both of them. And yours?"

"Both of them, too. I wonder if it could be the same sickness."

"I'm afraid it is."

"Will you do me a favor, Lamp-Wick?"

"Gladly! With my whole heart."

"Will you let me see your ears?"

"Why not? But before I show you mine, I want to see yours, dear Pinocchio."

"No. You must show yours first."

"No, my dear! Yours first, then mine."

"Well, then," said the Marionette, "let us make a contract."

"Let's hear the contract!"

"Let us take off our caps together. All right?"

"All right."

"Ready then!"

Pinocchio began to count, "One! Two! Three!"

At the word "Three!" the two boys pulled off their caps and threw them high in air.

And then a scene took place which is hard to believe, but it is all too true. The Marionette and his friend, Lamp-Wick, when they saw each other both stricken by the same misfortune, instead of feeling sorrowful and ashamed, began to poke fun at each other, and after much nonsense, they ended by bursting out into hearty laughter.

They laughed and laughed, and laughed again—laughed till they ached—laughed till they cried.

But all of a sudden Lamp-Wick stopped laughing. He tottered and almost fell. Pale as a ghost, he turned to Pinocchio and said:

"Help, help, Pinocchio!"

"What is the matter?"

"Oh, help me! I can no longer stand up."

"I can't either," cried Pinocchio; and his laughter turned to tears as he stumbled about helplessly.

They had hardly finished speaking, when both of them fell on all fours and began running and jumping around the room. As they ran, their arms turned into legs, their faces lengthened into snouts, and their backs became covered with long gray hairs.

This was humiliation enough, but the most horrible moment was the one in which the two poor creatures felt their tails appear. Overcome with shame and grief, they tried to cry and bemoan their fate.

But what is done can't be undone! Instead of moans and cries, they burst forth into loud donkey brays, which sounded very much like, "Haw! Haw! Haw!"

At that moment, a loud knocking was heard at the door and a voice called to them:

"Open! I am the Little Man, the driver of the wagon which brought you here. Open, I say, or beware!"

from The Silent Playmate
E. Nesbit

One of the first English writers of fine fantasy, Nesbit bases her fantasy of toys that come alive in the reality of two bored and inquisitive children. Rosamund and Fabian are based on two of her own children.

The Town in the Library

Rosamund and Fabian were left alone in the library. You may not believe this; but I advise you to believe everything I tell you, because it is true. Truth is stranger than story-books, and when you grow up you will hear people say this till you grow quite sick of listening to them: you will then want to write the strangest story that ever was—just to show that *some* stories can be stranger than truth.

Mother was obliged to leave the children alone, because Nurse was ill with measles, which seems a babyish thing for a grown-up nurse to have—but it is quite true. If I had wanted to make up anything I could have said she was ill of a broken heart or a brain-fever, which always happens in books. But I wish to speak the truth even if it sounds silly. And it *was* measles.

Mother could not stay with the children, because it was Christmas Eve, and on that day a lot of poor old people came up to get their Christmas presents, tea and snuff, and flannel petticoats, and warm capes, and boxes of needles and cottons and things like that. Generally the children helped to give out the presents, but this year Mother was afraid they might be going to have measles themselves, and measles is a nasty forward illness with no manners at all. You can catch it from a person before they know they've got it.

So the children were left alone. Before Mother went away she said, "Look here, dears, you may play with your bricks, or make pictures with your pretty blocks that kind Uncle Thomas gave you, but you must not touch the two top-drawers of the bureau. Now don't forget. And if you're good you shall have tea with me, and perhaps there will be cake. Now you *will* be good, won't you?"

Fabian and Rosamund promised faithfully that they would be *very* good and that they would not touch the two top-drawers, and Mother went away to see about the flannel petticoats and the tea and snuff and tobacco and things.

When the children were left alone, Fabian said, "I am going to be very good. I shall be

much more good than Mother expects me to."

"We *won't* look in the drawers," said Rosamund, stroking the shiny top of the bureau.

"We won't even *think* about the insides of the drawers," said Fabian. He stroked the bureau too and his fingers left four long streaks on it, because he had been eating toffee.

"I suppose," he said presently, "we may open the two *bottom* drawers? Mother couldn't have made a mistake—could she?"

So they opened the two bottom drawers just to be sure that Mother hadn't made a mistake, and to see whether there was anything in the bottom drawers that they ought not to look at.

But the bottom drawer of all had only old magazines in it. And the next to the bottom drawer had a lot of papers in it. The children knew at once by the look of the papers that they belonged to Father's great work about the Domestic Life of the Ancient Druids and they knew it was not right—or even interesting—to try to read other people's papers.

So they shut the drawers and looked at each other, and Fabian said, "I think it would be right to play with the bricks and the pretty blocks that Uncle Thomas gave us."

But Rosamund was younger than Fabian, and she said, "I am tired of the blocks, and I am tired of Uncle Thomas. I would rather look in the drawers."

"So would I," said Fabian. And they stood looking at the bureau.

Perhaps you don't know what a bureau is —children learn very little at school nowadays—so I will tell you that a bureau is a kind of chest of drawers. Sometimes it has a bookcase on the top of it, and instead of the two little top corner drawers like the chest of drawers in a bedroom it has a sloping lid, and when it is quite open you pull out two little boards underneath—and then it makes a sort of shelf for people to write letters on. The shelf lies quite flat, and lets you see little drawers inside with mother of pearl handles —and a row of pigeon holes—(which are not holes pigeons live in, but places for keeping the letters carrier-pigeons could carry round

"The Town in the Library" from NINE UNLIKELY TALES FOR CHILDREN by E. Nesbit. London: T. Fisher Unwin, 1901.

their necks if they liked). And there is very often a tiny cupboard in the middle of the bureau, with a pattern on the door in different coloured woods. So now you know.

Fabian stood first on one leg and then on the other, till Rosamund said, "Well, you might as well pull up your socks."

So he did. His socks were always just like a concertina or a very expensive photographic camera, but he used to say it was not his fault, and I suppose he knew best.

Then he said, "I say, Rom! Mother only said we weren't to *touch* the two top-drawers—"

"I *should* like to be good," said Rosamund.

"I *mean* to be good," said Fabian. "But if you took the little thin poker that is not kept for best you could put it through one of the brass handles and I could hold the other handle with the tongs. And then we could open the drawer without touching it."

"So we could! How clever you are, Fabe," said Rosamund. And she admired her brother very much. So they took the poker and the tongs. The front of the bureau got a little scratched, but the top drawer came open, and there they saw two boxes with glass tops and narrow gold paper going all round; though you could only see paper shavings through the glass they knew it was soldiers. Besides these boxes there was a doll and a donkey standing on a green grass plot that had wooden wheels, and a little wickerwork doll's cradle, and some brass cannons, and a bag that looked like marbles, and some flags, and a mouse that seemed as though it moved with clockwork; only, of course, they had promised not to touch the drawer, so they could not make sure. They looked at each other, and Fabian said:

"I wish it was tomorrow!"

You have seen that Fabian was quite a clever boy; and he knew at once that these were the Christmas presents which Santa Claus had brought for him and Rosamund. But Rosamund said, "Oh dear, I wish we hadn't!"

However, she consented to open the other drawer—without touching it, of course, because she had promised faithfully—and when, with the poker and tongs, the other drawer came open, there were large wooden boxes—the kind that hold raisins and figs—and round boxes with paper on—smooth on the top and folded in pleats round the edge; and the children knew what was inside without looking. Everyone knows what candied fruit looks like on the outside of the box. There were square boxes, too—the kind that have crackers in—with a cracker going off on the lid, very different in size and brightness from what it does really, for, as no doubt you know, a cracker very often comes in two quite calmly, without any pop at all, and then you only have the motto and the sweet, which is never nice. Of course, if there is anything else in the cracker, such as brooches or rings, you have to let the little girl who sits next to you at supper have it.

When they had pushed back the drawer Fabian said, "Let us pull out the writing drawer and make a castle."

So they pulled the drawer out and put it on the floor. Please do not try to do this if your father has a bureau, because it leads to trouble. It was only because this one was broken that they were able to do it.

Then they began to build. They had the two boxes of bricks—the wooden bricks with the pillars and the coloured glass windows, and the rational bricks which are made of clay like tiles. When all the bricks were used up they got the pretty picture blocks that kind Uncle Thomas gave them, and they built with these; but one box of blocks does not go far. Picture blocks are only good for building, except just at first. When you have made the pictures a few times you know exactly how they go, and then what's the good? This is a fault which belongs to many very expensive toys. These blocks had six pictures —Windsor Castle with the Royal Standard hoisted; ducks in a pond, with a very handsome green and blue drake; Rebecca at the well; a snowball fight—but none of the boys knew how to chuck a snowball; the Harvest Home; and the Death of Nelson.

These did not go far, as I said. There are six times as few blocks as there are pictures, because every block has six sides. If you don't understand this it shows they don't teach arithmetic at your school, or else that you don't do your home lessons.

But the best of a library is the books. Rosamund and Fabian made up with books. They got Shakespeare in fourteen volumes, and Rollin's *Ancient History* and Gibbon's *Decline and Fall,* and *The Beauties of Literature* in fifty-six fat little volumes, and they built not only a castle, but a town—and a big town—that presently towered high above them on the top of the bureau.

"It's almost big enough to get into," said Fabian, "if we had some steps." So they made steps with the *British Essayists,* the *Spectator* and the *Rambler,* and the *Observer,* and the *Tatler;* and when the steps were done they walked up them.

You may think that they could not have walked up these steps and into a town they had built themselves, but I assure you people have often done it, and anyway this is a true story. They had made a lovely gateway with two fat volumes of Macaulay and Milton's poetical works on top, and as they went through it they felt all the feelings which people have to feel when they are tourists and see really fine architecture. (Architecture means buildings, but it is a grander word, as you see.)

Rosamund and Fabian simply walked up the steps into the town they had built. Whether they got larger or the town got smaller, I do not pretend to say. When they had gone under the great gateway they found that they were in a street which they could not remember building. But they were not disagreeable about it, and they said it was a very nice street all the same.

There was a large square in the middle of the town, with seats, and there they sat down, in the town they had made, and wondered how they could have been so clever as to build it. Then they went to the walls of the town—high, strong walls built of the *Encyclopaedia* and the *Biographical Dictionary* —and far away over the brown plain of the carpet they saw a great thing like a square mountain. It was very shiny. And as they looked at it a great slice of it pushed itself out, and Fabian saw the brass handles shine, and he said:

"Why, Rom, that's the bureau."

"It's larger than I want it to be," said Rosamund, who was a little frightened. And indeed it did seem to be an extra size, for it was higher than the town.

The drawer of the great mountain bureau opened slowly, and the children could see something moving inside; then they saw the glass lid of one of the boxes go slowly up till it stood on end and looked like one side of the Crystal Palace, it was so large—and inside the box they saw something moving. The shavings and tissue-paper and the cotton-wool heaved and tossed like a sea when it is rough and you wish you had not come for a sail. And then from among the heaving whiteness came out a blue soldier, and another and another. They let themselves down from the drawer with ropes of shavings, and when they were all out there were fifty of them—foot soldiers with rifles and fixed bayonets, as well as a thin captain on a horse and a sergeant and a drummer.

The drummer beat his drum and the whole company formed fours and marched straight for the town. They seemed to be quite full-size soldiers—indeed, *extra large.*

The children were very frightened. They left the walls and ran up and down the streets of the town trying to find a place to hid.

"Oh, there's our very own house," cried Rosamund at last; "we shall be safe there." She was surprised as well as pleased to find their own house inside the town they had built.

So they ran in, and into the library, and there was the bureau and the town they had built, and it was all small and quite the proper size. But when they looked out of the window it was not their own street, but the one they had built; they could see two volumes of the *Beauties of Literature* and the head of Rebecca in the house opposite, and down the street was the Mausoleum they had built after the pattern given in the red and yellow book that went with the bricks. It was all very confusing.

Suddenly, as they stood looking out of the windows, they heard a shouting, and there were the blue soldiers coming along the street by twos, and when the Captain got opposite their house he called out, "Fabian! Rosamund! come down!"

And they had to, for they were very much frightened.

Then the Captain said, "We have taken this town, and you are our prisoners. Do not attempt to escape, or I don't know what will happen to you."

The children explained that they had built the town, so they thought it was theirs; but the captain said very politely, "That doesn't follow at all. It's our town now. And I want provisions for my soldiers."

"We haven't any," said Fabian, but Rosamund nudged him, and said, "Won't the soldiers be very fierce if they are hungry?"

The Blue Captain heard her, and said, "You are quite right, little girl. If you have any food, produce it. It will be a generous act, and may stop any unpleasantness. My soldiers *are* very fierce. Besides," he added in a lower tone, speaking behind his hand, "you need only feed the soldiers in the usual way."

When the children heard this their minds were made up.

"If you do not mind waiting a minute," said Fabian, politely, "I will bring down any little things I can find."

Then he took his tongs, and Rosamund took the poker, and they opened the drawer where the raisins and figs and dried fruits were—for everything in the library in the town was just the same as in the library at home—and they carried them out into the big square where the Captain had drawn up his blue regiment. And here the soldiers were fed. I suppose you know how tin soldiers are fed? But children learn so little at school nowadays that I daresay you don't, so I will tell you. You just put a bit of the fig or raisin, or whatever it is, on the soldier's tin bayonet—or his sword, if he is a cavalry man —and you let it stay on till you are tired of playing at giving the soldiers rations, and then of course *you eat it for him.* This was the way in which Fabian and Rosamund fed the starving blue soldiers. But when they had done so, the soldiers were as hungry as ever.

So then the Blue Captain, who had not had anything, even on the point of his sword, said, "More—more, my gallant men are fainting for lack of food."

So there was nothing for it but to bring out the candied fruits, and to feed the soldiers with them. So Fabian and Rosamund stuck bits of candied apricot and fig and pear and cherry and beetroot on the tops of the soldiers' bayonets, and when every soldier had a piece they put a fat candied cherry on the officer's sword. Then the children knew the soldiers would be quiet for a few minutes, and they ran back into their own house and into the library to talk to each other about what they had better do, for they both felt that the blue soldiers were a very hard-hearted set of men.

"They might shut us up in the dungeons," said Rosamund, "and then Mother might lock us in, when she shut up the lid of the bureau, and we should starve to death."

"I think it's all nonsense," said Fabian. But when they looked out of the window there was the house with Windsor Castle and the head of Rebecca just opposite.

"If we could only find Mother," said Rosamund; but they knew without looking that Mother was not in the house that they were in then.

"I wish we had that mouse that looked like clockwork—and the donkey, and the other box of soldiers—perhaps they are red ones, and they would fight the blue and lick them —because redcoats are English and they always win," said Fabian.

And then Rosamund said, "Oh, Fabe, I believe we could go into *this* town, too, if we tried!"

So they went to the bureau drawer, and Rosamund got out the other box of soldiers and the mouse—it *was* a clockwork one— and the donkey with panniers, and put them in the town, while Fabian ate up a few odd raisins that had dropped on the floor.

When all the soldiers (they *were* red) were arranged on the ramparts of the little town, Fabian said, "I'm sure we can get into this town," and sure enough they did, just as they had done into the first one. And it was exactly the same sort of town as the other.

So now they were in a town built in a library in a house in a town built in a library in a house in a town called London—and the town they were in now had red soldiers in it and they felt quite safe, and the Union Jack was stuck up over the gateway. It was a stiff little flag they had found with some others in the bureau drawer; it was meant to be stuck in the Christmas pudding, but they had stuck it between two blocks and put it over the gate of their town. They walked about this town and found their own house, just as before, and went in, and there was the toy town on the floor; and you will see that they might have walked into that town also, but they saw that it was no good, and that they couldn't get out that way, but would only get deeper and deeper into a nest of towns in libraries in houses in towns in libraries in houses in towns in . . . and so on for always—something like Chinese puzzle-boxes multiplied by millions and millions for ever and ever. And they did not like even to think of this, because of course they would be getting further and further from home every time. And when Fabian explained all this to Rosamund she said he made her head ache, and she began to cry.

Then Fabian thumped her on the back and told her not to be a little silly, for he was a very kind brother. And he said, "Come out and let's see if the soldiers can tell us what to do."

So they went out; but the red soldiers said they knew nothing but drill, and even the Red Captain said he really couldn't advise. Then they met the clockwork mouse. He was big like an elephant, and the donkey with panniers was as big as a mastodon or a megatherium. (If they teach you anything at school of course they have taught you all about the megatherium and the mastodon.)

The Mouse kindly stopped to speak to the children, and Rosamund burst into tears again and said she wanted to go home.

The great Mouse looked down at her and said, "I am sorry for *you*, but your brother is

the kind of child that overwinds clockwork mice the very first day he has them. I prefer to stay this size, and you to stay small."

Then Fabian said: "On my honour, I won't. If we get back home I'll give you to Rosamund. That is, supposing I get you for one of my Christmas presents."

The donkey with panniers said, "And you won't put coals in my panniers or unglue my feet from my green grass-plot because I look more natural without wheels?"

"I give you my word," said Fabian, "I wouldn't think of such a thing."

"Very well," said the Mouse, "then I will tell you. It is a great secret, but there is only one way to get out of this kind of town. You —I hardly know how to explain—you—you just *walk out of the gate*, you know."

"Dear me," said Rosamund; "I never thought of that!"

So they all went to the gate of the town and walked out, and there they were in the library again. But when they looked out of the window the Mausoleum was still to be seen, and the terrible blue soldiers.

"What are we to do now?" asked Rosamund; but the clockwork mouse and the donkey with panniers were their proper size again now (or else the children had got bigger. It is no use asking me which, for I do not know), and so of course they could not speak.

"We must walk out of this town as we did out of the other," said Fabian.

"Yes," Rosamund said; "only this town is full of blue soldiers and I am afraid of them. Don't you think it would do if we *ran* out?"

So out they ran and down the steps that were made of the *Spectator* and the *Rambler* and the *Tatler* and the *Observer*. And directly they stood on the brown library carpet they ran to the window and looked out, and they saw—instead of the building with Windsor Castle and Rebecca's head in it—they saw their own road with the trees without any leaves and the man was just going along lighting the lamps with the stick that the gaslight pops out of, like a bird, to roost in the glass cage at the top of the lamp-post. So they knew that they were safe at home again.

And as they stood looking out they heard the library door open, and Mother's voice saying, "What a dreadful muddle! And what have you done with the raisins and the candied fruits?" And her voice was very grave indeed.

Now you will see that it was quite impossible for Fabian and Rosamund to explain to their mother what they had done with the raisins and things, and how they had been in a town in a library in a house in a town they had built in their own library with the books and the bricks and the pretty picture blocks kind Uncle Thomas gave them. Because they were much younger than I am, and even I have found it rather hard to explain.

So Rosamund said, "Oh, Mother, my head does ache so," and began to cry. And Fabian said nothing, but he, also, began to cry.

And Mother said, "I don't wonder your head aches, after all those sweet things." And she looked as if she would like to cry too.

"I don't know what Daddy will say," said

Mother, and then she gave them each a nasty powder and put them both to bed.

"I wonder what he *will* say," said Fabian just before he went to sleep.

"*I* don't know," said Rosamund, and, strange to say, they don't know to this hour what Daddy said. Because next day they both had measles, and when they got better everyone had forgotten about what had happened on Christmas Eve. And Fabian and Rosamund had forgotten just as much as everybody else. So I should never have heard of it but for the clockwork mouse. It was he who told me the story, just as the children told it to him in the town in the library in the house in the town they built in their own library with the books and the bricks and the pretty picture blocks which were given to them by kind Uncle Thomas. And if you do not believe the story it is not my fault: I believe every word the mouse said, for I know the good character of that clockwork mouse, and I know it could not tell an untruth even if it tried.

Stories of Enchantment

 The magic and the fantasy of folklore are most closely approximated in the stories of enchantment, especially in the way in which magical objects or creatures impinge on the realistic world and its people. The miniature creatures who are Borrowers, the half-fairy child of *No Flying in the House,* the inexplicable enticement of movement in time, and the high fantasy of the struggle between good and evil in "Gurgi" stimulate and extend children's fertile imaginations. Although most of the stories in this category are not primarily humorous, humor is used effectively in many of them. These are the tales that most often make children wonder "What if this were true?" or "What would I do if this happened to me?"

The Real Princess
Hans Christian Andersen

One of the most engaging tales of the great Danish writer, this pokes fun at the idea that a princess is so delicate and sensitive that she can be kept awake by a tiny pea under a huge pile of bedding.

There was once a prince, and he wanted a princess, but then she must be a *real* princess. He travelled right round the world to find one, but there was always something wrong. There were plenty of princesses, but whether they were real princesses he had great difficulty in discovering; there was always something which was not quite right about them. So at last he had to come home again, and he was very sad because he wanted a real princess so badly.

One evening there was a terrible storm; it thundered and lightened and the rain poured down in torrents; indeed it was a fearful night.

In the middle of the storm somebody knocked at the town gate, and the old King himself went to open it.

It was a princess who stood outside, but she was in a terrible state from the rain and the storm. The water streamed out of her hair and her clothes, it ran in at the top of her shoes and out at the heel, but she said that she was a real princess.

"Well, we shall soon see if that is true," thought the old Queen, but she said nothing. She went into the bedroom, took all the bed-clothes off and laid a pea on the bedstead; then she took twenty mattresses and piled them on the top of the pea, and then twenty feather beds on the top of the mattresses. This was where the princess was to sleep that night. In the morning they asked her how she had slept.

"Oh, terribly badly!" said the princess. "I have hardly closed my eyes the whole night! Heaven knows what was in the bed. I seemed to be lying upon some hard thing, and my whole body is black and blue this morning. It is terrible!"

They saw at once that she must be a real princess when she had felt the pea through twenty mattresses and twenty feather beds. Nobody but a real princess could have such a delicate skin.

So the prince took her to be his wife, for now he was sure that he had found a real princess, and the pea was put into the Museum, where it may still be seen if no one has stolen it.

Now this is a true story.

"The Real Princess" from Hans Christian Andersen's FAIRY TALES translated by Mrs. Edgar Lucas. Reprinted by permission of J M Dent & Sons Ltd.

from **The Borrowers**
Mary Norton

Borrowers are tiny people who live a secret life in people's houses, and their ingenious adaptation of the objects they "borrow" delights children. The danger in this episode from Norton's popular story is that one of the borrowers has been seen by a human.

[Danger!]

Pod came in slowly, his sack on his back; he leaned his hat pin, with its dangling name-tape, against the wall and, on the middle of the kitchen table, he placed a doll's tea cup; it was the size of a mixing bowl.

"Why, Pod—" began Homily.

"Got the saucer too," he said. He swung down the sack and untied the neck. "Here you are," he said, drawing out the saucer. "Matches it."

He had a round, currant-bunny sort of face; tonight it looked flabby.

"Oh, Pod," said Homily, "you do look queer. Are you all right?"

Pod sat down. "I'm fair enough," he said.

"You went up the curtain," said Homily. "Oh, Pod, you shouldn't have. It's shaken you—"

Pod made a strange face, his eyes swiveled round toward Arrietty. Homily stared at him, her mouth open, and then she turned. "Come along, Arrietty," she said briskly, "you pop off to bed, now, like a good girl, and I'll bring you some supper."

"Oh," said Arrietty, "can't I see the rest of the borrowings?"

"Your father's got nothing now. Only food. Off you pop to bed. You've seen the cup and saucer."

Arrietty went into the sitting room to put away her diary, and took some time fixing her candle on the upturned drawing pin which served as a holder.

"Whatever are you doing?" grumbled Homily. "Give it here. There, that's the way. Now off to bed and fold your clothes, mind."

"Good night, Papa," said Arrietty, kissing his flat white cheek.

"Careful of the light," he said mechanically, and watched her with his round eyes until she had closed the door.

"Now, Pod," said Homily, when they were alone, "tell me. What's the matter?"

Pod looked at her blankly. "I been 'seen,' " he said.

Homily put out a groping hand for the edge of the table; she grasped it and lowered herself slowly on to the stool. "Oh, Pod," she said.

There was silence between them. Pod stared at Homily and Homily stared at the table. After a while she raised her white face. "Badly?" she asked.

Pod moved restlessly. "I don't know about badly. I been 'seen.' Ain't that bad enough?"

"No one," said Homily slowly, "hasn't never been 'seen' since Uncle Hendreary and he was the first they say for forty-five years." A thought struck her and she gripped the table. "It's no good, Pod, I won't emigrate!"

"No one's asked you to," said Pod.

"To go and live like Hendreary and Lupy in a badger's set! The other side of the world, that's where they say it is—all among the earthworms."

"It's two fields away, above the spinney," said Pod.

"Nuts, that's what they eat. And berries. I wouldn't wonder if they don't eat mice—"

"You've eaten mice yourself," Pod reminded her.

"All draughts and fresh air and the children growing up wild. Think of Arrietty!" said Homily. "Think of the way she's been brought up. An only child. She'd catch her death. It's different for Hendreary."

"Why?" asked Pod. "He's got four."

"That's why," explained Homily. "When you've got four, they're brought up rough. But never mind that now. . . . Who saw you?"

"A boy," said Pod.

"A what?" exclaimed Homily, staring.

"A boy." Pod sketched out a rough shape

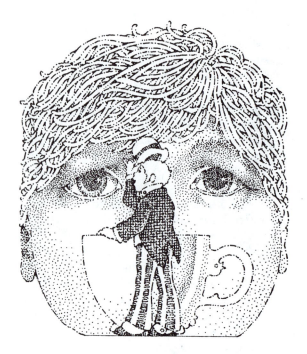

in the air with his hands. "You know, a boy."

"But there isn't—I mean, what sort of a boy?"

"I don't know what you mean 'what sort of a boy.' A boy in a night-shirt. A boy. You know what a boy is, don't you?"

"Yes," said Homily, "I know what a boy is. But there hasn't been a boy, not in this house, these twenty years."

"Well," said Pod, "there's one here now."

Homily stared at him in silence, and Pod met her eyes. "Where did he see you?" asked Homily at last.

"In the schoolroom."

"Oh," said Homily, "when you was getting the cup?"

"Yes," said Pod.

"Haven't you got eyes?" asked Homily. "Couldn't you have looked first?"

"There's never nobody in the schoolroom. And what's more," he went on, "there wasn't today."

"Then where was he?"

"In bed. In the night-nursery or whatever

it's called. That's where he was. Sitting up in bed. With the doors open."

"Well, you could have looked in the nursery."

"How could I—halfway up the curtain!"

"Is that where you was?"

"Yes."

"With the cup?"

"Yes. I couldn't get up or down."

"Oh, Pod," wailed Homily, "I should never have let you go. Not at your age!"

"Now, look here," said Pod, "don't mistake me. I got up all right. Got up like a bird, as you might say, bobbles or no bobbles. But"—he leaned toward her—"afterwards—with the cup in me hand, if you see what I mean. . . ." He picked it up off the table. "You see, it's heavy like. You can hold it by the handle, like this . . . but it drops or droops, as you might say. You should take a cup like this in your two hands. A bit of cheese off a shelf, or an apple—well, I drop that . . . give it a push and it falls and I climbs down in me own time and picks it up. But with a cup—you see what I mean? And coming down, you got to watch your feet. And, as I say, some of the bobbles was missing. You didn't know what you could hold on to, not safely. . . ."

"Oh, Pod," said Homily, her eyes full of tears, "what did you do?"

"Well," said Pod, sitting back again, "he took the cup."

"What do you mean?" exclaimed Homily, aghast.

Pod avoided her eyes. "Well, he'd been sitting up in bed there watching me. I'd been on that curtain a good ten minutes, because the hall clock had just struck the quarter—"

"But how do you mean—'he took the cup'?"

"Well, he'd got out of bed and there he was standing, looking up. 'I'll take the cup,' he said."

"Oh!" gasped Homily, her eyes staring, "and you give it him?"

"He took it," said Pod, "ever so gentle. And then, when I was down, he give it me." Homily put her face in her hands. "Now don't take on," said Pod uneasily.

"He might have caught you," shuddered Homily in a stifled voice.

"Yes," said Pod, "but he just give me the cup. 'Here you are,' he said."

Homily raised her face. "What are we going to do?" she asked.

Pod sighed. "Well, there isn't nothing we can do. Except—"

"Oh, no," exclaimed Homily, "not that. Not emigrate. Not that, Pod, now I've got the house so nice and a clock and all."

"We could take the clock," said Pod.

"And Arrietty? What about her? She's not like those cousins. She can *read*, Pod, and sew a treat—"

"He don't know where we live," said Pod.

"But they look," exclaimed Homily. "Remember Hendreary! They got the cat and—"

"Now, now," said Pod, "don't bring up the past."

"But you've got to think of it! They got the cat and—"

"Yes," said Pod, "but Eggletina was different."

"How different? She was Arrietty's age."

"Well, they hadn't told her, you see. That's where they went wrong. They tried to make her believe that there wasn't nothing but was under the floor. They never told her about Mrs. Driver or Crampfurl. Least of all about cats."

"There wasn't any cat," Homily pointed out, "not till Hendreary was 'seen.'"

"Well, there was, then," said Pod. "You got to tell them, that's what I say, or they try to find out for themselves."

"Pod," said Homily solemnly, "we haven't told Arrietty."

"Oh, she knows," said Pod; he moved uncomfortably. "She's got her grating."

"She doesn't know about Eggletina. She doesn't know about being 'seen.'"

"Well," said Pod, "we'll tell her. We always said we would. There's no hurry."

Homily stood up. "Pod," she said, "we're going to tell her now."

from My Father's Dragon
Ruth Gannett

In a story told by a boy, his father's adventures in his own childhood begin when a talkative cat entices him to run away to the island where the dragon lives.

My Father Meets the Cat

One cold rainy day when my father was a little boy, he met an old alley cat on his street. The cat was very drippy and uncomfortable so my father said, "Wouldn't you like to come home with me?"

This surprised the cat—she had never before met anyone who cared about old alley cats—but she said, "I'd be very much obliged if I could sit by a warm furnace, and perhaps have a saucer of milk."

"We have a very nice furnace to sit by," said my father, "and I'm sure my mother has an extra saucer of milk."

My father and the cat became good friends but my father's mother was very upset about the cat. She hated cats, particularly ugly old alley cats. "Elmer Elevator," she said to my father, "if you think I'm going to give that cat a saucer of milk, you're very wrong. Once you start feeding stray alley cats you might as well expect to feed every stray in town, and I am *not* going to do it!"

This made my father very sad, and he apologized to the cat because his mother had been so rude. He told the cat to stay anyway, and that somehow he would bring her a saucer of milk each day. My father fed the cat for three weeks, but one day his mother found the cat's saucer in the cellar and she was extremely angry. She whipped my father and threw the cat out the door, but later on my father sneaked out and found the cat. Together they went for a walk in the park and tried to think of nice things to talk about. My father said, "When I grow up I'm going to have an airplane. Wouldn't it be wonderful to fly just anywhere you might think of!"

"Would you like to fly very, very much?" asked the cat.

"I certainly would. I'd do anything if I could fly."

"Well," said the cat, "If you'd really like to fly that much, I think I know of a sort of a way you might get to fly while you're still a little boy."

"You mean you know where I could get an airplane?"

"Well, not exactly an airplane, but something even better. As you can see, I'm an old cat now, but in my younger days I was quite a traveler. My traveling days are over but last spring I took just one more trip and sailed to the Island of Tangerina, stopping at the port of Cranberry. Well, it just so happened that I missed the boat, and while waiting for the next I thought I'd look around a bit. I was particularly interested in a place called Wild Island, which we had passed on our way to Tangerina. Wild Island and Tangerina are joined together by a long string of rocks, but people never go to Wild Island because it's mostly jungle and inhabited by very wild animals. So, I decided to go across the rocks and explore it for myself. It certainly is an interesting place, but I saw something there that made me want to weep."

My Father Runs Away

"Wild Island is practically cut in two by a very wide and muddy river," continued the cat. "This river begins near one end of the island and flows into the ocean at the other. Now the animals there are very lazy, and they used to hate having to go all the way around the beginning of this river to get to the other side of the island. It made visiting inconvenient and mail deliveries slow, particularly during the Christmas rush. Crocodiles could have carried passengers and mail across the river, but crocodiles are very moody, and not the least bit dependable, and are always looking for something to eat. They don't care if the animals have to walk around the river, so that's just what the animals did for many years."

"But what does all this have to do with airplanes?" asked my father, who thought the cat was taking an awfully long time to explain.

"Be patient, Elmer," said the cat, and she went on with the story. "One day about four months before I arrived on Wild Island a baby dragon fell from a low-flying cloud onto the bank of the river. He was too young to fly very well, and besides, he had bruised one wing quite badly, so he couldn't get back to his cloud. The animals found him soon afterwards and everybody said, 'Why, this is just exactly what we've needed all these years!' They tied a big rope around his neck and waited for the wing to get well. This was going to end all their crossing-the-river troubles."

"I've never seen a dragon," said my father. "Did you see him? How big is he?"

"Oh, yes, indeed I saw the dragon. In fact, we became great friends," said the cat. "I used to hide in the bushes and talk to him when nobody was around. He's not a very big dragon, about the size of a large black bear, although I imagine he's grown quite a bit since I left. He's got a long tail and yellow and blue stripes. His horn and eyes and the bottoms of his feet are bright red, and he has gold-colored wings."

"Oh, how wonderful!" said my father. "What did the animals do with him when his wing got well?"

"They started training him to carry passengers, and even though he is just a baby dragon, they work him all day and all night too sometimes. They make him carry loads that are much too heavy, and if he complains, they twist his wings and beat him. He's always tied to a stake on a rope just long enough to go across the river. His only friends are the crocodiles, who say 'Hello' to him once a week if they don't forget. Really, he's the most miserable animal I've ever come across. When I left I promised I'd try to help him someday, although I couldn't see how. The rope around his neck is about the biggest, toughest rope you can imagine, with so many knots it would take days to untie them all.

"Anyway, when you were talking about airplanes you gave me a good idea. Now, I'm quite sure that if you were able to rescue the dragon, which wouldn't be the least bit easy, he'd let you ride him most anywhere provided you were nice to him, of course. How about trying it?"

"Oh, I'd love to," said my father, and he was so angry at his mother for being rude to the cat that he didn't feel the least bit sad about running away from home for a while.

That very afternoon my father and the cat went down to the docks to see about ships going to the Island of Tangerina. They found out that a ship would be sailing the next week, so right away they started planning for the rescue of the dragon. The cat was a great help in suggesting things for my father to take with him, and she told him everything she knew about Wild Island. Of course, she was too old to go along.

Everything had to be kept very secret, so when they found or bought anything to take on the trip they hid it behind a rock in the park. The night before my father sailed he borrowed his father's knapsack and he and the cat packed everything very carefully. He took chewing gum, two dozen pink lollipops, a package of rubber bands, black rubber boots, a compass, a tooth brush and a tube of tooth paste, six magnifying glasses, a very sharp jackknife, a comb and a hairbrush, seven hair ribbons of different colors, an empty grain bag with a label saying "Cranberry," some clean clothes, and enough food to last my father while he was on the ship. He couldn't live on mice, so he took twenty-five peanut butter and jelly sandwiches and six apples, because that's all the apples he could find in the pantry.

When everything was packed my father and the cat went down to the docks to the ship. A night watchman was on duty, so while the cat made loud queer noises to distract his attention, my father ran over the gangplank onto the ship. He went down into the hold and hid among some bags of wheat. The ship sailed early the next morning.

from The Book of Three
Lloyd Alexander

The cycle of five books that form the Prydain story begins with The Book of Three *and culminates in* The High King, *a Newbery Medal winner, in which the hero, Taran, shows his nobility. In this episode from the first book, Taran is a brash lad, and Gurgi is a toadying creature whose cadging ways and rhyming speech make him an instant favorite with children.*

Gurgi

By the time Taran woke, Gwydion had already saddled Melyngar. The cloak Taran had slept in was damp with dew. Every joint ached from his night on the hard ground. With Gwydion's urging, Taran stumbled toward the horse, a white blur in the gray-pink dawn. Gwydion hauled Taran into the saddle behind him, spoke a quiet command, and the white steed moved quickly into the rising mist.

Gwydion was seeking the spot where Taran had last seen Hen Wen. But long before they had reached it, he reined up Melyngar and dismounted. As Taran watched, Gwydion knelt and sighted along the turf.

"Luck is with us," he said. "I think we have struck her trail." Gwydion pointed to a faint circle of trampled grass. "Here she slept, and not too long ago." He strode a few paces forward, scanning every broken twig and blade of grass.

Despite Taran's disappointment at finding the Lord Gwydion dressed in a coarse jacket and mud-spattered boots, he followed the man with growing admiration. Nothing, Taran saw, escaped Gwydion's eyes. Like a lean, gray wolf, he moved silently and easily. A little way on, Gwydion stopped, raised his shaggy head and narrowed his eyes toward a distant ridge.

"The trail is not clear," he said, frowning. "I can only guess she might have gone down the slope."

"With all the forest to run in," Taran queried, "how can we begin to search? She might have gone anywhere in Prydain."

"Not quite," answered Gwydion. "I may not know where she went, but I can be sure where she did *not* go." He pulled a hunting knife from his belt. "Here, I will show you."

Gwydion knelt and quickly traced lines in the earth. "These are the Eagle Mountains," he said, with a touch of longing in his voice, "in my own land of the north. Here, Great Avren flows. See how it turns west before it reaches the sea. We may have to cross it before our search ends. And this is the River Ystrad. Its valley leads north to Caer Dathyl.

"But see here," Gwydion went on, pointing to the left of the line he had drawn for the River Ystrad, "here is Mount Dragon and the domain of Arawn. Hen Wen would shun this above all. She was too long a captive in Annuvin; she would never venture near it."

"Was Hen in Annuvin?" Taran asked with surprise. "But how . . ."

"Long ago," Gwydion said, "Hen Wen lived among the race of men. She belonged to a farmer who had no idea at all of her powers. And so she might have spent her days as any ordinary pig. But Arawn knew her to be far from ordinary, and of such value that he himself rode out of Annuvin and seized her. What dire things happened while she was prisoner of Arawn—it is better not to speak of them."

"Poor Hen," Taran said, "it must have been terrible for her. But how did she escape?"

"She did not escape," said Gwydion. "She was rescued. A warrior went alone into the depths of Annuvin and brought her back safely."

"That was a brave deed!" Taran cried. "I wish that I . . ."

"The bards of the north still sing of it," Gwydion said. "His name shall never be forgotten."

"Who was it?" Taran demanded.

Gwydion looked closely at him. "Do you not know?" he asked. "Dallben has neglected your education. It was Coll," he said. "Coll Son of Collfrewr."

"Coll!" Taran cried. "Not the same . . ."

"The same," said Gwydion.

"But . . . but . . . ," Taran stammered. "Coll? A hero? But . . . he's so bald!"

Gwydion laughed and shook his head. "Assistant Pig-Keeper," he said, "you have curious notions about heroes. I have never known courage to be judged by the length of a man's hair. Or, for the matter of that, whether he has any hair at all."

Crestfallen, Taran peered at Gwydion's map and said no more.

"Here," continued Gwydion, "not far from Annuvin, lies Spiral Castle. This, too, Hen Wen would avoid at all cost. It is the abode of Queen Achren. She is as dangerous as Arawn himself; as evil as she is beautiful. But there are secrets concerning Achren which are better left untold.

"I am sure," Gwydion went on, "Hen Wen will not go toward Annuvin or Spiral Castle. From what little I can see, she has run straight ahead. Quickly now, we shall try to pick up her trail."

Gwydion turned Melyngar toward the ridge. As they reached the bottom of the slope, Taran heard the waters of Great Avren rushing like wind in a summer storm.

"We must go again on foot," Gwydion said. "Her tracks may show somewhere along here, so we had best move slowly and carefully. Stay close behind me," he ordered. "If you start dashing ahead—and you seem to have that tendency—you will trample out any signs she might have left."

Taran obediently walked a few paces behind. Gwydion made no more sound than the shadow of a bird. Melyngar herself stepped quietly; hardly a twig snapped under her hoofs. Try as he would, Taran could not go as silently. The more careful he attempted to be, the louder the leaves rattled and crackled. Wherever he put his foot, there seemed to be a hole or spiteful branch to trip him up. Even Melyngar turned and gave him a reproachful look.

Taran grew so absorbed in not making noise that he soon lagged far behind Gwydion. On the slope, Taran believed he could make out something round and white. He yearned to be the first to find Hen Wen and he turned aside, clambered through the weeds—to discover nothing more than a boulder.

Disappointed, Taran hastened to catch up with Gwydion. Overhead, the branches rustled. As he stopped and looked up, something fell heavily to the ground behind him. Two hairy and powerful hands locked around his throat.

Whatever had seized him made barking and snorting noises. Taran forced out a cry for help. He struggled with his unseen opponent, twisting, flailing his legs, and throwing himself from one side to the other.

Suddenly he could breathe again. A shape sailed over his head and crashed against a tree trunk. Taran dropped to the ground and began rubbing his neck. Gwydion stood beside him. Sprawled under the tree was the strangest creature Taran had ever seen. He could not be sure whether it was animal or human. He decided it was both. Its hair was so matted and covered with leaves that it looked like an owl's nest in need of house-cleaning. It had long, skinny, woolly arms, and a pair of feet as flexible and grimy as its hands.

Gwydion was watching the creature with a look of severity and annoyance. "So it is you," he said. "I ordered you not to hinder me or anyone under my protection."

At this, the creature set up a loud and piteous whining, rolled his eyes, and beat the ground with his palms.

"It is only Gurgi," Gwydion said. "He is always lurking about one place or another. He is not half as ferocious as he looks, not a quarter as fierce as he should like to be, and more a nuisance than anything else. Somehow, he manages to see most of what happens, and he might be able to help us."

Taran had just begun to catch his breath. He was covered with Gurgi's shedding hair, in addition to the distressing odor of a wet wolfhound.

"O mighty prince," the creature wailed, "Gurgi is sorry; and now he will be smacked on his poor, tender head by the strong hands of this great lord, with fearsome smackings. Yes, yes, that is always the way of it with poor Gurgi. But what honor to be smacked by the greatest of warriors!"

"I have no intention of smacking your poor, tender head," said Gwydion. "But I may change my mind if you do not leave off that whining and sniveling."

"Yes, powerful lord!" Gurgi cried. "See how he obeys rapidly and instantly!" He began crawling about on hands and knees with great agility. Had Gurgi owned a tail, Taran was sure he would have wagged it frantically.

"Then," Gurgi pleaded, "the two strengthful heroes will give Gurgi something to eat? Oh joyous crunchings and munchings!"

"Afterward," said Gwydion. "When you have answered our questions."

"Oh, afterward!" cried Gurgi. "Poor Gurgi can wait, long, long for his crunchings and munchings. Many years from now, when the great princes revel in their halls—what feastings—they will remember hungry, wretched Gurgi waiting for them."

"How long you wait for your crunchings and munchings," Gwydion said, "depends on how quickly you tell us what we want to know. Have you seen a white pig this morning?"

A crafty look gleamed in Gurgi's close-set little eyes. "For the seeking of a piggy, there are many great lords in the forest, riding with frightening shouts. *They* would not be cruel to starving Gurgi—oh, no—they would feed him . . ."

"They would have your head off your shoulders before you could think twice about it," Gwydion said. "Did one of them wear an antlered mask?"

"Yes, yes!" Gurgi cried. "The great horns! You will save miserable Gurgi from hurtful choppings!" He set up a long and dreadful howling.

"I am losing patience with you," warned Gwydion. "Where is the pig?"

"Gurgi hears these mighty riders," the creature went on. "Oh, yes, with careful listenings from the trees. Gurgi is so quiet and clever, and no one cares about him. But he listens! These great warriors say they have gone to a certain place, but great fire turns them away. They are not pleased, and they still seek a piggy with outcries and horses."

"Gurgi," said Gwydion firmly, "where is the pig?"

"The piggy? Oh, terrible hunger pinches! Gurgi cannot remember. Was there a piggy? Gurgi is fainting and falling into the bushes, his poor, tender head is full of air from his empty belly."

Taran could no longer control his impatience. "Where is Hen Wen, you silly, hairy thing?" he burst out. "Tell us straight off! After the way you jumped on me, you deserve to have your head smacked."

With a moan, Gurgi rolled over on his back and covered his face with his arms.

Gwydion turned severely to Taran. "Had you followed my orders, you would not have been jumped on. Leave him to me. Do not make him any more frightened than he is." Gwydion looked down at Gurgi. "Very well," he asked calmly, "where is she?"

"Oh, fearful wrath!" Gurgi snuffled, "a

piggy has gone across the water with swimmings and splashings." He sat upright and waved a woolly arm toward Great Avren.

"If you are lying to me," said Gwydion, "I shall soon find out. Then I will surely come back with wrath."

"Crunchings and munchings now, mighty prince?" asked Gurgi in a high, tiny whimper.

"As I promised you," said Gwydion.

"Gurgi wants the smaller one for munchings," said the creature, with a beady glance at Taran.

"No, you do not," Gwydion said. "He is an Assistant Pig-Keeper and he would disagree with you violently." He unbuckled a saddlebag and pulled out a few strips of dried meat, which he tossed to Gurgi. "Be off now. Remember, I want no mischief from you."

Gurgi snatched the food, thrust it between his teeth, and scuttled up a tree trunk, leaping from tree to tree until he was out of sight.

"What a disgusting beast," said Taran. "What a nasty, vicious . . ."

"Oh, he is not bad at heart," Gwydion answered. "He would love to be wicked and terrifying, though he cannot quite manage it. He feels so sorry for himself that it is hard not to be angry with him. But there is no use in doing so."

"Was he telling the truth about Hen Wen?" asked Taran.

"I think he was," Gwydion said. "It is as I feared. The Horned King has ridden to Caer Dallben."

"He burned it!" Taran cried. Until now, he had paid little mind to his home. The thought of the white cottage in flames, his memory of Dallben's beard, and the heroic Coll's bald head touched him all at once. "Dallben and Coll are in peril!"

"Surely not," said Gwydion. "Dallben is an old fox. A beetle could not creep into Caer Dallben without his knowledge. No, I am certain the fire was something Dallben arranged for unexpected visitors.

"Hen Wen is the one in greatest peril. Our quest grows ever more urgent," Gwydion hastily continued. "The Horned King knows she is missing. He will pursue her."

"Then," Taran cried, "we must find her before he does!"

"Assistant Pig-Keeper," said Gwydion, "that has been, so far, your only sensible suggestion."

from **Tuck Everlasting**
Natalie Babbitt

In a tale that deftly blends fantasy and realism, Winnie meets the Tucks, an ordinary family except for the fact that they have discovered the secret of immortality. In a chapter that is followed by events that lead to a poignant conclusion, Winnie learns the truth.

It was the strangest story Winnie had ever heard. She soon suspected they had never told it before, except to each other—that she was their first real audience; for they gathered around her like children at their mother's knee, each trying to claim her attention, and sometimes they all talked at once, and interrupted each other, in their eagerness.

Eighty-seven years before, the Tucks had come from a long way to the east, looking for a place to settle. In those days the wood was not a wood, it was a forest, just as her grandmother had said: a forest that went on and on and on. They had thought they would start a farm, as soon as they came to the end of the trees. But the trees never seemed to end. When they came to the part that was now the wood, and turned from the trail to find a camping place, they happened on the spring. "It was real nice," said Jesse with a sigh. "It looked just the way it does now. A clearing, lots of sunshine, that big tree with all those knobby roots. We stopped and everyone took a drink, even the horse."

"No," said Mae, "the cat didn't drink. That's important."

"Yes," said Miles, "don't leave that out. We all had a drink, except for the cat."

"Well, anyway," Jesse went on, "the water tasted—sort of strange. But we camped there overnight. And Pa carved a T on the tree trunk, to mark where we'd been. And then we went on."

They had come out of the forest at last, many miles to the west, had found a thinly populated valley, had started their farm. "We put up a house for Ma and Pa," said Miles, "and a little shack for Jesse and me. We figured *we'd* be starting families of our own pretty soon and would want our own houses."

"That was the first time we figured there was something peculiar," said Mae. "Jesse fell out of a tree . . ."

"I was way up in the middle," Jesse interrupted, "trying to saw off some of the big branches before we cut her down. I lost my balance and I fell . . ."

"He landed plum on his head," said Mae with a shudder. "We thought for sure he'd broke his neck. But come to find out, it didn't hurt him a bit!"

"Not long after," Miles went on, "some hunters come by one day at sunset. The horse was out grazing by some trees and they shot him. Mistook him for a deer, they said. Can you fancy that? But the thing is, they didn't kill him. The bullet went right on through him, and didn't hardly even leave a mark."

"Then Pa got snake bite . . ."

"And Jesse ate the poison toadstools . . ."

"And I cut myself," said Mae. "Remember? Slicing bread."

But it was the passage of time that worried them most. They had worked the farm, settled down, made friends. But after ten years, then twenty, they had to face the fact that there was something terribly wrong. None of them was getting any older.

"I was more'n forty by then," said Miles sadly. "I was married. I had two children. But, from the look of me, I was still twenty-two. My wife, she finally made up her mind I'd sold my soul to the Devil. She left me. She went away and she took the children with her."

"I'm glad *I* never got married," Jesse put in.

"It was the same with our friends," said Mae. "They come to pull back from us. There was talk about witchcraft. Black magic. Well, you can't hardly blame them, but finally we had to leave the farm. We didn't know where to go. We started back the way we come, just wandering. We was like gypsies. When we got this far, it'd changed, of course. A lot of the trees was gone. There was people, and Treegap—it was a new village. The road was here, but in those days it was mostly just a cow path. We went on into what was left of the wood to make a camp, and when we got to the clearing and the tree and the spring, we remembered it from before."

"*It* hadn't changed, no more'n we had," said Miles. "And that was how we found out. Pa'd carved a T on the tree, remember, twenty years before, but the T was just where it'd been when he done it. That tree hadn't grown one whit in all that time. It was exactly the same. And the T he'd carved was as fresh as if it'd just been put there."

Then they had remembered drinking the water. They—and the horse. But not the cat. The cat had lived a long and happy life on the farm, but had died some ten years before. So they decided at last that the source of their changelessness was the spring.

"When we come to that conclusion," Mae went on, "Tuck said—that's my husband, Angus Tuck—he said he had to be sure, once and for all. He took his shotgun and he pointed it at hisself the best way he could, and before we could stop him, he pulled the trigger." There was a long pause. Mae's fingers, laced together in her lap, twisted with the tension of remembering. At last she said, "The shot knocked him down. Went into his heart. It *had* to, the way he aimed. And right on through him. It scarcely even left a mark. Just like—*you* know—like you shot a bullet through water. And he was just the same as if he'd never done it."

"After that we went sort of crazy," said Jesse, grinning at the memory. "Heck, we was going to live forever. Can you picture what it felt like to find that out?"

"But then we sat down and talked it over . . ." said Miles.

"We're still talking it over," Jesse added.

"And we figured it'd be very bad if everyone knowed about that spring," said Mae. "We begun to see what it would mean." She peered at Winnie. "Do you understand, child? That water—it stops you right where you are. If you'd had a drink of it today, you'd stay a little girl forever. You'd never grow up, not ever."

"We don't know how it works, or even why," said Miles.

"Pa thinks it's something left over from—well, from some other plan for the way the world should be," said Jesse. "Some plan that didn't work out too good. And so everything was changed. Except that the spring was passed over, somehow or other. Maybe he's right. *I* don't know. But you see, Winnie Foster, when I told you before I'm a hundred and four years old, I was telling the truth. But I'm really only seventeen. And, so far as I know, I'll stay seventeen till the end of the world."

from No Flying in the House
Betty Brock

Few contemporary authors are concerned with the child who has one mortal parent and one who was a fairy; here the orphaned Annabel is protected and taught by a fairy disguised as the small dog Gloria.

[I Can Fly!]

Christmas passed. The snows came, drifting on the terrace, icing the lawns and gardens with frosting as white as a wedding cake's. Using the terrace banisters as a ski slope, Gloria practiced jumps with her new Christmas skis. Annabel tried hers out on a gentler slope. Coasting with Beatrice took Annabel's

mind off flying. The closest she had come to flying was swooshing downhill on her red sled with Gloria perched on her shoulder. When the ice was black on the reservoir, Gloria taught Annabel to skate. Though Gloria rode around close to Annabel's ear like a small snowball, she knew how to land on her feet when Annabel fell down.

Sometimes when the weather was bad, Annabel roamed about the house alone, looking for the gold pieces of cat which Miss Peach had locked away. She tried drawers and closets and cupboards, but Miss Peach had hidden the pieces well. The one place she was never able to search—which was always kept locked—was the long chest in the stair hall. It was an old chest, used to store extra linen, carved all over with flowers and faces of mischievous elves. Since Mrs. Vancourt had found the pieces of golden cat in a pile in the stair hall, the chest was a logical place to store them, Annabel figured, and she had tried the lid a dozen times.

One afternoon in late February when the snows were melted and hard rain drummed against the terrace doors, Annabel thought of the cat. Its first visit on that rainy day seemed so long ago. Wandering into the stair hall, she jiggled the chest's carved lid. It was still locked. Kneeling down, Annabel squinted into the empty keyhole. Inside, it was black. She blew into the keyhole, making a little whistle. She tapped on the sides of the chest. She rattled the lid.

"Why don't you try holding your breath?" said a voice from the windowsill.

Annabel whirled around. Crouched on the sill, swishing its golden tail, was the cat! Carefully, she stood up, wanting very much to grab it before it could disappear, not daring to move nearer for fear of frightening it.

"It's all in the breathing," the cat went on. "If you want to open the chest, hold your breath, close your eyes; then breathe out slowly, and you'll get a surprise."

Annabel tried to speak calmly, as though finding the cat again didn't matter. "Holding my breath will only make my face turn red," she said. "I've tried it. I think you have me mixed up with someone else."

"If one of us is mixed up," said the cat, "it isn't I."

Afraid that the cat would disappear if she argued, she decided to try its suggestion. "Promise you won't go away if I close my eyes."

"I'll do no such thing," said the cat haughtily. "I come and go as I like."

"Oh, very well," said Annabel. She took a deep breath and closed her eyes, forgetting that she had no reason for wanting the chest open now.

"Not enough," said the cat. "Shallow breathing leads inevitably to failure. Take a really deep breath."

Annabel sucked in hard.

"Deeper."

Annabel felt like a balloon.

"Now," said the cat, "let it out slowly and wish on the chest."

Annabel felt as if her insides had turned to liquid honey flowing syrupy down a golden river, and as they flowed away she became lighter and lighter until she felt light enough to ride on a butterfly's wing.

She heard a click.

"Now open your eyes," said the cat.

There stood the chest, its lid wide open! But much more incredible, Annabel was floating three feet off the floor!

"I can fly!" she cried.

Immediately she collapsed on the floor with a thump.

The cat laughed.

Annabel rubbed her elbow. "I was flying. I know I was!" she exclaimed. "What happened?"

"Floating isn't flying," said the cat. "Flying takes practice. Floating is only the first step."

Annabel closed her eyes and breathed deeply again. When she opened them, she was once more floating.

"Keep your breathing regular and even," said the cat. "No shouting until you get the hang of it."

Soon Annabel was able to stretch out flat in the air and roll over. "For months I've tried to fly," she said. "Why couldn't I before?"

"You didn't really think you could," said the cat. "Isn't it amazing the things we don't

do simply because we think we can't do them? Wiggle your feet a bit. That's it. Away you go!"

To Annabel's delight, she shot up to the ceiling and sailed down again like a gull riding a fresh breeze.

"Can anyone be a fairy?" she asked. "My friend Beatrice Cox would be very interested—"

"Beatrice Cox is a mortal," said the cat.

"But so am I," said Annabel. Fortunately she was only a foot off the floor when she spoke, for immediately she fell.

The cat began to walk along the windowsill. "Stupid!" it spat at her.

"Don't leave!" called Annabel. "You always leave just when I want to ask you a question."

The cat sat down again. "If you weren't so stupid, you wouldn't need to ask questions."

Annabel decided to overlook its rudeness. "What you mean is if I believe I'm a fairy, I won't fall."

"Don't tell me what I mean," said the cat. "I know what I mean. You're the confused one."

"But if I'm a fairy now, wasn't I a mortal before? Like Beatrice?"

"How could you be?" asked the cat with a sneer. "Your mother is Princess Felicia of the Western Kingdom."

Annabel tingled all over with excitement. "My very own mother is a princess? A fairy princess?" She hugged herself. "So *that's* why I'm a fairy!"

"You're only half," said the cat. "Felicia made the mistake of marrying a mortal named Tippens when she could have chosen any prince in the realm."

Annabel nodded. "Beatrice *said* Tippens didn't sound like a fairy name. So I'm half-mortal like my father and half-fairy like my mother!"

"Unfortunately, yes," said the cat. "A most unsatisfactory arrangement for casting spells or disappearing. I doubt that you'll ever be a really first-rate fairy."

"What about my parents? Do you know where they are?"

"In exile, of course. Felicia's marriage angered her father, the King, so much he exiled her and her mortal spouse to an island far away."

"Someday they will return," said Annabel carefully. That was what Gloria had always told her. "But why can't Gloria talk about them?"

"They wanted you brought up as a mortal," said the cat. "That's why Felicia assigned Gloria to bring you up in the mortal world. Gloria has orders never to tell you that you are part-fairy."

So that was Gloria's secret! No wonder she never talked about Felicia. Suddenly Annabel felt very kindly toward the cat. "And but for you, dear cat, I would have grown up never knowing that I could fly!"

"I understand children," said the cat. "They all want to fly. With practice, you can fly as low as a dragonfly."

"High, you mean," said Annabel. "I want to fly high."

"Anybody can fly high," said the cat. "It's low flying that requires skill. Try hovering over a whitecapped sea without wetting your feet, or following a rabbit's trail up a cliff thick with bayberry without getting a scratch."

Annabel zoomed up to the ceiling and dipped down again, hovering a few inches above the carpet. Then she zoomed under a table. But, trying to maneuver through the legs of a chair, she became hopelessly entangled.

"I see what you mean," she said, getting back into the air. "Don't you think I'm too big to follow a rabbit's trail without getting a scratch?"

The cat didn't answer.

Looking down from the ceiling, Annabel couldn't see it anywhere. She flew down to investigate. On the windowsill, instead of the cat, glittered a neat pile of gold pieces, two of them studded with emeralds.

Thoughtfully, Annabel sifted the golden pieces through her fingers, listening to the clicking noise they made.

"It said it wasn't really a cat," she told herself, sweeping the golden pieces into her hand. Carefully, she placed them in the chest and closed the lid. Now it didn't matter about the cat. The discovery that she was half-fairy was enough. She didn't care if she never saw the cat again.

from Loretta Mason Potts
Mary Chase

Endangered by the Hill people, Loretta and her sisters and brother are rescued by their mother from the enchantment of the malevolent Countess and General.

Mother in the Tunnel

When Mother stepped out of the tunnel and found herself in a forest, she first thought, "I'm dreaming. I've fallen asleep and I'm dreaming."

But she remembered Colin had said the children were here. She looked around the forest and began to call them. At first her voice was low because she was puzzled and frightened. So she called softly, "Kathy, Sharon, Jerry, Loretta."

Nothing answered her. The leaves on the trees said nothing. The sun falling across the stone bridge at the end of the path was warm and yellow. Everything was silent.

She made her voice louder. She put her hands to her mouth and called louder and faster. "Kathy, Sharon, Jerry, Loretta! Come here." But no one answered.

She walked down the path to the stone bridge. They couldn't hide from her. She would find them, no matter how long it took. She stamped a foot on the stone bridge. "Kathy, come out here this minute! Sharon, Jerry, Loretta, where are you hiding?"

She started across the bridge. Then she thought she heard something like whispers in the wind. "Mother, don't come. Go back, Mother. Go back."

She stopped. She listened again. Now she heard nothing but the water flowing under the bridge. She looked down at it. It was green and glassy and it glistened as the sun shone down upon it.

If things were different, she would like to stay in just such a green forest spot as this, lean on that bridge and look down at that water a long time.

But she walked across the bridge, and she got so dizzy she had to hang onto the sides to keep from falling. She remembered she had eaten no breakfast. That was why she was dizzy.

She felt better when she looked up and saw the house. What a beautiful house! It was like a castle! With a stairway of broad stone steps going up to a big door. Where was she? Was this the Van Hummelwhite House, on the Canon Road? It must be. There was no house in town as big and beautiful. Still she was not sure. She didn't remember those stone steps. How had she gotten here? And if the children were here, what were they doing here?

She didn't know, but suddenly she began to feel better.

The terrible feeling of fear she had known when she walked into their empty bedrooms this morning began to leave her. Mrs. Van Hummelwhite was a very nice person, and if the children were here, then it was mysterious, but it was all right.

She saw someone waving at her. It was a man in a military uniform with a sword at his side. He was coming down the stone steps and he was holding out his hand. Mother wished she had remembered to wear a nicer dress.

"Mrs. Mason, good morning," he cried out, "what a nice surprise."

Mother thought, "Do I know him? He knows me."

So she said, "How nice to see you, what a lovely morning."

He came on down the steps, crooking his arm for her to lean on.

"The Countess will be delighted. You must have strawberries and cream with us."

The Countess? This surprised Mother. So Mrs. Van Hummelwhite was entertaining countesses these days. Still puzzled, she took the General's arm, however, and they walked up the steps.

"I'm looking for my children," she told him, still wondering who he was and how he knew her.

"How interesting!" He held the door open for her. "Do you do that sort of thing quite often?"

Then she was in a big beautiful room. She saw first a breakfast table in the center of the room and then, stepping out of the shadows, she saw a beautiful blond woman in ivory satin. When Mother first saw the beautiful woman she thought, "Oh, how beautiful she is." She next thought, "How shabby I am."

But the woman smiled at her so sweetly and suddenly she did not feel shabby. She felt beautiful and interesting and young and exciting.

"Mrs. Mason," the woman said, holding out a small white hand, "you didn't forget us. Thank you. Bless you." She led Mother to a chair.

Forget them? Then she must have met them. She wished she could remember where. But she must not offend them. So she said, "Forget you? How could I? How nice it is to be here." She looked at the table, set for breakfast and something odd ticked in her mind. Someone had been eating at this table. There was jelly dribbled across one of the plates. Jerry must not be the only one who did that with grape jelly—held it high and always let it dribble down.

The man and woman were watching her. "Have I interrupted your breakfast?" she asked them. "Do go on."

The woman poured a cup of coffee from a silver pot and handed it to her.

"Thank you, but I do not have time for coffee. I'm looking for my children. Tell me, have you seen three children, or possibly—four?"

The General nodded. "Many times. And I have seen twenty children, fifty children, a hundred children. Once at a circus, I saw five hundred."

"You see." The Countess smiled at Mother. "He always tells more than is asked of him. Don't you adore him?"

Mother looked at him. No, she didn't adore him. He had given her a silly answer. She frowned. "I mean only my children. They are missing and I am out looking for them."

The General rose and bowed. "I imagine you do that as you do everything else—charmingly."

Mother was getting a little impatient with him. "Have you seen them?" she asked. "Have they been playing around here? They ran away last night." She was beginning to get frightened again. "Perhaps Mrs. Van Hummelwhite has seen them."

"Perhaps," said the Countess. "I expect she has seen many things in her day. Do have some fresh strawberries."

Mother's voice was beginning to get tearful. "May I trouble you to speak to Mrs. Van Hummelwhite?"

"No trouble at all," the Countess smiled, "if she were here."

Mother was stunned. "But where is she?"

The Countess picked a rose out of a vase. "I wouldn't have the vaguest idea. General, do let me pin this flower in your buttonhole."

Mother was getting more and more impatient and frightened.

"Oh, do stop being so elegant and so charming, you two, and tell me. Have you seen my children, yes or no."

The Countess regarded her coldly, "My dear friend. Aren't you forgetting your manners?"

Mother's face got red. "I beg your pardon. I am so worried. But maybe you don't know how awful it is to run into their rooms to kiss your children and find—no one."

The Countess rose. "Stop," she cried. "This sentimental chatter bores me."

Mother started for the door. "I must go. I am wasting time here."

At the door she turned again and looked at the dribbled plate.

"A silly question," she said, "but I must ask it. Whoever did that jelly-dribbling on that plate?"

"Couldn't say," and here the General's eyes met those of the Countess. "We had guests for breakfast. I am not sure just which

one of them was a jelly dribbler. Do you know, Countess?"

The Countess's voice was firm. "To the best of my knowledge I have never met a jelly dribbler. But then, maybe I did and was not aware of it at the time. One meets many types these days."

"Good-bye," said Mother. "I'm sorry I troubled you."

The General was opening the door for her when Mother heard the noise. It was the noise of feet, like squirrels, scampering under the floor. She heard someone stumble and cry out.

Jerry! That was Jerry's voice coming from under the floor!

"Jerry!" she cried out. "Jerry, where are you?"

"Where is he?" She turned to the General, "I heard my little boy, Jerry. I know it."

The Countess held up her hand. "Yes, I heard something, too. It came—from out there." She looked toward the forest.

Mother believed her. "Did it?" she cried. She ran toward the door. The Countess breathed a sigh of relief.

But as Mother walked again over that rug, she heard again under it the sound of scampering feet.

"I heard it again," she told them, "and it's coming from down there." She pointed to the floor.

"Of course you did," the General smiled. "Dear lady, you heard the noise of the Countess's pet monkeys in the cellar. Would you care to see them?"

"Another time, perhaps," said Mother. "But now I must look in that forest for my children. Good-bye and thank you."

As Mother started out the door for the third time, she heard Kathy's voice. It came from the floor under her feet. Suddenly her spine grew cold. She could not speak at first from fear. She looked at the General. His hand was on his sword. She looked at the Countess and the soft beautiful eyes were now like blue flames. Whoever they were, wherever she was, Mother knew now that these people had her children!

When she could speak, she tried to make her voice sound easy. But when she heard it, it sounded strange and dry and a little as though it belonged to someone else.

She heard it say, "It's a lovely morning. A perfect morning for looking at pet monkeys. I believe I will see them after all."

"Certainly, Mrs. Mason." The Countess glared hatefully at Mother.

"Is this wise, my dear?" she heard the General whisper. But the Countess tossed her head.

"Wise or not, I will not be humiliated by this woman. Open the trap door."

With her heart beating, Mother saw the General lift a small rug off the floor and she saw a heavy iron ring. Just before he took hold of the ring to pull it up, the Countess said, "Wait!"

He stopped. She spoke to Mother.

"Mrs. Mason, do you love your home?"

"My home," said Mother. "Of course I love my home. I have a little green bedroom, high up under a chimney, with green leaves tapping at my window. I have a little china chandelier, made of pink and white flowers. In the dining room I have my grandmother's lace cloth. In the living room I have an oil painting of my father, a brick fireplace, a gold sofa with an ink stain. My home, I love every inch of the big rambling old place."

"Then think carefully," the Countess warned. "Once the General lifts this ring, you will never see your home again."

"Never see my home—" Well, Mother swallowed, but she thought of Kathy and Jerry and Sharon and Loretta and instantly made up her mind. If they lived in a boxcar, slept in hayfields, she would have her children.

"Lift the ring!" She threw up her head. And again the General touched the ring with his hand.

"Wait!" said the Countess. "There is someone else. Isn't there someone else across the bridge?"

Mother did not understand at first. Then she knew. She could read it in the Countess's eyes. Colin! Live without Colin! Colin live without her! Never!

The Countess was watching her. "I thought not," she said. "General, put back the rug. I think Mrs. Mason is leaving us after all."

Leaving? Leaving the children here! How would she explain this to Colin. "Colin, I have left your brother and sisters under a trap door to come back home to you." What would he think of her. No matter what he said, in his heart he would think, "Chicken! Cream puff! You left them, even the little ones, to come back here to me. Don't you know I could get along? I am the oldest. I am —a man. I can sell papers. I can work after school. I can grow up hard and tough. It will be lonely. It will be hard, but it will be better than sitting night after night in a warm dining room with a full meal with a mother who would go away and leave four children in a cellar under a rug."

"Oh, Colin," thought Mother, "you would be ashamed of a mother like that. And I would be ashamed of you if you weren't. So live, grow up, my boy, back there without us."

Mother turned to the Countess. "My son, Colin, would be ashamed of a cream puff for a mother. Lift up the ring."

The Countess was startled. She looked at the proud lift of Mother's head. She raised a nervous hand to her pearl necklace.

"But surely, Mrs. Mason," she said, "surely a boy that age needs his mother."

Mother turned her head away so that the Countess should not see the tears in her eyes. When she spoke she was not like a countess. She was like a queen.

"I hardly think, Countess," she answered, "I want to discuss my son with you. And now if you don't mind will you open that trap door and bring my children up out of that cellar."

"Oh no, Madam," the General growled, "it is you who will go down."

"And then," said the Countess, "after we have chained you, we will bring your children up. And I shall have my heart's desire, children—forever."

The General took hold of Mother to put her down the cellar, when suddenly the

Countess screamed. There was a huge finger pushing through the windows, moving blindly around, knocking over tables and chairs.

The General unsheathed his sword and rushed forward. "En garde!" he shouted, and plunged his sword into the finger.

Then they heard a bellowing voice outside, "Jeepers."

"Colin," Mother ran to the window and looked out. All she could see was an immense pair of legs in blue jeans, like two telegraph poles. But it was Colin's voice!

The finger was still moving. It had now encircled the Countess by the waist and was pulling her out through the windows and up into the air!

Peering out of the window to look, Mother saw the giant now more clearly.

"Colin," she cried out. "Colin, what are you doing? How dare you swell up like that? Stop it, this instant! I'll spank you."

"See what a fine, big son I have," she turned to the General. "I don't know how he got that big—but he did it anyway. So I don't think you will put me in any cellar now."

"Not so quickly," growled the General, and he took her by the arm and pulled her outside.

She was suddenly frightened speechless. She felt a tickling at her throat. It was the point of the General's sword!

Colin was looking at the figure of the Countess. How small she was as she lay in a dead faint on the roof of the house in her ivory satin dress. She looked exactly like one of his sisters' dolls, lying on the roof of a dollhouse.

When Colin had run through the tunnel a few moments ago, he had started to run across the bridge. Then, with one foot on it, he had remembered the last thing Mrs. Newby had said to him. "Don't cross the bridge. Walk upstream." So he had turned back.

At first he had seen nothing. Where was the house? What had happened?

Then he had looked down. There it lay. A dollhouse of a mansion with the broad stone steps no bigger than the width of his hand.

Why, he could step over and kick it with his foot and it would tumble down.

Then he leaned over and tried to look in. He put his finger inside. When he pulled it out, there was the Countess. Now he heard a noise like flies buzzing.

There at the doorway of the house, he saw the General and his mother—his own mother—ten inches tall! The General had hold of her. He was shouting.

Colin reached down to pick him up. Then he heard his mother's voice—so small and birdlike, "Don't, Colin. Don't. Stop! Stop!"

"One move and I'll kill her." He heard the tiny, angry voice. The General had his sword at Mother's throat. Gosh!

"Hello, Colin," he heard a voice say close to his ears. He turned and saw Mrs. Newby standing there. He had an idea.

"I'll call a truce," he told her. "You go in and tell him I will give him back his Countess for my mother and brothers and sisters."

Mrs. Newby was so pleased. "All my life I have wanted to be inside of a dollhouse. Yes, I'll do your negotiating. How do I get in there?"

"The bridge," said Colin. And then Mrs. Newby walked to the bridge, disappeared for a moment behind the trees at the side of it. In a minute he saw her coming across the bridge. She was ten inches high.

So that was what happened! Something in the center of the bridge. He saw her go up to Mother and the General, and the three of them went inside the house. He looked at the Countess on the roof and waited.

Inside now, Mrs. Newby was facing the General, who still held Mother firmly, her arms behind her back, his sword unsheathed.

"Those are the terms," she told him. "All of the Masons for your countess."

"Done," said the general, and he let go of Mother. "But Colin hands down the Countess first. Then I open the door for all of you to return across the bridge. My word of honor."

Mother was worried. "How do we know we can trust you?"

"You don't." His lip curled. "You must take my word of honor, as a soldier and a gentleman."

"Well," said Mrs. Newby, "that has a nice sound to it. What do you think, Mrs. Mason?"

Mother looked at the iron ring on the floor and then at the General's face. Both looked hard and cold.

"He may have a sense of honor," she decided. "Such things were fashionable once. We'll take the chance."

She ran outside and called up to Colin. "Colin, Colin." She cupped her hands around her mouth. "Put her down. Bring her back."

The Countess was coming to now and she stood upon the roof and stamped her tiny foot.

"Boor," she cried, "how dare you! Put me down—this instant."

Colin put his hand around her waist and gently lifted her off the roof. She squirmed and kicked like a small animal in his hand.

He sat her down at the top of the stone stairway. He saw her lift her head and sweep haughtily into the house, followed by Mother. Then he waited.

The Countess, as she passed Mother, said, "I will never forgive him, never, so it's no good your pleading for him."

The General hurried to her side. "Are you quite all right, my dear?" She nodded and walked to the fireplace to arrange her hair.

The General told her the agreement. She turned pale.

"Let them return! Now that they know? No one has ever learned our secret—and returned."

"I gave my word," he reminded her, "and my word is my life."

"Very well," she answered. "Let those who wish to go—go. Let those who wish to remain—remain."

The General took hold of the ring, pulled up the trap door, and the children, blinking from the darkness, climbed slowly up into the room. Jerry was first, then Sharon, then Kathy, and finally Loretta.

Jerry and Sharon and Kathy rushed to Mother and crowded around her like chicks around a hen. Loretta stood to one side, her face turned away.

"My darlings!" Mother hugged them so tight.

"Mother! Mother!" they cried out as they hugged her.

"Please," yawned the Countess, "do spare me this sentimental slush. I despise that word mother."

The children grew quiet. They did not look at the Countess now.

"Mother, we want to go home," they whispered.

"Come," and Mother took hold of Loretta's arm.

The Countess held her arms out to Loretta. "Loretta! Don't go. Not you. Don't leave me. Let me have one child of my own."

But Mother held Loretta. "Loretta, come with me."

"Why?" Loretta asked.

"Because I love you," said Mother.

"She loves me, too." Loretta pointed at the Countess. "And she will let me stay here and not send me back to the Pottses."

"That wicked creature," Mother looked at the Countess. "She stole you from me in the first place or you would never have left home at all. Yes, I understand it all now. And she has been trying to steal the others, too. It was not you, Loretta. It was she. Encouraging them to be naughty, just as she encouraged you. So please come with me now."

Now the Countess put her arms around Loretta.

"Don't go back over the bridge, dear child. Over there are many tears. Here there is always fun and laughter and music and dancing."

"Yes," Mother nodded, "there are tears over that bridge, but there are wonderful things, too. Remember, Loretta, how exciting it can be and how unexpected? Here everything is the same all the time. There, it is changing from sun to rain, rain to snow. One never knows what will happen next."

Loretta nodded. "Like the time Mr. Potts was hiding behind the door and popped me over the head with a rolled up *Saturday Evening Post.*"

The Countess laughed. "Dear Loretta! She is never dull."

Loretta leaned against her. The Countess stroked her hair.

"I will stay with you always," she said, "and laugh and dance and listen to your music."

"She has made her choice." The Countess smiled. "And now take your brood and go."

"No, no," Mother cried. "I love you, Loretta, please come home with me."

"We love you too, Loretta," cried Sharon and Jerry. "At first we didn't but now we do. Please come home with us."

"Please come home with us," said Kathy, "you are our very own big sister and I will let you play sometimes with Irene Irene Lavene."

Then she remembered. "Irene Irene!" and Kathy ran to the window and looked out at the bridge. "She's gone. She's gone. Where's Irene?"

Loretta ran to the window. "She's gone. Where is Irene Irene, Countess?"

The Countess was embarrassed. "I could not help it. I had to dispose of her. She was blocking our bridge. We set fire to her last night and swept the ashes into the stream this morning."

Before anyone could stop her, Loretta let out a cry of rage and made a grab for the Countess's hair. The Countess screamed but Loretta's hands were yanking her yellow curls and Loretta was screaming, "You burned Irene. You burned Irene. I hate you!"

"Help," cried the Countess to Mother. "Take her. Stop her. She's your child."

Mother had to take Loretta's arms and fasten them behind her back as she smiled at the Countess. "Loretta is never dull—remember?"

Then Mother pulled her to the door and Jerry and Sharon and Kathy followed.

There was a piercing sad cry from the Countess.

"Children! Children! Oh, why do you always leave me?" And she turned away her beautiful face and laid it on her arms in grief. The General bowed his head, in shame, and his sword hung limply from his side.

How sad and lonely they both looked!

No one said a word as they tiptoed out and hurried over the bridge as fast as they could.

For one second they all stood by the bank of the stream and looked across.

There it lay, dreaming in the sunlight, the little castle with the stone staircase, the little stone chimneys and the tiny door with the iron knocker in the shape of a lion's head.

It *was* a dear little thing!

From the bottom of the hill there came the sound of the cows mooing on the Potts farm.

The children said nothing. They knew they would never see the little castle again. Only Mrs. Newby spoke.

"If they had asked me to stay, I would have," she sighed. "All my life I have wanted to live in a dollhouse."

When they got back into the house again, Mother called the carpenter before she took off her hat.

"Come and board up a wall with strong wooden beams so nobody can ever get through it again."

Loretta was still crying. But she said nothing at all as the carpenter came and put nails into boards at the back of the closet.

Kathy looked at Irene Irene Lavene's little chair.

"Once, I had the most beautiful doll in the whole world."

"Me, too," said Loretta. "She was mine, too."

"She wasn't," said Kathy.

"She's gone forever," said Loretta. "And so she can be mine, too."

"Loretta is right," said Mother. "And it is sad about Irene Irene Lavene. But we had to pay for all of this some way. And we are all safe and we are all home. So let's be thankful."

Kathy said, "We will put a wreath of flowers on her little rocking chair and nobody will ever sit in that chair again."

Loretta and Kathy and Jerry and Sharon went out to get the flowers. But Colin stayed in the room and watched his mother as she went about the house singing and straightening things up. There was something he could not understand and would never understand.

Back there when he was so big and she was so small, he could have broken her in two with one hand. Yet, when she called him, his neck got hot and that same feeling came into the pit of his stomach. Size, he decided, had nothing to do with any of it.

And just to be sure, Mother often went into Kathy's old room—Loretta's room—and looked at the boards at the back of the closet. Once she held her ear down close to the wall and thought to herself, maybe it was all a dream anyway. But soon she jumped back. There was the faint sound of an orchestra playing dance music.

The Countess was giving a party over there!

Mother never listened at that wall again!

from Alice's Adventures in Wonderland
Lewis Carroll

Not all children respond to the capricious wonderland invented by Lewis Carroll, the pen name chosen by an Oxford lecturer, but the nonsensical humor of the tea party may entice them further.

A Mad Tea-Party

There was a table set out under a tree in front of the house, and the March Hare and the Hatter were having tea at it: a Dormouse was sitting between them, fast asleep, and the other two were using it as a cushion, resting their elbows on it, and talking over its head. "Very uncomfortable for the Dormouse," thought Alice; "only as it's asleep, I suppose it doesn't mind."

The table was a large one, but the three were all crowded together at one corner of it. "No room! No room!" they cried out when they saw Alice coming. "There's *plenty* of room!" said Alice indignantly, and she sat down in a large arm-chair at one end of the table.

"Have some wine," the March Hare said in an encouraging tone.

Alice looked all round the table, but there was nothing on it but tea. "I don't see any wine," she remarked.

"There isn't any," said the March Hare.

"Then it wasn't very civil of you to offer it," said Alice angrily.

"It wasn't very civil of you to sit down without being invited," said the March Hare.

"I didn't know it was *your* table," said Alice: "it's laid for a great many more than three."

"Your hair wants cutting," said the Hatter. He had been looking at Alice for some time with great curiosity, and this was his first speech.

"You should learn not to make personal remarks," Alice said with some severity: "it's very rude."

The Hatter opened his eyes very wide on hearing this; but all he *said* was "Why is a raven like a writing-desk?"

"Come, we shall have some fun now!" thought Alice. "I'm glad they've begun asking riddles—I believe I can guess that," she added aloud.

"Do you mean that you think you can find out the answer to it," said the March Hare.

"Exactly so," said Alice.

"Then you should say what you mean," the March Hare went on.

"I do," Alice hastily replied; "at least—at least I mean what I say—that's the same thing, you know."

"Not the same thing a bit!" said the Hatter. "Why, you might just as well say that 'I see what I eat' is the same thing as 'I eat what I see'!"

"You might just as well say," added the March Hare, "that 'I like what I get' is the same thing as 'I get what I like'!"

"You might just as well say," added the Dormouse, which seemed to be talking in its sleep, "that 'I breathe when I sleep' is the same thing as 'I sleep when I breathe!'"

"It *is* the same thing with you," said the Hatter, and here the conversation dropped, and the party sat silent for a minute, while Alice thought over all she could remember about ravens and writing-desks, which wasn't much.

The Hatter was the first to break the silence. "What day of the month is it?" he said,

"A Mad Tea-Party" from ALICE'S ADVENTURES IN WONDERLAND by Lewis Carroll (originally published 1865).

turning to Alice: he had taken his watch out of his pocket, and was looking at it uneasily, shaking it every now and then, and holding it to his ear.

Alice considered a little, and then said, "The fourth."

"Two days wrong!" sighed the Hatter. "I told you butter wouldn't suit the works!" he added, looking angrily at the March Hare.

"It was the *best* butter," the March Hare meekly replied.

"Yes, but some crumbs must have got in as well," the Hatter grumbled: "you shouldn't have put it in with the breadknife."

The March Hare took the watch and looked at it gloomily; then he dipped it into his cup of tea, and looked at it again: but he could think of nothing better to say than his first remark, "It was the *best* butter, you know."

Alice had been looking over his shoulder with some curiosity. "What a funny watch!" she remarked. "It tells the day of the month, and doesn't tell what o'clock it is!"

"Why should it?" muttered the Hatter. "Does *your* watch tell you what year it is?"

"Of course not," Alice replied very readily: "but that's because it stays the same year for such a long time together."

"Which is just the case with *mine,*" said the Hatter.

Alice felt dreadfully puzzled. The Hatter's remark seemed to her to have no sort of meaning in it, and yet it was certainly English. "I don't quite understand you," she said, as politely as she could.

"The Dormouse is asleep again," said the Hatter, and he poured a little hot tea upon its nose.

The Dormouse shook its head impatiently, and said, without opening its eyes, "Of course, of course: just what I was going to remark myself."

"Have you guessed the riddle yet?" the Hatter said, turning to Alice again.

"No, I give it up," Alice replied. "What's the answer?"

"I haven't the slightest idea," said the Hatter.

"Nor I," said the March Hare.

Alice sighed wearily. "I think you might do something better with the time," she said, "than wasting it in asking riddles that have no answers."

"If you knew Time as well as I do," said the Hatter, "you wouldn't talk about wasting *it.* It's *him.*"

"I don't know what you mean," said Alice.

"Of course you don't," the Hatter said, tossing his head contemptuously. "I dare say you never even spoke to Time!"

"Perhaps not," Alice cautiously replied; "but I know I have to beat time when I learn music."

"Ah! That accounts for it," said the Hatter. "He wo'n't stand beating. Now, if you only kept on good terms with him, he'd do almost anything you liked with the clock. For instance, suppose it were nine o'clock in the morning, just time to begin lessons: you'd only have to whisper a hint to Time, and round goes the clock in a twinkling! Half-past one, time for dinner!"

("I only wish it was," the March Hare said to itself in a whisper.)

"That would be grand, certainly," said Alice thoughtfully; "but then—I shouldn't be hungry for it, you know."

"Not at first, perhaps," said the Hatter: "but you could keep it to half-past one as long as you liked."

"Is that the way *you* manage?" Alice asked.

The Hatter shook his head mournfully. "Not I!" he replied. "We quarrelled last March— just before *he* went mad, you know—" (pointing with his teaspoon at the March Hare) "—it was at the great concert given by the Queen of Hearts, and I had to sing

'Twinkle, twinkle, little bat!
How I wonder what you're at!'

You know the song, perhaps?"

"I've heard something like it," said Alice.

"It goes on, you know," the Hatter continued, "in this way:—

'Up above the world you fly,
Like a tea tray in the sky.
      Twinkle, twinkle—' "

Here the Dormouse shook itself and began singing in its sleep *"Twinkle, twinkle, twinkle, twinkle—"* and went on so long that they had to pinch it to make it stop.

"Well, I'd hardly finished the first verse," said the Hatter, "when the Queen bawled out, 'He's murdering the time! Off with his head!'"

"How dreadfully savage!" exclaimed Alice.

"And ever since that," the Hatter went on in a mournful tone, "he wo'n't do a thing I ask! It's always six o'clock now."

A bright idea came into Alice's head. "Is that the reason so many tea-things are put out here?" she asked.

"Yes, that's it," said the Hatter with a sigh: "it's always tea-time, and we've no time to wash the things between whiles."

"Then you keep moving round, I suppose?" said Alice.

"Exactly so," said the Hatter: "as the things get used up."

"But what happens when you come to the beginning again?" Alice ventured to ask.

"Suppose we change the subject," the March Hare interrupted, yawning. "I'm getting tired of this. I vote the young lady tells us a story."

"I'm afraid I don't know one," said Alice, rather alarmed at the proposal.

"Then the Dormouse shall!" they both cried. "Wake up, Dormouse!" And they pinched it on both sides at once.

The Dormouse slowly opened its eyes. "I wasn't asleep," it said in a hoarse, feeble voice, "I heard every word you fellows were saying."

"Tell us a story!" said the March Hare.

"Yes, please do!" pleaded Alice.

"And be quick about it," added the Hatter, "or you'll be asleep again before it's done."

"Once upon a time there were three little sisters," the Dormouse began in a great hurry; "and their names were Elsie, Lacie, and Tillie; and they lived at the bottom of a well—"

"What did they live on?" said Alice, who always took a great interest in questions of eating and drinking.

"They lived on treacle," said the Dormouse, after thinking a minute or two.

"They couldn't have done that, you know," Alice gently remarked. "They'd have been ill."

"So they were," said the Dormouse; "*very* ill."

Alice tried a little to fancy to herself what such an extraordinary way of living would be like, but it puzzled her too much: so she went on: "But why did they live at the bottom of a well?"

"Take some more tea," the March Hare said to Alice, very earnestly.

"I've had nothing yet," Alice replied in an offended tone: "so I can't take more."

"You mean you can't take *less*," said the Hatter: "it's very easy to take *more* than nothing."

"Nobody asked *your* opinion," said Alice.

"Who's making personal remarks now?" the Hatter asked triumphantly.

Alice did not quite know what to say to this: so she helped herself to some tea and bread-and-butter, and then turned to the

Dormouse, and repeated her question. "Why did they live at the bottom of a well?"

The Dormouse again took a minute or two to think about it, and then said "It was a treacle-well."

"There's no such thing!" Alice was beginning very angrily, but the Hatter and the March Hare went "Sh! Sh!" and the Dormouse sulkily remarked "If you can't be civil, you'd better finish the story for yourself."

"No, please go on!" Alice said very humbly. "I won't interrupt you again. I dare say there may be *one*."

"One, indeed!" said the Dormouse indignantly. However, he consented to go on. "And so these three little sisters—they were learning to draw, you know—"

"What did they draw?" said Alice, quite forgetting her promise.

"Treacle," said the Dormouse, without considering at all, this time.

"I want a clean cup," interrupted the Hatter: "let's all move one place on."

He moved on as he spoke, and the Dormouse followed him: the March Hare moved into the Dormouse's place, and Alice rather unwillingly took the place of the March Hare. The Hatter was the only one who got any advantage from the change; and Alice was a good deal worse off than before, as the March Hare had just upset the milk-jug into his plate.

Alice did not wish to offend the Dormouse again, so she began very cautiously: "But I don't understand. Where did they draw the treacle from?"

"You can draw water out of a water-well," said the Hatter; "so I should think you could draw treacle out of a treacle-well—eh, stupid?"

"But they were *in* the well," Alice said to the Dormouse, not choosing to notice this last remark.

"Of course they were," said the Dormouse: "well in."

This answer so confused poor Alice, that she let the Dormouse go on for some time without interrupting it.

"They were learning to draw," the Dormouse went on, yawning and rubbing its eyes, for it was getting very sleepy; "and they drew all manner of things—everything that begins with an M—"

"Why with an M?" said Alice.

"Why not?" said the March Hare.

Alice was silent.

The Dormouse had closed its eyes by this time, and was going off into a doze; but, on being pinched by the Hatter, it woke up again with a little shriek, and went on: "—that begins with an M, such as mouse-traps, and the moon, and memory, and muchness—you know you say things are 'much of a muchness'—did you ever see such a thing as a drawing of a muchness?"

"Really, now you ask me," said Alice, very much confused, "I don't think—"

"Then you shouldn't talk," said the Hatter.

This piece of rudeness was more than Alice could bear: she got up in great disgust, and walked off: the Dormouse fell asleep instantly, and neither of the others took the least notice of her going, though she looked back once or twice, half hoping that they would call after her: the last time she saw them, they were trying to put the Dormouse into the teapot.

"At any rate I'll never go *there* again!" said Alice, as she picked her way through the wood. "It's the stupidest tea-party I ever was at in all my life!"

Just as she said this, she noticed that one of the trees had a door leading right into it. "That's very curious!" she thought. "But everything's curious to-day. I think I may as well go in at once." And in she went.

Once more she found herself in the long hall, and close to the little glass table. "Now, I'll manage better this time," she said to herself, and began by taking the little golden key, and unlocking the door that led into the garden. Then she set to work nibbling at the mushroom (she had kept a piece of it in her pocket) till she was about a foot high; then she walked down the little passage: and *then* —she found herself at last in the beautiful garden, among the bright flower-beds and the cool fountains.

from **Tom's Midnight Garden**
Philippa Pearce

In a time-slip fantasy that won the Carnegie Award in England, and is a stellar example of that genre, Tom's visits to the garden bring him into the childhood of Hatty, who is an old woman in his own time.

Through a Door

Every night now Tom slipped downstairs to the garden. At first he used to be afraid that it might not be there. Once, with his hand already upon the garden door to open it, he had turned back, sick with grief at the very thought of absence. He had not dared, then, to look; but, later the same night, he had forced himself to go again and open that door: there the garden was. It had not failed him.

He saw the garden at many times of its day, and at different seasons—its favourite season was summer, with perfect weather. In earliest summer hyacinths were still out in the crescent beds on the lawn, and wallflowers in the round ones. Then the hyacinths bowed and died; and the wallflowers were uprooted, and stocks and asters bloomed in their stead. There was a clipped box bush by the greenhouse, with a cavity like a great mouth cut into the side of it: this was stacked full of pots of geraniums in flower. Along the sundial path, heavy red poppies came out, and roses; and, in summer dusk, the evening primroses glimmered like little moons. In the latest summer the pears on the wall were muffled in muslin bags for safe ripening.

Tom was not a gardener, however; his first interest in a garden, as Peter's would have been, was tree-climbing. He always remembered his first tree in this garden—one of the yews round the lawn. He had never climbed a yew before, and was inclined to think ever afterwards that yews were best.

The first branches grew conveniently low, and the main trunk had bosses and crevices. With the toes of his left foot fitted into one of these last, Tom curved his hands round the branch over his head. Then he gave a push, a spring and a strong haul on the arms: his legs and feet were dangling free, and the branch was under his chest, and then under his middle. He drew himself still farther forward, at the same time twisting himself expertly: now he was sitting on the bough, a man's height above ground.

The rest of the ascent was easy but interesting: sometimes among the spreading, outermost branches; sometimes working close to the main trunk. Tom loved the dry feel of the bark on the main trunk. In places the bark had peeled away, and then a deep pink showed beneath, as though the tree were skin and flesh beneath its brown.

Up he went—up and up, and burst at last from the dim interior into an openness of blue and fiery gold. The sun was the gold, in a blue sky. All round him was a spreading, tufted surface of evergreen. He was on a level with all the yew-tree tops round the lawn; nearly on a level with the top of the tall south wall.

Tom was on a level, too, with the upper windows of the house, just across the lawn from him. His attention was caught by a movement inside one of the rooms: it came, he saw, from the same maid he had once seen in the hall. She was dusting a bedroom, and came now to the window to raise the sash and shake her duster outside. She looked casually across to the yewtrees as she did so, and Tom tried waving to her. It was like waving to the He in blindman's-buff.

The maid went back into the depths of the room, to her dusting. She left the window open behind her, and Tom could now see more. There was someone else in the room besides the maid—someone who stood against the far wall, facing the window. The maid evidently spoke to her companion occasionally as she worked, for Tom could hear the faint coming and going of voices. He could not see the other figure at all clearly, except that it was motionless, and there was the whiteness and shape of a face that was always turned in his direction. That stead-fastness of direction embarrassed Tom. Very gradually he began to draw his head down-wards, and then suddenly ducked it below tree-level altogether.

Tom saw more people later, in the garden itself. He stalked them warily, and yet—remembering his invisibility to the house-maid—with a certain confidence too.

He was pretty sure that the garden was used more often than he knew. He often had the feeling of people having just gone—and an uncomfortable feeling, out of which he tried to reason himself, again and again, of someone who had *not* gone: someone who, unobserved, observed him. It was a relief re-ally to see people, even when they ignored his presence: the maid, the gardener, and a severe-looking woman in a long dress of rus-tling purple silk, face to face with whom Tom once came unexpectedly, on a corner. She cut him dead.

Visibility . . . invisibility . . . If he were invisible to the people of the garden, he was not completely so at least to some of the other creatures. How truly they saw him he could not say; but birds cocked their heads at him, and flew away when he approached.

And had he any bodily weight in this gar-den, or had he not? At first, Tom thought not. When he climbed the yew-tree he had been startled to feel that no bough swung beneath him, and not a twig broke. Later—and this was a great disappointment to him—he found that he could not, by the ordinary grasping and pushing of his hand, open any of the doors in the garden, to go through them. He could not push open the door of the greenhouse or of the little heating-house behind it, or the door in the south wall by the sundial.

The doors shut against Tom were a check upon his curiosity, until he saw a simple way out: he would get through the doorways that interested him by following at the heels of the gardener. He regularly visited the green-house, the heating-house, and used the south wall door.

Tom concentrated upon getting through the south wall door. That entry promised to be the easiest, because the gardener went through so often, with his tools. There must be a tool-shed somewhere through there.

The gardener usually went through so quickly and shut the door so smartly behind him, that there was not time for anyone else to slip through as well. However, he would be slower with a wheelbarrow, Tom judged; and he waited patiently for that opportunity. Yet even then the man somehow only made a long arm to open the door ahead of the wheelbarrow, wheeled it very swiftly through, caught the door-edge with the toe of his boot as he passed and slammed the door in Tom's face.

Tom glared at the door that once more was his barrier. Once more, without hope, he raised his hand to the latch and pressed it. As usual, he could not move it: his fingers seemed to have no substance. Then, in anger, he pressed with all imaginable might: he knitted his brows, and brought all his will to bear upon the latch, until he felt that some-thing had to happen. It did: his fingers began to go through the latch, as though the latch, and not his fingers, now, were without sub-stance. His fingers went through the iron-work of the latch altogether, and his hand fell back into place by his side.

Tom stared down at that ever-memorable right hand. He felt it tenderly with his left, to see if it were bruised or broken: it was quite unhurt—quite as before. Then he looked at the latch: it looked as real as any latch he had ever seen anywhere.

Then the idea came to Tom that the door might be no more solid than the latch, if he really tried it.

Deliberately he set his side against the door, shoulder, hip and heel, and pressed. At first, nothing gave, either of himself or the door. Yet he continued the pressure, with still greater force and greater determination; and gradually he became aware of a strange sensation, that at first he thought was a numbness all down his side—but no, it was not that.

"I'm going through," Tom gasped, and was seized with alarm and delight.

On the other side of the wall, the gardener

had emptied his barrow-load of weeds and was sitting on the handle of his barrow, in front of a potting-shed, eating his midday dinner. If he had been able to see Tom at all he would have seen a most curious sight: a very thin slice of boy, from shoulder to foot, coming through a perfectly solid wooden door. At first the body came through evenly from top to bottom; then, the upper part seemed to stop, and the bottom part came through in its entirety, legs first. Then one arm came through, then another. Finally, everything was through except the head.

The truth was that Tom was now a little lacking courage. The passing through the door of so much of his body had not been without enormous effort and peculiar, if indescribable, sensations. "I'm just resting a minute," said Tom's head, on the garden side of the door; yet he knew that he was really delaying because he was nervous. His stomach, for instance, had felt most uncomfortable as it passed through the door; what would the experience be like for his head—his eyes, his ears?

On the other hand—and the new idea was even worse than the old—supposing that, like a locomotive-engine losing steam-pressure, he lost his present force of body and will-power in this delay? Then, he would be unable to move either forwards or backwards. He would be caught here by the neck, perhaps for ever. And just supposing someone came along, on the far side of the wall, who by some evil chance *could* see him—supposing a whole company came: they would see an entirely defenceless stern sticking out—an invitation to ridicule and attack.

With a convulsive effort, eyes closed, lips sealed, Tom dragged his head through the door, and stood, dizzy, dazed, but whole, on the far side of it.

When his vision cleared, he saw that he was standing directly in front of the potting-shed and the gardener. Tom had never been front to front with the gardener before: he was a large-framed young man, with a weather-reddened face, and eyes the colour of the sky itself—they now looked straight through Tom and far away. Into his mouth he was putting the last fragments of a thick bacon-and-bread sandwich. He finished the sandwich, closed his eyes and spoke aloud: "For all good things I thank the Lord; and may He keep me from all the works of the Devil that he hurt me not."

He spoke with a country voice, clipping short his *t*'s and widening his vowels, so that Tom had to listen attentively to understand him.

The gardener opened his eyes again, and, reaching behind him, brought out another sandwich. Tom wondered, in some surprise, whether he said grace after every sandwich. Perhaps he never knew how many he was going to eat.

The gardener went on eating, and Tom turned away to look around him. He was in an orchard, that also served for the keeping of hens, the pegging out of washing and the kindling of a bonfire. Beyond the orchard were meadows and trees, from among which rose the roofs of what must be a village.

While he looked, Tom was also keeping a sharp eye upon the gardener. When the man had really finished his meal he grasped the handles of his wheelbarrow, to return to his work in the garden. In a moment, Tom was beside him. He had not at all enjoyed the experience of going through a shut door, and he did not now intend to have to repeat it. This time there was an easy way through: he got nimbly up into the empty barrow and was wheeled back into the garden in comfort.

It was a long time before Tom literally forced his way through a door again. Anyway, he had seen the orchard, and that was enough in that direction; other doors could wait. Meanwhile, he climbed the low wall at the bottom of the garden and explored the wood beyond. On the third side of the garden he wormed his way through the hedge again and crossed the meadow. The only surprise there was the boundary: a river, clear, gentle-flowing, shallow, and green with reeds and water-plants.

The garden and its surroundings, then, were not, in themselves, outside the natural order of things; nor was Tom alarmed by his own unnatural abilities. Yet to some things his mind came back again and again, troubled: the constant fine weather, the rapid coming and going of the seasons and the times of day, the feeling of being watched.

One night all his uneasiness came to a head. He had gone from his bed in the flat upstairs and crept down to the hall at about midnight, as usual; he had opened the garden door. He had found for the first time that it was night, too, in the garden. The moon was up, but clouds fled continuously across its face. Although there was this movement in the upper air, down below there was none: a great stillness lay within the garden, and a heavier heat than at any noon. Tom felt it: he unbuttoned his pyjama jacket and let it flap open as he walked.

One could smell the storm coming. Before Tom had reached the bottom of the garden, the moon had disappeared, obscured altogether by cloud. In its place came another light that seemed instantaneously to split the sky from top to bottom, and a few seconds later came the thunder.

Tom turned back to the house. As he reached the porch, the winds broke out into the lower air, with heavy rain and a deathly chilling of the temperature. Demons of the air seemed let loose in that garden; and, with the increasing frequency of the lightning, Tom could watch the foliage of the trees ferociously tossed and torn at by the wind, and, at the corner of the lawn, the tall, tapering fir-tree swinging to and fro, its ivy-wreathed arms struggling wildly in the tempest like the arms of a swaddling-child.

To Tom it seemed that the fir-tree swung more widely each time. "It can't be blown over," thought Tom. "Strong trees are not often blown over."

As if in answer to this, and while the winds still tore, there came the loudest thunder, with a flash of lightning that was not to one side nor even above, but seemed to come down into the garden itself, to the tree. The glare was blinding, and Tom's eyes closed against it, although only for a part of a second. When he opened them again, he saw the tree like one flame, and falling. In the long instant while it fell, there seemed to be a horrified silence of all the winds; and, in that quiet, Tom heard something—a human cry—an "Oh!" of the terror he himself felt. It came from above him—from the window of one of the upper rooms.

Then the fir-tree fell, stretching its length—although Tom did not know this until much later—along the gravebeds of the asparagus in the kitchen-garden. It fell in darkness and the resumed rushing of wind and rain.

Tom was shaken by what he had seen and heard. He went back into the house and shut the garden door behind him. Inside, the grandfather clock ticked peacefully; the hall was still. He wondered if perhaps he had only imagined what he had seen outside. He opened the door again, and looked out. The summer storm was still raging. The flashes of lightning were distant now: they lit up the ugly gap in the trees round the lawn, where the fir-tree had stood.

The tree had fallen, that had been a sight terrible enough; but the cry from above troubled Tom more. On the next night came the greatest shock of all. He opened the garden door as usual, and surveyed the garden. At first, he did not understand what was odd in its appearance; then, he realized that its usual appearance was in itself an oddity. In the trees round the lawn there was no gap: the ivy-grown fir-tree still towered above them.

Hatty

Tom only rarely saw the three boys in the garden. They would come strolling out with the air-gun, or for fruit. They came for apples on the second occasion of Tom's seeing them, which was only a few days after the first.

With a terrier at their heels, they sauntered out of the house and—apparently aimlessly—took the path by the greenhouse, and so came into the kitchen-garden. Then, suddenly, they bunched together and closed upon a young tree of early ripening apples.

"We were only told not to pick any," said

Hubert, "Come on, lads! Shake the tree and make them fall!"

He and James set their hands to the tree-trunk and shook it to and fro. An apple dropped, and then several more. Edgar was gathering them up from the ground, when he paused, looked sharply across to the bushes, and cried: "Spying!" There stood the child, Hatty. She came out into the open, then, as concealment had become pointless.

"Give me an apple, please," she said.

"Or you'll tell, I suppose!" cried Edgar. "Spy and telltale!"

"Oh, give her an apple—she means no harm!" said James. As Edgar seemed unwilling, he himself threw one to her, and she caught it in the bottom of her pinafore held out in front of her. "Only don't leave the core on the lawn, Hatty, as you did last time, or you'll get yourself into trouble, and us too, perhaps."

She promised, and, eating her apple, drew nearer to the group. Each boy had an apple now, and they were eating them hurriedly, scuffling the earth with their feet as they came away from the tree, to confuse the tracks they had made.

Now they halted again—and it happened to be quite near Tom, but with their backs to him—while they finished their apples. The terrier snuffed his way round their legs and so came to Tom's side of the group. He was closer to Tom than he had ever been before, and became—in some degree—aware of him. So much was clear from the dog's behaviour: he faced Tom; his hackles rose; he growled again and again. Hubert said, "What is it, Pincher?" and turned; he looked at Tom, and never saw him.

Edgar had turned quickly, at the same time: he looked more searchingly, through and through Tom. Then James turned, and lastly even Hatty. They all four stared and stared through Tom, while the dog at their feet continued his growling.

It was very rude of them, Tom felt, and very stupid, too. Suddenly he lost patience with the lot of them. He felt the impulse to be rude back, and gave way to it—after all, no one could see him: he stuck out his tongue at them.

In retort, the girl Hatty darted out her tongue at Tom.

For a moment, Tom was so astounded that he almost believed he had imagined it; but he knew he had not. The girl had stuck out her tongue at him.

She could see him.

"What did you stick out your tongue for, Hatty?" asked Edgar, who must be able to see things even out of the corners of his eyes.

"My tongue was hot in my mouth," said Hatty, with a resourcefulness that took Tom by surprise. "It wanted to be cool—it wanted fresh air."

"Don't give pert, lying answers!"

"Let her be, Edgar," said James.

They lost interest in the dog's curious behaviour, and in Hatty's. They began to move back to the house. The dog skulked along nervously beside them, keeping them between himself and Tom, and still muttering to himself deep in his throat; the girl walked slightly ahead of them all.

Tom followed, seething with excitement, waiting his chance.

They went in single file by the narrow path between the greenhouse and the large box-bush. Hatty went first, then the three boys. Tom followed behind the four of them; but, when he emerged from the path and came on to the lawn, there were only the three boys ahead of him.

"Where's Hatty?" James was asking. He had been the last of the three.

"Slipped off somewhere among the trees," said Edgar, carelessly. The three boys continued upon their way back into the house.

Tom was left on the lawn, gazing about him in determination and anger. She thought she had slipped through his fingers, but she hadn't. He would find her. He would have this out with her.

He began his search. He looked everywhere that he could think of: among the bushes; up the trees; behind the heating-house; beyond the nut stubs; under the summerhouse arches; inside the gooseberry wire; beyond the beanpoles . . .

No . . . No . . . No . . . She was nowhere. At last, behind him, he heard her call, "Cooeee!"

She was standing there, only a few yards from him, staring at him. There was a silence. Then Tom—not knowing whether he was indeed speaking to ears that could hear him—said: "I knew you were hiding from me and watching me, just now."

She might have meant to pretend not to hear him, as, earlier, she must have pretended not to see him; but her vanity could not resist this opening. "Just now!" she cried, scornfully. "Why, I've hidden and watched you, often and often, before this! I saw you when you ran along by the nut stubs and then used my secret hedge tunnel into the meadow! I saw you when Susan was dusting and you waved from the top of the yew-tree! I saw you when you went right through the orchard door!" She hesitated, as though the memory upset her a little; but then went on. "Oh, I've seen you often—and often—and often—when you never knew it!"

So that was the meaning of the footprints on the grass, on that first day; that was the meaning of the shadowy form and face at the back of the bedroom, across the lawn; that, in short, was the meaning of the queer feeling of being watched, which Tom had had in the garden so often, that, in the end, he had come to accept it without speculation.

A kind of respect for the girl crept into Tom's mind. "You don't hide badly, for a girl," he said. He saw at once that the remark angered her, so he hurried on to introduce himself: "I'm Tom Long," he said. She said nothing, but looked as if she had little opinion of that, as a name. "Well," said Tom, nettled, "I know your name: Hatty—Hatty Something." Into the saying he threw a careless disdain: it was only tit for tat.

The little girl, with only the slightest hesitation, drew herself up into a stiffness, and said: "Princess Hatty, if you please: I am a Princess."

from The Hobbit
J. R. R. Tolkien

In this first episode of a beloved book, the staid little hobbit Bilbo Baggins meets the wizard through whom he is to have a series of adventures. Children enjoy Bilbo's unassuming heroism as well as his creator's easy, colloquial style.

An Unexpected Party

In a hole in the ground there lived a hobbit. Not a nasty, dirty, wet hole, filled with the ends of worms and an oozy smell, nor yet a dry, bare, sandy hole with nothing in it to sit down on or to eat: it was a hobbit-hole, and that means comfort.

It had a perfectly round door like a porthole, painted green, with a shiny yellow brass knob in the exact middle. The door opened on to a tube-shaped hall like a tunnel: a very comfortable tunnel without smoke, with panelled walls, and floors tiled and carpeted, provided with polished chairs, and lots and lots of pegs for hats and coats—the hobbit was fond of visitors. The tunnel wound on and on, going fairly but not quite straight into the side of the hill—The Hill, as all the people for many miles round called it—and many little round doors opened out of it, first on one side and then on another. No going upstairs for the hobbit: bedrooms, bathrooms, cellars, pantries (lots of these), wardrobes (he had whole rooms devoted to clothes), kitchens, diningrooms, all were on the same floor, and indeed on the same passage. The best rooms were all on the lefthand side (going in), for these were the only ones to have windows, deep-set round windows looking over his garden, and meadows beyond, sloping down to the river.

This hobbit was a very well-to-do hobbit, and his name was Baggins. The Bagginses had lived in the neighbourhood of The Hill for time out of mind, and people considered them very respectable, not only because most of them were rich, but also because they never had any adventures or did anything unexpected: you could tell what a Baggins would say on any question without the bother of asking him. This is a story of how a Baggins had an adventure, and found himself doing and saying things altogether unexpected. He may have lost the neighbors' respect, but he gained—well, you will see whether he gained anything in the end.

The mother of our particular hobbit—what is a hobbit? I suppose hobbits need some description nowadays, since they have become rare and shy of the Big People, as they call us. They are (or were) small people, smaller than dwarves (and they have no beards) but very much larger than lilliputians. There is little or no magic about them,

except the ordinary everyday sort which helps them to disappear quietly and quickly when large stupid folk like you and me come blundering along, making a noise like elephants which they can hear a mile off. They are inclined to be fat in the stomach; they dress in bright colours (chiefly green and yellow); wear no shoes, because their feet grow natural leathery soles and thick warm brown hair like the stuff on their heads (which is curly); have long clever brown fingers, good-natured faces, and laugh deep fruity laughs (especially after dinner, which they have twice a day when they can get it). Now you know enough to go on with. As I was saying, the mother of this hobbit—of Bilbo Baggins, that is—was the famous Belladonna Took, one of the three remarkable daughters of the Old Took, head of the hobbits who lived across The Water, the small river that ran at the foot of The Hill. It had always been said that long ago one or other of the Tooks had married into a fairy family (the less friendly said a goblin family); certainly there was still something not entirely hobbitlike about them, and once in a while members of the Took-clan would go and have adventures. They discreetly disappeared, and the family hushed it up; but the fact remained that the Tooks were not as respectable as the Bagginses, though they were undoubtedly richer.

Not that Belladonna Took ever had any adventures after she became Mrs. Bungo Baggins. Bungo, that was Bilbo's father, built the most luxurious hobbit-hole for her (and partly with her money) that was to be found either under The Hill or over The Hill or across The Water, and there they remained to the end of their days. Still it is probable that Bilbo, her only son, although he looked and behaved exactly like a second edition of his solid and comfortable father, got something a bit queer in his make-up from the Took side, something that only waited for a chance to come out. The chance never arrived, until Bilbo Baggins was grown up, being about fifty years old or so, and living in the beautiful hobbit-hole built by his father, which I have just described for you, until he had in fact apparently settled down immovably.

By some curious chance one morning long ago in the quiet of the world, when there was less noise and more green, and the hobbits were still numerous and prosperous, and Bilbo Baggins was standing at his door after breakfast smoking an enormous long wooden pipe that reached nearly down to his woolly toes (neatly brushed)—Gandalf came by. Gandalf! If you had heard only a quarter of what I have heard about him, and I have only heard very little of all there is to hear, you would be prepared for any sort of remarkable tale. Tales and adventures sprouted up all over the place wherever he went, in the most extraordinary fashion. He had not been down that way under The Hill for ages and ages, not since his friend the Old Took died, in fact, and the hobbits had almost forgotten what he looked like. He had been away over The Hill and across The Water on businesses of his own since they were all small hobbit-boys and hobbit-girls.

All that the unsuspecting Bilbo saw that morning was a little old man with a tall pointed blue hat, a long grey cloak, a silver scarf over which his long white beard hung down below his waist, and immense black boots.

"Good Morning!" said Bilbo, and he meant it. The sun was shining, and the grass was very green. But Gandalf looked at him from under long bushy eyebrows that stuck out further than the brim of his shady hat.

"What do you mean?" he said. "Do you wish me a good morning, or mean that it is a good morning whether I want it or not; or that you feel good this morning; or that it is a morning to be good on?"

"All of them at once," said Bilbo. "And a very fine morning for a pipe of tobacco out of doors, into the bargain. If you have a pipe about you, sit down and have a fill of mine! There's no hurry, we have all the day before

us!" Then Bilbo sat down on a seat by his door, crossed his legs, and blew out a beautiful grey ring of smoke that sailed up into the air without breaking and floated away over The Hill.

"Very pretty!" said Gandalf. "But I have no time to blow smoke-rings this morning. I am looking for someone to share in an adventure that I am arranging, and it's very difficult to find anyone."

"I should think so—in these parts! We are plain quiet folk and have no use for adventures. Nasty disturbing uncomfortable things! Make you late for dinner! I can't think what anybody sees in them," said our Mr. Baggins, and stuck one thumb behind his braces, and blew out another even bigger smoke-ring. Then he took out his morning letters, and began to read, pretending to take no more notice of the old man. He had decided that he was not quite his sort, and wanted him to go away. But the old man did not move. He stood leaning on his stick and gazing at the hobbit without saying anything, till Bilbo got quite uncomfortable and even a little cross.

"Good morning!" he said at last. "We don't want any adventures here, thank you! You might try over The Hill or across The Water." By this he meant that the conversation was at an end.

"What a lot of things you do use *Good morning* for!" said Gandalf. "Now you mean that you want to get rid of me, and that it won't be good till I move off."

"Not at all, not at all, my dear sir! Let me see, I don't think I know your name?"

"Yes, yes, my dear sir!—and I do know your name, Mr. Bilbo Baggins. And you do know my name, though you don't remember that I belong to it. I am Gandalf, and Gandalf means me! To think that I should have lived to be good-morninged by Belladonna Took's son, as if I was selling buttons at the door!"

"Gandalf, Gandalf! Good gracious me! Not the wandering wizard that gave Old Took a pair of magic diamond studs that fastened themselves and never came undone till ordered? Not the fellow who used to tell such wonderful tales at parties, about dragons and goblins and giants and the rescue of princesses and the unexpected luck of widows' sons? Not the man that used to make such particularly excellent fireworks! I remember those! Old Took used to have them on Midsummer's Eve. Splendid! They used to go up like great lilies and snapdragons and laburnums of fire and hang in the twilight all evening!" You will notice already that Mr. Baggins was not quite so prosy as he liked to believe, also that he was very fond of flowers. "Dear me!" he went on. "Not the Gandalf who was responsible for so many quiet lads and lasses going off into the Blue for mad adventures, anything from climbing trees to stowing away aboard the ships that sail to the Other Side? Bless me, life used to be quite inter—I mean, you used to upset things badly in these parts once upon a time. I beg your pardon, but I had no idea you were still in business."

"Where else should I be?" said the wizard. "All the same I am pleased to find you remember something about me. You seem to remember my fireworks kindly, at any rate, and that is not without hope. Indeed for your old grandfather Took's sake, and for the sake of poor Belladonna, I will give you what you asked for."

from Charlotte Sometimes
Penelope Farmer

Charlotte wakes one morning to find that, although she is in the same place, time has slipped backward and that she is not Charlotte, but Clare. The pace and suspense are nicely maintained in a story that stimulates children's imagination.

When in the World Am I?

Charlotte shot back down the bed, hiding her head beneath the covers. It must be a dream. If she counted ten before looking out again, she would find she had imagined it. As a little girl she had often lain like that under the bedclothes, counting, but hoping to open her eyes on a different world—a palace perhaps, herself a princess—whereas now she merely wanted things the same as yesterday, the red brick building, the shadowed room; no sun, no tree. Having counted to a hundred just to make sure, she peered out again to find the sun still there with its colored, dusty beams; also the cedar tree.

Slowly, reluctantly, she turned her head to look into the room itself. Her sun-dazzled eyes could tell scarcely more at first than its shape and color, both still apparently the same. She could see black iron bedsteads, too, four of them, but as her sight cleared, saw that against the wall opposite where the fifth bed should have been was a huge white-painted cupboard with drawers underneath. All the proper chests of drawers had gone, and their photographs and ornaments, their dogs and cats and gnomes, their calendars and combs and hairbrushes; so had the curtained cubicle and the wash-basin with its shining taps. In place of that a white enamel basin stood on a stand, a white enamel jug inside it. On the chair beside Charlotte's bed, where her new book should have been, lay a little prayerbook in a floppy leather cover and a rather shabby Bible with gold-edged pages.

Janet and Vanessa must have got up early, Charlotte thought wildly, for two of the beds were empty, their coverings smooth as if not slept in at all. They must have made their beds and gone out so quietly that no one had awakened.

But that did not explain why the cupboard stood where Elizabeth's bed should have been, nor why the hair on Susannah's pillow next to her own was no longer dark like Susannah's hair but a lightish brown.

The hump beneath the blankets stirred. There was a little groaning and sighing, and a hand reached out, curling itself and uncurling again, terrifying Charlotte, because if she did not know who the hand belonged to and the light brown hair, how would that person know who Charlotte was, and however was she to explain her presence there?

The hump spoke.

"Clare," it said crossly. *"Clare."*

Charlotte looked wildly about but found no one still to answer, except herself.

"Clare, are you awake?" demanded the hump, more crossly than ever.

"I'm awake," Charlotte said, which was true, without her having to admit she was not Clare, whoever Clare might be.

"Well then, why didn't you say so before?"

"I . . ." began Charlotte. "Because I . . ." And then, to her horror, the girl in the other bed sat up abruptly. She was quite a little girl, much smaller than Susannah. Indeed she looked smaller than anyone Charlotte had seen so far at boarding school, though she wore the regulation nightdress. She had long hair and a round face, puzzled rather than cross and red and creased-looking on the side nearest Charlotte on which she must have been lying.

She looked at Charlotte as if she saw just whom she expected to see and said, "Is it early, Clare? Has the bell gone? Have we got to get up?"

"But I'm not Clare," Charlotte began to say hopelessly, then stopped herself, explanation being impossible, especially since this girl seemed to think so incredibly that she was Clare.

"What's the matter with you, Clare?" the little girl cried. "Why don't you answer me? Is it time to get up, is it, is it, *is* it?"

"I haven't heard a bell yet," Charlotte said.

"Oh well, then it can't be time to get up. We mustn't be late. Aunt Dolly said we'd get into fearful trouble if we were late for breakfast at school."

Charlotte was scarcely listening, thinking, horrified, that perhaps she was not Charlotte any more but had changed into someone else. That would explain why the little girl had greeted her as Clare.

She held out her hands to see. They did not look any different, but she wondered suddenly if she knew them well enough to tell. They were quite ordinary hands with fingers of medium length and no scars or marks to

distinguish them. With her hands she stroked her hair, which was quite straight and fell some way below her shoulders just as it had done the day before. When she picked up a piece and drew it round, it seemed the same color, too, fairish, nondescript. She moved her hands rapidly over all her face—eyes, mouth, chin, cheeks, nose—and then again, more slowly. But it did not tell her very much. Could you just by feel, she wondered, recognize your own face? A blind person might, whose touch was sight, but she was not sure she could trust herself to do it. Her mouth, for instance, seemed wider than she'd thought; her nose felt narrower.

"What are you feeling your face for like that?" the little girl was asking curiously.

"Oh . . . oh . . . Nothing in particular. . . ." And at that moment, luckily, the bell went, an old-fashioned clanging bell, not the shrill electric one of the night before.

Charlotte jumped out of bed immediately, but the other huddled back into hers, saying, "I don't feel a bit like getting up, but of course you do what we ought, Clare, you always do."

Charlotte was so desperate by now that she did not care if the girl did find her odd. She ran to the only mirror in the room, a square, rather stained and pitted one hung just beside the door, and the relief that came when she saw her own face staring back at her was huger than she could have thought.

Except if she was Charlotte, why did the little girl take her for somebody else called Clare?

Just then the door opened and a woman came in; a tall, thin woman with her hair screwed up on her head under a white cap like a nurse's cap, her head very small like the knob on a knitting needle. Her big white apron was starched to shine; indeed, she shone all over as if newly polished: shoes, hair, apron, even her nose. Her skirt, Charlotte noticed, was so long that it stopped not far above her ankles.

"Emily? Isn't it?" she said to Charlotte. "Are you so vain, Emily, that you must stare at yourself before breakfast?"

Charlotte looked at her quite speechlessly,

but Emily shot up in bed and said indignantly, "She's not Emily, she's Clare. *I'm* Emily."

"I do beg your pardon then, Emily," said the woman sarcastically. "Just to remind you, *I* am Nurse Gregory. Did you not hear the bell, Emily? Get out of your bed at once. Just because you sleep here as a convenience—" ("And what does that mean?" thought Charlotte.) "Just because you sleep here as a convenience does not mean you may take liberties or disregard the rules."

"Oh, I don't think she meant to. I don't think she knew you had to get up at once." Charlotte found herself automatically defending Emily, just as she had always defended her own sister Emma at home.

"But it's a whole half hour to breakfast," Emily was protesting on her own behalf. "It doesn't take me half an hour to get dressed." The nurse looked from her to Charlotte with a smile that had a glitter but no friendliness.

"Do I take it then you are a dirty little girl and never properly wash yourself?"

"I wash very well, indeed," cried Emily indignantly. "Don't I, Clare? Our Aunt Dolly says I wash very well . . ."

"Does she not also tell you, Emily, that it is rude to answer back? I shall return then in fifteen minutes and expect to find you both ready, save your hair, which I shall braid myself today."

"Clare always braids my hair for me."

"No doubt," said Nurse Gregory, turning to the door. "But I shall do it for today."

If Emily was rebellious, Charlotte was relieved at this, never having braided hair before. She was also (foolishly she thought and irrelevantly) quite pleased at the idea of having her hair in braids, which she had always wanted secretly and never been allowed, for her grandfather, with whom she lived, did not like girls to wear their hair that way. To think foolish, irrelevant thoughts was more comfortable than fighting her way through the impossible ones: what was happening to her, and why and how.

The uniform she had to wear was not unlike the one she had worn yesterday, if less well-fitting. Under it, despite the blaze of sun, went a thick woolen vest and bodice, thick navy-blue knickers, and thick black stockings. Charlotte had not worn stockings the day before.

All the while she dressed herself and helped Emily do up her buttons, all the while Nurse Gregory was combing and braiding their hair—using the comb more as if to dissect heads—and while afterwards she and Emily knelt on the chilly linoleum to say their prayers, Charlotte was trying in her mind to describe how things seemed to her that morning: the room, Nurse Gregory, the clothes she wore. There was some particular word she wanted. She could not, in these confusions, think what it was. Nurse Gregory had pulled her hair so tightly into its single braid, tied ribbon so tightly at top and bottom, that her scalp ached and prickled still, which made her brain seem to ache and prickle, too. The more she hunted for this word, the more confused she felt.

Outside the room was the same—or it looked the same—horde of blue-clad girls whose faces she did not know, the same thud of feet and clatter of voices, the same mazed passages and stairs as yesterday, except that she thought (or had she dreamed it) that the walls had been white then, while today they were brown. Yesterday they had eaten in a large white-walled room but today went beyond it to breakfast in a smaller brown-paneled one, where a picture hung of a man with eyes black as buttons and a stiff white clergyman's collar. She thought she recognized the picture, though she did not recognize the room. The trouble was that she had found everything so strange and confusing yesterday in a new school that now, even when she shut her eyes and tried to remember, she could not really tell what had changed about her and what had not. She began to wonder whether perhaps she had dreamed before or even was dreaming today.

The porridge for breakfast was brought round by maids in uniform. There had been no maids yesterday, Charlotte was sure. The uniforms were black and white and looked, she thought, as Nurse Gregory's had—and again she fumbled for the right word, but this time it swam into her head quite easily—they looked a little old-fashioned. Their skirts were rather too long for one thing, like Nurse Gregory's. Of course, she thought, some people just did wear longish skirts and old-fashioned clothes—Miss Gozzling for example, her grandfather's housekeeper. Old-fashioned was the word she wanted anyway; the one her mind had chased so uselessly before. Everything this morning seemed old-fashioned: in obvious ways, such as there being no washbasin, no electric bell; and in other less obvious ways. But then her home, Aviary Hall, was just as old-fashioned, if not more so, having been decorated and furnished many years ago and scarcely altered since. No doubt this school was the same, she told herself firmly. A different explanation that slid into her mind was so huge and impossible that she could not believe it, did not want to even. It frightened her. She turned her mind wildly away, thinking, "How funny, I haven't heard any airplanes this morning. I wonder why?"

Humorous Tales

 Not every type of humor appeals to every child, but in this selection of comic fantasy are examples of the kinds of humor in which most children delight: the ludicrous quality of the Peterkin stories, not unlike the noodlehead tales of folklore; the sheer nonsense of Carl Sandburg; the realistic base of *The Future of Hooper Toote* with its single fanciful facet; the subtle irony of the stories by Lawson and Merrill. Because of their comic appeal, these are good choices for reading aloud, especially to children in a group.

The Emperor's New Clothes
Hans Christian Andersen

Available in many picture book versions, this comic and witty tale lampoons those whose credulous conformity makes them foolish.

Many years ago there was an Emperor who was so excessively fond of new clothes that he spent all his money on them. He cared nothing about his soldiers, nor for the theatre, nor for driving in the woods except for the sake of showing off his new clothes. He had a costume for every hour in the day, and instead of saying as one does about any other King or Emperor, "He is in his council chamber," here one always said, "The Emperor is in his dressing-room."

Life was very gay in the great town where he lived; hosts of strangers came to visit it every day, and among them one day two swindlers. They gave themselves out as weavers, and said that they knew how to weave the most beautiful stuffs imaginable. Not only were the colours and patterns unusually fine, but the clothes that were made of these stuffs had the peculiar quality of becoming invisible to every person who was not fit for the office he held, or if he was impossibly dull.

"Those must be splendid clothes," thought the Emperor. "By wearing them I should be able to discover which men in my kingdom are unfitted for their posts. I shall distinguish

"The Emperor's New Clothes" from Hans Christian Andersen's FAIRY TALES translated by Mrs. Edgar Lucas. Reprinted by permission of J M Dent & Sons Ltd.

the wise men from the fools. Yes, I certainly must order some of that stuff to be woven for me."

He paid the two swindlers a lot of money in advance so that they might begin their work at once.

They did put up two looms and pretended to weave, but they had nothing whatever upon their shuttles. At the outset they asked for a quantity of the finest silk and the purest gold thread, all of which they put into their own bags while they worked away at the empty looms far into the night.

"I should like to know how those weavers are getting on with the stuff," thought the Emperor; but he felt a little queer when he reflected that anyone who was stupid or unfit for his post would not be able to see it. He certainly thought that he need have no fears for himself, but still he thought he would send somebody else first to see how it was getting on. Everybody in the town knew what wonderful power the stuff possessed, and everyone was anxious to see how stupid his neighbor was.

"I will send my faithful old minister to the weavers," thought the Emperor. "He will be best able to see how the stuff looks, for he is a clever man and no one fulfils his duties better than he does!"

So the good old minister went into the room where the two swindlers sat working at the empty looms.

"Heaven preserve us!" thought the old minister, opening his eyes very wide. "Why, I can't see a thing!" But he took care not to say so.

Both the swindlers begged him to be good enough to step a little nearer, and asked if he did not think it a good pattern and beautiful colouring. They pointed to the empty loom, and the poor old minister stared as hard as he could but he could not see anything, for of course there was nothing to see.

"Good heavens!" thought he, "is it possible that I am a fool? I have never thought so and nobody must know it. Am I not fit for my post? It will never do to say that I cannot see the stuffs."

"Well, sir, you don't say anything about the stuff," said the one who was pretending to weave.

"Oh, it is beautiful! quite charming!" said the old minister looking through his spectacles; "this pattern and these colours! I will certainly tell the Emperor that the stuff pleases me very much."

"We are delighted to hear you say so," said the swindlers, and then they named all the colours and described the peculiar pattern. The old minister paid great attention to what they said, so as to be able to repeat it when he got home to the Emperor.

Then the swindlers went on to demand more money, more silk, and more gold, to be able to proceed with the weaving; but they put it all into their own pockets—not a single strand was ever put into the loom, but they went on as before weaving at the empty looms.

The Emperor soon sent another faithful official to see how the stuff was getting on, and if it would soon be ready. The same thing happened to him as to the minister; he looked and looked, but as there were only the empty looms, he could see nothing at all.

"Is not this a beautiful piece of stuff?" said both the swindlers, showing and explaining the beautiful pattern and colours which were not there to be seen.

"I know I am not a fool!" thought the man, "so it must be that I am unfit for my good post! It is very strange though! however, one must not let it appear!" So he praised the stuff he did not see, and assured them of his delight in the beautiful colours and the originality of the design. "It is absolutely charming!" he said to the Emperor. Everybody in the town was talking about this splendid stuff.

Now the Emperor thought he would like to see it while it was still on the loom. So, accompanied by a number of selected courtiers, among whom were the two faithful officials who had already seen the imaginary stuff, he went to visit the crafty impostors, who were working away as hard as ever they could at the empty looms.

"It is magnificent!" said both the honest officials. "Only see, Your Majesty, what a design! What colours!" And they pointed to the empty loom, for they thought no doubt the others could see the stuff.

"What!" thought the Emperor; "I see nothing at all! This is terrible! Am I a fool? Am I not fit to be Emperor? Why, nothing worse could happen to me!"

"Oh, it is beautiful!" said the Emperor. "It has my highest approval!" and he nodded his satisfaction as he gazed at the empty loom. Nothing would induce him to say that he could not see anything.

The whole suite gazed and gazed, but saw nothing more than all the others. However, they all exclaimed with His Majesty, "It is very beautiful!" and they advised him to wear a suit made of this wonderful cloth on the occasion of a great procession which was just about to take place. "It is magnificent! gorgeous! excellent!" went from mouth to mouth; they were all equally delighted with it. The Emperor gave each of the rogues an order of knighthood to be worn in their buttonholes and the title of "Gentlemen Weavers."

The swindlers sat up the whole night, before the day on which the procession was to take place, burning sixteen candles, so that people might see how anxious they were to get the Emperor's new clothes ready. They pretended to take the stuff off the loom. They cut it out in the air with a huge pair of scissors, and they stitched away with needles without any thread in them. At last they said, "Now the Emperor's new clothes are ready!"

The Emperor, with his grandest courtiers, went to them himself, and both the swindlers raised one arm in the air, as if they were holding something, and said, "See, these are the trousers, this is the coat, here is the mantle!" and so on. "It is as light as a spider's web. One might think one had nothing on, but that is the very beauty of it!"

"Yes!" said all the courtiers, but they could not see anything, for there was nothing to see.

"Will Your Imperial Majesty be graciously pleased to take off your clothes," said the impostors, "so that we may put on the new ones, along here before the great mirror."

The Emperor took off all his clothes, and the impostors pretended to give him one article of dress after the other, of the new ones which they had pretended to make. They pretended to fasten something round his waist and to tie on something; this was the train, and the Emperor turned round and round in front of the mirror.

"How well His Majesty looks in the new clothes! How becoming they are!" cried all the people round. "What a design, and what colours! They are most gorgeous robes!"

"The canopy is waiting outside which is to be carried over Your Majesty in the procession," said the master of the ceremonies.

"Well, I am quite ready," said the Emperor. "Don't the clothes fit well?" and then he turned round again in front of the mirror, so that he should seem to be looking at his grand things.

The chamberlains who were to carry the train stooped and pretended to lift it from the ground with both hands, and they walked along with their hands in the air. They dared not let it appear that they could not see anything.

Then the Emperor walked along in the procession under the gorgeous canopy, and everybody in the streets and at the windows exclaimed, "How beautiful the Emperor's new clothes are! What a splendid train! And they fit to perfection!" Nobody would let it appear that he could see nothing, for then he would not be fit for his post, or else he was a fool.

None of the Emperor's clothes had been so successful before.

"But he has got nothing on," said a little child.

"Oh, listen to the innocent," said its father; and one person whispered to the other what the child had said. "He has nothing on; a child says he has nothing on!"

"But he has nothing on!" at last cried all the people.

The Emperor writhed, for he knew it was true, but he thought "the procession must go on now," so he held himself stiffer than ever, and the chamberlains held up the invisible train.

from The Complete Peterkin Papers
Lucretia Hale

Readers tend to identify with the lady from Philadelphia, the voice of common sense who brings a solution to the problems of the noodlehead family, the Peterkins.

The Lady Who Put Salt in Her Coffee

This was Mrs. Peterkin. It was a mistake. She had poured out a delicious cup of coffee, and, just as she was helping herself to cream, she found she had put in salt instead of sugar! It tasted bad. What should she do? Of course she couldn't drink the coffee; so she called in the family, for she was sitting at a late breakfast all alone. The family came in; they all tasted, and looked, and wondered what should be done, and all sat down to think.

At last Agamemnon, who had been to college, said, "Why don't we go over and ask the advice of the chemist?" (For the chemist lived over the way, and was a very wise man.)

Mrs. Peterkin said, "Yes," and Mr. Peterkin said, "Very well," and all the children said they would go too. So the little boys put on their india-rubber boots, and over they went.

Now the chemist was just trying to find out something which should turn everything it touched into gold; and he had a large glass bottle into which he put all kinds of gold and silver, and many other valuable things, and melted them all up over the fire, till he had almost found what he wanted. He could turn things into almost gold. But just now he had used up all the gold that he had round the house, and gold was high. He had used up his wife's gold thimble and his great-grandfather's gold-bowed spectacles; and he had melted up the gold head of his great-great-grandfather's cane; and, just as the Peterkin family came in, he was down on his knees before his wife, asking her to let him have her wedding-ring to melt up with all the rest, because this time he knew he should succeed, and should be able to turn everything into gold; and then she could have a new wedding-ring of diamonds, all set in emeralds and rubies and topazes, and all the furniture could be turned into the finest of gold.

Now his wife was just consenting when the Peterkin family burst in. You can imagine how mad the chemist was! He came near

"The Lady Who Put Salt in Her Coffee" from THE COMPLETE PETERKIN PAPERS by Lucretia Hale (originally published 1880).

throwing his crucible—that was the name of his melting-pot—at their heads. But he didn't. He listened as calmly as he could to the story of how Mrs. Peterkin had put salt in her coffee.

At first he said he couldn't do anything about it; but when Agamemnon said they would pay in gold if he would only go, he packed up his bottles in a leather case, and went back with them all.

First he looked at the coffee, and then stirred it. Then he put in a little chlorate of potassium, and the family tried it all round; but it tasted no better. Then he stirred in a little bichlorate of magnesia. But Mrs. Peterkin didn't like that. Then he added some tartaric acid and some hypersulphate of lime. But no; it was no better. "I have it!" exclaimed the chemist,—"a little ammonia is just the thing!" No, it wasn't the thing at all.

Then he tried, each in turn, some oxalic, cyanic, acetic, phosphoric, chloric, hyperchloric, sulphuric, boracic, silicic, nitric, formic, nitrous nitric, and carbonic acids. Mrs. Peterkin tasted each, and said the flavor was pleasant, but not precisely that of coffee. So then he tried a little calcium, aluminum, barium, and strontium, a little clear bitumen, and a half of a third of a sixteenth of a grain of arsenic. This gave rather a pretty color; but still Mrs. Peterkin ungratefully said it tasted of anything but coffee. The chemist was not discouraged. He put in a little belladonna and atropine, some granulated hydrogen, some potash, and a very little antimony, finishing off with a little pure carbon. But still Mrs. Peterkin was not satisfied.

The chemist said that all he had done ought to have taken out the salt. The theory remained the same, although the experiment had failed. Perhaps a little starch would have some effect. If not, that was all the time he could give. He should like to be paid, and go. They were all much obliged to him, and willing to give him $1.37½ in gold. Gold was now 2.69¾, so Mr. Peterkin found in the newspaper. This gave Agamemnon a pretty little sum. He sat himself down to do it. But there was the coffee! All sat and thought awhile, till Elizabeth Eliza said, "Why don't we go to the herb-woman?" Elizabeth Eliza was the only daughter. She was named after her two aunts,—Elizabeth, from the sister of her father; Eliza, from her mother's sister. Now, the herb-woman was an old woman who came round to sell herbs, and knew a great deal. They all shouted with joy at the idea of asking her, and Solomon John and the younger children agreed to go and find her too. The herb-woman lived down at the very end of the street; so the boys put on their india-rubber boots again, and they set off. It was a long walk through the village, but they came at last to the herb-woman's house, at the foot of a high hill. They went through her little garden. Here she had marigolds and hollyhocks, and old maids and tall sunflowers, and all kinds of sweet-smelling herbs, so that the air was full of tansy-tea and elder-blow. Over the porch grew a hop-vine, and a brandy-cherry tree shaded the door, and a luxuriant cranberry-vine flung its delicious fruit across the window. They went into a small parlor, which smelt very spicy. All around hung little bags full of catnip, and peppermint, and all kinds of herbs; and dried stalks hung from the ceiling; and on the shelves were jars of rhubarb, senna, manna, and the like.

But there was no little old woman. She had gone up into the woods to get some more wild herbs, so they all thought they would follow her,—Elizabeth Eliza, Solomon John, and the little boys. They had to climb up over high rocks, and in among huckleberry-bushes and blackberry-vines. But the little boys had their india-rubber boots. At last they discovered the little old woman. They knew her by her hat. It was steeple-crowned, without any vane. They saw her digging with her trowel round a sassafras bush. They told her their story,—how their mother had put salt in her coffee, and how the chemist had made it worse instead of better, and how their mother couldn't drink it, and wouldn't she come and see what she could do? And she said she would, and took up her little old apron, with pockets all round, all filled with everlasting and pennyroyal, and went back to her house.

There she stopped, and stuffed her huge pockets with some of all the kinds of herbs. She took some tansy and peppermint, and caraway-seed and dill, spearmint and cloves, pennyroyal and sweet marjoram, basil and rosemary, wild thyme and some of the other time,—such as you have in clocks,—sappermint and oppermint, catnip, valerian, and hop; indeed, there isn't a kind of herb you can think of that the little old woman didn't have done up in her little paper bags, that had all been dried in her little Dutch-oven. She packed these all up, and then went back with the children, taking her stick.

Meanwhile Mrs. Peterkin was getting quite impatient for her coffee.

As soon as the little old woman came she had it set over the fire, and began to stir in the different herbs. First she put in a little hop for the bitter. Mrs. Peterkin said it tasted like hop-tea, and not at all like coffee. Then she tried a little flagroot and snakeroot, then some spruce gum, and some caraway and some dill, some rue and rosemary, some sweet marjoram and sour, some oppermint and sappermint, a little spearmint and peppermint, some wild thyme, and some of the other tame time, some tansy and basil, and catnip and valerian, and sassafras, ginger, and pennyroyal. The children tasted after each mixture, but made up dreadful faces. Mrs. Peterkin tasted, and did the same. The more the old woman stirred, and the more she put in, the worse it all seemed to taste.

So the old woman shook her head, and muttered a few words, and said she must go. She believed the coffee was bewitched. She bundled up her packets of herbs, and took her trowel, and her basket, and her stick, and went back to her root of sassafras, that she had left half in the air and half out. And all she would take for pay was five cents in currency.

Then the family were in despair, and all sat and thought a great while. It was growing late in the day, and Mrs. Peterkin hadn't had her cup of coffee. At last Elizabeth Eliza said, "They say that the lady from Philadelphia, who is staying in town, is very wise. Suppose I go and ask her what is best to be done." To this they all agreed, it was a great thought, and off Elizabeth Eliza went.

She told the lady from Philadelphia the whole story,—how her mother had put salt in the coffee; how the chemist had been called in; how he tried everything but could make it no better; and how they went for the little old herb-woman, and how she had tried in vain, for her mother couldn't drink the coffee. The lady from Philadelphia listened very attentively, and then said, "Why doesn't your mother make a fresh cup of coffee?" Elizabeth Eliza started with surprise. Solomon John shouted with joy; so did Agamemnon, who had just finished his sum; so did the little boys, who had followed on. "Why didn't we think of that?" said Elizabeth Eliza; and they all went back to their mother, and she had her cup of coffee.

from **Rootabaga Stories**
Carl Sandburg

Light nonsense, whimsy, and word play are combined in this and the other Rootabaga stories written by the poet for his children.

How They Bring Back the Village of Cream Puffs When the Wind Blows It Away

A girl named Wing Tip the Spick came to the Village of Liver-and-Onions to visit her uncle and her uncle's uncle on her mother's side and her uncle and her uncle's uncle on her father's side.

It was the first time the four uncles had a chance to see their little relation, their niece. Each one of the four uncles was proud of the blue eyes of Wing Tip the Spick.

The two uncles on her mother's side took a long deep look into her blue eyes and said, "Her eyes are so blue, such a clear light blue, they are the same as cornflowers with blue raindrops shining and dancing on silver leaves after a sun shower in any of the summer months."

And the two uncles on her father's side, after taking a long deep look into the eyes of Wing Tip the Spick, said, "Her eyes are so blue, such a clear light shining blue, they are the same as cornflowers with blue raindrops shining and dancing on the silver leaves after a sun shower in any of the summer months."

And though Wing Tip the Spick didn't listen and didn't hear what the uncles said about her blue eyes, she did say to herself when they were not listening, "I know these are sweet uncles and I am going to have a sweet time visiting my relations."

The four uncles said to her, "Will you let us ask you two questions, first the first question and second the second question?"

"I will let you ask me fifty questions this morning, fifty questions tomorrow morning, and fifty questions any morning. I like to listen to questions. They slip in one ear and slip out of the other."

Then the uncles asked her the first question first, "Where do you come from?" and the second question second, "Why do you have two freckles on your chin?"

"Answering your first question first," said Wing Tip the Spick, "I come from the Village of Cream Puffs, a little light village on the upland corn prairie. From a long ways off it looks like a little hat you could wear on the end of your thumb to keep the rain off your thumb."

"Tell us more," said one uncle. "Tell us much," said another uncle. "Tell it without stopping," added another uncle. "Interruptions nix nix," murmured the last of the uncles.

"It is a light little village on the upland corn prairie many miles past the sunset in the west," went on Wing Tip the Spick. "It is light the same as a cream puff is light. It sits all by itself on the big long prairie where the prairie goes up in a slope. There on the slope the winds play around the village. They sing it wind songs, summer wind songs in summer, winter wind songs in winter.

"And sometimes like an accident, the wind gets rough. And when the wind gets rough it picks up the little Village of Cream Puffs and blows it away off in the sky—all by itself."

"O-o-h-h," said one uncle. "Um-m-m-m," said the other three uncles.

"Now the people in the village all understand the winds with their wind songs in summer and winter. And they understand the rough wind who comes sometimes and picks up the village and blows it away off high in the sky all by itself.

"If you go to the public square in the middle of the village you will see a big roundhouse. If you take the top off the roundhouse you will see a big spool with a long string winding up around the spool.

"Now whenever the rough wind comes and picks up the village and blows it away off high in the sky all by itself then the string winds loose off the spool, because the village is fastened to the string. So the rough wind blows and blows and the string on the spool winds looser and looser the farther the village goes blowing away off into the sky all by itself.

"Then at last when the rough wind, so forgetful, so careless, has had all the fun it wants, then the people of the village all come together and begin to wind up the spool and bring back the village where it was before."

"O-o-h-h," said one uncle. "Um-m-m-m," said the other three uncles.

"And sometimes when you come to the village to see your little relation, your niece who has four such sweet uncles, maybe she will lead you through the middle of the city to the public square and show you the roundhouse. They call it the Roundhouse of the Big Spool. And they are proud because it was thought up and is there to show when visitors come."

"And now will you answer the second question second—why do you have two freckles on your chin?" interrupted the uncle who had said before, "Interruptions nix nix."

"The freckles are put on," answered Wing Tip the Spick. "When a girl goes away from the Village of Cream Puffs her mother puts on two freckles, on the chin. Each freckle must be the same as a little burnt cream puff kept in the oven too long. After the two freckles looking like two little burnt cream puffs are put on her chin, they remind the girl every morning when she combs her hair and looks in the looking glass. They remind her where she came from and she mustn't stay away too long."

"Oh-h-h-h," said one uncle. "Um-m-m-m," said the other three uncles. And they talked among each other afterward, the four uncles by themselves, saying:

"She has a gift. It is her eyes. They are so blue, such a clear light blue, the same as cornflowers with blue raindrops shining and dancing on silver leaves after a sun shower in any of the summer months."

At the same time Wing Tip the Spick was saying to herself, "I know for sure now these are sweet uncles and I am going to have a sweet time visiting my relations."

from The Future of Hooper Toote
Felice Holman

The trouble with Hooper is that his feet won't stay on the ground; he skims above it. In this airy fantasy with its solidly realistic base, Hooper has some difficulties when he starts school.

The day came to enter Hooper in the nearly new district school in the town of Central Westham. Mrs. Toote, holding his hand and enjoying, as always, the sensation of dancing with a light-footed partner, led him into the office to fill out the registration form.

"Seven," she wrote, after the question about age.

"Has already learned to read," she replied to the question of skills.

"None," she wrote in answer to the question, "Any physical reason to restrict school participation?"

But the new school clerk was walking circles about Hooper while Mrs. Toote was filling out the forms. Her eyes, Hooper thought, were marbles—lovely, glassy, absolutely perfect marbles. The fact is, the clerk's eyes were popping round only because she had come to the unavoidable conclusion that this lad applying for admission to the first grade was, so help her, *floating*. The clerk now dropped white lids over the blue marbles and squeezed them, hoping perhaps to erase an image on the delicate retina and block its path to the brain. Too late. She tiptoed into the principal's office.

"Mr. Dooey," she whispered, "I want to ask you, please, to come and look at one of the new kids. Something's wrong with him."

"How wrong?" asked Mr. Dooey, not looking up from the long list of figures that had to do with last year's fuel bills for the school heating system.

"I don't think . . ." the clerk started hesitantly. "I don't really think that he touches the floor, you know."

"Too short?" asked Mr. Dooey. "No problem. Teacher'll get him a lower chair. Several children in the same boat. One thousand and twenty-seven dollars and eighty-three cents!" He had finished adding the column of figures. "That's a twenty-three-dollar difference from the last time I added it."

"No, sir," said the clerk. "It's not that he's too short. He's . . . *off the floor, like*. Oh, please, come and see for yourself."

Mr. Dooey did not like to be diverted when he was figuring the cost of running a school efficiently. But he got up from his desk, flexed his knees, and followed the clerk into the outer office. The clerk led him across the room to the corner were Mrs. Toote was just filling in the last line of the registration form, and Hooper, neck craned, was patiently counting the squares of ceiling tile. The clerk started her circling Indian dance around Hooper, pointing to the floor as she did it, jerking her head to direct Mr. Dooey's eyes to the focus of interest—the several inches of space visible between the bottom of

Hooper's shoes and the varnished floor of the office.

Mr. Dooey's eyes still saw columns of black numerals in front of them, but even so he could not help but observe what the clerk insistently pointed out—there *was* a boy there who was certainly levitated. Mr. Dooey liked to think he had an open mind. Being in education, he had to keep it that way. And heaven knows, in these days, with people going to the moon and new diseases that never even existed when he was a boy . . .

"Madam," he addressed Mrs. Toote, who was just now looking up from the desk, "I wonder if you would step into my office for a moment?" Mrs. Toote smiled pleasantly and rose to follow him. Hooper started to follow, too. Mr. Dooey watched him with fascination, but then he said, "No, you wait out here, young man," and then he gave Hooper a second hard look before he led Mrs. Toote into his office.

"We shall have to consider the matter of where to place your son," said Mr. Dooey.

"He'll fit nicely into first grade for a while," said Mrs. Toote. "He is bright but a tiny bit lazy, I'm afraid."

"You don't understand," said Mr. Dooey. "I think we will have to put him in one of our . . . er . . . special classes, you know."

"How special?" asked Mrs. Toote.

"Well, the child *is* handicapped," said Mr. Dooey, deciding to come to the point.

"Handicapped! Hooper?" exclaimed Mrs. Toote.

"But surely if he can't, um . . . walk?"

"Oh, for heaven's sake!" said Mrs. Toote, relieved. "Is *that* what you mean? But why should he walk if he can *skim?*" she asked reasonably. "Why would anyone? Would you? Handicapped!" And she laughed without bitterness or derision. She was a generous person and could forgive people their narrow views.

It was a good thing that Mr. Dooey did have the open mind he had because if he hadn't, it might have taken him longer to see for himself that Hooper was in no way handicapped. For running messages (or rather, skimming messages) around the school, there was no one in a league with Hooper. Where other heavy-footed boys stomped through the halls with notices of early dismissal, health inspections, fire drills, et cetera, from teacher to teacher, Hooper glided quietly from class to class distracting no one from his work.

His own teacher prized him for erasing blackboards. He reached higher, did a neater, smoother job than anyone. As for Hooper, he was delighted to be excused, from time to time, from the more concentrated work of adding and subtracting. And he was very happy and outgoing. Always a gregarious boy, friendly, generous, and generally well-liked (except by the jealous), he was now surrounded by more people than he had ever known. Even the girls were nice to him. And he was popular when they jumped rope. He could beat anyone at jump rope.

As time went on, the practical aspects of skimming were apparent to anyone who would take a moment to think about it. Crossing mud puddles was just one, and Mrs. Toote appreciated it, especially since Hooper never made any muddy footprints on clean floors.

It was not until Hooper was ten that a very surprising thing happened. Hooper had his first attack. And for want of a better term, they were always called attacks after that. It was during a spelling bee. Hooper was one of the two boys left. The other boy was Morty Shwester. The word was "friable." Hooper started to think very hard. "F-R—" he began. He chewed his tongue and stared at a cobweb on the ceiling while the teacher's forefinger stiffly held the place on the page. Hooper thought, now was it Y, which is how you spell fry, of course, or was it . . . ? And Hooper continued to stare at the cobweb on the ceiling. Was it a cobweb or just some dust? It was hard to tell at this distance. He didn't see any spider. It was wispy, like a tiny cloud. A tiny cloud on the ceiling of the classroom. As Hooper stared at it, it seemed to get larger. He could see quite clearly now that it was a cobweb. Quite a big one and not as pretty as it looked at first. And at that moment his head hit the ceiling.

"Hey!" he said, and looked down.

All eyes were turned upward, all mouths agape, as they had been the whole time Hooper had been slowly skimming higher. As soon as she was able to speak, the teacher decided to take a firm tack.

"Hooper Toote," she said sternly. "You get down here right now."

"Yes ma'am," said Hooper, but try as he would he could not manage to think of a way to come down. He tried breathing in and he tried breathing out, but up he stayed.

"You heard me, Hooper," said his teacher. "This is a very shabby attention-getting device. If you can't spell a word, admit it. You don't have to carry on like that."

"No, ma'am," mumbled Hooper, a trifle embarrassed now. And he reached out absently and flicked the cobweb off the ceiling. It drifted softly down and fell onto the teacher's forefinger, which was still pointing firmly to the word "friable." Following the web's fall from his height, Hooper, squinting, thought that the next letter seemed to be an I. It didn't seem to branch out like a Y. Or did it? He felt like a cheat . . . horribly guilty, but before he could make up his mind, the teacher shook off the cobweb with annoyance and said, "Friable, Morty?"

"F-R-I-A-B-L-E, friable," said Morty Shwester, without any hesitation whatever. However, the cheers he would have received for his triumphant win were not so great as they might have been. Hooper was upstaging him.

"Very well. Come down now, Hooper," said the teacher.

"I can't," Hooper said. "The fact is, I don't know how I got up here and I don't know how to come down. It's the first time it's happened."

"Truly?" exclaimed the teacher, beginning to see she had been wrong in suspecting Hooper of merely bidding for her attention.

The class really came alive at this point. "Hey, Hooper!" cried Curly Green, "You're sure lucky this room has a ceiling!"

"Not as lucky as the kids in the class above us," said Morty Shwester, the brain. "If we didn't have a ceiling, they wouldn't have a floor!"

Hooper smiled down pleasantly, though a bit confused and embarrassed. And then the cheering, laughing, and delighted children were brought to the end of their school day by the bell.

"Dismissed!" cried the teacher, keeping her eyes on Hooper. "You stay right there," she said to him. "I'll go and tell Mr. Dooey."

And she did. And Mr. Dooey called Mrs. Toote, and Mrs. Toote hurried over.

"I'm sorry," Hooper apologized to his mother. "I don't know how it happened."

"What were you doing at the time?" asked Mrs. Toote, keeping her wits about her.

"Nothing, really," said Hooper. "I was just down there trying to think of how to spell 'friable' . . ."

"Friable!" exclaimed Mrs. Toote. "What kind of word is that for a ten-year-old boy!" She looked at the teacher questioningly.

". . . and I was thinking about it and not noticing anything until I hit my head," Hooper finished.

"Your head! Oh, Hooper, are you hurt?" Mrs. Toote's mother instinct was strong.

"Not a bit," said Hooper.

Mrs. Toote, relieved, turned her attention to the teacher. "How is Hooper doing?" she asked.

"Well, he's a bright boy," the teacher said, "but not overindustrious, let us say."

There was a laugh from the ceiling. "You all look pretty funny from here," Hooper said, seeming quite relaxed.

"It's not a laughing matter, Hooper," Mrs. Toote said.

"Now, now," said Mr. Dooey, in a quiet aside to Mrs. Toote. "Let's not seem to be showing him too much attention."

"Attention!" said Mrs. Toote. "But how is he to come home for supper?"

"Well, this problem is really not so difficult," said Mr. Dooey, taking over as an administrator should. "I'll get a ladder and take him down."

from **Ben and Me**
Robert Lawson

The story of Benjamin Franklin written by a mouse may cast no new light on a national hero, but it's devastatingly funny and perhaps just as memorable as a serious biography.

Electricity

Ben never thereafter mentioned my little adventure in printing, so I tried to be somewhat more lenient about his maxims.

Trying though they were, however, they were nothing compared to an enthusiasm which beset him about this time. This was the study of what he called "Electricity."

It all started with some glass tubes and a book of instructions sent him by a London friend. These tubes he would rub with a piece of silk or fur, thereby producing many strange and, to me, unpleasant effects. When a tube was sufficiently rubbed, small bits of paper would spring from the table and cling to it, or crackling sparks leap from it to the finger of anyone foolish enough to approach.

Ben derived great amusement from rubbing a tube and touching it to the tip of my tail. Thereupon a terrible shock would run through my body, every hair and whisker would stand on end and a convulsive contraction of all my muscles would throw me several inches in the air.

This was bad enough, but my final rebellion did not come until he, in his enthusiasm, used the fur cap to rub the tube. And *I* was in the cap.

"Ben," said I, "this has gone far enough. From now on, kindly omit me from these experiments. To me they seem a perfectly senseless waste of time, but if they amuse you, all right, go ahead with them. Just leave me out."

"I fear that you are not a person of vision,

Amos," said he. "You fail to grasp the world-wide, the epoch-making importance of these experiments. You do not realize the force—"

"Oh don't I?" I replied. "My tail is still tingling."

"I shall tear the lightning from the skies," he went on, "and harness it to do the bidding of man."

"Personally," said I, "I think the sky's an excellent place for it."

Nothing I could say, though, served to dampen Ben's enthusiasm.

Soon he received an elaborate machine that could produce much greater currents than the glass tubes. It was worked by a crank which he ground at happily for hours. Our room became cumbered with rods, wires, tubes, copper plates and glass jars filled with evil-smelling liquids. It was difficult to move about without touching something likely to produce one of those hair-stiffening shocks.

Ben even went so far as to organize a group of similarly obsessed people, calling it "the Philosophical Society." They gathered once a week, armed with their glass tubes, bits of silk and wires. They spent whole evenings fiddling with these things or listening to long speeches about the wonders of "electricity," mostly by Ben. I napped.

After he had played with the new apparatus for a few weeks and had it working well, Ben decided to give an exhibition of his achievements in this field.

A large hall having been secured for the occasion by the Philosophical Society, Ben spent several busy days arranging and testing his apparatus, planning various experiments, writing a speech and inviting prominent people.

Frankly, I was bored by the whole affair, but since Ben seemed rather hurt by my attitude I tried to take a little interest. I read his speech and the descriptions of all the various experiments. By noon I understood everything quite thoroughly.

While we ate a light lunch of bread and cheese I told Ben of my studies. He was delighted and quite touched by my interest.

In the afternoon he went to have his hair curled, leaving me in the hall, where I went on with my research. Determined that no errors should mar this performance, since it meant so much to Ben, I carefully went over each wire and piece of apparatus, comparing them with his diagrams and descriptions.

I discovered that he had apparently made several grave mistakes, for not a few of the wires were connected in a manner that seemed to me obviously incorrect. There were so many of these errors to rectify that I was kept quite busy all afternoon. My corrected arrangements seemed to leave several loose wires and copper plates with no place to go, so I just left them in one of the chairs on the stage. I was barely able to finish before Ben arrived from the hairdresser's.

As we hurried home for supper, he was so filled with pride and excitement that I had no opportunity to tell him how narrowly he had escaped ruining the exhibition by his carelessness.

When we arrived back at the hall in the evening the brilliantly lit auditorium was crowded. Seated in chairs on the stage were the Governor and his Lady; the Mayor; several of the clergy; and the Chief of the Volunteer Fire Brigade holding his silver trumpet.

Ben made his speech, and performed several simple experiments with the glass tubes. They were watched with great interest by the audience and generously applauded.

He then stepped to the new apparatus and signaled to a young apprentice from the print shop who was stationed at the crank. The lad turned with a will, and a loud humming sound came from the whirling wheel while blue sparks cracked about it.

"And now, my friends," said Ben proudly, "when I turn this knob you shall see, if my calculations are correct, a manifestation of electrical force never before witnessed on this continent."

They did.

As Ben turned the knob the Governor rose straight in the air in much the same manner that I used to when Ben applied the spark to my tail. His hair stood out just as my fur did. His second leap was higher and his hair even straighter. There was a noticeable odor of burning cloth.

On his third rising the copper plate flew from the chair, landing, unfortunately, in his Lady's lap. Her shriek, while slightly muffled by her wig, was, nevertheless, noteworthy.

The Fire Chief, gallantly advancing to their aid, inadvertently touched one of the wires with his silver trumpet. This at once became enveloped in a most unusual blue flame and gave off a strange clanging sound.

Ben leaped toward them, but I clamped on his ear. I had felt those shocks before.

"The boy—" I hissed. "Stop the machine!"

He sprang at the apprentice, who was still grinding merrily. The lad, not an admirer of the Governor, ceased his efforts with some reluctance.

The Governor was stiff and white in his chair, his Lady moaned faintly under her wig, the Fire Chief stared dazedly at his tarnished trumpet, and the audience was in an uproar.

"Never mind, Ben," I consoled as we walked home, "I feel certain that we'll succeed next time."

"Succeed!" shouted Ben. "SUCCEED! Why, Amos, don't you realize that I have just made the most successful, the most momentous experiment of the century? I have discovered the effects produced by applying strong electric shocks to human beings."

"Granted the Governor *is* one," I said, "we surely did."

from The Pushcart War
Jean Merrill

An amusing satire on some of the problems of city life is written with bland seriousness as though it were a scholarly report. The appeal of the victory of little people over those with power, and the humor of the concept and the characterization captivate most readers.

The Pea Shooter Campaign— Phase I

It took a week for the pushcart peddlers to prepare for their attack. Maxie Hammerman kept his shop open twenty-four hours a day, and the peddlers in teams of twenty men took turns putting the pins in peas.

Carlos made all five hundred and nine shooters himself. He cut them from a roll of yellow plastic tubing that a storekeeper had given him for taking away his cartons for ten years at no charge.

At last, everything was ready. The attack was set for the morning of March 23rd. The evening before, the peddlers all reported to Maxie Hammerman's shop to collect their shooters and twenty-four rounds of ammunition each.

General Anna outlined the plan of battle. Everyone was to go to the location where he usually did business. He was to wait there until 10:00 A.M., when the morning traffic would be well under way. At 10:00 sharp, he was to fire at the tires of any trucks that came in range.

Frank the Flower had wanted Wanda Gambling to fire the opening shot from in front of the Empire State Building, but General Anna felt that this would attract too much attention.

"Where there is a movie star," said General Anna, "There is a crowd. We do not want the trucks to know what is hitting them."

So the Pea Shooter Campaign began in quite an ordinary way. Between 10:05 A.M. and 10:10 A.M. on March 23rd, ninety-seven truck drivers in different parts of the city discovered that they had flat tires. Not one of the drivers knew what had hit him.

Ninety-seven hits (out of some five hundred pea-pins that were fired in the opening attack) is, according to the Amateur Weapons Association, a very good average, especially as many of the peddlers had never handled a pea shooter before. And there were a few, like Mr. Jerusalem, who had grave doubts about the whole idea.

Mr. Jerusalem's heart was not in the attack. Though he had voted with the other peddlers to fight the trucks, fighting of any sort went against his nature. Mr. Jerusalem's performance on the first morning of the Pea Shooter Campaign is, therefore, of special interest.

At the time of the Pushcart War, Mr. Jerusalem was already an old man. No one knew exactly how old. He was held in great respect by the other pushcart peddlers, because his cart was not only his business, but it was also his home.

Unlike the other peddlers, Mr. Jerusalem did not have a room where he went to sleep or cook his meals. Instead he had a small frying pan, a cup, and a tin plate which he hung neatly from the underside of his cart. He had a charcoal burner built into one corner of the cart so that he could cook for himself whenever he felt like a hot meal.

Mr. Jerusalem's favorite joke was: "Some people go out to dinner on special occasions. I eat out all the time." This was true. Mr. Jerusalem was often to be seen sitting on a curb eating a plate of beans or turnips that he had cooked himself.

At night Mr. Jerusalem dropped canvas sheets over the sides of his cart so that there was a sort of tent underneath the cart. Then he would park the cart under a tree or in a vacant lot, crawl under the cart, roll up in a quilt, and go to sleep. In the summer he often did not bother with the canvas sheets, but slept alongside the cart so that he could see the stars. He was usually the first peddler on the streets in the morning.

Mr. Jerusalem had lived this way for fifty or sixty years, and he had never picked a fight with anyone. His motto was: "I live the way I want. You don't bother me. And I won't bother you."

Having lived by this motto for so long, Mr. Jerusalem was not happy about the Pea Shooter Campaign. To be sure, he had a great deal more at stake than the other peddlers. In his case, it was not only his business, but his home that was in danger as long as the trucks continued to attack the pushcarts. Still it went against his deepest convictions to cause another man trouble.

"There are not troubles enough in the world?" he had asked himself as he had worked alongside the other peddlers, putting pins in the peas. "Why should I make more?"

Mr. Jerusalem was still asking himself this question as he set off down Delancey Street on the morning of March 23rd. Like the other peddlers, Mr. Jerusalem was fully armed, although no one walking down the street would have noticed.

Anyone glancing at Mr. Jerusalem would have taken the yellow plastic straw sticking from his coat pocket for a yellow pencil. And no one would have taken any notice at all of the two dozen peas with a pin stuck carefully through the center of each, which Mr. Jerusalem had pinned to the sleeve of his jacket.

Or, even if someone had noticed, he would have supposed that Mr. Jerusalem had twenty-four tiny sleeve buttons on his jacket. Mr. Jerusalem's clothes never looked like anyone else's anyway. He picked them up here and there, secondhand, and he had his own style of wearing them.

"A sleeveful of ammunition!" Mr. Jerusalem muttered to himself, as he set off on the morning of March 23rd to pick up a second-hand popcorn machine that he had arranged to buy. "Who would believe it?

"A man my age—going to war!" Mr. Jerusalem shook his head sadly. "I can hardly believe it myself.

"Fighting in the streets!" he continued. "A man of peace for eighty years is walking fully armed down Delancey Street. A man who does not care for fighting.

"It is not only that I do not care for fighting," he went on.

"Naturally, I do not care for fighting," he admitted. "But it is also that fighting a ten-ton truck with a pea shooter is a little crazy. I do not think it will work.

"But what else can we do?" he asked himself.

He could not think of anything else. "So I will fight," he said. "If I have to," he added.

All the same Mr. Jerusalem was relieved when at 10:00 o'clock, the hour the attack was to begin, there was no truck parked within a hundred feet of his cart. Mr. Jerusalem did not think he could hit the tire of a moving truck.

"Would General Anna want me to waste the ammunition?" he asked himself. "Or Maxie Hammerman? Or Miss Wanda Gambling who has been so kind as to pay for one ton of pins? Not to mention peas."

When Mr. Jerusalem arrived at the candy store where he was to pick up the popcorn machine, he parked his cart. He was just starting into the store, when someone shouted at him.

Mr. Jerusalem looked around and saw a Leaping Lema. The driver of the Leaping Lema was trying to back into a space in front of Mr. Jerusalem's cart. The truck was loaded with new glass-and-chromium popcorn machines.

Now if there was any kind of truck that Mr. Jerusalem did not like, it was a Leaping

Lema. The reason for this was that Mr. Jerusalem had known Louie Livergreen's father.

Louie's father had been, before his death, one of the most-respected pushcart peddlers in the secondhand-clothes line. Mr. Jerusalem had often made a cup of tea on his charcoal burner for Solomon Livergreen when he and Solomon were working on the same street.

Mr. Jerusalem should have been glad that Solomon's son was a big success—people said Louie Livergreen now owned one hundred big trucks. But Mr. Jerusalem held it against Louie Livergreen that from the day Louie had got his first truck, he had never come to see his father again. So every time Mr. Jerusalem saw a Leaping Lema on the streets, he thought, "They are breaking up family life."

As he watched the Leaping Lema backing into the curb on the first day of the Pea Shooter Campaign, Mr. Jerusalem wondered what his old friend Solomon Livergreen would have thought of the Pushcart War. Would Solomon, he wondered, have shot at a truck belonging to his own son, Louie Livergreen? And what would Solomon have wished his old friend Mr. Jerusalem to do?

"Shoot if you have to." That is what Solomon Livergreen would say, Mr. Jerusalem said to himself.

Mr. Jerusalem's conversation with Solomon Livergreen was interrupted by the driver of the Leaping Lema.

"Hey, Bud," shouted the driver. "Stop talking to yourself and move the baby buggy!" The driver was Little Miltie, a driver mentioned in the diary of Joey Kafflis.

Mr. Jerusalem frowned. It was bad enough that Little Miltie, a man one half the age of Mr. Jerusalem and not as tall, should call Mr. Jerusalem "Bud." But that Little Miltie should call Mr. Jerusalem's cart, which was also his home, a "baby buggy"—this was unnecessarily rude. However, Mr. Jerusalem answered courteously.

"I will only be a minute," he said.

"I can't wait a minute," said Little Miltie.

"I got to deliver a popcorn machine."

"Well," said Mr. Jerusalem, "I have to pick up a popcorn machine. And until I pick up this secondhand popcorn machine, there will be no room in the store for a new machine such as you wish to deliver." And he turned to go about his business.

But as Mr. Jerusalem started into the candy store, Little Miltie raced his motor. Mr. Jerusalem hesitated. He remembered what had happened to Morris the Florist. He glanced over his shoulder.

"I'm backing up, Bud," Little Miltie said.

Mr. Jerusalem sighed and walked back to move his cart to the other side of the street.

Little Miltie grinned. "That's a good boy, Buster."

Mr. Jerusalem did not reply, but as Little Miltie was backing into the place Mr. Jerusalem had left, the old peddler took out his pea shooter. He looked at it doubtfully.

"A man my age—with a *pea shooter!*" he sighed. "Such a craziness on Delancey Street." However, he inserted one of the pea-pins, took careful aim—and fired.

For a moment nothing happened. Mr. Jerusalem felt foolish. "All right, I admit it," he said. "We are all crazy."

Mr. Jerusalem was about to drop his pea shooter in the gutter when he heard a slight hissing sound—the sound of air escaping from a tire.

"Or perhaps not so crazy," said Mr. Jerusalem.

He put the pea shooter back in his pocket and went to collect the popcorn machine. When he came out of the candy store, one of Little Miltie's rear tires was quite flat. Little Miltie was stamping up and down in the street and speaking even more rudely to the tire than he had spoken to Mr. Jerusalem.

"What is the matter?" asked Mr. Jerusalem. "The Leaping Lema is not leaping so good? A little trouble maybe?"

But Little Miltie was too angry to reply.

"Believe me, Solomon, I had to do it," Mr. Jerusalem said, as if to his old friend Solomon Livergreen.

"The fact is, Solomon," he continued, as he roped the popcorn machine onto his cart, "to cause a little trouble now and then is maybe good for a man.

"But, Solomon," he asked as he set off down Delancey Street, "who would have thought a man of my age would be such a good shot?

"Naturally, it pays to use high-quality pins," he added.

Although Mr. Jerusalem knew where he could get a good price for the secondhand popcorn machine, he was now in no hurry to get there. He paused to look over every truck that had stopped for a traffic light or had pulled up to a curb to make a delivery.

Mr. Jerusalem chose his targets very carefully, and to his astonishment he hit four more trucks before he ran out of ammunition. At 2:30 in the afternoon, he headed back to Maxie Hammerman's for more peapins. He still had not got around to selling his popcorn machine.

Science Fiction

 Science fiction, which deals with the probable, and science fantasy, which suggests the improbable, differ from other forms of fantasy in being set in another world or time either in whole or in part. Almost always they reflect the imposition of imagination on a growing body of technological progress. Children in growing numbers respond to this genre, a blend of what is possible within humanity's experience and what may be possible beyond that experience, adventure, space flight and space vehicles, and often of larger issues such as the struggle between good and evil, the hope for one peaceful world, and the brotherhood of man.

from The Twenty-One Balloons
William Pène du Bois

This excerpt from a Newbery Medal book begins as Professor Sherman is taking a brief intermission during his long lecture about his adventures on the island of Krakatoa, part of a journey that began when he left the West Coast in one balloon and was picked up weeks later in the Atlantic with twenty.

Airy-Go-Round

During the intermission, the mayor and the Chief Surgeon of the San Francisco General Hospital rushed to Professor Sherman's bedside to see if he was all right. "Are you tired?" they asked in one voice. "Would you rather resume tomorrow?" asked the Mayor. "How do you feel?" asked the Chief Surgeon. "Is there anything we can do for you?"

"I feel fine," said Professor Sherman.

"Would you like one of the nurses to change the drinking water in your carafe?" asked the Chief Surgeon.

"I don't care, it tastes all right to me."

"Could I fetch you a little refreshment?" asked the Mayor. "Something to renew your strength?"

"If you insist," said the Professor. The

"Airy-Go-Round" from THE TWENTY-ONE BALLOONS by William Pène du Bois. Copyright 1947 by William Pène du Bois. Copyright renewed 1975 by William Pène du Bois. Used by permission of Viking Penguin Inc. and World's Work Ltd.

Mayor ran off at a fast puffing trot while the Chief Surgeon busied himself tucking in the comforter on the Professor's bed. It should have been obvious to anyone, even two such important personages as the Mayor and Chief Surgeon, that all Professor Sherman wanted during this intermission he had called was a few minutes of rest.

The Mayor came back with a nip and the Professor swallowed it in one gulp. Then, looking at the Mayor and Surgeon, he said with a smile on his face, "You know, Gentlemen, this to me is very funny. A little over a month ago, I was an insignificant arithmetic teacher who would have found it almost impossible to get to see either one of you. Now you are waiting on me like a pair of well-trained valets. I thank you for your kind attention. It goes to show how wonderful ballooning can be. You never can tell where the winds will blow you, what fantastic good fortune they can lead you to. *Long live balloons!*" he shouted. The Mayor and the Chief Surgeon joined in with a few sheepish giggles, then backed away.

By this time the fifteen minutes were up and Professor Sherman was gratified to see that the people of the audience had quietly returned to their seats and were sitting attentively. The packed auditorium wasn't making a sound. It was waiting anxiously to hear the end of his extraordinary story.

The Chief Surgeon saw, as before, that the Professor was comfortably propped up with pillows, and the Mayor walked over to the Professor's bedside. With one hand resting on the head of the bed, he turned to the audience and said:

"Again it gives me great pleasure to present Professor William Waterman Sherman."

The Professor thanked the Mayor, cleared his throat, and resumed his talk:

Mr. F. led me to the first invention he had promised to show me, the Balloon Merry-Go-Round. On our way I told Mr. F. that the name of the invention suggested something at an amusement park. "Just what is this invention for?"

"It is part of an amusement park," said Mr. F., "which the children of Krakatoa are planning for themselves. You see, our children now are between the ages of ten and fifteen. When we return from our trips to other countries, they help us unload our freighter with great interest. It suddenly dawned on them a year or so ago that it would be an excellent idea if a few boatloads were brought back full of supplies exclusively for them; for after all they do own a share in the mines, too. We agreed to give them two boatloads a year, so all of the children held a meeting to decide how best to fill their freighters. This amusement park they have started to build is the result of their planning. The Balloon Merry-Go-Round is their own invention, designed with but little help from us."

"Is there any school here?" I asked.

"The children have no formal schooling. We have taught them how to read and write, and we have tried to teach them a little arithmetic. They have all taken part in the building of our international houses—which is most educating in itself. But all in all, a school is sorely needed here. You aren't by any chance a teacher, are you? Just what does the title Professor stand for in your case?"

"Professor of, uh, Aeronautics," I stuttered. "I teach Balloon Theory at, uh, the San Francisco Lighter than Air School." I felt a flush of heat in my cheeks as I waded through this fabulous lie. I had no intention of getting involved again in teaching, the very thing from which this trip of mine was intended to take me.

"How interesting," said Mr. F. "That goes to show how quickly one gets out of touch with one's native city. I can't say that I even recall hearing of such an institution."

"It's one of the latest," I muttered, "practically brand new." Then quickly changing the subject, I asked what other forms of amusement could be found at the park.

"So far, they have just had time to design and build the Merry-Go-Round, but they have a lot more planned. Most of the usual rides found at amusement parks are impractical for Krakatoa because they are higher than the jungle life on the Island and would be visible from the sea. As a matter of fact, we only take rides on the Balloon Merry-Go-

Round after thoroughly scanning the horizon for passing ships. We never use it if anything is in sight. Do you see that tall pole in the distance?"

"Yes, I do," I said. The pole was straight and the same width at the bottom as at the top. It was threaded like a gigantic screw and it was about seventy-five feet tall.

"That's part of the Balloon Merry-Go-Round, the axle around which it revolves to give it its spin when it is gaining altitude."

"Can't that be seen from the ocean?"

"Yes, it can. But one lone pole isn't enough to attract much attention from passing ships."

We came to a little forest of palm trees, the same sort of neatly kept little forest I had seen the day before, with freshly cut lawn instead of the usual jungle underbrush. We walked through this forest for a hundred yards or so and then came upon a clearing. In the middle of this clearing was what was apparently the Balloon Merry-Go-Round. There were eight little boats around the base of the pole, all joined together bow to stern. In the place of oarlocks, there were two brass rings on these boats, and through these rings passed poles which all met at the main vertical pole of the Merry-Go-Round where they were screwed into the hub of another large brass ring around the pole, forming spokes of a giant wheel. Each boat was covered with a protective tarpaulin. Mr. F. removed one of the tarpaulins and showed me one. They were nice little centerboard sailboats, sturdy and quite seaworthy. The sails were neatly stowed in trim lockers. I didn't notice any masts, but there was definitely a place for them. Alongside of each of these boats was a large deflated balloon painted a pale sky-blue. Off to one side in the clearing there was a little shack made of bamboo which reminded me very much of my basket house. On its walls outside, eight silk hoses were hanging, neatly coiled up and in line. There was a bell on top of this little shack, which could be reached by climbing a ladder.

Mr. F. walked over to the shack, went inside, and came out again with a spyglass. He climbed up the ladder to the roof of the shack and carefully looked over the horizon around him, apparently for ships. "Would you care to risk a trip in it?" he asked me. "The weather today is ideal."

"As an ardent balloonist, I accept with enthusiasm; but as a sixty-six-year-old man I must confess that I accept with some trepidation. Is it safe?"

"Absolutely," answered Mr. F. "You don't believe that we would allow our children to make ascensions in dangerous contraptions, do you?"

"I guess not," I said, reassured. "I am sure that any invention using balloons and wind as motive power cannot but be enjoyable."

"Very well, then," said Mr. F. He then loudly rang the bell on top of the shack. This sound produced the same reaction, only considerably happier and more excited, as a school bell back home. We were shortly surrounded by children. These children didn't seem to need to be explained anything either; as soon as they arrived in the clearing they made themselves extremely busy readying the Balloon Merry-Go-Round. They took the tarpaulins off all the boats and rolled them up neatly. Four of the children ran into the shack where they prepared the hydrogen machine and pumps. Another eight each grabbed a silk hose, attached it to the hydrogen machine in the shack on one end, and to one of the balloons on the other. The balloons were all carefully unfolded and laid out flat on the ground, and the nets and ropes which attached them to the boats were carefully placed around and beside them so that they wouldn't get tangled up when the balloons were filled with gas. Slowly the balloons started to fill with hydrogen, the ones nearest the pumps filling faster than the others. They lazily lifted themselves off the ground with the children watching them carefully, constantly straightening the ropes so they wouldn't get tangled. Soon they were all full of hydrogen and straining at the boats which were roped to the ground. All forty children were present, working efficiently on the Merry-Go-Round, although it was apparent that there was only room for fourteen of them on this trip. There was room for two in each boat, making a total of sixteen seats, but Mr. F. and I were going to occupy two of the seats. There was no arguing among the children as to whose turn it was; they must have had some sort of passenger schedule they followed closely. I did notice that neither B-1 nor B-2 were among the children who climbed into the boats when they were ready. I suppose that this was because it was "B" Day of the Month of Lamb and they had plenty of work to do at their British chop house. I sat in a boat with Mr. F's son, F-1, and Mr. F. sat with a child in a boat which was on the opposite side of the big pole from ours. "This will make the Merry-Go-Round balance better," said F-1.

There were two children on the ground near each boat. When we were all aboard, they detached the silk hydrogen hoses and rolled them back up to the shack where they carefully hung them up. They then returned to us and one held a rope at the bow of each boat and the other held a rope at the boat's stern. One of the children passengers had a blank pistol, the sort used for starting races at track meets. He stood up and yelled in a high clear voice, *"Is everybody ready?"*

A shrill and deafening *"yes"* was heard, mixed with the deeper voices of Mr. F. and myself. At this signal, the children standing near the boats all gave their ropes a sharp pull, which seemed to unhook the boats from the ground, and they all ran around the pole in the direction we were heading, giving us a good fast start.

The boats were joined together to form the rim of a wheel. The poles going through the brass oarlocks of the boats formed the spokes of this wheel. The spokes were attached to a big brass ring, or hub of the wheel, and this whole gigantic Merry-Go-Round revolved around the seventy-five-foot pole which was pointing straight up to the sky and was threaded like a screw. The balloons lifted the boats around and around the huge screw up into the air. The Balloon Merry-Go-Round gained speed as it gained altitude. The pole was well greased so that by the time we neared the top we were going very fast. I asked F-1 what happened when we reached

the top of the pole. "Do we quickly deflate the balloons and revolve back down to the ground around the pole in the opposite direction?"

"Of course not," said F-1. "We fly right off the pole into the air."

"You'll see," he said.

We soon reached the top and the Merry-Go-Round lunged upward as it lost its grip on the pole. The wind immediately started to carry us off over the Island. We were gaining altitude fast and, of course, still spinning around at great speed. I must admit this was truly a delightful and exciting ride, unlike any other balloon experience I have ever had. I saw now how the boats were kept level. A child in each boat held the ripcord of his boat's balloon. Whenever a boat went a little higher than the others, the ripcord would be pulled releasing a little hydrogen until the boat was again on the same level.

"You must only be able to take short trips," I told F-1, "if you constantly have to release gas to keep the Merry-Go-Round level."

"That's right," he answered. "The length of our trips depends on many things such as the calmness of the weather, how well we distribute the weight in the boats, and how skillfully we control the ripcords. But you understand," he added, "the Balloon Merry-Go-Round wasn't built for travel but rather for short pleasure trips."

"Oh, of course," I said.

The Balloon Merry-Go-Round was heading directly for the mountain. I saw that we were going to fly over it. I asked F-1 if this were not dangerous.

"It isn't dangerous, but it's rather unfortunate because it always means a short trip."

"Why?" I asked.

"Because the huge crater of the volcanic mountain is full of hot air which forms sort of a vacuum. When we fly over the crater, the Merry-Go-Round is sucked downward rather violently and we always use up a lot of gas controlling it and keeping it level."

"Isn't this hazardous?" I asked.

"No," said F-1, "by the time we reach the mountain, we will be high enough to clear it by a great distance. The only danger in taking a ride in this is landing on the ground or on the mountain, or worst of all, in the mountain when the wind is calm. Krakatoa is a small island, and if there is any wind at all, it will carry the Merry-Go-Round out to sea. Once when we first got it, we took a trip on a very calm day. We went straight up, spun around a while, and gradually lost altitude, landing in a forest of palm trees. No one was hurt, but some of the boats were damaged and one of the balloons was torn. Since then, we have only risked trips when there is wind."

We were nearing the mountain and I leaned over the side of my boat to look down at the crater. There was a thick gray smoke crawling around inside. It was like looking into a horrible pit full of elephants. When we were directly over the mountain there was a sickening atmosphere of hot air permeated with sulphurous gases. The Merry-Go-Round started tossing around violently over the pit, and the children with the ripcords kept a careful watch directly across our giant wheel at opposite boats to keep the Merry-Go-Round as steady and level as possible. Hanging on tightly, I leaned over the side of the boat in order to have a direct look into the volcanic crater itself. In places where the smoke had cleared a bit I could see a lake of thick molten lava boiling and bubbling in slow motion. It was a sickening, frightening sight. As I was leaning over, the Merry-Go-Round suddenly plunged downward, then swayed from side to side as the children steadied it. I must have taken a deep gasp of breath, out of fear, I suppose, and my lungs were suddenly filled with hot sulphurous fumes. The Merry-Go-Round was still spinning fast, as well as pitching and rocking in the air. I hastily drew my head back into the boat, shut my eyes, and lay down on the bottom of the boat. I could hear the rumbling of the mountain beneath me mixed with the hissing noise of hydrogen being released from the balloons. I think I was as close to being sick then as it is possible for anyone to be. We were soon over the mountain, and in

fresh, calm air again and I sat up feeling considerably better.

"To tell you the truth, Sir," said F-1, who apparently could well see that I had nearly lost my British breakfast, "I was nearly sick myself that time. The mountain seems unusually violent this morning. I hope this isn't a bad sign."

I took this to be the remark of a younger balloonist comforting an older one who had nearly made a fool of himself. I told him that my behavior was quite inexcusable.

Flying over water in this spinning airship was completely enjoyable. The magnificent seascape of the Pacific Ocean passed before your eyes half of the time, and Krakatoa in its entirety was beneath you for your careful observation with each turn of the Merry-Go-Round. The Island looked beautiful from the air. Its vegetation was so rich, warm, and soft-looking. The mountain looked so fearful and exciting. The magnificent houses of all nations looked like extraordinary doll's houses on felt lawns, and the Krakatoan crystal house shone like a jewel. The contrast between the trimmed interior and untrimmed ring of jungle around the Island was easy to see from our boats. The Island looked like a formal garden surrounded by a bushy untrimmed hedge.

After a flight lasting approximately thirty-five minutes we were near the surface of the water. The children, controlling their ripcords like experts, lowered the Merry-Go-Round gently and smoothly into the Ocean. We made one complete turn in the water and came slowly to a stop. "Well," I exclaimed, "that was undoubtedly the most thrilling and unusual trip I have ever had the pleasure of taking."

The children in the boats, Mr. F., and I then all leaned back and relaxed a while in the sun, looking up at the balloons which were now half empty and bobbing back and forth with the wind. Suddenly one of the boys, the same one who had fired the starting gun, stood up and said, "All right, everybody, let's go."

At this command the rest of the children stood up and carefully deflated their balloons and folded them up in their boats without letting any part of them touch water. They folded them lengthwise first, then rolled them from the top toward the bottom where the gas escape was, thus forcing all of the gas out of them and making small neat bundles. They opened the little lockers in the boats, where the sails were, took the sails out, and replaced them with the folded balloons. Each boat had one mainsail.

"How do you sail these boats when they are all attached together like a wheel?" I asked. "And what do you use for masts?" These were foolish questions, I immediately realized, for while I was asking them I managed to figure out these problems for myself.

First of all, the children detached the boats one from the other at their bows and sterns. When this was done, they were still attached to each other by the poles which formed the spokes of the giant wheel. These poles were obviously the masts when the boats were used for sailing. The children, two on each pole, all pushed together toward the center hub until the poles slid out through the brass oarlock rings on their boats. Then, still working two on each pole, they unscrewed the poles from the brass hub in the center. They all unscrewed their poles except one boy, the boy who gave the commands. He pulled his pole in with the hub still attached to it, unscrewed the hub in his boat, and put it away in a separate locker. Now that they each had their masts, it was a simple problem to put them into the mast holes. Mr. F. and I did our best to work as efficiently as any of the other crew members. Soon the mainsail was rigged up and we were ready to sail back to the Island. Only the need for a boom was absent from this compact invention. We lowered centerboards and lined up. It was evidently the custom to race home. The boy who gave the signals took out his gun, fired it, and we were homeward bound as fast as the wind would take us. I am afraid I was more of a hindrance than a capable assistant to young F-1. We finished the race last by about seven minutes. The boats were moored to a dock near the freighter in the hidden inlet and we assembled on shore. F-1 explained to me that the boy who had given the signals was the "Captain of the Day," some sort of honor each child received in turn.

The Captain of the Day told the rest of us that since this was my first trip in the Balloon Merry-Go-Round, the results of the boat race wouldn't count on the Official Scoring Sheet. F-1 let out a whooping cheer at this which made me feel quite badly. The Captain of the Day then took me aside and told me, in a most polite way, that he thought it would be an excellent idea if I learned a bit about sailing since I now found myself to be a citizen of Krakatoa. I assured him that I would.

The Captain of the Day then closed the meeting by saying that the Merry-Go-Round would be reassembled around the flying pole right after supper. "And I want you all to be here and help," he said, looking sternly in my direction.

After forty years of schoolteaching I found myself being ordered about by a child. I couldn't help but find this heretofore impossible turnabout amusing. I was indeed far away from the usual dull school routines I so disliked.

"I'll be there!" I said in a loud voice, as everybody looked at me and laughed.

The whole trip had taken about five hours and we had therefore missed lunch. I devoured an excellent supper at the B's chop house, and then Mr. F. and I reported to the flying pole. The Captain of the Day rang the bell on top of the shack assembling all of the children and we were divided into eight groups of five. (B-1 and B-2 were still busy.) With five on each boat, we had the Merry-Go-Round reassembled and ready to go in less than half an hour. I will confess, though, that after this busy second day on the fabulous Island, I was well ready for bed and slept like a top.

from Space Cat
Ruthven Todd

Already an experienced space traveler, the cat Flyball joins a rocket trip to the moon.

After this flight, Flyball was, if possible, even more famous around the station. People would bend down to stroke him, or to give him an extra-specially tasty tidbit, saying, "Well, Flyball, you old rocketeer, how did you enjoy your flight, eh?"

Flyball, forgetting the discomfort of being squashed nearly flat, would wave his tail slowly, to show that, really, there was nothing to rocketflight which an intelligent and hardy cat, such as he was, could not accept without the least worry.

Now, when Captain Fred went to the rocket, which had been hauled back to the station from its landing place, miles away in the desert, Flyball went with him. On these visits he would inspect the equipment to make sure it was still in good order. All the workmen knew that Flyball was a highly critical overseer, and they did their best to make every joint in a pipe a perfect one. All the fittings were polished until the boss could see his gray face, yellow eyes and thin black whiskers as if in a mirror.

One day Captain Fred lifted Flyball and took him into the machine-shop.

"Joe," he said to one of the men working there, "see if you can fit Flyball out with a pressure-suit."

"You don't mean you want to take him along with you, Captain, do you?"

"Why not? He came through the trial flight without a suit, and if he could stand that he should be able to stand anything."

The man then measured Flyball carefully. He did not, really, much like being measured, any more than he liked the fittings which followed during the next few days, but if Captain Fred wanted him to have a pressure-suit, Flyball supposed he might as well give way to the wish. After all, he told himself, he was nothing if not an obliging cat.

Flyball was a great believer in listening to the conversation around the station. He collected a great deal of useful information in this way. Nowadays the conversation all seemed to be concerned with the subject of the Moon. Flyball gave no end of superior twitches of his whiskers. He knew all about the Moon and the Cat in the Moon. He knew that dogs, looking up at the full Moon, howled because there was a cat there and not a dog.

There were a thousand and one things that had to be done to the rocket before it was ready, and Flyball watched the slow progress with deep interest. He was particularly pleased with the small hammock, slung in the same way as the bigger seat on strong springs, which the men built beside Captain Fred's seat. He jounced up and down in it and was delighted with its springiness. The men, too, seemed to be glad that he approved of the work and they were forever trying him out in it.

Flyball was gratified by all the attention which he was receiving and he went about the station with his gray tail stuck up in the air at one end of him and his cool, damp nose at the other.

One day, when Flyball was lying curled up out of sight in a corner of the commanding officer's office, a man came in wearing the most tremendous amount of gold braid. The Colonel stood up stiffly and said, "Good morning, General."

Flyball examined the General out of a quarter-opened eye. He did not really like what he saw, which was a pink face and a white mustache which looked as if it had been blued in a washing-machine.

"What's all this I hear?" the General demanded. "I mean about Captain Stone wanting to take a cat along with him?"

The way he said the word "cat" made it sound awful and Flyball's whiskers twitched and the hair on his back stood up. The General better be careful or he would soon know all about cats and the way they could scratch.

Flyball unsheathed his claws and inspected them happily.

"Yes, sir," replied the Colonel. "I can see no objection to his doing so. Flyball is his own cat and ever since he stowed away on the trial, Stone has been sure that he's a lucky cat."

"There's nothing about it in the regulations," puffed the General. "I don't see that I can allow it."

The Colonel shrugged his shoulders. "I don't see that there's much we can do about it, sir. We've enough trouble with Stone as it is. He's a good pilot, but likes to do things his own way. If we forbid him to take his cat, he's quite capable of refusing to fly the rocket. And you know what it would cost, and how long it would take, to train another pilot!"

The General nodded his head. "Umm, yes. We don't want to have to start training another man now, with the flight so near. Don't you think you could argue with Stone and persuade him that it's stupid to take his cat along with him? One of the things that's worrying *them,*" he wagged his head vaguely, "is that we're bound to have all the Cruelty to Animals people down on our necks. You know what they are? They'll claim we're using the cat—what's his name—Flyball—for experimental purposes."

Flyball wondered how *they* could be so silly. It was just as if he had not made up his own mind to go to the Moon, just as if he had not been working for that very trip for all these months. Did *they* not know that he *wanted* to go, to see that everything went right?

"Try telling Stone about these people," the General went on, "and see if you can't get him to change his mind."

"No," the Colonel's voice was firm, "I'm not going to try to change his mind now. The flight's too near and I don't want to risk upsetting him in any way. He's going to be alone in space for several days and, if the flight's successful, he'll stand where man has never stood before. He'll be precious lonely and if having Flyball along will help him in any way, I'm not going to forbid it."

The General blew through his mustache and turned pinker. It looked for a moment as if he might burst. Then he took a deep breath.

"I suppose you're right," he said finally. "I never fly without my rabbit's foot myself. I'll tell *them* the Captain won't fly without his cat."

Flyball decided that this was the right moment to come forward. He padded softly toward the General with his tail stuck up in the air as straight as the flagpole he had climbed as a young kitten. At first the General did not notice him, so Flyball rubbed softly against his leg and said, "Miaow!"

"Hullo!" exclaimed the General, looking down. "This the cat?"

"Yes," said the Colonel, "that's Flyball."

"Well, he certainly is a beauty," the General stooped down and scratched him behind the ears. "Can't say I blame Stone for wanting to have him along."

With these kind words, Flyball felt glad that he had not given way to temptation and scratched the General when he had first started to speak.

At last the great day arrived. The flurry around the station reached its peak and Flyball was all over the place, checking to see that everything was being done correctly. He would allow no one to take things easy while he was around, and all the men seemed to work all the harder for his benevolent supervision. At the same time, he was careful not to let the Captain get out of sight for too long. One could never tell with these men when they'd plot something behind a cat's back.

Flyball was invited to sit up at dinner that night, and someone proposed a toast, "Here's to the luck of Flyball, the Rocketeer!"

Flyball looked round, nodding to show that he appreciated their good wishes. He did not himself drink out of the little glass which someone had placed before him. He smelled the stuff in the glass and as it did not smell in the least like milk decided that he would leave it alone.

After dinner Captain Stone, with Flyball following him slowly just to show that he went of his own free will, returned to his room.

There he unpacked Flyball's pressure-suit.

It was a most peculiar looking thing, with four floppy legs and a floppy tail. Flyball did not in the least like getting into it, but the Captain spoke to him softly, "Come on, Flyball. Last time you nearly finished up as flat as a waffle and this time it'll be much worse. If you don't get into this you can't come with me. Come on, old puss, come along."

Finally Flyball was encased in his new suit. Then the Captain blew it up and Flyball turned an anxious head to discover that he had grown several times as fat as he usually was. He tried to walk in the suit and found that it was really most inconvenient. The legs did not bend easily, as his own legs bent, and his tail looked like nothing so much as a fat frankfurter.

The Captain then put on his own suit and blew it up. Next, he opened a little box and took out a little plastic globe which he carefully fitted over Flyball's head, adjusting various tubes to a little pack on the back of the suit. Flyball found that breathing was simple inside the globe, for the compressed air meant that he did not have to breathe so strongly.

Captain Fred Stone finally put on his own helmet, made of the same clear plastic, and picked up Flyball, tucking him under a soft, fat arm. They went down the corridor and out toward the rocket. This time Flyball entered it along with Captain Fred and was placed in his little hammock and firmly strapped in. The port clanged shut and the Captain checked up on the belts that held him in his own seat.

"One minute," said the voice from the wall, "fifty-nine seconds. . . ."

Flyball, as a hardened flier, pretended that this had nothing to do with him but, all the same, he could not help feeling just a little excited as he lay in his hammock and purred:

Oh, I'm going to see the Cat in the Moon!
    Purr! Purr!
Oh, I'm going in a rocket, not a balloon!
    Purr! Purr!
When I come back I will tell you all
About the great big silvery ball!
    Purr!

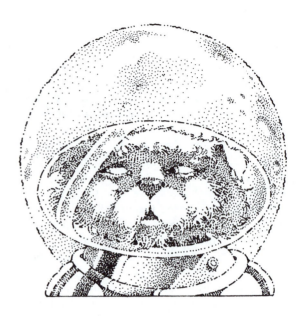

"Ten . . . nine . . ." said the voice, ". . . five . . . four . . . three . . . two . . . one . . . ZERO!"

Then there was the strong whoosh as they rose slowly into the air. The thin voice of the Captain said, "Well, Flyball, we've made it. We're off. Next stop—Moon!"

As the rocket gathered speed Flyball did not feel that he was being flattened, as he had done before. The springs on his hammock were pulled almost straight out, but he himself was quite comfortable. There did not seem to be anything for him to do, for the Captain was sitting back in his chair, paying no attention to the dials in front of him. So, uninterested in the dull business, Flyball went to sleep, feeling just a little strange as the hammock and the bulky suit prevented him curling up into his usual sleeping position.

When he awoke he became aware that the Captain was unstrapping himself. He undid Flyball's hammock-straps and took off his pressure-suit. He then let go in mid-air. Flyball scrabbled wildly with his paws, expecting that he would fall, but all that happened was that he whirled madly around and, before he knew where he was, he was upside-down in the middle of the cabin. Or at least, for he did not feel upside-down, the other way up from the Captain.

The Captain himself then climbed out of

his suit, but he kept on a pair of funny-looking boots. Then he stood up.

"Poor old Flyball!" he said, laughing, "we quite forgot to set you up with a pair of magnetic-boots!"

Flyball, who was still rolling madly around in the air, did not know exactly what this meant but, pushing himself off from a piece of gleaming copper tubing, he did allow that it was most odd to suddenly discover that one had no right way up or down. The Captain, anchored to the plating by his magnetized boots, reached out and caught Flyball, who was spinning past him in a slow roll.

"All right, Flyball," he said. "How about a drop of milk?"

He opened a little refrigerator and took out a paper milk-container. Flyball cheered up, forgetting the indignities to which he had been subjected by the absence of gravity.

The Captain next found a saucer in a closet and tried to pour out some of the milk. It would not flow! He hit the container a thump on the bottom, and some of the milk came out—but it did not go into the saucer or fall to the ground.

It just stayed floating around in the air. Captain Fred again let Flyball loose, and gave him a shove in the direction of the milk. It was, Flyball found, quite ordinary milk. At least it smelled like it and when he got some on his nose and whiskers it tasted like it. But it behaved as no milk had ever behaved before. When Flyball gave it a pat, it broke into drops, but the drops did not fall down. Instead they just stayed scattered in the air.

It was a long time before Flyball really managed to get a bite of it, and hold some in his mouth. Then he had to swallow extra hard, he found, for the milk did not flow smoothly down as it would have done on earth. At last, however, he managed the trick and succeeded in getting enough of the milk inside him to make him feel decently full. Then, lying upside down, he purred happily as he noticed that Fred Stone was also having a hard time eating.

The Captain, too, learned to eat, and, when he thought they had had enough, he twiddled some knobs and spoke into a microphone.

"Zee-Queue-Ex-One to Base," he said, "Zee-Queue-Ex-One to Base . . . Zee-Queue-Ex-One to Base. . . ."

He repeated this over and over again and, at last, very faintly, the speaker in the wall replied, "Base to Zee-Queue-Ex-One. Everything okay? Over."

"Zee-Queue-Ex-One to Base. Everything is okay," the Captain repeated, and then went on to give an account of the flight so far and told how Flyball was drifting around the cabin, batting at drops of milk as he passed them.

When he had finished he tore a sheet of paper from a scratch-pad on the wall and crumpled it into a ball. He tossed this in the air and gave Flyball a push toward it. In spite of being upside-down one moment and right-way up the next, Flyball started to enjoy himself. He quickly learned that, by giving a push against anything he ran into, he could shove himself in the direction in which he wanted to go.

After some time of this play, Captain Fred pressed a button and a steel plate slid aside to let them see through a thick glass window. Through this Flyball saw the Moon, but it was not the Moon he had first known as a kitten. It was much brighter, brighter than a new silver dollar, and much, much bigger. Besides, the Cat in the Moon seemed to have gone into hiding. Instead of his old wise face, Flyball saw lines and craters. The light outside the rocket was terribly bright and, after a moment or two, the Captain slid the plate shut again.

"I don't know about you," he said to Flyball, "but I'm all for another spot of shut-eye."

He caught Flyball by the tail and pulled him gently down. On Earth Flyball would have been most indignant and hurt by this, but here everything was strange and, funnily, being pulled by the tail was not in the least painful.

Once again they got into their hammocks, but this time without the pressure-suits. Captain Stone set an automatic pilot and an alarm and switched out the light that shone in what had once been the roof of the cabin, though, so far as Flyball was concerned, it might well have been the floor or one of the walls. Then they went to sleep.

Flyball had no idea how long he slept, but he was awakened by the Captain moving to turn on the light again.

This time they ate more carefully, and once more the Captain made his report to the base, but the answering voice was terribly weak, and he was forced, several times, to repeat his messages. He was silent for a moment when he had finished and then turned to Flyball.

"Looks as though we'll soon be right out of range. Let's hope they're keeping track of us with radar. We're on our own!"

Flyball was worried by none of this, but was perfectly happy rolling about the cabin in pursuit of his paper ball.

When they opened the shield again, the Moon was even bigger and even brighter. It was so dazzling, in fact, that Flyball had to close his eyes to slits to look at it.

Again they slept and again they woke up. It seemed to Flyball that they did this a great number of times, but then he never had been interested in counting, and he did not care now, for he had mastered the art of how to eat in space.

The last time they woke the glaring Moon seemed to fill the whole of the window. After eating they did not get into their hammock and chair at once. Captain Fred took Flyball's pressure-suit and put him back into it and then put on his own.

Now they were strapped in their places. The Captain watched the dials before him, while in turn Flyball watched him carefully, just to make sure that he made no mistakes. After a long time one of the dials showed a blue needle flickering on a red spot. The Captain pulled a lever and the rocket wobbled as it turned over, so that its tail was pointing toward the Moon. Then, some little time later, Fred Stone worked with a number of buttons and levers and once more Flyball heard the pulsing roar of the jets.

Suddenly Captain Fred flung a lever far over to one side and Flyball felt squashed, in spite of the sprung hammock and the pressure-suit. The rocket felt, for a moment, as if it was absolutely motionless. Then, slowly, braked by the pulsing jets, it started to fall again. There was a sudden bump and the rocket swayed slightly from side to side before it settled firmly down on its tail.

The Captain unstrapped himself from his chair and took Flyball out of the hammock. Then he moved slowly round the cabin, checking all the equipment which had brought them so far and which, they hoped, would take them back to Earth. It seemed to Flyball that Fred Stone took a long time in doing this but, at last, he had finished and he walked toward the port, after turning off the air in the cabin. He swung aside several large bars and pulled on a heavy handle.

The door swung slowly outward and Captain Fred Stone and Flyball looked down at the surface of the Moon, only a few feet below them.

from **The Fallen Spaceman**
Lee Harding

A small visitor from another planet has a confrontation with human beings who are terrified because the extraterrestrial creature is in an enormous, computer-operated spacesuit.

It had taken a long time for Tyro to get his spacesuit working. The fall had caused a lot of damage. But the computer checked everything out and made the necessary repairs, and when it had fixed everything it could, it told Tyro it was ready to move.

Tyro was pleased to hear the spacesuit whirring and humming for the first time since the fall. He was still uneasy about the sudden appearance of the Earth people. The first one had gone away and then a much bigger one had appeared.

Tyro shivered when he remembered how scared he had been when the huge, strange face had peered in through the faceplate.

He was much bigger than Tyro. And probably much stronger. Without his spacesuit Tyro would be helpless against such a giant. He was anxious to have his spacesuit working again, so that he need not fear these strangers.

The people outside had made no move to harm him, but there was no sense in taking chances. If they knew how small and helpless he was . . .

But everything was working now. There was no longer any need to feel afraid. He would soon be far away from here and hiding somewhere else.

He had a six-hour supply of air left. If the starship hadn't returned in that time, then he would have to open his helmet and let the unhealthy outside air in.

How long could he expect to breathe that air and remain alive? The computer could only guess. *About an hour,* it had said. It would take that long for the oxygen-rich air to strangle him. Long before that, of course, his body would begin to break down.

Tyro shuddered. It was not a pleasant thought.

When everything was ready to go, he cautiously touched the control levers. It wouldn't do to feed in too much power all at once. He would have to ease the spacesuit gently back to work.

His hands were soft and weak, but when he used the controls they became strong. The huge spacesuit faithfully followed his movements like a shadow. When it moved, there would be nothing on Earth that could stop it. But he would have to be careful not to harm anyone. It would not do for the Earth people to think him dangerous. . . .

A bright red light suddenly winked on the panel. Tyro was puzzled. It was a signal that the entrance hatch was open.

He felt a sudden stab of alarm. It must have been jarred open by the fall . . . and the outside air would have been leaking in ever since. No wonder he felt so strange in the head!

How had the computer missed it?

He was about to lean forward and press the switch that closed it manually, when the red light winked off.

The hatch was closed again.

Tyro breathed a sigh of relief. But just to be sure, he asked the computer to make a double check.

A second later the computer replied that all was well. The door *had* been jarred open but it was now closed.

Tyro nodded . . . and then frowned. The computer was making too many mistakes.

It was time to begin testing his damaged spacesuit. First he moved his great right hand. He fitted his own into a metal glove on the right of the control panel. Tiny wires in the glove made contact with his flesh and carried his movements to the computer, where they were coded and fed to the mighty engines. And all this happened in the smallest fraction of a second.

Tyro flexed his fingers inside the glove. Outside, the enormous right hand of the spacesuit copied his movements. It slowly raised itself a few inches from the floor of the forest and . . .

Stephen was first to see the spaceman move. "Dad!" he called out. "Look—over there! It's *moving.* . . ."

They crouched down near the edge of the clearing and waited.

The body of the spaceman remained still. But one hand had begun to move in a strangely human manner.

The huge fingers opened and closed, opened and closed, in a curious flexing gesture. The effect was quite startling.

Stephen huddled close to his father. "Dad, *what's happening? Is it—*"

Dad hushed him to be quiet. He was sick with fear now that the spaceman had stirred and was coming back to life. It seemed impossible that they could save Erik.

They continued to watch in wide-eyed wonder as the spaceman moved. . . .

The great right hand of the spaceman rose several feet from the ground. There was a loud whirring of machinery and then the other hand came into view. The giant held them aloft for several minutes, turning them over and around, as if he were inspecting them. Then very slowly they relaxed and came back to rest on the ground.

Stephen and his father listened with growing alarm to the deep growling sounds coming from inside the spacesuit.

"It sounds like a . . . a robot," Stephen whispered.

His father nodded, eyes narrowed. It did indeed. In which case his son might be safe for a while. The alien robot might not know he was inside. But it was such a slim chance. . . .

Of course, they were only close to the truth. The spacesuit was a mechanical being, true enough—but what they couldn't know was that inside this huge robot there was a small creature from another world, who looked a little like themselves and who was much more frightened of the situation than they!

It was time to get help. There was nothing they could do here, nothing at all. And they would have to hurry if they were to cut their way into the spaceman and rescue Erik before the robot began to move around.

At that moment there came a great groaning sound and the spaceman sat up.

The effect was quite strange. The bottom half of his metal body didn't move an inch, but from the waist up it rose with alarming suddenness. And that wasn't all. . . .

The spaceman began to *creak*. It was the kind of sound you would expect machinery to make when there wasn't enough oil on the bearings. The sound cut through the silence of the forest like a scythe.

Very slowly, the great helmeted head began to rotate. It moved around like a run-down turntable, with a strange jerky rhythm.

Three times it rotated. They could hear the busy little motors turning it around . . . and around . . . and around.

On the fourth rotation it came to a sudden stop. The darkened faceplate was pointing in their direction.

It seemed to be watching them, and they were too scared to move. Father and son were frozen to the spot.

Tyro studied the Earth people. One was quite large, the other much smaller. The tall one would be an adult, he thought. Such height made the little alien feel uncomfortable. He had never seen anyone so big in all his life, and he was glad to have his spacesuit working again. For a while there he had felt like a lost child, small and weak and lonely. *His* home and *his* parents were millions of miles away . . . and he might never see them again.

He had decided it was best not to make contact with the Earth people. He remembered starship gossip that said they were a very warlike race. Indeed, even from this distance the two natives looked rather fierce. And yet . . . he could feel no hostility directed at him. Only fear. This gave him confidence.

Tyro could read feelings as easily as Earth people read words. It was as natural for him as speech is for them. In this way his people were *very* different from the people of Earth.

So Tyro was puzzled. He did not feel that these people would harm him, but he thought it would be best to leave this area as fast as he could. He had no way of knowing what the rest of the natives would be like. Perhaps so far he had only been lucky.

The Earth people had not moved from the edge of the clearing. They seemed to be watching and waiting for something. He could sense their fear and felt sorry for them. He wanted to call out, *Do not be afraid. I will not harm you.* But of course they would never understand his strange musical speech.

Tyro made up his mind. It was time to get moving. He gave the computer full control and sat back in his seat. To wait.

In the brief silence before the atomic motors roared into life, Tyro thought he heard a strange sound. It was unlike anything he had ever heard, and it seemed to come from the entrance hatch, below and behind him.

Had something crawled inside his spacesuit when the hatch was open? Perhaps a small rodent, or some other forest animal?

For a moment he was alarmed. Then he shrugged his small shoulders. No need to worry. The air inside the spacesuit would soon put it to sleep. He was in no danger.

The sound was repeated again—a soft, hollow sound, like a child crying.

Tyro frowned. He was about to climb out of his protective webbing when the spacesuit roared louder than before. The control room shook and shuddered and the giant spacesuit lurched to its feet.

"Get back!" Dad cried. He pushed his son ahead of him, deeper into the forest.

The fallen spaceman stood up awkwardly, its great feet churning up the ground, showering the nearby trees with dirt and broken branches.

Strange sounds came from inside the spaceman, sounds like a truck with a broken gearbox. It waved its arms around like a madman.

Inside the spacesuit, Tyro groaned. All was not well! "Stop it!" he said to the computer. "You are feeding too much power to the treads! We want to move *quietly* away from here, not so loud that the whole world can hear us!"

The computer croaked out a reply. *My . . . mistake. There is still . . . much work . . . to be done.*

Tyro groaned again. "Just get us away from here, that's all! And do it *quietly*. We've drawn enough attention already from these curious natives."

He hoped that the computer, although damaged, would be able to perform the simple task of directing them away from the clearing. But the spacesuit roared and lurched toward the trees.

"Not that way!" Tyro cried. The damaged computer didn't reply.

The spacesuit crashed through the trees, sending them crashing to either side. Its great treads dug deeply into the ground and threw up a shower of dark earth, almost hiding it from view.

The enormous arms of the spacesuit were spread wide, pushing even the tallest trees to one side. The spacesuit roared on, cutting a deep tunnel through the dark forest.

It was out of control!

from A Wrinkle in Time
Madeleine L'Engle

Kindly beasts on a far planet care for Meg, the protagonist of a Newbery Medal fantasy, in which she and her companions fight against the malevolent entity, IT, when they travel into space through a tesseract, a wrinkle in time.

Aunt Beast

"No!" Mr. Murry said sharply. "Please put her down."

A sense of amusement seemed to emanate from the beasts. The tallest, who seemed to be the spokesman, said, "We frighten you?"

"What are you going to do with us?" Mr. Murry asked.

The beast said, "I'm sorry, we communicate better with the other one." He turned toward Calvin. "Who are you?"

"I'm Calvin O'Keefe."

"What's that?"

"I'm a boy. A—a young man."

"You, too, are afraid?"

"I'm—not sure."

"Tell me," the beast said. "What do you suppose you'd do if three of *us* suddenly arrived on your home planet."

"Shoot you, I guess," Calvin admitted.

"Then isn't that what we should do with you?"

Calvin's freckles seemed to deepen, but he answered quietly. "I'd really rather you didn't. I mean, the earth's my home, and I'd rather be there than anywhere in the world —I mean, the universe—and I can't wait to get back, but we make some awful bloopers there."

The smallest beast, the one holding Meg, said, "And perhaps they aren't used to visitors from other planets."

"Used to it!" Calvin exclaimed. "We've never had any, as far as I know."

"Why?"

"I don't know."

The middle beast, a tremor of trepidation in his words, said, "You aren't from a dark planet, are you?"

"No." Calvin shook his head firmly, though the beast couldn't see him. "We're—we're shadowed. But we're fighting the shadow."

The beast holding Meg questioned, "You three are fighting?"

"Yes," Calvin answered. "Now that we know about it."

The tall one turned back to Mr. Murry, speaking sternly. "You. The oldest. Man. From where have you come? Now."

Mr. Murry answered steadily. "From a planet called Camazotz." There was a mutter from the three beasts. "We do not belong there," Mr. Murry said, slowly and distinctly. "We were strangers there as we are here. I was a prisoner there, and these children rescued me. My youngest son, my baby, is still there, trapped in the dark mind of IT."

Meg tried to twist around in the beast's arms to glare at her father and Calvin. Why were they being so frank? Weren't they aware of the danger? But again her anger dissolved as the gentle warmth from the tentacles flowed through her. She realized that she could move her fingers and toes with comparative freedom, and the pain was no longer so acute.

"We must take this child back with us," the beast holding her said.

Meg shouted at her father. "Don't leave me the way you left Charles!" With this burst of terror a spasm of pain wracked her body and she gasped.

"Stop fighting," the beast told her. "You make it worse. Relax."

"That's what IT said," Meg cried. "Father! Calvin! Help!"

The beast turned toward Calvin and Mr. Murry. "This child is in danger. You must trust us."

"We have no alternative," Mr. Murry said. "Can you save her?"

"I think so."

"May I stay with her?"

"No. But you will not be far away. We feel that you are hungry, tired, that you would like to bathe and rest. And this little—what is the word?" the beast cocked its tentacles at Calvin.

"Girl," Calvin said.

"This little girl needs prompt and special care. The coldness of the—what is it you call it?"

"The Black Thing?"

"The Black Thing. Yes. The Black Thing burns unless it is counteracted properly." The three beasts stood around Meg, and it seemed that they were feeling into her with their softly waving tentacles. The movement of the tentacles was as rhythmic and flowing as the dance of an undersea plant, and lying there, cradled in the four strange arms, Meg, despite herself, felt a sense of security that was deeper than anything she had known since the days when she lay in her mother's arms in the old rocking chair and was sung to sleep. With her father's help she had been able to resist IT. Now she could hold out no longer. She leaned her head against the beast's chest, and realized that the gray body was covered with the softest, most delicate fur imaginable, and the fur had the same beautiful odor as the air.

I hope I don't smell awful to it, she thought. But then she knew with a deep sense of comfort that even if she did smell awful the beasts would forgive her. As the tall figure cradled her she could feel the frigid stiffness of her body relaxing against it. This bliss could not come to her from a thing like IT. IT could only give pain, never relieve it. The beasts must be good. They had to be good. She sighed deeply, like a very small child, and suddenly she was asleep.

When she came to herself again there was in the back of her mind a memory of pain, of agonizing pain. But the pain was over now and her body was lapped in comfort. She was lying on something wonderfully soft in an enclosed chamber. It was dark. All she could see were occasional tall moving shadows which she realized were beasts walking about. She had been stripped of her clothes, and something warm and pungent was gently being rubbed into her body. She sighed and stretched and discovered that she *could* stretch. She could move again, she was no longer paralyzed, and her body was bathed in waves of warmth. Her father had not saved her; the beasts had.

"So you are awake, little one?" The words came gently to her ears. "What a funny little tadpole you are! Is the pain gone now?"

"All gone."

"Are you warm and alive again?"

"Yes, I'm fine." She struggled to sit up.

"No, lie still, small one. You must not exert yourself as yet. We will have a fur garment for you in a moment, and then we will feed you. You must not even try to feed yourself. You must be as an infant again. The Black Thing does not relinquish its victims willingly."

"Where are Father and Calvin? Have they gone back for Charles Wallace?"

"They are eating and resting," the beast said, "and we are trying to learn about each other and see what is best to help you. We feel now that you are not dangerous, and that we will be allowed to help you."

"Why is it so dark in here?" Meg asked. She tried to look around, but all she could see was shadows. Nevertheless there was a sense of openness, a feel of a gentle breeze moving lightly about, that kept the darkness from being oppressive.

Perplexity came to her from the beast. "What is this dark? What is this light? We do not understand. Your father and the boy, Calvin, have asked this, too. They say that it is night now on our planet, and that they cannot see. They have told us that our atmosphere is what they call opaque, so that the stars are not visible, and then they were surprised that we know stars, that we know their music and the movements of their dance far better than beings like you who spend hours studying them through what you call telescopes. We do not understand what this means, *to see.*"

"Well, it's what things look like," Meg said helplessly.

"We do not know what things *look* like, as you say," the beast said. "We know what things *are* like. It must be a very limiting thing, this seeing."

"Oh, no!" Meg cried. "It's—it's the most wonderful thing in the world!"

"What a very strange world yours must be!" the beast said, "that such a peculiar-seeming thing should be of such importance. Try to tell me, what is this thing called *light* that you are able to do so little without?"

"Well, we can't see without it," Meg said, realizing that she was completely unable to explain vision and light and dark. How can you explain sight on a world where no one has ever seen and where there is no need of eyes? "Well, on this planet," she fumbled, "you have a sun, don't you?"

"A most wonderful sun, from which comes our warmth, and the rays which give us our flowers, our food, our music, and all the things which make life and growth."

"Well," Meg said, "when we are turned toward the sun—our earth, our planet, I mean, toward our sun—we receive its light. And when we're turned away from it, it is night. And if we want to see we have to use artificial lights."

"Artificial lights," the beast sighed. "How very complicated life on your planet must be. Later on you must try to explain some more to me."

"All right," Meg promised, and yet she knew that to try to explain anything that could be seen with the eyes would be impossible, because the beasts in some way saw, knew, understood, far more completely than she, or her parents, or Calvin, or even Charles Wallace.

"Charles Wallace!" she cried. "What are they doing about Charles Wallace? We don't know what IT's doing to him or making him do. Please, oh, please, help us!"

"Yes, yes, little one, of course we will help you. A meeting is in session right now to study what is best to do. We have never before been able to talk to anyone who has managed to escape from a dark planet, so although your father is blaming himself for everything that has happened, we feel that he must be quite an extraordinary person to get out of Camazotz with you at all. But the little boy, and I understand that he is a very special, a very important little boy—ah, my child, you must accept that this will not be easy. To go *back* through the Black Thing, *back* to Camazotz—I don't know. I don't know."

"But Father left him!" Meg said. "He's got to bring him back! He can't just abandon Charles Wallace!"

The beast's communication suddenly became crisp. "Nobody said anything about abandoning anybody. That is not our way. But we know that just because we want something does not mean that we will get what we want, and we still do not know *what* to do. And we cannot allow you, in your present state, to do anything that would jeopardize us all. I can see that you wish your father to go rushing back to Camazotz, and you could probably make him do this, and then where would we be? No. No. You must wait until you are more calm. Now, my darling, here is a robe for you to keep you warm and comfortable." Meg felt herself being lifted again, and a soft, light garment was slipped about her. "Don't worry about your little brother." The tentacles' musical words were soft against her. "We would *never* leave him behind the shadow. But for now you must relax, you must be happy, you must get well."

The gentle words, the feeling that this beast would be able to love her no matter what she said or did, lapped Meg in warmth and peace. She felt a delicate touch of tentacle to her cheek, as tender as her mother's kiss.

"It is so long since my own small ones were grown and gone," the beast said. "You are so tiny and vulnerable. Now I will feed you. You must eat slowly and quietly. I know that you are half starved, that you have been without food far too long, but you must not rush things or you will not get well."

Something completely and indescribably and incredibly delicious was put to Meg's lips, and she swallowed gratefully. With each swallow she felt strength returning to her body and she realized that she had had nothing to eat since the horrible fake turkey dinner on Camazotz which she had barely tasted. How long ago was her mother's stew? Time no longer had any meaning.

"How long does night last here?" she murmured sleepily. "It will be day again, won't it?"

"Hush," the beast said. "Eat, small one. During the coolness, which is now, we sleep. And, when you waken, there will be warmth again and many things to do. You must eat now, and sleep, and I will stay with you."

"What should I call you, please?" Meg asked.

"Well, now. First, try not to say any words for just a moment. Think within your own mind. Think of all the things you call people, different kinds of people."

While Meg thought, the beast murmured to her gently. "No, *mother* is a special, a one-name; and a father you have here. Not just friend, nor teacher, nor brother, nor sister. What is *acquaintance?* What a funny, hard word. *Aunt.* Maybe. Yes, perhaps that will do. And you think of such odd words about me. *Thing,* and *monster! Monster,* what a horrid sort of word. I really do not think I am a monster. *Beast.* That will do. *Aunt Beast."*

"Aunt Beast," Meg murmured sleepily, and laughed.

"Have I said something funny?" Aunt Beast asked in surprise. "Isn't Aunt Beast all right?"

"Aunt Beast is lovely," Meg said. "Please sing to me, Aunt Beast."

If it was impossible to describe sight to Aunt Beast, it would be even more impossible to describe the singing of Aunt Beast to a human being. It was a music even more glorious than the music of the singing creatures on Uriel. It was a music more tangible than form or sight. It had essence and structure. It supported Meg more firmly than the arms of Aunt Beast. It seemed to travel with her, to sweep her aloft in the power of song, so that she was moving in glory among the stars, and for a moment she, too, felt that the words Darkness and Light had no meaning, and only this melody was real.

Meg did not know when she fell asleep within the body of the music. When she wakened Aunt Beast was asleep, too, the softness of her furry, faceless head drooping. Night had gone and a dull gray light filled the room. But she realized now that here on this planet there was no need for color, that the grays and browns merging into each other were not what the beasts knew, and that what she, herself, saw was only the smallest fraction of what the planet was really like. It was she who was limited by her senses, not the blind beasts, for they must have senses of which she could not even dream.

She stirred slightly, and Aunt Beast bent over her immediately, "What a lovely sleep, my darling. Do you feel all right?"

"I feel wonderful," Meg said. "Aunt Beast, what is this planet called?"

"Oh, dear," Aunt Beast sighed. "I find it not easy at all to put things the way your mind shapes them. You call where you came from Camazotz?"

"Well, it's where we came from, but it's not our planet."

"You can call us Ixchel, I guess," Aunt Beast told her. "We share the same sun as lost Camazotz, but that, give thanks, is all we share."

"Are you fighting the Black Thing?" Meg asked.

"Oh, yes," Aunt Beast replied. "In doing that we can never relax. We are the called according to His purpose, and whom He calls, them He also justifies. Of course we have help, and without help it would be much more difficult."

"Who helps you?" Meg asked.

"Oh, dear, it is so difficult to explain things to you, small one. And I know now that it is not just because you are a child. The other two are as hard to reach into as you are. What can I tell you that will mean anything to you? Good helps us, the stars help us, perhaps what you would call *light* helps us, love helps us. Oh, my child, I cannot explain! This is

something you just have to know or not know."

"But—"

"We look not at the things which are what you would call seen, but at the things which are not seen. For the things which are seen are temporal. But the things which are not seen are eternal."

"Aunt Beast, do you know Mrs. Whatsit?" Meg asked with a sudden flooding of hope.

"Mrs. Whatsit?" Aunt Beast was puzzled. "Oh, child, your language is so utterly simple and limited that it has the effect of extreme complication." Her four arms, tentacles waving, were outflung in a gesture of helplessness. "Would you like me to take you to your father and your Calvin?"

"Oh, yes, please!"

"Let us go, then. They are waiting for you to make plans. And we thought you would enjoy eating—what is it you call it? oh, yes, breakfast—together. You will be too warm in that heavy fur, now. I will dress you in something lighter, and then we will go."

As though Meg were a baby, Aunt Beast bathed and dressed her, and this new garment, though it was made of a pale fur, was lighter than the lightest summer clothes on earth. Aunt Beast put one tentacled arm about Meg's waist and led her through long, dim corridors in which she could see only shadows, and shadows of shadows, until they reached a large, columned chamber. Shafts of light came in from an open skylight and converged about a huge, round, stone table. Here were seated several of the great beasts, and Calvin and Mr. Murry, on a stone bench that circled the table. Because the beasts were so tall, even Mr. Murry's feet did not touch the ground, and lanky Calvin's long legs dangled as though he were Charles Wallace. The hall was partially enclosed by vaulted arches leading to long, paved walks. There were no empty walls, no covering roofs, so that although the light was dull in comparison to earth's sunlight, Meg had no feeling of dark or of chill. As Aunt Beast led Meg in, Mr. Murry slid down from the bench and hurried to her, putting his arms about her tenderly.

"They promised us you were all right," he said.

While she had been in Aunt Beast's arms Meg had felt safe and secure. Now her worries about Charles Wallace and her disappointment in her father's human fallibility rose like gorge in her throat.

"I'm fine," she muttered, looking not at Calvin or her father, but at the beasts, for it was to them she turned now for help. It seemed to her that neither her father nor Calvin were properly concerned about Charles Wallace.

"Meg!" Calvin said gaily. "You've never tasted such food in your life! Come and eat!"

Aunt Beast lifted Meg up onto the bench and sat down beside her, then heaped a plate with food, strange fruits and breads that tasted unlike anything Meg had ever eaten. Everything was dull and colorless and unappetizing to look at, and at first, even remembering the meal Aunt Beast had fed her the night before, Meg hesitated to taste, but once she had managed the first bite she ate eagerly; it seemed that she would never

have her fill again.

The others waited until she slowed down. Then Mr. Murry said gravely, "We were trying to work out a plan to rescue Charles Wallace. Since I made such a mistake in tessering away from IT, we feel that it would not be wise for me to try to get back to Camazotz, even alone. If I missed the mark again I could easily get lost and wander forever from galaxy to galaxy, and that would be small help to anyone, least of all to Charles Wallace."

Such a wave of despondency came over Meg that she was no longer able to eat.

"Our friends here," he continued, "feel that it was only the fact that I still wore the glasses your Mrs. Who gave you that kept me within this solar system. Here are the glasses, Meg. But I am afraid that the virtue has gone from them and now they are only glass. Perhaps they were meant to help only once and only on Camazotz. Perhaps it was going through the Black Thing that did it." He pushed the glasses across the table at her.

"These people know about tessering," Calvin gestured at the circle of great beasts, "but they can't do it onto a dark planet."

"Have you tried to call Mrs. Whatsit?" Meg asked.

"Not yet," her father answered.

"But if you haven't thought of anything else, it's the *only* thing to do! Father, don't you care about Charles at all!"

At that Aunt Beast stood up, saying, "Child," in a reproving way. Mr. Murry said nothing and Meg could see that she had wounded him deeply. She reacted as she would have reacted to Mr. Jenkins. She scowled down at the table, saying, "We've *got* to ask them for help now. You're just stupid if you think we don't."

Aunt Beast spoke to the others. "The child is distraught. Don't judge her harshly. She was almost taken by the Black Thing. Sometimes we can't know what spiritual damage it leaves even when physical recovery is complete."

Meg looked angrily around the table. The beasts sat there, silent, motionless. She felt that she was being measured and found wanting.

Calvin swung away from her and hunched himself up. "Hasn't it occurred to you that we've been trying to tell them about our ladies? What do you think we've been up to all this time? Just stuffing our faces? Okay, you have a shot at it."

"Yes. Try, child." Aunt Beast seated herself again, and pulled Meg up beside her. "But I do not understand this feeling of anger I sense in you. What is it about? There is blame going on, and guilt. Why?"

"Aunt Beast, don't you know?"

"No," Aunt Beast said. "But this is not telling me about—whoever they are you want us to know. Try."

Meg tried. Blunderingly. Fumblingly. At first she described Mrs. Whatsit and her man's coat and multicolored shawls and scarves, Mrs. Who and her white robes and shimmering spectacles, Mrs. Which in her peaked cap and black gown quivering in and out of body. Then she realized that this was absurd. She was describing them only to herself. This wasn't Mrs. Whatsit or Mrs. Who or Mrs. Which. She might as well have described Mrs. Whatsit as she was when she took on the form of a flying creature of Uriel.

"Don't try to use words," Aunt Beast said soothingly. "You're just fighting yourself and me. Think about what they *are*. This *look* doesn't help us at all."

Meg tried again, but she could not get a visual concept out of her mind. She tried to think of Mrs. Whatsit explaining tessering. She tried to think of them in terms of mathematics. Every once in a while she thought she felt a flicker of understanding from Aunt Beast or one of the others, but most of the time all that emanated from them was gentle puzzlement.

"Angels!" Calvin shouted suddenly from across the table. "Guardian angels!" There was a moment's silence, and he shouted again, his face tense with concentration, "Messengers! Messengers of God!"

"I thought for a moment—" Aunt Beast started, then subsided, sighing. "No. It's not clear enough."

"How strange it is that they can't tell us what they themselves seem to know," a tall, thin beast murmured.

One of Aunt Beast's tentacled arms went around Meg's waist again. "They are very young. And on their earth, as they call it, they never communicate with other planets. They revolve about all alone in space."

"Oh," the thin beast said. "Aren't they *lonely?*"

Suddenly a thundering voice reverberated throughout the great hall:

"WWEEE ARRE HHERRE!"

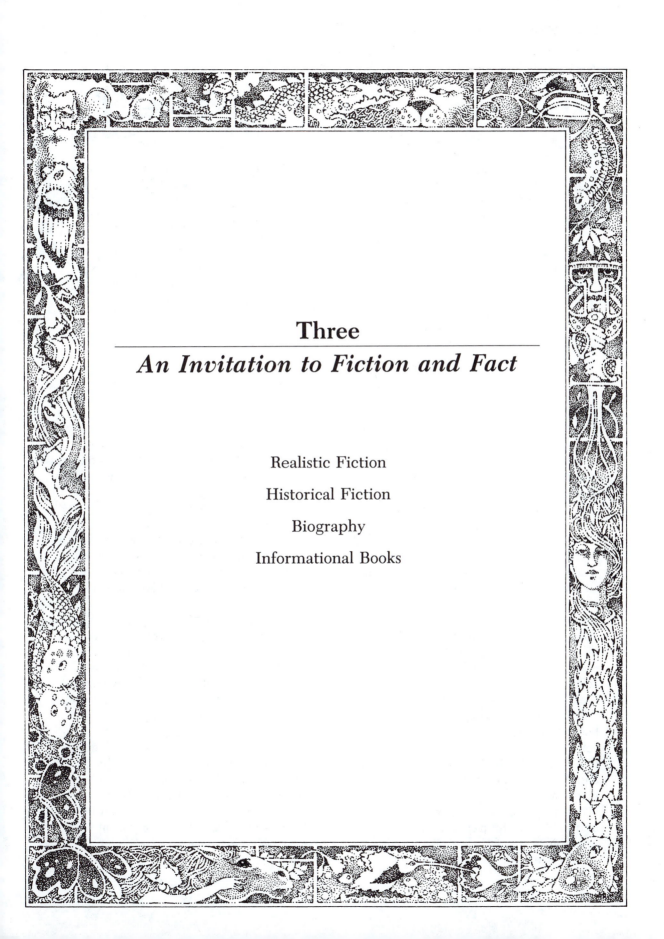

Three
An Invitation to Fiction and Fact

Realistic Fiction

Historical Fiction

Biography

Informational Books

Realistic Fiction

There is considerable dissension in the world of children's books today about the subject matter being handled in realistic books. Some adults reject out of hand the idea that juvenile fiction can—or should—deal with such subjects as a child murderer (*The Egypt Game* by Zilpha Snyder) or emotional disturbance (*Harriet the Spy* by Louise Fitzhugh). The same adults would probably reject children's books that deal with problems of divorce, alcoholism, and all social problems, whether they are brought about because of race, nationality, or religion.

Such adults think of themselves as protectors of the young. They are, in reality, merely protecting themselves from acknowledging the world around them as it exists today. They are also lacking in historical perspective, for many of the books they may most cherish were highly controversial when they were first published. *The Adventures of Tom Sawyer* and *The Adventures of Huckleberry Finn* were banned from libraries; even *Little Women* was considered, by some, unsuitable for children.

In the realm of realistic fiction, there has always been—in varying degree—controversy about didacticism in children's books, about whether it ought to be there at all, to what extent, and with what relative importance. Most critics today put stress on the importance of literary quality, readability, writing style, the inclusion of developmental values, and pace rather than on the didactic import of a story. What is appropriate for the reader of any age depends on such factors as reading ability and comprehension of concepts, subject interest, age and sex, and individual preferences for particular writing styles, subjects, or kinds of humor. When books portray characters who have fears or problems similar to those of the reader, they can help point the way to adjustment or solution, and they can ease the child reader's mind by showing that he or she is not alone in being afraid or resentful or discriminated against.

Children everywhere have the same needs and emotional responses. By seeing similarities and differences, children are laying the groundwork for a better understanding as adults. They can learn from books that the diversity of life is one of its miracles.

Life in the United States

 There are no fairy tales in realistic stories; their place is taken by realistic action and problems and solutions that today's children can apply to their own lives. When books portray characters who have fears or problems similar to those of the reader, they can help point the way to adjustment or solution, and they show the reader that he or she is not alone whatever the problem. Adherence to truth should be a part of all realistic fiction, whether the characters are animals or people. In the books in this section, children can see both similarities to, and differences from, their own lives, and thus lay the groundwork for a better understanding as adults, as people who see the similarities and differences in the lives of others.

from Did You Carry the Flag Today, Charley?
Rebecca Caudill

In Charley, Rebecca Caudill has created one of the most delightful characters of recent times—a boy who will appeal to all age groups.

[The Thing]

Of all the rooms at Little School, the one Charley liked best was Mr. Sizemore's. Charley's group went there the last half hour of every Wednesday.

In Mr. Sizemore's room the children made things of clay. They colored with crayons. They painted pictures with their fingers on big sheets of paper. They built houses and fences and calf pens with blocks. One day a boy built a mountain with blocks. On the mountain top he put a little flag.

The blocks were in a small room just off Mr. Sizemore's classroom. On a low shelf in that room stood big jars of clay of many colors.

One Wednesday afternoon, Mr. Sizemore said, "Suppose we paint today."

All the boys and girls liked to paint with their fingers. Whenever they sat at the tables to paint, Mr. Sizemore placed a piece of drawing paper in front of each of them. Then he took a large jar from a shelf, and went around the room pouring a blob of starch on each piece of paper.

Charley was sitting at the end of his table. He laid both hands flat in the blob of starch and smeared, and smeared, around and around. "It feels slick, like ice," he said, and he smeared some more.

"Ready for the blue stuff, Mr. Sizemore," he called.

"Is everyone ready?" asked Mr. Sizemore.

Around the room Mr. Sizemore went from table to table, sprinkling a few drops of tempera paint on each paper. He sprinkled blue paint on some papers, red paint on some, and yellow paint on some.

"I want some of every color, Mr. Sizemore," said Charley.

Mr. Sizemore sprinkled blue and red and yellow on Charley's paper.

"You know what I'm painting?" Charley said to Vinnie who sat next to him.

"No. What?" asked Vinnie.

"A rainbow," said Charley.

"I saw a rainbow one time," said Vinnie.

"Where was it?" asked Charley.

"In the sky, of course," said Vinnie. "Where'd you think it would be?"

"I saw a rainbow on the ground one time," said Charley.

"Mr. Sizemore," said Vinnie, "you know what Charley said? He said he saw a rainbow on the ground one time. He didn't, did he?"

"I did, too," said Charley.

"Where was it, Charley?" asked Mr. Sizemore.

"In a puddle," said Charley. "At a filling station."

"You could have seen one there," said Mr. Sizemore. "In an oil puddle. It wouldn't have been exactly like the rainbow you see in the sky, but it could have had some of the same colors."

"See?" Charley said to Vinnie.

Charley smeared and smeared.

"Done, Mr. Sizemore," he called.

Mr. Sizemore wrote on one corner of Charley's paper in big black letters, CHARLEY.

"Its name is Rainbow in a Puddle at a Filling Station," said Charley.

Mr. Sizemore wrote on one edge of the paper, RAINBOW IN A PUDDLE AT A FILLING STATION. With two clothespins he fastened Charley's picture on a cord stretched along the wall. When it was dry he would put it in a big folder labeled CHARLEY with all the other pictures Charley had painted. On the last day of school, Charley could take the folder home and show his mother all his pictures.

"Now I want to make something out of clay," Charley said.

"All right," said Mr. Sizemore. "You may get some clay off the shelf."

Charley went to the block room and chose some pink clay. Back at the table he pinched off a piece of the clay and rolled it in his hands till it was as thin as a toothpick. He took another piece and rolled it as thin as a pencil, and pinched one end of each of the two together to make a straight line. He rolled another piece just a bit thicker, and pinched one end of it to the end of the second piece. To keep it in a straight line, he had

to move Vinnie's paper.

"Quit that, Charley!" scolded Vinnie.

Charley rolled another piece of clay, a little thicker still. To pinch the end of it to the third piece, he had to move Carl's paper.

"Mr. Sizemore, make Charley quit!" complained Carl.

"What's Charley doing?" asked Mr. Sizemore as he walked over to the table.

"He thinks the whole table belongs to him," said Carl and Vinnie.

"What are you making, Charley?" asked Mr. Sizemore.

"A Thing," said Charley as he rolled another piece.

"You come with me," Mr. Sizemore said. "Bring your clay."

Mr. Sizemore led the way to the room where the blocks were kept. The other children went on painting.

"Since the Thing is so long, why don't you work in here by yourself?" asked Mr. Sizemore. "We'll spread a newspaper on the floor, and you can make your Thing on the paper."

"It'll have to be a long newspaper, Mr. Sizemore," Charley told him. "Because this sure is a long Thing I'm making."

Together Mr. Sizemore and Charley spread newspaper on the floor from the middle of the room up to the door. Then Mr. Sizemore went back into the classroom where the other boys and girls were painting.

Alone in the room, Charley looked at the row of jars of clay standing on the shelf. He took down the jar containing the pink clay and went to work, rolling and rolling, each piece a little thicker than the one before, and pinching the ends together.

Soon Charley had used up all the pink clay there was, and the Thing was not finished. He took down the jar of black clay and went to work again, rolling and rolling, each piece thicker than the one before. He used all the black clay there was. Then he took down the jar of yellow clay and began rolling.

The Thing was finally as big around as Charley's arm. It had reached almost to the door when the bell rang for the end of the school day.

Charley heard the children in the next room putting away their papers. He heard them getting in line in the hall. He heard Miss Amburgey say, "If you're going to meet that three o'clock bus at Elkhorn, Mr. Sizemore, you'll have to leave right away. I'll take care of your group."

Charley heard more talking and more shuffling of feet down the hall. Then everything grew still.

It was the best day he'd had at Little School. Here he was, all alone, with nobody to tell him "Do this" and "Do that." And the Thing was growing longer and thicker. It was now as thick as a baseball bat, its front end yellow, its middle black, its tail pink.

Charley heard footsteps in Mr. Sizemore's room. For a few seconds everything was quiet. Charley listened. Then he heard the footsteps go away down the hall. He heard Mr. Webb's voice. "Charley! Charley Cornett!"

He'd have to hurry, thought Charley to himself.

He took one more piece of yellow clay, shaped it broad and flat, and fastened it to the piece as thick as a baseball bat. That was the Thing's head. The Thing's head lay across the doorsill into Mr. Sizemore's classroom.

Charley stood up and looked at the Thing. He laughed as he thought how scared Mr. Sizemore would be when he walked into his room the next morning and saw the Thing looking at him over the doorsill.

The Thing ought to have a tongue, decided Charley. He took from the jar of red clay one tiny piece. He shaped it thin and short and flat, and fastened it to the Thing's head. The tongue curved upward. Charley stood up to admire it.

He heard steps coming along the hall toward Mr. Sizemore's room. He looked around. There stood Miss Amburgey in the doorway.

"Charley," she scolded, "where have you been?"

"Here," said Charley.

"All the time since the bell rang?"

"Yes'm."

"Why didn't you come with the other children?"

"I wasn't with the other children," said Charley. "They were out here and I was in there."

"But you heard the bell, didn't you?"

"Yes'm."

"Don't you know that when the bell rings it says you must come?" asked Miss Amburgey.

"Yes'm."

"Why didn't you come then?"

"I hadn't finished."

"What hadn't you finished?"

"A Thing I was making."

"Whether you've finished or not, when the bell rings you're to put everything away and come at once. You can finish the next day. Do you know the bus left fifteen minutes ago?"

Charley's face grew serious.

"But I wasn't done," he said.

"What were you doing," asked Miss Amburgey, "that you couldn't leave till tomorrow?"

"I told you, Miss Amburgey, I was making a Thing."

"What kind of thing?"

"Miss Amburgey," said Charley, "shut your eyes and I'll take your hand and lead you to see it. But you won't tell Mr. Sizemore, will you?"

"Charley," said Miss Amburgey sternly, "you know very well—"

She stopped and looked down at Charley.

"All right," she said, and she shut her eyes. Charley took her hand and led her to the door of the room where the blocks stayed.

"Open!" said Charley.

Miss Amburgey opened her eyes.

"Charley! What a snake!" she gasped. "It looks like a real one, except, of course, it is an odd color."

"You know what kind of snake it is?" asked Charley. "It's a yellowblackpink snake and it bites. I'm going to leave it here to scare Mr. Sizemore in the morning."

"Well," said Miss Amburgey, "since you've taken such pains to make the Thing, I guess you may leave it. But come along now. Since the bus has left you, I'll have to take you home myself."

Charley followed her out of the schoolhouse and climbed into her jeep beside her.

What a place school was! thought Charley. He had made the Thing to scare Mr. Sizemore and now he was going to go jeeping home along the blacktop.

As Miss Amburgey turned the key and stepped on the gas pedal, Charley braced himself and ordered, "Now, Miss Amburgey, let 'er tear!"

"You really ought to have to walk home," said Miss Amburgey.

Charley was silent.

"I told Mr. Mullins to stop and tell your mother we couldn't find you, but that, as soon as we did, I'd bring you home. If she weren't worried, I'd let you out right here and start you walking."

They drove along in silence for another minute.

"Miss Amburgey," asked Charley, "how can snakes run so fast when they don't have legs?"

"They're made that way," said Miss Amburgey.

"A rope's made that way too," said Charley, "but it can't run."

They drove another minute in silence.

"You want me to name all the snakes I know?" asked Charley.

"Let's hear them," said Miss Amburgey.

"Rattlesnake. Copperhead snake. Black snake. Chicken snake. Blue racer snake. Garter snake. Water moccasin snake."

"There are books in the library that tell all about snakes," Miss Amburgey said. "And all kinds of snakes that you don't know about, like boa constrictors, and king cobras, and sidewinders. I suspect they even tell how a snake can run fast when it hasn't any legs."

"Sure enough, Miss Amburgey? Books tell you that?"

"They do," said Miss Amburgey. "That's what books are written for."

"Is that what books really do?" asked Charley. "Tell you about things?"

"Books tell you almost anything you will ever want to know," said Miss Amburgey. "Some things, of course, you'll have to find out for yourself."

"When do I go to the library again?" asked Charley.

"This is Wednesday," said Miss Amburgey. "You go to the library day after tomorrow. On Friday."

Miss Amburgey stopped the jeep in front of the Cornetts' mailbox. All the Cornetts were waiting anxiously.

"No need asking," said Claude as Charley climbed out. "You didn't carry the flag today, Charley."

"No," said Charley. "But I made a Thing. Boy, you ought to see it!"

from The Secret Language
Ursula Nordstrom

This boarding school story has become a perennial favorite. The plight of the homesick Victoria engages the sympathy of any child who has felt that emotion.

New Girl

Sooner or later everyone has to go away from home for the first time. Sometimes it happens when a person is young. Sometimes it happens when a person is old. But sooner or later it does happen to everyone. It happened to Victoria North when she was eight.

The other children in the Coburn Home School bus shouted at each other, and pushed each other, and ran up and down the aisle. But Victoria sat alone looking out the window.

The bus turned down a country road, and suddenly one of the boys cried, "There's the old dump!"

"Coburn School! Coburn Home School!" the bus driver called. "All out!"

A pale, bony girl stood waiting for the bus. "Victoria North!" she yelled. "Victoria North Victoria North Victoria Victoria North North! I'm looking for a new girl named Victoria North! Any new kids on this bus?" She looked at Victoria. "That you? Well, I'm your roommate. My name is Ann Spear. Come on and I'll show you our room." She walked toward a large brick building, and Victoria followed her. Yellow leaves lay across the graveled path, and in the distance the hills were blue with mist.

"This is the girls' dormitory," Ann said as she opened the front door. "It's called Wingate Hall. The boys live in Shippen Hall. Do you like boys?"

Victoria looked at Ann. She was too homesick to speak.

"Well, I don't," Ann said flatly, and started up a flight of stairs. "But we just see them in classes. We have separate dining rooms. I've been here for two years and I'm supposed to tell you about everything. Anyhow, the boys at this school are all awful, if you ask me."

At the head of the stairs Ann turned and led Victoria down a long hall. "This is our corridor," Ann said. "Our housemother is Miss Mossman, and she is very very very strict." She opened a door. "Here's our room."

From THE SECRET LANGUAGE by Ursula Nordstrom. Copyright © 1960 by Ursula Nordstrom. By permission of Harper & Row, Publishers, Inc.

Victoria's trunk, which someone had unlocked for her, stood next to one of the beds.

"You better unpack now," Ann said. "I'm going back down to see what other old girls came back. See you later."

Victoria hung her hat and coat in the closet and slowly unpacked her trunk. On every article of clothing her mother had sewn a name-tape, in accordance with the instructions in the Coburn Home School catalogue. At home Victoria had liked the way her name looked woven in red on the white tape. But now, in this new place, the name-tapes made even her most familiar possessions seem strange to her.

When she hung up her flannel bathrobe she found a note from her mother pinned to it. In the note her mother asked her to remember to wear clean underwear every day and to say her prayers every night. And then her mother said Christmas vacation would come soon. The note made Victoria more homesick than she had been before. After she put on her new dark-blue dress she stood looking out the window, trying not to cry.

Ann came back in a little while. She looked at Victoria critically. "What's the matter with your *collar?*" she said impatiently. "My goodness, it's all twisted. Here, I'll fix it. My goodness, you can't even dress yourself yet!" Ann frowned as she pulled Victoria's collar straight.

There was a heavy knock at the door and a tall woman came in. "How do you do, Victoria?" she said. "I am your housemother, Miss Mossman." Miss Mossman was an ugly woman with straight black hair and little black eyes. "I'm glad to have you on my corridor," she said. "Ann will explain our rules and regulations to you, and I am sure you will find them easy to obey. I will see you at my table at supper."

Miss Mossman left, and Victoria sat down on her bed.

"We are not allowed to sit on the beds," Ann said sharply. "Sit on your chair. My goodness!"

Victoria went over to the window and carefully wrapped the cord of the shade around her thumb. She was trying not to cry in front of Ann.

In a few minutes a gong sounded, and Ann jumped up. "Come on," she said. "Supper! Hurry up!"

In the dining room Victoria followed Ann to one of the long tables and sat down next to her.

"Oh, you don't sit here, dopey," Ann said. "You're supposed to sit at Miss Mossman's table. She told you!"

Victoria stumbled to her feet. She didn't know which table was Miss Mossman's, and in the blur of strange faces she couldn't find the housemother. All the other children were at their places. At the sound of a bell all heads were lowered and grace was said aloud. "For what we are about to receive may the good Lord make us truly thankful." The words echoed around Victoria as she stood alone in the middle of the dining room. When grace was over, Victoria saw Miss Mossman beckoning to her.

"Girls," Miss Mossman said, "this is Victoria North, a new student this year. Victoria, there's your place, between Sue Burton and Eleanor Mindendorfer." She briefly introduced the other girls. Several of them looked up and said "Hi" as Victoria slid into her seat and stared at the plate of food in front of her. Sue Burton, who was fat and had red hair, said, "What's your name again?"

But Victoria didn't hear her.

"Please pass the bread," said Eleanor Mindendorfer loudly.

"How come you came back, Martha?" Sue said to a dark girl with bangs who sat opposite Victoria. "I thought you weren't coming back this year."

The dark girl scowled. "I'm probably only going to stay until Thanksgiving," she said.

"But I thought you weren't coming back at all this year," Sue insisted. "You did say you were going to live home. I remember. But I was sure you'd have to come back anyhow, though."

"M.Y.O.D.O.B. And that means Mind Your Own Dumb Old Business," Martha said clearly.

"Martha!" Miss Mossman said. "There is no need to be rude to Sue. Why, Victoria, you're not eating your supper. Here at Coburn School we eat what is placed in front of us, Victoria. Come, dear."

Victoria picked up her fork and tried to swallow some food.

"My little brother is coming to this school next year, Miss Mossman," Eleanor Mindendorfer announced.

"That's splendid, Eleanor. What is your brother's name?"

"His name is Sidney, and he's my little brother, and—"

"Oh, ick-en-spick," Martha said.

"What?" Eleanor looked at her. "What did you say, Martha?"

"I said ick-en-spick," Martha repeated.

"Oh, Martha, you're so funny!" Eleanor began to giggle.

But Sue was indignant. "What kind of talk is that?" she asked. "It's crazy."

"Well, it isn't crazy."

"It certainly sounds crazy, if you ask me," Sue said.

"I didn't ask you, and it isn't crazy. Neither is ankendosh. Neither is leebossa."

"Martha Sherman, what are you talking about?" Sue was puzzled.

"I'm talking about a secret language I just happen to know."

"What do you mean? What secret language?"

"It's just my secret language, that's all," Martha said.

"What was that funny word you said?"

"Ick-en-spick."

"What does it mean? And what did that other funny word you said mean?"

"Wouldn't you like to know?" said Martha, and she made a hideous face at Sue.

"Now, Martha," said Miss Mossman from the head of the table. "You must stop being rude. Stop it at once."

"She's a big fat dope," Martha said.

"Martha! You must behave yourself, or I will have to ask you to leave the table. Eleanor, I know you must be looking forward to having your little brother here next year."

"Yes, I am, Miss Mossman. He is a year and two months younger than I am, and his name is Sidney, and—"

"Well, what's so wonderful about that?"

Martha asked.

"Well! I guess I can talk about my brother if I want to!"

"Oh, all right. Tell some more. Go ahead." Martha shrugged. "His name is Sidney, and he's coming to this school next year."

"Yes, he is," Eleanor said.

"Poor old Sidney," said Martha heavily.

Everyone turned to look at the housemother. Two bright red spots appeared on Miss Mossman's cheeks, and her right eye began to twitch. She said sternly, "Martha, you may go to your room at once. Although you have been back at Coburn less than one day, I will have to give you a demerit. Now go to your room immediately. I'll talk to you later."

Martha folded her napkin, pushed back her chair, and left the dining room slowly. She was still scowling.

"She's an awful girl," Sue said to the rest of the table. "She's the worst girl in this whole school."

"That will be enough, Susan," Miss Mossman said severely.

"I think she is the worst girl here," Sue whispered to Victoria. "Some people in this school think she is so wonderful, and she thinks she is too, but I think she is awful."

Victoria didn't answer.

"Victoria, you haven't touched your food," Miss Mossman said. "Now finish your supper at once."

Victoria stared at her plate.

"Victoria, did you hear me? Eat your supper at once. The rest of us are waiting for you."

Tears suddenly spilled over Victoria's cheeks. They ran down her face and fell on her clasped hands. She lowered her head. Everyone at the table looked at her.

"Victoria," Miss Mossman said sharply. "Look at me, Victoria."

Slowly Victoria turned toward the head of the table. With her eyes shut and her mouth twisted, she wept soundlessly. Several of the girls began to giggle.

Miss Mossman saw that Victoria was indeed unable to eat. "You may clear," she said to the maid.

After supper the children sat on folding chairs in the drawing room for an hour of singing.

"Turn, please, to page eighty-seven, 'A Capital Ship,'" Miss Mossman said as Miss Douglass sat down at the piano.

"A Capital Ship" was a gay song, and everyone loved it.

Next Miss Mossman announced, "Page forty-one. 'Now the Day Is Over.'"

To Victoria, sitting in the front row next to Ann, the slow music and the words—"Now the day is over. Night is drawing nigh. Shadows of the evening steal across the sky"—seemed the saddest she had ever heard. In the middle of the song she started again to cry.

"Oh, stop it!" Ann whispered. "Stop crying!" And she shook the songbook in exasperation.

The next song was "The Harp That Once Through Tara's Halls." It, too, was a sad song, and Victoria continued to cry. Finally Miss Mossman motioned to Ann to take Victoria out. Behind her disgusted and resentful roommate, Victoria stumbled slowly from the room.

Upstairs Ann stood with her hands on her hips and glared at Victoria. "You're an awful crybaby," Ann said. She picked up her towel and washcloth and flounced out of the room.

Victoria pulled off her dress and her shoes and got into bed in her underwear and her socks. She was shivering, though it was not a cold night. She did not even think of saying her prayers.

Ann came back. "Aren't you going to get washed?" she asked.

Victoria was crying and she couldn't answer.

"Are you just going to leave your dress on the floor?"

There was no answer.

"You'll get a demerit," Ann said spitefully. "Don't say I didn't tell you. Miss Mossman may even give you two demerits. I don't care, though."

The singing was over. Girls came upstairs noisily to get ready for bed. They shouted to each other in the corridor, banged doors, ran back and forth to the bathrooms. Suddenly there was a loud blast on a whistle, and then there was silence. Ann snapped out the light and got into bed.

Victoria tried to be quiet. But she was crying so hard that she had to gasp when she tried to catch her breath. Every time Victoria did that, Ann turned over noisily in bed and heaved an irritated sigh. Finally Ann sat up and whispered crossly, "Oh, stop *bawling!*" Then she flopped back down in her bed and sighed loudly again. After a while Ann went to sleep.

This was the first night Victoria had ever spent away from her mother, and it was worse than the worst nightmare she had ever had. Her mother couldn't have known it would be like this! Gasping and choking, Victoria rolled over on her back, stared up into the dark, and wept. The tears rolled down her cheeks into her ears, and she turned over on her side and wiped her face and her ears on the stiff sheet. Today had been as awful as anything could be, and she had lived through it. She had lived through today, but what about tomorrow? What would she do tomorrow?

Finally, sobbing and gasping, she grew tired. After a long time, she turned over once more and put her head under the pillow. And then at last she fell asleep too.

The Secret Language

"Wake up!" Ann cried. She shook Victoria's shoulder. "The whistle just blew. Hurry up for inspection!"

Victoria pulled on her bathrobe and hurried into the hall behind her roommate. At the end of the corridor the housemother stood waiting to see that everyone was out of bed. When all the girls were lined up two by two in front of their doors, Miss Mossman called, "Dismissed!" and blew the whistle again.

"Breakfast in half an hour!" Ann yelled, and ran down the hall to the bathroom. Victoria followed her slowly.

"My, your eyes are all red," Sue Burton remarked, looking at Victoria in the mirror over the washbasins. "I guess you cry an awful lot. Don't you like it here?"

Victoria shook her head and bent over a basin. Sue began to talk across her to Ann. "Miss Mossman is just as mean as ever, with all those whistles and morning inspection and everything," Sue said.

"Yes." Ann sighed. "That standing in the hall gives me a pain. She must have been a jail-mother before, not a housemother."

Victoria finished brushing her teeth, and as she straightened up, Sue and Ann both looked at her and giggled. Several other girls did too. Suddenly Martha, the girl who had been dismissed from the table the night before, came in, dragging a towel. "What's so funny?" she asked.

"I guess that new girl's homesick," Sue said. "She was crying during singing last night, and Ann had to take her out, and her face looks funny."

"Oh, ankendosh," Martha said. "How old are you, anyhow?" she said to Victoria.

Martha sounded friendly, but Victoria hurried past her without speaking and went back to her room to get dressed.

The day wore on. Victoria went to the school hall with Ann and the others, and met the teachers. No class work was done, but books were distributed and desks were assigned.

After the last class was dismissed, Victoria walked out of the school hall behind Ann, who was whispering and giggling with Eleanor Mindendorfer. As they went out the door Ann turned to Victoria and said crossly, "Oh, hang off me, will you? You've been hanging on me all day! Just please hang off me!" Then Ann walked away with Eleanor and some of the other old girls.

Victoria stood by the school hall and looked around her. She didn't know where to go or what to do. In a few minutes Miss Blanchard, the arithmetic teacher, came out the door. "Hello," she said. "You're Victoria North, aren't you? I think Victoria is a pretty name."

Victoria looked up at her, but could think

of nothing to say.

"Why don't you go down to the swings for a while? That will be fun. In a few days you will know more of the other children and you'll be happier, Victoria. Really you will be. I know it is hard at first."

Victoria was silent, and finally Miss Blanchard turned and walked away. Victoria picked up some gravel and looked at it carefully, then let it fall slowly out of her hand. She examined the bark on a tree for a few minutes. Then she walked back to her room.

The first ten days at Coburn Home School were all lonely ones for Victoria. She didn't know anyone, and no one seemed to want to know her. Her mother wrote her every day, but the letters only made Victoria more homesick.

Then one afternoon, late in September, Victoria was alone down by the swings. Martha wandered by and saw her. "Hello," she said. She sat on the end of a slide. "That's some dumb table we're at," she added. "I wish I could be at Miss Blanchard's table."

Victoria was afraid to say something Martha might think was silly. So she said nothing. But she smiled.

"I hate this old school," Martha said.

"Oh, so do I!" Victoria said.

"I hate it," Martha repeated. "And it's worse than it was last year. But I only came back for a little while, anyhow. Pretty soon I'm going to live home and go to day school. Are you going home for Thanksgiving?"

Victoria shook her head. "I guess not."

"Well, I am, and I just bet I won't have to come back here. I'm going to tell my mother and father about this school. I'll tell them about the food. I'll tell them they give us horrible, disgusting, dirty, gluey purple stuff to eat and they call it oatmeal."

Victoria was startled but fascinated.

"Does your family live in New York?" Martha asked.

"My mother does, most of the time."

"What do you mean, most of the time?"

"Well, she has to go away once in a while. She works. That's why I can't go home for Thanksgiving."

"Where's she going?"

"Chicago."

"My father's an importer. What's yours?"

Victoria could hardly remember him. "I haven't any," she said.

"You just have a mother?"

"Yes."

"Oh. Lots of the kids here just have a mother, too. Or just a father. What's your favorite subject?"

"Reading. What's yours?"

"Arithmetic."

"Arithmetic!" Victoria was amazed. "Oh, I hate arithmetic!"

"Well, I hate reading," Martha said reasonably. "What are you going to be when you grow up?"

"I don't know yet. What are you?"

"Oh, I guess I'll be an inventor, or maybe a singer. Oh, I certainly hate this school," Martha repeated. "I hate all the buildings and all the rooms, and the food, and I even hate the swings, and I hate this dumb slide." She kicked the slide as she spoke.

"It's an awful old school," Victoria agreed. And she gave the slide a little kick too.

Suddenly Martha stood up and marched around one of the swings with her stomach stuck out in what seemed to Victoria an extremely amusing way. Then Martha sang in a piercing voice:

> "Two more months to vacation.
> Then I go to the station.
> Back to civilization.
> Back to Mother and Home."

"Did you make that up?" Victoria asked, impressed.

"Me? No! You never heard that before? I guess that's just because you never went to boarding school before. I can make up stuff, though, if I want to."

Victoria thought Martha was wonderful. They climbed up on a seesaw, and seesawed up and down in the darkening light. Then they went to the dormitory to get ready for dinner.

At the table that night Martha looked across at Victoria and said, "Hey, Vick, maybe we'll have ice cream tonight. That would be leebossa, wouldn't it?"

The other girls looked at Martha in surprise, and then at Victoria.

"Wouldn't it? Wouldn't it be leebossa?" Martha repeated, staring at Victoria.

"Yes, I guess so," Victoria said finally.

"After singing I'll tell you all about my secret language," Martha said. "But you'll have to promise you'll never tell anyone else!"

"I promise," said Victoria faintly.

The other girls looked at Victoria with new interest. Martha had never been so friendly to anyone else.

That night when singing was over, Martha waited in the hall for Victoria and they walked upstairs together.

"Ick-en-spick is for when something is silly," Martha explained. "Or like when someone is trying to get in good with a teacher, and is trying to be very sweet. You know. Goody-goody stuff is ick-en-spick."

Victoria nodded.

"Ankendosh," Martha went on, "is for something mean or disgusting. Ann Spear is usually very ankendosh."

"She certainly is," Victoria said.

"Now, leebossa is for when you like something. When something is just lovely or when something works out just right, it is leebossa. For anything especially nice you can say leeleeleeleebossa. But that's only for something really wonderful. Understand?"

"Yes, thank you for telling me. Are there any other words?"

"No. But maybe we can make up some more," Martha said.

"That would be leebossa," Victoria said, and Martha grinned at her.

From then on Martha and Victoria were friends. Whenever possible they did their homework with each other. They walked to and from the school hall together every day. And they sat next to each other at singing every night.

Being friends with Martha was wonderful, and Victoria was happier than she had been. But she was still afraid of Miss Mossman, and she still missed her mother, and she still counted the days to Christmas vacation.

from **Ramona and Her Father**
Beverly Cleary

It is the simplicity of Beverly Cleary's style, its natural flow and humor, that have made her so popular an author. In this amusing Christmas story, there is a nice balance of tender sentiment and comic relief.

Ramona and the Three Wise Persons

Suddenly, a few days before Christmas when the Quimby family least expected it, the telephone rang for Ramona's father. He had a job! The morning after New Year's Day he was to report for training as a checker in a chain of supermarkets. The pay was good, he would have to work some evenings, and maybe someday he would get to manage a market!

After that telephone call Mr. Quimby stopped reaching for cigarettes that were not there and began to whistle as he ran the vacuum cleaner and folded the clothes from the dryer. The worried frown disappeared from Mrs. Quimby's forehead. Beezus looked even more calm and serene. Ramona, however, made a mistake. She told her mother about her tight shoes. Mrs. Quimby then wasted a Saturday afternoon shopping for shoes when she could have been sewing on Ramona's costume. As a result, when they drove to church the night of the Christmas-carol program, Ramona was the only unhappy member of the family.

Mr. Quimby sang as he drove:

"There's a little wheel a-turning in my heart.
There's a little wheel a-turning in my heart."

Ramona loved that song because it made her think of Howie, who liked machines. Tonight, however, she was determined not to enjoy her father's singing.

Rain blew against the car, headlights shone on the pavement, the windshield wipers *splip-splopped.* Mrs. Quimby leaned back, tired but relaxed. Beezus smiled her gentle Virgin Mary smile that Ramona had found so annoying for the past three weeks.

Ramona sulked. Someplace above those cold, wet clouds the very same star was shining that had guided the Three Wise Men to Bethlehem. On a night like this they never would have made it.

Mr. Quimby sang on, "Oh, I feel like shouting in my heart. . . ."

Ramona interrupted her father's song. "I don't care what anybody says," she burst out. "If I can't be a good sheep, I am not going to be a sheep at all." She yanked off the white terry-cloth headdress with pink-lined ears that she was wearing and stuffed it into the pocket of her car coat. She started to pull her father's rolled-down socks from her hands because they didn't really look like hooves, but then she decided they kept her hands warm. She squirmed on the lumpy terry-cloth tail sewn to the seat of her pajamas. Ramona could not pretend that faded pajamas printed with an army of pink rabbits, half of them upside down, made her look like a sheep, and Ramona was usually good at pretending.

Mrs. Quimby's voice was tired. "Ramona, your tail and headdress were all I could manage, and I had to stay up late last night to finish those. I simply don't have time for complicated sewing."

Ramona knew that. Her family had been telling her so for the past three weeks.

"A sheep should be woolly," said Ramona. "A sheep should not be printed with pink bunnies."

"You can be a sheep that has been shorn," said Mr. Quimby, who was full of jokes now that he was going to work again. "Or how about a wolf in sheep's clothing?"

"You just want me to be miserable," said Ramona, not appreciating her father's humor and feeling that everyone in her family should be miserable because she was.

"She's worn out," said Mrs. Quimby, as if Ramona could not hear. "It's so hard to wait for Christmas at her age."

Ramona raised her voice. "I am *not* worn out! You know sheep don't wear pajamas."

"That's show biz," said Mr. Quimby.

"Daddy!" Beezus-Mary was shocked. "It's church!"

"And don't forget, Ramona," said Mr. Quimby, "as my grandmother would have said, 'Those pink bunnies will never be noticed from a trotting horse.'"

Ramona disliked her father's grandmother even more. Besides, nobody rode trotting horses in church.

The sight of light shining through the stained-glass window of the big stone church diverted Ramona for a moment. The window looked beautiful, as if it were made of jewels.

Mr. Quimby backed the car into a parking space. "Ho-ho-ho!" he said, as he turned off the ignition. "'Tis the season to be jolly."

Jolly was the last thing Ramona was going to be. Leaving the car, she stooped down inside her car coat to hide as many rabbits as possible. Black branches clawed at the sky, and the wind was raw.

"Stand up straight," said Ramona's heartless father.

"I'll get wet," said Ramona. "I might catch cold, and then you'd be sorry."

"Run between the drops," said Mr. Quimby.

"They're too close together," answered Ramona.

"Oh, you two," said Mrs. Quimby with a tired little laugh, as she backed out of the car and tried to open her umbrella at the same time.

"I will not be in it," Ramona defied her family once and for all. "They can give the program without me."

Her father's answer was a surprise. "Suit yourself," he said. "You're not going to spoil our evening."

Mrs. Quimby gave the seat of Ramona's pajamas an affectionate pat. "Run along, little lamb, wagging your tail behind you."

Ramona walked stiff-legged so that her tail would not wag.

At the church door the family parted, the girls going downstairs to the Sunday-school room, which was a confusion of chattering children piling coats and raincoats on chairs. Ramona found a corner behind the Christmas tree, where Santa would pass out candy canes after the program. She sat down on the floor with her car coat pulled over her bent knees.

Through the branches Ramona watched carolers putting on their white robes. Girls were tying tinsel around one another's heads while Mrs. Russo searched out boys and tied tinsel around their heads, too. "It's all right for boys to wear tinsel," Mrs. Russo assured them. Some looked as if they were not certain they believed her.

One boy climbed on a chair. "I'm an angel. Watch me fly," he announced and jumped off, flapping the wide sleeves of his choir robe. All the carolers turned into flapping angels.

Nobody noticed Ramona. Everyone was having too much fun. Shepherds found their cloaks, which were made from old cotton bedspreads. Beezus's friend, Henry Huggins, arrived and put on the dark robe he was to wear in the part of Joseph.

The other two sheep appeared. Howie's acrylic sheep suit, with the zipper on the front, was as thick and as fluffy as Ramona knew it would be. Ramona longed to pet Howie; he looked so soft. Davy's flannel suit was fastened with safety pins, and there was something wrong about the ears. If his tail had been longer, he could have passed for a kitten, but he did not seem to mind. Both boys wore brown mittens. Davy, who was a thin little sheep, jumped up and down to make his tail wag, which surprised Ramona. At school he was always so shy. Maybe he felt brave inside his sheep suit. Howie, a chunky sheep, made his tail wag, too. My ears are as good as theirs, Ramona told herself. The floor felt cold through the seat of her thin pajamas.

"Look at the little lambs!" cried an angel. "Aren't they darling?"

"Ba-a, ba-a!" bleated Davy and Howie.

Ramona longed to be there with them, jumping and ba-a-ing and wagging her tail, too. Maybe the faded rabbits didn't show as much as she had thought. She sat hunched and miserable. She had told her father she would *not* be a sheep, and she couldn't back down now. She hoped God was too busy to notice her, and then she changed her mind. Please, God, prayed Ramona, in case He wasn't too busy to listen to a miserable little sheep, I don't really mean to be horrid. It just works out that way. She was frightened, she discovered, for when the program began, she would be left alone in the church basement. The lights might even be turned out, a scary thought, for the big stone church filled Ramona with awe, and she did not want to be left alone in the dark with her awe. Please, God, prayed Ramona, get me out of this mess.

Beezus, in a long blue robe with a white scarf over her head and carrying a baby's blanket and a big flashlight, found her little sister. "Come out, Ramona," she coaxed. "Nobody will notice your costume. You know Mother would have made you a whole sheep suit if she had time. Be a good sport. Please."

Ramona shook her head and blinked to keep tears from falling. "I told Daddy I wouldn't be in the program, and I won't."

"Well, OK, if that's the way you feel," said Beezus, forgetting to act like Mary. She left her little sister to her misery.

Ramona sniffed and wiped her eyes on her hoof. Why didn't some grown-up come along and *make* her join the other sheep? No grown-up came. No one seemed to remember there were supposed to be three sheep, not even Howie, who played with her almost every day.

Ramona's eye caught the reflection of her face distorted in a green Christmas ornament. She was shocked to see her nose look huge, her mouth and red-rimmed eyes tiny. I can't really look like that, thought Ramona in despair. I'm really a nice person. It's just that nobody understands.

Ramona mopped her eyes on her hoof again, and as she did she noticed three big girls, so tall they were probably in the eighth grade, putting on robes made from better bedspreads than the shepherd's robes. That's funny, she thought. Nothing she had learned in Sunday school told her anything about girls in long robes in the Nativity scene. Could they be Jesus's aunts?

One of the girls began to dab tan cream from a little jar on her face and to smear it around while another girl held up a pocket mirror. The third girl, holding her own mirror, used an eyebrow pencil to give herself heavy brows.

Makeup, thought Ramona with interest, wishing she could wear it. The girls took turns darkening their faces and brows. They looked like different people. Ramona got to her knees and peered over the lower branches of the Christmas tree for a better view.

One of the girls noticed her. "Hi, there," she said. "Why are you hiding back there?"

"Because," was Ramona's all-purpose answer. "Are you Jesus's aunts?" she asked.

The girls found the question funny. "No," answered one. "We're the Three Wise Persons."

Ramona was puzzled. "I thought they were supposed to be wise *men,*" she said.

"The boys backed out at the last minute," explained the girl with the blackest eyebrows. "Mrs. Russo said women can be wise too, so tonight we are the Three Wise Persons."

This idea seemed like a good one to Ramona, who wished she were big enough to be a wise person hiding behind makeup so nobody would know who she was.

"Are you supposed to be in the program?" asked one of the girls.

"I was supposed to be a sheep, but I changed my mind," said Ramona, changing it back again. She pulled out her sheep headdress and put it on.

"Isn't she adorable?" said one of the wise persons.

Ramona was surprised. She had never been called adorable before. Bright, lively, yes; adorable, no. She smiled and felt more lovable. Maybe pink-lined ears helped.

"Why don't you want to be a sheep?" asked a wise person.

Ramona had an inspiration. "Because I don't have any makeup."

"Makeup on a *sheep!*" exclaimed a wise person and giggled.

Ramona persisted. "Sheep have black noses," she hinted. "Maybe I could have a black nose."

The girls looked at one another. "Don't tell my mother," said one, "but I have some mascara. We could make her nose black."

"Please!" begged Ramona, getting to her feet and coming out from behind the Christmas tree.

The owner of the mascara fumbled in her shoulder bag, which was hanging on a chair, and brought out a tiny box. "Let's go in the kitchen where there's a sink," she said, and when Ramona followed her, she moistened an elf-sized brush, which she rubbed on the mascara in the box. Then she began to brush it onto Ramona's nose. It tickled, but Ramona held still. "It feels like brushing my teeth only on my nose," she remarked. The wise person stood back to look at her work and then applied another coat of mascara to Ramona's nose. "There," she said at last. "Now you look like a real sheep."

Ramona felt like a real sheep. "Ba-a-a," she bleated, a sheep's way of saying thank you. Ramona felt so much better, she could almost pretend she was woolly. She peeled off her coat and found that the faded pink rabbits really didn't show much in the dim light. She pranced off among the angels, who had been handed little flashlights, which they were supposed to hold like candles. Instead they were shining them into their mouths to show one another how weird they looked with light showing through their cheeks. The other two sheep stopped jumping when they saw her.

"You don't look like Ramona," said Howie.

"B-a-a. I'm not Ramona. I'm a sheep." The boys did not say one word about Ramona's pajamas. They wanted black noses too, and when Ramona told them where she got hers, they ran off to find the wise persons. When they returned, they no longer looked like Howie and Davy in sheep suits. They looked like strangers in sheep suits. So I must really look like somebody else, thought Ramona with increasing happiness. Now she could be in the program, and her parents wouldn't know because they wouldn't recognize her.

"B-a-a!" bleated three prancing, black-nosed sheep. "B-a-a, b-a-a."

Mrs. Russo clapped her hands. "Quiet, everybody!" she ordered. "All right, Mary and Joseph, up by the front stairs. Shepherds and sheep next and then wise persons. Angels line up by the back stairs."

The three sheep pranced over to the shepherds, one of whom said, "Look what we get to herd," and nudged Ramona with his crook.

"You cut that out," said Ramona.

"Quietly, everyone," said Mrs. Russo.

Ramona's heart began to pound as if something exciting were about to happen. Up the stairs she tiptoed and through the arched door. The only light came from candelabra on either side of the chancel and from a streetlight shining through a stained-glass window. Ramona had never seen the church look so beautiful or so mysterious.

Beezus sat down on a low stool in the center of the chancel and arranged the baby's blanket around the flashlight. Henry stood behind her. The sheep got down on their hands and knees in front of the shepherds, and the Three Wise Persons stood off to one side, holding bath-salts jars that looked as if they really could hold frankincense and myrhh. An electric star suspended above the organ began to shine. Beezus turned on the big flashlight inside the baby's blanket and light shone up on her face, making her look like a picture of Mary on a Christmas card. From the rear door a wobbly procession of kindergarten angels, holding their small flashlights like candles, led the way, glimmering, two by two. "Ah . . ." breathed the congregation.

"Hark, the herald angels sing," the advancing angels caroled. They looked nothing like the jumping, flapping mob with flashlights shining through their cheeks that Ramona had watched downstairs. They looked good and serious and . . . holy.

A shivery feeling ran down Ramona's backbone, as if magic were taking place. She looked up at Beezus, smiling tenderly down at the flashlight, and it seemed as if Baby Jesus really could be inside the blanket. Why, thought Ramona with a feeling of shock, Beezus looks nice. Kind and—sort of pretty. Ramona had never thought of her sister as anything but—well, a plain old big sister, who got to do everything first. Ramona was suddenly proud of Beezus. Maybe they did fight a lot when Beezus wasn't going around acting like Mary, but Beezus was never really mean.

As the carolers bore more light into the church, Ramona found her parents in the second row. They were smiling gently, proud of Beezus, too. This gave Ramona an aching feeling inside. They would not know her in her makeup. Maybe they would think she was some other sheep, and she didn't want to be some other sheep. She wanted to be their sheep. She wanted them to be proud of her, too.

Ramona saw her father look away from Beezus and look directly at her. Did he recognize her? Yes, he did. Mr. Quimby winked. Ramona was shocked. Winking in church! How could her father do such a thing? He winked again and this time held up his thumb and forefinger in a circle. Ramona understood. Her father was telling her he was proud of her, too.

"Joy to the newborn King!" sang the angels, as they mounted the steps on either side of the chancel.

Ramona was filled with joy. Christmas was the most beautiful, magic time of the whole year. Her parents loved her, and she loved them, and Beezus, too. At home there was a Christmas tree and under it, presents, fewer than at past Christmases, but presents all the same. Ramona could not contain her feelings. "B-a-a," she bleated joyfully.

She felt the nudge of a shepherd's crook on the seat of her pajamas and heard her shepherd whisper through clenched teeth, "You be quiet!" Ramona did not bleat again. She wiggled her seat to make her tail wag.

from **The Middle Moffat**
Eleanor Estes

What starts as a game between Jane and old Mr. Buckle develops into a real friendship in this selection. The ingenuous tone of the writing, the warmth and simplicity of the relationship, and Estes' ability to identify with the child's point of view have made the Moffats minor classics.

An Afternoon With the Oldest Inhabitant

Jane took the short cut across the huge, empty lot to the library. She was in a hurry because she had just gotten the idea that it would be fine to read every book in the library. Of course not all at once; just one at a time. She arrived there hot and panting. The best way to go about reading every book in the library, she thought, was to go to a certain section, take down the first book on the first shelf, get it stamped, take it home, read it, bring it back, and take out the very next book. In this way she would not miss one single book. She tiptoed over to one of the sections, took down the first book without looking to see what it was, and had it stamped at the desk. As she was about to leave she noticed Mr. Buckle in an armchair by the window.

"What book did you take, mysterious middle Moffat?" he asked her.

Jane showed him her book. She saw for the first time it was called "The Story of Lumber."

"H-m-m-m, 'The Story of Lumber' . . . very mystifying," he said, and he put his forefinger on the side of his nose like Hawkshaw, the detective.

Jane played her part, too; then she backed out on tiptoes, waving a reassuring good-by

to Miss Lamb, the librarian, who watched her with a truly mystified expression.

Jane read "The Story of Lumber" as rapidly as possible. It was not very interesting. But if she were going to read every book in the library, she would have to take the bad along with the good. She brought "The Story of Lumber" back the next day and took the next book. The oldest inhabitant was sitting in the same place by the window. His soft white hair shone in the sunshine.

Again Jane showed him the new book she had borrowed and saw with a trace of dismay that this one was called "The Story of Cotton."

" 'The Story of Cotton' . . . more mystifying than ever," whispered Mr. Buckle.

Jane played Hawkshaw a trifle absent-mindedly. She sat down on the granite steps outside the library and read for a while. This book also was far from interesting. Evidently she had chosen the wrong section to begin on. Where were all the books like "Heidi"? Still if she read the bad ones first, the good ones would be like dessert.

When she brought back "The Story of Cotton" and saw that the next book was "The Story of Sugar," she decided to try something different. She still planned to read every book in the library but she would take the best ones first. Then, by the time she finished all the good ones, she would be such a good reader she could just tear through things like "The Story of Sugar" in a few minutes.

She chose a bound volume of *St. Nicholas* magazine. This was full of good things. As she left the library she met Mr. Buckle coming up the granite steps. He was supporting himself by means of the brass railing.

"Hello, Mr. Buckle," said Jane. "I am going to read every book in the library," she added, feeling exuberant again now that she had something good.

Mr. Buckle nodded his head up and down, beaming. He was out of breath and he was hanging onto the brass railing.

"Is it cheating," Jane demanded, "if I don't

read every word in this big book? It's not really a book. It's a lot of magazines."

"Did you say to yourself, I am going to read every book and every magazine?"

"No . . . every book."

"Well, then, it's not cheating."

"But maybe a whole lot of magazines together makes a book."

"It is very mystifying," agreed Mr. Buckle, "but I think once a magazine, always a magazine."

Jane ran home the long way so she could race the trolley car to Ashbellows Place. She was a good runner and almost always beat the trolley to her corner. Running around to the back yard and climbing onto the high board fence, she peered through the apple trees. She hoped that Nancy Stokes would have come home from her piano lesson by now. But Nancy was nowhere in sight. She must have had to go somewhere with her mother.

So Jane went around front and sat down on the little square porch to read her *St. Nicholas.* The first story began, "In the middle of the night . . ."

In the middle of the night . . . It reminded Jane of her own position in the Moffat family. It was now definitely established that she was the middle Moffat. Mama introduced her as "Jane, the middle Moffat" not only to the Gillespie girls but also to the new curate of the church for whom she was making vestments and cassocks.

Of course the only person to whom she had made that mistake about being the mysterious middle Moffat was Mr. Buckle. And, as it turned out, this had not proved to be such a grave error anyway. In fact, he seemed to enjoy the game of Hawkshaw, the detective, very much. And if he liked it, and he was the oldest inhabitant and the most important person in the town, it certainly had not done any harm, this calling herself the mysterious middle Moffat. It might even, by keeping him in such good spirits, help him live to be one hundred.

Jane was doing all she could about that. For instance, she sometimes followed him from a distance to see that he crossed the street safely and that no dogs jumped out at him unexpectedly and made him lose his balance. Whenever she heard of a new family moving to Cranbury, she checked up immediately to find out how old the oldest person in that family was. When she found that there was no one ninety-nine or over, she quickly told Mr. Buckle so he would know he was still the oldest inhabitant in town.

Janey tried to be near by whenever the oldest inhabitant was shuffling past the firehouse, because the Cranbury fire alarm was the loudest in the whole state. What a blast when it went off! And it was so sudden! There was no warning at all. Jane always said politely when she joined him here, "Don't we have the loudest fire alarm here in Cranbury?" This was just to remind him to be on guard and steel himself in case it blew.

Yes, she was doing everything she could to help him reach one hundred. Just this afternoon running home from the library, she had kicked aside a fallen branch, a broken bottle, an orange peel, so the way would be clear when Mr. Buckle came home. She even occasionally carried around an old umbrella so that he would not get caught in the rain. Of course she could not spend her whole time this way, but she did as much as she could.

Once she had seen Mr. Buckle go out and she had followed at a distance with the Moffats' big old umbrella. She really thought it might rain because the sparrows were chattering in the big elm tree in front of the house. Somebody told her once this was a sure sign of rain. When she reached the Green, there he was blowing cotton to the birds. Puffs of cotton on the grass looked like dandelions gone to seed.

Just as Janey arrived, the sky actually, all of a sudden, did turn black all over. The rain came marching up the street. She reached the oldest inhabitant and opened the umbrella over his head just as the big drops started to fall on his side of the street.

"This is very mysterious," he said, "your being on hand with the umbrella." And they had walked home together in the rain.

Now, while Jane was rocking back and forth in the green rocker, and reading her *St.*

Nicholas magazine, a fog began to roll in from the Sound. Jane looked up from her book. A fog! And it seemed to be growing thicker and thicker. She put her book down and watched it roll in. Soon she could hardly see the lot across the street. This was going to be a really heavy fog, perhaps as good a fog as they had in London.

She ran down the steps and up and down the Moffats' long lawn trying to separate the fog, as though it were a gauzy curtain. Then she could see what was going on in the world. As she reached the sidewalk, she slipped on some damp autumn leaves and ran into Miss Buckle, the daughter of the oldest inhabitant, who caught her in her arms.

"Goodness, Jane. What a start you gave me. I'm afraid I'm going to be late to P'fessor Fairweather's Browning Society. . . . Goodby, child."

And she set Jane firmly on the walk. Jane watched the oldest inhabitant's daughter disappear in the fog. P'fessor Fairweather . . . Jane liked the way she said that. She never said *Pro*fessor Fairweather. Just P'fessor Fairweather, very fast. That was nice, the way she talked. Everything she said sounded so important.

Well! Miss Buckle was going to the Browning Society, leaving the oldest inhabitant all alone. Jane hoped he had gotten home from the library in the fog safely. Supposing some witch who was exactly one hundred was jealous of him and had snatched him down under the squash vines that grew so thickly all over one corner of the lot. That's the way it might be if this were a fairy tale and not Ashbellows Place. However, fairy tale or not, she decided to spend the afternoon with the oldest inhabitant so he would not be tempted to go out in the fog.

Once the oldest inhabitant had said to her:

"Come in and see my chicken-bone furniture some day."

Today would be a good chance to do this. Of course she would not say she had come to call on him to keep him from getting lost in the fog. But she would say she had come to see his chicken-bone furniture. Besides she really owed him a visit since he had come to

her organ recital.

Jane ran into her house to get her knitting, for she intended to stay with the oldest inhabitant until the fog lifted. Then she marched up the street and onto Mr. Buckle's porch. She walked right in. She tiptoed through the little parlor with the black horse-hair chairs and sofa, and she went into the sitting-room, where the oldest inhabitant was bent over a big book. He balanced it halfway on his knees and halfway on the little oval-shaped table beside him.

"Hello, Mr. Buckle," said Jane politely.

"Hello, Jane," said the oldest inhabitant.

"I've come to see the bones," said Jane.

"Ah, yes," said the oldest inhabitant. "The chicken-bone furniture . . ."

Jane glanced around the room. She had never been in this house before. On one wall was a picture of the ruins of Pompeii, and on another was a picture of a lot of sheep huddled together in a blizzard. There was a picture exactly like this in Nancy's house. Jane preferred colored pictures such as the one the Moffats had in their green and white parlor of a milkmaid leading home the cows.

The oldest inhabitant showed her a little glass cabinet in a corner of the room. This held the furniture he had carved out of chicken bones. Jane stood with her hands behind her back so Mr. Buckle would not think she would touch things and break them. She looked at the chicken-bone furniture in amazement. What lovely little things! Tiny tables, chairs, cupboards, beds, a sofa, a bookcase with what looked like real little books, and even the tiniest of clocks!

"Oh, how nice!" exclaimed Jane.

"Yes . . . those are all carved out of chicken bones. Every piece. I did them all by hand."

"My," said Jane. "What a lot of chickens you must have eaten!"

"Yes . . ." said the oldest inhabitant. "They are very famous. Peabody Museum is asking for them all the time. My daughter frequently suggests that I give them to the Museum, but I like to keep them here."

Jane admired the chicken-bone furniture for quite some while. The oldest inhabitant sat down in his little rocking chair again.

Now that Jane had seen the chicken-bone furniture, she wondered if the oldest inhabitant expected her to go home. He had gone home after the organ recital. But first they had had cookies and grape juice. He might think if she stayed longer that she wanted something to eat. But she had resolved to stay until the fog lifted or Miss Buckle came home. However, she couldn't look at the chicken-bone furniture the whole afternoon. And he might get alarmed if she sat down and took out her knitting. He might think, "Goodness! Is she going to stay all day?"

That's what the Moffats always thought when Mrs. Price arrived and sat down with her knitting. For she usually did spend the entire afternoon there, while everybody was wanting to do something else.

Fortunately the oldest inhabitant spoke just then and relieved Jane of her embarrassment. "Well, middle Moffat. Now we have seen the chicken-bone furniture. How would you like to look at pictures through the stereoscope?"

"That would be nice," agreed Jane.

The oldest inhabitant went to a little closet in the corner and came back with a pile of pictures and the stereoscope. He put the pile of pictures on the table beside him and sat down. Jane pulled up a chair.

"Now you fit the pictures in and we'll look," said Mr. Buckle.

So Jane fitted a picture in the stereoscope and passed it to the oldest inhabitant, who adjusted it to his eyes. He peered at it with his white head thrust a little forward. Then he handed it to Jane and she adjusted it to her eyes. One by one they went through all the pictures this way. When it was Jane's turn to look, she never knew exactly how long she should look. She didn't want to look too long and make the oldest inhabitant tired of waiting for the next picture. And she didn't want to look too little and give the impression she was not appreciating the beauty of the scene. At length she decided to count up to ten, slowly. There! That was a good polite time to look at each one, she thought.

It really was funny how these two same pictures on the cards jumped together into

one picture when you looked at them through the stereoscope. In real life they looked like picture post cards with two identical pictures separated by a line down the middle. But through the stereoscope the two pictures hopped together into one.

How the man, walking along the woody path, suddenly jumped out at you! A real man in a straw hat! The mountains stood out from one another, and the waterfall looked as though it might splash you. A castle hidden in the trees suddenly emerged. You could almost pick the flowers, especially the edelweiss! There was a nearness and a farness to the pictures, as though you were standing on the top of Shingle Hill and looking at real scenery. But of course these scenes were of the Alps, not Shingle Hill. One picture showed an old Swiss with a long white beard sitting in front of his mountain cottage. Goats were nibbling the grass.

"Maybe the alms-uncle in 'Heidi,'" thought Jane.

"Another oldest inhabitant," said Mr. Buckle, laughing.

Jane smiled at him and looked a longer time, counting up to fifteen at this one.

When they had finished looking at the pictures, the oldest inhabitant said, "I see you have brought your knitting."

"Yes," said Jane. "A scarf for the soldiers in France."

She held it up for him to see. She wished she could knit red rows and blue rows for a change. Maybe she could change it into a helmet. It was not long enough for a scarf yet, but it was nearly long enough for a helmet.

"Would you change this into a helmet?" she asked the oldest inhabitant.

"It's supposed to be a scarf?"

"Yes."

"My goodness! Changing scarves into helmets! The mysterious middle Moffat!" exclaimed the oldest inhabitant.

Jane laughed, and whoops! she lost a stitch!

"Catch it! Catch it!" shouted the oldest inhabitant as though it were a runaway horse.

Jane sat down and clumsily recaptured the stitch.

"Narrow escape," said Mr. Buckle.

"My goodness," thought Jane. "He shouldn't shout like that. I better not drop any more stitches."

She knit one or two rows in silence. The oldest inhabitant watched her for a while and then he bent his head over his book. All you could hear now in the house was the sound of Janey's knitting needles clicking together, the soft breathing of the oldest inhabitant, and the tick-tock of the comfortable clock on the mantel. Mr. Buckle breathed in to the clock's tick and out to the clock's tock.

Jane knit and the clock tick-tocked. The quiet made her sleepy. She heard coal being dumped into Clara Pringle's cellar. Bag after bag rattled down the chute. What a lot of bags of coal they were getting, good hard black coal! Must be enough for a year at least. In the Moffats' house they never had more than one bag of coal at a time . . . She heard an occasional horse and wagon joggle by. Clop, clop. And she heard Joey call, "Ru-fus! Mama wants you to come home." All these noises sounded miles away.

Jane thought she would like to stretch her legs now and look out of the window, and see if she could see any of these things that were going on out there in the fog. But of course she did not do this. The oldest inhabitant might get it into his head that she did not like sitting here, or that he should offer her something to eat.

She looked at the oldest inhabitant to see if he had gone to sleep. But he hadn't, and he surprised her very much by saying, "How about a good game of double solitaire now?"

Double solitaire! Her favorite game! She and Joey and Rufus played it all the time. She nodded her head up and down. She would play slowly and let him win, she thought. She was the quickest double solitaire player of the Moffats. That was one thing, like running, that she was very good at. It made Rufus mad, she went so fast. She would be careful and not go too fast for the oldest inhabitant.

Mr. Buckle pushed aside the lamp, a small plaster model of the Yale Bowl, a copy of the *National Geographic*, and the red-fringed tablecloth. This table had a white marble top, wonderful for games! He pulled out a little drawer that was ordinarily hidden by the tablecloth and took out two decks of playing cards. Jane pulled her chair around opposite him, and they were ready to begin.

He gave her one deck of cards. "Shuffle!" he bade her.

Jane separated her pack of cards into two piles and shuffled one into the other. The oldest inhabitant did not like the way she shuffled.

"That is not the way to shuffle," he said. "This is the way to shuffle."

And he held the pack in his left hand, took some of the cards out with his right hand, and shuffled them back and forth so fast you couldn't see them. He was the fastest shuffler Jane had ever known.

"There," he said. "Now! We are ready to begin."

They laid out the cards neatly for the game and all was ready.

"Start!"

The oldest inhabitant bit out the words like a sergeant giving a command.

Start! The cards flew! Slap down the ace of hearts! Who would get the two on first? The oldest inhabitant! Slap on the three . . . the four. Ace of spades! Slap down the two . . . the three. Who'd get the four on first?

The oldest inhabitant!

He flipped the cards through the air between plays! The cards were flying! Slap on the jack . . . the queen . . . the king! Look at the diamonds! Build up the diamond pile. Who had the seven?

Janey!

Put it on quick. Down with the eight . . . the nine. The oldest inhabitant got his card there first almost every time. When he didn't, he put the card on the edge of the table, flipped it lightly in the air, making it turn a somersault, caught it neatly between thumb and forefinger, and returned it to its proper place while Jane was racing for the next card. Flying through the air, aces, spades, hearts, twos, threes, jacks, queens, everything!

Jane's head spun! Her eyes felt crossed. She played faster than she had ever played in her whole life in order to uphold the honor of the

Moffats. Let the oldest inhabitant win! Pooh! Not to be licked hollow the way she licked Clara Pringle, that's all she hoped for now.

The oldest inhabitant was winning! And not because she was letting him either. Letting him! What a foolish thought! The oldest inhabitant, a veteran of the Civil War, who sat on the reviewing stand for every important occasion, and gave out the diplomas at graduation . . . soon to be one hundred years old. . . . What had she been thinking? Letting him win! Of course a man such as this would win.

Mr. Buckle flipped his last card, the king of hearts, into the air. It turned a neat somersault right smack down on the heart pile.

The oldest inhabitant had won!

"There!" he beamed, rocking back and forth in his chair, his hands on his knees, watching while Jane finished up her last cards.

"Gee . . ." gasped Jane. "You're some player!"

"Shall we have another game?" he asked. "Or is it time for Nellie? She doesn't like me to play doubles."

And at that very moment the front door opened. The oldest inhabitant swept all the cards into the little drawer, yanked the tablecloth back into place, and the Yale Bowl, too! Just in time!

"Hello, Father. And, why, hello, Jane!" said Miss Buckle, bustling into the room, the cherries on her hat shaking and rattling together. "I declare . . . P'fessor Fairweather. . . . What an inspiration! My . . ."

Jane backed out of the room and out of the house, scarcely able to say good-by. Goodness! What a game! Her head was whirling and she still felt dizzy. She must practice that card trick. The one in which you flipped the card off the edge of the table and caught it neatly between thumb and forefinger. That would impress Joey and Rufus, and Nancy Stokes, too.

"Watch me!" she'd say. And the cards would flip through the air the way they had for the oldest inhabitant.

from Baseball Fever
Johanna Hurwitz

A historian with an interest in sociology, Ezra's scholarly father goes to his first baseball game, since Ezra has been trying to convince him that baseball is not a waste of time. This gently humorous book shows that a father and son can understand each other's interests even if they don't share them.

Mr. Feldman, the Rookie Baseball Fan

"I'll be glad to explain everything to you again," offered Ezra the afternoon they went to the baseball game together. He thought he had probably explained the game a dozen times over the past couple of years. Perhaps now his father was ready to understand.

"Not now," said Mr. Feldman. "I want to look around." He watched the people entering the ball park. He was fascinated to see that there were people of all ages and ethnic backgrounds in the stadium. "This is a wonderful cross section of American society," he said to Ezra.

Ezra had been thinking how best to describe the game to his father. He hit on the idea of comparing baseball to a game of chess. Each player, like each chessman, had certain moves to make. He tried to draw a chart comparing the pitchers on each baseball team to the kings. Then he decided that it would be better to compare the pitchers to the queens. After all, in some games there might be several pitchers, and queens could be replaced. But there is only one king. Perhaps the king would be equivalent to a manager. On the other hand, sometimes managers get thrown out of the game by the umpire. Ezra decided that he was just confusing himself. He would probably confuse his father too. So instead, he watched the players as they warmed up. He was happy to be at the game, and he hoped his father would enjoy it too.

Mr. Feldman didn't look at the field at all. "Do you mind if I ask you a few questions?" he said to a man on his left. "How often do you attend games, and how many games do you watch on TV?"

"What are you, a nut or something?" asked the man.

"No, no. I'm a historian with an interest in sociology," explained Mr. Feldman.

The man didn't seem to understand the difference, but eventually Mr. Feldman was able to engage him in conversation. He talked with him for a long time and took many notes. Then he offered to go and buy Ezra a hot dog. "Don't bother, Dad," said Ezra. "The game is just about to begin, and you don't want to miss any of it. Besides, they'll be coming around to sell them to us right here in a little while."

Nevertheless, Mr. Feldman went downstairs to get hot dogs. He returned with two of them and some information that he found astounding. "Do you know," he said, "I saw people watching the game and listening to it on portable radios at the same time!"

"Sure," said Ezra, "lots of people do that, so they can hear the descriptions of all the plays. Look over there." He pointed to a man sitting across the aisle.

"I can't believe it!" Mr. Feldman was stunned. The man had a small, battery-powered television set.

"Why does he bother to come?" Mr. Feldman asked Ezra. "I must go and interview him."

"No, Dad," said Ezra, "don't bother him. He won't want to talk during the game. He wants the TV set so he can see the instant replays of close calls."

"What is that?" asked Mr. Feldman. "This game is so complicated! But it speaks well of American intelligence that all these people can follow what is going on."

He sat staring at the field. Sometimes Ezra

cheered. Sometimes he clapped his hands in rhythm and shouted, "We want a hit!" Sometimes Ezra groaned. Ezra explained that the Mets were losing.

Mr. Feldman wrote quietly through it all. He filled page after page in his notebook. "I think I'll write an article about this," he said.

"No, Dad, you can't possibly write anything until you understand what is going on."

"You're right," agreed Mr. Feldman. "But I'll stick with it until I understand. There must be a reason why people pay good money to sit here. As soon as I understand it, I'll write about it—from a sociological point of view of course."

During the seventh-inning stretch, Mr. Feldman tried to interview a young couple sitting in front of them. The fellow was wearing a shirt that said M.I.T. (Monsters in Trousers, thought Ezra).

"You look as if you've had some education," Mr. Feldman said. "Perhaps you can explain why you would spend a Sunday sitting here watching all this." He waved his hand toward the playing area.

Instead of taking offense, as Ezra feared, the young man said, "When I watch a baseball game, it's all that matters. I don't have to worry about pollution, inflation, recession, communism, cancer, crime, or anything else. All I do is watch the ball." He looked at Mr. Feldman, who was writing down the words as fast as he could.

"Mister, you'd be a happier person if you threw away your pen and just watched that ball."

Mr. Feldman tried. From time to time, during the weeks that followed, he sat down beside Ezra as he watched a game on television. And Ezra, to show his appreciation of his father's new attitude toward baseball, continued to offer to play him a game of chess. After his one loss to his son, Mr. Feldman beat him as before, but Ezra didn't mind as much as he used to. And he noticed that his father had to work a little harder to get his win these days.

So by the time October rolled around that year, life was a whole new ball game for Ezra. Mr. Feldman had received a letter notifying him that he was awarded the grant that he had applied for in the spring. To celebrate, the Feldmans had dined at Chopmeat Charlie's, and that night even Ezra had steak.

The Mets had a good reason to celebrate too. They weren't in last place the way they'd often been in the past. This year they were in next-to-last place. It was an improvement. Mr. Feldman still didn't understand baseball. Yet he was trying harder to understand Ezra. He was much more relaxed about the time his son spent watching, thinking, and talking about baseball. He stopped complaining about Ezra's baseball-card collection, which now filled three shoe boxes.

Sometimes, to show that he was interested, he would come up to Ezra and ask, "Any FBI's lately?"

"FBI?" asked Ezra. "Don't you mean RBI?"

"What about the grand bangs?" asked Mr. Feldman, realizing that he had made another error.

"Grand slams," corrected Ezra. He smiled.

Mr. Feldman still didn't like pumpkin pie either.

"It's all right," Mrs. Feldman explained to her son. "It makes the world a much more interesting place if people have different interests and different tastes. Besides, this way there is more pie for you and me."

"And Harris, if he comes home," said Ezra.

"The important thing," she added, "is that you try to understand and respect each other, not whether you understand baseball or history or whatever."

Ezra realized that his father might never learn to understand and *speak* baseball. But as long as he didn't make fun of it, it wouldn't matter. Like speaking Greek, Ezra thought, some people could do it and some couldn't.

And when the baseball season ended that year, Ezra decided that he would read a book of chess openings. He had a good memory, like his father, and it would be the beginning of something new. Reading about chess would be something to pass the time till the next baseball season.

from How Many Miles to Babylon
Paula Fox

James is a lonely child who lives with his three aunts while his mother is in the hospital. Trapped by gang members in the solitary game of make-believe that comforts him, James is held captive. The mood and suspense of this selection are equally dramatic.

[Trapped by the Gang]

"James Douglas! You're sleeping!" cried Miss Meadowsweet.

His hand was damp where his cheek had rested against it. For a second, he couldn't see clearly. Everyone was laughing except the teacher. "The fours," she said.

"Four times one is four," said James, still in a daze.

An eraser hit him. "Who did that?" Miss Meadowsweet shouted; the children roared.

"Four times two is eight," James said, brushing the chalk dust off his shirt.

No one heard him. Perhaps he had wakened up into a little corner of a dream. But he saw the dark scars on his desk, the faces drawn with red ink, the carved words, the little ditch for a pencil.

Then the milk and crackers came and he didn't have to finish the fours. What were fours for? Why did he get so sleepy every morning about this time? He yawned.

"Cover your mouth with your hand when you yawn," said Miss Meadowsweet. He didn't see how she could spot him yawning in a room full of kids—dozens, fifty maybe. He didn't even know half of them. There were Buddy and Karen and Lucky who sat right near him, and a new boy in front of him who couldn't even speak English. The children called him *"Mira,"* because that's what he was always saying.

Lucky wasn't often in school because he liked to set the wastebasket on fire and he was always being sent home. Karen cried a lot. She cried when she got something wrong. She'd put her head down on her desk and say, "But I know the answer." Her notebook was full of gold stars and still she'd howl if she made just one little mistake. Buddy had used the masking tape Miss Meadowsweet kept on her desk to tape a knife to his arm. It was only a little knife but James could see where it bulged. Buddy would say, "You do what I say, James, or I cut you!" James didn't pay any attention because he knew it would take Buddy too long to get the masking tape off and get at the knife.

Then there was Ben. He was the biggest boy in the class. He wore a blue jacket and a necktie and he worked hard all the time. Ben never fooled around. He was Miss Meadowsweet's favorite—everybody knew that—but he didn't seem to care. She smiled at him, but Ben didn't smile at her. He just worked. At the end of the day he put his books in his canvas bag and he walked out of school, not looking to his left or right. He had such a stern expression on his face that even the older children made way for him in the corridors, and behind his back they called Ben "Deacon."

The Deacon was a different color from anyone else. There were light brown children in James' class, dark brown children like James and just a few white children. But Ben was pale brown as though he'd faded from some darker color, and he had golden freckles on his nose and his hair was reddish. James had seen him once in the church Aunt Grace and Aunt Althea took him to on Sunday. The church was just a little room you walked into right off the street and the Deacon had been sitting in the back. Right next to him was a little window with colored pieces of glass stuck into it, and the light fell on the Deacon's face so that his hair looked blue and his skin red.

After church, James saw the Deacon walking away between his father and mother. They were all dressed up in clothes that looked new, not like the clothes Aunt Grace and Aunt Althea brought back from the places where they worked. Aunt Paul never brought him old things. She said he had to have his own new clothes. She said she didn't want James walking around in somebody else's old raggedy pants and Aunt Althea had called her a dreamer.

It was reading time now. James opened his book. He didn't care much about clothes; it bothered him though when the pants were too big and slid down his hips, or when the shirts smelled funny as if they had been in the bottom of some dusty old bag.

"James Douglas! Come back to us!" He jumped in his seat and fumbled for his book which fell out of his hands to the floor.

"You leave it on the floor or I fix you," whispered Buddy. James paid no attention to him. Karen reached over and showed him the place where he was supposed to read. "Look, Jane, Look!" he read. Someone had drawn a little figure wearing a tall hat falling out of the window of Jane's and Dick's house. James made a mistake.

"Not *her*, James, but *here*. Come up to the blackboard and write out both words," said Miss Meadowsweet.

When he got to the blackboard he couldn't find any chalk.

"James, go to Mr. Johnson's room and ask Mr. Johnson to give you some chalk. Politely now!" said Miss Meadowsweet.

James left his classroom feeling sleepier

than ever. He must have waked up last night. He remembered now that he had seen Aunt Paul and Aunt Grace sitting in two straight chairs in front of the television set. The light from the screen had fallen on their faces and had made them look scary, like people made of wood.

What was it that had waked him? Was it Aunt Grace pointing at something he couldn't see on the screen and whispering, "Look at that! Look at the way those people behave themselves." But he was used to the Aunts whispering all night long, back and forth across the room, until the sound was like a song that rocked him back to sleep. Maybe it was the noise next door, right up against the wall where his bed was, a noise like furniture breaking.

Mr. Johnson's room was way down at the end of the corridor near the school entrance. Sometimes a policeman stood there and leaned up against the door with his hat tipped over half his face. He was a special policeman, not like the ones who directed traffic or the ones who sometimes came at night to James' building. He wore a thick black leather holster strapped to his hip. It was hard for James to imagine real feet inside the policeman's shoes.

He shivered. The policeman wasn't there today.

James felt suddenly wide awake. He hardly thought about what he was doing, but he walked right past Mr. Johnson's room and out through the front door onto the street.

The sunlight was pale yellow now, the gray clouds all swept away into one corner of the sky, like the dust Aunt Grace swept into a corner of their room every evening. He was cold but he couldn't go back to get his jacket. No, he couldn't walk into the classroom and say to Miss Meadowsweet, "I've come to get my jacket before I go." Perhaps he'd never be able to get his jacket.

Right across the street there was a row of buildings just like the one he lived in. Two yellow dogs chased a gray cat under an old black car, and all the people leaning up against the steps laughed.

What if Miss Meadowsweet came with a policeman and chased him while his three Aunts stood and watched and cried into their hands? He wouldn't be able to dive under a car like that cat. But they wouldn't find him, not where he was going. He felt in his pocket to make sure the ring was still there and then set off along the avenue.

He was a good walker. He had discovered that if he told himself stories, he could cover a lot of ground without noticing how much time it took. Once last year, all the subways in New York had stopped running because the men who ran the trains went on strike, and Aunt Paul had had to walk miles because the lady she worked for every day wouldn't pay her wages if she didn't show up. The subway workers wanted more money. That was easy for James to understand; everybody he knew wanted more money.

James' school was closed during the strike because the teachers couldn't get to it. So he and Aunt Paul had left early one morning, when the sun was barely up, and they had walked toward Flatbush Avenue with hundreds of people. When they finally got to the big apartment house where she worked, Aunt Paul said that she was just sick and hardly knew how she'd get through the day thinking about walking all the way back home. For the first time he could remember, Aunt Paul had been cross with him. She had told him to sit down on a chair in the lady's kitchen and *not move* until she said he could.

Walking away from school now, looking at his feet as they moved, first one, then the other, he told himself the story of that day. He had sat in the kitchen with all those green plants lined up on the window sill and looked at everything until the toaster and the coffee pot and all the pots and pans and the stove became one big silver blur. Then Aunt Paul had come in and said the Missus had gone out and he could look at the other rooms. The whole place was like a big store except that there were no price tags on anything. All the time he was looking, his Aunt Paul was wiping furniture or running the vacuum cleaner, or carrying a pail of water and a mop somewhere.

She had told him not to touch anything, but he did. He touched two white keys on the piano and he picked up a little carved sheep made out of some kind of white stone. The sheep had a bell that really rang tied around its neck. James wanted to put it in his pocket and take it home. Aunt Paul told him to put it right down. "She's very particular about her things," she had said. "If she catch you playing with that, I don't know what she'd do!"

Right inside that apartment there were two bathrooms, and so many closed doors he wondered if other families lived there. But most of the doors led to closets. "You can go into the boy's room," his Aunt had said, "but you stand right in the middle of the floor and don't hardly move."

The boy's room had shelves of toys and other shelves of books and a bicycle with its own stand in a corner. He couldn't bear that room, not while he had to be so still in the middle of the floor.

He had a piece of chocolate cake after his lunch. "Don't try to get it all in your mouth at once, Little Bits. There's plenty more," Aunt Paul had said.

Later that day the lady came back. She had on gloves and she patted his head. "Well . . . so this is *her* son," the lady had said to Aunt Paul. "Yes, ma'am. That's him," Aunt Paul had said. "Nice-looking," said the lady and she took a bunch of flowers from a vase and gave them to Aunt Paul. "You might catch a ride," she said. "I saw a lot of trucks stopping for people. Isn't it awful how this strike can tie up the whole city?" "Yes, ma'am," said Aunt Paul.

Aunt Paul filled her shopping bag with other paper bags and some balls of string, and she stuck the flowers in on top. Then they went down to the wide street which ran along beside a big park. They caught a ride too. A big truck with canvas flaps at the back stopped for them, and a lot of arms reached out and pulled them both in behind the flaps. James was so tired he had leaned against his Aunt. "That's where your mother worked before she got sick and had to go to the hospi-

tal," she said. The words woke him up. His mother had been in that same place and had known all about the bicycle and the little stone sheep with the bell. He sat in the dark thinking about those rooms with his mother walking through them, wondering why she had never told him about it, and smelling the funny sour smell of the flowers the lady had given Aunt Paul.

James had told himself the story of that day many times and each time he was able to remember more clearly what things had felt like and tasted like, how they had looked. It was the same with all the stories he told himself—whether they had really happened or not, they seemed to get clearer as he thought about them.

James looked up.

He had come to the street which his Aunts had told him never to cross. It was a different part of town, they said. On the other side of the street were little apartment houses, light brown, with curtains in the windows and little skinny black fire escapes zig-zagging down to the street. Last time he had been here, he had seen some children his own age playing ball on the sidewalk. Some of them had hair the color of margarine. Aunt Paul had said that this was the kind of place she'd like to live in, and Aunt Althea had laughed and declared that Aunt Paul's mind was leaving her.

He turned right and walked two blocks and then right again and there was the empty house. James had found it almost a month ago, right after his birthday and two months after his mother had gone away. It was a real house made of wood with a sagging wooden porch and a doorbell hanging out on its wire near the door. It had a peaked roof and most of the windows were broken. There was a little rusty fence like a line of written "m's" all around the front, and a soft old black tire inside where there were little tufts of yellowed grass.

Before he took a step on the path, James looked up and down the street. A woman was pushing a baby carriage around the corner. The two gray buildings on either side of the house showed no sign of life. Nobody leaned out of the windows like people did in his building. Across the street was a place where you took laundry. He could see some women sitting in front of the washing machines looking at magazines. The only living thing on the street at the moment was a little brown dog tied up to a bus-stop sign by a long rope. The dog watched him silently.

James wished the dog was not looking at him. He didn't want to be seen going into the house, even by a dog. He *knew* he shouldn't go into the house—it wasn't his house. But that wasn't the reason why he wanted the street to be empty when he walked up the little path. What he knew and what he felt were two different things. He felt that going into that house had to be something he did secretly, as though it were night and he moved among shadows.

The door was open enough to let him slip in without pushing it. Sunlight didn't penetrate the dirty windows, so he stood still until his eyes grew accustomed to the darkness. Then, as he smelled the dusty old rooms and the dampness of the wallpaper that was peeling off the walls, other things he felt came swimming toward him through the gloom like fish.

James knew that his mother had gotten so sick one night that she had had to go away to a hospital. He knew that she couldn't write to him because she had to wait until she got better before she could do anything except lie flat and still. Sometimes Aunt Grace got a letter from the hospital telling how she was coming along. He knew that he had once lived in another room where there had been only three people, his father, his mother and himself, and that his father was mostly home and his mother was out working, and that one night the light which had hung from the middle of the ceiling, like the light in his Aunt's room, had never gone out. His mother had spent that night standing next to the window looking into the street. After that he had not seen his father again, and when he asked his mother about him she had said,

"Gone, gone, gone. . . ." just like that, three times. Then they had moved in with the three Aunts, who were not really his Aunts but his father's. That same day someone had given him a bag of jelly beans.

That was the story of what had happened. But James had discovered another story hidden just beneath it. It was different from the first, but if he felt it, wasn't it true? When his Aunts talked about his mother being in the hospital, he wanted to tell them she was in Africa. Yet when he was walking along somewhere, thinking, or sitting at his desk in school, picturing her there in Africa, something in *him* said, no, she was sick and in the hospital. It was like having his arms yanked by two people going in different directions. But when he came to this house, the stories came together and were one.

Then James knew and felt the same thing! He was being guarded by those three old women so that no harm would come to him. His mother had gone across the ocean to their real country, and until she came back, no one was supposed to know who he really was. She had to fix everything. She had to see the people who lived in the deserts and the mountains, in the forests and the cities and tell them about him. But he knew he was not the only prince. He knew there were others. When everything was all right, all the princes would come together in a great clearing dressed in their long bright robes and their feathers, and after that everything would be different.

James knew how a prince would dress. He had seen pictures of princes and the villages they lived in. He had seen them dance on television and in the movies, but his mother had told him how the real life of all those princes had come to an end long ago, how they had been made to march for days and weeks through the wild forests, with their hands chained and their necks in ropes, until they came to a river where they were put in boats which carried them across the water.

Even though James had a good memory, he couldn't recall his mother ever telling him any other story except that one. She didn't talk much. But sitting there one morning across the table from him she had just begun, even though he wasn't looking at her. It was pouring rain outside and they were alone in the room. "What happened then?" he had asked her, because he was so afraid she would stop and not say any more, just get quiet the way she usually was and watch him and not speak. But she had gone on. She said that all those people would never recognize each other again, and no one knew who his own grandparents were.

But his mother must have found a secret paper that told all about James' great-great-great-grandfather who had been a king. She had left the ring for him so that he would know how hard she was working to make everything fine.

"King," he whispered to himself as he felt his way down the stairs to the basement. The word gave him courage. He hadn't gotten used to that basement yet, and some of the things he *knew* scared him: rats cannonballing out of corners, fanged like snakes, damp and gray; or the people who really owned the house suddenly coming back and finding him there, tying him up and sending him away to jail.

The basement was very cold. He fumbled around in the dark until his knees bumped up against the orange crate, then he reached in his pocket and took out a book of matches. He lit one and saw the soup can with the candle stub stuck in it. There was a strong draft blowing through the basement, so he had to light a lot of matches before he got the candle lit.

Great shadows swelled and sprang at the walls or shrank into dense black pools on the floor. James opened the box next to the can and took out the things he needed. There were some feathers from a duster, a little bottle of white paste and tubes and little jars of paint, blue and red and gray and white, that Aunt Althea had brought home one day in her shopping bag. There was a piece of red curtain he had found upstairs and a band with some feathers pasted on it and a pair of old slippers that Aunt Paul had thrown away.

When he had first come to the house, he had been able to go barefoot. But now it was too cold and the floor felt wet as though water had leaked in from the ground. The only sound he heard was the little noise he made opening jars. He began to paint his face, a line down his nose, across his forehead, slanting across his cheeks, but he didn't use very much because later he would have to rub it all off on the red curtain so that his Aunts wouldn't find a trace of it. Then he tied the band around his head, and the feathers hung down and tickled his cheeks. He stopped his work for a minute and ate a cheese cracker he found in his pocket. He wasn't scared now. He had even begun to feel quite warm. He tied the curtain around himself, making a big knot around his neck from two of the ends and pulling the other two in at his waist with a rope he'd found in the bathroom one morning. He took off his shoes and slid his feet into the slippers. Then, his heart beating faster, he took candle and ring and walked back to the other end of the basement.

The flicker of light showed him first the giant black boots, then the huge red-clothed legs, then the black belt with the silver buckle, then the white beard almost covering the face, the two apple cheeks, the small gleaming eyes, then the cap with the bell disappearing into the darkness above. He held the candle up high until he could see the whole giant cardboard figure, three times taller than he was, leaning up against the wall, the eyes staring straight ahead.

He put the candle down, placed the ring in front of the figure and clapped his hands softly, then harder. James began to dance, hopping on one foot and then the other, brushing his slippered feet on the floor, bending back and forward as far as he could. He never quite took his glance from the bright eyes of the figure. If the dance was right, those eyes would see him, recognize him, and his mother would know he had found the ring. Slowly his clapping grew louder; he bent and whirled until it seemed to him he was dancing before an immense fire that warmed and comforted him.

Then just when James thought the eyes had found him at last, he heard such a shriek that he spun on his heels and leapt back until he had fallen against the figure, his arms flung out, the feathered band falling over his face.

There was a second shriek, then shouts, and James realized that what he had heard was laughter.

"Look at—look at!" said a voice. "We got a Sandy Claus in our house!"

"Yeah. He got his dwarf with him too," said a second.

"Sandy Claus and his dwarf," said the first.

Two figures emerged from the darkness. One was tall and skinny and had a black cloth wrapped around his head. One earring gleamed in his ear. The other was short and plump and carried a torn umbrella, one of its metal ribs sticking straight out.

"Well, well, you never know, do you, Blue?" said the tall skinny one.

"No, Stick, you never do know."

"Can I go?" cried James, his voice trembling.

"The dwarf speaks English. Here I thought it'd speak Sandy Claus," said Stick.

"Yeah. That's just what I thought. Say a word in Sandy Claus, dwarf," said Blue.

"Please. Can I go?" pleaded James.

They stared down at him. They weren't so much bigger than he was after all, but big enough. Stick turned his head toward Blue.

"I just got an idea," said Stick. "We can use him to get the dogs."

"A whole idea?" said Blue. "You improving."

"We could use us a dwarf," said Stick, grinning.

"What's your name, dwarf?" asked Blue.

Thinking suddenly of his mother, her black hair tumbling down her back, dressed in a long white gown, stronger than anyone, thinking of the big clearing where all the people would come together, of the princes who would be there, James darted forward and picked up the ring. He held it out above the candle so they could see it. For a second he forgot what he knew, and only said what he felt.

"I'm a prince," he cried.

The two of them threw back their heads and shouted with laughter. They clutched themselves around their middles and staggered and stamped on the floor with their feet.

"A prince!" howled Blue.

"Yeah. A little black prince," yelled Stick. "Wait'll Gino hear this." Then they both stopped laughing at the same moment and Stick reached out and grabbed the ring from James' hand.

"Look here, he got himself a ring from a candy box. A ring for a black prince," said Stick.

"Let's see that valuable ring. Look at that! They let us in the subway for free if we flash this ring," said Blue. Then he threw the ring into the farthest corner of the basement.

James tore off the red curtain and ran for the stairs, but the big slippers tripped him up and Stick caught hold of his arm.

"No, no, Prince," said Blue. "You going to stay with us. We got work for you to do. If you be good, maybe we'll make you a king. We got the power, Prince. If you don't be good, we keep you a dwarf."

"Go get Gino," said Stick. "We got to change our plan."

from **Give Us a Great Big Smile, Rosy Cole**
Sheila Greenwald

Despite its gentle humor, this story of a child who can't be pushed into the family mold has a strong message about individuality, as Rosy resists family pressures.

My name is Rosy Cole and I'm in a lot of trouble. I've been in trouble now for six weeks, starting when I turned ten. I have two older sisters named Anitra and Pippa, a mother and a father named Sue and Mike, a cat named Pie, and an uncle Ralph, who is a successful photographer.

Because of Uncle Ralph we are a famous family.

My sister Anitra is thirteen. She studies ballet at the American School of Ballet. Three years ago when she was ten, Uncle Ralph did a book all about her. It was called *Anitra Dances.* It featured photographs of my sister looking cute and adorable and graceful in her tutu and leotard. The words in the book were supposed to sound like Anitra. I'll give you an idea of how this worked out.

In the book, when Anitra finds she didn't get the part of Mary in *The Nutcracker,* she says, "I am always a little sad when I don't get a part I try out for, but then I can learn so much from the person who does get the part because she must be better than I am, and I can improve myself so I'll be ready when my turn comes."

In real life, the day Anitra didn't get the part, she slammed the door and yelled, "That klutz Zora Slonim got the role in *The Nutcracker.* She can't dance her way out of a can of nuts. Pull, it's all pull. She moves like a spastic giraffe."

My sister Pippa is twelve. She is an equestrian. She loves to ride her horse, Doobie,

more than anything. Two years ago, when she was ten, Uncle Ralph did a book all about Pippa. It was called *Pippa Prances.* It showed beautiful photographs of Pippa in shows, jumping and galloping and fondling her horse, Doobie.

I have the two books in front of me on my desk. They are big and beautiful and have made my sisters famous and Uncle Ralph "in the dough."

They make me nervous and frequently depressed. *Anitra Dances* and *Pippa Prances.* For three years now I have been thinking, what does Rosy do? Take Chances? Give Cockeyed Glances?

Okay, so everything was moving along in its normal way until about six weeks ago, when I turned ten. I'm sure you can imagine that ten has been an important birthday in my family. The birth of a new celebrity.

As usual, this landmark event was celebrated at a restaurant called Gino's on the Park. We were all there. Mom, Dad, Anitra, Pippa, Uncle Ralph, and the Nikon. I blew out the candles.

Uncle Ralph aimed his camera and said, "Hey, Rose, Toots, are you or are you not going to be my next best-seller?"

Right then and there I realized I couldn't consider eating my own birthday cake. The piece of icing in my mouth simply stuck there like Crazy Glue. I excused myself to go to the ladies' room. I was only three feet from the table when I heard Uncle Ralph say to Mom, "Hey, Sis, has she pulled her act together?"

And I heard Mom say, "She's awfully good at drawing pictures, Ralph."

Ralph said, "Doesn't sound very visual. I mean, does she play tennis or swim or—you know what I mean, Sis."

"No, what do you mean, Ralph?"

"I mean I need another book real bad. I mean I am temporarily broke."

"You mean you've gone and lost at the track again," Mom said. "Honestly, Ralph, you are hopeless."

By then I was out of earshot. I spat my icing into the toilet and washed my face and began to cry.

A lady came into the washroom, so I sat down in one of the booths and closed the door and cried privately for the next three minutes. Those were the last good three minutes I can remember. As I walked up to the table, everybody was looking at me.

Mom said, "Rose, sweetheart, would you mind if Uncle Ralph goes over to watch you when you take your violin lessons this week?"

I didn't answer right away.

Uncle Ralph said, "I just want to see how it looks, Rose, Bush Babes. Just get the feel of it."

Now the truth of the matter is this: I have been taking violin lessons for two years. I go twice a week. I try to miss at least one lesson and arrive late for the other. The first lesson is a quartet. We play chamber music. It's me on violin, Debbie Prusock on viola, Hermione Wong on cello, and Linda Dildine on piano.

Ms. Radzinoff, who runs the School of Music, is an old friend of my mom's from college. Me and Ms. Radzinoff have a secret. We both know that the only reason she keeps teaching me is that my mom is an old friend. I didn't want anybody to learn this secret.

My next lesson was on Tuesday. Monday night I prayed that I would wake up with a terrible cold or a high fever. My prayers were not answered.

"Rosamond, don't forget you're meeting Uncle Ralph at music school," my mother reminded me at breakfast. "I called T.R."—that's Radzinoff—"to make sure it was all right."

Ever since I turned ten, I noticed my family called me Rosamond instead of Rosy.

I go to the Read School. It is a medium-sized private school on one of the side streets on the Upper East Side. I can walk to school. Anitra and Pippa are at a professional children's school. They used to go to Read.

Most mornings I walk to school with Hermione Wong. She is the same Hermione Wong who plays cello at Ms. Radzinoff's chamber-music class. Lately she has been super-friendly to me.

"Hi, Hermione," I said. "I thought you wouldn't have waited. I'm five minutes late." Hermione is a nut about being prompt.

"That's okay," she said. "I'd rather be late and walk with you. You are my best friend."

"Really?" This was news to me. I always thought I was more her most convenient friend. But I let this pass. We walked for half a block and didn't say anything because there was such a sharp April wind in our faces it was hard to talk.

Then Hermione said, "Say, Rosy, now that you are ten, isn't your uncle Ralph going to do a book about you?"

"I don't know," I said.

"Well, if he does, and I bet he does," Hermione chirped on, "I hope you remember I'm your best friend, and I'd love it if he got a picture of us together, just walking along to school or just talking in the lobby or maybe at my house or maybe just a picture of me carrying my book bag, waiting for you in the lobby."

"He could do a whole book on you," I said, "and call it *A Very Young Bag Lady.*"

Hermione pinched her lips together and shot me a very unfriendly look. We did not have any more to say to each other.

from Peter and Veronica
Marilyn Sachs

Peter and Veronica first met in an earlier book, Veronica Ganz. *After their original enmity, they have become close friends.*

[A Small Miracle]

"Are you sure it's all right if I come?" Veronica asked.

"Sure I'm sure," Peter said, even though he wasn't sure at all. With only three weeks to go now, he and his family were still deadlocked over Veronica. He had spoken to

Rabbi Weiss, and of course Rabbi Weiss had only said he must respect his parents' wishes. He had drawn Rosalie into the argument, and she had sided with him. But still his mother said no. Every night at his house there were more arguments, more scenes, more tears. The whole atmosphere began to feel more like a funeral, Peter thought, than a bar mitzvah.

So now, on this Friday afternoon, he had just gone ahead and invited her anyway. If his parents persisted in refusing to allow her to come, he had decided that he would ask them to call the whole thing off. But there was no point in going into details with Veronica. She knew how his mother felt about her. He knew how her mother (and Stanley), felt about him. Ever since their conversation on the library steps, it hadn't seemed necessary to discuss family matters any further.

"I mean—nobody'll mind if I come?" Veronica said carefully.

"Look," said Peter, "this is my party, and if I can't invite my friends, then it won't be much of a party. And I especially want you to come. As a matter of fact," Peter clenched his fists, "I want you to come more than anybody else. O.K.?"

"Well, thanks," Veronica said, her face thoughtful. "But what do I do? Where do I go?"

"First you come to the synagogue at nine o'clock in the morning. And then, after the services, you come to my house for the party."

"I've never been inside a synagogue before," Veronica said, twisting up her face. "Stop pulling my hand, Stanley! What do I have to do?"

"Nothing special. Just come and sit down. Oh, wear a hat and maybe a nice dress."

"Like church." Veronica nodded. "But what do I do inside?"

"It's easy. Sit down, and take a prayer book, and just do what everybody else is doing."

"Well, you know, Peter, I'm Lutheran, and I don't know if I'm supposed to do what everybody else is doing in a synagogue."

"Oh, that's right," said Peter. "Well, I guess you don't have to say or do anything if you don't want to. Some of the other kids who are coming aren't Jewish either. Just read the book or look around."

"What do you do?"

"I'm up in the front with the rabbi and the other boy who's being bar mitzvahed. The two of us read selections in Hebrew from the Torah—that's the first five books of the Bible —and then we make speeches."

"In front of everybody?"

"Uh, huh."

"Aren't you scared?"

"Nope." And he wasn't. Not about making the speech. It was going to be a good one, that he knew. Most bar-mitzvah speeches dealt with the debt of gratitude the boy owed to his parents and his teacher. Peter's speech would also contain the expected words of gratitude, but he had some other ideas he thought he might also like to include. This part of his speech he had not discussed with his teacher, preferring to develop it all by himself. The idea for it had actually grown out of his friendship with Veronica, and his struggle in her behalf. He had some polishing up to do, but by and large, the speech was completed. He was proud of it and of himself. It would be somewhat different from other bar-mitzvah speeches he had heard, somewhat more important, he thought. Of course, the way matters stood now, he might never get to give it at all.

"You just be there," he said grimly.

Stanley's skates skidded out from under him and he flopped down on the ground.

On this particular Friday, Stanley had again joined them, on skates, this time, and was occupied at present with clutching Veronica's hands, legs, skirts—whatever he could reach.

Veronica turned her attention to him. "Get up, Stanley, and don't hang on to me. You'll never learn to skate if you hang on."

Stanley remained seated on the ground. "If I don't hold on to you, you'll run away," he said pathetically.

"All right. I promise I won't run away. Now stand up. Here." She held out a hand to him. Stanley grabbed it with both hands and staggered to his feet.

"Now—let go!"

Stanley let go, swayed, skidded, and flopped again to the ground. He began hiccuping.

"Why don't we put him between us," Peter said, "and each of us hold one of his hands. That way we can balance him better."

"I'm not going to hold your hand," Stanley said, turning his special look of loathing on Peter.

"Now look," Veronica said sharply, "nobody wanted you along today, but you said you were just dying to skate. So get up, and you're going to skate whether you like it or not."

She pulled him to his feet, grabbed one hand, and motioned for him to give Peter his other hand. But Stanley's arm hung limply by his side. Peter put out his hand, took Stanley's, and Stanley clenched his fist so that Peter ended up holding his thumb. The three of them began moving along, Veronica and Peter supporting Stanley between them.

"Who else is going to be there?" Veronica asked, continuing the conversation.

"Marv, and Paul, and I have to ask Bill, and I guess some of the girls, and . . ."

"I'm not coming," Stanley said, lurching into Veronica.

"Nobody asked you," Veronica said, yanking him upright.

Around the corner came Roslyn Gellert and Reba Fleming. Reba began giggling as soon as she saw them, and Roslyn seemed to be studying something in another direction. There was strength in numbers, and Peter decided that this would be a fine time to invite Roslyn to his bar mitzvah. And since one should not harbor thoughts of malice at such an important occasion, he might as well ask that drip, Reba, too.

"Hey, Roslyn, Reba," he yelled, letting go of Stanley's hand and skating in their direction.

Stanley's feet flew out from under him and he fell down.

"Aw," said Reba, "the poor little kid."

She and Roslyn hurried over and helped Stanley up.

"Hello, Veronica," Roslyn said. "Is this your brother?"

"Yeah."

"What a cute little boy!"

Stanley grabbed hold of Roslyn and held on for dear life.

"Roslyn," said Peter, "I'd like you to come to my bar mitzvah. It's three weeks from tomorrow. You too, Reba."

"Thanks," said Reba. "I can come."

Stanley had one arm around Roslyn's neck and the other around her waist.

"There you are, honey," Roslyn cooed. "You won't fall. Just let go of my neck."

"Let go of her neck, Stanley," Veronica ordered.

But Stanley hung paralyzed where he was.

"You're choking me," gasped Roslyn.

Veronica grabbed Stanley and pulled. He hung on. She pulled harder.

"I can't breathe," Roslyn gurgled.

"Let go, Stanley," Peter yelled, and he tried to unfasten Stanley's fingers.

A strong yank from Veronica, and then Stanley came loose, and the two of them were rolling on top of each other on the ground.

"Roslyn," Peter repeated, "I'd like you to come to my bar mitzvah. It's going to be three weeks from tomorrow."

Roslyn's face was very pink. She looked at Stanley and Veronica twisted up together like a pretzel on the ground and suddenly began laughing. Peter followed her gaze. They sure did look funny, wrapped up in each other that way. He began snickering, too, and then Roslyn looked at him, and they smiled at each other, and it was all very comfortable and friendly again.

"I'd love to come Peter. Thanks. I'm sure I can make it."

"Swell," Peter said enthusiastically, and then he added quickly, "How's everything? How are you doing in math?"

"O.K., I guess."

"Well now, don't forget, if you need any help, just ask me."

Roslyn looked away. "Thanks, Peter," she said softly, "I will." She took Reba's arm. " 'By now, 'By Veronica, 'By Stanley."

The living knot had disentangled itself and began to assume the vertical. Veronica's face was angry.

"Come on, Stanley, we're going home." She pulled Stanley to his feet and began skating away from Peter.

"Hey, wait," Peter yelled, going after her. "What's wrong?"

"You laughed," Veronica said sullenly.

"Well, so what? You sure looked funny, the two of you."

"If it was you, you wouldn't think it was so funny. I'm going home."

Peter put an arm on Veronica's shoulder. "Don't be like that, Veronica. I'm sorry if I laughed, but—here—this is what you looked like."

He began lurching back and forth, making crazy, clownlike gestures. Finally he let one skate skid and went down, twisting himself up as he went.

Veronica looked down at him coldly.

He crossed his eyes at her.

She pursed up her lips in disdain.

He made Mortimer Snerd noises at her. She blinked. Then he began waggling his tongue and trying to lick his nose. Veronica burst out laughing, and Stanley said sadly, "Aren't we going home, Veronica?"

Peter leaned back on his hands and smiled fondly at Stanley. The kid had his good points after all, and now Roslyn and he were friends again.

"Come on, Stanley, let's skate," said Peter. He stood up, reached for Stanley's thumb where it hung limply at the end of an unresponsive arm, and the three of them were off again.

They came to a big hill, leading down to a busy thoroughfare. He and Veronica had zoomed down it many a time, turning sharply at the end of it to avoid the heavy traffic that always whizzed along the cross street. They stood on the crest, looking down hungrily, and Veronica said, "You sit here, Stanley, and we'll be back up in a second."

"No!" said Stanley.

She took him by both arms and sat him down, protesting, on the pavement.

"Let's go," she cried, and she and Peter flew down the hill with the wind and Stanley's cries spurring them on. At the bottom, each turned sharply in different directions, finding anchorage in the parked cars along the curb.

They climbed back up the hill and Stanley was waiting for them.

"I want to go down too," he said.

"No," said Veronica. "You can't even skate."

"You take me."

"No!"

Stanley hicced, and Peter said generously, grateful for Stanley's presence today, "Look, if I hold him by one hand and you hold him by the other, we can do it."

"No!"

"I wanna go," shouted Stanley. "I wanna go."

He offered his thumb to Peter, and Veronica smiled and said, "Well . . ."

"I wanna go."

"O.K.," said Veronica, "but don't fall."

The three of them stood poised at the top of the hill.

"Get ready," said Peter, "get set."

"Go," shouted Stanley.

And they were off. Peter tried hard to keep a tight grip on Stanley's thumb, but it kept wiggling. Stanley managed to skim along with them though, and at the bottom he yanked his thumb out of Peter's hand. Thinking that Stanley had gone along with Veronica, Peter made his sharp turn, anchored himself around a parked car, and turned, smiling, to look at Veronica and Stanley. There was only Veronica on the opposite side of the street, leaning against a parked car and looking at him in horror.

"Didn't he go with you?" she shouted.

"No—didn't he go with you?"

"Oh—no!"

For a moment he couldn't look. He just couldn't. All those cars and buses whizzing along, and little Stanley, poor, little Stanley who couldn't skate, somewhere lost under them.

And then Veronica began screaming, "Stanley! Stanley! Stanley!"

Peter took a deep, terrified breath and looked. The cars were still whizzing along, and from across the broad, busy street, Stanley stood on the sidewalk, waving and laughing and marvelously safe.

Peter got across first. "Are you all right?" he cried. "What happened?"

And then Veronica was there. She grabbed Stanley, and pulled him close to her, and said, "Stanley, Stanley, oh, Stanley!"

"I can skate," Stanley said, pushing her away. "Now, I can skate. Come on, Peter. Let's do it again."

He offered Peter his whole hand this time, which was, in this afternoon of miracles, the greatest miracle of all.

from From the Mixed-Up Files of Mrs. Basil E. Frankweiler
Elaine Konigsburg

The winner of the 1968 Newbery Medal is this story of Claudia Kincaid and her brother Jamie, who hide out in the Metropolitan Museum of Art in New York City so that Claudia's absence will, she hopes, cause her family to appreciate her.

["Checking-in" at the Met]

On Monday afternoon Claudia told Jamie at the school bus stop that she wanted him to sit with her because she had something important to tell him. Usually, the four Kincaid children neither waited for each other nor walked together, except for Kevin who was somebody's charge each week. School had begun on the Wednesday after Labor Day. Therefore, their "fiscal week" as Claudia chose to call it began always on Wednesday. Kevin was only six and in the first grade and was made much over by everyone, especially by Mrs. Kincaid, Claudia thought. Claudia also thought that he was terribly babied and

impossibly spoiled. You would think that her parents would know something about raising children by the time Kevin, their fourth, came along. But her parents hadn't learned. She couldn't remember being anyone's charge when she was in the first grade. Her mother had simply met her at the bus stop every day.

Jamie wanted to sit with his buddy, Bruce. They played cards on the bus; each day meant a continuation of the day before. (The game was nothing very complicated, Saxonberg. Nothing terribly refined. They played *war,* that simple game where each player puts down a card, and the higher card takes both. If the cards are the same, there is a war which involves putting down more cards; winner then takes all the war cards.) Every night when Bruce got off at his stop, he'd take his stack of cards home with him. Jamie would do the same. They always took a vow not to shuffle. At the stop before Bruce's house, they would stop playing, wrap a rubber band around each pile, hold the stack under each other's chin and spit on each other's deck saying, "Thou shalt not shuffle." Then each tapped his deck and put it in his pocket.

Claudia found the whole procedure disgusting, so she suffered no feelings of guilt when she pulled Jamie away from his precious game. Jamie was mad, though. He was in no mood to listen to Claudia. He sat slumped in his seat with his lips pooched out and his eyebrows pulled down on top of his eyes. He looked like a miniature, clean-shaven Neanderthal man. Claudia didn't say anything. She waited for him to cool off.

Jamie spoke first, "Gosh, Claude, why don't you pick on Steve?"

Claudia answered, "I thought, Jamie, that you'd see that it's obvious I don't want Steve."

"Well," Jamie pleaded, "want him! Want him!"

Claudia had planned her speech. "I want you, Jamie, for the greatest adventure in our lives."

Jamie muttered. "Well, I wouldn't mind if you'd pick on someone else."

Claudia looked out the window and didn't answer. Jamie said, "As long as you've got me here, tell me."

Claudia still said nothing and still looked out the window. Jamie became impatient. "I said that as long as you've got me here, you may as well tell me."

Claudia remained silent. Jamie erupted, "What's the matter with you, Claude? First you bust up my card game, then you don't tell me. It's undecent."

"Break up, not bust up. Indecent, not undecent," Claudia corrected.

"Oh, boloney! You know what I mean. Now tell me," he demanded.

"I've picked you to accompany me on the greatest adventure of our mutual lives," Claudia repeated.

"You said that." He clenched his teeth. "Now tell me."

"I've decided to run away from home, and I've chosen you to accompany me."

"Why pick on me? Why not pick on Steve?" he asked.

Claudia sighed, "I don't want Steve. Steve is one of the things in my life that I'm running away from. I want you."

Despite himself, Jamie felt flattered. (Flattery is as important a machine as the lever, isn't it, Saxonberg? Give it a proper place to rest, and it can move the world.) It moved Jamie. He stopped thinking, "Why pick on me?" and started thinking, "I am chosen." He sat up in his seat, unzipped his jacket, put one foot up on the seat, placed his hands over his bent knee and said out of the corner of his mouth, "O.K., Claude, when do we bust out of here? And how?"

Claudia stifled the urge to correct his grammar again. "On Wednesday. Here's the plan. Listen carefully."

Jamie squinted his eyes and said, "Make it complicated, Claude. I like complications."

Claudia laughed. "It's got to be simple to work. We'll go on Wednesday because

Wednesday is music lesson day. I'm taking my violin out of its case and am packing it full of clothes. You do the same with your trumpet case. Take as much clean underwear as possible and socks and at least one other shirt with you."

"All in a trumpet case? I should have taken up the bass fiddle."

"You can use some of the room in my case. Also use your book bag. Take your transistor radio."

"Can I wear sneakers?" Jamie asked.

Claudia answered, "Of course. Wearing shoes all the time is one of the tyrannies you'll escape by coming with me."

Jamie smiled, and Claudia knew that now was the correct time to ask. She almost managed to sound casual. "And bring all your money." She cleared her throat. "By the way, how much money do you have?"

Jamie put his foot back down on the floor, looked out the window and said, "Why do you want to know?"

"For goodness' sake, Jamie, if we're in this together, then we're together. I've got to know. How much do you have?"

"Can I trust you not to talk?" he asked.

Claudia was getting mad. "Did *I* ask *you* if I could trust you not to talk?" She clamped her mouth shut and let out twin whiffs of air through her nostrils; had she done it any harder or any louder, it would have been called a snort.

"Well, you see, Claude," Jamie whispered, "I have quite a lot of money."

Claudia thought that old Jamie would end up being a business tycoon someday. Or at least a tax attorney like their grandfather. She said nothing to Jamie.

Jamie continued, "Claude, don't tell Mom or Dad, but I gamble. I play those card games with Bruce for money. Every Friday we count our cards, and he pays me. Two cents for every card I have more than he has and five cents for every ace. And I always have more cards than he has and at least one more ace."

Claudia lost all patience. "Tell me how much you have! Four dollars? Five? How much?"

Jamie nuzzled himself further into the corner of the bus seat and sang, "Twenty-four dollars and forty-three cents." Claudia gasped, and Jamie, enjoying her reaction, added, "Hang around until Friday and I'll make it twenty-five even."

"How can you do that? Your allowance is only twenty-five cents. Twenty-four forty-three plus twenty-five cents makes only twenty-four dollars and sixty-eight cents." Details never escaped Claudia.

"I'll win the rest from Bruce."

"C'mon now, James, how can you know on Monday that you'll win on Friday?"

"I just know that I will," he answered.

"How do you know?"

"I'll never tell." He looked straight at Claudia to see her reaction. She looked puzzled. He smiled, and so did she, for she then felt more certain than ever that she had chosen the correct brother for a partner in escape. They complemented each other perfectly. She was cautious (about everything but money) and poor; he was adventurous (about everything but money) and rich. More than twenty-four dollars. That would be quite a nice boodle to put in their knapsacks if they were using knapsacks instead of instrument cases. She already had four dollars and eighteen cents. They would escape in comfort.

Jamie waited while she thought. "Well? What do you say? Want to wait until Friday?"

Claudia hesitated only a minute more before deciding, "No, we have to go on Wednesday. I'll write you full details of my plan. You must show the plan to no one. Memorize all the details; then destroy my note."

"Do I have to eat it?" Jamie asked.

"Tearing it up and putting it in the trash would be much simpler. No one in our family but me ever goes through the trash. And I only do if it is not sloppy and not full of pencil sharpener shavings. Or ashes."

"I'll eat it. I like complications," Jamie said.

"You must also like wood pulp," Claudia said. "That's what paper is made of, you know."

"I know. I know," Jamie answered. They spoke no more until they got off the bus at their stop. Steve got off the bus after Jamie and Claudia.

Steve yelled, "Claude! Claude! It's your turn to take Kevin. I'll tell Mom if you forget."

Claudia who had been walking up ahead with Jamie stopped short, ran back, grabbed Kevin's hand and started retracing her steps, pulling him along to the side and slightly behind.

"I wanna walk with Stevie," Kevin cried.

"That would be just fine with me, Kevin Brat," Claudia answered. "But today you happen to be my responsibility."

"Whose 'sponsibility am I next?" he asked.

"Wednesday starts Steve's turn," Claudia answered.

"I wish it could be Steve's turn every week," Kevin whined.

"You just may get your wish."

Kevin never realized then or ever that he had been given a clue, and he pouted all the way home.

On Tuesday night Jamie found his list of instructions under his pillow pinned to his pajamas. His first instruction was to forget his homework; get ready for the trip instead. I wholeheartedly admire Claudia's thoroughness. Her concern for delicate details is as well developed as mine. Her note to Jamie even included a suggestion for hiding his trumpet when he took it out of its case. He was to roll it up in his extra blanket, which was always placed at the foot of his bed.

After he had followed all the instructions on the list, Jamie took a big glass of water from the bathroom and sat cross-legged on the bed. He bit off a large corner of the list. The paper tasted like the bubble gum he had once saved and chewed for five days; it was just as tasteless and only slightly harder. Since the ink was not waterproof, it turned his teeth blue. He tried only one more bite before he tore up the note, crumpled the pieces, and threw them into the trash. Then he brushed his teeth.

The next morning Claudia and Jamie boarded the school bus as usual, according to plan. They sat together in the back and continued sitting there when they arrived at school and everyone got out of the bus. No one was supposed to notice this, and no one did. There was so much jostling and searching for homework papers and mittens that no one paid any attention to anything except personal possessions until they were well up the walk to school. Claudia had instructed Jamie to pull his feet up and crouch his head down so that Herbert, the driver, couldn't see him. He did, and she did the same. If they were spotted, the plan was to go to school and fake out their schedules as best they could, having neither books in their bags nor musical instruments in their cases.

They lay over their book bags and over the trumpet and violin cases. Each held his breath for a long time, and each resisted at least four temptations to peek up and see what was going on. Claudia pretended that she was blind and had to depend upon her senses of hearing, touch, and smell. When they heard the last of the feet going down the steps and the motor start again, they lifted their chins slightly and smiled—at each other.

Herbert would now take the bus to the lot on the Boston Post Road where the school buses parked. Then he would get out of the bus and get into his car and go wherever else he always went. James and Claudia practiced silence all during the ragged ride to the parking lot. The bus bounced along like an empty cracker box on wheels—almost empty. Fortunately, the bumps made it noisy. Otherwise, Claudia would have worried for fear the driver could hear her heart, for it sounded to her like their electric percolator brewing the morning's coffee. She didn't like keeping her head down so long. Perspiration was causing her cheek to stick to the plastic seat; she was convinced that she would develop a medium-serious skin disease within five minutes after she got off the bus.

The bus came to a stop. They heard the door open. Just a few backward steps by Herbert, and they would be discovered. They held their breath until they heard him walk down the steps and out of the bus. Then they heard the door close. After he got out, Herbert reached in from the small side window to operate the lever that closed the door.

Claudia slowly pulled her arm in front of her and glanced at her watch. She would give Herbert seven minutes before she would lift her head. When the time was up, both of them knew that they could get up, but both wanted to see if they could hold out a little bit longer, and they did. They stayed crouched down for about forty-five more seconds, but being cramped and uncomfortable, it seemed like forty-five more minutes.

When they got up, both were grinning. They peeked out of the window of the bus, and saw that the coast was clear. There was no need to hurry so they slowly made their way up to the front, Claudia leading. The door lever was left of the driver's seat, and as she walked toward it, she heard an awful racket behind her.

"Jamie," she whispered, "what's all that racket?"

Jamie stopped, and so did the noise. "What racket?" he demanded.

"You," she said. "You are the racket. What in the world are you wearing? Chain mail?"

"I'm just wearing my usual. Starting from the bottom, I have B.V.D. briefs, size ten, one tee shirt . . ."

"Oh, for goodness' sake, I know all that. What are you wearing that makes so much noise?"

"Twenty-four dollars and forty-three cents."

Claudia saw then that his pockets were so heavy they were pulling his pants down. There was a gap of an inch and a half between the bottom hem of his shirt and the top of his pants. A line of winter white skin was punctuated by his navel.

"How come all your money is in change? It rattles."

"Bruce pays off in pennies and nickels. What did you expect him to pay me in? Traveler's checks?"

"O.K. O.K.," Claudia said. "What's that hanging from your belt?"

"My compass. Got it for my birthday last year."

"Why did you bother bringing that? You're carrying enough weight around already."

"You need a compass to find your way in the woods. Out of the woods, too. Everyone uses a compass for that."

"What woods?" Claudia asked.

"The woods we'll be hiding out in," Jamie answered.

"Hiding *out in?* What kind of language is that?"

"English language. That's what kind."

"Who ever told you that we were going to hide out in the woods?" Claudia demanded.

"There! You said it. You said it!" Jamie shrieked.

"Said what? I never said we're going to hide out in the woods." Now Claudia was yelling, too.

"No! you said '*hide out in.*'"

"I did not!"

Jamie exploded. "You did, too. You said, 'Who ever told you that we're going to *hide out in* the woods?' You said that."

"O.K. O.K." Claudia replied. She was trying hard to remain calm, for she knew that a group leader must never lose control of herself, even if the group she leads consists of only herself and one brother brat. "O.K.," she repeated. "I *may* have said hide *out in,* but I didn't say *the woods.*"

"Yes, sir. You said, 'Who ever told you that . . .'"

Claudia didn't give him a chance to finish. "I know. I know. Now, let's begin by my saying that we are going to hide out in the Metropolitan Museum of Art in New York City."

Jamie said, "See! See! you said it again."

"I did not! I said, 'The Metropolitan Museum of Art.'"

"You said *hide out in* again."

"All right. Let's forget the English language lessons. We are going to the Metropolitan Museum of Art in Manhattan."

For the first time, the meaning instead of the grammar of what Claudia had said penetrated.

"The Metropolitan Museum of Art! Boloney!" he exclaimed. "What kind of crazy idea is that?"

Claudia now felt that she had control of herself and Jamie and the situation. For the past few minutes they had forgotten that they were stowaways on the school bus and had behaved as they always did at home. She said, "Let's get off this bus and on the train, and I'll tell you about it."

Once again James Kincaid felt cheated. "The train! Can't we even hitchhike to New York?"

"Hitchhike? and take a chance of getting kidnapped or robbed? Or we could even get mugged," Claudia replied.

"Robbed? Why are you worried about that? It's mostly my money," Jamie told her.

"We're in this together. It's mostly your money we're using, but it's all my idea we're using. We'll take the train."

"Of all the sissy ways to run away and of all the sissy places to run away to. . . ." Jamie mumbled.

He didn't mumble quite softly enough. Claudia turned on him, "Run *away to?* How can you run *away* and *to?* What kind of language is that?" Claudia asked.

"The American language," Jamie answered. "American James Kincaidian language." And they both left the bus forgetting caution and remembering only their quarrel.

They were not discovered.

On the way to the train station Claudia mailed two letters.

"What were those?" Jamie asked.

"One was a note to Mom and Dad to tell them that we are leaving home and not to call the FBI. They'll get it tomorrow or the day after."

"And the other?"

"The other was two box tops from corn flakes. They send you twenty-five cents if you mail them two box tops with stars on the tops. For milk money, it said."

"You should have sent that in before. We could use twenty-five cents more."

"We just finished eating the second box of corn flakes this morning," Claudia informed him.

They arrived at the Greenwich station in time to catch the 10:42 local. The train was not filled with either commuters or lady shoppers, so Claudia walked up the aisles of one car and then another until she found a pair of chairs that dissatisfied her the least with regard to the amount of dust and lint on the blue velvet mohair covers. Jamie spent seven of the twenty-eight-and-a-half railroad miles trying to convince his sister that they should try hiding in Central Park. Claudia appointed him treasurer; he would not only hold all the money, he would also keep track of it and pass judgment on all expenditures. Then Jamie began to feel that the Metropolitan offered several advantages and would provide adventure enough.

And in the course of those miles Claudia stopped regretting bringing Jamie along. In fact when they emerged from the train at Grand Central into the underworld of cement and steel that leads to the terminal, Claudia felt that having Jamie there was important. (Ah, how well I know those feelings of hot and hollow that come from that dimly lit concrete ramp.) And his money and radio were not the only reasons. Manhattan called for the courage of at least two Kincaids.

from Queenie Peavy
Robert Burch

Set in rural Georgia during the Great Depression, Queenie's story reflects the impact of hard times on a community, but it is primarily a perceptive portrayal of a child molded by circumstance and rising above it by her own efforts.

The Pride of the County

The next afternoon Queenie didn't try to catch Persimmon the way she had been doing. She decided not to risk making matters worse by getting into another scrap. She

was still hurt that he had done her such a mean turn, but it was not nearly so important to her now. The thing that mattered was that her father had been paroled, and she hurried home to see him.

Her mother had taken half a day off from the canning plant, and was with her father in the house. They were sitting in her mother's room—only from now on it would be her father's room, too.

"Pa!" cried Queenie excitedly. "You're home!" She ran over to the rocking chair where he sat, planning to kiss him. But he did not reach out to her and she stopped abruptly and stood in front of him. She didn't know what to say next, so she said again, "You're home." This time she said it as if she couldn't quite believe it.

"Yes, I'm home," said her father, smiling at her.

"I'm glad you are," said Queenie. "I sure am glad you are."

"Me, too," said her father. "Anything beats the penitentiary." He got to his feet, and she thought maybe he was going to put his arms around her. Maybe he had been so overcome by seeing her again that he'd been too happy to know what to do at first. But he started toward the kitchen. "I'm thirsty," he said. "Is the bucket still in the same place?"

"I'll get you a dipperful," said Queenie, hurrying to bring him the gourd filled with water.

When he took it, he noticed his daughter's height and said, "You get lankier and lankier, don't you, String Bean?"

Queenie laughed. "I sure do, Pa. Lankier and lankier."

"She's getting prettier," said her mother, while Mr. Peavy drank the water. "Why can't you tell her that?"

Her father handed back the dipper. "Cain't tell her anything I ain't noticed," he said, slapping Queenie on the back. Both of them laughed, but her mother did not. Her father continued, "Go do your night work, Queenie. We're gonna eat supper early and go into town."

"Are we really?" asked Queenie.

"Just your ma and me. We got to see some

folks."

Queenie's smile disappeared as she started out. "Don't you want to come with me and see how the chickens are looking and all?"

"Cain't say that I do," said her father, sitting back in the rocker.

Queenie left, but she was sorry to be urged out of the house. She wanted to talk with her father—and just get to look at him for a while, too. And besides, it was early for doing the chores. She told Ol' Dominick, after she had fed the chickens, "You think I'm going crazy, don't you?—doing the night work ahead of time. And unless you tell 'em better, those dumb hens will be so confused they'll decide it's time to go to roost." He flew onto the post that held the clothesline, flapped his wings, and crowed. Queenie reached up and patted him. "Tell 'em again!" she said, and he crowed once more as she walked away.

Sweetheart was not at the gate or anywhere in sight, and Queenie walked down into the pasture. She brooded over being sent from the house until she thought of the most likely reason her father and mother were going into town. She guessed they would call on Sheriff Townsend and Deputy Ellins, and Judge Lewis, if they got there before he left his office, and maybe Cravey Mason's father, too, since it seemed that he was one of the main ones agitating for something to be done about her. She imagined her father was going to ask everybody to leave his daughter alone. He would assure them that his girl would be so good, now that he was home, that everyone in these parts would be proud of her. Queenie Peavy would be the pride of the county.

That's what she was thinking when she finally located Sweetheart on the far side of the pasture, eating kudzu through the barbed-wire fence. Amaryllis was there, too, and Queenie drove both cows to the barn. By the time she got there it was almost the usual milking time.

Elgin Corry came along soon, followed by Dover, Avis, and Matilda. Avis and Dover swung on the door of one of the stables and Matilda sat and watched them. Elgin said, "Children, don't make me have to tell you again that you're too heavy for such as that. You'll ruin the hinges." They went into another part of the barn and a few moments later the squeaking sounds of the feed-room door opening and closing indicated that they were swinging on it. But Elgin did not call to them. Instead, he told Queenie, "I hate to stay on 'em all the time. I can remember when I was their age it came natural to always be swinging on anything that would move."

Queenie got up from her milking stool to pour a pan of milk into the bucket. When she sat down again, she said, "Pa's home. Did you know that?"

"I heard he was coming. How's he getting along?"

"He's fine," she answered cheerily. "He sure is glad to get home and see me and Mamma again."

She waited for Elgin to say how pleased he was to hear the news; but instead he called to Avis and Dover, "Come here a minute, I want to talk to you." They came over and stood near him and he continued, "Queenie tells me that Mr. Peavy is home."

"Yes, sir," said Avis. "We heard. We were sitting over there in the feed room all the time."

Elgin laughed. "You were swinging on the feed-room door, you mean. But that's not why I called you. I want to remind you that you're not to be playing near Queenie's house any more. Do you hear me?"

"How come?" asked Dover.

" 'Cause I said not to," answered Elgin sternly. "And 'cause Mr. Peavy might not like it if you yell and holler and carry on with a lot of noise. His nerves may not be too good after all he's been through and—"

Queenie interrupted. "Oh, Pa's nerves are just fine. And if you suspect he's apt to get mad and chase Dover and Avis off, I'm sure he won't. Oh, I know some folks claim Pa's got a mean streak, but they don't know him, that's all."

Someone in the doorway of the barn said, "You tell 'em, String Bean!" and Queenie looked up to see her father coming inside. He spoke to Elgin, who had got up to turn Amaryllis into the lot.

"Howdy," greeted Elgin.

Queenie's father asked, "How's it going?"

"Fine, I reckon. Glad to see you back."

Dover and Avis began edging away, but Elgin stopped them. "Children," he said, "say 'hello' to Mr. Peavy."

Dover said, "Howdy-do, Mr. Peavy," but bashfulness suddenly came on Avis and she looked down at the ground and would not lift her head.

Queenie said, "They've grown a heap since you saw them, haven't they, Pa?"

"Not as much as you," he said pleasantly. "But I came to tell you that your ma and I are leaving for town."

"But what about your supper?"

"After you were so long getting back, we went ahead and ate."

"I had to hunt for Sweetheart," explained Queenie as her father left the stable.

He called back to her, "Your supper's on the stove."

Queenie felt cheated. Here he was home and she had barely seen or talked to him. She reminded herself, however, that it was probably on her account that he was so anxious to go into town. He must not be able to wait another minute to get started. She called after him, "Bye, Pa. Have a good time in town!" But if he heard her he did not turn around to answer.

Queenie ate supper by herself and then put away the dishes from the kitchen table and brought out her books. She planned to excel in her school work tomorrow. And she would behave so well, too, that everybody would see right off the change that had come over her the minute her father got home. Nobody was apt to say anything that would make her mad, she knew, since the remarks that unloosed her temper always had to do with her father's being in prison. Now that he was home, nobody could irritate her about it. But even if they could, she decided, she wouldn't let it upset her—because she was going to improve so drastically. She intended to astound everyone: Queenie Peavy would definitely be the pride of the county!

She studied her algebra problems for the next day, reworking each one until she understood it clearly, and then stopped to think more about her own situation. She wondered where her parents were at that moment. Had they seen Sheriff Townsend already? Had they arrived in town before Judge Lewis left? What about Cravey's father? She bet they would talk sense into everybody before the night was over, and she wouldn't any more have to go off to that ol' reformatory than a jack rabbit.

She got out her notebook and began writing sentences for English homework. "My rooster's name is Ol' Dominick," she wrote first. It showed the apostrophe being used to denote possession in one instance and to take the place of an omitted letter in another. "Well, how about that!" she said to herself, pleased that she had come across the second example accidentally.

Next, she began to read her science book. She read beyond the pages assigned for the lesson because she was not sleepy—and, too, she wanted to stay awake until her parents came home.

After a while she had studied her lessons until she was well prepared in all of them. But her mother and father were not home yet and she began to wonder what was taking them such a long time. She left her English book open on the table in front of her, and whenever she heard any kind of noise outside, she would bend over the book and appear to be reading it, deep in concentration. She wanted her parents to think she was sitting up late because she still had homework to do instead of because she was curious to find out what had happened in town. But the noises outside always turned out to be false alarms, twigs breaking or perhaps animals from the woods scurrying about, not the return of Mr. and Mrs. Peavy.

At first she was not sleepy, but gradually she began to nod. Then suddenly there was a crackling noise on the dried leaves near the side of the house and she was wide awake once more. She bent over the English book and waited.

Several minutes passed and nothing happened. Then she heard the crackling noise again and could not pretend to study any longer. She ran to the door and opened it. "Ma?" she called into the yard. "Pa? Are you there?"

No answer came and then she saw the Corrys' hound standing near the steps. "Aw, Matilda!" she said dejectedly, "was that you crunching around out there?" and went back inside.

She gave up then, and got into bed. It was so long past her usual bedtime that she went to sleep almost by the time she pulled the cover under her chin.

During the night she heard, or thought she heard, her mother and father coming into the house, but she was too sleepy to rouse herself to say anything. Soon she drifted back to sleep, thinking she was overhearing them talk. Such phrases as "out of your mind drinking even one drop of whisky when you're on parole" and "no firearms" came from her mother. Her father's voice, sounding gruff, was low. He seemed to be telling his wife that he wished she would not nag at him on his first day home.

In the morning, Queenie overslept. She usually woke up the moment daylight came into the room, but this time the sun had cleared the horizon before she knew it had even begun to rise. She dressed quickly, got a fire started in the cookstove, and then hurried to the barn to do the milking—after tiptoeing into the next room and waking her mother.

It was a beautiful morning, and she felt refreshed and good until the thoughts came back to her about the conversations in the night. Then she decided she hadn't really heard them. She must have only dreamed them, the way she sometimes did when she was too anxious about anything.

Smoke was coming out of the chimney at Elgin Corry's house and Queenie could smell ham cooking. Nothing smelled quite as good on a crisp, clear morning. Elgin was leaving the barn when Queenie got to it. "Good morning," he said. "Sun-up comes early, don't it?"

Queenie smiled. "I thought I was later than I am." She was relieved to find that he wasn't too far ahead of her with his work. She bet he never overslept.

When she got home with the milk, her mother was in the kitchen. The fire was roaring hot now, and fatback and eggs were frying on top of the stove while biscuits from the day before were being warmed in the oven. Only two plates were on the table, and Queenie laughed. "You forgot to set a place for Pa!"

"He's still sleeping," answered Mrs. Peavy. "We'd better not wake him this time." She put the breakfast on the table and the two of them sat down.

Talking softly, so as not to wake her father, Queenie asked, "What did you find out last night?"

"About what?"

"About me. Is anybody still saying I need to be sent off? Wasn't that what you and Pa went to town about?"

Mrs. Peavy looked up. "No," she said. "That wasn't it. Your father wanted to see a few old friends. And you may just as well know it, he also wanted to see a few old enemies—ones he thinks should have lied in court to keep him out of jail." She broke the yellow of a fried egg and sopped at it with a biscuit. Then she continued the conversation. "But I've been trying all along to persuade the sheriff that the charges against you ought to be dropped. I had hoped to convince him that you'd do all right from now on."

"Did you sway him? Can't he see what a good effect Pa's being home will have on me?"

Her mother shook her head. "If your father obeys his parole officer and goes by the rules, it will help all of us in the long run. Of course, your behavior will count, too." She added slowly, "And I just as well . . ." She stopped there, as if she dreaded to say more. "Have some butter and pass it to me," she said briskly. "Let's finish breakfast."

Queenie ate in silence and then began getting ready for school. "I left my civics book on a chair in yonder," she said, motioning toward the other room.

"Tiptoe in and get it," said Mrs. Peavy, putting pieces of the fatback between biscuits for a lunch for Queenie and one for herself to take to the canning plant.

Queenie entered the other room quietly. Her father turned over in the bed as if he might be awake, but soon he was breathing heavily and she knew he was still asleep. She eased over to the corner where she had left the book. Her father's work jacket was hung on the back of the chair, and she reached over it and lifted the book without making a sound. But suddenly she saw something that made her gasp. She straightened up and stood motionless.

A second later she looked over at her father, but he had not awakened. Her gaze then returned to what had startled her. The sun shone in through the window and she saw clearly that she had not been mistaken. Sticking out of the jacket pocket was the handle of a pistol.

Queenie backed away from it—as if it were a snake or a wild animal that might not strike if she managed to back out of range without attracting its attention. At the door, she turned and hurried to the kitchen table.

"Ma!" she said, sitting down in one of the chairs.

"Here's your lunch," said Mrs. Peavy. "And your father's breakfast is in the warming closet. I'd better be on my way."

"Ma," said Queenie, "we better do all we can to help Pa not break any of his parole rules or anything."

"Yes, we'd better," agreed her mother, wrapping a piece of newspaper around her own lunch. "And before I leave, there's something else . . ." She hesitated, then started over. "I've been trying to tell you— the sheriff says his investigation of you proves there'll have to be a trial or a court hearing or something."

Queenie looked as if she had been slapped. Her eyes widened and her mouth dropped open and she put her hands to her head. She said nothing for a few seconds. Then she asked, "Will they put me in jail?"

"No," answered Mrs. Peavy. "I signed an appearance bond, which means I promised them you won't run away and that you'll appear at the hearing or the trial, whichever they decide to have."

from The Cybil War
Betsy Byars

In a fourth-grade rivalry for the attention of Cybil, Simon learns to cope with the fact that Tony, a classmate and rival, is an inveterate liar. The deep issues are handled with candor and light humor.

Being Ms. Indigestion

Simon was at his desk, slumped, staring at the dull wood. Someone had once carved "I hate school" in the wood, and over the years others had worked on the letters so that now they were as deep as a motto in stone.

Simon sighed. His teacher, clipboard in hand, was choosing the cast of a nutrition play. She had already cast Tony Angotti as the dill pickle, which meant that Simon, another of her non-favorites, would probably be the Swiss cheese. The thought of himself in a yellow box full of holes made him miserable. He had never been one for costumes— even at Halloween he limited himself to a mask—and now this. Well, he would just have to be absent that day.

Miss McFawn cast Laura Goode and Melissa Holbrook as the green beans.

"Good casting," Tony Angotti said. "You guys look like green beans when you turn sideways."

Simon smiled.

"Frontways you look like spaghetti."

Simon laughed, and Laura Goode hit him on the arm with her music book.

"I didn't say it," Simon protested.

"You laughed."

He turned away. "Violence is not characteristic of the green bean," he said coldly. His arm hurt but he refused to rub it.

He waited, without hope, while Miss McFawn cast Billy Bonfili as the hot dog, Wanda Sanchez as the bun. Slowly he realized that the entire play had been cast. Bananas, tacos, onions, pecans surrounded him. He alone had no role.

"Let's see," Miss McFawn said, "who can we get to be Mr. Indigestion?"

Mr. Indigestion! Simon couldn't believe it. This was the lead role. She could only be doing it out of spite, he knew that, but still he really wanted to be Mr. Indigestion. He who had walked along in misery last Halloween in his Jimmy Carter mask while Tony Angotti romped beside him in his mother's dress stuffed with balloons, *he* now actually wanted to put on a black cape and mustache and twirl on stage as Mr. Indigestion. He was surprised at himself.

"Oh, yes," she said. "Simon can be Mr. Indigestion." She made a note on her clipboard. "Simon will be the perfect indigestion."

"It takes one to know one," Tony Angotti muttered.

Everyone around Tony snickered, and Miss McFawn looked at him. Miss McFawn could stare down a cobra. In three seconds Tony's eyes were on his desk.

In the pause that followed, Cybil Ackerman called from the back of the room. "Miss McFawn?"

Miss McFawn's eyes were still on Tony Angotti in case he was fool enough to look up again. He was not, and Miss McFawn's eyes shifted to Cybil.

"Miss McFawn?"

"Yes, Cybil, what is it?"

"Well, every time we have a play, the boys get all the good parts. When we did the ecology play, the girls had to be trees and flowers while the boys got to be forest fires and strip mines and nuclear waste. And when we did the geography parade, the boys got to be countries like Russia and China, and we had to be Holland and the Virgin Islands. It's not fair."

"What do you suggest, Cybil?"

"I think we ought to have a *Ms.* Indigestion."

Simon swirled around in his seat. He felt as cheated as a dog deprived of a sirloin steak. His mouth was open. He tried to give her a McFawn stare-down, but she was looking over his head.

"We could vote on it," she said nicely.

"That's not fair," Simon said. There were seventeen girls in the room and only fourteen boys. He turned back to Miss McFawn. "All the girls will vote for Ms. Indigestion, and—"

"We will not!" the girls said in a chorus. They were used to voting in a bloc.

"All right, that's a good idea. We'll vote," Miss McFawn said. Simon thought she looked at him with satisfaction. "How many of you would like to have Ms. Indigestion?"

Seventeen girls raised their hands.

"How many for Mr. Indigestion?"

Fourteen boys raised their hands. Tony Angotti had two hands up, one positioned to appear to be Wanda Sanchez's, but Miss McFawn was not fooled.

"Ms. Indigestion it is," Miss McFawn said in a pleased voice. She crossed out Simon's name on her list. "Let's see. Cybil, would you like to be Ms. Indigestion?"

"Yes!"

"So what's Simon going to be?" Tony Angotti asked. He was not going to be the dill pickle unless everybody was something.

"He can have my part," Cybil offered.

"Or mine," Tony said. "I have the feeling I'm going to be absent that day."

"No, Tony, I especially want you to be the dill pickle." Miss McFawn checked her list of players and foods. "Let's see, we can use another starch. All right, Simon, you can either be a macaroni and cheese pie or—what were you, Cybil?"

"A jar of peanut butter."

Simon kept his eyes on his desk. He stared at the phrase "I hate school" so hard that he expected the words to catch fire.

"I'll have to have your decision, Simon."

He did not move. He felt betrayed. For the first time in his life, he had actually been willing to put on a costume, come out on-stage, twirling his mustache, even saying, "I am the dreaded Mr. Indigestion," only to have it taken away.

"Simon," she prompted.

He mumbled something without taking his eyes from the letters on his desk. Now he was actually willing them to catch fire, like Superman.

"I'm sorry, Simon, I didn't hear you. You'll have to speak up. What do you want to be?"

"A jar of peanut butter!"

"Violence is not characteristic of peanut butter," Laura Goode sneered.

Simon struck at her, hitting his hand on the back of her desk. Pain shot all the way up to his shoulder.

"Miss McFawn, Simon hit me," Laura called happily.

"Simon, I'm not going to have violence in my classroom."

Simon looked up at Miss McFawn. He stared at her with the same intensity and hatred he had stared at the letters on his desk.

For the first time that anyone could remember, it was Miss McFawn who looked away.

"Rehearsal Friday," she reminded them as she shifted the papers on her desk.

Arbor Day Is for the Birds

Simon, eyes on his book, felt his face burn. He had made a fool of himself, and over nothing. Over being Mr. Indigestion, which nobody in his right mind would want to be.

"Tony, will you explain what the poet means?" Miss McFawn was asking.

"He means," Tony said slowly, stalling for time, "he *means,* now, wait a minute—"

"Wanda?"

"He means that things are not what they seem."

"Very good!"

And what really hurt, Simon told himself—he was sitting with his eyes on the wrong page, finger marking the wrong poem—what really hurt was that Cybil Ackerman had a part in his humiliation. And he was in love with Cybil Ackerman, had been for three years.

He had fallen in love with her in the room right below this one. It was Arbor Day, and their teacher, Miss Ellis, made a big thing out of it. She gave every student a little tree to take home and plant, and the celebration was capped off with the writing and reading of tributes to trees.

Simon had been careful with his baby tree. Some of the other boys were using theirs in whip battles and trying to see how high they could throw them. Not Simon. He was taking his home in the crook of his arm, like a real baby, so his father could help him plant it. It was the first time he had something he was sure his father would want to do.

He went in the house, and his mother was standing in the kitchen. He said, "Look, I've got this baby tree, and Dad and I are going to plant it and watch it grow and—"

"Your dad cannot help you plant that tree," his mother said tiredly. "Your dad is gone."

"Well, I'll wait till he gets back. I'll put the tree in a little bucket. I'll water it. I'll—"

"Simon, look at me." She sat down on a chair so that their heads were level. "Now your dad is gone. We've been over this and over this. No, don't turn away. Your dad is gone and I do not know where he is or when he's coming back. Do you understand me?"

He tried to look away, but she held his head in place with her hand. He blinked uneasily. He was aware his mom had been talking to him about his father's absence, probably for days, but for the first time he realized what she was talking about.

"When will he be back?"

"I don't know."

"Well, where has he gone?"

"All I know is this. He is gone. His clothes are gone. The car is gone. The camping equipment is gone. Half the money in our bank account is gone."

"It's business—it's vacation—" he stuttered.

"No, he's gone."

It was more than he could stand—that his father, the only person he could not live without, could actually decide to live without him. The earth seemed to tremble with a terrible inner quake.

"Maybe he's dead," he said, his voice reflecting the quivering world.

"He's not dead."

"How do you know? He could be. People die. Their bodies are never found."

"It turns out he's been talking to Mitch Wilson about leaving for months."

"What did he say?"

"Oh, he talked about solitude and about getting away from the confusion and corruption of the world and going back to the simple way of life and about living off the land and about—"

"It has to be more than that. It has to be!"

Suddenly Simon turned, pulling away from his mother. He looked down. He was clutching the baby tree in both hands as if he were trying to choke it. He ran from the room.

"Simon, he'll be back sometime. I know he will," his mother called. "It's just something he's going through, and we'll get along." She followed him to the back door. "Simon, I can't give you answers because he didn't give them to me!"

Simon ran into the yard and threw his baby tree as far as he could. He didn't see it land because his hands were over his eyes, but in his mind that baby tree went so high and so far nobody ever saw it again.

When it came to the reading of tributes to trees, Simon was the first to volunteer. He read in a loud, hard voice.

> "I hate Arbor Day. I hate trees. I'm
> going to chop down every tree I see."

He had to lean close to read his writing. He had pressed down so hard with his pencil that he'd gone through the paper in three places.

There was a gasp from Miss Ellis. "That is enough!" She made her way to the front of the room in three steps. She took the paper from him so violently that she tore off the corner. Then she ripped the rest into pieces and threw them into the wastebasket.

"Sit, Simon," she said.

He had heard kinder tones used on dogs. He walked back to his desk with his head held so high he stumbled over Billy Bonfili's foot.

In a voice still trembling with rage, Miss Ellis called on Wanda Sanchez. Wanda made a lot of noise walking to the front of the room because she, too, was outraged about Simon's tribute to trees.

Her composition went:

> "The tree is a gift from God. It gives
> us shade. It gives us wood. It gives
> us food. Thank you, God, for trees."

"Thank *you*, Wanda," Miss Ellis said.

"You're *welcome*, Miss Ellis."

When all the kids had read their tributes, Miss Ellis announced they would have a vote on whose paper was the best. Wanda Sanchez, the favorite, got nine votes. Tony Angotti got five. He had written a comic tribute to trees, pointing out that if there were no trees, birds would have to build nests on top of people's heads.

"Oh, Miss Ellis," Cybil Ackerman called from the back of the room when the voting was over.

"Yes, Cybil?"

"You forgot to call Simon's name."

There was a pause while Miss Ellis inhaled and exhaled. "I don't think anyone wants to vote for Simon's paper," she said, "do they?"

She sounded as if she were asking if anyone wanted to vote for a fungus infection.

Simon put his hand up so high his arm hurt.

There was another icy pause. "Simon Newton—two votes." It was if the North Pole had spoken.

Simon swirled around in his seat. He could not believe he had gotten another vote. Who would dare risk Miss Ellis's displeasure?

Cybil's hand was in the air. As Simon looked at her, she grinned and crossed her eyes.

Love washed over him with the force of a tidal wave. He turned back to the front of the room. He lowered his hand and put it over his chest. He had not known it was possible to love like this.

His eyes blurred. His heart was beating so hard he expected to look down and actually see it pounding, like in cartoons.

He glanced back once again at Cybil Ackerman and knew he would love her until the day he died.

"Simon! *Simon!*"

He looked up. "What?"

"Would you like to tell the class the meaning of the next poem?"

Simon was sitting with his hand on his chest, over the very spot that had pounded so hard years ago. He was surprised to see it was Miss McFawn in front of the class instead of Miss Ellis.

"Would you like to tell the class the meaning of the next poem?" she repeated.

He looked down at the blurred image of his English book. He decided to tell the truth. "No," he said.

from A Dog on Barkham Street
Mary Stolz

Edward Frost wants two things from life: a dog, and Martin Hastings, the bully next door, to disappear from his world. Mary Stolz, long recognized as an outstanding writer of stories for teenage girls, here turns her attention to a real boy with real problems.

[Edward Cleans His Room]

Edward stood at the window and watched the rain tossing in sudden gusts along the street when the wind caught it, then falling straight again. Once in a while a car went by, its tires hissing, and once a wet, ruffled robin bounded across the grass and then took to its wings and flew, apparently, over the roof.

Now a dog came running along, its nose to the ground, its back quite sleek with water. Edward watched it hopefully. There were no end of stories in which the boy wanted a dog but didn't get one until a wonderful dog came along and selected *him.* In the stories these dogs were either stray ones, or the peo-

ple who owned them saw how the boy and the dog loved each other and gave the dog up.

In the stories the parents agreed to keep the dog, even if they'd been very much against the idea before.

Edward was always looking around for some dog that would follow him home from school and refuse to leave. In a case like that, he didn't see how his mother could refuse. He had even, a couple of times, tried to lure a dog to follow him. Whistling at it, snapping his fingers, running in a tempting way. But he must have picked dogs that already had homes and liked them. Now if this dog, this wet dog running along by itself in the rain, should suddenly stop at his house, and come up to the door and cry to be let in . . . wouldn't his mother be *sure* to let Edward have him? You couldn't leave a dog out in the rain, could you? The dog ran across the street, ran back, dashed halfway over the lawn, stopped to shove its nose in a puddling flowerpot, backed off sneezing, sat down and scratched its chin.

Edward held his breath, waiting. After a moment he tapped lightly on the windowpane. The dog cocked its head in an asking gesture, got to its feet, then wheeled around and continued down the street. Edward sighed. He was not at all surprised—the dog had a collar with at least four license tags dangling from it—but still he sighed. He was pretty sure he'd forgotten to make his bed and suspected that a hammer he'd been using yesterday was now lying in the back yard getting pretty wet. Mr. Frost was particular about his tools, and Edward felt that dogs, if they weren't getting further away from him, certainly weren't coming any nearer. He decided to go up and make his bed. He didn't see what there was to do about the hammer just now, since his mother would notice if he went out in the rain to get it.

The mailman turned the corner, and Edward lingered to watch him. Mr. Dudley had his mail sack and a tremendous black umbrella to juggle. He wore a black slicker that glistened in the rain and shining mud-splashed rubbers and a plastic cover on his hat. He was late already but he moved slowly, as if he were tired.

"Mr. Dudley's coming," Edward said, as his mother came in the room.

Mrs. Frost came over to the window. "Poor man," she said. "Stay and ask him if he'd like to come in for a cup of coffee."

Edward waited, and when Mr. Dudley turned up their walk, he ran to the front door and opened it. "Mother says do you want some coffee, Mr. Dudley," he asked, as he took the mail.

"Well now, that's a handsome offer," Mr. Dudley said, frowning down at his rubbers, "but does your mother know I'm just this side of drowned?"

"Oh, that's all right," Edward said cheerfully. "You take off your rubbers and raincoat here on the porch."

Mr. Dudley laid down the mail sack and his huge black umbrella. "Can't say a cup of coffee won't be welcome," he observed, as he and Edward made for the kitchen.

Mrs. Frost gave the mailman a sweet bun with his coffee, and Edward a cup of cocoa. They sat in the breakfast nook and the rain beat against the window, making things quite snug. Edward glanced out in the back yard. There was the hammer, all right. In perfectly plain view. He guessed his mother hadn't noticed it yet, and decided that rain or no rain he was going to have to go after it. It was too good a hammer to leave there until his father got home and saw it.

"Notice you have a letter there from Arizona, Mrs. Frost," said Mr. Dudley. He licked the sugar daintily from his fingers and Edward watched with admiring envy. He wondered if Mr. Dudley's mother had told him, when he was a little boy, "Don't lick your fingers, dear, use the napkin." He decided she probably had and now Mr. Dudley, all grown up, was doing as he pleased. It was satisfying to watch and look forward to. Edward was really looking forward to growing up. And the first thing I'll do, he said to himself now, is move to some city that Martin Hastings never heard of.

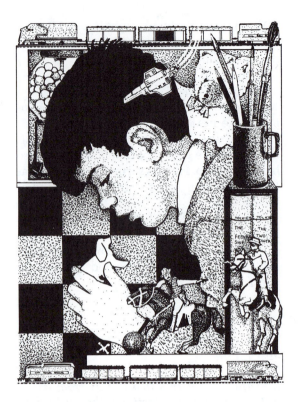

Mrs. Frost had picked up the letter from Arizona. Her forehead wrinkled the way it did when a pie came out of the oven not looking as she'd planned it to. Edward and Mr. Dudley waited for her to say who it was from. Or, perhaps, "How strange—who can it be from?" Or, "So it is—a letter from Arizona." But she said none of these things. She frowned at the letter, and then, in a funny gesture, put the other letters on top of it, and asked Mr. Dudley if he wanted another cup of coffee.

After the mailman had gone, Edward began to say, "Who is that letter from—" but his mother interrupted him. This was something she practically never did, since she was always telling Edward how he shouldn't, and it made him begin to be very curious about the letter. His mother asked if he'd made his bed and he said maybe he ought to go up and see, so he climbed the stairs to his room, wondering all the way (about the letter, not the bed), and found that sure enough everything was rumpled and tossed around just as he had left it.

Suddenly, because that possible dog was on his mind, and because there was nothing else to do, Edward decided to make a tremendous gesture. He would clean his entire room. He would stack the books that lay around so carelessly. He would straighten his toys and his clothes. He'd get out the vacuum and do the rug. Maybe he'd even clean the closet. Yes, that was a great idea. He'd never cleaned the closet in his life. His mother would be so bowled over she'd probably offer him a St. Bernard on the spot.

He plunged in at once, dragging out clothes, books, fishing equipment, old forgotten trucks and games. He put the clothes on the still-unmade bed, shoved everything else out on the floor. It seemed to take an awfully long time to get the closet emptied, and then when he thought he was done he looked up, saw the shelves, and wished he'd never started.

They were absolutely jammed with junk. Well, maybe it wasn't all junk, but it looked it. And now his room was filled to brimming with things that would have to be put away again. He sat on his heels and stared around, thinking that the whole idea of cleaning up was pretty silly. Everything was just going to have to be put back in the closet, so what was the point of taking it out in the first place?

"My word, Edward," said his mother at the door, "what are you doing?"

"Cleaning my room," he said glumly.

"That's a good idea," she said, coming in. "Did all that come out of the closet?"

Edward nodded. "And it all has to go back," he said. "And I was just thinking, what's the point? I mean, where do you get *ahead?* I don't think I'll clean it after all."

"You can't leave it this way," said Mrs. Frost.

She picked up a battered green dump truck. "Do you ever use this?" When Edward said he didn't suppose so, at least he hadn't in a long time, she said, "Why don't you get a box from the cellar and put the things you don't really want in it, and we'll give it to the Salvation Army? They're marvelous at fixing things up for Christmas. It seems to me there must be a lot of things you've outgrown. When you get all that sorted out, you won't have so much to put back, and you'll be neater, *and* ahead. Sweep the closet out before you put your things away, of course, and put them away tidily. I see you hadn't made your bed after all."

There was no reasonable answer to this, so Edward stumped down to the basement for a box, wondering if dogs appreciated what people had to go through to get them. He paused at the cellar door, looking out. The rain hadn't slackened any. Or had it? He leaned forward, pressing his nose to the glass. He wasn't fifteen feet from that hammer, and his mother was busy upstairs, so if he just dashed out . . .

Pulling his sweater up so that it partly covered his head, he opened the door and dashed. The grass was sopping, the earth beneath it marshy, and, though he got the hammer all right, his shoulders and feet were drenched even in so short a run. Back in the cellar, he dried the hammer thoughtfully and stared at his shoes. Finally he removed them. The socks were dry enough. He took a towel from the hamper and rubbed his head and the sweater. Picking up the box, he went upstairs in his stocking feet, hoping his mother wouldn't notice anything.

"Here's the box," he said in a loud cheerful voice. "Think it's big enough?"

His mother had her back to him. She was on a chair, getting things down from the shelves. "I thought," she said, not turning around yet, "that I'd help you out a little. This is really quite a big job. Here, you take these things, and I'll hand you down some more—" She glanced around and stopped talking. Her eyes went from his head to his feet.

"I suppose," she said, "you had some reason for going out in the pouring rain? Aside from its nuisance value, that is?"

Edward wiggled his shoulders. He disliked that kind of remark, and would have preferred to have her come right out and ask what the heck he thought he was doing. But just saying something right out was a thing grownups rarely did. In this, as in so many matters concerning adults, Edward failed to see the reason but accepted the fact.

"Somebody had left the hammer out in the rain," he mumbled. "It might've got rusty."

"Somebody?" said Mrs. Frost, lifting one eyebrow.

Edward debated, and then said with inspiration, "Well, *I'm* somebody, aren't I?"

Mrs. Frost began to scowl, looked at the ceiling, half-smiled, turned back to the closet, and said, "How about all these jigsaw puzzles?"

"They're a bit on the simple side," said Edward. He almost added that they could get him some harder ones, but decided this wasn't the best time for requests of any sort. His mother was being very nice about the rain and the hammer, so there was no point in annoying her.

It was a funny thing, he mused, piling things in the box for the Salvation Army, that lots of times he asked for things not really much wanting them at all. For instance, jigsaw puzzles. He didn't actually want any, he didn't even like doing them very much when he got them, but the habit of *asking* was just one he sort of had. He asked for Good Humors if the Good Humor man happened to be around, clothes if he happened to be in a store where they sold them, toys if he happened to see them in an advertisement or a shop window. He guessed that one way and another he asked for something or other every single day whether he wanted it or not. Sometimes he got the thing and sometimes he didn't but anyone could see that the asking annoyed parents. Rod said he'd found that, too. Once Mr. Frost had said, "Edward, don't you ever bore yourself with these constant requests?" and Edward had said he didn't think so.

Still, thinking it over now, he wondered if it wouldn't be wiser to limit all the asking to a dog. If he concentrated on that, one of several things might happen. Either he'd wear them down so that at last they'd give in, or he'd impress them so much with how he wanted a dog and nothing else that they'd give in, or they'd get to be so sorry for him

that they'd give in. Or—he had to admit—they'd get so irritated that he'd never see a dog until he was grown-up himself. He piled a fleet of little trucks in the box, and sat back on his heels to think.

"Problems?" said his mother, coming away from the closet to inspect the box. Edward nodded. "Could I help?" Mrs. Frost asked.

"Probably not," he said sadly. Then he looked up and met his mother's blue, friendly eyes. "*How* responsible do I have to be before I can have a dog?"

"Quite a bit, I'm afraid. Now, Edward . . . look at today. Bed unmade again, hammer out in the rain, *you* out in the rain—"

"But I'm cleaning my whole room," he protested.

"You started to," his mother reminded him. "If you recall, you got everything out and then changed your mind."

"When I grow up," Edward said, "my boy will have a dog as soon as he asks for it. In fact, I bet having the dog will *teach* him to be responsible," he added hopefully.

"But suppose it doesn't? Suppose you get the dog, and he doesn't take care of it at all?"

"I wouldn't mind taking care of it myself."

"Well, that's where you and I differ," said Mrs. Frost. "I would mind."

Edward, realizing that he hadn't handled his end of the argument well at all, gave up for the time being.

So now he could either get on with the room because he'd started and ought to finish, or he could get on with it because his mother was perfectly sure to make him. He decided on the former, and, in as responsible a voice as he could manage, he said, "Guess I might as well finish up here, eh?"

"I guess you might as well," said Mrs. Frost with a smile. "I'll have to leave you. I'm making a lemon meringue pie."

"You are?" said Edward with pleasure. There were few things he preferred to lemon meringue pie. "Gee, that's great." He went and fetched the vacuum cleaner and set to work in a good humor, the matter of dogs dwindling to the back of his mind.

Even people who wanted something badly couldn't think about it every single minute.

from The Adventures of Tom Sawyer
Mark Twain

This excerpt is one of the most famous scenes in American literature, and it should lead children to the book.

[The Glorious Whitewasher]

Saturday morning was come, and all the summer world was bright and fresh, and brimming with life. There was a song in every heart; and if the heart was young the music issued at the lips. There was cheer in every face and a spring in every step. The locust-trees were in bloom and the fragrance of the blossoms filled the air. Cardiff Hill, beyond the village and above it, was green with vegetation, and it lay just far enough away to seem a Delectable Land, dreamy, reposeful, and inviting.

Tom appeared on the sidewalk with a bucket of whitewash and a long-handled brush. He surveyed the fence, and all gladness left him and a deep melancholy settled down upon his spirit. Thirty yards of board fence nine feet high. Life to him seemed hollow, and existence but a burden. Sighing, he dipped his brush and passed it along the topmost plank; repeated the operation; did it again; compared the insignificant whitewashed streak with the far-reaching continent of unwhitewashed fence, and sat down on a tree-box discouraged. Jim came skipping out at the gate with a tin pail, and singing *Buffalo Gals.* Bringing water from the town pump had always been hateful work in Tom's eyes, before, but now it did not strike him so. He remembered that there was company at the pump. White, mulatto, and negro boys and girls were always there waiting their turns, resting, trading playthings, quarrelling, fighting, skylarking. And he remembered that although the pump was only a hundred and fifty yards off, Jim never got

"The Glorious Whitewasher" from THE ADVENTURES OF TOM SAWYER by Mark Twain. Reprinted by permission of Harper & Row, Publishers, Inc.

back with a bucket of water under an hour—and even then somebody generally had to go after him. Tom said:

"Say, Jim, I'll fetch the water if you'll whitewash some."

Jim shook his head and said:

"Can't, Mars Tom. Ole missis, she tole me I got to go an' git dis water an' not stop foolin' roun' wid anybody. She say she spec' Mars Tom gwine to ax me to whitewash, an' so she tole me go 'long an' 'tend to my own business—she 'lowed *she'd* 'tend to de whitewashin'."

"Oh, never you mind what she said, Jim. That's the way she always talks. Gimme the bucket—I won't be gone only a minute. *She* won't ever know."

"Oh, I dasn't, Mars Tom. Ole missis she'd take an' tar de head off'n me. 'Deed she would."

"*She!* She never licks anybody—whacks 'em over the head with her thimble—and who cares for that, I'd like to know. She talks awful, but talk don't hurt—anyways it don't if she don't cry. Jim, I'll give you a marvel. I'll give you a white alley!"

Jim began to waver.

"White alley, Jim! And it's a bully taw."

"My! Dat's a mighty gay marvel, *I* tell you! But Mars Tom, I's powerful 'fraid ole missis—"

"And besides, if you will I'll show you my sore toe."

Jim was only human—this attraction was too much for him. He put down his pail, took the white alley, and bent over the toe with absorbing interest while the bandage was being unwound. In another moment he was flying down the street with his pail and a tingling rear, Tom was whitewashing with vigor, and Aunt Polly was retiring from the field with a slipper in her hand and triumph in her eye.

But Tom's energy did not last. He began to think of the fun he had planned for this day, and his sorrows multiplied. Soon the free boys would come tripping along on all sorts of delicious expeditions, and they would make a world of fun of him for having to work—the very thought of it burnt him like fire. He got out his worldly wealth and examined it—bits of toys, marbles, and trash; enough to buy an exchange of *work,* maybe, but not half enough to buy so much as half an hour of pure freedom. So he returned his straitened means to his pocket, and gave up the idea of trying to buy the boys. At this dark and hopeless moment an inspiration burst upon him! Nothing less than a great, magnificent inspiration.

He took up his brush and went tranquilly to work. Ben Rogers hove in sight presently—the very boy, of all boys, whose ridicule he had been dreading. Ben's gait was the hop-skip-and-jump—proof enough that his heart was light and his anticipations high. He was eating an apple, and giving a long, melodious whoop, at intervals, followed by a deep-toned ding-dong-dong, ding-dong-dong, for he was personating a steamboat. As he drew near, he slackened speed, took the middle of the street, leaned far over to starboard and rounded to ponderously and with laborious pomp and circumstance—for he was personating the *Big Missouri,* and considered himself to be drawing nine feet of water. He was boat and captain and engine-bells combined, so he had to imagine himself standing on his own hurricane-deck giving the orders and executing them:

"Stop her, sir! Ting-a-ling-ling!" The headway ran almost out, and he drew up slowly toward the sidewalk.

"Ship up to back! Ting-a-ling-ling!" His arms straightened and stiffened down his sides.

"Set her back on the stabboard! Ting-a-ling-ling! Chow! ch-chow-wow! Chow!" His right hand, meantime, describing stately circles—for it was representing a forty-foot wheel.

"Let her go back on the labboard! Ting-a-ling-ling! Chow-ch-chow-chow!" The left hand began to describe circles.

"Stop the stabboard! Ting-a-ling-ling! Stop the labboard! Come ahead on the stabboard! Stop her! Let your outside turn over slow! Ting-a-ling-ling! Chow-ow-ow! Get out that head-line! *Lively* now! Come—out with your spring-line—what're you about there! Take a turn round that stump with the bight of it! Stand by that stage, now—let her go! Done with the engines, sir! Ting-a-ling-ling! *Sh't! s'h't! sh't!*" (trying the gauge-cocks).

Tom went on whitewashing—paid no attention to the steamboat. Ben stared a moment and then said:

"Hi-*yi! You're* up a stump, ain't you!"

No answer. Tom surveyed his last touch with the eye of an artist, then he gave his brush another gentle sweep and surveyed the result, as before. Ben ranged up alongside of him. Tom's mouth watered for the apple, but he stuck to his work. Ben said:

"Hello, old chap, you got to work, hey?"

Tom wheeled suddenly and said:

"Why, it's you, Ben! I warn't noticing."

"Say—*I'm* going in a-swimming, *I* am. Don't you wish you could? But of course you'd druther *work*—wouldn't you? Course you would!"

Tom contemplated the boy a bit, and said:

"What do you call work?"

"Why, ain't *that* work?"

Tom resumed his whitewashing, and answered carelessly:

"Well, maybe it is, and maybe it ain't. All I know, is, it suits Tom Sawyer."

"Oh come, now, you don't mean to let on that you *like* it?"

The brush continued to move.

"Like it? Well, I don't see why I oughtn't to like it. Does a boy get a chance to white-wash a fence every day?"

That put the thing in a new light. Ben stopped nibbling his apple. Tom swept his brush daintily back and forth—stepped back to note the effect—added a touch here and there—criticised the effect again—Ben watching every move and getting more and more interested, more and more absorbed. Presently he said:

"Say, Tom, let *me* whitewash a little."

Tom considered, was about to consent; but he altered his mind:

"No—no—I reckon it wouldn't hardly do, Ben. You see, Aunt Polly's awful particular about this fence—right here on the street, you know—but if it was the back fence I wouldn't mind and *she* wouldn't. Yes, she's awful particular about this fence; it's got to be done very careful; I reckon there ain't one boy in a thousand, maybe two thousand, that can do it the way it's got to be done."

"No—is that so? Oh come, now—lemme just try. Only just a little—I'd let *you*, if you was me, Tom."

"Ben, I'd like to, honest injun; but Aunt Polly—well, Jim wanted to do it, but she wouldn't let him; Sid wanted to do it, and she wouldn't let Sid. Now don't you see how I'm fixed? If you was to tackle this fence and anything was to happen to it—"

"Oh, shucks, I'll be just as careful. Now lemme try. Say—I'll give you the core of my apple."

"Well, here— No, Ben, now don't. I'm afeard—"

"I'll give you *all* of it!"

Tom gave up the brush with reluctance in his face, but alacrity in his heart. And while the late steamer *Big Missouri* worked and sweated in the sun, the retired artist sat on a barrel in the shade close by, dangled his legs, munched his apple, and planned the slaughter of more innocents. There was no lack of material; boys happened along every little while; they came to jeer, but remained to whitewash. By the time Ben was fagged out, Tom had traded the next chance to Billy Fisher for a kite, in good repair; and when *he* played out, Johnny Miller bought in for a dead rat and a string to swing it with—and so on, and so on, hour after hour. And when the middle of the afternoon came, from being a poor poverty-stricken boy in the morning, Tom was literally rolling in wealth. He had besides the things before mentioned, twelve marbles, part of a jews-harp, a piece of blue bottle-glass to look through, a spool cannon, a key that wouldn't unlock anything, a fragment of chalk, a glass stopper of a decanter, a tin soldier, a couple of tadpoles, six fire-crackers, a kitten with only one eye, a brass doorknob, a dog-collar—but no dog—the handle of a knife, four pieces of orange-peel, and a dilapidated old window sash.

He had had a nice, good, idle time all the while—plenty of company—and the fence had three coats of whitewash on it! If he hadn't run out of whitewash he would have bankrupted every boy in the village.

Tom said to himself that it was not such a hollow world, after all. He had discovered a great law of human action, without knowing it—namely, that in order to make a man or a boy covet a thing, it is only necessary to make the thing difficult to attain. If he had been a great and wise philosopher, like the writer of this book, he would now have comprehended that Work consists of whatever a body is *obliged* to do, and that Play consists of whatever a body is not obliged to do. And this would help him to understand why constructing artificial flowers or performing on a tread-mill is work, while rolling ten-pins or climbing Mont Blanc is only amusement. There are wealthy gentlemen in England who drive four-horse passenger-coaches twenty or thirty miles on a daily line, in the summer, because the privilege costs them considerable money; but if they were offered wages for the service, that would turn it into work and then they would resign.

The boy mused awhile over the substantial change which had taken place in his worldly circumstances, and then wended toward headquarters to report.

from Harriet the Spy
Louise Fitzhugh

The arrival of Harriet the Spy *into the book world created a major furor; some adults strongly object to the book, while other adults and most children find Harriet believable and unforgettable. In this chapter Harriet objects to being sent to dancing school.*

[Harriet Changes Her Mind]

That night at dinner everything was going along as usual, that is, Mr. and Mrs. Welsch were having an interminable, rambling conversation about nothing in particular while Harriet watched it all like a tennis match, when suddenly Harriet leaped to her feet as though she had just then remembered, and screamed, "I'll be *damned* if I'll go to dancing school."

"Harriet!" Mrs. Welsch was appalled. "How dare you use words like that at the table."

"Or any other place, dear," interjected Mr. Welsch calmly.

"All right, I'll be FINKED if I'll go to dancing school." Harriet stood and screamed this solidly. She was throwing a fit. She only threw fits as a last resort, so that even as she did it she had a tiny feeling in the back of her brain that she had already lost. She wouldn't, however, have it said that she went down without a try.

"Where in the world did you learn a word like that?" Mrs. Welsch's eyebrows were raised almost to her hairline.

"It's not a verb, anyway," said Mr. Welsch. They both sat looking at Harriet as though she were a curiosity put on television to entertain them.

"I *will not,* I *will not,* I *will not,*" shouted Harriet at the top of her lungs. She wasn't getting the right reaction. Something was wrong.

"Oh, but you will," said Mrs. Welsch calmly. "It really isn't so bad. You don't even know what it's like."

"I hated it," said Mr. Welsch and went back to his dinner.

"I *do so* know what's it's like." Harriet was getting tired of standing up and screaming. She wished she could sit down but it wouldn't have done. It would have looked like giving up. "I went there once on a visit with Beth Ellen because she had to go and I was spending the night, and you have to wear party dresses and all the boys are too short and you feel like a *hippopotamus.*" She said this all in one breath and screamed "hippopotamus."

Mr. Welsch laughed. "An accurate description, you must admit."

"Darling, the boys get taller as you go along."

"I just *won't.*" Somehow, indefinably, Harriet felt she was losing ground all the time.

"It isn't so bad." Mrs. Welsch went back to her dinner.

This was too much. The point wasn't coming across at all. They had to be roused out of their complacency. Harriet took a deep breath, and in as loud a voice as she could, repeated, "I'll be *damned* if I'll go!"

"All right, that does it." Mrs. Welsch stood up. She was furious. "You're getting your mouth washed out with soap, young lady. Miss Golly, Miss Golly, step in here a minute." When there was no response, Mrs. Welsch rang the little silver dinner bell and in a moment Cook appeared.

Harriet stood petrified. *Soap!*

"Cook, will you tell Miss Golly to step in here a minute." Mrs. Welsch stood looking at Harriet as though she were a worm, as Cook departed. "Now Harriet, to your room. Miss Golly will be up shortly."

"But . . ."

"Your *room,*" said Mrs. Welsch firmly, pointing to the door.

Feeling rather like an idiot, Harriet left the dining room. She thought for half a second about waiting around and listening outside but decided it was too risky.

She went up to her room and waited. Ole Golly came in a few minutes later.

"Well, now, what is this about dancing school?" she asked amiably.

"I'm not going," Harriet said meekly. There was something that made her feel ridiculous when she shouted at Ole Golly. Maybe because she never got the feeling with Ole Golly that she did with her parents that they never heard anything.

"Why not?" Ole Golly asked sensibly.

Harriet thought a minute. The other reasons weren't really it. It was that the thought of being in dancing school somehow made her feel undignified. Finally she had it. "*Spies* don't go to dancing school," she said triumphantly.

"Oh, but they do," said Ole Golly.

"They do *not,*" said Harriet rudely.

"Harriet"—Ole Golly took a deep breath and sat down—"have you ever thought about how spies are trained?"

"Yes. They learn languages and guerrilla fighting and everything about a country so if they're captured they'll know all the old football scores and things like that."

"That's *boy* spies, Harriet. You're not thinking."

Harriet hated more than anything else to be told by Ole Golly that she wasn't thinking. It was worse than any soap. "What do you mean?" she asked quietly.

"What about *girl* spies? What are they taught?"

"The same things."

"The same things and a few more. Remember that movie we saw about Mata Hari one night on television?"

"Yes . . ."

"Well, think about that. Where did she operate? Not in the woods guerrilla fighting, right? She went to parties, right? And remember that scene with the general or whatever he was—she was dancing, right? Now how are you going to be a spy if you don't know how to dance?"

There must be some answer to this, thought Harriet as she sat there silently. She couldn't think of a thing. She went "Hmmmph" rather loudly. Then she thought of something. "Well, do I have to wear those silly dresses? Couldn't I wear my spy clothes? They're better to learn to dance in anyway. In school we wear our gym suits to learn to dance."

"Of course not. Can you see Mata Hari in a gym suit? First of all, if you wear your spy clothes everyone knows you're a spy, so what have you gained? No, you have to look like everyone else, then you'll get by and no one will suspect you."

"That's true," said Harriet miserably. She couldn't see Mata Hari in a gym suit either.

"Now"—Ole Golly stood up—"you better march downstairs and tell them you changed your mind."

"What'll I say?" Harriet felt embarrassed.

"Just say you've changed your mind."

Harriet stood up resolutely and marched down the steps to the dining room. Her parents were having coffee. She stood in the doorway and said in a loud voice, "I've changed my mind!" They looked at her in a startled way. She turned and left the doorway abruptly. There was nothing further to be said. As she went back up the steps she heard them burst out laughing and then her father say, "Boy, that Miss Golly is magic, sheer magic. I wonder where we'd be without her?"

Harriet didn't know how to approach Janie about her defection, but she decided she must. At lunch Sport and Janie sat laughing over the new edition of *The Gregory News* which had just come out. *The Gregory News* was the school paper. There was a page reserved for every grade in the Middle School and every grade in the Upper School. The Lower School were such idiots they didn't need a page.

"Look at that. It's ridiculous." Janie was talking about Marion Hawthorne's editorial about candy wrappers everywhere.

"She just did that because Miss Whitehead talked about them on opening day," Harriet sneered.

"Well, what else? She hasn't got the sense to think of anything original." Sport bit into a hard-boiled egg. Sport made his own lunch and it was usually hard-boiled eggs.

"But it's so dumb and boring," Harriet said. "Listen to this: 'We must not drop our candy wrappers on the ground. They must be put into the wastebaskets provided for this purpose.' It's not even news; we hear it practically every day."

"I'll put *her* in a wastebasket," said Janie with satisfaction.

"My father says you have to catch the reader's attention right at first and then hold it," said Sport.

"Well, she just lost it," said Harriet.

"You oughta write it, Harriet, you're a writer," said Sport.

"I wouldn't do it now if they paid me. They

can have their dumb paper." Harriet finished her sandwich with a frown.

"They should be blown up," said Janie.

They ate in silence for a moment.

"Janie . . ." Harriet hesitated so long that they both looked up at her. "I think they've got me," she said sadly.

"What? Was that sandwich poisoned?" Janie stood up. The egg fell right out of Sport's mouth.

"No," Harriet said quickly. Now it was anticlimactic. "I mean dancing school," Harriet said grimly.

Janie sat down and looked away as though Harriet had been impolite.

"Dancing school?" Sport squeaked, picking the egg out of his lap.

"Yes," said Janie grimly.

"Oh, boy, am I glad. My father never even *heard* of that." Sport grinned around his egg.

"Well," said Harriet sadly, "it looks like I'm gonna have to if I'm gonna be a spy."

"Who ever heard of a dancing spy?" Janie was so furious she wouldn't even look at Harriet.

"Mati Hari," Harriet said quietly; then when Janie didn't turn around she added very loudly, "I can't *help* it, Janie."

Janie turned and looked at her. "I know," she said sadly, "I'm going too."

It was all right then, and Harriet ate her other tomato sandwich happily.

After school, when Harriet went home for her cake and milk, she remembered that it was Thursday and that Thursday was Ole Golly's night out. As she was running down the steps to the kitchen she was struck by a thought so interesting that it made her stop still on the steps. If Ole Golly had a boy friend and she went out on her night out—wouldn't she meet the boy friend? And . . . if she were to meet the boy friend—couldn't Harriet follow her and see what he looked like? Extraordinary thought. She decided that she would have to be extra careful and terribly crafty to find out when, where, and with whom Ole Golly was spending her free evening. If Ole Golly went to places like the Welsches did, like night clubs, Harriet wouldn't be able to

follow. Out of the question. She would have to wait until she was Mata Hari for that.

But *IF*, for instance, this boy friend were to come to the house and pick up Ole Golly, *THEN* Harriet could at least see what he looked like. She decided to pursue this as she clattered down the rest of the way into the kitchen. Ole Golly was having her tea. The cook put out the cake and milk as Harriet slipped into place at the table.

"Well," said Ole Golly in a friendly manner.

"Well?" said Harriet. She was looking at Ole Golly in a new way. What was it like for Ole Golly to have a boy friend? Did she like him the way Harriet liked Sport?

"Well, iffen it don't rain, it'll be a long dry spell," Ole Golly said softly, then smiled into her tea.

Harriet looked at her curiously. That was one thing about Ole Golly, thought Harriet, she never, never said dull things like, 'How was school today?' or 'How did you do in arithmetic?' or 'Going out to play?' All of these were unanswerable questions, and she supposed that Ole Golly was the only grown-up that knew that.

from Little Men
Louisa May Alcott

This sequel to Little Women *reflects both the post-Civil War era in which it was published and the beliefs of Bronson Alcott and his family in the ways in which children should be raised and taught.*

A Firebrand

"Please, ma'am, could I speak to you? It is something *very* important," said Nat, popping his head in at the door of Mrs. Bhaer's room.

It was the fifth head which had popped in during the last half-hour; but Mrs. Jo was

"A Firebrand" from LITTLE MEN by Louisa May Alcott (originally published 1871).

used to it, so she looked up, and said briskly:

"What is it, my lad?"

Nat came in, shut the door carefully behind him, and said, in an eager, anxious tone:

"Dan has come."

"Who is Dan?"

"He's a boy I used to know when I fiddled round the streets. He sold papers, and he was kind to me, and I saw him the other day in town, and told him how nice it was here, and he's come."

"But, my dear boy, that is rather a sudden way to pay a visit."

"Oh, it isn't a visit, he wants to stay if you will let him!" said Nat innocently.

"Well, but I don't know about that," began Mrs. Bhaer, rather startled by the coolness of the proposition.

"Why, I thought you liked to have poor boys come and live with you, and be kind to 'em as you were to me," said Nat, looking surprised and alarmed.

"So I do, but I like to know something about them first. I have to choose them, because there are so many. I have not room for all. I wish I had."

"I told him to come because I thought you'd like it, but if there isn't room he can go away again," said Nat sorrowfully.

The boy's confidence in her hospitality touched Mrs. Bhaer, and she could not find the heart to disappoint his hope, and spoil his kind little plan, so she said:

"Tell me about this Dan."

"I don't know anything, only he hasn't got any folks, and he's poor, and he was good to me, so I'd like to be good to him if I could."

"Excellent reasons every one; but really, Nat, the house is full, and I don't know where I could put him," said Mrs. Bhaer, more and more inclined to prove herself the haven of refuge he seemed to think her.

"He could have my bed, and I could sleep in the barn. It isn't cold now, and I don't mind; I used to sleep anywhere with father," said Nat eagerly.

Something in his speech and face made Mrs. Jo put her hand on his shoulder, and say, in her kindest tone:

"Bring in your friend, Nat; I think we must find room for him without giving him your place."

Nat joyfully ran off, and soon returned, followed by a most unprepossessing boy, who slouched in and stood looking about him, with a half-bold, half-sullen look, which made Mrs. Bhaer say to herself, after one glance:

"A bad specimen, I am afraid."

"This is Dan," said Nat, presenting him as if sure of his welcome.

"Nat tells me you would like to come and stay with us," began Mrs. Jo, in a friendly tone.

"Yes," was the gruff reply.

"Have you no friends to take care of you?"

"No."

"Say, 'No, ma'am,'" whispered Nat.

"Shan't neither," muttered Dan.

"How old are you?"

"About fourteen."

"You look older. What can you do?"

"Most anything."

"If you stay here we shall want you to do as the others do, work and study as well as play. Are you willing to agree to that?"

"Don't mind trying."

"Well, you can stay a few days, and we will see how we get on together. Take him out, Nat, and amuse him till Mr. Bhaer comes home, when we will settle about the matter," said Mrs. Jo, finding it rather difficult to get on with this cool young person, who fixed his big black eyes on her with a hard, suspicious expression, sorrowfully unboyish.

"Come on, Nat," he said, and slouched out again.

"Thank you, ma'am," added Nat, as he followed him, feeling without quite understanding the difference in the welcome given to him and to his ungracious friend.

"The fellows are having a circus out in the barn; don't you want to come and see it?" he asked, as they came down the wide steps on to the lawn.

"Are they big fellows?" said Dan.

"No; the big ones are gone fishing."

"Fire away, then," said Dan.

Nat led him to the great barn and introduced him to his set, who were disporting themselves among the half-empty lofts. A large circle was marked out with hay on the wide floor, and in the middle stood Demi with a long whip, while Tommy, mounted on the much enduring Toby, pranced about the circle playing being a monkey.

"You must pay a pin apiece, or you can't see the show," said Stuffy, who stood by the wheelbarrow in which sat the band, consisting of a pocket-comb blown upon by Ned, and a toy drum beaten spasmodically by Rob.

"He's company, so I'll pay for both," said Nat, handsomely, as he stuck two crooked pins in the dried mushroom which served as money-box.

With a nod to the company they seated themselves on a couple of boards, and the performance went on. After the monkey act, Ned gave them a fine specimen of his agility by jumping over an old chair, and running up and down ladders, sailor fashion. Then Demi danced a jig with a gravity beautiful to behold. Nat was called upon to wrestle with Stuffy, and speedily laid that stout youth upon the ground. After this, Tommy proudly advanced to turn a somersault, an accomplishment which he had acquired by painful perseverance, practising in private till every joint of his little frame was black and blue. His feats were received with great applause, and he was about to retire, flushed with pride and a rush of blood to the head, when a scornful voice in the audience was heard to say:

"Ho! that ain't anything!"

"Say that again, will you?" and Tommy bristled up like an angry turkey-cock.

"Do you want to fight?" said Dan, promptly descending from the barrel and doubling up his fists in a business-like manner.

"No, I don't"; and the candid Thomas retired a step, rather taken aback by the proposition.

"Fighting isn't allowed!" cried the others, much excited.

"You're a nice lot," sneered Dan.

"Come, if you don't behave, you shan't stay," said Nat, firing up at that insult to his friends.

"I'd like to see him do better than I did, that's all," observed Tommy, with a swagger.

"Clear the way then!" And without the slightest preparation Dan turned three somersaults one after the other and came upon his feet.

"You can't beat that, Tom; you always hit your head and tumble flat," said Nat, pleased at his friend's success.

Before he could say any more the audience were electrified by three more somersaults backwards, and a short promenade on the hands, head down, feet up. This brought down the house, and Tommy joined in the admiring cries which greeted the accomplished gymnast as he righted himself, and looked at them with an air of calm superiority.

"Do you think I could learn to do it without its hurting me very much?" Tom meekly asked, as he rubbed the elbows which still smarted after the last attempt.

"What will you give me if I'll teach you?" said Dan.

"My new jack-knife; it's got five blades, and only one is broken."

"Give it here then."

Tommy handed it over with an affectionate look at its smooth handle. Dan examined it carefully, then putting it into his pocket, walked off, saying with a wink:

"Keep it up till you learn, that's all."

A howl of wrath from Tommy was followed by a general uproar, which did not subside till Dan, finding himself in a minority, proposed that they should play stick-knife, and whichever won should have the treasure. Tommy agreed, and the game was played in a circle of excited faces, which all wore an expression of satisfaction when Tommy won, and secured the knife in the depth of his safest pocket.

"You come off with me, and I'll show you round," said Nat, feeling that he must have a little serious conversation with his friend in private.

What passed between them no one knew, but when they appeared again Dan was more respectful to everyone, though still gruff in his speech and rough in his manner; and what else could be expected of the poor lad, who had been knocking about the world all his short life with no one to teach him any better?

The boys had decided that they did not like him, and so they left him to Nat, who soon felt rather oppressed by the responsibility, but was too kind-hearted to desert him.

Tommy, however, felt that, in spite of the jack-knife transaction, there was a bond of sympathy between them, and longed to return to the interesting subject of somersaults. He soon found an opportunity, for Dan, seeing how much he admired him, grew more amiable, and by the end of the first week was quite intimate with the lively Tom.

Mr. Bhaer when he heard the story and saw Dan shook his head, but only said quietly:

"The experiment may cost us something, but we will try it."

If Dan felt any gratitude for his protection, he did not show it, and took without thanks all that was given him. He was ignorant, but very quick to learn when he chose; had sharp eyes to watch what went on about him; a saucy tongue, rough manners, and a temper that was fierce and sullen by turns. He played with all his might, and played well at almost all the games. He was silent and gruff before grown people, and only now and then was thoroughly social among the lads. Few of them really liked him, but few could help admiring his courage and strength, for nothing daunted him, and he knocked tall Franz flat on one occasion with an ease that caused all the others to keep at a respectful distance from his fists. Mr. Bhaer watched him silently, and did his best to tame the "Wild Boy," as they called him, but in private the worthy man shook his head, and said soberly, "I *hope* the experiment will turn out well, but I am a little afraid it may cost too much."

Mrs. Bhaer lost her patience with him half a dozen times a day, yet never gave him up, and always insisted that there was something good in the lad after all; for he was kinder to animals than to people, he liked to rove about in the woods, and, best of all, little Ted was fond of him. What the secret was no one could discover, but baby took to him at once —gabbled and crowed whenever he saw him —preferred his strong back to ride on to any of the others—and called him "My Danny" out of his own little head. Teddy was the only creature to whom Dan showed any affection, and this was only manifested when he thought no one else could see it; but mothers' eyes are quick, and motherly hearts instinctively divine who love their babies. So Mrs. Jo soon saw and felt that there *was* a soft spot in rough Dan, and bided her time to touch and win him.

But an unexpected and decidedly alarming event upset all their plans, and banished Dan from Plumfield.

Tommy, Nat, and Demi began by patronizing Dan, because the other lads rather slighted him; but soon they each felt there was a certain fascination about the bad boy, and from looking down upon him they came to looking up, each for a different reason. Tommy admired his skill and courage; Nat was grateful for past kindness; and Demi regarded him as a sort of animated story-book, for when he chose Dan could tell his adventures in a most interesting way. It pleased Dan to have the three favourites like him, and he exerted himself to be agreeable, which was the secret of his success.

The Bhaers were surprised, but hoped the lads would have a good influence over Dan, and waited with some anxiety, trusting that no harm would come of it.

Dan felt they did not quite trust him, and never showed them his best side, but took a wilful pleasure in trying their patience and thwarting their hopes as far as he dared.

Mr. Bhaer did not approve of fighting, and did not think it a proof of either manliness or courage for two lads to pommel one another for the amusement of the rest. All sorts of hardy games and exercises were encouraged, and the boys were expected to take hard knocks and tumbles without whining; but black eyes and bloody noses given for the fun of it were forbidden as a foolish and a brutal play.

Dan laughed at this rule, and told such exciting tales of his own valour, and the many frays that he had been in, that some of the lads were fired with a desire to have a regular good "mill."

"Don't tell, and I'll show you how," said Dan; and, getting half a dozen of the lads together behind the barn, he gave them a lesson in boxing, which quite satisfied the ardour of most of them. Emil, however, could not submit to be beaten by a fellow younger than himself—for Emil was past fourteen, and a plucky fellow—so he challenged Dan to a fight. Dan accepted at once, and the others looked on with intense interest.

What little bird carried the news to headquarters no one ever knew, but, in the very hottest of the fray, when Dan and Emil were fighting like a pair of young bulldogs, and the others with fierce, excited faces were cheering them on, Mr. Bhaer walked into the ring, plucked the combatants apart with a strong hand, and said, in the voice they seldom heard:

"I can't allow this, boys! Stop it at once; and never let me see it again. I keep a school for boys, not for wild beasts. Look at each other and be ashamed of yourselves."

"You let me go, and I'll knock him down again," shouted Dan, sparring away in spite of the grip on his collar.

"Come on, come on, I ain't thrashed yet!" cried Emil, who had been down five times, but did not know when he was beaten.

"They are playing be gladdy—what-you-call-'ems, like the Romans, Uncle Fritz," called out Demi, whose eyes were bigger than ever with the excitement of this new pastime.

"They were a fine set of brutes; but we have learned something since then I hope, and I cannot have you make my barn a Colosseum. Who proposed this?" asked Mr. Bhaer.

"Dan," answered several voices.

"Don't you know that it is forbidden?"

"Yes," growled Dan sullenly.

"Then why break the rule?"

"They'll all be molly-coddles, if they don't know how to fight."

"Have you found Emil a molly-coddle? He doesn't look much like one," and Mr. Bhaer brought the two face to face. Dan had a black eye, and his jacket was torn to rags; but Emil's face was covered with blood from a cut lip and a bruised nose, while a bump on his forehead was already as purple as a plum. In spite of his wounds, however, he still glared upon his foe, and evidently panted to renew the fight.

"He'd make a first-rater if he was taught," said Dan, unable to withhold the praise from the boy who made it necessary for him to do his best.

"He'll be taught to fence and box by and by, and till then I think he will do very well without any lessons in mauling. Go and wash your faces; and remember, Dan, if you break any more of the rules again, you will be sent away. That was the bargain; do your part and we will do ours."

The lads went off, and after a few more words to the spectators, Mr. Bhaer followed to bind up the wounds of the young gladiators. Emil went to bed sick, and Dan was an unpleasant spectacle for a week.

But the lawless lad had no thought of obeying, and soon transgressed again.

One Saturday afternoon as a party of the boys went out to play, Tommy said:

"Let's go down to the river, and cut a lot of new fishpoles."

"Take Toby to drag them back, and one of us can ride him down," proposed Stuffy, who hated to walk.

"That means *you*, I suppose; well, hurry up, lazy-bones," said Dan.

Away they went, and having got the poles, were about to go home, when Demi unluckily said to Tommy, who was on Toby with a long rod in his hand:

"You look like the picture of the man in the bullfight, only you haven't got a red cloth, or pretty clothes on."

"I'd like to see one; wouldn't you?" said Tommy, shaking his lance.

"Let's have one; there's old Buttercup in the big meadow, ride at her Tom, and see her run," proposed Dan, bent on mischief.

"No, you mustn't," began Demi, who was learning to distrust Dan's propositions.

"Why, not, little fuss-button?" demanded Dan.

"I don't think Uncle Fritz would like it."

"Did he ever say we must not have a bullfight?"

"No, I don't think he ever did," admitted Demi.

"Then hold your tongue. Drive on, Tom, and here's a red rag to flap at the old thing. I'll help you to stir her up"; and over the wall went Dan, full of the new game, and the rest followed like a flock of sheep—even Demi, who sat upon the bars, and watched the fun with interest.

Poor Buttercup was not in a very good mood, for she had been lately bereft of her calf, and mourned for the little thing most dismally. Just now she regarded all mankind as her enemies (and I do not blame her), so when the matador came prancing towards her with the red handkerchief flying at the end of his long lance, she threw up her head, and gave a most appropriate "Moo!" Tommy rode gallantly at her, and Toby, recognizing an old friend, was quite willing to approach; but when the lance came down on her back with a loud whack, both cow and donkey were surprised and disgusted. Toby backed with a bray of remonstrance, and Buttercup lowered her horns angrily.

"At her again, Tom; she's jolly cross, and will do it capitally!" called Dan, coming up behind with another rod, while Jack and Ned followed his example.

Seeing herself thus beset, and treated with such disrespect, Buttercup trotted round the field, getting more and more bewildered and excited every moment, for whichever way she turned, there was a dreadful boy, yelling and brandishing a new and very disagreeable sort of whip. It was great fun for them, but real misery for her, till she lost patience and turned the tables in the most unexpected manner. All at once she wheeled short round, and charged full at her old friend Toby, whose conduct cut her to the heart. Poor slow Toby backed so precipitately that he tripped over a stone, and down went horse, matador, and all, in one ignominious heap, while distracted Buttercup took a surprising leap over the wall, and galloped wildly out of sight down the road.

"Catch her, stop her, head her off! Run, boys, run!" shouted Dan, tearing after her at his best pace, for she was Mr. Bhaer's pet Alderney, and if anything happened to her, Dan feared it would be all over with him. Such a running, and racing, and bawling, and puffing as there was before she was caught! The fish-poles were left behind; Toby was trotted nearly off his legs in the chase; and every boy was red, breathless, and scared. They found poor Buttercup at last in a flower-garden, where she had taken refuge, worn out with the long run. Borrowing a rope for a halter, Dan led her home, followed by a party of very sober young gentlemen, for the cow was in a sad state, having strained her shoulder in jumping, so that she limped, her eyes looked wild, and her glossy coat was wet and muddy.

"You'll catch it this time, Dan," said Tommy, as he led the wheezing donkey beside the maltreated cow.

"So will you, for you helped."

"We all did, but Demi," added Jack.

"He put it into our heads," said Ned.

"I told you not to do it," cried Demi, who was most broken-hearted at poor Buttercup's state.

"Old Bhaer will send me off, I guess. Don't care if he does," muttered Dan, looking worried in spite of his words.

"We'll ask him not to, all of us," said Demi, and the others assented with the exception of Stuffy, who cherished the hope that all the punishment might fall on one guilty head. Dan only said: 'Don't bother about me'; but he never forgot it, even though he led the lads astray again as soon as the temptation came.

When Mr. Bhaer saw the animal, and

heard the story, he said very little, evidently fearing that he should say too much in the first moments of impatience. Buttercup was made comfortable in her stall, and the boys sent to their rooms till supper-time. This brief respite gave them time to think the matter over, to wonder what the penalty would be, and to try to imagine where Dan would be sent. He whistled briskly in his room, so that no one should think he cared a bit; but while he waited to know his fate, the longing to stay grew stronger and stronger, the more he recalled the comfort and kindness he had known here, the hardship and neglect he had felt elsewhere. He knew they tried to help him, and at the bottom of his heart he was grateful, but his rough life had made him hard and careless, suspicious and wilful. He hated restraint of any sort, and fought against it like an untamed creature, even while he knew it was kindly meant, and dimly felt that he would be the better for it. He made up his mind to be turned adrift again, to knock about the city as he had done nearly all his life; a prospect that made him knit his black brows, and look about the cosy little room with a wistful expression that would have touched a much harder heart than Mr. Bhaer's if he had seen it. It vanished instantly, however, when the good man came in, and said in his accustomed grave way:

"I have heard all about it, Dan, and, though you have broken the rules again, I am going to give you one more trial, to please Mother Bhaer."

Dan flushed up to his forehead at this unexpected reprieve, but he only said in his gruff way:

"I didn't know there was any rule about bullfighting."

"As I never expected to have any at Plumfield, I never did make such a rule," answered Mr. Bhaer, smiling in spite of himself at the boy's excuse. Then he added gravely: "But one of the first and most important of our few laws is the law of kindness to every dumb creature on the place. I want everybody and everything to be happy here, to love and trust and serve us, as we try to love

and trust and serve them faithfully and willingly. I have often said that you were kinder to the animals than any of the other boys, and Mrs. Bhaer liked that trait in you very much, because she thought it showed a good heart. But you have disappointed us in that, and we are sorry, for we hoped to make you quite one of us. Shall we try again?"

Dan's eyes had been on the floor, and his hands nervously picking at the bit of wood he had been whittling as Mr. Bhaer came in, but when he heard the kind voice ask that question, he looked up quickly, and said in a more respectful tone than he had ever used before:

"Yes, please."

"Very well then, we will say no more, only you will stay at home from the walk to-morrow, as the other boys will, and all of you must wait on poor Buttercup till she is well again."

"I will."

"Now, go down to supper, and do your best, my boy, more for your own sake than for ours." Then Mr. Bhaer shook hands with him, and Dan went down more tamed by kindness than he would have been by the good whipping which Asia had strongly recommended.

Dan did try for a day or two, but not being used to it, he soon tired and relapsed into his old wilful ways. Mr. Bhaer was called from home on business one day, and the boys had no lessons. They liked this, and played hard till bedtime, when most of them turned in and slept like dormice. Dan, however, had a plan in his head, and when he and Nat were alone he unfolded it.

"Look here!" he said, taking from under his bed a bottle, a cigar, and a pack of cards, "I'm going to have some fun, and do as I used to do with the fellows in town. Here's some beer, I got it of the old man at the station, and this cigar; you can pay for 'em, or Tommy will, he's got heaps of money, and I haven't a cent. I'm going to ask him in; no, you go, they won't mind you."

"The folks won't like it," began Nat.

"They won't know. Daddy Bhaer is away, and Mrs. Bhaer's busy with Ted; he's got croup or something, and she can't leave him.

We shan't sit up late or make any noise, so where's the harm?"

"Asia will know if we burn the lamp long, she always does."

"No, she won't, I've got the dark lantern on purpose; it don't give much light, and we can shut it quick if we hear anyone coming," said Dan.

This idea struck Nat as a fine one, and lent an air of romance to the thing. He started off to tell Tommy, but put his head in again to say:

"You want Demi, too, don't you?"

"No, I don't; the Deacon will roll up eyes and preach if you tell him. He will be asleep, so just tip the wink to Tom and cut back again."

Nat obeyed, and returned in a minute with Tommy half-dressed, rather tousled about the head and very sleepy, but quite ready for fun as usual.

"Now, keep quiet, and I'll show you how to play a first-rate game called 'Poker,'" said Dan, as the three revellers gathered round the table, on which were set forth the bottle, the cigar, and the cards. "First, we'll all have a drink, then we'll take a go at the 'weed,' and then we'll play. That's the way men do, and it's jolly fun."

The beer circulated in a mug, and all three smacked their lips over it, though Nat and Tommy did not like the bitter stuff. The cigar was worse still, but they dared not say so, and each puffed away till he was dizzy or choked, when he passed the "weed" on to his neighbor. Dan liked it, for it seemed like old times when he now and then had a chance to imitate the low men who surrounded him. He drank, and smoked, and swaggered as much like them as he could, and, getting into the spirit of the part he assumed, he soon began to swear under his breath for fear someone should hear him. "You mustn't: it's wicked to say 'Damn!'" cried Tommy, who had followed his leader so far.

"Oh, hang! don't you preach, but play away; it's part of the fun to swear."

"I'd rather say 'thunder—turtles,'" said Tommy, who had composed this interesting exclamation and was very proud of it.

"And I'll say 'The Devil'; that sounds well," added Nat, much impressed by Dan's manly ways.

Dan scoffed at their "nonsense," and swore stoutly as he tried to teach them the new game.

But Tommy was very sleepy, and Nat's head began to ache with the beer and the smoke, so neither of them was very quick to learn, and the game dragged. The room was nearly dark, for the lantern burned badly; they could not laugh loud nor move about much, for Silas slept next door in the shed-chamber, and altogether the party was dull. In the middle of a deal Dan stopped suddenly, called out, "Who's that?" in a startled tone, and at the same moment drew the slide over the light. A voice in the darkness said, tremulously, "I can't find Tommy," and then there was the quick patter of bare feet running away down the entry that led from the wing to the main house.

"It's Demi! he's gone to call someone; cut into bed, Tom, and don't tell!" cried Dan, whisking all signs of the revel out of sight, and beginning to tear off his clothes, while Nat did the same.

Tommy flew to his room and dived into bed, where he lay laughing till something burned his hand, when he discovered that he was still clutching the stump of the festive cigar, which he happened to be smoking when the revel broke up.

It was nearly out, and he was about to extinguish it carefully when Nursey's voice was heard, and fearing it would betray him if he hid it in the bed, he threw it underneath, after a final pinch which he thought finished it.

Nursey came in with Demi, who looked much amazed to see the red face of Tommy reposing peacefully upon his pillow.

"He wasn't there just now, because I woke up and could not find him anywhere," said Demi, pouncing on him.

"What mischief are you at now, bad child?" asked Nursey, with a good-natured shake, which made the sleeper open his eye to say, meekly:

"I only ran into Nat's room to see him

about something. Go away, and let me alone; I'm awful sleepy."

Nursey tucked Demi in, and went off to reconnoiter, but only found two boys slumbering peacefully in Dan's room. "Some little frolic," she thought, and as there was no harm done she said nothing to Mrs. Bhaer, who was busy and worried over little Teddy.

Tommy was sleepy, and, telling Demi to mind his own business and not ask questions, he was snoring in ten minutes, little dreaming what was going on under his bed. The cigar did not go out, but smouldered away on the straw carpet till it was nicely on fire, and a hungry little flame went creeping along till the dimity bed-cover caught, then the sheets, and then the bed itself. The beer made Tommy sleep heavily, and the smoke stupefied Demi, so they slept on till the fire began to scorch them, and they were in danger of being burned to death.

Franz was sitting up to study, and as he left the schoolroom he smelt the smoke, dashed upstairs, and saw it coming in a cloud from the left wing of the house. Without stopping to call anyone, he ran into the room, dragged the boys from the blazing bed, and splashed all the water he could find at hand on to the flames. It checked but did not quench the fire, and the children, wakened on being tumbled topsy-turvy into a cold hall, began to roar at the top of their voices. Mrs. Bhaer instantly appeared, and a minute after Silas burst out of his room shouting "Fire!" in a tone that raised the whole house. A flock of white goblins with scared faces crowded into the hall, and for a minute everyone was panic-stricken.

Then Mrs. Bhaer found her wits, bade Nursey see to the burnt boys, and sent Franz and Silas downstairs for some tubs of wet clothes, which she flung on to the bed, over the carpet, and up against the curtains, now burning finely, and threatening to kindle the walls.

Most of the boys stood dumbly looking on, but Dan and Emil worked bravely, running to and fro with water from the bath-room, and helping to pull down the dangerous curtains.

The peril was soon over, and ordering the boys all back to bed, and leaving Silas to watch lest the fire broke out again, Mrs. Bhaer and Franz went to see how the poor boys got on. Demi had escaped with one burn and a grand scare, but Tommy had not only most of his hair scorched off his head, but a great burn on his arm, that made him half crazy with the pain. Demi was soon made cosy, and Franz took him away to his own bed, where the kind lad soothed his fright and hummed him to sleep as cosily as a woman. Nursey watched over poor Tommy all night, trying to ease his misery, and Mrs. Bhaer vibrated between him and little Teddy with oil and cotton, paregoric and squills, saying to herself from time to time, as if she found great amusement in the thought, "I always *knew* Tommy would set the house on fire, and now he has done it!"

When Mr. Bhaer got home next morning he found a nice state of things. Tommy in bed, Teddy wheezing like a little grampus, Mrs. Jo quite used up, and the whole flock of boys so excited that they all talked at once, and almost dragged him by main force to view the ruins. Under his quiet management things soon fell into order, for everyone felt that he was equal to a dozen conflagrations, and worked with a will at whatever task he gave them.

There was no school that morning, but by afternoon the damaged room was put to rights, the invalids were better, and there was time to hear and judge the little culprits quietly. Nat and Tommy told their parts in the mischief, and were honestly sorry for the danger they had brought to the dear old house and all in it. But Dan put on his devil-may-care look, and would not own that there was much harm done.

Now, of all things, Mr. Bhaer hated drinking, gambling, and swearing; smoking he had given up that the lads might not be tempted to try it, and it grieved and angered him deeply to find that the boy, with whom he had tried to be most forbearing, should take advantage of his absence to introduce these forbidden vices, and teach his innocent little lads to think it manly and pleasant to indulge in them. He talked long and earnestly to the assembled boys, and ended by saying, with an air of mingled firmness and regret:

"I think Tommy is punished enough, and that scar on his arm will remind him for a long time to let these things alone. Nat's fright will do for him, for he is really sorry, and does try to obey me. But you, Dan, have been many times forgiven, and yet it does not good. I cannot have my boys hurt by your bad example, nor my time wasted in talking to deaf ears, so you can say good-bye to them all, and tell Nursey to put up your things in my little black bag."

"Oh! sir, where is he going?" cried Nat.

"To a pleasant place up in the country, where I sometimes send boys when they don't do well here. Mr. Page is a kind man, and Dan will be happy there if he chooses to do his best."

"Will he ever come back?" asked Demi.

"That will depend on himself; I hope so."

As he spoke, Mr. Bhaer left the room to write his letter to Mr. Page, and the boys crowded round Dan very much as people do about a man who is going on a long and perilous journey to unknown regions.

"I wonder if you'll like it," began Jack.

"Shan't stay if I don't," said Dan coolly.

"Where will you go?" asked Nat.

"I may go to sea, or out West, or take a look at California," answered Dan, with a reckless air that quite took away the breath of the little boys.

"Oh, don't! Stay with Mr. Page a while and then come back here; do, Dan," pleaded Nat, much affected at the whole affair.

"I don't care where I go, or how long I stay, and I'll be hanged if I ever come back here," with which wrathful speech Dan went away to put up his things, every one of which Mr. Bhaer had given him.

That was the only good-bye he gave the boys, for they were all talking the matter over in the barn when he came down, and he told Nat not to call them. The wagon stood at the door, and Mrs. Bhaer came out to speak to Dan, looking so sad that his heart smote

him, and he said in a low tone:

"May I say good-bye to Teddy?"

"Yes, dear; go in and kiss him. He will miss his Danny very much."

No one saw the look in Dan's eyes as he stooped over the crib, and saw the little face light up at first sight of him, but he heard Mrs. Bhaer say pleadingly:

"Can't we give the poor lad *one* more trial, Fritz?" and Mr. Bhaer answered in his steady way:

"My dear, it is not best, so let him go where he can do no harm to others, while they do good to him, and by and by he shall come back, I promise you."

"He's the only boy we ever failed with, and I am so grieved, for I thought there was the making of a fine man in him, spite of his faults."

Dan heard Mrs. Bhaer sigh, and he wanted to ask for *one more* trial himself, but his pride would not let him, and he came out with the hard look on his face, shook hands without a word, and drove away with Mr. Bhaer, leaving Nat and Mrs. Jo to look after him with tears in their eyes.

A few days afterwards they received a letter from Mr. Page, saying that Dan was doing well, whereat they all rejoiced. But three weeks later came another letter, saying that Dan had run away, and nothing had been heard of him, whereat they all looked sober, and Mr. Bhaer said:

"Perhaps I ought to have given him another chance."

Mrs. Bhaer, however, nodded wisely and answered: "Don't be troubled, Fritz; the boy will come back to us, I'm sure of it."

But time went on and no Dan came.

Hatsuno's Great-Grandmother
Florence Crannell Means

This excerpt is from Told Under the Stars and Stripes, *a collection of stories that reflects the many racial and religious groups living together under the flag of the United States.*

Hatsuno Noda walked alone in the crowd of girls and boys pouring out of school. She held her head so straight that her chubby black braids spatted her trim shoulders, and her step was so brisk that you would have thought she enjoyed walking by herself. Hatsuno could not bear to let anyone guess how lonesome she felt in the gay throng.

Brother Harry and six-year-old brother Teddy were deep in clumps of their schoolmates, but the girls from Hattie's class streamed by her without pausing. Behind her Patty White, whom she liked best of all, skipped along between Sue and Phyllis, giggling and talking. Hattie wondered what they were talking about. Often they were chattering about Hattie's secret dream; but today it sounded as if they were discussing the Mother's Day tea next month. This morning the teacher had appointed Patty chairman of the decorating committee.

Hattie could have helped decorate. Her slim fingers knew how to fold amazing Japanese paper birds, flowers, dolls. And at the old school the teacher would have had her do colored drawings on the blackboard, along with Tommy Lin, who was Chinese, and Consuelo, who was Mexican. The three drew better than any of the "plain Americans." But in this new school, where almost all were "plain Americans," no one knew what Hattie's fingers could do.

No, the girls were not talking about the tea.

"If you join now," Patty was saying, "you can go up to camp this summer—"

Oh, if only Patty were saying it to Hatsuno! But she wasn't. She broke off as she danced past with the others.

"Hi, Hattie!" she called, wrinkling her uptilted nose in a smile and tossing back her thistledown curls.

Hattie smiled a small, stiff smile, though she ached to shout "Hi!" and fall in step with Patty. Then maybe Patty would think to ask her.

"Join"—"camp": those words were the keys to one of Hattie's dearest dreams.

Hatsuno had never been in the mountains. All her life she had lived where she could see them, stretching like a purple wall across the end of the dingy downtown street. They were beautiful, with snow-capped peaks shining pink and lavender and gold in the sunrise, and Hatsuno had always longed to explore them; but though they looked so near, they were miles and miles away.

The new school had given her hope. In the new school there was a Camp Fire group; and every summer it spent a few days at a camp far up in the mountains. Hattie had seen pictures of its bark-covered lodges climbing steeply among the tall evergreens beside a sparkling stream. She had heard Patty tell of the campfires and the horse-back rides. For Patty was a Camp Fire girl, and Patty's mother was the guardian of the group. Yet, friendly though Patty was, she never spoke of Hattie's joining. And Hattie was far too shy to bring up the subject.

In her old home she had not been so shy; but the old house had grown too small, and they had had to move to a larger one. Hattie, the first Noda baby, had been followed by five boys, and, as Harry said, each child shrunk the house a little bit more. This spring brought not only a new baby but a new grandmother, and the house was as small as Hattie's year-before-last coat. Even Mother couldn't let out its hems enough to make it do.

Mother could manage almost anything. During the depression, when Father was out of work, Mother had kept the children neat as wax and even stylish. She was always up, working, when Hattie woke in the morning, always up, mending and making over, when Hattie went to sleep at night. Mother was proud that even in the bad years Denver had few Japanese Americans "on relief": almost as few as in jail.

Even Mother could not stretch the house enough for the new baby and Great-Grandmother. So the Nodas had moved, uprooting the children from neighborhood and school.

"Hatsuno's Great-Grandmother" by Florence Crannell Means, from TOLD UNDER THE STARS AND STRIPES, copyright 1945 The Macmillan Company, New York, New York. Reprinted by permission of the author and the Association for Childhood Education International, 3615 Wisconsin Avenue, N.W., Washington, DC 20016.

The new school was pleasant; Hattie's teacher, Miss Bender, was lovely; Patty White was the gayest, prettiest girl Hattie had ever met. But Hattie didn't fit in.

So here she was, walking home alone, with Camp Fire and the mountains as far away as ever. Teddy overtook her, making noises like a machine gun—like a railway train—like an airplane. Teddy's face was as round as a button, his eyes as black as coal, his teeth as white as rice.

"Last one home's a lame duck!" he chirped at her.

She did not hurry as once she would have done. Home was a changed place now; changed by Grandmother as well as by the new house.

Though Great-Grandmother had come from Japan ten years ago, Hattie had never seen her till this month. Great-Grandmother had lived with Aunt Kiku in San Francisco, until Aunt Kiku's death had left Grandmother alone.

She was not at all what Hattie had expected; not at all like grandmothers in books, comfortable, plump people who loved to spoil their grandchildren. No, Grandmother was not that kind.

Hattie slowly opened the door, which still quivered from Teddy's banging it. Little gray Grandmother sat stiffly erect, only her head bent toward the sock she was darning, her small feet dangling.

"How do you do, Grandmother?" said Hattie.

"How do you do, Elder Daughter?" Grandmother responded. There is no easy way to say "granddaughter" in Japanese.

Under their folded lids Grandmother's eyes traveled down Hattie. Hattie, feeling prickly, smoothed her hair, straightened her collar, twitched her checked skirt, and finally shifted her weight to one knee as Grandmother reached her feet.

"A cold day for bare legs," Grandmother observed. Hattie thought her look added, *And a great girl twelve years old should wear long stockings.*

Self-consciously Hattie's eyes pulled free from Grandmother's. "Oh," she cried,

"Dicky's climbed on the piano again." She ran over and replaced the box of satiny white wood in which her latest—and last—doll always stood on view, fairly safe from the six boys. It was an enchanting doll, with glossy black hair and a silk kimono. "The other boys at least keep off the piano," Hattie scolded, "but not Dicky."

Grandmother's cool eyes seemed to say, *Boys have to be excused, since they're so much more important than girls. And why should a great girl of twelve care about dolls?*

Hatti hurried on into the good-smelling kitchen. "Mother," she complained, "Grandmother doesn't understand that we're Americans, not Japanese. I bet she'd like me to flop down on my knees and bump my head on the floor the way you used to have to, and say, 'Honorable Grandmother, I have returned.'"

"Wash your hands," said Mother, "and help me get dinner on the table."

Hattie slapped her shoes down hard, as she went to the sink to wash. She wished her heels weren't rubber; they didn't make enough noise to express her feelings.

"Of course you will give proper courtesy to the old," Mother said quietly.

"Why? She doesn't even like me." The question was useless. Hattie had grown up knowing that politeness to the old was as much a law as honesty, industry, self-control —and minding parents.

Mother only said, "Stop and buy grapefruit on your way from school. Be sure to pick out heavy ones."

"Of course," Hattie grumbled. Hadn't she known how to choose good fruit and vegetables since she was nine?

Dinner was Japanese American. Seven Nodas—and Grandmother—crowded around an ordinary American table; but the utensils were chopsticks instead of knives and forks. The fish soup and the pickled radish were Japanese; the *pakkai* were American spareribs and the fluffy white rice was international. Bread and butter were pure American, and the dessert was Japanese gelatin, too firm to quiver. "It's not so nervous as American jelly," Harry said, and made

Teddy laugh till his eyes went shut.

Only Grandmother seemed all Japanese; in the way she sipped her soup and tea, with a noise that was polite in Japan but not in America; in the way she refused bread and butter; in the way she greeted an old neighbor of the Nodas', who came in as they were finishing the meal.

Grandmother shuffled across the room, toeing in, because for sixty-five of her seventy-five years she had worn clogs; and she bowed the deep bow of old Japan, her withered hands sliding down to her knees. Why couldn't Grandmother be more American?

The neighbor had come to remind them that tonight was the festival called Buddha's Birthday. Grandmother's eyes brightened at the news. But Mother apologized: she could not go with Grandmother, for Saburo the new baby was feverish, and she could never bear to leave her babies when they were sick. Father? He had to work tonight. Thoughtfully Grandmother looked at Hattie. Hattie excused herself and hurried back to school.

Right up to the time school opened, she kept seeing Grandmother's eyes brighten and grow dull. If Hattie had been with Patty and the others on the schoolground, as she longed to be, she might have forgotten Grandmother. But sitting lonesomely at her desk, pretending to read, she could not forget.

Maybe it was good, after all, to have a rule about being kind to old people whether they like you or not. Hattie thought of Mother, taking care of her and her brothers when they were young and helpless. How dreadful if, when Mother grew old and helpless, they did not take turn about and care for her! Hattie frowned at her book, thinking.

"Mad, Hattie? My, but you're scowling!" teased Patty, pausing as she came in from the schoolground.

Hattie shook her head and smiled. If only Patty would sit down beside her and say the thrilling words, "Oh, Hattie, wouldn't you like to join Camp Fire?" If she would even say, "Can't you come over after school?"

But after school Hattie walked home alone, as usual, stopping for the grapefruit on her way. When she had put them in the home cooler, she hunted up Grandmother, and ducked her head in a shy bow. "Grandmother," she said, "if you want to go to Buddha's Birthday tonight, I'm sure Mother will let Harry and me go with you."

The Nodas were Methodists, so the Buddhist church was strange to Hattie and Harry. Tonight it was crowded, and all through the program small children trotted in and out and climbed over people's feet, with nobody minding. There were songs and dances and pantomimes, graceful kimonos, stately poses, dignified steps; and voices in the high falsetto which was the proper tone for Japanese actors, but which gave Hattie a funny, embarrassed feeling. "Such squeaky doors!" Harry whispered comically.

Coming home by street-car and bus, the three arrived so late that the house was all sleeping. Harry bade Grandmother goodnight and stumbled drowsily to his room, but Grandmother lingered, eyes bright and cheeks flushed.

Hattie hunted for something to say. "The dancing was lovely," she said. "And the kimonos."

"I have one old kimono," Grandmother said, turning toward her door. With Hattie at her heels, she opened a dresser drawer and took out a silken bundle which she unfolded and held out, smiling faintly at Hattie's gasp of admiration.

"Chrysanthemums, for your aunt's name, Kiku, Chrysanthemum," said Grandmother. Gorgeous blossoms in many rich colors grew across the heavy blue crepe. "It was the only one saved from the great San Francisco fire. She wrapped it round one of her doll boxes." Grandmother motioned toward the drawer and a white wood box that lay there.

"Could I see?" Hattie stuttered.

"You may," Grandmother answered.

When Hattie slid open the box the breath of the Orient puffed out into her nostrils. She lifted the bag that protected the doll's hair and face, and gazed at the miniature lady, exquisitely moulded, and robed in brocades, padded, corded, embroidered. Clasping the box to her breast with one hand, Hattie

pulled out a chair for Grandmother. "I don't know much about the doll festival," she coaxed shyly. "Here in Denver we don't."

She curled up on the floor at Grandmother's feet. "O Kiku San brought her doll set with her," Grandmother said, "when she married and came to America. This one is more than a hundred years old. We were taught to take care of things. The girls' festival—O Hina Matsuri—was a great day. It was play, but it taught us history and manners."

Looking from the doll to Grandmother, Hattie listened with all her might. She missed some words, for the Japanese the Nodas used at home was simple, and, to Hattie's relief, there had been no Japanese Language School for some years now. Still, she could follow the story, and it made pictures for her in the quiet night: little-girl-Grandmother wearing enchanting kimonos, in charming rooms carpeted with cushiony mats; spending long hours learning to serve tea just so, to arrange flowers just so, to paint the difficult Japanese letters just so; learning to hold her face and voice calm no matter how she felt. Girl-Grandmother, writing poems with her friends and going to view the full moon, valuing beauty above riches. Grandmother, hearing about America, and longing to go where life was free for women. Grandmother, never able to come until she was too old to fit herself into this new land.

When the parlor clock struck one, Grandmother stopped short. "A girl of twelve should be asleep!" she said severely.

Next morning Hattie wondered if she had dreamed that companionable midnight visit, for Grandmother looked coldly at Hattie's bare knees and said, "Since you must run and jump like a boy, I suppose those ugly short clothes are necessary." But even while Hattie was biting her lip uncomfortably, Grandmother added, "Hatsuno, the chrysanthemum kimono and the doll are to be yours. After all, you are our only girl."

Home was beginning to seem homelike again.

That was fortunate for Hattie, since neighborhood and school were still strange. It was a relief to go back to their old district on Sundays, to the Japanese Methodist Church. And once Mother took the older children to an evening carnival at their old school. On the way they stopped at the store where they used to buy Japanese food, dishes, cloth. Clean and bright itself, it was jammed in among grimy second-hand stores and pawn shops. It was queer, Hattie thought, but no matter how clean people were, or what good citizens, if they happened to be born Chinese or Japanese or Mexican, they were expected to live down on these dirty, crowded streets, with the trucks roaring past. Yes, the new neighborhood and school were far pleasanter than the old—if only Hatsuno could fit in.

As Mother's Day approached, Hattie felt lonelier than ever. When she came into school two days before the tea, Patty, Sue and Phyllis were huddled round the teacher's desk. Miss Bender smiled approvingly at Hattie, who was already top student in Seventh Grade. Patty smiled, too, and looked at her expectantly. Hattie's heart thumped with the wish to push herself in amongst them. But how could she? She smoothed her starched skirt under her, sat down, and pretended to clean out her desk.

"It's such a late spring," Miss Bender was saying, "the lilacs aren't out. But I'll bring sprays of cherry-blossoms. And we must find out how many mothers to expect. I hope your mother is coming, Hattie."

"No, ma'am," Hattie said soberly. "The baby has chickenpox, and Mother just won't leave a sick baby."

"Haven't you an aunt or grandmother who could come in her place?"

Oh, dear! Grandmother would be so different from the rest. What would Patty think of her? Then Hattie's head came up. "I'll ask Great-Grandmother," she said.

She thought Grandmother would refuse. She hoped Grandmother would refuse. Instead, Grandmother asked, "Every girl should have mother or grandmother at this tea?"

"Yes, Grandmother."

"And your mother will not leave the baby. Elder daughter, you went with me to Buddha's Birthday. I go with you to school."

Hattie swallowed a lump in her throat. Grandmother was doing this because she thought Hattie wished it. Tea—Grandmother would sip it in Japanese fashion. Would she notice if the girls giggled? She would hide the fact if she did. Hattie thought of Grandmother's long training in the concealment of pain or disappointment. Well, that was a good heritage for anybody. Hattie would use it now. "Thank you, Grandmother," she said. "I will come and get you Friday, after school."

When the two came into the schoolroom that afternoon, the mothers were all there and having their tea, and it seemed to Hattie that everyone stopped talking and turned to gaze. Well, she and Grandmother must look pretty funny, Hattie thought.

Hattie was dressed like the other girls, in white sweater and short white skirt, her white anklets folded neatly above her oxfords, and her black hair out of its braids and done in another favorite style of the season. Grandmother, as short and slim as Hattie, wore a dress nicely made over from a kimono, but looking a little strange; and her gray hair was combed straight back from the withered little face with its slanting eyes.

Politely Hattie introduced Miss Bender to Grandmother, and pulled up one of the visitor's chairs, since Grandmother had never been to a tea where people stood up and balanced the dishes on their hands. Patty brought her a plate, Phyllis the sandwiches, Sue a cup of tea. Then Patty returned, pulling her mother after her. "Mom," she said, "here's Hattie. And here's her great-grandma." Patty dropped her mother's hand and stood beaming.

Hattie looked anxiously at Grandmother. She could not speak a word of English, nor the others a word of Japanese. But, instead of words, Seventh Grade and its mothers were bringing sandwiches and cakes till Grandmother's plate was heaped. And Grandmother sat there, as stately and self-possessed and smiling as if she went to seven teas a week.

Hattie studied her more closely. Others might think Grandmother's little face a mask, but Hattie saw that the eyes were bright again, and that the wrinkled cheeks were pink. Grandmother liked it! Grandmother felt happy and at home!

Maybe even a great-grandmother could be lonesome, especially when she was too old to learn the ways of a new land. Thinking so happily of Grandmother that she forgot all about her own shyness, Hattie squeezed Patty's arm, just as she might have squeezed Teddy's on some rare occasion when he was sweet instead of maddening.

Patty squeezed back—quickly, as if she had been waiting for the chance. "Mother!" she stuttered, in a voice that matched her gay fluff of curls. "Mother, I think maybe I was mistaken. I think Hattie might like to—" She looked eagerly up into her mother's questioning eyes—"You ask her, Mother!" she begged.

"About Camp Fire? Hattie, would you like to join our Camp Fire group?"

Hattie was silent from pure joy and astonishment.

"If I got your name in this week," Mrs. White continued, "you could go to camp with us. A camp in the mountains; do you know about it?"

"Oh, yes, ma'am, I know," Hattie said with shining eyes. "Oh, yes, ma'am!"

from **Ellen Grae**
Vera and Bill Cleaver

In Ellen Grae, *the authors have written a short but provocative book that is humorous and at the same time seriously explores the question of moral responsibility.*

[Ellen Tells a Story and Hears a Story]

Mrs. McGruder isn't a religious person especially, although she and Mr. McGruder attend the Methodist Church every Sunday and when I live with her I have to leave off being a Pantheist and turn Methodist too. But she likes to have people talk to her about religion.

So, wanting to please her, I told her that I had learned to be most truly, humbly grateful for all the benevolences God had seen fit to bestow upon me.

She turned a light green gaze upon me and asked, "Oh? What brought that on?"

"Nothing brought it on," I explained. "I just started feeling grateful toward Him. I feel grateful toward you too, Mrs. McGruder. For letting me come back down here and stay with you while I go to school. I vow that I've changed since last year and won't be as much trouble to you this year as I was last."

She said, "Well, if that's true it'll be my turn to be grateful. Like what, for instance, have you changed?"

"Well, for one thing I take a bath every night now without anybody hollering at me to do it and for another I've stopped swearing. I don't even say hell any more. I think that the use of profanity is a vocabulary deficiency, don't you?"

"At the moment I can't think," Mrs. McGruder said, handing me a freshly sugared doughnut. "I'm too busy counting my blessings."

"I know a girl whose father, they said,

dropped dead from swearing. Her name's Opal Gridley. Her father's name was Fortis Alonzo and I think that's what killed him."

"I'm really trying but I don't get the connection," Mrs. McGruder said.

"You will in a minute. Well, anyway, he was a meter reader for the gas company and I guess that and his having a name like Fortis Alonzo burdened him heavily and made him feel unimportant."

"I think Fortis Alonzo is rather a pretty name," Mrs. McGruder murmured.

"Do you? Well, that's what it was. Fortis Alonzo Gridley. He used to drive around with all the windows in his car rolled up. Even when everybody else was standing around pouring sweat and with their tongues hanging out having trouble breathing because it was so hot, Mr. Gridley would get in his car and roll up all the windows and drive around and wave to people."

"I'm still trying," Mrs. McGruder said.

"His wife was fat and could sing Italian. She practiced every night after supper. If you listened it was sadly pretty but nobody did. They'd all come out on their porches and stand around and laugh and this made Mr. Gridley mad. He'd run out of his house and shake his fist at them and swear. When he died everybody said that's what caused it. They said God struck him dead for swearing so much. But do you know something?"

"I'm beginning to think not," Mrs. McGruder said.

"Mr. Fortis Alonzo Gridley died at his own hand. Trying to make people think he was rich enough to have an air-conditioned car. He didn't have it though and that's what killed him. The heat and no air at all. I was the one who got to him first the night he collapsed. Gridley's house was next door to ours and when I saw Mr. Gridley drive up weaving and wobbling I ran over and jerked the door of his car open and he fell out. He didn't have time to say one word. Just blew a bubble and died."

"What do you mean he blew a bubble?"

"He blew a bubble while he was dying. It looked like glass. Mrs. McGruder?"

"Yes, Ellen Grae?"

"Was that telegram that came a few minutes ago from Rosemary?"

"It was from her father. She'll be in on the ten o'clock train. Are you ready for more breakfast now?"

"No thanks. I still hate breakfast; I haven't changed that much. Will I have to room with her again?"

"That's my plan. Why?"

"Oh, nothing. It's just that I was thinking it might be better if I could have a room to myself this year. I forgot to tell you and I'll bet Grace did too that lately I have these strange seizures."

"Seizures? What kind of seizures?"

"Seizures. You know. They always come at night. I get up and crash around and cry out. I know when I'm doing it but I can't stop myself. Jeff says it's a very frightening thing to watch. He says it's almost as if I was disembodied. I was just thinking it might be better if Rosemary could be spared the sight. You know how frail she is."

"No, I hadn't noticed," Mrs. McGruder said, setting two scrambled eggs and a glass of milk in front of me. "I'll be on the lookout for one of your attacks but in the meantime could you just oblige me and eat so that we can get on to more important things?"

Mrs. McGruder is a MORE person. Everything, no matter what it is, always should be MORE.

Together we went down the hall to the room that I was again to share with Rosemary and Mrs. McGruder looked at my bed and said that the sheets and spread could stand a little MORE smoothing and the pillow a little MORE plumping. Then she watched while I finished unpacking my suitcases which contained MORE books than clothes and said that I should have brought MORE dresses and that those I did bring needed MORE starch.

She looked at my white shoes and made a noise with her tongue against the roof of her mouth. "Who polished these shoes, Ellen Grae?"

"I did. Don't they look nice?"

"Yes. Except they've got MORE white on the soles than on the tops."

About ten o'clock we drove down to the village of Thicket to meet Rosemary's train but as usual it was late. Mrs. McGruder parked the car off to one side and tried to settle down to reading a magazine which she had had the foresight to bring along but couldn't because I was there.

"Goodness, Ellen Grae. Stop fidgeting."

"I'm not fidgeting. I'm itching myself. It's all those baths I've been taking. Wouldn't some boiled peanuts taste good right about now? Just to take our minds off things?"

Mrs. McGruder frowned but when she turned her head to look at me there was a gentleness in her eyes. "Oh, honey, you don't really want any boiled peanuts now, do you?"

"Some nice, salty, juicy ones. The way Ira fixes them. While we're just sitting here waiting for Rosemary I could just hop over to his stand and get us a couple of bags. I'd hurry."

Mrs. McGruder sighed but reached into her handbag and found her change purse and extracted a quarter. "All right but don't make me come after you. And watch when you cross the street."

She meant for cars, of course, but there were only three parked ones. First Street lay hot and quiet under the September sun. The only humans in sight were the clerk from Sangster's Grocery Store who was busy letting down the green window awnings, a man in white coveralls who had his head stuck in the door of the barber shop, and Ira who was setting up his stand in its customary oak-shaded spot.

A lot of people in Thicket think that Ira is crazy but he's not. He's just different. He never wears shoes even when the cold winds come sweeping down from the north, he can't read or write and he lives in a two-room tin shack down near the river bend all by himself. Mrs. McGruder told me that once upon a time Ira had a mother and father, at least a stepfather, but that one day they just picked up and left and never came back. Nobody knows how old Ira is. Mrs. McGruder says maybe thirty but I think maybe he's older because he's got white in his black hair and sometimes his dark eyes have a very old man's sadness in them. Ira lives on what money he can make selling boiled and parched peanuts and sometimes somebody patient will pay him to mow a yard. He could make a lot of money mowing yards because he's neat and careful but he won't talk to people. He just nods and points which makes everybody nervous. Even when he goes into a store to buy something that's all he does. Mrs. McGruder told me that in all the years she's been seeing Ira around town she's never heard him speak. I reckon nobody has except me. He talks to me all the time.

I skipped up to his stand and whacked the board that was his counter and said, "Hey, Ira."

He turned around and gave me his slow, quiet look. "Hey, Ellen Grae. I wuz hopin' you'd come by to see me this mornin'. I saw you yistiddy when you come on the train."

"You did? I didn't see you. Why didn't you holler?"

"They wuz people around. Ellen Grae, I got me a goat now."

"Oh, Ira, that's wonderful!"

"When can you come and see her?"

"I don't know. Maybe Sunday after church. I'll get Grover to come with me. I brought back a whole pile of books with me. If you want me to I'll bring one when I come and read you a story. What's your goat's name?"

"Missouri."

"Missouri? That's a funny name for a goat."

"My mother's name wuz Missouri," Ira explained softly, setting two waxed paper bags of boiled peanuts up on the counter. "My goat reminds me of my mother. Did I ever tell you what happened to my mother, Ellen Grae?"

I laid my quarter on the counter and waited for Ira to lay back a nickel change but he didn't. Which wasn't unusual. Ira didn't know how to make change. If you handed him a dollar for one bag of peanuts he'd keep the whole thing. But, by the same token, if you only handed him a penny for a half dozen bags that was all right too. So, if you traded with him for any length of time, things kind of evened themselves out.

"Yes, you told me what happened to your

mother, Ira. Listen, I have to go now. Mrs. McGruder and I just came down to the train station to meet Rosemary. When Grover and I come over Sunday afternoon I'll read to you."

"She died in the swamp, she and her husband. While they wuz tryin' to run away from me. They had 'em this ol' rattler in a box and they wuz draggin' me alongside an' pokin' at him with a stick but instead of bitin' me like he wuz suppose' to, she stuck his ol' head out 'n bit 'em. They swoll up and threshed around some afterward but they wa'n't nothing I could do for 'em. We wuz too far back in the swamp. So I buried 'em 'longside of that ol' snake. I killed the snake first so he wouldn't bite 'em no more. I didn't tell you 'bout this before, did I, Ellen Grae?"

"No, I reckon this is the first time, Ira. Listen, I'll see you Sunday." I picked up the two bags of peanuts and started to turn away and leave but something in the way Ira looked caused me to turn back. "Listen, Ira, you feel all right, don't you? You aren't sick or anything, are you?"

For a second I thought there were tears on Ira's black lashes but it was only the sun glinting on them. He said, "No, I'm not sick, Ellen Grae. Just tuckered out from talkin' so much."

Poor Ira. He has these hallucinations.

from The Egypt Game
Zilpha K. Snyder

Once launched into the "Egypt Game," Melanie and her brother Marshall meet April. The two girls plunge themselves into imaginative games with youthful enthusiasm.

Enter Melanie—and Marshall

On that same day in August, just a few minutes before twelve, Melanie Ross arrived at the door of Mrs. Hall's apartment on the third floor. Melanie was eleven years old and she had lived in the Casa Rosada since she was only seven. During that time she'd welcomed a lot of new people to the apartment house. Apartment dwellers, particularly near a university, are apt to come and go. Melanie always looked forward to meeting new tenants, and today was going to be especially interesting. Today, Melanie had been sent up to get Mrs. Hall's granddaughter to come down and have lunch with the Rosses. Melanie didn't know much about the new girl except that her name was April and that she had come from Hollywood to live with Mrs. Hall who was her grandmother.

It would be neat if she turned out to be a real friend. There hadn't been any girls the right age in the Casa Rosada lately. To have a handy friend again, for spur-of-the-moment visiting, would be great. However, she had overheard something that didn't sound too promising. Just the other day she'd heard Mrs. Hall telling Mom that April was a strange little thing because she'd been brought up all over everywhere and never had much of a chance to associate with other children. You wouldn't know what to expect of someone like that. But then, you never knew what to expect of any new kid, not really. So Melanie knocked hopefully at the door of apartment 312.

Meeting people had always been easy for Melanie. Most people she liked right away, and they usually seemed to feel the same way about her. But when the door to 312 opened that morning, for just a moment she was almost speechless. Surprise can do that to a person, and at first glance April really was a surprise. Her hair was stacked up in a pile that seemed to be more pins than hair, and the whole thing teetered forward over her thin pale face. She was wearing a big, yellowish-white fur thing around her shoulders, and carrying a plastic purse almost as big as a suitcase. But most of all it was the eyelashes. They were black and bushy looking, and the ones on her left eye were higher up and sloped in a different direction. Melanie's mouth opened and closed a few times before anything came out.

April adjusted Dorothea's old fur stole, patted up some sliding strands of hair and waited—warily. She didn't expect this Melanie to like her—kids hardly ever did—but she *did* intend to make a very definite impression; and she could see that she'd done that all right.

"Hi," Melanie managed after that first speechless moment. "I'm Melanie Ross. You're supposed to have lunch with us, I think. Aren't you April Hall?"

"April Dawn," April corrected with an offhand sort of smile. "I was expecting you. My grandmother informed me that—uh, she said you'd be up."

It occurred to Melanie that maybe kids dressed differently in Hollywood. As they started down the hall she asked, "Are you going to stay with your grandmother for very long?"

"Oh no," April said. "Just till my mother finishes this tour she's on. Then she'll send for me to come home."

"Tour?"

"Yes, you see my mother is Dorothea Dawn—" she paused and Melanie racked her brain. She could tell she was supposed to know who Dorothea Dawn was. "Well, I guess you haven't happened to hear of her way up here, but she's a singer and in the movies, and stuff like that. But right now she's singing with this band that travels around to different places."

"Neat!" Melanie said. "You mean your mother's in the movies?"

But just then they arrived at the Ross's apartment. Marshall met them at the door, dragging Security by one of his eight legs.

"That's my brother, Marshall," Melanie said.

"Hi, Marshall," April said. "What in the heck is that?"

Melanie grinned. "That's Security. Marshall takes him everywhere. So my dad named him Security. You know. Like some little kids have a blanket."

"Security's an octopus," Marshall said very clearly. He didn't talk very much, but when he did he always said exactly what he wanted

"Enter Melanie—and Marshall" from THE EGYPT GAME by Zilpha Keatley Snyder. Copyright © 1967 by Zilpha Keatley Snyder (New York: Atheneum, 1967). Reprinted with the permission of Atheneum Publishers.

to without any trouble. He never had fooled around with baby talk.

Melanie's mother was in the kitchen putting hot dog sandwiches and fruit salad on the table. When Melanie introduced April she could tell that her mother was surprised by the eyelashes and hairdo and everything. She probably didn't realize that kids dressed a little differently in Hollywood.

"April's mother is a movie star," Melanie explained.

Melanie's mother smiled. "Is that right, April?" she asked.

April looked at Melanie's mother carefully through narrowed eyes. Mrs. Ross looked sharp and neat, with a smart-looking very short hairdo like a soft black cap, and high winging eyebrows, like Melanie's. But her smile was a little different. April was good at figuring out what adults meant by the things they didn't quite say—and Mrs. Ross's smile meant that she wasn't going to be easy to snow.

"Well," April admitted, "not a star, really. She's mostly a vocalist. So far she's only been an extra in the movies. But she almost had a supporting role once, and Nick, that's her agent, says he has a big part almost all lined up."

"Gee, that's neat!" Melanie said. "We've never known anyone before whose mother was an extra in the movies, have we Mom?"

"Not a soul," Mrs. Ross said, still smiling.

During lunch, April talked a lot about Hollywood, and the movie stars she'd met and the big parties her mother gave and things like that. She knew she was overdoing it a bit but something made her keep on. Mrs. Ross went right on smiling in that knowing way, and Melanie went right on being so eager and encouraging that April thought she must be kidding. She wasn't sure though. You never could tell with kids—they didn't do things in a pattern, the way grown-ups did.

Actually Melanie knew that April was being pretty braggy, but it occurred to her that it was probably because of homesickness. It was easy to see how much she'd like to be back in Hollywood with her mother.

While they were having dessert of ice cream and cookies, Mrs. Ross suggested that April might like to look over Melanie's books to see if there was anything she'd like to borrow.

"Do you like to read?" Melanie asked. "Reading is my favorite occupation."

"That's for sure." Mrs. Ross laughed. "A full-time occupation with overtime. Your grandmother tells me that you do a lot of reading, too."

"Well, of course, I'm usually pretty busy, with all the parties and everything. I do read some though, when I have a chance."

But after lunch when Melanie showed April her library, a whole bookcase full in her bedroom, she could tell that April liked books more than just a little. She could tell just by the way April picked a book up and handled it, and by the way she forgot about acting so grown-up and Hollywoodish. She plopped herself down on the floor in front of the bookcase and started looking at books like crazy. For a while she seemed to forget all about Melanie. As she read she kept propping up her eyelashes with one finger.

All of a sudden she said, "Could you help me get these darn things off? I must not have put them on the right place or something. When I look down to read I can't even see the words."

So Melanie scratched the ends of the eyelashes loose with her longest fingernail, and then April pulled them the rest of the way off. They were on pretty tight, and she said, "Ouch!" several times and a couple of other words that Melanie wasn't allowed to say.

"——!" said April, looking in the mirror. "I think I pulled out most of my real ones. Does it look like it to you?"

"I don't think so," Melanie said. "I still see some. Is this the first time you've worn them? The false ones, I mean?"

April put back on her haughty face. "Of course not. Nearly everybody wears them in Hollywood. My mother wears them all the time. It's just that these are new ones, and they must be a different kind."

April put her eyelashes away carefully in her big bag and they went back to looking at books. Melanie showed her some of her favorites, and April picked out a couple to borrow. It was then that April took a very special book off the shelf.

It was a very dull-looking old geography book that no one would be interested in. That was why Melanie used it to hide something very special and secret. As April opened the book some cutout paper people fell out on the floor.

"What are those?" April asked.

"Just some old things of mine," Melanie said, holding out her hand for the book, but April kept on turning the pages and finding more bunches of paper people.

"Do you really still play with paper dolls?" April asked in just the tone of voice that Melanie had feared she would use. Not just because she was April, either. It was the tone of voice that nearly anyone would use about a sixth grade girl who still played with ordinary paper dolls.

"But they're not really paper dolls," Melanie said, "and I don't really play with them. Not like moving them around and dressing them up and everything. They're just sort of a record for a game I play. I make up a family and then I find people who look like them in magazines and catalogues. Just so I'll remember them better. I have fourteen families now. See they all have their names and ages written on the back. I make up stuff about their personalities and what they do. Sometimes I write it down like a story, but usually I just make it up."

April's scornful look was dissolving. "Like what?"

"Well," Melanie said, "this is the Brewster family. Mr. Brewster is a detective. I had to cut him out of the newspaper because he was the only man I could find who looked like a detective. Don't you think he does?"

"Yeah, pretty much."

"Well anyway, he just—that is, I just made up about how he solved this very hard mystery and caught some dangerous criminals. And then the criminals escaped and were going to get revenge on Mr. Brewster. So the whole family had to go into hiding and wear disguises and everything."

April spread the Brewsters out on the floor. Her eyes were shining and without the eyelashes they were pretty, wide and blue. "Have they caught the criminals yet?" she asked. Melanie shook her head. "Well, how about if the kids catch them. They could just happen to find out where the criminals were hiding?"

"Neat!" Melanie said. "Maybe Ted," she pointed to the smallest paper Brewster, "could come home and tell the other kids how he thinks he saw one of the criminals, going into a certain house."

"And then," April interrupted, "the girls could go to the house pretending to sell Girl Scout cookies, to see if it really was the crooks."

From the Girl-Scout-cookies caper, the game moved into even more exciting escapades, and when Mrs. Ross came in to say that Marshall was down for his nap and that she was leaving for the university where she was taking a summer course for school-teachers, the criminals were just escaping, taking one of the Brewster children with them as a hostage. An hour later, when Marshall came in sleepy-eyed and dragging Security, several of the other paper families had been brought into the plot. Marshall seemed content to sit and listen, so the game went on with daring adventures, narrow escapes, tragic illnesses and even a romance or two. At last, right in the middle of a shipwreck on a desert island, April noticed the time and said she'd have to go home so she'd be there when Caroline got back from work.

As they walked to the door Melanie said, "Do you want to play some more tomorrow?"

April was adjusting her fur stole around her shoulders for the trip upstairs. "Oh, I guess so," she said with a sudden return to haughtiness.

But Melanie was beginning to understand about April's frozen spells, and how to thaw her out. You just had to let her know she couldn't make you stop liking her that easily. "None of my friends know how to play imagining games the way you do," Melanie said. "Some of them can do it a little bit but they mostly don't have any very good ideas. And a lot of them only like ball games or other things that are already made up. But I like imagining games better than anything."

April was being very busy trying to get her stole to stay on because the clasp was a little bit broken. All at once she pulled it off, wadded it all up and tucked it under her arm. She looked right straight at Melanie and said, "You know what? I never did call them that before, but imagining games are just about all I ever play because most of the time I never have anybody to play with."

She started off up the hall. Then she turned around and walked backward waving her fur stole around her head like a lasso. "You've got lots of good ideas, too," she yelled.

from **The Flea Market Mystery**
Virginia Evansen

A brother and sister who are Mexican-Americans investigate a mystery at a senior citizens' co-op from which their grandmother's knitted goods have been stolen.

The October air felt nippy as I hurried the six blocks from school to my grandparents' house. It had been a bad day, as had been all of the days since school started. My cheeks still burned from the embarrassment I had suffered during English class. I'd known the answer to Mrs. Bunton's question; I just couldn't get it out. The giggles from the girl sitting next to me hadn't helped, either.

I hurried through the door, heading for the comfort of the warm kitchen and the cookie jar. "Where are you, *Abuelita?*" I called. "I'm hungry."

"Out here." Grandmother was in the kitchen, sitting at the table. Tears were streaming down her cheeks.

I stopped just inside the door. I had never seen my grandmother cry before, and I felt as if the floor had tilted under my feet. I sort

of tippy-toed over to her, put out my hand, and then let it fall to my side.

I looked at *mi abuelo.* My grandfather was pacing back and forth across the big, old-fashioned kitchen, setting down each foot with an angry stamp. His tall, thin frame was tense, his usually pleasant face furrowed with lines.

"What's the matter? What happened?" I asked.

"Some thieves broke into the Co-op Store and took almost everything there, Nancy. All of your grandmother's sweaters and afghans," he answered.

I moved closer to my grandmother and put my arm around her shoulder. I knew how happy my grandparents had been when the Senior Citizens' Cooperative Store had opened during the summer. They had both worked hard to make things to sell there on consignment.

"All of your grandfather's leather purses and belts were taken, too. I don't know what we are going to do. We needed the money for a new roof," Grandmother said. Her voice sounded hopeless.

"You can make more, *Abuelita.* You crochet so fast."

"No, Nancy. I can't spare the extra money for the yarn. When I sell an afghan, I buy yarn for the next one. The profit goes into the roof fund."

I looked longingly at the cookie jar. I was always hungry after school, but I didn't think that mentioning cookies would be a good idea when my grandparents were so upset. I wished I could do something to help—something besides giving Grandmother a hug. I wanted to buy a pile of yarn as big as a mountain for her.

"Maybe Tomás will know what to do," I said. "He'll be here soon. My brother always has good ideas."

"What can a fifteen-year-old boy do that the police can't?" Grandfather asked scornfully.

I hadn't thought about the police. "*They'll* find the robbers and get everything back. It will be all right." I patted Grandmother's shoulder.

"Mrs. Lancet, the manager, called the police first thing this morning when she opened the store and discovered the robbery. They told her that the stolen goods had probably been taken to Los Angeles to be sold. They held little hope of getting anything back. We aren't the only victims. Bill Jackson lost over three hundred dollars' worth of his handmade jewelry," Grandfather said.

Mr. Jackson was a long-time friend and neighbor. He had taken up jewelry-making as a hobby after he retired from the post office. I remembered hearing him say that his sales helped pay his taxes.

"Maybe your things are right here in Santo Rosario. The police should look around," I protested. "Anyway, I'm going to walk toward the high school to meet Tomás. He might have an idea."

I ran out of the house and down the steps. I just couldn't stay in the kitchen a moment longer watching my grandmother cry. I had never seen her look defeated before. She was tiny and always busy, and so quick that she reminded me of a miniature whirlwind. Her hair, piled high on her head, was thick and still almost all black. She had large brown eyes that could snap when we misbehaved. She was a beautiful grandmother—*una abuela muy linda.*

When I reached the sidewalk, I turned and looked at the house. The white paint around the windows gleamed against the gray siding. The ornate gingerbread trim on the porch was clean, dusted by my grandmother each week. The eight-room house was really too large for my grandparents but I knew that they loved it and wouldn't be happy living anywhere else. The house had been built by my grandfather's grandfather almost a hundred years ago. One of the oldest houses in Santo Rosario, it was known as the Pérez House.

I sighed and started down the street which was lined with acacia trees, walking slowly past the old Victorian houses toward the high school. For almost as long as I could remember I had been going to my grandparents' house after school. My mother worked as a supervisor at an electronics plant and my father owned a florist shop. They picked us up around six each evening. On week nights they often didn't stop in but just waved to my grandparents, because Mom was anxious to get home and start dinner. Usually we spent part of our Sundays together.

At times I wished I could go to my own home after school as Jean Lewis, my best friend, did—to my own room where I could play records or just lie on my bed and look at the flowered wallpaper and let my thoughts drift. When school started, a month ago, I told my mother that now that I was thirteen I was old enough to come home after school and that I could help her by starting dinner.

"No, Nancy," Mom said in the firm voice that meant no arguing. "Thirteen's still young. When you are at Grandmother Pérez's house, I don't worry about you. Besides, you need to keep up your Spanish."

That sounded funny coming from my red-haired Irish mother who knew only a few words of Spanish. She always claimed she was going to take a night-school course in the language if she ever found the time. But she had insisted that we grow up bilingual, so we had learned Spanish from our grandparents. While both of them spoke English well, in their home they spoke nothing but Spanish unless they had guests. Tomás and I had learned the language in self-defense. We called our grandparents *Abuelo* and *Abuelita,* Grandfather and Little Grandmother.

The memory of *Abuelita's* tears quickened my steps as I turned the corner. Halfway down the block I saw Tomás walking slowly with Pete Higgins and Jim Block. I hurried up to them and told my brother I had to talk to him.

He waved me away. "Later," he said. "We're busy now."

"This is important," I insisted. "We have to talk before we reach *Abuelita's* house." I made it plain that I wanted to speak to my brother privately. I wasn't going to discuss family business in front of his friends, even though I had known Pete Higgins ever since I could remember. Jim Block was new in town and I didn't like him, although Tomás said he was an okay guy.

"Better listen to the kid's problem. That's what big brothers are for. She probably busted her doll buggy and wants you to fix it," Jim said, then doubled up with laughter over what he thought was a terrific joke.

I mentally pictured him as a horned toad with warts growing out of warts. "Come on, Tomás," I said. "This is serious."

We walked away from the two boys, and I told Tomás about the robbery. "*Abuelita's* whole world is broken," I finished. "They need that money to fix the roof. We have to do something *pronto.*"

By this time we had reached the house. Tomás removed the headband he had taken to wearing during school hours. In the last couple of months he had become extremely ancestor conscious. He insisted that we call him Tomás instead of the Thomas he had been christened. He had taken to reading all kinds of books about early California history and studying Apache lore. That accounted for the headband.

"We must have some Indian ancestors," he had said. "I have a better right to wear a headband than lots of guys I know."

Grandfather Pérez had gone through the roof the first time Tomás came up with that theory. "My ancestors were soldiers who came to Santo Rosario with the Mission Fathers. There are records that Alvardo Pérez came to this city in 1791. And before that his father came from Spain to Mexico."

I could understand Grandfather's pride in his name, but I couldn't follow Tomás' reasoning. We were of Mexican and Irish descent. If he insisted on wearing a headband, it seemed logical to me that he should carry a shillelagh, too.

Anyway, Grandfather ruled in his own house so Tomás always took off the headband before he went inside. Now he leaned against the porch pillar and looked at me thoughtfully.

"So the police don't offer much hope," he said. "That's typical. Ever see a cop around when you need one?"

Since I had never needed a police officer, I couldn't see what the remark had to do with our problem and I told Tomás so. "We must figure out a way to help them."

"Maybe the parents can come up with the money for the roof."

"Yes, and if they did, you know that Grandfather would refuse it," I answered, impatient with a suggestion that I knew was impractical. My grandfather was a proud man.

Tomás looked at the house. I knew he had the same thoughts as I. We knew every nook and cranny from the attic stuffed with chests, trunks, and barrels to the basement, unusual in Santo Rosario dwellings, where Grandfather kept his leatherworking tools. We had spent so much of our time there that it was home to us.

"I'll just bet the loot is right here in Santo Rosario," Tomás said. "I can't imagine that a big gang of crooks with a truck would bother with a small operation like the Senior Citizens' Co-op here."

"You'd be surprised at how much some of the things sell for," I answered. "*Abuelita's* sweaters and afghans were priced at fifty to one hundred and twenty dollars. And there were Grandfather's leather belts and Mr. Jackson's jewelry. Remember that hammered silver bracelet I wanted? Forty-five dollars. There's no way I could save up for it with an allowance of only three dollars a week."

"That's it!" Tomás cried. "Our allowances. We can give your three and my five to Grandmother. Then she can buy yarn with the money."

I shook my head. "I don't think she'd take it. Besides, what would we do for lunch money?"

"It won't hurt us to go without. The Indians used to fast. They believed it benefitted the body and spirit."

"You and your ideas. Going without lunch would mean you'd clean out Grandmother's refrigerator after school."

Tomás opened the front door. "Speaking of food, what's the condition of the cookie jar?"

"It didn't seem appropriate to ask *Abuelita* for cookies when she was crying. Don't you go doing it," I warned.

"That's dumb. We need to get her mind off her troubles." With that Tomás roared into the house like an Apache brave. He pulled Grandmother off her chair, gave her a big kiss, and told her his stomach was screaming for food. "They had tacos in the cafeteria at lunch," he said. "Imagine serving a Pérez tacos so bad that my taste buds convulsed. You'll have to go over there and give the cooks a lesson in taco-making."

Grandmother brightened. She poured two glasses of milk and set out a plate of cookies while Tomás questioned Grandfather about the robbery.

"It seems that the cops are taking the easy way out," Tomás argued, reaching for a cookie. "If they decide the thieves are hundreds of miles away, they won't have to spend time looking for them here."

"The police know what they are doing," Grandfather said. "Besides, no one would dare to sell the items in Santo Rosario."

"This is a tourist town with dozens of shops handling artsy-craftsy goods. If you spread the things out among the stores, no one would recognize them as stolen," Tomás insisted.

"I would. I'd know my afghans anywhere. Your grandfather's belts, too." Grandmother's dark eyes flashed as she looked at Tomás.

I knew she was right. She made her own patterns, adapting them from Mexican and Indian designs. She finished the edges with a special stitch and signed each piece with a tiny monogram in the corner. That was why her sweaters and afghans brought so much money.

Tomás polished off the cookies while we waited for our parents. As soon as we were in the car, I told Mom and Dad about the burglary. "We have to do something," I finished. "Grandmother needs that money for a new roof."

"Stealing from anyone is a crime, but stealing from old people who live on pensions is hideous," Dad said in a furious voice. "I'd like to get my hands on them. I'd teach them not to take other people's property if I had to break every one of their fingers into ten pieces."

"That won't help your parents," Mom said. She was silent for a couple of blocks. I looked out at the darkening sky and fear gathered behind my chest. My parents *had* to come up with a solution. They had always had the answers before.

"We could take the money out of the college fund, Juan," Mom said to my father. "We have a few years before Tomás starts college, and I'll save some extra dollars each week to make it up."

"You know as well as I do, *machree*, that my father's stubborn Spanish pride wouldn't permit him to take a penny from us." The affectionate Irish word always sounded strange coming from my father's lips. Somehow I always expected him to say *querida* or *mi novia*, but he called her *machree* or some other Irish endearment.

"You could insist," my mother said gently. "Families should help in times of trouble."

"No, I couldn't. Father's a proud man. *Mucho hombre.*"

"Please, Juan. We must help them. You could offer to lend them the money," Mom insisted.

"All right. We'll be pinched because our property taxes went up twenty per cent and are due in December, but I'll try to make Father accept the money as a loan."

As soon as the car stopped, I dashed into the kitchen and started setting the table for dinner. My head felt like a food blender with thoughts splashing against my skull. What were we going to do? I knew that my grandfather would refuse the money. I had heard him say too many times that he owed no man and was proud of it. If Mom and Dad couldn't help, Tomás and I would have to find the stolen goods or a way to make money. But how?

from Guests in the Promised Land
Kristin Hunter

"Two's Enough of a Crowd," a short story for older children, is both funny and tender; a love story in which two black

adolescents find each other. It is also a plea against conformity that has a useful application.

Two's Enough of a Crowd

I used to blame all my troubles on being a nondancer. I thought if I could learn to wiggle and shake, I'd be popular.

One flashy minute on the floor, and whammo! I'd be the Dream Lover. Instead of a tall, skinny, nervous cat who's always trying to disappear into a wall.

It took Amy to show me I was different in other ways, too.

Like my name. Most black cats are named James or William or Leroy. And they're called Cool Breeze or Poor Boy or Pots and Pans.

Nobody black is named Maurice. Except me. And nobody ever called me anything else.

(Of course, nobody black is named *Amy*, either. Now that there's two of us, it's not so bad.)

But in the old days, I felt mighty sorry for myself. I thought I was the only black person in the world with two left feet and no sense of rhythm.

If you're white, you don't have to dance. All you got to do is talk that talk, program them computers, and count that money.

But to be black and a nondancer is like being a blind brain surgeon. Or a one-armed violinist.

Most black kids are born knowing how to dance. They boogaloo into this world and funky chicken into their mothers' arms. Even in my family.

At twelve months my little brother started walking. At fourteen months, he was slopping. I was so disgusted, I never spoke to the little monster again.

Here I thought my bad dancing was something I'd *inherited*, like a long head and pointed ears.

"Two's Enough of a Crowd" from Kristin Hunter, GUESTS IN THE PROMISED LAND. Copyright © 1968, 1972, 1973 by Kristin E. Lattany (New York: Charles Scribner's Sons, 1973). Reprinted with the permission of Charles Scribner's Sons and the Harold Matson Company, Inc.

Don't tell me dancing isn't important. Old folks always say that. They say not dancing leaves you more time to study. Well, that just shows how much *they* know. I'd sell my straight A average tomorrow if I could do the monkey.

Don't tell me to take dancing lessons, either. I tried. I found out three things.

One, only the first lesson is free. After that, they charge you a fortune.

Two, they only teach nowhere dances like the fox-trot and the samba.

Three, ain't no school in the world can teach soul dancing. Sure, they can draw marks on the floor to show where your feet go. But those marks don't show you how to move the rest of your body. And *that's* where it's at, baby.

The knees and the hips and the waist and the arms are all part of the action. And they all got to move *together*. You're either born knowing how, or you're not. If you got it, flaunt it.

If you haven't got it, hide behind the biggest piece of furniture. Which is what I usually do at parties.

At Keeno Robinson's Christmas party, I headed for the Christmas tree as soon as the first record started playing. The tree was only five feet high, and I'm six-one. But by scrunching down, I managed to hide.

Then I peered through the branches. The floor was frantic. Every couple deserved to be on TV. But the best were Stretch Hankins and LaTanya Harris.

LaTanya is the world's foxiest chick. She wears extra hair, false eyelashes, and skin-tight sweaters. I don't really like her. But I'd have given anything to dance with her the way Stretch was doing.

The only time I danced with LaTanya, I stepped on her foot. She laughed at me. I haven't asked her to dance since.

I thought I was the only one at the party not dancing. Then I spotted someone else. I couldn't believe my eyes.

Over in the opposite corner sat this *beautiful* girl. All by herself. *Reading.*

Crossing the floor to get to her wasn't easy. It was like walking through a roomful of guided missiles. But I managed to get there without any bruises.

She looked just as good close up. And it was all real. Hair, eyelashes, everything. "What's your name?" I asked.

"Amy, Amy Livingston."

I told her mine. Then I asked what she was reading.

"Oh, just a book."

"Why did you hide it when I came over?"

"I thought you might laugh at me. It's not relevant."

Now, "relevant" is a very big word in our crowd. If a thing isn't relevant, it's nowhere. As far as I can figure out, "relevant" means something you know already. Like how to comb a natural, and where to buy neck bones.

I finally got the title out of her. *Green Mansions*, by W. H. Hudson.

"It's just a romantic story about a girl who lives in the woods. There aren't any black people in it or anything. It isn't even about anything that could have really happened. It's not at *all* relevant."

"Do you like it?" I asked.

"Very much."

"Well then," I said, "it's relevant to *you.*"

She smiled. It was delightful. All pearls and dimples. "Thank you for saying that. I never thought of that before."

"But why aren't you dancing?" I wanted to know.

"Oh, nobody ever asks me to dance." She wasn't feeling sorry for herself. She just said it straight. Like, "Oh, it never rains around here in October."

But she had to be putting me on. She looked like somebody on a magazine cover.

Idiot that I am, I couldn't resist. "Well, someone is now." Here we go, Mister Clumsy Chump, I thought.

"We'll have to wait for a slow record," she said. And looked down sideways, toward her right foot.

I saw that she had on a heavy, built-up shoe. "I was born with one leg shorter than the other," she explained.

"Just be glad you were born," I said. It came out sounding hard and tough. I hadn't meant it to.

So I added, "Because *I* am."

I got the full, dazzling smile that time. It almost blinded me.

"Oh, what a nice thing to say. I *am* glad. Especially now that I can walk. I couldn't always, you know."

The athletes and acrobats were finally taking a rest. A slow record started playing. And we started moving around the floor.

It was just as easy as that. I found I didn't have to worry about the beat. She dragged one foot slowly. So I dragged both of mine. It left me free to concentrate on other things, like her perfume. It smelled like lilacs, and got me a little drunk.

"You're a great dancer," she said afterward.

Now, anyone who tells me *that* has a friend for life. But the trouble with me is I'm honest.

"Girl, you're a lovely liar," I said. "I can't dance at all."

"Really?" she said with a mischievous grin. "What else can't you do?"

I gave it some serious thought. Finally I admitted, "I can't curse."

It's quite a problem. Most of my friends turn the air blue with every other sentence. But *my* folks are so strict, I have trouble saying heck and darn.

"You think that's bad? I can't even use *slang,*" she said.

She really had my sympathy. First of all, it's not "slang," it's "jive talk." And in our crowd, it's your first language. English is your second.

"I had eight operations," she explained. "I spent four years in the hospital, off and on. Nobody to talk to but white doctors and nurses. Now all the kids say I talk white. They make fun of me. So I mostly keep quiet."

"I love the way you talk. Don't you dare stop," I said.

It was jungle time again. James Brown was grunting and shouting over three speakers.

And LaTanya was going into her act. She danced so violently you'd have thought she was in a hurricane.

Keeno appointed himself a one-man cheering section. "Work out, mama," he urged. "Take it easy, but go greasy. Shake it but don't break it, cause if you bruise it, you can't use it! Oh, I feel so *attitudinous!* My vines are fine, my choppers shine, I'm full of wine, and this pad is *mine!* Pull back your jibs, peasants, and let me pass! Oobydooby-shoobyOW!"

"I think he's happy," I translated for Amy.

"Monkeys love bananas. Maybe somebody just gave him one," she said with a giggle.

I laughed too. Suddenly, the crowd at the party didn't seem like the World's Most Important People. They were just people.

Another person was what made the difference. Or so I was discovering. When you're alone, the center of the crowd seems like the only place to be.

But when there are two of you, you can sit back and watch without feeling left out. You feel very cozy because you've got your *own* crowd.

"Do you like soul food?" I asked. Some platters were appearing.

"I hate it," she said. "All that grease. *Ugh.*"

My sentiments exactly. Why had I been forcing myself to swallow it all those years?

Because I had been alone, that's why. And, alone, I didn't have the courage to say "no thank you."

I was getting curious about this girl. I asked her more questions. "Do you hate honkies?"

"What are they?" she asked.

Too much. Too everlasting much. I explained.

She shuddered. "Oh, no. My doctor is white. He *helped* me. Besides, I don't hate anybody."

"But don't you feel oppressed?"

"I guess I *should,*" she said, looking troubled. "But the truth is, I feel free as a bird. Ever since I started walking."

"Do you like James Brown?" was my next question.

"No," she admitted. "He doesn't sing. He screams."

Now, James Brown is the High Priest of What's Happening. The Sultan of Soul. Not liking him is like drawing a funny mustache on a picture of Malcolm X.

I cheered her courage. "Hooray. Who *is* your favorite musician?"

"Schubert," she said. "And after him, Brahms."

Too unbelievable much! "What else do you like that's unrelevant?"

"The word is *irrelevant,*" she corrected gently. "And the answer is 'everything.'"

The steamy odor of stewed innards was filling Keeno's rec room. Our host was about to pass out the chitlins. "Wrinkled steads, everybody!" he hollered gleefully.

"It's not polite to refuse food," I said. "Let's go, before they make us *eat* those horrible things."

Boy, I felt brave. And free. Like it was 1865, and I'd just kicked off my chains. The ones put on me by my own people.

Amy's house was just like Amy. Different. There were no zebra-striped pillows. No plaster heads of Africans. No orange ceramic cats. Strangest of all, no plastic slipcovers. And no wall-to-wall Spanish-style stereo.

Just worn, comfortable furniture. Old, soft rugs. Lots of books. And a fine, foreign turntable sitting on top of a speaker.

It worked too, which is more than I can say for some stereos. The *Great Symphony* by Schubert lived up to its name. So did the *Fantastic* one by Berlioz.

When they had finished playing, I said, "You're a brave girl, to be so different."

"Not really," she said. "If you're different, you just *are*. You can't be any other way. You have no choice."

So it was as simple as that! After all those years of hiding and pretending to be like the crowd. This girl was amazing.

"But how did you get to be this way?"

"I told you. I had all those operations. They put me behind in school. I've never had much time to run with the crowd. I have to read and study a lot, if I want to catch up and go to college."

"What do you plan to take up? Black studies?"

"Promise not to tell."

I promised.

"English writers. The early ones. Like Chaucer."

Now, how irrelevant can you get? I almost kissed her *then.* "Why did you make me promise not to tell?" I asked.

"Because they'd put me down."

"Who?"

"Keeno. And Cool Breeze. And Sheryl. And Stretch. And LaTanya."

"Well, who put them in charge of the world?" I asked. "Who made *them* the dictators?"

"Nobody. But they *are.*"

"Let me tell you about me," I said. "I have this thing about cells and germs. I love to look at them under a microscope."

"Maybe you'll discover a cure for sickle cell anemia. That's a disease only black people have. That would be relevant."

"Maybe *you'll* discover Chaucer was black."

We laughed ourselves absolutely silly over that one.

Then we got serious. We promised never to let the others know our secrets. Not that we're scared or ashamed. It's just more fun that way.

"Listen, Amy," I said. "This spring my class is having a prom. Not my scene at all. I wasn't planning to go. But I will if you'll go with me."

"I'd love to, Maurice," she said. She made my name sound better than a nickname. When all those years, I'd wished for one.

"I warn you," I said. "I can't do the slop, the wobble, the monkey, or the funky chicken."

"My favorite dance," she said, "is the waltz."

I *had* to kiss her that time. First, for being so different. Second, for showing me I was, too. Third, for proving it didn't matter. Because there were *two* of us now, and we didn't need the dictators. We didn't need to dance, either. How important is dancing, compared to walking?

So we'll go to the prom. And when the others rap and rave, we'll keep quiet. While they jump and shake, we'll sit on the sidelines and smile. And keep our secrets.

Because we've found out that nothing's as relevant as love.

Life in Other Lands

One of the appeals for children in reading about children in other countries is the fascination of learning about other customs and ways of life, and another is almost the opposite: learning that people in other countries have the same problems, share the same joys, and delight in the same accomplishments as they do themselves. The familial relationships of "In the Middle of the Night" by Philippa Pearce could happen in an American as well as an English family; the dramatic setting for A. Rutgers van der Loeff's *Avalanche!* may be exotic to many readers, but the emotions and motivation will be comprehensible to all of them.

from **Hello, Aurora**
Anne-Cath Vestly

This selection is one of the many humorous episodes in this story of a Norwegian family; its quality of warmth is typical of this delightful story.

Father in the Laundry Room

Mother had gone to work, and Father was doing his best to find the things that needed washing. "Let's see, here are the sheets and towels and so on, and here are all our sweaters, Mummy's heavy ski sweater and mine, too. We'll take them all, because those large machines can take a big load, you know. I'll have to make several trips with them, and we'll have Socrates with us too."

"There's an awful lot," said Aurora.

"Listen, I'll go down first with the sheets and put them in the machine, and you can wait here. Then we'll feed and change Socrates, and you can take him out in his baby carriage while I'm in the laundry room."

"All right," said Aurora.

Father went off with a heavy suitcase full of laundry, and Aurora was left behind. Maybe she could try to do the dishes while he was away. She was sure he'd be pleased.

Aurora got a nice, solid kitchen chair to stand on. She tied on an apron and put the right amount of soap in the water. There was plenty of hot water in this building, so doing the dishes was fun, and it would be nice to surprise Daddy.

Just as she was getting started, there was a ring at the door. She gave an impatient little sigh. There seemed to be no peace. Anyway, should she open the door when she was alone? Daddy hadn't said anything about that. If only she had had one of those peep-

holes in the door now, she could have seen who was standing outside.

The bell rang again and Aurora said: "Who is it?"

"It's Nusse's mother," said a voice outside.

That was safe enough. Aurora managed to open the door although her fingers were covered with soap and slipped on the smooth handle.

"Hello, Aurora," said Nusse's mother. Aurora hadn't seen her since the time when she was going into town with Brit-Karen and Nusse, and was so angry because Nusse had been playing in the sandbox. But she certainly wasn't thinking of that today.

"I wondered if you would come up and keep Nusse company while I go shopping?"

"Oh, no," said Aurora. "I can't today."

"Perhaps Nusse could come up here?" said her mother. "She can be up for a little while even if she isn't allowed to go out."

"No," said Aurora, "because I won't be here. I have to take Socrates out while Daddy is in the laundry room."

"Oh, is that so? Can't you take him—what was it you called him?"

"Socrates," said Aurora.

"Socrates, yes. Can't you take Socrates up to Nusse? She has such a bad cold I don't dare take her shopping with me, but she doesn't like being alone, you know."

Aurora understood that very well. Nobody liked to be left alone when the grownups went shopping. Still, everybody had to put up with it when they were sick.

"What about Brit-Karen?" said Aurora. "She can come and stay with Nusse, can't she?"

"Her parents are afraid of her catching cold," said Nusse's mother, "so Brit-Karen isn't allowed to come. I went to ask her first for they are supposed to be such good friends, but no luck. Her mother was quite upset at the idea and wouldn't let Brit-Karen go. But then we thought that maybe you would come, since you are alone so much."

Aurora looked at Nusse's mother. Her eyes were hard, too, just like the other woman's had been. She wanted Aurora to stay with Nusse and take Socrates with her. But Nusse had a cold, and Mommy had said that she must be very careful to keep Socrates away from anyone who was coughing and sneezing, because it was no laughing matter when such tiny babies caught a cold.

"No, I can't," said Aurora.

"But it will only be for a little while, while I'm at the store," said Nusse's mother. "Surely you can do me that little service." Aurora felt desperate; it was so confusing. But then she remembered her mother saying that Daddy and Socrates and she and Mommy were a group on their own, and must look after each other, and so she said: "No, I can't, because there are things called cold germs and they mustn't come near Socrates."

"Oh well, I just thought you might enjoy getting out for a little while," said Nusse's mother, "but I won't press you, of course."

She turned and went. Aurora could see from her back that she wasn't pleased. The dishes didn't seem so much fun now, either.

A little later, Father came upstairs at full speed. "So far so good," he said. "I hope I've done it right. There were instructions but it all seemed so complicated. Anyway, the clothes can go on washing themselves while I check on Socrates. Why, bless your heart. Have you begun the dishes?"

"They would be finished if the doorbell hadn't rung," said Aurora.

"Was it someone selling raffle tickets for the Sausage Eaters' Association?" said Father.

"It was Nusse's mother," Aurora answered. "She wanted me to keep Nusse company while she went shopping."

"Of course you couldn't," said Father, and went around snatching up more dirty clothes.

Socrates obviously sensed that Father was extra busy today, for he wasn't in a good mood. He kicked and screamed, and Father had to stop and say "bsbsbsbsbsbsbs" many times before he calmed down. Not until Aurora brought his bottle did he become really good-tempered and smiling.

"We're helping Daddy do the washing," said Aurora, "so you must be a good boy when I take you out in the baby carriage, understand?"

Socrates looked as if he wanted to think about it first, but then he drank his milk, burped twice, and seemed to have no objection to being put in his baby carriage.

"Now I'll carry the suitcase with the sweaters and we'll put the bag of dirty linen on top of you, Socrates. Wrap up well, Aurora, it's cold outside."

It was a long way to the laundry room and they had a heavy load, but fortunately Socrates didn't seem to mind his carriage being used as a laundry truck. When they came to the door of the laundry room, Father said: "Well, so long, Aurora. Don't go too far."

He didn't look happy as he went off with his load.

"It's only for today, you know," said Aurora, wheeling Socrates away.

Father came into the laundry room and was dismayed to see a stream of soapsuds flowing from the washing machine he was using.

Luckily there was a woman there who was doing her washing, too, and she calmed Father down and said he had just used too much soap powder. She showed him how to set the machine for rinsing, and finally she helped him to put the clothes in the spin dryer to get most of the water out. Everything was all right as long as the woman was there. She was calm and collected and Father understood everything she said. But unfortunately she had finished her own washing. She had started early in the morning and was ready to go now. Father thought the place seemed deserted after she had gone. But she had done a lot already. Soon he could put all their sweaters in the machine. He had to laugh when he remembered how last year Mother had struggled to wash the thick sweaters in a small tub. She hadn't had much water either, poor soul. No, this really was much better.

These machines weren't bad when you got used to them. Father began to whistle to himself, and to think about how people washed clothes in the olden days and in many parts of the world today. The women stood on the riverbank and beat the clothes clean, and stooped down to rinse them. Perhaps they sang too. Father could picture the women doing the washing for him while he sat and watched them and thought about it all.

He wondered what Aurora was doing now. He put the sweaters in the machine, turned the knobs to set it going, and went out to look for her.

Aurora had been wheeling Socrates up and down for quite a long time. Now and then she had peeped into the low windows of the laundry room and seen her father standing in front of the washing machine, but he hadn't seen her for he was so terribly busy. Socrates was quiet because he was asleep.

"Hello, Aurora," said Father. "All right?"

"Yes," whispered Aurora. "Will you be finished soon?"

"No, not for a while," said Father. "Our sweaters are being washed this very minute. Are you tired of pushing the carriage? If you want to you can leave it for a few minutes and play in the snow."

"Mmmn," said Aurora. There was a lot of snow here. Perhaps she could make something really important; a snowman, or maybe an animal that she could sit on would be better. Lovely. She began to roll the snow into big round balls, working away with all her might, and Father went in to his washing.

He stood for a minute looking at the machine that was washing the sweaters. He ought to rinse them now, but he had to get rid of the soapy water first. The water that came out was boiling hot. Oh dear! He had set the machine at boiling. Maybe that wasn't right for washing woolens. Of course it made them nice and clean, but he would keep quiet about it all the same. The washing that was hanging in the drying cupboard was already dry enough for ironing, so he would have to start that. It was an electric mangle iron and there was something that had to be turned on here, too. The rollers had some kind of material around them, and Father set

the iron going to see if they really did turn by themselves.

They did, but apparently they didn't like to have nothing to iron, for suddenly there was a very hot smell. Father was so frightened that he turned the iron off as fast as he could. He went out to Aurora. "That iron is hard to use," he said. "I wonder if the super is around."

Aurora looked up from the large snow animal she was making. She didn't see the superintendent, but she saw that Father looked upset. Then she caught sight of Knut. He was coming home from school with some other boys. She tried to wave to him without the others noticing. Clearly, he had seen her, for he went a little farther and then suddenly jumped, shouting something or other, ran back the way he had come, sprang quickly to one side, and made for the laundry room.

"Do you know where the super is, Knut?" asked Father. "I can't figure out how to work that iron."

"I can," said Knut proudly. "I've done the washing several times when Mother was too busy."

"Are you allowed in the laundry room?" asked Aurora.

"It's only small children who aren't allowed," answered Knut. He went in with Father, and Aurora stood outside and thought how lucky it was that Knut knew all about knobs. He showed Father what to do and stayed with him until all the ironing was finished.

The woolens were ready to come out of the spin dryer. Father took one garment out after another and Knut said: "Aurora and Socrates have a lot of sweaters."

"Well, yes, but these are not only theirs," said Father. "There are ski sweaters belonging to my wife and me as well."

"Oh," said Knut, looking at the sweaters Father was talking about. They were just the right size for Aurora and even Socrates.

"Hmmn," said Father. "They do seem to be smaller. Maybe they'll stretch again while they're drying. That's probably what happens."

Knut looked at Father. "Did you boil them?" he asked.

Father was embarrassed, but he looked Knut straight in the eyes and said: "That's just what I did."

"They've shrunk," said Knut. "I did that the first time, too."

"Oh dear, what can we do about it?" said Father.

"You can dry them in my apartment," said Knut. "and then we can . . ." He whispered, although there were only the two of them in the laundry room now.

"Yes," said Father, "and then we can buy Mother a new sweater for Christmas. Thank you for all your help, Knut. I don't know what I would have done if you hadn't been here."

That, thought Knut, was a thing worth hearing. He helped Father carry all the washing upstairs.

Aurora was working on the animal she was making. She was not sure what kind of animal it was, because on one side it was a little like a camel and on the other it was more like a sheep.

"It's most like a camel," she said to herself, "and now I'm riding my camel over the desert, and there are camels in front of me and behind me, too. We stick together so we won't be attacked by desert robbers."

She didn't notice the two boys who were standing there looking at her.

"What's that ugly thing?" said one of them. "It spoils the looks of the whole building."

"Be quiet," said Aurora, "you'll wake up Socrates."

"I'll talk as much as I want. We live here, too, you know."

"Mmmn," said Aurora. She sat quiet as a mouse on her splendid camel and didn't dare say any more. Then Knut appeared.

Aurora remembered what he had said, so she petted her camel's head and didn't look at him at all.

"Hi, Knurre, will you help us knock down the scarecrow this kid has made?"

"That's a silly game," said Knut. His voice sounded quite different now than when he spoke to Aurora and her father. "No—come on, you guys, let's go and see if the slide behind the building is any good."

They ran off and Aurora went home with Socrates. She found her father there. "Isn't Knut with you?" he said. "I promised him an extra good lunch today because he was such a help."

"He had to help me with some boys," said Aurora, "so he went away with them."

"That's too bad," said Father.

He and Aurora were eating their sandwiches, and Socrates was lying in his carriage thinking about his last bottle, when Knut arrived.

"I'm a little late," he said, "but I couldn't get here any sooner."

"Lunch is served," said Father. "I really am glad there are some men living in this building, Knut."

"So am I," said Knut, and he took a large bite of bread and cheese.

from **From Anna**
Jean Little

A new country, Canada, a new school, a new language—all terrify Anna. After her initial fears, Anna finds herself among sympathetic classmates and befriended by a kindly doctor and a teacher who understood how much patience and understanding a disabled child might need.

The Second Day

Anna watched her feet walking along.

One . . . two . . . one . . . two . . .

Soon she would be at the school. Maybe she could even see it now if she looked up. She did not look up.

It was a long walk but there was no way to get lost. You just kept going straight ahead after you got to the first big street and turned left. Mama had watched until Anna had made that first turn safely. So she was not lost.

She felt lost though.

One . . . two . . . one . . . two . . .

Yesterday at school they had been nice but she was new yesterday. Today she would probably be Awkward Anna again. Miss Williams would not smile.

Today she'll want me to read from a book, Anna told herself, getting ready for the worst.

"Hi, Anna," a boy's voice called.

Anna looked up without stopping to think. The next instant, she felt silly. Nobody knew her. There must be another Anna. She glanced around quickly. There were no other girls in sight. Only a tall boy coming along the sidewalk from the opposite direction.

Anna dropped her gaze hastily and quickened her steps. She was almost sure he had been looking right at her and smiling but her new glasses must be playing tricks. She did not know that boy.

They met where the walk led into the school building.

"What's the matter? You deaf?" the boy asked.

He was laughing a little.

Anna darted another glance up at him and then stared at her shoes again.

It's Bernard, she thought, feeling sick.

She was not positive, but she had better answer. Bernard was Rudi's size exactly.

"I am not deaf," she told him.

Her voice was thin and small.

"Good," the boy said. "Hey, why don't you look at me."

Obediently, Anna lifted her head. He was still laughing. Sometimes when Rudi teased, he laughed too.

"That's better," the boy said. "Now I'm going to do you a favor."

Anna had no idea what he was talking about. She was certain now, though, that he was Bernard. She longed to run but something firm in the way he spoke to her made her stay facing him, waiting.

"This will be your first lesson in being a good Canadian," he went on.

"Lesson?" Anna repeated like a parrot.

Her voice was a little stronger now.

"Yeah, lesson. When you hear somebody say 'Hi, Anna,' the way I did, you say 'Hi' back again."

He paused. Anna stared up at him.

"You say 'Hi, Bernard!'" he prompted.

Anna just stood, still not understanding, still not quite brave enough to run.

"Come on or we're both going to be late," he urged. "Just say, 'Hi, Bernard.' That's not so hard to say, is it?"

"Hi," Anna heard herself whisper.

She could not manage to add his name. What did "Hi" mean anyway?

Bernard grinned.

"That's a start," he said. "See you in class, kid."

He loped up the walk, leaving her behind. Anna followed slowly.

Somehow she had done the right thing. Bernard had not been mean. But what had it all been about?

She was so puzzled that she was inside the school before she remembered how afraid she was.

Then the nightmare began. She could not find the right classroom. She wandered up one long hall, down another. Through open doorways, she caught sight of groups of children but she recognized nobody. Several boys and girls hurried past her. They all knew exactly where they were going. If one had stopped long enough, she might have been able to ask the way but nobody seemed to see her.

A bell clanged. Anna jumped. Then everywhere the doors were closed.

She went on walking past the tall shut doors. She tried not to think of Papa. She tried not to think at all. She just walked and walked and walked.

"Anna! Anna! This way!"

Footsteps clattered after her. Angel footsteps! But the angel was Isobel, her ringlets bouncing, her eyes warm with sympathy.

"Bernard said he'd seen you so we guessed you must be lost," she explained.

She grabbed Anna's cold hand and squeezed it.

"I know exactly how you feel," she told the new girl, tugging her along, not seeming to mind that Anna could not speak a word in return. "I got lost six times my first week here. This school is so big and all the halls look the same. At recess, I'll show you a sure way to remember. You just have to come in the right door, climb two sets of stairs, turn right and you're there. Here, I mean," she finished.

Before them, like a miracle, was the right door. It stood open. Nobody was working. Benjamin wasn't even in his desk. He was at the door watching for them. In an instant, Miss Williams was there too.

"Oh, Anna, I'm sorry I wasn't there to meet you," she said.

Anna let Isobel lead her to her desk. She sank into her seat. She listened. Apparently everyone in the class had been lost at least once in the school building. Nobody blamed Anna. Not once did anyone say, "How stupid of you not to have paid better attention yesterday!"

"I got lost once just coming back from the bathroom," Ben said and blushed.

The rest laughed. Ben didn't seem to mind. He smiled himself.

"I expect you were daydreaming, Ben," Miss Williams commented.

"I was figuring out whether a person could dig a tunnel under the Atlantic Ocean," Benjamin admitted.

The class laughed again. Anna stopped trembling. Here in Canada, she thought, maybe it is all right to make mistakes.

"Now it's time we stopped gossiping," Miss Williams told them. "Take your place, Ben."

Ben went to his desk. Miss Williams moved to stand at the front of the room. As she opened her mouth to begin, a voice spoke up.

"Hi, Anna," Bernard said.

Anna looked at him. Then she looked at the teacher. Miss Williams was smiling, waiting. Anna gripped the edge of her desk.

"Hi, Bernard," she said, still in a whisper.

"I'm teaching her to be a Canadian," Bernard explained.

Miss Williams did not look surprised.

"Good," she said simply. "Class, stand."

When it was time for recess, Isobel did not forget. Ben came along too. They took Anna

to the door through which she would enter the school.

"It's the door you'd come to naturally, walking from your place," Isobel said.

Anna's surprise showed on her face. How did Isobel know where the Soldens lived?

"I heard Dr. Schumacher tell Miss Williams your address yesterday," Isobel confessed. "I live on the same street, two blocks this way. Now listen, you come in here . . ."

"Cross-eyed . . . cross-eyed!" a voice in the playground sang out.

Anna did not know what the words meant. Until she saw her stiffen, she did not know they had anything to do with Isobel.

"Ignore them, Isobel," Ben urged. "Pretend you don't even hear, like Miss Williams said."

"Four-eyes . . . four-eyes!" another voice took up the mocking chant.

Isobel let the school door close, shutting the three of them safely inside. She smiled shakily at Ben.

"Ignore them yourself, Benjamin," she advised.

"I hate them!" Ben said, through clenched teeth.

"Me too . . . but hating doesn't help," Isobel said. "It would if we were a lot bigger."

She caught the bewilderment on Anna's face.

"She doesn't know what they mean," she said to Ben.

She explained about crossed eyes. Anna did not get all the words but she understood the gestures. Isobel's eyes did cross sometimes but they were nice eyes, brown and kind. Anna remembered the brightness in them that morning when Isobel had found her. She, like Ben, hated whoever called Isobel names.

"Four-eyes" meant glasses. Ben pointed to his eyes and then to each of his round lenses, counting them up.

"Four," he finished.

Anna looked at his earnest face. She hesitated. Could she make herself understood? Then she tried.

"Maybe I was it," she told him.

Ben looked at Isobel for help.

"What did you say?" Isobel asked Anna.

That hateful English! She should have known better than to attempt it. Then in a flash, Anna knew what to do. She imitated Ben, pointing to her own eyes and lenses as she counted.

"Ohhhh," Ben and Isobel said together. They laughed, the tension leaving their faces.

"Join the crowd," Isobel said.

As she spoke, she put her arm around Anna's shoulders and hugged her quickly, lightly.

"Come on. We're showing her how to find the room," Ben reminded them.

Anna followed her guides. She did not know what "join the crowd" meant exactly, but she was suddenly glad she had tried out her English.

Then, as she climbed the stairs with the other two, she remembered the tormenting singsong voices outside and she scowled. So there were boys like Rudi in Canada too. She had been wrong about Bernard, but there were others.

She had been very wrong about Bernard. He spoke to her again that afternoon when school was over and he was about to leave.

"So long, Anna," he said.

Anna did not know it but she reminded Bernard of a stray cat. He had rescued so many stray cats that his mother had refused to let him in the door with one ever again. Now he waited for Anna to answer him. He did not hurry her. You had to be gentle and patient with strays.

At last Anna responded.

"So long?" she said, making a question out of it.

"It just means 'Good-bye till later,'" the boy explained. She understood—it meant *"Auf wiedersehen."*

He smiled at her and left, forgetting her the moment she was out of sight.

Anna did not forget. All the way to Papa's store, she thought and thought about Bernard.

A bell chimed when she opened the door. Anna listened for it. It was as though the store said "Hi, Anna."

It is a Canadian store, she thought.

Papa was busy. Anna did not mind. She drifted back to a shadowy corner and perched on an upended orange crate. Already she had chosen this dim room, so crowded with things and yet so peaceful, as a refuge. Even Papa did not have a lot of time to notice her here. Sometimes it was nice not being noticed. Sometimes you had things to think about, private things.

She could see Papa weighing some cheese for a plump lady. She watched him count oranges into a bag. But she was not thinking about him.

"Hi, Bernard," whispered Anna. "So long, Bernard."

Now Papa was climbing up a set of steps to get down a mousetrap.

I could say it to the others too maybe, Anna thought. Hi, Isobel. So long, Ben.

She gasped at her own daring. Yet one of these days, she might.

The stout lady said, "Thank you, Mr. Solden," and went out.

Isobel put her arm around me, remembered Anna.

Papa was the only person who hugged her. When anyone else tried, she went stiff and jerked away. She could not help it. Sometimes she did not even want to. But she still did.

"Anna's not a loving child," Mama had said once to Aunt Tania when Anna had squirmed away from a kiss.

But today, with Isobel, it had been different.

No fuss, thought Anna. Just nice.

Papa had turned. He was peering through the shadows, looking for her. Anna waited for him to find her in her corner. They smiled at each other across the store.

"Good afternoon, Anna," her father said.

She looked at him. In all her world, he was the kindest person. He would not laugh at her even if she got it wrong. Papa never laughed at her when he knew she was serious. She took a deep breath.

"Hi, Papa," said Anna in a loud, brave voice.

It sounded fine.

from **Heidi**
Johanna Spyri

In this classic children's story, Heidi arrives at her grandfather's and gets acquainted with him and his surroundings. This is a reassuring book and Heidi's gallant spirit is unforgettable.

At the Grandfather's

After Dete had disappeared, the uncle sat down again on the bench and blew great clouds of smoke from his pipe, while he kept his eyes fixed on the ground without saying a word. Meanwhile Heidi was content to look about her. She discovered the goats' shed built near the hut and peeped into it. It was empty.

The child continued hunting about and came to the fir trees behind the hut. The wind was blowing hard, and it whistled and roared through the branches, high up in the tops. Heidi stood still and listened. When it stopped somewhat she went round to the other side of the hut and came back to her grandfather. When she found him in the same place where she had left him, she placed herself in front of him, put her hands behind her, and gazed at him. Her grandfather looked up.

"What do you want to do?" he asked, as the child continued standing in front of him without moving.

"I want to see what you have in the hut," said Heidi.

"Come along, then!" and the grandfather rose and started to go into the hut.

"Bring your bundle of clothes," he said as he entered.

"I shan't want them any more," replied Heidi.

The old man turned round and looked sharply at the child, whose black eyes shone in expectation of what might be inside the hut.

"She's not lacking in brains," he said half to himself. "Why won't you need them any more?" he asked aloud.

"I'd rather go like the goats, with their swift little legs."

"So you shall, but bring the things along," commanded the grandfather; "they can be put into the cupboard."

Heidi obeyed. The old man opened the door, and Heidi followed him into a good-sized room, which occupied the whole hut. In it were a table and a chair; in one corner was the grandfather's bed, in another the fireplace where hung the large kettle; on the other side, in the wall, was a large door, which the grandfather opened; it was the cupboard. There hung his clothes, and on one shelf lay his shirts, stockings, and linen; on another were plates, cups, and glasses, and on the topmost a loaf of bread, smoked meat, and cheese. Everything the Alm-Uncle owned and needed for his living was kept in this closet. As soon as he had opened the door, Heidi came running with her bundle and pushed it in, as far back of her grandfather's clothes as possible, that it might not be easy to find it again. Then she looked carefully round the room and said:

"Where shall I sleep, grandfather?"

"Wherever you like," he replied.

This was quite to Heidi's mind. She looked into every nook and corner to see where would be the best place for her to sleep. In the corner by her grandfather's bed stood a little ladder, which led to the hayloft. Heidi climbed this. There lay a fresh, fragrant heap of hay, and through a round window one could look far down into the valley below.

"This is where I will sleep," Heidi called down; "it is lovely! Just come and see how lovely it is up here, grandfather!"

"I know all about it," sounded from below.

"I am going to make a bed," called out the child again as she ran busily to and fro in the loft; "but you must come up here and bring a sheet, for the bed must have a sheet for me to sleep on."

"Well, well," said the grandfather below; and after a few moments he went to the cupboard and rummaged about; then he drew out from under his shirts a long, coarse piece of cloth, which might serve for a sheet. He came up the ladder and found that a very neat little bed had been made in the hayloft; the hay was piled up higher at one end to form the pillow, and the bed was placed in such a way that one could look from it straight out through the round open window.

"That is made very nicely," said the grandfather; "next comes the sheet; but wait a moment,"—and he took up a good armful of hay and made the bed as thick again, in order that the hard floor might not be felt through it; "there, now put it on."

Heidi quickly took hold of the sheet, but was unable to lift it, it was so heavy; however, this made it all the better because the sharp wisps of hay could not push through the firm cloth. Then the two together spread the sheet over the hay, and where it was too broad or too long Heidi quickly tucked it under. Now it appeared quite trim and neat, and Heidi stood looking at it thoughtfully.

"We have forgotten one thing, grandfather," she said.

"What is that?" he asked.

"The coverlet; when we go to bed we creep in between the sheet and the coverlet."

"Is that so? But supposing I haven't any?" asked the old man.

"Oh, then it's no matter," said Heidi soothingly; "we can take more hay for a coverlet"; and she was about to run to the haymow again, but her grandfather prevented her.

"Wait a moment," he said, and went down the ladder to his own bed. Then he came back and laid a large, heavy linen bag on the floor.

"Isn't that better than hay?" he asked. Heidi pulled at the bag with all her might and main, trying to unfold it, but her little hands could not manage the heavy thing. Her grandfather helped, and when it was finally spread out on the bed, it all looked very neat and comfortable, and Heidi, looking at her new resting-place admiringly, said:

"That is a splendid coverlet, and the whole bed is lovely! How I wish it were night so that I could lie down in it!"

"I think we might have something to eat first," said the grandfather. "What do you say?"

In her eagerness over the bed, Heidi had forgotten everything else; but now that eating was suggested to her, a great feeling of hunger rose within her, for she had taken nothing all day, except a piece of bread and a cup of weak coffee early in the morning, and afterward she had made the long journey. So Heidi heartily agreed, saying:

"Yes, I think so too."

"Well, let us go down, since we are agreed," said the old man and followed close upon the child's steps. He went to the fireplace, pushed the large kettle aside and drew forward the little one that hung on the chain, sat down on the three-legged wooden stool with the round seat and kindled a bright fire. Almost immediately the kettle began to boil, and the old man held over the fire a large piece of cheese on the end of a long iron fork. He moved it this way and that, until it was golden yellow on all sides. Heidi looked on with eager attention. Suddenly a new idea came to her mind; she jumped up and ran to the cupboard, and kept going back and forth. When the grandfather brought the toasted cheese to the table, it was already nicely laid with the round loaf of bread, two plates, and two knives, for Heidi had noticed everything in the cupboard, and knew that all would be needed for the meal.

"That is right, to think of doing something yourself," said the grandfather, laying the cheese on the bread and putting the teapot on the table; "but there is something still lacking."

Heidi saw how invitingly the steam came out of the pot, and ran quickly back to the cupboard. But there was only one little bowl there. Heidi was not long puzzled; behind it stood two glasses; the child immediately came back with the bowl and glasses and placed them on the table.

"Very good. You know how to help yourself; but where are you going to sit?"

The grandfather himself was sitting in the only chair. Heidi shot like an arrow to the fireplace, brought back the little three-legged stool and sat down on it.

"Well, you have a seat, sure enough, only it is rather low," said the grandfather; "but in my chair also you would be too short to reach the table; still you must have something anyway, so come!"

Saying which he rose, filled the little bowl with milk, placed it on the chair, and pushed it close to the three-legged stool, so that Heidi had a table in front of her. The grandfather laid a large slice of bread and a piece of the golden cheese on the chair and said:

"Now eat!"

He seated himself on the corner of the table and began his dinner. Heidi grasped her bowl and drank and drank without stopping for all the thirst of her long journey came back to her. Then she drew a long breath and set down the bowl.

"Do you like the milk?" asked her grandfather.

"I never tasted such good milk before," answered Heidi.

"Then you must have some more"; and the grandfather filled the bowl again to the brim and placed it before the child, who looked quite content as she began to eat her bread, after it had been spread with the toasted cheese soft as butter. The combination tasted very good, with frequent drinks of milk.

When the meal was over, the grandfather went out to the goat-shed to put it in order, and Heidi watched him closely as he first swept it clean with a broom and then laid down fresh straw for the animals to sleep on. Then he went to his little shop, cut some round sticks, shaped a board, made some holes in it, put the round sticks into them, and suddenly it was a stool like his own, only much higher. Heidi was speechless with amazement as she saw his work.

"What is this, Heidi?" asked the grandfather.

"It is a stool for me, because it is so high; you made it all at once," said the child, still deeply astonished.

"She knows what she sees; her eyes are in the right place," remarked the grandfather to himself as he went round the hut driving a nail here and there; then he repaired something about the door, and went from place to place with hammer, nails, and pieces of wood, mending and clearing away wherever it was needed. Heidi followed him step by step and watched him with the closest attention, and everything he did interested her very much.

Evening was coming on. It was beginning to blow harder in the old fir trees, for a

mighty wind had sprung up and was whistling and moaning through their thick tops. It sounded so beautiful in Heidi's ears and heart that she was quite delighted, and skipped and jumped under the firs as if she were feeling the greatest pleasure of her life. The grandfather stood in the doorway and watched the child.

A shrill whistle sounded. Heidi stopped her jumping, and the grandfather stepped outside. Down from above came goat after goat, leaping like a hunting train, and Peter in the midst of them. With a shout of joy Heidi rushed in among the flock and greeted her old friends of the morning one after the other.

When they reached the hut, they all stood still, and two lovely slender goats—one white, the other brown—came out from the others to the grandfather and licked his hands, in which he held some salt to welcome them. This he did each evening. Peter disappeared with his flock. Heidi gently stroked first one goat and then the other and ran round them to stroke them on the other side; she was perfectly delighted with the little creatures.

"Are they ours, grandfather? Are they both ours? Will they go into the shed? Will they stay with us always?" asked Heidi, one question following the other in her delight. When the goats had finished licking their salt, the old man said:

"Go and bring out your little bowl and the bread."

Heidi obeyed, and came back at once. The grandfather milked the goat and filled the bowl and cut off a piece of bread, saying:

"Now eat your supper and then go up to bed! Your Aunt Dete left a bundle for you; your nightgowns and other things are in it. You will find it downstairs in the closet if you need it. I must attend to the goats now; so sleep well!"

"Good night, grandfather! Good night— what are their names, grandfather? what are their names?" cried the child, running after

the old man and the goats as they disappeared into the shed.

"The white one is named Schwänli[1] and the brown one Bärli,"[2] answered the grandfather.

"Good night, Schwänli! good night, Bärli!" called Heidi at the top of her voice. Then Heidi sat down on the bench and ate her bread and drank her milk; but the strong wind almost blew her off the seat; so she finished hastily, then went in and climbed up to her bed, in which she immediately fell asleep and slept as soundly and well as if she had been in the loveliest bed of some royal princess.

Not long after, even before it was entirely dark, the grandfather also went to bed; for he was always up with the sun, and it came climbing over the mountain very early in the summer time. In the night the wind blew with such force that its blasts made the whole hut tremble, and every rafter creaked. It howled and groaned down the chimney like voices in distress, and outside in the fir trees it raged with such fury that now and then a bough was broken off.

In the middle of the night the grandfather rose and said half aloud to himself:

"She may be afraid."

He climbed the ladder and went to Heidi's bedside. The moon outside shone brightly in the sky for a moment and then disappeared behind the driving clouds, and everything grew dark. Then the moonlight came again brightly through the round opening and fell directly on Heidi's couch. Her cheeks were fiery red as she slept under the heavy coverlet, and she lay perfectly calm and peaceful on her little round arm. She must have been dreaming happy dreams, for a look of happiness was on her face. The grandfather gazed long at the sweetly sleeping child until the moon went behind a cloud again and it was dark. Then he went back to his own bed.

[1]Schwänli = little swan
[2]Bärli = litte bear

from **What the Neighbors Did**
Philippa Pearce

One of England's major stylists, Pearce shows her command of the short story form in this tale, both lively and touching, of a child who cannot sleep and is comforted by his older sister.

[In the Middle of the Night]

In the middle of the night a fly woke Charlie. At first he lay listening, half-asleep, while it swooped about the room. Sometimes it was far; sometimes it was near—that was what had woken him; and occasionally it was very near indeed. It was very, very near when the buzzing stopped; the fly had alighted on his face. He jerked his head up; the fly buzzed off. Now he was really awake.

The fly buzzed widely about the room, but it was thinking of Charlie all the time. It swooped nearer and nearer. Nearer. . . .

Charlie pulled his head down under the bedclothes. All of him under the bedclothes, he was completely protected; but he could hear nothing except his heartbeats and his breathing. He was overwhelmed by the smell of warm bedding, warm pajamas, warm himself. He was going to suffocate. So he rose suddenly up out of the bedclothes; and the fly was waiting for him. It dashed at him. He beat at it with his hands. At the same time he appealed to his younger brother, Wilson, in the next bed: "Wilson, there's a fly!"

Wilson, unstirring, slept on.

Now Charlie and the fly were pitting their wits against each other: Charlie pouncing on the air where he thought the fly must be; the fly sliding under his guard towards his face. Again and again the fly reached Charlie; again and again, almost simultaneously, Charlie dislodged him. Once he hit the fly—or, at least, hit where the fly had been a second before, on the side of his head; the blow was so hard that his head sang with it afterwards.

Then suddenly the fight was over; no more buzzing. His blows—or rather, one of them—must have told.

He laid his head back on the pillow, thinking of going to sleep again. But he was also thinking of the fly, and now he noticed a tickling in the ear he turned to the pillow.

It must be—it *was*—the fly.

He rose in such panic that the waking of Wilson really seemed to him a possible thing, and useful. He shook him repeatedly. "Wilson—Wilson, I tell you, there's a fly in my ear!"

Wilson groaned, turned over very slowly like a seal in water, and slept on.

The tickling in Charlie's ear continued. He could just imagine the fly struggling in some passageway too narrow for its wingspan. He longed to put his finger into his ear and rattle it around, like a stick in a rabbit hole; but he was afraid of driving the fly deeper into his ear.

Wilson slept on.

Charlie stood in the middle of the bedroom floor, quivering and trying to think. He needed to see down his ear, or to get someone else to see down it. Wilson wouldn't do; perhaps Margaret would.

Margaret's room was next door. Charlie turned on the light as he entered: Margaret's bed was empty. He was startled, and then thought that she must have gone to the bathroom. But there was no light from there. He listened carefully: there was no sound from anywhere, except for the usual snuffling moans from the hall, where Floss slept and dreamed of dog biscuits. The empty bed was mystifying; but Charlie had his ear to worry about. It sounded as if there were a pigeon inside it now.

Wilson asleep; Margaret vanished; that left Alison. But Alison was bossy, just because she was the eldest; and anyway she would probably only wake Mum. He might as well wake Mum himself.

Down the passage and through the door always left ajar. "Mum," he said. She woke, or at least half-woke, at once. "Who is it? Who? Who? What's the matter? What?—"

"I've a fly in my ear."

"You can't have."

"It flew in."

She switched on the bedside light, and as she did so, Dad plunged beneath the bed-clothes with an exclamation and lay still again.

Charlie knelt at his mother's side of the bed, and she looked into his ear. "There's nothing."

"Something crackles."

"It's wax in your ear."

"It tickles."

"There's no fly there. Go back to bed and stop imagining things."

His father's arm came up from below the bedclothes. The hand waved about, settled on the bedside light, and clicked it out. There was an upheaval of bedclothes and a comfort-able grunt.

"Good night," said Mum from the dark-ness. She was already allowing herself to sink back into sleep again.

"Good night," Charlie said sadly. Then an idea occurred to him. He repeated his good night loudly and added some coughing, to cover the fact that he was closing the bed-room door behind him—the door that Mum kept open so that she could listen for her children. They had outgrown all that kind of attention, except possibly for Wilson. Charlie had shut the door against Mum's hearing be-cause he intended to slip downstairs for a drink of water—well, for a drink and perhaps a snack. That fly business had woken him up and also weakened him; he needed some-thing.

He crept downstairs, trusting to Floss's good sense not to make a row. He turned the foot of the staircase towards the kitchen, and there had not been the faintest whimper from her, far less a bark. He was passing the dog basket when he had the most unnerving sensation of something being wrong there—

something unusual, at least. He could not have said whether he had heard something or smelled something—he could certainly have seen nothing in the blackness; perhaps some extra sense warned him.

"Floss?" he whispered, and there was the usual little scrabble and snuffle. He held out his fingers low down for Floss to lick. As she did not do so at once, he moved them to-wards her, met some obstruction—

"Don't poke your fingers in my eye!" a voice said, very low-toned and cross. Charlie's first, confused thought was that Floss had spoken: the voice was familiar—but then a voice from Floss should *not* be familiar; it should be strangely new to him—

He took an uncertain little step towards the voice, tripped over the obstruction, which was quite wrong in shape and size to be Floss, and sat down. Two things now happened. Floss, apparently having climbed over the obstruction, reached his lap and began to lick his face. At the same time a human hand fumbled over his face, among the slappings of Floss's tongue, and settled over his mouth. "Don't make a row! Keep quiet!" said the same voice. Charlie's mind cleared; he knew, although without understanding, that he was sitting on the floor in the dark with Floss on his knee and Margaret beside him.

Her hand came off his mouth.

"What are you doing here anyway, Charlie?"

"I like that! What about you? There was a fly in my ear."

"Go on!"

"There was."

"Why does that make you come down-stairs?"

"I wanted a drink of water."

"There's water in the bathroom."

"Well, I'm a bit hungry."

"If Mum catches you. . . ."

"Look here," Charlie said, "you tell me what you're doing down here."

Margaret sighed. "Just sitting with Floss."

"You can't come down and just sit with Floss in the middle of the night."

"Yes, I can. I keep her company. Only at weekends, of course. No one seemed to realize what it was like for her when those puppies went. She just couldn't get to sleep for loneliness."

"But the last puppy went weeks ago. You haven't been keeping Floss company every Saturday night since then."

"Why not?"

Charlie gave up. "I'm going to get my food and drink," he said. He went into the kitchen, followed by Margaret, followed by Floss.

They all had a quick drink of water. Then Charlie and Margaret looked into the larder: the remains of a joint; a very large quantity of mashed potato; most of a loaf; eggs; butter; cheese . . .

"I suppose it'll have to be just bread and butter and a bit of cheese," said Charlie. "Else Mum might notice."

"Something hot," said Margaret. "I'm cold from sitting in the hall comforting Floss. I need hot cocoa, I think." She poured some milk into a saucepan and put it on the hot plate. Then she began a search for the cocoa. Charlie, standing by the cooker, was already absorbed in the making of a rough cheese sandwich.

The milk in the pan began to steam. Given time, it rose in the saucepan, peered over the top, and boiled over on to the hot plate, where it sizzled loudly. Margaret rushed back and pulled the saucepan to one side. "Well, really, Charlie! Now there's that awful smell! It'll still be here in the morning, too."

"Set the fan going," Charlie suggested.

The fan drew the smell from the cooker up and away through a pipe to the outside. It also made a loud roaring noise. Not loud enough to reach their parents, who slept on the other side of the house—that was all that Charlie and Margaret thought of.

Alison's bedroom, however, was immediately above the kitchen. Charlie was eating his bread and cheese, Margaret was drinking her cocoa, when the kitchen door opened and there stood Alison. Only Floss was pleased to see her.

"Well!" she said.

Charlie muttered something about a fly in his ear, but Margaret said nothing. Alison had caught them red-handed. She would call Mum downstairs, that was obvious. There would be an awful row.

Alison stood there. She liked commanding a situation.

Then, instead of taking a step backwards to call up the stairs to Mum, she took a step forward into the kitchen. "What are you having, anyway?" she asked. She glanced with scorn at Charlie's poor piece of bread and cheese and at Margaret's cocoa. She moved over to the larder, flung open the door, and looked searchingly inside. In such a way must Napoleon have viewed a battlefield before the victory.

Her gaze fell upon the bowl of mashed potato. "I shall make potato cakes," said Alison.

They watched while she brought the mashed potato to the kitchen table. She switched on the oven, fetched her other ingredients, and began mixing.

"Mum'll notice if you take much of that potato," said Margaret.

But Alison thought big. "She may notice if some potato is missing," she agreed. "But if there's none at all, and if the bowl it was in is washed and dried and stacked away with the others, then she's going to think she must have made a mistake. There just can never have been any mashed potato."

Alison rolled out her mixture and cut it into cakes; then she set the cakes on a baking tin and put it in the oven.

Now she did the washing up. Throughout the time they were in the kitchen, Alison washed up and put away as she went along. She wanted no one's help. She was very methodical, and she did everything herself to be sure that nothing was left undone. In the morning there must be no trace left of the cooking in the middle of the night.

"And now," said Alison, "I think we should fetch Wilson."

The other two were aghast at the idea; but Alison was firm in her reasons. "It's better if we're all in this together, Wilson as well. Then, if the worst comes to the worst, it won't be just us three caught out, with Wilson hanging on to Mum's apron strings, smiling innocence. We'll all be for it together; and Mum'll be softer with us if we've got Wilson."

They saw that, at once. But Margaret still objected. "Wilson will tell. He just always tells everything. He can't help it."

Alison said, "He always tells everything. Right. We'll give him something *to* tell, and then see if Mum believes him. We'll do an entertainment for him. Get an umbrella from the hall and Wilson's sou'wester and a blanket or a rug or something. Go on."

They would not obey Alison's orders until they had heard her plan; then they did. They fetched the umbrella and the hat, and lastly they fetched Wilson, still sound asleep, slung between the two of them in his eiderdown. They propped him in a chair at the kitchen table, where he still slept.

By now the potato cakes were done. Alison took them out of the oven and set them on the table before Wilson. She buttered them, handing them in turn to Charlie and Margaret and helping herself. One was set aside to cool for Floss.

The smell of fresh-cooked, buttery potato cake woke Wilson, as was to be expected. First his nose sipped the air; then his eyes opened; his gaze settled on the potato cakes.

"Like one?" Alison asked.

Wilson opened his mouth wide, and Alison put a potato cake inside, whole.

"They're paradise cakes," Alison said.

"Potato cakes?" said Wilson, recognizing the taste.

"No, paradise cakes, Wilson," and then, stepping aside, she gave him a clear view of Charlie's and Margaret's entertainment, with the umbrella and the sou'wester hat and his eiderdown. "Look, Wilson, look."

Wilson watched with wide-open eyes, and into his wide-open mouth Alison put, one by one, the potato cakes that were his share.

But, as they had foreseen, Wilson did not stay awake for very long. When there were no more potato cakes, he yawned, drowsed, and suddenly was deeply asleep. Charlie and Margaret put him back into his eiderdown and took him upstairs to bed again. They came down to return the umbrella and the sou'wester to their proper places, and to see Floss back into her basket. Alison, last out of the kitchen, made sure that everything was in its place.

The next morning Mum was down first. On Sunday she always cooked a proper breakfast for anyone there in time. Dad was always there in time; but this morning Mum was still looking for a bowl of mashed potato when he appeared.

"I can't think where it's gone," she said. "I can't think."

"I'll have the bacon and eggs without the potato," said Dad; and he did. While he ate, Mum went back to searching.

Wilson came down, and was sent upstairs again to put on a dressing gown. On his return he said that Charlie was still asleep and there was no sound from the girls' rooms either. He said he thought they were tired out. He went on talking while he ate his breakfast. Dad was reading the paper and Mum had gone back to poking about in the larder for the bowl of mashed potato, but Wilson liked talking even if no one would listen. When Mum came out of the larder for a moment, still without her potato, Wilson was saying: ". . . and Charlie sat in an umbrella boat on an eiderdown sea, and Margaret pretended to be a sea serpent, and Alison gave us paradise cakes to eat. Floss had one too, but it was too hot for her. What are paradise cakes? Dad, what's a paradise cake?"

"Don't know," said Dad, reading.

"Mum, what's a paradise cake?"

"Oh, Wilson, don't bother so when I'm looking for something. . . . When did you eat this cake, anyway?"

"I told you. Charlie sat in his umbrella boat on an eiderdown sea and Margaret was a sea serpent and Alison—"

"Wilson," said his mother, "you've been dreaming."

"No, really—really!" Wilson cried.

But his mother paid no further attention. "I give up," she said. "That mashed potato; it must have been last weekend. . . ." She went out of the kitchen to call the others. "Charlie! Margaret! Alison!"

Wilson, in the kitchen, said to his father, "I wasn't dreaming. And Charlie said there was a fly in his ear."

Dad had been quarter-listening; now he put down his paper. "What?"

"Charlie had a fly in his ear."

Dad stared at Wilson. "And what did you say that Alison fed you with?"

"Paradise cakes. She'd just made them, I think, in the middle of the night."

"What were they like?"

"Lovely. Hot, with butter. Lovely."

"But were they—well, could they have had any mashed potato in them, for instance?"

In the hall Mum was finishing her calling. "Charlie! Margaret! Alison! I warn you now!"

"I don't know about that," Wilson said. "They were paradise cakes. They tasted a bit like the potato cakes Mum makes, but Alison said they weren't. She specially said they were paradise cakes."

Dad nodded. "You've finished your breakfast. Go up and get dressed, and you can take this"—he took a coin from his pocket—"straight off to the sweetshop. Go on."

Mum met Wilson at the kitchen door. "Where's he off to in such a hurry?"

"I gave him something to buy sweets with," said Dad. "I wanted a quiet breakfast. He talks too much."

from The Family Under the Bridge
Natalie Savage Carlson

After World War II, there was a time in Paris when there were not enough houses and apartments for people to live in. The poor lived in tents, slept in doorways, or made homes for themselves under bridges. In this selection, old Armand, the hobo, first encounters the children.

[A Hobo Adventure]

Once there was an old hobo named Armand who wouldn't have lived anywhere but in Paris. So that is where he lived.

Everything that he owned could be pushed around in an old baby buggy without any hood, so he had no worries about rents or burglars. All the ragged clothing he owned was on his back, so he didn't need to bother with trunks or dry-cleaners.

It was easy for him to move from one hidey-hole to another so that is what he was doing one late morning in December. It was a cold day with the gray sky hanging on the very chimney pots of Paris. But Armand did not mind because he had a tickly feeling that something new and exciting was going to happen to him today.

He hummed a gay tune to himself as he pushed his buggy through the flower market at the side of Notre Dame cathedral. The flowers reminded him that someday it would be spring even though it wasn't bad winter yet.

There were pots of fragile hyacinths and tulips crowded together on planks in front of the stalls. There were pink carnations and oleanders in great tin pails. Most of all there were bouquets of red-beaded holly, clumps of white-pearled mistletoe and little green fir trees because it would soon be Christmas.

Armand's keen eye caught sight of a pile of broken branches and wilted flowers swept away from one stall. "Anabel" was the name written over the stall, and Armand touched his black beret to the stocky woman whose blue work apron hung below her wooly coat.

"By your leave and in gratitude for your generosity, madame," he said to the woman who was surely Anabel. He piled the broken branches on top of his belongings in the baby buggy. Then he fastidiously picked a sprig of dried holly from the litter and pulled it through his torn buttonhole. He wanted to look his best for whatever gay adventure was waiting for him this day.

The woman who must have been Anabel only frowned at Armand as he trundled his buggy toward the Rue de Corse. Past the ancient buildings he shuffled, his buggy headed for the far branch of the Seine River.

But as he entered the square in front of Notre Dame, a hand grasped his arm from behind.

"Your fortune, monsieur," wheedled a musical voice. "You will meet with adventure today."

Armand let go of the handle of the buggy and whirled around to face a gypsy woman in a short fur coat and full, flowered skirt.

He gave her a gap-toothed smile. "You, Mireli," he greeted her. "Your people are back in Paris for the winter?"

The gypsy woman's dark face beamed under the blue scarf. "Doesn't one always spend the winters in Paris?" she asked, as if she were a woman of fashion. "But have you taken to the streets so early?"

Armand shrugged his shoulders under the long overcoat that almost reached to his ankles. "It's back under the bridge for me," he answered. "I've had enough of the crowded corners and tight alleys in the Place Maubert. And I'm tired of sorting rags for that junk dealer. I'm ready for that adventure you're promising me."

Mireli could understand. "That courtyard we rent seems like a cage after the freedom of the long, winding roads," she said, "but the men have found plenty of work for the winter. A city with as many restaurants as Paris has more than enough pots and pans to be mended. Of course the children can talk of nothing but the fields and woods of spring."

"I can't abide children," grumped Armand. "Starlings they are. Witless, twittering, little pests."

Mireli shook her finger at him. "You think you don't like children," she said, "but it is only that you are afraid of them. You're afraid the sly little things will steal your heart if they find out you have one."

Armand grunted and took the handle of the buggy again. Mireli waved him away, swaying on bare feet squeezed into tarnished silver sandals. "If you change your mind

about the bridge, you can come to live with us," she invited. "We're beyond the Halles—where they're tearing down the buildings near the old Court of Miracles."

Armand tramped under the black, leafless trees and around the cathedral by the river side without even giving it a glance.

In the green park behind the flying buttresses, some street urchins were loitering. Two of them played at dueling while a third smaller one watched, munching a red apple. The swordsmen, holding out imaginary swords, circled each other. Closer and closer came the clenched fists, then the boys forgot their imaginary swords and began punching each other.

They stopped their play as Armand went by. "Look at the funny old tramp!" one cried to his playmates.

Armand looked around because he wanted to see the funny old tramp too. It must be that droll Louis with his tall black hat and baggy pants. Then he realized that he was the funny old tramp.

"Keep a civil tongue in your head, starling," he ordered. He fingered the holly in his lapel. "If you don't, I'll tell my friend Father Christmas about your rude manners. Then you'll get nothing but a bunch of sticks like these on my buggy."

The boys looked at him with awe. Father Christmas is the Santa Claus of France. He rides down from the north on his little gray donkey and leaves presents for good children.

The small boy held out his half-eaten apple. "Are you hungry, monsieur?" he asked. "Would you like the rest of this apple?"

But the biggest boy mockingly punched the air with his fist. "Pouf!" he scoffed. "There's no Father Christmas. He's just make-believe."

"If you doubt my word," said Armand with dignity, "just take a look in the Louvre store. You'll find him on the mezzanine floor."

He grinned like one of the roguish gargoyles on the cathedral. There really was a Father Christmas and it was his friend Camille, who felt the urge to work when the weather turned cold.

"I believe you, monsieur," said the boy with the apple. "I saw Father Christmas outside the store yesterday. He was eating hot chestnuts on the street."

Armand hunched his shoulders and quickly walked toward the bridge. Mireli was right. These starlings would steal your heart if you didn't keep it well hidden. And he wanted nothing to do with children. They meant homes and responsibility and regular work—all the things he had turned his back on so long ago. And he was looking for adventure.

Down a few blocks was the bridge under which he lived when the weather wasn't too raw. And plenty of company he had during the summer with all the homeless of Paris staking their claims to this space or that.

"But first I must have dinner," he told himself, looking up at the restaurant across the street. He licked his thumb and held it up. "The wind is just right," he decided.

So he parked his buggy beside the low wall and settled himself in the breeze that came from the restaurant. He pulled all the kitchen smells deep into his lungs. "Ah, steak broiled over charcoal," he gloated. "And the sauce is just right. But they scorched the potatoes."

For two hours Armand sat on the curb enjoying the food smells because that is the length of time a Frenchman allows himself for lunch in the middle of the day.

Then he daintily wiped his whiskered lips with his cuff and rose to his knobby shoes. "And just keep the change, waiter," he said generously, although there wasn't a white-uniformed waiter in sight. "You'll need it for Christmas."

He started down the steps that dropped from the street to the quay beside the Seine. He bounced the back wheels of the buggy down each step. "I am really quite stuffed," he told himself, "but I wish I had taken that apple. It would have been the right dessert after such a rich sauce."

Down the quay he pushed the buggy toward the bridge tunnel that ran along the shore. On the cobbled quay a man was washing his car with the free Seine water. A

woman in a fur coat was airing her French poodle. A long barge, sleek as a black seal, slid through the river. It was like coming home after a long absence, thought Armand. And anything exciting could happen under a Paris bridge.

As he neared the tunnel, his eyes widened with surprise and anger. A gray canvas was propped over the niche that had always been his own. And a market pushcart was parked by the pillar.

He raced his buggy across the cobblestones toward the arch. When he arrived there, he reached up and angrily tore down the canvas with one swoop of his arm. Then he jumped back in surprise and horror.

"Oh, là, là!" he cried. "Starlings! A nest full of them!"

Because three startled children snuggled into a worn quilt looked up at him with eyes as surprised as his own. The little girl and the boy cowered deeper into the quilt. But the older girl quickly jumped to her feet. She had direct blue eyes and they matched her determined chin and snubbed nose and bright red hair.

"You can't take us away," she cried, clenching her fists. "We're going to stay together because we're a family, and families have to stick together. That's what mama says."

As Armand glared at the children, a shaggy dog that should have been white came

bounding across the quay. It protectively jumped between the tramp and the children, barking fiercely at Armand. The hobo quickly maneuvered his buggy between himself and the dog.

"If that beast bites me," he cried, "I'll sue you for ten thousand francs."

The girl called the dog to her. "Here, Jojo! Come, Jojo! He won't take us away. He's only an old tramp."

The dog stopped barking and sniffed at the wheels of Armand's baby buggy.

The man was insulted. "I'll have you know that I'm not just any old tramp," he said. And he wasn't. "I'm not friendless, and I could be a workingman right now if I wanted. But where are your parents and who are you hiding from? The police?"

He studied the children closely. Redheads they were, all of them, and their clothes had the mismatched, ill-fitting look of poverty.

The older girl's eyes burned a deep blue. "Our landlady put us out because we don't have enough money to pay for the room since papa died," she explained. "So mama brought us here because we haven't any home now. And she told us to hide behind the canvas so nobody could see us, or they'd take us away from her and put us in a home for poor children. But we're a family, so we want to stay together. I'm Suzy and they're Paul and Evelyne."

The boy swaggered a little. "If I was bigger, I'd find a new place for us to live," he boasted.

"It looks to me like you've already found a new place," said Armand, "and it's my old place. You've put me out of my home just like that landlady did to you."

Suzy was apologetic. She moved the push-cart over and measured Armand with one eye closed. Then she carefully drew a long rectangle on the concrete with a piece of soft coal.

"That's your room," she said. "You can live with us." On second thought, she scrawled a small checkered square at the foot of the rectangle. "There's a window," she said gravely, "so you can look out and see the river."

Armand grumbled to himself and pulled his coat tighter across his chest as if to hide his heart. Oh, this starling was a dangerous one. He'd better move on. Paris was full of bridges, the way the Seine meandered through it. No trouble finding another one. But as he started away, the girl ran over and clutched him by his torn sleeve.

"Please stay," she begged. "We'll pretend you're our grandfather."

Armand snorted. "Little one," he said, "next to a millionaire, a grandfather is the last thing I hope to be." But even as he grumbled, he began unpacking his belongings.

He stacked the branches and twigs, and made a pile of the dead leaves he had gathered. He pulled out a dirty canvas and a rusty iron hook. He set a blackened can with a handle near the leaves. He sorted some bent spoons and knives. Last of all, he pulled out an old shoe with a hole in the sole.

"Might come across its mate one of these days," he explained to the children. "And it fits me just right."

The children wanted to help him. Oh, these starlings were clever. They knew how to get around an old man. Lucky he wasn't their grandfather. But he laid his canvas over the rectangle Suzy had made for him.

He started a fire with the branches and dead leaves. Then he hung a big can over the fire. Into it he dropped scraps of food he unwrapped from pieces of newspaper.

"In the good old days of Paris," he told the children, "they used to ring bells in the market places at the close of day so the tramps would know they were welcome to gather up the leftovers. But no more. Nowadays we have to look after ourselves."

They watched him eating his food. Even the dog that should have been white watched each morsel that went into his mouth and drooled on the concrete. Armand wriggled uneasily. "What's the matter?" he asked gruffly. "Haven't you ever seen anybody eat before?" They said nothing in reply, but four pairs of eyes followed each move of his tin spoon. "I suppose you're hungry," he growled. "Starlings always have to be eating. Get your tinware."

Suzy pulled some stained, cracked bowls

and twisted spoons from the pushcart. Armand carefully divided the food, even counting in the dog.

It was dark by the time the children's mother joined them. The lights of Paris were floating in the river, but the only light in the tunnel flickered from a tiny fire Armand had made. He could not see the woman's face well, but he felt the edge of her tongue.

"What are you doing here?" she demanded of the hobo.

Armand was angered. "And I might ask you the same, madame," he retorted. "You have taken my piece of the bridge."

"The bridges don't belong to anybody," said the woman. "They're the only free shelter in Paris."

Suzy tried to make peace. "He's a nice, friendly old tramp, mama," she explained, "and he's going to live with us."

"I'm not a friendly old tramp," said Armand indignantly. "I'm a mean, cranky old tramp, and I hate children and dogs and women."

"Then if you hate us," said Paul, "why did you give us some of your food?"

"Because I'm a stupid old tramp," replied Armand. "Because I'm a stupid, soft-hearted old tramp." Oh, là, là! There it was. He had let slip that he really had a heart. Now this homeless family would surely be after that too.

The mother was displeased to hear that the children had accepted the hobo's food. "We are not beggars," she reminded them. "I have a steady job at the laundry, and that is more than he can say."

She went to work warming a pan of soup and breaking a long loaf of bread that she had brought with her. Armand sat in the rectangle marked by Suzy and thought that this woman's trouble was pride, and that pride and life under the bridge weren't going to work out well together.

By the dying light of the fire, the woman went back and forth to her pushcart, pulling out moth-eaten blankets and making bed-places on the concrete. Just overhead the automobiles roared, lights garlanded the bridge and people walking along the higher quay

laughed lightly. But it could have been a million miles away from the little group under the bridge.

"You ought to put the starlings in some charity home until you find a place of your own, madame," suggested Armand, after the children had dropped off to sleep. "This life is not for them. Now, you wouldn't want them to end up like me, would you?"

"Families should stick together through the lean times as well as the fat," replied the woman. "And I have hopes. I'm going to see my sister-in-law soon. She may know of a place for us out in Clichy."

Armand stretched out on his canvas without bothering about any covering. He was used to the cold. He never felt it any more. But he was sure these children would feel it. As he lay on the hard concrete an uneasy thought worried him, like a mouse gnawing at his shoestring. Now that he had befriended these starlings, his life would never again be completely his own.

from The Power of Light
Isaac Bashevis Singer

A tender, touching story of the love between two blind children in a Polish poorhouse is outstanding both because of the writing style and the gentle innocence of Menashe and Rachel.

Menashe and Rachel

The poorhouse in Lublin had a special room for children—orphans, sick ones, and cripples. Menashe and Rachel were brought up there. Both of them were orphans and blind. Rachel was born blind and Menashe became blind from smallpox when he was three years old. Every day a tutor came to teach the children prayers, as well as a chapter of the five books of Moses. The older ones also learned

"Menashe and Rachel" from THE POWER OF LIGHT: EIGHT STORIES FOR HANUKKAH by Isaac Bashevis Singer, with illustrations by Irene Lieblich. Text copyright © 1980 by Isaac Bashevis Singer. Reprinted by permission of Farrar, Straus & Giroux, Inc. and the author.

passages of the Talmud. Menashe was now barely nine years old, but already he was known as a prodigy. He knew twenty chapters of the Holy Book by heart. Rachel, who was eight years old, could recite "I Thank Thee" in the morning, the Shema before going to sleep, make benedictions over food, and she also remembered a few supplications in Yiddish.

On Hanukkah the tutor blessed the Hanukkah lights for the children, and every child got Hanukkah money and a dreidel from the poorhouse warden. Rich women brought them pancakes sprinkled with sugar and cinnamon.

Some of the charity women maintained that the two blind children should not spend too much time together. First of all, Menashe was already a half-grown boy and a scholar, and there was no sense in his playing around with a little girl. Second, it's better for blind children to associate with seeing ones, who can help them find their way in the eternal darkness in which they live. But Menashe and Rachel were so very deeply attached to each other that no one could keep them apart.

Menashe was not only good at studying the Torah but also talented with his hands. All the other children got tin dreidels for Hanukkah, but Menashe carved two wooden ones for Rachel and himself. When Menashe was telling stories, even the grownups came to listen. Not only Rachel, but all the children in the poorhouse were eager to hear his stories. Some his mother had told him when she was still alive. Others he invented. He was unusually deft. In the summer he went with the other children to the river and did handstands and somersaults in the water. In the winter when a lot of snow fell, Menashe, together with other children, built a snowman with two coals for eyes.

Menashe had black hair. His eyes used to be black, too, but now they had whitish cataracts. Rachel was known as a beauty. She had golden hair and eyes as blue as cornflowers. Those who knew her could not believe that such shining eyes could be blind.

The love between Menashe and Rachel was spoken of not only in the poorhouse but in the whole neighborhood. Both children said openly that when they grew up they would marry. Some of the inmates in the poorhouse called them bride and groom. There were some do-gooders who believed the two children should be parted by force, but Rachel said that if she was taken away from Menashe she would drown herself in a well. Menashe warned that he would bite the hand that tried to separate him from Rachel. The poorhouse warden went to ask the advice of the Lublin rabbi, and the rabbi said that the children should be left in peace.

One Hanukkah evening the children got their Hanukkah money and ate the tasty pancakes; then they sat down and played dreidel. It was the sixth night of Hanukkah. Six lights burned in the brass lamp in the window. Until tonight Menashe and Rachel had played together with the other children. But tonight Menashe said to Rachel, "Rachel, I have no desire to play."

"Neither have I," Rachel answered. "But what shall we do?"

"Let's sit down near the Hanukkah lamp and just be together."

Menashe led Rachel to the Hanukkah lamp. They followed the sweet smell of the oil in which the wicks were burning. They sat down on a bench. For a while both of them were silently enjoying each other's company as well as the warmth that radiated from the little flames. Then Rachel said, "Menashe, tell me a story."

"Again? I have told you all my stories already."

"Make up a new one," Rachel said.

"If I tell you all my stories now, what will I do when we marry and become husband and wife? I must save some stories for our future."

"Don't worry. By then you will have many new stories."

"Do you know what?" Menashe proposed. "You tell me a story this time."

"I have no story," Rachel said.

"How do you know that you don't have any? Just say whatever comes to your mind. This is what I do. When I'm asked to tell a story I begin to talk, not knowing what will come out. But somehow a story crops up by itself."

"With me nothing will crop up."

"Try."

"You will laugh at me."

"No, Rachel, I won't laugh."

It grew quiet. One could hear the wood burning in the clay stove. Rachel seemed to hesitate. She wet her lips with the tip of her tongue. Then she began, "Once there was a boy and a girl—"

"Aha."

"He was called Menashe and she Rachel."

"Yes."

"Everyone thought that Menashe and Rachel were blind, but they saw. I know for sure that Rachel saw."

"What did she see?" Menashe asked in astonishment.

"Other children see from the outside, but Rachel saw from the inside. Because of this people called her blind. It wasn't true. When people sleep, their eyes are closed, but in their dreams they can see boys, girls, horses, trees, goats, birds. So it was with Rachel. She saw everything deep in her head, many beautiful things."

"Could she see colors?" Menashe asked.

"Yes, green, blue, yellow, and other colors, I don't know what to call them. Sometimes they jumped around and formed little figures, dolls, flowers. Once, she saw an angel with six wings. He flew up high and the sky opened its golden doors for him."

"Could she see the Hanukkah lights?" Menashe asked.

"Not the ones from the outside, but those in her head. Don't you see anything, Menashe?"

"I, too, see things inside me," Menashe said after a long pause. "I see my father and my mother and also my grandparents. I never told you this, but I remember things from the time I could still see."

"What do you remember?" Rachel asked.

"Oh, I was sick and the room was full of sunshine. A doctor came, a tall man in a high hat. He told mother to pull down the curtain because he thought I was sick with the measles and it is not good when there is too much light in the room if you have measles."

"Why didn't you tell me this before?" Rachel asked.

"I thought you wouldn't understand."

"Menashe. I understand everything. Sometimes when I lie in bed at night and cannot fall asleep, I see faces and animals and children dancing in a circle. I see mountains, fields, rivers, gardens, and the moon shining over them."

"How does the moon look?"

"Like a face with eyes and a nose and a mouth."

"True. I remember the moon," Menashe said. "Sometimes at night when I lie awake I see many, many things and I don't know whether they are real or I'm only imagining. Once I saw a giant so tall his head reached the clouds. He had huge horns and a nose as big as the trunk of an elephant. He walked in the sea but the water only reached to his knees. I tried to tell the warden what I saw and he said I was lying. But I was telling the truth."

For some time both children were silent. Then Menashe said, "Rachel, as long as we are small we should never tell these secrets to anybody. People wouldn't believe us. They might think we were making them up. But when we grow up we will tell. It is written in the Bible, 'For the Lord seeth not as man seeth; for man looketh on the outward appearance but the Lord looketh on the heart.'"

"Who said this?"

"The prophet Samuel."

"Oh, Menashe, I wish we could grow up quickly and become husband and wife," Rachel said. "We will have children that see both from the outside and from the inside. You will kindle Hanukkah lights and I will fry pancakes. You will carve dreidels for our children to play with, and when they go to bed we will tell them stories. Later, when they fall asleep, they will dream about these stories."

"We will dream also," Menashe said. "I about you and you about me."

"Oh, I dream about you all the time. I see you in my dreams so clearly—your white skin, chiseled nose, black hair, beautiful eyes."

"I see you too—a golden girl."

Again there was silence. Then Rachel said, "I'd like to ask you something, but I am ashamed to say it."

"What is it?"

"Give me a kiss."

"Are you crazy? It's not allowed. Besides, when a boy kisses a girl they call him a sissy."

"No one will see."

"God sees," Menashe said.

"You said before that God looks into the heart. In my heart we are already grown up and I am your wife."

"The other children are going to laugh at us."

"They are busy with the dreidels. Kiss me! Just once."

Menashe took Rachel's hand and kissed her quickly. His heart was beating like a little hammer. She kissed him back and both of their faces were hot. After a while Menashe said, "It cannot be such a terrible sin, because it is written in the book of Genesis that Jacob loved Rachel and he kissed her when they met. Your name is Rachel, too."

The poorhouse warden came over. "Children, why are you sitting alone?"

"Menashe has just told me a story," Rachel answered.

"It's not true, she told me a story," Menashe said.

"Was it a nice story?" the warden asked.

"The most beautiful story in the whole world," Rachel said.

"What was it about?" the warden asked, and Menashe said, "About an island far away in the ocean full of lions, leopards, monkeys, as well as eagles and pheasants with golden feathers and silver beaks. There were many trees on the island—fig trees, date trees, pomegranate trees, and a stream with fresh water. There was a boy and a girl there who saved themselves from a shipwreck by clinging to a log. They were like Adam and Eve in Paradise, but there was no serpent and—"

"The children are fighting over the dreidel. Let me see what's going on," the warden said. "You can tell me the rest of the story tomorrow." He rushed to the table.

"Oh, you made up a new story," Rachel said. "What happened next?"

"They loved one another and got married," Menashe said.

"Alone on the island forever?" Rachel asked.

"Why alone?" Menashe said. "They had many children, six boys and six girls. Besides, one day a sailboat landed there and the whole family was rescued and taken to the land of Israel."

from Avalanche!
A. Rutgers van der Loeff

This excerpt is about the aftermath of an avalanche in a Swiss village. Werner asks the question we all ask, "Why do all these things happen?" The answer he receives provides one of the most important messages in juvenile literature within the framework of a thoroughly spellbinding story.

Where Do We Go from Here?

When he came to, he was lying on his camp bed in the station restaurant at Brachen. It was broad daylight and only one or two people here and there were sitting or lying on their beds. The place seemed less full than before. He looked at the corner over by the coffee machines to see if Klaus were lying there, but the bed had been taken away.

He looked round slowly. He had a queer, lightheaded feeling and wondered how long he had been asleep.

Paolo was in the next bed. He was asleep, but his hands moved restlessly on the coverlet, and now and then he muttered something. Farther along, Nikolai and Giuseppe lay fast asleep.

The camp beds of the others had been tidily made. They were empty. The boys must have gone off to the village. Werner raised himself on one elbow and gave a little grunt of pain. All his muscles hurt. He looked round a bit farther. Then he saw Hans Peter sitting behind him a little distance away. He was sitting on a pile of knapsacks between two beds with his back against the wall, staring gloomily before him. Werner beckoned, but Hans Peter did not see. He was sunk in thought.

Was he angry at their having gone off without him? He would have been a great help, but he could never have given Mr. Hutamäki the slip like the rest of them. Would he know how Klaus and Marie were? And whether their parents had been found?

Werner heaved himself up a bit farther and all his muscles seemed to protest. He was aching everywhere—back, shoulders, arms.

"Hans Peter!" he said in an urgent whisper.

Hans Peter jumped. He stood up rather reluctantly and came over to Werner's bed. "How do you feel?" he asked gruffly.

"I'm fine. How are the others?"

"I've been left here as watchdog," said Hans Peter. "You're none of you to get up till the doctor says you may. He's coming back this afternoon. There was no room for you in the hospital."

"But there's nothing wrong with us!" exclaimed Werner in surprise.

Hans Peter did not answer.

"How long have we been asleep?" asked Werner.

"Two nights and a day and a half."

Werner's jaw dropped.

"They gave you injections to make you sleep. You were suffering from exhaustion or something. They made quite a song and dance about you."

"But I feel fine," protested Werner. "My muscles ache a bit, that's all."

Hans Peter shrugged his shoulders. "Well, you looked pretty moldy, all the lot of you, when they brought you in here the day before yesterday. You all had jabs at the hospital. You looked more dead than alive, I can tell you, and Hutamäki had the scare of his life. It was a mean trick you played us, creeping out while we were asleep, instead of taking us with you."

"We couldn't help that," said Werner. "Mr. Hutamäki would never have approved of your coming and you might have let on to him about us."

"Honestly, I don't know what I should have done," Hans Peter admitted. He was not so gruff now. "But I've never been so angry in all my life."

Werner glanced over to the corner where he had expected to see Klaus. He hesitated and then asked, "How are Klaus and his sister?"

Hans Peter looked uncomfortable. He began to say something and then stopped, looking away so as not to meet Werner's eyes.

"D'you mean it was all for nothing?" Werner asked suddenly, with his heart in his mouth.

Hans Peter shook his head. "Marie's alive, but they don't know if she'll pull through." He paused. "They found the parents; they were both dead." He paused again and it was a minute before he added, "And Klaus is very ill. He's delirious."

Werner felt the blood beating in his temples. His heart was thumping. He felt dizzy and lay down again on his back.

"Everyone here is getting on fine," Hans Peter went on presently, in a flat, expressionless voice. "Most of them are out now. It's visiting time at the hospital. And the trains are running again. A lot of the evacuees have left."

But Werner was not listening any more. He could see Klaus, and Marie's pinched white face. Should not he and the other boys have done what they did? Had they just been crazy fools?

Then he remembered Klaus when he was brought in that evening, sobbing and kicking because he had had to leave the place where his parents were buried. He had kept on shouting, but no one had listened to him. He had known they had been searching in the wrong place. In his helplessness there was nothing Klaus could do but howl. But later he had dug frantically for hours.

And had it all been wrong? Had they just caused more misery? Klaus was delirious, his parents were dead after all, and Marie. . . .

"What exactly is wrong with Marie?" he asked. Hans Peter hesitated, but after a bit he answered. "She bled an awful lot inside," he said. "She's got to have an operation. They wanted to do it yesterday afternoon, but they couldn't because they hadn't any blood for her."

"No blood?" asked Werner, puzzled.

"She's got to have a blood transfusion before the operation, and after it's over. But they couldn't find anyone that had exactly the same kind of blood. As a rule it isn't so tricky, but with Marie it was very difficult. A lot of us went over to let them test our blood. They tried me and Mr. Hutamäki and Bartel. But our blood wasn't right either. There were two doctors and three nurses working on us, and word kept on coming up from the lab that it wasn't the right kind of blood. And you'll never guess who had the right kind in the end."

"Who?" demanded Werner excitedly.

"Your Aunt Augusta. First they wouldn't try her. They said she was too old and her blood pressure wasn't high enough, or something. She was so cross with the doctors when they wouldn't try her that they gave in. And then they found she had exactly the right kind."

"Well, what happened?" Werner asked. "Were they in time?"

"I'm not quite sure about what happened after that. They took Aunt Augusta away with them and we were all sent back here."

"Have they operated on Marie?"

"Yesterday evening, but they don't know yet if it was successful or not. It should have been done much sooner. Your aunt had to stay in the hospital."

Werner lay quite still on his back. It was all too much for him to take in at once. Aunt Augusta and Marie . . . it was all so wonderful. He knew just what his father would have said about it—"It was meant."

He tried to think. If he and his father had not brought the boys down from the hut above Urteli, they would not have been evacuated together. If they had not come here to Brachen, Klaus would not have been able to take them up to his home. In that case Marie would be dead by now, for she could have lasted only a couple of hours longer. And if Aunt Augusta had not been evacuated with them she would not have been able to give her blood. It was meant!

But what about the avalanches? Were they meant too? That could not be right. There must be something wrong somewhere. All those people killed and injured, all that grief and suffering! His whole heart revolted against the idea of so much pain. It was senseless for the snow to come hurtling down from the mountains. Why did it happen? Why? Why? Why did Klaus and Marie have to lose their father and mother?

"*I* don't know," he muttered suddenly half aloud.

"What is it?" asked Hans Peter. "What don't you know?"

"Why do all these things happen? Why can't people just live happy and ordinary lives?"

"Happy and ordinary aren't the same," said Hans Peter slowly. "I believe you're only happy if you *know* you're happy. And you only know that after you've been miserable. A lot of us in the Children's Village have learned that."

Werner said nothing. Hans Peter went on rather uncertainly, "The head of our Village told us something once. He said misfortune shakes you awake, and it's only when you're awake that life becomes quite real, because then you've learned what it's worth."

from **The Incredible Journey**
Sheila Burnford

This is the story of three heroic animals—a young Labrador retriever, a Siamese cat, and an old bull terrier—who travel through two hundred and fifty miles of Canadian wilderness to the place and people that mean home and love to them.

[The Beginning of the Journey]

There was a slight mist when John Longridge rose early the following morning, having fought a losing battle for the middle of the bed with his uninvited bedfellow. He shaved and dressed quickly, watching the mist roll back over the fields and the early morning sun break through. It would be a perfect fall day, an Indian summer day, warm and mellow. Downstairs he found the animals waiting patiently by the door for their early morning run. He let them out, then cooked and ate his solitary breakfast. He was out in the driveway, loading up his car when the dogs and cat returned from the fields. He fetched some biscuits for them and they lay by the wall of the house in the early sun, watching him. He threw the last item into the back of the car, thankful that he had already packed the guns and hunting equipment before the Labrador had seen them, then walked over and patted the heads of his audience, one by one.

"Be good," he said. "Mrs. Oakes will be here soon. Good-by, Luath," he said to the Labrador, "I wish I could have taken you with me, but there wouldn't be room in the canoe for three of us." He put his hand under the young dog's soft muzzle. The golden-brown eyes looked steadily into his, and then the dog did an unexpected thing: he lifted his right paw and placed it in the man's hand. Longridge had seen him do this many a time to his own master and he was curiously touched and affected by the trust it conveyed, almost wishing he did not have to leave immediately just after the dog had shown his first responsive gesture.

He looked at his watch and realized he was already late. He had no worries about leaving the animals alone outside, as they had never attempted to stray beyond the large garden and the adjacent fields; and they could return inside the house if they wished, for the kitchen door was the kind that closed slowly on a spring. All that he had to do was shoot the inside bolt while the door was open, and after that it did not close properly and could be pushed open from the outside. They looked contented enough, too—the cat was washing methodically behind his ears—the old dog sat on his haunches, panting after his run, his long pink tongue lolling out of his grinning mouth; and the Labrador lay quietly by his side.

Longridge started the car and waved to them out of the window as he drove slowly down the drive, feeling rather foolish as he did so. "What do I expect them to do in return?" he asked himself with a smile, "Wave back? Or shout 'Good-by'? The trouble is I've lived too long alone with them and I'm becoming far too attached to them."

The car turned around the bend at the end of the long tree-lined drive and the animals heard the sound of the engine receding in the distance. The cat transferred his attention to a hind leg; the old dog stopped panting and lay down; the young dog remained stretched out, only his eyes moving and an occasional twitch of his nose.

Twenty minutes passed by and no move was made; then suddenly the young dog rose, stretched himself, and stood looking intently down the drive. He remained like this for several minutes, while the cat watched closely, one leg still pointing upwards; then slowly the Labrador walked down the driveway and stood at the curve, looking back as though inviting the others to come. The old dog rose too, now, somewhat stiffly, and followed. Together they turned the corner, out of sight.

The cat remained utterly still for a full minute, blue eyes blazing in the dark mask. Then, with a curious hesitating run, he set off in pursuit. The dogs were waiting by the gate when he turned the corner, the old dog peering wistfully back, as though he hoped to see his friend Mrs. Oakes materialize with a juicy bone; but when the Labrador started up the road he followed. The cat still paused by the gate, one paw lifted delicately in the air— undecided, questioning, hesitant; until suddenly, some inner decision reached, he followed the dogs. Presently all three disappeared from sight down the dusty road, trotting briskly and with purpose.

About an hour later Mrs. Oakes walked up the driveway from her cottage, carrying a string bag with her working shoes and apron, and a little parcel of tidbits for the animals. Her placid, gentle face wore a rather disappointed look, because the dogs usually spied her long before she got to the house and would rush to greet her.

"I expect Mr. Longridge left them shut inside the house if he was leaving early," she consoled herself. But when she pushed open the kitchen door and walked inside, everything seemed very silent and still. She stood at the foot of the stairs and called them, but there was no answering patter of running feet, only the steady tick-tock of the old clock in the hallway. She walked through the silent house and out into the front garden and stood there calling with a puzzled frown.

"Oh, well," she spoke her thoughts aloud to the empty, sunny garden, "perhaps they've gone up to the school. . . . It's a funny thing, though," she continued, sitting on a kitchen chair a few minutes later and tying her shoelaces, "that Puss isn't here—he's usually sitting on the window sill at this time of the day. Oh, well, he's probably out hunting —I've never known a cat like that for hunting, doesn't seem natural somehow!"

She washed and put away the few dishes, then took her cleaning materials into the sitting room. There her eye was caught by a sparkle on the floor by the desk, and she found the glass paperweight, and after that

the remaining sheet of the note on the desk. She read it through to where it said: "I will be taking the dogs (and Tao too of course!) . . . ," then looked for the remainder. "That's odd," she thought, "now where would he take them? That cat must have knocked the paperweight off last night—the rest of the note must be somewhere in the room."

She searched the room but it was not until she was emptying an ash tray into the fireplace that she noticed the charred curl of paper in the hearth. She bent down and picked it up carefully, for it was obviously very brittle, but even then most of it crumbled away and she was left with a fragment which bore the initials J. R. L.

"Now, isn't that the queerest thing," she said to the fireplace, rubbing vigorously at the black marks on the tiles. "He must mean he's taking them all to Heron Lake with him. But why would he suddenly do that, after all the arrangements we made? He never said a word about it on the telephone—but wait a minute, I remember now—he was just going to say something about them when the line went dead; perhaps he was just going to tell me."

While Mrs. Oakes was amazed that Longridge would take the animals on his vacation, it did not occur to her to be astonished that a cat should go along too, for she was aware that the cat loved the car and always went with the dogs when Longridge drove them anywhere or took them farther afield for walks. Like many Siamese cats, he was as obedient and as trained to go on walks as most dogs, and would always return to a whistle.

Mrs. Oakes swept and dusted and talked to the house, locked it and returned home to her cottage. She would have been horrified to the depths of her kindly, well-ordered soul if she had known the truth. Far from sitting sedately in the back of a car traveling north with John Longridge, as she so fondly visualized, the animals were by now many miles away on a deserted country road that ran westward.

They had kept a fairly steady pace for the first hour or so, falling into an order which was not to vary for many miles or days; the Labrador ran always by the left shoulder of the old dog, for the bull terrier was very nearly blind in the left eye, and they jogged along fairly steadily together—the bull terrier with his odd, rolling, sailorlike gait, and the Labrador in a slow lope. Some ten yards behind came the cat, whose attention was frequently distracted, when he would stop for a few minutes and then catch up again. But, in between these halts, he ran swiftly and steadily, his long slim body and tail low to the ground.

When it was obvious that the old dog was flagging, the Labrador turned off the quiet, graveled road and into the shade of a pinewood beside a clear, fast-running creek. The old dog drank deeply, standing up to his chest in the cold water; the cat picked his way delicately to the edge of an overhanging rock. Afterwards they rested in the deep pine needles under the trees, the terrier panting heavily with his eyes half closed, and the cat busy with his eternal washing. They lay there for nearly an hour, until the sun struck through the branches above them. The young dog rose and stretched, then walked towards the road. The old dog rose too, stiff-legged, his head low. He walked toward the waiting Labrador, limping slightly

and wagging his tail at the cat, who suddenly danced into a patch of sunlight, struck at a drifting leaf, then ran straight at the dogs, swerving at the last moment, and as suddenly sitting down again.

They trotted steadily on, all that afternoon —mostly traveling on the grassy verge at the side of the country road; sometimes in the low overgrown ditch that ran alongside, if the acute hearing of the young dog warned them of an approaching car.

By the time the afternoon sun lay in long, barred shadows across the road, the cat was still traveling in smooth, swift bursts, and the young dog was comparatively fresh. But the old dog was very weary, and his pace had dropped to a limping walk. They turned off the road into the bush at the side, and walked slowly through a clearing in the trees, pushing their way through the tangled undergrowth at the far end. They came out upon a small open place where a giant spruce had crashed to the ground and left a hollow where the roots had been, filled now with drifted dry leaves and spruce needles.

The late afternoon sun slanted through the branches overhead, and it looked invitingly snug and secure. The old dog stood for a minute, his heavy head hanging, and his tired body swaying slightly, then lay down on his side in the hollow. The cat, after a good deal of wary observation, made a little hollow among the spruce needles and curled around in it, purring softly. The young dog disappeared into the undergrowth and reappeared presently, his smooth coat dripping water, to lie down a little away apart from the others.

The old dog continued to pant exhaustedly for a long time, one hind leg shaking badly, until his eyes closed at last, the labored breaths came further and further apart, and he was sleeping—still, save for an occasional long shudder.

Later on, when darkness fell, the young dog moved over and stretched out closely at his side and the cat stalked over to lie between his paws; and so, warmed and comforted by their closeness, the old dog slept, momentarily unconscious of his aching, tired body or his hunger.

In the nearby hills a timber wolf howled mournfully; owls called and answered and glided silently by with great outspread wings; and there were faint whispers of movement and small rustling noises around all through the night. Once an eerie wail like a baby's crying woke the old dog and brought him shivering and whining to his feet; but it was only a porcupine, who scrambled noisily and clumsily down a nearby tree trunk and waddled away, still crying softly. When he lay down again the cat was gone from his side —another small night hunter slipping through the unquiet shadows that froze to stillness at his passing.

The young dog slept in fitful, uneasy starts, his muscles twitching, constantly lifting his head and growling softly. Once he sprang to his feet with a full-throated roar which brought a sudden splash in the distance, then silence—and who knows what else unknown, unseen or unheard passed through his mind to disturb him further? Only one thing was clear and certain—that at all costs he was going home, home to his own beloved master. Home lay to the west, his instinct told him; but he could not leave the other two— so somehow he must take them with him all the way.

Historical Fiction

For many children, historical fiction is more appealing reading than history, since it is lightened both by imaginary people and events, and since it contains invented dialogue. The best historical fiction, however, is solidly based on accurate historical details and takes no liberties with those historical personages who appear in the story, nor with historical fact. In whatever period the story is set, life is depicted in accurate detail and with dialogue that is appropriate to the characters and the period.

In this section of the anthology, the second world war has been used as a chronological dividing line, and a focus on the period as a criterion. Unlike the excerpt from *Little Men* in the previous section, the stories chosen here are shaped and colored by the time and the events they reflect; in other words, in this section are the stories that were written as historical fiction, rather than stories that were written in another period but do not reflect or focus upon historical events.

Historical fiction for younger readers must be chosen carefully so that it makes no demands on the reader that cannot be satisfied. Younger children who do not have as finely developed a time sense as they later will, and who have less historical background at their command, need a story like Judith Griffin's *Phoebe and the General* to catch and hold their interest. It is not historically complex, it is simply written, and it focuses on people rather than unfamiliar events. For older readers, it is possible to introduce both the background for historical events and the conflicting patterns that led to stress without making the story historically burdensome. Indeed, the best historical fiction presents characters and events with an apparent spontaneity that brings them to life so vividly that readers feel no sense of distance.

from Ellen and the Queen
Gillian Avery

Since her mother is lodgekeeper for the Earl, Ellen is sure that she'll have a chance to see Queen Victoria when she comes to visit. A daring child, Ellen takes matters into her own hands in her determination.

Queen Victoria was coming, she really was, with Prince Albert and four of their children, to spend a night at the Great House. The Earl was so grand and his house so big that he could do things like this. The village was very proud of him, and they pitied other places that had only a plain "Mr." or just a "Sir" for a landlord, and were scornful about "great houses" that were too poverty-struck for the Queen to visit. There were tremendous preparations going on at their own Great House, and the fathers of many of the children at school were working up there, building, painting, getting the gardens into shape. So every day the girls in Ellen's class could contribute a new wonder their fathers had told them—while Ellen had nothing at all to tell. Joe worked in the Great House stables, but he had nothing much of interest to tell about that, and Ellen didn't even see the wagons of workmen and materials from Salisbury passing through her gates, because they used a separate entrance.

"Never mind," Joe comforted her when she complained loudly. "You'll be seeing it soon, I daresay. There's talk of them putting up tents in the park when the Queen comes, and giving us all tea there."

But so far as Ellen was concerned, the Countess and Miss Higgs decided otherwise. It happened like this.

It was on a May morning when everything was bright and shining outside, and she was aching all over with having to sit still at school. She was supposed to be writing her copies at the long desk under the window while other children were called up to Miss Higgs's table to read. The babies were gabbling their alphabet, first forward, then backward, over and over again, and everybody was busy except Ellen. She had written "Procrastination is the thief of time" four times, each time worse than the one above, and had no wish to write it a fifth. So she poked Eliza Moon with her elbow.

"Why do you write with your tongue sticking out? Our old cat does that if you tickle behind his ears. Shall I tickle behind your ears?"

But Eliza wrote steadily on.

"Or I'll ink your tongue if you like, so's you can write with it." Ellen jabbed her pen into the ink pot, dragged it out full and pointed it at Eliza, who gave a bleat and jerked herself away.

"Who is that making a disturbance down there? Ellen Timms. I thought so. Come out to the front with your copybook." Miss Higgs took out her ruler meaningly, and laid it in front of her.

Everybody watched while Ellen went up. The babies, still gabbling ZYXWV, stared at her with huge round eyes. The writers held their pens poised over their copies. The group around Miss Higgs's table, clutching their books, fell back to let her pass.

"Disgusting, as I thought," said Miss Higgs, glancing at the copy, in which "procrastination" had been spelled four different ways, and which was lavishly spattered with blots. Then Miss Higgs produced the label "Empty vessels make the most sound"—it was worn by Ellen more than by anybody else in the school—and pinned it to her back.

But Ellen scarcely noticed this time, for she was staring out of the window behind Miss Higgs's back. There was a carriage drawing up outside the school, and a man in splendid dark-green livery had jumped down to open the door.

"Get up on the stool, Ellen," commanded Miss Higgs.

"Oh, but . . ." began Ellen.

"Ellen Timms, do as I say at once," said Miss Higgs, scandalized.

But just as Ellen had climbed onto the stool in the corner, the schoolroom door opened and the Countess swept in.

They all scrambled to their feet and stood staring. They had never seen her so close before. She was so big. She was not only tall, but broad; not just comfortably fat like most of their mothers, but all tightly bound up like the staves of a barrel. As she sailed down the room she seemed to dwarf everything in it. And in her wake, like a duckling behind a barge, followed a little girl of about seven, in a green dress with a little matching cape and a green silk bonnet.

"Miss Higgs, I presume?" said the Countess. "I am sorry that I have not been able to pay an earlier visit to this school which our family founded. The Earl and I propose to take a keen interest in it. I have brought my daughter, Lady Mary, so that she also may see the children."

"Your ladyship," said Miss Higgs, hurrying forward, confused, "if I had known . . ."

The Countess waved a large gloved hand, and Miss Higgs sank into silence. She looked about her. "Nice neat hair, I am glad to see. Though one or two of your children could do with tighter braids. I see curls here and there, and curls are things that I will not stand for in my servants, nor at our school. Perhaps you will correct the matter before my next visit."

Miss Higgs swallowed and twisted her hands nervously. "Oh, yes, your ladyship, certainly, your ladyship."

"They are all good children, I hope?" The Countess scrutinized them again. "And they know their Catechism? Well, then, I am going to tell them of a great treat. Her Majesty the Queen . . ." Here the Countess paused impressively. "Her Majesty the Queen has graciously consented to pass a night at the Great House—as many of you may know. And the Earl and I thought that if the children had been good children—but only on that condition, mind—they should come up to the main entrance of the house to see her alight from her carriage."

There was an excited murmuring among the children, and Miss Higgs stepped for-ward. "I am sure we all thank his lordship and her ladyship for their kind thought for the school, don't we, children?"

The Countess waved her hand once more, as if to dismiss further talk. Her eye roved around the schoolroom, and then fell on Ellen for the first time. She pointed an awful finger at her.

"And why, may I ask, is that child there?" She held a pair of glasses up to her eyes. "She has the most unruly hair I have ever seen on a child. She cannot help its color, but those curls can, and must be, controlled."

"Ellen Timms, do you hear what her ladyship says? You had better get down and show her your label." Miss Higgs unpinned it, put it into Ellen's hands, and gave her a little push forward.

" 'Empty vessels make the most sound,' " read out the Countess. "You have been talking in class?"

Ellen hung her head.

"You see, Mary, what becomes of naughty children in this school," remarked the Countess to the little girl at her side.

"Yes, Mamma."

Through lowered eyelashes Ellen looked at the little girl. And she noticed that under the green silk bonnet there was hair like her own. It was certainly very smooth, and it was not so bright, but it was red. At the same time she saw the little girl staring back at her—and she seemed to be the one sympathetic person in the room.

When the huge bulk of the Countess had made its stately departure, Miss Higgs told Ellen how she had disgraced the school. "And of course," she finished, "I cannot dream of allowing you to go up to the Great House with the school. Her ladyship said 'good children only.' "

"Who was going to see ever so much of The Family—more than any of us?" they taunted her in the playground afterward. "And now she's not even going to be allowed in the park!"

"I wouldn't be going with you for anything," said Ellen loftily. "Going two by two with Miss Higgs! I shall be going by myself."

Little Lucy Baines took no part in any of

this talk. "She *was* on wheels—her ladyship —under all them skirts," she said dreamily. "She just rolled along so smooth."

Ellen told the schoolchildren so many times in the next few weeks of how she was going to see the Queen that in the end she came to believe it herself.

She needed to console herself somehow, after all, for the talk now at school and up and down the village was of nothing but the Queen. The children were practicing their curtsies and learning all the verses of "God Save the Queen," and stitching the banners that were to decorate the village street, and wondering which of the little princes and princesses would be coming and what they would be wearing. The village women were scouring and polishing their cottages. "You never know, her carriage might just break down outside, and I'd never get over the shame of it if everything weren't just apple-pie order in here," they told each other. They were trimming up their bonnets, too, with every bit of finery they could lay hands on, for on the evening of the Queen's visit there was to be roast beef and plum pudding served in tents in the park to everybody in the village who chose to come.

"It's going to rain," said Ellen with savage satisfaction as they came out of school the afternoon before the great day. "The sun rose red as red this morning."

"But then you'll get wet when the Queen comes," said Lucy Baines, wide-eyed. "You're going, too, you said you were."

For the moment Ellen had forgotten all about her boastings. "Oh, I shall be inside," she said haughtily, "not like you, standing out in the wet."

"You'll be inside, locked in the pigsty," taunted Sarah Jarvis. "Don't forget to see if the ladies have . . . legs," she added daringly, and then ran away because Miss Higgs was looking out of her window and might have heard her.

But when Ellen woke next morning and heard rain dripping from the gutter, from the porch, and pattering on the plants in the garden, she did not feel glad at all. At that moment she would willingly have tossed away all her proud boastings and gone with the school to see the Queen, and the fact that it was a gray, soaking day only made her feel gloomier than ever. What was she going to do with herself? Everybody else had their plans, but she had a whole, dreary, wet day to fill all alone.

Her mother had no sympathy. "No, you're certainly not going to be outside with me opening the gate for the Queen. If you're too naughty to go up with the school, then you're certainly too naughty for that. Whatever would the Countess say? You should have thought of all this before—it isn't as if I haven't told you till I'm tired. You'd better stay in the back and keep Moll and Martie quiet."

But Ellen got tired of the four-year-old twins, who wanted to play by themselves, not with her. Sulkily she went out onto the porch and stared at the gray haze of rain that was sweeping over the park. There were footsteps coming down the road. She turned and saw Lucy and Mary Ann Baines, sheltering under a huge green umbrella.

"What are you doing, Ellen Timms?" called Mary Ann. "Waiting for the Queen?"

"We're going to school," said Lucy eagerly. "To meet the others, and then we're all marching up that drive." She pointed to the avenue beyond the gates.

"I was just setting out," said Ellen coolly. "You'll get very wet, but I shall be indoors."

She reached for her mother's shawl, which hung by the door. Mam wouldn't need it today; she would be wearing her Sunday one. Then she went down the path to the little garden gate, let herself out, and with a wary eye on the windows of the Lodge she opened the huge iron gates into the forbidden territory beyond. She didn't bother to close them, but turned and waved to the Baines sisters, who were huddled under their umbrella, staring at her. Then she trotted on under the dripping trees.

She was alarmed at what she was doing, but she wasn't going back, not yet, anyway. The avenue went on and on in the shadow of the enormous beech trees. The rain pattered on the leaves overhead and splashed onto her in big cold drops. But she didn't care, she told herself—she was walking along the way the Queen was going to come.

Then the beech trees ended and she was out in the open. In front of her lay a huge house, as big as a whole village, with hundreds of windows in it and such a rolling carpet of grass in front and such flower beds. Ellen did come to a stop now, frightened by her own daring. There might be all sorts of people behind those windows, staring out at her. Even outside she could see plenty of people, running to and fro in the rain, between carts that stood on the gravel ahead of her and tents in the distance.

Any of the other village children would have run away, but Ellen had always had a bold nature to match her red hair. She. was also very proud. If she turned back now she would have nothing to tell them at school. She would also probably run straight into the whole school party headed by Miss Higgs. So forward she marched.

from **Phoebe and the General**
Judith Berry Griffin

Thirteen-year-old Phoebe has a chance to save the life of General George Washington when he dines at her father's tavern in New York in 1776.

In 1776, the year Phoebe Fraunces was thirteen years old, her father gave her a very dangerous job. Phoebe was going to be a spy.

At that time most black people in New York were slaves. But Phoebe and her family had always been free. Phoebe's father, Samuel Fraunces, owned the Queen's Head Tavern. The Queen's Head was a popular eating and meeting place. George Washington (who was now General George Washington, commander in chief of the American Army) had dinner there when he visited New York. So did John Adams.

Many people met there because they knew it was a safe place to talk. In 1776 the war had begun, and there could be trouble if a person were caught talking against the

king. But the Patriots knew that Samuel Fraunces could be trusted. So they held meetings at his tavern and discussed their secret plans, and Sam Fraunces never let on that he knew any of them.

One morning in April, 1776, Sam and his daughter Phoebe were sitting side by side in the long dining room of the Queen's Head. There was to be a big dinner that night, and they were getting the room ready—polishing the pewter plates and candlesticks and laying out fresh candles.

Phoebe loved the Queen's Head from its broad front steps all the way up to its bright red-tiled roof. But this room—called the Long Room—was the room she loved best, with its neat tables and chairs, its fireplaces and its big windows. From the window seat where she sat she could see clear to the harbor. The water was dotted with big white-sailed ships, their tall masts pointing at the sky like fingers.

"Phoebe," her father began.

"Yes, sir," Phoebe answered. Her father did not respond, and Phoebe looked up at him, smiling. She thought him very handsome, with his curly hair powdered and drawn back and his smooth brown skin and dark eyes.

"Phoebe, I've something important to say to you this day," he said. "It's a bad time in this country."

Phoebe stopped smiling when she saw he was so serious.

"It's hard to find a person you can trust with a secret—especially a dangerous secret," he went on. "I'm glad to know I can trust you. Young as you are, you've learned from your father how to listen well and talk little."

Something in her father's voice made Phoebe put down the candlestick she was holding. She sat quite still, waiting for him to go on, watching the polishing cloth in his hands go around and around.

"I have a great fear in me," he said slowly,

"that our General Washington is in dread, dread danger. It is he who is keeping the colonies together. But there are those who'd like to see the colonies separated and so ruled more easily by the king. And if something were to happen to the general, it would be a hard, hard job to find another such as he, to pull the colonies together and throw off the king. Indeed, such a man might not be found at all, and the king would rule on."

There was silence for a time. The sunlight, stronger now, pushed warm fingers through the windows, glittering against the candlesticks.

"New York is full of soldiers," he continued. "Some are only out for money. To them it makes no difference what side they're on. They'd even take money from the enemy and do anything they'd ask. Some such scoundrel might be paid to kill the general. I heard something."

Phoebe closed her eyes, seeing her father moving like a shadow among his guests, gracious, smiling, pouring wine and exchanging greetings. It was so easy for him to hear secrets without seeming to listen!

"What I heard could cost my life, Daughter, and the general's as well," her father said quietly. "Phoebe, I need your help."

Phoebe opened her mouth to speak, but her voice would only whisper. "What must I do?" she asked.

Her father put down the candlestick and took her hand in his. "I want you to do a big job, Phoebe," he said gravely. "General Washington has let me know he's arriving in New York with his household in seven days' time. He's to move into Mortier House on Richmond Hill, and I promised to find him a housekeeper. I want you to live there and be his housekeeper, Phoebe. I know you will be a good one. But your real job will be to watch —to listen—to spy out every bit of information you can. I want you to find out if there is someone planning to kill him and how he plans to do it. Your real job will be to save General Washington's life."

Phoebe was very frightened. General Washington was a great soldier! How could she save his life, if his whole army could not?

She wouldn't know who to look for. She was not even strong enough to fight anyone! And what if she failed?

Her father spoke again, as if he had read her thoughts. "I'm asking only that you try, Daughter," he said. "I have no proof of a plot against the general's life. I know only what I heard. If I tell, his enemies would only hide themselves and wait for a safer time."

Phoebe shook her head. Could this really be happening? But her father's voice was real. "You'll tell no one who you are. You'll listen as you serve the officers of the Army. You must watch for a member of General Washington's bodyguard—someone whose name begins with T. It is this man who is supposed to carry out the plan. Every day you and I will meet down by the market, and you can tell me what news you have.

"Now hear me well, Phoebe. You are to do nothing by yourself—nothing that would put you in danger. You are only to listen and tell me what you hear. Trust no one. No one." He picked up his candlestick and began to polish it once more. When he spoke this time, his voice sounded sad, but Phoebe heard more than sadness. Her father was angry.

"You know, Phoebe," he said, "'tis a strange freedom we're fighting for, alongside George Washington."

Phoebe nodded. She knew what her father meant. How could a man lead an army to win freedom if he himself owned slaves? For General Washington did own slaves. It was said he treated them well. But still, they were slaves.

"And 'tis stranger yet that you and I will save him," Samuel went on. "And those like us will have no share in that freedom he's fighting for!"

"But maybe," Phoebe said, "when the Patriots win their freedom, they'll let the slaves go free, too. Maybe then everyone will be free!"

Samuel shook his head. "I think not, Daughter," he said. "But maybe, one day...." Then he looked at Phoebe and smiled. "Here, now! Get on with your polishing! It won't do to have tonight's dinner set off by dull candlesticks!"

And so it was that a few days later Phoebe packed two clean aprons and a bottle of her father's best cider into a bundle, said goodbye to her family, and set off to save George Washington's life.

from One Day in Ancient Rome
G. B. Kirtland

The place is Rome, the time is 75 A.D., and the story is both funny and informative as it reflects the setting and the period in a light style that is particularly skilled in its incorporation of Latin words.

It is very early in the morning, and something is walking under your bed. You open your eyes to see what it is, and it is exactly what you thought it was.

"*Salve,* you silly monkey," you say, which is the way to say good morning to silly mon-

keys, and then you climb down the steps from the bed and put on your *soleae.* If you don't wear *soleae,* your feet will freeze because the floor is made of colored stones, and, although it is fine for checkers and hopscotch, it is very cold for feet.

"It is today!" you call to your brother. "Wake up! At last, it is today!" The monkey prances all about and turns somersaults because even he knows that this is a special day, but your brother still sleeps. And so you have to do something important. You have to fetch the *hydria* that is full of water and pour some on him.

"Oh!" says your brother, awake at last. "I was dreaming. I dreamed I was a soldier with Caesar in Africa and that a crocodile was splashing water on me. But I see it is only you."

"It is finally today!" you say.

"*Eje! Eja! Evoe!*" shouts your brother, and, jumping down from his bed, he puts the marble table under the window, the stool on top of the table, and the book-box on top of the stool. "Come quickly," he says. "Let us see where Apollo is." And up you climb to look for Apollo, the Sun-God, who drives the sun across the sky in his chariot every day.

"*Salve, liberi,* and *salve* to you, too, silly monkey," says your mother from the doorway. "If you are looking for Apollo, he is halfway up the sky."

"*Salve, Mater!*"

"For Diana's sake!" says *Mater,* coming into your room. "Do you mean to tell me you are still in your *vestes nocturnae?* Well, you had better get into your tunics immediately, this very minute, and go eat your *jentaculum.* Surely you haven't forgotten what a special day this is?"

"*Hecate,* no!" you say. "Do you think there will be elephants, *Mater?*"

"Oh, yes," says *Mater.* "There are always elephants." Downstairs there is such a hustle and such a bustle that you can scarcely make your way to the dining room. The cooks and

the waiters, the kitchenboys and the pastrymakers, the wood carriers and the hairdressers are going one way, while the dancing master and the steward, the barber and the physician, the doorkeeper and the butler are going another.

"Festina lente!" shrills the parrot, which means "Take it easy." He says it again and again: *"Festina lente! Festina lente!"* but nobody listens to him.

Here comes a pageboy who bumps into a secretary who bumps into a chambermaid, and down fall the feather dusters, the sponges, and the palm-leaf brooms. It is all rather a commotion, but then you can hardly expect to have fifty people living in the house without a little noise and traffic.

There are two people at the breakfast table. The large one is Nurse. The small one with honey all over its face is the baby. You sit down in front of your napkin and spoon, and you eat bread and honey and raisins and olives, and you drink wine.

Nurse eats a great many olives, and, like the parrot, she says one thing over and over again. She says: "Do not spill your wine. Do not spill your wine. Do not spill your wine."

After *jentaculum,* you look in at your father's office. It is so crowded that at first you cannot see him.

"Salve, liberi!" he says, and there he is on his couch, reading a scroll, while the barber shaves him and the physician paces around him and his secretaries write and his visitors talk.

"Salve, Pater!" you say, and now you hurry upstairs to *schola.*

"I wish there were couches in the schoolroom," says your brother.

"Just wait. When you are a man, you will have all the couches you want," you tell him, and it is true. Grownups lie down when they read and when they talk and even when they eat. Here is the tutor. *Pater* bought him on a trip to Greece. The tutor teaches you reading, writing, and arithmetic. Sometimes he is cross, but mostly he is not.

"Salve," you say.

"Salve," he says.

This is the scroll of papyrus to read poems and stories from.

This is the abacus to add numbers on. (XXVI and XXV makes LI.)

This is the stylus to write on wax tablets with. A stylus is also fine for sword fights, but only when the tutor is not looking.

You recite Horace's poem about the Town Mouse and the Country Mouse, and your brother practices making a speech.

"I am proud to be a Roman citizen," he says. *"Et cetera, et cetera, et cetera."*

The tutor laughs. "All right," he says. "All right, that will be all for today. I have not forgotten that this is a special day."

"Do you think there will be elephants?" you say.

"Oh, yes," says the tutor. "There are always elephants."

"Come," your brother says. "We must do something important. We must find *Mater* immediately."

"Yes," you say. "We must find *Mater* at once."

You run into the weaving room, but she is not there. You run to the picture gallery, but she is not there. You run to the *solarium,* and there she is, taking a sun bath.

"*Salve, Mater,*" you say.

"*Salve, liberi,*" she says.

"Is it time to go?" your brother asks.

"No, of course it is not time to go," she says.

"*Vale, Mater,*" you say, which is the way to say good-by.

"*Vale, liberi,*" Mater says. Now somebody is crying.

"It is the baby," you say.

"Who else?" says your brother, and you go into the nursery.

"Don't cry, little one," you say, and you rock her cradle, but she does not care for that.

"Don't cry, little one," says your brother, and he gives her a wolf's tooth to bite on, but she does not care for that.

"She probably wants to see the *animales,*" you say, and so your brother points to the camelopard and the tiger and the rhinoceros parading on the wall, but she does not care for that.

Nurse comes in.

"Oh, *Nutrix,*" you say. "The baby is crying."

"Who else?" says *Nutrix.* She picks the baby up, and the baby stops crying at once because she does care for that.

"I have something to ask you, *Nutrix,*" you say.

"And what is it?"

"Do you think there will be elephants?"

"Oh, yes," says *Nutrix.* "There are always elephants."

"Is it time to go?" asks your brother.

"No, of course it is not time to go," says *Nutrix.* "But your *mater* needs turtle doves for the banquet tonight, so you may come shopping with me later."

"But we have nothing to do now."

"Nonsense. You can play. That is something to do."

"But there is nothing to play with."

"Nonsense. There is a great deal to play with," says *Nutrix* and, as it sometimes happens, she is quite right.

from Save Queen of Sheba
Louise Moeri

Having survived a Sioux Indian raid on the trail to Oregon, King David and his little sister, Queen of Sheba, are hoping to be reunited with their wagon train. King David then realizes what it means to the Sioux to have white settlers on their land.

The rain stopped just before daybreak. King David, sleeping lightly, heard the pounding rush of the rain dwindle and finally cease, but he waited a little longer before crawling out from under the quilt. At the dusky back of the cave, Maggie was sleeping on her feet, her head hanging low, one big hind hoof tilted on its rim. Her harness lay nearby, spread out on a couple of boulders, and the silver balls on the hames gleamed in the dimness.

A pale gray light was creeping in under the overhang by the time King David slid carefully away from Queen of Sheba, so as not to wake her, and stood in the opening behind the big boulders. It was still too dark to see much, but it seemed that the storm was over. Great pearl-colored rifts were appearing in the clouds, and the wind had gentled to become only a fitful breeze. There was a heavy scent of wet earth and sage in the air, and a meadowlark was just beginning to sing.

King David's clothes were still a little damp from the rain, and he would have liked to wrap the quilt around him, but of course he could not do that. He had to leave it tucked around Queen of Sheba to keep her warm. Once again he was swept by a powerful surge of fury and frustration that chance had left her to him to take care of.

It would have been so much easier if he had been left alone, with only himself to feed and shelter. Queen of Sheba was like the loose flap of skin that had been on his wound —he had had to cut it off because of the infection it caused, or it would have killed him. He hoped Queen of Sheba would not prove to be a burden too heavy for him to carry, and cause the death of both of them.

Grudgingly King David left Queen of Sheba asleep and carefully made his way up over the rimrock, where for half an hour he busied himself pulling grass for the mare. The grass was wet but it was better than no feed at all, and the mare seemed to have hollow legs—she ate ravenously all the grass he could gather and then would look around hungrily for more. Even so, she was gaunt. She needed grain to keep up her strength, although they were not really working her that hard.

They had been taking turns riding the horse, although King David's turns had been few and far between. He rode only when his knees threatened to buckle under him, and he was afraid he would collapse and leave Queen of Sheba alone.

Queen of Sheba did not really like riding the mare, and she complained endlessly because Maggie was a workhorse—broad-backed and heavy—and the harness was uncomfortable to sit on. But King David would not take the harness off the horse. He suspected that Maggie was more used to being in harness than to being ridden bareback, and she was flighty enough now, without making her worse. They did indeed look peculiar, journeying along all alone across the prairie with a horse fully harnessed right down to the blinkers on her bridle, and no cart or wagon hitched to her tugs. But peculiar or not, the harness gave him more control over her, and that's what counted most.

After King David fed the horse, he started a very small fire, cooked the last of the bacon and boiled some cornmeal and water. As soon as possible, he put the fire out and fanned the smoke with his coat to disperse it. Although they had not sighted any Indians since the raid, there was no point in taking chances. He still had seven bullets left in the bullet pouch, and enough caps to fire them, but he knew he couldn't load and fire the Sharps fast enough, especially under attack, to do them much good. At best he might get off one, maybe two, good shots. And after that . . .

Queen of Sheba awoke, cranky and peevish. She was very hungry but did not want bacon or boiled cornmeal.

"I want a hot biscuit," she said, "with butter on. And honey—"

"We ain't got none."

"I want fried potatoes."

"We ain't got no potatoes. Eat your bacon and cornmeal."

"Ma don't make me eat no old cornmeal— I want Ma—I want Ma to fix me something to eat—"

King David smothered his exasperation. He was trying—hard—to think, and Queen of Sheba's whining aggravated him till his head started to ache. He couldn't allow anything to distract him—he had to think everything through very carefully, plan their next move. There would be no room for mistakes out here, and no second chances.

On the one hand, they could stay here at the cave, a little safer probably than out on open ground, and try to hold out in case a rescue party came back looking for survivors or maybe another wagon train came through. He had heard that several trains were making the trek this summer, and there was a slight chance that there would be one maybe a few weeks behind theirs, although there was no guarantee that he might be able to sight it from here. The main trail to Oregon was north of them, near the Platte River, but by now he did not know how far away it was. In the meantime, their food supply was dwindling, although they might make it last another three or four days at most. Game was scarce here, mostly antelope that stayed out of range of his rifle, but there was a chance he might be able to shoot some more rabbits.

Equally likely with the arrival of white men, however, was the possibility that Indians might appear. He knew they were all around this territory, and he knew that even though he and Queen of Sheba were hidden in the shallow cave, it wouldn't take Indians long to find them if they should happen to pass this way. For all he knew, the cave might well be a regular stopping place for tribes moving through the area—it had plainly sheltered people many times before this.

Balanced against the possibility of staying in the cave was the possibility of moving out, searching for the tracks of the wagon train, and making a last attempt to either catch up with Pa and Ma and the others or make it alone to Fort Laramie.

He had no illusions about their chances. They were both weak and half starved. Cornmeal and water, even with a little bacon, didn't put much strength into your bones and muscles. He had lost quite a bit of blood, and the fever caused by his wound had weakened him. Queen of Sheba was not a strong child at best—that was one of the reasons why Ma had always favored her so much.

He could see that Queen of Sheba had lost weight these last few days, and even the possibility of getting back to Ma, that he dangled in front of her, barely drove her on. It wasn't impossible that she might just lie down and refuse to move again, and his reduced strength would make it very hard for him to save her then. Given just the right set of conditions, the small package of bone and muscle that made up Queen of Sheba could easily turn into a burden of such intolerable weight that neither of them would live to make it out of this wilderness. . . .

But as the last of the smoke from the little fire drifted away on the breeze, and the sun came out from behind the broken clouds, it seemed that the various possibilities changed into probabilities. The more he thought about it, the more convinced he became that they must go on. Chance of rescue if they waited here was too slim to gamble on. No—

they would have to push on—try to make the fort or the wagons before their last supplies of food and ammunition and their remaining strength gave out.

King David forced Queen of Sheba to choke down a few bites of the soggy cornmeal and then ate all she left. He harnessed Maggie and led her out from under the overhang and then boosted Queen of Sheba up onto her broad back. With some regret, he looked back once into the shelter of the cave and then led Maggie down the slope, in what he hoped would be the right direction.

By late morning, they were no more than five or six miles from the cave. King David had realized that he must make every effort to locate the tracks of the wagon train because they could not afford to waste time going the wrong way. As the sky cleared, he quickly got his directions from the sun, and he knew that the wagons had to be moving toward the northwest.

Accordingly, when they set out, he had set for his course a half circle, hoping to cut across the track and follow it in. The farther west they traveled, the more broken the country became, slowly rising, he supposed, into the higher country that flanked the massive ranges of the Rocky Mountains ahead. With the rain over, the wet ground would dry fast, and he was fairly sure that the tracks of the wagons would still be visible enough to follow.

Queen of Sheba bobbed along on the horse without saying much. Her face was drawn, and her silence made him nervous.

"Look, Queen of Sheba," he tried to arouse her, "way over there—some antelope. Sure wish I could shoot one. Then we'd eat good."

"I'm hungry," the child said listlessly.

"I know. When we catch up with the wagons you'll have something good to eat. Biscuits and honey, maybe, or beans—"

"My legs hurt."

He paused to look where she pointed and was dismayed at the sight. Both of her bony legs were bruised and raw where the horse's harness rubbed the skin as she rode. No wonder she complained so much about riding the mare. Maybe if he let her walk awhile she would hush up about that one misery at least.

"All right," he said, lifting her down. "I'll let you walk awhile. Why don't you eat an apple? We still got some left."

Queen of Sheba accepted an apple and settled into a shuffling walk. King David had tied the strings of her sunbonnet under her chin to protect her face from the sun and keep the heat from tiring her as long as possible. Her shoes, he noted, were beginning to show heavy wear from the stony ground and abrasive sand; the toes were scuffed and a button was missing from the left one. Margaret Anne Beecham's pa might have more money than Pa, but he didn't buy very good shoes for his daughter.

King David took one of the remaining apples and climbed onto the horse. Maggie snorted and raised a foot to kick, but as soon as he was astride she settled into her usual plodding walk.

As they pushed ahead, the land was becoming rougher, with low rocky ridges and shallow swales, and a dry stream bed, that made it hard to see very far in any direction. Once he got off and left the mare, with Queen of Sheba holding the rope, standing just under the crest of a hill so he could go forward and reconnoiter without exposing them to view.

Luke Skinner's hat was so big on him that he had to tilt his head far back to see out from under the brim. Queen of Sheba stared at him. "Why don't you take that hat off?" she muttered. "You look silly."

"Can't do that," he told her. "A hawk just flew by, and if she looked down and saw this hole in my head, she might think it looked like a hole in a hollow tree and decide to build a nest in it. And what would I do with baby birds hatching out inside my head?" Queen of Sheba only stared silently at him.

"Well, come on," he said flatly. "Let's git moving. I'll ride the horse—you can walk if you'd rather, but keep close behind me, now—"

It was past the middle of the afternoon when King David's eyes, blurring again with fatigue, picked out a faint mark across the next grassy hill. Eagerly he pressed forward, pushing the mare along. Yes—there was another mark farther on. Wagon tracks—no doubt about it—wagon tracks! He jerked the mare to a halt and slid off to peer closely at the crushed grass.

"It's their tracks!" he called excitedly over his shoulder to Queen of Sheba. "We done it! Now all we got to do is follow their tracks!"

Filled once more with hope and energy, he climbed back onto the mare and kicked her sides to get her moving as fast as possible. "Come on—walk as fast as you can. Let's see how far we can go before dark—"

His head was pounding again, but King David pushed forward. Sighting the wagon tracks had flooded him with optimism. He could believe once more that they would make it now—yes, they would make it now.

He did not know how much time had gone by since they struck the trail of the wagons, but suddenly the leveling rays of the sun made King David look up from the wagon tracks. The tired mare thudded to a stop, lowered her head, snorted up a puff of dust from the ground, and grabbed a mouthful of the scanty grass that grew among the red and yellow flowering prickly pears. They had just crossed a low rise and were dropping down into a swale where clumps of tall sage were clustered.

"Guess we'll take cover in that high brush over there," said King David as he slid off the mare. "Be dark soon. Got to eat a little, get some sleep. You tired, Queen of Sheba?"

He looked around, expecting a peevish reply from the child. But behind the horse lay only an empty reach of grass and stunted sage, spotted here and there with buffalo wallows. All he could see were the horse's tracks. Nothing more.

Queen of Sheba was gone.

from The Winter When Time Was Frozen
Els Pelgrom

In Holland, during the last months of World War II, a girl of twelve and her father find sanctuary with a farm family.

Klaphek Farm

Klaphek Farm lay hidden by woods, not far from Heuven Hill. When you walked down to the end of First Beech Lane, you could take a narrow winding path to the right across the heath to Klinger Wood, and then you were in Zemst. But when you stood there at the end of Beech Lane and took the path that led straight ahead through the heath, you came to the village of Ulsten. But, if you walked all the way down Second Beech Lane, the heath lay big and wide all the way to the hills in the north, as far as one could see.

Till September, 1944, Noortje and her father had been living in the center of Arnhem, just the two of them in an apartment. Noortje's mother had died several years before the war broke out. Noortje was still very small then.

She had always liked living with her father in the city. True, she'd been alone a lot, and it also became more and more difficult to find enough food because of the war.

When the British lost the battle of Arnhem, all the Arnhemers had to leave the city. Noortje and her father threw some clothes, a few blankets and some books into bags and suitcases, tied them onto their bicycles, and pedaled out into the big moving stream of refugees.

All those people who were forced to leave their houses were not a very pretty sight. They saw a man and woman pushing a hand-cart on which someone sick lay. And old people, gray with fatigue, shuffling along, only a small bundle of clothes in their hands, because they weren't strong enough to carry heavy suitcases. One mother pushed a carriage with three small children in it. The people walked with set faces, staring straight

ahead. They each had enough trouble of their own and didn't pay much attention to the others. There had also been many Germans on the road, trucks going up and down and troops of singing soldiers marching in the direction of the city.

Soon the farms situated on the sides of the roads, and also the barns belonging to them, were filled up with evacuees. That's what the people who were chased out of their city were called. Noortje bicycled north with her father; they were looking for a good spot to stay for a few days. But there were lots of people all over already, and together with twenty others they'd slept in an empty schoolroom.

There were refugees not only in the farms they passed, but also in the houses of the towns and villages they came through. They couldn't stop anywhere longer than a few days. And food got scarcer and scarcer. There was very little to be gotten with their rationing cards, and the Germans confiscated the farmers' supplies. Noortje and her father both got even thinner than they already were; there wasn't a single day when they really had enough to eat.

"We're straying much too far away from home," Father said one day in November. "We should be turning back. And if they still don't allow us to enter the city, we'll stay near it. The war can't last much longer!"

They rode back and a few days later arrived at the first houses of the city. There they ran into a guard station and had to get off their bikes. The Germans searched their bags and suitcases and found the half roll, all the food they had. They took it. Then they were told to turn around and get out of there fast. No one was allowed in the city.

"We should be glad they didn't grab our bikes," Father said, after they rode side by side in silence for a while. They both were tired, from the long journey, from hunger, and especially from the disappointment.

There were lots of soldiers on the road, but no civilians to be seen anywhere. They hadn't gone far when Father said, "I've had enough cobblestones and singing Germans for today. Come on, Noortje, let's go left here, into these beautiful woods. Then we'll forget all this misery and just pretend we're on a vacation."

Noortje was so tired she couldn't even laugh. They took a sandy path and came through a beautiful wood and then to the heath. It was wonderfully quiet there, not a single human being. You could see that autumn was already far along, and it was getting dark early. The sun set behind the hills, and the small, naked birch trees caught its last rays. They looked as if there were no such thing as a war going on, and as if all the terrible things of the last years hadn't really happened.

And so Noortje and her father first came to Beech Lane with its wagon ruts running between the thick, smooth tree trunks. A layer of gleaming wet leaves lay on the moss that grew on the ground.

"Let's go in here," Noortje called out. "It's lovely here, and who knows where it will lead to!" And so they found Klaphek.

Past the bend in Beech Lane, they suddenly saw the farm lying there. They hadn't expected to find a house so far away from the world of people, and Father said, "Maybe they'll let us sleep in the hay there for a night. And then we'll see what's next in the morning."

They ended up in the small kitchen, eating bread and bacon, as much of it as they wanted. That same evening Farmer Everingen said to Mr. Vanderhook, "The wife and I have been thinking. If you would like, the two of you can stay here. It cannot last very much longer now, and if we all move ourselves a little closer together, there'll be space enough."

Everingen and his wife went to sleep with their children in the small sleeping alcove, so that Mr. Vanderhook and Noortje could have their own bedroom.

There was already one other guest at the farm when they came there—Theo. They didn't see him till the next morning. Sometimes, when the sun shone, he walked outside for a while, but he never came into the kitchen. He slept in the maid's room, which was called that because the maid used to live there. For the last few years now, there hadn't been a maid at Klaphek and all the work was done by Everingen, Aunt Janna, and Henk, the farmhand. When Noortje was awake during the night, she could hear Theo coughing in the room above. Theo was sick.

The first days at Klaphek, Noortje had the feeling she was in a dream. And when she woke up she would be back on her bike trekking from one village to the next. Or she would be in their apartment in the city, where she'd been alone so often. There was nobody to talk with there when she got home from school. She had to remember the events of the whole day, so she could tell them to her father when he came home from work.

Here at Klaphek she didn't have to go up a long staircase first to be at home. And aside from having her own father, there was another father, and a mother, and two brothers, and a sister. And then there were horses and cows, chickens and geese, pigs, and a nanny goat and a billy goat, a dog, and a whole bunch of cats.

The feeling that she was dreaming hadn't lasted very long. No, now it was just the other way around; her former life seemed very long ago, as if it hadn't really been hers, but the life of a different girl she'd once been told about.

The autumn went by and winter had begun, and they still couldn't go back home. Arnhem was an empty city, and they didn't know what it looked like there.

The Germans still occupied the greater part of the Netherlands. Life became very difficult for the Dutch people; the German armies had to eat too, and they took whatever they could use. There was hardly anything left for the Dutch.

Not a day passed without someone knocking at the door asking for something to eat. At each midday meal there were always strangers at the table sharing the food. These were people on a food-foraging trip who were lucky enough to arrive at Klaphek just at dinnertime. For Aunt Janna cooked at least twice as much as they needed for themselves, because she didn't want to send anyone away with an empty stomach.

On New Year's Day it started snowing. It snowed and froze almost every day. A thick layer of frozen snow covered the world, making everything around them beautiful and mysterious, as in an old tale.

The evening they'd been outside so late with the sled, Noortje and Evert, sleepy from the warmth of the kitchen, were sitting with the others around the table. There wasn't much talk. Aunt Janna was mending a sock.

"I wonder how Henk is doing," said Mr. Vanderhook. "What time will he be back?"

"Yes, who knows. . . . I would have gone myself, but he felt he had to do it. They just order you around, the Germans. Bring this here, take that there!" Farmer Everingen said.

"Yes, Chris, but if one doesn't do it, they would make it even worse," Aunt Janna put in.

And Everingen said, "If I say 'no' I'll be taken away. And then who would see to the work here and look after the cattle? And quite a few people wouldn't be eating then."

"Still, it's very risky for Henk," Mr. Vanderhook said. "He's a healthy young fellow. They may very well send him off to Germany."

"That's exactly the point. They already know he's here. And now they use him in this way."

"Well, I won't get a wink of sleep till I hear him coming in," Aunt Janna said. "He's a good boy. You don't get many like him anymore these days."

"Yeah, he's strong as a horse. Come, we might as well get ready for bed." Everingen rose from his creaking wicker chair.

They said good night to each other. In the shed, it was ever so dark now. Noortje and her father had to grope their way past the wooden partition to the toilet. There they waited for each other.

Noortje could hear the cows chewing. Something rustled above her head in the hay. Now it was her turn to go to the toilet. "You'll wait for me, won't you?" she said to her father.

The toilet plank was cold. She finished as fast as she could. When they walked through the dark shed, they took each other's hand. Close to the pump stood a beet cutter. You had to watch out for it.

"Mind the cutting machine," Noor whispered. "Ow! I hit myself on that bar again."

The bedroom had become very cold. The stove must have been dead for hours, and the wind was rattling the shutters. She undressed quickly. The sheets in the old wooden bed were clammy and cold. Noortje crept close against her father. She fell asleep immediately.

But Mr. Vanderhook did not sleep. He lay listening to his daughter's quiet breathing, thinking that she was a real child of the war. Almost twelve years old, he thought, and what things she'd gone through already! What would she have been like if these had been normal times? Would she have been less serious and more childlike then?

He heard Theo's coughing in the room above. He sounded badly congested, and the coughing lasted a long time. And then finally, hours later, there was the sound of the big door rattling. Rachel, the old sheepdog, softly whimpered. The horse was taken to its stall where the Fox greeted him with one quiet snort. Henk kicked off his clogs at the bottom of the ladder, before climbing up to his little loft room.

In the alcove room Aunt Janna turned herself over. The farmer was snoring and the children slept quietly. Now she could close her eyes too.

No Need to Tell Sarah

That year spring didn't seem to want to arrive. It stayed cold and was often stormy. The buds on the trees and bushes were already quite swollen. They looked as if all they needed was one warm day and they would burst open. How much more friendly the earth would look if only the sun would shine a little more often.

The grassland still had its somber winter color, and there was some snow left here and there. Even the birds were later than normal that year. You couldn't hear the wood pigeon cooing in the wood yet, and the meadow birds, the lapwings and the herons, hadn't returned from the south. They knew quite well the cold hadn't been driven off and that it wasn't safe to go back to their old nests. In the woods, the woodpecker was hammering away for hours on the bark of the beech tree, looking for insects that also were later than usual. In that last winter of the war there was much suffering, much hunger and cold, both for the people and the animals.

From time to time they heard the latest war news, but they didn't know what to believe of all those stories. The people who came to the door to ask for some milk or potatoes told whatever they knew about the way the war was going. Those stories weren't very cheerful.

In the west of the country, the situation was getting worse and worse. If the war were to continue much longer, no one would survive it there. One boiled potato cost five dollars on the black market. The Allies were advancing very slowly. The south of the country had been liberated, but the area between the rivers was a kind of no-man's-land, and no one could live there anymore. All the bridges were blown up. How could the English and the Americans ever reach the Veluwe, where Klaphek was, and the northern part of the country? What if they forgot about that small piece of the Netherlands? Perhaps they would just turn their backs on it and go directly to fight in Germany.

At Klaphek, too, they were looking forward to the end of the war impatiently. The grownups especially got a bit testy sometimes because of all the tension. It wasn't easy to live for so long in a few small rooms with so many people. And yet, comparatively, they didn't have such a difficult time of it. At least they had something to eat. Because there was nothing to do in the evenings, they went to

bed earlier and earlier. Usually the Wolthuis family and Granny went first.

One evening Mr. Vanderhook and Noortje were sitting around talking with Everingen, Aunt Janna, and Evert. They were in the kitchen. Suddenly Henk stood in the doorway, eyes cast down, silent. They hadn't even heard the latch of the door when he came in. He held the sack with the panful of food, the bag with bread, and a bottle of milk in his hands. He stood there blinking, his hands trembling as he very slowly placed the bread on the table. Aunt Janna had risen from her chair and looked at him with a very tense face.

Then Henk took the bottle out of the bag and set it down next to the bread. The bottle was still full of milk. They all stared at it, no one saying anything. Henk sat down, took off his cap, and buried his face in his hands.

Noortje couldn't bear the silence any longer. "Henk," she said, "what's happened? Say something, Henk!"

Aunt Janna was the first to move again. She took the bread off the table and put it on the sink. She set the pan with food and the milk bottle next to it.

"Leave Henk alone for a moment, child," she said.

Then finally Henk began. As on any other evening, he had made the trip to the wood. With most of the snow melted, he didn't have to fear leaving prints so much anymore, but the branches were creaking more loudly under his feet. It wasn't terribly dark, not as dark as on some other evenings. How else would he have been able to notice from a distance that the entrance to the hole was open? Branches had been broken off the thick fir tree and the dark-brown piece of cloth that hung before the entrance was gone. The earth around it was all rooted up as if many people or animals had tramped the soil there.

He'd thought that strange and careless, but didn't yet understand what had happened. Stopping in front of the hole, Henk called out softly. No answer came. Then he crawled in; it was dark down there and dead quiet. He had asked whispering, "Are you there?"

And then, because he heard nothing, Henk called out in a voice much too loud, "Say something! Where are you?"

And only then did he strike a match and light the lantern with shaky hands. That lantern had the very last bit of real kerosene, which they'd kept for these trips.

The hole was empty. The people were not there. The young woman, not yet very strong after the birth of her child, gone. Mr. Meyer, too, gone. And the two little boys were not there either. The crates and the beds were kicked all over the place. In one corner there still were some clothes. The fire in the cooking pot was out.

And suddenly Henk was afraid. As fast as he could he ran home through the wood, giving no thought at all to the noise he was making. Not until he was halfway down Beech Lane did he stop to listen for someone following him. But no one was. He heard nothing but the wind in the trees high above his head, rising and falling. There was no other sound. Rachel had come to meet him and stayed right with him. And even that had been strange, for Rachel knew very well that she wasn't allowed to come on those trips through the wood in the evening. She'd never done so before.

For a long time, no one in the kitchen spoke. The farmer heaved a few sighs, and Aunt Janna wiped her eyes. Her mouth twisted very strangely as if she were going to cry, but she didn't. Noortje's father sat nervously drumming his fingers on the table, his eyebrows lifted high, and didn't look at anyone. He always did that when he felt at a loss. The silence became so oppressive that Noortje had to speak up, whether she wanted to or not.

"What could have happened?" she asked, her voice sounding strangely loud. "Shouldn't we go look for them?"

"Who would do such a crazy thing? Go look for them!" Everingen said curtly. "Come on, wife. We're going to bed."

Aunt Janna silently prepared Sarah's bottle and gave it to Noortje. "Noor, you'd better give it to her tonight," she said.

The others went to bed; Noortje and her father took the little oil light with them to the parlor. The stove was almost out there, and it was unpleasantly chilly. The flame in the glass spread a small circle of yellow light. Around its rim everything was darkness. Only the table and the chairs were visible. The room might well be quite large, with all sorts of bad things hiding in the corners. On other nights Noortje wasn't really bothered by that. She had never been afraid of the dark. But now she had the feeling that something in the room threatened her, something invisible that wanted to harm her and little Sarah.

Noortje's father had seized a chair and gone to sit in front of the stove close to Sarah's basket. He bent over the fire and threw a log on it. Soon the red and orange flames shone through the mica windows, making the big room a little cheerier. Sarah gurgled while she drank.

"Actually we ought to tell her what has happened," Noortje said. "Only she can't understand it yet. So there's no need to tell Sarah."

Her father didn't answer. He cleared his throat a few times. The room was quiet. Noortje wanted to know exactly what had happened, and there was no one she could ask but her father. She cleared her throat a few times just like him. Then she asked, "What do you think happened?"

It was a difficult moment for Mr. Vanderhook. How does one tell one's daughter about the terrible things of the world? Who wouldn't much rather wish to keep them hidden from her? "I think you already know," he said, "for you've heard it talked about so often. You know that the Meyers are Jewish, don't you?"

Noortje couldn't say anything. She could hear the silence in the whole house. Sarah had fallen asleep on her lap.

After a while her father started again, "I'm afraid the worst has happened, the worst thing that could have happened to them. The Germans found them."

"That's impossible. No one could find them there."

"Maybe someone discovered them by accident and betrayed them to the Germans. That's happened before. Not everybody is like our Farmer Everingen and Aunt Janna."

"But who could have done it? Do you know? Not a soul ever came into that part of the woods! How is it possible?"

"I don't know, Noortje. I just don't know."

"What are the Germans going to do with them?"

"What they do with all the Jews, I think. Send them away to a sort of camp."

"You mean a prison?"

"Yes, something like that. I'm afraid it will be very bad."

Sarah's bottle was empty. Noortje held the baby upright with her warm head against her cheek, because she still had to be burped. She didn't burp.

"You know, Father," she said. "I wish I had a rifle. Oh, how I wish I had a rifle! And if one German soldier had the guts to come in here, you know what I'd do? I'd shoot him right in the head."

"Ah, my child," her father said, "you'd better give Sarah a clean diaper. There's nothing else we can do now."

from **Calico Bush**
Rachel Field

Set at the time of the French and Indian War, this story of a French girl who is the servant of a pioneer family in Maine reflects, in Marguerite's loneliness at Christmas, the isolation of the setting.

Winter

It was a fairly warm day for December and she went out with Debby to watch him split the wood. It was pleasant to see his ax come down so swift and sure each time, and sometimes when he paused to rest he would talk to her for a minute or two. The baby was so well wrapped in a woolen shawl that she

looked like a brownish caterpillar with a pink nose and tufts of light hair showing at one end.

"What time of year is it now?" Marguerite asked as Ira stopped to draw his sleeve across his streaming forehead.

"Let's see," he answered going over to the post where he still made his daily notches, dividing the months by means of long horizontal strokes. "Well, I declare, if it ain't got to be the middle o' December! Yes, tomorrow's the seventeenth, time I finished that beaver cap I promised Abby."

"Is it for Christmas?" asked Marguerite.

But he shook his head. "No," he said. "Our folks don't hold with such foolishness. We went to meetin' back in Marblehead on Christmas, I recollect, but there was a Dutch boy I knew told me how they had all kinds o' doin's where he come from."

"You mean, it will be no different from other days?" Marguerite's eyes grew wide with disappointment. "No carols, and no cakes, and no gifts from one to another?"

"I guess that's about right," he told her and went on with the chopping.

If Ira gave her no encouragement in Christmas festivities she knew it would be useless to expect more of Dolly and Joel Sargent. She tried to put the thought from her mind, but as each day came bringing it nearer she found herself remembering more and more the happy preparations for it she had helped to make at home. She dreamed of the Christmas cakes Grand'mère had always baked with such pride, of the seeded raisins and the picked nut-meats stirred ceremoniously in the rich batter. And then there were the carols, with the Sisters in the convent beating time and making sure that not a single "Noël" was left out when all their pupils' voices were lifted together. She tried to tell the children of the tiny carved statues of the Virgin and Joseph and the little Christ Child in the manger, with cattle and sheep and shepherds all painted as perfectly as life, that were brought out on Christmas Eve in the candle-lit chapel. Unfortunately Dolly had overheard part of this recital and had chided her roundly.

"I'll thank you to keep your Popishness to yourself," she had told her. "We may be in too God-forsaken a spot for a meetin' house, but that's no reason to put ideas in the children's heads."

And so it came to be Christmas Eve in the log cabin on Sargents' point with no smell of spice cakes, or incense, or candles, and none to feel the lack of them but Marguerite Ledoux.

She had been out to the post herself that noon, counting the month's notchings to be sure. There could be no doubt—tomorrow would make twenty-five. She would not have missed the holiday preparations so much, she thought, if she might have gone over to see Aunt Hepsa; but she knew there was no chance of this with such a high sea running and snow left in patches from last week's fall. It was rare, Joel had said, to have much fall near the sea. A bad winter ahead, Seth Jordan had predicted, and it looked as if he were right. Frost had covered the little square panes of glass with such feathery patternings, it required much breathing and scratching to make even a little hole to see out. Marguerite was tired of doing this. The room was almost dark, but she knew that outside there was still half an hour or so left of twilight. She went over to the pegs behind the door and took down the brown cloak and hood.

"What are you doin'?" Dolly asked her as she had her hand on the door.

"I'm—I want to bring more cones," she hazarded, grasping at the first idea that came into her head. "There are not so many left in the basket."

"Well, all right, then," Dolly told her, "only don't fetch in the wet ones that make the fire smoke. Pick 'em from underneath. No, Jacob," she added at a question from the child, "you can't go along—it's too cold."

Marguerite buckled on the shoes Aunt Hepsa had given her, tied on her cloak, and went out basket in hand. Once she shut the door behind her some of the depression which had weighed upon her spirit all day left her. It was impossible to feel so sad out in the snow with the pointed trees and all their shiny dark-green needles. They

smelled of Christmas to her. There had been branches of evergreen in the chapel sometimes. Perhaps if she hunted at the edge of the tall woods behind the spring she might find some red partridge berries to bring back to the children. It was bad luck if you gave nothing on Christmas, and they need not know the reason for such a gift.

As she turned into the wood path behind the house she looked across the water to Sunday Island. White places showed on the cleared field round the Jordan house where the snow remained, and the trees above it on the upper pasture where she and Aunt Hepsa had gathered bayberry looked more dark and bristling than ever in the winter twilight. She was glad that a curl of smoke rose from the chimney. Aunt Hepsa must be cooking supper, she told herself, and she paused to send her a Christmas wish across the water.

"I wonder if she's begun her new quilt yet?" she thought as she struck into the wood path. "She had the indigo dye Ethan brought her all ready to make a blue pot."

There were no red berries under the snow in the clearing by the spring where she had hoped to find them, so she went on farther along the blazed trail. It was very still there, with only a light wind stirring the spruce and fir boughs overhead. The light stayed longer there than she had expected, for the snow helped prolong the winter afternoon. Sometimes she stooped to gather cones, taking care to shake off the snow as Dolly Sargent had bidden her. The cold was intense, but her blood was quick and the old homespun cloak and hood enveloped her warmly. There was no sound except her footfalls in the snow. A sudden impulse came upon her to sing one of the carols which she knew the Sisters in the convent must even then be teaching other voices to raise.

She set down the half-filled basket of cones, folded her hands piously under the cloak, and began the first simple little chant that she had ever learned.

"Noël—Noël—Noël!"

Her own voice startled her in the stillness. Then at the sound of the familiar words she

grew confident and began the one that had
been Grand'mère's favorite because she also
had sung it when she was a girl in the little
village where she had lived.

> "J'entends le ciel retentir
> Des cantiques des Saints Anges,
> Et la terre tressaillir
> Des transports de lours louanges.
> C'est l'Oinct qui devoit venir,
> Il est déjà dans ses langes.
> Miracle! prodige nouveau,
> Le fils de Dieu dans le berceau!
> Mais plus grand prodige encore,
> Ce grand Roi, que le ciel adore,
> Doit expirer sur un poteau.
> Noël! Noël! Noël!"*

As she sang there in the deepening twilight, she felt strangely comforted. The
French words that had lain so long forgotten
welled up out of her mind as easily as if she
had been with the Sisters in the candle-lit
chapel and not alone these thousands of
miles away in a snowy wood.

"Noël! Noël!" she cried once more to the
ranks of spruces, and then as she turned to
retrace her steps something dark and swift
moved towards her from behind a tree
trunk.

There was not time enough to run away.
The words were hardly cool on her lips before he stood beside her—a tall Indian in
skins, with a musket that went oddly with his
fringes and bright feathers. So silently did he
come that not a twig snapped under his foot.
He seemed not to dent the snow as he moved
over it. His eyes showed bright in the copper
of his skin, and a deep scar ran crookedly
across one cheek. He came so close that she
saw it plainly, and yet she could not move so
much as an inch. Her feet seemed rooted in
the snow, and if her heart continued to beat,

*This old carol may be freely rendered as follows:

> I hear the heavens resound
> To such angelic song
> That trembling stirs the ground,
> While rolls the news along—
> The Heavenly Child is found,
> To Whom all praise belong.
> Oh! wondrous miracle,
> A God in his cradle!
> Yet must we wonder more,
> This King the heavens adore
> Must die upon a cross.

she could not feel it. For what seemed like
ages he continued to regard her fixedly with
his black, unblinking eyes, while she waited
for him to seize the tomahawk from his belt
and make an end of her. But he did not move
to do so. Instead, his lips parted in a queer
smile.

"Noël!" he said, pronouncing the word
carefully in a deep, guttural voice. "Noël!"

Marguerite felt her heart begin to beat
again, though her knees were still numb and
she continued to stare at him incredulously.
Surely this must be a miracle, more extraordinary than any bestowed on Saint Catherine
or Saint Elizabeth! A savage had come out of
the woods to greet her in her own tongue on
Christmas Eve! She forced herself to smile
back and answer him.

His words were meager and hard to catch,
but she made out from them and his signs
that he had lived with the French in Quebec.
He was bound there now, or so she guessed
from his pointing finger. She could not tell
how many of her words he understood, but
whenever she said "Noël" his eyes would
brighten with recognition and he would repeat it after her. "Les Pères Gris," he told
her, had cured him. He touched the scar as
he spoke and crossed his two lean forefingers
to make a cross.

It was almost dark now; only a faint light
lingered between the spruces. Pumpkin
barked in the distance and Marguerite knew
she must hurry back lest they grow alarmed.
What would they think, Joel and Dolly Sargent and the rest, if they should come upon
her there in the woods holding converse with
an Indian? Prompted by an impulse she
pulled the cord out from under her dress and
jerked off Oncle Pierre's gilt button. It glittered in her hand as she held it out to the tall
figure before her.

"Pour un souvenir de Noël," she said as she
laid it in his hand before she turned and sped
off towards the clearing.

Her heart was still pounding as she came
out of the woods and in sight of the log house.
Pumpkin bounded to meet her as she paused
to put back the cord and its only remaining
treasure. She had not thought to make such

a Christmas gift, but surely she could not have done less. She could not but feel that somehow it was a fortunate sign, this strange meeting. Perhaps Le Bon Dieu had Himself arranged it that she might be less lonely on Christmas Eve. But she knew there must not be a word of it to the rest. She would never be able to make them understand what she scarcely understood herself. As for Caleb, she could well guess what he would say and that he would think ill of her ever after.

Dolly Sargent scolded her roundly for staying away so long.

"I declare you deserve a beatin'," she told her hotly, "strayin' so far at this time o' night. I vow Debby's got more sense 'n you show sometimes."

There was no mention made of Christmas next day save that Joel asked a lengthier blessing over their breakfast cornmeal than was usual with him. But Marguerite no longer minded. Had she not had her miracle the night before?

from **Master Rosalind**
John and Patricia Beatty

In a tale of the Elizabethan period, Rosalind, kidnapped and taken to London while dressed as a boy, is known as Robin by the theatrical people with whom she has found work.

Copyist

The famous bells of Saint Saviour's Church greeted Rosalind as she and Thomas Pope rode westward along the south bank of the Thames past the brick palace of the Bishop of Winchester and down several of Southwark's meandering streets. She judged from the many red lattices she saw that they traveled streets of taverns. "Do men drink much wine and ale here, Master Pope?"

"Oh, lad, they do. Southwark is not a place of good reputation according to the sour folk who preach in London, but Dame Willingson and I like it well enough, for all that there are five prisons here. May you never see one of

them from the wrong side of their gates, Robin. They are very terrible."

The actor's horse chose its wary way across a plank set over a ditch. Southwark, Rosalind noticed, was a place of swamps, criss-crossed with ditches and small bridges. She looked westward across the marshes to where she saw some tall wooden buildings much like the Curtain and the Theater. "Master Pope, is one of those the Bear Garden?" She'd heard of it from Dickon.

"Aye, lad, the other is a playhouse belonging to the Lord Admiral's Men, our rivals. We are the Lord Chamberlain's Men, you know. As for the Bear Garden, you would scent the stink of the bears and bulls if this were a warm day. Be glad that it is not."

They came to the end of a street and stopped before a house finer by far than Moll's in Whitefriars. Thomas Pope, for all of his talk about being a "poor player," was no poor man. His three-storied house even boasted a carved front. On each side of the house were gardens with tall limes rearing their green limbs above neat brick walls. Pope dismounted and handed his reins to a little lad who seemingly materialized out of the earth. Rosalind, too, slid down.

"Come," ordered the player, as the boy took the horse behind the house through a gate. "I will take you to Mistress Willingson. She will not find a pastor's grandson unseemly. You will know your catechism, and that will please her."

Like all London houses, Pope's was narrow with a pantry, buttery, and kitchen on the ground floor. Unlike Moll's, the air was fragrant here. Rosalind scented sweet herbs as the player shouted, "Dame Gillet! Dame!"

A woman came slowly down the dark hallway with a pan of burning herbs in her hands. She curtseyed to Pope, the pan held out before her, smoking, and gazed at Rosalind. Mistress Willingson was a handsome woman with dark hair, pulled back under a caul of gold and black wires. Her eyes were large and dark and her face white, but not painted as Rosalind had noticed those of so many London ladies were. Her clothing was good, a kirtle of milk-and-water blue, a black lawn apron, and a bodice of the same pale blue as her skirt. She said, "I try to ward off the plague with sweet herbs, Master Pope." She gestured with the herb pan. Then she asked him, "Who, pray, is this? Another player lad?" It seemed to Rosalind that she spoke as if Pope fetched home strange lads every day of the week. The woman went on, "This one does not have the look of a rogue about him, but I would say he has the evil smell of Whitefriars. He will be bathed first. Then he will be fed."

Suddenly frightened of the prospect of a bath, Rosalind blurted, "I do not need to be bathed."

"You do, indeed," said Mistress Willingson.

"No!" Rosalind felt the blood rising to her face. What if Master Pope or Dame Gillet were with her while she bathed? She started for the open door, but Pope caught her by the arm.

She heard his roar of laughter. "Dame, see how he can blush. He will have no need for paint if he ever plays a shy maiden's part. See to it that he bathes in private. He is of gentle birth, reads Latin and Greek, and is the grandson of a pastor."

"All the same a ball of sweet soap would not be amiss for him." The woman smiled and motioned for Rosalind to follow her. Clearly Mistress Willingson's approval was important to Pope. Rosalind wondered as she followed behind the thin, perfumed trail of herb and smoke, embarrassed by her "evil smell," how many lads the old actor had brought home to be bathed. How many had stayed servants to him? How many had become players?

Rosalind splashed in the dim kitchen before the warmth of the large brick oven in a deep wooden tub with a ball of scented soap. While she spluttered, washing her head, Dame Gillet came in, threw a large towel at her, and left, saying, "Put this about you and call me, shy Robin, when you are clean. Do not forget to wash your ears and neck."

When she was wrapped in the towel, Rosalind cried out "Dame" and Mistress Willingson came in with clothing for her. There was a blue doublet, blue breeches and hose, and a small ruff, all somewhat worn, Rosalind noted, as she donned them after the woman had gone out again. But they were clean and they fit her well enough. The sight of them pleased her. They were a good omen. If she was to be a servant, she was not to be a common one. Common servants wore canvas doublets, not good woolen ones, and certainly not fashionably padded doublets like this one.

As Dame Gillet later yanked a comb through her wet hair, she said, "You will sup with the stable lad, the servingman, and the maids in the kitchen. You will sleep in the attic. I have chars for you to do for me in the morning. You will go shopping with me and carry my basket."

Pope came into the kitchen at that moment, puffing on his pipe. "No, dame, Robin will have the chamber the last lad slept in. Robin goes back to the Curtain with me tonight."

"Hah! Little use I shall have of him then. I mark your game. Another son, Master Pope? Yet *another*?" Dame Gillet sighed.

Rosalind supped that evening far more grandly than ever before. The food was marvelous and came not from wooden trenchers but from heavy pewter dishes. The two young maids piled her plate high and vowed she ate as heartily as the brawny young servingman. Then they sent her climbing through the well-furnished house to inspect the bedchamber on the third floor. To her way of thinking, the "last lad" in this house had been no servant. Had he been a player? This chamber was better than hers in Cowley. It had a featherbed and a walnut bedstead with blue canopy and hangings, a table and brass ewer, and, to her utter astonishment, a looking glass. She had never seen such a wondrous thing before. She spent long moments gazing by candlelight at her clean face. Yes, she made a passing fair boy, slim, with the square jaw of the Broomes, as her grandfather had told her, and the same dark brows. And Moll had cut her hair well. She had misled people in Oxfordshire and the rogues, too. But now she had gulled the practiced eyes of players into thinking she was Robin, not Rosalind. She laughed for an instant, then thought of Helen and Ned, caught that morning in the goldsmith's house. She thought of her flight through Blackfriars, of the forger, of Moll's friendship and Tom o' Bedlam's wrath, of the Earl of Essex, the play, Master Gulliford, and now Thomas Pope. What a day it had been! Yet she was not tired. She had never felt so alive in all her days.

Suddenly her mirror gazing was interrupted by Pope's shouting from below. "Robin, 'tis time to ride back to the playhouse."

Rosalind found the stage of the Curtain lit by candles set on the floor outlining its rim and by many torches in sconces at its rear. It was chill inside for all that it was late summer. Ice-white stars glittered through the opening at the Curtain's top. She was grateful for the warmth of the cloak Dame Gillet had given her, as she went about the chars Pope set her. In the tiring room she learned that an efficient company of players readied properties and costumes long before a play was performed. Tonight while the tiring men ironed and mended garments, Rosalind dusted off and repainted the face of the severed head she'd seen earlier that day. As she daubed paint on it, she watched Master Burbage striding about rehearsing gestures. He was crowned with a gilt circle, adorned with a false gray beard, and clad in the long scarlet gown of a king. What king, Rosalind had no idea. Then as she finished the head, she was called by Pope to attend Master Gulliford, who required his face to be painted again for another lady's part.

"What do I use?" she asked Gulliford as she looked bewildered at the many ointment pots on the table before him.

Seated on a high stool, he giggled. "The white paint. The white is the jawbones of a sow, burned, then mixed with oil of white poppy. Paint me first with the white. I shall darken my eyes with kohl and drop bel-

ladonna into them with this feather." He held up a white pigeon's feather, then glared across the tiring room at his uncle, who spoke with Master Will. Gulliford went on, "When I have donned my wig, I trust these players will think me a great lady enough for this old play. We only rehearse tonight. Master Burbage says he wishes to see how I will suit the lady's part. It is a new part for me."

As Rosalind began to stroke white onto the boy's face, she said, "I have met Dame Gillet. She is all that you say she is."

The boy player nodded sagely. "Do as I told you, Robin. Carry yourself cleverly. Master Pope may make a player of you yet. We have some need of boy players now. There are often too few of us. We come here as small lads and play women's roles until we are twenty years, if we can manage our voices that long. Some of us grow too tall much too quickly and grow beards." He smiled into the looking glass at his reflection. "Other boy players depart the company."

"Do all boys live with older players?"

"Aye, all do. I am older than you, Robin, near to sixteen. I shall not play court ladies much longer. I grow too old. I must have an eye to my future."

Rosalind had not guessed him to be so old. He was not tall. She went on smoothing the white stuff over his face, then asked, "Why do boys play women's parts?"

Gulliford did a strange thing. He pinched his stark white nose with his fingers and said, whining through it, "'Boys must play women's parts. 'Tis a more scandalous thing for a woman to play a woman's part.' This is how many churchmen of London preach against us from their churches. They hate plays and players, but still we play. Someone must play women's parts. Authors keep writing parts into plays for women and girls. So boys and men must play them. Lads play pretty maidens and queens. Men play old women." He laughed. "You should see your good Master Pope play a fat old hag. You would not know him to be Master Pope at all."

Rosalind's work done with the white paint, the boy player waved her aside, motioned

toward a scroll of paper, and then pulled a small pot of vermilion to him and began to paint his cheeks and lips with a brush. "Master Pope tells me you can read. I want to practice my lines for this play. Hear me recite them to you, Robin."

Rosalind unrolled the scroll. It was made up of sheets of paper pasted together. She saw lines of writing on it and in the left-hand margin instructions, "Enter," "Exit."

"Give me my cues," Gulliford commanded.

She felt helpless. "I do not know what cues are."

"They are the other player's closing lines to their speeches. Commence with the fourth line from the top. It should say, 'I'll win this Lady Margaret. For whom? Why, for my king. Tush! That's a wooden thing!'"

After Rosalind recited, Gulliford spoke his lines in an ice-sweet girlish treble. "'He talks of wood; it is some carpenter!' Now, Robin, you read the next line you see to me. After you have read it, I speak again."

For a half hour Rosalind coached Master Gulliford, who complained more than once that he was "slow of study." Then, snatching up a fan, the player, garbed as a dazzling, bewigged lady in a violet gown, swept out of the tiring room onto the stage.

All had gone out there now except for the tiring men, who folded costumes into chests. They paid no heed to Rosalind as she took up a candle and began to wander around the playhouse. First she read the pasteboard plot of *The Taming of the Shrew* hanging from a peg, listing the players' names. Then she found stairs leading down below the stage. There, as she listened to Burbage's resonant voice from above, she saw more steps. These steps led up to a trapdoor cut into the stage floor. Rosalind yearned to open it and poke her head through it to surprise the players but discarded the idea. She suspected Burbage would not approve if she interrupted his rehearsal. Because it was dark and gloomy under the stage, she soon left. She went back to the tiring room and began to climb another set of stairs she'd also spied out. They led above the stage to the hut. In it over the stage's ceiling, which was painted to represent a blue but clouded sky, she found a remarkable variety of things—a winch and a chairlike throne on ropes, a gray rain cloud of painted canvas, gunpowder in small casks, cannonballs, and a small cannon.

Also to her surprise she found Master Will seated at a small table, writing, flanked by two candles blowing slant-wise in the August breeze.

Rosalind apologized, backing toward the steep flight of steps. "I did not mean to disturb you, sir."

He put his finger to his lips. "Do not tell anyone that I am here. I came up without their knowing it. They think I have gone home. Here I have some peace. In the tiring room I am besieged by players who say to me 'Alter this line for me' or 'Why have you given me but one song to sing in your new play?'" He laughed, then asked, "How do you fare with Master Pope?"

"I like him very well. I hope he may make a player of me. I would rather be a player than a servant."

The playwright nodded. "He has made players of other boys before. I am told you are a pastor's grandson, of good birth, read and write, and know Latin and Greek."

Rosalind felt her face grow hot. She could only nod. Master Pope had said much of her to the company in a very short time, it seemed, while she had repainted the earl's cut-off head.

He pushed a piece of blank paper over to her, then offered her his quill and ink. "Write these words for me as I speak them, Robin. Write in your very fairest hand."

Leaning over his table, Rosalind wrote as fast as she could in the hand her grandfather had taught her.

> But when the blast of war blows in our ears,
> Then imitate the action of the tiger;
> Stiffen the sinews, summon up the blood.

Master Will took the paper, looked at it, then nodded. "It is a fair secretary hand, the Italian hand. I write but the common English hand. Yours is by far the clearest I have seen of this company, and it is well spelled, too. Tell Master Pope for me that I shall require you to copy out the players' parts for the cue sheets for the play I now write."

Rosalind felt a pang of disappointment. First servant's work, now a clerk's.

"You do not wish to be a copyist for me?" Master Will seemed to have read her mind.

"If I am to be a servant to one player and a copyist to another, when am I to be a player?"

The playwright laughed. "Before you are a player, you will do many, many things. You will learn to starch ruffs, take playbills to the printer, nail them up on London Bridge, send this throne of the gods down out of our painted heavens by means of the winch, and push ghosts up through the trapdoor so their draperies will not get caught on the steps. Perhaps you will even set flame to the touch-hole of our cannon when the play calls for cannon fire, though I trust you will not send a ball through the roof or set the playhouse afire. Players must know all about the theater." The dark-eyed man rose, went to one end of the hut, and with his foot sent the cannonball rolling noisily across the floor. He put his finger to his lips again for silence.

"You up there in the hut! Cease that. We require no thunder in this play!" came Richard Burbage's angry roaring from the stage below.

Master Will waited until Rosalind had stopped laughing, then said, "Tell Dame Gillet to have your face washed well at the moon's wane with elder leaves distilled in May. You have country freckles, Robin."

Rosalind grinned; he but teased her. "'Tis near September now, and I'm not often out-of-doors. Freckles will go away."

"Yes, it is near autumn. Soon the Queen will return to London to spend the winter. She goes from London in the summer when the plague is most fierce."

"Do common folk ever see her, Master Will?"

"All London may see her if they choose to when she returns. She comes riding into the city with her court about her."

"Lord Essex, too? I saw him today."

The man's wise eyes were fixed on her face. "Aye, Essex, too. I do not know what business brought him here today. He is mostly with the Queen. You love him then?"

"Yes, he is the greatest man in England. My father was in Spain with him."

"Aye, the greatest man in England." His face grave, Master Will looked down at the papers of his unfinished play. "Many young men and all London lads love Essex well today. Tomorrow he may not fare so well."

from Johnny Tremain
Esther Forbes

In this excerpt from a Newbery Medal book, Forbes draws a convincing and stirring picture of the motivation and the patriotism of the Boston leaders of the American Revolution, and of the way in which their discussion stirs young Johnny Tremain.

[That a Man Can Stand Up]

It was fall, and for the last time Sam Adams bade Johnny summon the Observers for eight o'clock that night.

"After this we will not meet again, for I believe Gage knows all about us. He might be moved to arrest Mr. Lorne. He might send soldiers to arrest us all."

"I hardly think they would hang the whole club, sir. Only you and Mr. Hancock."

Johnny had meant this for a compliment, but Sam Adams looked more startled than pleased.

"It has been noticed that every so often many of us are seen going up and down Salt Lane, entering the printing shop. We must, in the future, meet in small groups. But once more, and for the last time . . . And make as good a punch for us as you can."

As Johnny went from house to house talking about unpaid bills of eight shillings, he was thinking of the punch. Not one ship had come into Boston for five months except British ships. Only the British officers had limes, lemons, and oranges these days—they and their friends among the Boston Tories. Miss Lyte had God's plenty of friends among the British officers. He'd get his tropical fruit there.

Mrs. Bessie listened to him.

"And who's going to eat these fruits or drink them, if I do give you some?"

"Well . . . Sam Adams for one."

"Don't say any more. Give me your dispatch bag, Johnny." She returned with it bulging.

"No limes, though. Izzy eats them all."

"Does she do tricks for them? Like she used to for the sailors along Hancock's Wharf?"

"*Tricks?* Does she do tricks? Lieutenant Stranger has taught her a rigmarole about poor Nell Gwyn selling fruit at a theater. I don't need to tell you how she carries on."

"What happened to that Cousin Sewall?"

"Gone to Worcester. Joined up with the Minute Men."

"But he's too fat and . . ."

"Soft? No. From now on nobody's too fat nor soft nor old nor young. The time's coming."

It would be a small meeting, for of the twenty-two original members many had already left town to get away from the threat of arrest by the British. Josiah Quincy was in England. Of the three revolutionary doctors, only Church and Warren remained. Doctor Young had gone to a safer spot. James Otis was at the moment in Boston. Johnny had not notified him, although he had founded this club in the first place. Ever since he had grown so queer, the other members did not wish him about, even in his lucid periods. He talked and talked. Nobody could get a word in edgewise when James Otis talked.

This, the last meeting, started with the punch bowl on the table instead of ending with it. There was no chairman nor was there any time when the two boys were supposed to withdraw. They were talking about how Gage had at last dared send out a sortie beyond the gate of Boston and, before the Minute Men got word of their plans, they had seized cannon and gunpowder over in Charlestown, got into their boats and back to Boston. Not one shot had been fired and it was all too late when the alarm had been spread and thousands of armed farmers had arrived. By then the British were safe home again. Yet, Sam Adams protested, this rising up of an army of a thousand from the very soil of New England had badly frightened General Gage. Once the alarm spread that the British had left Boston, the system of calling up the Minute Men had worked well indeed. The trouble had been in Boston itself.

"In other words, gentlemen, it was our fault. If we could have known but an hour, two hours, in advance what the British were intending, our men would have been there before the British troops arrived instead of a half-hour after they left."

Johnny had been told off to carry letters for the British officers, to keep on good terms with their grooms and stable boys over at the Afric Queen. Somehow he had failed. He hadn't known. Nobody had known that two hundred and sixty redcoats were getting into boats, slipping off up the Mystic, seizing Yankee gunpowder, and rowing it back to Castle Island for themselves.

Paul Revere was saying, "We must organize a better system of watching their movements—but in such a way that they will not realize they are being watched."

Sam and John Adams were standing and the other members were crowding about them, shaking hands with them, wishing them success at the Continental Congress in Philadelphia. They were starting the next day. Everyone was ready to give them advice whom to see, what to say, or to prophesy the outcome of this Congress. Paul Revere and Joseph Warren were apart a little, making plans for that spy system which was needed badly. They called Johnny to them, but he could hear one of the men standing about the two Adamses saying, "But there must be some hope we can still patch up our differences with England. Sir, you will work for peace?"

Sam Adams said nothing for a moment. He trusted these men about him as he trusted no one else in the world.

"No. That time is past. I will work for war: the complete freedom of these colonies from any European power. We can have that freedom only by fighting for it. God grant we fight soon. For ten years we've tried this and we've tried that. We've tried to placate them and they to placate us. Gentlemen, you know it has not worked. I will not work for peace. 'Peace, peace—and there is no peace.' But I will, in Philadelphia, play a cautious part—not throw all my cards on the table—oh, no. But nevertheless I will work for but one thing. War—bloody and terrible death and destruction. But out of it shall come such a country as was never seen on this earth before. We will fight . . ."

There was a heavy footstep across the floor of the shop below. Rab leaped to the ladder's head.

"James Otis," he reported to the men standing about Adams.

"Well," said Sam Adams, a little crossly, "no one needs stay and listen to *him*. He shot

his bolt years ago. Still talking about the natural rights of man—and the glories of the British Empire! You and I, John, had as well go home and get a good night's sleep before leaving at dawn tomorrow."

Otis pulled his bulk up the ladder. If no one was glad to see him, at least no one was so discourteous as to leave. Mr. Otis was immediately shown every honor, given a comfortable armchair and a tankard of punch. Seemingly he was not in a talkative mood tonight. The broad, ruddy, good-natured face turned left and right, nodding casually to his friends, taking it for granted that he was still a great man among them, instead of a milestone they all believed they had passed years before.

He sniffed at his punch and sipped a little.

"Sammy," he said to Sam Adams, "my coming interrupted something you were saying . . . 'We will fight,' you had got that far."

"Why, yes. That's no secret."

"For what will we fight?"

"To free Boston from those infernal redcoats and . . ."

"No," said Otis. "Boy, give me more punch. That's not enough reason for going into a war. Did any occupied city ever have better treatment than we've had from the British? Has one rebellious newspaper been stopped—one treasonable speech? Where are the firing squads, the jails jammed with political prisoners? What about the gallows for you, Sam Adams, and you, John Hancock? It has never been set up. I hate those infernal British troops spread all over my town as much as you do. Can't move these days without stepping on a soldier. But we are not going off into a civil war merely to get them out of Boston. Why are we going to fight? Why, why?"

There was an embarrassed silence. Sam Adams was the acknowledged ringleader. It was for him to speak now.

"We will fight for the rights of Americans. England cannot take our money away by taxes."

"No, no. For something more important than the pocketbooks of our American citizens."

Rab said, "For the rights of Englishmen—everywhere."

"Why stop with Englishmen?" Otis was warming up. He had a wide mouth, crooked and generous. He settled back in his chair and then he began to talk. It was such talk as Johnny had never heard before. The words surged up through the big body, flowed out of the broad mouth. He never raised his voice, and he went on and on. Sometimes Johnny felt so intoxicated by the mere sound of the words that he hardly followed the sense. That soft, low voice flowed over him: submerged him.

". . . For men and women and children all over the world," he said. "You were right, you tall, dark boy, for even as we shoot down the British soldiers we are fighting for rights such as they will be enjoying a hundred years from now.

". . . There shall be no more tyranny. A handful of men cannot seize power over thousands. A man shall choose who it is shall rule over him.

". . . The peasants of France, the serfs of Russia. Hardly more than animals now. But because we fight, they shall see freedom like a new sun rising in the west. Those natural rights God has given to every man, no matter how humble . . ." He smiled suddenly and said . . . "or crazy," and took a good pull at his tankard.

". . . The battle we win over the worst in England shall benefit the best in England. How well are they over there represented when it comes to taxes? Not very well. It will be better for them when we have won this war.

"Will French peasants go on forever pulling off their caps and saying 'Oui, Monsieur,' when the gold coaches run down their children? They will not. Italy. And all those German states. Are they nothing but soldiers? Will no one show them the rights of good citizens? So we hold up our torch—and do not forget it was lighted upon the fires of England—and we will set it as a new sun to lighten a world . . ."

Sam Adams, anxious to get that good night's sleep before starting next day for Philadelphia, was smiling slightly, nodding his gray head, seeming to agree. He was bored. It does not matter, he was thinking, what James Otis says these days—sane or crazy.

Joseph Warren's fair, responsive face was aflame. The torch Otis had been talking about seemed reflected in his eyes.

"We are lucky men," he murmured, "for we have a cause worth dying for. This honor is not given to every generation."

"Boy," said Otis to Johnny, "fill my tankard."

It was not until he had drained it and wiped his mouth on the back of his hand that he spoke again. All sat silently waiting for him. He had, and not for the first time, cast a spell upon them.

"They say," he began again, "my wits left me after I got hit on the head by that customs official. That's what you think, eh, Mr. Adams?"

"Oh, no, no, indeed, Mr. Otis."

"Some of us will give our wits," he said, "some of us all our property. Heh, John Hancock, did you hear that? *Property*—that hurts, eh? To give one's silver wine-coolers, one's coach and four, and the gold buttons off one's sprigged satin waistcoats?"

Hancock looked him straight in the face and Johnny had never before liked him so well.

"I am ready," he said. "I can get along without all that."

"You, Paul Revere, you'll give up that silvercraft you love. God made you to make silver, not war."

Revere smiled. "There's a time for the casting of silver and a time for the casting of cannon. If that's not in the Bible, it should be."

"Doctor Warren, you've a young family. You know quite well, if you get killed they may literally starve."

Warren said, "I've thought of all that long ago."

"And you, John Adams. You've built up a very nice little law practice, stealing away my clients, I notice. Ah, well, so it goes. Each shall give according to his own abilities, and some—" he turned directly to Rab—"some will give their lives. All the years of their maturity. All the children they never live to have. The serenity of old age. To die so young is more than merely dying; it is to lose so large a part of life."

Rab was looking straight at Otis. His arms were folded across his chest. His head flung back a little. His lips parted as though he would speak, but he did not.

"Even you, my old friend—my old enemy? How shall I call you, Sam Adams? Even you will give the best you have—a genius for politics. Oh, go to Philadelphia! Pull all the wool, pull all the strings and all the wires. Yes, go, go! And God go with you. We need you, Sam. We must fight this war. You'll play your part —but what it is really about . . . you'll never know."

James Otis was on his feet, his head close against the rafters that cut down into the attic, making it the shape of a tent. Otis put out his arms.

"It is all so much simpler than you think," he said. He lifted his hands and pushed against the rafters.

"We give all we have, lives, property, safety, skills . . . we fight, we die, for a simple thing. Only that a man can stand up."

With a curt nod, he was gone.

Johnny was standing close to Rab. It had frightened him when Mr. Otis had said, "Some will give their lives," and looked straight at Rab. Die so that "a man can stand up."

Once more Sam Adams had the center of attention. He was again buttoning up his coat, preparing to leave, but first he turned to Revere.

"Now *he* is gone, we can talk a moment about that spy system you think you can organize in Boston."

Paul Revere, like his friend, Joseph Warren, was still slightly under the spell of James Otis.

"I had not thought about it that way before," he said, not answering Sam Adams's words. "You know my father had to fly France because of the tyranny over there. He was only a child. But now, in a way, I'm

fighting for that child . . . that no frightened lost child ever is sent out a refugee from his own country because of race or religion." Then he pulled himself together and answered Sam Adams's remarks about the spy system.

That night, when the boys were both in bed, Johnny heard Rab, usually a heavy sleeper, turning and turning.

"Johnny," he said at last, "are you awake?"

"Yes."

"What was it he said?"

"That a man can stand up."

Rab sighed and stopped turning. In a few moments he was asleep. As often had happened before, it was the younger boy who lay wide-eyed in the darkness.

"That a man can stand up."

He'd never forget Otis with his hands pushed up against the cramping rafters over his head.

"That a man can stand up"—as simple as that.

And the strange new sun rising in the west. A sun that was to illumine a world to come.

from Shackleton's Epic Voyage
Michael Brown

Marooned on desolate Elephant's Island, the British explorer Shackleton and five other men make a grim voyage across the icy seas to reach a whaling settlement after their ship has foundered.

"Stand by to abandon ship!"

The command rang out over the Antarctic seas, and it meant the end of all Ernest Shackleton's plans. He was the leader of an expedition which had set out to cross the unknown continent of Antarctica. It was a journey no one before him had ever attempted.

For months his ship, the *Endurance*, had been trapped in ice. It drifted helplessly in the Weddell Sea, over 400 miles east of the

From SHACKLETON'S EPIC VOYAGE by Michael Brown. Text copyright © 1969 by Showell Styles. Reprinted by permission of the publisher, Hamish Hamilton Ltd.

Antarctic mainland and 1,200 miles south of the southernmost tip of South America. The pressure on the hull of the *Endurance* was extreme, and the ship's timbers groaned under the strain.

Now Shackleton's first goal was to lead his men to safety. They would try to cross the polar sea on foot, head for the nearest tiny island, 250 miles to the west.

Slowly the men climbed overboard with the ship's stores. Shackleton, a gaunt bearded figure, gave the order "Hoist out the boats!" There were three, and they would be needed if the ice thawed.

Two days later, on October 30th, 1915, the *Endurance* broke up and sank beneath the ice. In the bitter cold, the chances of survival seemed small. But spurred on by Shackleton the 27 men set off, dragging their stores and the ship's boats on sledges across the uneven ice.

For five months the crew of the *Endurance* pushed their way slowly northwest across the frozen seas. Sometimes they dragged the sledges painfully behind them. Sometimes they drifted on large ice floes that slowly split into smaller and smaller pieces until they had to be abandoned. At times they took to the boats and sailed or rowed through melting ice. At last, in April 1916, they reached Elephant Island—a tiny, barren, rocky outcrop 540 miles from the nearest inhabited land, Port Stanley in the Falkland Islands.

By now the situation was grim. Food and other supplies were low. Still worse, five months of constant cold and hardship had weakened all of the men. They were in poor condition to face the coming winter.

Seeing this, Shackleton knew that he and his crew could not last much longer. He decided on a desperate attempt to find help before winter set in. He turned to the men. "We will make our camp here. Six of us will take the *James Caird* and try to reach Stromness. It's our only chance." Stromness was a whaling base on the island of South Georgia, 800 miles N.E. of Elephant Island. To reach it they must cross some of the stormiest seas in the world.

The *James Caird* was the biggest of the ship's boats. Even so she looked pitifully small to face the great grey seas of the southern ocean. Shackleton had the keel strengthened and added make-shift decking to give more shelter.

By April 24th all was ready, and the *James Caird* was launched from the beach. Some of the crew were soaked to the skin as they worked; this could be deadly in the bitter cold and wind so they changed clothes with those who were to stay behind. Shackleton shook hands with the men he was leaving, and then amidst cheers the *James Caird* set sail.

The little knot of men left behind was dwarfed by the high peaks of Elephant Island, and was soon lost from sight.

The *James Caird* was alone on the vast heaving seas. With one arm gripping the mast, Shackleton guided the boat through the ice floes that threatened to hole the sides. At last they were in clear water and, with a fair wind, set their course for South Georgia.

Now began a fierce ordeal for the crew of the *James Caird*. The boat was small and crowded. It was almost impossible for the men to find space among the stores and the rocks carried for ballast. All cooking must be done over a single primus stove that needed three men to handle it. One held a lamp, the other two lifted the cooking pot off whenever the violent pitching of the boat threatened to upset it. A fine spray of water constantly soaked its way through the flimsy decking.

There were storms, and seas so big that in the trough of a wave the boat seemed surrounded by mountains of water. The waves towering above cut off the wind so that the sails flapped uselessly.

Four days passed. A gale sprang up that threatened to swamp the *James Caird* and hurl her crew into the icy seas. "Lower the sails," shouted Shackleton, above the roar of the wind. "We'll heave-to under bare poles and lie to the sea anchor." The sea anchor was a triangular canvas bag at the end of a long line which held the bows of the boat into the wind. If the seas hit them sideways on, they would capsize.

No man aboard had faced such waves before. Sometimes looking out abeam they could see a great tunnel formed as the crest of a towering wave hung toppling over its base, then broke. Time after time it seemed they *must* be overwhelmed, but they survived.

The spray shot at them like burning arrows. It froze thick on the canvas decks and the bare masts, and would soon make the boat top-heavy. Shackleton saw the danger. "We must get the ice off, or we'll capsize," he warned.

Some of the men struggled on to the heaving deck and chipped ice away with axes to free the boat of the deadly weight. Others hurled things overboard—spare oars and sleeping bags—anything they could do without that would lighten the load.

At last on the morning of the seventh day, the wind dropped. The sea calmed, the skies cleared, and for the first time the sun shone. Thankfully, the men dragged out sleeping bags and sodden clothes and hung them in the rigging to dry. Cape pigeons flew overhead and porpoises played in the sea alongside. Shackleton and his men lay on deck soaking up the warmth. Hope surged in them; life was not so miserable after all.

from Samurai of Gold Hill
Yoshiko Uchida

After the collapse of the Japanese feudal system, a samurai and his son come to California in 1869 to establish a colony where they hope to welcome the feudal lord they have served.

The Secret Plan

It was the fourth month of the Year of the Serpent, 1869, and a fine spring rain fell softly over the town of Wakamatsu deep in the Bandai-Azuma mountains of Japan.

In a farmhouse at the edge of town, Koichi peered out at the rainy evening wondering why his father was so late. Taking a paper umbrella and a lantern, he slipped into his straw sandals and went to look down the dark road. Suppose something had happened to Father. Koichi felt once more the cold weight of fear that had overwhelmed him so often since the terrible battle for the castle last fall.

He rubbed his nose with the back of his hand and pulled his homespun kimono close around him. Then, almost without thinking, he looked toward the great black shadow that was the castle of Lord Matsudaira who had ruled over their town. In the darkness he could not see the bullet marks on the white plaster walls or the charred timbers of the massive gates, but he knew that the castle that had soared over their town like a beautiful gold-crested eagle was no longer the proud fort that once protected them. Like the rest of the town it had been badly battered by the southern clans, but at least it still stood.

Koichi thought of the cluster of samurai homes just beyond the granite base and moat of the castle. They were now only charred piles of rubble and Koichi's home was among them. Koichi shuddered as he remembered the futile battle when, for seven terrible days, the castle and the Aizu Clan had lain in siege. They had been bombarded night and day by the artillery of the southern clans, who, after many years of rule by the Shogunate, wanted the Emperor returned to power. They mercilessly attacked those northern clans who believed that it was the Shogun who should continue to rule. Even now, Koichi could smell the death and defeat that had hovered over everything then.

Father had ridden off to that battle, brave and noble, in his armor and helmet, proudly wearing his two samurai swords and carrying a spear bearing the Matsudaira banner. The last thing he had said before he rode off on his black stallion was, "Be very careful, Koichi, and take good care of Grandmother."

Koichi had nodded solemnly, wishing more than anything else that he could ride off to battle with his father as his older brother had done. But if he had, he would not be here now, for his brother and the entire White Tiger Unit of boys not even seventeen had died in battle.

Koichi and his grandmother had escaped to a farmhouse at the edge of town where Father came back to them with a terrible wound in his left arm and a glazed emptiness in his eyes. The southern clans had stripped him of his armor and his weapons and his steed. He was no longer a proud samurai warrior, but only an exhausted, defeated soldier, whose lord and commander had been captured and sentenced to imprisonment. It was a miracle that Father was still alive.

Koichi prayed each morning for the soul of his mother, who had died when he was born, and now he prayed for the soul of his sixteen-year-old brother, who had died in battle. He did not want to have to pray for the soul of his father as well.

Father had gone off early in the morning, saying only that he had some urgent business to attend to and that he was going with Lord Matsudaira's advisor, Herr Schnell. Koichi wasn't sure he could trust the big green-eyed Prussian. He had sold arms to Lord Matsudaira and had even married the daughter of one of the court samurai, but still, even Father seemed to have some doubts about him.

Koichi wondered if the two of them had gone somewhere to plot the recapture of the castle and the rescue of Lord Matsudaira. If ever there was to be another battle for the castle, Koichi thought, he would be there. He was only twelve, but he was strong and as brave as any samurai son. He had been trained at the castle school to fight with sword and spear. He knew how to use a bow and arrow with grace and skill, and could handle a horse as well as his older brother. He had been trained, furthermore, to think and act as a samurai. He would be brave and dignified at all times and, above all, loyal to his lord. If he captured an enemy warrior, he would permit the man to die with honor, by his own sword. If only he could have a chance to show his skill, Koichi thought forlornly.

He was about to turn back to the farm-house now, when he saw the faint flicker of a lantern coming toward him. He hurried down the road, slippery and soggy from the rain, and waited for the bobbing lantern to approach. Soon he heard the sound of sandals stepping into the sucking mud and the heavy breathing of one who had walked a long way.

"Father?" Koichi called into the darkness.

"Yes. I have returned."

Koichi sighed with relief. "I'm glad you're back," he said. And they hurried toward the farmhouse together.

Grandmother was sitting close to the oil lamp, which lent only a feeble light to the mending she did. Both she and the farmer's wife worked into the night until it was time to get the quilts from the cupboard and spread them on the floor to sleep. The farmer's wife was weaving hemp and the farmer too was hard at work, twisting strands of rope from rice straw. They all stopped their work when they heard Father's voice at the entrance, and Grandmother hurried to the entrance to help him with his rain-soaked straw cape.

"Mah, mah," she said sympathetically, "you must be weary." And she urged him to come inside quickly.

The farmer's wife stirred the charcoal in the open hearth and heated the black pot that hung over it. Grandmother poured hot water into the pot of fragrant green tea, and the farmer brought Father's tobacco box so he might refresh himself with a smoke.

They were all eager to hear what had happened, for they knew Father had been on an important mission, but first, they attended to his comfort. When Father had eaten two steaming bowls of buckwheat noodles and had some pickled radish with his tea, he began to speak, and they all leaned close to listen.

"Herr Schnell has a plan," he began. "It is a most ambitious plan—one that makes my head swim and my heart anxious."

"Then it is not good?" Koichi asked.

Father thought a moment. "It may hold great good if it is successful," he said carefully, "but for now, we do only what seems best for Lord Matsudaira."

"You have seen him then?" the farmer wondered.

"No, we could not," Father explained, "but Herr Schnell has communicated with him and knows his wishes." Father stopped now, as though not quite sure how much more to tell.

The farmer and his wife lowered their eyes and did not look at Father. He was a samurai, high in Lord Matsudaira's court, while they were only peasants. They did not wish to be unseemly in their curiosity. And Grandmother, although she was of the noble class, did not speak either, for she was only a woman. As for Koichi, he knew that a child listened and did not question.

They waited for Father to speak when he was ready, and he seemed to be sorting the words in his head before he spoke. Finally, looking at the farmer and his wife he said, "You have been most kind to us since the day of the terrible battle. You took in my mother and son and then myself. You allowed us to share the little you possessed. I shall always be grateful."

Koichi wiggled his toes impatiently. He wished Father would hurry and say what he had to say.

"But now," Father went on, "the time has come for my son and me to leave."

"Leave?" The word burst from Koichi like an explosion in the night.

Grandmother caught her breath and put a hand to her mouth. She had noticed that Father had not included her.

"Koichi and I must go on a long journey," Father continued, and then he spoke gently to Grandmother. "Good Mother, I must ask you to wait here for the time being. The plan entails long days of weariness which I cannot ask you to undertake."

Grandmother nodded. "I understand, my son," she said. "When will you and Koichi leave?"

"Very soon now," Father answered. "There is little time and much to do."

Long after the embers in the hearth had been covered with ash and the lamps blown out, Koichi, like each of the others, lay awake on his quilt. Father had not said where they were going, but he had asked Grandmother to prepare enough food and clothing for a long journey. Could they be going as far as Tokyo, the capital city, where now the Emperor reigned instead of the Shogun? Could it be that they were going to join in another battle?

Koichi had never been outside of Wakamatsu before. His heart began to pound at the mere thought of such a trip and he really had to know now. He sat up on his quilts and glanced toward his father, but the only sound coming from his quilts were those of sleep, and Koichi slid back into his own, filled with impatient curiosity.

The next day Father was gone again, and this time when he returned, he had a horse. He also carried a small drawstring leather bag which he immediately put away with great care.

"Is that sad-looking horse taking us on our journey?" Koichi asked. He had never seen a more pitiful creature, but horses were hard to find now, for the southern warriors had taken away most of those that hadn't been killed in battle.

"That is our hope," Father said with a wan smile. "I hope he will be up to it."

"How far will he have to go?" Koichi asked quickly, seeing that it was a good time to find out where they were going.

"To Tokyo," Father answered.

"To ask the Emperor to give the castle back to Lord Matsudaira?"

Koichi asked the question, knowing even as he did, that such a thing was impossible. One would have to be a very great lord and one who had supported the southern clans to even get near the Emperor's court.

Father shook his head quickly. "You can be sure our plan has nothing to do with His Imperial Majesty, Koichi," he said. And then he added, "We will go on from Tokyo to Yokohama."

"To the port city?" Koichi asked. "Why?"

But Father was not ready to tell him anything more, and Koichi was left with an even bigger puzzle than the night before. All he could do now was get ready to leave and that was easily done, for Koichi possessed scarcely more than the clothes on his back.

Grandmother, however, had planned carefully. For many days before the enemy attacked, she had been preparing the things she would take if it became necessary to flee from their house. She had wrapped everything in large heavy silk *furoshiki* bundles. She took one of them out now and removed Father's and Koichi's black silk kimonos bearing their family crest. She also took out a long box that contained Grandfather's samurai swords.

"You are now the only remaining son of the Matsuzaka family, Koichi," she said gravely. "These swords are yours. But for the journey take only one and keep it in remembrance of your grandfather and me."

Koichi knew then that Grandmother must know more than he did, for she spoke as though she might not see him again.

"But we will be back one day, won't we, Grandmother?" Koichi asked.

Grandmother held a thin hand over her mouth, covering the teeth she had carefully blackened, as was the custom, on the day she was married. "Perhaps, my child, perhaps," she said softly, but she said nothing more.

Now she placed the beautiful sheathed sword on top of Koichi's formal kimono, and wrapped them together in a silk *furoshiki*. Then, bowing as she would have done to Father, she slid the packet across the matted floor to Koichi.

"Thank you, Grandmother," Koichi said.

Although he did not know it then, it was to be his Grandmother's last gift to him.

from **Petros' War**
Alki Zei

In a story of World War II, an Athenian boy of ten works with the Underground to help defeat the German invaders of Greece, and Petros learns the bitterness of defeat.

"Within the Gates" from PETROS' WAR by Alki Zei, translated by Edward Fenton from the Greek. English translation © 1972 by Edward Fenton. Reprinted by permission of the publisher, E. P. Dutton.

Within the Gates

A thin ray of light crept between the bars of the shutters and rested on Petros' bed; then it traveled on to caress Theodore's domed shell. Petros had brought the tortoise up to his room the night before because everyone said that at any moment now the Germans would be entering Athens. It was not that Theodore was in any special danger; Petros just wanted him for company. The odd thing was that Antigone made no objection when Petros suggested it.

Petros opened his eyes and watched the dust motes stirring in the rays of sunlight. It was Sunday. But with the war on, one day was no longer any different from another. Sunday, Monday, Tuesday: they were all the same, workday or holiday. That, Petros reflected, was one good thing about going to school. With school, Sunday was special, something you waited for eagerly. Now, if it weren't for the calendar in their room, with Sunday marked on it in red, you'd never even notice when it arrived. Every morning, whoever woke up first could tear off the page with the date and read the verse or the proverb that was printed on the back of it. He glanced over at Antigone's bed. She wasn't there. She must be up. Petros hastened to tear off the page before she could get back to the room and do it.

SUNDAY
27
APRIL
1941

The proverb for today was a funny one: "Either the compass is out of order or else the boat is going in the wrong direction."

He was one up on Antigone, he thought, and hid the bit of paper in a book.

Theodore was wandering about the room, bumping his shell against the furniture. Petros stretched his arms, yawned, and gave the bedclothes a kick. Then he had an inspiration.

He leapt out of bed, searched furiously among Antigone's paints, found a tube of red paint, grabbed Theodore, who was trying vainly to squeeze under the chest of drawers, and, with a brush, he wrote on Theodore's shell: *April 27, 1941.* Then he set the tortoise down on the floor. It was a great idea to have a living calendar roaming around the room! It might even amuse Antigone so much that she wouldn't make him take Theodore back down to the cellar. . . . What had happened to make his sister get up so early?

From the dining room came the sound of the radio. They were playing the national anthem at full blast.

"Grandfather," a voice called, "turn it down! You'll have the whole neighborhood on its feet." Petros heard the rush of footsteps. He turned and saw Mama and Antigone standing in the doorway. Antigone had her hair pulled back, and it was tied with a black ribbon. Where, Petros wondered, was the cauliflower coiffure like Deanna Durbin's this morning? He started to say something, but Mama's frightened voice broke in.

"Can you hear it?"

Antigone ran to the window and listened.

"It sounds like the tanks," she whispered.

"The Germans are coming!" Petros cried. And he too ran toward the window. He started to fling open the shutters.

"No!" his mother cried. "Leave them closed!"

They pressed together and peered through the bars. The streets were deserted. All the shutters in all the houses were closed. Except that you knew that behind those shutters other eyes were staring out.

"*. . . When the victorious Marcus Claudius Marcellus entered the city, he found the houses barred and the streets deserted. There was not even a single dog, or a cat, not a living soul. . . . He was aware only of thousands of eyes watching them from behind the pierced shutters. And then Marcus Claudius Marcellus understood that the enemy without arms, the enemy with hatred in its eyes, is the most powerful. . . .*"

Petros remembered reading that, in some book at school, in history class. And for a moment, he felt as though he were in ancient Syracuse when the conquering Romans took over the city.

Everyone in the house was silent. You'd think the enemy was hidden in every corner, watching. His father took down the map with the little flags and tore it into pieces. The radio went silent: it was as though it too refused to surrender. With no one daring to utter a word, it was like having an invalid in the house. He remembered how, just before Sotiris' grandfather died, everyone had gone about on tiptoe. Sotiris had walked in stocking feet.

There was a sudden sound of rapping.

Everyone started.

It was Theodore, who had reached the door.

"Look at that!" exclaimed Antigone, pointing at Theodore's shell. Then she said that tortoises are supposed to live for a hundred years; and so everyone would recall, a century later, that it was on that day the Germans entered Athens.

For the first three days no one left the house. Petros went back and forth between their apartment and Sotiris', where the two boys stayed in a tiny room that just barely held Sotiris' bed. They climbed up on it and peered between the bars of the shutters at the German soldiers in the street, with their green uniforms, their shaved heads, and their blank eyes.

On the morning of the second day Petros and Sotiris climbed secretly out onto the balcony, by way of the spiral iron service staircase. The house was on a small rise; from the balcony they could see the whole city, as far as the Acropolis.

"Look!" Sotiris cried. "What's happening to the flag?"

The wind was blowing. The flag that hung from a thin pole at the eastern end of the Acropolis seemed no larger than a dot. The wind blew stronger, and suddenly the flag was blown out so that the whole of it could be seen.

"Holy Mother of God!" Sotiris exclaimed.

Instead of the white and sky-blue emblem of Greece spread out on the wind, the flag they beheld was red with an enormous black swastika, like the claws of an angry bird of prey, in its center.

They stared out at it, their hearts strange and heavy in their chests. Then they crept down from the balcony on tiptoe so as not to be seen.

During those days the grown-ups all went about with swollen eyes. No one dared mention Uncle Angelos' name because then Grandfather's hands started to tremble and he looked a hundred years old. Sotiris' father had not come back from the front either.

And Antigone had begun to write poetry. She sat on her bed with a notebook on her knees, a big notebook with a cherry-colored cover. Of course she never showed Petros what she was writing. But once in a while she would ask him a question.

"Tell me a word that rhymes with 'conquered.'"

Petros couldn't think of one. The only words that came to his mind didn't rhyme, like "barley" and "lentils." They were eating lentils for the third day. Every time she reheated them, Mama added more water; and they kept getting more and more tasteless. No one had any appetite at meals and yet Petros was always hungry. He was ashamed that nothing seemed to stem his appetite; not even the stamping of German boots on the sidewalk outside, under the windows.

The evening when he and Sotiris saw a German car come to a halt outside their door, they held their breaths. Their eyes nearly popping out of their heads, they watched while a husky German soldier jumped out, held open the rear door of the car, and stood there like a ramrod.

Out of the car stepped Mrs. Leventi's daughter Lela, her hair bleached yellow as straw; and another German, an officer with pale blond hair. The chauffeur followed them into the house, carrying a huge cardboard carton that looked just like the ones that Michael, Lela's English fiancé, used to bring.

Petros left Sotiris there and ran off to tell the news to Antigone. As he pelted down the stairs he heard the sound of footsteps coming up. He bent over the railing to see who was coming. A Greek soldier in a ragged uniform with a rough stubble of beard on his face waved a grimy hand at him. The soldier's eyes were bloodshot. Petros felt a shiver of fear. He started running back up the stairs to Sotiris'.

"Petraki!"

He turned. Then he leaped into the arms of the ragged, dirty soldier.

The soldier pushed him away.

"Don't," he said. "You'll only catch my lice."

The glittering medals, the shiny boots, the white horse, the sword flashing like lightning, the victories and the valorous deeds of heroism that Petros had awaited with the return of his uncle, all swept across his mind and vanished.

"Well," Angelos asked in a weary voice, "aren't you glad to see me?"

Then Petros noticed that one of his uncle's feet was bandaged in filthy rags. With a single bound he reached the door of their apartment and banged at it with his fists.

"Open the door!" he shouted. "Open up! Uncle Angelos has come home!"

A man with hollow, freshly shaven cheeks and red sunken eyes sat on Grandfather's couch. He was wearing Papa's pajamas. They seemed much too big for him. One stockingless foot was stuffed into a green slipper of Mama's (Papa was wearing his and there wasn't another pair in the house) with his heel sticking out of it. The other foot was bare, the big toe bandaged in clean gauze.

What could Petros say now to Sotiris, who was waiting impatiently to hear all about Uncle Angelos' valiant deeds at the front? How could he tell Sotiris that all Angelos could talk about were the woolen stockings and sweaters that never reached the front lines, the shoes into which the water leaked, and the chilblains? Angelos didn't say, "The bullets slaughtered us." What he said was, "It was the frostbite that knocked us out." How could Petros admit that Angelos had made his way home covered with lice, his boots in shreds, going from village to village begging for bread? And in those villages, others had been there before him. The villages had been stripped bare of food—or else the villagers were hiding what was left. Could he tell Sotiris that Angelos had swapped Rita's gold locket for half a loaf of stale bread?

"All the same," Petros said stubbornly, "we beat the Italians!"

"That's all over now," Uncle Angelos said in a tired voice. Then he asked if he could go into the bedroom now and lie down, because he hadn't slept for days.

Petros would tell Sotiris that Angelos hadn't told them any of his feats of war because he had been too tired. Or he'd make up something himself: how his uncle had returned on a horse—fortunately Sotiris hadn't seen him when he arrived—and described to them how he had whirled his sword around his head and the Italians had fled like rabbits.

But there was no need to lie to Sotiris. The next day when they went outdoors the streets were full of ragged soldiers begging for old clothes or a little food. But Sotiris' father never came back, not even in rags or crippled.

"What are we going to say to Rita?" Antigone asked Petros when they were getting ready for bed and she was tying up her hair in curling rags.

"About her locket?" Petros asked.

"No. About his not coming home a hero."

"If he had been wounded in battle, that wouldn't be so bad," Petros reflected. "But to get frostbite!"

They turned off the light. But before they fell asleep, they jumped up. From Mama's bedroom they could hear a hoarse wild voice: "The machine gun—get the machine gun! It's to the right!" And then came Mama's soothing voice: "Calm yourself, Angelos."

"He did fight, all the same," Antigone whispered happily.

"He's having nightmares about the battle," Petros rejoined enthusiastically.

After that they both fell into a deep, peaceful sleep, and they didn't hear Uncle Angelos shout, "Don't! Don't beat him! He's a prisoner!"

Biography

If there is one area of literature for children that has improved over the years, it is probably biography. In the past, and especially in biographical series, there was a strong tendency to idealize the subjects of the books, to ignore their faults or motives that were self-seeking, and in some cases to focus on their childhoods rather than on that part of their lives in which they made those contributions to society for which they became famous. Even in the first half of the twentieth century, most biographies for children were unbalanced, undocumented, and laudatory in tone, and most of them were written about the lives of comparatively few people: the same national heroes, primarily men, were written about over and over.

There are two major changes in the field today. One is that biographies for young readers are often carefully documented and based on thorough research, and are much more candid. A second is that there is a much broader range of subjects: not yet another book on George Washington or Benjamin Franklin, but books about people of all races, many jobs and professions, and varying degrees of status. There are also many more biographies about women.

In a good biography, whether it is intended for an adult or a child, certain literary criteria must be met. First, biographical details must be accurate, both in provision of concrete details and in reflecting the period in which the subject lived, the speech patterns of that period, and the concepts which the biographical subject would have held depending on the circumstances of his or her life. The writing should be objective insofar as is possible, never offering personal opinions of the writer as fact. While no biographer can include every detail of a subject's life, detail should be chosen to give a balanced and honest picture of the subjects, both in depicting their personalities and their accomplishments. Although it is not customary to include footnotes in biographies for children, there should be evidence of research through appended notes or a bibliography; finally, there should be no laudatory tone in the writing: the author should let the words and deeds of the subject speak for themselves.

Most biographies for children are fictionalized in various degrees, in order to make the writing more vivid. While some leeway is permissible in biographical fiction, in which the format is biographical but the approach fictional, more care must be exercised in fictionalized biography, in which the emphasis is on fact. In the rich assortment of excellent biographies now available, children can get a realistic view of some of the many careers they may choose to pursue as adults; of some of the men and women who have made, and are making, signal contributions to society; and of the fact that such men and women, in addition to their small or great achievements, were or are vibrant, complex, and fallible human beings.

from Laura Ingalls Wilder
Gwenda Blair

For children who are already Wilder fans, this story of the family's move from Wisconsin to Kansas will have special appeal, but the book should also interest readers as a biography of a child in a pioneer family.

"Here we are, little half pint of cider half drunk up," Pa said to Laura and stopped the wagon. "Here is where we'll build our house."

Laura and her older sister Mary scrambled down from the covered wagon. They rode in it all the way from their cabin in the Big Woods of Wisconsin to the wide Kansas prairie that was still Indian Territory. Ma always sat straight and quiet in the wagon, but Laura squirmed and fidgeted. It is hard to sit still when there is so much to see and do and hear.

Laura Ingalls was born on February 7, 1867. People in the United States had just finished fighting the long, terrible Civil War with each other. Pioneers looking for better lives were pushing west. Two-and-a-half-year-old Laura was sad to leave the Big Woods in Wisconsin. But Pa said they had to go because all the people moving there were scaring away the wild animals, and the family depended on the animals for food. Besides, he told Laura, she might see a papoose, an Indian baby, in Kansas.

Now Pa built a cabin and a barn with the help of their new neighbor, Mr. Edwards. Laura knew that they had found the right spot, because at night Pa played his fiddle and sang her favorite song:

Oh I am a Gypsy King!
I come and go as I please!
I pull my old nightcap down,
And take the world at my ease!

As she fell asleep, it seemed to Laura that everything, even the moon and stars, was dancing to Pa's music.

Laura and Mary were pioneer girls. Their family was always one of the first to move into a new area. Their food came from their own fields and the wild animals that Pa hunted. The family made everything by hand. Pa made their house and the furniture too. Ma made all their clothes. She also cooked, washed and cleaned.

Ma taught Laura and Mary to be young ladies. "Wash your hands and faces, girls," she told them every morning when they woke up. Then they put on clean dresses and combed their hair. They helped make breakfast and wash up afterwards. When they went out to play, they wore sunbonnets to protect their skin.

It was a funny thing about those sunbonnets. Mary's always seemed to stay right in place on top of her beautiful golden curls, but Laura's had a way of sliding off her head and down over her long, straight brown hair.

Every day new things happened. Some were fun, like finding birds' nests or wading in the creek, or picking delicious blackberries. But some were scary. When Indians came to call, or wolves and panthers prowled nearby, Laura didn't like it. Pa said the Indians were friendly, but they looked scary to Laura. She was afraid whenever Pa went away on the four-day trip to town for supplies. Once the whole family was so sick that no one could move. They didn't know it, but they had caught malaria from the mosquitoes around the creek.

Christmas that year almost didn't come. The creek flooded and their presents were on the other side. But Mr. Edwards actually swam across with the presents and delivered them. In her stocking Laura found a shiny new tin cup, a stick of candy, a bright new penny, and a heart-shaped little cake that seemed the sweetest thing she had ever eaten. There had never been such a Christmas—never!

from Truth on Trial: The Story of Galileo Galilei
Vicki Cobb

This is a good example of careful fictionalization, as Cobb puts into the dialogue many of the recorded ideas of the great scientist who challenged many of the accepted theories of his time and was tried by the Inquisition for his daring.

A Challenging Talk, A Daring Thought

The lecture hall was packed, as usual. The students were watching intently, completely caught up in the magic of the lesson. On the platform at the end of the room was a stocky young professor with a reddish beard named Galileo Galilei. Galileo had followed his father's wishes and gone to the university in Pisa, where he had started on a program in medicine. Soon, however, his first love, mathematics, took over. When he graduated, he took a job teaching mathematics in Pisa. It paid poorly as his father had predicted. That had been especially hard on his family. His father had died seven years before, and they were short on money. But for the past six years he had been teaching here in Padua, in the Republic of Venice, 150 miles from home, and this position had been good for him. He was still not paid very well, but there was an air of freedom in Padua, and Galileo had blossomed as a daring and original thinker and a first-rate teacher.

In the seventeenth century, Italy was not one nation as it is now, but rather was divided into many small states. Some, like the Republic of Venice, were under control of the people who lived there. Such local control encouraged free thinking. Other states, like Tuscany, where Galileo had grown up, were under control of the Church of Rome, so that the Pope was the head of the government as well as the Church. The Church was powerful enough to smother ideas it disagreed with.

As he spoke in the lecture hall, Galileo was obviously enjoying his ideas. Although he had not become a doctor, his father would have been proud of him. His lectures had a very strong effect on students, and it was easy to see why. Galileo talked as if he were looking for an argument. Very few students were willing to take him on. The ones who did took their chances, since Galileo had a way of tripping up even careful and intelligent speakers.

Galileo was weaving a spell over his audience. His eyes glittered as he paced back and forth.

"Let me tell you what happened to me when I was a student at Pisa. I was looking at something all of you have seen hundreds of times in your lives—but I'm sure none of you noticed what I did."

Everyone was caught up in the excitement of Galileo's thinking.

"I was in church," Galileo was saying. "An overhead lamp had just been lit. The lamplighter had set it in motion and it was swinging back and forth." Galileo put his hands on his hips and faced the group squarely. "Now let's do some hard thinking about the motion of a swinging lamp. How would you describe it?" Silence. Galileo let his piercing eyes search around the room for some poor volunteer.

Today no one dared answer, so the professor answered his own question. "A swinging lamp is a pendulum. It cuts an arc as it moves back and forth. After a while the arc gets smaller and smaller until the pendulum comes to rest. Sometimes this takes a long time." Again Galileo challenged his students.

"At first, the pendulum cuts a wide arc. Eventually it cuts a small one. Which arc takes longer?" Galileo waited. At first no one answered. Then a few students called out.

"The long path."

"It takes longer to make a big arc."

Galileo smiled. He knew he had them in the palm of his hand.

"But a pendulum is moving faster when it is cutting a long arc," he responded.

Some students reconsidered their answer.

"Then it must take longer to make a small arc."

The professor shook his finger at his class.

"You don't know the answer, do you? If you learn nothing else from me, never be ashamed of not knowing! I know I've asked what seems to be a simple question. I found the truth by experimenting. I watched the lamp. Suddenly I realized that the swings could be timed by my pulse, since it has a regular beat. So I put my fingers on my wrist and counted, and I found that the long swings took *exactly* as much time as the short ones.

"Here, I'll show you." Galileo took two lengths of chain from behind his desk. A small iron ball hung from the end of each chain.

"You will notice that these chains are the same length and the bobs are exactly the same weight."

He hung the chains on two pegs sticking out of a beam on the wall behind him.

"I want all the students on the left side of the room to clap to the beat of this pendulum." Galileo drew one of the pendulums aside so it was completely horizontal. He let it drop so it swung back and forth in a wide arc. Then he gently pushed the other pendulum to set it moving in a small arc. He signaled the other half of the room to clap to the beat of its small swing. The sound grew strong. Suddenly everyone realized that the entire room was clapping in a steady beat together! Galileo's experiment revealed the truth. The size of the swing of a pendulum did not affect the time it took to make it.

Galileo raised his hands. The clapping stopped.

"Gentlemen, my point is made."

This time the hands joined in a round of applause. The lesson for the day was over. Galileo waited patiently for the room to clear. When he looked up, he saw his favorite former student, Sagredo, leaning against the wall, watching him.

"Sagredo, you devil! What are you doing here?" Galileo rushed forward to greet his friend.

"I'm in Padua for a few days on business and I thought I'd drop by. I see you're still using your old material."

"Listen, my friend. Some ideas get better with time," laughed Galileo. "But it is good to see you. So you think I have nothing new to say? Come home with me to dinner. We'll see if there is nothing new to discuss."

Sagredo accepted with pleasure. He had many fond memories of good food, wine, and talk at his old teacher's home.

This night proved to be no exception. Several of Galileo's students boarded at his house, as Sagredo had done in his student days. The university didn't pay enough for Galileo to make ends meet, so he opened his home to boarders. Dinner conversation was lively. Sagredo told stories of his wild student days and some of the fun he and Galileo had. One thing was certain. Galileo was not a stuffy professor. He liked good times like most young men.

After dinner, Sagredo and Galileo went into his study.

"So, my friend," said Sagredo, "what's the cause of your new excitement?"

"This book," said Galileo, picking up a heavy leather-bound volume. "It's more than fifty years old. It was written by a Polish churchman named Nicolaus Copernicus. He spent his life studying the heavens and put all his findings in this book. What he says about the universe goes against everything the scholars at the universities and the Church of Rome state as the truth. I discovered it in my early student days and have been thinking about it for a long time."

"Are you telling me," Sagredo said slowly, "that you believe in this book and that you are going to do something so others will believe it also?"

"You know me too well, Sagredo. There is no question that people are afraid of the new ideas in this book. Even Copernicus knew his truth would stir people up. He was afraid to have his book published. Look, in the introduction he says, 'I feared I would be laughed off the stage.' He even dedicated the book to the Pope, hoping the Pope wouldn't ban the book. And he waited until he was an old man before he gave his book to the printer. Imagine! He first saw his book on his deathbed."

"What are his ideas, anyway, that they can make the Church so angry?" asked Sagredo.

"Well, you know we all teach about the universe the way Aristotle and Ptolemy did. The earth is at the center and the sun, moon, planets, and stars all move in crystal balls around us. Copernicus dares to say that the *sun*, not the earth, is at the center. And the earth is just another planet. Look, here he says the earth is moving: 'In the middle of all sits the sun, like a king. From here he can light all the planets at once. The sun sits as if on a throne ruling his children, the planets which circle him.' "

"How do you know that his system is the truth?" asked Sagredo. "After all, the evidence is that the heavenly bodies move around us. You can *see* that happening."

"You always were one of my best students, Sagredo. The fact is that there is no proof that Copernicus is right! I just have a hunch he is. For one thing, his system is much simpler than Ptolemy's. You know the paths of the planets are not simple like the sun, moon, and stars. Planets sometimes have a backward motion. Under the present system we add extra circles to the planetary motions so that their paths look like curlicues. Copernicus gets rid of the curlicues and makes their paths simple circles again. He can do this because he says the earth is *passing* another planet as they both move around the sun. This makes the other planet *seem* to be moving backward. All the planets are moving in the same direction in circular paths around the sun, including earth."

"What about the path of the sun across the sky in the daytime and the paths of the moon and stars at night?" asked Sagredo.

"Copernicus says the earth has two ways of moving. It spins like a top while it moves around the sun. It is this spinning motion that makes the sun appear to move across the sky by day and the moon and stars *appear* to move across the sky at night. Actually we are the ones who move, though we feel no motion. I tell you, Sagredo," Galileo added with feeling, "the man is right. His system is beautifully simple. And it's based on more than thirty years of carefully tracking the paths of all the heavenly bodies."

"Then why isn't it accepted? Why aren't people arguing over it?"

"First, as I said, there is no proof Copernicus is correct. Right now, it's only his opinion. Secondly, his book is hard to read. It requires careful study. It's not widely known, so it's not yet a threat to the Church. But mark my words, my friend. Someday soon there will be proof Copernicus is right. And I will not be shy about speaking out. You can count on that!"

Sagredo glanced out the window into the night. Venus, called the evening star, was rising in the east. Perhaps Galileo's star was rising, too.

from Where Do You Think You're Going, Christopher Columbus?
Jean Fritz

With a smooth incorporation of theory into the text, this biography of Columbus is distinctive in its style and distinguished by the lucidity with which Fritz uses accurate data in a lively, fluent narrative.

It was lucky that Christopher Columbus was born where he was or he might never have gone to sea. The city of Genoa sat smack on the west coast of Italy with the sea right outside its front door. Its harbors rocked with ships; its sailors sailed wherever men dared to sail. Of course some people (like Christopher's father, a master weaver) were content to stay in Genoa all their lives. But not Christopher Columbus. Whenever he had a chance, off he'd sail, his red stocking cap pulled down over his red hair, his gray eyes squinting to see all that he could see. Sailing, he said, made a person "wish to learn the secrets of the world."

And in 1451, when Columbus was born, there were still many secrets. Most people agreed that the world was round like a ball, but they didn't agree on how big the world was or how wide the ocean. Still, they did know that far away in the east there was a fabulous place called the Indies, which was overflowing with gold and jewels and spices. They had even bought these treasures from merchants who traded with other merchants in a long overland trail that stretched over thousands of miles of mountains and deserts.

Then, in 1453, when Christopher Columbus was two years old, the merchants suddenly had to stop trading. The Turks, who had been fighting the Christians for centuries, put an end to overland travel, so now there'd be no more gold or spices unless someone could figure out another way of getting to the Indies.

Portugal was the country where people were figuring the hardest. So, of course, that was a good place for anyone interested in learning the secrets of the world. Christopher Columbus got there by accident. In 1476, when he was twenty-five years old, he was sailing past Portugal on a trading trip when all at once his ship was attacked by an enemy. He was wounded. Then he was flung into the sea, six miles from shore. His ship went down in flames; his friends drowned. Christopher Columbus would have drowned too except that he was lucky. He grabbed an oar floating by and slowly kicked his way to shore.

And there he was in Portugal. And there he stayed, off and on for nine years, running a store that sold maps, making trips to far-away places, listening to talk about the world's secrets. He stayed until he had learned what he thought he needed to know and until he had decided what he wanted to do.

He was going to beat everyone in the race to the Indies. The king of Portugal was going about it the wrong way, he decided. The king was instructing his ships to sail around Africa and then head east, but his ships kept turning back. Oh, it was too far, the sailors moaned, and it was too scary. No one had ever sailed so far south. No one knew where Africa ended.

Columbus thought all this was a big waste of time. Why not take a short cut? Why not sail *west* to the Indies? Straight across the Ocean Sea.

Japan. And Japan was the place in the Indies where Columbus most wanted to go.

Columbus had read all about the Indies in a well-known travel book written by Marco Polo, who had gone there on the overland route about two hundred years before. His stories about the riches and splendor of the Great Khan's court in China were so fantastic that he was accused of exaggerating. But Columbus believed him. Especially when he talked about the island of Japan (or Cipangu, as he called it) which supposedly had so much gold that whole palaces were built of it.

Japan was one of 7,448 islands in the Indies, Marco Polo said. An English travel writer, Sir John Mandeville, also wrote about the islands of the Indies. He claimed to have seen men with umbrella feet, people whose eyes were on their shoulders, griffons (half-lion, half-eagles), and ants that dug for gold. Actually, Mandeville was an out-and-out faker who had never been near the Indies, but many people (including Columbus) accepted his stories. Why wouldn't unknown parts of the world contain unknown forms of life?

So Columbus read, but it was not just books that finally convinced him. He believed that God Himself had revealed the secrets of the world to him. Indeed, God had arranged his life so that *he* would be the one to find the way to the Indies by sea. Nothing had been an accident. Not his birthplace, not his shipwreck, not even his name. In Latin the name Christopher means "Christ-bearing," and so obviously he was meant to take the Christian religion across the Ocean Sea and convert the people there. God had even arranged a useful marriage for him. In 1478, two years after he had landed in Portugal, he had married a young lady who came from a noble family with friends at court. So now Christopher Columbus was not just a common seaman. There was nothing to stop him from going to the king of Portugal and asking for ships and money for his trip to the Indies.

In 1484 that is just what he did. Columbus was thirty-three years old now, a tall-standing, well-built man with ruddy cheeks and

Why not? Well, there were plenty of people to tell him why not. The Ocean Sea was no short cut, they said; it was a big place. It would take three years to cross it. You would run out of food and water. And how would you get back? Not with the wind. It didn't blow that way, people said. Even if it did, how could it blow you uphill? And it would have to. The world was round, wasn't it? Downhill, one way; uphill, the other. People laughed. That Christopher Columbus had some crazy ideas! If God had wanted His Ocean Sea crossed, He would have seen to it long ago. Not now. Not so late in the world's history.

But Columbus read books and found a few that agreed with him. (If they didn't agree, he stopped reading.) One writer said that a man could walk around the whole world in four years, sixteen weeks, and two days. Since Columbus was only going to the Indies and wouldn't be walking, he figured he didn't have far to go at all. Indeed, it was a "small sea" between Spain and India, according to an ancient Greek philosopher. This seemed reasonable to Columbus. How could nature be so unorderly, he asked, as to have more water than land? Dr. Toscanelli, a famous Italian scholar, estimated that there were only 3000 nautical miles between the Canary Islands (southwest of Portugal) and hair that was turning gray. He was too proud to be "soft of speech," as he, himself, admitted, so when he spoke to King John of Portugal, he spoke right out. He didn't *believe* he'd find the way to the Indies by going west; he *knew* he would. He didn't *hope* to bring back gold; he *promised* to bring it back.

In the end the king decided that Christopher Columbus was just a big talker and his counselors agreed. So King John told Columbus, No, thank you; the Portuguese would stick to the African route. And that was that.

The next year Columbus went to Spain. His wife had died, leaving him with a son, Diego, whom he put in the care of monks in a Spanish monastery. Then he went to see King Ferdinand and Queen Isabella. He was particularly hopeful that the queen would help him. After all, she was such an enthusiastic Christian that she insisted everyone in Spain be a Christian too. At the moment she was fighting a war with the Moors of southern Spain, who had the bad luck to be Mohammedans; later she would banish Jews from the country. Indeed, she was so religious that if she even found Christians who were not sincere Christians, she had them burned at the stake. (Choir boys sang during the burning so Isabella wouldn't have to hear the screams.) So, of course, Columbus was hopeful. The queen was one person who should understand that crossing the Ocean Sea to the Indies was not only the way to make Spain richer, but the way to turn more people into Christians.

The trouble was that Queen Isabella was too busy to think about the Indies. It was a year before Columbus could even see her, and then she didn't say yes. But she didn't say no either. She told Columbus to wait. So he waited. Week after week. Month after month. The longer he waited, the bigger he talked, until people began laughing and making jokes about him. Naturally this made Columbus mad, and when he got mad, he got red in the face and he said, "By San Fernando!" (He never swore.)

After two years of waiting, he was very red in the face and he decided, by San Fernando, he'd go back to Portugal! Maybe he could change King John's mind. But in Portugal everyone was celebrating the return of Bartholomew Diaz from Africa. He'd sailed all the way down the African coast and clear around the cape at the southern end. With such good news, King John couldn't bother with the silly schemes of Christopher Columbus.

Columbus returned to Spain. It was 1489 now and he had three more years to wait until the queen finished her war and beat the Moors. Only then did she think about the Indies. Only then did she finally say yes. She would help Columbus.

Pleased as he was, Columbus couldn't forget the wasted years and the jokes. He was forty-one years old now and he decided the queen would have to pay well for his services. He wasn't going to give away the riches of the Indies for nothing. He stated his terms. If he was successful, he must be knighted. He must be given the title of Admiral of the Ocean Sea, made viceroy and governor-general of all the lands he discovered, and granted one-tenth of the treasure brought back to Spain. Furthermore, these rights were to be passed down in his family.

The queen could hardly believe it. Who did Columbus think he was? If he was going to be so high and mighty, she said, he could just forget the whole thing. She was through with him.

But she wasn't through. At the very last minute the queen changed her mind. Columbus was already on his way to see the king of France when the queen called him back. She didn't want the king of France to get those riches. She would accept the terms, she said. After all, what could she lose? If Columbus didn't succeed, he'd get nothing. If he did succeed, let him have his terms; it would be worth it. So the contract was signed. All Columbus had to do now was to succeed.

from **The Real Tom Thumb**
Helen Reeder Cross

Discovered at the age of five by P. T. Barnum, the midget Charles Stratton became a famous performer under the name of "Tom Thumb." In the chapter included here, Tom Thumb is at the start of his career.

Suddenly Barnum had an idea. Why not take Tom to England to visit the queen? That would make the world sit up and take notice. To understand why, you have to remember that it was 1843. America had just beaten England again, in the War of 1812. That's part of why "Yankee Doodle" was such a popular song! If an American general could win the heart of the English queen, it would give people something to talk about for years to come.

It was an outrageous idea. Royalty didn't speak to commoners in those days—and Barnum and Tom Thumb were in show business! Why, when the Beatles were knighted by Queen Elizabeth, more than 125 years later, people would think it a scandal!

Barnum flew into action, writing to the English newspapers, making arrangements, and trying to wangle an invitation to Buckingham Palace.

Tom's ma was asked to travel with her son. His pa went along to manage the money. A teacher was hired to give Tom lessons from proper school books (but Barnum would teach Tom all of the proper manners for visiting the queen—once he'd learned them himself).

They all arrived at the New York docks on a bright January day in 1844, ready to board the *Yorkshire* and sail for England. There had been much ballyhoo in the papers, of course, but even Barnum was surprised by the size of the crowd. Thousands of people lined the pier to wave farewell to their beloved Tom Thumb.

"Good-bye, Little General! We will miss you. Give our greetings to the queen!" they shouted. A brass band, hired by Barnum, struck up "Yankee Doodle." As a joke, and to please the people, Tom did his "Yankee Doodle" act right there on the ship's upper deck. Phineas was delighted. He could already see the headlines—on both sides of the Atlantic! But it wasn't that easy.

Though messages had been sent ahead, the docks were empty when they landed in England. To make matters worse, P. T. Barnum and General Tom Thumb hadn't been invited to Buckingham Palace.

Those English needed to see the Prince of Hokum in action!

So Barnum rented a handsome house on a fashionable street and paid a great deal of money for it. He felt perfectly sure that the "golden showers" would come just as soon as his general had the chance to visit the queen.

He sent invitations for teas and supper parties to the finest lords and ladies of the realm. These read:

PHINEAS TAYLOR BARNUM, ESQUIRE,
of New York, U.S.A.,
invites
Lord and Lady such-and-such
to high tea on Tuesday afternoon
at half after four o'clock
to meet
GENERAL TOM THUMB,
the toast of America.

Here was a new kind of party. The lords and ladies laughed. Still, they came out of curiosity. It might be amusing to see this crude American showman and his "general." To their own surprise they stayed to marvel. The pretty child was not only clever, he had fine manners. They went home to tell their children about tiny Tom Thumb.

Finally the queen's curiosity got the best of her. A shining coach drew up to Barnum's front door. Out stepped one of the queen's Life Guards in full dress. He had a message from the royal lady herself. It said:

Her Majesty, Victoria, Queen of England,
commands an audience with
Mr. Phineas Taylor Barnum
and his General Tom Thumb
on the twenty-third of March,
at eight-thirty in the evening,
at Buckingham Palace.

When the door closed behind the footman, Phineas and Tom danced around the room. All of Barnum's plans had worked—the queen was curious.

The next few days were a flurry of preparations. Tom's court suit must be fitted and stitched. It was to be made of brown velvet and must have knee britches. There were to be silver buttons on the coat, silver buckles on the shoes, and a frill of lace under Tom's chin. He was also fitted with a powdered curly wig.

"American boys don't wear lace on their shirts!" Tom stormed. "They don't wear wigs either!"

"American boys don't often appear at the queen's court," Phineas replied.

There were more important things to worry about than lace under a boy's chin. Tom must learn a new dance and a long poem called *The Boy Stood on the Burning Deck.* It was all the rage back in America.

He had to learn to sing a new song, called "Blow, Bugle, Blow!" To top it off, Tom had to practice posing like a tiny Napoleon.

Phineas felt pretty sure Tom could do these acts well enough to delight any queen. But how about the child's manners? Could a six-year-old boy master a proper courtly bow? Would he learn how to leave the Queen's Royal Presence?

Barnum studied the rules for visiting the queen, and then he drilled them with Tom.

You must bow at every fourth step. Coming and going.

Never turn your back upon the queen. That meant backing slowly out of the throne room with a deep bow at every fourth step.

Never begin a conversation with a queen. Would Tom remember not to speak unless first spoken to? After all, the child had been brought up in free and easy America, and he was a famous star to boot.

"When you address the queen for the first time, say 'Your Majesty and ladies and gentlemen of the court,'" Barnum repeated time and again.

It was most unlike the showman to worry about such formalities, and there was some comfort in the fact that Queen Victoria had sent word that she wished "to see the little general in his natural state."

Still, Barnum had never before appeared in the queen of England's throne room. He himself had been born a simple Yankee boy. Now he wondered if his own manners would be polished enough for Buckingham Palace.

Tom knew that Queen Victoria had two children, and he was excited by the prospect of meeting them. He imagined that a prince would be too noble to laugh at a midget or tease him for being small. It was Tom's great hope to find a friend at the palace.

At last it was the twenty-third and the hours ticked by. Phineas pulled his snow-white gloves off and on, nervously waiting for the royal coach. When it came, pulled by four white horses, Tom was as cool as a spring morning. He twirled his tiny cane with the silver knob and looked out the windows as the coach traveled through the darkening streets of London.

They cantered through the gates of Buckingham Palace, passing the royal guards in their scarlet coats and high fur hats. Then they stopped at the palace itself.

A lord-in-waiting opened the door to the coach with a flourish. With great ceremony, P. T. Barnum and the general were announced to the queen of England.

Huge carved doors swung open. Tom gasped and shivered a bit. By now Phineas had grown calm, as he always did before appearing on stage. He put his steady hand for a moment on Tom's shoulder and said, "Easy does it, lad. Just remember your manners: they're the manners of a fine American boy."

The floor of the throne room looked like a lake of shimmering water, its marble shone so. At its end was a high throne. On the throne, not wearing a crown at all, sat a little lady dressed plainly. She looked for all the world like someone's mother, which she was. She held a small white poodle on her lap. The lords and ladies surrounding her were far more elegant!

Tom and Phineas approached Queen Victoria's throne. They had practiced for days just how to do this. Still, Phineas knew it was hard for Tom's short legs to match his own long strides. At every fourth step, the two Americans paused and bowed from the waist in the proper way.

At last they reached the throne, where they bowed low again.

The queen spoke first, as was the rule. "Sirs," she said, "you may entertain us."

It was time for Tom to recite his poem and do a bit of dancing. To begin with, he completely forgot to say the proper words. Instead, the six-year-old boy gave the greeting he always used in his act at the American Museum.

"Good evening, ladies and gentlemen," Tom said grandly. Phineas gasped and so did the lords and ladies, but the queen did not look shocked. She waved her hand for him to continue.

Phineas held his breath while Tom recited his poem, sang the bugle song, and danced the "Victoria Slide." It had been Barnum's idea to give the queen's own name to the dance.

As he knew they would, the English loved the sight of Tom posing as a miniature French Napoleon.

When the act was over, there was a polite patter of applause. Tom beamed, and Phineas found that he could breathe again. The queen looked pleased. She took Tom by the hand and led the child around the great room.

"What do you think of all these pictures, my little man?" she asked him.

"Why, I think they're first rate, ma'am," he said cheerfully. "Only I thought you had some children to show me. Where are they?"

"The little prince and princess are in bed at this hour, where you should also be," Queen Victoria told Tom. "You shall come again and meet them at tea another day."

Then it was time to leave. The queen surprised everyone by bending to kiss General Tom Thumb good-bye. No one had ever heard of such a thing. There was a murmur as the queen sat back on her throne, taking her poodle back on her lap.

This time Tom remembered his lessons in courtly manners. Still, backing his way over that shining floor was not easy. It felt like slippery ice under his feet. At every fourth step, Tom took a quick look behind him at Phineas. His tall friend's long legs stepped three times farther than his own short ones. Tom was horrified to see that Barnum would reach the door of the throne room long before he did.

The thought of being the only American left in Buckingham Palace, even for a minute, made Tom's head swim. He forgot the command, "*Never* turn your back upon a queen!" Instead, Tom backed three more steps, made his bow, then turned and *ran* as fast as his little legs would carry him, to catch up with Mr. Barnum.

He turned again to face the queen. "Step, step, step, bow—then *turn and run like mad!*" he told himself. "Step, step, step, bow —then *turn and run like mad!*"

Suddenly Tom realized that people were laughing—laughing at him—when he was being most polite and not trying to be funny at all! Just as suddenly the poodle jumped from the queen's lap. No one knows why. Perhaps the dog was jealous. Yapping loudly, it began nipping Tom's heels.

This was too much. A boy must protect himself from a nipping dog, even when that dog belongs to a queen. So Tom began hitting the creature with his cane.

"Stop him! Stop him!" someone shouted. Did that mean stop Tom Thumb or stop the dog? No one knew, but in a thrice, a lord-in-waiting swooped down on the furious pet. The poodle was taken back to Her Majesty's lap.

Tom's last glimpse of the royal court of

England caught the queen and her lords and ladies laughing merrily—at him! Tom's pride was hurt and he was angry.

Of course the newspapers of London wrote stories about that court visit. "Queen Pleased with Tiny American General!" the headlines screamed on every street corner. "Queen's Dog Jealous of Miniature Man," said another. Tom blushed to see them. For three days Phineas tried to tempt him outdoors, but Tom wouldn't go. He even gave Tom a beautiful little boat to sail on the lake in St. James's Park. At any other time, Tom would have loved sailing that boat, but now he wouldn't budge. Someone might laugh at him.

Phineas tried again to soothe Tom's feelings.

"Our visit to the queen went well, my boy. They won't forget you at the court of England. Mark my words."

He was right, as Barnum so often was. Next morning the royal coach again stopped at the Barnum door. This time the Life Guard brought a present from the queen herself to the "Little General." It was a sack of gold coins and another invitation to the palace. This time it was for high tea with the Prince of Wales, named "Bertie," and his sister, the Princess Royal, who was called "Pussy" by her family.

When he saw them, Tom was disappointed. He thought them "babies," for they were only about half his own age. They could talk of nothing but a new rocking horse and a doll that could nod its head.

To this visit Tom took his red plush sofa. He politely invited the little princess to sit beside him, which she did. He also measured himself beside the prince. Later he told Mr. Barnum, "The prince is taller than I am, but I feel as big as anybody."

Queen Victoria talked with the children while they took their tea. It was plain nursery food: bread and milk and treacle tarts. Tom had expected something much finer.

"Do you draw, my little man?" the queen asked Tom.

"Yes, I frequently draw and can do it very well," he replied.

Queen Victoria did not know that Tom and Barnum often played games with words. He was punning. Tom always "drew" crowds to see him sing and dance.

Next morning another present arrived at the Barnum house. It was a fine mahogany and silver box filled with artists' pencils and brushes. With it there was a note in the queen's own handwriting. It said, "So that some of the tiny general's art may be framed and hung on the wall for all to see."

Tom and Phineas laughed at the "drawing" joke. Secretly Tom had hoped for a pony, but he sent the queen a message, saying "I am very much obliged and will keep this present as long as I live."

"That's the spirit," Phineas declared. "It's time we rented a hall—a big one—and began showing you to all the people. They'll batter down the door to see the diminutive Tom Thumb—the American general who has charmed their queen. We've found the pot of gold at the foot of the rainbow, Tom, or I miss my guess."

Then P. T. Barnum hired a large hall where he and Tom played all their old acts and several new ones. People came in droves. They were as happy to pay their English shillings as New Yorkers had been to part with their quarters. Overnight Tom Thumb became the pet of London. Money poured in. Sometimes Mr. Stratton had to hire a special cab to take the heavy money bags to the bank.

Phineas and Tom were fast becoming rich.

The city became "Tom Thumb crazy." There were soon Tom Thumb paper dolls in toy-shop windows. A new sweet, called "Tom Thumb Sugar Plums," was sold on the street. Miniature milk jugs shaped like the little general appeared on shop shelves. Dancing masters began teaching a new step called the "Tom Thumb Polka." One day Tom saw a puppet show about himself. It was being shown to English children in Kensington Garden. Suddenly his own life seemed a fairy tale, which, in a way, it was.

It was like this everywhere they went in Europe. In France he was hailed as *"Le Petit Pouce,"* which meant "Little Thumb." He had a quick ear for language and starred in a play, *Le Petit Pouce,* which had been written expressly for him—in French. He was feted by the king, who raced toy sailboats with him on the lake in the Tuileries Palace garden. He watched bullfights in Spain from a royal perch—on the young Queen Isabella's lap.

No wonder Tom began to feel, as his pa said, "Too big for his britches."

Phineas glowed with pride. "I am the goose, my boy, and you are my golden egg!"

Tom had been showered with presents at every turn. One of the best was a surprise designed by Barnum. It was a miniature Cinderella coach, all red, white, and blue. On its doors were the American eagle and the British lion. In large letters were the words "GO AHEAD!"

Four matched Shetland ponies pulled the tiny coach through the streets and countryside. On its roof sat two seven-year-old boys, small for their age, but not midgets. One was coachman, the other footman. They wore cocked hats, curly powdered wigs, and sky-blue coats with red knee britches. Wigs on other boys especially delighted Tom, and, for a time, the boys were friendly to their midget master.

Sometimes they would travel by stagecoach, while Tom's tiny coach rode along in a van. But whenever Tom whirled along the roads in his little carriage, people dashed out of their doors to see the astonishing sight.

"Is the tiny boy a prince?" asked one man.

With his tongue in his cheek, P. T. Barnum replied. "Yes, indeed. He's Prince Charles the First, of the dukedom of Bridgeport, in the kingdom of Connecticut."

The man bowed deeply, then ran to tell his friends of the marvel, unaware that he'd just been talking to the Prince of Hokum.

By the time Barnum was known as "The Greatest Showman on Earth," Tom's coachman and footman had outgrown their uniforms. They began to look a bit ridiculous perched atop the tiny coach. Other small boys took their places. Then there were others. It did precious little good to keep hiring new small friends for Tom. They could not be kept from growing. By now the general was

eight years old, though the public thought he was fifteen. Posters had begun calling him "The Twenty-five-Inch Man!" He had grown a little, though scarcely enough to notice. Tom Thumb would be a midget all his life.

Tom and Phineas began to feel a little homesick. It was time to return to America.

from **The Helen Keller Story**
Catherine Owens Peare

One of the best-known and certainly one of the most dramatic stories of triumph over physical handicaps is the life of Helen Keller, blind and deaf, whose courage and intelligence were disclosed through the efforts of her wise and patient teacher, Anne Sullivan.

Pupil and Teacher

The baby was pretty and bright and quick. At six months she was almost talking. "Tea, tea, tea!" she said, or "wah-wah! wah-wah!" when she wanted a drink of water. By the time she was a year old she was trying to walk, a few steps and a tumble, a few steps and a tumble.

In the long, mild summers of the South, where shrubs and flowers grew luxuriantly, she learned quickly to love the out-of-doors. She reached out for dancing leaves, buried her nose in the roses, or cocked her head at the song of a bird.

"My daughter will be a lovely young lady some day," said her mother, holding the baby high. "She's a Boston Adams on my side, and her father is a Southern gentleman of distinction."

Captain Arthur Keller looked the part of a distinguished Southerner with his full mustache and goatee and straight posture. He had been an officer in the Confederate Army during the Civil War, and he was distantly related to Robert E. Lee.

"I can scarcely believe he is twenty years older than I," Kate Adams Keller thought as she handed him his jouncing, lively daughter.

"My first little girl," he said, as the child tugged at his whiskers, "has a mind of her own."

Captain Keller already had two sons by a former marriage: James who was nineteen, almost as old as his stepmother; and Simpson who was in his early teens.

The little girl with a mind of her own had been born on June 27, 1880, in the town of Tuscumbia, Alabama, in a two-room house on the Keller farmlands where her parents were spending the first few years of their married life. The rest of the Keller family lived very near by in the main house, "Ivy Green."

"What will you call her?" had been the question of family and neighbors who crowded into the little annex to see the new baby.

"She is to be named after my mother, Helen Everett," said Mrs. Keller.

"I like the name of Mildred," said Captain Keller, but his remark was lost in the gay confusion.

When the day of the baby's christening arrived, Kate Keller looked proudly at her husband as he stood before the minister holding the tiny creature in a long white dress. But when the minister asked the baby's name, Captain Keller had a lapse of memory. He could remember only that she was to be named for her grandmother.

"She is to be called Helen Adams Keller," he told the minister, and Helen Adams Keller she became.

Kate Keller sighed and resigned herself to the error. Apparently her husband had a keen enough memory to be editor of their paper, the *North Alabamian,* but not keen enough to remember his own daughter's name.

Helen thrived and grew rapidly, passed her first summer, then her second, and her mother recited the old superstition, "When a baby passes its second summer, it is safe."

"Tea, tea, tea!" the baby chattered, as she became more and more aware of the world around her. "Wah-wah! Wah-wah!"

It was during Helen's second winter, in February, that she was stricken and lay in her bed burning with fever.

"Acute congestion of the stomach and brain," was the diagnosis of the family doctor, which told them nothing at all. "I will not deceive you," he added. "I doubt very much that she will recover."

Kate Keller stayed with her baby day and night, soothed Helen's hot forehead with cool, wet cloths, whispered and hummed to her when she fretted. By some miracle the baby did recover, so far as anyone could see at the time, but the Kellers soon realized that the fever had destroyed Helen's sight and hearing.

Helen Keller became another kind of child. Since she could not hear, she could not learn to talk, and only emitted an occasional squeal or cry. Since she could not see, she became baffled by her environment, and would walk only when she could cling to her mother's long skirts. Because she was baffled, she became bad-tempered, contrary, hostile, unmanageable.

As she passed her second, third, and fourth birthdays, her disposition grew worse and worse. She wanted to communicate with the world around her and could not. She had devised a few signs of her own. She would nod for *yes* and shake her head for *no.* If she wanted bread and butter, she would act out the slicing of bread with a knife. If she wanted her mother, she stroked her cheek.

"She has intelligence," the heartbroken mother insisted. "I can see that she has intelligence."

But there were others who thought differently.

"You ought to have her put away, Kate," said one relative. "She's too odd to have around. The sight of her makes everyone unhappy."

She was certainly not a pleasant sight, even though she was a healthy, husky child, quite tall for her age. She was sullen and disheveled, often refusing to let anyone comb her hair or straighten her clothing.

"Pupil and Teacher" and "Miracle at the Pump House" from THE HELEN KELLER STORY by Catherine Owens Peare. Copyright © 1959 by Catherine Owens Peare. Reprinted by permission of Thomas Y. Crowell Company.

All the while Kate and her husband inquired in every direction for doctors and specialists, the child's temper tantrums grew more violent, and her acts of mischief more dangerous.

Kate knew in her heart that she could expect to have the child taken away from her. What happened to a child that was "taken away"? Where would she be placed? Who would endure her willfulness like her own mother?

Captain and Mrs. Keller had moved out of the annex into the main house by the time Helen was five. Surely there was plenty of room for one handicapped child! And Mr. Keller had been appointed marshal of northern Alabama, which increased their income. Surely they could afford to give Helen some kind of care.

When Helen was six Mrs. Keller had a second child, Mildred.

Helen, surrounded by darkness and silence, was used to rushing to her mother's arms and her mother's lap whenever she felt insecure or lost or aggrieved. Suddenly there was another child in Mother's lap. Helen was accustomed to Mother's time whenever she wished, and now Mother was dividing her time, even pushing Helen away when she was attending to the new creature.

One day in a fit of resentment Helen darted at Mildred's cradle and tipped it over, sending Mildred tumbling out. Maybe the new child would break, the way her dolls sometimes broke when she dashed them to the floor.

Then, while the stamping and remorseless Helen felt hands pulling her away and guiding her out of the room, the distraught mother had to listen once more to the grim advice.

"You ought to put her away, Kate. She's mentally defective."

"No, no, no! She's intelligent. She learns easily. I can tell."

Something had to be done. The situation had to be faced and solved.

In the quiet of a late evening, when Mr. and Mrs. Keller were sitting in the living room and both children were asleep, an idea suddenly did occur to Mrs. Keller. She had been reading Charles Dickens's *American Notes.*

"Listen to this!" she said suddenly to her husband. "When Charles Dickens was in Boston he visited a place called the Perkins Institution for the Blind. He says, 'The children were at their daily tasks in different rooms, except a few who were already dismissed, and were at play. . . . Good order, cleanliness, and comfort pervaded every corner of the building. The various classes, who were gathered round their teachers, answered the questions put to them with readiness and intelligence, and in a spirit of cheerful contest for precedence which pleased me very much. . . . In a portion of the building set apart for that purpose are workshops for blind persons whose education is finished, and who have acquired a trade. . . . Several people were at work here, making brushes, mattresses, and so forth; and the cheerfulness, industry, and good order discernible in every other part of the building extended to this department also. On the ringing of a bell, the pupils all repaired, without any guide or leader, to a spacious music-hall, where they took their seats . . . and listened with manifest delight to a voluntary on the organ.' "

"My dear!" her husband interrupted her. "Have you forgotten that Helen is also deaf? Bells? Music halls? Organs? She could not be reached in that way."

"I know, I know!" replied Kate Keller. "But there's more. Dickens discovered something else. Listen to this."

Mrs. Keller read on: " 'The thought occurred to me as I sat down in another room, before a girl, blind, deaf, and dumb; destitute of smell, and nearly so of taste: before a fair young creature with every human faculty, and hope, and power of goodness and affection, enclosed within her delicate frame, and but one outward sense—the sense of touch. There she was, before me; built up, as it were, in a marble cell, impervious to any ray of light or particle of sound; with her poor white hand peeping through a chink in the wall, beckoning to some good man for help, that an immortal soul might be awakened.

. . . Her face was radiant with intelligence and pleasure. Her hair, braided by her own hands, was bound about a head whose intellectual capacity and development were beautifully expressed in its graceful outline and its broad open brow; her dress, arranged by herself, was a pattern of neatness and simplicity. The work she had knitted lay beside her; her writing-book was on the desk she leaned upon. . . . She was seated in a little enclosure, made by school-desks and forms, writing her daily journal. . . . Her name is Laura Bridgman.' "

Arthur Keller had put down his own book and was looking off into space, thinking deeply as he listened.

"How did they communicate with her?" he asked.

"With a finger alphabet of some sort—entirely through her sense of touch, which is about all Laura Bridgman has. Helen is not as afflicted as Laura. Helen can taste and smell."

"I don't know," said Captain Keller. "Charles Dickens likes to dramatize things to the hilt. I think it would be wise to check up on the Perkins Institution in some other way."

A few days later a peddler came through town selling harnesses, and he knocked at the door of "Ivy Green." The minute Mrs. Keller heard his accent she asked, "Are you from New England?"

"Boston, ma'am."

"Have you ever heard of the Perkins Institution for the Blind?"

"No, ma'am, but I'll inquire about it when I return home," he promised.

Maybe he kept his promise; maybe he forgot. Anyway, the Kellers never heard from him again.

In a town as small as Tuscumbia everyone knew everyone else, and many of the neighbors worried about the deaf-blind child who was growing up half wild.

"I've heard of an eye specialist in Baltimore, a Dr. Chisholm," one of them dropped by to say. "He has cured many cases of blindness that were thought to be hopeless. Why don't you take your little girl to see him?"

Anxiously Kate Keller and the Captain took Helen on the long train trip to Baltimore, only to have Dr. Chisholm say, "I can do nothing for her. She is permanently blind."

"But what becomes of people like Helen?" Mrs. Keller asked in desperation. "She won't always have us."

"While you are this far north," said Dr. Chisholm, "why don't you stop at the national capital on the way home and see Alexander Graham Bell? He knows a great deal about the teaching of deaf children, and he is a very sympathetic and understanding man."

With fading courage they went on to Washington, scarcely speaking a word to one another on the way, so sunken were they in black despair. A first child, a lovely child with silken, wavy hair, yet not a child, not really a human being.

Kate Keller thought Dr. Bell the kindliest man she had ever met. He was tall and attractive, with black hair and beard and large eyes. Not yet forty, he had ten years earlier demonstrated his telephone at the Philadelphia Centennial.

Dr. Bell put the Kellers at their ease at once and lifted the little girl to his knee while he talked with them.

"She's obviously a bright child, a very teachable child," said Dr. Bell as Helen explored his vest buttons with her fingers.

"Yes, Dr. Bell, but how? How?" begged Mrs. Keller, and she was almost in tears.

"Have you ever heard of the Perkins Institution in Boston?" he asked.

Kate and Arthur Keller looked at each other. Yes, they had!

"My wife read about it in Dickens's *American Notes*," the Captain told Dr. Bell.

"Oh, then you know of the case of Laura Bridgman?"

They nodded.

"The man who taught Laura Bridgman, Dr. Samuel Gridley Howe, is dead, but his successor, Mr. Michael Anagnos, is doing splendid work with handicapped children. I suggest that you write to him about Helen."

Both Kellers thanked him profusely. Their

spirits had risen steadily from the moment they had begun to talk with him.

"How did you happen to become interested in this sort of thing, Dr. Bell?" asked Mrs. Keller.

"My grandfather, my father, and I have all been interested in speech, in elocution, and in teaching articulation to deaf persons."

"It must be frightful to be deaf or blind," said Mrs. Keller.

"Oh, not necessarily," replied Dr. Bell in a very matter-of-fact tone. "My wife has been deaf since she was four, when she lost her hearing as a result of scarlet fever. We are very happy."

Kate Keller could have bitten off her own tongue for having said such a careless thing, but Dr. Bell didn't seem perturbed.

"The only thing we have to fear," he went on, "is ignorance, Mrs. Keller. In olden times the deaf-blind were legally classified as idiots, because no one understood them. We are beginning to overcome our ignorance of these matters. We are beginning to learn that what the handicapped need is education at the hands of well-trained and sympathetic teachers. Beethoven lost his hearing, you will remember, but he went right on composing music. Homer, the Greek poet, was blind. John Milton wrote his greatest poetry after he had lost his sight. And Thomas Edison, who has perfected the electric light bulb and is developing the electric power plant, is quite deaf. When he and his wife go to the theater, she taps out the dialogue on his knee in Morse code. We really don't need all of our senses to live successfully."

Dr. Bell smiled at the little girl sitting on his knee, and he set his watch so that its alarm would ring and placed it in her hands. When she felt the vibration in her finger tips, she began to jounce and swing her feet happily.

"I can easily detect a great deal of intelligence in this little brown head," said Dr. Bell. "I am sure she can be educated. She is certainly bright enough to learn the finger alphabet."

The Kellers left his office filled with hope.

"Write the letter to Mr. Anagnos immediately," Mrs. Keller said as soon as they were home.

Captain Keller did just that, sending a detailed description of Helen, and a reply came from Perkins Institution very soon after. Before the summer ended, Mr. Anagnos had selected one of his own former students, twenty-year-old Anne Sullivan, to be Helen Keller's governess.

Anne Sullivan had come to Perkins as a blind child, he explained to the Kellers, and later her vision had been partially restored by surgery. She wanted to spend the winter weeks studying Dr. Howe's records on Laura Bridgman, before going to Alabama, and so they could expect her on the first of March.

"Just a few more months," thought Kate Keller. "Just a few more months, and there will be someone to take care of my little girl."

And while the robust and undisciplined Helen tyrannized the household with her pranks—locking doors and hiding keys, yanking tablecloths filled with dishes to the floor—Kate Keller fastened her hopes on Anne Sullivan and the first of March.

"James will drive you to the station to meet her," said the Captain when the day came.

Anxious and tense, Mrs. Keller sat on the front seat of the carriage beside her stepson. He allowed the reins to lie slack on the back of the motionless horse, and they both stared along the railway tracks watching for that first puff of soft-coal smoke in the distance.

"How will we know her?" Mrs. Keller wondered aloud.

"She will probably be the only passenger, Mother. It will be all right. Don't worry."

"She is coming such a long way to help us!"

James noticed the train first.

"There it is," he said and climbed out of the carriage.

The train pulled in and ground to a stop before the little wooden station house. A man in the baggage compartment tossed a sack of mail to the local agent, and the train pulled out. No passenger disembarked.

Without a word James Keller climbed back into his seat, jerked the reins, and turned the horse's head toward home. Kate Keller fumbled for a handkerchief and began to cry.

"What can you expect from a Yankee?" James snapped. "I hope she never sets foot in Alabama."

"There's another train this afternoon, and we are going to meet it!" declared Mrs. Keller firmly.

Anne Sullivan didn't appear on the first of March, nor on the second.

"We are going to meet every train until she comes!" insisted Helen's mother.

On the third of March, 1887, Kate and James sat in the carriage at the railway station once more, waiting for a late afternoon train. This time a passenger did get off, a young girl dressed in burdensome woolen clothing, looking frightened and tired, her eyes red from weeping and the irritation of the soft-coal dust.

"Miss Sullivan?"

"Yes."

James helped her into the carriage, and placed her bag and trunk in the back.

"We were afraid you weren't coming," said Mrs. Keller.

"I am sorry," said Anne Sullivan. "I had the wrong kind of ticket somehow, and I had to change trains at Philadelphia and Baltimore. Then I had to wait over a whole day at Washington for a train coming to Tuscumbia."

"Oh, that is too bad."

"It's all right, now," said Miss Sullivan. "I'm only thinking of your little girl. I want to see my pupil as soon as possible."

The carriage drew into the yard at last and Captain Keller came forward to help them down. Miss Sullivan didn't seem to be listening to the introduction. She was looking at the open doorway of the house where a young mortal stood—blank-faced and hostile —nearly seven years old.

Miss Sullivan left the Kellers and hurried forward to gather the little "phantom" into her arms.

Miracle at the Pump House

"Phantom"—Helen Keller's own name for herself as a child—stood in the doorway sensing the excitement of a new arrival. She felt the vibration of a strange footstep on the porch, then another footstep, coming closer. Strangers were often enemies. She bent her head down and charged into the newcomer, and the newcomer fell back. Again the footsteps came toward her, and the stranger tried to put arms around her. Helen drove off Miss Sullivan's embrace with kicks and punches.

She discovered that the stranger had a bag, and she grabbed the bag and darted into the house. When her mother caught up with her and tried to take the bag away she fought, because she knew her mother would give in. Mother always gave in.

But Anne Sullivan encouraged her to keep the bag and carry it up the stairs. Soon a trunk was brought into the room, and Helen flung herself against it, exploring the lid with her fingers until she found the lock. Miss Sullivan gave her the key and allowed her to unlock it and lift the lid. Helen plunged her hands down into the contents, feeling everything.

The newcomer lifted a doll out of the trunk and laid it in Helen's arms, and after that she did something very strange indeed. She held one of Helen's hands and in its palm formed curious figures with her own fingers. First she held her own thumb and middle finger together while her index finger stood upright. Then she formed a circle by joining her thumb and first finger, and finally she spread her thumb and index finger as far apart as they would go.

With a sudden wild leap Helen darted for the door, but the stranger caught hold of her and brought her back, forcing her into a chair. Helen fought and raged, but the stranger was strong. She did not give in like family and servants. Helen was startled to feel a piece of cake being placed in her hand, and she gobbled it down quickly before it could be taken away. The stranger did another trick with her fingers. On Helen's palm she formed an open circle with thumb and first finger, next closed her fist for a moment, following that by placing her thumb between her second and third fingers and curling her last two fingers under, and finally held all her finger tips together against her thumb.

That was enough! Helen tore loose and bolted out of the room and down the stairs, to Mother, to Father, to her stepbrother, to the cook, to anybody whom she could manage.

But at dinner the stranger sat next to her. Helen had her own way of eating, and no one had ever tried to stop her. She stumbled and groped her way from place to place, snatching and grabbing from other people's plates, sticking her fingers into anything at all. When she came to the visitor, her hand was slapped away. Helen reached out for the visitor's plate again. Another slap! She flung herself forward and was lifted bodily back. Now she was being forced into her own chair again, being made to sit there, and once more she was raging, fighting, kicking. She broke away and found all the other chairs empty. Her family had deserted her, left her alone with this enemy!

Again the enemy took hold of her, made her sit down, forced a spoon into her hand, made her eat from her own plate.

When the ordeal finally ended, she broke away and ran out of the dining room—to Mother, to Mother's arms. Mother's eyes were wet. Mother was crying. Mother was sorry.

Every day there were battles with the newcomer. There were battles when she had to take her bath, comb her hair, button her shoes. And always those finger tricks; even Mother and Father were doing them. Since the trick for cake usually brought her a piece of cake, Helen shrewdly began to learn others.

If battles with her new governess grew too unbearable, Helen could seek out Martha Washington, a child her own age, daughter of their Negro cook, and bully and boss her. Martha's pigtails were short because Helen had once clipped them off with a pair of scissors.

Or she could simply romp with her father's hunting dogs and forget there was such a thing in the house as a governess. She could help feed the turkey gobblers, or go hunting for the nests of the guinea hens in the tall grass. She loved to burrow her way in amongst the big flowering shrubs; completely surrounded by the prickly leaves of the mimosa she felt safe and protected.

There was real comfort in revenge. She knew about keys and locks, and she found a day when she could lock the awful intruder in her room and run away with the key. The big day of revenge came when, in one of the enemy's unguarded moments, Helen raised her fists in the air and brought them down on Miss Sullivan's face. Two teeth snapped off.

An abrupt change occurred in her life right after that.

Miss Sullivan took her by the hand and they went for a carriage drive. When the carriage stopped, they alighted and entered a different house. Helen groped her way about the room, recognizing nothing, until her companion placed one of her own dolls in her arms. She clung to the familiar thing. But as soon as Helen realized that she was alone with the stranger in a strange place, that no amount of rubbing her cheek would bring her mother, she flung the doll away in a rage. She refused to eat, refused to wash, and gave the governess a long, violent tussle when it came time to go to bed.

The governess did not seem very tall, but she was strong and stubborn, and for the first time in her life Helen began to experience defeat. She grew tired, wanted to lie down and sleep, but still she struggled against the stranger's will. She would sleep on the floor, or in the chair! But each time she was dragged back to the bed. At last Helen felt herself giving in, and, exhausted by her own efforts, and huddled close to the farthest edge of the big double bed, she fell asleep.

When Helen awoke in the morning, she flung herself out of bed prepared to give further resistance, but somehow her face was washed with less effort than the night before, and after she had dressed and eaten her breakfast she felt her companion's determined but gentle hands guiding her fingers over some soft, coarse yarn, guiding them again along a thin bone shaft with a hooked end. In a very little while Helen had grasped the idea of crocheting, and as she became interested in making a chain she forgot to hate Anne Sullivan.

Each day in the new house after that brought new skills to be learned—cards to sew, beads to string.

After about two weeks, Helen had begun to accept her routine, her table manners, her tasks, her companion. The whole world seemed to grow gentler as her own raging disposition subsided.

She cocked her head suddenly one afternoon and sniffed the air, detecting a new odor in the room, something familiar—one of her father's dogs! Helen groped about until she found the silken, long-haired setter, Belle. Of all the dogs on the farm, Belle was Helen's favorite, and she quickly lifted one of Belle's paws and began to move the dog's toes in one of the finger tricks. Miss Sullivan patted Helen's head, and the approval made her feel almost happy.

Miss Sullivan soon took her by the hand and led her out the door, across a yard, to some front steps, and instantly Helen realized where she was. She was home! She had been in the little annex near home all this time. Mother and Father had not been far away. She raced up the steps and into the house and flung herself at one adult after another. She was home! Scrambling up the stairs to the second floor, she found her own room just the same, and when she felt Miss Sullivan standing behind her she turned impulsively and pointed a finger at her and then at her own palm. Who was she?

"T-e-a-c-h-e-r," Anne Sullivan spelled into her hand.

But the finger trick was too long to be learned at once.

Every day after that Teacher and Helen were constant companions indoors and out, and gradually Helen learned to see with her fingers. Teacher showed her how to explore plants and animals without damaging them —chickens, grasshoppers, rabbits, squirrels, frogs, wildflowers, butterflies, trees. Grasshoppers had smooth, clear wings; the wings of a butterfly were powdery. The bark of a tree had a curious odor, and through its huge trunk ran a gentle humming vibration.

Hand-in-hand they wandered for miles over the countryside, sometimes as far as the Tennessee River where the water rushed and churned over the mussel shoals.

For everything she felt or did there was a finger trick: wings, petals, river boats—walking, running, standing, drinking.

One morning when she was washing her face and hands, Helen pointed to the water in the basin, and Teacher spelled into her hand: "w-a-t-e-r." At the breakfast table later Helen pointed to her mug of milk, and Teacher spelled: "m-i-l-k." But Helen became confused. "D-r-i-n-k" was milk, she insisted. Helen pointed to her milk again and Teacher spelled, "m-u-g." Was m-u-g d-r-i-n-k? In another second Helen's mind was a jumble of wiggling fingers. She was frustrated, bewildered, angry, a bird trapped in a cage and beating her wings against the bars.

Quickly Teacher placed an empty mug in her hand and led her out-of-doors to a pump that stood under a shed in the yard. Helen stood before the pump, mug in hand, as Teacher indicated, and felt the rush of cold water over her hands. Teacher took one of her hands and spelled, "w-a-t-e-r." While water rushed over one hand Helen felt the letters, w-a-t-e-r, in the other.

Suddenly Helen was transfixed, and she let her mug crash to the ground forgotten. A new, wonderful idea . . . back into her memory rushed that infant's word she had once spoken: "wah-wah." She grew excited, her pulse raced, as understanding lighted her mind. Wah-wah was w-a-t-e-r. It was a word! These finger tricks were words! There were words for everything. That was what Teacher was trying to tell her.

She felt Teacher rush to her and hug her, and Teacher was as excited as she, crying and laughing, because at last Helen understood the concept of words.

Joyfully they ran back into the house, and Helen was surrounded by an excited household. All the rest of the day she demanded words, words, words. What was this? What was that? Even the infant Mildred? What was that? "B-a-b-y." And once more Helen pointed a persistent finger at Miss Sullivan and demanded the word that would identify *her.*

"T-e-a-c-h-e-r," Anne Sullivan spelled. "T-e-a-c-h-e-r."

The last shred of hostility and hate vanished from Helen's soul as she glowed with her sudden happiness. She felt her fingers being lifted to Teacher's face to explore its expression. The corners of the mouth were drawn up and the cheeks were crinkled. Helen imitated the expression, and when she did her face was no longer blank, because Helen Keller was smiling.

When bedtime finally arrived, she put her hand willingly into Teacher's and mounted the stairs, and before climbing into bed she slipped her arms around Teacher's neck and kissed her—for the first time.

from Harriet Tubman: Conductor on the Underground Railroad
Ann Petry

Born a slave, Harriet Tubman escaped in 1849 and went to Philadelphia. She devoted her life to the dangerous mission of returning to the South repeatedly to help other slaves escape, becoming the best known "conductor" on the escape route known as the Underground Railroad.

Minta Becomes Harriet

There was panic in the quarter. The master was dead. Would the slaves be sold? Would all these families be separated and scattered about the countryside? The older slaves whispered to each other, saying: "Did he free us as he promised?"

Harriet, conscience-stricken, believing that her prayers had killed Edward Brodas, ignored the fear in the voices, the faces, of

the slaves. She said, later, of this period, "It appeared like I would give the world full of silver and gold, if I had it, to bring that poor soul back. . . . I would give *myself*; I would give everything!"

The slaves were quickly reassured. The overseer told them that the plantation was to remain intact. It had been willed to an heir who was too young to administer it. It would be managed by the young master's guardian, Dr. Anthony Thompson, a minister in Bucktown. According to the master's will, none of the slaves could be sold outside the state of Maryland.

This information ended the whispered, panicky conversations in the quarter. It did nothing to end Harriet's feeling of guilt. Her common sense told her that her prayers could not possibly have killed the master. Yet she was not quite certain. This incident of the master's death following so swiftly after her reiterated plea, *Kill him, Lord,* left her with the conviction that prayer was always answered.

She was uneasy, too. She knew that she was no longer regarded as a desirable slave. There was always the possibility that Dr. Thompson, once he heard the story of the way in which she had defied an overseer, would decide to sell her, lest she transmit to the other slaves the same spirit of rebellion.

Once again she toyed with the idea of running away. Somehow the urgency was gone. Old Rit and Ben were here on the plantation. So were her brothers and sisters. All of them had joyously accepted the announcement that nothing was to be changed.

But who could be certain? The master had promised to free Old Rit, but he hadn't. He had never been cruel to his slaves. But he hired them out to men who were cruel. He sold them whenever the need arose. He had tried to sell her when she was sick and worthless. No one could know what this temporary master, Doc Thompson, as he was known in Bucktown, would be like. He would probably continue the old master's practice of hiring out slaves.

She knew what it was like to be hired out.

One moment she had been a laughing child, running through the woods, chasing rabbits, playing with the other small children in the quarter, and the next moment she had been picked up and taken to the house of James Cook and set to work doing jobs that a child should not have been expected to do.

She would always remember Miss Susan and the whip that she kept on the little shelf behind her bed, always remember how desperately tired she got because she never had enough sleep. She could see herself a child, rocking a baby in a cradle, rock, rock, rock; could see herself sick with the measles, walking the length of Cook's trap line, in winter, shivering, eyes watering. She remembered how she had hated the scaly tails of the muskrats, the wild smell of them, and yet did not want to find them caught fast in the traps.

Long afterward, she said of this period in her life, "They [the slaveholders] don't know any better, it's the way they were brought up. 'Make the little slaves mind you, or flog them,' was what they said to their children, and they were brought up with the whip in their hands. Now that wasn't the way on all plantations; there were good masters and mistresses, as I've heard tell, but I didn't happen to come across any of them."

After the terrible wound in her head had healed, she became aware of the admiration of the other slaves. Even the old ones listened to her opinions, deferred to her. Though Old Rit continued to deplore the audacity, the boldness in Harriet that made her defy an overseer, she stopped calling her Minta or Minty. So did the others.

She was Harriet now to all of them. It was as though the pet names, the diminutives, were no longer suitable for a teen-aged girl who bore on her forehead a great scar, ineradicable evidence of the kind of courage rarely displayed by a grownup.

Though the wound in her head had healed, she was subject to periods of troubled sleep, she had strange dreams which recurred night after night. These dreams had a three-dimensional quality in which people and places were seen more clearly, more sharply than in her waking moments. At night, in the quarter, she described these dreams or visions, as she called them, to the other slaves. Even in the telling, something of the reality of the dream came through to the others, so that they were awed by her.

As soon as she was able to work again, Doc Thompson hired out Harriet and her father, Ben, to John Stewart, a builder. At first Harriet worked in his house, doing the housework that she despised.

There was no question but what she was well enough to work, though she sometimes had severe headaches, especially if she got very tired. Then the ache was like a pounding inside her skull. The headaches did not bother her as much as the sudden onset of that deep trancelike sleep which still occurred without warning.

Whenever she thought of running away, not so often now, the knowledge of this awful weakness stopped her. She knew that she might be found asleep by the side of the road, and brought back immediately. The deep scar on her forehead made her easily recognized.

She was afraid to leave and yet she could not bear the life she led, inside all day, sweeping and dusting, making beds, washing clothes. The house was so near the woods that she could hear the ring of the axes, hear the crash as a great tree came down.

After three months of housework, she asked Stewart, her temporary master, if she could work in the woods with the men. "I always did field work," she explained. "So I can swing a ax just like a man."

Stewart knew she was strong. He had seen her bring in big logs for the fireplaces, had once stopped to watch in unconcealed amazement as she carried a tremendous iron caldron filled with hot water from the cookhouse to a nearby stream. He did not have to pay her old master, Doc Thompson, very much for her hire because she was a woman. If she could do a man's work, felling trees, splitting logs, he'd be getting a bargain.

"We can try it," he said. "If it don't work out, why you'll have to go back to cooking and cleaning."

But it did work out. Harriet was delighted.

She knew that Stewart was pleased with the new arrangement, for shortly afterward he allowed her to "hire her time." This was a privilege which was extended to trustworthy slaves who were good workers. It meant that Harriet could find jobs for herself, and would pay Stewart fifty or sixty dollars a year. Whatever she earned over and beyond this sum, she was allowed to keep.

She sought and found jobs that would keep her out of doors. She hauled logs, plowed fields, drove an oxcart. She became a familiar figure in the fields—a slender, muscular young woman, with her skirts looped up around her waist and a vivid bandanna tied on her head. Dressed in this fashion, she did the rough hard work of a prime field hand.

During this period, she often worked with Ben, her father. John Stewart placed Ben in charge of the slaves who cut the timber which was to be sent by boat to the Baltimore shipyard. For weeks at a time Harriet swung a broadax in the woods as part of Ben's crew, cutting half a cord of wood a day just like a man.

She learned most of the woods lore that she knew from Ben: the names of birds, which berries were good to eat and which were poisonous, where to look for water lilies, how to identify the hemlocks and the plant that he called cranebill, wild geranium or crane's bill. For these things—bark of hemlock, root of water lily, leaf of crane's bill—had medicinal value. The slaves used them to cure all sorts of ailments, fevers and intestinal disorders.

Harriet was an apt pupil. Ben said that her eyes were sharper than his. She said, "No. It's not just my eyes. It's my hands, too." She thought her hands seemed to locate the root or herb she was seeking before she actually saw it.

Ben taught her how to pick a path through the woods, even through the underbrush, without making a sound. He said, "Any old body can go through a woods crashing and mashing things down like a cow. That's easy. You practice doing it the hard way—move so quiet even a bird on a nest don't hear you and fly up."

Neither of them ever discussed the reasons why it was desirable to be able to go through the woods soundlessly. Discussion wasn't necessary. Deep inside herself Harriet knew what Ben was doing. He was, in his own fashion, training her for the day when she might become a runaway, and a successful flight would depend on the stealth of her movements through the woods that bordered all the roads.

When she was nineteen, Ben rewarded her efforts with praise. She had followed him through the woods and though he moved quietly himself, he had not heard her, although she was close behind him. When they reached a clearing, she came up in back of him and touched him lightly on the arm. He jumped, startled, and then laughed when he saw Harriet standing beside him.

He said, "Hat, you walk like a Injun. Not even a leaf make a rustle, not even a twig crack back on itself when you come through there."

She was tremendously pleased by this. She thought if only her master, John Stewart, would stop having her exhibit her strength for the entertainment of his guests, she would be content to spend the rest of her life on this plantation hiring herself out. The work was hard, yes, but now that she was grown, she could do the most back-breaking jobs without effort. Besides the workday was lightened and shortened by moments of fun, by words of praise like those of Ben's, by the endless wonder and beauty of the woods.

Unfortunately, Stewart had long since discovered that she was as strong as any of the men on the plantation. She could lift barrels of produce, could shoulder heavy timbers. Whenever he had visitors, he gave orders that she was to be hitched to a boat loaded with stone and was to drag it behind her as she walked along the edge of the river. She could hear cries of astonishment, laughter, applause from the men who stood on the bank watching. This audience of fashionably dressed planters made her feel that she was little better than a trained animal, brought out for their amusement.

Though Stewart continued to have her

perform for his friends, she remained with him, hiring her time, for six years.

> In Boston, on October 21, 1835, William Lloyd Garrison, publisher of *The Liberator,* was rescued from a mob of some two thousand well-dressed, eminently respectable men who were intent on hanging him. The mayor and the constables got Garrison away from the crowd and finally lodged him in the Leverett Street Jail for safety.
>
> That night, thin, bespectacled William Lloyd Garrison wrote on the wall of his cell: "William Lloyd Garrison was put into this cell on Monday afternoon, October 21, 1835, to save him from the violence of a respectable and influential mob, who sought to destroy him for preaching the abominable and dangerous doctrine that all men are created equal, and that all oppression is odious in the sight of God."

The Patchwork Quilt

In 1843, Harriet Ross began to make a patchwork quilt. She had trouble finding the brilliantly colored pieces of cotton cloth she needed. Sewing the quilt together was even harder.

The needle kept slipping through her fingers. Sometimes she did not know that she had lost it, until she tried to take a stitch and found that she held only a long piece of thread. Time and again she hunted for the needle on the dirt floor of the cabin. It was difficult to find it there, difficult for fingers accustomed to grasping the handle of a broadax to pick up an object as tiny as a needle.

It seemed as though she would never be able to master the art of sewing, to make the needle go through the material in the places where she wanted it to go. It was the hardest task she had ever undertaken.

Yet as the quilt pattern developed, she thought it was as beautiful as the wild flowers that grew in the woods and along the edge of the roads. The yellow was like the Jerusalem flower, and the purple suggested motherwort, and the white pieces were like water lily, and the varying shades of green represented the leaves of all the plants, and the eternal green of the pine trees.

For this was no ordinary quilt. It would be trousseau, and the entire contents of what under different circumstances would have been a hope chest. Harriet had fallen in love. She was going to marry a young man named John Tubman. He was a tall, well-built fellow, with a ready laugh, and a clear lilting whistle.

When she worked on the quilt, head bent, awkward fingers guiding the needle carefully through the material, she experienced a strange, tender feeling that was new to her. The quilt became a symbol of the life that she would share with John. She thought about him while she sewed, how tall he was, how sweet the sound of his whistling. She was so short she had to look up to him. She looked up to him for another reason, too. He was free. He had always been free. Yet he wanted to marry her and she was a slave. So she felt humble, too.

They were married in 1844. Harriet went to live in his cabin, taking with her her one beautiful possession, the patchwork quilt.

The knowledge that she was still a slave bothered her more and more. If she were sold, she would be separated from John. She truly loved him. She had asked him how he came to be free. He said it was because his mother and father had been freed by their master, at the time of the master's death.

This made Harriet wonder about her own family, especially about Old Rit, who was forever talking about the promises of freedom that had been made to her. She paid five dollars to a lawyer to look up the wills of the various masters to whom Old Rit had belonged. It had taken her years to save five dollars; she had hoarded pennies to accumulate such a sum. But it seemed to her the information she received was well worth the cost. She found that Old Rit had originally been willed to a young woman named Mary Patterson, with the provision that she was to be freed when she was forty-five. Mary Patterson died shortly afterward, still unmarried. According to the lawyer, Old Rit should have been freed long ago. Instead she remained a slave, and so, of course, her children were slaves. Old Rit had been sold and resold many times.

After this, Harriet grew more and more discontented. She felt that she was a slave only because Old Rit had been tricked and deceived, years ago.

Times were hard the year that Harriet married John Tubman. And the next year, too. In the quarter she heard a great deal of talk about the reasons for this. One of the house servants said the trouble was due to the difference in the price of cotton. Dr. Thompson had said so. He said cotton brought thirteen cents a pound in 1837, and when it was high, the slave traders paid as much as a thousand dollars for prime field hands. Then cotton started going down, down, down, until now in 1845 it was bringing only five cents a pound, and the slave traders gave less than five hundred dollars for young strong slaves.

Harriet decided that from the dilapidated look of the plantation—fields lying fallow, the Big House in need of repair—Doc Thompson would soon be selling slaves again. He wouldn't be able to get much for them in Maryland, so in spite of the old master's will, he would sell them South.

She told John Tubman this. Every time she said it, she spoke of going North, of running away, following the North Star.

He warned her against such foolishness. What would she find there that she didn't have here? She hired her time, and so she always had a little money of her own. They had a cabin to themselves. Maryland was a good place to live. It never got too cold. There were all the coves and creeks where one could fish and set traps.

He said that if she went North, she'd freeze to death. Besides, what happened to the ones who went there? None of them came back to tell what it was like. Why was that? Because they couldn't. They died there. They must have. If they were still alive, they would have returned to show the way to some of the rest of the slaves. None returned. None sent back word. What would she have there that she didn't have here?

Her reply was always the same: "I'd be free."

She told him about the dreams she had, how night after night, she dreamed that men on horseback came riding into the quarter, and then she heard the shrieks and screams of women and children, as they were put into the chain gang, that the screaming of the women made her wake up. She would lie there in the dark of the cabin, sweating, feeling cold because the fire was out, and the chill from the dirt floor seemed to have reached her very bones, and, though awake, she could still hear the echo of screams.

When she went back to sleep she would dream again. This time she was flying. She flew over cotton fields and cornfields, and the corn was ripe, the tassels waving all golden brown in the wind, and then she flew over Cambridge and the Choptank River, and she could see the gleam of the water, like a mirror, far down, under her, and then she came to a mountain and flew over that. At last she reached a barrier, sometimes it was a fence, sometimes a river, and she couldn't fly over it.

She said, "It appeared like I wouldn't have the strength, and just as I was sinking down, there would be ladies all dressed in white over there, and they would put out their arms and pull me across—"

John Tubman disliked these dreams. When she retold them, her husky voice pitched low, she made them sound as though they had really happened. He thought this showed how restless and impatient she had become. He laughed at her, finally. He said that she must be related to Old Cudjo, who was so slow-witted he never laughed at a funny story until a half hour after it was told. Because only a slow-witted person would have the same dream all the time.

In spite of his derision, she kept telling him about her dreams. She said that on clear nights the North Star seemed to beckon to her. She was sure she could follow that star. They could go North together. Then she would be free too. Nothing could part them then.

He decided he would put an end to this talk of escape, of the North, and freedom. He asked what she would do when the sky was dark. Then how would she know which way was North? She couldn't read the signs along the road. She wouldn't know which way to go. He would not go with her. He was perfectly satisfied where he was. She would be alone, in the dark, in the silence of the deep woods. What would she eat? Where would she get food?

She started to say: in the woods. She could live a long time on the edible berries and fruit that she had long ago learned to recognize. And yet—she had seen many a half-starved runaway brought back in chains, not enough flesh left on him to provide a decent meal for a buzzard. Perhaps she, too, would starve. She remembered the time she ran away from Miss Susan's and crawled into a pigpen, remembered the squealing and grunting of the pigs, the slops thrown into the trough, and fighting with the pigs, pushing them away, to get at the trough. After four days she had been indistinguishable from the pigs, filthy, foul-smelling—and starving. So she had gone back to Miss Susan. The memory of this experience made her avoid John's eyes, not answer him.

Perhaps her silence made him angry. He may have interpreted it as evidence of her stubbornness, her willfulness, her utter disregard of all his warnings, and so made a threat which would put a stop to this crazy talk about freedom.

He shouted at her, "You take off and I'll tell the Master. I'll tell the Master right quick."

She stared at him, shocked, thinking, he couldn't, he wouldn't. If he told the master that she was missing, she would be caught before she got off the plantation. John knew what happened to runaways who were caught and brought back. Surely he would not betray his own wife.

And yet—she knew that there were slaves who had betrayed other slaves when they tried to escape. Sometimes they told because they were afraid of the master, it was always hard on the ones who were left behind.

Sometimes the house servants were the betrayers, they were closest to the masters, known to be tattletales, certain to be rewarded because of their talebearing.

But John Tubman was free. And free Negroes helped the runaways. It was one of the reasons the masters disliked and distrusted them. Surely John would not deny freedom to her, when he had it himself. Perhaps he was afraid he would be held responsible for her escape, afraid the master would think John had incited her to run away. Besides, he was satisfied here, he had said so, and men disliked change, or so Old Rit had told her, saying also that women thrived on it.

Then she thought, frowning, but if a man really loved a woman, wouldn't he be willing to take risks to help her to safety? She shook her head. He must have been joking, or speaking through a sudden uncontrollable anger.

"You don't mean that," she said slowly. But he did mean it. She could tell by the way he looked at her.

For the tall young man with the gay laugh, and the merry whistle, had been replaced by a hostile stranger, who glared at her as he said, "You just start and see."

She knew that no matter what words she might hear during the rest of her life, she would never again hear anything said that hurt like this. It was as though he had deliberately tried to kill all the trust and the love and the deep devotion she had for him.

That night as she lay beside him on the floor of the cabin, she felt that he was watching her, waiting to see if this was the night when she would try to leave.

From that night on, she was afraid of him.

In the spring of the same year, Thomas Garrett, Quaker, who since 1822 had been offering food and shelter to runaway slaves in Wilmington, Delaware, was tried and found guilty of breaking the law covering fugitive slaves. Found guilty with him was John Hunn, a stationmaster of the Underground Railroad in Middletown, Delaware, and a much younger man.

The trial was held in the May Term of the

United States Court, at New Castle, before Chief Justice Taney and Judge Hall.

The fines and damages that Garrett had to pay took every dollar of his property. His household effects and all his belongings were sold at public auction. The sheriff who conducted the sale turned to Garrett and said, "Thomas, I hope you'll never be caught at this again."

Garrett, who was then sixty years old, answered: "Friend, I haven't a dollar in the world, but if thee knows a fugitive anywhere on the face of the earth who needs a breakfast, send him to me."

During the operation of the Underground Railroad, twenty-five hundred slaves passed through Garrett's "station" in Wilmington.

from Dr. Elizabeth: A Biography of the First Woman Doctor
Patricia Clapp

A biography of Elizabeth Blackwell, the first woman doctor, is written in the first person, which gives an immediacy to the text and permits readers to see the feelings aroused by her struggles to enter a field hitherto reserved for men.

The Decision

I have written a number of letters to doctors known by my family and me in various parts of the country, and there have been two points on which all my correspondents have agreed. First, that the entire prospect of a woman becoming a doctor is unsuitable, unfeminine, distasteful, and impossible. Second, that if I were foolhardy enough to pursue this course I would soon discover that no American school would accept me as a student. Oh dear, that is *not* the way to discourage Elizabeth Blackwell! The more I am told "no," the more I think "yes."

But if I cannot study in the United States, then where can I? I have asked this question of several physicians, and the guarded answer has come back—well, possibly Paris. I had an opportunity to talk with a well-known Cincinnati physician, Dr. Muzzey, and broached the possibility to him, knowing he had spent some time working in French hospitals. I thought his sparse hair would stand up straight on his shocked head!

"Miss Blackwell! You surely are not serious!"

"But I am," I assured him. "Why should I not be?"

"The very thought of a woman going into the Parisian schools horrifies me! It's impossible!"

"But *why?*" I persisted.

"It would be offensive to both of us for me to go into detail," he said firmly. "I will simply say that the method of instruction is such that no American or English lady could stay there for six weeks!"

And I could get no more information out of him.

I talk to everyone who will listen! One of my closest friends is a gay and happy and clever woman named Harriet Beecher, who has married a very dull and stolid man named Stowe, and what they find in common I can't imagine, though there must be something for they have quite a number of children. When I mentioned my idea to Harriet she was stunned.

"Oh, Elizabeth! How could you ever do it? It's—it's so impracticable!"

"So I am constantly being told," I said. "But if I *could*, Harriet. What then?"

"If you could, I think it would be the very greatest boon to women!"

"I'm not sure what you mean."

"I mean women who are ill—or even just having babies, as I do—would feel so much more at ease with a female physician! And women who want to—to kick over the tight traces that tie them down would have an example to follow! But—how could you ever do it, Elizabeth?"

"I don't know," I confessed, "but I think I am going to try."

We have another family friend, an educated, intelligent man, James Perkins. When I mentioned the idea to him he neither gasped nor blushed, but simply asked me several succinct questions which I answered. When I had done, he said, with a very bright face, "I do wish you would take the matter up, if you have the courage—and you have courage, I know!"

At that moment I felt I could conquer the world! How far a little encouragement can go! He gave me a copy of Jackson's Memoirs which deals with medical training, especially in French schools. I am eager to read it!

A few days ago I did read it. What am I getting myself into? The immensity of the field before me is unbelievable! But someday some woman is going to do it. Why should I not be the one? I am gradually coming up to the resolution.

Enough of shilly-shallying! I have made the decision (Heaven help me!) and my family is in accord. I Will Become A Doctor!

My first necessity is money for my studies, though where and when those will take place I have no idea. For this reason I have accepted the position of music teacher in a school in Asheville, North Carolina. Teaching again! Ugh! But it is the only way I know to raise enough money to carry on this plan I have committed myself to follow. My main reason for accepting this particular offer was that the Reverend John Dickson, who is the principal of the school, was formerly a doctor and will start me on a medical education.

Mother would not accept the idea of her undersized chick making the journey to Asheville alone, so Samuel and Henry are to drive me there. I must admit I am relieved! I hear the roads through Kentucky are little traveled, and there are rivers to ford and mountains to cross—rather like the course I have set myself!—and it will take a good eleven days to make the trip. Henry is twenty now, and Samuel a year older, and they are such good company I look forward to this interlude with them.

Everyone in the family has been gathering books and other small comforts for me to take, and the carriage has been packed and repacked. Tomorrow, June 16, 1845, we will leave! I have never been so far from home before, and now, even before we start, I can feel the throat-tightening pangs of homesickness. But I feel something more, too. A deep, strong, inevitable force that leads me on, a purpose I must accomplish.

May God go with me.

The Preparation

I have arrived. There were times, as Sam and Henry and I jolted our way over the Alleghenies, or forded a frighteningly rapid river, when I doubted we would ever see the end of the journey. Yet what fun it was! We sang, and talked, and picnicked by the roadside (where there were roads), and I feel I know my two oldest brothers better than ever before. As we came down from the last stretch of mountain onto the beautiful plateau where Asheville lies, I wished devoutly that the shared journey could go on, that Samuel and Henry would not have to leave me here —a forlorn little music teacher in a strange town, dedicated to a most dubious course.

I was very kindly welcomed by Reverend Dickson and his wife, and shown to my room, and for a while all was easy talk and hospitality. But then, that evening, no matter how I tried to hold it back, the moment came when I had to say good-bye to Sam and Henry, who were to start back at first light the next morning. Standing outside in the tranquil summer night I could find nothing to say that did not make the tears start in my voice, and at last I just kissed each of them and felt them hug me tightly for a minute, before I ran in the house and upstairs to my room.

I dropped to my knees before the open window. The surrounding mountains were dimly visible in the starlight, blurred by my tears, seeming to shut me away from all I knew or cared for, and suddenly I was terrified of what I was undertaking. I held tight to the windowsill, closing my eyes in an agony of despair, and whispering over and over, "Oh God, help me, support me! Lord Jesus, guide and enlighten me!" I must have crouched there for several minutes, praying, weeping, holding my loneliness and doubts deep within myself, yet reaching out for help, and then, suddenly, I felt as though my whole soul were flooded with brilliance! I felt a—*something*—around me, an influence, a presence, that was so gentle, so joyful, yet so powerful that all doubt disappeared! I can't explain this. There was nothing to be seen— I opened my eyes, but the room, the dark night, the dim mountains had not changed. Only I had changed, for I knew then, quite positively, that however insignificant my individual effort might be, it was in a right direction, and there was no more need to hesitate.

It was a most marvelous occurrence! I went to bed and to sleep, and in the days that have passed since then, this new assurance has never left me.

Now that I dare to speak openly of my intention of becoming a doctor, it has resulted in benefits as well as teasing. Reverend Dickson has opened his medical library to me, and I read until my eyes are red with weariness, trying to remember the strange new terms and words—like a new language! —studying the charts and diagrams, and listening as this kind man patiently explains some of the myriad things I don't understand. I suppose it is an amusing contrast. During the day Miss Blackwell thumps away on the piano, guiding awkward young hands, asking for the same notes to be given over and over. During the evening Medical Student Blackwell mumbles her way through the muscular system, repeating the terminology over and over. I do not know which is more likely, that my students will learn to play well, or that I shall learn to be a doctor!

Just yesterday I came close to discarding the whole idea. Another young woman teacher, who knows of my "unbelievable" ambition, brought me a large beetle, a cockchafer, thoroughly dead from having been smothered between her pocket handkerchiefs, and offered it to me as a first subject for dissection. Trying to look very businesslike, I placed the creature in a small shell and

held it with a hairpin, while I poised my mother-of-pearl-handled penknife for the incision. It was impossible! The idea of penetrating that small carcass was so repugnant to me that I could feel my hair growing damp with perspiration, and see my hand shake. My friend stood gleefully waiting, and I was on the verge of giving up when I suddenly knew quite simply that, like it or not, I had to do it. So I did. The knife point went in gently but firmly, and all it revealed was a little yellowish dust. After a moment, faint with relief, I felt larger than the mountains that surround me here! One small "beetle battle" had been won, and by me.

But what in heaven's name will I do when it is something more than a cockchafer into which I must thrust my knife?

Life here in Asheville is quite pleasant, and people are very friendly. Last week I attended a party with Reverend and Mrs. Dickson—rather reluctantly, I must admit, since parties have never been my particular forte—and to my amazement I found myself to be quite a social success! This was so unusual that it must have made me a little giddy, for I found myself chattering away vivaciously over the ice cream and whips and cakes and jellies; playing the piano with the top up and the bass pedal down; and even performing some tricks of logic, the sort of thing we do often at home, such as transporting the cannibals and missionaries across the stream.

There was one young gentleman from New York, attractive enough, but full of the silly, twaddling conversation that has always irritated me. He seemed quite beguiled by all my goings on, and insisted on escorting me home.

"You come from Cincinnati?" he asked, as we walked through the soft southern night. I admitted I did. "If I had only known!" he said. "I should have made the trip from New York to Cincinnati, just to accompany you here!"

He was tall and I am short and fortunately my bonnet brim hid the smile on my face. I could think of nothing duller than having him for a traveling companion!

"And you are teaching piano?" he went on.

"For a while," I said, and then could not resist the temptation to add, "I am going to become a doctor."

He stopped dead on the path. "A *doctor?*" he repeated, and his voice sounded a trifle weak. "What—er—what sort of doctor?"

"A physician," I announced calmly. "A surgeon, I expect."

He started walking again, but he said nothing for several minutes. At last he murmured, "Well! That's—er—that's very unusual, isn't it? I don't recall ever having known a—a lady doctor before."

"That's not surprising," I said with satisfaction. "There has never been one."

from Sadat, The Man Who Changed Mid-East History
George Sullivan

In a biography that gives readers a great deal of information about contemporary Egypt, Sullivan traces the life of the peasant boy who became president of his country, a leader in world politics, and a recipient of the Nobel Peace Prize.

The childhood of the Egyptian *fellahin* was Anwar el-Sadat's childhood. He was born on December 25, 1918, in Mit Abul-Kum, a small village in the Nile Delta about sixty miles from Cairo. He was one of thirteen children. Anwar's father so much admired Kemal Atatürk, the cofounder of modern Turkey, that he named his sons after Turkish officers. Anwar's mother, from the Sudan, could neither read nor write.

When Anwar was still very young, his father, a military hospital clerk, was sent to the Sudan. With his father away, Anwar's grandmother became the head of the family. Although his grandmother was illiterate, she was one of the most respected members of the village. She could solve personal and family problems with her wisdom. She could cure the sick with herbal medicines based on ancient Arab recipes. When she passed through the streets of the village, with young Anwar trailing after her, barefooted, wearing his long white Arab dress over a calico shirt, men would rise as she approached and greet her warmly.

"How I loved that woman," Sadat has said of her.

Egypt was controlled by the British at this time. Although the British recognized Egypt as an independent state beginning in 1922 and Sultan Ahmed Fuad reigned as king, British troops remained in the country. There was constant strife between British soldiers and Egyptian people. Young Anwar was well aware that his were troublesome times. At bedtime as he and his brothers lay stretched out on top of the family's huge mud-brick oven, along with their rabbits, their mother or grandmother would tell them stories of Egyptian patriots who had been imprisoned, beaten, or hanged by the British.

The tale that affected young Anwar the most told of Zahran, the hero of Denshway, a village only three miles away from Mit Abul-Kum. One day British soldiers were shooting pigeons in Denshway when a stray bullet set fire to a silo filled with wheat. When local farmers gathered to try to put out the blaze, a British soldier fired at them. The soldier ran away. The farmers ran after him. In the scuffle that followed, the soldier was killed.

The British wasted no time in seeking to avenge the soldier's death. Many villagers were arrested and promptly brought to trial. But even before the trials were completed and sentences handed down, the British started erecting platforms for hangings. A number of farmers were hanged. Other farmers were whipped.

Zahran was the hero of the tale. He was the first of the villagers to be hanged. The story told of Zahran's courage in battle, his pride, and how he walked with his head held high to the scaffold.

Young Anwar listened to the ballad night after night. His imagination played with the image. He often saw Zahran and lived his heroism. "I wished I was Zahran," Sadat has said.

Anwar was not so young that he did not realize that there was something wrong. How was it that the people of Denshway could be killed and beaten?

Anwar's grandfather could read and write, "a rare accomplishment," as Sadat himself has said. He wanted his son to be an educated man, and thus Sadat's father was sent to school. Since the British were occupying Egypt at the time, students were taught in English.

Anwar's father was the first of the villagers to complete grade school and receive a General Certificate of Primary Education. By so doing, he achieved high status in the village. Throughout his life, Mr. Sadat was known as "the *effendi*," a title of respect reserved for the well educated or members of the aristocracy. Anwar's grandmother was known as "the *effendi*'s mother."

Anwar's grandmother wanted him to receive an education as his father had. She enrolled young Anwar in a religious training school in the village, where he was taught to read and write. He also learned the Koran, memorizing it from front to back. The Koran is the sacred text of Islam, the foundation of Muslim religion, law, culture, and politics.

Anwar and the other students would sit on the classroom floor, each holding a notebook and writing with a reed pen, their only tools of learning. Anwar's long Arab dress had a big pocket. In the morning as he was leaving home for school, he would fill the pocket with bread crusts and pieces of dry cheese. He would munch on them during lessons or between classes.

Sheikh Abdul-Hamid was Anwar's teacher at the school. He helped to instill in Anwar a love of learning and the spirit of the Muslim faith.

When his Koranic schooling was completed, his grandmother enrolled Anwar in a Coptic school in Toukh, about a half a mile from the village where he lived. The Copts are descendants of the ancient Egyptians who were converted to Christianity in the A.D. 100s and 200s. Today slightly more than one million Egyptians still belong to the Coptic church. Sadat did not attend the Coptic school for a very long period. About all he remembers of the school is that he and his fellow students both loved and feared their teacher.

But school occupied only a part of young Anwar's time. At sunrise, before the broiling heat of the day, he and scores of boys and men would head out into the fields with their oxen, water buffaloes, and other beasts of burden. There were seeds to be sown, fields to be irrigated, and wheat, cotton, and dates to be harvested. Anwar would be assigned to take the cattle to drink from the canal. He would help in picking cotton or operate the ox-driven thrashing machine.

None of this was ever drudgery for young Anwar. Each family helped the others cultivate the land. In the winter the special canal that served Sadat's village was filled to overflowing, but only for about two weeks. During that period, all the land in the village had to be irrigated. The men of the village had to work quickly. They would toil on one person's land for an entire day, and the next day they would move on to another's.

The water was lifted from one level to another by means of the threads of an Archimedes' screw, or *tunbar,* which consisted of a spiral passage resting within an inclined tube. When the screw was turned, the water would be raised from the tube bottom to the top. The villagers used any *tunbar* that happened to be available. It didn't matter to whom it belonged. The main thing was to be sure that the entire village was irrigated by the end of the two-week period.

Such sharing affected almost every aspect of village life. Seldom did any one family have enough farm animals to plow and cultivate their fields. No matter. A buffalo would be borrowed. Or a plow. Or either would be cheerfully lent to a neighbor.

One day when Anwar was still attending the Coptic school, his father suddenly announced that the family was moving to

Cairo. Thus the Sadats were made to endure the same anxieties that *fellahin* of the present day suffer when they exchange their placid village lives for the harshness of the city. Sadat himself did not take easily to his new life. In the village people depended on one another, indeed, belonged to one another. There was a spirit of mutual love. But in the city people were concerned with their wealth, power, and possessions.

Anwar's father chose a private school for him to attend. The family had barely enough money for food, and the fact that the school was not an expensive one was one of the chief reasons it was selected.

The new school was not far from Anwar's home, so he walked to it and back every day. In so doing, he passed Al-Qubbah, one of the royal palaces of King Fuad, the reigning monarch at the time. Sometimes Anwar and his friends would pluck a few apricots from the palace orchard. They would do so quickly and silently, their hearts pounding, for even to touch anything belonging to the king could spell death. Of course, Sadat did not know, nor did anyone else, that one day he would cross the threshold of the palace and sit on the very chair occupied by King Fuad and later by his successor, King Farouk.

When Anwar was twelve years old, he received his General Certificate of Primary Education, just as his father had. He and his brother Tal'at, the oldest of the Sadat boys, then went on to the Fuad I Secondary School.

By the standards of the Sadat family, it was a very expensive school to attend. Anwar's first tuition payment was £16 (about $38), a sum equal to his father's salary for an entire month. But Mr. Sadat gave his son the money. Anwar took it to school and made the payment.

Tal'at was given the same amount. But Tal'at took the money, ran away, spent it all, and then returned home to announce that he didn't care to continue his education.

Sadat has said that this incident might be taken as evidence of the workings of destiny. Sadat's father, because of his small income,

would never have been able to keep both sons in school. And when the choice came as to which son could continue, Tal'at, because he was the eldest, would surely have been picked.

At secondary school Anwar was constantly reminded that he was a member of the Egyptian lower class. Some of his fellow students, the sons of government officials, came to school by car and dressed stylishly. At the school canteen they bought candies and chocolate. All Anwar could afford was a daily cup of milky tea.

Yet Anwar had no bitterness toward his wealthier classmates. He never wished to possess what they had. Instead he felt proud of the house and cattle the Sadats had owned and the fact that he belonged to the land.

Sadat had several heroes at this time, mostly individuals who were seeking to liberate their homelands. Mohandas K. (Mahatma) Gandhi was one. Several times the leader of the Indian National Congress, Gandhi was seeking to throw off the yoke of British rule and obtain independence for his country by means of nonviolent resistance. More than once he had been able to exact political concessions from the British by threatening "fasts unto death."

In 1932, when Sadat was fourteen, Gandhi passed through Egypt on his way to England. Articles about him and his struggle to oust the British from his country filled the Egyptian newspapers. Sadat fell in love with Gandhi and his image, and began to imitate him. He retreated to the roof of the Sadat home in Cairo. In imitation of Gandhi's practice of self-denial, Anwar refused all food and would not speak to anyone. Anwar's father finally persuaded him to give up the charade. It was winter and growing relatively cold. What benefit would it be to Egypt and to himself to get pneumonia, his father argued.

Kemal Atatürk, leader of the young Turk revolution in 1908, was another of Sadat's heroes. There was a picture of Atatürk in the Sadat home in Cairo, and Anwar's father described him as "a great man." Anwar's opinion of the Turkish leader was the same.

Later, when Anwar studied the Turkish revolution and the role Atatürk played in it, he would be deeply influenced by H. C. Armstrong's book, *The Grey Wolf,* which delved deeply into the personality of the Turkish leader.

Mit Abul-Kum, the village where Sadat grew up, is changing. The primitive huts are being replaced by stone houses. The construction is being financed by royalties from Sadat's autobiography. He has erected a two-story villa at the spot where the Sadat family lived until he was six.

Sadat cherishes his peasant beginnings. The love of prayer, the willingness to endure hardship, a closeness to the earth, a native shrewdness—all of these facets of Sadat's character are rooted in Mit Abul-Kum. He returns there often to pray at the local mosque and mingle with the tradespeople.

Mit Abul-Kum gave Sadat his sense of being, of belonging. In his book he puts it this way: ". . . wherever I go, wherever I happen to be, I shall always know where I really am. I can never lose my way because I know I have living roots there, deep down in the soil of the village, in that land out of which I grew, like the trees and the plants."

His grandmother holds a special place in Sadat's memories of his early years. When I was preparing this book, I wrote to Sadat and asked him to cite the one person who most influenced his life. ". . . my grandmother, a simple countrywoman" was the person he cited.

In his letter to me, Sadat spoke of the enormous influence wrought by the legends and stories his grandmother narrated. The story of Zahran, Sadat said, became "deeply rooted in my heart."

While what was expressly stated in the legends was important, of even greater influence was what the legends implied. These stories of heroes and heroism, said Sadat, "turned out to be an embodiment of such virtues as honor, fidelity, and sacrifice." In the years to come, they would help to shape Sadat's thoughts and actions.

from **Penn**
Elizabeth Janet Gray

In this excerpt from the biography of the man for whom Pennsylvania was named, the trial scene gives readers a clear picture of the beliefs that led William Penn to become a Quaker in a country in which that faith was not tolerated and from which he later fled to the freedom of the New World.

The Trial

On Thursday the first of September 1670, a sergeant and his yeomen came early in the morning to escort Penn and Mead out of Newgate and down the street called the Old Bailey to the Sessions House, where the court sat at seven. It was a "fair and stately building," with large galleries for spectators.

There were ten justices on the bench. Several of them young William Penn already knew. Sir Samuel Starling was Chief Justice. The Admiral's "buffle-headed" old friend, Sir John Robinson, the Lord Lieutenant of the Tower, was another—and good reason William had for remembering him! A third, Sir Richard Brown, had been particularly brutal in his raids on the Friends' meeting-houses a few years ago, and two more were well known as zealous churchmen and persecutors of Non-Conformists. Altogether they were about as arrogant, puffing, choleric, muddleheaded, prejudiced a lot of judges as one could find anywhere.

The jury was sworn in, twelve slow-witted, plain citizens, with good plain English names, John and James and William and Henry. There was an Edward Bushell, and Thomas Veer was foreman.

The prisoners were brought before the bar, and the indictment read. It was an astonishing piece of writing: a single sentence of two hundred and fifty words looped and bunched together in alternately legal and hysterical phrases. The gist of it was that "William Penn, gent., and William Mead, linen-draper, the fifteenth day of August, with force and arms unlawfully and tumultuously did assemble, and the aforesaid William Penn by agreement between him and William Mead before made, then and there in the open street did take upon himself to preach and speak, by reason whereof a great concourse and tumult of people in the street, a long time did remain and continue in contempt of the Lord the King and of his law, to the great disturbance of his peace and to the great terror of many of his liege subjects."

The Clerk then asked: "What say you, William Penn and William Mead? Are you guilty as you stand indicted, or not guilty?"

They pleaded "Not guilty," and the court was adjourned till afternoon.

While they were waiting, they discussed the errors in the indictment. To begin with, the date was wrong; the day of the meeting was Sunday the fourteenth of August, not the fifteenth. In the second place, they did not meet with force and arms. Nobody had arms except the soldiers. Nobody used force except the soldiers. Then, since they had never seen each other before, they obviously could not have met by agreement before made. And finally, they did not remain and continue in contempt of the King and his law, for the chief officer who came to take them had allowed the meeting to go on after Mead promised that Penn would go with them at the end of it.

In the afternoon they were brought back to the Sessions House, but instead of going on with their trial, the court, "both to affront and to tire them," kept them waiting there for five long hours while trials of felons and murderers were held, and at the end of the time adjourned.

September second they cooled their heels in Newgate.

September third was a Saturday. The sergeant and his yeomen came for them again before seven. Just as they went into the courtroom one of the officers, on a kindly impulse, took off their hats for them. Sir Samuel Starling was quick to see.

"Sirrah," he thundered, "who bid you put their hats off? Put them on again."

So, hats on, they stood before the bar. Ten judges in wigs and robes sat in a portentous row upon the bench and looked down with hostile eyes, while the chief among them proceeded solemnly to fine the prisoners forty marks apiece for wearing their hats in court.

It was childish; it was contemptible. William Penn, who was twenty-five, looked straight into all those hard and prejudiced old eyes, and said calmly: "I desire it may be observed that we came into the court with our hats off (that is, taken off), and if they have been put on since, it was by order from the Bench, and therefore not we, but the Bench, should be fined."

There being no answer to that, the jury was sworn again. Sir John Robinson objected to the way Edward Bushell took the oath. Bushell was known to be a man of tender conscience and tough will, and the judges were a little uneasy about him. They had no good excuse, however, for getting rid of him, and so the trial went forward.

The first witness was called and sworn to tell "the truth, the whole truth, and nothing but the truth, so help me God."

Lieutenant Cook, in command of the soldiers, testified that he saw Mr. Penn speaking to the people but could not hear what he said. Two others said that they saw Penn preaching to some four hundred people and Mead talking to Lieutenant Cook, but could not hear what either Penn or Mead said. There was no further evidence.

Then Penn spoke up and said: "I desire you would let me know by what law it is you prosecute me, and upon what law you ground my indictment."

The Recorder of London, who was the legal expert on the case, answered promptly: "The common law."

At once Penn asked: "What is that common law?" but the legal expert could not produce a definition or an example of it. The other justices on the bench began to shout at Penn, and the Recorder snapped:

"The Trial" from PENN by Elizabeth Janet Gray. Copyright 1938 by Elizabeth Janet Gray. Copyright renewed 1966 by Elizabeth Gray Vining. Used by permission of Viking Penguin Inc.

"The question is whether you are guilty of this indictment."

Penn corrected him. "The question is not whether I am guilty of this indictment, but whether the indictment be legal." He pointed out that if the common law was so hard to understand it was very far from being common, and he quoted Coke and the Magna Carta.

The Recorder, losing his temper completely, shouted: "Sir, you are an arrogant fellow, and it is not for the honor of the court to suffer you to go on!" To which Penn answered mildly: "I have asked but one question, and you have not answered me; though the rights and privileges of every Englishman are concerned in it."

"If I should suffer you to ask questions till tomorrow morning," replied the Recorder huffily, "you would never be the wiser."

And young Penn could not resist the temptation to retort: "That is according as the answers are."

That was too much for the judges; they turned purple with rage.

"I desire no affront to the court but to be heard in my just plea. . . ."

The Mayor and the Recorder both broke out in indignant shouts: "Take him away! Take him away! Turn him into the bale-dock."

The bale-dock was a sort of pen at the far end of the courtroom, open at the top but enclosed by high palings so that the prisoners could not see or hear what was going on. Before he was dragged off to this coop, William Penn delivered a ringing challenge:

"Is this justice or true judgment? Must I therefore be taken away because I plead for the fundamental laws of England? However, this I leave upon your consciences, who are of the jury and my sole judges, that if these ancient fundamental laws which relate to liberty and property (and are not limited to particular persuasions in the matter of religion) must not be indispensably maintained and observed, who can say he hath a right to the coat upon his back?"

"Be silent there."

"I am not to be silent in a case wherein I am so much concerned, and not only myself but many ten thousand families besides."

Roughly they pulled him off to the bale-dock. Mead had his turn, stood his ground well, quoted a Latin tag, defined a riot, and was also consigned for his pains to the bale-dock.

There, stuck away in the dimness, they could not hear what was going on in the court, but one of the officers whispered to them that the Recorder was charging the jury. It was absolutely against the law to charge the jury in the absence of the prisoners. Penn flung himself on the palings and pulled himself up so that he could shout over the top of them:

"I appeal to the jury who are my judges!" Loudly as he could, he quoted the law, and he called to the jury to take notice that he had not been heard in his own defense.

"Pull that fellow down, pull him down," bawled the Recorder.

The people in the galleries craned their necks and rustled and buzzed.

"I say these are barbarous and unjust proceedings!" shouted Penn, clinging to the side of the bale-dock.

"Take them away to the hole," commanded the Recorder.

To the hole they went, a sort of dungeon in the Sessions House, a stinking hole, Penn said, and one that the Lord Mayor would not consider a fit sty for his swine. There they stayed while the jury deliberated.

They were a long time at it. After an hour and a half, eight of them returned to the court, and four who disagreed remained in the jury chamber above. The four, of whom Edward Bushell was recognized as the leader, were brought down and scolded and threatened by the court. All twelve of them were then sent back to reach a conclusion, and this time, after more deliberation, they brought the unanimous verdict that William Penn was guilty of speaking in Gracechurch Street.

This of course was equal to an acquittal. There was no law against speaking in Gracechurch Street. The Mayor tried to make them say "speaking to an unlawful assembly," but they refused. Determined to have a different verdict, he ordered them back to the jury chamber, and they asked for pen, ink, and paper to take with them.

In a little more than half an hour they returned, Penn and Mead were brought back to the bar, and the jury handed in its verdict again, this time written and signed. "We do find William Penn to be guilty of speaking or preaching to an assembly met together in Gracechurch Street, the fourteenth of August last, 1670, and that William Mead is not guilty of the said indictment."

Whereupon the Mayor called Bushell "an impudent, canting fellow," and the Recorder told them all:

"Gentlemen, you shall not be dismissed till we have a verdict the court will accept; and you shall be locked up without meat, drink, fire, and tobacco. You shall not think thus to abuse the court; we will have a verdict, or by the help of God you shall starve for it."

Before the jury departed again, Penn got his word in, and the voice of this young man of twenty-five, whom the Lord Mayor later called "that wild, rambling colt," was the only calm and authoritative voice in the whole amazing, hysterical courtroom.

"My jury, who are my judges, ought not to be thus menaced. Their verdict should be free and not compelled. The bench ought to wait upon them but not forestall them."

But the court was ready to break up for the day and "huddle the prisoners to the jail and the jury to their chamber." As the second day of the trial ended, Penn turned to the jury and said:

"You are Englishmen; mind your privileges, give not away your right."

To which Bushell stanchly made reply: "Nor will we ever do it."

And that night the jury was shut up without "meat, drink, fire, nor any other accommodation."

The next day was Sunday, and it was illegal to hold court. Nevertheless, at seven, the court sat.

The foreman of the jury read the verdict again: "William Penn is guilty of speaking in Gracechurch Street."

The Mayor prompted him: "To an unlawful assembly?" and Edward Bushell answered for him: "No, my lord, we give no other verdict than what we gave last night; we have no other verdict to give."

Another of the justices, Sir Thomas Bludworth, commented gloomily: "I knew Mr. Bushell would not yield," and the Recorder threatened again: "I will have a positive verdict, or you will starve for it." After the night they had just spent, the jury could not look on this as an empty threat.

Penn desired to ask one question: Did the court accept the verdict "Not guilty," given of William Mead?

"It cannot be a verdict," said the Recorder, "because you are indicted for a conspiracy; and one being found guilty and not the other, it could not be a verdict."

Penn's answer was quick. "If not guilty be not a verdict, then you make of the jury and Magna Carta a mere nose of wax. . . . And if

William Mead be not guilty, it consequently follows that I am clear, since you have indicted us of a conspiracy, and I could not possibly conspire alone."

But for the third time the verdict was rejected and the jury sent back to find another. Again it returned with the one answer it had to give.

The court was well-nigh beside itself with rage. It threatened to set a mark on Edward Bushell, to have an eye on him, to cut his nose. And now Penn's voice rings out:

"It is intolerable that my jury should be thus menaced. Is this according to the fundamental law? Are they not my proper judges by the great charter of England? What hope is there of ever having justice done, when juries are threatened and their verdicts rejected? I am concerned to speak and grieved to see such arbitrary proceedings. Did not the Lieutenant of the Tower render one of them worse than a felon? And do you not plainly seem to condemn such for factious fellows who answer not your ends? Unhappy are those juries who are threatened to be fined and starved and ruined if they give not in their verdicts contrary to their consciences."

The Recorder had nothing to say in answer but: "My lord, you must take a course with that fellow."

"Jailer, bring fetters," commanded the Chief Justice, "and stake him to the ground."

"Do your pleasure," replied Penn superbly, "I matter not your fetters."

And now the Recorder's rage did what Penn was later to tell his children anger always does: it threw him into a desperate inconvenience. He made a speech that echoed around London and that he bitterly regretted afterwards.

"Till now," he said, "I never understood the reason of the policy and prudence of the Spaniards in suffering the Inquisition among them. And certainly it will never be well with us till something like the Spanish Inquisition be in England."

It was a dreadful thing to say. The torture and terror of the Spanish Inquisition were fresh in men's minds—Penn's grandfather,

Giles Penn, had suffered from it—and in England Popery was more feared and detested than non-conformity.

For the fourth time the jury was ordered to go find another verdict; this time they refused to go, saying there was no other verdict. The Recorder in a passion left the bench, sputtering: "I protest I will sit here no longer to hear these things," but the Mayor called to him to stay while he uttered a few more threats, had the sheriff take the jury up to their room, and adjourned the court.

The prisoners were sent back to Newgate, where at least they had more freedom and comfort than the jury.

At seven o'clock on the morning of Monday, September fifth, the court sat again. The jury staggered in, wan, white, hungry, thirsty, and disheveled.

"Look upon the prisoners," said the Clerk. "What say you, is William Penn guilty or not guilty?"

"Not guilty."

"What say you? Is William Mead guilty, or not guilty?"

"Not guilty."

It was plain and definite this time. There was nothing the Bench could do except to call the roll and make each juror give his verdict separately. Everyone answered firmly: "Not guilty."

The people in the galleries were pleased, so pleased that they "made a kind of hymn about it." All over the courtroom there were little murmurs of satisfaction.

But the affair was not over. The Recorder had his last word. "I am sorry, gentlemen, you have followed your own judgments and opinions rather than the good and wholesome advice which was given you. God keep my life out of your hands: but for this the court fines you forty marks a man, and imprisonment till paid."

They had been threatened with fines and imprisonment, they had faced the ugly temper of the Bench, they must have known this was coming. But forty marks was a lot of money, about twenty-six pounds sterling, in a day when a lieutenant in the Plymouth colony, for instance, got an annual salary of twenty marks, and women worked in the hayfields for a penny a day.

Penn then stepped up toward the Bench and demanded his liberty. He was told that he too was in for fines—the forty mark fine imposed at the beginning of the session for wearing his hat. He began to quote the Magna Carta again, but the Recorder had had all he could stand. "Take him away," he implored, "take him away, take him out of the court."

But before he went young William Penn had one thing more to say. He said it. "I can never urge the fundamental laws of England but you cry: 'Take him away, take him away.' But it is no wonder, since the Spanish Inquisition hath so great a place in the Recorder's heart. God Almighty, who is just, will judge you for these things."

So the prisoners who had been acquitted, and the jury who had acquitted them, went together to Newgate prison.

That night Penn wrote to his father. "Because I cannot come, I write." He told him the story of the trial, ending: "I am more concerned at thy distemper and the pains that attend it, than at my own mere imprisonment, which works for the best."

The next day he wrote: "I entreat thee not to purchase my liberty. They will repent them of their proceedings. I am now a prisoner notoriously against law."

And the next: "I am persuaded some clearer way will suddenly be found to obtain my liberty, which is no way so desirable to me as on the account of being with thee. . . . My present restraint is so far from being humor that I would rather perish than release myself by so indirect a course as to satiate their revengeful, avaricious appetites. The advantage of such freedom would fall very far short of the trouble of accepting it."

To pay the fine would be to admit its justice. What he wanted was either to be released by the court, or to bring suit against the judges for illegal imprisonment. In this way a principle could be established. This was the course the jury was taking. Every six hours they demanded their freedom, and when at length they were released on bail, they brought suit against the judges—and won their case. The whole body of judges in the King's Bench Court decided that no jury could be fined for its verdict. So it was that as a result of the trial of William Penn the sacredness of trial by jury was established for all time.

But that was nearly a year later.

The Admiral could not wait. He was dying, and he wanted to see his beloved son William again. He secretly paid his fine, and Mead's too, and they were set free.

Informational Books

Perhaps the easiest group of children's books for adults to evaluate is informational books. The criteria are specific; the adult can, with varying degrees of expertise, judge the vocabulary difficulty and the clarity of the writing; the readers have an expressed or prescribed interest in the subject; and the authors and editors of the best books usually have taken great care to see that the format, the scope, and the illustrations are appropriate for the reading level of the intended audience.

The same improvement in these books as was noted for biographies has come about in the last few decades. Far fewer books have that unmistakable air of being put together by a commissioned writer; far more of them are written by authors who are experts qualified to write about the subject, and the manuscripts are often sent to other subject experts or to specialists in children's literature to be checked for accuracy, authenticity, clarity, and style. Certainly accuracy is a primary criterion for informational books, but even a compilation of accurate facts can be misleading or at least confusing if the text

is poorly organized. It should move from the general to the specific, from the known to the unknown; it should be so divided—by chapters or topic headings—as to facilitate use and comprehension.

For some subjects, it is important that the material be current; this is particularly true for most scientific subjects. In all informational books, it should be made clear that knowledge is usually based on the work of others as well as the insight or diligence of the individual, and that, for most subjects, there are no final answers. While many good informational books are written with no distinction of style, the best of them add that quality while fulfilling all of the other criteria by which they may be judged.

For no other kind of book is the quality and placement of the illustrations so important. Illustrative material such as charts, graphs, maps, and diagrams should be placed in as close as possible a position in relation to the text to which they refer or which they amplify, and the captions or coding for such material must be accurate and explicit. Here, too, appended material such as chronological listings or glossaries may be important in their amplification or clarification of the text.

Like adults, children read informational books for several reasons: to learn how to do or make something, to fulfill an assignment, to satisfy curiosity, or to pursue a subject interest. The best books satisfy their needs, exemplify the scientific method, are reliable in their accuracy, hold their interest because of good writing style, and encourage them to pursue the subject further.

from **Here Come the Dolphins**
Alice E. Goudey

In a good example of lucid and lively science writing for younger readers, Goudey introduces action but adheres to accuracy and gives the dolphins individual characteristics by using anthropomorphism.

[A Baby Is Born]

Small waves ripple quietly across the blue-green water of the ocean.

The air is clear and the first rays of morning sunlight dance on the waves like a million twinkling lights.

Three kittiwakes fly above the sparkling water.

"Kittiwake! Kittiwake! Kittiwake!" they call, as if glad to be alive on such a wonderful day.

Suddenly a dolphin leaps from the quiet surface of the water. Then another one leaps into the air. Soon, all about, dolphins are leaping high in the air.

Young, happy looking dolphins of different sizes chase one another and then leap upward.

Mother dolphins join the young ones.

Even Old Scarsides, who is almost twelve feet long, leaps out, showing the scars of many battles on his gray, rubbery skin.

But one dolphin, Grayback, does not join the others in their play. She stays quietly by herself a short distance away.

Two companions stay with Grayback. They swim slowly around her. Now and then they touch her with their noses as if uneasy about her safety.

It is almost noon before the dolphin herd leaves the open water and starts swimming toward the bay. With strong downward movements of their flat tails, or flukes, they send their streamlined bodies through the water.

Up and down, up and down, their dark gray backs move through the water with even, rolling motions.

When they enter the bay the laughing gulls see the dolphins as their rounded backs break the surface of the water.

"Keeow! Keeow! Keeow!" The gulls scream their noisy greeting.

Grayback is the last to enter the bay. Her companions swim close beside her.

Not far away two long, gray, shadowy forms circle slowly about.

Old Scarsides makes a clapping sound with his powerful jaws when he sees them.

Two hungry tiger sharks!

But he will leave them alone as long as they do not bother any member of the herd.

The dolphins are hungry now. They have not eaten since early morning.

Just ahead of them they hear a school of little mullets.

Flip! Flip! Splash! The little fish flop in and out of the water.

The dolphins dash in among them and snap them up as they jump above the water.

The hungry dolphins swallow the mullets in one gulp. Even though they have almost a hundred teeth in their jaws they seldom use them for chewing. They use their teeth for catching and holding their prey or for nipping and biting one another and their enemies.

The laughing gulls swoop down on outstretched wings. They, too, gobble up the little fish when they flop out of the water.

It is almost sundown when the gulls look down into the clear water of the bay and see a little dolphin by Grayback's side.

Grayback's first baby has been born!

"Keeow! Keeow! Keeow!" the gulls scream.

We might imagine the gulls are saying, "Just another big fish. Just another big fish in the ocean. Too big for us to swallow. *Much* too big for us to swallow."

It is true that Grayback's baby looks like a big fish. But he does not belong to the fish family. He belongs to the great family of mammals.

He cannot get oxygen from the air dissolved in water as the fishes do. He must get his oxygen from the air above the water.

Now the gulls see him swim quickly toward the surface of the water. Grayback swims just below him, ready to push him up if he needs her help. If he does not get air quickly he cannot live.

The gulls see his small, rounded head come above the water.

At last he is breathing!

He draws the fresh air into his lungs through a hole on the top of his head. It is called a *blow hole.*

When the baby dolphin has filled his lungs with air he closes his little blow hole and goes beneath the water again to rest quietly at his mother's side.

If he did not close his blow hole, water would run into his lungs and he would drown.

But he does not rest for long. In about thirty seconds he rises to the surface again.

Woo-OOf! Woo-oof! He blows the old air out of his lungs with a rushing sound and again draws in fresh, clean air.

Like all dolphins, he could stay under the water for about six minutes but he, and all the dolphin family, usually come up for air two or three times each minute.

Grayback and her companions stay close beside the baby. It is well that they do because, as night comes on, the two shadowy forms of the tiger sharks circle closer and closer to them.

The sharks are not alone. Little pilot fish swim close to them. The pilot fish are waiting to gobble up bits of food that the sharks drop while they are eating.

Also, two shark suckers cling to the sides of the sharks and get a free ride. These strange creatures hold onto the sharks' rough skin with little suction discs on the tops of their heads. They, too, snatch up bits of food that the sharks drop.

A baby dolphin would make a good meal for the sharks, the pilot fish and the shark suckers!

The sharks make quick turns and swim in figure eights, turning this way and that way, as if hunting for something.

They cannot see very well but their sense of smell leads them toward Grayback and her baby.

Now their turns become quicker and quicker and more frantic and their small eyes glitter with excitement.

Grayback and her companions encircle the baby dolphin, and Old Scarsides whistles shrilly as the sharks dart toward them.

Then the whole herd of dolphins shoot through the water like torpedoes. They are upon the sharks in an instant, ramming them with their hard, bony snouts and slamming them with their tails.

Water flies in all directions!

The dolphins whistle shrilly and Old Scarsides snaps his powerful jaws again and again as he rushes forward for another poke with his snout.

The noise of the battle can be heard across the bay.

A night heron, flying across the bay, hears it.

"Quok! Quok!" he cries.

The gulls, rocking on the water, hear it and fly up and circle about and sound their alarm cry.

And the fish under the water scoot away to a safer place.

One of the sharks sinks his notched saw-teeth in the side of a dolphin. Blood flows from the wound and stains the water.

The taste and smell of the blood makes the sharks fight more wildly than ever.

At last Old Scarsides strikes one of the

sharks a hard blow behind one of his gills. The shark sinks to the bottom of the bay.

When this happens the other shark whirls quickly and heads out toward the open water.

Grayback's baby is safe at last.

But it takes some time for the dolphins to quiet down. They are uneasy and swim about, whistling and snapping their jaws.

It is not very often that they must fight the sharks in the ocean. It is usually only when a baby dolphin is born or when a dolphin is wounded and there is the taste and smell of blood in the water.

The sharks are quick, and their saw-teeth are dangerous, but they do not have hard, bony skeletons to protect their bodies. Their skeletons are of cartilage which is somewhat like gristle and much softer than the hard bones of the dolphins. The blows of the dolphins' snouts can send them to the bottom of the ocean.

Now that the battle is over, the dolphin herd is tired and, like all other animals, needs sleep.

They take little catnaps, never sleeping for long at a time. Even while sleeping, with their eyes partly or completely closed, they swim slowly about just below the surface of the water. With slow movements of their flat tails they go up and down, up and down as they rise to the surface to breathe.

The moon throws her light across the water and all is quiet as the dolphins rest.

from **The Fisherman Who Needed a Knife**
Marie Winn

The narrative form and the use of dialogue are nicely gauged to catch and hold children's interest in this clear explanation of why it is easier to use money as a medium of exchange than to barter.

Long, long ago, before people used money, everybody traded different things. A fisherman traded the fish he caught for the other things he needed. A baker traded his bread. A hatmaker traded his hats. A potter traded his pots.

Once upon a time, long, long ago, a fisherman needed a sharp knife. Since there was no money long ago, he could not go out and buy one.

So he took one of his fish and wrapped it up to keep it fresh. He took the fish to the knifemaker's house.

"Here is a fresh fish I caught today," he said to the knifemaker. "I will give you the fish if you give me a sharp knife that I need."

"I would be glad to trade with you," said the knifemaker, "but this very morning a man brought me a large fish and traded it for a knife. Now I don't need another fish. What I need is a new hat. My old hat fell into the fire yesterday."

The fisherman took his fish and went to the hatmaker's house.

"Here is a fresh fish," he said to the hatmaker. "I will give you the fish if you give me a hat. Then I can give the hat to the knifemaker and trade it for a sharp knife that I need."

"Sorry," said the hatmaker. "I already have a nice fish for my supper. A boy brought it this morning and traded it for a cap. But I have no more bread in the house. What I need is a crusty loaf of bread."

The fisherman took his fish and went to the baker's house.

"Here is a fresh fish," he said to the baker. "I will give you the fish if you give me a crusty loaf of bread. Then I can give the bread to the hatmaker and trade it for a hat. Then I can take the hat to the knifemaker and trade it for a sharp knife that I need."

"I'm afraid I don't need any fish today," said the baker. "This morning my wife went fishing, just for fun, and she caught an enormous fish. But my best pot has a crack in it. What I need is a new pot."

Once more the fisherman went off with his fish. He went to the potter's house.

"Here is a fresh fish," he said to the potter. "I will give you the fish if you give me a pot. Then I can give the pot to the baker and trade it for a loaf of bread. Then I can take the bread to the hatmaker and trade it for a hat. And then I can give the hat to the knifemaker and trade it for a sharp knife that I need."

The potter looked at the fish. He sniffed it with his nose. He picked it up to feel how heavy it was.

"This is a good fish," he said. "It would make a delicious supper, fried over the fire. I will be happy to trade you a pot for this fine fish."

The fisherman gave the fish to the potter and traded it for a strong, round pot.

The fisherman took the pot to the baker and traded it for a crusty loaf of bread.

Then the fisherman took the bread to the hatmaker and traded it for a soft leather hat.

At last the fisherman took the hat and went to the knifemaker's house.

He said to the knifemaker, "First I traded my fish for a pot. Then I traded the pot for a loaf of bread. Then I traded the bread for this hat. And now I would like to trade this hat for a sharp knife that I need."

The knifemaker took the hat and tried it on. It fit him very well and kept the sun out of his eyes. He picked out a knife he had made and gave it to the fisherman.

"Here is my best, sharpest knife," said the knifemaker. "But what a lot of trouble you had getting this knife. You had to make so many trades! You had to go to so many people before you found someone who needed your fish!"

"Yes," said the fisherman, "everybody needs *something*, but it's not always a fish that they need."

"I have the same trouble," said the knifemaker. "Sometimes I have to make many trades before I get the things I need. Sometimes trading takes so much time that I hardly have time left to make knives."

The fisherman thought very hard and then he had an idea.

"Wouldn't it be good if there were some easier way for us to get the things we need?" the fisherman asked. "Instead of everybody trading different things—fish and pots and bread and knives—wouldn't it be easier if people used one special thing for trading?"

"What kind of special thing could people use?" asked the knifemaker.

"It would have to be something really special, something you couldn't find just anywhere. Otherwise people would not need to work to get it.

"It might be special, colored seashells, or little bits of gold or silver or copper. It might be almost anything, just so long as everyone used the same special thing," said the fisherman.

"That is a fine idea," said the knifemaker to the fisherman. "That is a great idea! We wouldn't have to do all that trading."

The fisherman and the knifemaker talked to all the people who lived and worked in their village. They told them their idea.

"A great idea," everybody agreed. "Why didn't we think of it before?"

They picked small pieces of metal to be their special thing for trading. Everybody used the same pieces of metal. And life was much easier and better for everyone.

from **Oh, Boy! Babies!**
Alison Herzig and Jane Mali

A photo-essay about a group of fifth and sixth grade boys who have enrolled in a class on infant care has a lively spontaneity. This excerpt, from the end of the book, gives a clear indication of how much the boys have learned and how much they have enjoyed the babies for whom they cared.

The Sixth Wednesday

I'm going to be nice to my children. Every father wants to add something of his own experience. I'd encourage a good education, but if they wanted to give up in one subject, like English for example . . . if they thought they knew their stuff, I'd let them watch TV.

—Smith

I'm probably more capable at baby-sitting than a girl is. No offense. Girls get hysterical. They fidget. When things go wrong they don't know what to do. I get irritated when the babies cry, but you just keep whispering and patting and playing and eventually they stop.

—Seth

The only thing that makes you a good baby-sitter whether you're a girl or a boy is if you can stand them.

—Rick

When I grow up and have kids, I'm going to help my wife, because I want to and I should. When the baby's crying it isn't always hers and when it's laughing, it isn't always mine.

—Douglas

I've always loved babies. I think they're the smallest most cutest things you can have.

—Luke

"Hey, Joey, have you told her yet?" Luke leaned back on his hands, but he kept an eye on Andrew, who prowled around Caroline. Andrew had his eye on Caroline's toy toaster that popped up toy toast. Nearby, Smith was teaching Emily some basic calisthenics. On the other big mat Michael was trying to show Todd how to sit up straight, using Freddy as an example.

Joey beamed up at Mrs. Maher from under the visor of his baseball cap. "I've got a baby brother," he said.

"Wonderful, Joey!" said Mrs. Maher. "That's really terrific news! Have you seen him yet?"

"Yeah. He and my mom came home last night. I got to hold him, too. He's all red and wrinkled, and his legs are as long as his arms."

"Is your mom going to bring him in today?" asked Forrest.

"Well, no. My mom didn't remember he'd be so small. But she's *definitely* bringing him in next term."

"Next term? Oh, no! Hey, Mrs. uh . . . Mrs. . . . Caroline's mother? This isn't the last class, is it?" asked Forrest.

"Yes," said Mrs. Maher. "I'm afraid so."

"Are we going to get our certificates today?" asked Gordon and Rick at the same time.

"I'm going to start baby-sitting as soon as I get mine," said Luke. "I'm tired of walking dogs."

"Did everyone, you know, pass?" asked Joey. Mrs. Maher didn't seem to hear him. She was busy at the sink unloading paper cups, bottles of soda, and tinfoil packages from two brown bags.

"I hope I fail. I hope I don't get my certificate," Dylan whispered to Henry. "I hope I have to repeat. That would be fun."

"I've got to get mine," said Joey. "To show my mom. Forrest, do you think Mrs. . . . ah, Mrs. Ma . . . counts for trying? Nothing really bad has happened since that time Brooke fell on her head."

"What's the 7-Up for?" asked Luke. "Are we having a party?"

"What's with all the questions?" countered Mrs. Maher, attempting to conceal the 7-Up behind the empty grocery bags. "At the moment the only thing we're having is a class, and you've got to be really with it today. You've got to take care of five babies, listen to me, and think, all at the same time."

"Think? About what?" asked Rick in a muffled voice. He was taking off Freddy's sneakers.

"About hazards and precautions," answered Mrs. Maher, moving to the middle of the room. "And more about the importance of questions, what to ask when you go baby-sitting. Before the parents leave you should find out where they can be reached, the name and telephone number of their pediatrician, and the names and numbers of friends or neighbors who could help if you had a problem."

"What about the poison-control number?" asked Gordon.

"Police? Fire?" added Smith.

"Turn on channel six. They have all the numbers," said Douglas.

"Only if you have cable," said Seth.

"You can find all those emergency numbers listed on the inside front cover of the telephone book. Okay? You should also check out front and back doors and emergency exits," said Mrs. Maher.

"Closets too. That's fun," said Forrest.

"Now. The parents have their coats on and they're half out the door," said Mrs. Maher. "What else do you need to know?"

"Things about the baby?"

"Special instructions," said Seth.

"What time she goes to bed? Does she have an allergy?"

"When the parents will be back?"

"And whether there's only health food in the refrigerator," said Luke under his breath. "If so, I'm not baby-sitting."

"Exactly," said Mrs. Maher. "And one more thing. Find out whether the parents are expecting any visitors while they're gone. If not, you answer the phone, of course, and take messages, but you don't open the door to anyone."

"Not even if it's Uncle Fester," said Rick.

"All right," Mrs. Maher went on. "Let's say the parents have left. You're on your own. What are some hazards you have to guard against?"

Forrest lay on his side without moving, watching Caroline clamber up his back and down his front like a small bulldozer. Todd slowly listed toward the mat. "Babies are so loose," observed Michael, straightening him up again.

"Electrical plugs," said Luke without looking at Mrs. Maher. He took the toy toaster away from Andrew and gave it back to Caroline. "You gotta make sure they've put those little stopper things over them. Watch out, Seth. Watch out. Andrew's coming. Now he's after Freddy's bottle."

"Things on the floor that they can pick up and put in their mouths," said Rick.

"My cat eats dust balls," said Forrest.

"If they pull over a lamp, they could start a fire."

"Pins."

"Paper clips. Staples."

"Little trays with poisonous plants on them."

"Ropes. You shouldn't leave ropes around."

"Cigarette butts."

"Well, they could, you know," said Joey, "be sort of . . . or anything could happen."

"My mother said I used to pick used gum off the ground," said Rick.

"Match tips," said Forrest.

"Match tips?"

"Yes. I loved them. I still do. They're delicious."

"Right. All those things and more," said Mrs. Maher. "Crawlers and toddlers can find trouble anywhere. With infants your major concern is that they will roll over unexpectedly and fall off things. But for older babies, there is potential danger in every room. Take the kitchen, for example. . . ."

"Open windows."

"Window guards are good," said Seth. "I had those."

"They could turn the gas on in the stove," suggested Gordon.

"Or pull down pots of boiling water on their heads," said Douglas.

"Good thinking," said Mrs. Maher. "If you have to cook, keep the pots on the back burners or, at the very least, keep their handles turned in."

"Wet floors. They're slippery," said Rick.

"That's another good one," agreed Mrs. Maher. "If it's not too cold, I think bare feet are healthier and safer. They can grip the floor better whether it's wet or not."

"I knew it," said Rick. "I hate to walk around in clunky shoes, and I figure babies hate it too."

"You've got to watch out for the dryer," said Joey. "It's hot and gloomy in there."

"What about under the kitchen sink?" asked Mrs. Maher.

"Oh. Right. Floor waxes."

"Sprays."

"Pills. They think they're candy."

"Detergents."

"Deodorants," said Forrest.

"You should keep them high up so they

can't get them," said Dylan.

"They can get anything. They can climb," said Joey. "I had a cousin once who climbed into a cabinet. It was no bigger than a drawer. They found her, but only finally."

"Face it," said Seth. "The deal is you have to watch little kids all the time."

"You've got it," said Mrs. Maher. "That's it in a nutshell. Time to break out the 7-Up."

There were cheers and clapping.

"A party?" asked Luke. "What's there to eat?"

"Double trouble. Homemade brownies stuffed with chocolate chips," said Mrs. Maher. "And donuts and some other stuff. It's hidden behind the bags. Don't forget to offer some to the mothers."

"The certificates? What about them? Do we get them today?" asked Gordon.

"What certificates?"

"The diploma. The paper that says we've worked hard and deserve better," said Forrest. "The paper that says we're qualified."

Mrs. Maher bent her head and rummaged through her shoulder bag. "Ah ha," she said, pulling a manila envelope out of a side pocket. "This looks promising." Inside the envelope was a sheaf of papers. Rick tried to sneak a look at them, but Mrs. Maher held them close to her chest. "Documents," she said. "Definitely what we're after. The first one has your name on it, Seth. Congratulations." She handed him the certificate and shook his hand. Douglas was next and then Rick. "You did really well," she said. "Luke? Luke?"

"Just a sec. I've got to get this wad of Kleenex out of Caroline's mouth. Open your mouth, silly girl. Slobber. Slobber. Oh, gross, drool. You know what I mean? You feel a little wetness."

"Odel, odel, odel, odel, odel," said Caroline.

"Listen. She's learned to yodel," said Luke.

"That's nothing," said Smith. "Andrew can say 'queen,' 'kiss,' 'let,' and 'nine.' I'm sure I heard 'nine.' Or 'mime.'"

"Try Ricky." Rick put his face close to Andrew's and mouthed at him. "Ricky. Ricky. Ricky. Try Nicky. Maybe that's easier. Nicky. Nicky. Nicky."

Mrs. Maher put Luke's certificate to one side and shook hands with Michael and Gordon. Joey brushed the hair off his forehead and realigned his baseball cap. The visor was down to his eyebrows.

Luke was still dealing with Caroline so Mrs. Maher looked to see whose certificate was next. Just at that moment she was interrupted by a woman who pushed through the crowd of onlookers in the doorway and crossed the room to whisper in her ear.

"Boys . . . boys," Mrs. Maher raised a hand. "We've got a request. Does anyone want to baby-sit? After school?"

Almost all the boys raised their hands and some of them waved certificates.

"Okay. Let me see. All right, Seth. I saw your hand first. You're on. In the basement, the teacher's lounge, at 3:15. Now, who was I up to? Luke, are you ready?"

"Yes. Hey, Rick, watch Caroline for me."

Caroline grabbed the leg of a chair and tried to pull herself up.

"Hold on. Hold on! You're tilting," said Rick. "Yes! She stands! By herself. I've got to stick with her now."

"Can I take her for a walk?" asked Seth.

"No. She's mine, all mine. Go get your own baby."

Seth picked up a brownie for himself and a bottle of juice for Todd.

"I wonder how much that woman will pay me," Seth said between bites. "If she offers me a dollar, I can say, 'No, I've taken this course.' I can say, 'I get a dollar-fifty.'"

"Then she'll just go hire someone else," said Rick.

"Then I'll take the dollar."

"I'd even do it for free," Rick said.

Mrs. Maher shook hands with Luke. Joey put his hands in his pockets. There were only a few certificates left. Mrs. Maher congratulated Forrest, Smith, and Dylan. Joey strolled over to the sink and helped himself to a brownie and some 7-Up.

"Joey? Joey? Where are you?" called Mrs. Maher. "You were right here a minute ago.

Don't tell me he's left without his certificate."

Joey dropped his brownie. He hurried back across the room wiping the crumbs off his mouth with the back of his hand. Then he wiped his hand on his pants before he held it out to Mrs. Maher.

"You learned a lot, Joey," said Mrs. Maher. "You're going to have a ball with your new baby brother."

Joey read his typed certificate. His name appeared twice, penned in by a calligrapher, and Mrs. Maher had signed her full name at the bottom, right above an official seal. The seal was dazzlingly red with serrated edges and embossed with the school's motto and crest. Joey ran his fingers over the raised surface. "How are we supposed to carry this thing around with us?" he asked Luke.

"Fold it, you fool," said Luke.

"I don't want to," said Joey. "I'm going to get it framed."

The brownies and donuts were disappearing fast, and the 7-Up was all gone. The only thing left to drink was a bottle of unsweetened natural apricot juice.

"Who brought this stuff in?" Douglas wanted to know. He helped himself to another brownie.

"These look like the best brownies I've ever tasted," said the boy from "Walls."

"Hey! Get your greasy fingers out of there! This is our party," said Luke. "There aren't even enough for the mothers."

The boy from "Walls" put the brownie back, minus a bite. "I've signed up for this course next term," he said. "I put it first and third. Can I have an animal cracker?"

"They're for the babies," Luke told him.

"What am I going to give Andrew, besides this apricot juice?" Seth asked Mrs. Maher. "These cookies have sugar in them. I read the label."

Mrs. Maher produced some raisins in a plastic sandwich bag and Seth held one out to Andrew. Andrew took the raisin and ran. Seth followed him out the door and into the hall.

"I want to give Freddy one more stroll,"

said Luke. "Down to the water fountain and back. He likes to investigate. Where's his hot rod?"

On the way out Luke and Freddy passed Seth and Andrew coming in. Seth walked backward, luring Andrew with raisins.

"It was amazing," said Seth. "He charged right into Mr. Jacob's office. I've seen a lot of people wanting to get out of there but no one ever wanting to get in before."

Andrew's diaper sagged.

"We could try and change him," Joey said to Smith. "Want to risk it? What've we got to lose?"

"Sure. I'm game. First we've got to catch him."

"Right," said Joey. "Go for it."

The bell clanged in the hallway. "I'm afraid it's time, boys," said Mrs. Maher.

Gordon carried Emily over to where her mother was standing. "I'll zip her into the front pack for you," he said. "I know where her legs go and everything."

"I don't want this class to end," said Forrest. "I want to change Todd one last time. Quick. Where's a diaper?"

Michael was trying to fold up one of the big mats singlehandedly, but Caroline thought it was a game.

"Caroline, if you'll just let go so I can finish this, I'll show you something," said Michael.

Forrest handed over Todd, freshly diapered and dressed, and Luke relinquished the stroller to Freddy's mother. "I'm sorry, Fred," he said. "Your animal cracker broke into three parts."

"Thank you, mothers," said Gordon.

"Yes," said Luke. "Thank you. And thank you, Mrs. Mahurst."

Todd and Freddy were gone. Andrew's mother trailed Andrew out the door. Only Caroline and Emily were left.

Luke gave Emily a last hug.

Michael sat on the floor with Caroline and showed her the seal of his certificate. Mrs. Maher picked up Caroline's bottle and the last of her toys. Boys began to push the desks back into rows. Forrest watched the space around Michael and Caroline shrink.

"I'm going to beg and beg them to let me take the class again," Forrest said. "I'm going to sign up again even if I have to get down on my knees. I just love babies. I mean, I'm going to get down on my knees and beg them."

from The First Travel Guide to the Moon: What to Pack, How to Go, and What to See When You Get There
Rhoda Blumberg

Brisk, imaginative, and funny, this bland spoof of travel literature uses an unusual form for informational writing, but all of the information about space flight lunar conditions is factual.

All Aboard!

Check in at a hotel near the Earthport the night before your flight. You need a good night's rest before you're outward bound.

Wake-up time is 5:30 A.M. After breakfast at the coffee shop, a bus takes you to your Earthport. You should arrive at least an hour before blast-off, which is usually at 8:00 A.M. (weather permitting).

After you hand in your ticket, your luggage is weighed and sent separately to your space shuttle. A small bus takes you to the launch pad, where an outside elevator lifts you thirty stories to the top of the rocket ship. After crossing a short bridge, you climb down a ladder into the shuttle. A flight attendant helps you find your seat.

The latest-model shuttle carries seventy tourists. The crew consists of the pilot, a copilot, a flight engineer, and five attendants. The shuttle, a double-winged craft with three engines, goes back and forth between an Earthport and Space Base. Two huge rockets are attached to the ship, one on each side. The shuttle rides piggyback on an enormous fuel tank.

Place your hand luggage in the zipper pocket under your contour chair. Then fasten your safety belts—all of them: ankle strap, thigh strap, waist strap, shoulder strap. They prevent you from floating around. Eyeglasses must be strapped around your head to keep them from floating. You feel as though you're wearing a straitjacket, but you must buckle down to fly right! An attendant comes by to make sure all safety belts are buckled.

You must remain in your seat at all times during the short shuttle trip. Don't fidget. It usually takes about one hour before you are anchored at Space Base, where you transfer to the plane that goes to the Moon.

LIFT-OFF

Ready for take off? The control tower broadcasts the countdown over the ship's loudspeakers.

Brace yourself at number 10. At number 3 you hear noise that sounds as though you're sitting underneath Niagara Falls. The ship shudders and shakes.

At zero it's up and away. You roar into space, as you watch the takeoff on the small TV screen in front of your seat. You're riding on huge flames, rocketing away.

After a few minutes, when you're up twenty-five miles, you feel a jolt. If you look outside you'll see the two large rockets dropping off the ship. The plane seems to be falling apart!

Don't panic. During every flight the pilot releases these rockets which descend by parachute into the ocean. They are picked up by Earthport ships, hauled in, fixed up, and used again for other shuttle flights.

Shortly after the rockets are released you'll feel another thud. Although you seem to be floating, your heart may be sinking when you see the fuel tank fall off, and there's sudden silence. The motors have stopped.

Relax. The tank is being dumped because all the fuel has been used up. There's no need for fuel as the ship starts orbiting Earth.

Look outside. You'll see with your own eyes: the Earth is round.

Although the sun is brighter than you ever saw it, the sky is jet black. (You won't see a blue sky again until you return to the atmosphere, the blanket of air that surrounds our globe.) Stars shine everywhere.

Of course, your nose is pressed against your window as you start circling planet Earth at 17,500 miles per hour. If you're lucky you may see China's Great Wall.

Before you complete one orbit of the Earth, the pilot uses small rockets to steer the shuttle to Space Base, three hundred miles above earth.

DOCKING AT SPACE BASE

It takes about ten minutes for your ship to hook onto Space Base, the human-made satellite used as a way station to the Moon. You feel a bump when the shuttle locks into its dock. A circular ring on the shuttle fits a sealing ring on the harbor. Magnetic clamps grip the ship, and steel claws lock into each other.

Outside your window you see dockworkers in space suits guiding your shuttle to a perfect landing. The workers are tethered to Space Base by long lifelines. These lines keep them from drifting away and going into orbit forever after.

When the shuttle is safely moored, green lights flash above your seat. Wait until the pilot announces that it's time to unbuckle.

Grab handrails along the walls of the ship, or use the guide ropes stretched along the aisles. You must hold on to something or you will float. Don't hurry, and don't push. Pull yourself to the open hatch. Then, holding guide ropes, "walk" with your hands through a short tunnel into port.

SPACE BASE

Space Base, three hundred miles above Earth, is the stopover for lunar tourists. Supply ships headed for the Moon stop here, too.

Stevedores carry bulky but weightless cargo that comes up from Earth in unmanned robot ships. They transfer the freight into large containers which are then shot by giant cannons to a supply depot on the Moon.

You wait for your Moonliner in a room called Windows of the World. The room is a semicircle of glass with window seats for everyone. Once again, you must be strapped in so that you don't float around, for you are still in zero gravity. Chairs are on the floor and the ceiling. Reserve an "upper." You won't feel odd hanging with your head down because there's no gravity to pull blood to your head. And although you don't feel topsy-turvy, the experience is offbeat.

You relax at Space Base for one and a half hours, the time it takes the base to orbit Earth once.

Around the world in ninety-three minutes! It takes only ten minutes to cross the United States, and twenty-five to fly over the Pacific Ocean. Because orbits don't always go the same route, you never know what you'll see.

A telescope in front of each seat has attachments for your camera. You may be able to zoom in on Egypt's pyramids, Russia's Kremlin, or India's Taj Mahal. Use color film. The Sahara and Gobi deserts show up in vivid reds, golds, oranges, and browns. Oceans are swirls of greens and blues. Icebergs and polar caps are a dazzling blue-white. When orbiting you see both day and night. Earth at night shows forest fires, lightning streaks, and city lights that sparkle like jewels. Keep clicking your camera. If Earth isn't socked in by pollution or by clouds, you'll have marvelous photos to show the folks back home.

Although Lunar Trip officials prefer that you remain seated during most of your stay at Space Base, you can leave your chair to float around, climb the walls, and walk along the ceiling. There are lots of tricks you can try in zero gravity, but be patient. You'll have plenty of time to amuse yourself during your two-day journey to the Moon.

The Moon, at Last!

Moonliner lands gently in the middle of Clavius Crater. Unfasten your safety harnesses. You no longer float, because the Moon has gravity. It's six times weaker than Earth's gravity, and, therefore, you feel six times lighter than you did at home.

Divide your weight by about six. If you tip the scales back home at two hundred pounds, you weigh 33.3 pounds on the Moon. No crash diets needed to feel slim, svelte, and springy.

Once Moonliner has landed and taxied to its moorings, it's down the hatch, through a tunnel, and into the large, underground Moon Central Station. Here escorts are waiting to lead you to minibuses which ride through underground shopping arcades connecting Moon Central Station with all hotels. You'll have plenty of time to shop here during your holiday.

Check into your room as soon as possible. You must rest and give your mind and body time to become adjusted to a new world.

HOTELS

You have a choice of four hotels, each rated from one to five stars. The number of stars, awarded by the Lunar Tourist Bureau, is based upon comfort, service, and luxury.

The *Zodiac* (★) attracts astrology and astronomy conventions. *Honeymoon Haven* (★★★★) gets the carefree rocket set, formerly called the jet set. The *Milky Way*

Lodge (★★) attracts a family crowd and caters to school groups on class trips. *Crescent Earth Inn* (★★★) is the most popular and the oldest of the tourist resorts.

Although built and managed by Americans, Chinese, and Russians, who were the Moon's first immigrants, the hotels are not owned by any nation or private company. Article XI of the United Nations Outer Space Treaty states:

> . . . neither the surface nor the subsurface of the Moon shall become the property of any State.

Hotels are underground. The rocky crust of the Moon is excellent protection against harmful radiation and against the extreme temperatures of hot and cold. All rooms are pressurized and air-conditioned. Although the Moon has been pocked by meteorites, the chances of being hit by one are about as small as the chance of being struck by lightning on Earth. You're as safe as you'd be in your own home.

Bedrooms are comfortable. No worries about lumpy mattresses, because there aren't any. You sleep on a plastic platform that feels as soft as a cushion because your body doesn't press down the way it does in Earth's gravity. Elastic plastic sheets are snapped around the bed. They hug you and make you feel a bit heavier and less spacey. All furniture is plastic, metal, glass, or ceramic. There aren't any Moon forests, so don't expect to knock on wood. Closet shelves go to the ceiling. You can reach the top with a hop. The ceiling is padded, in case you jump too high.

There is color television in every room, offering a variety of entertainment. Tune in to a local lunar station, or turn the dial to your favorite program back home. The SBC (Satellite Broadcasting Company) brings you TV broadcasts from Moscow, Madrid, Montreal, Paris, Peking, Peoria, and hundreds of other places around the globe.

Be sure to read the notices posted in every room: "In case of emergency, oxygen masks will be released from the ceiling. You will receive instructions by loudspeaker." All announcements are in Arabic, Chinese, English, French, Russian, and Spanish—the official languages of the United Nations. Translating computers installed in the walls change messages into forty-seven additional languages. You'll know what's going on whether you come from Burma or Bulgaria. Just press the button next to your country's flag, put on the attached earphones, and listen carefully.

Even though hotels are from two to four stories tall, there aren't any elevators. Ramps lead from floor to floor. In addition, halls have poles like those in firehouses. Just hoist yourself up. You only weigh as much as an earthling infant. Slide down. You slip slowly.

NEWSPAPERS

The *Daily Planet* and the *Morning Moon* are at newstands in your hotel lobby.

Pick up a free copy of "This Week on the Moon," which is usually stacked at the front desk. It lists entertainment and special events.

ENTERTAINMENT

The huge underground Astro Center has theaters, sports arenas, and gymnasiums.

Visiting actors present the best Broadway and London hits. Ballet companies are star attractions. Dancers delight in leaps, twirls, and midair spins that are superhuman by Earth's standards. Toe dancers don't need slippers; they dance barefoot. (You, too, can dance on tiptoe due to weak gravity.)

Dancers perform to taped music. Because different muscle power and pressure are necessary, the usual instruments are not tuned for heavenly harmonies. New instruments are being designed. Until they are perfected all lunar symphony concerts are televised from Earth, by satellite.

Every once in a blue Earth a troop of acrobats who call themselves "The Astrobats" visits outer space. Don't miss them! They perform trapeze acts over the audience's heads, clowning as they throw each other from one end of the room to the other.

LOUNGES

All hotels have ramps to Pleasure Domes, above ground glass-domed observation lounges made with a special type of glass that has been mined on the Moon. The glass is perfect protection against the outside, and it's tinted to shield your eyes against the fierce rays of the searing sun. (Moon glass is becoming easier and cheaper to mine and mold. A hotel on the drawingboards will be an above ground glass structure. It's to be called the *Star Scraper,* and it will probably be the first deluxe five-star hotel.)

Some of your finest hours will be spent in the Pleasure Dome Lunar Lounges. You will see more stars than you ever saw in your life. They shine twenty times brighter than they do when seen from Earth, and they don't twinkle because there's no air to make them shimmer and blink.

Earth shines in the sky above, a beautiful blue ball that appears four times bigger and eighty times brighter than your at-home Moon. It has phases exactly like the Moon's. How romantic it is to see crescent Earth! What poetry and music have been inspired by half Earth! Full Earth, always seen in the Moon's midnight sky, is mind-boggling. (Some people insist it can cause insanity, but this is merely a superstition.)

from **There Really Was a Dodo**
Esther and Bernard Gordon

A description of the flightless bird, now extinct, that once thrived on the island of Mauritius, serves as a good example of the ways in which living things adapt to their environment and of the ways in which a species can become extinct.

No one is sure how the dodo got its name. The Dutch word "dodoor" means slow, and the Portuguese word "doudo" means silly, crazy or foolish. The dodo, with its fat body and waddling walk, was slow, and it looked foolish. The birds were given several names, but dodo is the one that stuck.

In 1644, people from Holland came to settle on Mauritius. They brought goats, pigs, dogs and cats, and these were new dangers for the dodo. Soon the animals ran all over the island chasing the slow, fat, flightless bird.

When the animals found one of the nests, they would chase away the dodos and eat the egg. So, with the nests destroyed and the eggs smashed and eaten, not many chicks were hatched. Every year there were fewer and fewer dodos.

When the sailors returned to Europe, they described the strange big birds that could not fly, and people wanted to see them. Several dodos were shipped back and shown in Holland, Germany, England, and Italy.

All these dodos died. One of the dead ones was bought by John Tradescant who had a museum in London. He stuffed it and put it on display there, and it was later moved to the Ashmolean Museum at Oxford, England. After a while it was thrown out. Only the head and one foot were saved.

Meanwhile, the dodos on Mauritius completely died out. Records show that there were dodos there until 1681, but since that time no one has seen a living dodo.

After a hundred years or so, with no more living dodos, people started to think that there might never have been a dodo. They thought perhaps the dodo was only imaginary, like a dragon or a unicorn. The dodo head and foot were in the museum in England, but there was no full skeleton to show what the bird looked like or to prove that it really existed.

In Lewis Carroll's book *Alice in Wonderland,* which was published in 1865, a dodo appears. Alice meets the bird in Wonderland, and it gives her a thimble. But this didn't help to show that the dodo had really existed.

Since then, people have gone to Mauritius to search for proof that the dodo was real. They have found bones buried in swamps and mud pools. Scientists have dug them up, examined them and put them together into dodo skeletons—proof that these birds really did exist. There are dodo skeletons in the American Museum of Natural History in New York City, the British Museum and the Paris Museum.

Scientists also found that there were two other kinds of dodos besides the one on Mauritius. The white dodo lived on the island of Réunion, and the Solitaire, another dodo, was found on the island of Rodriguez. Both kinds are extinct today too.

The dodo became extinct within about one hundred and fifty years from the time we first saw it. For hundreds of years before, the dodo had lived on Mauritius, Réunion, and Rodriguez. But people and the animals they brought caught and killed so many dodos, and destroyed so many dodo eggs, that in a very short time, there were no dodos left.

Because of carelessness through the years, many kinds of birds and animals have become extinct. Today, the whooping crane, the orangutan, and the blue whale are in danger of dying out. Our natural resources must be protected and used wisely. If our plants and animals are carelessly destroyed, we all may become as "dead as a dodo."

from The Coral Reef: What Lives There
Gilda Berger

In a good study of the intricate relationships within a narrow environment, the text describes the plants and animals that form a coral reef and its inhabitants' adjustment to each other in an underwater community.

Swim out over a coral reef, and you see coral shaped like rocks, stars, fingers or fans. There is coral shaped like animal horns and antlers, even like trees and bushes. There is coral of all colors—tan, orange, yellow, purple, green and pink.

A coral reef is an underwater range of stone hills. It forms in the shallow, warm oceans of the world. The warm temperature of the water and a good supply of sunlight are needed for the coral to grow. It is built up, bit by bit, over thousands of years, by the remains of sea plants and animals. The largest coral reef in the world is the Great Barrier Reef off the coast of Australia. It is hundreds of feet wide and over one thousand miles long.

Coral reefs take a constant pounding from the waves that hit against them. But these moving waters make the reef a wonderful place for plants and animals to live. They bring to the reef a rich supply of food and oxygen. And they carry away from the reef carbon dioxide and other waste products.

Dive down, and you see thousands of different sea plants growing in, on and around the reef. There are many more that you cannot see. These are tiny, invisible specks floating in the water.

Meet the many animals that live around the reef. There are sponges, anemones and clams that are fixed to one place on the coral. They depend on the rushing waters to bring them food. There are starfish, sea urchins, lobsters and crabs that creep and crawl over the reef looking for food among the coral. And there are fish who swim in and out of the tunnels, caves and passages in the coral.

As you get to know the plants and animals on a coral reef you find that

—each has its place on the reef.

—each is fit for its way of life on the reef.

—each depends on the reef.

—each depends on others that live on the reef.

All coral reefs are made up of layer upon layer of the stony skeletons of animals and plants that once lived there. But covering the skeletons is a thick layer of small, living animals known as coral polyps. The coral polyps are the most important animals on the reef. They are the reef builders.

A reef begins to form when one floating polyp attaches itself to a piece of rock in the water. The polyp is a small colorless blob of jelly, no bigger than your fingernail. As soon as it is in place, the polyp starts to grow a skeleton around itself.

This skeleton takes the shape of a little cup around the lower part of the polyp. It protects the polyp like a suit of armor protects a knight. It is made of a kind of stone called limestone. The limestone skeleton is made from chemicals that the animal takes in from the water.

During the day the polyp stays safely inside its skeleton. But at night it stretches out its tiny arms, or tentacles, and catches and eats the smallest animals that drift by in the water.

After a while the coral polyp sends out a branch, or bud. The bud attaches itself to the rock next to the parent polyp. It starts to grow. It builds its own cuplike skeleton.

More and more polyp buds form. They build their stone houses alongside the others. Soon the mass of coral skeletons grows quite large. New polyps start to grow on top of the older polyps. The older ones die as they are covered over by the new ones. But their skeletons remain. These layers of polyp skeletons make up most of the coral reef.

But a reef made up only of coral skeletons would not be very strong. It would crumble under the battering of the ocean waves. Other animals and plants that come to live on the reef help to make it stronger.

But life on a reef is full of danger. Most of the fish on a reef eat other fish who live there. The biggest fish, the sharks and the barracuda, eat the snappers. The snappers eat the smaller mackerel, the mackerel eat the still smaller herring, and the herring eat the very small fry.

And many kinds of fish eat the coral polyps.

The parrot fish scrapes and bites the coral all day looking for the juicy polyps. The bumpfish looks for polyps in the pieces of coral which it knocks off the reef with the noselike bump on its head. Worms, snails and starfish make holes in the reef as they search for the polyps.

Raging storms and pounding waves also break off pieces of coral. Sewage and other pollution are more recent dangers to the reefs. Where the polyps die, the reefs are often torn apart.

A coral reef is one of the most varied, crowded, busy, exciting and challenging environments on earth. It is an ever-changing wonderland of colors and shapes and forms. It is rough and rugged, and at the same time it is delicate and fragile. But most of all, a coral reef is a closely woven community of millions of well-adapted plants and animals that depend on each other and on the reef for their survival.

from The Mystery of Stonehenge
Franklyn M. Branley

A distinguished scientist explains how contemporary research has led to theories of the function of the Stonehenge circle, carefully drawing a line between fact and supposition, and investing the text with the challenge of a suspense story.

For 300 years archeologists have tried to find out why Stonehenge was built—as have anthropologists, engineers, and other scientists. Many astronomers believe that the stones were used to keep track of time, and thus represent a sort of calendar.

In 1960, Gerald Hawkins, an astronomer who came to America from England, became intensely interested in Stonehenge. After years of study, he developed the following theory about why it was built:

The sun was extremely important in the lives of Stone Age people. And so the priests and kings of the tribes would have been much concerned about its coming and going. Anyone who could tell, months ahead, where the sun would appear in the morning or set in the evening would be greatly respected.

Dr. Hawkins reasoned that Stone Age men must have considered the sun and moon to be gods—for they brought good to the people. The sun created warmth, and the moon lighted the way at night. When the sun or moon disappeared from the sky, as during an eclipse, people must have been frightened, thinking that the gods were displeased and that they were leaving the sky forever. Anyone who could warn the people of such a disaster would naturally hold a position of importance.

Perhaps Stonehenge was intended as a device to tell when there would be an eclipse of the sun or moon.

Dr. Hawkins first studied those eclipses that occurred around the time Stonehenge

From THE MYSTERY OF STONEHENGE by Franklyn M. Branley. Copyright © 1969 by Franklyn M. Branley. By permission of Thomas Y. Crowell, Publishers.

was built. He figured out where in the sky the eclipses took place. Then he numbered all the stones as well as the Aubrey Holes and fed these numbers into an electronic computer. The computer matched, wherever possible, the positions and alignments of the stones and holes against the times and locations of the eclipses.

Dr. Hawkins discovered that the 56 Aubrey Holes, just inside the ditch and mound that mark the outer boundary of the Stonehenge site, could be used to predict eclipses. He found that if in 1591 B.C. six stones had been placed in the Aubrey Holes at the locations he numbered 56, 47, 38, 28, 19, and 10, and if each stone had been moved to the next hole once a year after that, an important lunar event would have occurred whenever a stone came around to Hole number 56. This is the hole that is situated on a straight line connecting the Heel Stone and the Altar Stone.

In the years between 1591 and 1452 B.C. there were 21 eclipses. At the time of each eclipse, there would have been a stone in Aubrey Hole number 56, had this system been followed. And most of the eclipses would have occurred in a direct line with the Heel Stone.

Since anthropologists know that eclipses have always caused alarm among primitive peoples, it is reasonable to suppose that the design of Stonehenge may be related to happenings in the sky.

Stonehenge might also have been used to predict when the sun would return to a high place in the sky (summer) and bring back once again warmth and plentiful food.

In a six-month period, the place where the sun rises and sets changes a great deal. In summer the sun rises far north of east, and in winter it rises far south of east. Notice carefully where the sun rises or sets today. Then check the location a week or two from now —and you will see that, even in this short time, the sun appears farther north or south, depending upon the season.

The location where the moon rises and sets also changes a great deal. Within a single month the shift can be from north of the equator to south—the direction, again, depending upon the season of the year.

With great care Dr. Hawkins recorded the positions of the Sarsen Stones and the stones of the inner horseshoe. Then he measured the distances between them and the angles of one stone relative to another. He also figured out where the sun and the moon rose and set over the Salisbury Plain 4,000 years ago. He gathered hundreds of measurements of the stones and sky positions of the sun and moon. Then the astronomer fed this information into the computer in order to match, wherever possible, the positions and alignments of the stones against the different rising and setting locations of the sun and moon.

Although the computer failed to find a relationship in many cases, it also showed that there were dozens of connections between the placements of the stones and the events occurring in the sky. One startling example is the following:

If a viewer stood at the center of Stonehenge on February 5 and November 8 and looked over Stone number 91, he would see the sunrise. And if he looked toward Stone number 93 on May 6 and August 8, he would see the sunset.

These four sightings could have been used to mark the passage of the seasons. The beginnings of our seasons of spring and fall are determined by those moments when the sun is directly over the equator. Our summer begins when the sun is at its farthest point north of the equator, and winter starts when the sun is farthest south of the equator. The dates when the four seasons begin are December 21, March 21, June 21, and September 21— or close to them. The dates of sunrise and sunset mentioned in the preceding paragraph are February 5, May 6, August 8, and November 8. Each of these is about 45 days before or after the beginning of our summer or winter. It seems that such a division could not be accidental:

November 8 (44 days before December 21)—
   Sunrise above Stone number 91
February 5 (47 days after December 21)—

Sunrise above Stone number 91
May 6 (47 days before June 21)—
Sunset above Stone number 93
August 8 (49 days after June 21)—
Sunset above Stone number 93

The place where the summer sun rises above Stonehenge was also predicted by the computer.

Even today, a person standing on the fallen Altar Stone at the center of Stonehenge can look right through the two pillars of the Sarsen Circle that form the entrance. Beyond the circle he can see the Heel Stone, framed within the space once set off by the two Slaughter Stones. From the viewer's position, the top of the Heel Stone is exactly even with the horizon. On the first day of summer, the rising sun rests momentarily atop the Heel Stone—then continues across the sky. For the people of the Stone Age this day may have been the most important of all. It was the day in each year when the sun reached its highest point in the sky.

Gerald Hawkins and his computer seem to have shown that the stones of Stonehenge are arranged for a definite purpose. It is hard to believe that the large number of occasions when their locations have been related to events in the sky could be accidental.

But astronomers, archeologists, anthropologists, engineers, and nonscientists do not all agree about Stonehenge.

Some think the massive rocks and pillars are the remains of a sacred temple; some believe the monument was built by men of Greek descent who lived in England some three or four thousand years ago; many are convinced that the stones were brought to the Salisbury Plain from faraway places. But all still wonder why Stonehenge was built at this particular place, and what its purpose could have been. Was it a place of worship? Or was it a calendar that would forewarn the kings and priests of events relating to the sun and moon?

Scientists from around the world have pondered such questions. They have studied the site, using test tubes, microscopes, computers—the many tools of modern science. They have dug into the ground, probed beneath the pillars, explored different avenues to unravel its mysteries. But Stonehenge remains a challenge. Its mysteries may be locked forever within the silent stones.

from **The Sports**
Leonard Everett Fisher

One of the author's series of books about aspects of life in nineteenth-century America, this is a good example of both the candor and the research that marks today's best informational books.

According to the ancient Greeks, the Elysian Fields were beyond this world, a glorious place where deserving heroes, selected by the gods, could live through all eternity. In the classical Greek mind, athletic heroes, like military heroes and others, never died. The ancient hero so rewarded went from this world to Elysium—to the Elysian Fields—where life continued out of the vulgar sight of ordinary mortals, in joyous and perfect surroundings, forever. Every Greek aspired to such a wondrous reward. It was the ultimate prize.

Many Americans, caught up in the blissful pursuit of life, liberty, and happiness at the onset of the 19th century, viewed their entire country as Elysium, as Paradise. They had already won the ultimate prize and were about to build a nation in the place.

Thomas Jefferson himself had fired the imagination for things Greek. He saw the American political system as being the heir of 5th century B.C. Greek democracy. Moreover, he encouraged the idea that new government buildings in Washington, D.C., the nation's new capital, reflect the Greek lineage of American politics and culture in their architectural splendor.

As far as the amateur Knickerbocker Ball Club of New York was concerned, the Elysian Fields in 1845 were definitely not in another world; nor could they be confused with the territory and promise of the United States. They were in this world—in Hoboken, New Jersey—a dreamy, romantic, but very real flat and grassy meadow surrounded by lush picnic groves and a cluster of thirst-quenching taverns. All this across the Hudson River from Manhattan.

A private park, the Elysian Fields was owned by inventor John Stevens, who helped introduce steam locomotives and railroads, among other things, to America. There, in the unspoiled, scenic New Jersey countryside of 1845, Alexander Cartwright and friends—28 fun-loving cronies with steady jobs and leisure time who socialized as the Knickerbocker Ball Club of New York—indulged their ball-playing passion in peace, far from the rush of New York City civilization which had now reached as far north as 27th Street.

And there, on the Elysian Fields of Hoboken, in sight of strolling lovers brought to the picturesque spot by John Stevens' ferryboats, the Knickerbockers continued what they had started doing three years earlier on another meadow in Lower Manhattan, since buried under advancing civilization.

They, not Abner Doubleday, forged the rules of modern baseball and played the game—give or take a few refinements—much as it is played today. The Knickerbockers revised and made more adult and energetic a schoolboy game called town ball, or rounders, its British counterpart. Western Plains Indians beyond the Mississippi River still played a comparatively crude bat and ball game that was not too far removed from the idea of baseball. There, a batter stood in a circle and swatted a stuffed rawhide ball at any number of fielders. The fielder who caught the ball on the fly had the privilege of throwing it at the batter. If he managed to hit the batter, the batter was knocked out of the circle and became a fielder. The thrower became the batter.

In any case, town ball, or rounders, sometimes called baseball, and often called one o' cat, two o' cat, three o' cat, and four o' cat, depending on the number of bases used, had been played in Boston, Philadelphia, and New York in a variety of haphazard ways since before 1800. Gaining some momentum after the War of 1812, during which time English sailors impressed American seamen and English soldiers burned down the White House, American baseball gradually replaced the very popular British cricket, a game introduced to the colonies by the English about 1750.

Cricket incorporated rules and equipment seemingly similar to those in town ball, making it a distant ancestral cousin to the game of baseball being developed in the United States. The fact is, however, that cricket faded rapidly after 1820, not so much because most Americans did not think too highly of anything British after the war, but because cricket was not suitable to the American temperament. It was too slow, too courteous and genteel. Americans were more interested in speed, arguments, and excitement. Many a skillful American cricketeer became a baseball player by midcentury.

Alexander Cartwright was not only the manager, umpire, player, organizer, and chief inventive spirit of the Knickerbocker Base Ball Club of New York, he was also a gentleman surveyor. In 1845, he decided that bases had to be 90 feet apart in a perfect square and that the pitcher's position must be fixed exactly 60 feet from "home." There, at home, or "home base," the batters had stood for years ready to "knock the stuffing" out of stuffed leather balls.

The Knickerbockers changed several other practices. No longer would players run clockwise around the bases. Now they would run counterclockwise around the "diamond." And no longer could a fielder put a batter "out" by "plugging" or hitting him with the ball as he ran around the bases. The Knickerbockers continued to play as many innings as was necessary to roll up the required scores of either 11 or 21 runs. The team that scored 21 or more, or 11 or more, runs in an inning, and whose total score was more than that of the opposition, won the ball game. The Knickerbockers came to their games in uniform—blue floppy pants, white shirts, and straw hats—revolutionizing the look of the game.

On September 23, 1845, the Knicks drew up a set of bylaws and organized themselves into the first formal baseball team in America, and introduced the first fixed schedule of games. In addition, they invented the game book to record in detail every game played, the first of these being on October 6, 1845. As in the past, they played themselves. Cartwright's side lost. The score was 11–8 in three innings.

On June 19, 1846, the Knickerbockers did another remarkable thing. They played another team, the New Yorks. It was the first match game in baseball history. The Knicks lost 23–1, playing according to the rules they themselves had devised and developed. There was much swearing, umpire-baiting—Cartwright was the umpire—and arguing. The game was beginning to lose its good breeding. Two other notable firsts concocted by the Knicks were the system of nine-player teams with substitutes called "muffins," and the fining of ball players for sundry infractions, including swearing.

By 1858, there were at least two dozen baseball clubs in the New York City area—the Gothams, Brooklyn Eagles, Brooklyn Eckfords, Jamaica Atlantics, Long Island Pastimes, Manahattans, and more. The players on these clubs, chiefly policemen, bartenders, mechanics, laborers, and assorted toughs, met in convention to simplify and standardize the rules which varied from place to place. After much wrangling, they adopted the rules used by the Knickerbockers, who continued to lose more games than they won. They disappeared from the scene some ten or eleven years later, having done their work—establishing the modern game of baseball.

All during the Civil War (1861–1865),

nearly every rest from the carnage of battle resulted in a baseball game. The mania was everywhere among Union troops. These Northerners brought the game south with them when they were carted off as prisoners-of-war. They introduced the game to their guards and wardens in the prison camps. By the time the war had ended, baseball had spread all over America. By 1870, the game had become professional. The Cincinnati Red Stockings, managed by an ex-cricketeer, centerfielder Harry Wright, were paid to beat everyone else. Only one of their hired players was from Cincinnati, first baseman Charles Gould.

In 1876, America celebrated 100 years of independence; Wild Bill Hickok, a federal marshal, was shot in the back in South

Dakota; General George Armstrong Custer and his troopers died at the hands of Chief Sitting Bull and his warriors at the Battle of the Little Big Horn in Montana; Democrat Samuel J. Tilden received the most votes for President of the United States but lost the election to Rutherford B. Hayes; and the baseball pros founded the National League in New York. Five years before, however, on St. Patrick's Day, 1871, nine teams had formed the National Association of Professional Baseball Players—the first playing league. Those paying the $10 membership fee that day were the Boston Red Stockings, Chicago White Stockings, Cleveland Forest Citys, Fort Wayne Kekiongas, New York Mutuals, Philadelphia Athletics, Rockford Forest Citys, Washington Nationals, and the Washington Olympics.

Riddled with crime and corruption, the league did not last four years. It was replaced by the National League with Hartford, Connecticut, businessman Morgan G. Bulkeley as its first president, and organized baseball became a more tightly supervised sport. Tickets cost about fifty cents a game. Modern baseball, a generation old in 1876—the game itself in all its recognized forms had been played for at least a half century—was beginning to live up to the promise and prophecy of one midcentury, forgotten author: "This game . . . bids fair to become our national pastime. . . ."

Without doubt baseball had quickly become a national craze among the American male population. The game certainly involved the largest number of participants—organized and unorganized, amateur and professional, boys and men. The game or sport of baseball became a distinctive and unique American institution, whatever its origins, before the 19th century had run its course.

from
ECIDUJERP–PREJUDICE: Either Way It Doesn't Make Sense
Irene Gersten and Betsy Bliss

Since the authors use an actual class experiment to illustrate the destructive nature of biased behavior, this text on the causes, effects, and solutions of prejudice can serve as a good springboard for group discussion.

HOW DOES PREJUDICE FEEL? Recently a fourth-grade teacher decided that she wanted her students to really understand how prejudice works and how it feels. These students had heard a great deal about prejudice, but none of them had ever experienced it. They lived in a small town in Iowa. Most of the people in their town looked pretty much alike, had the same background, and seemed to share most of the same values and goals. Their problem was to find or create a situation in which they would be able to experience the effects of prejudice. Their teacher, Jane Elliot, helped them by pointing out that one difference among them was eye color. People had for years been treated unfairly because of their skin color, type of hair, and religion, so why not use eye color? The students agreed, and so they were separated into a blue-eyed group and a brown-eyed group.

Since the teacher was blue-eyed, she decided that on the first day of the experiment the blue-eyed students would be better, and on the next day they would change roles and the brown-eyed students would be better. This way both groups had the chance to experience what it felt like to be "superior" and "inferior."

The class felt at first that the experiment would be fun. They laughed together and looked forward to the first day of the experiment. On the first day, all the blue-eyed students were allowed to sit in the front of the room, while the brown-eyed students were forced to sit in the back. To make sure that the brown-eyed students stayed in their place and didn't pretend to be blue-eyed, they had to wear collars around their necks. As the class began, the blue-eyed teacher started calling on the brown-eyed students and making fun of them when they didn't know the right answers. Soon the brown-eyed students became very nervous when the teacher called on them. They were afraid that she would make fun of them in front of the whole class. They began to mumble their answers and forget information they had known very clearly only that morning. At recess time, only the blue-eyed students were allowed to use the playground. The brown-eyed students had to stay inside. The teacher also gave the blue-eyed students five extra minutes of play. At lunch, the brown-eyed students had to wait behind the blue-eyed students in the line. The teacher told them they couldn't have seconds, but the blue-eyed students could have extras if they wanted.

By afternoon, it was clear that experimenting with prejudice was no fun at all.

During the lunch period, the blue-eyed students started calling the brown-eyed students "brownies." They made fun of the "brownies" by calling them lazy, stupid, and dirty. The brown-eyed students were angry, but they were hurt, too. It was hard to believe that only yesterday they had all been friends. The brown-eyed students started to fight back. Several students were involved in fistfights and shoving matches.

When the students went back to the classroom after lunch, things did not improve. The teacher was very angry with the brown-eyed students for fighting. She made fun of them again in front of the whole class. When they began doing their schoolwork, it became clear to everybody that the brown-eyed students couldn't keep up with the blue-eyed students. This was very strange because before the experiment with prejudice the entire class was able to work at just about the same level. The brown-eyed students were really unhappy now, and the blue-eyed students really felt that they were better. The fighting and anger between the two groups continued for the rest of the afternoon.

Everybody was happy when the day was over—the teacher, the brown-eyed group, and even the blue-eyed group.

Members of the blue-eyed group were happy during the beginning of the experiment. One boy said that he was happy because he felt like a king and that he was "ruling" over the brown-eyed people. Generally the blue-eyed people felt happy because they felt that they were superior. They liked getting all the special attention, they liked feeling smarter and better than the other students. Yet when they bullied the "brownies" and called them names, they felt mean and nasty. After a while they began to miss their friends in the brown-eyed group. Finally they just felt unhappy and lonely.

The brown-eyed people felt terrible throughout the whole experiment. They realized from the beginning when Mrs. Elliot put the collars around their necks to prevent them from passing for "bluies" that they weren't going to get any fun out of the experiment at all. At first they tried to protect themselves by arguing whenever Mrs. Elliot or one of the "bluies" said something bad about brown-eyed people. But nobody paid any attention to them. And so they just accepted all the bad comments after a while. It seemed to the "brownies" that their teacher and the rest of the class had simply stopped looking at them. They were the same boys and girls they had been the day before, but nobody in the class seemed to care about that after they started wearing their collars. All of the "brownies" felt completely left out and they were hurt, unhappy, and angry. They also felt helpless, since no matter what they did the "bluies" treated them the same way. Finally, one by one, they just "gave up" and went along with the situation. This made them feel even worse and they began to hate themselves for not fighting back. There just didn't seem to be any way out of the problem.

On the second day of the experiment, the rules were switched—the brown-eyed students became "superior" and the blue-eyed students became "inferior." The same thing happened.

The teacher found the whole experiment very educational and yet frightening at the same time. She thought it was educational because she learned that victims of prejudice did indeed become "dumb" when they were treated as if they were "dumb." She saw bright students, who the day before had done very well in math and spelling, fail math and spelling tests. She saw students, who knew their studies very well, suddenly lose confidence in themselves and become frightened of being called on.

She was frightened because she saw students, who had always been cooperative and well-mannered, suddenly change overnight and become mean little bullies. She felt the experiment proved that all of us are capable of prejudiced behavior, and that frightened her very much.

Another experiment was performed with teachers. In this experiment, two teachers were given classes to teach. Both classes were at the same level of progress and the students in each of these classes had received the same kinds of grades.

But the teachers were told that one class was stupid and one class was smart.

Then they began to teach their separate classes.

After some time they were asked to report on the progress of their classes. The teacher who thought she had a smart class reported that her class was doing good work, and that the students were performing well.

The teacher who thought her class was stupid reported that her students were slow. She said they were unable to keep up with their work, they had trouble answering questions in class, and, in general, they were poor students.

Both of these classes were tested when the experiment was over. The class that was labeled "smart" had stayed at exactly the same level as before the experiment began, but the class that was labeled "slow" had really become slow. In some cases the individual I.Q. test levels of students had actually dropped.

What had happened was that the teacher who thought her class was smart treated her students as if they were smart. The teacher who thought her class was slow treated her students as if they were stupid.

The conclusion of the experimenters was exactly the same conclusion that Mrs. Elliot and her class came to: when you are treated in an unfair way, you begin to feel and even act as if you are not as good as other people.

PREJUDICE HURTS EVERYONE. The experience of practicing and feeling prejudice shows very clearly that prejudice is a two-way street: it twists the prejudiced person as well as the victim. These experiments prove that prejudice not only hurts, but really changes the way you act, the way you think about yourself, and the way you do your work.

When these experiments were over, the students who took part in them had new answers to many questions, questions like these:

If you knew that no matter how hard you worked you would be called "dumb," would that make you try your hardest and do your best work?

If being treated unfairly in school made you feel angry or left out, would you want to go to school?

What would you feel like if you were told, over and over again, that you were "bad," "dirty," or "lazy"?

Is it any better to judge a person by the color of his skin or by his religion than by the color of his eyes?

These experiments were a very hard way to find out about prejudice. Yet all these students learned a great deal about themselves and about people in general.

They learned that we must never be afraid to look at ourselves and at each other. They learned that we must always try to see ourselves and others as we really are. And most important, they learned that only in this way can we really be free.

from Burrowing Birds
Anita Gustafson

Since this text focuses on a comparatively narrow area of biological science, it has minor reference use and gives good coverage of the topic, as is evident in this chapter on the kinds of birds that burrow underground in order to nest.

The Underground Birds

Who are the underground birds?

Some of them are "squatters." They take over another animal's burrow.

If rabbits leave their burrow in a sand dune, a pair of Shelduck may move in. Sweeping marks on the sand at ebb tide say a Shelduck is around. The bird finds its food by sweeping its bill back and forth in an arc in shallow water, leaving marks in the sand. Not far away, in the burrow, the female Shelduck may shelter up to sixteen white eggs.

A few birds that have found "squatting" convenient stay with certain digging animals. Pika are small burrowing rodents that live in mountains. They dig their burrows close together, making Pika towns. Around every Pika town in the high mountains of Tibet are Snow Finches. These Tibetan finches move into any vacant burrows.

Sometimes "squatters" are a part of a large underground community. The Burrowing Owl is one of these birds. In dry grasslands, like the southwestern plains of the United States, there are few large trees and many predators. So the Burrowing Owl joins snakes and ferrets and prairie dogs underground where there is safety from the large animals that walk the surface.

Burrowing Owls can dig their own burrows if they want to. Unlike most other burrowing birds, these owls use only their feet to dig. But usually they don't bother. They move into a burrow abandoned by another member of their underground community. Sometimes their new home is too small. Then the Burrowing Owls will make it larger by scraping away the earth and kicking it outside into a mound.

But the most intriguing underground birds are the ones that do all their own digging—the burrowing birds.

Some don't dig very deeply. In New Zealand, the parrot Kakapo and the pear-shaped Kiwi search around tree roots. When they find a hole already there, they dig it out a little more.

Both these birds live their entire lives on the ground. They can't fly. The Kiwi's wings don't work at all. The Kakapo's wings merely help it flutter *down* from a rock or tree it has *climbed.* Hiding in a burrow helps protect the birds from enemies such as dogs and cats.

A bird doesn't have to be flightless to be a burrowing bird, however. Surprisingly, many birds that are expert fliers are also expert diggers. Some of the best aviators in the bird world can burrow as far as fifteen feet into the earth!

A few birds are expert excavating engineers. On Whero Island off New Zealand, five different kinds of petrels and shearwaters burrow. Each kind digs its nest into a different layer of the soil. Whero Island is a real underground city! Instead of high-rise apartments, the island has deep-down burrows.

There are underground birds with familiar names. Some starlings, woodpeckers, and pigeons burrow. Kingfishers and their relatives dig down to nest. Most gulls and terns lay their eggs in scrapes in sand or on the bare shore, but the Inca Tern *(Larosterna inca)* may use niches, hollows, rock caverns, or underground burrows it has enlarged itself.

There are burrowing birds that perch and sing. Perching birds, or passerines, are the most numerous group of birds, and most passerines are songbirds. The Sand Martins of England and Europe are the same species as our Bank Swallow. They are songbirds, and they nest underground. In England, all the Sand Martins in a community help dig each other's burrows. When all the burrows are finished, each pair of Sand Martins pays attention to only what's happening in its own burrow.

There are burrowing birds that like to wade. The Crab Plover, a wading bird from Africa, burrows into sandbanks. Young Crab Plovers are born with a coat of down. They can run right after they hatch. But their parents still bring crabs and other crunchy things to feed them in their burrows.

There are burrowing birds that love the sea. Puffins burrow into cliffs and under grass sod in the north. One kind of penguin burrows in the south. Prions and storm-petrels and shearwaters live most of their lives at sea. All these sea-loving birds come to land for only one reason—to go into a burrow and nest.

All these and more are burrowing birds. They use their bills as pickaxes and their feet as shovels. They dig a tunnel that ends in a room, a larger nesting chamber. They were born knowing how to do this.

A burrow nest is a secret place. It's meant to hide what's inside. And the burrowing birds like it that way. A dark underground nest is the only place they will raise a family.

from Sky Stars: The History of Women in Aviation
Ann Hodgman and Rudy Djabbaroff

From a history of women flyers that gives international coverage and includes the contributions of women aviators to military and scientific projects, this excerpt describes the achievements of some of the women who flew at the beginning of the twentieth century.

The first American woman to make a solo flight was Blanche Stuart Scott, nicknamed Betty, from Rochester, New York. Betty

"The First Women in Airplanes" from SKY STARS: THE HISTORY OF WOMEN IN AVIATION by Ann Hodgman and Rudy Djabbaroff. Copyright © 1981 by Rudy Djabbaroff (New York: Atheneum, 1981). Reprinted with the permission of Atheneum Publishers and Curtis Brown Associates, Ltd.

Scott was not encouraged to fly. In fact, her friends were openly discouraging, warning her that she would become dizzy high up in the air and that there would be no steadying male nearby to help her down to the ground. "I do not intend to get myself killed by trying foolish stunts," she answered, and she was so sure of this that she managed to convince Glenn Curtiss, the celebrated American aviator, airplane designer, and inventor, to teach her to fly.

Blanche Scott's first solo flight was on September 2, 1910, but it was unintentional. She was sitting in the plane while Curtiss gave her a lesson. As she began to practice driving the plane back and forth across the field, a sudden gust of wind lifted the plane into the air. Because the engine was on at the same time, and because airplanes in those days were lighter than they are now, the plane was soon forty feet in the air. That is not very high, but it can seem a terrible distance to a novice pilot. Fortunately Scott kept her head, perhaps remembering her staunch answer to her friends' misgivings. She landed the plane smoothly. Glenn Curtiss had been teaching her for only three days, but he decided she was clearly ready to begin flying. He never did become convinced that women should fly at all, although he continued to teach Scott; after that he never had another woman pupil.

Another American woman named Bessica Raiche was learning to fly at the same time as Blanche Scott. Bessica had left Beloit, Wisconsin to study music in Paris and while there had become fascinated by stories about the French aviators. While in Paris she also met and married Frank Raiche, an airplane designer. The newlyweds returned to America, and Bessica began to study aviation instead of music. She was an exceptionally fast learner. Two weeks after Blanche Scott first soloed, so did Bessica Raiche. She could only get the plane a few feet off the ground, but in another two weeks she managed to fly it at a more respectable height.

Because Blanche Scott's solo flight had been made possible by a trick of the wind, the Aeronautical Society decided that the first solo honors should go to Bessica Raiche. It must have been a little hard on Blanche Scott that on October 13, 1910, a formal dinner was given for Raiche by the Society. She was awarded a gold medal studded with diamonds; on it was inscribed, "First Woman Aviator of America, Bessica Raiche."

Raiche then began to devote her time to helping her husband design and construct airplanes. The Raiches were especially interested in making planes lighter, and they were the first to use piano wire rather than iron stove wire in airplane construction. In addition they introduced bamboo and Chinese silk—lighter than wood and canvas—into the American aviation industry.

Eventually Bessica Raiche was forced to give up flying because it was a strain on her health. By the time she had recovered her health, she had lost her interest in flying. Instead she began to study medicine and became a practising physician. In medicine she finally found a lasting career, and she never returned to aviation.

Neither Bessica Raiche nor Blanche Scott had a flying license. Licenses had not been necessary when they were taught to fly. Although the Aero Club soon forbade new pilots to fly without licenses, it did not require existing pilots to obtain them. Blanche Scott thought the requirements for being licensed were too strict to make it worth trying for, so she went on flying without one.

The first American to receive a pilot's license was the strikingly beautiful Harriet Quimby. Quimby was the dramatic editor of *Leslie's Weekly* when she began learning to fly in April, 1911. Unlike some other aviators, Quimby was not boastful about flying. In fact she was determined to keep her lessons on Long Island completely secret. They were secret for a little while, secret in a dashing and romantic way. Quimby worked with her flying instructor just after dawn; she always wore an aviator's suit and shrouded her face in a deep hood. Her cover was ruined when she was forced to make a crash landing after only a few weeks of training. The accident—from which she escaped safely—made all the

front pages, and Quimby was discovered. She continued to study, though, until she had received her license in August.

By December, Harriet Quimby had learned enough about flying to be a stunt pilot at the inauguration of the president of Mexico. But she wanted more than that. She began to plan, again in complete secrecy, to be the first woman to cross the English Channel in an airplane. There was a reason for the secrecy this time: Harriet Quimby did not want any other woman to find out her plans and try to beat her across the Channel. She arranged to meet Louis Bleriot for lessons in flying one of the planes he'd designed, and she arranged as well to have a plane like the one she had been flying in America shipped to Dover, where she was planning to take off. Unfortunately the plane was spotted on its way to her. People became suspicious. If the plane was being shipped secretly, someone must have big plans for it.

Eleanor Trehawk Davis, a British woman, evidently suspected what those plans might be. On April 2, 1912, Davis flew across the Channel as a passenger, something that no woman had ever done; the record became hers, and some of the fun went out of Harriet Quimby's preparations.

Now it was up to Quimby to become the

first woman actually to pilot across the Channel. She worked furiously for two more weeks before deciding that she was ready. But the weather had never been good enough for her to test the Bleriot airplane she planned to fly in. This was another blow, and to add to it, Quimby was told that if she flew even five miles off course, she would end up in the North Sea. No one thought she should attempt the trip. One pilot (the one who had flown Eleanor Davis across the Channel) told Quimby frankly that she had no chance at all. Wouldn't she like to let him wear her clothes, he suggested, so that he could make the flight in her place? Then he would let her have all the credit.

But Harriet Quimby was not afraid. "My heart was not in my mouth," she said firmly. "I felt impatient to realize this project on which I was determined, despite the protests of my best friends. For the first time I was to fly a Bleriot monoplane. For the first time I was to fly by compass. For the first time I was to fly across water. For the first time I was to fly on the other side of the Atlantic. My anxiety was to get off quickly."

Her clothes for the flight had been chosen almost as carefully as her airplane. She wore her customary purple satin suit, to start with, and under it she wore two pairs of silk long underwear. Then on top came a wool coat and a raincoat, and finally a huge sealskin stole. Just as she was ready to go, her friends forced her to take a hot water bottle as well, which her advisor "insisted on tying to my waist like an enormous locket." Thus laden down, she climbed into the plane and took off.

In half a minute Quimby was fifteen hundred feet above the choppy Channel waves. Briefly she noticed the crowd of reporters far below her, and then the fog came up and she saw nothing but fog. She was forced to use her compass for guidance, the compass she had never used before. Quimby kept her composure, and in twenty minutes the fog lifted. There below her Quimby could see land and she was filled with disappointment; she must have flown in circles, she thought

disgustedly, and have stayed above England the whole time. How could she face the people down on the ground?

But Harriet Quimby was not above England. She was above Calais, she had succeeded, and she was the first woman in the world to have flown herself across the Channel. When she landed on the beach beside a fishing village, the townspeople were so delighted to see her that they brought coffee right down to her plane.

As Quimby wrote later, the detail that had been so annoying at the beginning of the trip —that hot water bottle—had been helpful after all. "I did not suffer from cold while crossing for the excitement stimulated my warmth, but I noticed when I landed that the hot water bag was cold as ice. It surely saved me something."

Harriet Quimby was famous not only for her flying but also for her sense of style. Her purple satin flying costume attracted a lot of attention, and after crossing the Channel she returned to the United States with an all-white Bleriot airplane as well. But she was not to savor her fame very long. On July 1, 1912, less than three months after crossing the Channel, Quimby took a passenger, William Willard, for a short flight near Boston. She was trying to break a speed record, and perhaps it was the plane's tremendous speed that caused the accident.

As Quimby and Willard flew above Dorchester Bay their plane dove downward. Neither of the passengers was wearing a seat belt, and Willard was thrown out of his seat. A second later Harriet fell out too. Both landed in four feet of water and died instantly.

Blanche Scott, flying over Boston, had seen Harriet Quimby die, and she was so horrified that she landed her plane and collapsed.

No one knew what had caused the crash. Perhaps Willard had moved suddenly and caused the plane to lurch; perhaps Quimby had fainted; perhaps a sudden gust of wind had jarred the plane. In any case one of the world's most popular pilots was dead.

from Wrapped for Eternity: The Story of the Egyptian Mummy
Mildred Mastin Pace

The vigorous, almost conversational style adds to the pleasure of a book that is based on deftly incorporated research and that has almost a detective-story appeal in its investigation of the process of mummification, myths about mummies, and the depredations by tomb robbers.

Where Did All the Mummies Go?

A mummy must be pretty tough.

We have seen how the thirty royal mummies survived the damage by graverobbers, the hasty rewrapping by tomb priests, a hurried transfer to another tomb in antiquity, and finally, in modern times, the trip by boat to Cairo. Even unwrapped, a mummy will continue to exist if kept with reasonable care, the temperature constant, humidity low.

Why then, out of the tremendous number of mummies made by the ancient Egyptians over a period of twenty-five centuries, are there only a comparatively few left? Obviously, they were destroyed.

Some were destroyed by carelessness and ignorance, some by accident. A few, a very few, were destroyed in scientific study and experimentation. But many were destroyed on purpose, for profit.

The greatest destruction of mummies for profit occurred over a period of four hundred years, when mummies were used as medicine. From the early thirteenth century A.D. well into the seventeenth century, Egyptian tombs were stripped of their mummies, the mummies chopped up and sold in Europe to be fed to the sick and ailing.

While the ancient thieves favored the tombs of the royal and the rich, these later looters took any and all mummies they could find. For them, the communal tombs of the poor, stacked with mummies, were bonanzas.

Taking "mummy" to cure their ills was not just a practice of the superstitious and ignorant. Far from it! Sir Francis Bacon, the great English philosopher of Shakespeare's day, took it and recommended it particularly "for the staunching of blood." Whether Shakespeare used it or not, we don't know. But he mentions it as medicine in several of his plays. And it is one of the magic ingredients in the witches' brew in *Macbeth*.

King François I of France always carried a little packet of mummy in case of sudden illness or an accident.

Most all the doctors of those centuries prescribed it and believed in it as a cure for many diseases.

The loathsome practice would never have gotten started if people had known how mummies were really made. They thought bitumen—a kind of mineral pitch—was used in the wrappings to preserve the bodies. It never was. What they saw in the wrappings was not bitumen but resins that had turned black and glasslike, resembling the mineral.

For several centuries before they began using cut-up mummies for medicine, pure bitumen was prized as a cure-all. However, it was hard to get. There was a mountain in Persia where bitumen, called *mummia* by the Persians, oozed out of cracks in the rocks. It was considered so precious, the mountain was guarded night and day and the mineral was stored in the Royal Treasury. There were other sources—the Dead Sea, for one. But these sources were very difficult to work, and the amounts extracted after tremendous hard labor were small.

Doctors, apothecaries, the sick, and the suffering demanded it. Merchants dishonestly stretched the precious stuff by mixing it with pitch. Smugglers and thieves trafficked in it. Another source was desperately needed.

Then came the rumor, wild and inaccurate: In Egypt there were thousands, probably hundreds of thousands, of ancient bodies wrapped in bandages that were heavy with bitumen. Travelers had seen them. Why not remove the bandages and reclaim the substance?

At the very first this is what was done. The body itself was not used. And because the Persians called the substance mummia, the Arabs began calling the bandaged body a mummy. Thus the word mummy was never known to the Egyptians who practiced mummification. It was coined in the early centuries after Christ. It is actually a misnomer for a wrapped corpse.

As soon as the "bitumen" (which was really resin) from the wrappings came into use, doctors and surgeons everywhere proclaimed it far better, far more effective, than the natural bitumen, or mummia, had ever been. It was believed that the human body around which it had been wrapped gave the drug, in some unknown way, greater curing powers. Now the doctors asked: If this is so, why not go one step further and use the entire wrapped body?

Without doubt, those who dealt in the drug found it much easier to chop up the whole mummy. It must have been a bit difficult to unwrap the body, soak the bandages, and reclaim the hard black substance. Also, there would be a much greater volume of salable drug if the whole body were used.

A lot was needed! Not only did doctors prescribe mummy for all kinds of ailments and diseases, but also for bone fractures, concussions, paralysis—even as an antidote for poison. It became a standard drug on the shelves of apothecary shops all over Europe.

Demand was so great, so many mummies were being destroyed to make the drug, that Egyptian officials finally realized along in the late sixteenth century that their land would soon be mummyless if steps weren't taken. So it was made illegal to transport mummies. They must be left in their tombs.

This led to a most unsavory fraud, practiced on a wide and dangerous scale in Egypt. Greedy and dishonest men began to manufacture mummies. They took any bod-

ies they could lay their hands on. Some were executed criminals. Others were slaves who had died and whose bodies had not been claimed. Some were paupers who had died without funds or friends to bury them.

These facts mattered not at all to the mummy manufacturers as they went about the business of making a mummy. First they filled the body's natural openings with a cheap blackish material, asphaltum. Then incisions were cut in the muscular part of the limbs and asphaltum packed in. The bodies were then tightly bound up and placed in the sun. The heat of the sun and the arid atmosphere dried them out sufficiently so they looked like mummies. And as mummies they were sold.

A prominent French physician, visiting Egypt late in the sixteenth century, saw one of these "mummy factories." He reported that he saw forty or more mummies newly

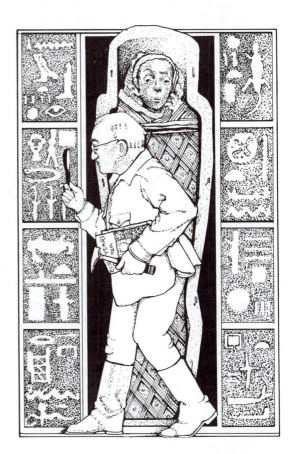

made and ready for sale. He asked the owner of the factory if any of these people had died of infectious diseases, especially the plague. The owner said he neither knew nor cared. As long as he could get the bodies, it mattered not to him how the person died. These were the bodies that would turn up as mummies in apothecary jars in Europe!

When the physician returned to France, he told a friend, a well-known surgeon, what he had seen. They both publicly denounced the use of mummy as medicine and refused to prescribe it. Whether they influenced others in their profession is not known.

In any event, the use of mummy as medicine was on its way out. But not because the medical men and their patients had lost faith in it as a cure-all.

The fraudulent mummy-makers in Egypt were in trouble. It started in one small town where money was sorely needed to meet local expenses. The town officials learned that a certain citizen was getting rich making false mummies and transporting them for sale. They had him arrested, fined him a large sum, and let him go. But not for long. A few mummies later he was again arrested and again the fine was a big one.

Other towns and cities heard of this simple method of raising funds and tried it—with success. Soon the heavy fines became too much for the crooks. They could not afford to continue their mummy hoax and went out of business. With no mummies available—real or false—mummy as medicine gradually disappeared.

But for a long time after, the mummia from Mummy Mountain in Persia was still considered magical and more precious than gold. In 1809 the King of Persia, wishing to bestow an important gift on the Queen of England and the Empress of Russia, sent each lady a small gold box full of the bitumen. While traveling in Persia a few years later, Sir William Ouseley, an English writer, met a trader who offered a dab of the mountain's mummia—about enough to fill an English walnut shell—for the price of eight pounds sterling. He did not buy it. The price was too high.

from The Story of Mankind
Hendrik Willem Van Loon

As this chapter indicates, the organization of this Newbery Medal book is based on major events or discoveries that changed history, rather than the usual chronological arrangement. The book brings history to life by relating, in fine narrative style, historical events to the changes they brought to the people of their time.

The Age of the Engine

BUT WHILE THE PEOPLE OF EUROPE WERE FIGHTING FOR THEIR NATIONAL INDEPENDENCE, THE WORLD IN WHICH THEY LIVED HAD BEEN ENTIRELY CHANGED BY A SERIES OF INVENTIONS, WHICH HAD MADE THE CLUMSY OLD STEAM ENGINE OF THE 18TH CENTURY THE MOST FAITHFUL AND EFFICIENT SLAVE OF MAN

The greatest benefactor of the human race died more than half a million years ago. He was a hairy creature with a low brow and sunken eyes, a heavy jaw and strong tiger-like teeth. He would not have looked well in a gathering of modern scientists, but they would have honoured him as their master. For he had used a stone to break a nut and a stick to lift up a heavy boulder. He was the inventor of the hammer and the lever, our first tools, and he did more than any human being who came after him to give man his enormous advantage over the other animals with whom he shares this planet.

Ever since, man has tried to make his life easier by the use of a greater number of tools. The first wheel (a round disc made out of an old tree) created as much stir in the communities of 100,000 B.C. as the flying machine did only a few years ago.

In Washington, the story is told of a director of the Patent Office who in the early thirties of the last century suggested that the Patent Office be abolished, because "everything that possibly could be invented had been invented." A similar feeling must have spread through the prehistoric world when the first sail was hoisted on a raft and the people were able to move from place to place without rowing or punting or pulling from the shore.

Indeed one of the most interesting chapters of history is the effort of man to let some one else or something else do his work for him, while he enjoyed his leisure, sitting in the sun or painting pictures on rocks, or training young wolves and little tigers to behave like peaceful domestic animals.

Of course in the very olden days, it was always possible to enslave a weaker neighbour and force him to do the unpleasant tasks of life. One of the reasons why the Greeks and Romans, who were quite as intelligent as we are, failed to devise more interesting machinery, was to be found in the widespread existence of slavery. Why should a great mathematician waste his time upon wires and pulleys and cogs and fill the air with noise and smoke when he could go to the marketplace and buy all the slaves he needed at a very small expense?

And during the Middle-Ages, although slavery had been abolished and only a mild form of serfdom survived, the guilds discouraged the idea of using machinery because they thought this would throw a large number of their brethren out of work. Besides, the Middle-Ages were not at all interested in producing large quantities of goods. Their tailors and butchers and carpenters worked for the immediate needs of the small community in which they lived and had no desire to compete with their neighbours, or to produce more than was strictly necessary.

During the Renaissance, when the prejudices of the Church against scientific investigations could no longer be enforced as rigidly as before, a large number of men began to devote their lives to mathematics and astronomy and physics and chemistry. Two years before the beginning of the Thirty Years War, John Napier, a Scotchman, had published his little book which described the new invention of logarithms. During the war itself, Gottfried Leibnitz of Leipzig had perfected the system of infinitesimal calculus. Eight years before the peace of Westphalia, Newton, the great English natural philosopher, was born, and in that same year Galileo, the Italian astronomer, died. Meanwhile the Thirty Years War had destroyed the prosperity of central Europe and there was a sudden but very general interest in "alchemy," the strange pseudo-science of the middle-ages by which people hoped to turn base metals into gold. This proved to be impossible but the alchemists in their laboratories stumbled upon many new ideas and greatly helped the work of the chemists who were their successors.

The work of all these men provided the world with a solid scientific foundation upon which it was possible to build even the most complicated of engines, and a number of practical men made good use of it. The Middle-Ages had used wood for the few bits of necessary machinery. But wood wore out easily. Iron was a much better material, but iron was scarce except in England. In England therefore most of the smelting was done. To smelt iron, huge fires were needed. In the beginning, these fires had been made of wood, but gradually the forests had been used up. Then "stone coal" (the petrified trees of prehistoric times) was used. But coal as you know has to be dug out of the ground and it has to be transported to the smelting ovens and the mines have to be kept dry from the ever invading waters.

These were two problems which had to be solved at once. For the time being, horses could still be used to haul the coal-wagons, but the pumping question demanded the application of special machinery. Several inventors were busy trying to solve the difficulty. They all knew that steam would have to be used in their new engine. The idea of the steam engine was very old. Hero of Alexandria, who lived in the first century before Christ, has described to us several bits of machinery which were driven by steam. The people of the Renaissance had played with the notion of steam-driven war chariots. The Marquis of Worcester, a contemporary of Newton, in his book of inventions, tells of a steam engine. A little later, in the year 1698, Thomas Savery of London applied for a patent for a pumping engine. At the same time, a Hollander, Christian Huygens, was trying to perfect an engine in which gun-powder was used to cause regular explosions in much the same way as we use gasoline in our motors.

All over Europe, people were busy with the idea. Denis Papin, a Frenchman, friend and assistant of Huygens, was making experiments with steam engines in several countries. He invented a little wagon that was driven by steam, and a paddle-wheel boat. But when he tried to take a trip in his vessel, it was confiscated by the authorities on a complaint of the boatmen's union, who feared that such a craft would deprive them of their livelihood. Papin finally died in London in great poverty, having wasted all his money on his inventions. But at the time of his death, another mechanical enthusiast, Thomas Newcomen, was working on the problem of a new steam-pump. Fifty years later his engine was improved upon by James Watt, a Glasgow instrument maker. In the year 1777, he gave the world the first steam engine that proved of real practical value.

But during the centuries of experiments with a "heat-engine," the political world had greatly changed. The British people had succeeded the Dutch as the common-carriers of the world's trade. They had opened up new colonies. They took the raw materials which the colonies produced to England, and there they turned them into finished products, and then they exported the finished goods to the four corners of the world. During the seventeenth century, the people of Georgia and the Carolinas had begun to grow a new shrub which gave a strange sort of woolly substance, the so-called "cotton wool." After this had been plucked, it was sent to England and there the people of Lancashire wove it into cloth. This weaving was done by hand and in the homes of the workmen. Very soon a number of improvements were made in the process of weaving. In the year 1730, John Kay invented the "fly shuttle." In 1770, James Hargreaves got a patent on his "spinning jenny." Eli Whitney, an American, invented the cotton-gin which separated the cotton from its seeds, a job which had previously been done by hand at the rate of only a pound a day. Finally Richard Arkwright and the Reverend Edmund Cartwright invented large weaving machines, which were driven by water power. And then, in the eighties of the eighteenth century, just when the Estates General of France had begun those famous meetings which were to revolutionise the political system of Europe, the engines of Watt were arranged in such a way that they could drive the weaving machines of Arkwright, and this created an economic and social revolution which has changed human relationship in almost every part of the world.

As soon as the stationary engine had proved a success, the inventors turned their attention to the problem of propelling boats and carts with the help of a mechanical contrivance. Watt himself designed plans for a "steam locomotive," but ere he had perfected his ideas, in the year 1804, a locomotive made by Richard Trevithick carried a load of twenty tons at Pen-y-darran in the Wales mining district.

At the same time an American jeweller and portrait-painter by the name of Robert Fulton was in Paris, trying to convince Napoleon that with the use of his submarine boat, the "Nautilus," and his "steam-boat," the French might be able to destroy the naval supremacy of England.

Fulton's idea of a steamboat was not original. He had undoubtedly copied it from John Fitch, a mechanical genius of Connecticut whose cleverly constructed steamer had first navigated the Delaware river as early as the year 1787. But Napoleon and his scientific advisers did not believe in the practical possibility of a self-propelled boat, and although the Scotchbuilt engine of the little craft puffed merrily on the Seine, the great Emperor neglected to avail himself of this formidable weapon which might have given him his revenge for Trafalgar.

As for Fulton, he returned to the United States and, being a practical man of business, he organised a successful steamboat company together with Robert R. Livingston, a signer of the Declaration of Independence, who was American Minister to France when Fulton was in Paris, trying to sell his invention. The first steamer of this new company, the "Clermont," which was given a monopoly of all the waters of New York State, equipped with an engine built by Boulton and Watt of Birmingham in England, began a regular service between New York and Albany in the year 1807.

As for poor John Fitch, the man who long before any one else had used the "steamboat" for commercial purposes, he came to a sad death. Broken in health and empty of purse, he had come to the end of his resources when his fifth boat, which was propelled by means of a screw-propeller, had been destroyed. His neighbours jeered at him as they were to laugh a hundred years later when Professor Langley constructed his funny flying machines. Fitch had hoped to give his country an easy access to the broad rivers of the west and his countrymen preferred to travel in flat-boats or go on foot. In the year 1798, in utter despair and misery, Fitch killed himself by taking poison.

But twenty years later, the "Savannah," a steamer of 1850 tons and making six knots an hour, (the Mauretania goes just four times as fast,) crossed the ocean from Savannah to Liverpool in the record time of twenty-five days. Then there was an end to the derision of the multitude and in their enthusiasm the people gave the credit for the invention to the wrong man.

Six years later, George Stephenson, a Scotchman, who had been building locomotives for the purpose of hauling coal from the mine-pit to smelting ovens and cotton factories, built his famous "travelling engine" which reduced the price of coal by almost seventy per cent and which made it possible to establish the first regular passenger service between Manchester and Liverpool, when people were whisked from city to city at the unheard-of speed of fifteen miles per hour. A dozen years later, this speed had been increased to twenty miles per hour. At the present time, any well-behaved flivver (the direct descendant of the puny little motor-driven machines of Daimler and Levassor of the eighties of the last century) can do better than these early "Puffing Billies."

But while these practically-minded engineers were improving upon their rattling "heat engines," a group of "pure" scientists (men who devote fourteen hours of each day to the study of those "theoretical" scientific phenomena without which no mechanical progress would be possible) were following a new scent which promised to lead them into the most secret and hidden domains of Nature.

Two thousand years ago, a number of Greek and Roman philosophers (notably Thales of Miletus and Pliny who was killed while trying to study the eruption of Vesuvius of the year 79 when Pompeii and Herculaneum were buried beneath the ashes) had noticed the strange antics of bits of straw and of feather which were held near a piece of amber which was being rubbed with a bit of wool. The schoolmen of the Middle Ages had not been interested in this mysterious "electric" power. But immediately after the Renaissance, William Gilbert, the private physician of Queen Elizabeth, wrote his famous treatise on the character and behaviour of Magnets. During the Thirty Years War Otto von Guericke, the burgomaster of Magdeburg and the inventor of the air-pump, constructed the first electrical machine. During the next century a large number of scientists devoted themselves to the study of electricity. Not less than three professors invented the famous Leyden Jar in the year 1795. At the same time, Benjamin Franklin, the most universal genius of America next to Benjamin Thomson (who after his flight from New Hampshire on account of his pro-British sympathies became known as Count Rumford) was devoting his attention to this subject. He discovered that lightning and the electric spark were manifestations of the same electric power and continued his electric studies until the end of his busy and useful life. Then came Volta with his famous "electric pile" and Galvani and Day and the Danish professor Hans Christian Oersted and Ampère and Arago and Faraday, all of them diligent searchers after the true nature of the electric forces.

They freely gave their discoveries to the world and Samuel Morse (who like Fulton began his career as an artist) thought that he could use this new electric current to transmit messages from one city to another. He intended to use copper wire and a little machine which he had invented. People laughed at him. Morse therefore was obliged to finance his own experiments and soon he had spent all his money and then he was very poor and people laughed even louder. He then asked Congress to help him and a special Committee on Commerce promised him their support. But the members of Congress were not at all interested and Morse had to wait twelve years before he was given a small congressional appropriation. He then built a "telegraph" between Baltimore and Washington. In the year 1837 he had shown his first successful "telegraph" in one of the lecture halls of New York University. Finally, on the 24th of May of the year 1844 the first long-distance message was sent from Washington to Baltimore and to-day the whole world is covered with telegraph wires and we can send news from Europe to Asia in a few seconds. Twenty-three years later Alexander Graham Bell used the electric current for his telephone. And half a century afterwards Marconi improved upon these ideas by inventing a system of sending messages which did away entirely with the old-fashioned wires.

While Morse, the New Englander, was working on his "telegraph," Michael Faraday, the Yorkshire-man, had constructed the first "dynamo." This tiny little machine was completed in the year 1831 when Europe was still trembling as a result of the great July revolutions which had so severely upset the plans of the Congress of Vienna. The first dynamo grew and grew and grew and to-day it provides us with heat and with light (you know the little incandescent bulbs which Edison, building upon French and English experiments of the forties and fifties, first made in 1878) and with power for all sorts of machines. If I am not mistaken the electric-engine will soon entirely drive out the "heat engine" just as in the olden days the more highly-organised prehistoric animals drove out their less efficient neighbours.

Personally (but I know nothing about machinery) this will make me very happy. For the electric engine which can be run by waterpower is a clean and companionable servant of mankind but the "heat-engine," the marvel of the eighteenth century, is a noisy and dirty creature for ever filling the world with ridiculous smoke-stacks and with dust and soot and asking that it be fed with coal which has to be dug out of mines at great inconvenience and risk to thousands of people.

And if I were a novelist and not a historian, who must stick to facts and may not use his imagination, I would describe the happy day when the last steam locomotive shall be taken to the Museum of Natural History to be placed next to the skeleton of the Dinosaur and the Pterodactyl and the other extinct creatures of a by-gone age.

from True Escape and Survival Stories
Gurney Williams III

For readers who prefer fiction, a collection of true stories that have excitement and action is often the best way to gain information. In this account of a space flight adventure, the experience of the astronauts on Apollo 13 is no less dramatic for being completely factual.

Lifeboat in Space

The spaceship carrying three men to the moon shuddered as if it had bumped into something.

The shudder made no sense. There was nothing to bump into, 205,000 miles away from earth in black space. Astronaut Fred W. Haise was floating between two cabins in the ship when he felt the bump. He pulled himself quickly into the main cabin, called the command module. The ship continued to shake up and down. Haise's heart was beating twice as fast as usual.

There was no gravity in space, so Haise appeared to be floating through the air. Quickly he pulled himself to his seat. Another astronaut, John L. Swigert, slammed the door shut, sealing off the cabin.

Now all three were sitting in a small compartment, about as big as a three-man tent. It was a little after 9:00 P.M. on Monday, April 13, 1970, somewhere between earth and the moon.

Sealed into their cramped quarters, the men tried to figure out what had happened by reading dials in front of them. The whole ship was wobbling now, something like a car with a flat tire. The men's eyes raced over the lighted boards.

A few of the dials were behaving wildly. Some showed the ship was losing electrical power. Capt. James A. Lovell tried to stop the wobbling by firing small rockets outside the ship. It didn't work. Then suddenly he hit on the problem. One of the instruments was like a fuel gauge on a car. It showed how much fuel—called oxygen—was left in one of the large tanks. The fuel was used to make electrical power to run the ship. Just as important, it helped fuel the men: oxygen was a vital part of the air they breathed. Without fuel, the ship—and the men running it—would die.

Lovell radioed the earth about what he had found. "Our oxygen number two tank is reading zero," he said.

Then Lovell got out of his seat and glided to a window so he could see the outside of Apollo 13. He turned to the section of the ship called the service module. That was a large cylinder containing the fuel tanks and the main rocket engine. The service module

was connected to one end of the command module where the men lived. In the black night of space, Lovell saw a ghostly cloud coming out of the side of the service module.

Lovell got back on the radio, flashing the news to the gray-walled mission control room in Texas. "It looks to me that we are venting something," he said.

The ship, Apollo 13, pride of America, had soared into the sky two days before. Now like an old boat it was leaking, or "venting." One of its round, silvery fuel tanks had exploded, blasting a hole right through the side of the service module. Fuel was disappearing into space. Every two seconds the ship moved a mile closer to the moon, farther from earth.

Dozens of people on the ground tried to figure out what to do. What they needed was a lifeboat, another rocket ship with its own supply of oxygen, its own rocket engine, to bring the men home.

Well, in a way, Apollo 13 had a lifeboat. Its name was Aquarius. Aquarius was a small but complete rocket ship attached to the command module where the men lived. It had been designed to break away from the command module and carry two men to the surface of the moon, and then back up to the command module. It had its own air supply. It had its own rocket engine.

What it didn't have was space. There was no room to sit down in Aquarius. It had about as much space as a small closet. Aquarius also lacked strength. It was built to land on the moon—not on the earth. If the astronauts tried to ride it all the way home into the earth's air, it would burn to cinders. The command module was the only part of Apollo 13 designed to survive the fiery plunge back to earth.

The people on the ground argued and sweated over what to do. Finally, they agreed on a plan. They radioed the idea into space: Turn off everything in the command module to save what fuel is left. Climb into Aquarius. Use the Aquarius air supply and the Aquarius rocket to get home. Then when you get close to earth, climb back into the command module to protect yourselves when things get hot during landing.

Haise was the first to enter Aquarius. There were no lights except his flashlight. He floated into the dark little cabin. Closer and closer he moved to instruments covering the walls, closer to two triangular windows that had been designed for a view of the moon's surface. There were no seats. Haise turned on some of the switches. Soon the cramped lifeboat was filling with its own supply of oxygen.

Lovell joined Haise. Swigert stayed behind in the command module for a few minutes. He turned everything off, saving the little fuel left for the earth landing. Then he followed the other two into Aquarius. There was no chance now that Aquarius would land on the moon. It now had a new mission, a more important one: to keep three men alive.

Apollo 13, its crew huddled in one end, hurtled on toward the moon. The ship curved around the back side of the moon, out of sight of the earth. The gray lunar surface, pocked with craters, unrolled beneath the ship at about ten times the speed of a fast jet plane on earth. Then the earth, a blue green ball, appeared again. It was time to see whether the small rocket on Aquarius could blast the whole ship into a good course back home to Earth. If the course adjustment failed, Apollo could miss the earth completely. The crew wouldn't survive long, and the ship would carry their bodies on an endless trip through space.

"Mark!" said a man in Texas, telling Lovell he had forty seconds to go before firing. Lovell put his hand on the firing button. "Five . . . four . . . three . . . two . . . one." At exactly the right time, the rocket began to fire. No one could hear the explosion. Sound couldn't pass through empty space. But the astronauts could feel the movement. The little rocket on Aquarius kept pushing the whole ship into line. It fired on, a four-minute explosion. Then a computer took over. It turned the rocket off at precisely the right instant.

Men in space and on the ground anxiously checked the course. The rocket had done its job. The ship was aimed for a landing in the Pacific Ocean, a quarter of a million miles away. At least the ship was headed in the right direction. Whether it would splash down safely, no one knew.

Other problems crowded in on the men in the crippled ship.

Since fuel was low, there was not enough energy to keep Aquarius warm. The temperature was dropping. And there were no winter clothes on Apollo 13.

Fuel had been used to make water, so now water supplies were low, too. Like desert explorers, the men had carried some of the water from the main supply in the command module to Aquarius in plastic juice bags. But the supply was still low. Their constant thirst was making it hard for the men to concentrate.

The air was bad. Back in the command module, a machine cleaned the air of dangerous gases. Aquarius had no such machine. Scientists on the ground suggested that the men try to build an air cleaner out of scraps aboard the ship—plastic bags, a hose, some cards, and tape. No one knew whether the contraption would work.

By now, millions of people on earth were worried about the voyagers from the moon. Concern had spread around the world. Thirteen countries offered to help in recovering the ship if it made it back to earth. People gathered on streets to watch TV reports, and in churches and synagogues to pray.

In space, it was cold and quiet. By early Wednesday morning, the temperature in Aquarius had dropped to fifty-five degrees. No one aboard could sleep. The men stayed awake, thirsty, tired, cold, moving around restlessly like animals in a small cage.

"You got up kind of early, didn't you?" the ground radioed. The men said it was impossible to sleep. Temperatures were headed for the forties.

The air got worse. Before noon on Wednesday, a yellow light in Aquarius warned suddenly that it wasn't safe to breathe. Lovell turned on the taped-up contraption. It began to suck air through the filter.

Clean air flooded the cabin. The light went off. They would be okay as long as the makeshift air cleaner worked.

The double impact of thirst and cold was making it ever more difficult to think. At one point, Lovell was looking out the window. "The moon passed by," he said, watching a ball move slowly in front of the window. Then he corrected himself. "No, that's the earth." For an instant, the astronaut hadn't been able to tell them apart.

A sharp mind was now critical. The ship bore in on the earth like a bullet. The men had to begin moving back into the command module to prepare to land. Landing was complicated because most of Apollo 13 had to be thrown away in space before it was safe to come down. The command module had a solid round shield on its bottom to help it survive the heat when it plunged into the earth's air. The service module and Aquarius had no such protection. One of the astronauts' first jobs was to separate the command module from Aquarius and the service module.

The service module was the first to go. Explosive charges pushed it away from the command module. The module was spinning away into space when Lovell spotted the damage caused by the fuel tank explosion. "There's one whole side of that spacecraft missing," he said. Haise saw it too. "It's really a mess," he reported. The service module shrank to a dot in the blackness.

As it disappeared in the distance, the crew aboard Apollo began to worry about something else, more dangerous than anything that had happened. The fuel tank explosion had damaged the service module just a few feet from the heat shield that would protect the men during the last few minutes of the flight. Suppose the explosion had also damaged the heat shield. Would the command module stand the shock of re-entering Earth's atmosphere? No one talked about the possibility. The earth seemed to grow steadily, a big, blue ball out the spaceship's window.

Lovell was the last to leave Aquarius. By the time he had eased his way back through a tunnel into the command module, Aquarius was filled with debris from the flight. The men switched over to the remaining oxygen in the command module. They sealed off the compartment in Aquarius. Then they blasted away from their lifeboat.

They were falling now, in the command module cone, at about 15,000 miles an hour. In less than an hour, they would either land, or burn up.

No one was talking much. Men on the ground were plotting the cone's course. There was little that could be done now. The command module was picking up speed. 17,000 miles an hour. 18,000. In a few minutes it reached 20,000 miles an hour. That meant the end of radio contact was near. The ship-to-ground radios couldn't work through the fire that would soon surround the command module. People on the ground talked nervously with the astronauts about a party they would have after the mission was ended. Swigert said he wished he could be there for it.

About 400,000 feet above the earth, the capsule began heating up. Soon flames whipped around it and the radio went dead. Ground scientists expected radio contact to be broken for about three and a half minutes.

But at the end of three and a half minutes, there was still no word. Another half-minute ticked by. Apollo 13 remained silent. And then another half-minute. Some people began to lose hope.

"Okay, Joe." The voice was Swigert's. He was on the air again. Within minutes, white-and-orange parachutes rose like giant party balloons over the little command module. It splashed into the sea and the men were picked up from their bobbing ship, still so cold inside you could see your breath. They had survived.

And what of Aquarius? The lifeboat had continued to send radio signals long after it had been separated from the men it had saved. "Where did she go?" one of the astronauts had asked just before radio contact was broken.

"Oh I don't know," replied one of the ground crew. "She's up there somewhere." A radio aboard the deserted lifeboat sputtered out one dying signal. Then lifeboat Aquarius plunged into the earth's atmosphere and burned to ashes.

Four
An Invitation to Children's Literature

Milestones in Children's Literature

1484 Aesop's Fables, translated and printed by William Caxton

Illustration by William Caxton for *Aesop's Fables*

These fables were originally intended for adult reading, but the children probably heard them read aloud and took them over. Later, in 1692, Sir Roger l'Estrange put out a special children's edition.

c. 1600 Hornbooks and battledores

From the fifteenth through the eighteenth centuries these were used to teach children the alphabet and numbers. Their importance lies in the fact that for the first time printed, educational material was put into children's own hands.

1646 Spiritual Milk for Boston Babes, John Cotton

This tedious theological treatise in catechism form was designed, alas, for the edification of the young; it is important only because it was one of the earliest children's books to be imported from England.

1657 or 1658 Orbis Pictus, Comenius

Generally considered to be the earliest picture book for children, *Orbis Pictus (The World Illustrated)* was certainly the first book we know to use explanatory pictures to amplify a word's meaning, much as the modern primer does.

[1]These dates have been checked and double-checked, but agreement over precise dates is apparently impossible because some sources give the date of writing, others the date of copyrighting or first publication or publication in the United States.

1678 Pilgrim's Progress, John Bunyan

Children probably skipped the long, moralizing interludes and read with pleasure the dramatic story which was intended for adults. For generations it inspired children to act out its episodes and artists to illustrate many editions.

1691 The New England Primer

Almost as depressing as the *Spiritual Milk,* this little primer inducted New England children into the joys of reading.

1697 Contes de ma Mère l'Oye, Perrault

In France appeared *Histoires ou Contes du Temps Passé avec des Moralités,* popularly called *Contes de ma Mère l'Oye.* These eight famous folk tales—The Sleeping Beauty, Cinderella, Puss in Boots, Little Red Riding Hood, Bluebeard, Riquet with the Tuft, Little Thumb, Toads and Diamonds—are still beloved by children.

1715 Divine and Moral Songs for Children, Isaac Watts

Realizing that poetry makes words easily remembered, Watts fashioned moralistic verses and wonderful hymns, the former for children, the latter for all ages. *Divine and Moral Songs* was originally titled *Divine Songs Attempted in Easy Language for the Use of Children.*

1719 Robinson Crusoe, Daniel Defoe

Adventure at last! Defoe, pamphleteer and satirist, in trouble politically and religiously most of his life, turned out the memorable story of a lone man, marooned on an island, creating and controlling a savage world.

1726 Gulliver's Travels, Jonathan Swift

A political satire by the famous Dean of the Dublin Cathedral, *Gulliver's Travels* was not intended for children, but was appropriated by them, in part at least. The miniature world of the Lilliputians is their favorite section and the double meanings do not trouble them.

1729 **Tales of Mother Goose (first English translation of Perrault's Contes de ma Mère l'Oye)**

Perhaps it was from this pioneer translation of the popular folk tales that John Newbery got the idea for the title of his nursery rhyme book.

1744 **A Little Pretty Pocket-Book**

John Newbery's famous first venture into the field of book publishing for children was highly successful. This little miscellany included games, proverbs, fables, a rhymed alphabet, and two moral letters to children signed by Jack the Giant-Killer.

1765 **Mother Goose's Melody, or Sonnets for the Cradle**

The publication date of this work has been open to question, but the Opies *(Oxford Dictionary of Nursery Rhymes)* place it as 1765. However, no copy earlier than T. Carmen's edition of 1780 survives.

1765 **The History of Little Goody Two-Shoes**

Almost as famous as *A Little Pretty Pocket-Book* and *Mother Goose* is this little novel of the life, sufferings, and successes of the enterprising Margery Meanwell.

1779 **A Pretty Book of Pictures for Little Masters and Misses; or, Tommy Trip's History of Beasts and Birds, Thomas Bewick**

Bewick's woodcuts were the first book illustrations of high artistic quality and skill for children.

1785 **Mother Goose's Melodies (Isaiah Thomas edition)**

Publisher W. H. Whitmore vouches for the fact that this was the first American edition of Mother Goose, pirated from Newbery. The 1899 Whitmore edition was titled *The Original Mother Goose's Melody.*

1789 **Songs of Innocence, William Blake**

Authentic poetry began for children with William Blake's remarkable book. It was followed by *Songs of Experience* in 1794.

1803 **First public library for children**

Caleb Bingham, author of school texts, remembering the lack of books in his own childhood, gave a children's library to Salisbury, Connecticut. By 1900, many public libraries had children's rooms directed by such great pioneers as Anne Carroll Moore, Caroline Hewins, and Frances Jenkins Olcott.

1804 **Original Poems for Infant Minds, Ann and Jane Taylor**

In the gently moralistic vein of Isaac Watts, these sisters wrote children's verses that were much loved in their day. In 1806 *Rhymes for the Nursery* appeared.

1822 **A Visit from St. Nicholas, Clement C. Moore**

This lively narrative poem has attracted many major artists whose imaginative illustrations have proved as spellbinding as the spirited verse. It was written in 1822, but not published until 1823.

1823 **Grimm's Popular Stories (translated into English by Edgar Taylor)**

Published in two volumes between the years 1823 and 1826, these unforgettable old tales caught the imagination of English children and of adults as well. The books contained etchings by George Cruikshank, the first English artist to combine fine drawing with imaginative humor in illustrations for children.

1843 **A Christmas Carol, Charles Dickens**

Perhaps this classic was intended for adults, but how wise children are when they appropriate books that speak to them.

1846 **Book of Nonsense, Edward Lear**

Illustration from Edward Lear's *Book of Nonsense*

Hilarious jingles with equally absurd pictures constituted England's first contribution to laughter in the evolution of children's books.

1846   **Fairy Tales, Hans Christian Andersen (first English translation)**
These beautiful stories, sometimes adaptations of folk themes, sometimes completely original, mark the beginning of the modern fanciful tale.

1846   **Struwwelpeter, Heinrich Hoffmann**
Translated from the German in 1848, *Slovenly Peter* added its humorous exaggerations both in picture and verse to the child's sense of the comic. Here was tongue-in-cheek moralizing about untidiness or fussiness or haughtiness that set both children and grownups chuckling.

1852   **A Wonder-Book for Girls and Boys, Nathaniel Hawthorne**
Hawthorne's famous retelling of the Greek myths, popular for a long time because of its imaginative and storytelling qualities, is now little used, perhaps because the author reduced the Olympians to child size, sacrificing the stern adult meanings.

1865   **Alice's Adventures in Wonderland, Lewis Carroll (Charles Lutwidge Dodgson)**

Illustration by Sir John Tenniel for *Through the Looking-Glass* by Lewis Carroll

One of the world's great fantasies came from an Oxford don, a lecturer in logic and mathematics. The nonsensical adventures of Alice in her mad world have a curious logic that is not wholly childlike.

1865   **Hans Brinker, or the Silver Skates, Mary Mapes Dodge**

Written by an American who had never been to Holland, this story of Dutch life and adventure is still good reading and has enjoyed long popularity.

1865–1876   **Sing a Song of Sixpence, illustrated by Walter Crane**
Since Crane's Toy Books were never dated, 1865–1876 is only an approximation of the years in which his picture books appeared. his work marked the beginning of modern color printing and fine design applied to children's books.

1868–1869   **Little Women, Louisa May Alcott**
This notably realistic classic of family life has been read, reread, laughed and cried over by girls for generations. Issued originally in two parts.

1872   **Sing-Song, Christina Rossetti**
A gifted poet wrote these tender and lovely lyrics for children, their first collection of lyric verse since William Blake.

1873   **St. Nicholas Magazine**
This monthly magazine, edited by Mary Mapes Dodge and published until 1940, was the all-time outstanding periodical for children. It was distinguished for the high quality of its fiction and for its policy of not sermonizing. Alcott, Burnett, Palmer Cox, Kipling, Pyle, Longfellow, and Lucretia Hale were some of the well-known contributors.

1876   **The Adventures of Tom Sawyer, Mark Twain (Samuel Clemens)**
Here is realism and Americana for young readers, written in the vernacular by a great humorist who, in Tom, remembered his own boyhood.

1877   **Black Beauty, Anna Sewell**
Although the horse is overly humanized, this famous book marks the beginning of the popularity of stories about the vicissitudes of animals, both pets and wild creatures.

1878   **Under the Window, Kate Greenaway**
Undistinguished verses about children's play activities are recorded on pages that are pictorial lyrics. The quaint costumes of the char-

acters influenced children's clothes over much of the world.

1878 **The House That Jack Built and The Diverting History of John Gilpin, illustrated by Randolph Caldecott**

Illustration from *Randolph Caldecott's Picture Book*

Continuing in the tradition of Walter Crane, Randolph Caldecott brought the picture book new distinction with his illustrations.

1880 **The Peterkin Papers, Lucretia Hale**
Told with a straight face, these "moron stories" are as fantastic as any of the "Clever Elsies" or sillies of the folk tales.

1880 **The Adventures of Pinocchio, Carlo Lorenzini (pseudonym, C. Collodi)**

From *Le Adventure di Pinocchio* by C. Collodi, illustration by Attilio Mussino. C/E Giunti Bemporad Marzocco, Florence, Italy

This is the children's own epic, themselves in wood, first translated into English and pub-

lished in the United States in 1892. The beautiful Italian edition illustrated by Attilio Mussino was published in 1929 in this country, opening the way to the rich international exchange of children's books.

1883 **Treasure Island, Robert Louis Stevenson**
Mystery, unforgettable characters, and hair-raising action make this absorbing story by a great storyteller as spellbinding today as ever.

1883 **Nights with Uncle Remus, Joel Chandler Harris**

UNCLE REMUS: HIS SONGS AND SAYINGS by Joel Chandler Harris. Copyright 1895, 1880 by D. Appleton & Co. Copyright 1908, 1921, 1935, 1963 by Esther LaRose Harris. Published by E. P. Dutton.

These stories of quickwitted, mischievous Brer Rabbit and his pranks are reminiscent of talking-beast tales of other countries.

1883 **The Merry Adventures of Robin Hood, Howard Pyle**

Illustration by Howard Pyle for *The Merry Adventures of Robin Hood* by Howard Pyle, Charles Scribner's Sons

For years this was the favorite version of these enchanting hero tales. Pyle's meticulous and beautiful illustrations greatly enhanced the book.

1884   Heidi, Johanna Spyri (date of English translation)

The story of the little Swiss girl, her grandfather, and her goats has become a classic. Heidi's great love for the peace and beauty of her mountains speaks to every young reader.

1884   The Adventures of Huckleberry Finn, Mark Twain (Samuel Clemens)

This work is considered by many critics to be the greatest of all Twain's books, but *Tom Sawyer* still holds first place with most young readers.

1885   A Child's Garden of Verses, Robert Louis Stevenson

Said to have been inspired by one of Kate Greenaway's little books, *A Child's Garden of Verses* contains poems as fresh today as ever. Their singing quality and the universal subject matter make the book a real treasure.

1889   The Blue Fairy Book, Andrew Lang

This was the first of Andrew Lang's long series of folk tale collections, named for various colors. His excellent versions popularized the tales.

1894   The Jungle Book, Rudyard Kipling

Children were fascinated by this tale of a boy who was raised by wolves and who knew the languages and laws of the jungle.

1901   The Tale of Peter Rabbit, Beatrix Potter

Because this book was written and circulated before the idea of publication occurred to the author, there is a conflict about the original dates. Percy Muir *(English Children's Books)* insists that the author's own date, 1900, is wrong and that 1901 is correct. We know at least that this small picture story is written and illustrated with consummate skill.

1903   Johnny Crow's Garden, L. Leslie Brooke

Illustration "And the Pig Danced a Jig" from JOHNNY CROW'S GARDEN by L. Leslie Brooke, published by Frederick Warne (Publishers) Ltd.

Leslie Brooke is known for this and for *Ring o' Roses,* a delightful Mother Goose book. Sly humor, excellent drawing, and good use of color mark his picture books.

1908   Wind in the Willows, Kenneth Grahame

Written by a master of prose style, *Wind in the Willows* is pure enchantment. It is rich in sensory appeal, peopled with unforgettable characters, full of humor, kindliness, and warmth.

1919   First children's book department in the United States

Macmillan was the first American publisher to set up a separate children's book department and Louise Seaman Bechtel was its first editor.

1919   Children's Book Week

This week, initiated by Franklin K. Matthews, Chief Librarian of the Boy Scouts, and Frederic G. Melcher of the American Booksellers Association, is still observed annually in schools, libraries, and bookstores.

1921   The Story of Mankind, Hendrik Willem van Loon

The first book to receive the Newbery Medal tells the history of humanity's slow march toward civilization. Van Loon brought to informational writing a whole new approach.

1922   Newbery Medal

Frederic G. Melcher, an American editor and publisher, created this award, which is given annually to the author of the year's "most distinguished contribution to American literature for children," and he named it appropriately for John Newbery, first English publisher of books for children.

1924   When We Were Very Young, A. A. Milne

With these deft verses, Christopher Robin joined the juvenile immortals and went gaily on through *Now We Are Six* (1927).

1926   Winnie-the-Pooh, A. A. Milne

From THE HOUSE AT POOH CORNER by A. A. Milne, illustrations by Ernest H. Shepard. Copyright 1928 by E. P. Dutton & Co.; renewal © 1956 by A. A. Milne. Reproduced by permission of the publishers, E. P. Dutton and McClelland and Steward Ltd.

Line illustration by E. H. Shepard, copyright under the Berne convention. Reproduced by permission of Curtis Brown Ltd., London.

After the first book of verse, Christopher Robin and Pooh Bear set off on a series of prose adventures that are the essence of straight-faced humor. *The House at Pooh Corner* followed in 1928.

1928   Millions of Cats, Wanda Gág

Reprinted by permission of Coward, McCann and Geoghegan, Inc., from MILLIONS OF CATS by Wanda Gág. Copyright 1928 by Coward-McCann, Inc. Copyright renewed 1956 by Robert Janssen.

Told and illustrated by an artist steeped in folk tales, *Millions of Cats* paved the way for the "golden years" of the thirties when picture books achieved a new importance.

1932   Little House in the Big Woods, Laura Ingalls Wilder

This is the first of a series of eight books which describe the pioneer experiences of the Ingalls family. The series was reissued in 1953 with splendid, authentic illustrations by Garth Williams.

1937   The Hobbit, J. R. R. Tolkien

In this book, which stands as a milestone in fantasy, and in the succeeding trilogy, *Lord of the Rings,* Tolkien has created an ancient world of small people which is completely fascinating to young and adult readers alike.

1937   Carnegie Medal

Named in honor of Andrew Carnegie and given annually by the British Library Association since 1937, for a children's book of outstanding merit published in the United Kingdom in the preceding year.

1938   Caldecott Medal

Named in honor of Randolph Caldecott, the English artist and illustrator, this award is given annually to the illustrator of the year's "most distinguished American picture book for children."

1941   George Washington's World, Genevieve Foster

This is the first of the author's *World* books which give a horizontal view of life around the world at the different periods of each man's life. These books provide children with a rounded sense of period, seldom found in a textbook.

1941   Paddle-to-the-Sea, Holling C. Holling

With simple and dramatic text and glowing illustrations there are combined anthropology, geography, science, history, and imagination, all of which give Holling's books timeless interest and values.

1943   Johnny Tremain, Esther Forbes

The story of a silversmith's apprentice during the Revolutionary War marks a high point in American historical fiction for children.

1947   Canadian Library Awards
Given annually to outstanding children's books, one in English and, since 1954, one in French. An award for illustration was added in 1971.

1950   The Lion, the Witch, and the Wardrobe, C. S. Lewis
C. S. Lewis, English scholar and theologian, wrote seven entrancing fantasies (this is the first) about the mythical land of Narnia.

1952   Charlotte's Web, E. B. White

Illustration (page 95) from CHARLOTTE'S WEB by E. B. White. Illustrations copyright 1952, renewed 1980 by Garth Williams. Reprinted by permission of Harper & Row, Publishers, Inc.

Quite probably the best-loved American book for children written this century! The warmth, humor, and pathos of the story of Charlotte's efforts to save Wilbur have endeared it to all ages.

1952   Anne Frank: Diary of a Young Girl
It is possible that this haunting diary of a little Jewish girl who lived from her thirteenth to fifteenth year in a wretched hideout and finally died in the Nazi camp at Bergen-Belsen will be too poignant for some young readers to endure.

1954   Laura Ingalls Wilder Award
Given at five-year intervals to an author or illustrator whose books published in the United States have made a lasting contribution to literature for children, this award was first presented to Laura Ingalls Wilder for her "Little House" books.

1956   Hans Christian Andersen Award
The first international book award was established to be presented every two years to a living author who has made an outstanding contribution to children's literature. In 1966 the award was expanded to include an illustrator as well.

1957   The Cat in the Hat, Dr. Seuss (pseudonym for Theodor Seuss Geisel)

From THE CAT IN THE HAT by Dr. Seuss. Copyright © 1957 by Dr. Seuss. Reprinted by permission of Random House, Inc. and Collins Publishers Ltd., London.

This preposterous fantasy pioneered the way for easy-to-read books, which aim to give readers a sense of fluency and a growing confidence in their own ability.

1957   Kate Greenaway Medal
Named in honor of Kate Greenaway, the award has been given annually, since 1957, by the British Library Association for the most distinguished work in the illustration of children's books published in the United Kingdom in the preceding year.

1960s   Children's paperback books
Flexibility, wide choice, economy, and informality are some of the reasons for the great impact of paperbacks on children's reading, a growing trend that began in the '60s.

1962   The Snowy Day, Ezra Jack Keats
The innovative illustrations in this book won the Caldecott Award for the author artist; however, of more significance was the fact that this was one of the first picture books with which black children could identify.

1962   The Work of Meindert DeJong
For the body of his work, DeJong was awarded the Hans Christian Andersen Medal.

1963   Where the Wild Things Are, Maurice Sendak

Specified illustration from WHERE THE WILD THINGS ARE by Maurice Sendak. Copyright © 1963 by Maurice Sendak. Reprinted by permission of Harper & Row, Publishers, Inc. and The Bodley Head.

The delightful monsters that inhabit an imaginary land in which an unhappy child takes refuge have captivated a generation of children. The book won the Caldecott Award.

1964   The Book of Three, Lloyd Alexander
In this first book and the succeeding ones in the series about the mythical kingdom of Prydain, Lloyd Alexander has written some of the finest fantasy of our time. The fifth and final book, *The High King,* won the Newbery Award.

1964   Harriet the Spy, Louise Fitzhugh
Completely contemporaneous! Harriet is popular with children and heartily disliked by some adults. Whether or not Harriet survives is not important; it is her very immediacy that gives her significance.

1964   Consultant in Children's Literature, Library of Congress
The establishment of this position gave national recognition to the importance of the field of children's literature.

1966   Mildred L. Batchelder Award
The American Library Association established an annual award for the most outstanding translation of a book first published in a foreign language in a foreign country.

1970   The Work of Maurice Sendak
For the body of his work, Sendak was awarded the Hans Christian Andersen Medal.

1972   The Work of Scott O'Dell
For the body of his work, O'Dell was awarded the Hans Christian Andersen Medal.

1974   M. C. Higgins, the Great, Virginia Hamilton
This was the first book to win both the Newbery Medal and the National Book Award.

1975   International Reading Association Children's Book Award
Given for the first time in 1975, the award is conferred annually to an author who shows, in his or her first or second book, unusual promise in the children's book field.

1977   National Council of Teachers of English Award for Excellence in Poetry for Children
First presented in 1977, the award is given annually to a living American poet in recognition of his or her aggregate work.

1978   The Work of Paula Fox
For the body of her work, Paula Fox was awarded the Hans Christian Andersen Medal.

What Literature Can Do for Children

Rebecca Lukens

Some years ago, just after the Soviet Union shocked us all by putting into space a satellite called Sputnik, we were suddenly struck by all the facts in the world that needed to be known. Concepts, principles, and information obsessed us. The idea of "All there is to know—and I know so little!" seemed to have captured and threatened us all. A great flood of books on every conceivable concrete object and elemental principle came rushing off American presses. All-about-this and the-complete-book-of-that inundated us; bookshelves, advertising flyers, encyclopedia series after series—all were filled with facts we must absolutely know. And Right Now.

At this period, publishers of books for children often turned down fantasy as irrelevant; realistic fiction seemed to appear only if it were top-heavy with instructively factual information. Thank heaven, we have survived that panic, and have returned to the realization that human life is not merely the facts of how, where, and with what we live, but even more important, what we are, whom we live with or among, and how we relate to elements of our environment as well as to other human beings. We have not so much rediscovered our human qualities as recognized that science and technology are not the simple answers to complex human problems. Our awe at scientific change—all change, we now know, is not progress—shifted to wondering why, if we could put a man on the moon, we were so foot-dragging about understanding and solving the human problems of racism, poverty, old age, mental health, and others.

Now, fortunately for us all, there are again available for children as well as adults both new and old stories and poems that concern the human spirit—its joys and playfulness, its yearnings and triumphs, its sorrows and despairs, every variety of human relationship, every kind of personal search for independence.

These are the discoveries we want for today's children, discoveries they can make through literature, and that are summarized in the words *pleasure* and *understanding.* All of us want to enjoy reading, in fact to be so intrigued and engrossed that we cannot put the piece down—unless, of course, we wish to absorb and contemplate what we have just read. We also want to understand people. Our wish for recognition that we are part of the human race, that we are like others, is universal. And yet, we wish for individuality to be recognized and accepted. Reading stories about other human beings helps us to accept ourselves and others, and to understand why we and our friends or acquaintances behave as we do. This recognition is the source of our understanding of human beings.

More specifically, what can literature actually do for children? Literature for children differs from literature for adults in degree but not in kind. Like all literature, it can open to children a world of new understandings.

Literature *shows human motives* for what they are, inviting children to identify with or to react to a fictional character. We see into the mind of a character, or even into the subconscious unknown to the character. By noting, as we do in Hans Christian Andersen's "The Real Princess," the writer's choice of details from the prince's environment and his imaginary world, as well as the chosen details about the smallest of actions or speeches, we understand human motivation, other people's as well as our own.

Literature provides *form for experience.* Certain events in our own lives have greater significance than others. In retrospect, "the day Uncle Joe visited us," or "that time I read your diary" made a difference in our lives.

Something happened then. Days, months, years which usually fall into some clouded continuum of chronology, a disorder without significance, now have their significance highlighted in the depiction of certain events or conversations.

For children, as for all of us, life is made up of emotional pulls and tugs in all directions: "I want to help Daddy, but my friends are waiting." "I'd like to save my Halloween candy, but I want to eat it now." Literature *reveals for readers this fragmentation in our lives.* And, at the same time, literature *helps us to focus on essentials.* In looking back, we realize that life does not distribute events in order of their mounting intensity or their cumulative effects upon us. Literature, however, because it ignores the irrelevant and focuses on the essentials, does make significance clear. Because we are detached as we read about others, we can see more clearly events and their possible influences. We can know the challenge of making choices, feel the excitement of suspense, and glow with the warmth of accomplishment.

As we all know, society pervades and invades our private lives. Literature can *reveal the institutions of society.* A group called an institution can be the family, the class, or that great abstraction called the system. Every week new regulations affect our personal lives: higher gasoline taxes, no-left-turn signs where we have always turned left, the canceling of our favorite TV show. The occasional fear that such institutions will close in on us and restrict us completely balances with the recognition that some restrictions are essential to our survival. Literature assists us all, clarifying our reactions to institutions, showing us where we must give in and where we can, may, or ought to struggle against them.

Institutions are not alone in affecting our lives; nature, too, influences us. Literature *reveals nature as a force,* sometimes simply by nudging us to a simple awareness of the pleasures of a lazy summer day, or by forcing us to recognize the life and death necessity to struggle against extreme cold.

And finally, literature *introduces us to writers-creators* whose sure artistry and understanding of us all make us wish to know them better, to discover what further understanding they can foster for our pleasure in other stories and poems.

Wealth: The Great Variety of Literature for Children

Like literature for adults, literature for children offers infinite variety. It can be of equal beauty, significance, and artistry. Like literature for adults, literature for children comes in an infinite variety of kinds and types called "genres." In fact, adults are far more limited in what they like and don't like than are children. Adults are quickly bored: Just notice how we weary from reading the same bedtime story over and over, and how infinite is the patience of the listening child. Even more relevant, however, is our feeling that fables are for children, folk and fairy tales are for children, even fantasy is for children. As adults we tend to limit ourselves to one or two kinds of literature. We are fond of science fiction and read only science fiction. Or we are devoted to Gothic tales and read only Gothic tales. Young adult women may become addicted to romances, and young adult men to sports or adventure stories.

Children, however, find vast varieties of literature interesting. And, lucky for them, there are many, many kinds available. It is that wealth that we can tap.

Of course, we have found that some children have favorite kinds of stories: fairy tales, or stories about animals that talk. But since a classroom holds all these different children with all their differing tastes, it is important that all possible kinds of literature be introduced to them. Once they have heard read aloud or read for themselves some, or better still many, of the kinds of literature, they may then begin to specialize, to go on their own binges of preference. If we are to introduce literature to children, however, it is our responsibility to forget our own adult preferences for "nothing but"—historical fiction or humorous stories—and open the world to our small charges.

What are these kinds of literature?

Poetry, included in the first section of this anthology, is a great delight to children, no matter what we may feel as adults. We will speak of it more fully in later pages. There are many kinds of prose literature for children; they come to us from the pens and typewriters of Victorian and contemporary writers, and from the tradition of storytelling. *Folk tales,* in the days before books and libraries and the widespread capacity to read, were heard by the teller and retold in the teller's own words. As we know from our own experience in hearing and telling jokes, some tellers are far more skillful than others. As one tells the story more often, skill increases—or one abandons storytelling. Some tellers show high skill; they entertain us continually, using phrases and rhymes that become familiar and that continue to please. Although in many folk tales the characters are similar, their predictability appeals to children. Notice, for example, because we know that a witch is intrinsically bad, we must designate others as "good witches." Children, who like the justice of folk tales, want the world to run in an orderly fashion: the good win, the cruel are punished. Folk tales are not all alike, although our selective memories may have forgotten the cumulative ones, or all but the humorous or the romantic. Variety in the folk tales is one of their many assets, because there is something for everyone, for any day, every mood, any age. Small children may like "The Story of the Three Bears," others "The Pancake," and still others may prefer the romantic ones like "The Sleeping Beauty in the Wood." Some want magic tales like "East o' the Sun and West o' the Moon," and others prefer those with animals that outwit people, like "The Bremen Town Musicians." Since the folk tales of every continent and region are represented in this anthology, the opportunities are endless for reading them aloud or for telling them in conjunction with other classes or lessons, or simply for the variety they offer in the classroom.

Children dislike being preached to, just as we all do. But one of the virtues of the *fable* is that the brief incident illustrates quickly some moral point. We all remember being told not to be "a dog in the manger," or that no one will come when we really need them if we continually "cry wolf." The child whose arithmetic paper is slowly completed but whose work is correct may hear with great satisfaction that, as the hare and the tortoise prove, "slow but sure wins the race."

Myths, although they are too often ignored, also have their place. If we read and think of them as ways that earlier peoples used to explain events and concepts they could not understand, myths can have their places in many kinds of classes. The spider web is explained in "Arachne," the constellations by "The Golden Fleece," and thunder by "How Thor Found His Hammer." It is important in choosing myths for children that they be told with dignity and simplicity, so that we do not demean the culture so creative as to try to answer the unanswerable.

Epics and hero tales often grew up, and still do, around a historical person or event, like Charlemagne's battles in the story of "Roland and Oliver." They may have as central truth the existence of the person or event like Robin Hood and Little John, but finally they become the narratives embroidered by admiring storytellers. Children like —and need—to hear about people who are bigger than life, grandly heroic, truly sacrificial in their motives. Unlike the heroes of television or of their video games, these people are worthy of being called heroes.

Stretching the imagination enlarges a child's world, the sense of potential, the awareness of all that is out there to find out about. Our greatest scientific and social changes have come from the alliance of facts with imagination, with fantasy. *Modern fantasy* comes in many forms. Letting the real world grow into an ideal one, or one where animals talk and toys become like people, releases children's imaginations, gives them not only ideas for further dreams, but also the vital permission to dream and create. *Tuck Everlasting* responds to the wish to live forever, but goes far beyond that into "But what would happen if I did?" Some literary fantasy has been around for a long time, and each time we reread it, we are delighted with new discoveries. The younger child reading, for example, *Alice's Adventures in Wonderland,* may find only the fantastic situations and be either amused or frightened. The older child will see the absurdity of the Mad Hatter's moving around the tea table to find a cleaner space, one just vacated by the Dormouse in search of a cleaner place. Still later that same reader, now older and wiser, may be wonder-struck by the verbal wit Lewis Carroll packs into his stories. Fantasy exists on many levels, for many ages. Its releasing of imagination is essential to children's emotional and intellectual growth.

Realistic fiction for children comes in several varieties, and each variety has its place in awakening pleasure and contributing to a child's understanding of all that goes on in the real world. In these stories, the outcome is reasonable and plausible, cause produces effect, and characters seem to have qualities common to most of us. Recently, issues other than mere everyday life have been introduced into fiction for children, and new kinds of realistic stories called problem realism and social issues realism are available for children. Physical handicaps, divorced parents, problems with drugs or sex are personal issues, yet not universal personal issues like the search for friendship. In social issues realism the protagonist faces a problem engendered by society—like racism, sexism, or social position. One selection included in this anthology might be called problem realism; James in *How Many Miles to Babylon* is trapped into helping a dog-stealing gang. Other selections deal with *Ramona* and her unemployed father, and the Jew-Gentile friendship in *Peter and Veronica.* The important issue in judging whether a story is a good one is whether character and plot are inextricably interrelated. Given the source of con-

flict, solutions to genuine problems ought not to be made too easy; the characters ought to behave in a plausible manner.

There are still other varieties of realism. Animal realism, in contrast to animal fantasy, is about animals that behave as animals; *The Incredible Journey* offers an excellent example. Children, who love their pets, enjoy stories in which such pets are the central characters, and in which the reader makes some discovery about animal behavior and their relationship to human beings. Still another kind of realism makes us aware of what it is to grow up in other lands or in other times, perhaps with other ways of structuring the family. The Norwegian story *Hello, Aurora,* and the Swiss *Heidi* show clearly that although lives can be different, people are the same, with the same wishes and needs. The important criterion for a story about life in other lands is that the characters have universal human traits, despite living in other times and countries. These faraway places and unusual customs are important means by which the past becomes credible or other regions become realities. Such stories awaken the child's awareness of a great and diverse world and of vast periods of changing times in which people remain the same.

The great variety of kinds of stories for children means that the adult can find for each individual child a book that satisfies curiosity, and also creates understanding of people and how they live and work together.

The Elements of Literature

Character

Children do know about character, about what people are like, and can catch the subtleties of human nature. Even infants respond differently to different people, hiding in a mother's skirts from one visitor and holding up arms to be held by another. They know that people are consistent, and can respond to fakery by refusing to speak to the effusive newcomer. Since children, even the smallest, are aware of personality in people around them, it seems sensible that they respond to people in stories, expecting consistency there as well. We have mentioned understanding as one of the greatest effects of good literature; even in the simplest stories it is possible to find characters that verify truth about human nature, meeting them in actions that seem part of their natures.

We find great pleasure in reading about people like ourselves, beings both wise and foolish, brave and cowardly, frightened and confident, lonely and secure. It is this pleasure of recognition that leads to understanding. Children as much as adults, or perhaps even more than adults, need the discovery of themselves as part of humanity. Conversely, they need the discovery that humanity exists in themselves. If literature is to help children understand the nature of human beings, we need reality in the portrayal of character. Nothing—not style nor conflict, nor adventure, nor vivid setting, nor laughter nor tears —nothing can substitute for solid character development in creating a pleasurable and lasting literature for children as well as for adults.

Plot

Children want what most adults want in literature: action, happenings, questions that need answers, answers that fit questions, glimpses of happy and unhappy outcomes, discovery of how events grow and turn. Everyday happenings are not all children need; they soon come to expect that life is more exciting in a story than in their own experience. "What if?" the big question of all literature, lets children lose themselves in action and reaction.

Some kind of conflict, events described in narrative order that children of different ages and maturity can follow, suspense to pull the reader along, foreshadowing to raise anticipation and make outcomes credible, and some climax or resolution to make the plot interesting—all are important. And yet, children do not demand high drama and ex-

citement; they are often content or even engrossed in stories where tension derives from the protagonist's finding a friend as in *Charlotte's Web,* or being valued for achievement in *Johnny Tremain,* or being accepted in *Calico Bush.* Sentimentality, the emotion we feel a bit embarrassed about because we know we are overreacting, flaws some stories. Children fed on sentimentality do not develop the sensitivity essential to recognize what is truly moving. Sentimentality results in great loss: the diminished understanding of people.

Plots that combine tension with real people carry readers back to the book, back to the library, back to sharing their reading with friends. Children, like adults, do not finish dull stories.

Setting

Setting for a story may be either a backdrop for the plot, like the generalized backdrop of a city, street, or forest against which we see the action of a play. Or it may be so essential to our understanding of this plot, these characters, and these themes, that we must experience it with our senses. Setting in folk tales is mere backdrop for the fast-moving action, but an integral setting in other kinds of stories not only may clarify the conflict, but also may help the reader understand character, act as the force against which the main character struggles, or influence mood. Often the sense of place and time prepares the reader to accept the story and the writer's personal view of life and its significance. If setting is essential to our understanding, the writer must make the reader see, hear, touch, and perhaps even smell the setting. A good description of setting in either paragraphs or in phrases woven into action, by details of color, sound, or figurative comparisons does much to add to the reader's involvement in the story. Our knowing how the Queen's Head Tavern looks inside, how the Long Room with its long tables and its chairs faces the harbor in *Phoebe and the General* helps us picture the action and live for a time with

Phoebe and her father during the Revolutionary War. In *The Incredible Journey* we must see the terrain over which the Siamese cat, the Labrador, and the old English bull must travel: fast-running creeks, dense pinewoods, low, overgrown ditches, overhanging rocks. Only the writer's description of the rugged Canadian wilderness convinces us of the difficulty of the animals' journey.

Theme

In literature, the theme is the idea that holds the story together, such as a comment about society, human nature, or the human condition. It is the main idea or central meaning of a piece of writing. Stated either explicitly or implicitly, theme is essential to a children's story if it is to merit the title "literature." A narrative with action and people but without theme is a story without meaning that leaves the reader wondering at the close, "So what?" The theme we take to become part of ourselves is the one that enlarges our understanding, the one we discover for ourselves—not the one underlined and delivered preachily by the author. In the chapters from novels included in this anthology, we may not find the theme as clearly as we will when we read the book in its entirety. The themes in *Charlotte's Web,* for example, distinguish the nature of friendship as reciprocal, as slow in its growth, as the giving of oneself. The themes of *Queenie Peavy* suggest that one's personal worth does not depend upon money or status, but upon what one thinks of oneself.

Point of View

Point of view is an integral part of storytelling; it determines the view the readers get of events, of character motivation, of suspense and climax, as well as of theme. In *Master Rosalind,* for example, Rosalind's feelings about masquerading as a boy, taking a boy's part in productions at the Globe Theater, are important to our understanding the times and their attitudes toward women and the theater. In *The Family Under the Bridge,* the hobo Armand's thoughts are told to us: he hates children, calls them starlings. Knowing his attitudes heightens our interest in his meeting the homeless children as he tries at first to chase them from his home under the bridge. Point of view plays a highly important part in our coming to understand what makes people do, think, and feel as they do.

Style

The skilled writer chooses words that best describe setting and plot and best illumine character and theme to make a piece of literature. Style is *how* the author says something as opposed to *what* the author says. The writer chooses the best words for a particular story, each story needing different "best words" than others. Style is not something applied to a finished piece of writing, since it *is* the writing, conveying both the idea and the writer's view of the idea. The content of the story and how the story is told are inseparable; each word and punctuation mark directly contribute to meaning, and are therefore parts of style. The best stories for children are never trite but fresh, vivid, and surprising, each speaker using words true to that personality. Janie Moffat in *The Middle Moffat* speaks the best words to convey the kind of innocent but mischievous child she is, and how she thinks and feels about the Oldest Resident of the town.

Any good story is words, many words, selected and arranged in a manner that best creates characters, draws setting, recounts conflict, builds suspense to a climax, and ties it all together with some thematic significance. Words, the best possible words for this story, are not merely the style of the story; they are the story itself.

Tone

In our speech we vary tone to assist the words in conveying meaning. We may pull a rebellious child into the classroom, saying "Come on!" Or encourage a child to try a new number puzzle, saying "Come on!" Or reject a long-winded excuse from the child who is avoiding cleaning up a messy work table, saying "Come on!" Our tone influences our meaning. The writer, too, uses tone to convey meaning. Notice, for example, the different attitudes of the writer of *Queenie Peavy* who writes in a serious tone, and the writer of *From the Mixed-Up Files of Mrs. Basil E. Frankweiler* who writes in a humorous tone. There are, of course, all kinds of tones available to the writer, as many tones as there are attitudes. And yet, many adults think humor is the only kind of tone children can respond to. Humor when combined with affection in *The Borrowers* increases our pleasure, and yet not all fantasy is humorous, as *Tuck Everlasting* demonstrates. *Roland and Oliver*, a very dissimilar story, tells of mutually admiring warriors and is serious but filled with the warmth of admiration.

Poorly written stories for children may use a condescending tone: "You're too little to understand, so I'll explain it all to you," or, more likely, overexplain. Such condescension is particularly offensive in the retelling of the myths and hero tales, stories both serious and important to the people who first told and heard them. The writer does both readers and stories an injustice by adopting a condescending tone, or by preachiness and didacticism. Some writers seem to approach their stories with an attitude of "I'll teach these children to shape up," then surround the preachiness with a shallow story, hoping the didactic point will be more palatable if disguised as story. "It's good for you" has won few children over to eating spinach, and it will win even fewer over to reading.

How Early Does Literature Begin?

A young parent can find article after essay after questionnaire on child rearing. The days have come and gone when parents were told not to encourage children to learn before they begin school. And that is good news. What is sometimes bewildering is the question of what activities can put small children on the learning path. Teachers are often asked such questions.

Begin with object books, ABC books, number books, those made of durable linen. Don't be tempted to keep a child quiet in the classroom or the supermarket by buying a cheap book off the rack. And don't spend "big money" on a book until you find one you know the child will read and reread, a book that will please every time he or she turns to it. Get into the library habit, and let children help in choosing what is to be read aloud. Then read aloud at regular times, before naps, before dinner, and at bedtime, never making reading aloud contingent upon being good. Reading aloud should be an integral part of life, one of the pleasures of family living.

There are things a parent can do at home, long before classes are part of a child's life. In talking with parents, teachers should defend to the teeth the nursery rhymes of Mother Goose. Periodically the rhymes are castigated as bad verse and bad example. But considered seriously, how many children have cut off the tails of three blind mice? How many cats have been tossed in the well because of Johnny Green? How often has Dapple Gray been whipped and slashed?

Ask parents to remember their own childhoods, and the many rhymes they knew as youngsters. Perhaps they hardly know they remember them still, until a toddler sits on a comfortable lap and the rhymes rise from deepest adult memory. One by one they come back, until parents realize they remember, after all. When old friends Little Jack Horner and Old King Cole become new friends for the child, adult and child sit together longer and longer in the evenings, poring over the Mother Goose book. On Saturday mornings, over workbench or laundry, parents start a rhyme and let the child finish it. They take turns.

The values the parent believes in are embodied in many of these rhymes, waiting quietly in the verses for today's children. The pleasure of imitation and achievement comes with pat-a-cake. Stretching a plump foot for "This Little Piggy," the child shows an awareness of self nourished by the rhythms and actions, and shares the excitement of learning and performing. Although "Deedle, Deedle Dumpling, my son John" may sound to a child like "mice on John," showing him or her own "one shoe off and one shoe on" and saying the appropriate words give the child great delight in accomplishment.

Before children enter kindergarten, they can find in the rhymes of Mother Goose an unexplored world no spaceship can reach. With a little effort and the help of parents, they can make this world their own. In these simple verses they discover laughter, truth, and delight in the inevitable.

Commonplace things become important and mysterious in the Mother Goose rhymes, because in each verse there is the unique integration of technique and content. "Humpty Dumpty," the child discovers, is what happens to an egg when it topples. "Higgledy, Piggledy" is responsible for the breakfast omelet. "Home again, home again, jiggetty jig" is the tune for a trip home with Father from the A & P.

Adventures, real and fantastic, await the child in the first rhymes. Not every "garden grow," after all, belongs to Mistress Mary. Even dishes and spoons are capable of the extraordinary: Two of them did run away together, didn't they? A child who hears rhymes from parents just before going to sleep may be lucky enough some night to catch sight of a cow in the middle of a moon-jump. To land on the moon in a spaceship is, no doubt, a grand accomplishment. But can it be compared to jumping over the moon—with all four legs?

People with limited perspectives may be good people, but often they measure time by funerals and inevitably know the number of rainy days this month, or how badly their street is maintained. The children who grow up with nursery rhymes aren't likely to become those kinds of adults; they are more likely to become optimists. After all, rain goes away and comes again another day, leaving sunshine in between. All the world isn't cruel. Didn't Johnny Stout pull poor pussy out? True, Georgie Porgie was a lemon, but there is no use thinking everyone is sweet. New lemons ripen every day.

Laughter is the way many adults keep their sanity. And laughter can become part of a child's way of dealing with life—if the nonsense of Mother Goose begins early. There is the barber who shaved a pig and made of 24 hairs a wig. And that foolish Doctor Foster who didn't go back to Gloucester because he "stepped in a puddle up to his middle."

There are other gains, too, from nursery rhymes. Early development of muscle coordination, as well as the recognition of aural pleasures begin with Mother Goose. "Jack, be nimble" makes easy the leap into bed. Unpleasant matters exist in life, and children can be eased into knowing them. We remember finding the dead bird in the shrubbery beneath the window; "Who Killed Cock Robin?" tells the whole sad story. Dishonesty has painful rewards: "Tom, the Piper's Son" knows that. Most parents have rows at one time or another, but breakfast arguments aren't cataclysmic when parents remember affectionately for their children that "My little old man and I fell out." Matters that are handy to know, the days of the week and the numbers of days in the months, register for children who learn "Thirty days has September," and "Monday's child is fair of face; Tuesday's child is full of grace." A rhyme, not a list, makes such facts easy to assimilate.

On and on through the rhymes of Mother Goose a child can go, learning without having to put up with preachiness or boredom, without even being aware that he or she is learning. The rhymes assure the possibility that children will grow up with minds open to new ideas, that they may learn rapidly, for they know the self-esteem that accompanies achievement. In such a child, the education of mind and spirit begins simply, pleasurably, and effectively.

Poetry: The Neglected Literature

Once little children leave behind them the nursery or Mother Goose rhymes, they are often deprived of just the pleasures that had first introduced them to literature: the music of words, the bounce of rhythms, the echoes of rhymes, as well as the serious or nonsensical ideas of ancient folk verses. But there is a vast body of delight out there for them—if their teachers and parents will only gird their loins, seek and find the courage to try poetry, real poetry.

As we have noted, children first meet literature in infancy, when they are making valiant efforts to pat-a-cake. From nursery rhymes and nonsense it is a short step to poetry—if we will only take that step. Something about the possibility of getting meaning beyond amusement from brief groups of words in short lines, each line or phrase usually beginning at the left margin, seems to frighten adult readers. Strange to say, we can read along easily in paragraphed pages, but if the same words are placed in stanza form, and if the meaning is not quickly apparent, we are lost. Perhaps, at some time in our childhoods, poetry has been made forbidding by adults who seemed puzzled, and that puzzlement is passed from generation to generation.

Differences in Poetry and Prose

The difference between poetry and prose is not as great as it may seem. Flow or cadence in prose may become more regular in poetry and be called rhythm or meter. Sound patterns in prose also exist in poetry, but are used to a greater degree. Connotative or implied meaning in prose acquires heightened significance in poetry. Figurative language, stated and implied comparisons between unlike things, occurs in prose but occurs more frequently in poetry. What seems to take us by surprise and to make us feel that the two forms are totally different lies elsewhere.

Several characteristics set poetry apart from prose. The principal difference between the two is *compactness.* A single word in a poem may say far more than a single word in prose; the connotations and images or sensory appeals hint at, imply, and suggest other meanings. In a sense, like the chemist who is a distiller, making a product free from impurities, the poet is making the expression in words brief but vivid, packed with meaning, although at times ambiguous. Economy and suggestion evoke our responses. This compactness, achieved through the compressed expression in words, and combined with the use of rhythm, sound patterns, and figurative language, creates *emotional intensity.* Children, as emotionally intense a group as any in all humanity, surely are familiar with the compression of intensity into small units of words and sounds.

What sets poetry for children apart from poetry for adults is largely subject matter. Adult interests include the passing of time, the confronting of death, the sense of loss, or the seizure of the moment. But the concerns of children's poetry are the concerns of childhood. Since much of childhood is spent in play or in wonder at what is common and yet not commonplace, in marveling at what surrounds them in their constantly unfolding world, these are the subject matter of children's poetry.

Many have tried to define poetry, and most have found such definitions difficult. Most definitions, however, return to at least one central idea derived from the Greek origin of the word. A poet is a maker, and poetry is *made:* every word counts.

Unlike the word "created," which implies mystery and inspiration, the term "made" suggests materials and effort. Poetry does not emerge perfect from the writer's pen. Like anything made, poetry follows a pattern of development: conception, effort, technical discipline, and refining and polishing before the maker is pleased with the thing made. Most likely the poem is written and rewritten; words are crossed out, substituted, perhaps replaced with earlier words, rewritten, crossed out, substituted again—until the maker-poet feels the poem is finally right. Of course, effort alone does not make a poem, any more than it makes good fiction. Skill, patience, and the critical judgment of the disciplined mind are a more likely combination.

First, let us note that there is a difference between poetry and the verse we sometimes call poetry. Some maintain that while poetry is an end in itself, verse has a specific purpose. T. S. Eliot, for example, contrasts the two by saying that feeling and imaginative power are found in real poetry, but verse is merely a matter of structure, formal metrical order, and rhyme pattern. Furthermore, its structure often seems more important than its meaning. "Red sky at morning/ Sailors take warning," has more purpose or form than emotional intensity. Chewing-gum commercials and greeting-card verse we sense are not really poetry, but unless they are truly incongruous we may thoughtlessly call them poetry rather than verse, and poor verse at that.

So, what's the matter with verse?

Nothing, so long as we know that it has its limitations. Verses can be pleasant and entertaining, but often their agreeable sentiments are expressed tritely and awkwardly, in useless and throwaway words, with rigid metrical structure, ordinary images, obvious rhymes, or phrases twisted to produce forced rhymes. These verses are not "the distilled and imaginative expression of feeling" that Eliot describes. The difference lies in distillation of language and intensification of feeling.

All this differentiation leads to a simple conclusion. Children need poetry as well as rhymes and verses. They are deprived if their experience is limited to verse, for they miss a great deal of pleasure. Neat, tricky, inventive verses can delight us in one way, and poetry in quite another.

"Mrs. Peck-Pigeon" by Eleanor Farjeon from ELEANOR FARJEON'S POEMS FOR CHILDREN. Poems copyright 1933, © 1961 by Eleanor Farjeon. Reprinted by permission of J. B. Lippincott, Publishers, and Harold Ober Associates Incorporated.

Rhythm

The recurrence of stress is called rhythm. It may occur in cadenced prose, but when it is set to a more regular pattern as it is in verse or poetry, we call it meter. The poet uses rhythm to enhance and reinforce the feeling that the poet's words express. In choosing the rhythm for a poem, whether it be unvarying metrical form or more freely flowing lines, the poet makes several common-sense choices. When we are happy, we speak quickly; when we are sad or serious or matter-of-fact, our words come more slowly. The poet, in the same way, uses a quickly moving line and many unaccented syllables and short vowels to express light-heartedness in lines that move quickly. When the poet is expressing serious thoughts, the rhythm moves more slowly with longer vowels and a higher proportion of accented syllables. Within the line, rhythm may also vary as the poet wishes to stress an idea or a single word. And within the poem the rhythm slows or quickens to vary the mood or shift the tone. The best poetry uses rhythm to add meaning to words. Look, for example, at Eleanor Farjeon's "Mrs. Peck-Pigeon."

Mrs. Peck-Pigeon
Is picking for bread,
Bob-bob-bob
Goes her little round head.
Tame as a pussy-cat
In the street,
Step-step-step
Go her little red feet.
With her little red feet
And her little round head,
Mrs. Peck-Pigeon
Goes picking for bread.

The stiffly bobbing motions of a pigeon, and the rhythmic stepping are carefully duplicated in the rhythm of the short lines, and the short consonants and vowels. The poem's rhythm duplicates the motions of the pictured pigeon.

Sound Patterns

In the poem "Fog," Carl Sandburg, using musical devices and sound patterns that are exceptionally helpful in reinforcing meaning, compares the fog to a cat, a creature known for its quiet stealth.

The fog comes
on little cat feet.

It sits looking
over harbor and city
on silent haunches
and then moves on.

The long sounds of the words "fog," "comes," "looking," "over," "harbor," "haunches," and "moves" all create the feeling of slowness and stealth. None of the words are brisk or sharp, but rather are slow-moving, quiet. The result is sound that duplicates meaning, reinforces it, adds to the intensity of the short poem. As for rhythm, stressed syllables in "Fog" are far more frequent than unstressed syllables, and the effect is a slowly moving poem—movement like that of the fog slowly drifting, settling, then stealing off. One of the most quoted and remembered of poems from childhood, "Fog" is not only a comparison that is memorable, but demonstrates clearly that a poem's sounds are an integral part of comparison.

Figurativeness

Figurative language is a means by which a writer says one thing in terms of another, and by which the writer makes comparisons. It is this quality which Christopher Fry speaks of when he says that poetry "has the virtue of being able to say twice as much as prose in half the time, and the drawback, if you do not . . . give it your full attention, of seeming to say half as much in twice the time." Personification which compares nonhuman things to human beings, similes which state comparisons of unlikes by using "like" and "as," and metaphors which make implied comparisons are the most common figurative devices in children's poetry.

When a poem makes either implied or explicit comparisons, the images called up may acquire connotative meaning, or may be seen in a fresh way. For example, when May Swenson writes about a tourist coming in from outer space and seeing the freeway with its line of cars, she carefully compares each part of the car—"the creatures of this star," as the tourist surmises—to something like and yet unlike what earth people know as feet, or eyes, or "guts." In "Southbound on the Freeway," the highway looks to the space tourist from Orbitville like a measuring tape with spaced inches. The sound of the car wheels is a "hiss," and the creature with five eyes, one "a red eye turning/on the top of his head" is, of course, the patrol car. Every comparison is clear and consistent. Nothing irrelevant or impossible to see as comparison interrupts our understanding of a space traveling tourist's puzzling vision.

The poet's use of figurative language may delay our discovery of meaning, but at the same time, these comparisons make the poem more intriguing and the final discovery of meaning more exciting. Sometimes we may be puzzled by the figurative language in a poem; in fact, the more complex the poem, the more slowly we may comprehend the figurative possibilities. The simplest way to check the meaning and suitability of the comparisons is by means of simple "this = that" equations. The similes and metaphors of Swenson's "Southbound on the Freeway" form a series of figurative equations: creatures of this star = people of the earth; transparent parts = windows; feet, round and rolling = wheels; measuring tapes = marked highway. And so on, through the poem.

Imagery

Imagery or verbal appeals to the senses further stretch our perceptions to see details and figurative comparisons. Bats are mouse-like but winged, cling upside down to rafters, and fly in swift but unpredictable swoops. Look, however, at how Theodore Roethke tells us these facts—and far more—in "The Bat."

By day the bat is cousin to the mouse.
He likes the attic of an aging house.

His fingers make a hat about his head.
His pulse beat is so slow we think him dead.

He loops in crazy figures half the night
Among the trees that face the corner light.

But when he brushes up against a screen,
We are afraid of what our eyes have seen:

For something is amiss or out of place
When mice with wings can wear a human
*   face.*

The value of such images lies in their making much more vivid our mental picture of bats —or any other topic that is the poetic focus. Poetry, as Herbert Read says, "is not made up of words like pride and pity, or love and beauty. . . . The poet distrusts such words and always tries to use words that have a suggestion of outline and shape, and represent things seen as clear and precise as crystal."

The connotatively rich words of a poem add further dimensions of meaning to words we have always known. When the connotations of words are distracting, however, they have been poorly chosen. The best choices are helpful in uncovering and expanding the meaning of the poem.

Compactness

Poetry exists for itself, an end in itself. It has no mission or message beyond discovery, beyond the emotion and thought of the reader as he or she explores the lines. A poem is best

said in few and artfully chosen lines; it follows that if we change a word, we change the poem. Langston Hughes' poem, "Mother to Son," a poem rich in connotative words, a striking and consistently developed metaphor, and clear visual images, has not a word more than Hughes needs to convey the meaning.

Well, son, I'll tell you:
Life for me ain't been no crystal stair.
It's had tacks in it,
And splinters,
And boards torn up,
And places with no carpet on the floor—
Bare.
But all the time
I'se been a-climbin' on,
And reachin' landin's,
And turnin' corners,
And sometimes goin' in the dark
Where there ain't been no light.
So, boy, don't you turn back.
Don't you set down on the steps
'Cause you finds it kinder hard.
Don't you fall now—
For I'se still goin', honey,
I'se still climbin'
And life for me ain't been no crystal stair.

Brevity heightens the impact of the poem. Were we to explain in prose what the experiences of this woman have been, the roughness and sorrows, the despair and courage, we would expend far more words with less impact. The compactness of the poem caused by the connotatively rich word choices describes vividly the black mother's experiences; briefly, we even share them.

Emotional Intensity

Like fiction at its best, poetry at its best lets us enjoy an old experience with new insight, or understand one that we have never met. Even more than fiction, poetry condenses the experience, involving the reader briefly but intensely. Looking back over even the small number of quoted examples in these past few pages, "The Bat," "Fog," "Mrs. Peck-Pigeon," "Southbound on the Freeway," and "Mother to Son," we can notice how brief each poem is, how much it tells, how intense the impression we get. That is the greatest virtue of poetry: So little says so much.

Teachers and parents need not be afraid of poetry. It is just made up of words, words we already know. The lines may be shorter, but that makes their reading an intriguing experience because we can look carefully at each word to see what the poet says or implies, and why the poet breaks the lines where he or she does. If we approach the poem with a sense of search, of curiosity, or even of puzzlement, we find it opens for us its meaning. That meaning so carefully and thoughtfully discovered gathers great significance. Children who respond to rhythm and rhyme and sound effects of rhymes and verse can also appreciate poetry. Once they learn that poetry, however, is more than rhythm, rhyme, and sound effects, that its meaning can be found, and that the process of finding that meaning can itself be pleasurable, children are hooked. They can very early become devoted to poetry.

What to do with poetry in the classroom? Read it aloud. Again and again. As the subject suits the day: Rainy days are days for mud-puddle and rainbow poems, winter days for cold fingers, frosty windows, and snowy landscapes. Show-and-tell yields numerous possibilities for reading poems aloud; included in this anthology are poems for many topics. Make a class anthology of children's favorites. Let children read their favorites aloud. Let them memorize those they wish to hang on to. Print them for the bulletin board where children will read and reread them. Send children to this anthology and others to find poems on topics that interest them. Illustrate the poems, dramatize their stories, dance to their rhythms.

But read them, aloud, again and again. And again. Talk about them if the children want to. But read them.

Biography: The Worship of Real Heroes

In the child's world dominated by television and radio, where disc jockeys sing the praises of so-called pop "artists," and where make-believe heroes achieve approval by being flashy and sassy, children find few people worth emulating. Although such entertainers may, in private life, be admirable human beings, they rarely play admirable roles for children to acquire inspiration from. For this reason biography is essential to children's growing aware of the possibilities for their own development and achievement. In the lives of frontierspeople, of presidents, of composers, and liberation leaders and crusaders for all kinds of justice, there is evidence that all of us, simple though our origins, can contribute something. This is perhaps the greatest contribution of biography to child readers.

Biographies are available for children of all ages. The youngest child can read Gwenda Blair's biography of Laura Ingalls Wilder, recognizing through the narrative of Laura's life that her experiences were those not only of the frontier and of the constantly moving settlers, but also of an ordinary little girl whose family loved and enfolded her. Frontier experience we cannot now acquire, but we might, any of us, act on a wish to write of our experiences as Laura Ingalls Wilder did in her Little House books.

Older children can be stirred by such true stories as that of the courageous William Penn who stood by his right to free speech and to a fair trial, and of the jury members who refused to convict Penn despite the intimidation they experienced in the courtroom. Such dogged and successful insistence upon justice confirms children's faith in the legal process at the same time as it presents a fiery and dramatic story for their enjoyment. Ann Petry has written of Harriet Tubman's work in *Harriet Tubman, Conductor on the Underground Railroad*, saving countless slaves by starting them off on the route to safety in the North. Petry, in brief references to historical happenings occurring at the time of Tubman's life, reminds young readers that there were principled whites who also struggled to free slaves. Such examples of commitment to life and principle, at risk of their own lives, are valuable additions to children's recognition of the strength of the human spirit. Great scientists like Galileo come alive; determined explorers like Columbus show their dedication to an idea; international peacemakers like Anwar Sadat treasure their simple village origins.

The best biography for children works information into story form, using either dialogue found recorded by those who knew the subject, or, if that is not available, credible dialogue invented by the writer to show the nature of the subject. Greater license to manufacture dialogue does not, however, mean that incident or character may be changed. Since biography is history, the history of the life of an individual, the writer is obligated to be truthful, and herein lies another problem. In the writer's zeal to present a historical figure worthy of being written and read about, the writer may be tempted to omit mention of negative traits. The result is a less-than-human being, one so perfect that the child reader finds no similarity to real people, and therefore no possibility of either understanding them or taking inspiration from them.

In good biography, as in literature of all kinds, there is pleasure in the reading. Understanding of how people behave and think and feel, of what motivates them, how they behave in groups, how their early lives affect their later achievements contributes greatly to children's lives.

Reading Aloud and Its Payoff

As teachers of children, we are interested not only in their learning to read—so they can read the backs of cereal boxes and assembly instructions for paper toys—but their read-

ing of far more significant words.

We want to foster a love of reading.

Necessity forces today's child to learn to read; pleasure keeps children reading. And that pleasure divides the readers from the nonreaders.

Nonreaders are those who don't *like* to read. Perhaps no one at home reads, and therefore no one reads to them. Perhaps they have not been read to often enough to discover very early that reading is a marvelously exciting way to live in other times, in other places, and even in other people's skins. In some homes adults assume that once a child can read 150 or so words of first-grade vocabulary, there is no point in reading aloud anymore. But, really now, how much fascination can a child find in the basic one- and two-syllable vocabulary?

With 40,000 books for children in print, and ten times as many books published for children now as in 1880, 2500 new titles each year, perhaps a child has a bookcase full at home—none of them interesting. Try reading the books aloud; usually if they bore you, they will bore children. Dull books make nonreaders.

What benefits besides pleasure accrue from reading aloud? Increased vocabulary, greater linguistic competence, keen observation skills, lengthened attention spans follow. Inevitably, as child and adult pore over a book together, they talk of what they see, using words they otherwise might not speak. Pointing out objects and patterns in illustrations, they stretch the child's understanding, say things in different phrasing, question and explore meanings, check connotations. Together they imagine happenings and extend stories, stimulating each other to new ideas.

The earliest pleasure comes, of course, from oral language, from as we have noted, nursery rhymes that tell of cows jumping over moons and blackbirds in a pie, or fishing in a pail. By the time a child reaches school, his or her language education may be six years old, and books are long overdue: The picture story books with imaginative illustration and, most important, with skillful use of language begin it all. Peter Rabbit, and the millions of cats who eat each other up, and Max and his Wild Things. Each story stimulates talk and holds the child entranced. Scritch, scratch, scrrritch! Millions and billions and trillions of cats. Grrrr, I'll eat you up! Listening, the child fastens down new words, discovers new meanings for old ones, and together shares with the adult.

As an adult you may have forgotten how that favorite teacher held you spellbound as you listened to that story after recess. Listen to the delight of language skillfully written, perfect for reading aloud, in Kipling's "The Elephant's Child."

The original oral stories were the folk tales, and this anthology has a wide assortment from many lands. Universally, we yearn to be discovered like Cinderella, or loved despite our homeliness like the Beast. We dream of happily-ever-after lives. We know the special love between fathers and daughters, mothers and sons; folk tales show these loves as universal. Didn't we all envy older siblings and want the youngest—us—to win? We all feared monsters and ogres and trolls and loved to hear of their defeat, each monster no more fearful than our imaginations were capable of picturing. Bruno Bettelheim, child psychologist, assures us such stories are valuable; without them children invent monsters vastly more frightening than those folk literature describes. Furthermore, says Bettelheim, every child deserves to hear tales of optimism, predicting happiness, security, acceptance, love, even wealth. Folk tales, since they originated in oral tradition, are perfect for reading aloud.

But don't stop with folk tales; move on to tales of heroes: Theseus who saved the Athenians from their regular sacrifice of their finest men to the monster Minotaur. Struggling with the Minotaur, he struck a mighty blow to its jaw, pinned it to the floor of its den, and saved his people.

Reading aloud a fantasy, suspending disbelief to share a world so intriguing everyone wishes it were real, has rewards, too. Immediately post-Sputnik, as we have noted,

adults felt there was so much information to learn that fantasy was irrelevant, perhaps even worse than a waste of time, even destructive. But imagination has envisioned all kinds of change that has come to pass, from laser beams to microcomputers. Stimulate a child's imagination and it goes on to create and innovate.

Fantasy confronts the greatest issues of human life. As Charlotte and Wilbur reassure each other and are patient and devoted, the listening child sees how friendship develops, how commitments makes it bloom. Even that imponderable death facing us all, old and young, E. B. White faces squarely. But the music of oral language is never discounted, no matter what the subject, whether it be the predawn silence of a barn or the diet of a bloodthirsty spider. Sometimes the world seems short on contentment, warmth, hospitality, and security. Few homes are warmer or more inviting than that of Bilbo Baggins the hobbit.

Every child has been the Ugly Duckling. Like most of us, the duckling spills some things and runs into others, can't swim right or walk straight, can't find friends or siblings who accept him. Read that story aloud to any child; make him or her feel part of the human race through the greatest allegory of childhood, one that ends in the triumph of maturity and acceptance. A world of tiny people—something children have always fantasized about—is nowhere more convincingly described than in *The Borrowers*. Children who wonder why they never see those imaginary people will know why: they panic at the possibility of discovery in their home beneath the floorboards. Worlds of other kinds exist in fantasy for children, and great numbers of benefits accrue to those who journey there in imagination.

Realism is an excitement of another kind. Real people in the real world struggle against significant forces, and yet they manage without supernatural powers. The story of *Queenie Peavy* moves children into a world few of them ever experience, that of the poor black in the South. The stringbean daughter of a parolee, Queenie is trying to maintain some dignity and develop some pride despite her father's reputation and behavior. Because Robert Burch so skillfully manages dialogue that reveals the personalities of his characters, listeners and adults see and understand motives and worries they might not otherwise meet. And who can fail to sympathize with and enjoy *Harriet the Spy* as she throws a fit: "I'll be FINKED if I'll go to dancing school!" Reading aloud this defiance, and laughing together over its vehemence, make children feel their own strong feelings are acceptable and normal. There's nothing wrong with that.

To summarize, what can reading literature aloud do for children?

1. Children learn from their reader's attention to the literature how much pleasure a good story or poem can bring.
2. The obvious delight of the reader reveals how absorbing reading can be.
3. The voice inflection of the reader expresses the varieties of emotion evoked by the selection.
4. Language development increases as children hear words unknown to their daily conversation. All studies confirm the fact that high linguistic competence inevitably occurs where children are read to.
5. Poring over a book causes reader and child to talk about what they see and hear. Verbal skills increase.
6. Illustrations carefully examined and talked about increase the child's powers of observation.
7. Listeners stretch to understand questioning words, exploring meanings, checking to see whether words mean what they think they mean.
8. Children discover the great variety of literature available to them; their own tastes are uncovered and developed, as well as broadened.

As Charlotte Huck has said, the reading interests children bring to school with them are the teacher's opportunity; the reading interests children leave school with are the teacher's responsibility. But, lest the word "responsibility" put us off, just keep in mind all the pleasures involved for children *and* for the helpful adults who see literature as the great opener of the world for us all.

Children's Literature in the Classroom

Sue Woestehoff Peterson

Involving Children in Literature: The Classroom Environment

"Give us books," say the children; "Give us wings. You who are powerful and strong, help us to escape into the faraway. Build us azure palaces in the midst of enchanted gardens. Show us fairies strolling about in the moonlight. We are willing to learn everything that we are taught at school, but, please, let us keep our dreams."[1]

Paul Hazard

Unlike the flight of Icarus, the winged flight into the world of children's literature is a journey of sustenance and survival. It is a journey that feeds the emotions, the intellects, and the creative and artistic sensibilities of our youth.

But what kinds of classrooms launch such flights, where children enthusiastically embark on literary journeys? These classrooms do not happen by chance. They are the creations of dedicated teachers who, too, savor the journey; teachers who are readers by choice, lovers of literature, persons who can share this literary excitement with children.

These teachers surround children with fine literature of all types, provide time for books in their classrooms, and respect both the reader and the literature. They are readers and tellers of poems and tales, and offer many other ways for children to experience literature in their classrooms. These teachers view the journey as more important than the destination, the travel as more important than the travelogue.

[1] Hazard, Paul. *Books, Children and Men.* Boston: The Horn Book, Inc., 1960, page 4.

A Roomful of Books

Whether they are working with young preschool children or mature teen-agers, teachers who give children "wings" are ones who surround them with literature. Their classrooms are brimming with books! Their chalkboards and window ledges are lined with them. Shelves are stuffed with books. Books are opened on display tables. Personal favorites are tucked into every desk in the room, including the teacher's. Favorite poems or other literary passages speak from posters or bulletin boards, or perhaps are taped to desks, or even hanging from the ceiling! These teachers recognize that children are stimulated by an environment where literature is all around them.

Classroom Reading Centers. Because they know that children can also enjoy and benefit from a special spot in the classroom devoted specifically to literature and reading, many teachers have created classroom reading centers. These centers serve as self-contained libraries as well as feeders for the books throughout the room.

The most effective of these reading centers are both inviting spots for quiet reading and well-stocked storehouses of fine literature. They are available to children throughout the school day as places to privately escape into books, as gathering spots for groups of youngsters wishing to discuss books, and as centers for browsing and choosing books for leisure reading.

Teachers and children usually prefer reading centers that are separated from the major traffic patterns of the classroom. A corner in the back of the room, set apart by bookcase dividers, or perhaps an unused coatroom can provide an ideal spot. Some teachers, short of floor space, have even elicited the help of school students, friends, parents, and grandparents in building reading lofts, complete with stairs and railings. Wherever the space is found, the reading center that appeals to children is one that is attractive and comfortable. The teacher might cover the floor with carpet squares or a used carpet piece. Old couches, stuffed chairs, rocking chairs, bean-bag chairs, and floor pillows might be added. Aged bathtubs on legs, painted, perhaps decorated, and stuffed with pillows can provide ideal nooks for quiet reading. Other such spots can be made with overturned appliance boxes modeled into miniature rooms or carrels. Or perhaps the bookcases and furniture of the reading center, creatively arranged, can provide small and quiet "cubbies" for readers.

Children like to participate in the design, decoration, and operation of their reading centers. They may want to add book-inspired murals or mobiles, or perhaps pillow covers or curtains done in cloth and permanent markers or fabric paints; or a comfortable quilt with each square decorated by a child wanting to commemorate a favorite book. Children may enjoy designing book jackets for those books neglected by readers because their own covers look tired and limp.

However arranged, however decorated, to be effective the reading center must be an inviting environment. And, an inviting environment includes books, scores of them! As the classroom storehouse of literature, the reading center must be stocked with books that meet the varied interests and tastes of all of the children in the classroom. This includes anthologies and individual books containing literature of many topics, styles, and reading levels. It includes traditional and modern fantasy, poetry, many types of realistic fiction, and informational books. It includes books with beautiful artwork, inviting children to pore over their fine illustrations.

While many of these books will be part of the permanent classroom collection, the creative teacher will supplement this collection with an ever-changing array of books from the school and public libraries, and perhaps with books donated for temporary circulation by class members.

Of necessity, most of these books will be arranged side-by-side in bookcases with their spines facing out. But books that are prominently displayed are more likely to be picked up and read. Therefore, children and teachers will want to experiment with various book arrangements, standing some books face out on top of low bookcases, tables, or other convenient spots in the reading center. Some of these books should be placed strategically around the classroom. A collection of them near the front door will encourage children to browse as they congregate to leave for home, perhaps even to snatch a book to read for evening pleasure. These "featured" books should be changed on a regular basis to appeal to the variety of reading tastes in the classroom.

The reading center can house a record-keeping system to keep track of class books checked out and returned. Children and teachers should together devise and monitor this system. Of course, any system can have drawbacks, and a check-out system, rigidly adhered to, can, in certain situations, inhibit book circulation. Books grabbed on the run as children are leaving for home, might, for example, be excluded from a formal check-out procedure. Classrooms where books are prized, breed children who take care of them. And, the replacement cost of an occasional lost book, resulting from a flexible check-out system, is a small price to pay for the added hours of reading enjoyment for the children.

Students enjoy taking turns as class librarians. In this role, they oversee the check-out procedure and the arrangement of books and book-related materials. They might solicit lists, perhaps on index cards, of books that classmates wish to recommend to others. They might organize storytelling and reading sessions, or informal book discussions or book talks.

We do not need researchers to tell us, though they will, that a comfortable class environment, rich in books, spawns readers. The lucky children who find themselves in these environs can indeed say, "We have wings! We can 'keep our dreams!'"

A Time for Books

Readers need time! Time to read for pleasure; time to enjoy new pieces of literature, and time to return to comfortable favorites. They need time to ponder difficult pieces and time to escape with easy ones.

It is surprising how many teachers, who would never think of overlooking skill instruction in the teaching of reading, do overlook some important purposes of this instruction: to help children to get pleasure from the printed page and to develop in them a lifelong interest in literature. Many joyless readers emerge from these classrooms where time was never freely given to reading for pleasure. Reading habits *are* influenced by our teachers, and those who set aside class time for recreational reading are helping to foster habits that will stay with the children for a lifetime.

Silent Reading Time. Many teachers develop silent recreational reading times as a regular part of the daily class schedule. In these rooms, a brief block of time, perhaps fifteen to twenty minutes, is set aside each day for silent reading. In the best of situations, everyone in the classroom, including the teacher, reads during this period, just for the pure pleasure of it. In some schools, everyone in the building participates in the silent reading. The principal, the custodian, the secretary, a visiting parent, all take a reading break! The message the participating adults give by actually reading in front of their students, and enjoying it, is much stronger than any message said through words.

Scheduled silent reading programs are easy to institute. Each classroom will probably want to develop a few simple rules such as: Have something good to read, several books if you wish; do not distract other readers; do not use silent reading time to catch up on other school work. It is a time to read and to enjoy books. This latter rule may be a reminder more for the teacher than the students. This is not a time to catch up on paperwork. Nor is it a time to ask laggard children to finish yesterday's paper on long division, or this morning's phonics worksheet. Some of these children may be the ones who do little recreational reading outside of the classroom and who would benefit the most from the opportunity. Furthermore, the message that they might receive from this practice is that long division or phonics exercises are more important than the reading experience itself.

Children at all age and reading levels can benefit from classroom silent reading periods. To be sure, some children may be "reading" pictures rather than texts. And some may need to absorb literature through their ears, rather than their eyes, using headphones and taped or recorded interpretations of stories and poems. But *all* children, whether reading pictures or text, whether using the eyes or the ears, need a time *just* for literature.

Of course, in addition to scheduled silent reading periods, children should be allowed and encouraged to use any free class time for recreational reading. And, if they have been surrounded by a roomful of books, these lucky children cannot lament, "We have nothing to read!"

A Respect for the Reader

Consider the following monologue. Mary, an adult reader, is talking to her friend Jane:

> I just read *Sophie's Choice.* I expect you to read it. Please finish the book in two weeks because I'll be giving you a test on it then.

It's about time we set up a personal reading program for you. When you finish *Sophie's Choice*, read the rest of the literary selections on this list. You'd better read at least three of these each month.

Here are some book report forms that ask you to describe and analyze each selection you read. You must complete a form for each book you read. And, by the way, I expect you to *accurately* interpret each book in your analysis.

I'm organizing a book competition among my friends. Your names will all be listed on a chart and we'll add a star to the chart next to your name everytime you read a book and fill out a book report form on it. The person who wins this year's competition will be awarded a special prize.

Absurd, isn't it? Yet, change Mary to a teacher, and Jane to a child, and the monologue sounds all too familiar. Now consider the following statement by Mary:

Jane, I just finished reading *Sophie's Choice*, and I found it superb! I think you'd like it, too. Let me know if you read the book and want to talk about it. I'd like to know what you think of it. In fact, I'd like to compare some of my perceptions of the story with yours. By the way, let me know also if you run across any books that I might enjoy. I'm always looking for new titles.

What is the difference? Whether Mary is teacher or friend, which scenario is apt to inspire the Janes of the world to read?

Adult readers respect each other. They respect the personal nature of book selection, response, and interpretation. They should afford this same courtesy of respect to the children in their charge.

This respect for the reader is the base upon which all effective classroom reading programs must be built and the foundation for the following recommendations on ways of bringing children and literature together in the classroom.

Bringing Children and Literature Together.
To be effective conduits connecting children with literature, teachers must know and enjoy children's books. Of course, they need to be familiar with the classroom literature collection, but they also must keep up with the ever-changing collections in the school and public libraries. Only if they really *know* literature, can teachers guide children's choices.

Teachers will want to approach children with the same respect they show their friends: "Jason, I just finished a great book about dragons. I bet you'd like it. If you read it, let me know what you think and whether you think others in the class might enjoy the book," or "Amy, this anthology selection by Gwenda Blair on Laura Ingalls Wilder might be just the thing to put with the display you're preparing on Wilder." Teachers need to be ready to spontaneously suggest literature for leisure time reading as well as literature that might extend the children's understanding of the curriculum.

Note that teachers should *suggest*, they should *encourage*, they should not force-feed. Consider the reaction of the child who is force fed spinach because it is "good for you." Force-feeding breeds rebellion. We would never force-feed our adult friends either spinach or literature.

Teachers guiding children's reading experiences often find that children readers go on binges, absorbing every book in sight on a certain topic. This is of little consequence. All readers binge, and one type of binge frequently replaces another. A teacher concerned about varying a child's reading diet might give gentle nudges. Becky, an avid reader of books on horses, had a teacher who fed her the best horse books around but who also slipped in some other books that she thought Becky would enjoy. The teacher felt a small victory the day Becky exclaimed, "I just read that book you told me about. It didn't have any horses in it, but you know, I actually liked it!"

Most schools house libraries that are accessible to children on an individual basis during the week and that regularly provide specific library periods for individual classrooms. This special library period should not be considered as a coffee-break time for teachers but rather as an opportunity to aid the school librarian in recommending books for individual children. After all, teachers know the interests, tastes, and abilities of the children in their classrooms far better than the librarians who must serve every child in the school. During the library period, teachers and librarians may want to introduce the whole class to some special books and then provide time for book browsing and selection. The adults should circulate among the children, giving book suggestions where needed and encouraging children to help each other make choices.

Back in the classroom, a few minutes should be provided after the library period for children to informally share their finds with each other. Holding up children's choices for others to see, teachers can add valuable comments, "Brian just found one of my favorite books. It's called *Tuck Everlasting* and it's written by a fine author, Natalie Babbit." Such comments can serve many purposes: They introduce the whole class to titles and authors; Brian feels proud of his selection and is more likely to read the story; other children, hearing about Brian's choice, may ask him about it as they consider future book choices, "What was *Tuck Everlasting* about? Is it a good book? Do you think I'd like it?"

Peer recommendations are often more highly prized than teacher recommendations. Wise teachers realize this and provide informal set-ups for this kind of interaction. Some also formalize the peer recommendation process by regularly offering a few minutes, perhaps at the class meeting time, for children to voluntarily share literature recommendations with each other.

Considering Literary Choices and Responses. Many children like to keep personal records of stories and poems they have read and enjoyed. These can be kept in special reading folders on personalized lists, perhaps as entries in individual journals. Teachers should keep abreast of what their students are reading. Scheduled student-teacher conferences can be beneficial. A student brings to the conference the personalized list of literature read. The teacher conducts the conference as one genuinely interested in what the student has read, using the "I'm curious to hear about what you've been reading lately," approach. The ensuing dialogue will not be unlike that of two friends talking over a story or poem. Perceptive teachers will learn much from the dialogue and will hope for responsive partners.

However, teachers should not demand a response on a particular piece of literature. Some literary experiences are too personal or perhaps too painful to share. Sometimes a child needs time before formulating a response. A piece of music may need to be played over and over before a listener forms an opinion about it. Likewise, a piece of literature may need to be read and reread.

Nor should teachers expect uniformity of response or interpretation among children. Each reader brings different perspectives to the printed page, and each reader injects a personal meaning into the literature based on a lifetime of experiences. Jeff's interpretation of a text may be quite different from Sam's. Yet their interpretations may be equally valid. Sarah's favorite book may not appeal to Monica. Yet we respect each child's right to an honest response.

Sometimes individuals respond selectively to a literary piece. A person listening to a great symphony may intuitively respond to a single movement yet not be at all touched by the rest of the piece. A single image in a poem, a single passage in a book, may move a reader in untold ways. The experience provided by a bit or piece of literature may be far more significant than comprehension or attraction to the whole piece.

In eliciting responses to literature, wise teachers are cautious about asking children to analyze what they have read. As poet John Ciardi has noted, "It is the *experience*, not the final examination which counts."[2] Whether the analysis or "final examination" comes in the form of oral questions, report

[2] Ciardi, John. *How Does a Poem Mean?* Cambridge, MA: The Riverside Press, 1959, page 23.

writing, or a written test, it can cause children to read books for the wrong reasons. The essence and joy of the reading experience may be lost. Would you willingly read in your spare time if you knew that a book analysis awaited you at the closing of every final page?

Sharing Literature. Book lovers, whether children or adults, are often ardent evangelists. They want to share perceptions and reactions of their reading with others. And lucky this is, because enthusiasm for literature is contagious. Effective evangelists attract followers.

Some mechanisms for recommending and discussing literature have already been cited. Creative teachers and children will think of others. While mechanisms of this sort should always be considered voluntary, in an enthusiastic classroom, it is quite likely that every child will want to recommend stories and poems to friends and talk with them about favorites.

Reading corners are ideal places to keep student-written lists or files of literature children want to recommend to each other. A file box of children's recommendations recorded on index cards is a useful addition to the corner. If children think that their classmates would enjoy a particular selection, they can choose to write a brief description of it on an index card. A typical card might look like this:

Charlotte's Web by E. B. White
This story is about a barnyard full of animals but especially about Charlotte, a spider, and how she saved the life of her friend, Wilbur, the pig. This is the best book I ever read!

by Tanya Jones

Note that the card is simply written, containing information that Tanya thinks will be useful to others. Tanya includes her name on the card in case her classmates want further information about *Charlotte's Web*.

Rather than annotating index cards, children may prefer simply to keep running lists

of recommended selections. If desired, these can be arranged according to topics. Lists might have such titles as "Poetry Books," "Mysteries," or "Stories and Poems About Horses." Entries on the list of mysteries, for example, might be recorded in the following manner:

> Raskin, Ellen   *The Tattooed Potato and Other Clues*
> For information, see Peter Eide
>
> Winterfeld, Henry   *Detectives in Togas*
> For information, see Leah King
>
> Aiken, Joan   *The Wolves of Willoughby Chase*
> For information, see Katie Decker and Jenny Burroughs

Such lists may be compiled into booklets or recorded on shelf paper and attached to the classroom walls. Young children may need to dictate their recommendations for the teacher to record.

Any recommendation system developed by children should be kept strictly voluntary and should be limited purely to the recommendation function. It should not turn into a competitive device, highlighting the accomplishments of prolific readers.

Sometimes, well-meaning teachers and librarians devise competitive reading charts in their desire to increase recreational reading among their students. Beside their names, children add stars, perhaps pictures of rocket ships or miniature books, or segments of "bookworms" each time they complete a book. Consider what happens. Emily and Greg are avid readers. They add star after star after their names, each hoping to be the contest winner. Jessica, for any number of reasons, does not engage in much recreational reading. She sees the stars piling up next to the names of Emily and Greg, and knows the futility of competing with them. To save face, she assumes a defensive stance, "I'm not playing that stupid game." The very child who needs support and encouragement to read for pleasure is turned further away from it.

What is happening to Emily and Greg is

not much better. In order to amass stars, they turn to short, easy-to-read books. They shun anything long or demanding. They become satisfied with the "quick take" in literature, becoming prolific but lazy readers, giving little of themselves to the act of reading. Emily and Greg don't take the time to savor favorite passages or to ponder difficult ones. They measure success on the number of books read, not on the quality of the reading experience. And, although we know that highly literate people read their favorite books again and again, we can be sure that Emily and Greg would not do that even though they would probably find it a far more enriching experience to read *Tom's Midnight Garden* ten times over than to read a dozen books on the Hardy Boys. Of course, these children might also not stop to examine individual stories or poems in anthologies or isolated segments from other books. Are there *any* winners in this race?

Consider one more "no win" practice. Ask a group of adults to recall childhood experiences about writing traditional book reports and you will probably hear tales of staying up until three o'clock in the morning to finish a book so that a report could be written (and probably hating a book that might be enjoyed under other circumstances); or of reading the book-jacket copy rather than the book to fill out a form; or of searching for short books to read for these assignments. Among this group, it is unlikely that you will hear an endearing word about personal book report experiences. Reading should be an end in itself, not a means to something else. In the eyes of many children, reading is simply a means to fill out the book report.

To be sure, there are many creative and worthwhile written and oral language experiences that extend the enjoyment and understanding of literature for children and that allow them to share ideas and feelings about the books they have read. Some of these will be explored later in the section on Extending Literature: Children's Literature in the Curriculum.

Teachers who love literature want children to take their reading beyond the four walls of the classroom. For that reason, they may want to use their own knowledge of children's books as well as student book recommendations as bases for compiling lists to be periodically sent home with children. These lists are particularly welcome at the end of the school year to guide and encourage summer leisure reading. These teachers may also want to organize book talks and book clubs for parents to involve them in their children's reading.

Supportive parents and teachers who respect child readers and who offer them a wealth of literature and a time for literature are placing the cornerstones for many lifetimes of happy reading.

The Magic of the Book: Reading Aloud

A fourth-grade teacher, wishing to assess her effectiveness in various areas, polled her students using an anonymous questionnaire. She asked the children to rank order, in terms of interest, their school-day subjects and experiences. All components of the children's day were included on the questionnaire including the traditional school subjects, as well as noninstructional activities such as recess and lunch time. It was no surprise to the teacher when the "first-place winner" on the poll turned out to be the time of the day she regularly devoted to reading aloud to her class. The teacher was an avid fan of good literature and it was obvious that her students had been infected by her enthusiasm.

Why Read Aloud? Perhaps the pleasure children derive from being read to is reason enough for its inclusion in the school curriculum. Yet, there *are* many other convincing arguments for including a read-aloud time in every classroom.

For some, the time when the teacher reads aloud to the class may be the first or only exposure to the world of fine literature. For many, this exposure awakens a desire for independent reading. Research tells us that children who are regularly read to are more likely to learn to read with ease and more likely to want to read than children deprived of this experience.

When children are read to, their worlds and horizons are expanded. Some learn to laugh, some to cry. Some come to understand different value systems and different ways of life. Some enter, for the first time, the literary world of make-believe—and are allowed to dream. Others first come to understand stark realities of life. As teachers read to children, they feed their imaginations and their emotions. As they listen to literature, children learn much about others, but they also learn a great deal about themselves.

What to Read Aloud.   What kinds of literature read well aloud? There are many considerations in selecting oral reading material. One of the first and most important is that the reader genuinely like the literary selection. It is unlikely that a reader will project, with enthusiasm, a piece considered limp or dull or obscure. A second consideration is that the selection be a fine piece of literature. We should give our children the *best* that we can find.

Children generally favor fast-paced stories and poems that both speak to and extend their experiences, pieces that may help them to see the familiar in new and exciting ways. They like well-styled pieces with pleasing rhythms and sound patterns. Memorable characters, infused with life, also attract listeners.

Readers need to know their audiences since group interests, tastes, and comprehension abilities are all considerations in selection. Humorous literature, both prose and poetry, is often appealing to children and can serve the added advantage of "breaking the ice" between readers and listeners unfamiliar with each other. Substitute teachers in new surroundings, or teachers reading to their classes on the first day of school, like to fill their knapsacks with humorous literature.

Some literature does not read well aloud. Prose and poetry pieces with extended descriptions or difficult passages that require

time to be absorbed and, perhaps several readings for their impact, are generally more appropriate for silent reading times. Some literature, particularly stories of contemporary realistic fiction, appeals to children because of the seemingly private interaction developed between the main character (or perhaps the author) and the reader. Children often experience uneasiness or discomfort when adult readers intrude upon this relationship.

On occasion, an oral reading selection will be chosen that, for any number of reasons, does not appeal to a particular group. One teacher chose a favorite book of hers to share with the class. The group proved to be not quite ready for the selection. Rather than continuing on, and perhaps turning children away from the book forever, she stopped. She encouraged those few who were enjoying the book to consider it as a silent reading choice. To the others she observed, "I think you'll enjoy this book in a few years and I hope you'll remember the title and think of coming back to it." If a piece of literature does not catch on, readers should not be afraid to stop and perhaps to hold it for another time or another situation.

Children often request old favorites to be read again and again. Teachers should hope for and honor these requests. Children find comfort in the familiar and are often pleasantly surprised when they pick up an image or idea, or catch a rhythmical phrase not noticed in earlier readings.

Most of the selections presented in this anthology provide fine examples of literature for oral reading experiences. There should be many other appropriate poems and stories housed in every classroom's storehouse of literature.

When to Read Aloud.   Teachers at all grade levels recognize the need to build both spontaneous and scheduled oral reading experiences into the school day. Spontaneous readings can occur at any time. Consider the possibilities using selections from this anthology. A particularly troublesome mathematics lesson might be lightened by the reading of

"Arithmetic" by Carl Sandburg (page 32). The imagery in Robert Francis' poem, "The Base Stealer" (page 91) is likely to appeal to young baseball players as they leave for, or return from, a big game. A rainy April day, casting gloom on the class, can be brightened by Langston Hughes' "April Rain Song" (page 124). The perfect accompaniment to children molding fanciful clay creations during an art class might be "The Thing" from Rebecca Caudill's story, *Did You Carry the Flag Today, Charley?* (page 575). Frequent and spontaneous readings during the school day help children to view stories and poems as a natural part of life.

In addition to spontaneous readings, effective teachers set aside specific times during the day devoted exclusively to reading literature aloud to children. Teachers of young children may schedule two or three brief read-aloud periods each day. Those working with older children commonly schedule one longer period. Many teachers discover favorite times for reading aloud and build these times into the daily schedule. Children find comfort and security from a set reading time that they can anticipate and count on. Some teachers regularly read to their children the first thing each morning, providing a pleasing entry into the school day. Others may schedule time immediately after lunch or prior to the children's departure for home. Teachers in busy classrooms sometimes find this latter choice an unwise one. Time runs out on them. At 3 P.M. they are reluctant to call a halt to a group science experiment just as some exciting discovery is about to be made. Literature saved until the end of the day often loses its spot in the curriculum.

Techniques of Reading Aloud. One does not need to be a dramatist to become an effective oral reader. One must simply be attached and responsive to the members of the listening audience and have the need and desire to share best-loved pieces of literature with them.

There are, however, various preparations and techniques that are useful for effective readers to consider. The following comments

are geared toward material read for preplanned read-aloud sessions. It is recognized that spontaneous readings might necessarily not have undergone some of the rigors of preparation suggested for preplanned interpretations.

Background preparation prior to a reading is important in developing effective oral skills. The reader must have close familiarity with the text and should certainly have preread the whole piece. In perusing the text, the reader will want to single out words or sections for emphasis, consider elements of rhythm and tempo, and in texts with characterization, work on understanding and voicing the various characters. It is useful to practice a piece out loud before presenting it to a group. Poems and short literary selections should be practiced in their entirety. In longer prose pieces, the reader can try out a representative segment.

When the reader is ready to begin, the listeners should be gathered into a comfortable area, free from distractions. The reader may want to share information about the author or poet of the chosen selection and perhaps set a background or tone for the reading with suitable comments. Troublesome words that might not be picked up in the context of the material should be introduced, particularly if they will cause confusion and break the continuity of the reading. The reader might simply begin with a comment such as, "I found a new book that I like and I can't wait to share it with you."

If the presenter is well prepared, the reading, once begun, should flow smoothly and appear effortless. The reader who knows the text well can move with the audience, changing pace and otherwise altering the delivery of the reading as deemed appropriate.

Reading time for very young children is often centered around the picture storybook, a book where text and pictures are equally necessary for the story's interpretation. Children hearing picture storybooks should be close enough to the reader to take in the pictures as the accompanying words are being read. Teachers should sit on low chairs, or even on the floor, to be close to the children. During the reading they should slowly move the book, if necessary, to allow all children to absorb the illustrations. When the reading is completed, the book should be available to children to look at, and, if desired, to reread.

Teachers who are reading longer full-length stories to older children usually read the book in sections, offering a chapter or other self-contained excerpt each day during the scheduled class reading time. Since illustrations in these books are usually too small for an entire class group to see at once, teachers often reserve the viewing of these until after the selection has been completed. They then slowly circulate among the children showing them the pictures, or perhaps they pass the book around the class. As in the younger classrooms, the book should be available to children after the reading session. Some teachers ask children not to read ahead in the chosen read-aloud book. Perhaps this is a selfish act of teachers who want to be in on the excitement of discovery that comes with the reading or hearing of new literature. Teachers who allow children to read ahead will testify that this practice of some children often engenders enthusiasm for the book and for the subsequent oral reading sessions. Commonly heard in these children's classrooms are exclamations such as, "Boy! Wait until you hear what happens to Tom and Becky today!"

During poetry readings, teachers will want to be armed with several selections to share. Each poem should be readily accessible, allowing for smooth transitions between pieces. Teachers should have prepared enough selections to read to meet the common cry, "Read some more!"

Of course, prose and poetry are often mixed in oral reading sessions and many teachers regularly include short verses in the reading times. Some poems are natural companion pieces to prose selections. Consider, for example, Eloise Greenfield's poem, "Harriet Tubman" (page 139) as an accompaniment to selections from Ann Petry's biography, *Harriet Tubman, Conductor on the Underground Railroad* (page 745).

Whether children have heard stories or poems, an important part of the reading and listening experience comes after the last word of the piece has been read. At this point, listeners often need and want to sit in silence, perhaps to contemplate what they've just experienced, perhaps to let the mood of the piece linger. Verbal responses, if they need come at all, can wait until later. Teachers should resist the temptation to jump in with questions of fact or queries on response lest the magic of the literature be lost.

To Weave a Tale: Storytelling

> This is my story which I have related. If it be sweet, or if it be not sweet, take some elsewhere, and let some come back to me.[3]

Long before stories were committed to paper, they were committed to the memories of storytellers who offered their literary riches to kith and to kin. The spells created by these early weavers of tales are still being cast today when masterful storytellers engage receptive audiences.

A storyteller *tells* rather than reads a tale. The tale is "possessed," so to speak, by the teller rather than by the bound pages of a book. The tale comes to life through the words and actions of a storyteller, touching the imaginations of listeners. An accomplished storyteller can create a bond with the listening audience that is unsurpassed in any other form of communication.

One does not need to be any more of a dramatist to tell a story than to read one. Tellers must simply enjoy children and be so taken by tales that they need to release them.

Choosing Tales to Tell. The weaver of a tale is quite like the weaver of a tapestry. In the beginning, both artists seek the finest materials available. Perhaps the richest source for the weaver of tales is the traditional literature, particularly the storehouse of folk tales from around the world. Folk tales

[3]Haley, Gail E. *A Story, a Story.* New York: Antheneum, 1979.

began in the oral tradition and were passed on from generation to generation, from one community to another, by word of mouth. The mere fact that these tales survived orally for centuries before finally being written down attests to their suitability as stories to tell. They have, quite literally, "stood the test of time."

A story that survives many retellings is generally one that is fast-paced, logically sequenced, full of action, and devoid of lengthy descriptions or obscure passages. These stories are relatively easy for the storyteller to learn and for the listeners to comprehend and remember.

In addition to the folk tales, myths and fables, as well as some short selections from modern literature, can be suitable sources for storytellers. However, selections that rely on extended descriptions or other extended stylistic devices for their effectiveness would be better read than told.

The storyteller will need, of course, to know the composition of the audience in order to select passages of appropriate length and content. Every teacher should be a storyteller, prepared with stories of all kinds to share both spontaneously and in preplanned class sessions. A story learned well will stay with a teller for a lifetime. If teachers learn a few new tales each year, they will, before long, possess a repertoire of riches.

Preparing and Telling a Story.   To weave a tapestry, one must first prepare materials, dress the loom, and consider a design. Careful preparation is just as essential to the weaver of tales.

Beginning storytellers should locate brief, simple tales with uncomplicated plot structures. A perfect tale to start with is "The Three Billy-Goats Gruff" (page 227). You can use this tale to take yourself through the preparatory stages for storytelling. To begin, give several thoughtful readings to the tale. Consider its plot structure. Organize it into segments. Determine the introduction and the conclusion. Divide the development of the tale into scenes.

The beautifully compact introduction in "The Three Billy-Goats Gruff" comes in its first two paragraphs. This introduction is an easy one to learn because it simply answers the questions who, what, when, where, why, and how. It establishes the conflict and leads the reader directly into the development of the body of the story.

The body of the story divides nicely into three segments. The first begins, "So first of all came the youngest billy-goat Gruff to cross the bridge." It presents the encounter of the young goat with the troll, and ends, "Well, be off with you," said the troll. The second segment is almost identical, beginning, "A little while after came the second billy-goat Gruff to cross the bridge." After a similar goat-troll encounter, it concludes, " 'Very well! be off with you,' said the troll." The introduction to the third segment is much like the other two, but the ending solves the conflict with the big billy-goat's victory over the troll, "That was what the big billy-goat said; and so he flew at the troll, and poked his eyes out with his horns, and crushed him to bits, body and bones, and tossed him into the burn, and after that he went up to the hillside."

As you consider each segment, you will notice an economy of words and action. Look at the parallel structures of the segments. As in many folk tales, there is a repetition of words, phrases, and events. The second and third scenes basically repeat the first, with a slight change and growth of the text to reflect the growth and intensity of the billy-goats. Once one lives through one scene with a billy-goat, the others are relatively easy to remember.

Most folk tales also have decisive and abrupt conclusions. This one is no exception. As soon as the conflict is resolved, the tale is quickly concluded. Memorable phrases such as "And they lived happily ever after," or "Snip, snap, snout. This tale's told out," signal to the audience that the story is over.

Next, carefully visualize the scenes and characters. Place yourself on the hill with the billy-goats and under the bridge with the troll. Form clear images. What colors and shapes do you see? What smells are in the air? Is the troll tall and skinny . . . or round and scraggly? Is he sitting, or standing, or crouching? How long is the bridge? Is it narrow or wide? Is it built from wooden planks or logs? Consider the billy-goats. Does each have a distinct personality and appearance? Do they have different voices? Where are the goats positioned when you enter the story? In what direction do they move? Are they quick-footed? Know the season, the weather, the time of day, the colors of the trees. Of course, many of these details are not and never will be in the text itself. They have been supplied by the prospective storyteller who really has "been there." Placing oneself in the story is essential to the learning and remembering of it; but it is also essential when bringing listeners to the hillside.

When the setting, characters, action, and structure of the story are clearly understood and internalized, go back over the text to consider elements of emphasis and pacing. For example, the little billy-goat's plea, "Oh no! pray don't take me. I'm too little, that I am," almost begs to be read in a high, hushed tone. In contrast, "IT'S I! THE BIG BILLY-GOAT GRUFF" demands a loud, hoarse interpretation. Similarly, the light "Trip, trap! trip, trap!" of the little goat's feet might be expressed in a quick, quiet voice, quite different from the slow, heavy interpretation suggested by the sound of the big billy-goat, "TRIP, TRAP! TRIP, TRAP! TRIP, TRAP!"

After this careful perusal and preparation of the text, try telling the story to yourself, silently at first perhaps, but eventually practice it aloud. Tape yourself and evaluate your attempt.

Oral tales are fluid tales. Each time they are told, they undergo change. The storyteller who knows the story, who has entered the scene and internalized the actions, and who understands its structure, should be able to tell the story effectively, to relate its settings, its moods, its characters, and events.

The fluidity, the pleasure and magic of weaving a tapestry is lost when the artist is commissioned to produce identical copies of the original. In the same way, the exact reproduction or memorization of a tale often interferes with the storytelling process. The teller who strictly adheres to a memorized version often cannot establish an effective relationship with the audience, adding or eliminating details, changing words, embellishing a point, or otherwise changing a tale as a situation demands. It is also easier to forget sections of memorized tales, thus breaking the bond between teller and listener. However, some storytellers do like to commit simple sections to memory—perhaps quick introductions and conclusions and short rhymed passages in the text. These are easy to learn and retain and often add to the appeal of the oral interpretation.

If a story has been well prepared, its delivery should come naturally. A certain response or cue from the audience may cause the teller to change the weaving, to add a new and unexpected thread to the creation, perhaps to lengthen the tale, to repeat a pattern; or perhaps to remove a section because the tale would be more beautiful without it.

Once released, a well-woven tale, just as a well-woven tapestry, is not static. It lives on in the imaginations and memories of others. And each time this creation is offered to a receptive audience, it provides new pleasures and new discoveries.

Extending Literature: Children's Literature in the Curriculum

. . . one of the priceless possessions of childhood is the ability to take delight in a thing for its own sake, and not as a means to an end.[4]

While it is true that stories and poems can serve as means to wonderful ends, this literature should be offered to children, first and foremost, as something of delight. It should exist for its own sake. If a child wants to use literature as a springboard to a classroom ac-

[4]Viguers, Ruth Hill. *Margin for Surprise.* Boston: Little, Brown and Company, 1974, page 32.

tivity, fine, but such activities should never be forced on children nor should they take on such dimensions that they become more important than the reading of literature itself. Book-related activities should be designed so that they increase the child's appreciation of literature rather than detract from it, and inspire children to want to do more reading, rather than less. Following are examples of ways literature might be effectively connected to selected areas of the elementary curriculum.

The Sounds of Literature: Oral Interpretation

The young child chanting as she rocks atop her wooden horse, "Ride a cock horse to Banbury Cross . . . ," the girl skipping rope to "Teddy Bear, Teddy Bear, turn around . . . ," and the lad playing with his infant sister, "This little piggy went to market . . ." are all orally interpreting favorite verses. This natural delight in the sounds of literature will be tapped by effective teachers and used as a basis for building choral speaking experiences into elementary language arts programs.

Choral speaking, as used here, will refer to oral group interpretations of literature through either the reading, or telling from memory, a story or poem. Choral speaking experiences provide important exposure to children to fine literature. If handled appropriately, children become active participants in the literature, they internalize it, find delight in it, and become attuned to the words and sounds of their language. Choral speaking stimulates imaginations and emotions. It develops expressive voice qualities of pitch, tempo, and volume. Group speaking experiences provide comfortable avenues of oral expression for the shy or insecure child and skills of listening and cooperation are enhanced.

Techniques of preparation and delivery of choral speaking pieces are similar to those used in learning to sing a song. Children first need to hear the song several times, to be exposed to its melody and words. They don't learn it cold, line by line, without a sense of the entire piece. And, if they dislike the song, their interpretation may be flat and lifeless. In the same way, a choral speaking experience must begin with exposure to the literature chosen for interpretation. A piece should never be put through the interpretive process unless children already know it well and enjoy it.

Teachers usually begin choral speaking experiences with poetry. They choose a simple, familiar, and well-liked poem to introduce various elements of interpretation. Perhaps even a nursery rhyme:

Hey, diddle, diddle!
The cat and the fiddle
The cow jumped over the moon;
The little dog laughed
to see such sport,
And the dish ran away with the spoon.

Teachers might begin by reciting the verse, perhaps several times, inviting children to join in as they wish. It is usually helpful, even if the children know the piece by heart, to have it written out on the chalkboard or on a large sheet of paper. Children should be asked to suggest ways of interpreting the piece. If not freely offered, teachers will want to draw out comments about the ways we can vary our voices through pitch, tempo, and volume. Then the children should be allowed to make decisions on how to orchestrate the piece. The group may, for example, decide to interpret, "Hey, diddle, diddle! The cat and the fiddle," with a high pitch and quick tempo and, conversely, recite, "The cow jumped over the moon" in low, slow voices. (They may even want to reverse these interpretations, noting the humor and incongruity of low, sluggish voices talking about a cat who plays a fiddle and high, quick voices introducing the cow.) Children could choose to turn the rhyme's volume up and down, merrily shouting, "The little dog laughed to see such sport," and then whispering, "And the dish ran away with the spoon."

Children discover that they already know

and use techniques of oral interpretation in their daily lives and that they can draw on these skills to make literature come to life. It is important for children to recognize that the variations for orally interpreting a literary piece are endless and that they can create many versions in trying to come up with a favorite.

Children usually find unison choral speaking experiences the easiest and most comfortable. With everyone in the group speaking the same words, unison pieces do require cooperative group efforts to be effective. To help the group with its interpretation, the teacher or a volunteer student may need to serve as a conductor of the group. David McCord's "The Pickety Fence" (page 36) is a wonderful piece for a unison interpretation. It reads almost like a tongue twister and is particularly appealing to children when they are allowed to play with its tempo. They might begin the verse slowly, but then quickly increase the speed of the reading until they are chanting the final, "Pickety Pickety Pickety Pick" as fast as they can. A conductor or group leader can help the group stay together as well as signal variations in pitch and volume.

After children have had some experiences with choral speaking in unison, they may want to divide a selection into parts and assign the parts to different groups. A poem such as Christina Rossetti's "Who has seen the wind?" (page 134) is a perfect poem for two groups, with one asking the question, "Who has seen the wind?" and the second responding with Rossetti's answer. Sometimes speakers divide into sound groups. In Rossetti's poem, for example, the group asking the question might do so in low, pitched voices. The second group could respond in normal speaking voices.

Poems containing characters engaged in dialogue work well with sound group interpretations. "Hiding" by Dorothy Aldis (page 87) contains three characters. Benny, the

child narrator in the poem, could be voiced by one group in high-pitched tones, his mother in middle-ranged tones, and his father with a lower sound. If children are working with a text such as "Hiding," where the groups switch regularly, sometimes even in the middle of a line, they will probably need to prepare the script in advance underlining or highlighting each group's section in different colors.

Sometimes single children, or small groups of two or three, speak individual lines for an effective interpretation. Children have used this format to provide beautiful renderings of Myra Cohn Livingston's "The Sun Is Stuck":

	Group
The sun is stuck.	1
I mean, it won't move.	2
I mean it's hot, man, and we need a red-hot poker to pry it loose.	3
Give it a good shove and roll it across the sky	4
And make it go down	5
So we can be cool,	6
Man.	7

After becoming familiar with the entire poem, each group develops an interpretation for its particular line. Group 4, for example, might decide to emphasize and draw out the words "good" and "roll" in order to vocally depict the action. After each group has determined its interpretation, the piece can be put together for total group response and evaluation. Sometimes children like to add simple gestures or movements to a choral speaking piece. When the "sun is stuck" it seems almost natural to push against it with one's hands.

Background chants can add life to a choral speaking piece. e. e. cummings' "Hist Whist" (page 102) can be accompanied by eerie ghostlike sounds, perhaps even becoming part of a Halloween celebration. Sometimes vocal or instrumental background sounds are also added. Experienced choral speakers might even try to speak a "round," having groups stagger their entries into the chorus.

Some stories work well as choral speaking pieces. The best are brief ones containing several characters engaged in lively dialogue. A story such as "Jack and the Robbers" (page 358) is ideal. It is action-packed and contains interesting conversations and sounds. It can be easily divided into parts with individuals assuming the roles of the narrator, Jack, and the robbers. The animal characters might be assigned to single children or to small groups of them. Scripts will need to be prepared for longer pieces such as this one, highlighting the parts of all participants. "Danger!" from Mary Norton's fantasy, *The Borrowers,* (page 503) and Lewis Carroll's "A Mad Tea Party" (page 522) would also make fine choices. Children need to put themselves into the literary selection to effectively interpret it. Some of the techniques recommended to the storyteller in entering the land of "The Three Billy-Goats Gruff" would work with choral speakers as well.

As children become involved with literature, they want to share it, sometimes even to play with it. Choral speaking allows them this. They recognize the endless possibilities for variation and interpretation of spoken literature and take pleasure in discovering that literature can come to life through sounds of their own making.

Movement and Literature: The Dramatic Arts

Children immersed in a choral speaking experience often begin to intuitively move with the story or poem. This physical involvement with literature is natural. Dramatic activities, built upon these intuitive responses, are effective in helping children to internalize literature, thereby gaining an increased understanding and appreciation of it.

Dramatic activities take many forms. The most popular form used with children is creative dramatics. Creative dramatics involves improvisation. The drama may be pre-planned but it is acted out spontaneously, being created on the spot.

Creative Dramatics. Young children often engage in dramatic play. They assume roles that reflect people or book characters they have known. They play out scenes that are familiar to them. Creative dramatics experiences that draw upon known characters or events in real life or in literature are often the easiest for beginners. Those that draw from the riches of literature will be considered here.

Children are usually most comfortable when dramatic sessions start with group interpretations where all of the children in the group dramatize the same material at the same time. The inhibited child, in particular, takes comfort in not being singled out but in being one of many dramatists. In unison improvisations children are all working with the same material, however, they each create their own impromptu interpretations of it.

Teachers can draw upon literary characters, situations, or movements suggested by literature in planning whole group improvisation sessions. Young children, in particular, often delight in interpreting the movements of animals. Many poems offer vivid and precise images of animals in action. Sometimes small bits of poems suggest movement experiences. Lewis Carroll's "slithy toves" and "mimsy borogoves" from "Jabberwocky" (page 120) can come to life for children through dramatic interpretations. Children delight in defining these creatures and actions for themselves, perhaps first through discussing plausible interpretations and then through acting them out.

Given lots of space, perhaps the gymnasium floor, children can become William Jay Smith's "Seal" (page 69). After hearing the poem several times, they should be able to offer dramatic interpretations for individual movements suggested by the poem to "See how he darts Through his watery room . . ."

or "See how he swims with a swerve and a twist . . ." They may want to combine these individual movements to act out the entire poem as the teacher, or perhaps a volunteer student, recites the poem. In this case the whole class can improvise in unison the actions offered by the narrator. Or children can divide into groups, each choosing one of the seal's actions to interpret as it is presented by the narrator.

Real and fanciful people can be released from the pages of a book through creative dramatics. The stern and haughty stepsisters in Perrault's version of Cinderella (page 200) are popular characters for whole group dramatization. Children can benefit from talking about the evil sisters, considering ways to use small and large dramatic movements to "become" one of them. They might play with darting eye movements, quick jerks of the head, and rigid postures in their character portrayals.

Literature provides many other unique and memorable characters for group improvisation experiences. Consider folk tale heroes such as Rumpelstiltzkin (page 185) or Pecos Bill (page 365). Modern prose pieces offer hundreds of popularly dramatized characters including Templeton, the rat, from *Charlotte's Web*, the Mad Hatter of *Alice's Adventures in Wonderland* (page 522), the proud emperor in Hans Christian Andersen's "The Emperor's New Clothes" (page 537), Amos, the electrically charged mouse in *Ben and Me* (page 547), and Aunt Beast from the delightful fantasy, *A Wrinkle in Time* (page 565). Consider also the wonderful characters housed in poems such as T. S. Eliot's "Macavity: The Mystery Cat" (page 60), "The Grand Old Duke of York" (page 113) of Mother Goose, and the mighty American folk hero from the ballad of "John Henry" (page 28).

Once children have been successful in dramatically interpreting movements and characters, they will want to try out brief situations found in the literature. The fox in "The Fox and the Grapes" (page 411) can be

the impetus for a situational dramatization with child foxes in unison striving unsuccessfully to reach imaginary grapes, and then walking away, with noses in the air.

Improvisations in unison are not possible when a situation from a literary selection calls upon the interaction of several characters for a dramatic rendering. When this occurs, volunteers can assume different roles as might be done in the wonderful sequence where Mark Twain has Tom Sawyer convincing his friends, one by one, that it is a special honor to whitewash a fence (page 625). This selection almost demands the inclusion of spontaneous dialogue although some selections containing several characters may be effective if strictly pantomimed.

After a number of creative dramatic experiences interpreting individual movements, characters, or brief situations from literary texts, children will be ready to improvise whole stories. Although spontaneous, these improvisations will require preplanning. First, children will need to try on various parts. In "The Three Billy-Goats Gruff," for example, they can all become the youngest billy-goat and practice various movements and mannerisms. Then collectively, the dramatists should "try on" all of the other characters before choosing individual parts. They will also want to visualize the story's setting and discuss the various events and movements in the selection, dividing the story into logical and memorable segments. Children may want whole group participation in a single story dramatization. In "The Three Billy-Goats Gruff," some may choose to be trees or even additional goats grazing on the hillside. Perhaps the troll under the bridge is a many-headed one played by several children at once. Children will need to decide which, if any, of the characters should have speaking parts.

Beginners may be uncomfortable with dialogue, but eventually they will choose to include it. Since the dialogue in creative dramatics is spontaneous, children will need to literally "think on their feet." If children have prepared well and if they really know and understand and can internalize their characters, the dialogue should come with relative ease.

Sometimes children enjoy going beyond the basic material of a literary text in an improvisation. They often choose to extend or alter a plot. This can happen spontaneously, but often it is preplanned. A plot may be moved backward in time, for example, as when children set up a scene depicting the swindlers in the planning stages of their deceptive act in "The Emperor's New Clothes" (page 537). Children improvising the relief and subsequent celebration of the three billy-goats after they outwitted the troll, are extending a plot beyond the time of the tale.

Experienced child dramatists like to create "what if" spin-offs from favorite tales to use as material for improvisation. Here are some examples:

What if Cinderella's fairy godmother was really her stepsister in disguise?

What if Little Miss Muffet really liked spiders?

What if the crocodile hadn't pulled the elephant's trunk in Kipling's "The Elephant's Child" (page 487)? How else might the elephant's trunk have been created?

What if the cow bumped into the moon in her attempt to jump over it?

What if "Sarah Cynthia Sylvia Stout" (page 115) had a godmother who turned all her garbage into gumdrops?

What if "The Husband Who Was to Mind the House" (page 235) turned out to be a better housekeeper than his wife?

What if the crow had not sung for the fox in Aesop's, "The Fox and the Crow" (page 410)? How might the fox have gotten the cheese then?

Sometimes children like to place themselves in scenes, showing how they would respond to a particular situation, perhaps in a way different from that suggested by the literature, such as:

What if you were the mother in "Tom Tit Tot" (page 153)? What would you tell the king about your foolish "darter"?

What if you were Hans Christian Andersen's "The Real Princess" (page 502)? Show how you would react to the lump under your mattress.

What if you were the ant in "The Ant and the Grasshopper" (page 409)? How would you treat the starving grasshopper in the winter?

Of course the possibilities for extending literature are limitless. Children familiar with literature will have no difficulty thinking of material for improvisation.

Children's Theater.   Creative dramatics is a form of drama which emphasizes process—its value lies in the dramatic experience itself and it is generally not performed for an audience. Children's theater is a more formal dramatic experience that involves the production of a play for an audience. Productions are scripted rather than improvised. They involve extensive preparation including script making, staging, costuming, and rehearsing. Children's theater performances are perhaps best suited to professional theater groups and older, experienced children. Teachers may occasionally want to attempt this form of drama in their classrooms but only if it does not take too much time away from other dramatic and literary experiences.

Puppetry.   Puppets have been used for centuries to interpret literature. Many individuals, in fact, feel more comfortable interpreting literature through puppets than through their own improvisations.

The same ideas and techniques used to prepare for creative dramatics can be used to prepare a puppet dramatization. Some puppetry experiences will be completely spontaneous. Such as when children at their desks, or perhaps in the reading center, engage their puppets in brief dialogues. Whole story dramatization with puppets, however, takes preplanning. Children will need to identify necessary characters, find or make appropriate puppets, and manipulate their puppets, trying out different movements and voices, attempting to get the right personalities. They will want to visualize the story's setting and perhaps make scenery for the puppet stage. The story to be dramatized should be read several times through, and considered scene by scene. Children will need to become comfortable with the stage and will want to practice moving puppets on and off of it.

Once the dramatization is underway, the dialogue can assume the same spontaneous quality of creative dramatics dialogue. Some groups may prefer staging a production with a single narrator, or perhaps with several children orally interpreting the text while others simply manipulate the puppets. More experienced children may want to memorize lines. However, they should know the story well enough to furnish impromptu dialogue if their memory fails them.

Handmade puppets, representing literary characters, can be easily created by children. Finger puppets made from felt or heavy paper can be effective. Rod puppets are easy to construct with flat sticks and heavy paper or cardboard, even with paper plates and popsicle sticks. Hand puppets are perhaps the most fun for children to manipulate because they offer greater movement possibilities than finger or rod puppets. Hand puppets can be made from discarded socks or perhaps from sewn cloth. Papier-mâché, or styrofoam heads are often added. Because marionettes are difficult for young children to handle, they should probably be discouraged in elementary classrooms.

Many teachers have elaborate puppet stages constructed from wood. Children can make their own stages from large cardboard boxes. However, a table turned on its side can become an effective stage. And children can even enjoy improvising with their puppets with no stage at all.

Whatever dramatic form is used with literature, the wise teacher recognizes that the drama should add to the awareness and enjoyment of the literature. If it does, children will willingly bring their favorite stories and poems to the dramatic experience. And they may also be led further into the world of books in search of good literature to dramatize.

Literature in the Writing Program

Children who read widely become better writers than their nonreading friends. Because they know the pleasure of the printed word, avid readers are usually more motivated to write for themselves and for others. And, child writers, with no direct instruction, often pick up the literary styles of their favorite authors and use these styles in their own compositions. So even without teacher intervention, the writing program can be influenced by what, and by how much, children read. But children can also learn much about reading through writing. Creative writing motivators can help children to see a book in a new way, perhaps to understand characterization or thematic elements, perhaps to become aware of specific stylistic devices used by a writer. To be effective, these writing activities should go beyond the traditional "write a book report" assignments that ask for dry facts and analyses.

If children engage in book-related writing, they should have a number of options to choose from—both in terms of writing forms or approaches and in terms of the literature to be used for the writing experience. Following are some examples of writing activities that many children enjoy and that can be used to extend the literature program.

> Pretend you are a specific book character. Write a letter to a character from another book. Have that character reply to your letter.

> Write diary entries as though you were a specific book character.

A book character who is applying for a job has just asked you to write a letter of support to accompany this application. What would you write?

Your book character is running for a political office. Write a speech or brochure in support of your character's candidacy.

You have magical powers that can take book characters forward or backward in time. Write a story chronicling the characters' adventures in a different time zone.

Write and present a singing telegram to celebrate a favorite book. Your words can be written to the tune of a familiar song if you wish.

Get together with your friends and write and share riddles about book characters.

Adapt any of the "what if" dramatic situations to writing.

Contribute to a class newspaper focusing on literature. The content of your copy will vary since you will be incorporating books and characters from your own reading. However, you can include entries such as the following:

As court reporter, write an account of the trial of the knave of hearts from *Alice's Adventures in Wonderland.*

You have just interviewed several people who witnessed a strange object flying over the island of Krakatoa (see *The Twenty-One Balloons,* page 552). Write an article using this interview material.

Write a lost and found advertisement entitled, "Found: One Magic Lamp."

Write an obituary for a book character such as Charlotte the spider or the Wicked Witch of the West.

Write a help wanted ad such as: "Wanted, someone who can spin flax into gold."

Use book characters as bases for an advice column.
"Dear Aunt Gabby,
    My stepsisters are impossible to live with . . ."

Write a feature article on Beverly Cleary's Ramona (page 584).

Design cartoons featuring book-related characters.

Write advertisements related to children's books such as "We spin the finest cloth. We are currently working on clothes for our Emperor."

Write an engagement announcement for two book characters. . . . "Tom Sawyer to wed Harriet the Spy."

Write bona fide reviews of good books you have read.

Choose a particular form of literature and try to reproduce it:

"Rumpelstiltzkin" (page 185) and "Tom Tit Tot" (page 153) are variants of the same tale emerging from different cultures. Write another version of this tale as it might emerge from your culture.

Write your own fable. Make sure to include a moral.

Create your own tall tale hero and write of his or her adventures.

Write an autobiography of yourself or a biography of a friend or relative.

Create your own gods and goddesses and write a myth.

Choose a poetry form that you like and try it yourself.

Writing motivators can be recorded on cards and housed in the reading center. Creative children will think of many other ways to share literary responses and information through writing. They may want to record these ideas to be filed with those of the teacher. Book-related writing motivators should be available to children for the times when they want to use literature as the basis for a private or shared piece of writing or when they want to use writing as a basis to better understand and appreciate what they have read.

Literature and the Visual Arts

Three-year-old Jonathan had the chance to choose, on his own, a free book from one of many offered in a preschool program. After the choice was made, he ran to his mother who was waiting outside. When she asked him about his choice, he responded with a smile, "I don't know what it's called, but I just know it's a Ezra Jack Keats book 'cause he took some of that neat stuff off the pages of *The Snowy Day* and put it in this book!" Holding up *Whistle for Willie,* Jonathan continued, "I know I picked a good one mommy! Let's go sit in the car and read it!"

At three years of age, Jonathan already recognizes and appreciates the beautiful artwork found in children's books. For many children, books serve as their first and most important exposure to fine art. Young children do not need to be taught about the art in their books, they absorb it, tuning into fine details and techniques.

Just as illustrated literature can feed children's artistic sensibilities, so can book-related art experiences feed their literary sensibilities. Examples of possible book-related art experiences follow. Some of these activities make reference to specific books. Children should, of course, make their own book choices and adapt these types of activities, if they like, to their own reading.

Consider any of the following art projects as a possibility for interpreting and sharing a favorite book:

Make mobiles containing objects or images suggested by a book.

Paint a mural containing book scenes.

Design a book inspired bulletin board.

Prepare and tell a story on a flannelboard.

Make shadowboxes containing book scenes.

Design and construct puppets, dolls, or stuffed animals depicting book characters.

Form papier-mâché characters or objects suggested by books.

Draw book scenes or characters on cloth with permanent markers or paint. Use the fabric for such things as clothing, table runners, curtains, quilts, and room dividers.

Design book jackets for favorite books.

Use various forms of stitchery to make wall hangings with book themes.

Design bookmarkers.

Arrange a display to commemorate a favorite book.

Think of different themes for the classroom reading center. Periodically feature books related to these themes and design appropriate props. (Themes such as outer space, fantasy land, and frontier days are appropriate.)

Attempt various artistic renderings suggested by the artwork or text of specific children's books:

Examine the beautiful woodcuts in Marcia Brown's *All Butterflies* and *Once a Mouse.* Use blunt pencils to make impressions on styrofoam meat trays. Roll ink over the tray and press it to paper to make your own design.

After hearing *Jenny's Hat* by Ezra Jack Keats, design your own collage hat or make a real hat out of scrap materials.

Make your own wordless picture book.

Design your own alphabet or counting book.

Read Sylvia Plath's *The Bed Book.* Design your own fanciful bed.

Using poems from Mary O'Neill's *Hailstones and Halibut Bones* as an impetus, make a montage using many tones of a single color.

Design a mask to transform you into a character from Maurice Sendak's *Where the Wild Things Are.*

Make a web by pasting yarn or string on construction paper. Think of a word to describe Wilbur to spin into your web just as Charlotte did in *Charlotte's Web.*

You are Cinderella's fairy godmother. Draw a rendering of the dress you have created for her.

Using a cardboard base or a shoe box, make a miniature home for the family from *The Borrowers.*

The possibilities for using art to extend reading experiences are endless. Children often turn to art as a means of sharing their excitement for books with others.

If handled with care, stories, poems, and informational literature can be effectively connected to the entire curriculum: to the social and the natural sciences, to the language arts, and the fine arts. Literature has something of a symbiotic relationship with the other subjects taught in school. Literature can extend the disciplines, and the disciplines can extend literature. Literature can inspire children to create time lines and maps, to cook and to sew, to experiment with scientific and mathematical principles, to write, to draw, to act, and to make music. Likewise, the disciplines can inspire children to turn to literature. A girl who enjoys writing, and a boy who enjoys painting, may both return to literature for material to feed their craft. A child fascinated with history will seek stories of historical fiction for both pleasure and knowledge. But first children must be surrounded with literature, have time to read, and be living in an environment that creates an enthusiasm to read for both pleasure and understanding and to share the fruits of this reading with those around them.

Illustrations in Children's Books

Patricia J. Cianciolo

Almost two decades ago Bettina Hürlimann said in the introductory pages of *Picture Book World* that among the many books from all quarters of the globe that she examined, she found some illustrated with magnificent pictures and their splendor defied description.[1] One wonders what this internationally distinguished author, editor, and publisher would think about the accomplished picture books and other illustrated books that are now available or about the many serious artists who are devoting their talents to illustrating books for children. What we see in chil-

dren's books whose story is told by an integration of text and pictures represents an image of our technical progress and the taste and spirit of our time. The process of photography, the camera work in offset printing, the paper, and the effect of the professional book designer's influence on book production are only a few of the advances that have influenced the quality of children's illustrated books as we see them today.

Admittedly, one will find books filled with pictures that appear to be intended to fulfill self-indulging purposes. It is apparent that some illustrators have used the children's book as the means to satisfy their desires for creative activity, of self-expression, or as a

[1]Bettina Hürlimann. *Picture Book World.* Translated and edited by Brian W. Alderson. (Cleveland: World Publishing Co., 1969), p. 4. (First published under the title *Die Welt im Bilderbuch* by Atlantis Verlag, Zurich, 1965.)

catharsis of some peculiar preoccupation or obsession. There seem to be a number of picture books in which the art work in content and form is vacuous or seem designed to make caustic and cynical comments about life or the state of the world. There are also among the thousands of children's illustrated books published each year a gratifying number of books with pictures that are truly handsome and original, that reflect refined, sophisticated graphic accomplishments. Picture books from all over the world are addressed to readers of all ages, not just to the preschool and early childhood age group as was the case in past years. In these books there are illustrations that are understandable, evoke emotional identification and intense emotional response, that allow room for the exercise of the reader's own imagination, that provide the reader with a new, wholesome, and vital way of looking at the world and at life.

The recent edition of O. Henry's (William Sidney Porter) classic romantic tale *The Gift of the Magi,* illustrated with eleven full-color expressionistic paintings by Lisbeth Zwerger and calligraphy by Michael Neugebauer exemplifies bookmaking at its best. Each page of this illustrated version of the memorable short story about a poor young couple who each sold their most treasured possession to buy one another Christmas gifts is splendidly designed, uncluttered, delicate, and absolutely elegant. The full color pictures transmit the timelessness and universality of the story itself, although occasionally the text is deeply rooted in the early 1900s. All of the pictures are uniform in size, appear on the right-hand pages, and have a generous margin all around. The book jacket and the hand-sewn hard cover are laminated.

Another fine example of accomplished modern bookmaking is *Yeh-Shen: A Cinderella Story from China* retold by Ai Ling Louie. It is illustrated by Ed Young with impressionistic pictures created with pastels and watercolor on panels in a style typical of Chinese screen paintings. With careful examination of the illustrations, one will notice a fish on each page; sometimes it is obvious, other times it appears through the artistic techniques of negative space and skillful shading of the forms of other figures. In this variant of the tale about the beautiful girl who overcomes the wickedness of her stepmother and stepsister to become the bride of a member of royalty, the fish which she caught and raised and confided in possesses the magical spirit that helps her get to the ball, properly attired. The loss of her slipper subsequently leads her to meet the man she ultimately marries and with whom she lives happily ever after. The size and the placement of the illustrations vary considerably from page to page. The right-hand page is definitely not the only focus: full-page illustrations can be found on both the left-hand and right-hand pages, sometimes they appear over the text, are started in one panel, burst out of the panel frames or stop abruptly at the point of a panel frame and begin again at the edge of the next frame. It is a decidely modern and calculated iconoclastic design. The story told in Chinese calligraphy by Jeanyee Wong precedes the English text. The laminated book jacket and the cloth-bound hard cover both depict the fish motif.

These books are but two examples from among the many fresh and appealing picture books now available. Because of their artistic originality, graphic integrity and charm, they are likely to endure and please young readers for many years to come.

Correlation of Text and Illustration

The intention to express on paper one's thoughts and feelings determines a mental attitude of its own. When these thoughts and feelings are expressed in the text and graphic forms, careful deliberation occurs. Book designers, with the cooperative efforts of the illustrator, the art editor, the plate maker, the printer, the marketing manager, and many other specialists involved in aspects of publishing, all affect the final visual outcome of the making of an illustrated book. The layout and format of a book is an aesthetic consideration; it is also a psychological and intellectual consideration.

A well-made book does not turn out that way accidently. It involves considerable skill, time, talent, communication, and cooperation on the part of people associated with myriad aspects of publishing and printing. If the creative expression of the authors and artists of picture books or profusely illustrated books are to be communicated to the readers, the craftsmen responsible for the many facets of book production must achieve a faithfulness of reproduction of both text and illustration.

A good book is not the same as a good effort. In all the books in which the story is accompanied by illustration throughout, word and picture form an interdependent, integrated, complex work of visual art. Any evaluation of the illustrations as one of the two elements that make up a picture book would consider the extent to which the illustrations (a) relate to the text; (b) influence the interpretation of the text; (c) clarify the interpretation of the text; and (d) comment on the impact, mood, and intention of the text. The combination of the illustration and word constitute one form of art, namely a picture book. Each complements the other. Each creates conditions of dependence and interdependence. The full meaning of the illustration can only be revealed in this context. The old adage that the whole is greater than the sum of the parts has definite application here. In this multidimensional role the book illustration amounts to far more than it would when viewed as a picture, even though a single illustration, in-and-of-itself, is beautiful and appears to be as complete and comprehensive a work of art as any gallery painting could be. Each one of the fifteen abstract impressionistic paintings Leonard Everett Fisher created for the thirteen-stanza poem *A Circle of Seasons* by Myra Cohn Livingston would serve as a valuable gallery painting. When considered as an illustration designed to express the poetic elements voiced in the stanza facing it, its perspective changes. The gestalt functions and the painting exudes greater depth and

breath in mood, rhythm, and meaning. When all fifteen paintings and the thirteen-stanza poem are viewed as one phenomenon, namely a picture book, the result is a smashing sophisticated literary masterpiece. It took daring and an appreciation of the arts (literature, graphics, and painting) to publish this unique book. *A Circle of Seasons* is truly a distinguished picture book, as complete and comprehensive a work of art as any gallery painting could be.

A correlation exists between aesthetic creativeness and quality and the empathy that the illustrator has for the deeper layers of the story. Consider the full color impressionistic paintings (some almost surrealistic)

Isadora offers a sophisticated and personal interpretation of this classic fairy tale by Hoffman. The full color, impressionistic paintings (some of them almost surrealistic) literally transport the viewer into a fantasy world. Done in gouache, each illustration is suggestive of a "still picture" in a scene of a ballet performance. The artist varies the amount of detail used to form the figures in the pictures. In some pictures the shapes and features are carefully defined, in others the lack of details on the figures give an ethereal effect.

that Rachel Isadora created for her retelling of *The Nutcracker*, Ernst Theodor Amadeus Hoffman's classic ballet. The combination of polished, rich language used to tell this story about the little girl who travels with the Nutcracker Prince to the Land of Cake and Honey matches the opulence and splendor presented in each double-page picture. Isadora's effective use of shading and color creates the illusion of sitting through a theatrical spectacle, seeing the action that is described in the text being performed by the ballet dancers on a stage bedecked with a magnificent array of props and costumes for each scene. Isadora has accomplished in her picture book version of *The Nutcracker* a weaving together, an alliance between the verbal and the visual modes. This is not easily achieved, for the combination of these two modes is an involved task. Careful examination of this provocative and sophisticated picture book will reveal how competently and imaginatively she has managed to accommodate the range of possibilities and limitations to advantages.

The combination of the verbal with the visual in a picture book or illustrated book does not mean that the contents and meanings can be translated from one medium to the other. (No communication in any medium is ever exactly translatable into any other.) By its very nature and purpose an illustration must go well beyond the levels of translation. A sensitive intertwining of the skills of the writer and the artist have created in *We Be Warm Till Springtime Comes*, a picture book which expresses reality and feeling. Through Lillie Chaffin's strong, picturesque language, powerful use of metaphor and allusion, and a hint of Appalachian dialect combined with Lloyd Bloom's energetic black-and-white oil paintings, the deep love within the family, their utter poverty, and the vulnerability to weather conditions are expressed. One finds in the verbal and visual modes of this picture book artistic values that are noteworthy and when presented together evoke sincere and aesthetic responses on the part of children and adults who are exposed to them. Together, they present a

Lloyd Bloom's vigorous impressionistic paintings in black-and-white oil exude a definite sense of place and intense feelings by his effective use of shadow and light. The features and shapes of the objects inside and outside the house and the facial expressions of the characters are at times quite definite; in contrast, they are at other times only vaguely suggested.

moving and memorable story, one that is characterized by dramatic energy and originality seldom found in a picture book, or, for that matter, in some of the contemporary novels for children. The artist's use of black-and-white oils rather than a multiplicity of color, his ability to implement effectively this sophisticated and abstract art style plus the content that he included in each of his pictures offer a truly believable world in a refreshingly inventive way. It is a world that children (and adults, too!) will most certainly long remember and maybe might even respond to with a sympathetic consciousness of others' distress and be moved to want to do something that will alleviate such plights.

The decision to use only black-and-white illustrations was a wise one, for the black-and-white reinforces the atmospheric perspective of this tale. The effects of the penetrating cold on an impoverished family without a well-stocked fuel supply is more effectively made with the black-and-white than it would ever be with full-color illustrations. The black-and-white relays a more intense aura of starkness and discomfort experienced by the members of this loving family. It also allows the reader to use his or her imagination to create with greater depth the images put forth in the text and in the illustrations.

We Be Warm Till Springtime Comes is an exceptional picture book. One that is multidimensional, one that evokes sincere emotional responses on the part of the readers (children and adults), one that will be thought about and "seen" again and again long after the last page is turned and the book is returned to the shelf.

Both the verbal mode and the visual mode of expression that make up a picture book include more than can be detected in them by any one reader or viewer. They are understood on different levels of meaning and looked at from different angles and responded to with different degrees of emotional identification and involvement. One person reading *Pettranella* by Betty Waterton and illustrated by Ann Blades will consider this picture book a slight story about a family who came to Canada long ago from a country far away. That same person would consider the full-page naive-style paintings "colorful" but would not take time and effort to examine them in terms of the details they include, much less in terms of how effectively the artist uses her medium and, implements this particular art style to enrich the text.

Another person reading *Pettranella* would recognize it as depth portrayal of the motivation, mixed emotions expressed by persons leaving relatives and friends, as well as the immense hardships and humbling experiences they had to endure to get from their homeland to North America in addition to the fantastic amount of fortitude and effort they must have had to put forth to homestead on the grant of land in Manitoba, Canada. The author refers briefly to each of these aspects of a family's immigration to a new land. The full-page paintings provide innumerable factual details and considerably more depth of feeling to the author's words. The reader knows so much more from the illustrations what it was like for Pettranella's family to live in a crowded, smoke-filled city (in Eastern Europe—probably German Mennonites from Ukrania), and the turmoil the girl and her family felt when her father announced to his family that they were going to Canada to homestead—to claim some land, clear it and build their home, and farm their own land. The text and especially the illustrations emphasize some important facts and concepts about the attitudes concerning the fragile and the elderly immigrants, what it was like to travel by ship across the ocean pass, the ordeal with the immigration officials, to travel again inland across Canada to the settlement where they got the homestead papers, to find the homestead and work on it.

Color and shading may be a goal in preparing illustrations, but at times monochromatic illustrations serve the purpose of expressing the components of a story even better. When one examines the illustrated books, including, of course, picture books, that were included in the "Children's Choices,"[2] by far the majority of the books contain colorful illustrations. This is *not* to say that black-and-white illustrations or even line drawings and silhouettes and monochromatic pictures were rejected by the children, for indeed, there are a number of these among their choices, too. Colorful illustrations might well attract the children's attention to the book initially, but the "holding power," the crucial

[2]"Children's Choices" is the annual project of the International Reading Association and the Children's Book Council (IRA-CBC) Joint Committee. Since the 1974–75 school year teams of children have read new children's tradebooks (books other than textbooks) as they were published and voted for their favorites. Each year five teams, each from a different geographical area of the United States and including approximately 2,000 children on each team cast votes. Books receiving the highest number of votes subsequently are identified as "Children's Choices."

factors pertaining to the illustrations that help to hold children's attention and keep them reading the book until it is finished, apparently are the subject or topics of the illustrations and the shape of the content (the art style). The major aim of color is to serve an expressive rather than a representational or realistic color sense. Most book illustrators realize that absolute imitation of color can scarcely be called art because it expresses so little of the human mind. Therefore, relatively few contemporary book artists try to imitate the colors in nature. In fact, most book artists use tones and shades of color freely for they believe that free use of color permits them to express their own feelings and emotions toward their subjects.

In his illustrations for *Dawn,* Uri Shulevitz has blended shades of blue, green, black, yellow, and lavender to subtly portray the drama of a pastoral dawn. In this serene mood book, one sees an old man and his

Chris Van Allsburg's surrealistic illustrations are done with Conté dust and Conté pencil. Notice how competently the artist has made use of this medium. He has rendered subtle, varied tones of black, gray, and white. He uses dramatic manipulation of scale, perspective, and distance so that the objects and people in his pictures look frozen, even sculptured, giving them a feeling of permanence; yet they seem unreal or dreamlike.

From JUMANJI by Chris Van Allsburg. Copyright © 1981 by Chris Van Allsburg. Reprinted by permission of Houghton Mifflin Company.

young grandson asleep, curled up in their blankets in the quiet, moonlit night under a tree by the lake. The visual images of the night and the gradual change to early morning daylight are literally breathtaking. One can hardly imagine that such a sustained mood could have been created by using colors other than those chosen. Of particular importance is the way Shulevitz uses shape and color to introduce and develop the mood. Starting with a small glimpse of deep blue night, he slowly enlarges the focus on each page by gradually increasing the shape and the amount of color, adding more details to each picture, i.e., moonlight on the rocks, a rowboat, mountains in the distance, and the rippled lake water until the dawn bursts forth and the page is filled with resplendent colors.

The 1982 Caldecott Medal book, *Jumanji,* by Chris Van Allsburg, is illustrated in black-and-white surrealistic drawings. Each incredibly meticulous and three dimensional full-page picture was made with Conté dust and Conté pencil. Van Allsburg has set objects close to the picture plane and created a strong sense of depth and space by careful placement of objects. These techniques bring the viewer directly into each scene. As a result our imagination is so highly charged we create our own array of colors for each scene. The incredibly effective use of light and shade for composition, plus the variety of shapes and sizes of the objects included in the pictures demonstrate Van Allsburg's highly artistic sense of creative design. These striking illustrations are not at all dependent upon color. In fact, if color had been added by the artist, the reader would probably not have the wonderful flights into fantasy and would not have the opportunities to experience the satisfying imaginative thinking they have now when responding to the black-and-white pictures.

Book jackets and title page design are important in contemporary bookmaking. Most novels today contain no illustrations. More picture books have black-and-white illustrations than full color. The exhilaration which is experienced on first seeing a cover of a

Mercer Mayer's large, full-page surrealistic, muted watercolor paintings are faithful to the tone poem text in their fluid gentleness. The detailed dreamlike paintings are strongly suggestive of Salvador Dali.

Illustration from AMANDA, DREAMING by Barbara Wersba, illustrated by Mercer Mayer, Atheneum 1973, New York. Text Copyright © by Barbara Wersba. Illustrations copyright © 1973 by Mercer Mayer.

book or a title page must be held at a high point when leafing through the rest of a book. It should be as though the book artist had sought not merely to attract the eye of the potential reader by a brilliant beginning, but to set the theme and mood of the decor and content of the entire book. Any number of artists and book designers have met this challenge and accomplished it with distinction. One need only examine the book jackets and covers of some picture books to realize how effectively this was done. Consider the book jacket Mercer Mayer created for *Amanda, Dreaming*, Barbara Wersba's surrealistic reaction to the phenomenon of dreams. The full-color surrealistic painting tends to suggest the climax of the child's dream. This picture is only the beginning of the marvelous flight into a sensuous dream world that Mayer's highly sophisticated surrealistic full-color paintings inside the book

will provide. The textured, expressionistic line and watercolor wash illustration on the book jacket designed by Charles Mikolaycak reiterates the theme of the place of freedom in an enduring friendship that is stressed in the classic Japanese folk tale *Perfect Crane*, retold by Anne Laurin. Like Mercer Mayer's book jacket picture, the one that appears on the jacket Charles Mikolaycak created is not a repeat of a picture that is included in the book. It is a forecast of the style and media he uses to make the illustrations inside the book covers and it is a statement of the theme of the story. The book jacket and front cover

Charles Mikolaycak's textured line and watercolor wash expressionistic paintings are boldly conceived. That he was inspired by the Japanese master draftsman Katsushika Hokusai is apparent: His lines are clear and penetrating in form and spirit; they display a healthy vigor. The details included in the styles of clothes, hair styles, patterns embroidered or painted on the kimonos and other articles of clothing are comparable to those of Hokusai's era. Even Mikolaycak's use of the black, gray, white, and mustard in his illustrations is suggestive of some of Hokusai's famous prints.

Illustration on page 30 from PERFECT CRANE by Anne Laurin. Illustrations copyright © 1981 by Charles Mikolaycak. Reprinted by permission of Harper & Row, Publishers, Inc.

Variety in design and layout is the major characteristic of the black-and-white illustrations Rachel Isadora created for this realistic story. Vibrating jazz rhythms and beat are visually interpreted in sophisticated graphics: the silhouettes (seen above) create the semblance of the various movements made by a trumpeter in the way Isadora uses the technique called "continuous narrative" to represent the stages of split-second action. One will find in this award-winning picture book fine line contour figure drawings, cityscapes, portraits done in crosshatching, collages and montages, art deco designs, aerial views, and so much more displayed on full- and double-page spreads.

Illustration from BEN'S TRUMPET by Rachel Isadora, published by Greenwillow Books. Copyright © 1979 by Rachel Isadora Maiorano. Reprinted by permission of the author and Angus & Robertson Publishers, Sydney, Australia.

that Rachel Isadora designed for *Ben's Trumpet* are sophisticated highlights of incidents in the story. The book jacket of this 1980 Caldecott Award Honor book is done in silver and black creating a monochromatic effect. The figures on the cover are silhouettes; these figures and the lettering for the title present a shadow effect. On the front of the book jacket the silver silhouetted figure of the adult trumpeter is poised playing his real instrument and partially imposed on him (looking like his shadow image—just as the attitude of the boy actually was in this story) is a black silhouetted figure of the boy "playing" his imaginative trumpet. On the back of the book jacket is a black silhouette of city buildings reiterating what is said in-

side by way of text and illustrations that the setting for this story is in a crowded section of a big city. On the hardbound cover which is charcoal gray is pressed a contour line drawing of the jazz combo that the boy loved to listen to when they practiced and when they played for the patrons of the Zig Zag Jazz Club at night. This same picture appears inside the book against a white background depicting the musicians practicing during the day. Repeating it on the dark gray background (but on a smaller scale) suggests that they were playing at night.

The designs that appear on book jackets are varied to say the very least. Some make use of graphic devices, hand-drawn lettering, wood block prints, photographs, water color paintings, or pen drawings. Others use purely topical designs that are in keeping or in direct contrast with the inside of the book. Any of these can be used to advantage. The three discussed above hardly serve to demonstrate the marvelous variety found on the book jackets and covers of contemporary picture books. They only whet one's appetite and encourage the student of literature to be more observant and notice other accomplished and effectively designed book jackets on the children's books that are now available.

Artistic Elements of Illustrations

"There is no real distinction between 'art' and illustration."[3] Thus one is justified in this study of book illustrations to examine the artistic elements that make up an illustration and to incorporate these elements into the criteria for evaluating the artistic excellence of illustration in picture books and other illustrated books for young people.

The first point to emphasize in this discussion of the artistic elements of illustrations pertains to *the illusion* in art. It is important

[3]Uri Shulevitz. "Caldecott Acceptance Speech: *The Fool of the World and the Flying Ship,*" *Newbery and Caldecott Medal Books: 1966–1975.* Edited by Lee Kingman (Boston: The Horn Book, Inc., 1975), p. 212.

to recognize that artistic excellence is not identical with photographic accuracy. Works of art—book art or gallery art—are not mirrors of reality. They do share with mirrors the elusive magic of transformation of reality, but this transformation or representation need not be art.

What is expressed about a person or a situation in handmade visual statements—paintings, drawings, or woodblock prints—is a selective interpretation; it is an illusion rather than a miniature of the reality[4] depicted in the story.

Most modern artists have rebelled against a mere transcript of nature, against something that attempts even an approximation to photographic accuracy. Similarly, most book artists do not try to transcribe what they see in reality itself or in the reality depicted in the author's text, for the "essence of art is not imitation but expression."[5] Furthermore, the reality can be depicted only within the terms of the medium that the artist uses and only within the range of the tones which the medium will yield. The artist therefore, cannot copy a reality, but each artist can and does suggest it—each in his or her own way. Exactly *how* this is done in any particular instance is the artist's secret, a secret the artist is quite unable to verbalize. The word of power which makes this visual expression by the artist so unique and captivating and moving is "relationship."[6] That is to say the relationship of the elements that make up the grammar and the semantics of the language of art.

No two artists will interpret a reality or express their thoughts and feelings about this reality in exactly the same way. Unique qualities of each artist are recognizable by an experienced eye. It is in the artist's movement and shapes that the connoisseur will find the personal accent of an artist. The personal accent of an artist's language (grammar and usage) is not made up of the individual tricks of hand which can be isolated and described. It is a question of relationships, of the interaction of countless personal reactions, a matter of distribution and sequences which we see as a whole and are unable to name the elements in combination.[7]

This explains quite clearly why we find the refreshing diversity in the illustrations in picture books and other illustrated books. It explains why diversity exists when illustrators even of comparable talent and experience use the same media, employ the same style of art, or illustrate the same story. How fortunate we are that this human element operates. Without this diversity how dull and stifling our world would be! Without it there would be no art of any kind. There would be no literature, no picture books, no music, or dance. As it is we have available to us some very fine picture books and illustrated books created by accomplished highly talented authors and artists. Consider the illustrations in *The Hundred Penny Box*, written by Sharon Bell Mathis, and illustrated by Leo and Diane Dillon; *Panda*, written and illustrated by Susan Bonners; and *Star Boy*, written and illustrated by Paul Goble. Each of these books is illustrated with watercolor paintings. Each reflects the unique artistic talents of its illustrator. Ten full-page representational watercolor paintings adorn *The Hundred Penny Box*, a profusely illustrated short story about a boy's love for his hundred-year-old great-great aunt. This ancient relative, Aunt Dew, has a story to go with the year stamped on each of the one hundred pennies in her "old, cracked-up, wacky dacky box" and Michael loves to hear her tell these stories. It is the presence of Aunt Dew in the house, her rambling reminiscences and her obsession with the old box that provokes Michael's mother's resolve to replace the old box with a new one, and causes a conflict between the boy and his mother. The sepia pictures that accompany this carefully written story are masterfully effective. The illustrators' treatment of the subject matter and

[4]Susan Sontag. *On Photography* (New York: Farrar, Straus & Giroux, 1977), pp. 4–7.

[5]E. H. Gombrich. *Art and Illusion: A Study of the Psychology of Pictorial Representation* (Princeton, N. J.: Princeton University Press, 1969), p. 356.

[6]Gombrich, pp. 34–38.

[7]Gombrich, p. 336.

the media they make use of to create their visuals provide fare for a fascinating study. Their two-color art is rendered with watercolors applied with cotton, their arrangements and treatment of light and dark parts to get different tones of the same color (chiaroscuro) is created with water and bleach applied with a brush and the use of an air brush. They also use an air brush to create the frames for each picture.

Susan Bonners reveals an awe of and reverence for life in *Panda,* a captivating and lovely picture book in which she has detailed the life cycle of the panda. Bonners makes use of the continuous narrative technique to create the illusion of motion and time passing before the viewer's eyes. To represent the

Susan Bonners uses watercolor and gouache on paper soaked in water to create the monochromatic paintings in this nonfiction life-cycle story. The result is that a textural quality is created for everything: the bears and other furry animals look soft and fuzzy, the snow covering the trees and mountainous terrain appears soft and cold and the blue rushing water looks icy and fresh.

Excerpted from the book PANDA by Susan Bonners. Copyright © 1978 by Susan Bonners. Used by permission of DELACORTE PRESS.

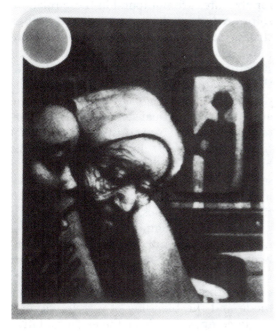

Leo and Diane Dillon's full-page representational watercolor paintings are printed in sepia. The artists applied the watercolors with cotton. They created the light areas with water and bleach applied with a brush; some areas were softened by using an air brush. They also used the air brush to create the frames around each picture. This technique of framing the illustrations emphasizes not only the dramatic function of the illustration but encourages reader response to be "reader-viewer" or "participant observer" rather than merely that of literal reading.

From THE HUNDRED PENNY BOX by Sharon Bell Mathis. Illustrated by Leo and Diane Dillon. Illustrations Copyright © 1975 by Leo and Diane Dillon. Reprinted by permission of Viking Penguin Inc.

growth of the panda cub, six different pictures of the cub, each one a little bigger and more mature looking than the next, appear on one double-page spread. To show the panda rolling playfully, pictures of the cub in three different positions appear in sequence on one full page. The continuous narrative demands to be "read" in a certain direction. Only when this direction is accepted by the viewer can the picture be perceived and understood correctly.[8] These and other antics of this endearing creature of southwestern China, the scenes of the icy mountains, the wild flowers, and the bamboo thickets are depicted with artistic excellence in blue, black, and white watercolor and gouache paintings made on wet paper.

The crispness and clarity of Paul Goble's full-color India ink and watercolor and very fine line illustrations combine with the polished straightforward text tell the story of *Star Boy,* a Blackfoot Indian legend about a

[8]For an extensive discussion of this technique and some excellent examples of children's illustrated books in which it is used see *Ways of the Illustrator* by Joseph H. Schwarcz (Chicago: American Library Association, 1982), pp. 23–33.

boy who gains the Sun's forgiveness for his mother's disobedience and is allowed to return to the Sky World. The amassing of numerous authentic details about the Blackfoot Indian ways and the flora and fauna of the Great Plains contribute significantly to the credibility of this tale: the tipi designs are divided into a bottom border which represents the earth, the top representing the sky with stars. The animals, birds, and people in between have their feet on earth and their heads under the sky—mortal yet aspiring. Each design is divinely inspired. Each of the geometric designs on the tipis serves a purpose and is symbolic, nothing is merely decorative: the gila monster is the sign of the desert, the lightning snake symbolizes the giver of water, the beaver suggests industriousness, the sun symbols refer to happiness, and the sun rays refer to constancy. Much of the mythology of the Blackfoot Indians concerns the Sky World. They believe that when a person dies his spirit walks along the Milky Way to the world above and that some of the stars are their ancestors who were changed to stars long ago. Caldecott Medalist Paul Goble researched the origin of his story and the design motif for *Star Boy.* Obviously he was meticulous when creating each of the detailed representational paintings that illustrate this authentic retelling. The expert use of the watercolor art medium and his distinctive sense of design so noticeable in each picture, and the interesting and multidimensional content expressed in each picture in *Star Boy* all add up to a distinguished picture book.

From these three examples of picture books illustrated with pictures made from watercolor we can readily see how an artist's visual statement is influenced by the interaction and relationship of the book artist's image (perception and visual memory of his or her reality), the choice of and skill in using the medium to express aspects of the story in question, as well as the artist's facility with the grammar and semantics of the language of art (shape, line, texture, color) used to express the nature of the reactions to the reality that is the subject of the painting or drawing. Furthermore, the relationship of the artist's personality and temperament, his or her selective preferences and sensitivities to aspects of his world and to the story being illustrated, as well as his or her creative and artistic talent in general will finally determine the *visual* representation and translation (the picture) of the author's *verbal* representation and translation (the text) that is the subject and focus of the story.

Styles of Art

Visual expression is intimately connected with form. One cannot charge a definite shape or color with an expressive meaning, for absolutes are not found in these relationships. Art does, however, operate with a structured style that is governed by technique and the schemata of tradition. This structure limits the parameters (establishes the constants) for each of the components that make up the language of art used by the artist to make a visual statement. To this extent the language of art exists independent of the individual artist and limits the creative liberty of the artist. Yet, a truly creative and self-confident artist will follow his or her own inclinations and talents within certain limitations of the traditions.

There are any number of ways of classifying the drawings and paintings that illustrate books (or hang on walls in the home or art gallery). No designation can be precise because of the great variations within a style or mode and the blending of a style within a single composition. Nonetheless, a tentative classification based on consistent structural elements serves as a means for a clearer perception and understanding of the possibilities of artistic expression through drawing and painting. It also serves as a general basis for the judging of quality in the examples of book illustrations which are reproductions of paintings and drawings. In the discussion that follows, several styles of art employed by book artists to illustrate children's prose and poetry literary selections are described briefly: representational art or realistic art, expressionistic art, cartoon art, naive art, folk art, impressionistic art, collage art, and surrealistic art. Some specific titles of children's books in which the illustrations are done in these art styles will be identified.

Representational Art or Realistic Art

A painting or drawing in the representational art or realistic art style can be, at the most, an interpretation of some aspect of life as depicted by an author of fiction or poetry. It is not a miniature of this subject nor is it a mirror image of a subject or a faithful recording of it. A representational illustration contains specific visual details and facts about an object or aspect of reality; these details are three dimensional and are depicted in proportions and from the perspective that suggests the way one sees it in real life. The shapes are exact and precise, yet lines are vital and free flowing to permit a vitality; they do not give the impression of being frozen in time and space. It transmits a feeling of formality and a here-and-now stance. Although a limited amount of distortion of the object or action occurs in order to express feelings and thoughts, the realist stays fairly close to the appearance of the subject. Because the artist, like any other person, selects and abstracts thought from experience, perceives it, and reacts to it, he or she will interpret it and thus create a visual expression about it so that the end result does differ from the reality to which it refers.

Full-color watercolor paintings in the realistic art style were created by Barbara Firth to illustrate *The Spider* by Margaret Lane. In this exceptionally beautiful factual book, the concise, informative text combined with twelve double-page paintings provide a wealth of intriguing facts about different species of the spider: what they look like, where they live, how they spin their webs and trap their food, who their natural enemies are,

and so much more. Each lush and meticulously detailed painting, be it a landscape or close-up view of a corner or particular kind of web, contains a recognizable species of spider in its natural habitats—under stones, on berry trees, on the leaves of flowers, on a flower petal, or underwater. Along with the intricate realness expressed in each picture there is an aura of awesomeness and vitality in the brush marks and ink lines and in the handling of the watercolor itself.

The crosshatch, line, and watercolor wash overlays that were employed by Lynne Cherry to create the illustrations in the poem *The Snail's Spell* by Joanne Ryder are in the realistic style but have an entirely different effect than those described above. These double page pictures are close-up views of the plants, animals, and insects in an everchanging garden, all of which are seen from the perspective of a garden snail crawling on the ground among them. The poet-author invites the young reader to pretend he or she is a snail. From that point, while turning the pages of the book, the child gradually gets smaller until he or she is the size of a snail and able to see things from that perspective, too. Since the artist has depicted the child as "everychild" rather than specify it as a boy or girl, the reader will perhaps more readily identify with the child, and live for a short time like a different creature. The artist shows the child in approximately the same positions as the snail, another effective technique for involving the child more completely so he or she will more quickly and willingly imitate as a tiny snail: soft with no bones, gliding up and down through the garden eating bits of lettuce, stretching its feelers, tucking them inside its head, drawing the body inside the shell and finally, sleeping. At first glance the pages look dreadfully cluttered, but in actual fact the artist has done a superb job of employing the technique of representing the spatial relation of the many things in the garden as they might appear to the snail. Using a representational or realistic art style helps to involve the reader more completely in this refreshing pretense.

Lynne Cherry's detailed realistic pictures are in full color. They are filled with a phenomenal variety of flowers, vegetables, birds, insects, and woodland animals and, of course, the snail and the child who are constantly changing their positions as they glide through the garden. Each picture, a double-page spread, is to be looked at carefully over and over for a surprising tableau of living things will be seen in the ever-changing garden.

Crosshatching, a technique which employs thousands of short, varied lines, is used to form the objects, to create texture, and to suggest perspective. Watercolor wash is then added.

Illustration from THE SNAIL'S SPELL. Copyright © 1982 by Lynne Cherry, reproduced by permission of Frederick Warne and Co., Inc.

Naive Art

The drawings created by the naive artist suggest the artist is untrained, for he or she creates forms outside the rules of "accepted" aesthetic principles. The naive artist creates with the same passion as the trained artist, but without a formal knowledge of method. Every inch of the page seems to be filled with extremely detailed, intricate patterns. Brilliant saturated colors rather than the more subtle mixture of tones available to the trained craftsman are often used by the naive artist. One will notice also a characteristic absence of perspective, which creates the illusion that the figures are anchored in space, are floating in deep still space, or are frozen in motion. The figures are either shown in full face or in a fairly strict profile; seldom, if ever, are they shown from the back.

Mattie Lou O'Kelley's vibrant paintings for the lyrical prose poem *A Winter Place* by Ruth Yaffe Radin constitute a perfect example of naive art. It has fifteen richly detailed landscape scenes of a remote mountainous area. Each scene (a full-page picture) documents the route the family took during an outing on a winter afternoon. They made their way arduously up and down the mountains, through villages, farmland and forests, stopped at a frozen lake hidden high in the hills, ice skated, and watched men ice fishing. The family is then shown on their trek back to their cozy home where they settle down for hot drinks and cookies. This is not a book to look through hastily. Indeed, the story begins with the full-page picture that faces the title page and the child's sense of discovery is challenged from that point forward. Each figure—buildings, animals, people, trees, trains, and pieces of furniture—resembles miniatures crafted and assembled by a child. The full-page pictures oftentimes reveal a carefully calculated symmetrical balance: two trees arranged equidistanced from the left and right margins of the picture; three or four rolling hills, each the same size as the next one; and a blazing campfire at each end of the frozen lake.

Full page watercolor paintings by Vera B. Williams in her realistic story *A Chair for My Mother* are done primarily in the naive art style but some of them also evidence some aspects of the expressionistic art style. Each centimeter of the colorful pictures is filled with rich color and uninhibited, crudely shaped forms. The pictures are all placed on the left-hand page and are framed with decorative borders of motifs that reflect the setting, action, or point of interest expressed in a picture. The borders carry over to the facing page that is covered with a light wash of a complementary color and contain the text of this first person narrative. *A Chair for My Mother* is an expression of the uninhibited and joyful giving of love a child has for her mother and grandmother and their mutual expression of love for her.

Folk Art

One finds frequently in the illustrations in picture book versions of folk tales artistic expressions of folk cultures produced in every part of the world. These culture groups are often found in rural or peasant communities but include many ethnic groups, national groups, or religious groups that are isolated from the principal centers of culture and thus have developed a continuous tradition. Folk art is not comparable to naive art, nor is it an artificial or unconventional form of sophisticated art. Expressed in folk art are the ideals, beliefs, needs, and tastes of an entire cultural group. These expressions of a particular and singular community are intimately related to their everyday life. The folk artist pays close attention to the form and decoration a culture group puts on their clothing, useful implements, and religious ceremonial objects. The motifs, symbols, and decorative patterns associated with the diversified aspects of a cultural community are retained in the work of a folk artist, although they are often reintroduced with minor adaptations. One of the outstanding characteristics of a drawing or painting modeled after a cultural community is the simplification of line and color, volume, and space. There is also a tendency, at least by contemporary artists whose illustrations are suggestive of folk art, toward a surface ornamental quality.

Perfected craftsmanship characterize Ed Young's Persian miniatures created for *The Girl Who Loved the Wind* by Jane Yolen. Typical of Persian drawings, and reflected in Young's collage illustration and so suggestive of Persian art, is its perfectionism. Every detail in each of Young's pictures is as perfect as is possible. The brickwork, tile, and the patterns of the carpets and fabrics of the clothing are meticulously detailed. The colors are in warm creamy tones and rich pigments. A tensity permeates the whole set of illustrations in this special picture bock; the figures are stiff and they look stiff with excitement. The figures are disposed in different planes in what is known as the "high horizon" convention, so that each can be seen separately. Ed Young's Persian miniatures are elaborate yet uncomplicated. Their strongest appeal probably is their vitality. There seems to be no overt didacticism beneath their exquisite form and color. It appears that Ed Young's chief aim—over and above that of illustrating this fairy tale about a lovely Princess whose father wished to protect her from life's harsh realities—is to give pleasure by making the most beautiful and effective illustrations he possibly can. Since it took the artist approximately seven years to illustrate this story, to suggest that one of his major motivations was to create the most beautiful illustrations he was capable of, should not appear to be too presumptuous.

Marcia Brown's splendid collage and gouache paint illustrations for *Shadow,* a poem by Blaise Cendrars, reflect the exotic atmosphere and the dramatic qualities of the text. Much of the African aura that is created in the illustrations results from the inclusion of animals and vegetation common to various parts of Africa, especially East Africa. For example, seen throughout the book are wildebeest (gnu), impala, elephant, hyena, zebra, gazelle, crocodile, and the ever-present vultures. There are the snakes, lizards, centipedes, and spiders. One also will recognize the acacia or "flame" tree and the baobab tree. Brown has captured the very essence of the red sun of the open plains, the dreadfully parched and desolate expanse of desert wastes, and contrasts this with the impenetrable tropical rain forests where the sky is obstructed by giant trees. Folk art of Africa tends to be expressed in dance, music, and wooden sculpture. Interestingly, Marcia Brown's human figures and their shadows strongly suggest dance sequences and body movement associated with the drumming music played during African tribal events. Wood carving predominates the visual arts in Africa and Brown has included in her pictures numerous wooden ritual masks and dance masks. Marcia Brown's translation of Cendrars' poem from the French and her professional and talented manipulation of the various artistic elements that make up the accomplished illustrations result in an artistic and authentic interpretation of African beliefs, folk art, and literary heritage.

Impressionistic Art

The impressionistic artist does not seem to be concerned with recording minute factual details about the subject of the drawing or painting. Since the eye, in one moment, cannot absorb detail, the momentary impression is what the impressionist puts on canvas or paper. The main concern then is the attempt to record the spontaneous, personal, and individualistic perception and response to a specific situation. This impressionistic statement is expressed through the use of "broken color," usually applying dots and slashes of color in close juxtaposition. These colors are then modified by the colors surrounding them. The colors are actually mixed on the canvas or paper by placing them next to each other rather than by scientifically mixing them. The impressionistic picture must be viewed either from a distance or through squinted eyes, for if looked at too closely, only the artist's dots and slashes or strokes will be more apparent than the generalized shape and details of the object. It is the viewer's eye that then recomposes the color.

The sense of immediacy and vivacity so typical of the impressionistic art is seen in illustrations of Beni Montresor and Stephen Gammell. The full-page illustrations in Oscar Wilde's *The Birthday of the Infanta and Other Tales* are elegant impressionistic pictures created by combining various techniques and media—pen-and-ink crosshatch drawings with watercolor wash and pastels. Each of the many oversized, full-page and double-page pictures is a superbly executed graphic art piece. Each illustration contains rich, clear jeweled-toned hues that stand in innovative counterpoint to the text. Montresor's skillful use of color and shading gives depth to each of his pictures. His illustrations create the illusion of observing a theatrical performance of the action depicted in them.

Stephen Gammell's full- and double-page grease pencil drawings are in the impressionistic art style. Innumerable pencil strokes varying in length and width give form, build patterns, and give an aura of texture and action to the figures that make up each illustration. This artist's keen sense of design effects an awareness of the dramatic strength and thundering rumble of the stampeding buffaloes. He creates a sense of distance and spaciousness by diminishing the shapes of the animals and contour of the plains.

Illustration from WHERE THE BUFFALOES BEGIN. Copyright © 1981 by Stephen Gammell, reproduced by permission of Frederick Warne and Co., Inc.

The picture book version of a Blackfoot Indian legend told by Olaf Baker, *Where the Buffaloes Begin,* is illustrated by Stephen Gammell with grease pencil drawings done in the impressionistic style and reproduced in black-and-white. Gammell has effectively expressed, through this art style and in the content and action of the pictures, the beliefs and lore of these Indian people. He has expressed in his drawings the storytelling qualities unique to this legend that tells about Little Wolf, a young boy who went off with his pony to search for the great lake where the buffaloes begin. The boy found the lake and saw the buffaloes rise out of the lake; at the same time he also saw that the Assiniboins, the deadly enemy of his tribe, were about to attack his people while they slept. With a piercing, shrill cry that excited the stampeding buffaloes even more, he caused them to bear down on the Assiniboins and trample them, thus saving his own people. The prose used by Baker to tell this Blackfoot Indian legend is elegant, at times poetic. Gammell's illustrations strongly express but do not detail specific features of the setting, or the actions and emotions of the protagonist. This is quite in keeping with an art style as abstract and spontaneous in its intent to express an instantaneous emotional or feeling response to an experience as impressionism is known to be. *Where the Buffaloes Begin* was named a 1982 Caldecott Honor Award Book.

Expressionistic Art

Expressionistic art, which leans heavily toward abstraction, is a form of impressionism. When compared to representational art or impressionism it may seem to be more undisciplined. There seems to be a concern about the essence of the subject depicted, for attention is focused more on the general structural qualities rather than on the minute outward aspects. The emphasis is on the artist's uninhibited emotional expression about his or her response to reality than the formal or traditional aspects. The figures tend to be distorted in proportion, they are lacking in detail, and somewhat out-of-line with the perspective and proportion of reality. These characteristics suggest an uninhibited communication of the artist's inner self with nature; it denounces the artist who expresses response and relationship with reality in a controlled and calculating manner. The work of an expressionistic artist suggests a free-spirited personality.

Marcia Sewall's masterfully accomplished black-and-white scratchboard drawings for Richard Kennedy's *Song of the Horse* offer an excellent example of expressionistic art. The strong, graceful free-flowing lines depicting the girl and her horse express so perfectly the exalted enthusiasm that typifies the style of the author's language. The quality of line reflects so well the changing moods in this story and the relationship between this spirited twosome. The illustrations, as

Marcia Sewall's robust scratchboard drawings printed in black and white reveal a strong sense of design. In each superbly executed expressionistic picture, be it a full- or double-page spread, there is a clear sense of focus and direction in composition. The facing pages are brought together with line and shape in the close-ups and in the panoramic views. Sewall's control of line and white space varying the amount, shape, and direction of each, creates a sense of the changing moods felt by the girl and the horse, ranging from the serene to the expectant, to the bursts of power and energy, to the rushing and ecstatic, then leading to satisfaction and self-containment.

Illustration from SONG OF THE HORSE by Richard Kennedy, illustrated by Marcia Sewall. Text copyright © 1981 by Richard Kennedy. Illustrations copyright © 1981 by Marcia Sewall, published by E. P. Dutton, Inc.

with the text, are a study in contrasts: the young rider and her horse are depicted in closeups and in panoramic views. The drawings are made up of long sweeping lines and short swishes, and undisciplined crosshatching contrasted with spaces of solid black and solid white. Every detail of this book, from the book jacket portraying the horse in a tense, expectant pose, to the title and copyright pages showing the girl and the horse gleefully galloping across the expansive land, to the carefully designed full-page and double-page spreads and then the understated and serene concluding pages. *Song of the Horse* is truly an elegant and sophisticated picture book.

Although the illustrations created by Freire Wright and Michael Foreman for Oscar Wilde's sad fairy tale *The Nightingale and the Rose* differ considerably from Marcia Sewall's, they still can be classified as expressionistic art. Wright and Foreman's use of line, shape, texture, and mood express the fanciful and cynical qualities of this story of unrequited love between a student of philosophy and the nightingale that sacrificed its life in vain. The shift from delicate, ethereal paintings designating the student's fantasies about the young woman he loves dancing at the Prince's ball, to the dark solid colors reflecting the reality of the nightingale's suffering. With its breast against the thorn of the rose tree, it sang all night and all the while pressing closer against the thorn; its life blood ebbed away from it but the pale rose on the topmost spray of the Rose-tree gradually became crimson from the Nightingale's heart's blood. The expanse of space between the student and his surroundings, showing him so very small in relation to anyone else and everything he comes in contact with emphasizes how vulnerable he is to the materialistic values of people significant to him, his lack of pride in his own self-worth, his cynicism about the unpredictability of relationships with people, escaping ultimately to the safe, thoroughly predictable, and practical world of Philosophy and Metaphysics. The use of watercolor as the medium to illustrate this memorable short story makes the pensive, melancholy mood created by the superb design and stylistic art employed by the artist even more pronounced.

Collage Art

A collage picture is made up of figures created by pasting on to paper materials of different textures, usually materials not associated with painting. Occasionally the form of the figure is completed with a linear structure drawn on top of these multitextured surfaces. Collage is a form of expressionism. Helme Heine and Eric Carle are two of the

There is no relation between color and the specific objects in reality included in Eric Carle's handsomely designed illustrations. He applies paint in swashes, sploshes, and spatters of color on large sheets of rice paper. He then makes cutouts from these into the simple shapes he wants and combines them with other shapes to create an object. Placing the cutouts on stark white, heavy paper creates the illusion of texture and dimension and even animation. The pages in this mul-

tifaceted informational book are all graduated in size as the hungry caterpillar each day of the week eats through an assortment of food metamorphosing into a cocoon and then into a stunning butterfly made only as Carle can by combining explosions of vibrant colors of paint and collage.

Illustration from THE VERY HUNGRY CATERPILLAR by Eric Carle reprinted by permission of Philomel Books.

growing number of contemporary illustrators of children's books who use this technique. Clever collage illustrations by Helme Heine introduce *King Bounce the 1st,* a monarch so dedicated to the concerns of his kingdom that when he finally goes to bed each night he cannot sleep. He solves his problem by bouncing on his bed until his worries slip away and then he sleeps peacefully. What happens when this unkingly activity is discovered and the eventual resolve of the conflict are amusingly portrayed by collages of such diverse colors and textures that they, of themselves, contribute to the humor of this spirited tale. Heine makes collage art look like a fun technique. He has made his pictures with generous shapes, does not get lost in details,

and uses quite extraordinary colors throughout. He makes his work as a collage artist look so easy, but in actual fact considerable effort and talent had to have gone into the making of these accomplished and refreshingly upbeat collage pictures.

Surprise-filled and strikingly colorful collage pictures characterize the collage illustrations that Eric Carle creates for his picture books. He makes the figures in his pictures by pasting pieces of rice paper splashed or splattered with paint on paperboard and then uses a *minimum* amount of gouache paint on top of these surfaces to complete the figure. One of his perennial favorite picture books is *The Very Hungry Caterpillar.* His designs are characterized by their simple understatement, creating the effect of a zest for life and an awesome attitude about all it has to offer. This story about a caterpillar who eats an amazing variety and quantity of foods contains Carle's typical super collages in full color plus clever die cuts that record the path that the caterpillar follows during his gluttonous escapade, consuming an amazing variety and quantity of food before he makes a cocoon around himself and goes to sleep, to wake up a few weeks later transformed into a strikingly colorful butterfly. As with Eric Carle's other picture books, *The Very Hungry Caterpillar* is multifaceted. As the caterpillar eats his way through various foods the reader learns to count and to identify the days of the week and learns about the life cycle of this creature. The end pages show colorful abstract shapes with holes in them, carrying forth the theme of the ravenous caterpillar. The book jacket and front hardboard cover show this wide-eyed and very healthy looking caterpillar which again highlights the cheerful mood of this book.

Cartoon Art

Cartoon art may be classified as a form of expressionistic art. The cartoonist employs the playful distortion of the basic structure of an object or the anatomy of an individual or animal, or juxtaposes the circumstances of a particular situation. The purpose of engaging in this particular kind of distortion or juxtaposition is to evoke humor or laughter, and sometimes mockery. The two basic qualities that the cartoon artist uses to evoke his or her particular brand of humor are incongruous and incompatible characteristics or situations. When depicting these qualities a cartoonist employs slapstick, the absurd, or exaggeration.

By far the majority of picture books addressed to the younger reader seem to be illustrated in the cartoon art style. Unfortunately, the majority of these stories and the illustrations used in them tend to be sadly lacking in literary and artistic excellence.

However, there are some picture books illustrated in this art style that reveal depth of feeling, do not insult the intelligence and the level of sophistication of their audience, and exemplify accomplished and skillful use of pen-and-ink and watercolor or crayon. Two cartoon artists especially worthy of note are James Marshall and Steven Kellogg.

James Marshall's cartoon illustrations for his own amusing book *George and Martha* are black pen-and-ink drawings with four-color overlays. His cartoon drawings are deceptively casual. The addition of the gentle, clean colors (red, yellow, and olive) to the deft ink line drawings tend to reinforce the light, open feeling of the pictures and the gentle humor which pervades these five short stories that offer a special view of friendship between two appealing hippos. Each story, the essence of humanness and simplicity, is introduced by a brief but perfectly appropriate title. Mr. Marshall hand

James Marshall's visual wit is accomplished by his particular style of caricatures and graphic techniques. His perky cartoon drawings are rather childlike. They are outlined in thin black lines and contain few details. A minimal amount of texture is added to the clean, flat surfaces and a line or two added in what appears to be a most casual manner suggests a range of emotions—surprise, annoyance, or pleasure.

lettered the title page and the titles for each of the five stories. The casualness of his letters are perfectly compatible with his drawings. The portraits of the two protagonists on the jacket with the artist's hand lettering for the title combined with the traditional typeface at the bottom of the page indicating who created the book cause one to smile even before looking inside. The full-page illustration of George and Martha on the back of the jacket offers a firm reminder that these two friends do indeed enjoy being together and the reader need only look inside the book to see the wonderful relationship they have established with one another.

Steven Kellogg achieves an overall charm in its admirable simplicity in the illustrations for his book *The Mysterious Tadpole.* His cartoon illustrations are pen-and-ink drawings with a wash overlay. They are quite detailed, so much so they literally demand close scrutiny. The page layout varies considerably as one moves through this whimsical fantasy.

Still another fine example of surrealistic illustration is Michael Foreman's *War and Peas.* This surrealistic collage and watercolor painting is striking in the bold form given to each figure, the explosion of color, the animated facial expressions and posture of the king, and the out-of-scale gargantuan, and delicious-looking cakes, pies, and fruits. This sophisticated style of art and the page composition is perfectly in keeping with this satirical fable.

One page will consist of two rectangular pictures each different in size, facing it will be a full-page drawing; another will consist of a full-page drawing and facing it will be another full-page drawing. This variety in layout surprises the reader just as the events in the story and the expressions on the faces of Alphonse the tadpole, Louis the young protagonist, his family, and friends. The picture on the front of the book jacket and the front cover foreshadows what Louis' gift from his Uncle McAllister will amount to; the picture on the back of the book jacket foreshadows what will happen with the next thing he was given by his ingenious, gift-giving relative. The story begins on the title page, moves on to copyright page, then the dedication page and onward through the rest of the book. The result is a fantastic adventure story, imaginative and original and refreshingly wholesome in its humor.

Surrealistic Art

In its literary and visual aspects, surrealism is an attempt to work out techniques and methods of tapping the store of images hidden beyond the conscious image. Its basic purpose is to find such images through a penetration of the irrational through hypnotic states, hallucination, dreams, nightmares, and pursuit of the supernatural. In order to make these kinds of images more concrete and believable the surrealist artist resorts to a sharp-focused realism. Surrealistic drawings or paintings are often highly romantic or fanciful in character; they are executed with knowing skill. The surrealist artist often resorts to ambiguities and strange overtones for as Max Ernst once said, it is in these "fortuitous meetings of distant realities" that many meanings are found. The surrealist also tends to flaunt tradition and moderation, thus combining colors, forms, and textures that are truly iconoclastic. Symbolic visual references are often used by the surrealistic artist. Two book artists who have used surrealistic art in children's book illustrations are Etienne Delessert and Patrick Couratin. Moderately surrealistic paintings by Etienne Delessert for Eugene Ionesco's *Story Number 1*, translated by Calvin K. Towle, effectively express the surrealistic wordplay story about a three-year-old who strives to get the attention of her sleepy, hung-over parent and the maid early in the morning. Delessert employs the grotesque absurdities typical of this art style masterfully: the luminous psychedelic colors, the amusing literal projections—the gargantuan tray of food, with the little girl in the middle of it and about the same size as the biscuit barrel she peers into so greedily, carried by the much smaller maid and viewed from above; the huge cat checking his watch in which a mouse rather than the traditional cuckoo pops out to announce the quarter hour, the little girl's face on every object, animal, and person she says is named Jacqueline (which is her name); the incredibly close-up views of people's eyes, each of which is reflecting images of people and things mentioned in the text; grotesque animals (a monkey with huge humanlike ears, a beetle with the head of a parrot, a boar with butterfly wings).

The perfectly square-shaped book entitled *Shhh!* written and illustrated by Patrick Couratin epitomizes the iconoclastic stance of the surrealist. The message of this picture book is stated in oversized type on the last page, "Shhh! Moral: Don't believe everything you read. Or see. Or hear."

The illustrations of these two surreal artists are boldly imaginative and are brightened by humorous details. They reflect the active mind of each artist. These texts and especially the pictures that illustrate the texts offer marvelous nonsense for children—one does not always have to get meaning from things read. These books focus our attention on the many possible meanings of each color and form—much in the way which a successful pun may make us aware of the function of

words and their meaning; they are fine examples of how a play on words can be expressed in the visual mode.

Children's Responses to Illustrations

At times children's responses to art (be it literary art, painting, or drawing) are different from adults', especially the adult critic. An adult can look at a literary selection (picture book, novel, or poem) or a painting or drawing as though it were created for everyman. But what is the image of everyman, or rather everychild, that adult critics can use when trying to assess picture books for children and how accurate will they be for all or indeed any children? The critic of an adult book or gallery painting can always test out his image of everyman on his own literary or artistic needs and skills. The adult critic of children's picture books, inevitably separated because of his own experience from the actual needs and tastes of children, must instead turn to intuition and experience as a guide. Some can do this effectively, but it is still a necessarily inexact and somewhat wayward criterion on which to base literary judgments.[9] Nonetheless, one can engage in this kind of guesswork. There is a certain amount known already about children's capacity to think and feel at certain developmental stages. This fund of information can be incorporated into other successful criteria when it comes to assessing how successfully or ambitiously a picture book will communicate with its audience.

There are problems when one attempts to study children's responses to book illustrations. The difficulties of working with children cause some researchers to make use of "models of picture analysis." These models are heavily dependent upon linguistics and semantics in their terminology and discus-

[9]Nicholas Tucker, "Can We Ever Know the Reader's Response?" *Approaches to Research in Children's Literature.* Michael Benton (editor). (Southampton, England: Faculty of Education, University of Southampton, 1980), p. 3.

sion. Those researchers who work directly with children acknowledge the pressing need to perfect the methodology for really getting at the heart of children's responses. To their dismay the kinds of inquiry into children's responses to illustrations in picture books (and to literature in general for that matter) are all too dependent on codings that pertain primarily to the isolated visual elements of the pictures (line, shape, color, and balance). All too frequently the codings are the subjective decision of the experimental designer. In reality, children's comments about their reactions to the pictures in their books are not easily pigeonholed into precise grids of categories of response.[10] Perusal of studies of children's responses to the illustrations in picture books reveals some patterns. These patterns of response along with an attempt to state the implications of these patterns of response to picture-book selection and use of picture books will be discussed briefly.

There are eight categories for the research pertaining to children's responses to illustrations in children's books: Visual Literacy, Oral Language, Reading Skills, Content, Interests and Preferences, Writing Skills, Imaginative Thinking, and Historical Studies. By far, the most common kind of research was that which reflected a preoccupation of educators with the kind of contribution (the extent to which) the illustrations contribute to the growth of understanding. (Understanding seen in limited, mechanistic terms of the schoolroom.) They view the illustration—all literature for that matter—as an agent from some cause external to the illustrations of literature itself.

Content Analysis.   The content analysis research studies focus on external aspects of the illustrations. Descriptive studies in which the illustrations were analyzed to determine the extent to which sex-role and racial stereotypes are present in picture books were very common. In some cases the descriptive studies were combined with an experimental research component to determine what effect the presence or absence of these stereotypes would have on the behavior and self-concepts of children. Typical titles of studies which focus on the *content* of the illustrations would be descriptive and experimental studies that pertain to racial concerns and sex-role stereotyping.

Visual Literacy.   Any number of studies focused on using illustrations to assess different kinds or levels of thinking when children "read" the illustrations. Most frequently these were illustrations in wordless books. For example, one researcher studied the effect of illustrations on children's interpretations of a fairy tale; thus addressing his study to aspects of imaginative thinking. Another researcher got an idea of children's inferential thinking when responding to a wordless book.

Reading Skills.   There is no paucity of studies focusing on assessing the use of illustrations in children's books to instruct children in reading, especially decoding skills. A number of studies demonstrated that illustrations in picture books (or basal readers) do not contribute significantly to the child's ability to decode. On the other hand, some researchers reported that illustrations did serve to spark or increase reading interests. Researchers reported also that when wordless books were used in reading experiences, especially in language experience approaches to the teaching of reading, there was significant growth in such reading skills as vocabulary development, comprehension, total reading scores, and critical reading.

Oral Language and Written Language. Studies in which one appraised the impact of the use of illustrations in oral and written language facility might be classified as visual literacy studies. But the emphasis on lan-

[10]Celia Berridge, "Notes Towards a Critical Method of Appraising Picture Books Produced for a Child Audience," *Further Approaches to Research in Children's Literature.* Peter Hunt (editor). (Cardiff, Wales: Department of English, University of Wales, Institute of Science and Technology, 1982), pp. 26–27.

guage facility rather than on the visual reading skills per se justified a separate category here. Numerous studies demonstrated that the use of wordless books, also non-narrated films and picture books which contained illustrations that depicted action, children and people, resulted in significant growth in oral and written language facility.

Preferences. The studies examining responses to illustrations in terms of their interests and preferences pertained to the (1) subjects (topics) depicted in the pictures; (2) the physical makeup of the illustrations (color preferences if the illustrations are in color, black-and-white pictures or full-color pictures, silhouettes or line drawings); and (3) styles of art. There are several subjective factors which influence how one can respond to the functions of illustrations. These subjective factors affect the child's process of perception and reception of the illustration. These factors include: the child's maturity at a given age, the way in which the child is prepared for the experience of seeing an illustration, their emotional state at the particular moment in question, and the number of times the child returns to the picture.

It was evident that most of the researchers expected children to become sensitive to the visual arts—paintings and illustrations—to acquire artistic understandings merely by having children examine them. Numerous studies—the most important of these by Howard Gardner—demonstrate *how* children's understandings of different art forms, concepts, and processes develop. This is to say, children's understandings about the source of art, the production of art, the medium and style of art, the formal properties of art, and criteria for evaluating art. Some of these researchers indicated *what is,* but did not go beyond this point, by default perhaps suggesting *what could be.* Only a few preference studies dealt with how one might educate and foster the development of the reader's eye to an artistic awareness. This suggests, perhaps, that they think less about the content of the illustrations and evaluate them on stylistic terms such as complexity, balance,

and composition. These studies demonstrate quite solidly that taste is educable and that graphic design (book design, in particular) offers a fine resource which might be used to educate children in artistic awareness and a high level of artistic discrimination.

Responding to Picture Books as a Work of Art: An Aesthetic Experience

The love of beauty is a natural feeling. As human beings we have an instinctive drive, or an *appetite* for the beautiful. This is not to say that we have the *aptitude* for the beautiful. Actually, one cannot fulfill this drive for the beautiful until one has had an opportunity to be exposed to it and this exposure occurs in different ways. The means used to expose children to the beautiful in literature should allow children to discern the beautiful from the mediocre or pedestrian. Literature that is read aloud to children or recommended to them for their private reading should result in a satisfying artistic or aesthetic literary experience. The ability to recognize excellent literature, to discern the beautiful from the ordinary, involves some degree of adventuring. There must be many opportunities for self-exploration and discovering. To accomplish this, children should be allowed to look leisurely at the picture books in their classroom libraries. They need large blocks of time to examine the books on the shelves in their school or public libraries. In addition to experiencing the beautiful and discovering it through exploring on their own, someone (parents, teachers, librarians, even their own peers) must help children recognize the characteristics that typify "quality" in a picture book and quality in literature in general.

Children seldom talk specifically about the separate aspects of their aesthetic literary experiences. They might well say that they were really saddened by a story; the story made them tremble with fright. They might comment that the artist's choice of colors in an illustration depicting a child caught in the crevice of a mountain slope was just right for depicting that character's anguish, or that the artist knew just when to draw a picture showing the character's action close at hand and when to show him or her from a considerable distance.

Literature is one of the fine arts and the reading of literature can be an artistic or aesthetic experience. The illustrated book, especially the picture book, is a special kind of literature. Because of its unique blending of illustrations and words, a picture book is considered a genre apart from other kinds of literature. But because it is basically a genre of literature, it can be read and responded to as an art form. As an art form a picture book has the potential of providing the reader with an aesthetic literary experience.

To some extent, an identifiable behavior occurs when one has (is having) an aesthetic literary experience. In actual fact, one cannot ever really know all of the actual details about the immediate or delayed thoughts, feelings, images, or associations a reader conjures up in response to reading a picture book. There are, however, some behavioral signs to look for that suggest the reader is indeed enjoying what is read or is having an aesthetic literary experience.

A Personal Response

I cannot verbalize exactly and completely what went on in my mind and within my whole self for that matter, while I read certain memorable picture books. Nor can I verbalize about this now, when I think about them. I do know I was moved by them, that I was profoundly affected by them. Some personal associational thoughts and feelings did accompany my responses to aspects of these books—some I can and do verbalize, others for one reason or another, I cannot or choose not to verbalize. These responses were shaped by many factors: my background of experience, my personality, the values to which I subscribe and live by, my experiences with literature and paintings, and so much more. So it is with everyone else and the ways they respond aesthetically to literature and to picture books in particular.

A description of my personal aesthetic response to one picture book, namely, *Hiroshima No Pika* by Toshi Maruki, might clarify what happens when one responds aesthetically to this kind of literature as an art form.

An Intense Internal Happening. One convincing, overt sign of an intense happening in response to reading a picture book is that the reader looks at the pictures closely while reading the story, and will oftentimes want to reread the story and reexamine the illustrations even more carefully in subsequent readings. Depending on the personality of the child, the nature of the topic of the book, and of course, the rapport the child has with the adult or peer that is close at hand, the child will talk about his or her opinions of the story and specific aspects of the illustrations, sharing his or her enthusiasm. Since intensity grows directly out of real or vicarious experience, the reader will conjure up the details for the faces, actions, atmosphere, and so on to fit his or her personal undirected response, special meaning of the story as a whole, or for separate episodes in the story. Intensity tends toward excitement and vividness of experience.

When first seeing the 1983 Batchelder award-winning picture book, *Hiroshima No Pika,* I found I was compelled to look at the full-page expressionistic paintings that illustrate this first-person account of the dropping of the atomic bomb on Hiroshima in 1945, even before reading the text. Each illustration depicting the turmoil, devastation, and human suffering during and long after the bombing occurred, resulted in a series of unforgettable and insightful images of what it would be like to experience this or any other nuclear bombing. Each time I look at the illustrations in this book, I not only see more, but I react more intensely to the author/artist's graphic and verbal portrayal of "the Flash" that occurred in Hiroshima, Japan, August 6, 1945, 8:15 in the morning.

A Tangible Object or Structure.   In the aesthetic response to literature the reader relates consciously or subconsciously to the basic structure in the work. This does not mean that the reader of the picture book needs to consciously identify the structure of the work (the type of literature it is, the balance and interaction that exists between text and pictures, or the characteristics of the art style or medium of art used by the artist to create the illustrations). It does mean that the reader must be open to the structure. Even though the reader is not yet able to analyze it, he or she does have an intuitive albeit inarticulate grasp. The details of a work will be noted and there may be an awareness (be it only a slight awareness) that these details relate to each other or affect one

The accomplished expressionistic paintings by Toshi Maruki create intensely moving and memorable comment about some of the shocking and horror-filled realitites of nuclear holocaust that occurred with the dropping of the atomic bomb on Hiroshima on August 6, 1945. Heavy, definite lines used to create the human figures in motion, the exaggerated proportions, the twisted positions of their bodies, and their facial expressions that dramatize the terror that was so pervasive. The artist made astute use of color (black, gray, dark green, blue, and red) to allude to the intense pain and suffering and death that resulted from the incredible force of the explosion, the searing heat, and the release of the radiation rays.

Illustration from HIROSHIMA NO PIKA, by Toshi Maruki, published by Lothrop, Lee & Shepard Books, New York. Copyright © 1980 by Toshi Maruki.

another. Along with perceiving and creating sensory images, the reader will realize the emotional atmosphere that is derived from them.[11]

So it was when I read *Hiroshima No Pika*. In this account of what happened when the bomb was dropped, one's attention focuses on the members of a single family, especially seven-year-old Mii. Although the numerous separate episodes involving Mii seem to predominate in my memory about this account, there are others that come readily to mind: the overall effects of the bombing on the residents of Hiroshima described by the author and Mii's family's response to these effects, too, all come together to form a story organized on a structured basis. During the course of telling her story (in words, in words combined with pictures, and in the sequence of the pictures alone) one recognizes the introduction, the exciting force, the rising action that comes to a climax of tension, and a conclusion. This story opens with a description of a normal day in Hiroshima in 1945, the people well aware of the war but not yet in the midst of it and Mii's family breakfasting together (this is the Introduction). The "Flash" occurred (the exciting force is presented). There follows a series of pictures depicting the horrifying effects of the bomb: buildings trembled, collapsed, and burst into flames, with people (including Mii and her mother) rushing about in a hysterical frenzy or lying about severely injured or dead (the climax occurs here). There then is offered a grim detailing of the aftereffects: Mii, some thirty-five years after, is still the same size and of the same mental capacity she was when she was seven years old. Her mother is still removing bits of glass that were embedded in Mii's scalp when the bomb went off and occasionally work their way to the surface. Her father and numerous others like him recovered from their wounds but died of the radiation sickness (this constitutes the falling tension). The people are described and pictured in the traditional memorial cel-

[11]Bruce E. Miller. *Teaching the Art of Literature* (Urbana: National Council of Teachers of English, 1980), pp. 49–51.

ebration that occurs each year on August 6. Mii's mother watches as Mii carries two lanterns—one in memory of her father and the other in memory of the little swallow she saw after the bombing, its wings burned; it couldn't fly but could hop about on its feet (this brings the story to its conclusion).

Multiple Meanings.   An aesthetic response to a picture book will result in a recognition of several dimensions or levels of meaning. Attentive and involved reading will most likely result in the recognition of at least some of the themes in a literary and graphic work of art. Some deep and personal associations in relation to these themes may occur at this point. Literary works can offer messages about the world. The meanings one gets from the selection may result in action in a self-referential way. It is quite possible that the reader will identify meanings that neither the author or the artist ever thought about expressing in the picture book.

One theme that is present in *Hiroshima No Pika* is expressed directly by the author's words in the dialogue. Mii's mother says as Mii participates in the memorial service, "It can't happen again, if no one drops the bomb." But the multiple meanings in a literary selection and in paintings also result from implication. A theme can be arrived at by the reader making generalizations that are gleaned from the various incidents described in the text and depicted in the paintings, from the behavior of the characters as they respond to the major conflict upon which the action is focused and developed. One is bound to realize, in this way, the horrific consequences of war, especially a nuclear war. It emphasizes the fact that children and adults—all of humanity (and even a little swallow!) are the innocent victims of war. These themes become more apparent, more profoundly significant each time one looks at Maruki's expressionistic paintings. Her use of contrasts—focusing in one picture on one or two individuals, in another picture focusing on massive groups of people. Her use of detailed and clean line drawings; also making use of swashes of color in abstract paintings

to denote the dehumanizing, if not obscene, effects of nuclear warfare. The use of cool colors and then warm colors to denote calm, violence, turmoil, despair, and acceptance. The implications of Maruki's talented use of the artistic elements that form her expressionistic paintings, as well as the content of the paintings, allow considerably more thought and feeling about the various meanings in this story to be evoked and compacted during, and most certainly, long after the reading of the book than ordinary discourse could possibly accomplish.

This variety in meanings gleaned from a picture book does not occur immediately. It requires prolonged and repeated thinking about the story and illustrations. To respond in this way one goes back to the work again and again, rereading the text and reexamining the pictures, each time reviewing separate episodes, choice illustrations, reviewing the key aspects of the story and the overall statement it appears to be making.

Contemporary Trends in Book Illustration

In the pictorial material in contemporary books for children there tends to be a healthy amount of variety, vigor, intricacy, and idiosyncrasy. These characteristics of present trends in book illustration offer wonderfully imaginative fare to the child's mind; at the same time they make greater demands on the child. This all tends to suggest the creators of books for children, the publishers, and certainly the people who buy books for children (parents, librarians, or teachers) believe the children for whom the books are intended are quite capable of interpreting and enjoying the sophisticated, multidimensional qualities inherent in the book illustrations (and the texts they express).

Variety and Individuality in Interpretation Prevail.   The proliferation of art styles in children's books, coupled with the many different artists who are employing these styles in their individual way (if not idiosyncrati-

Iwasaki uses soft watercolors with control and the composition of her impressionistic paintings is unobtrusive and spare. She seldom uses line to outline the figures, thus there are no harsh edges. When she does use line it is used cautiously to create a suggestion of shape and depth; these lines are made with soft pencil, so they blend well with the delicate and fluidal watercolor paintings.

Illustration from STAYING HOME ON A RAINY DAY, by Chihiro Iwasaki, published by McGraw-Hill Book Co. Reproduced by permission. ©1986 Shiko-Sha. All Rights Reserved. Printed in Japan.

cally), means that a child has to adjust to a different stylistic expression with almost every illustrated book he or she picks up. Experience has demonstrated that children tend to be more flexible and respond to change more easily than do adults. Perhaps the demands on the child to adapt to a variety of techniques and styles might well be taken in stride. On the other hand, there is a substantial amount of valid research to demonstrate that at first glance children tend to reject what is new or different (in artwork) but will soon accept it and enjoy it after repeated exposure to it. It is not too unusual for one child to read over a short period of time and to thoroughly appreciate the illustrations in: Chihiro Iwasaki's *Staying Home Alone on a Rainy Day,* illustrated by the author with beautifully evocative impressionistic watercolor paintings; Rachel Isadora's

Ben's Trumpet, a highly sophisticated and thoroughly modern picture book illustrated with black-and-white pen-and-ink drawings —the style used to create each picture changes from page to page; Shirley Hughes' *Alfie Gets in First* which contains full-color realistic illustrations that detail the humorous, believable story; the Grimm Brothers' imaginative folktale *The Bearskinner* illustrated by the late Felix Hoffmann with preliminary color studies and expressionistic brush drawings; Barbara Cohen's *I Am Joseph,* the retelling of the Old Testament

The expressionistic pictures created by Hoffmann are mostly preliminary studies and brush drawings. Notice how the changing thickness of his line from a thin waver to a thick spread of ink creates a feeling of different textures, energy, and vitality. Clear vibrant watercolor paint is applied in uninhibited strokes over the angular lines. The total effect of these illustrations is a wonderfully spontaneous quality seldom found in contemporary book art.

Illustration by Felix Hoffmann from *The Bearskinner* by the Brothers Grimm. A Margaret K. McElderry Book, reproduced with the permission of Atheneum Publishers. Illustrations copyright © 1977 by Sauerlander AG Aarau. Translation copyright © 1978 by Atheneum Publishers.

story from the Book of Genesis, illustrated by Charles Mikolaycak with massive realistic paintings in full color; and Eric Carle's *The Tiny Seed* in which superb collages are combined with poetic prose to portray the beauty of the changing seasons and the life cycle of a flowering plant.

One positive result of this diversity and proliferation in styles of illustration is that the child's imagination is stimulated and he or she is provided with a wealth of new experiences (vicarious experiences about aspects of life plus actual experiences with the visual art of illustrations) that are needed for productive and original imaginative or creative thinking. This diversity and proliferation can also liberate the viewer from his or her own narrowness and improve the viewer's perception of the world, if not the understanding, enjoyment, and appreciation of the visual art of paintings and drawings.

One possible result of this proliferation is that the reader will resort to superficial viewing of the illustrations. This is especially likely to happen if there are too many illustrations in the book (or even on one page), if the illustrations vary too little in content, size, and shape from page to page or if the illustrations amount to little more than a literal and superficial expression of the text. The wordless picture book *The Snowman* created by Raymond Briggs is offered to serve as an example of one kind of proliferation. When taken individually, each cartoon-style picture done with colored grease pencil and occasionally gouache is expertly executed. But as one proceeds through the wordless story, however, the task of "reading" the visuals imaginatively may become not only tiresome but quite impossible. The artist provided too many details. The proliferation of the pictures simply does not allow for imaginative and expansive thinking; it restricts the responses to literalness and superficiality at the most. Quite likely, too, the closer the child gets to the end of the story the more superficial will be his or her examination of each of the pictures.

Viewed from a positive position, the flexibility of individual expression displayed in the illustrations of especially gifted artists can be taken in stride by the children as they read their picture books. This prevalence of quality illustrations might cause children to be less tolerant of the commonplace, mediocre book art one finds in mass-market bookstores or supermarkets. It might even have a more comprehensive effect and help them to be more accepting of the diversities in our culture, and more cosmopolitan in their attitudes and relationships with people.

Picture-Book Audience Covers Wide Age Range.   No longer can we generalize about the age range of the picture-book audience. Picture books are no longer just for the preschool and early primary school-age child. Nor are they all easy-to-read books. Some of the picture books are multileveled, which is to say that younger children will read them and get several levels of meaning from the

Brodsky-McDermott's bright, full-color paintings created with gouache, watercolor, dye, and ink on watercolor paper are done in the expressionistic art style; at times they are cubistic. Her figures are massive and angular; they are varied in texture. Throughout one will notice effective placement and use of the symbols of the Hebrew alphabet to express their corresponding magical qualitites according to the Cabalists, the Jewish mystics.

illustrations and text; an older child, adolescent, or adult will read the same book and get several more levels of meaning. One of the many examples of a picture book for the older reader is *The Golem,* retold and illustrated by Beverly Brodsky McDermott. This retelling of a Jewish legend stressing that hope for a better world is tempered by the reality of human limitations, is presented in large-sized, sophisticated (at times quite abstract) expressionistic paintings. The artist uses gouache, watercolor, dye, and ink on watercolor paper. Another example of a picture book for the mature reader is *The Unique World of Mitsumasa Anno: Selected Works and Graphics.* The paintings and graphics contained in this book are only a sampling of the work this illusionist book artist has done over a period of ten years. They demonstrate the versatility of his work, his ability to dramatize the real meaning of "representational truth," and his ability to play with perspective, to use concepts to advantage, and to use the visual paradoxes and optical illusions. Instead of giving verbal explanations for his pictures, Anno quoted relevant passages from the words of famous authors. These quotes are designed to motivate the readers to return to the illustrations again and again, each time discovering something new or more profound.

Increase in Number of Wordless Books and Toy Books.   Some people refer to the wordless books as "visual literature," which is quite an appropriate descriptor for this kind of picture book. Fernando Krahn's black-and-white, cartoon-styled illustrations in *Here Comes Alex Pumpernickel!* detail the slapstick incidents that happen to a curious, well-intentioned, but catastrophe-prone boy during the course of one mighty full day.

Also, pop-up books and books with moving parts have multiplied considerably in the past two or three years. Some of this proliferation of "toy books" is due probably to the fact that the buying power of trade books has shifted, because of the cutbacks in government-subsidized funds, from school and public libraries to the general public who buy books from bookstores instead of book jobbers or directly from the publishers. The selection criteria of the general public are naturally not professionally oriented, and indeed tend to be based on what they "remember" they liked to have had when they were children. So, there is also a certain element of nostalgia that motivates their purchases. The desire to buy books "like the good old days" (whether these times were as good as the people think they were is not the issue here) is very prevalent. The important point of emphasis is that current predisposition of the book buyers toward nostalgia motivates many of them to purchase the "toy books" for their children. Some of the "toy books" are facsimiles of antique books, others are newly created books based on the old books. A unique participation book (toy book) created by Robert Crowther is exactly what the title says it is—*The Most Amazing Hide-and-Seek Counting Book.* As one pulls up or down or sideways as the arrows indicate, one finds a fascinating array of things to count: one toadstool and two spiders on it; five water lilies and six jumping frogs; eleven flowers and twelve bees; nineteen eggs and twenty turtles; thirty leaves and ninety ants, and one hundred little creatures to bring the book to a challenging conclusion. Each number is written in the form of the figure and the word; the name of each object pictured is also written. A reproduction of an antique revolving picture book by Ernest Nister entitled *Magic Windows* contains a collection of poems illustrated with line drawings and full color representational or realistic paintings that revolve when one moves the ribbon tab back and forth. All of these books are examples of accomplished paper engineering. Probably none of them would last very long in a classroom or public library but they would be fine for use in a home with only a few children using them—many times over with considerable pleasure each time.

In this expressionistic painting for the fanciful and cynical short story about unrequited love, Freire Wright and Michael Foreman use dark, solid colors to reflect the reality of the nightingale's suffering as its heart's blood crimsoned the pale rose. The artists' use of color, line, shape, and texture express a melancholy mood and emphasize how alone and vulnerable the nightingale was in its futile and wasted sacrifice.

The colors in Mattie Lou O'Kelley's vigorous naive paintings are clean and crisp. Each full-page scene detailing the family's winter outing is framed with a precise, firm, fine line. The traditional technique of framing the illustrations tends to encourage the reader to take on the spectator's role, to view life through the eyes of the book artist (and in the case of this book, through the words of the author, too). The full-page illustration is symmetrically balanced with the objects arranged equidistant from the margins of the picture. The figures are shaped awkwardly; often their anatomy appears wooden and out of proportion. Everything is given a concreteness and detail so as to effect an aura of perfection.

The artist's calculated use of space, color, and line results in iconoclastic composition. This impressionistic full-color picture was created with pastels and watercolor. The use of the panels suggests the traditional Chinese screen paintings. The fish which functions as a unifying symbol in this variant of Cinderella is subtly included as the background of this picture, as it is throughout this brilliantly conceived picture book.

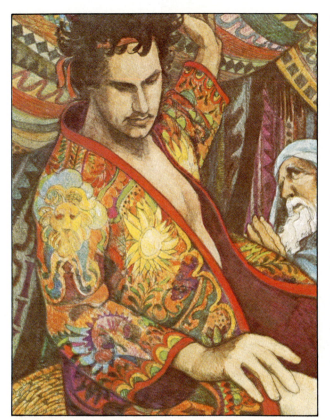

Charles Mikolaycak used colored pencil with oil glazes to create the realistic pictures in this version of the Biblical story of Joseph. The fabric designs on the draperies which make up the background in this picture and the designs on Joseph's glorious coat (the proverbial "coat of many colors") evidence the careful research of the era and culture the artist engaged in so his illustration would contain authentic details. Mikolaycak's lines display a firm and vigorous movement of pen and brush and expert draftsmanship; he uses shading effectively to create a three-dimensional quality and a realistic feeling of depth and texture.

Suekichi Akaba's full-color illustrations, done in the style of the traditional Japanese brush watercolor paintings on rice paper, are timeless in appeal. The composition and design of the picture suggest uninhibited brush movement and a flair for innovation. Except for the occasional expressionistic figures drawn with bold, firm line, the style used throughout this book is impressionistic, suggesting tenuous images.

Illustration from I AM JOSEPH by Barbara Cohen, illustrated by Charles Mikolaycak. Published by Lothrop, Lee & Shepard Books. Text copyright © 1980 by Barbara Cohen. Illustrations copyright © 1980 by Charles Mikolaycak. From SUHO AND THE WHITE HORSE—A Legend of Mongolia by Y. Otsuka. Copyright © 1967 by Fukuinkan Shoten, English translation copyright © 1969 by Fukuinkan Shoten Publishers. Reprinted with permission of The Bobbs-Merrill Company, Inc., U.S. distributor.

Even the end pages are important in Peter Spier's detailed, impressionistic ink sketches and watercolor wash graphics that were motivated by the narrative poem about the age-old story of Noah's Ark and the Great Flood. The innumerable sketches of a fascinating array of animals, plants, people, and landscapes not only embellish the story, but create the impression that Noah and his family, as well as the animals that sailed with him on the Ark, still have much work to do now that they are back on land.

The full-color naïve paintings by Ann Blades in this story about an immigrant family show a flair for design and an eye for the emotional effect of color. The full-page illustrations were done with watercolors.

Illustration reproduced from NOAH'S ARK illustrated by Peter Spier. Copyright © 1977 by Peter Spier. Reprinted by permission of Doubleday & Co., Inc. Illustration from PETTRANELLA by Betty Waterton, with illustrations by Ann Blades. Published by Vanguard Press Inc., New York. Text copyright © by Betty Waterton, 1980. Illustrations copyright © by Ann Blades, 1980.

Shirley Hughes uses ink and watercolor wash to make the detailed realistic full-color paintings for this upbeat here-and-now story. The animated expressions of the characters embellish and illuminate the dramatic and very human domestic encounter focused on in this narrative. The illustrator's use of media, space, and technique gives the reader a sense of place as well as a feel for the degree of frustration the characters are experiencing.

Crayons, ink, and paint are used by John Burningham to create the expressionistic illustrations for this refreshingly credible and unique multidimensional story. The little girl's fantasy world (in sharp contrast with her real world) is depicted as exciting and action-filled in the full-page illustrations containing skillfully drawn scenes, every inch of which is filled with splashes of bright hues and bold lines.

Illustration from ALFIE GET IN FIRST by Shirley Hughes. Copyright © 1981 by Shirley Hughes. Reprinted by permission of Lothrop, Lee & Shepard and The Bodley Head.   Illustration from TIME TO GET OUT OF THE BATH, SHIRLEY by John Burningham (Thomas Y. Crowell). Illustrated by the author. Copyright © 1978 by John Burningham. Reprinted by permission by Harper & Row, Publishers, Inc.

The gaily colored illustrations by Ed Young, collages with mixed media and printed in five colors, are in the style of the classic Persian miniatures. Incorporated in this exceptional artwork are all of the major iharacteristics traditionally associated with this ethnic art: richness of color, meticulous attention to detail, calculated proportion, and perspective.

Illustrated by Ed Young from THE GIRL WHO LOVED THE WIND by Jane Yolen. Thomas Y. Crowell, 1972. Reprinted by permission of Harper & Row, Publishers, Inc. © Ed Young 1972 from THE GIRL WHO LOVED THE WIND, published by Collins.

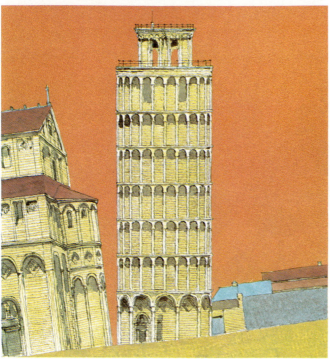

Mitsumasa Anno resorts to the optical trick (visual joke is perhaps the better descriptor) to make the well-known tower of Pisa perpendicular, causing everything surrounding it to tilt precariously. The effect challenges the visual literacy skills of the viewer; regardless of age each viewer must determine the accuracy or the truth perceived by the eye. Anno's amusing, two-dimensional visuals are made with pen and ink and watercolor wash.

Reprinted by permission of Philomel Books: illustration from THE UNIQUE WORLD OF MITSUMASA ANNO by Mitsumasa Anno. Copyright © 1977 by Mitsumasa Anno, copyright © 1980 by Philomel Books, © Kodansha Ltd.

This large, abstract impressionistic acrylic painting by Leonard Everett Fisher captures the essence of Spring: its unpredictable mood and character, the imagery and prevailing colors so artfully described in the quatrain by Myra Cohn Livingston printed opposite it. Placed off center on the page and surrounded by a generous amount of white space, the splashes of color and geometric shapes that comprise this distinctive work are highlighted. The calculated patterns made by the bold brush strokes which vary in width, length, and amount of color combined with the perfect choice of colors result in superb design and a unique, pleasing sense of balance.

Uri Shulevitz's impressionistic watercolor painting of a misty pastoral dawn creates a lingering mood of happy serenity. The spaciously proportioned page design, a silhouetted, free-formed cameo framed in white, shows off the purity of the hues and the simplicity of the shapes of the people and the landscape.

In this retelling of the myth of how the sacred knowledge of the Sun Dance was given to the Blackfoot Indians, Paul Goble created the illustrations with India ink and watercolor, achieving a flat appearance, a technique influenced by Indian hide and ledgerbook painting. There is no attempt made at perspective and shading. The decorations on the girl's dress and shoes are in the style used by these nomadic people who traveled and hunted over the northern plains of North America. The discs at the top of the picture represent the stars. Each star represents a person who was changed to a star long ago.

Marcia Brown's dynamic full-color illustration constitutes an innovative combination of collages, woodblock prints, and paintings. The content of the illustration, the colors and shapes create a strong sense of time, place, and culture. The stark black, opaque silhouetted figures of the people express the explosive energy of their dance and song. The woodblock prints of the ritual dance masks and the eerie, ever-present shifting shadow are printed in white on translucent paper and suggest ghosts and spirit images.

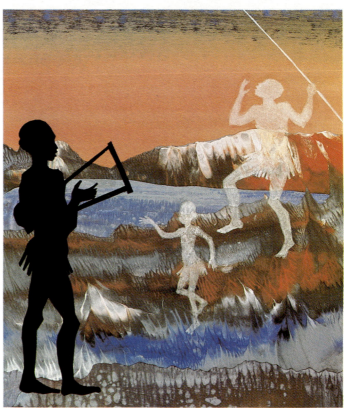

Hand-drawn frames enclose the excellent soft pencil and pen-and-ink cartoon line drawings which develop Krahn's fast-paced, slapstick, wordless picture book. Expressive caricatures of the characters are accomplished by exaggerating their features and grossly exaggerating their antics. Krahn's cartoon sketches will engage the children's imagination; they need only look over (and read) his unique brand of cartoons to benefit from his crazy sense of humor.

From HERE COMES ALEX PUMPERNICKEL! by Fernando Krahn. Copyright © 1981 by Fernando Krahn. Reprinted by permission of Little, Brown and Company in association with the Atlantic Monthly Press and the Harriet Wasserman Literary Agency as agent for the author.

Translations and International Co-Productions Prevail. The children's picture books currently being published in the United States (and in other countries around the world) reflect international influences. Examination of book holdings in school and public libraries and in bookstores around the world will reveal that children from all over the world are reading (or have available to them) many of the same literary selections. This means that gradually some facets of people's literary heritage may be the same among people from all over the world. One need only examine some issues of *Graphis* which are devoted wholly to the illustrations of children's books[12] for dramatic and convincing proof that children around the world

are reading in their native languages (and in foreign languages) many of the same picture books or different picture books illustrated by the same book artists.

The list of picture books published in translation or created by authors and artists from English-speaking countries and published in other English-speaking countries is literally endless. Only a few representative titles will be cited here. There is a German version of Eric Carle's *All About Arthur*, also *Treehorn's Treasure* written by Florence Heide and illustrated by Edward Gorey. Japanese and English versions of *Staying Home Alone on a Rainy Day* written and illustrated by Chihiro Iwasaki are available, as is *Suho and the White Horse* written by Yuzo Otsuka and illustrated by Suekichi Akaba, the Hans Christian Andersen award-winning artist.

[12]*Graphis* # 200, published in 1979; *Graphis* # 177, published in 1975, and *Graphis* # 155, published in 1971.

Gorey's pen-and-ink cartoon drawings printed in strong black ink against stark white paper emphasize the black humor and irony of Treehorn's situation. Master draftsmanship of Gorey's touch, and his skillful use of the pen to depict action and humor are readily apparent. The juxtaposition of size of things in his pictures emphasizes quite directly in graphic form what the author implied that Treehorn's flights into fantasy are larger and more worthly of his attention than is his real world.

British editions of books originally published in the United States are available, i.e., *Panda* written and illustrated by Susan Bonners, and Peter Spier's Caldecott Medal Award book *Noah's Ark* is sold in England under the title *The Great Flood.* Many picture books created by English and Australian authors are available in the United States: the picture books by Shirley Hughes, Kate Greenaway Medal winner, have been published in the United States. Some of these are *Alfie Gets in First, David and Dog* (published in England under the title *Dogger*), and *George, the Babysitter* (published in England under the title *The Helper*). Two fun-filled fantasies by John Burningham, *Time to Get Out of the Bath, Shirley* and *Time to Get Out of the Water, Shirley,* originated in England and are available to American children. The upbeat, here-and-now wordless books *Sunshine* and *Moonlight* created and illustrated by Jan Ormerod originated in Australia and are much enjoyed by American children.

Fewer Illustrations Are in Full Color.   Because of rising production costs, more books are illustrated with black-and-white pictures or are limited to two colors, occasionally three colors, but far less often does one find full- or four-color illustrations. Occasionally there will be a combination of black-and-white and colored illustrations—usually facing pages of color, the next two pages of black-and-white, alternating in this manner throughout the book.

When the books are illustrated in full color, the title often represents a sure sale. This means that the book is illustrated by an author and/or artist that is already well established in the field; the story is established as a classic or is a known folk tale; or an international co-production—a picture book that was published simultaneously in several countries at one time (usually only the text has to be translated or minor adjustments are made to accommodate idiosyncratic terminology, but the same plates might be used to print the pictures). Oftentimes, the international co-productions are books that have been cited for an award in the country where they originated. They were chosen for translation or co-production for American children because their excellence and perhaps even their potential marketing success were already demonstrated.

To some extent, the trend toward less color is a decided advantage for the child. Considerably more opportunity is given the child to create his or her own images, to embellish, extend, and enrich the artist's interpretation of the text.

Another rather happy result has occurred as a result of less color. Artists have demonstrated far more uniqueness and seem so much more creative. It seems so many more artists are reflecting the mood of the stories more decidedly and dramatically than they did before. Or it might be that editors are selecting "mood" books more freely now and the book illustrators are responding to this opportunity to express their talents through these books. Whatever, one does find many more books (especially mood books) illustrated dramatically and very effectively with black-and-white or nonchromatic illustrations. A number of these books have been discussed already—*Jumanji* by Chris Van Allsburg, *Ben's Trumpet* by Rachel Isadora, and *We Be Warm Till Springtime Comes* written by Lillie Chaffin and illustrated by Lloyd Bloom, are three among the many.

Summary

The children's literature selections cited in this essay on illustrations are those this writer thought were truly handsome graphic arts and literary accomplishments. They are offered as examples of modern bookmaking at its best. Diverse aspects of book illustration were identified and elaborated upon. That there should exist a correlation between text and illustration may seem self-evident but it is important for the book selector to be aware how and the extent to which the illustrations influence, clarify, at times even determine the reader's interpretation of the text. The book artist's role goes well beyond that of merely translating the contents and meanings of the text to the graphic art form. The verbal mode and the visual mode of expression are understood and looked at subjectively by each reader. This means each reader understands a picture book at different perspectives. Each reader responds to the picture book with different degrees of emotional identification and involvement.

The role of color and shading or the lack of it as a goal in preparing illustrations was described. The importance of the book jacket and title page in contemporary bookmaking was discussed briefly, focusing on their role in setting the theme and mood of the decor and content of the entire book.

Artistic elements of illustrations were examined and were incorporated into the criteria for evaluating and determining the degree of artistic excellence of the illustrations in children's literature selections. The reasons for the diversity one sees in artists' visual statements (diversity in their use of artistic media, expression of styles of art, even the content of their illustrations for the same stories) were identified as the result of interaction and relationship of a number of factors. Some of the factors discussed included the book artist's image (one's perception and visual memory of one's reality), the choice of and skill in using the art medium used to create the picture, and the artistic facility in aspects of the language of art (shape, line, texture, color), the artist's personality and temperament, his or her creative and artistic talent, and so on.

As a way of classifying drawings and paintings, the major styles of art were identified, defined briefly in terms of their structural elements, and specific books in which artists used these art styles were named.

The nature of children's responses to illustrations was discussed; some patterns of children's responses to illustrations revealed in related research were identified. Response to the picture book as an aesthetic experience, as "a work of art" was discussed also.

The essay concluded by identifying some contemporary trends in book illustration. The trends discussed pertained to the variety and individuality in interpretation, the wide age range of the picture-book audience, the increase in the number of wordless and toy books, the proliferation of translations and international co-productions, and the reduction in the number of full-color illustrations.

Bibliography of Children's Books Cited

ANNO, MITSUMASA. *The Unique World of Mitsumasa Anno: Selected Works and Graphics* (1968–1977); Translated from the Japanese and adapted by Samuel Crowell Morse; Foreword by Martin Gardner; Illustrated by Mitsumasa Anno; New York: Philomel Books, 1980.

BAKER, OLAF. *Where the Buffaloes Begin;* Illustrated by Stephen Gammell; New York: Frederick Warne, 1981.

BONNERS, SUSAN. *Panda;* Illustrated by Susan Bonners; New York: Delacorte Press, 1978.

BRIGGS, RAYMOND. *The Snowman;* Illustrated by Raymond Briggs; New York: Random House, 1978.

BURNINGHAM, JOHN. *Time to Get Out of the Bath, Shirley;* Illustrated by John Burningham. New York: Thomas Y. Crowell, 1978.

———. *Time to Get Out of the Water, Shirley;* Illustrated by John Burningham; New York: Thomas Y. Crowell, 1977.

CARLE, ERIC. *The Tiny Seed;* Illustrated by Eric Carle; New York: Thomas Y. Crowell, 1970.

——. *The Very Hungry Caterpillar;* Illustrated by Eric Carle; New York: Philomel Books (formerly Collins-World), 1972.

CENDRARS, BLAISE. *Shadow;* Translated from the French and illustrated by Marcia Brown; New York: Charles Scribner's Sons, 1982.

CHAFFIN, LILLIE. *We Be Warm Till Springtime Comes;* Illustrated by Lloyd Bloom; New York: Macmillan, 1980.

COHEN, BARBARA. *I Am Joseph;* Illustrated by Charles Mikolaycak; New York: Lothrop, Lee and Shepard, 1980.

COURATIN, PATRICK. *Shhh!* Illustrated by Patrick Couratin; New York: Harlin Quist, 1974.

CROWTHER, ROBERT. *The Most Amazing Hide-and-Seek Counting Book;* Illustrated by Robert Crowther; Kestrel/Viking, 1981.

FOREMAN, MICHAEL. *War and Peas.* Illustrated by Michael Foreman; New York: Thomas Y. Crowell, 1974.

GOBLE, PAUL. *Star Boy;* Illustrated by Paul Goble; Scarsdale: Bradbury Press, 1983.

GRIMM, JACOB and WILHELM. *The Bearskinner;* Retold and illustrated by Felix Hoffmann; New York: A Margaret K. McElderry Book/Atheneum, 1978.

HEIDE, FLORENCE. *Treehorn's Treasure;* Illustrated by Edward Gorey; New York: Holiday House, 1981.

HEINE, HELME. *King Bounce the 1st;* Illustrated by Helme Heine (English edition). London: Neugebauer Press, 1982. (Distributed in the U.S. by Alphabet Press. First published in Austria by Neugebauer Press, Bad Goisern under the original title *König Hupf Der 1,* 1976.)

HUGHES, SHIRLEY. *Alfie Gets in First;* Illustrated by Shirley Hughes; New York: Lothrop, Lee and Shepard, 1981.

——. *David and Dog;* Illustrated by Shirley Hughes; Englewood Cliffs, N.J.: Prentice-Hall, 1978.

——. *George, the Babysitter;* Illustrated by Shirley Hughes; Englewood Cliffs, N.J.: Prentice-Hall, 1977.

IONESCO, EUGENE. *Story Number 1;* Translated by Calvin K. Towle; Illustrated by Etienne Delessert; New York: Harlin Quist, 1968.

ISADORA, RACHEL. *Ben's Trumpet;* Illustrated by Rachel Isadora; New York: Greenwillow Books, 1979.

——. *The Nutcracker;* Illustrated by Rachel Isadora; New York: Macmillan, 1981.

IWASAKI, CHIHIRO. *Staying Home Alone on a Rainy Day;* Illustrated by Chihiro Iwasaki; New York: McGraw-Hill, 1968.

KELLOGG, STEVEN. *The Mysterious Tadpole;* Illustrated by Steven Kellogg; New York: Dial Press, 1977.

KENNEDY, RICHARD. *Song of the Horse;* Illustrated by Marcia Sewall; New York: A Unicorn Book/E. P. Dutton, 1981.

KRAHN, FERNANDO. *Here Comes Alex Pumpernickel!* Illustrated by Fernando Krahn; Boston: Atlantic/Little, Brown, 1981.

LANE, MARGARET. *The Spider;* Illustrated by Barbara Firth; New York: Dial Press, 1982.

LAURIN, ANNE. *Perfect Crane;* Illustrated by Charles Mikolaycak; New York: Harper & Row, 1981.

LIVINGSTON, MYRA COHN. *A Circle of Seasons;* Illustrated by Leonard Everett Fisher; New York: Holiday House, 1982.

LOUIS, AI LING. *Yeh-Shen: A Cinderella Story from China;* Illustrated by Ed Young; New York: Philomel, 1982.

MARSHALL, JAMES. *George and Martha;* Illustrated by James Marshall; Boston: Houghton Mifflin, 1972.

MARUKI, TOSHI. *Hiroshima No Pika;* Illustrated by Toshi Maruki; New York: Lothrop, Lee and Shepard, 1982.

MATHIS, SHARON BELL. *The Hundred Penny Box;* Illustrated by Leo and Diane Dillon; New York: Viking Press, 1975.

MCDERMOTT, BEVERLY BRODSKY. *The Golem;* Illustrated by Beverly Brodsky McDermott; New York: Lippincott, 1976.

NISTER, ERNEST. *Magic Windows;* New York: Philomel Books, 1981.

O. HENRY (WILLIAM SIDNEY PORTER). *The Gift of the Magi;* Illustrated by Lisbeth Zwerger; London: Neugebauer Press, 1982 (Distributed in the U.S. by Alphabet Press, Boston).

ORMEROD, JAN. *Moonlight;* Illustrated by Jan Ormerod; New York: Lothrop, Lee and Shepard, 1982.

——. *Sunshine;* Illustrated by Jan Ormerod; New York: Lothrop, Lee and Shepard, 1981.

OTSUKA, YUZO. *Suho and the White Horse;* Adapted from the translation by Ann Herring; Illustrated by Suekichi Akaba; New York: Viking Press, 1981. (Original title *Suho no shiroi uma.* Illustrations copyright 1967.)

RADIN, RUTH YAFFE. *A Winter Place;* Illustrated by Mattie Lou O'Kelley; Boston: Atlantic/Little, Brown, 1982.

RYDER, JOANNE. *The Snail's Spell;* Illustrated by Lynne Cherry; New York: Frederick Warne, 1982.

SHULEVITZ, URI. *Dawn;* Illustrated by Uri Shulevitz; New York: Farrar, Straus and Giroux, 1974.

SPIER, PETER. *Noah's Ark;* Illustrated by Peter Spier; New York: Doubleday, 1977.

VAN ALLSBURG, CHRIS. *Jumanji;* Illustrated by Chris Van Allsburg; Boston: Houghton Mifflin, 1981.

WATERTON, BETTY. *Pettranella;* Illustrated by Ann Blades; New York: Vanguard Press, 1980.

WERSBA, BARBARA. *Amanda, Dreaming;* Illustrated by Mercer Mayer; Atheneum, 1973.

WILDE, OSCAR. *The Birthday of the Infanta and Other Tales;* Abridged and illustrated by Beni Montresor; New York: Atheneum, 1982.

——. *The Nightingale and the Rose;* Illustrated by Freire Wright and Michael Foreman; New York: Oxford University Press, 1981.

WILLIAMS, VERA B. *A Chair for My Mother;* Illustrated by Vera B. Williams; New York: Greenwillow Books, 1982.

YOLEN, JANE. *The Girl Who Loved the Wind;* Illustrated by Ed Young; New York: Thomas Y. Crowell Company, 1972.

Bibliography

The numbers at the ends of the entries indicate the age range for the books, although adults should always remember that there are individual differences among children of the same age level and that what is appropriate, for example, for one ten-year-old may be too hard or too easy for another. Some out-of-print titles are included for the reason that they are classics and are still available in many libraries. The symbol ♪ denotes collections of folk songs with music or single songs in picture-book form. A list of publishers with their addresses appears on page 971.

The Bibliography is organized under the same categories as the anthology with the addition of several groups of adult references. The table of contents below shows the organization and should help you find your way more easily through the following pages.

Adult References

General References

ARBUTHNOT, MAY HILL, *Children's Reading in the Home*, Scott, Foresman, 1969. Especially designed to help parents guide their children's reading.

BADER, BARBARA, *American Picture Books: From Noah's Ark to the Beast Within*, Macmillan, 1976. An extensive survey of the development of the genre is notable for its informed criticism.

BLOUNT, MARGARET, *Animal Land: The Creatures of Children's Fiction*, Morrow, 1975. A thoughtful discussion and analysis of types of animal stories.

BRODERICK, DOROTHY M., *Image of the Black in Children's Fiction*, Bowker, 1973. A literary and historical analysis of the portrait of the black in children's books published between 1827 and 1967.

CHUKOVSKY, KORNEI, *From Two to Five*, tr. and ed. by Miriam Morton, Univ. of Calif. Pr., 1963. This work, by a great Russian educator, critic, and writer, was first published in Russia in 1925 and was addressed to teachers and parents. It stresses the importance of poetry, folk tales, and fantasy in the development of imagination and creativity.

DREYER, SHARON, *The Bookfinder*, American Guidance Service, 1977. Horizontally cut pages facilitate the matching of headings and annotations of books.

DUFF, ANNIS, *"Bequest of Wings": A Family's Pleasures with Books*, Viking, 1944. A charming and intimate account of one family's experience with books. The discussion of poetry and fairy tales is of special value. The author also has much to say on reading aloud and discussing books with children.

EGOFF, SHEILA, G. T. STUBBS, and L. F. ASHLEY, eds., *Only Connect: Readings on Children's Literature*, Oxford Univ. Pr., 1969. A discriminating and often provocative selection of articles by and about illustrators and authors on a broad range of topics.

FISHER, MARGERY, *Intent upon Reading*, rev. ed., Watts, 1964. A work which discusses, with perception and great insight, every kind of fiction for children. The author was for many years a reviewer of children's books for a national magazine in England and mentions no book that she has not read. Bibliographies cover mainly the period from 1930 to 1960.
Matters of Fact; Aspects of Non-Fiction for Children, T. Crowell, 1972. A critic of international standing discusses the criteria for evaluation of nonfiction, examining critically books within each subject area. Useful information about the books discussed; firm guidelines for future book selection.

FRYE, NORTHROP, *The Educated Imagination*, Ind. Univ. Pr., 1964. A book concerned with the study and teaching of literature.

GERSONI, DIANE, ed., *Sexism and Youth*, Bowker, 1974. An excellent variety of articles on social attitudes and sex roles in children's books.

HAVILAND, VIRGINIA, *Children and Literature: Views and Reviews*, Scott, Foresman, 1973. A choice collection of essays and criticism concerning trends and theories in children's literature.
Children's Literature: A Guide to Reference Sources, Library of Congress, 1966. An "annotated bibliography which describes books, articles, and pamphlets selected on the basis of their estimated usefulness to adults concerned with the creation, reading, or study of children's books" (preface).

HAZARD, PAUL, *Books, Children and Men*, tr. by Marguerite Mitchell, 4th ed., Horn Book, 1960. An eminent member of the French Academy discusses national traits in relation to children's books and gives special attention to folklore, fairy tales, nursery rhymes, and poetry.

HEARNE, BETSY, *Choosing Books for Children: A Commonsense Guide*, Delacorte, 1981. A practical, thoughtful, and authoritative book that should be especially useful to parents.

HEARNE, BETSY, and MARILYN KAYE, eds., *Celebrating Children's Books: Essays on Children's Literature in Honor of Zena Sutherland*, Lothrop, 1981. A collection of memorable essays by authors, artists, editors, and librarians of several countries.

HUCK, CHARLOTTE S., *Children's Literature in the Elementary School*, 3rd ed., Holt, 1979. A critique of books for children based on the psychology of child growth and development at different age levels.

JACOBS, LELAND B., ed., *Using Literature with Young Children*, Teachers College Pr., 1965. A collection of papers on relating literature to school experiences.

JORDAN, ALICE M., *From Rollo to Tom Sawyer and Other Papers*, decorated by Nora S. Unwin, Horn Book, 1949. A survey of American children's literature from early days through the nineteenth century.

KIEFER, MONICA, *American Children Through Their Books, 1700–1835*, Univ. of Pa. Pr., 1970. This book will be of special value to students interested in the history of American books for children. Miss Kiefer's book is carefully documented and indexed.

KIRKPATRICK, DANIEL, ed., *Twentieth-Century Children's Writers*, St. Martin's, 1978. A massive compilation of essays, informative and critical.

LUKENS, REBECCA, *A Critical Handbook of Children's Literature*, 2nd ed., Scott, Foresman, 1982. A discussion of the elements of imaginative literature for children.

LYSTAD, MARY, *From Dr. Mather to Dr. Seuss: 200 Years of American Books for Children*, G. K. Hall, 1980. An exploration of the social values that have been reflected in children's books since Colonial times.

MAC CANN, DONNARAE, and OLGA RICHARD, *The Child's First Books; A Critical Study of Pictures and Texts*, Wilson, 1973. A perceptive and authoritative discussion of the qualities that distinguish picture books.

MEEK, MARGARET, AIDAN WARLOW, and GRISELDA BARTON, eds., *The Cool Web: The Pattern of Children's Reading*, Atheneum, 1978. Myriad aspects of children's reading are covered in a selection of papers that are distinctive for their polish and perception.

MEIGS, CORNELIA, ANNE THAXTER EATON, ELIZABETH NESBITT, and RUTH HILL VIGUERS, *A Critical History of Children's Literature*, rev. ed., Macmillan, 1969. A chronological survey of children's books in English from the earliest times to the present.

MORTON, MIRIAM, ed., *A Harvest of Russian Children's Literature*, Univ. of Calif. Pr., 1967. An outstanding effort to bring to children, librarians, and teachers of the U.S. a sampling of the reading of Russian children. One hundred selections published from 1825 to the present.

PELLOWSKI, ANNE, *The World of Children's Literature*, Bowker, 1968. Brings together annotated bibliographic references of monographs, articles, and periodicals that trace the development of children's literature in 106 countries.

SMITH, LILLIAN, *The Unreluctant Years: A Critical Approach to Children's Literature*, ALA, 1953. An excellent book on all types of literature for children by a distinguished librarian.

SUTHERLAND, ZENA, DIANNE MONSON, and MAY HILL ARBUTHNOT, *Children & Books*, 6th ed., Scott, Foresman, 1981. A broad and comprehensive survey of all areas of children's books and how to use them with children.

TOWNSEND, JOHN ROWE, *Written for Children: An Outline of English Children's Literature*, rev. ed., Lippincott, 1975. "A brief, readable account of English prose fiction for children from its beginnings to the present day."

Biographical References

BARNES, WALTER, *The Children's Poets*, World, 1924. Interesting notes about the older poets of childhood.

BENÉT, LAURA, *Famous American Poets*, ill. with photos, Dodd, 1950; *Famous Poets for Young People*, Dodd, 1964. Biographical sketches of American and British poets of the nineteenth and twentieth centuries.

COMMIRE, ANNE, *Something About the Author: Facts and Pictures About Contemporary Authors and Illustrators of Books for Young People*, Gale Research, almost 30 volumes. A series of biographical listings that includes other sources of information, examples of illustrators' work, photographs, references to work in progress, and a cumulative index.

DARTON, F. J. HARVEY, *Children's Books in England; Five Centuries of Social Life*, 2nd ed., Cambridge Univ. Pr., 1958. First published in 1932, this classic in the field of children's literature is primarily a history of children's books in England, but it also contains invaluable biographical information.

DE MONTREVILLE, DORIS, and DONNA HILL, *Third Book of Junior Authors*, Wilson, 1972. A supplement to the Kunitz and the Fuller titles, this includes biographical and autobiographical sketches for each author listed, and photographs.

FULLER, MURIEL, ed., *More Junior Authors*, Wilson, 1963. Short biographical sketches of authors who have become known since the publication of *The Junior Book of Authors*, ed. by Stanley J. Kunitz and Howard Haycroft (see below).

GREEN, ROGER LANCELYN, *Tellers of Tales: Children's Books and Their Authors from 1800–1968*, rev. ed., Watts, 1965. This survey of British authors of children's books gives an excellent historical perspective.

HOFFMAN, MIRIAM, and EVA SAMUELS, eds., *Authors and Illustrators of Children's Books; Writings on Their Lives and Works*, Bowker, 1972. A compilation of articles from magazines gives more depth than many of the briefer entries in other sources, although the coverage is not as broad. Editorial notes add information.

HÜRLIMANN, BETTINA, *Three Centuries of Children's Books in Europe*, World, 1968, first published in Switzerland in 1959, tr. and ed. by Brian W. Alderson. A historical survey that includes discussion of contemporary authors and illustrators as well as those of the past.

KINGMAN, LEE, ed., *Newbery and Caldecott Medal Books: 1956–1965*, Horn Book, 1965. A biographical sketch of each author or illustrator, along with his or her acceptance paper and related material from *The Horn Book*.

KUNITZ, STANLEY J., and HOWARD HAYCROFT, *American Authors, 1600–1900*, Wilson, 1938. A biographical dictionary of American literature, complete in one volume.

The Junior Book of Authors, 2nd ed. rev., Wilson, 1951. Includes biographical or autobiographical sketches of authors of both classic and contemporary juvenile literature.

Twentieth Century Authors, Wilson, 1942. A biographical dictionary of modern literature. Gives information about writers of this century of all nations. First suppl. 1955.

MAHONY, BERTHA (Bertha Mahony Miller), LOUISE PAYSON LATIMER, and BEULAH FOLMSBEE, *Illustrators of Children's Books, 1744–1945*, Horn Book, 1947. Includes articles on illustration, biographical sketches, and bibliographies of authors and illustrators.

MILLER, BERTHA MAHONY, and ELINOR WHITNEY FIELD, eds., *Newbery Medal Books: 1922–1955*, Horn Book, 1957. In addition to a biographical note on each author, his or her acceptance paper and related material from *The Horn Book* are included.

Caldecott Medal Books: 1938–1957, Horn Book, 1957. In this volume, the biographical material is devoted to the illustrators, many of whom also were authors of the prize-winning books.

TOWNSEND, JOHN ROWE, *A Sense of Story: Essays on Contemporary Writers for Children*, Lippincott, 1971. Each of the nineteen essays on contemporary English-language writers for children is accompanied by a brief autobiographical note.

VIGUERS, RUTH HILL, MARCIA DALPHIN, and BERTHA MAHONY MILLER, *Illustrators of Children's Books, 1946–1956*, Horn Book, 1958. In the same format as the Mahony title cited above.

Book Selection Aids

Review Magazines

Appraisal: Children's Science Books, Harvard Graduate School of Education, Cambridge, Mass. Published three times each year. Around 50 books reviewed in each issue, all rated on a five-point scale by both a librarian and a science specialist.

The Bulletin of the Center for Children's Books, Graduate Library School, University of Chicago. This is a highly selective list which does not hesitate to indicate books which are *not recommended*. The reviews are careful, authoritative, and based not only on the critical analyses by librarians but on the evaluations of classroom teachers and subject specialists. Published every month except August.

Canadian Children's Literature, Canadian Children's Press/Canadian Children's Literature Association. A quarterly journal that includes articles, reviews, and bibliographies.

The Horn Book Magazine, Horn Book. Devoted wholly to children's books, with many fine articles about writers, illustrators, and special areas of literature and reading. Many children's books are selectively reviewed. Published six times a year.

In Review; Canadian Books for Children, Provincial Library Service, Ontario, Canada. Published quarterly, a journal that reviews both recommended and not recommended books. Reviews are in English for English language books, in French for French language books.

Kirkus Reviews, The Kirkus Service. Punched loose-leaf sheets are published twice a month; reviews are divided and grouped by age level.

Language Arts, Nat. Council of Teachers of English. Besides a regular column reviewing children's books, this journal has articles on children's reading and related subjects.

School Library Journal, Bowker. A journal for librarians especially, it is published monthly, September through May. Approximately fifteen hundred titles are reviewed, sometimes with dissenting opinions. There are also many articles on library services, books, and reading for children and young people.

Science Books: A Quarterly Review, Am. Assoc. for the Advancement of Science. Reviews around 100 science and mathematics books, elementary through college and beyond. Reviews are by specialists in the field.

Annual Booklists

Children's Books, Library of Congress. An annotated list of about 200 of the best books published during the year for preschool through junior high school.

Fanfare: The Horn Book Honor List, Horn Book. Books chosen by the editors of *The Horn Book Magazine* as the best books published during the preceding year. The list appears annually in the October issue of the magazine.

Growing Up with Books, Bowker. Two hundred fifty to three hundred best children's books are briefly annotated. Old and new books are included.

Notable Children's Books, ALA. Also appears in the April issue of the *ALA Bulletin.* Fifty or so titles are selected by a committee of the Children's Services Division as the best books for children published during the preceding year.

Standard Lists

ARBUTHNOT, MAY HILL, et al., *Children's Books Too Good to Miss,* Case Western Reserve Univ. Pr., rev. ed., 1971. A reliable guide to new and old books for children. It features sample illustrations from some of the more outstanding titles.

Choosing a Child's Book, Children's Book Council, 67 Irving Place, New York, N.Y. 10003. General lists and lists in specific categories. Regularly updated.

HUUS, HELEN, *Children's Books to Enrich the Social Studies,* Nat. Council for the Social Studies, 1966. A graded, annotated list arranged under general topics with many subheads. Emphasizes nonfiction and books for younger children.

SUTHERLAND, ZENA, ed., *The Best in Children's Books; The University of Chicago Guide to Children's Literature 1973–1978,* Univ. of Chicago Pr., 1980. 1400 reviews selected from some of the best books reviewed in the *Bulletin of the Center for Children's Books.* Graded and annotated, with indexes to curricular uses and developmental values, reading levels, and types of literature.

Storytelling and Reading Aloud[1]

BAKER, AUGUSTA, and ELLIN GREENE, *Storytelling: Art and Technique,* Bowker, 1977. An excellent source of information for storytellers, especially for beginners.

BROWN, JENNIFER, "Reading Aloud," *Elementary English,* April 1973, pages 635–36. An annotated bibliography follows a discussion of the values of reading aloud.

CATHON, LAURA E., and others, eds. *Stories to Tell to Children,* 8th ed., Carnegie Library of Pittsburgh, 4400 Forbes Ave., Pittsburgh, Pa. 15213, 1974. "A selected list for use by libraries, schools, clubs, and by radio and television storytellers, with a special listing of stories for holiday programs."

GREENE, ELLIN, comp., *Stories; A List of Stories to Tell and to Read Aloud,* 6th ed., New York Public Library, 1972. An excellent aid for the beginning storyteller. Contains an annotated list of stories and their sources, a list of poetry and books for reading aloud, a bibliography for the storyteller, a subject index, and a name index.

HARDENDORFF, JEANNE B., ed., *Stories to Tell: A List of Stories with Annotations,* 5th ed., Enoch Pratt Free Library, 400 Cathedral St., Baltimore, Md. 21201, 1965. In addition to a well-annotated list of stories for telling, this book contains a list of picture books for TV storytelling, suggested programs for story hours, a list of stories by subject, and a list of poetry collections.

MOORE, VARDINE, *The Pre-School Story Hour,* 2nd ed., Scarecrow, 1972. Gives the basic necessities for planning and conducting story hours in all kinds of libraries. Especially useful for its listings of finger games, recordings, and picture books. A practical and authoritative work, unfortunately marred by an abundance of typographical errors.

PELLOWSKI, ANNE, *The World of Storytelling,* Bowker, 1977. A survey of techniques and traditions of storytellers in countries all over the world.

SAWYER, RUTH, *The Way of the Storyteller,* rev. ed., Viking, 1962. A great storyteller discusses the art and technique of successful storytelling and shares eleven of her best stories.

---

[1] For additional discussion of storytelling and reading aloud, see the Sutherland, Duff, and Huck titles in "General References" (p. 880).

SHEDLOCK, MARIE, *The Art of the Story-Teller*, 3rd ed., bibl. by Eulalie Steinmetz, Dover, 1951. A master British storyteller discusses the techniques of storytelling and presents eighteen stories as she would tell them.

WILLCOX, ISOBEL, *Reading Aloud with Elementary School Children*, Teachers Practical Press, Atherton, 1963. Designed especially for the classroom teacher, this brief booklet discusses various aspects of reading aloud. In addition, it contains useful suggestions for scheduling and recommends appropriate post-reading activities.

Sources of Audiovisual Materials

School personnel, librarians, and parents who wish to know what literature has been presented on recordings, films, or filmstrips often find it difficult to ascertain just what is available. Further, it is difficult to obtain information about its quality or the value it may have for the particular situation in which they propose to use it. Recently more periodicals have begun reviewing current productions, and *Previews*, published by R. R. Bowker from September through May, reviews nonprint software and hardware. Four basic types of listings which give information about media are available: producers' catalogs, indexes, bibliographies, and periodical reviews.

Producers' catalogs are usually free upon request and are easily kept up-to-date since the old catalog can be discarded when the new one arrives. As a source of information as to what is available they are moderately helpful. They generally describe the item quite accurately as to content, length of time, color, and other such details. However, no producer can be expected to give a dispassionate evaluative report on the product he is in business to sell. For the individual interested in keeping abreast of the total range of material, even in the field of literature, such catalogs soon become very cumbersome to search through. Catalogs from agencies that distribute materials from other sources give a broader range. Two useful ones are *Social Studies School Service*, distributed by the firm of the same name, and Baker & Taylor's *Guide to the Selection of Books and Media for the Elementary School Library*; both of these are revised annually. The *Media Review Digest* (formerly *Multi-Media Reviews Index*) is an annual volume published by the Pierian Press that culls and gives ratings to reviews from many periodicals.

Indexes are easier to use than producers' catalogs when one needs to locate and compare what is available on a certain topic or when one needs to locate all the forms in which a folk tale or work of literature has been presented. The NICEM *Indexes* published by the R. R. Bowker Company are designed to serve the media field in much the same manner in which *Books in Print* has served the book trade for many years. (NICEM is the acronym for National Information Center for Educational Media located at the University of Southern California.) The *Index to 16 mm Educational Films* (2nd ed.) lists more than 30,000 films; the *Index to 8 mm Educational Motion Cartridges* lists approximately 9000 films; and the *Index to 35 mm Educational Filmstrips* lists about 25,000 items. The annotations are descriptive, not evaluative, and the inclusion of an item in the index should not be considered an indication of quality or worth.

Another index which covers motion pictures and filmstrips since 1953 is the *Library of Congress Catalog: Motion Pictures and Filmstrips*. It is issued quarterly with quinquennial cumulations. Each volume is arranged alphabetically by title with a detailed subject index. Entries include a brief descriptive annotation. The *Library of Congress Catalog: Music and Phonorecords* has also been issued since 1953 and is similar in format to the motion picture and filmstrip catalog.

Although parents and teachers may find relatively little need to consult the indexes described above they should be aware of them and of their usefulness in locating materials.

The bibliographies and catalogs described below are of greater value to those in search of material since they provide both description and evaluation of the items included. Indeed the fact of their inclusion is for most of the listings an evaluation since the compilers aim to include only worthwhile and high quality productions.

One of the best bibliographies of recordings is *An Annotated List of Recordings in the Language Arts*, compiled and edited by Morris Schreiber, published by the National Council of Teachers of English, nineteen hundred and sixty-four. This guide is divided into sections for elementary, secondary, and higher education. The 125 entries for elementary schools include poetry, rhymes, folk songs, literary fairy tales, folk tales, musical plays, and a few recordings for use with social studies.

The Elementary School Library Collection; A Guide to Books and Other Media: Phases 1-2-3 is published by the Brodart Company and is revised biennially. Each revision has included more entries for the various media. It is reassuring to note that media based on books are not included unless the book itself is recommended.

Films for Children, published by the Educational Film Library Association is a list of 272 16 mm entertainment films which includes among its thirteen categories those of: fables, legends, fairy tales, and story films.

Films for Children: A Selected List, prepared and published by the New York Library Association, lists 70 16 mm entertainment films which represent a wide range of subjects. The annotations also suggest books and recordings which may be used with a film to make a complete program.

Folk Music: A Catalog of Folk Songs, Ballads, Dances, Instrumental Pieces and Folk Tales of the United States and Latin America on Phonograph Records is a list of the choicest recordings in the Archive of Folk Song of the Library of Congress. The catalog is arranged by subject with variuous indexes. All recordings listed are for sale by the Library of Congress.

Recordings for Children: A Selected List, regularly revised and published by the New York Library Association, lists about 500 of the best recordings for home and recreational use. It includes among its many categories: spoken records of poetry, folk tales, fairy tales, as well as music.

Spoken Records, 3rd ed. by Helen Roach, Scarecrow Press, 1970, includes recordings of children's literature among its 500 entries. Inclusion on this list is based upon literary or historical merit, interest and entertainment values, and excellence of production.

Some periodicals which formerly reviewed only printed materials have broadened their coverage to include nonprint productions. *Booklist,* which is published twice monthly, except August, by the American Library Association, has included a quarterly review of films suitable for public library use for several years. In September 1969, it began coverage of 35 mm filmstrips and 8 mm motion film loops and in September 1970 began reviews of 16 mm films in each issue and also added nonmusical recordings (discs, tapes, and tape cassettes). The reviews include media in all fields: science, social science, literature, and the arts.

There are several periodicals devoted solely to audiovisual education and media which review new material. *Landers Film Review* covers from 50 to 60 current productions each month. The *Film News,* published bimonthly, has a regular "New Films" department which gives brief descriptive annotations of recent productions. It also provides coverage of filmstrips and recordings. The *Educational Screen and AV Guide,* published monthly, includes regular columns on motion pictures, recordings, and filmstrips. Among the periodicals that are devoted to the field of audiovisual materials are *Educational Technology,* the *Audio Visual Language Journal,* and *Audiovisual Instruction,* which occasionally publishes supplements to the *Media Review Digest* mentioned above.

In addition to the publications listed above there are many which give extensive coverage to a limited field. An example of such coverage is: *An Audio Visual Guide to Shakespeare,* or, *African Film Bibliography.* Readers who wish to learn more about the specialized lists available in the audiovisual field are advised to consult *Guides to Newer Educational Media,* 4th ed. by Margaret Rufsuold and Carolyn Guss.

Poetry

Mother Goose and Nursery Rhymes

AMERICAN MOTHER GOOSE, THE, Ray Wood, ed., with a foreword by John A. Lomax, ill. by Ed Hargis, Lippincott, 1938.

APPLEY DAPPLY'S NURSERY RHYMES, Beatrix Potter, Warne, 1917.

BABY'S LAP BOOK, THE, Kay Chorao, comp., ill. by the author, Dutton, 1977.

BEARS, BEES AND BIRCH TREES, RUSSIAN RIDDLES AND RHYMES, Norma B. Green, adapt. and trans., Doubleday, 1973.

BOOK OF SCOTTISH NURSERY RHYMES, A, Norah and William Montgomerie, comps., ill. by T. Ritchie and N. Montgomery, Oxford, 1965.

BRIAN WILDSMITH'S MOTHER GOOSE: A COLLECTION OF NURSERY RHYMES, Watts, 1964.

BURNIE'S HILL, A TRADITIONAL RHYME, ill. by Erik Blegvad (Northern England and Scotland), Atheneum, 1977.

CAKES & CUSTARD, CHILDREN'S RHYMES, Brian Alderson, ed., ill. by Helen Oxenbury, Morrow, 1975.

CAT CAME FIDDLING, AND OTHER RHYMES OF CHILDHOOD, A, adapted and made into songs by Paul Kapp, ill. by Irene Haas, introduction by Burl Ives, Harcourt, 1956.

CECILY PARSLEY'S NURSERY RHYMES, Beatrix Potter, Warne, n.d.

CHINESE MOTHER GOOSE, Robert Wyndham, ed., ill. by Ed Young, Collins, 1968.

COURTSHIP, MERRY MARRIAGE AND FEAST OF COCK ROBIN AND JENNY WREN TO WHICH IS ADDED THE DOLEFUL DEATH OF COCK ROBIN, THE, ill. by Barbara Cooney, Scribner's, 1965.

FUN IN AMERICAN FOLK RHYMES, Ray Wood ed., with drawings by Ed Hargis and an introduction by Carl Carmer, Lippincott, 1952.

GRANFA' GRIG HAD A PIG AND OTHER RHYMES WITHOUT REASON FROM MOTHER GOOSE, compiled and ill. by Wallace Tripp, Little, 1976.

GRAY GOOSE AND GANDER AND OTHER MOTHER GOOSE RHYMES, ill. by Anne Rockwell, Crowell, 1980.

GREAT BIG UGLY MAN CAME UP AND TIED HIS HORSE TO ME, A BOOK OF NONSENSE VERSE, A, Wallace Tripp, comp., ill. by the author, Little, 1973.

HECTOR PROTECTOR AND AS I WENT OVER THE WATER, TWO NURSERY RHYMES, ill. by Maurice Sendak, Harper, 1965.

IT'S RAINING, SAID JOHN TWAINING, DANISH NURSERY RHYMES, trans. and ill. by N. M. Bodecker, Atheneum, 1973.

JAMES MARSHALL'S MOTHER GOOSE, Farrar, 1979.

KELLYBURN BRAES, Sorche Nic Leodhas, ill. by Evaline Ness (Scotland), Holt, 1968.

LAVENDER'S BLUE, A BOOK OF NURSERY RHYMES, Kathleen Lines, comp., ill. by Harold Jones, Watts, 1954.

LONDON BRIDGE IS FALLING DOWN, ill. by Peter Spier, Doubleday, 1967.

MARGUERITE DE ANGELI'S BOOK OF NURSERY AND MOTHER GOOSE RHYMES, Doubleday, 1954.

MITTENS FOR KITTENS AND OTHER RHYMES ABOUT CATS, Lenore Blegvad, comp., ill. by Erik Blegvad, Atheneum, 1974.

MOON-UNCLE, MOON-UNCLE, RHYMES FROM INDIA, sel. and trans. by Sylvia Cassedy and Parvathi Thampi, ill. by Susanne Suba, Doubleday, 1973.

MOTHER GOOSE ABROAD, NURSERY RHYMES, Nicholas Tucker, comp., ill. by Trevor Stubley (France, Spain, Germany, Belgium, and Holland), Crowell, 1975.

MOTHER GOOSE AND NURSERY RHYMES, wood engravings by Philip Reed, Atheneum, 1966.

MOTHER GOOSE BOOK, THE, ill. by Alice and Martin Provenson, Random House, 1976.

MOTHER GOOSE ON THE RIO GRANDE, Frances Alexander, ill. by Charlotte Baker (Spanish/English), Skokie, Illinois: National Textbook Co., 1976.

MOTHER GOOSE TREASURY, ill. by Raymond Briggs, Coward, 1966.

OLD MOTHER HUBBARD AND HER DOG, ill. by Paul Galdone, McGraw-Hill, 1960.

OXFORD NURSERY RHYME BOOK, THE, Iona and Peter Opie, ill. by Joan Hassall, Oxford, 1955.

OVER IN THE MEADOW, John Langstaff, ill. by Feodor Rojanovsky, Harcourt, 1957.

PRANCING PONY, NURSERY RHYMES FROM JAPAN, THE, adapted into English verse for children by Charlotte B. DeForest with "Kusa-e," ill. by Keiko Hida, Walker, 1968.

R. CALDECOTT'S COLLECTION OF PICTURES & SONGS, ill. by Randolph Caldecott, London, Warne, n.d.

R. CALDECOTT'S SECOND COLLECTION OF PICTURES & SONGS, ill. by Randolph Caldecott, London, Warne, n.d.

REAL MOTHER GOOSE, THE, ill. by Blanche Fisher Wright, Rand McNally, 1965.

RING O' ROSES, A NURSERY RHYME PICTURE BOOK, ill. by L. Leslie Brooke, Warne, 1923.

THREE JOVIAL HUNTSMEN, adapted and ill. by Susan Jeffers, Bradbury Press, 1973.

WHAT DO YOU FEED YOUR DONKEY ON? RHYMES FROM A BELFAST CHILDHOOD, Collette O'Hare, ill. by Jenny Rodwell (Ireland), Collins, 1978.

Books of Interest to Adults

AUSLANDER, JOSEPH, and FRANK ERNEST HILL, comps., *The Winged Horse Anthology,* Doubleday, 1929.
The Winged Horse, the Story of the Poets and Their Poetry, with decorations by Paul Honoré and a bibliography by Theresa Elmendorf, Doubleday, 1927.

BARING-GOULD, WILLIAM S., and CECIL BARING-GOULD, *The Annotated Mother Goose, Nursery Rhymes Old and New, Arranged and Explained,* ill. by Walter Crane, Randolph Caldecott, Kate Greenaway, Arthur Rackham, Maxfield Parrish, and early historical woodcuts; with chapter decorations by E.M. Simon, Bramhall House, 1962.

BEHN, HARRY, *Chrysalis, Concerning Children and Poetry,* Harcourt, 1968.

BREWTON, JOHN E., and SARA W. BREWTON, comps., *Index to Children's Poetry,* Wilson, 1942.
Index to Children's Poetry; First Supplement, Wilson, 1953.
Index to Children's Poetry; Second Supplement, Wilson, 1965.

BREWTON, JOHN E., and G. MEREDITH BLACKBURN III, comps., *Index to Poetry for Children and Young People, 1964–1969,* Wilson, 1972.

BREWTON, JOHN E., G. MEREDITH BLACKBURN III, and LORRAINE A. BLACKBURN, *Index to Poetry for Children and Young People, 1970–1975,* Wilson, 1978.

BROOKS, CLEANTH, and ROBERT PENN WARREN, *Understanding Poetry,* 3d ed., Holt, 1960.

CAMMAERTS, EMILE, *The Poetry of Nonsense,* Dutton, 1926.

CHUKOVSKY, KORNEI, *From Two to Five,* tr. and ed. by Miriam Morton, Foreword by Frances Clarke Sayers, Univ. of California Press, 1963.

CIARDI, JOHN, and MILLER WILLIAMS, *How Does a Poem Mean?* 2d ed., Houghton, 1975.

DEUTSCH, BABETTE, *Poetry Handbook; a Dictionary of Terms,* Funk & Wagnalls, 1962.

EMRICH, DUNCAN, comp., *American Folk Poetry, an Anthology.* Little, 1974.

HAVILAND, VIRGINIA, and WILLIAM JAY SMITH, comps., *Children and Poetry, a Selective, Annotated Bibliography,* 2d ed. rev., Library of Congress, 1979.

HENDERSON, HAROLD G. trans. and ed., *An Introduction to Haiku; an Anthology of Poems and Poets from Basho to Shiki,* Doubleday, 1958.

HOUSMAN, A.E., *The Name and Nature of Poetry,* Macmillan, 1956.

HUGHES, TED, *Poetry Is,* Doubleday, 1970.

KENNEDY, X. J., *An Introduction to Poetry,* 4th ed., Little, 1978.

MAC LEISH, ARCHIBALD, *Poetry and Experience,* Houghton, 1961.

NIMS, JOHN FREDERICK, *Western Wind: An Introduction to Poetry,* Random House, 1974.

OPIE, IONA, and PETER OPIE, eds., *The Oxford Book of Children's Verse,* Oxford, 1973.
The Oxford Dictionary of Nursery Rhymes, Oxford, 1951.

SEWELL, ELIZABETH, *The Field of Nonsense,* Chatto & Windus, 1952.

SHAW, JOHN MACKEY, notes and index by, *Childhood in Poetry, a Catalogue with Biographical Critical Annotations of the Books of English and American Poets, Comprising the Shaw Childhood in Poetry Collection in the Library of the Florida State University with Lists of Poems that Relate to Childhood,* Gale, 1967, 5 vols.

Subject Index to Poetry for Children and Young People by Violet Sell, et al., American Library Association, 1957.

Subject Index to Poetry for Children and Young People, 1957–1975, comp. by Dorothy B. Frizzell Smith and Eva L. Andrews, American Library Association, 1977.

Individual Poets

ADOFF, ARNOLD, *I Am the Running Girl,* pictures by Ronald Himler, Harper, 1979. Adoff's patterned verse is appropriate to the energy he feels existing in the child. Here, as in other books, he seeks to convey the joys of family and individual. Others include:
Black is Brown is Tan, pictures by Emily Arnold McCully, Harper, 1973.
Eats, ill. by Susan Russo, Lothrop, 1979.
Make a Circle Keep Us In, ill. by Ronald Himler, Delacorte, 1975.
Tornado! Poems, ill. by Ronald Himler, Delacorte, 1977.
Where Wild Willie, ill. by Emily Arnold McCully, Harper, 1978.

AIKEN, CONRAD, *Cats and Bats and Things with Wings, Poems,* drawings by Milton Glaser, Atheneum, 1965. A collection of happy verses about animals.

AIKEN, JOAN, *The Skin Spinners, Poems,* drawings by Ken Rinciari, Viking, 1976. Complex thoughts and words abound to make the reader stretch both mind and imagination in a brilliant array of haunting and humorous poetry.

ALDIS, DOROTHY, *All Together: A Child's Treasury of Verse,* ill. by Helen D. Jameson, Marjorie Flack, and Margaret Freeman, Putnam, 1952. Verses for young children about their discoveries, joys, and surprises in the pleasant environment of early and mid-twentieth century America.

BEHN, HARRY, *All Kinds of Time,* ill. by the author, Harcourt, 1950. One of the best poets writing for children, Behn's emphasis is on the world of nature and the relationship of the child to his environment. Others include:
The Golden Hive, ill. by the author, Harcourt, 1966.
The Little Hill, ill. by the author, Harcourt, 1949.
Windy Morning, ill. by the author, Harcourt, 1953.
The Wizard in the Well: Poems and Pictures by Harry Behn. Harcourt, 1956.

BELLOC, HILAIRE, *The Bad Child's Book of Beasts,* pictures by B.T.B., Knopf, 1965. Frances Clarke Sayer's introduction and Basil T. Blackwood's illustrations enliven Belloc's hilarious bestiary which was originally published in 1896. Others include:

Cautionary Verses, illus. album edition with the original pictures by B.T.B. and Nicholas Bently, Knopf, 1951.

More Beasts for Worse Children, pictures by B.T.B., Knopf, 1966.

BELTING, NATALIA, *Calendar Moon,* ill. by Bernarda Bryson, Holt, 1964. Free verse renderings of legends and traditions about the moon from many cultures and traditions.

The Sun Is a Golden Earring, ill. by Bernarda Bryson, Holt, 1962.

BENÉT, ROSEMARY, and STEVEN VINCENT BENÉT, *A Book of Americans,* ill. by Charles Child, Holt, 1933. Fifty-six verses about famous men and women from Columbus to P.T. Barnum.

BISHOP, ELIZABETH, *The Ballad of the Burglar of Babylon,* woodcuts by Ann Grifalconi, Farrar, 1968. Set in Rio de Janeiro and based on the true story of Micuçú, this is a beautifully told literary ballad enhanced by the picture book format.

BLAKE, WILLIAM, *Poems of William Blake,* sel. by Amelia H. Munson, ill. by William Blake, Crowell, 1964. A biographical introduction to Blake's poetry from *Poetical Sketches, Songs of Innocence/Songs of Experience* and others.

Songs of Innocence, music and ill. by Ellen Raskin, Doubleday, 1956.

BODECKER, N. M., *Hurry, Hurry Mary Dear! and Other Nonsense Poems,* ill. by the author, Atheneum, 1976. Forty-three outstanding rhyming verses of nonsense and delight. Others include:

Let's Marry! Said the Cherry! and Other Nonsense Poems, ill. by the author, Atheneum, 1974.

Pigeon Cubes and Other Verses, ill. by the author, Atheneum, 1982.

BROOKE, L. LESLIE, *Johnny Crow's Garden, a Picture Book,* drawn by the author. Frederick Warne, 1903. Bestial nonsense in rhyme; a classic for the younger reader, with delightful drawings by the author.

Johnny Crow's New Garden, Warne, 1935.

Johnny Crow's Party, Warne, 1907.

BROOKS, GWENDOLYN, *Bronzeville Boys and Girls,* pictures by Ronni Solbert, Harper, 1956. A classic book of poetry about black children in the city by a poet widely respected in the field of adult poetry.

BROWNING, ROBERT, *Poems,* selected by Rosemary Sprague, drawings by Robert Galster, Crowell, 1964. One of the Crowell Poets series, this offers a biographical introduction as well as lyrics and some of the dramatic monologues.

BURNS, ROBERT, *Hand in Hand We'll Go,* ill. by Nonny Hogrogian, Crowell, 1965. Handsome cheerful woodcuts illustrate ten poems by Burns. A glossary helps interpret his warm, happy and nostalgic poems.

Poems of Robert Burns, selected by Lloyd Frankenberg, drawings by Joseph Low, Thomas Y. Crowell, 1967.

CARROLL, LEWIS, *Poems of Lewis Carroll,* selected by Myra Cohn Livingston, with ill. by John Tenniel, Harry Furniss, Henry Holiday, Arthur B. Frost, and Lewis Carroll, from the original editions, Crowell, 1973. The introduction, the selections, not only from *Alice* books, but also others not known as well, together with the original illustrations and illuminating notes make this a valuable work for young and old.

Individual poems of Carroll's, illustrated by a variety of artists are to be found in many other books including:

The Hunting of the Snark, pictures by Helen Oxenbury, Watts, 1970.

Jabberwocky, ill. by Jane Breskin Zalben, with annotations by Humpty Dumpty, Warne, 1977.

Jabberwocky and Other Frabjous Nonsense, pictures by Simms Taback, Harlin Quist, 1967.

The Pig-Tale, ill. by Leonard B. Labin, Little, Brown, 1975.

The Walrus and the Carpenter and Other Poems, pictures by Gerald Rose, Dutton, 1969.

CAUDILL, REBECCA, *Wind, Sand and Sky,* ill. by Donald Carrick, Dutton, 1976. Three line verses, some alone, some together like lyrics, all about the Arizona desert. Large lovely landscapes fill the pages with soft muted watercolors.

Come Along, ill. by Ellen Raskin, Holt, 1969.

CAUSLEY, CHARLES, *Figgie Hobbin,* ill. by Trina Schart Hyman, intro. by Ethel L. Heins, Walker, 1974. Thirteen poems by a fine craftsman, touching on the humorous and serious.

CHAUCER, GEOFFREY, *A Taste of Chaucer: Selections from "The Canterbury Tales"* chosen and edited by Anne Malcolmson, ill. by Enrico Arno, Harcourt, 1964. Fine introduction for young people to the world of Chaucer.

CIARDI, JOHN, *The Reason for the Pelican,* ill. by Madeleine Gekiere, Lippincott, 1959. Winner of the 1982 NCTE Award for Poetry for Children, Ciardi's rhymes and poems are outstanding in craftsmanship, their humor appealing to young children and adults alike. Others include:

Fast and Slow, Poems for Advanced Children and Beginning Parents, ill. by Becky Gaver, Houghton Mifflin, 1975.

I Met a Man, ill. by Robert Osborn, Houghton Mifflin, 1961.

John J. Plenty and Fiddler Dan, a New Fable of the Grasshopper and the Ant, ill. by Madeleine Gekiere, Lippincott, 1963.

The Man Who Sang the Sillies, drawings by Edward Gorey, Lippincott, 1961.

Someone Could Win a Polar Bear, drawings by Edward Gorey, Lippincott, 1970.

You Read to Me and I'll Read to You, drawings by Edward Gorey, Lippincott, 1962.

CLARE, JOHN, *The Wood is Sweet, Poems for Young Readers,* sel. by David Powell, introduction by Edmund Blunden, ill. by John O'Connor, Watts, 1966. A good introduction to a poet who wrote chiefly about nature during the first half of the nineteenth century.

CLIFTON, LUCILLE, *Some of the Days of Everett Anderson,* ill. by Evaline Ness, Holt, 1970. A six-year-old black child's life is told in simple, but effective free verse. Others include:

Everett Anderson's Friend, ill. by Ann Grifalconi, Holt, 1976.

Everett Anderson's Year, ill. by Ann Grifalconi, Holt, 1974.

The Times They Used to Be, ill. by Susan Jeschke, Holt, 1974.

COATSWORTH, ELIZABETH, *The Sparrow Bush,* ill. by Stefan Martin, Norton, 1966. Nature is predominant

in these lovely verses. Others include:
Down Half the World, ill. by Zena Bernstein, Macmillan, 1968.
Summer Green, ill. by Nona S. Unwin, Macmillan, 1948.
Under the Green Willow, ill. by Janina Domanska, Macmillan, 1971.

COLERIDGE, SAMUEL TAYLOR, *Poems of Samuel Taylor Coleridge,* sel. by Babette Deutsch, woodcuts by Jacques Hnizdovsky, Crowell, 1967. A biography serves as an introduction to selections of the poet's work.

CULLEN, COUNTEE, *The Lost Zoo: Christopher Cat and Countee Cullen,* ill. by Joseph Low, Follett, 1968. Narrative verse about fantastically named creatures by one of America's finest black poets.

DE GASZTOLD, CARMEN BERNOS, *Prayers from the Ark,* trans. from the French by Rumer Godden, ill. by Jean Primrose, Viking, 1962. Twenty-seven free verse poems addressed to the Creator by a variety of animals.
The Creatures' Choir, trans. from the French by Rumer Godden, ill. by Jean Primrose, Viking, 1965.

DE LA MARE, WALTER, *Rhymes and Verses, Collected Poems for Children,* drawings by Elinore Blaisdell, Holt, 1947. The collected poems of de la Mare who lives in both fantasy and reality. Others include:
Bells and Grass, ill. by Dorothy Lathrop, Viking, 1963.
Peacock Pie, ill. by Barbara Cooney, Knopf, 1961.

DE REGNIERS, BEATRICE SCHENK, *Something Special,* drawings by Irene Haas, Harcourt, 1958. Small book of nine poems and a chanting game, pleasant and imaginative.

DICKINSON, EMILY, *Poems of Emily Dickinson,* sel. by Helen Plotz, drawings by Robert Kipniss, Crowell, 1964. Dickinson's most appealing poems for children including some riddles, selected by a distinguished anthologist. Others include: *I'm Nobody! Who are You? Poems of Emily Dickinson for Children,* ill. by Rex Schneider, with an introduction by Richard B. Sewall, Stemmer House, 1978. *Letter to the World, Poems for Young Readers,* sel. by Rumer Godden, ill. by Prudence Seward, Macmillan, 1968.

ELIOT, T. S., *Old Possum's Book of Practical Cats,* Harcourt, 1967. T. S. Eliot in a playful mood, conjuring up a variety of irresistible cats.

FARBER, NORMA, *As I Was Crossing Boston Common,* ill. by Arnold Lobel, Dutton, 1973. An alphabetical parade across and around the Boston Commons of a most uncommon group of real animals with very strange names. Others include:
How Does it Feel to Be Old? ill. by Trina Schart Hyman, Dutton, 1979.
Never Say Ugh to a Bug, ill. by Jose Aruego, Greenwillow, 1979.
Small Wonders, woodcuts by Kazue Mizumura, Coward, 1979.

FARJEON, ELEANOR, *The Children's Bells, a Selection of Poems,* ill. by Peggy Fortnum, Walck, 1960. First published in 1957 in England, this is a selection made by the author of her own verse from previous books. Others include:
Eleanor Farjeon's Poems for Children, Lippincott, 1951.

Then There Were Three, Being Cherrystones, The Mulberry Bush, The Starry Floor; Verses, ill. by Isobel and John Morton-Sale, Lippincott, 1965.

FIELD, RACHEL LYMAN, *Poems,* ill. by the author, Macmillan, 1957. Poems about the everyday younger child and his reaction to his environment.
Taxis and Toadstools. Macmillan, 1926.

FISHER, AILEEN, *Out in the Dark and Daylight,* drawings by Gail Owens. Harper, 1980. The 1978 winner of the NCTE Award for Poetry for Children, Aileen Fisher's work from many previous books are included in this collection. Others include:
Cricket in a Thicket, ill. by Feodor Rojanovsky, Scribner's, 1963.
Do Bears Have Mothers Too? ill. by Eric Carle, Crowell, 1973.
In the Middle of the Night, ill. by Adrienne Adams, Cromwell, 1965.
In the Woods, In the Meadow, In the Sky, ill. by Margot Tomes, Scribner's, 1965.
Listen Rabbit, ill. by Symeon Shimin, Crowell, 1964.
My Cat Has Eyes of Sapphire Blue, ill. by Marie Angel, Crowell, 1973.

FOX, SIV CEDERING, *The Blue Horse and Other Night Poems,* ill. by Donald Carrick, Seabury, 1979. Dream poems written in free verse.

FROMAN, ROBERT, *Seeing Things, a Book of Poems,* lettering by Ray Farber, Crowell, 1974. Shape poetry in which the words become the illustrations.
Street Poems, McCall, 1971.

FROST, ROBERT, *You Come Too, Favorite Poems for Young Readers,* with wood engravings by Thomas W. Nason, Holt, 1959. About fifty of Frost's favorites for his own children with a warm and personal introduction by a young friend, Hyde Cox.

GARDNER, JOHN, *A Child's Bestiary,* with additional poems by Lucy Gardner and Eugene Rudzewicz and drawings by Lucy, Joel, Joan, and John Gardner, Knopf, 1977. Funny poems in alphabetical order from African Wild Dog to Zebra, of course with line drawings.

GILBERT, W. S., *Poems of W. S. Gilbert,* sel. by William Cole, ill. by W. S. Gilbert "Bab," Crowell, 1967. A biographical introduction with notes on the selections, most of which are from the Gilbert and Sullivan operettas.

GIOVANNI, NIKKI, *Spin a Soft Black Song, Poems for Children,* ill. by Charles Bible, Hill and Wang, 1971. Poems about black children in this picture book format are simple and moving. Others include:
Ego-Tripping and Other Poems for Young People, ill. by George Ford, Lawrence Hill, 1974.
Vacation Time: Poems for Children, ill. by Marisabina Russo, Morrow, 1980.

GRAVES, ROBERT, *The Penny Fiddle,* ill. by Edward Ardizzone, Doubleday, 1960. A collection of outstanding poems by a fine poet, written for children.

GREENFIELD, ELOISE, *Honey, I Love, and Other Love Poems,* ill. by Diane and Leo Dillon, Crowell, 1978. The love poems of a child for her family and delight in the life around her.

HARDY, THOMAS, *The Pinnacled Tower,* ed. by Helen Plotz, wood engravings by Clare Leighton, Macmillan, 1975. A biographical introduction to Hardy's poetry and a selection of his poetry by a noted anthologist.

HOBAN, RUSSELL, *The Pedaling Man*, drawings by Lillian Hoban, Norton, 1968. A writer who brings to life the inanimate and quickens the innards of life in its stillness.
Egg Thoughts and Other Frances Songs, ill. by Lillian Hoban, Harper, 1972.
HOBERMAN, MARY ANN, *The Raucous Auk, a Menagerie of Poems*, ill. by Joseph Low, Viking, 1973. Humorous verse about a variety of animals like auks, bandicoots, and whales.
Bugs, ill. by Victoria Chess, Viking, 1976.
HOLMAN, FELICE, *At the Top of My Voice and Other Poems*, ill. by Edward Gorey, Norton, 1970. A child's perception of the world, done in excellent verse with humor.
I Hear You Smiling and Other Poems, ill. by Laszlo Kubinyi, Scribner's, 1973.
HUGHES, LANGSTON, *Don't You Turn Back, Poems*, sel. by Lee Bennett Hopkins, woodcuts by Ann Grifalconi, Knopf, 1970. A discriminating selection of the work of one of America's finest black poets.
The Dream Keeper and Other Poems, ill. by Helen Sewell, Knopf, 1932.
HUGHES, TED, *Season Songs*, ill. by Leonard Baskin, Viking Press, 1975. Provocative poems about the seasons or events that occur during the year. Others include:
Meet My Folks, ill. by Mila Lazarevich, Bobbs-Merrill, 1973.
Moon Whales and Other Moon Poems, drawings by Leonard Baskin, Viking, 1976.
ISSA, et al., *Don't Tell the Scarecrow and Other Japanese Poems by Issa, Yayu, Kikaku, and Other Japanese Poets*, ill. by Talivaldis Stubis, Four Winds, 1969. Simple, expressive haiku in a picture book format.
A Few Flies and I, Haiku by Issa, sel. by Jean Merrill and Ronni Solbert from translations by R. H. Blyth and Nobuyuki Yuasa, ill. by Ronni Solbert, Pantheon, 1969.
JARRELL, RANDALL, *The Bat Poet*, Macmillan, 1964. A must for reading aloud to children who are interested in the writing of poetry.
JORDAN, JUNE, *Who Look at Me?* ill. with 27 paintings, Crowell, 1969. For the child who seeks identification as a black.
KEATS, JOHN, *Poems*, sel. by Stanley Kunitz, woodcuts by Jacques Hnizdovsky, Crowell, 1964. An introduction to the poet through his poetry and excerpts from his letters.
KENNEDY, X. J., *One Winter Night in August and Other Nonsense Jingles*, ill. by David McPhail, Atheneum, 1975. Nonsense and wordplay by one of our wittiest poets.
The Phantom Ice Cream Man: More Nonsense Verse. Atheneum, 1979.
KHERDIAN, DAVID, *Country Cat, City Cat*, woodcuts by Nonny Hogrogian, Four Winds, 1978. Brief imagist poetry and experimental forms characterize this group of poems.
KUSKIN, KARLA, *Dogs & Dragons, Trees & Dreams, a Collection of Poems*, Harper, 1980. Winner of the 1979 NCTE Award for Poetry for Children, this collection includes poetry written between 1958 and 1975. The poet's notes introduce some of the poems. Others include:
Alexander Soames: His Poems, Harper, 1962.
Any Me I Want to Be: Poems, Harper, 1972.

Near the Window Tree, Poems and Notes, Harper, 1975.
LEAR, EDWARD, *The Complete Nonsense Book*, ed. by Lady Strachey, introduction by the Earl of Cromer, Dodd, 1948. One of the masters of nonsense and verse, this volume includes most of Lear's works. Others include:
The Dong with the Luminous Nose, drawings by Edward Gorey, Young Scott, 1959.
How Pleasant to Know Mr. Lear, sel. by Myra Cohn Livingston, Holiday House, 1982.
The Jumblies, drawings by Edward Gorey, Young Scott, 1968.
The Jumblies and Other Nonsense Verses, drawings by Leslie Brooke, Warne, 1959.
The Owl and the Pussycat, ill. by William Pène DuBois, Doubleday, 1962.
The Owl and the Pussycat, ill. by Gwen Fulton, Atheneum, 1977.
The Pelican Chorus, ill. by Harold Berson, Parents Magazine Press, 1967.
The Scroobious Pip, completed by Ogden Nash, ill. by Nancy Ekholm Burkert, Harper, 1968.
Two Laughable Lyrics: The Pobble Who Has No Toes; The Quangle Wangle's Hat, ill. by Paul Galdone, Putnam, 1966.
LEE, DENNIS, *Alligator Pie*, ill. by Peter Newfield, Houghton, 1975. Nonsense rhyming verses with a Canadian twist.
Garbage Delight, ill. by Frank Newfield, Houghton, 1978.
LEODHAS, SORCHE NIC, *Always Room for One More*, ill. by Nonny Hogrogian, Holt, 1965. The humor of the Scots and the mists of Scotland are reflected in this charming picture book.
LINDSAY, VACHEL, *Johnny Appleseed and Other Poems*, ill. by George Richards, Macmillan, 1928. (Children's Classic) Robust verse which is always best read aloud.
LIVINGSTON, MYRA COHN, *The Malibu and Other Poems*, ill. by James Spanfeller, Atheneum, 1972. Winner of the 1980 NCTE Award for Poetry for Children, this book includes poems and verses about contemporary children and their attitudes toward their world. Others include:
A Crazy Flight and Other Poems, ill. by James Spanfeller, Harcourt, 1969.
Four Way Stop & Other Poems, ill. by James Spanfeller, Atheneum, 1976.
A Lollygag of Limericks, drawings by Joseph Low, Atheneum, 1978.
The Moon and a Star, ill. by Judith Shahn, Harcourt, 1965.
No Way of Knowing: Dallas Poems, Atheneum, 1980.
O Sliver of Liver, Together with Other Triolets, Cinquains, Haiku, Verses, and a Dash of Poems, ill. by Iris Van Rynbach, Atheneum, 1979.
The Way Things Are, and Other Poems, ill. by Jenni Oliver, Atheneum, 1974.
MC CORD, DAVID, *One at a Time, His Collected Poems for the Young*, ill. by Henry B. Kane, Little, 1977. Recipient of the first NCTE Award for Poetry for Children in 1977, McCord has gathered together his poems and verses from five previous books. Others include:
Every Time I Climb a Tree, ill. by Marc Simont, Little, 1967.
Speak Up: More Rhymes of the Never Was and Always

Is, ill. by Marc Simont, Little, 1980.

The Star in the Pail, ill. by Marc Simont, Little, 1975.

MAHER, RAMONA, *Alice Yazzie's Year,* drawings by Stephen Gammell, Coward, 1977. Poems for each month of modern Navajo Alice Yazzie's year.

MERRIAM, EVE, *It Doesn't Always Have to Rhyme,* drawings by Malcolm Spooner, Atheneum, 1964. Poetry which revels in word play and commentary on contemporary life. Eve Merriam is the recipient of the NCTE Award for Poetry for Children for 1981. Others include:

Catch a Little Rhyme, ill. by Imero Gobbato, Atheneum, 1969.

Finding a Poem, ill. by Seymour Chwast, Atheneum, 1970.

Independent Voices, ill. by Arivs Stewart, Atheneum, 1968.

Out Loud, designed by Harriet Sherman, Atheneum, 1973.

Rainbow Writing, Atheneum, 1976.

There is No Rhyme for Silver, drawings by Joseph Schindelman, Atheneum, 1966.

MILLAY, EDNA ST. VINCENT, *Edna St. Vincent Millay's Poems, Selected for Young People,* woodcuts by Ronald Keller, Harper, 1979. An attractive selection from several of the author's previous books.

MILNE, A. A., *When We Were Very Young,* ill. by Ernest H. Shepard, Dutton, 1924. Light verse that has been popular for over fifty years with both children and adults.

Now We Are Six, ill. by Ernest H. Shepard, Dutton, 1927.

MIZUMURA, KAZUE, *Flower, Moon, Snow, a Book of Haiku,* woodcuts by the author, Crowell, 1977. Thirty poems in the spirit of haiku with a beautiful sense of imagery.

I See the Winds, Crowell, 1966.

MOORE, LILIAN, *Something New Begins,* decorated by Mary Jane Dunton, Atheneum, 1982. Filled with the joy of discovery in both country and city, these are poems from other books by Moore as well as fifteen new poems. Others include:

I Feel the Same Way, ill. by Robert Quackenbush, Atheneum, 1968.

I Thought I Heard the City, collage by Mary Jane Dunton, Atheneum, 1969.

Little Raccoon and Poems from the Woods, ill. by Gioia Flammenghi, McGraw, 1975.

Sam's Place, Poems from the Country, drawings by Talivaldis Stubis, Atheneum, 1973.

See My Lovely Poison Ivy, and Other Verses about Witches, Ghosts and Things, ill. by Diane Dawson, Atheneum, 1975.

Think of Shadows, ill. by Deborah Robison, Atheneum, 1980.

MORRISON, LILLIAN, *The Sidewalk Racer and Other Poems of Sports and Motion,* Lothrop, 1977. All kinds of sports from boxing to surfing and tennis are subjects of Morrison's fine poetry. Others include:

Overheard in a Bubble Chamber and Other Science Poems, Lothrop, 1981.

Who Would Marry a Mineral? Riddles, Runes and Love Tunes, decorations by Rita Floden Leydon, Lothrop, 1978.

NASH, OGDEN, *Custard and Company,* sel. and ill. by Quentin Blake, Little, Brown, 1980. A rollicking collection of the best of Nashinanity.

The New Nutcracker Suite and Other Innocent Verses, Little, 1967.

NORRIS, LESLIE, *Merlin and the Snake's Egg: Poems,* ill. by Ted Lewin, Viking, 1978. Beautiful poems about animals and natural things as well as magic by the contemporary Welsh poet.

O'NEILL, MARY, *Hailstones and Halibut Bones: Adventures in Color,* ill. by Leonard Weisgard, Doubleday, 1961. Simple verses introduce colors to children in a popular book. Others include:

Take a Number, Doubleday, 1968.

What Is That Sound? Atheneum, 1966.

POE, EDGAR ALLAN, *Poems,* sel. by Dwight Macdonald, drawings by Ellen Raskin, Crowell, 1965. Another in the Crowell Poets series which serves as introduction to the works of Poe.

POMERANTZ, CHARLOTTE, *The Tamarindo Puppy and Other Poems,* ill. by Byron Barton, Greenwillow, 1980. Thirteen poems with some Spanish words throughout, all readily understandable in context. Some bilingual poems in English and Spanish.

PRELUTSKY, JACK, *The Sheriff of Rottenshot,* ill. by Victoria Chess, Greenwillow, 1982. A master of the rollicking anapestic line and many subject matters, Prelutsky is at his best in this book. Others include:

The Headless Horseman Rides Again, More Poems to Trouble Your Sleep, ill. by Arnold Lobel. Greenwillow, 1980.

It's Halloween, ill. by Marilyn Hafner, Greenwillow, 1977.

Nightmares, Poems to Trouble Your Sleep, ill. by Arnold Lobel, Greenwillow, 1976.

The Queen of Eene, Poems, ill. by Victoria Chess. Greenwillow, 1978.

The Snopp on the Sidewalk, and Other Poems, ill. by Byron Barton, Greenwillow, 1977.

REEVES, JAMES, *The Blackbird in the Lilac, Verses for Children,* ill. by Edward Ardizzone, Dutton, 1959. Graceful rhyming verses, both witty and bright, done by a superb craftsman. Others include:

Prefabulous Animiles, ill. by Edward Ardizzone, Dutton, 1960.

The Wandering Moon, ill. by Edward Ardizzone, Dutton, 1960.

RICHARDS, LAURA E., *Tirra Lirra, Rhymes Old and New,* foreword by May Hill Arbuthnot, ill. by Marguerite Davis, Little, 1955. Using the "broad back of her current baby as a writing board," Richards turned out multitudinous nonsense rhymes for many years. This is a selection of the best.

RIEU, E. V., *The Flattered Flying Fish, and Other Poems,* ill. by E. H. Shepard, Dutton, 1962. A translator of classics, his more "serious efforts during some thirty years" produced this volume of delightful rhyming verse.

ROBERTS, ELIZABETH MADOX, *Under the Tree,* ill. by R. D. Bedford, Viking, 1922. The language of the child beautifully rendered in traditional form with response to the world around. A classic.

ROETHKE, THEODORE, *Dirty Dinky, and Other Creatures,* sel. by Beatrice Roethke and Stephen Lushington, ill. by Julie Brinckloe, Doubleday, 1973. A selection of Roethke's poetry for the young.

ROSSETTI, CHRISTINA, *Goblin Market,* ill. by Arthur Rackham, Watts, 1969. A rich, evocative poem, a classic in its field. Others include:

Doves and Pomegranates, Poems for Young Readers, sel. by David Powell, introduction by Naomi Lewis, Macmillan, 1969.

Sing-Song, a Nursery Rhyme Book for Children, Macmillan, 1924.

SANDBURG, CARL, *Rainbows Are Made: Poems by Carl Sandburg,* sel. by Lee Bennett Hopkins, Harcourt, 1982. A selection of Sandburg's poems that speak to young people. Others include:

Early Moon, ill. by James Daugherty, Harcourt, 1930.

Wind Song, ill. by William S. Smith, Harcourt, 1960.

SENDAK, MAURICE, *The Nutshell Library:* v. 1 *Alligators All Around;* v. 2 *Chicken Soup with Rice;* v. 3 *One Was Johnny;* v. 4 *Pierre,* Harper, 1962. Four small rhyming books of joyous verse, especially the modern cautionary tale of Pierre.

SERRAILLIER, IAN, *Suppose You Met a Witch,* ill. by Ed Emberley, Little, Brown, 1973. A poetic interpretation of the folktale about two children who escape the witch Grimblegrum. Others include:

Beowulf the Warrior, ill. by Severin, Walck, 1961.

Happily Ever After, ill. by Brian Wildsmith, Oxford, 1963.

Thomas and the Sparrow, ill. by Severin, Oxford, 1951.

SHAKESPEARE, WILLIAM, *Poems of William Shakespeare,* sel. by Lloyd Frankenberg, etchings by Nonny Hogrogian, Crowell, 1966. A biographical introduction to Shakespeare, his sonnets, poetry, and songs from the plays.

SHELLEY, PERCY BYSSHE, *Poems of Percy Bysshe Shelley,* sel. by Leo Gurko, ill. by Lars Bo, Crowell, 1968. An introduction to the power and emotion of the Romantic poet.

SILVERSTEIN, SHEL, *Where the Sidewalk Ends, the Poems and Drawings of Shel Silverstein,* Harper, 1974. Zany light verse with a popular appeal for children.

A Light in the Attic, Poems and Drawings by Shel Silverstein, Harper, 1981.

SMITH, WILLIAM JAY, *Laughing Time,* ill. by Fernando Krahn, Delacorte, 1980. A selection of the best of Smith's nonsense verse for children culled from earlier books.

Boy Blue's Book of Beasts, Little, 1957.

Mr. Smith and Other Nonsense, ill. by Don Bolognese, Delacorte, 1968.

Typewriter Town, E. P. Dutton, 1960.

SNYDER, ZILPHA KEATLEY, *Today is Saturday,* photography by John Arms, Atheneum, 1969. Poems about the contemporary child in his own world of Saturday and a time of action and dreaming.

STARBIRD, KAYE, *Don't Ever Cross a Crocodile,* ill. by Kit Dalton, Lippincott, 1963. Narrative portraits are a staple in this poetry, both in a humorous and serious vein. Wit and perception distinguish the work. Others include:

The Covered Bridge House, ill. by Jim Aronsky, Four Winds, 1979.

The Pheasant on Route Seven, ill. by Victoria de Larrea, Lippincott, 1968.

A Snail's a Failure Socially; and Other Poems, ill. by Kit Dalton, Lippincott, 1966.

Speaking of Cows, ill. by Rita Fava, Lippincott, 1960.

STEVENSON, ROBERT LOUIS, *A Child's Garden of Verses,* ill. by Jessie Willcox Smith, Scribner's, 1905. One of the first books of verse to celebrate the world of the child, this collection still speaks convincingly of a children's world. This is the best of dozens of editions which vary as to format and illustration.

Poems of Robert Louis Stevenson, sel. by Helen Plotz, drawings by Charles Attebery, Crowell, 1973.

SWENSON, MAY, *Poems to Solve,* Scribner's, 1966. Riddle poems in which the subjects reveal themselves through exciting imagery and original form.

More Poems to Solve, Scribner's, 1971.

TAGORE, *Moon, for What Do You Wait?* ed. by Richard Lewis, ill. by Ashley Bryan, Atheneum, 1967. Provocative two-line verse reprinted from *Stray Birds* by Rabindranath Tagore, one of India's greatest poets and winner of the Nobel Prize for Literature.

TEASDALE, SARA, *Stars To-night: Verses New and Old for Boys and Girls,* ill. by Dorothy P. Lathrop, Macmillan, 1930. A look at nature from the perspective of an older girl.

TENNYSON, ALFRED, *Poems,* sel. by Ruth Greiner Rausen, ill. by Virgil Burnett, Crowell, 1964. An introductory selection of Tennyson's work; another in the Crowell Poets Series.

THURMAN, JUDITH, *Flashlight and Other Poems,* ill. by Reina Rubel, Atheneum, 1976. Free verse about everyday things with a simplicity of metaphor that startles the reader with its freshness.

TOLKIEN, J. R. R., *The Adventures of Tom Bombadil, and Other Verses from the Red Book,* ill. by Pauline Baynes, Houghton, 1963. The verse of Middle Earth for anyone who enjoys the world of the Hobbits.

UPDIKE, JOHN, *A Child's Calendar,* ill. by Nancy Ekholm Burkert, Knopf, 1965. Joyful verse depicting the symbols for each month of the year.

WATSON, CLYDE, *Father Fox's Pennyrhymes,* ill. by Wendy Watson, Crowell, 1971. These sprightly, humorous, original nonsense rhymes are almost an American Mother Goose.

Catch Me, Kiss Me and Say It Again: Rhymes, ill. by Wendy Watson, Collins, 1978.

WATSON, NANCY DINGMAN, *Blueberries Lavender: Songs of the Farmer's Children: Poems,* ill. by Erik Blegvad, Addison-Wesley, 1977. Contemporary verse celebrating quiet moments on a Northern farm.

WHITMAN, WALT, *Leaves of Grass: Poems,* sel. by Lawrence Clark Powell, woodcuts by John Ross and Clare Romano, Crowell, 1964. Poetry and excerpts from the longer poems chosen by an enthusiastic admirer and scholar; one of the Crowell Poets Series.

Overhead the Sun: Lines from Walt Whitman, woodcuts by Antonio Frasconi, Farrar, 1969.

WILBUR, RICHARD, *Opposites,* ill. by the author, Harcourt, 1973. Verses by one of America's finest poets in a witty and humorous mood.

WORDSWORTH, WILLIAM, *Poems,* sel. by Elinor Parker, wood engravings by Diana Bloomfield, Crowell, 1964. A biographical introduction to the poet and his works: one of the Crowell Poets Series.

WORTH, VALERIE, *Small Poems,* ill. by Natalie Babbitt, Farrar, 1972. One of the finest poets for children whose sense of metaphor is unique and haunting.

More Small Poems, ill. by Natalie Babbitt, Farrar, 1976.

Still More Small Poems, ill. by Natalie Babbitt, Farrar, 1978.

YEATS, WILLIAM BUTLER, *Running to Paradise: An Introductory Selection,* sel. by Kevin Crossley-Holland, ill. by Judith Valpy, Macmillan, 1967. A selection of the poems of Yeats with an introduction inviting the young reader to learn how childhood shaped his writing.

YOLEN, JANE, *How Beastly! a Menagerie of Nonsense Poems,* ill. by James Marshall, Collins, 1980. Newly created beasts immortalized in Learish fashion with typical insouciant illustrations by Marshall.

ZOLOTOW, CHARLOTTE, *River Winding,* ill. by Kazue Mizumura, Crowell, 1978. Brief verses about seasons, feelings, and intimate moments.

Poetry Anthologies

ABDUL, RAOUL, *The Magic of Black Poetry,* ill. by Dane Burr, Dodd, 1972. A fine introduction to poetry written by blacks from all over the world.

ADAMS, ADRIENNE, comp., *Poetry of the Earth,* ill. by the author, Scribner's, 1972. Handsomely illustrated collection of 33 poems about nature in all its aspects.

ADOFF, ARNOLD, ed., *Black Out Loud: An Anthology of Modern Poems by Black Americans,* drawings by Alvin Hollingsworth, Macmillan, 1970. A modern black poetry anthology in celebration of black people. Adoff's anthologies focus on the black experience in America and include biographical information on the poets. Others include:
Celebrations, a New Anthology of Black American Poetry, introduced by Quincy Troupe, Follett, 1977.
I Am the Darker Brother: An Anthology of Modern Poems by Negro Americans, drawings by Benny Andrews, Foreword by Charlemae Rollins, Macmillan, 1968.
It Is the Poem Singing into Your Eyes, Anthology of New Young Poets, Harper, 1971.
My Black Me, a Beginning Book of Black Poetry, Dutton, 1974.
The Poetry of Black America: An Anthology of the 20th Century, Harper, 1973.

ADSHEAD, GLADYS L., and ANNIS DUFF, comps., *An Inheritance of Poetry,* with decorations by Nora S. Unwin, Houghton, 1948. A classic collection of English and American poetry, including a source index and index of musical settings as well as author, title, and first line.

AGREE, ROSE, sel., *How To Eat a Poem and Other Morsels: Food Poems for Children,* ill. by Peggy Wilson, Pantheon, 1967. A cheerful collection of poems about food.

ALLEN, SAMUEL, ed., *Poems from Africa,* ill. by Romare Bearden, Crowell, 1973. An overview of poetry in Africa from the past and of contemporary time.

ALLEN, TERRY, ed., *The Whispering Wind, Poetry by Young American Indians,* with an introduction by Mae J. Durham, Doubleday, 1973. The work of students at the Institute of American Indian Arts in Santa Fe, New Mexico, with biographical information included.

BARON, VIRGINIA OLSEN, ed., *The Seasons of Time, Tanka Poetry of Ancient Japan,* ill. by Yuuhide Koba-shi, Dial Press, 1968. Tanka between 759 and 905 A.D. in a picture-book format.
Sunset in a Spider Web, Sijo Poetry of Ancient Korea, adapted from translations by Chung Seuk Park, ill. by Minja Park Kim, Holt, 1974.

BEHN, HARRY, comp., *Cricket Songs, Japanese Haiku,* translated by Harry Behn, pictures selected from Sesshu and other Japanese masters, Harcourt, 1964. Haiku by Issa, Basho, and others rendered in the traditional seventeen-syllable pattern.
More Cricket Songs, Japanese Haiku, translated by Harry Behn, illustrated with pictures by Japanese masters, Harcourt, 1971.

BELTING, NATALIA, comp., *Our Fathers Had Powerful Songs,* ill. by Laszlo Kubinyi, Dutton, 1974. Nine poems from one Canadian and several American Indian tribes are a celebration of song and legend.
Whirlwind is a Ghost Dancing, ill. by Leo and Diane Dillon, Dutton, 1974.

BENEDETTI, MARIO, ed., *Unstill Life/Naturalez Viva: An Introduction to the Spanish Poetry of Latin America,* translated by Darwin Flakoll and Claribel Alegría, ill. by Antonio Frasconi, Harcourt, 1969. A sampling of the rich poetry from South America in a bilingual format.

BIERHORST, JOHN, ed., *In the Trail of the Wind, American Indian Poems and Ritual Orations,* Farrar, 1971. Poems taken from the oral literature of about forty tribes of Indians in North, Central, and South America as well as from the Eskimos.

BLISHEN, EDWARD, comp., *Oxford Book of Poetry for Children,* ill. by Brian Wildsmith, Watts, 1964. A rounded traditional assortment of poetry enriched by vivid watercolors.

BOGAN, LOUISE, and WILLIAM JAY SMITH, comps., *The Golden Journey, Poems for Young People,* woodcuts by Fritz Kredel, Reilly and Lee, 1965. A traditional collection of English and American poets.

BONTEMPS, ARNA, ed., *Golden Slippers, an Anthology of Negro Poetry for Young Readers,* drawings by Henrietta Bruce Sharon. Harper, 1941. A representative collection of traditional black American poetry selected by a fine poet. Also:
Hold Fast to Dream: Poems Old and New, Follett, 1969.

BREWTON, SARA, and JOHN E. BREWTON, comps., *America Forever New: A Book of Poems,* drawings by Ann Grifalconi, Crowell, 1968. A fresh anthology of American poets covering many aspects of American life from history to tall tales as well as regional poems about the land. Other Brewton anthologies include:
Birthday Candles Burning Bright, decorations by Vera Bock, Macmillan, 1960.

BREWTON, SARA, JOHN E. BREWTON, and G. MEREDITH BLACKBURN III, comps., *My Tang's Tungled and Other Ridiculous Situations,* ill. by Graham Booth, Harper, 1973.

BREWTON, SARA, JOHN E. BREWTON, and JOHN BREWTON BLACKBURN, *Of Quarks, Quasars, and Other Quirks, Quizzical Poems for the Supersonic Age,* ill. by Quentin Blake, Crowell, 1977.

BREWTON, SARA, and JOHN E. BREWTON, sel., *Shrieks at Midnight, Macabre Poems, Eerie and Humorous,* drawings by Ellen Raskin, Crowell, 1969.

BREWTON, JOHN E., LORRAINE A. BLACKBURN, GEORGE

M. BLACKBURN III, comps., *In the Witch's Kitchen,* Crowell, 1980.

BREWTON, JOHN E., and LORRAINE A. BLACKBURN, comps., *They've Discovered a Head in the Box for the Bread and Other Laughable Limericks,* ill. by Fernando Krahn, Crowell, 1978.

CARLISLE, OLGA, and ROSE STYRON, trans. and eds., *Modern Russian Poetry,* Viking, 1972. Biographical material and poems of Russian poets from 1880 to 1940.

CAUSLEY, CHARLES, comp., *Modern Ballads and Story Poems,* chosen and introduced by Charles Causley, drawings by Anne Netherwood, Watts, 1965. Forty ballads by contemporary writers.

CLYMER, THEODORE, sel., *Four Corners of the Sky: Poems, Chants and Oratory,* ill. by Marc Brown, Little, 1975. Poems and chants from the American Indian oral tradition with notes to explain some of the poems.

COLE, WILLIAM, comp., *Beastly Boys and Ghastly Girls: Poems,* drawings by Tomi Ungerer, Collins, 1964. A favorite of children who see themselves reflected in other boys and girls. William Cole, a prolific anthologist, has gathered a variety of verse and poetry to compile many thematic anthologies. Other anthologies include:
The Birds and the Beasts Were There: Animal Poems, woodcuts by Helen Siegel, World, 1963.
An Arkful of Animals, ill. by Lynn Munsinger, Houghton Mifflin, 1978.
A Book of Animal Poems, ill. by Robert Andrew Parker, Viking, 1973.
A Book of Love Poems, ill. by Lars Bo, Viking, 1965.
Dinosaurs and Beasts of Yore, ill. by Susanna Natti, Collins, 1979.
Oh, What Nonsense! drawings by Tomi Ungerer, Viking, 1966.
Pick Me Up, a Book of Short Poems, Macmillan, 1972.
Poems from Ireland, drawings by William Stobbs, Crowell, 1972.
Poems of Magic and Spells, ill. by Peggy Bacon, World, 1960.
The Poetry of Horses, ill. by Ruth Sanderson, Scribner's, 1979.
The Poet's Tales; a New Book of Story Poems, ill. by Charles Keeping, World, 1971.
The Sea, Ships and Sailors, Poems, Songs and Shanties, drawings by Robin Jacques, Viking, 1967.

COLUM, PADRAIC, ed., *Roofs of Gold, Poems to Read Aloud,* Macmillan, 1964. A traditional collection of personal favorites chosen by a master.

DE FOREST, CHARLOTTE B., ad., *The Prancing Pony: Nursery Rhymes from Japan,* adapted into English verse for children, ill. by Keike Hida, Walker, 1968. Simple verses of pleasure to the young.

DE GEREZ, TONI, comp., *Two Rabbit, Seven Wind, Poems from Ancient Mexico, retold from Nahuatl texts,* Viking, 1971. An attractive and interesting collection "from the codices of the Nuhuatl-speaking."

DE LA MARE, WALTER, ed., *Come Hither, a Collection of Rhymes and Poems for the Young of All Ages,* decorations by Warren Chappell, Knopf, 1957. First published in 1923, this is a collection of about 500 traditional poems chosen by a distinguished poet. Extensive notes, some like essays, add immeasurably to the work.

Tom Tiddler's Ground, a Book of Poetry for Children, chosen and annotated by De La Mare with a foreword by Leonard Clark and drawings by Margery Gill, Knopf, 1961.

DOOB, LEONARD W., ed., *A Crocodile Has Me by the Leg,* ill. by Solomon Irein Wangboje, Walker, 1967. Fifty verses from the African oral tradition collected by travelers and scholars in African languages.

DOWNIE, MARY ALICE, comp., *The Wind Has Wings, Poems from Canada,* ill. by Elizabeth Cleaver, Walck, 1968. A varied collection of Canadian poets' works ranging from English to translations from Yiddish, French, and Eskimo.

DUNNING, STEPHEN, EDWARD LUEDERS, and HUGH SMITH, comps., *Reflections on a Gift of Watermelon Pickle . . . and Other Modern Verse,* Lothrop, 1967. Pairings of 114 contemporary poems with photographs selected by three English teachers.
Some Haystacks Don't Even Have Any Needles and Other Complete Modern Poems. Scott, Foresman, 1969.

EATON, ANNE THAXTER, comp., *Welcome Christmas! A Garland of Poems,* decorated by Valenti Angelo, Viking, 1955. About fifty poems and carols, largely traditional.

EMRICH, DUNCAN, comp., *The Nonsense Book of Riddles, Rhymes, Tongue Twisters, Puzzles, and Jokes from American Folklore,* ill. by Ib Ohlsson, Four Winds, 1970. A great many American folk rhymes chosen by a respected compiler.

GREGORY, HORACE, and MARYA ZATURENSKA, eds., *The Silver Swan, Poems of Romance and Mystery,* wood engravings by Diane Bloomfield, Holt, 1966. Mystic, romantic, and mysterious lyrics, songs, and elegies from the past and the present, chosen by two outstanding poets. Also:
The Crystal Cabinet, an Invitation to Poetry, wood engravings by Diana Bloomfield, Holt, 1962.

GRIGSON, GEOFFREY, comp., *The Cherry Tree, a Collection of Poems,* Vanguard Press, 1959. A large anthology with a good introduction to much rarely anthologized English verse. Also:
Rainbows, Fleas and Flowers, a Nature Anthology, decorations by Glynn Thomas, John Baker, 1971.

HANNUM, SARA, and GWENDOLYN E. REED, comps., *Lean Out the Window, an Anthology of Modern Poetry,* introduction by Siddie Joe Johnson, decorations by Ragna Tischler, Atheneum, 1965. A series of traditional and contemporary poems to introduce young readers to modern poetry. Others include:

HANNUM, SARA, and JOHN TERRY CHASE, comps., *To Play Man Number One,* ill. by Erwin Schachner, Atheneum, 1969.
The Wind is Round, ill. by Ron Bowen, Atheneum, 1970.

HAYDEN, ROBERT, ed., *Kaleidoscope: Poems by American Negro Poets,* Harcourt, 1967. An outstanding black poet selects his favorite poetry for the young.

HILL, HELEN, AGNES PERKINS, and ALETHEA HELBIG, comps., *Straight on Till Morning, Poems of the Imaginary World,* ill. by Ted Lewin, Crowell, 1977. A fine selection of modern poetry about the world of imagination. Also:

HILL, HELEN, and AGNES PERKINS, *New Coasts and Strange Harbors, Discovering Poems,* ill. by Clare Romano and John Ross, Crowell, 1974.

HOPKINS, LEE BENNETT, sel., *I Am the Cat*, ill. by Linda Rochester Richards, Harcourt, 1981. Lee Bennett Hopkins has compiled many anthologies with focus on a particular theme. Others include:
And God Bless Me, Prayers, Lullabies and Dream Poems, Knopf, 1982.
By Myself, ill. by Glo Coalson, Crowell, 1980.
Easter Buds are Springing: Poems for Easter, ill. by Tomie de Paola, Harcourt, 1979.
The City Spreads Its Wings, ill. by Moneta Barnett, Watts, 1970.
Go to Bed! A Book of Bedtime Poems, ill. by Rosekrans Hoffman, Knopf, 1979.
Good Morning to You, Valentine, ill. by Tomie de Paola, Harcourt, 1975.
Hey-How for Halloween, ill. by Janet McCaffery, Harcourt, 1974.
Merrily Comes Our Harvest In: Poems for Thanksgiving, ill. by Ben Schecter, Harcourt, 1978.
Moments: Poems About the Seasons, ill. by Michael Hague, Harcourt, 1980.
Morning Noon and Nighttime, Too, ill. by Nancy Hannans, Harper, 1980.
To Look at Any Thing, photographs by John Earl, Harcourt, 1978.
Sing Hey for Christmas Day! ill. by Laura Jean Allen, Harcourt, 1975.
HOUSTON, JAMES, ed., *Songs of the Dream People, Chants and Images from the Indians and Eskimos of North America*, ill. by the author, Atheneum, 1972. Brief poems from the Eskimos and the Indians of the Northwest Coast, the Central Plains, and the Eastern Woodland.
JANECZKO, PAUL B., ed., *Don't Forget to Fly: A Cycle of Modern Poems*, Bradbury Press, 1981. Al Young's line is the title for this splendid collection.
Postcard Poems: A Collection of Poetry for Sharing, Bradbury Press, 1979.
JONES, HETTIE, comp., *The Trees Stand Shining, Poetry of the North American Indians*, paintings by Robert Andrew Parker, Dial Press, 1971. Songs of the American Indian including prayers, short stories, lullabies, and war chants.
KHERDIAN, DAVID, ed., *The Dog Writes on the Window With His Nose and Other Poems*, pictures by Nonny Hogrogian, Four Winds, 1977. Twenty-two brief poems by contemporary poets. Others include:
If Dragon Flies Made Honey: Poems, ill. by Jose Aruego and Ariane Dewey, Greenwillow, 1977.
Visions of America, by the Poets of Our Time, ill. by Nonny Hogrogian, Macmillan, 1973.
LANGSTAFF, JOHN, *Hot Cross Buns, and Other Old Street Cries*, ill. by Nancy Winslow Parker, Atheneum, 1978. Thirty traditional street cries with music. Also: and CAROL LANGSTAFF, comps., *Shimmy Shimmy Coke-ca pop! A Collection of City Children's Street Games and Rhymes*, photographs by Don MacSorley, Doubleday, 1973.
LARRICK, NANCY, sel., *Crazy to Be Alive in Such a Strange World, Poems About People*, photographs by Alexander L. Crosby, M. Evans, 1977. Larrick is the compiler of many anthologies of both traditional and contemporary verse and poetry. Others include:
Bring Me All Your Dreams, M. Evans, 1979.
Green is Like a Meadow of Grass: An Anthology of Children's Pleasure in Poetry, Garrard, 1968.

More Poetry for Holidays, drawings by Harold Berson, Garrard, 1973.
On City Streets, photography by David Sagarin, M. Evans, 1968.
Piper, Pipe That Song Again! Poems for Boys and Girls, ill. by Kelly Oeschli, Random House, 1965.
Piping Down the Valleys Wild, Poetry for the Young of All Ages, ill. by Ellen Raskin, Delacorte Press, 1968.
Poetry for Holidays, drawings by Kelly Oechsli, Garrard, 1966.
Room For Me and a Mountain Lion, Poetry of Open Space, ill. with photographs, M. Evans, 1974.
Tambourines! Tambourines to Glory! Prayers and Poems, drawings by Geri Greinke, Westminster, 1982.
LEWIS, RICHARD, ed., *I Breathe a New Song, Poems of the Eskimo*, ill. by Oonark with an introduction by Edmund Carpenter, Simon & Schuster, 1971. A collection of primitive Eskimo verse from the journals of Arctic explorers and others. Others include:
In a Spring Garden, ill. by Ezra Jack Keats, Dial Press, 1965.
The Moment of Wonder, a Collection of Chinese and Japanese Poetry, ill. with paintings by Chinese and Japanese masters, Dial Press, 1964.
Out of the Earth I Sing: Poetry and Songs of Primitive Peoples of the World, Norton, 1968.
LIVINGSTON, MYRA COHN, ed., *A Tune Beyond Us, a Collection of Poetry*, ill. by James J. Spanfeller, Harcourt, 1968. A collection of world-wide traditional and contemporary poetry in its original language as well as English. Others by Livingston include:
Callooh! Callay! Holiday Poems for Young Readers, ill. by Janet Stevens, Atheneum, 1978.
Listen, Children, Listen, an Anthology of Poems for the Very Young, ill. by Trina Schart Hyman, Harcourt, 1972.
O Frabjous Day! Poetry for Holidays and Special Occasions, Atheneum, 1977.
One Little Room, an Everywhere: Poems of Love, ill. by Antonio Frasconi, Atheneum, 1975.
Poems of Christmas, Atheneum, 1980.
Speak Roughly to Your Little Boy, a Collection of Parodies and Burlesques, Together with Original Poems, Chosen and Annotated for Young People, ill. by Joseph Low, Harcourt, 1971.
What a Wonderful Bird the Frog Are: An Assortment of Humorous Poetry and Verse, Harcourt, 1973.
Why Am I Grown So Cold? Poems of the Unknowable, Atheneum, 1982.
LOVE, KATHERINE, ed., *A Pocketful of Rhymes*, ill. by Henrietta Jones, Crowell, 1946. A favorite selection of verse and poetry for younger children.
A Little Laughter, ill. by Walter H. Lorraine, Crowell, 1957.
LUEDERS, EDWARD, and PRIMUS ST. JOHN, comps., *Zero Makes Me Hungry, a Collection of Poems for Today*, art and design by John Reuter Pacyna, Lothrop, 1976. A collection of contemporary poetry on contemporary subjects.
MC DONALD, GERALD D., comp., *A Way of Knowing: A Collection of Poetry for Boys*, ill. by Clare and John Ross, Crowell, 1959. A varied and rich selection appealing to both girls and boys.
MAC KAY, DAVID, *A Flock of Words, an Anthology of Poetry for Children and Others*, collected and introduced and annotated by David MacKay, drawings by

Margery Gill, Harcourt, 1969. A personal and refreshing collection from all countries and ages.

MANNING-SANDERS, RUTH, comp., *A Bundle of Ballads,* ill. by William Stobbs, Lippincott, 1959. A collection of traditional folk ballads.

MEZEY, ROBERT, sel., *Poems from the Hebrew,* etchings by Moishe Smith, Crowell, 1973. Hebrew poetry from Biblical to modern times.

MOORE, LILIAN, comp., *Go with the Poem: A New Collection,* McGraw, 1979. Contemporary subjects treated by contemporary American poets, reflecting children's interests.

MOORE, LILIAN, and JUDITH THURMAN, comps., *To See the World Afresh,* Atheneum, 1974.

MORRISON, LILLIAN, comp., *Sprints and Distances, Sports in Poetry and Poetry in Sport,* ill. by Clare and John Ross, Crowell, 1965. Traditional and contemporary poetry about sports. Others include:
Remember Me When This You See, a New Collection of Autograph Verses, ill. by Marjorie Bauerschmidt, Crowell, 1961.
Touch Blue, Signs, Spells, Love Charms and Chants, Auguries and Old Beliefs in Rhyme, ill. by Doris Lee, Crowell, 1958.
Yours Till Niagara Falls, ill. by Marjorie Bauerschmidt, Crowell, 1950.

MORSE, DAVID, *Grandfather Rock, the New Poetry and the Old,* Delacorte Press, 1972. Rock lyrics and counterparts in classical poetry with commentaries by Morse, a teacher.

NASH, OGDEN, comp., *The Moon is Shining Bright as Day: An Anthology of Good-Humored Verse,* Lippincott, 1953. A traditional selection verse, not all humorous.

NESS, EVALINE, *Amelia Mixed the Mustard and Other Poems,* selected and illustrated by Evaline Ness, Scribner's, 1975. Twenty poems in varying mood about unusual girls.

OPIE, IONA, and PETER, eds., *The Oxford Book of Children's Verse,* Oxford, 1973. More of a reference book for adults than for children.

PARKER, ELINOR, sel., *Four Seasons, Five Senses,* ill. by Diane De Groat, Scribner's, 1974. Traditional verses about the seasons selected by a fine anthologist. Others include:
Here and There, 100 Poems About Places, ill. by Peter Spier, Crowell, 1967.
100 Story Poems, ill. by Henry C. Pitz, Crowell, 1951.
Poets and the English Scene, Scribner's, 1975.
The Singing and the Gold, Poems Translated from World Literature, wood engravings by Clare Leighton, Crowell, 1962.

PLOTZ, HELEN, ed., *Imagination's Other Place: Poems of Science and Mathematics,* ill. by Clare Leighton, Crowell, 1955. A fine anthology chosen by one of the outstanding anthologists for young people. Others include:
As I Walked Out One Evening, a Book of Ballads, Greenwillow, 1976.
The Earth is the Lord's, Poems of the Spirit, ill. with wood engravings by Clare Leighton, Crowell, 1965.
The Gift Outright, America to Her Poets, Greenwillow, 1977.
Life Hungers to Abound, Poems of the Family, Greenwillow, 1978.
The Marvelous Light, Poets and Poetry, Crowell, 1970.
This Powerful Rhyme: A Book of Sonnets, Greenwillow, 1979.
Untune the Sky, Poems of Music and the Dance, ill. by wood engravings by Clare Leighton, Crowell, 1957.

READ, HERBERT, ed., *This Way Delight, a Book of Poetry for the Young,* ill. by Juliet Kepes, Pantheon, 1956. One of the first anthologies to introduce a mixture of traditional and contemporary poetry with a fine essay on "What Is Poetry?"

REED, GWENDOLYN, comp., *Out of the Ark, an Anthology of Animal Verse,* drawings by Gabrille Margules, Atheneum, 1968. A menagerie of creatures from ancient as well as modern times.

REIT, ANN, sel., *Alone Amid All This Noise, a Collection of Women's Poetry,* Four Winds, 1976. Women poets from many ages and countries present "an aspect of the poet's image of herself."

RESNICK, SEYMOUR, ed., *Spanish American Poetry, a Bilingual Selection,* Harvey House, 1964. Notes and an introduction form a solid base for this collection which presents poems in both English and Spanish.

SMITH, JOHN, comp., *My Kind of Verse,* decorations by Uri Shulevitz, Macmillan, 1968. An attractive variety of old and new verse for many ages.

SMITH, WILLIAM JAY, ed., *Poems from France,* ill. by Roger Duvoisin, Crowell, 1967. A bilingual selection from many centuries of French poetry.

STEELE, MARY Q. ed., *The Fifth Day,* decorations by Janina Domanska, Greenwillow, 1978. A collection of poetry about only those things which were present on the fifth day of creation.

TALBOT, TOBY, comp., *Coplas, Folk Poems in Spanish and English,* ill. with woodcuts by Rocco Negri, Four Winds Press, 1972. Brief verse in Spanish, translated into English.

THOMPSON, BLANCHE JENNINGS, ed., *All the Silver Pennies;* combining *Silver Pennies* and *More Silver Pennies,* decorations by Ursula Arndt, Macmillan, 1967. Verse and poetry for children originally selected in 1925 and 1938, reissued in one volume.

TOWNSEND, JOHN ROWE, comp., *Modern Poetry,* ill. with photographs by Barbara Pfeffer, Lippincott, 1974. Three decades of poetry well chosen.

UNTERMEYER, LOUIS, ed., *Rainbow in the Sky,* ill. by Reginald Birch, Harcourt, 1935. More than 500 poems from Mother Goose to Jane Taylor, this is a comfortable collection of familiar rhymes.
This Singing World, ill. by Florence Wyman Ivins, Harcourt, 1923.

WALLACE, DAISY, ed., *Witch Poems,* ill. by Trina Schart Hyman, Holiday House, 1976. A specialized anthology about witches. Others include:
Fairy Poems, ill. by Trina Schart Hyman, Holiday House, 1980.
Giant Poems, ill. by Margot Tomes, Holiday House, 1978.

WEISS, RENEE KAROL, comp., *A Paper Zoo,* ill. by Ellen Raskin, Macmillan, 1968. Poems about animals in a delightful picture book setting.

WILNER, ISABEL, comp., *The Poetry Troupe, an Anthology of Poems to Read Aloud,* decorations by the author, Scribner's, 1977. Poetry to read aloud, chosen by the anthologist for performance in the schools.

WITHERS, CARL, comp., *A Rocket in My Pocket, the Rhymes and Chants of Young Americans,* ill. by Susanne Suba, Holt, 1948. Four hundred rhymes, chants, games, and jingles collected from American children from the cities to the suburbs and rural areas.

WOOD, NANCY, comp., *Hollering Sun,* photographs by Myron Wood, Simon & Schuster, 1972. Ideas and thoughts of the Taos Indians interpreted by the author as "poems, aphorisms, and sayings." Not all poetry. *War Cry on a Prayer Feather: Prose and Poetry of the Ute Indians,* Doubleday, 1979.

Folk Tales

Worldwide Collections: General

ASSOCIATION FOR CHILDHOOD EDUCATION, *Told Under the Green Umbrella,* ill. by Grace Gilkison, Macmillan, 1962. Twenty-six excellent tales for reading aloud or storytelling.   5–7

BAKER, AUGUSTA, comp., *The Golden Lynx and Other Tales,* ill. by Johannes Troyer, Lippincott, 1960. *The Talking Tree and Other Stories,* ill. by Johannes Troyer, Lippincott, 1955. The compiler, a storyteller of distinction, selected from her own repertoire and from out-of-print sources forty-four stories of proven interest to children.   8–11

CHILD STUDY ASSOCIATION OF AMERICA, *Castles and Dragons: Read-to-Yourself Fairy Tales for Boys and Girls,* ill. by William Pène du Bois, Crowell, 1958. Eighteen amusingly illustrated stories selected for their interest to the young independent reader.   9–12

COLE, JOANNA, comp., *Best-Loved Folktales of the World,* Doubleday, 1982. Two hundred old favorites and less known stories, arranged by broad geographical area.   9–11

DE LA MARE, WALTER, *Tales Told Again,* ill. by Alan Howard, Knopf, 1959. Felicitously worded versions of nineteen widely known stories. A valuable book for the storyteller.   9–12

DORSON, RICHARD, ed. *Folktales Told Around the World,* University of Chicago, 1975. Motif and type indexes add to the usefulness of this well-chosen selection of over a hundred stories.   10–13

FENNER, PHYLLIS R., comp., *Adventure, Rare and Magical,* ill. by Henry C. Pitz, Knopf, 1945. *Giants and Witches and a Dragon or Two,* ill. by Henry C. Pitz, Knopf, 1943. Excellent collections for the reader and storyteller.   9–12

FILLMORE, PARKER, *The Shepherd's Nosegay, Stories from Finland and Czechoslovakia,* ed. by Katherine Love, ill. by Enrico Arno, Harcourt, 1958. Favorites selected from three of the author's out-of-print books.   9–13

JACOBS, JOSEPH, *The Pied Piper and Other Tales,* ill. by James Hill, Macmillan, 1963. An attractive edition with good illustrations and large print.   10–12

LANG, ANDREW, ed., *Fifty Favorite Fairy Tales,* ill. by Margery Gill, Watts, 1964. Selected from the many volumes collected by this great folklorist. (Andrew Lang's "color fairy books" are still in print and include such titles as *Blue Fairy Book, Crimson Fairy Book, Green Fairy Book,* and *Yellow Fairy Book.* McGraw-Hill and Dover have undertaken publication of facsimile editions of the twelve original titles. Users should be aware that a few stories in the original editions are unacceptable to minority groups.) Note new editions edited by the British critic Brian Alderson, published by Kestrel/Viking.   9–12

MANNING-SANDERS, RUTH, comp., *A Choice of Magic,* ill. by Robin Jacques, Dutton, 1971. Most of the tales, retold in fluent style, are from Europe.   9–11 *Tortoise Tales,* ill. by Donald Chaffin, Nelson, 1974. Short tales particularly useful for young children.   5–8

SHEEHAN, ETHNA, comp., *Folk and Fairy Tales from Around the World,* ill. by Mircea Vasiliu, Dodd, 1970. Includes suggestions for the storyteller.   9–11

UNITED NATIONS WOMEN'S GUILD, *Ride with the Sun: An Anthology of Folk Tales and Stories from the United Nations,* ed. by Harold Courlander, ill. by Roger Duvoisin, McGraw, 1955. Each of the sixty tales included was approved by the U.N. delegate of the country from which it comes.   10–12

WITHERS, CARL, comp., *A World of Nonsense; Strange and Humorous Tales from Many Lands,* ill. by John E. Johnson, Holt, 1968. An outstanding collection of nonsense stories.   9–11

Worldwide Collections: Special Topics

BELTING, NATALIA M., *Cat Tales,* ill. by Leo Summers, Holt, 1959. *The Earth Is on a Fish's Back: Tales of Beginnings,* ill. by Esta Nesbitt, Holt, 1965. Two excellent collections.   8–12

DE LA MARE, WALTER, *Animal Stories,* Scribner's, 1940. This valuable collection for storytellers contains forty-two stories and forty-six rhymes and ballads about animals.   10–up

JAGENDORF, M. A., and C. H. TILLHAGEN, *The Gypsies' Fiddle and Other Gypsy Tales,* ill. by Hans Helweg, Vanguard, 1956. A unique and useful collection of stories gathered from Gypsy sources.   9–12

LEACH, MARIA, *How the People Sang the Mountains Up: How and Why Stories,* ill. by Glen Rounds, Viking, 1967. Imaginative tales from primitive cultures, retold by one of America's well-known folklorists. Sources and backgrounds are explained in the notes.   9–12

LURIE, ALISON, ad., *Clever Gretchen and Other Forgotten Folktales,* ill. by Margot Tomes, Crowell, 1980. Stories that stress the valor and ingenuity of their female protagonists.   9–11

MC CARTY, TONI, comp., *The Skull in the Snow and Other Folktales,* ill. by Katherine Coville, Delacorte, 1981. A lively collection of tales about the female folk hero.   9–11

MANNING-SANDERS, RUTH, *A Book of Charms and Changelings,* ill. by Robin Jacques, Dutton, 1972.   9–11 *A Book of Mermaids,* ill. by Robin Jacques, Dutton, 1968.

A Book of Witches, ill. by Robin Jacques, Dutton, 1966. Excellently illustrated collections.   8–12

The Red King and the Witch: Gypsy Folk and Fairy Tales, ill. by Victor G. Ambrus, Roy, 1965. Entertaining versions of familiar tales.   9–11

A Book of Spooks and Spectres, Dutton, 1979.

MINARD, ROSEMARY, ed., *Womenfolk and Fairytales,* ill. by Suzanna Klein, Houghton, 1975. Eighteen tales of clever, decisive women. Time-tested material in a timely anthology.   9–11

SAWYER, RUTH, *Joy to the World: Christmas Legends,* ill. by Trina Schart Hyman, Little, 1966.

The Long Christmas, ill. by Valenti Angelo, Viking, 1941.

Two fine collections of stories well told by a master storyteller.   8–12

Europe

Jewish Folk Tales

HIRSH, MARILYN, ad., *Could Anything Be Worse?* ill. by author, Holiday, 1974. A humorous tale of rabbinical wisdom.   5–8

SIMON, SOLOMON, *The Wise Men of Helm,* ill. by Lillian Fischel, Behrman, 1945. Funny tales about a mythical Jewish community in Poland.   10–12

SINGER, ISAAC BASHEVIS, *The Fools of Chelm and Their History,* ill. by Uri Shulevitz, tr. by the author and Elizabeth Shub, Farrar, 1973.   10–12

When Shlemiel Went to Warsaw and Other Stories, tr. by Elizabeth Shub and the author, ill. by Margot Zemach, Farrar, 1968. Eight lively, appealing stories.   9–up

Zlateh the Goat and Other Stories, tr. by Elizabeth Shub and the author, ill. by Maurice Sendak, Harper, 1966. Seven skillfully told stories.   10–up

Naftali the Storyteller and His Horse, Sus, and Other Stories, ill. by Margot Zemach, Farrar, 1976.   10–up

ZEMACH, MARGOT, ad., *It Could Always Be Worse: a Yiddish Folk Tale,* ill. by author, Farrar, 1976. A crowded house makes a complaining man realize how much better it was before he took a rabbi's advice.   5–8

British Isles: General Collections

MANNING-SANDERS, RUTH, ed., *A Bundle of Ballads,* ill. by William Stobbs, Oxford (in U.S. by Lippincott), 1959. A fine compilation of ballads from the British Isles.   11–15

PICARD, BARBARA LEONIE, *Tales of the British People,* ill. by Eric Fraser, Criterion, 1961. Nine stories which represent the lore of the various peoples who invaded the British Isles.   10–12

♪ RITCHIE, JEAN, *From Fair to Fair: Folk Songs of the British Isles,* photos by George Pickow, piano arrangements by Edward Tripp, Walck, 1966. Sixteen songs woven together by a story about Jock, a wandering minstrel. The piano and guitar arrangements add to the value of this volume.   9–13

British Isles: Cornwall and Wales

CLIMO, SHIRLEY, ad. *Piskies, Spriggans, and Other Magic Beings: Tales from the Droll-Teller,* ill. by Joyce dos Santos, Crowell, 1981. Tales of the ancient, magical beings that haunt the moors and caves of Cornwall.   9–11

JONES, GWYN, *Welsh Legends and Folk-Tales,* ill. by Joan Kiddell-Monroe, Walck, 1955. Retellings of ancient sagas as well as folk and fairy tales are included.   11–14

MANNING-SANDERS, RUTH, *Peter and the Piskies: Cornish Folk and Fairy Tales,* ill. by Raymond Briggs, Roy, 1966. A sprightly and diversified group of Celtic tales filled with the deeds of the spriggans, demons, knockers, piskies, and other supernatural beings.   8–11

PUGH, ELLEN, *Tales from the Welsh Hills,* ill. by Joan Sandin, Dodd, 1968. Tales told by the author's grandmother and nicely adapted from Mrs. Pugh's notes.   9–11

SHUB, ELIZABETH, ad., *Seeing Is Believing,* ill. by Rachel Isadora, Greenwillow, 1979. A Cornish and an Irish tale are simply told for young readers.   6–8

TREGARTHEN, ENYS, *Piskey Folk; A Book of Cornish Legends,* collected by Elizabeth Yates, Day, 1940. A rare compilation of Cornish tales. Although out of print, the book is available in many public libraries.   9–11

ZEMACH, HARVE, ad., *Duffy and the Devil,* ill. by Margot Zemach, Farrar, 1973. An entertaining Cornish version of "Rumpelstiltskin" and winner of the Caldecott Medal.   5–8

British Isles: England

BROOKE, L. LESLIE, ed., *The Golden Goose Book,* ill. by editor, Warne, n.d. Contains "The Golden Goose," "The Three Bears," "The Three Little Pigs," and "Tom Thumb."   5–7

CARRICK, MALCOLM, ad., *The Wise Men of Gotham,* ill. by author, Viking, 1975. A selection of tales from the chapbook version of *The Foles of Gotyam.*   9–11

CHAUCER, GEOFFREY, *Chanticleer and the Fox,* adapted and ill. by Barbara Cooney, T. Crowell, 1958. Caldecott Medal.   6–9

CROSSLEY-HOLLAND, KEVIN, *The Pedlar of Swaffham,* ill. by Margaret Gordon, Seabury, 1971. A dream comes true.   9–11

Dick Whittington and His Cat, adapted and ill. by Marcia Brown, Scribner's, 1950.   4–8

HAVILAND, VIRGINIA, ad., *Favorite Fairy Tales Told in England,* ill. by Bettina, Little, 1959. Bland and simplified retellings of six folk tales.   8–10

JACOBS, JOSEPH, ed., *English Folk and Fairy Tales,* ill. by John Batten, Putnam, n.d. A good source for the favorite tales, appealing in format and illustration.   9–12

King of the Cats, ad. and ill. by Paul Galdone, Houghton, 1980. This version has the dialect removed.   5–8

Mr. Miacca, an English Folktale, ill. by Evaline Ness, Holt, 1967.   5–7

Tom Tit Tot, ill. by Evaline Ness, Scribner's, 1965.   5–8

♪ *London Bridge Is Falling Down,* ill. by Ed Emberley, Little, 1967. The verses, the tune, the rules, and the historical background of this favorite game accented with glowing illustrations.   5–8

♪ *London Bridge Is Falling Down!* ill. by Peter Spier, Doubleday, 1967. Eighteenth-century London lives again in this splendid picture book.   6–8

SEWALL, MARCIA, ill. *Master of All Masters; An English Folktale,* Atlantic, 1972. The master's a Ms!   8–10

STEEL, FLORA ANNIE, *English Fairy Tales,* ill. by Arthur Rackham, Macmillan, 1962. First published in 1918. Although the style is somewhat more formal and literary than that of Joseph Jacobs, the book is an excellent one for both readers and storytellers.   9–12

British Isles: Ireland

COLUM, PADRAIC, *The King of Ireland's Son,* ill. by Willy Pogány, Macmillan, 1962, 1944, 1916. Each exciting story in this volume is concerned with the daring deeds of the King's son.   10–12

DANAHER, KEVIN, *Folktales of the Irish Countryside,* ill. by Harold Berson, White, 1970. Delightful style and wit, and a good source for storytelling.   10–12

HAVILAND, VIRGINIA, ed., *Favorite Fairy Tales Told in Ireland,* retold from Irish storytellers, ill. by Artur Marokvia, Little, 1961.   7–10

JACOBS, JOSEPH, ed., *Celtic Fairy Tales,* ill. by John D. Batten, Putnam, n.d.

More Celtic Fairy Tales, ill. by John D. Batten, Putnam, n.d.

Both volumes include Welsh, Scotch, Cornish, and Irish tales.   9–12

Munachar and Manachar; An Irish Story, ill. by Anne Rockwell, T. Crowell, 1970. Nonsense humor.   5–7

MACMANUS, SEUMAS, *The Bold Heroes of Hungry Hill,* ill. by Jay Chollick, Farrar, 1951.

Hibernian Nights, ill. by Paul Kennedy, Macmillan, 1963.

Fascinating tales which the author collected. Three out-of-print collections worth seeking in libraries are: *Donegal Fairy Stories, Donegal Wonder Book,* and *In Chimney Corners.*   10–up

O'FAOLAIN, EILEEN, *Children of the Salmon and Other Irish Folktales,* selected and tr. by the author, ill. by Trina Schart Hyman, Little, 1965.

Irish Sagas and Folk-Tales, ill. by Joan Kiddell-Monroe, Walck, 1954.

Two useful books. The cadence of the Gaelic has been preserved in the latter.   10–up

PICARD, BARBARA LEONIE, *Celtic Tales: Legends of Tall Warriors and Old Enchantments,* ill. by John G. Galsworthy, Criterion, 1965. Source and background are given for each story.   10–12

YOUNG, ELLA, *The Unicorn with Silver Shoes,* ill. by Robert Lawson, McKay, 1957. The tale of Ballor, the King's son, and his adventures in the Land of the Ever Young is told in beautifully cadenced prose.   9–12

British Isles: Scotland

HAVILAND, VIRGINIA, ed., *Favorite Fairy Tales Told in Scotland,* ill. by Adrienne Adams, Little, 1963. Six action-packed stories retold with simplicity.   7–10

NIC LEODHAS, SORCHE (pseud. of LeClaire Alger), *By Loch and by Lin: Tales of the Scottish Ballads,* ill. by Vera Bock, Holt, 1969.

Claymore and Kilt: Tales of Scottish Kings and Castles, ill. by Leo and Diane Dillon, Holt, 1967.

Gaelic Ghosts, ill. by Nonny Hogrogian, Holt, 1964.

Heather and Broom: Tales of the Scottish Highlands, ill. by Consuelo Joerns, Holt, 1960.

Sea-Spell and Moor Magic: Tales of the Western Isles, ill. by Vera Bock, Holt, 1968.

Thistle and Thyme: Tales and Legends from Scotland, ill. by Evaline Ness, Holt, 1962.

These delightful volumes have made a great body of Scottish lore accessible to children.   9–12

Sorche Nic Leodhas has also written for younger children four picture books based on folklore of Scotland: *All in the Morning Early,* ill. by Evaline Ness, 1963; *Always Room for One More,* ill. by Nonny Hogrogian, 1965; *Kellyburn Braes,* ill. by Evaline Ness, 1968; *The Laird of Cockpen,* ill. by Adrienne Adams, 1969. All published by Holt.   5–8

SHEPPARD-JONES, ELISABETH, *Scottish Legendary Tales,* ill. by Paul Hogarth, Nelson, 1962. An extensive compilation of stories about the fairy people and other small folk of Scotland.   10–13

WILSON, BARBARA KER, *Scottish Folk-Tales and Legends,* ill. by Joan Kiddell-Monroe, Walck, 1954. Contains examples of many types of Scottish folk tales.   11–13

Finland

BOWMAN, JAMES CLOYD, and MARGERY BIANCO, *Seven Silly Wise Men,* from a tr. by Aili Kolehmainen, ill. by John Faulkner, Whitman, 1964. A picture-book version of a story often called "The Wise Men of Holmola."   5–8

Tales from a Finnish Tupa, from a tr. by Aili Kolehmainen, ill. by Laura Bannon, Whitman, 1936, 1964. An interesting group of Finnish tales.   10–14

France

BERSON, HAROLD, ad., *How the Devil Gets His Due,* ill. by author, Crown, 1972. Adapted from the story in *Le Meunier Garçon,* this is a tale in which justice triumphs.   9–10

The Thief Who Hugged a Moonbeam, ill. by author, Seabury, 1972. First published in the 12th century, the story of a gullible knave trapped by his intended victim.   8–10

BROWN, MARCIA, *Stone Soup,* ill. by author, Scribner's, 1947.   5–8

CARLSON, NATALIE, ad., *King of the Cats and Other Tales,* ill. by David Frampton, Doubleday, 1980. Eight stories about the legendary creatures of Brittany.
                                                                  8–10

D'AULNOY, COMTESSE, *The White Cat and Other Old French Fairy Tales,* ed. and tr. by Rachel Field, Macmillan, 1967, 1928. A fine collection that has long deserved republication.   8–11

LANG, ANDREW, *The Twelve Dancing Princesses,* ill. by Adrienne Adams, Holt, 1966. This version of the tale, drawn from French sources, is more elaborate and fanciful in tone than that recorded by the Grimms.
                                                                  5–9

PERRAULT, CHARLES, *Cinderella; or The Little Glass Slipper,* ill. by Marcia Brown, Scribner's, 1954. Caldecott Medal.   5–9

Perrault's Complete Fairy Tales, tr. by A. E. Johnson and others, ill. by W. Heath Robinson, Dodd, 1961. This edition is not very attractive to children, but adults should know of it because the "moralities" of Perrault are included and the illustrations are excellent.   10–up

Puss in Boots, ill. by Marcia Brown, Scribner's, 1952.   6–9

Puss in Boots, adapted and ill. by Hans Fischer, Harcourt, 1959.   5–8

PICARD, BARBARA LEONIE, *French Legends, Tales, and Fairy Stories,* ill. by Joan Kiddell-Monroe, Walck, 1955. A rich source of French folklore.   10–14

Germany

A Boy Went Out to Gather Pears, ill. by Felix Hoffmann, Harcourt, 1966. An outstanding pictorial interpretation of this cumulative verse-tale.   5–8

GRIMM, JACOB and WILHELM, *The Brave Little Tailor,* adapted by Audrey Claus, ill. by E. Probst, McGraw, 1965.   6–9

The Bearskinner, ill. by Felix Hoffmann, Atheneum, 1978.   5–8

The Brothers Grimm Popular Folk Tales, tr. by Brian Alderson, ill. by Michael Foreman, Doubleday, 1978.
                                                                  9–11

The Complete Grimm's Fairy Tales, ill. by Josef Scharl, Pantheon, 1974. A reissue of the 1944 edition based on the Margaret Hunt translation. Includes a full folkloristic commentary by Joseph Campbell, and is useful to adults as well as children.   9–11

The Fisherman and His Wife, ill. by Margot Zemach, Norton, 1966.   6–8

The Four Clever Brothers, ill. by Felix Hoffmann, Harcourt, 1967.   5–8

Grimm's Fairy Tales, based on the Frances Jenkins Olcott edition of the English translation by Margaret Hunt, Follett, 1968. This beautiful edition is notable for its illustrations, which were chosen from artwork submitted by children of many nations. Frances Clarke Sayers, author and storyteller of distinction, has contributed an eloquent foreword.   7–up

Grimm's Tales for Young and Old, tr. by Ralph Manheim, Doubleday, 1977.   9–11

The Juniper Tree and Other Tales from Grimm, selected by Lore Segal and Maurice Sendak, tr. by Lore Segal with four tales tr. by Randall Jarrell, ill. by Maurice Sendak, Farrar, 1973. A two-volume edition distinguished both for the translations and the illustrations.   9–up

Rapunzel, ill. by Felix Hoffmann, Harcourt, 1961.
                                                                  6–8

The Seven Ravens, ill. by Felix Hoffmann, Harcourt, 1963.   6–9

Rapunzel, ad. by Barbara Rogasky, ill. by Trina Schart Hyman, Holiday, 1982.   8–10

The Shoemaker and the Elves, ill. by Adrienne Adams, Scribner's, 1960.   5–9

The Sleeping Beauty, ill. by Felix Hoffmann, Harcourt, 1960.   6–11

Snow-White and the Seven Dwarfs, tr. by Randall Jarrell, ill. by Nancy Ekholm Burkert, Farrar, 1972.
                                                                  8–11

Tales from Grimm, freely tr. and ill. by Wanda Gág, Coward, 1936.   8–11

JAGENDORF, M. A., *Tyll Ulenspiegel's Merry Pranks,* ill. by Fritz Eichenberg, Vanguard, 1938. A large collection of tales about the exploits of that legendary figure who championed the cause of the underdog and embarrassed his enemies with jokes and pranks.   9–11

PICARD, BARBARA LEONIE, *German Hero-Sagas and Folk-Tales,* ill. by Joan Kiddell-Monroe, Walck, 1958. Despite the title of this volume from the Oxford Myths and Legends series, the content is predominantly folklore.   10–12

VAN WOERKOM, DOROTHY, ad., *The Queen Who Couldn't Bake Gingerbread,* ill. by Paul Galdone, Knopf, 1975. A romping tale of role reversal, with amusing pictures.   5–8

Italy

BASILE, GIOVANNI BATTISTA, *Old Neapolitan Fairy Tales,* selected and retold by Rose Laura Mincieli, ill. by Beni Montresor, Knopf, 1963. These stories are retold from a seventeenth-century collection, *Il Pentamerone.* Children will enjoy the variants of "Cinderella" and "Rapunzel."   8–10

CALVINO, ITALO, ad., *Italian Folk Tales,* trans. by George Martin, Harcourt, 1980. A robust and often funny anthology representing all regions.   10–up

DE PAOLA, TOMIE, ad., *The Prince of the Dolomites,* ill. by author, Harcourt, 1980. A love story as well as a "why" story that explains the beauty of the Dolomite mountains.   5–8

HAVILAND, VIRGINIA, *Favorite Fairy Tales Told in Italy,* ill. by Evaline Ness, Little, 1965. Two of the six tales in this collection are variations on the themes of "Cinderella" and "The Three Little Pigs."   7–11

JAGENDORF, MORITZ ADOLF, *The Priceless Cats and Other Italian Folk Stories,* ill. by Gioia Fiammenghi, Vanguard, 1956. An attractive, gaily illustrated collection which children will enjoy reading for themselves.
                                                                  10–13

VITTORINI, DOMENICO, *Old Italian Tales,* ill. by Kathryn L. Fligg, McKay, 1958. Twenty short tales alive with humor and wisdom.   7–12

Poland

BORSKI, LUCIA M., and KATE B. MILLER, *The Jolly Tailor, and Other Fairy Tales Translated from the Polish*, ill. by Kazimir Klepacki, McKay, 1928, 1956. An excellent source for the storyteller, but tales should be selected from this collection with discretion, for some may offend minority groups.   9–12

DOMANSKA, JANINA, ad., *King Krakus and the Dragon*, ill. by author, Greenwillow, 1979. A clever man in ancient times outwits a dragon in this beautifully illustrated story.   5–8

PELLOWSKI, ANNE, ad., *The Nine Crying Dolls: A Story from Poland*, ill. by Charles Mikolaycak, Philomel, 1980. Papercut collage pictures illustrate a tale about the crying epidemic among Polish babies.   5–8

TURSKA, KRYSTYNA, ad., *The Woodcutter's Duck*, ill. by author, Macmillan, 1973. Nicely retold and beautifully illustrated, a story of virtue rewarded.   5–8

Scandinavian Countries

ASBJÖRNSEN, PETER, ad., *The Squire's Bride*, ill. by Marcia Sewall, Atheneum, 1975. A Norwegian tale about a girl who fools an obdurate, elderly suitor has comedy in text and pictures.   8–10

ASBJÖRNSEN, PETER C., and JÖRGEN E. MOE, *East of the Sun and West of the Moon, and Other Tales*, ill. by Tom Vroman, Macmillan, 1963. The unsurpassed tales of Scandinavia that were collected in mid-nineteenth century by the scholarly authors and translated by Sir George Dasent.   10–14
Norwegian Folk Tales, tr. by Pat Shaw Iversen and Carl Norman, ill. by Erik Werenskiold and Theodor Kittelsen, Viking, 1960. Excellent stories and some of the incomparable illustrations of earlier Scandinavian artists. Invaluable to the storyteller.   10–up
The Three Billy-Goats Gruff, ill. by Marcia Brown, Harcourt, 1957.   7–9

D'AULAIRE, INGRI and EDGAR PARIN, eds., *East of the Sun and West of the Moon*, ill. by eds., Viking, 1969. Reissue of an earlier edition, also based upon work of P. C. Asbjörnsen and J. E. Moe.   8–12

HATCH, MARY C., *13 Danish Tales*, ill. by Edgun (pseud.), Harcourt, 1947.
More Danish Tales, ill. by Edgun (pseud.), Harcourt, 1949.
Two fine compilations of amusing and wittily illustrated stories.   9–12

JONES, GWYN, *Scandinavian Legends and Folk-Tales*, ill. by Joan Kiddell-Monroe, Walck, 1956. Contains a few well-known stories along with hero tales and some unusual examples of folklore.   8–12

LUNDBERGH, HOLGER, tr., *Great Swedish Fairy Tales*, ill. by John Bauer, Delacorte/Seymour Lawrence, 1973. The tales have a gentle quality that is echoed by the romantic pictures by one of Sweden's greatest illustrators.   9–11

THORNE-THOMSEN, GUDRUN, *East o' the Sun and West o' the Moon*, rev. ed., ill. by Gregory Orloff, Row, 1946. Though out of print, this book is included because it is an outstanding rendition of Norwegian folk tales by a storyteller who represented the highest and most artistic achievement in her field. It is available in many libraries.   9–13

Spain

BOGGS, RALPH STEELE, and MARY GOULD DAVIS, *Three Golden Oranges and Other Spanish Folk Tales*, ill. by Emma Brock, McKay, 1936, 1964. Romantic and exciting stories for older children. Includes one remarkable ghost story.   10–12

DAVIS, ROBERT, *Padre Porko, the Gentlemanly Pig*, ill. by Fritz Eichenberg, Holiday, 1948. The activities of the kindly pig who delights in helping his friends, both human and animal, are retold in eleven tales.   8–12

DUFF, MAGGIE, ad., *The Princess and the Pumpkin*, ill. by Catherine Stock, Macmillan, 1980. A frothy Majorcan tale about a princess who could not laugh.   5–8

HAVILAND, VIRGINIA, ed., *Favorite Fairy Tales Told in Spain*, ill. by Barbara Cooney, Little, 1963. Six of the best-loved stories of the Spanish people.   7–10

Turkey[2]

DOWNING, CHARLES, *Tales of the Hodja*, ill. by William Papas, Walck, 1965. Nasreddin Hodja, the invincible, half-wise, half-foolish personality from Turkey, is the hero of each of these short tales.   8–11

EKREM, SELMA, comp., *Turkish Fairy Tales*, ill. by Liba Bayrak, Van Nostrand, 1964. These twelve Turkish tales, never before published in the U.S., were heard by the Turkish-born author from her nurse in Istanbul.   9–12

KELSEY, ALICE GEER, *Once the Hodja*, ill. by Frank Dobias, Longmans, 1943. Humorous tales about Nasred-Din Hodja, who combines wisdom and foolishness but always manages to come out on top.   8–11

WALKER, BARBARA K., *Hilili and Dilili*, adapted from a tr. by Mrs. Neriman Hizir, ill. by Bill Barss, Follett, 1964.
Just Say Hic! adapted from a tr. by Mrs. Neriman Hizir, ill. by Don Bolognese, Follett, 1965.   5–7
The Round Sultan and the Straight Answer, ill. by Friso Henstra, Parents, 1970. A humorous tale of sage advice.   5–8

Union of Soviet Socialist Republics[3]

AFANASIEV, ALEKSANDR, *Soldier and Tsar in the Forest; A Russian Tale*, tr. by Richard Lourie, ill. by Uri Shulevitz, Farrar, 1972. A lively adaptation.   5–8

AFANASIEV, ALEKSANDR, comp., *Russian Folk Tales*, ill. by Ivan Bilibin, tr. by Robert Chandler, Shambhala/Random, 1980. Superb pictures illustrate the great basic Russian collection.   9–11

---

[2]Included in this section are stories from Asian Turkey.

[3]Included in this section are stories from Asian sections of the Union of Soviet Socialist Republics.

DANIELS, GUY, tr., *Foma the Terrible; A Russian Folktale,* ill. by Imero Gobbato, Delacorte, 1970. A merry tale adapted from the Afanasyev collection.   5–8

DE REGNIERS, BEATRICE, ad., *Everyone Is Good for Something,* ill. by Margot Tomes, Houghton/Clarion, 1980. A Slavic folk tale, retold with zest and humor, shows how a child gains self-esteem.   7–8

DEUTSCH, BABETTE, and AVRAHM YARMOLINSKY, eds., *Tales of Faraway Folk,* ill. by Irene Lorentowicz, Harper, 1952.
More Tales of Faraway Folk, ill. by Janina Domanska, Harpers, 1963.
These unique collections come mainly from Russia and other Asiatic lands.   7–11

DOWNING, CHARLES, *Russian Tales and Legends,* ill. by Joan Kiddell-Monroe, Walck, 1957. Authoritative versions of Russian tales.   9–11

DURHAM, MAE, *Tit for Tat and Other Latvian Folk Tales,* retold from the tr. of Skaidrite Rubene-Koo, ill. by Harriet Pincus, Harcourt, 1967. Twenty-two distinctive stories which portray the Latvian peasant's philosophy of life.   9–11

GINSBURG, MIRRA, tr., *The Kaha Bird; Tales from the Steppes of Central Asia,* ill. by Richard Cuffari, Crown, 1971. Non-Russian tales from Russia are told with vigor.   9–11
How Wilka Went to Sea, ill. by Charles Mikolaycak, Crown, 1975. Nine tales of creatures with magical powers.   9–11

HODGES, MARGARET, comp., *The Little Humpbacked Horse,* ill. by Chris Conover, Farrar, 1980. A fluent retelling of the adventures through which Ivan the Fool became Ivan the Tsar.   8–10

HOGROGIAN, NONNY, ill., *One Fine Day,* Macmillan, 1971. A cumulative tale with pictures, based on an Armenian tale, awarded the Caldecott Medal.
4–7

HUGGINS, EDWARD, ad., *Blue and Green Wonders and Other Latvian Tales,* ill. by Owen Wood, Simon, 1971. Told with true folktale cadence, a varied selection.
9–11

RANSOME, ARTHUR, *Old Peter's Russian Tales,* ill. by Dimitri Mitrokhin, Nelson, 1917. This is the teacher's most practical source for the Russian tales.   8–12
The Fool of the World and the Flying Ship; A Russian Tale, retold; ill. by Uri Shulevitz, Farrar, 1968. Caldecott Medal.   8–11

TASHJIAN, VIRGINIA A., *Once There Was and Was Not,* based on stories by H. Toumanian, ill. by Nonny Hogrogian, Little, 1966. A captivating array of Armenian tales, all of which deserve to be better known.
9–12
Three Apples Fell from Heaven, ill. by Nonny Hogrogian, Little, 1971.   9–12

TOLSTOY, LEO, *Russian Stories and Legends,* tr. by Louise and Aylmer Maude, ill. by Alexander Alexeieff, Pantheon, 1967. Eight folk tales grouped around the theme of brotherhood.   10–up

WHITNEY, THOMAS P., tr. *Vasilisa the Beautiful,* ill. by Nonny Hogrogian, Macmillan, 1970. A version of the Cinderella story from the Afanasyev collection.
9–11

In a Certain Kingdom; Twelve Russian Fairy Tales, ill. by Dieter Lange, Macmillan, 1972. Illustrations in woodcut style echo the sturdy, humorous qualities of traditional tales.   9–11

WYNDHAM, LEE, comp., *Tales the People Tell in Russia,* ill. by Andrew Antal, Messner, 1970. Told with gusto.
8–10

Other Countries of Europe

AIKEN, JOAN, comp., *The Kingdom Under the Sea and Other Stories,* ill. by Jan Pienkowski, Cape, 1979. Eleven folk tales from Eastern Europe are told in a graceful, witty style.   10–12

AMBRUS, VICTOR G., *Brave Soldier Janosh,* ill. by author, Harcourt, 1967.
The Three Poor Tailors, ill. by author, Harcourt, 1965. Two Hungarian tales. Both books are notable for glowing illustrations.   5–9

CURCIJA, PRODANOVIC NADA, *Heroes of Serbia,* ill. by Dusan Ristic, Walck, 1964. An excellent contribution to the study of folklore. Scholarly comments on background and sources.   11–up
Yugoslav Folk-Tales, ill. by Joan Kiddell-Monroe, Walck, 1957. One of the books in the Oxford Myths and Legends series.   10–14

DEUTSCH, BABETTE, and YARMOLINSKY, AVRAHM, comp., *Tales of Faraway Folk,* ill. by Trena Lorentowicz, Harper, 1952. Ten well-told tales from Eastern Europe and Central Asia.   8–11

MANNING-SANDERS, RUTH, *Damian and the Dragon; Modern Greek Folk-Tales,* ill. by William Papas, Roy, 1966. Superior and extremely interesting retellings of several gay tales in which the brave, steadfast, and wise are aided by a variety of magical creatures.
9–11

MÜLLER-GUGGENBÜHL, FRITZ, *Swiss-Alpine Folk-Tales,* tr. by Katharine Potts, ill. by Joan Kiddell-Monroe, Walck, 1958. One of the collections in the useful Oxford Myths and Legends series.   10–14

PRIDHAM, RADOST, *A Gift from the Heart: Folk Tales from Bulgaria,* ill. by Pauline Baynes, World, 1967. A good collection of tales that reflect the Oriental and Western heritage of the Bulgarian people. The introduction provides background for the stories.   9–11

SEVERO, EMOKE DE PAPP, tr., *The Good-Hearted Youngest Brother,* ill. by Diane Goode, Bradbury, 1981. A Hungarian folk tale shows kindness rewarded.
8–10

STALDER, VALERIE, ed., *Even the Devil Is Afraid of a Shrew; A Folktale of Lapland,* ill. by Richard Brown, Addison, 1972. Told with quiet, sly humor.   5–8

Africa

AARDEMA, VERNA, *Behind the Back of the Mountain; Black Folktales from Southern Africa,* ill. by Leo and Diane Dillon, Dial, 1973. Smoothly written, a varied collection.   9–11
Tales from the Story Hat: African Folk Tales, ill. by Elton Fax, Coward, 1960. In West Africa the storyteller wears a broad-brimmed hat from which dangle tiny objects representing his tales of magic, wonder, and fun.   7–11
Why Mosquitoes Buzz in People's Ears, ill. by Leo and Diane Dillon, Dial, 1974. A "why" story that won the Caldecott Award.   5–8

APPIAH, PEGGY, *Ananse the Spider: Tales from an Ashanti Village*, ill. by Peggy Wilson, Pantheon, 1966. These interesting stories are a trifle more formal than those of Courlander and will appeal to older readers.
11–14

ARKHURST, JOYCE COOPER, *The Adventures of Spider: West African Folk Tales*, ill. by Jerry Pinkney, Little, 1964. A book of amusing folk tales, dashingly illustrated, which many youngsters will be able to read for themselves.
7–10

BRYAN, ASHLEY, comp., *Beat the Story Drum, Pum-Pum*, ill. by author, Atheneum, 1980. Humorous animal tales, strikingly illustrated.
8–10

BURTON, W. F. P., *The Magic Drum; Tales from Central Africa*, ill. by Ralph Thompson, Criterion, 1962. Thirty-eight tales heard from storytellers in Congo villages during the author's service as a missionary.
9–12

CARPENTER, FRANCES, *African Wonder Tales*, ill. by Joseph Escourido, Doubleday, 1963. Twenty-four tales from various parts of Africa. Includes a pronunciation guide for African names.
8–11

COURLANDER, HAROLD, *The King's Drum and Other African Stories*, ill. by Enrico Arno, Harcourt, 1962.
9–11

COURLANDER, HAROLD, and GEORGE HERZOG, *The Cow-Tail Switch, and Other West African Stories*, ill. by Madye Lee Chastain, Holt, 1947.
10–12

COURLANDER, HAROLD, and ALBERT PREMPEH, comp., *The Hat-Shaking Dance, and Other Tales from the Gold Coast*, ill. by Enrico Arno, Harcourt, 1957. From the Ashanti, twenty-one stories about the trickster-hero Anansi.
9–11

DAVIS, RUSSELL, and BRENT ASHABRANNER, *The Lion's Whiskers: Tales of High Africa*, ill. by James Teason, Little, 1959. Thirty-one tales from Ethiopia and its borderlands.
11–15

FUJA, ABAYOMI, comp., *Fourteen Hundred Cowries; And Other African Tales*, ill. by Ademola Olugebefola, Lothrop, 1971. An anthology of Yoruba tales.
9–12

GILSTRAP, ROBERT, and IRENE ESTABROOK, *The Sultan's Fool and Other North African Tales*, ill. by Robert Greco, Holt, 1958. Eleven stories concerned with the deeds of sultans, caliphs, camel drovers, merchants, and scheming wives.
10–12

GUILLOT, RENÉ, *Guillot's African Folk Tales*, ill. by William Papas, Watts, 1965. Tales of the days when men and animals, trees and plants, and the sun and the moon walked and talked with one another.   11–up

GUIRMA, FREDERIC, *Princess of the Full Moon*, ill. by author, tr. by John Garrett, Macmillan, 1970. Good triumphs over evil in a tale from the Upper Volta.
9–11

HARMAN, HUMPHREY, comp., *Tales Told Near a Crocodile: Stories from Nyanza*, ill. by George Ford, Viking, 1967. Tales gathered from the storytellers of six tribes who live in the vicinity of Lake Victoria.   9–11

HEADY, ELEANOR B., *Jambo Sungura! Tales from East Africa*, ill. by Robert Frankenberg, Norton, 1965.
7–11

When the Stones Were Soft; East African Fireside Tales, ill. by Tom Feelings, Funk, 1968.   9–12
These collections feature stories about the animals of East Africa and contain some *why* stories of the region.

PITCHER, DIANA, *Tokoloshi: African Folk Tales Retold*, ill. by Meg Rutherford, Dawne-Leigh, 1981. Chiefly from Bantu sources, a varied and impressive selection of tales.
9–11

ROBINSON, ADJAI, *Singing Tales of Africa*, ill. by Christine Price, Scribner's, 1974. Tales from Sierra Leone and Nigeria.
9–11

Asia

General Collections

CARPENTER, FRANCES, *The Elephant's Bathtub; Wonder Tales from the Far East*, ill. by Hans Guggenheim, Doubleday, 1962. An entertaining group of twenty-four tales gathered from Oriental sources. Each carries the atmosphere of the country in which it originated.
9–11

COURLANDER, HAROLD, *The Tiger's Whisker and Other Tales and Legends from Asia and the Pacific*, ill. by Enrico Arno, Harcourt, 1959. Brevity and simple concepts make these tales suitable for telling to groups in which the children vary widely in age.   9–12

Arabian Countries

COLUM, PADRAIC, *The Arabian Nights: Tales of Wonder and Magnificence*, ill. by Lynd Ward, Macmillan, 1953. This attractive group of stories, selected by a noted storyteller, will appeal to older readers.
10–14

DAWOOD, N. J., ad., *Tales from the Arabian Nights*, ill. by Ed Young, Doubleday, 1978. A collection that includes some stories never before used in collections intended for children.
10–13

EL-SHAMY, HASAN, ed., *Folktales of Egypt*, University of Chicago Press, 1980. A large and varied collection includes extensive notes and an index of motifs.
11–up

KELSEY, ALICE GEER, *Once the Mullah*, ill. by Kurt Werth, McKay, 1954. Stories told by the Mullah give insight into Persian life and folklore and are often exceedingly funny.
9–12

LANG, ANDREW, ed., *Arabian Nights*, ill. by Vera Bock, McKay, 1946. Attractive format, fine design and illustrations.
10–12

MEHDEVI, ANNE SINCLAIR, *Persian Folk and Fairy Tales*, ill. by Paul E. Kennedy, Knopf, 1965. Stories authentically Persian in their portrayal of character but universal in topic.
9–12

SPICER, DOROTHY GLADYS, *The Kneeling Tree; and Other Folktales from the Middle East*, ill. by Barbara Morrow. Coward, 1971. Retold in a lively, fluent style.
9–12

TRAVERS, PAMELA, ad., *Two Pairs of Shoes*, ill. by Leo and Diane Dillon, Viking, 1980. Two tales, one humorous and one courtly, from Middle Eastern sources.
9–11

VAN WOERKOM, DOROTHY, ad., *Abu Ali: Three Tales of the Middle East*, ill. by Harold Berson, Macmillan, 1976. Breezy noodlehead stories.
7–8

China

CARPENTER, FRANCES, *Tales of a Chinese Grandmother,* ill. by Malthé Hasselriis, Doubleday, 1937. Thirty folk tales, told with quiet charm, reveal customs, beliefs, and home life in the China of long ago.   8–11

JAGENDORF, MORITZ, and WENG, VIRGINIA, eds., *The Magic Boat and Other Chinese Folk Stories,* ill. by Wan-go Weng, Vanguard, 1980. A varied selection of tales chosen to represent the diversity of peoples in China.   9–12

KNIGHT, MARY, *The Fox That Wanted Nine Golden Tails,* ill. by Brigitte Bryan, Macmillan, 1969.   7–10

LIN, ADET, *The Milky Way, and Other Chinese Folk Tales,* ill. by Enrico Arno, Harcourt, 1961. A collection of twelve stories translated from original sources.   9–12

WOLKSTEIN, DIANE, ad., *White Wave: A Chinese Tale,* ill. by Ed Young, Crowell, 1979. A Taoist tale of the goddess who emerges from the shell of a moon snail.   8–11

WYNDHAM, ROBERT, *Tales the People Tell in China,* ill. by Jay Yang, Messner, 1971. A varied collection.   9–11

India

BABBITT, ELLEN C., *The Jataka Tales,* ill. by Ellsworth Young, Appleton, 1912.
More Jataka Tales, ill. by Ellsworth Young, Appleton, 1912.
These fables from India have more elaborate plots and characterization than Aesop's fables, and they are often rather humorous.   6–10

CROUCH, MARCUS, ad., *The Ivory City and Other Tales from India and Pakistan,* ill. by William Stobbs, Pelham, 1981. Line drawings add elegance to a many-faceted selection.   9–11

GRAY, JOHN E. B., *India's Tales and Legends,* ill. by Joan Kiddell-Monroe, Walck, 1961. Skillfully told and well-illustrated tales and fables from the ancient epics and folklore of India.

JACOBS, JOSEPH, ed., *Indian Folk and Fairy Tales,* ill. by John D. Batten, Putnam, n.d. First published in 1892 with the title *Indian Fairy Tales.*   9–11

MACFARLANE, IRIS, *Tales and Legends from India,* ill. by Eric Thomas, Watts, 1966. Tales retold with respect for their basic humor and the ancient oral tradition of the village storytellers.   8–11

REED, GWENDOLYN, *The Talkative Beasts: Myths, Fables, and Poems of India,* ill. with photographs by Stella Snead, Lothrop, 1969. The culture of India is reflected in this volume.   All ages

SHIVKUMAR, K., *The King's Choice,* ill. by Yoko Mitsuhashi, Parents, 1971. An animal tale with a moral.   5–8

Indonesia

BRO, MARGUERITTE HARMON, *How the Mouse Deer Became King,* ill. by Joseph Low, Doubleday, 1966. An excellent collection of eleven stories about Kantjil, the mouse deer, Indonesian counterpart of Brer Rabbit.   9–11

COURLANDER, HAROLD, *Kantchil's Lime Pit, and Other Stories from Indonesia,* ill. by Robert W. Kane, Harcourt, 1950. Twenty-three tales with notes on their origins and a glossary and pronunciation guide.   9–11

DELEEUW, ADÈLE L., *Indonesian Legends and Folk Tales,* ill. by Ronni Solbert, Nelson, 1961. An enjoyable collection gathered from the storytellers of Indonesia.   10–11

Japan

CARPENTER, FRANCES, *People from the Sky; Ainu Tales of Northern Japan,* ill. by Betty Fraser, Doubleday, 1972. A contemporary storyteller, Ekashi, remembers the tales of his childhood.   9–11

ISHII, MOMOKO, *Issun Boshi, the Inchling, an Old Tale of Japan,* tr. by Yone Mizuta, ill. by Fuku Akino, Walker, 1967.   7–9

MC ALPINE, HELEN and WILLIAM, *Japanese Tales and Legends,* ill. by Joan Kiddell-Monroe, Walck, 1959. Traditional tales of Japan's legendary past, folk tales, and the epic of the Heike.   10–15

MOSEL, ARLENE, ad., *The Funny Little Woman,* ill. by Blair Lent, Dutton, 1972. A Caldecott Award book.   5–8

STAMM, CLAUS, ed., *Three Strong Women: A Tall Tale from Japan,* ill. by Kazue Mizumura, Viking, 1962. Hilarious story of the wrestler who trained with three women of superhuman strength.   6–10

UCHIDA, YOSHIKO, *The Dancing Kettle and Other Japanese Folk Tales,* ill. by Richard C. Jones, Harcourt, 1949.
The Magic Listening Cap, ill. by author, Harcourt, 1955.
Tales in the two books are well told, moralistic, and full of magic.   9–12
The Sea of Gold and Other Tales from Japan, ill. by Marianne Yamaguchi, Scribner's, 1965. A handsome book in which the tales reflect age-old concepts of morality.   9–11

WINTHROP, ELIZABETH, ad., *Journey to the Bright Kingdom,* ill. by Charles Mikolaycak, Holiday, 1979. An adaptation of the tale of "The Rolling Rice Cakes," reminiscent of the Greek myth of Persephone.   8–10

YAGAWA, SUMIKO, ad., *The Crane Wife,* trans. by Katherine Paterson, ill. by Suekichi Akaba, Morrow, 1981. A familiar folk tale theme, the animal-spouse, is beautifully illustrated by the winner of the Hans Christian Andersen Medal.   8–10

Other Countries of Asia

HITCHCOCK, PATRICIA, *The King Who Rides a Tiger, and Other Folk Tales from Nepal,* ill. by Lillian Sader, Parnassus, 1966. A dozen Nepalese folk tales were selected and handsomely illustrated for this volume.   10–12

JEWETT, ELEANORE MYERS, *Which Was Witch? Tales of Ghosts and Magic from Korea,* ill. by Taro Yashima, Viking, 1953. Fourteen stories with sparkle and suspense, excellent for storytelling.   9–12

MERRILL, JEAN, *High, Wide, and Handsome*, adapted from a Burmese folk tale, ill. by Ronni Solbert, W. R. Scott, 1964.   7–9
Shan's Lucky Knife, ill. by Ronni Solbert, W. R. Scott, 1960. A Burmese folk tale.   7–11
SIDDIQUI, ASHRAF, and MARILYN LERCH, *Toontoony Pie and Other Tales from Pakistan*, ill. by Jan Fairservis, World, 1961. Twenty-two authentic tales from the regions of the Punjab and Bengal.   8–11

Oceania and Australia

BATES, DAISY, *Tales Told to Kabbarli; Aboriginal Legends*, retold by Barbara Ker Wilson, ill. by Harold Thomas, Crown, 1972. Tales of the first humans on earth.   10–up
BROWN, MARCIA, *Backbone of the King*, ill. by author, Scribner's, 1966. Linoleum-block prints enhance this presentation of an old Hawaiian legend.   10–12
COLUM, PADRAIC, *Legends of Hawaii*, ill. by Don Forrer, Yale Univ. Pr., 1937. Nineteen tales, some selected from the author's *At the Gateways of the Day* and *The Bright Islands*.   11–up
HOLDING, JAMES, *The Sky-Eater and Other South Sea Tales*, ill. by Charles Keeping, Abelard, 1955. Tales of the origin of the moon, the mango, and the coconut, and other stories with the flavor of the South Seas.
                                                    6–9
MARALNGURA, N., and others, *Djugurba: Tales from the Spirit Time*, Indiana University Press, 1976. Tales collected by Aborigine students have the cadence of the oral tradition.   8–10
SECHRIST, ELIZABETH HOUGH, *Once in the First Times*, ill. by John Sheppard, Macrae, 1969. Fifty folk tales from the Philippine Islands.   8–12
THOMPSON, VIVIAN L., *Hawaiian Myths of Earth, Sea, and Sky*, ill. by Leonard Weisgard, Holiday, 1966. Twelve nature myths retold with artful simplicity.
                                                    8–10
WILLIAMS, JAY, ad., *The Surprising Things Maui Did*, ill. by Charles Mikolaycak, Four Winds, 1979. Some of the many tales about a folk hero with magical powers are simply told in a book with striking illustrations.
                                                    5–9

North and South America

General Collections

COTHRAN, JEAN, *The Magic Calabash: Folk Tales from America's Islands and Alaska*, ill. by Clifford N. Geary, McKay, 1956. A useful collection of tales from Hawaii, Puerto Rico, the Virgin Islands, and Alaska.
                                                    8–10
LEACH, MARIA, *The Rainbow Book of American Folk Tales and Legends*, ill. by Marc Simont, World, 1958. Tall tales, Indian legends, and scary stories from all regions of North and South America.   9–12

North America: Indian and Eskimo Tales

BAKER, BETTY, *At the Center of the World; Based on Papago and Pima Myths*, ill. by Murray Tinkelman,

Macmillan, 1973. A reverent integration and interpretation.   9–11
BAYLOR, BYRD, comp., *And It Is Still That Way: Tales Told by Arizona Indian Children*, Scribner's, 1976. Simply told tales from several Native American tribes.
                                                    7–9
BELTING, NATALIA, *The Long-Tailed Bear, and Other Indian Legends*, ill. by Louis F. Cary, Bobbs, 1961. Twenty-three animal legends retold from the lore of various Indian tribes. Bibliography and notes on tribal sources are included.   7–9
CURRY, JANE LOUISE, *Down from the Lonely Mountain: California Indian Tales*, ill. by Enrico Arno, Harcourt, 1965. Twelve tales concerning the creation, the way men obtained fire, and the outwitting of enemies.
                                                    8–10
CURTIS, EDWARD, comp., *The Girl Who Married a Ghost and Other Tales from the North American Indian*, ed. by John Bierhorst, Four Winds, 1978. Told with flair, nine tales from six geographical regions.   10–up
DE WIT, DOROTHY, ed., *The Talking Stone: An Anthology of Native American Tales and Legends*, ill. by Donald Crews, Greenwillow, 1979. Hero tales, comic tales and "why" stories are included in a well-balanced anthology.   10–12
ERDOES, RICHARD, ed., *The Sound of Flutes and Other Indian Legends*, ill. by Paul Goble, Pantheon, 1976. Historical material is included in a broad and varied collection.   10–12
FISHER, ANNE B., *Stories California Indians Told*, ill. by Ruth Robbins, Parnassus, 1957. Legends collected by an eminent anthropologist, Dr. C. Hart Merriam, who in turn related them to the author.   8–12
FRITZ, JEAN, ad., *The Good Giants and the Bad Pukwudgies*, ill. by Tomie de Paola, Putnam, 1982. Several tales of the Wampanoag Indians are combined into a story of the good giant Maushop.   5–8
GILLHAM, CHARLES EDWARD, *Beyond the Clapping Mountains: Eskimo Stories from Alaska*, ill. by Chanimun, Macmillan, 1943. Unusual and highly imaginative tales of the animals and folk heroes of the Eskimos. Unfortunately, the author's language tends to detract from the dignity of the stories.   9–10
HARRIS, CHRISTIE, *Once Upon a Totem*, ill. by John Frazer Mills, Atheneum, 1963. Five tales of the Northwest Indians which will help boys and girls understand an interesting people.   10–13
The Trouble with Princesses, ill. by Douglas Tait, Atheneum, 1980. Seven tales of Indian princesses of the Northwest include the familiar figures, Mouse Woman and Raven.   10–up
HILL, KAY, *Glooscap and His Magic: Legends of the Wabanaki Indians*, ill. by Robert Frankenberg, Dodd, 1963. Amusing stories of the mythical Indian hero, his people, and his animals.   8–11
HOFMANN, CHARLES, *American Indians Sing*, ill. by Nicholas Amorosi, Day, 1967. An excellent introduction to the ceremonials of American Indians by a collector of folk materials for the Library of Congress. Includes transcribed music and a recording. 10–14
HOUSTON, JAMES, *Tikta'liktak: An Eskimo Legend*, ill. by author, Harcourt, 1965.
The White Archer: An Eskimo Legend, ill. by author, Harcourt, 1967.
Stories that reflect the Eskimo's courage and his will to survive adversity.   9–11

MAC MILLAN, CYRUS, comp., *Glooskap's Country: And Other Indian Tales,* ill. by John Hall, Oxford, 1956. The hero-figure of the Micmac Indians helps his people in the days before the settlers came.   9–12

MARTIN, FRAN, *Nine Tales of Coyote,* ill. by Dorothy McEntee, Harper, 1950.
Raven-Who-Sets-Things-Right, ill. by Dorothy McEntee, Harper, 1975.
The first volume draws upon the legends of the Nez Percé Indians; the second upon the tales which came via the Eskimos and Canadian Indians.   9–11

REID, DOROTHY N., *Tales of Nanabozho,* ill. by Donald Grant, Walck, 1963. Twenty-one short Indian tales about the great creator-magician, Nanabozho (Hiawatha) of the Ojibwas. Pronunciation guide and extensive bibliography.   9–12

TOYE, WILLIAM, ad., *The Fire Stealer,* ill. by Elizabeth Cleaver, Oxford, 1980. Bright collage pictures illustrate one of the many tales about Nanabozho, hero of many Canadian Indian legends.   5–8

Canada

BARBEAU, MARIUS, *The Golden Phoenix, and Other French-Canadian Fairy Tales,* retold by Michael Hornyansky, ill. by Arthur Price, Walck, 1958. These stories are quite easily recognized as variants of well-known European tales, and little about them is distinctively French-Canadian.   9–11

CARLSON, NATALIE, *The Talking Cat and Other Stories of French Canada,* ill. by Roger Duvoisin, Harper, 1952. This array of genuinely funny stories has been adapted from tales told within the author's family circle.   9–11

HOOKE, HILDA MARY, *Thunder in the Mountains; Legends of Canada,* ill. by Clare Bice, Walck, 1947. Seventeen tales which draw upon three major sources: Indian legends, stories of the coming of white men, and variants of European tales.   9–12

Latin America

AARDEMA, VERNA, tr., *The Riddle of the Drum: A Tale from Tizapan, Mexico,* ill. by Tony Chen, Four Winds, 1979. The hand of a princess goes to him who can solve a riddle.   5–8

BARLOW, GENEVIEVE, *Latin American Tales: From the Pampas to the Pyramids of Mexico,* ill. by William M. Hutchinson, Rand, 1966. Most of these stories, translated from Spanish sources which are cited, come from the Indian tribes of South America. Four have not previously been published.   8–11

BRENNER, ANITA, *The Boy Who Could Do Anything, and Other Mexican Folk Tales,* ill. by Jean Charlot, W. R. Scott, 1942. These curious tales are distinguished for their authentic idiom. They evoke the setting and style of Mexico and its people.   9–11

CARTER, DOROTHY SHARP, ad., *The Enchanted Orchard; And Other Folktales of Central America,* ill. by W. T. Mars, Harcourt, 1973. A colloquial retelling, with notes.   10–12

FINGER, CHARLES J., *Tales from Silver Lands,* ill. by Paul Honore, Doubleday, 1924. Nineteen Indian legends and folk tales from South America transcribed as the author heard them on his travels. Newbery Medal.   10–12

JAGENDORF, M. A., and RALPH S. BOGGS, *The King of the Mountains: A Treasury of Latin American Folk Stories,* ill. by Carybé, Vanguard, 1960. An impressive gathering of sixty-five tales.   9–12

YURCHENCO, HENRIETTA, *A Fiesta of Folk Songs from Spain and Latin America,* ill. by Jules Maidoff, Putnam, 1967. Over thirty folk songs and singing games from Spain and the Spanish-speaking American nations. Melody line and chords are indicated for accompaniment.   5–11

United States: General Collections

COTHRAN, JEAN, ed., *With a Wig, With a Wag, and Other American Folk Tales,* ill. by Clifford N. Geary, McKay, 1954. Fifteen stories gleaned from many parts of the United States, felicitously worded for telling or reading aloud.   8–10

FIELD, RACHEL, ed., *American Folk and Fairy Tales,* ill. by Margaret Freeman, Scribner's, 1929. A highly satisfactory collection of Indian legends, Negro stories, Louisiana folk tales, mountain stories, and tall tales.   12–13

JAGENDORF, MORITZ ADOLF, ed., *Folk Stories of the South,* ill. by Michael Parks, Vanguard, 1973. Broad humor.   9–12
The Ghost of Peg-Leg Peter and Other Stories of Old New York, ill. by Lino S. Lipinsky, songs of old New York selected by June Lazare, Vanguard, 1966. An amusing potpourri of tales about one of our greatest cities.   10–13

United States: Black Tales

COURLANDER, HAROLD, *Terrapin's Pot of Sense,* ill. by Elton Fax, Holt, 1957. American Negro stories collected in several widely spaced rural areas of the U.S. Notes give sources of different versions of the stories.   8–11

FAULKNER, WILLIAM, *The Days When the Animals Talked: Black American Folktales and How They Came to Be,* ill. by Troy Howell, Follett, 1977. Animal tales and anecdotes about the days of slavery.   10–up

HARRIS, JOEL CHANDLER, *Brer Rabbit: Stories from Uncle Remus,* adapted by Margaret Wise Brown with the A. B. Frost pictures redrawn for reproduction by Victor Dowling, Harper, 1941. Twenty-four stories suitable for younger children. The dialect has been modified slightly to make it easier for the young reader.   8–11

JAQUITH, PRISCILLA, ad., *Bo Rabbit Smart for True: Folktales from the Gullah,* ill. by Ed Young, Philomel, 1981. Text and dramatic pictures are beautifully integrated for four tales told in the distinctive Gullah speech patterns.   5–9

LESTER, JULIUS, ad., *The Knee-High Man, and Other Tales,* ill. by Ralph Pinto, Dial, 1972. Six animal stories, retold with simplicity.   5–7

REES, ENNIS, ad., *Brer Rabbit and His Tricks,* ill. by Edward Gorey, Scott/Addison, 1967, and *More of Brer Rabbit's Tricks,* ill. by Edward Gorey, Scott/Addison, 1968. Rhyme without dialect, simple style, droll pictures.   5–8

United States: Tall Tales

BLAIR, WALTER, *Tall Tale America: A Legendary History of Our Humorous Heroes,* ill. by Glen Rounds, Coward, 1944. The authenticity is questionable but this should not detract from enjoyment of the book.   10–14

BOWMAN, JAMES CLOYD, *Mike Fink,* ill. by Leonard Fisher, Little, 1957.   11–15
Pecos Bill, ill. by Laura Bannon, Whitman, 1937. Collections of tales about two American superheroes whose folk origins are doubtful.   11–15

CARMER, CARL, *The Hurricane's Children,* ill. by Elizabeth Black Carmer, McKay, 1967. A reissue of an excellent collection of American tall tales first published in 1937.   9–11

CREDLE, ELLIS, *Tall Tales from the High Hills, and Other Stories,* ill. by Richard Bennett, Nelson, 1957. Twenty amusing tales from the Blue Ridge Mountains.   9–12

FELTON, HAROLD W., *Bowleg Bill, Seagoing Cowpuncher,* ill. by William Moyers, Prentice, 1957.   8–10
Mike Fink, Best of the Keelboatmen, ill. by Aldren Watson, Dodd, 1960.   10–12

MALCOLMSON, ANNE, *Yankee Doodle's Cousins,* ill. by Robert McCloskey, Houghton, 1941. This is one of the finest and most satisfying collections of real and made-up heroes from all sections of the United States.   10–14

ROUNDS, GLEN, *Ol' Paul the Mighty Logger,* ill. by author, Holiday, 1949. Paul Bunyan stories retold with an earthy, exuberant zest.   10–adult
Mr. Yowder and the Train Robbers, ill. by author, Holiday, 1981. A very funny story in which some rattlesnakes help their friend Mr. Yowder recover mail stolen by some criminals.   8–10

STOUTENBERG, ADRIEN, *American Tall Tales,* ill. by Richard M. Powers, Viking, 1966. Covers many of the characters found in Malcolmson's *Yankee Doodle's Cousins* but is more modestly written.   9–11

YORK, CAROL, ad., *Mike Fink,* ill. by Ed Parker, Troll, 1980. A breezy account of the toughest riverboat man who ever sailed down the Mississippi.   8–10

United States: Variants of European Folk Tales

BARTH, EDNA, *Jack-O'-Lantern,* ill. by Paul Galdone, Seabury, 1974. The Devil is outwitted by Mean Jack.   8–10

CHASE, RICHARD, ed., *Grandfather Tales,* ill. by Berkeley Williams, Jr., Houghton, 1948.
The Jack Tales, ill. by Berkeley Williams, Jr., Houghton, 1943.
Two fine collections of tales from the Southern mountains. Priceless contributions to American folklore.   10–up

JAGENDORF, MORITZ ADOLF, *New England Bean-Pot; American Folk Stories to Read and to Tell,* ill. by Donald McKay, Vanguard, 1948. The dry humor characteristic of the New England people is found in these folk tales from six states.   10–13

SAWYER, RUTH, *Journey Cake, Ho!* ill. by Robert McCloskey, Viking, 1953.   6–10

West Indies

CARTER, DOROTHY SHARP, ad., *Greedy Mariani; And Other Folktales of the Antilles,* ill. by Trina Schart Hyman, Atheneum, 1974. Marvelous style and humor.   9–11

COURLANDER, HAROLD, *The Piece of Fire: And Other Haitian Tales,* ill. by Beth and Joe Krush, Harcourt, 1964. Twenty-six tales which capture the humor and mischief of this island people.   9–11
Uncle Bouqui of Haiti, ill. by Lucy Herndon Crockett, Morrow, 1942. This delightful array of folk tales from Haiti is now out of print. It should, however, be available in some libraries and is well worth searching out, for the tales reflect the happy collision of African and European folklore.   9–11

SHERLOCK, PHILIP M., *Anansi, the Spider Man,* ill. by Marcia Brown, T. Crowell, 1954. These stories, told by Jamaicans, have their roots in Africa.   9–12
West Indian Folk-Tales, Retold, ill. by Joan Kiddell-Monroe, Walck, 1966. Twenty-one West Indian *how* and *why* stories, eight of them new tales about the wily spider man, Anansi.   9–11

WOLKSTEIN, DIANE, comp., *The Magic Orange Tree and Other Haitian Folktales,* ill. by Elsa Henriquez, Knopf, 1978. Local color, flavorful dialogue, and a communicated relish distinguish the retelling.   10–up

Fables

AESOP, *The Miller, His Son, and Their Donkey,* ill. by Roger Duvoisin, McGraw, 1962.   5–9

AESOP, *Aesop's Fables,* ill. by Heidi Holder, Viking, 1981. Nine fables are illustrated by intricate, colorful, and meticulously designed paintings.   9–up

ARTZYBASHEFF, BORIS, ed., *Aesop's Fables,* ill. by editor, Viking, 1933. Ninety fables selected by the editor-illustrator and embellished with beautiful wood engravings.   12–14

ATIL, ESIN, ed., *Kalila wa Dimna: Fables from a Fourteenth-Century Arabic Manuscript,* Smithsonian Institution Press, 1981. The theme of the parables, animal fables, and longer tales is that all creatures share a common fate.   10–up

BROWN, MARCIA, *Once a Mouse . . . ,* Scribner's, 1961. A fable from *The Hitopadesa,* illustrated with vivid woodcuts. Caldecott Medal.   5–9

GAER, JOSEPH, *The Fables of India,* ill. by Randy Monk, Little, 1955. Selected from three collections of Indian fables—*The Panchatantra, The Hitopadesa,* and the *Jatakas.*   10–14

JACOBS, JOSEPH, ed., *The Fables of Aesop,* ill. by David Levine, Macmillan, 1964. Contains over eighty fables and Jacobs' history of them.   9–11

KRYLOV, IVAN ANDREEVICH, *Fifteen Fables of Krylov,* tr. by Guy Daniels, ill. by David Pascal, Macmillan, 1965. The translator has rendered these fables into sophisticated English verse.   12–up

LA FONTAINE, *The Hare and the Tortoise,* ill. by Brian Wildsmith, Watts, 1967.
The Lion and the Rat, ill. by Brian Wildsmith, Watts, 1963.
The Rich Man and the Shoemaker, ill. by Brian Wildsmith, Watts, 1966.
Each of the above fables is beautifully illustrated in glowing colors.   5–8

UNTERMEYER, LOUIS, ed., *Aesop's Fables,* selected and adapted by editor, ill. by Alice and Martin Provensen, Golden Pr., 1965. Forty fables in a large picture book with refreshing illustrations.   6–9

WHITE, ANNE TERRY, *Aesop's Fables,* retold; ill. by Helen Siegl, Random, 1964. These fables are retold in an easy, contemporary style.   8–10

WRIGGINS, SALLY, ad., *White Monkey King: A Chinese Fable,* ill. by Ronni Solbert, Pantheon, 1977. A portion of a longer Chinese classic about the arrogant prankster who must serve five hundred years of penance.   9–11

Myths, Epics, and Hero Tales

General Collections

ASIMOV, ISAAC, *Words from the Myths,* ill. by William Barss, Houghton, 1961. Explains the mythological origins of many words in common usage and thus deepens the reader's understanding of the myths and their pervasive influence in literature and art.   9–14

GREEN, ROGER LANCELYN, ed., *A Book of Myths,* selected and retold by editor, ill. by Joan Kiddell-Monroe, Dutton, 1965. A useful reference for children because it gives parallels and variants of myths from many ancient lands.   9–12

HAMILTON, EDITH, *Mythology,* ill. by Steele Savage, Little, 1942. Probably the most valuable single source of information for the reader who needs background in the myths.   12–up

HAZELTINE, ALICE I., ed., *Hero Tales from Many Lands,* ill. by Gordon Laite, Abingdon, 1961. A judicious selection from well-known retellings of the stories about great epic heroes. Includes sources, background notes, a glossary, a pronunciation guide, an index, and a bibliography.   10–14

LURIE, ALISON, ad., *The Heavenly Zoo: Legends and Tales of the Stars,* ill. by Monika Beisner, Farrar, 1980. Smoothly retold legends about animal constellations.   9–11

UDEN, GRANT, ad., *Hero Tales from the Age of Chivalry; Retold from the Froissart Chronicles,* ill. by Doreen Roberts, World, 1969. Twelve dramatic stories.   11–13

Babylonian Epic

BRYSON, BERNARDA, *Gilgamesh,* ill. by author, Holt, 1967. An exceptionally fine retelling of the ancient story of the proud King Gilgamesh.   11–up

FEAGLES, ANITA, ed., *He Who Saw Everything: The Epic of Gilgamesh,* ill. by Xavier Gonzáles, W. R. Scott, 1967. This epic antedates the earliest Hebrew and Greek writers by at least fifteen centuries.   9–13

Greek and Roman Myths and Epics

BARTH, EDNA, ad., *Cupid and Psyche: A Love Story,* ill. by Ati Forberg, Seabury, 1976. Drawings that incorporate ancient motifs illustrate a moving story, smoothly retold.   9–11

BULFINCH, THOMAS, *A Book of Myths,* selections from Bulfinch's *Age of Fable,* ill. by Helen Sewell, Macmillan, 1942. Striking illustrations suggestive of ballet postures and movement distinguish this collection.   10–14

COLUM, PADRAIC, *The Children's Homer,* ill. by Willy Pogány, Macmillan, 1918, 1962. A distinguished version in cadenced prose.   10–14
The Golden Fleece and the Heroes Who Lived Before Achilles, ill. by Willy Pogány, Macmillan, 1962. A good-looking modern edition of this famous retelling.   11–15

COOLIDGE, OLIVIA E., *Greek Myths,* ill. by Edouard Sandoz, Houghton, 1949. A retelling of the most widely known Greek myths. Here the gods are not idealized —indeed the book opens with an unappealing tale of trickery—but the stories have authenticity.   10–14

D'AULAIRE, INGRI and EDGAR PARIN, *Ingri and Edgar Parin d'Aulaire's Book of Greek Myths,* ill. by authors, Doubleday, 1962. A book with appeal for younger readers. The Greek myths are told in a simple narrative beginning with the Titans and finishing with the heroes. A large volume illustrated with beautiful lithographs.   8–11

EVSLIN, BERNARD, *Greeks Bearing Gifts: the Epics of Achilles and Ulysses,* ill. by Lucy Bitzer, Four Winds, 1976. The fluent, witty style gives fresh life to the ancient story.   11–up

GARFIELD, LEON, and EDWARD BLISHEN, *The God Beneath the Sea,* ill. by Zevi Blum, Pantheon, 1971, and *The Golden Shadow,* ill. by Charles Keeping, Pantheon, 1973. Myths woven together into a continuous story in each book, superb in style, cohesive and dramatic.   12–up

GRAVES, ROBERT, *Greek Gods and Heroes,* ill. by Dimitris Davis, Doubleday, 1960. This sardonic interpretation is excellent for young people who are familiar with the standard treatments of the myths.   12–up

HAWTHORNE, NATHANIEL, *The Complete Greek Stories of Nathaniel Hawthorne,* ill. by Harold Jones, Watts, 1963. Hawthorne's treatment of the myths, though often criticized, has helped to interest many children in mythology.   10–12

KINGSLEY, CHARLES, *The Heroes,* ill. by Joan Kiddell-Monroe, Dutton, 1963. Narrative versions of Hercules' twelve labors and of the legends about Perseus, the Argonauts, and Theseus.   10–14
The Heroes, ill. by Vera Bock, Macmillan, 1954. Thirty tales are beautifully retold and make a fine cycle for the storyteller.   10–14

PRODDOW, PENELOPE, tr., *Hermes, Lord of Robbers; Homeric Hymn Number Four,* ill. by Barbara Cooney,

Doubleday, 1971. Smoothly told, handsomely illustrated.   9–11

SELLEW, CATHARINE F., *Adventures with the Gods*, ill. by George and Doris Hauman, Little, 1945. Sixteen popular myths are included in this volume.   9–11

SERRAILLIER, IAN, *The Clashing Rocks; the Story of Jason*, ill. by William Stobbs, Walck, 1964.
A Fall from the Sky; the Story of Daedalus, ill. by William Stobbs, Walck, 1966.
The handling of these legends is direct and vigorous, and the illustrations are dramatically strong.   10–up

TOMAINO, SARAH F., ad., *Persephone, Bringer of Spring*, ill. by Ati Forberg, T. Crowell, 1971. Dramatic.
    8–10

VAUTIER, GHISLAINE, ad., *The Shining Stars: Greek Legends of the Zodiac*, ill. by Jacqueline Bezencon, Cambridge University Press, 1981. These are simplified retellings of those myths on which the constellations' names are based.   8–10

WISE, WILLIAM, ad., *Monster Myths of Ancient Greece*, ill. by Jerry Pinkney, Putnam, 1981. An introduction gives background that can help readers understand the intricacies of the Greek pantheon.   8–10

Norse Myths and Epics

BARTH, EDNA, ad., *Balder and the Mistletoe*, ill. by Richard Cuffari, Seabury, 1979. Based on the Sturluson version of the Icelandic Edda, this tells of the death of the god Balder and his being sentenced to live in the underworld.   9–11

COLUM, PADRAIC, *The Children of Odin: The Book of Northern Myths*, ill. by Willy Pogány, Macmillan, 1920, 1962. This incomparable retelling of Norse mythology has been given a new format and new type, but the distinctive Pogány illustrations remain.
    11–15

D' AULAIRE, INGRI and EDGAR PARIN, *Norse Gods and Giants*, ill. by authors, Doubleday, 1967. Retells for younger children the dramatic, exciting, and often humorous tales of Norse mythology.   8–11

HOSFORD, DOROTHY G., *Thunder of the Gods*, ill. by Claire and George Louden, Holt, 1952. The author successfully combines the dramatic form of the folk tale and the formal language appropriate to the myths.   9–11

SELLEW, CATHARINE F., *Adventures with the Giants*, ill. by Steele Savage, Little, 1950. A discriminating selection of stories for younger readers.   8–11
Adventures with the Heroes, ill. by Steele Savage, Little, 1954. The Volsung saga retold in simple language.
    9–12

English Epics and Hero Tales

HIEATT, CONSTANCE, ad., *The Sword and the Grail*, ill. by David Palladini, T. Crowell, 1972. One of the best of Hieatt's Arthurian retellings is this tale of Percival.
    10–12

HOSFORD, DOROTHY, *By His Own Might; the Battles of Beowulf*, ill. by Laszlo Matulay, Holt, 1947. A retelling especially suitable for children in upper grades of elementary school.   10–12

LANIER, SIDNEY, *The Boy's King Arthur*, ill. by N. C. Wyeth, Scribner's, 1942. An authoritative and popular version, the best one to use for reading or telling.
    10–14

MAC LEOD, MARY, *The Book of King Arthur and His Noble Knights*, ill. by Henry C. Pitz, Lippincott, 1949. A version, faithful to the original, which presents the legend in an easily understood manner. (Other editions by this author were published by Dodd, 1953; Macmillan, 1963; World, 1950.)   9–13

MALCOLMSON, ANNE, ed., *Song of Robin Hood*, music arr. by Grace Castagnetta, ill. by Virginia Lee Burton, Houghton, 1947. A handsome book containing eighteen songs.   11–14

PICARD, BARBARA LEONIE, *Hero Tales of the British Isles*, ill. by John G. Galsworthy, Criterion, 1963. Eleven stories about the ancient heroes of the Isles. Helpful notes give perspective on each hero's place in history and folklore.   10–13
Stories of King Arthur and His Knights, ill. by Roy Morgan, Walck, 1955. An absorbing retelling that evokes the atmosphere and spirit of the Middle Ages without the use of archaic language.   10–12

PYLE, HOWARD, *The Merry Adventures of Robin Hood of Great Renown in Nottinghamshire*, ill. by author, Scribner's, 1946. This version has gone through many editions and remains a favorite with readers. A fine source for reading aloud.   12–14
The Story of King Arthur and His Knights, ill. by author, Scribner's, 1903. One of the great versions of the Arthurian legends. Also available in paperback edition from Dover.   10–12

SUTCLIFF, ROSEMARY, *Beowulf*, ill. by Charles Keeping, Dutton, 1962. The battles with Grendel and Grendel's mother, and the final combat with the fire-drake are covered in this account.   12–14
The Light Beyond the Forest: The Quest for the Holy Grail, Dutton, 1980. Distinguished retelling of the Arthurian legend.   10–12
The Sword and the Circle: King Arthur and the Knights of the Round Table, Dutton, 1981.   11–13

Irish Epics and Hero Tales

EVSLIN, BERNARD, ad., *The Green Hero: Early Adventures of Finn McCool*, ill. by Barbara Bascove, Four Winds, 1975. A witty and fluent retelling of Finn's struggles against his enemies.   11–14

SUTCLIFF, ROSEMARY, *The High Deeds of Finn Mac Cool*, ill. by Michael Charlton, Dutton, 1967. A vivid recounting of the legends of the Fianna by a superb storyteller.   11–14
The Hound of Ulster, ill. by Victor Ambrus, Dutton, 1964. A finely written account which incorporates the many legends about Cuchulain into one consecutive narrative.   11–14

YOUNG, ELLA, *The Tangle-Coated Horse and Other Tales*, ill. by Vera Bock, Longmans, 1929. Tales of Finn told by one of Ireland's most gifted storytellers.
    11–14
The Wonder Smith and His Son, a Tale from the Golden Childhood of the World, ill. by Boris Artzybasheff, McKay, 1957. Fourteen tales from the Gaelic told with incomparable verve and beauty by one who had the poet's touch.   10–13

Other National Epics and Hero Tales

ALMEDINGEN, EDITH MARTHA, *The Knights of the Golden Table*, ill. by Charles Keeping, Lippincott, 1964. These twelve stories about Prince Vladimir of Kiev and his knights are filled with the color and flavor of early Russia.   12–14

BERTOL, ROLAND, ad., *Sundiata, the Epic of the Lion King*, ill. by Gregorio Prestopino, T. Crowell, 1970. Story of the founder of the African kingdom of Mali.   9–12

DAVIS, RUSSELL, and BRENT K. ASHABRANNER, *Ten Thousand Desert Swords: the Epic Story of a Great Bedouin Tribe*, ill. by Leonard Everett Fisher, Little, 1960. Eleven tales from the great group of legends surrounding the Bani Hilal, a powerful tribe of Bedouin warriors.   11–13

DEUTSCH, BABETTE, *Heroes of the Kalevala*, ill. by Fritz Eichenberg, Messner, 1940. A version with literary distinction and continuity.   10–14

GAER, JOSEPH, *The Adventures of Rama*, ill. by Randy Monk, Little, 1954. This is a retelling of one of the best-loved epics of India.   12–14

GOLDSTON, ROBERT C., *The Legend of the Cid*, ill. by Stephane, Bobbs, 1963. The adventures and brave deeds of this Spanish hero are presented in a simple prose narrative enhanced by strong illustrations.   10–13

PICARD, BARBARA, ad., *German Hero-Sagas and Folk Tales*, ill. by Joan Kiddell-Monroe, Walck, 1976. Vigorous and smooth retellings of twenty stories.   9–11

SYNGE, URSULA, ad., *Land of Heroes: A Retelling of the Kalevala*, Atheneum, 1978. A splendid version of the great Finnish epic.   11–up

THOMPSON, VIVIAN L., ad., *Hawaiian Tales of Heroes and Champions*, ill. by Herbert Kawainui Kane, Holiday, 1971. Good style, and useful for storytelling.   9–11

Adult References: Folk Tales, Fables, Myths, Epics, and Hero Tales[4]

AUSUBEL, NATHAN, ed., *A Treasury of Jewish Folklore*, Crown, 1948. A lengthy compilation of over seven hundred stories and seventy-five songs of the Jewish people.

BARBER, RICHARD, *A Companion to World Mythology*, ill. by Pauline Baynes, Delacorte, 1980. Broad scope and comprehensive coverage distinguish an alphabetical, annotated listing of the gods of the major myths of the world.   10–up

BAUGHMAN, ERNEST, *A Type and Motif Index of the Folktales of England and North America*, Indiana University Pr., 1966.

♪ BONI, MARGARET BRADFORD, ed., *Favorite American Songs*, arr. by Norman Lloyd, ill. by Aurelius Battaglia, Simon, 1956.   10–up

[4]In addition to the books listed here, many of the entries in "General References" (p. 880) include discussions specifically concerned with folk tales, fables, myths, and epics. See especially the Arbuthnot and Sutherland, Chukovsky, Duff, Hazard, Huck and Kuhn, Morton, Pickard, and Smith titles.

Numbers at the end of an entry marked ♪ in this section suggest the age level of the children with whom the songs in that collection can best be used.

♪ *Fireside Book of Folk Songs*, sel. and ed. by Margaret Bradford Boni, arr. by Norman Lloyd, ill. by Alice and Martin Provensen, Simon, 1947, 1966.   10–up

BOTKIN, BENJAMIN A., ed., *A Treasury of American Folklore*, Crown, 1944. The stories, ballads, and traditions of the people are grouped under such headings as "Heroes and Boasters," "Boosters and Knockers," "Songs and Rhymes."
A Treasury of New England Folklore, Crown, n.d.
A Treasury of Western Folklore, Crown, 1951.
A Treasury of Southern Folklore, Crown, 1949.

BRAND, OSCAR, *The Ballad Mongers; Rise of the Modern Folk Song*, Funk, 1962. An excellent historical survey.

♪ BRAND, OSCAR, ed., *Singing Holidays*, music arr. by Douglas Townsend, ill. by Roberta Moynihan, Knopf, 1957. Ninety interesting folk songs for American holidays.   12–up

BRUNVAND, JAN H., *The Study of American Folklore, An Introduction*, Norton, 1968. A good text and bibliographies.

BULFINCH, THOMAS, *Bulfinch's Mythology: The Age of Fable; The Age of Chivalry; Legends of Charlemagne*, ill. by Elinore Blaisdell, T. Crowell, n.d., 3 vols. in 1. This adult work, first published in 1855, has much value as a basic reference.

♪ CARMER, CARL, comp., *America Sings*, music arr. by Edwin John Stringham, ill. by Elizabeth Black Carmer, Knopf, 1942.   11–16

♪ CHASE, RICHARD, *American Folk Tales and Songs*, New Am. Lib., n.d. This excellent contribution to American folklore, by a renowned collector and teller of tales, has been given new life by its recent reissue in a paperback edition.

CLARKSON, ATELIA, and GILBERT CROSS, *World Folktales: A Scribner Resource Collection*, Scribner's, 1980. The extensive notes, index to motifs, index to tale types, and notes on classroom use indicate the book's appropriateness in a research collection, although the over sixty stories can be enjoyed by children.   11–up

COLUM, PADRAIC, ed., *A Treasury of Irish Folklore*, 2nd rev. ed., Crown, 1967. The legends, ballads, stories, and superstitions of the Irish people, compiled and edited by an eminent authority on the subject.

COOK, ELIZABETH, *The Ordinary and the Fabulous; An Introduction to Myths, Legends, and Fairy Tales for Teachers and Storytellers*, Cambridge Univ. Pr., 1969.

DIETZ, BETTY WARNER, and THOMAS CHOONBAI PARK, eds., *Folk Songs of China, Japan, Korea*, Day, 1964. A valuable volume for teachers and others who are interested in helping children understand the culture of the Orient. Many of the songs can be effectively used with the folk tales of the countries named in the title.

DORSON, RICHARD, *American Folklore*, Univ. of Chicago Pr., 1959. A volume in the Chicago History of American Civilization series, this work surveys the entire field of American folklore from colonization to mass culture. Based upon field collection and research, the text includes folkways, jests, boasts, tall tales, folk and legendary heroes, and ballads.
Buying the Wind: Regional Folklore in the United States, Univ. of Chicago Pr., 1964. A supplement to *American Folklore*. Includes the folklore of Maine Down Easters, the Pennsylvania Dutch, Southwest Mexicans, Utah Mormons, southern mountaineers, Louisiana Cajuns, and Illinois Egyptians. For each re-

gional group, the text provides narratives, proverbs, riddles, beliefs, folk dramas, and folk songs.

EASTMAN, MARY HUSE, *Index to Fairy Tales, Myths, and Legends,* Faxon, 1926. First supplement, 1937. Second supplement, 1952. Useful for locating various sources in which individual tales may be found. There are geographical and racial groupings and lists for storytellers.

♪ ENGVICK, WILLIAM, ed., *Lullabies and Night Songs,* music by Alec Wilder, ill. by Maurice Sendak, Harper, 1965. 4–8

♪ FELTON, HAROLD W., ed., *Cowboy Jamboree: Western Songs and Lore,* arr. by Edward S. Breck, ill. by Aldren A. Watson, Knopf, 1951. 9–15

♪ FUKUDA, HANAKO, comp. and tr., *Favorite Songs of Japanese Children,* ill. by Katsuya Kay Nishi, Highland Music Company, 1965. Fifteen delightful songs presented with dancing, dramatization, and games, just as they would be performed in Japan. 6–10

♪ GLAZER, TOM, comp., *Treasury of Folk Songs,* ill. by Art Seiden, arr. for piano by Stanley Lock and Herbert Haufrecht, Grosset, 1964. All ages

♪ HAYWOOD, CHARLES, ed., *Folk Songs of the World,* ill. by Carl Smith, Day, 1966. Songs in this global array are presented in their native languages and in English. Notes add commentary on the musical life of each country and a description of each song. Chords for instrumental accompaniment are also indicated. 10–up

♪ HURD, MICHAEL, *Sailors' Songs and Shanties,* ill. by John Miller, Walck, 1965. Includes a brief but informative discussion of the purposes and origins of various sea shanties. 10–up

JOURNAL OF AMERICAN FOLKLORE, *Folklore in America,* sel. and ed. by Tristram P. Coffin and Hennig Cohen, Doubleday, 1966. This interesting compilation of verified folk pieces, reprinted from the *Journal of American Folklore,* is divided into the following categories: tales, songs, superstitions, proverbs, riddles, games, folk dramas, and folk festivals.

JUNG, CARL, and others, eds., *Man and His Symbols,* Doubleday, 1964. The chapter "Ancient Myths and Modern Man" should be read for the insight which it gives into the importance of myth. This book serves as the best introduction to Jung's psychology to have appeared so far.

♪ KNUDSEN, LYNNE, comp., *Lullabies from Around the World,* arr. by Carl Bosley, ill. by Jacqueline Tomes, Follett, 1967. This very specialized collection is excellent for use with young children. Guitar and simple piano accompaniments are included, and a brief, informative introduction precedes each song. 3–6

♪ KRONE, BEA and MAX, *Cantemos, Ninos,* Neil Kjos, 1961. A compilation of folk songs, singing games, and dances. Lyrics are printed in Spanish and in English. Simple accompaniments and chords for guitar and autoharp are included. Excellent for use with stories from Spain and Latin American countries. 10–up

LEACH, MARIA, ed., *Funk and Wagnalls Standard Dictionary of General Folklore, Mythology and Legend,* 2 vols., Funk, 1949–1950. The tremendous extent and variety of the world's folklore is made known in this fine reference work which serves the general reader as well as the expert.

♪ LOMAX, ALAN, *The Folk Songs of North America,* Doubleday, 1960. 12–up

♪ LOMAX, ALAN, and ELIZABETH POSTON, *Penguin Book of American Folk Songs,* Penguin, 1964. 12–up

MUNCH, PETER A., *Norse Mythology, Legends of Gods and Heroes,* rev. by Magnus Olsen, tr. by Sigurd Hustvedt, Singing Tree, 1968. Material on sources.

OPIE, IONA and PETER, *The Classic Fairy Tales,* ill., Oxford, 1974. Although primarily for adult students of folk literature, the 24 stories can be used for children. *The Oxford Dictionary of Nursery Rhymes,* Oxford, 1951. An authoritative and highly interesting work which gives much of the folklore surrounding the nursery rhymes.

PAZ, ELENA, *Favorite Spanish Folk Songs,* Oak, 1965. Forty-five traditional songs from Spain and Latin America. Included are literal English translations, notes on the songs, and guitar chords. 10–up

RITCHIE, JEAN, *Folk Songs of the Southern Appalachians,* Oak, 1965. 10–up

♪ *Jean Ritchie's Swapping Song Book,* piano arr. by A. K. Fossner and Edward Tripp, ill. by George Pickow, Walck, 1952. 9–12

♪ *Singing Family of the Cumberlands,* Oak, 1963. 10–up

RYDER, ARTHUR W., tr., *The Panchatantra,* Univ. of Chicago Pr., 1925. Adult students will be interested in discovering in these Indian fables the sources of many Aesop and La Fontaine fables.

♪ SANDBURG, CARL, ed., *American Song Bag,* Harcourt, 1927. *New American Song Bag,* Broadcast Music Inc., 1950. 10–up

SAWYER, RUTH, *The Way of the Storyteller,* Viking, 1942, 1962. The history and techniques of storytelling.

♪ SEEGER, PETE, *American Favorite Ballads,* Oak, 1961. Eighty-four traditional songs as sung by this noted wandering minstrel. 12–up

♪ SEEGER, RUTH CRAWFORD, *American Folk Songs for Children,* ill. by Barbara Cooney, Doubleday, 1948. 5–12

♪ *American Folk Songs for Christmas,* ill. by Barbara Cooney, Doubleday, 1953. 5–12

♪ *Animal Folk Songs for Children; Traditional American Songs,* ill. by Barbara Cooney, Doubleday, 1950. These three books should assuredly form the nucleus of any collection of folk songs for children. The tunes and piano accompaniments are simple and appealing. *American Folk Songs for Children* contains an especially helpful discussion on the values and uses of folk songs. Each book includes a classified index and an index of titles and first lines. 5–12

SHEDLOCK, MARIE, *Art of the Storyteller,* 3rd ed., Dover, 1951. Guide to selection and use of materials.

♪ SHEKERJIAN, HAIG and REGINA, *A Book of Ballads, Songs and Snatches,* Harper, 1966. A book that is graphically beautiful and musically excellent. Many unusual and little-known songs can be found here. Piano arrangements are tasteful and guitar chords are given. The coverage is international. 10–up

♪ SILBER, IRWIN, and E. ROBINSON, *Songs of the Great American West,* Macmillan, 1967. Each of eight chapters is prefaced by a short historical essay. In addition, documentary notes on sources are provided for the ninety-two songs, which cover the decades from 1840 through the 1920's. Adult

THOMPSON, STITH, *The Folktale,* Holt, 1960 (Dryden Pr., 1946). The author, one of the world's foremost authorities on the subject, discusses the universality of the folk tales, and analyzes types of tales and their place in a primitive culture. The final section concerns ways of studying the folk tale on a worldwide basis. *Motif-Index of Folk Literature,* ed. by Stith Thompson, rev. and enl. ed., 5 vols., Indiana Univ. Pr., 1955. A reference work valuable for analyzing and categorizing folk literature of the world. Volume I includes a bibliography of all works examined for motifs.

TOOR, FRANCES, *A Treasury of Mexican Folkways,* ill. by Carlos Merida, Crown, 1947. Although published over twenty years ago, this comprehensive book has much of value on the customs, myths, fiestas, dances, and songs of the Mexican people.

TOOZE, RUTH, *Storytelling,* Prentice, 1959. Suggests titles, methods, and criteria for selection.

♪ WEAVERS, THE, eds., *The Weavers' Song Book,* arr. by Robert De Cormier, Harper, 1960.   10–up
Travelin' On with The Weavers, arr. for piano and guitar by Herbert Haufrecht, Harper, 1966.   10–up

♪ WHITE, FLORENCE, and KAZUO AKIYAMA, *Children's Songs from Japan,* ill. by Toshihiko Suzuki, Edward B. Marks Music Corp., 1960. Approximately fifty songs make up this interesting collection.   6–10

♪ WINN, MARIE, and ALLAN MILLER, *The Fireside Book of Children's Songs,* arr. by Allan Miller, ill. by John Alcorn, Simon, 1966.   6–10

Modern Fantasy

ADAMS, RICHARD, *Watership Down,* Macmillan, 1974.   12–up

AIKEN, JOAN, *Nightbirds on Nantucket,* ill. by Robin Jacques, Doubleday, 1966.
The Wolves of Willoughby Chase, ill. by Pat Marriott, Doubleday, 1963. In these engagingly melodramatic and fantastic stories, the author demonstrates her mastery of a writing style which seems to poke sly fun at Victorian novels.   9–12
The Stolen Lake, Delacorte, 1981. A fanciful romp in which a girl of twelve finds the descendants of ancient Britons in an imaginary South American country.   10–13

ALCOCK, VIVIEN, *The Haunting of Cassie Palmer,* Delacorte, 1982. Daughter of a medium, Cassie is horrified when, taking a dare, she raises a ghost who proceeds to make her life miserable.   10–13

ALEXANDER, LLOYD, *The Book of Three,* Holt, 1964.
The Black Cauldron, Holt, 1965.
The Castle of Llyr, Holt, 1966.
Taran Wanderer, Holt, 1967.
The High King, Holt, 1968.
These five spirited chronicles, set in the imaginary kingdom of Prydain, follow the adventures of Assistant Pig-Keeper Taran as he grows to manhood. *The High King* received the Newbery Medal.   10–up
Coll and His White Pig, ill. by Evaline Ness, Holt, 1965. Coll, once warrior, now farmer, wants only to be left to his garden. But when Hen Wen, a pig with oracular power, is spirited away, Coll sets out to rescue her from the land of death. This story is also set in the imaginary kingdom of Prydain.   7–9
The Kestrel, Dutton, 1982, and *Westmark,* Dutton, 1981. Companion volumes tell exciting stories of high adventure in a mythical land.   10–13

ANDERSEN, HANS CHRISTIAN, *Andersen's Fairy Tales,* ill. by Lawrence Beall Smith, Macmillan, 1963. An attractive and useful edition containing sixteen stories.   8–11
The Complete Fairy Tales and Stories, tr. by Erik Christian Haugaard, Doubleday, 1974. A fine translation by an author equally fluent in Danish and English.   9–11
The Emperor and the Nightingale, retold and ill. by Bill Sokol, Pantheon, 1959. Retold with sensitivity and illustrated with striking pictures.   9–12
The Emperor's New Clothes, ill. by Virginia Lee Burton, Houghton, 1949, 1962. An enchanting edition of Andersen's funniest story. Children and adults find the pictures as irresistible as the story.   7–10
It's Perfectly True: And Other Stories, tr. by Paul Leyssac, ill. by Richard Bennett, Harcourt, 1938. This collection, translated by a well-known Danish actor, is most highly recommended for the storyteller. The tales are written in the conversational tone in which Andersen liked to tell his stories.   9–12
The Nightingale, tr. by Eva Le Gallienne, designed and ill. by Nancy Ekholm Burkert, Harper, 1965. A beautifully designed book in every detail. The translation flows smoothly, and the illustrations faithfully echo the gemlike quality of the story.   9–11
Seven Tales, tr. and adapted by Eva Le Gallienne, ill. by Maurice Sendak, Harper, 1959. Pleasant, appreciative versions of some of Andersen's simpler tales, illustrated in a medieval style. Large print and wide margins add to the appeal of this volume.   8–12
The Steadfast Tin Soldier, tr. by M. R. James, ill. by Marcia Brown, Scribner's, 1953. Beautiful pastel illustrations enhance this poignant tale.   6–10
The Swineherd, tr. and ill. by Erik Blegvad, Harcourt, 1958.   5–9

ANDERSON, LONZO, *Two Hundred Rabbits,* ill. by Adrienne Adams, Viking, 1968. A gentle, beautifully illustrated tale of a boy and his magical wooden whistle, which summoned all the rabbits in the wood to parade before the king.   5–8

ASSOCIATION FOR CHILDHOOD EDUCATION INTERNATIONAL, *Told Under the Magic Umbrella,* ill. by Elizabeth Orton Jones, Macmillan, 1962. A fine collection of modern fairy tales for storytelling or reading aloud.   6–9

BABBITT, NATALIE, *The Devil's Storybook,* ill. by author, Farrar, 1974. Ten brief tales about a plump, vain Devil.   9–11
Kneeknock Rise, ill. by author, Farrar, 1970. A lively, suspenseful fantasy which examines the nature of truth and its meaning for various people.   9–12
The Something, ill. by author, Farrar, 1970. What's the "something" a little cavedweller fears? A child of today, and they meet in dreams.   4–6
Tuck Everlasting, Farrar, 1975. A fine blend of fantasy and realism, in a deftly written story about immortality.   9–11

BAILEY, CAROLYN SHERWIN, *Finnegan II: His Nine Lives,* ill. by Kate Seredy, Viking, 1953. The story of how Finnegan II lost one after another of his lives in one short year but lived to scoff at the legend that a cat has only nine lives.   9–11
Miss Hickory, ill. by Ruth Gannett, Viking, 1946. The story of a homemade doll and her remarkable adventures in Boston. Newbery Medal.   9–11

BARRIE, J. M., *Peter Pan in Kensington Gardens,* retold by May Byron, ill. by Arthur Rackham, Scribner's, 1930. This is a simplified version. The illustrations are considered by some critics to be the richest and most imaginative work of this noted illustrator.   8–10
Peter Pan, ill. by Nora Unwin, Scribner's, 1950. Peter Pan, the boy who never grew up, and all his delightful companions are beautifully pictured in this edition.   9–12

BAUM, LYMAN FRANK, *The Wizard of Oz,* new ed., ill. by W. W. Denslow, Reilly, 1964. The story of Dorothy and Toto's visit to the Land of Oz is perennially popular with children since it was first published in 1900. Many sequels are also available from the publisher listed above. Other editions are available from Dutton and Parents Magazine Press and in various paperback versions.   8–11

BELLAIRS, JOHN, *The House with a Clock in Its Walls,* ill. by Edward Gorey, Dial, 1973. This and its sequel, *The Figure in the Shadows* (ill. by Mercer Mayer, Dial, 1974), describe the adventures of a boy who lives with an amiable uncle who's a wizard.   10–12

BIANCO, MARGERY WILLIAMS, *The Velveteen Rabbit,* ill. by William Nicholson, Doubleday, 1926, 1958. How a very old velveteen rabbit, with the aid of the Fairy of Old Toys, becomes real and goes off into the real world.   4–7

BIEGEL, PAUL, *The King of the Copper Mountains,* English version by Gillian Hume and author, ill. by Babs Van Wely, Watts, 1969. A series of tales told by animals help keep the King alive. Dutch Children's Book Award winner.   9–11

BISHOP, CLAIRE H., *The Five Chinese Brothers,* ill. by Kurt Wiese, Coward, 1938. Told in folk-tale style, this very funny story has been a favorite of kindergartners for many years.   5–8

BOND, MICHAEL, *A Bear Called Paddington,* ill. by Peggy Fortnum, Houghton, 1960. This and the subsequent books in the series chronicle the adventures of Paddington, a Peruvian brown bear, whom the Brown family found wandering in Paddington Railway Station in London. He became a member of the family and complicated its life ever after.   6–10
The Tales of Olga da Polga, ill. by Hans Helweg, Macmillan, 1973. A humorous tale of a guinea pig. 9–10

BOSTON, LUCY MARIA, *The Castle of Yew,* ill. by Margery Gill, Harcourt, 1965. This brief tale involves the imaginative play of two boys who suddenly find themselves small enough to inhabit the castle of a topiary yew chess set. This book is for children younger than the readers of the author's *Green Knowe* stories. 8–10
The Children of Green Knowe, ill. by Peter Boston, Harcourt, 1955.   9–11
Treasure of Green Knowe, ill. by Peter Boston, Harcourt, 1958.
The River at Green Knowe, ill. by Peter Boston, Harcourt, 1959.
An Enemy at Green Knowe, ill. by Peter Boston, Harcourt, 1964.
Beautifully written fantasies that skillfully blend present and past.   9–12
The Sea Egg, ill. by Peter Boston, Harcourt, 1967. A finely written fantasy woven around an episode in the lives of two boys on vacation at the seaside. The egg-shaped stone which they place in a tide pool disappears, and a few days later they observe a child merman playing with the seals.   8–10

BRAND, CHRISTIANNA, *Nurse Matilda,* ill. by Edward Ardizzone, Dutton, 1964.
Nurse Matilda Goes to Town, ill. by Edward Ardizzone, Dutton, 1968.
Although Nurse Matilda is not as attractive a character as Mary Poppins, she also has some marvelous ways of exacting obedience, and incredibly naughty children are soon brought into line.   7–10

BRIGGS, RAYMOND, *Father Christmas,* ill. by author, Coward, 1973. A series of cartoon-style frames show a grumbling Santa making heavy weather of his job.   5–8

BRINK, CAROL R., *Andy Buckram's Tin Men,* ill. by W. T. Mars, Viking, 1966. Andy builds four robots to help with his routine farm chores. When danger threatens, the robots rise to the challenge and perform heroically.   9–11

BROCK, BETTY, *No Flying in the House,* ill. by Wallace Tripp, Harper, 1970. Half a fairy, Annabel can fly!   7–9

BROOKS, WALTER, *Freddy Goes to Florida,* ill. by Kurt Wiese, Knopf, 1927, 1949.
Freddy and the Dragon, ill. by Kurt Wiese, Knopf, 1958. Between these two books lies a long series (twenty-one titles) of *Freddy* stories that enjoy enormous popularity.   9–12

BRUNHOFF, JEAN DE, *The Story of Babar, the Little Elephant,* tr. by Merle Haas, ill. by author, Random, 1933. This delightful story about the young elephant who was reared by an elderly lady has long been a favorite with young children. Many titles follow in the series, but some lack the charm and appeal of the first. The author's son, Laurent de Brunhoff, has carried on the series and has added another memorable animal character—Serafina, the giraffe.   4–7

BUCHWALD, EMILIE, *Gildaen: The Heroic Adventures of a Most Unusual Rabbit,* ill. by Barbara Flynn, Harcourt, 1973. Magic and humor in a lively story.   9–11

BURNETT, FRANCES H., *Racketty-Packetty House,* ill. by Harrison Cady, Dodd, 1961. An old-fashioned story of dolls and their house.   6–9

BURTON, VIRGINIA, *Katy and the Big Snow,* ill. by author, Houghton, 1943.
The Little House, ill. by author, Houghton, 1942. Caldecott Medal.
Mike Mulligan and His Steam Shovel, ill. by author, Houghton, 1939.
These fanciful stories, which have as their real heroes an enormous tractor, an old-fashioned house, and a steam shovel, respectively, have delighted three generations of children and will probably survive to amuse several more.   5–8

BUTTERWORTH, OLIVER, *The Enormous Egg,* ill. by Louis Darling, Little, 1956. A tale of the fantastic complications that develop for twelve-year-old Nate Twitchell when a baby Triceratops emerges from a giant egg found in the family henhouse.   9–11
The Trouble with Jenny's Ear, ill. by Julian de Miskey, Little, 1960. When her two brothers discover that Jenny has an unusually sensitive ear that can hear thoughts, they arrange her appearance on a TV quiz show.   9–11

CAMERON, ELEANOR, *The Court of the Stone Children,* Dutton, 1973. Mystery and fantasy deftly blended.

National Book Award. 10–12

The Wonderful Flight to the Mushroom Planet, ill. by Robert Henneberger, Little, 1954.

Stowaway to the Mushroom Planet, ill. by Robert Henneberger, Little, 1956.

A Mystery for Mr. Bass, ill. by Leonard Shortall, Little, 1960.

Time and Mr. Bass: A Mushroom Planet Book, ill. by Fred Meise, Little, 1967.

These four books, which relate the adventures of David and Chuck on the Mushroom Planet, are an interesting mixture of fantasy and science fiction. 9–11

The Terrible Churnadryne, ill. by Beth and Joe Krush, Little, 1959. Fast-paced, suspenseful writing marks this story, which moves convincingly on the border between realism and fantasy. 9–11

CARROLL, LEWIS (pseud. for Charles Lutwidge Dodgson), *Alice's Adventures in Wonderland* and *Through the Looking Glass*. Many editions are available.
10–up

CERVANTES, MIGUEL DE, *The Adventures of Don Quixote de la Mancha*, adapted by Leighton Barret from the Motteux translation, ill. by Warren Chappell, Knopf, 1945, 1960. 12–up

CHASE, MARY, *The Wicked Pigeon Ladies in the Garden*, ill. by Don Bolognese, Knopf, 1968. A delightfully scary fantasy about a neighborhood pest and how she incurs the anger of seven evil sisters who haunt an abandoned mansion in the guise of pigeons. 9–12

Loretta Mason Potts, ill. by Harold Berson, Lippincott, 1959. An absorbing tale of a naughty child and the fantasy world which she inhabits. 9–12

CHRISMAN, ARTHUR B., *Shen of the Sea*, ill. by Elsie Hasselriis, Dutton, 1925, 1968. These original fairy tales, set in China, seem very similar to folk tales and are told with glee and subtle humor. Newbery Medal.
10–12

CHRISTOPHER, JOHN, *The Guardians*, Macmillan, 1970. Superior science fiction set in 21st century England.
11–14

The Prince in Waiting, Macmillan, 1970. First in a trilogy (*Beyond the Burning Lands*, 1971; *Sword of the Spirits*, 1972) of England returned to feudalism.
11–14

The White Mountains and its sequels, *The City of Gold and Lead*, Macmillan, 1967, and *The Pool of Fire*, 1968. Exciting science fiction. Supposedly, earth has been invaded from outer space, and men are controlled by means of wire-mesh caps permanently attached to their scalps at the age of fourteen. The books are concerned with the adventures of three boys who decide to evade the capping ceremony. 10–13

CLEARY, BEVERLY, *The Mouse and the Motorcycle*, ill. by Louis Darling, Morrow, 1965. A delightful fantasy about a mouse who makes friends with a boy and learns how to ride a toy motorcycle. 7–9

Runaway Ralph, ill. by Louis Darling, Morrow, 1970. In this lively sequel to the book listed above, Ralph makes a daring bid for freedom. 8–10

COATSWORTH, ELIZABETH, *The Cat Who Went to Heaven*, ill. by Lynd Ward, Macmillan, 1930, 1967. A humble Japanese artist risks his future to include the portrait of his cat in a painting for the temple. A miraculous change in the picture rewards his unselfish act. Newbery Medal. 9–12

COBLENTZ, CATHERINE CATE, *The Blue Cat of Castle Town*, ill. by Janice Holland, McKay, 1949. The blue Kitten, born under a blue moon, learned the river's song, "Enchantment is made of three things—of beauty, peace and content." 9–12

COLLODI, See LORENZINI

COOPER, SUSAN, *Over Sea, Under Stone*, ill. by Margery Gill, Harcourt, 1966. An unusual story which melds mystery, Arthurian legend, and allegory. Two children, aided by an old uncle, follow the clues found on an ancient parchment and find themselves involved in the age-old struggle between good and evil. *Greenwitch*, Atheneum, 1974, *The Dark Is Rising*, 1973, and *Grey King*, 1975, are sequels. 10–12

CORBETT, SCOTT, *Ever Ride a Dinosaur?* ill. by Mircea Vasiliu, Holt, 1969. Charlie rides a dinosaur whose one ambition is to see a museum dinosaur exhibit—which is easy if you can make yourself invisible. 9–11

The Lemonade Trick, ill. by Paul Galdone, Little, 1960. First in a series of "Trick" books about the magic powers of a chemistry set. All bouncy and amusing.
8–11

CRAIG, M. JEAN, *The Dragon in the Clock Box*, ill. by Kelly Oechsli, Norton, 1962. While not fantasy in the usual sense of the word, this is a highly fanciful story that is concerned with the amusing imaginative play of a child. 5–7

CRESSWELL, HELEN, *The Bongleweed*, Macmillan, 1973. Fantasy adroitly integrated with the reality of a family desperately resisting a plant that takes over. 9–11

CUNNINGHAM, JULIA, *Candle Tales*, ill. by Evaline Ness, Pantheon, 1964. A story within a story made up of the rhyming tales which six little animals tell to a rather crabbed candlemaker each evening. Happily, the lonely old man enjoys the stories so much that he invites the animals to live with him. 8–10

Dorp Dead, ill. by James Spanfeller, Pantheon, 1965. A memorable story of an orphan boy who is sent from the orphanage to live with a seemingly pleasant carpenter. With growing terror the boy, Gilly, discerns that the carpenter's true purpose is to make him into an utterly submissive slave. A sharp mixture of hard reality and allegory well worth introducing to youngsters. 10–up

CURRY, JANE LOUISE, *Beneath the Hill*, ill. by Imero Gobbato, Harcourt, 1967. A group of Pennsylvania children attempt to aid Welsh elfin folk in their struggle against the evil forces released by a strip-mining operation. 9–11

DAHL, ROALD, *Charlie and the Chocolate Factory*, ill. by Joseph Schindelman, Knopf, 1964. Charlie, who lives in dire poverty, is one of five children chosen to visit a chocolate factory whose eccentric owner is seeking an heir. When tests finally eliminate the other children, Charlie is chosen to inherit the bizarre and wonderful factory. 10–11

James and the Giant Peach, ill. by Nancy Ekholm Burkert, Knopf, 1961. When his parents were devoured in "thirty-five seconds flat" by an angry rhinoceros, James was sent to live with two very unpleasant aunts. After three years of misery he made his escape across the Atlantic in a giant peach, which also carried some very strange insect companions.
9–11

The Magic Finger, ill. by William Pène du Bois, Harper, 1966. An original and intriguing fantasy in which an eight-year-old girl, whose right forefinger acquires magic powers whenever she becomes angry, turns a teacher into a cat and a family of hunters into the hunted.   8–10

DAUGHERTY, JAMES, *Andy and the Lion,* ill. by author, Viking, 1938. Young Andy had read about lions but never expected to meet one. The encounter ends in adventure for both of them and for the reader.   6–8

DE LA MARE, WALTER, *A Penny a Day,* ill. by Paul Kennedy, Knopf, 1960. Six tales of fantasy which offer choice reading aloud. Followed by a companion volume, *The Magic Jacket* (1962).   10–13
The Three Royal Monkeys, ill. by M. E. Eldridge, Knopf, 1948. Originally published as *The Three Mulla-Mulgars,* this distinguished fantasy is a long story of the adventures of three young monkeys who go in search of their father, a prince from the valley of Tishner.   12–up
Mr. Bumps and His Monkey, ill. by Dorothy Lathrop, Holt, 1942. The story of the monkey who came to London from Africa, learned to speak English, affected the dress of a British gentleman, and eventually became the toast of the theater.   8–11

DEL REY, LESTER, *The Runaway Robot,* Westminster, 1965. Convincing science-fiction account of a sixteen-year-old boy and his companion robot, Rex, who refuse to be separated when the boy's family is to be transferred back to earth.   12–15

DEUTSCH, BABETTE, and AVRAHM YARMOLINSKY, *The Steel Flea,* adapted from the Russian of Nicholas Leskov, ill. by Janina Domanska, Harper, 1964. A humorous account of the dancing steel flea that was made by English craftsmen for Alexander, Czar of Russia.   8–10

DICKENS, CHARLES, *Captain Boldheart and The Magic Fishbone,* ill. by Hilary Knight, Macmillan, 1964. Two comedies presented in picture-book format. Boldheart was certainly the bravest ten-year-old pirate ever to set foot on a ship. "The Magic Fishbone," the story of a princess and her eighteen brothers and sisters, will delight girls.   8–10
A Christmas Carol, ill. by Arthur Rackham, Lippincott, 1956. The story of Ebenezer Scrooge and his discovery of the true meaning of Christmas has timeless appeal for both young and old.   8–up
The Magic Fishbone, ill. by Louis Slobodkin, Vanguard, 1953. Slobodkin's illustrations enhance this charming fairy tale.   8–10

DICKINSON, PETER, *The Devil's Children,* Little, 1970.
Heartsease, ill. by Nathan Goldstein, Little, 1969.
The Weathermonger, Little, 1969. A trilogy, set in England, which explores a future in which machines have been outlawed, superstitious belief in witchcraft is prevalent, and only the courage and faith of the young seem to hold promise for mankind.   10–14
The Gift, Little, 1974. Davy's Welsh grandmother has the gift, and he too can read minds—an ability that leads him into a dangerous adventure.   10–14

DOLBIER, MAURICE, *Torten's Christmas Secret,* ill. by Robert Henneberger, Little, 1951. This gay Christmas story involves Santa's toy factory, hard-working gnomes, lists of good and bad children, and lovely glimpses of Santa's frosty, sparkling Arctic world.   4–8

DRURY, ROGER W., *The Finches' Fabulous Furnace,* ill. by Erik Blegvad, Little, 1971. It's not easy to keep a family from learning that the furnace is really a very small, quite active, volcano.   9–11

DU BOIS, WILLIAM PÈNE, *The Alligator Case,* ill. by author, Harper, 1965. The story of an unusually alert boy detective who starts working on the case before the crime is committed.   8–10
Bear Party, ill. by author, Viking, 1951, 1963. A wise old koala bear gives a costume party which serves to reunite all the bears and make them stop quarreling. Delightful fantasy with allegorical overtones.   5–7
Elisabeth the Cow Ghost, ill. by author, Viking, 1936, 1964. The story of gentle Elisabeth, who decided to reveal her true, fiery nature after her death and returned to haunt her former master.   5–8
The Horse in the Camel Suit, ill. by author, Harper, 1967. The boy detective who solved the *Alligator Case* pits his skill against a troupe of entertainers who turn out to be horse thieves in disguise.   8–10
The Twenty-One Balloons, ill. by author, Viking, 1947. Newbery Medal.   11–up

DUVOISIN, ROGER, *Petunia,* ill. by author, Knopf, 1950. *Petunia, I Love You,* ill. by author, Knopf, 1965. Between these two titles the author has given us four other humorous stories about the doings of this adventurous and silly goose.   5–8
Veronica, ill. by author, Knopf, 1961. As with Petunia, the author has told the adventures of Veronica, an extremely versatile hippopotamus, in several amusingly illustrated picture books.   5–8

EAGER, EDWARD M., *Half Magic,* ill. by N. M. Bodecker, Harcourt, 1954.
Magic by the Lake, ill. by N. M. Bodecker, Harcourt, 1957.
Magic or Not? ill. by N. M. Bodecker, Harcourt, 1959.
The Well-Wishers, ill. by N. M. Bodecker, Harcourt, 1960. Although the above titles do not comprise a series in the usual sense of the word, they do have many elements in common: lively, somewhat bookish children, humor, magic, and lighthearted satire of the current scene.   9–11

ENGDAHL, SYLVIA LOUISE, *Beyond the Tomorrow Mountains,* ill. by Richard Cuffari, Atheneum, 1973. A sequel to *This Star Shall Abide* (1972) continues the story of a young man's maturing in a world that is rebuilding after Earth is doomed.   11–14
Journey Between Worlds, ill. by James and Ruth McCrea, Atheneum, 1970. A story of the pioneers of the future and their life on Mars.   12–14

ENRIGHT, ELIZABETH, *Tatsinda,* ill. by Irene Haas, Harcourt, 1963. This original, strikingly illustrated fairy tale on the topic of unreasoning conformity offers children penetrating social comment, coupled with the delight and suspense of a well-told tale.   8–11
Zeee, ill. by Irene Haas, Harcourt, 1965. Glowingly illustrated and expertly told, this humorous fairy tale with allegorical overtones concerns the efforts of an irritable fairy to find a suitable home.   7–9

ESTES, ELEANOR, *The Witch Family,* ill. by Edward Ardizzone, Harcourt, 1960. The witches created by Amy and Clarissa with crayons and paper take on an independent life of their own. The result is a fine blend of reality and fantasy.   6–10

ETS, MARIE HALL, *Mister Penny,* ill. by author, Viking, 1935. Mr. Penny's good-for-nothing animals did nothing to help themselves or their master. But after they

ate up old Thunderstorm's garden, they redeemed themselves and saved Mr. Penny from a life of toil.
6–8

Mister Penny's Race Horse, ill. by author, Viking, 1956. Further adventures of Mr. Penny and his animals.
6–8

Mr. T. W. Anthony Woo, ill. by author, Viking, 1951. Mr. Woo and his cat, dog, and mouse live together, but not too happily. When Mr. Woo's meddling sister moves in with the idea of reforming them, they unite against the common enemy and learn to live peacefully. Humorous pictures add to the fun.
7–9

FARJEON, ELEANOR, *The Glass Slipper,* ill. by Ernest H. Shepard, Viking, 1956. An extension of the story of Cinderella into a full-length book.
8–11

The Little Bookroom, ill. by Edward Ardizzone, Walck, 1956. Twenty-seven stories with the author's unique blend of reality and fantasy, humor and wisdom. Most of them are excellent for reading aloud.
6–10

The Silver Curlew, ill. by Ernest H. Shepard, Viking, 1954. An expansion of the story of Tom Tit Tot, to which Shepard's humorous illustrations add a great deal.
8–11

FARMER, PENELOPE, *The Summer Birds,* ill. by James J. Spanfeller, Harcourt, 1962. The children of a small English village are faced with a difficult decision when the boy who has taught them to fly asks them to go with him to save his race from extinction. Followed by *Emma in Winter,* ill. by James J. Spanfeller, Harcourt, 1966.
9–12

William and Mary; A Story, Atheneum, 1974. Two children are transported to other times and places when they hold a magic shell. Fine style and characterization.
10–12

FATIO, LOUISE, *The Happy Lion,* ill. by Roger Duvoisin, McGraw, 1954. An unlocked gate inspires the amiable lion in a little French zoo to return the calls of the villagers. The results are amusing. Roger Duvoisin's drawings are humorous and full of atmosphere. This first story about the Happy Lion has been followed by others equally hilarious and popular: *The Happy Lion in Africa* (1955), *The Happy Lion Roars* (1957), *The Happy Lion's Rabbits* (1974), and others.
5–8

FIELD, RACHEL, *Hitty, Her First Hundred Years,* ill. by Dorothy P. Lathrop, Macmillan, 1929. Hitty was a doll of real character, and the adventures of her first hundred years are varied and satisfying to little girls. Newbery Medal.
10–13

FISK, NICHOLAS, *Grinny,* Nelson, 1974. The sweet old lady at Tim's door announces she's Great-aunt Emma but Tim's little sister calls her "Grinny" and suspects the malevolence of the lady with metal bones.
10–12

Trillions, Pantheon, 1973. One of the few science fiction books for children that have the theme of invasion from outer space.
11–13

FLACK, MARJORIE, *Walter the Lazy Mouse,* ill. by Cyndy Szekeres, Doubleday, 1939, 1963. A whimsical tale about a lazy mouse whose family forgot him when they moved.
6–8

FLEISCHMAN, SID, *McBroom Tells the Truth,* ill. by Kurt Werth, Norton, 1966.

McBroom and the Big Wind, ill. by Kurt Werth, Norton, 1967.

McBroom the Rainmaker, ill. by Kurt Werth, Grosset, 1973.
Tall tales spun by an author with a great sense of the ridiculous and the ability to make it seem plausible.
7–10

FLEMING, IAN, *Chitty-Chitty-Bang-Bang,* ill. by John Burningham, Random, 1964. The Potts, owners of a magic auto, took a sea voyage in it and stumbled onto a gangster's cave. When they were surrounded by danger, Chitty-Chitty-Bang-Bang took over.
9–11

FLORA, JAMES, *Grandpa's Farm,* ill. by author, Harcourt, 1965. This book is sure to bring chortles of delight from the children who hear about the time the cow's tail got cut off and Grandma's marvelous ointment, applied to each part, causes a new tail to grow on the cow and a new cow on the tail!
5–8

FREEMAN, BARBARA C., *Broom-Adelaide,* ill. by author, Little, 1965. A convincing tale of magic and mystery in which the evil powers of a feared and abhorred governess are revealed and destroyed.
8–10

FRITZ, JEAN, *Magic to Burn,* ill. by Beth and Joe Krush, Coward, 1964. An amusing tale, excellently illustrated, in which an English boggart causes his hosts much trouble when he decides to return to America with them.
9–11

GÁG, WANDA, *The Funny Thing,* ill. by author, Coward, 1920.
Millions of Cats, ill. by author, Coward, 1938.
Nothing at All, ill. by author, Coward, 1941.
These three picture books, by a noted author-illustrator, contain fun, suspense, and incredible happenings of great appeal to children.
4–9

GAGE, WILSON, *Miss Osborne-the-Mop,* ill. by Paul Galdone, World, 1963. When Jody accidentally turns her cousin into a squirrel, her magic powers seem quite delightful; but when a mop comes alive and begins to direct the children's activities, the youngsters take a different view.
9–11

GARD, JOYCE, *Talargain,* Holt, 1965. The story that Talargain, who wanders the seas as a member of a band of seals, tells to Lucilla, a young girl of today, concerns his life as a human in the seventh century.
11–up

GARNER, ALAN, *Elidor,* Walck, 1967. A convincing, eerie, atmospheric fantasy in which four English children are transported backward in time to a war-torn medieval kingdom and become involved with the forces of evil that are striving to destroy the realm.
9–11

The Moon of Gomrath, Walck, 1967. This original story has its sources in the mythology of the British, Celtic, and Scandinavian peoples. A child, aided by dwarfs and elves, battles against the evil forces called to life by the power of an ancient bracelet.
10–12

The Owl Service, Walck, 1968. A story of suspense and beauty in which three youths of today are caught up in the mystery of an ancient Welsh legend and are seemingly forced to reenact it.
13–up

GATES, DORIS, *The Cat and Mrs. Cary,* ill. by Peggy Bacon, Viking, 1962. A story which moves quite convincingly on the border between realism and fantasy. The only fantastic element is a talking cat who talks to no one but Mrs. Cary.
8–11

GEISEL, THEODOR SEUSS (pseud., Dr. Seuss), *And to Think That I Saw It on Mulberry Street,* ill. by author,

Vanguard, 1937.

The 500 Hats of Bartholomew Cubbins, ill. by author, Vanguard, 1938.

Horton Hatches the Egg, ill. by author, Random, 1940.

The King's Stilts, ill. by author, Random, 1939.

This prolific author has written and illustrated more than twenty books for children. All feature improbable creatures performing incredible feats. Probably, Dr. Seuss will be remembered best for his imaginative use of language and his facility in inventing descriptive names for the creatures of his imagination. In general, his earlier books are superior to his later ones. The titles listed above are among his best. 4–10

GODDEN, RUMER, *Candy Floss,* ill. by Adrienne Adams, Viking, 1960. Candy Floss, a doll with compelling powers, is stolen by a spoiled child, but is eventually returned to the carnival worker to whom she belongs. 7–10

The Doll's House, ill. by Tasha Tudor, Viking, 1962. A completely enthralling book about the adventures of Tottie, a Dutch farthing doll. 7–10

The Dragon of Og, ill. by Pauline Baynes, Viking, 1981. Shy and gentle, a young dragon is revived after being slain and becomes the good luck symbol of the castle and its folk. 9–12

Impunity Jane, ill. by Adrienne Adams, Viking, 1954. An excellent doll story that boys will enjoy. 8–10

Mouse House, ill. by Adrienne Adams, Viking, 1957. An enchanting and brief story that tells how a little mouse, crowded out of the nest, finds a comfortable new home. 7–10

The Story of Holly and Ivy, ill. by Adrienne Adams, Viking, 1958. A fanciful tale of the fortuitous way in which a doll, an orphan, and a lonely woman are united at Christmas time. 7–10

GOODALL, JOHN S., *The Adventures of Paddy Pork,* ill. by author, Harcourt, 1968. This delightful fantasy depicts, without text, the adventures of a brash young pig who runs off to join the circus. 4–7

The Ballooning Adventures of Paddy Pork, Harcourt, 1969. Another picture story, this one showing the rescue of a pretty young piglet from the pot under which some cannibal gorillas are ready to light a fire. 5–7

GOUDGE, ELIZABETH, *The Little White Horse,* ill. by C. Walter Hodges, Coward, 1947. This memorable mystery story, set in the west of England more than a century ago, contains a rare blend of fantasy and realism. 12–15

Linnets and Valerians, ill. by Ian Robbins, Coward, 1964. A rather special concoction of witchcraft, fantasy, and reality. Four children run away from their stern grandmother, only to be taken in by their great-uncle who is equally strict in a different way. 10–12

GOULD, JOAN, *Otherborn,* Coward, 1980. Cast ashore on a tropical island, two children find a race that is born old and gets younger and younger as death nears. 11–14

GRAHAME, KENNETH, *The Reluctant Dragon,* ill. by Ernest H. Shepard, Holiday, 1938, 1953. A subtly amusing tale about a boy who made friends with a dragon and contrived to have him meet and fight St. George. 10–12

The Wind in the Willows, ill. by Ernest Shepard, Scribner's, 1953. 9–12

GRAMATKY, HARDIE, *Hercules,* ill. by author, Putnam, 1940.

Little Toot, ill. by author, Putnam, 1939.

Loopy, ill. by author, Putnam, 1941. An ancient fire engine, a tugboat, and a very early model airplane are amusingly personified in these ever popular picture books. 4–9

GRAY, GENEVIEVE, *Ghost Story,* ill. by Greta Matus, Lothrop, 1975. When a bum moves into the house they're haunting, Mama feels he's a bad influence on the kids. A blithe tale in breezy style. 8–10

GRAY, NICHOLAS STUART, *Mainly in Moonlight,* ill. by Charles Keeping, Merdith, 1967. A group of original stories with appeal for children who are a bit older than the usual fairy-tale age. The settings are traditional, but the language and colloquial expressions used are very modern. 10–14

GRIPE, MARIA, *The Glassblower's Children,* tr. by Sheila La Farge, ill. by Harald Gripe, Delacorte, 1973. A tale of good and evil in the Gothic vein. 9–11

GROSSER, MORTON, *The Snake Horn,* ill. by David Stone, Atheneum, 1973. Playing the tartöld, a snake-shaped horn, brought its owner from the 17th century into Danny's room. 10–12

HALE, LUCRETIA, *The Complete Peterkin Papers,* Houghton, 1960. 10–12

HAMILTON, VIRGINIA, *Justice and Her Brothers,* Greenwillow, 1978; *Dustland,* Greenwillow, 1980; and *The Gathering,* Greenwillow, 1981. A stunning trilogy about a group of black children who test their psychic powers as they travel in time and space. 12–15

Sweet Whispers, Brother Rush, Philomel, 1982. A fantasy element is smoothly merged with the touching story of an adolescent girl's protective love for an older brother, gentle and retarded. 11–14

HARRIS, ROSEMARY, *The Moon in the Cloud,* Macmillan, 1968. A humorous, much-embroidered retelling of the story of Noah's ark. 10–up

The Seal-Singing, Macmillan, 1971. A smooth blend of realism and the supernatural, set in Scotland. 11–14

The Shadow on the Sun, Macmillan, 1970. In the sequel to the book first listed above, Reuben and Thamar return to Egypt for a visit. 10–up

HAUFF, WILHELM, *Dwarf Long-Nose,* tr. by Doris Orgel, ill. by Maurice Sendak, Random, 1960. This is the well-known German fairy tale about the shoemaker's son who was "herb-enchanted" by an evil fairy. It is given new life by Sendak's illustrations. 9–11

HEINLEIN, ROBERT A., *Farmer in the Sky,* ill. by Clifford Geary, Scribner's, 1950. 11–13

Have Space Suit—Will Travel, Scribner's, 1958.

Podkayne of Mars; Her Life and Times, Putnam, 1963. One of the few science fiction stories with a female protagonist, and a cracking good one. 11–14

Rocket Ship Galileo, ill. by Thomas Voter, Scribner's, 1947.

Space Cadet, ill. by Clifford N. Geary, Scribner's, 1948. All of Heinlein's science-fiction novels are written for the teen-ager or adult. Those listed above are also suitable for a younger age group. 11–up

HENDERSON, LEGRAND. *See* LeGrand.

HOBAN, LILLIAN and PHOEBE, *The Laziest Robot in Zone One,* ill. by Lillian Hoban, Harper, 1983. A brisk story about a little robot and his friends. 4–8

HOBAN, RUSSELL, *Bedtime for Frances,* ill. by Garth Williams, Harper, 1960. The first of a series of books about a small badger, all delightful. 3–6

The Mouse and His Child, ill. by Lillian Hoban, Harper, 1967. A tender and delicate fantasy about a wind-up tin toy, a father and child with paws attached. 9–11

HODGES, ELIZABETH JAMISON, *Serendipity Tales,* retold; ill. by June Atkin Corwin, Atheneum, 1966. Seven well-written, carefully plotted fairy tales set in Persia. They recount the victories of faith, hope, and steadfastness over the worst deeds of men and gods. 9–11

The Three Princes of Serendip, retold; ill. by Joan Berg, Atheneum, 1964. The three princes are sent into the world by their father to finish their education and to find a way of ridding the seas of monsters. 10–12

HOLMAN, FELICE, *The Escape of the Giant Hogstalk,* ill. by Ben Shecter, Scribner's, 1974. A blithe, nonsensical tale of a giant plant that runs amok. 8–11

The Future of Hooper Toote, ill. by Gahan Wilson, Scribner's, 1972. A very funny story about a boy whose feet just won't stay on the ground. 9–12

HOLT, ISABELLA, *The Adventures of Rinaldo,* ill. by Erik Blegvad, Little, 1959. A rather old and worn, albeit courageous, knight seeks and wins a wife and castle. A jaunty tale in the manner of *Don Quixote.* 10–13

HOOVER, H. M. *Children of Morrow,* Four Winds, 1973. Telepathy is used to rescue two children from a cruel culture in a fast-paced science fiction story. 10–13

HOWE, DEBORAH and JAMES, *Bunnicula: A Rabbit-Tale of Mystery,* ill. by Alan Daniel, Atheneum, 1979. Chester, the Monroe's literate and suspicious cat, is convinced that the new pet rabbit is a vampire, in a hilarious and witty story. 9–11

HUDDY, DELIA, *Time Piper,* Greenwillow, 1979. A medieval legend is brought to life in a science fantasy written with depth and perception. 11–13

HUNTER, MOLLIE, *The Haunted Mountain,* ill. by Laszlo Kubinyi, Harper, 1972. Brave McAllister defies the blind ghost that guards the treasure of the mountain. 10–12

The Kelpie's Pearls, ill. by Joseph Cellini, Funk, 1966. When old Morag saved the kelpie's life, she set in motion a chain of happenings. A convincing, suspenseful fantasy in which humane values triumph over fear and avarice. 9–12

The Smartest Man in Ireland, ill. by Charles Keeping, Funk, 1965. A modern fairy tale about a boaster who bragged that he was smart enough to outwit the little people. When they stole his son away, he had to make good on his boasting. 9–11

The Walking Stones, ill. by Trina Schart Hyman, Harper, 1970. Once a century, the stones walk, and an old Highlander staves off the building of a dam to let it happen just once more. Eerie yet convincing. 10–12

JANSSON, TOVE, *The Exploits of Moominpappa,* tr. by Thomas Warburton, ill. by author, Walck, 1966.

Finn Family Moomintroll, tr. by Elizabeth Portch, ill. by author, Walck, 1965.

Moominland Midwinter, tr. by Thomas Warburton, ill. by author, Walck, 1962.

Moominpappa at Sea, tr. by Kingsley Hart, ill. by author, Walck, 1967.

Moominsummer Madness, tr. by Thomas Warburton, ill. by author, Walck, 1961.

Moominvalley in November, tr. by Kingsley Hart, ill. by author, Walck, 1971.

Tales from Moominvalley, tr. by Thomas Warburton, ill. by author, Walck, 1964.

These highly imaginative fantasies have been largely ignored in this country. Since, however, the author received the 1966 Hans Christian Andersen Award, it is likely that more librarians and teachers will read these engaging stories and bring them to the attention of children. 9–12

JARRELL, RANDALL, *The Animal Family,* ill. by Maurice Sendak, Pantheon, 1965. A memorable story of a solitary hunter who takes unto himself some remarkable companions: a mermaid, a bear cub, a lynx, and a little boy. How they adjust to each other and become a loving family is perceptively told. 10–up

The Bat-Poet, ill. by Maurice Sendak, Macmillan, 1967. A beautiful tale about a little brown bat who does not conform to the habits of bats. Instead, he opens his eyes in the daytime and awakens to a whole world previously unknown to him. For the sensitive reader who likes to daydream. 10–up

JESCHKE, SUSAN, *Firerose,* ill. by author, Holt, 1974. A fresh, amusing tale of a foundling who can't be admitted to school because she has a dragon's tail. 5–8

JOHNSON, CROCKETT (pseud. of David Leisk), *Ellen's Lion,* ill. by author, Harper, 1959. Twelve whimsical stories about Ellen's conversations with her stuffed toy lion—talk which, though seemingly absurd, carries bits of wisdom. This author's stories about Harold, especially *Harold and the Purple Crayon* (Harper, 1955) and *Harold's Trip to the Sky* (Harper, 1957), are also popular with children. 5–8

JOHNSON, SALLY PATRICK, ed., *The Harper Book of Princes,* ill. by Janina Domanska, Harper, 1964. Twelve enjoyable stories, each of which describes the training of the mind and heart of a prince and the testing of these qualities. The book contains biographical notes on each author. 9–12

The Princesses, ill. by Beni Montresor, Harper, 1962. Well-chosen selections, most given in their complete and original form, which encompass a variety of plots and styles. Includes biographical notes on each author. 9–11

JONES, ELIZABETH ORTON, *Big Susan,* ill. by author, Macmillan, 1967. An entrancing little story about the happenings in a dollhouse on the one night of the year when dolls can come alive and speak. 8–10

JUSTER, MORTON, *The Phantom Tollbooth,* ill. by Jules Feiffer, Random, 1961. An extensive, well-written fantasy with much clever play on words and ironic social comment. Milo, a very bored boy, puts together a gift, which proves to be a tollbooth. After he pays his toll, he finds himself in an exceedingly strange land where he encounters many unusual characters and has some extraordinary adventures. 10–up

KAHL, VIRGINIA, *Away Went Wolfgang!* ill. by author, Scribner's, 1954. Wolfgang was the least useful dog in an Austrian village, until the housewives discovered that when Wolfgang ran, he could churn a whole cartful of milk into butter! 5–8

The Duchess Bakes a Cake, ill. by author, Scribner's, 1955. A humorous, rhymed story of the duchess who was carried skyward atop the light fluffy cake she had baked.   6–10

The Perfect Pancake, ill. by author, Scribner's, 1960. A lighthearted rhymed story about the good wife who limited her "feathery, fluffy, and flavory" pancakes one to a person.   6–10

KÄSTNER, ERICH, *The Little Man*, ill. by Rick Schreiter, tr. by James Kirkup, Knopf, 1966. An extremely funny fantasy about a two-inch-high circus artist who plans not only his own rescue from kidnapers but also the subsequent arrest of his abductors.   9–11

The Little Man and the Big Thief, ill. by Stanley Mack, tr. by James Kirkup, Knopf, 1970. An interesting sequel which ties up some of the unsolved problems of the earlier book and introduces a possible wife for Maxie.   9–up

KENDALL, CAROL, *The Gammage Cup*, ill. by Erik Blegvad, Harcourt, 1959. A compelling well-written fantasy about the Minnipins, or Small Ones, who dwell in the land between the mountains.   10–12

KING-SMITH, DICK, *Pigs Might Fly*, ill. by Mary Rayner, Viking, 1982. Daggie, the runt of a pig litter, becomes a hero by rescuing the other pigs during a flash flood; Daggie can't fly, but he has learned to swim, in this witty and entertaining tale.   9–11

KINGSLEY, CHARLES, *The Water Babies*, ed. by Kathleen Lines, ill. by Harold Jones, Watts, 1961. A judicious cutting of this lengthy, Victorian, moralistic fairy tale has resulted in a readable version for today's children.   8–12

KIPLING, RUDYARD, *The Jungle Book*, ill. by Philip Hays, Doubleday, 1964. Stories of India and the jungle life of the boy Mowgli, who was adopted by the wolf pack.   9–13

The Jungle Books, ill. by Robert Shore, Macmillan, 1964. A selection of fourteen stories from *The Jungle Book* and *The Second Jungle Book*.   9–13

Just So Stories, ill. by author and Joseph M. Gleeson, Doubleday, 1932. Other editions are available from various publishers.   7–10

The Second Jungle Book, ill. by J. L. Kipling, Doubleday, 1923, 1946.   9–13

KOOIKER, LEONIE, *The Magic Stone*, ill. by Carl Hollander, tr. from the Dutch by Richard and Clara Winston, Morrow, 1978. The pretty stone that Chris finds proves to be a magical object of great power.   8–10

KRAUS, ROBERT, *Leo the Late Bloomer*, ill. by Jose Aruego, Windmill, 1971. Some lion cubs start slowly but, like Leo, they soon can do everything.   3–5

Owliver, ill. by Jose Aruego and Araine Dewey, Windmill, 1974. An owlet with ambitious parents chooses his own surprising career.   3–5

LAGERLÖF, SELMA, *The Wonderful Adventures of Nils*, tr. by Velma Swanston Howard, ill. by H. Baumhauer, Pantheon, 1947. Nils rides astride the gray goose and so learns about the geography, customs, and folklore of his country, Sweden.   9–12

LAMORISSE, ALBERT, *The Red Balloon*, ill. with colored photos from the film of the same title, Doubleday, 1957. A captivating story about a little boy who catches a magic red balloon and pursues it through the streets of Paris.   6–10

LAMPMAN, EVELYN SIBLEY, *The City Under the Back Steps*, ill. by Honore Valintcourt, Doubleday, 1960. Jill and Craig suffer many indignities and adventures when they are reduced to ant size and taken prisoner by the ants. Scientific detail is accurate.   9–11

The Shy Stegosaurus of Indian Springs, ill. by Paul Galdone, Doubleday, 1962. The Brown twins renew their friendship with George, the shy stegosaurus, who is an English-speaking, modern dinosaur. Preceded by *The Shy Stegosaurus of Cricket Creek* (1955).   10–12

LANGTON, JANE, *The Fledgling*, Harper, 1980. Adroit in its blending of the real and fanciful, this poignant story is about a shy child who learns the joy of flying from a solitary Canada goose.   10–12

LANIER, STERLING E., *The War for the Lot: A Tale of Fantasy and Terror*, ill. by Robert Baumgartner, Follett, 1969. Alec strives to help defeat a horde of rats intent upon invading the territory of some small friends. A story of communication and rapport between men and animals.   8–12

LAUGHLIN, FLORENCE, *The Little Leftover Witch*, ill. by Sheila Greenwald, Macmillan, 1960. How a stubborn little witch, accidentally left behind on Halloween, is gradually transformed by the human family which takes her in.   7–9

LAURENCE, MARGARET, *Jason's Quest*, ill. by Staffan Torell, Knopf, 1970. An episodic, humorous tale of a band of animals who seek a cure for fatal ennui.
                                                9–11

LAWSON, JOHN, *The Spring Rider*, T. Crowell, 1968. A fine, dreamlike fantasy in which a boy and his sister mingle with the soldiers who fought a Civil War battle on the area that is now farmed by their family.
                                                12–14

You Better Come Home With Me, ill. by Arnold Spilka, T. Crowell, 1966. A fantastic tale which blends into the realistic setting of rural Appalachia as an orphaned boy seeks through the mountains for clues to his real identity.   10–up

LAWSON, ROBERT, *Edward, Hoppy, and Joe*, ill. by author, Knopf, 1952. When Edward, a rabbit, needed educating, Hoppy Toad and Joe Possum did plenty of mischief, but Benjamin Beaver came to the rescue and turned their pranks into constructive action.
                                                6–8

Mr. Revere and I, ill. by author, Little, 1953. A unique view of some events of the American Revolution as related by Paul Revere's horse, Scheherazade. A good story for reading aloud.   9–12

Rabbit Hill, ill. by author, Viking, 1944. Newbery Medal.   8–11

The Tough Winter, ill. by author, Viking, 1954. Sequel to *Rabbit Hill*. This book carries the story of the animal inhabitants of Rabbit Hill through a long and severe winter during which the Big House is left in charge of a dour caretaker who owns a very mean dog.
                                                8–11

LE GRAND (pseud. for LeGrand Henderson), *Cats for Kansas*, ill. by author, Abingdon, 1948.

How Baseball Began in Brooklyn, ill. by author, Abingdon, 1958.

Why Cowboys Sing in Texas, ill. by author, Abingdon, 1950.

Three tall tales with a folklore flavor. Good for reading aloud.   5–8

LE GUIN, URSULA K., *A Wizard of Earthsea*, ill. by Ruth Robbins, Parnassus, 1968. An extraordinary allegory

that explores the nature of evil. Ged, a young apprentice sorcerer, unintentionally releases a malignant force, which he must then struggle to overcome.
                                                    12–up

The Farthest Shore, ill. by Gail Garraty, Atheneum, 1972.

The Tombs of Atuan, ill. by Gail Garraty, Atheneum, 1971.
Sequels to *A Wizard of Earthsea,* equally intricate.
                                                    12–up

LEICHMAN, SEYMOUR, *The Boy Who Could Sing Pictures,* ill. by author, Doubleday, 1968. A brief but profound fairy tale that explores the problems created for the unhappy citizens of a kingdom whose ruler fights a succession of "just wars."   8–11

L'ENGLE, MADELEINE, *A Wrinkle in Time,* Farrar, 1962. Newbery Medal.   11–14

LEWIS, CLIVE STAPLES, *The Lion, the Witch, and the Wardrobe,* ill. by Pauline Baynes, Macmillan, 1951. Other titles in the Narnia series, in order of appearance, are: *Prince Caspian* (1951), *The Voyage of the Dawn Treader* (1952), *The Silver Chair* (1953), *The Horse and His Boy* (1954), *The Magician's Nephew* (1955), and *The Last Battle* (1956).   9–13

LIFTON, BETTY JEAN, *The Cock and the Ghost Cat,* ill. by Fuku Akino, Atheneum, 1965. An outstanding book that tells of the sacrifice made by the cock to save his master from the demon cat.   6–10

The Rice-Cake Rabbit, ill. by Eiichi Mitsui, Norton, 1966. Despising his success as a baker of rice cakes, the rabbit became a swordsman, won a fencing contest, and was rewarded by being made Samurai of the Moon.   6–8

LINDGREN, ASTRID, *Pippi Longstocking,* tr. by Florence Lamborn, ill. by Louis Glanzman, Viking, 1950. For sheer outrageous hilarity, Pippi the superchild takes all prizes. Sequels are: *Pippi Goes on Board* (1957) and *Pippi in the South Seas* (1959).   8–11

LIONNI, LEO, *Inch by Inch,* ill. by author, Astor, 1962. A truly distinguished picture book, with glowing illustrations, tells a clever tale of the inchworm who escaped great danger by literally measuring his enemies.   5–7

Swimmy, ill. by author, Pantheon, 1963. A picture book of flawless design. It tells how a little orphan fish finds a way to protect himself and his newly adopted family from the dangers of the deep.   5–7

Alexander and the Wind-up Mouse, ill. by author, Pantheon, 1969. An allegory of love and friendship in which a young mouse learns that real life with all its dangers is preferable to life as a toy.   5–8

LIPKIND, WILLIAM, *The Magic Feather Duster,* ill. by Nicolas Mordvinoff, Harcourt, 1958. The story of four brothers who covet a unique feather duster which can produce anything desired with but a flick.   5–8

LIPKIND, WILLIAM, and NICOLAS MORDVINOFF, *Finders Keepers,* Harcourt, 1951. Written in folk-tale style, this is the rollicking fable of two dogs who solve, with admirable commonsense, the problem of who shall keep the bone.   4–8

LITTLE, JANE, *Sneaker Hill,* ill. by Nancy Grossman, Atheneum, 1967. When Matthew's mother decides to take the test for membership in the Sisterhood of Witches before she is eligible, her owl, Shadow, Matthew, and his cousin Susan attempt to rescue the would-be witch.   9–11

LIVELY, PENELOPE, *The Ghost of Thomas Kempe,* ill. by Antony Maitland, Dutton, 1973. A mischievous ghost leaves notes for which poor James is blamed. Winner of the Carnegie Award.   9–11

The House in Norham Gardens, Dutton, 1974. Time-shift sequences are smoothly woven into the setting of an old house where Clare lives with two beloved great aunts.   11–14

The Revenge of Samuel Stokes, Dutton, 1981. An irritated ghost wreaks havoc because he's annoyed by the changes in the estate he'd landscaped centuries before.   10–12

The Voyage of QV 66, ill. by Harold Jones, Dutton, 1979. In a story told by a dog, this fantasy adventure takes place after a worldwide flood has left only animals alive.   9–11

LOBEL, ARNOLD, *Frog and Toad Are Friends,* ill. by author, Harper, 1970. Five short stories, simple and charming, tell the ups and downs of friendship, as do those in its sequel, *Frog and Toad Together,* 1972.
                                                    6–7

Ming Lo Moves the Mountain, ill. by author, Greenwillow, 1982. A tale set in ancient China is written in the style of a folktale, and is illustrated with soft pastel scenes.   5–8

LOFTING, HUGH, *The Story of Doctor Dolittle,* ill. by author, Lippincott, 1920.

The Voyages of Doctor Dolittle, ill. by author, Lippincott, 1922.
There are seven more books in the *Doctor Dolittle* series, but these first two remain the favorites. Some volumes include racially offensive material.   8–12

The Story of Mrs. Tubbs, Lippincott, 1923, 1968.
                                                    6–8

Twilight of Magic, ill. by Lois Lenski, Lippincott, 1930, 1967. Entirely different from the Dr. Dolittle tales, this story tells of a magic shell and its influence upon two children of medieval days.   9–12

LORENZINI, CARLO, *The Adventures of Pinocchio,* tr. by Carol Della Chiesa, with ill. after Attilio Mussino, Macmillan, 1951.   9–11

LUENN, NANCY, *The Dragon Kite,* ill. by Michael Hague, Harcourt, 1982. Fluent and simple in style, the story of a kite that comes alive and comes to the rescue of its maker is beautifully illustrated with paintings of the Chinese setting.   5–9

MC AFFREY, ANNE, *Dragonsong,* Atheneum, 1976. In a fantasy world that is cohesive and imaginative in its conception, a young girl longs to be a harper, a career deemed unseemly for a girl. In the sequels, *Dragonsinger* (1977) and *Dragondrums* (1979) she becomes a master harper and acquires a young scamp as her pupil.   11–14

MC CLOSKEY, ROBERT, *Burt Dow: Deep-Water Man,* ill. by author, Viking, 1963. This handsomely illustrated tall tale recounts the adventures of a weather-beaten fisherman who was lucky enough to catch a whale by the tail.   7–9

MAC DONALD, GEORGE, *At the Back of the North Wind,* ill. by Harvey Dinnerstein, Macmillan, 1964. A fine edition of this Victorian fairy tale, which tells of a little boy's relationship with the North Wind and of the many ways in which she appears to him. (Available in another edition, ill. by E. H. Shepard, Dutton.)
                                                    10–12

The Light Princess, ill. by William Pène du Bois, Crowell, 1962. The lovely pastel illustrations add greatly to the appeal of this whimsical story about the princess who floated away unless tied down. (Available in another edition, beautifully illustrated by Maurice Sendak, Farrar, 1969.)   7–11

The Princess and Curdie, ill. by Nora Unwin, Macmillan, 1954. Curdie, son of a silver miner, is commanded by a strange witchlike woman to seek the land of Gwyntystorm where the king is very ill. Along the way he encounters and overcomes much evil until at last the enemy is vanquished and justice established. *The Princess and the Goblin,* ill. by Nora S. Unwin, Macmillan, 1951, 1967.

Excellent editions of the two books immediately above are also available from Dutton, ill. by Charles Folkard.   9–11

MC GINLEY, PHYLLIS, *The Horse Who Lived Upstairs,* ill. by Helen Stone, Lippincott, 1944.

The Horse Who Had His Picture in the Paper, ill. by Helen Stone, Lippincott, 1951.

In the first book, a trip to the country teaches discontented Joey that he is a true city dweller at heart. The second book finds Joey again restless, this time yearning for publicity that will silence the policeman's boastful horse. The climax is utterly satisfying.   4–8

MAC GREGOR, ELLEN, *Miss Pickerell and the Geiger Counter,* ill. by Paul Galdone, McGraw, 1953.

Miss Pickerell Goes to Mars, ill. by Paul Galdone, McGraw, 1951.

Miss Pickerell Goes to the Arctic, ill. by Paul Galdone, McGraw, 1954.

Miss Pickerell Goes Undersea, ill. by Paul Galdone, McGraw, 1953.

Miss Pickerell is a plainspoken, elderly spinster with a remarkable flair for attracting adventure wherever she goes. The author combines some scientific information with suspense and nonsense in a way that pleases young readers.   9–11

MC HARGUE, GEORGESS, *Hot & Cold Running Cities,* Holt, 1974. An anthology of tales about the future.
                                          11–up

MAC KELLAR, WILLIAM, *Ghost in the Castle,* ill. by Richard Bennett, McKay, 1960. The hero of the story did not believe in ghosts. To prove his point and to demonstrate his courage, he went to Craigie Castle—and came face to face with Mr. MacSpurtle, the ghost.
                                          9–11

MC KENZIE, ELLEN K., *Taash and the Jesters,* Holt, 1968. A complicated and absorbing tale of adventure, witchcraft, and malice in an imaginary kingdom. By returning a kidnaped prince to the palace, Taash and his allies defeat the power of the witches.   9–12

MC LEOD, EMILIE, *Clancy's Witch,* ill. by Lisl Weil, Little, 1959. Nine-year-old Clancy has the startling experience of having a witch for a neighbor!   7–10

MC NEILL, JANET, *Tom's Tower,* ill. by Mary Russon, Little, 1967. A beguiling fantasy with appeal for both boys and girls. The hero, Tom, is suddenly transported to a strange country where he is made to serve as guardian of the castle treasure.   9–11

MAYER, MERCER, *The Great Cat Chase,* ill. by author, Four Winds, 1975. Raffish children, plenty of action in a wordless picture book.   2–5

Frog, Where Are You? ill. by author, Dial, 1969. One of a series of very funny wordless books about a frog, a dog, and a boy.   2–5

MAYNE, WILLIAM, *Earthfasts,* Dutton, 1966. An engrossing fantasy in which inhabitants of a sedate British community become involved with legendary characters from the past. Supernatural and everyday events are woven into an exciting, convincing tale with appeal for the above-average reader.   10–14

A Game of Dark, Dutton, 1971. Time-shift at its eeriest, in a story with psychological depths.   10–13

A Grass Rope, ill. by Lynton Lamb, Dutton, 1962. Four children follow clues in an old legend concerned with lost treasure and a unicorn, and solve a local mystery of long standing.   9–12

The Hill Road, Dutton, 1969. Three contemporary young people, riding their ponies on the Yorkshire moors, become involved in the lives of ancient Britons and Saxons.   10–up

MERRILL, JEAN, *The Pushcart War,* ill. by Ronni Solbert, W. R. Scott, 1964.   10–12

The Superlative Horse, ill. by Ronni Solbert, W. R. Scott, 1961. An imaginative tale set in ancient China.
                                          9–11

MILNE, ALAN ALEXANDER, *The House at Pooh Corner,* ill. by Ernest H. Shepard, Dutton, 1961. Concerned with the adventures of Christopher Robin and all his toys: Eeyore, Tigger, Winnie-the-Pooh, and others. Full of the same whimsical humor as *Winnie-the-Pooh.*   5–10

Prince Rabbit and the Princess Who Could Not Laugh, ill. by Mary Shepard, Dutton, 1966. Two amusing fairy tales, each a variation on the contest theme. In the first are tests of skill and intelligence. The second contains a trial for the hand of the princess.   7–10

Winnie-the-Pooh, ill. by Ernest Shepard, Dutton, 1974.   4–9

The World of Pooh, ill. by E. H. Shepard, Dutton, 1957. Distinctive color illustrations lend a festive air to this large-print volume containing *Winnie-the-Pooh* and *The House at Pooh Corner.*   5–10

MINARIK, ELSE H., *Father Bear Comes Home,* ill. by Maurice Sendak, Harper, 1959.

A Kiss for Little Bear, ill. by Maurice Sendak, Harper, 1968.

Little Bear, ill. by Maurice Sendak, Harper, 1957.

Little Bear's Friend, ill. by Maurice Sendak, Harper, 1960.

Little Bear's Visit, ill. by Maurice Sendak, Harper, 1961. These are books for children in primary grades to read for themselves, but the stories are also worth reading aloud to the preschool child.   4–8

MOON, SHEILA, *Knee-Deep in Thunder,* ill. by Peter Parnall, Atheneum, 1967. A most unusual fantasy in which the characters seem to have been brought together by some mysterious force in order to travel and struggle toward an unseen goal. Gradually a purpose is revealed to them, and when it is fulfilled, after much toil, pain, and death, each is released to go his way.
                                          12–up

MULOCK, DINAH M., *The Little Lame Prince,* ill. by John Nielsen, World, 1948. A fascinating tale, first published in 1893, in which a lonely prince visits strange lands and sees marvelous sights while wrapped within a wonderful traveling cloak.   9–11

NESBIT, E., *The Enchanted Castle,* ill. by Cecil Leslie, Dutton, 1964. The story of a beautiful house and garden and of the many strange adventures caused by the power of a wishing ring.   10–12

The Story of the Treasure Seekers: Being the Adventures of the Bastable Children in Search of a Fortune, ill. by Gordon Browne, Dover, 1958. Although the young Bastables have little success in regaining the family fortune, their quest offers the reader much amusement.   8–10

This author also wrote a number of stories which feature plucky, resourceful children who find themselves in strange situations brought on by the forces of magic. The better-known titles are:

Five Children and It, Random, 1959; Dover, 1965.
                                                          8–up

Harding's Luck, ill. by H. R. Millar, Dover, 1961.
                                                          8–10

House of Arden, Dutton, 1968; Dover, 1958.   8–13

The Magic City, Dover, 1958.   7–9

The Magic World, Dover, 1959.   7–9

Wet Magic, Dover, 1958.   7–9

The Wonderful Garden, Dover, 1959.   7–9

NICHOLS, RUTH, *A Walk out of the World,* ill. by Trina Schart Hyman, Harcourt, 1969. An absorbing fantasy in which a brother and sister are carried into the world of their royal ancestors and help bring about the end of a usurper's reign.   10–12

NORTH, JOAN, *The Light Maze,* Farrar, 1971. A witty depiction of village life in England is a foil for a trip outside time and space.   11–14

NORTON, ANDRE (pseud. of Alice Mary Norton), *Catseye,* Harcourt, 1961. This teen-age science-fiction story, set in the future, tells of the adventures of Troy Horan, who is demoted and exiled from his native planet.
                                                          11–14

Key out of Time, World, 1963. A group of Terran explorers are sent ten thousand years backward in time to probe the past of a beautiful but now uninhabited planet. Like the author's other science-fiction stories, this is a well-written, fast-moving adventure fantasy.   11–15

NORTON, MARY, *Bed-Knob and Broomstick,* ill. by Erik Blegvad, Harcourt, 1957. The three Wilson children have some exciting times after they discover a lonely spinster who is studying to become a witch and who gives them some magic powers.   8–11

The Borrowers, ill. by Beth and Joe Krush, Harcourt, 1953.   8–11

The Borrowers Avenged, ill. by Beth and Joe Krush, Harcourt, 1982.

NOSTLINGER, CHRISTINE, *Konrad,* tr. by Anthea Bell, ill. by Carol Niclaus, Watts, 1977. A factory-made child, insufferably perfect, is mistakenly delivered to a charming, eccentric woman.   9–11

NOURSE, ALAN, *Rx for Tomorrow; Tales of Science Fiction, Fantasy, and Medicine,* McKay, 1971. A varied anthology with emphasis on medicine, written by a physician.   11–15

OAKLEY, GRAHAM, *The Church Mouse,* ill. by author, Atheneum, 1972. Bland style, lively plot and humor.
                                                          5–7

O'BRIEN, ROBERT C., *Mrs. Frisby and the Rats of NIMH,* ill. by Zena Bernstein, Atheneum, 1971. Ex-laboratory rats try to improve their image. Newbery Medal.
                                                          9–11

Z for Zachariah, Atheneum, 1975. A taut science fiction story of the last people left in the world.
                                                          11–up

ORMONDROYD, EDWARD, *Broderick,* ill. by John Larrecq, Parnassus, 1969. A dashing mouse rides to fame by reason of his exploits on a surfboard.   5–9

Castaways on Long Ago, ill. by Ruth Robbins, Parnassus, 1973. A mystery-fantasy concocted with suspense.
                                                          9–11

Time at the Top, ill. by Peggy Bach, Parnassus, 1963.
                                                          11–13

PARK, RUTH, *Playing Beatie Bow,* Atheneum, 1982. Abigail sees children playing a game called "Beatie Bow" but doesn't know, until she's gone back in time, who Beatie is. A finely crafted Australian story.   10–13

PARKER, EDGAR, *The Enchantress,* ill. by author, Pantheon, 1960. A princess-enchantress, in the form of an owl, tries in vain to deter a young knight from performing three dangerous tasks in order to win her hand. A happy change from the standard fairy tale.
                                                          8–11

PARKER, RICHARD, *A Time to Choose; A Story of Suspense,* Harper, 1974. A nicely knit story of movement between two periods of time, one the far future.
                                                          11–14

PARRISH, ANNE, *Floating Island,* ill. by author, Harper, 1930. An unusually imaginative tale about the adventures of Mr. and Mrs. Doll and their family while shipwrecked on a tropical island.   8–12

PEARCE, ANN PHILIPPA, *A Dog So Small,* ill. by Antony Maitland, Lippincott, 1963. The child who is the central figure of the story lives in a dream world of his own devising. It is a world he has created by meticulous research, intense concentration, and the exclusion of everyday reality. In the end he returns to reality, slowly and painfully, as he recovers from an accident.   10–11

Mrs. Cockle's Cat, ill. by Antony Maitland, Lippincott, 1962. Mrs. Cockle's cat, Peter, deserts her because fish are scarce and too expensive for her to buy. Grieving for her pet, she grows extremely thin. One day a strong wind lifts her, along with the balloons she is trying to sell, into the sky. When the wind drops, Mrs. Cockle is unexpectedly reunited with Peter.   7–9

The Squirrel Wife, ill. by Derek Collard, T. Crowell, 1972. An original story in pure fairy-tale tradition, in which good and justice triumph.   8–10

Tom's Midnight Garden, ill. by Susan Einzig, Lippincott, 1959.   10–12

PECK, RICHARD, *The Ghost Belonged to Me,* Viking, 1975. Turn-of-the-century flavor, a restless ghost, and a boy with powers of precognition are merged in a lively and amusing story.   10–13

PEET, BILL, *The Wump World,* ill. by author, Harcourt, 1970. Through this story about the despoliation of an imaginary planet, the author provides effective satire and comment on the pollution of the earth.   6–up

PESEK, LUDEK, *The Earth Is Near,* tr. by Anthea Bell, Bradbury, 1974. A striking story of a Mars expedition, stressing the problems of the astronauts.   11–up

PEYTON, K. M., *A Pattern of Roses,* T. Crowell, 1973. This combines deftly the theme of adolescent independence and identification with a long-dead boy.
                                                          11–14

PICARD, BARBARA LEONIE, *The Faun and the Woodcutter's Daughter,* ill. by Charles Stewart, Criterion, 1965.

The Goldfinch Garden, ill. by Anne Linton, Criterion, 1965.

The Lady of the Linden Tree, ill. by Charles Stewart, Criterion, 1962.
Three books of delightful, original fairy tales with special appeal to slightly romantic little girls. 9–12
The Mermaid and the Simpleton, ill. by Philip Gough, Criterion, 1970. Beautifully written and carefully plotted, these fifteen original fairy tales are excellent for reading aloud. 10–13

PINKWATER, DANIEL, *The Magic Moscow,* ill. by author, Four Winds, 1980. A romping fantasy tall tale about the owner of an ice cream shop who's smitten by a television program. 9–11

POOLE, JOSEPHINE, *Moon Eyes,* ill. by Trina Schart Hyman, Little, 1967. An eerie, suspenseful tale of witchcraft in a modern English setting. The victims are a fifteen-year-old girl and her five-year-old mute brother. 10–12

POTTER, BEATRIX, *The Tale of Peter Rabbit,* ill. by author, Warne, 1903. A favorite nursery classic followed by many more books about the little animals which the author-artist observed so lovingly and reproduced in meticulous watercolors. 4–8
The Fairy Caravan, new ed., ill. by author, Warne, 1952. This amusing collection of stories tells about the adventures of an extremely long-haired guinea pig who joins a traveling circus. The delightful illustrations are in Potter's usual style, though only a few are in color. 8–10

PREUSSLER, OTFRIED, *The Little Witch,* tr. by Anthea Bell, ill. by Winnie Gayler, Abelard, 1961. Too young to join in the annual Walpurgis Night dance, the little witch sneaks in. As punishment she is sentenced to be a good witch all year. At the end of the time she finds herself a pariah because the only good witch is a bad witch. 7–10
The Satanic Mill, tr. by Anthea Bell, Macmillan, 1973. An evil magician traps all his apprentices until one escapes through the power of love. 11–14

PROKOFIEFF, SERGE, *Peter and the Wolf,* ill. by Warren Chappell, Knopf, 1940. This is a delightful version of the well-known story. 7–12

PROYSEN, ALF, *Little Old Mrs. Pepperpot,* tr. by Marianne Helwig, ill. by Björn Berg, Obolensky, 1959. 8–10
Mrs. Pepperpot to the Rescue, ill. by Björn Berg, Pantheon, 1964. An engaging story about the further adventures of an old woman who found herself shrunken to the size of a pepperpot at unexpected moments. 7–11

PYLE, HOWARD, *Pepper and Salt, or Seasoning for Young Folks,* ill. by author, Harper, 1885, 1923. This charming book of eight fairy tales, wittily retold and well-illustrated, is apt to be overlooked in the flood of new material that appears each year. However, it deserves continued use by teachers and storytellers. 9–11
The Wonder Clock, ill. by author, Harper, 1887, 1943. This volume of twenty-four delightful tales, "one for each hour of the day," is a companion volume to the one above. 9–11

RASKIN, ELLEN, *Figgs & Phantoms,* ill. by author, Dutton, 1974. Hilarious nonsense about a family of odd personalities moves into fantasy—or is it a dream? 9–11

REY, H. A., *Curious George Gets a Medal,* ill. by author, Houghton, 1957. Curious George, the little monkey hero of many popular tales, rockets into space and wins a medal for his courage. Other popular titles are *Curious George Rides a Bike,* Houghton, 1952, and by Margaret Rey, *Curious George Flies a Kite,* Houghton, 1958. 5–8

RODGERS, MARY, *Freaky Friday,* Harper, 1972. What would a girl do if she woke one morning and found she'd turned into her mother? Annabel tells us what. 9–11
A Billion for Boris, Harper, 1974. Annabel and her friend Boris find a television set that gives the news of the next day. Including stockmarket prices! 9–11

ROSS, EULALIE STEINMETZ, ed., *The Lost Half-Hour: A Collection of Stories,* ill. by Enrico Arno, Harcourt, 1963. This excellent collection, compiled by a noted storyteller, contains both traditional and modern fanciful stories, especially selected for their appeal when told aloud. 9–11

RUSKIN, JOHN, *The King of the Golden River, or the Black Brothers,* ill. by Fritz Kredel, World, 1946. A well-written, genuinely dramatic story in the old fairy-tale style. Other editions are available from various publishers. 10–14

SACHS, MARILYN, *Fleet-Footed Florence,* ill. by Charles Robinson, Doubleday, 1981. A yeasty spoof, a feminist baseball story, about a woman player who sets the record for RCIs, Runs Carried In. 5–8

SANCHEZ-SILVA, JOSÉ MARIA, *The Boy and the Whale,* tr. by Michael Heron, ill. by Margery Gill, McGraw, 1964. Santiago, small boy of Madrid, loved his imaginary whale very much and they had many wonderful adventures together before she swam away forever. 7–10

SANDBURG, CARL, *Rootabaga Stories,* ill. by Maud and Miska Petersham, Harcourt, 1936. 9–12
The Wedding Procession of the Rag Doll and the Broom Handle and Who Was in It, ill. by Harriet Pincus, Harcourt, 1967. One of Sandburg's delightful *Rootabaga Stories* has been transformed into an eye-filling picture book which captures the unique humor and invention of the author. 4–8

SARGENT, SARAH, *Weird Henry Berg,* Crown, 1980. In a story with a goofy pace, Henry and an elderly friend solve the problem of what to do about the little dragon that's hatched from an ancient egg. 9–11

SAUER, JULIA L., *Fog Magic,* Viking, 1943. A sensitive and beautifully written story of a little girl who goes back in time to a people and a village which no longer exist. The day comes when she knows that her "fog magic" must end. 10–12

SAWYER, RUTH, *The Enchanted Schoolhouse,* ill. by Hugh Troy, Viking, 1956. A tale of the wonderful enchantment which an Irish leprechaun and a timid young immigrant worked on the town taxpayers. 9–11
This Way to Christmas, rev. ed., ill. by Maginel Wright Barney, Harper, 1967. When a stranded boy takes a fairy's suggestion that he visit each of his neighbors, he receives a wonderful Christmas gift from each of them. A fine Christmas story. 9–11
The Year of the Christmas Dragon, ill. by Hugh Troy, Viking, 1960. A charming original story concerning the origin of Mexican Christmas customs. The tale begins in China, where a small boy becomes friendly with a great dragon. Together they fly to Mexico, and there the dragon hibernates for hundreds of years. 8–11

SCHLEIN, MIRIAM, *The Raggle Taggle Fellow*, ill. by Harvey Weiss, Hale, 1959. Written in folk-tale style, this engaging story of Dick, a wandering musician, holds wisdom and entertainment for the story hour.   7–10
The Big Cheese, ill. by Joseph Low, W. R. Scott, 1958. A story about a farmer who made an excellent cheese and decided to take it as a gift to the king. Each of the many characters he met along the way persuaded him to part with a sliver, and in the end there was nothing left for the king.   5–8

SELDEN, GEORGE (pseud. of George Selden Thompson), *The Cricket in Times Square*, ill. by Garth Williams, Farrar, 1960. This engaging modern-day fantasy features Chester, a cricket with perfect pitch. Once this fact is discovered, he is launched on a concert career.   8–10
Harry Cat's Pet Puppy, ill. by Garth Williams, Farrar, 1974. Everybody but Chester Cricket is back in New York and preoccupied with a stray puppy.   8–11
Tucker's Countryside, ill. by Garth Williams, Farrar, 1969. Some of the engaging city-bred animals first met in *Cricket in Times Square* appear in this adventure set in rural Connecticut.   8–11

SENDAK, MAURICE, *Higglety Pigglety Pop: Or, There Must Be More to Life*, ill. by author, Harper, 1967. An extremely amusing tale of a Sealyham terrier, Jennie, who leaves home to go in search of EXPERIENCE. A playful use of language.   6–up
In the Night Kitchen, ill. by author, Harper, 1970. Mickey falls out of his bed and into the night kitchen, amid the singing bakers and their work. An unusual and highly fantastic story which provides a rich evocation of the sensory enjoyment to be found in the textures, tastes, and smells of food.   4–8
Where the Wild Things Are, ill. by author, Harper, 1963. This perceptively written and illustrated book portrays the fearsome monsters of a child's imagination. Caldecott Medal.   3–7
Outside Over There, ill. by author, Harper, 1981. A beautifully illustrated fantasy about a small girl who rescues her baby sister from malevolent goblins.   5–8

SEREDY, KATE, *The White Stag*, ill. by author, Viking, 1937. This hero tale of the founding of Hungary was awarded the Newbery Medal. Illustrated with interpretive drawings of great beauty.   9–12

SEUSS, DR. *See* Theodor Seuss Geisel.

SHARMAT, MARJORIE WEINMAN, *Walter the Wolf*, ill. by Kelly Oechsli, Holiday, 1975. Blithe style, vigorous pictures, and sly humor enliven the story of a *very* good wolf.   5–7
The Trolls of Twelfth Street, ill. by Ben Shecter, Coward, 1979. Every hundred years, Eldred the troll leaves his cave to see what it's like above ground in Manhattan, and in this very funny story he finds how difficult it is to understand those oddities, People.   6–8

SHARP, MARGERY, *The Rescuers*, ill. by Garth Williams, Little, 1959. A clever fantasy concerning the adventures of three mice who attempt to rescue a Norwegian poet from the dungeon of a Black Castle. Adults catch the satire, while children enjoy the story. The charming drawings of the mice capture the essence of their courage and daring. Followed by: *Miss Bianca* (1962), *The Turret* (1963), *Miss Bianca in the Salt Mines* (1966).   9–up

SHURA, MARY FRANCES, *The Nearsighted Knight*, ill. by Adrienne Adams, Knopf, 1964. This easy-to-read fantasy features some improbable characters: a rotund witch, a congenial dragon, a homely princess, and the nearsighted knight. The plot is rather weak but beginning readers may enjoy it.   6–9
Simple Spigott, ill. by Jacqueline Tomes, Knopf, 1960. A friendly Scottish spook proves a wonderful guide and companion to three American children who visit Scotland. A first-person narrative that happily blends fantasy and realism.   7–10

SILVERBERG, ROBERT, *The Calibrated Alligator: and Other Science Fiction Stories*, Holt, 1969. Nine imaginative tales in a varied collection.   11–15
Time of the Great Freeze, Holt, 1964. A story set in the ice age of the future, circa A.D. 2300. A seventeen-year-old boy accompanies his father, a scientist, and several other men on an expedition. They travel by solar-powered sled and hope to establish contact with other isolated communities of the world.   11–14

SINGER, ISAAC BASHEVIS, *The Fearsome Inn*, tr. by author and Elizabeth Shub, ill. by Nonny Hogrogian, Scribner's, 1967. A tale of witchcraft and evil conquered by magic and fast thinking. Beautifully executed illustrations.   7–11

SKURZYNSKI, GLORIA, *The Poltergeist of Jason Morey*, Dodd, 1975. Two girls find that the quiet young cousin who's come to live with them brings a destructive poltergeist along.   10–13

SLEIGH, BARBARA, *Carbonel, the King of the Cats*, ill. by V. H. Drummond, Bobbs, 1957. Humorous magical tale of two children who rescue the king of cats from the spell of an old witch. Followed by *The Kingdom of Carbonel*, ill. by D. M. Leonard, Bobbs, 1960.   9–12

SLOBODKIN, LOUIS, *The Space Ship Under the Apple Tree*, ill. by author, Macmillan, 1952, 1967. Things begin to happen when a strange little man is found in Grandmother's apple orchard. A good combination of activity, country fun, and pseudoscience. Followed by *Space Ship Returns to the Apple Tree* (1958) and *The Three-Seated Space Ship* (1964).   8–10

SLOBODKINA, ESPHYR, *Caps for Sale*, ill. by author, W. R. Scott, 1947. This merry little story, with its engaging monkeys, is always popular with younger children.   5–7

SLOTE, ALFRED, *C.O.L.A.R.: A Tale of Outer Space*, ill. by Anthony Kramer, Lippincott, 1981. Jack and his robot twin Danny run out of fuel and land on an uncharted planet.   8–10
My Trip to Alpha I, ill. by Harold Berson, Lippincott, 1978. There's pace and suspense in a story in which people are put in cold storage while their computer-produced duplicates do the traveling.   9–12

SMITH, EMMA, *Emily's Voyage*, ill. by Irene Haas, Harcourt, 1966. An appealing short fantasy about a proper, respectable guinea pig who is periodically given to wanderlust. This tale is concerned with her adventures on a voyage which ended with shipwreck on a tropical island.   8–10

SNYDER, ZILPHA K., *Below the Root*, ill. by Alton Raible, Atheneum, 1975. A science fantasy set in a community of tree-dwellers has depths of meaning below the surface events.   10–12
Black and Blue Magic, ill. by Gene Holtan, Atheneum, 1966. Modern-day San Francisco is the

setting for this story. Lonely, awkward Harry Houdini Marco meets a fascinating stranger who gives him a magic lotion that enables him to grow wings. His nocturnal wanderings are most amusing. 8–11

STEELE, MARY Q., *Journey Outside*, ill. by Rocco Negri, Viking, 1969. Dilar, a young boy who has always lived on a raft floating endlessly on a subterranean river, undergoes many trials and adventures when he leaves his people to search for a better place. 9–12

STEELE, WILLIAM O., *Andy Jackson's Water Well*, ill. by Michael Ramus, Harcourt, 1959. When a terrible drought hit frontier Nashville, Andrew Jackson, attorney-at-law, and his friend, Chief Ticklepitcher, went east to get water. Their hilarious and exaggerated experiences are told with dry humor. 9–14

The No-Name Man of the Mountain, ill. by Jack Davis, Harcourt, 1964. This hilarious tall tale may bring tears of laughter when read aloud. 9–up

STEIG, WILLIAM, *Dominic*, ill. by author, Farrar, 1972. Dominic is a dog with heart of gold and nerves of steel who swashes and buckles through a beguiling tale of derring-do. 9–11

Sylvester and the Magic Pebble, ill. by author, Simon, 1969. An amusing tale of a donkey who, while trying to escape from a hungry lion, uses a magic pebble to turn himself into a rock. Caldecott Medal. 5–7

STEVENSON, JAMES, *The Night After Christmas*, ill. by author, Greenwillow, 1981. Two toys that have been discarded by their owners are taken in by a kindly dog who finds a solution for their loneliness. 4–7

The Wish Card Ran Out, ill. by author, Greenwillow, 1981. In a spoof of the age of the credit card, Charlie and his dog are pursued by a roomful of computers. 4–7

STOCKTON, FRANK R., *The Bee-Man of Orn*, ill. by Maurice Sendak, Holt, 1964. Stockton's amusing story of the man who set out to discover his original form is given new life with Sendak's illustrations. 10–up

Casting Away of Mrs. Lecks and Mrs. Aleshine, ill. by George Richards, Meredith, 1933. The absurd adventures of two prosaic matrons on a desert isle, where they kept house with the same meticulous precision which had characterized their life in a New England village.

The Griffin and the Minor Canon, ill. by Maurice Sendak, Holt, 1963. A humorous tale about the friendship which develops between a young minor canon and a griffin who takes up residence in a cathedral town in order to observe his likeness over the church door. 8–10

The Storyteller's Pack, ill. by Bernarda Bryson, Scribner's, 1968. A collection of twenty short stories, representative of the author's best work. Includes ghost stories, comic fantasy, and fairy tales. 12–up

STOLZ, MARY, *Belling the Tiger*, ill. by Beni Montresor, Harper, 1961.

The Great Rebellion, ill. by Beni Montresor, Harper, 1961.

Siri the Conquistador, ill. by Beni Montresor, Harper, 1963.

Maximilian's World, ill. by Uri Shulevitz, Harper, 1966. These gently satirical little fantasies will amuse children on one level and adults on another. 7–10

Frédou, ill. by Tomi Ungerer, Harper, 1962. The story of a Parisian cat who manages a hotel and does it supremely well. 6–9

THACKERAY, W. M., and CHARLES DICKENS, *The Rose and the Ring; The Magic Fishbone*, ill. by W. M. Thackeray, John Gilbert, and Paul Hogarth, Dutton, 1959. In the Thackeray story, the fairy's gift of a "little misfortune" gives rise to one hilarious error after another in the Court of Paflagonia. "The Magic Fishbone" is also available in other editions. (*See* Charles Dickens.) 9–12

THURBER, JAMES, *The Great Quillow*, ill. by Doris Lee, Harcourt, 1944. In this delightful story with an old, old theme, Quillow, the shortest man in town, triumphs over the giant, Hunder. 8–11

Many Moons, ill. by Louis Slobodkin, Harcourt, 1943. Told in fairy-tale style, this is the appealing story of a little princess who yearned for the moon but learned to be satisfied with less. Caldecott Medal. 7–10

The White Deer, ill. by author and Don Freeman, Harcourt, 1945. An amusing satire on red tape and official regulations. 10–up

TITUS, EVE, *Anatole and the Cat*, ill. by Paul Galdone, McGraw, 1957. An alert French mouse outwits the cat who interferes with his duties as Cheese Taster in M'sieu Duval's cheese factory. Other adventures of this dauntless mouse are related in: *Anatole* (1956), *Anatole and the Robot* (1960), *Anatole over Paris* (1961), *Anatole and the Poodle* (1965), *Anatole and the Piano* (1966). 5–7

Basil and the Pygmy Cats, ill. by Paul Galdone, McGraw, 1971. The great mouse detective, Basil of Baker Street, hero of other breathless and nonsensical tales of brilliant snooping, goes to the Far East. 8–10

TODD, RUTHVEN, *Space Cat*, ill. by Paul Galdone, Scribner's, 1952. An amusingly illustrated story about Flyball, a daring kitten, and his adventures in space. Followed by: *Space Cat Visits Venus* (1955), *Space Cat Meets Mars* (1957), *Space Cat and the Kittens* (1958). 8–10

TOLKIEN, J. R. R., *Farmer Giles of Ham*, ill. by Pauline Diana Baynes, Houghton, 1962. The story of how Farmer Giles, the reluctant dragon hunter, subdues the dragon, gets a large share of his treasure, and manages peaceful coexistence with his erstwhile enemy. 10–up

The Hobbit, ill. by author, Houghton, 1938. An enthralling account of the great quest which took Bilbo Baggins from his comfortable Hobbit hole out into the great world of evil, danger, and magic. 10–up

TRAVERS, PAMELA L., *Mary Poppins*, ill. by Mary Shepard, Harcourt, 1934. The story of the many remarkable things that happened to Jane and Michael Banks while their wind-borne nurse, Mary Poppins, held sway in their nursery. These adventures are continued in the succeeding books: *Mary Poppins Comes Back* (1935), *Mary Poppins Opens the Door* (1943), *Mary Poppins in the Park* (1952). 8–12

TRESSELT, ALVIN R., *The World in the Candy Egg*, ill. by Roger Duvoisin, Lothrop, 1967. The magic world inside a spun-sugar Easter egg is witnessed first by the animals in a toy shop window, and finally by the small girl who receives the egg as a gift. 4–8

UNGERER, TOMI, *Crictor*, ill. by author, Harper, 1958. An original and very nonsensical tale about the boa constrictor who became a pet of Madame Bodot, schoolteacher in a little French town. 5–8

Emile, ill. by author, Harper, 1960. The originator of

Crictor and the Mellops now introduces another uncommon picture-book character—an engaging octopus.   5–8

Moon Man, ill. by author, Harper, 1967. This oversize picture book, with special appeal for small boys, depicts the adventures of Moon Man on a visit to earth.   4–8

UTTLEY, ALISON, *A Traveler in Time*, ill. by Christine Price, Viking, 1964. A story set in a marvelous old manor house which Penelope, a girl of sixteen, comes to visit. Gradually she becomes aware that she is living in two worlds—the modern world and that of three hundred years earlier.   11–up

WABER, BERNARD, *"You Look Ridiculous," Said the Rhinoceros to the Hippopotamus*, ill. by author, Houghton, 1966. A hippopotamus grows more and more depressed as each of her animal friends tells her she looks ridiculous. They say this only because she does not possess the features which distinguish each of them.   5–7

Waber has created another remarkable and fantastic animal character, Lyle, the Crocodile. His adventures are related in: *The House on East 88th Street; Lyle, Lyle, the Crocodile; Lyle and the Birthday Party;* and *Lyle Finds His Mother*, ill. by author, Houghton, 1962, 1965, 1966, and 1974.   4–7

WALDEN, DANIEL, *The Nutcracker*, ill. by Harold Berson, Lippincott, 1959. This retelling of the familiar Nutcracker ballet is marked by grace and delicacy in both text and pictures.   8–12

WATSON, SALLY, *Magic at Wychwood*, ill. by Frank Bozo, Knopf, 1970. The Princess Elaine's search for magic shakes her royal family's composure. A story which has appeal for girls of all ages.   8–up

WELLS, ROSEMARY, *Morris's Disappearing Bag*, ill. by author, Dial, 1975. Told he's too young to play with his siblings' Christmas presents, a small rabbit is delighted when they envy the last gift he opens: a bag that makes him invisible.   4–6

WHITE, ANNE H., *Junket*, ill. by Robert McCloskey, Viking, 1955. The story of a strong-minded airedale who succeeded in teaching the new city folks, who had purchased his master's farm, just how a farm should be run. Despite the new owner's verdict that there be no animals, Junket manages to have all the animals which had belonged to the farm returned one by one.
                                                    8–11

The Story of Serapina, ill. by Tony Palazzo, Viking, 1951. Serapina, the cat who could carry milk bottles with her tail, both disciplined and entertained the children. This is a modern tall tale of great originality. It is also very funny.   8–12

WHITE, E. B., *Charlotte's Web*, ill. by Garth Williams, Harper, 1952.   8–10

Stuart Little, ill. by Garth Williams, Harper, 1945. It is unusual for a mouse to be born to an apartment-dwelling Park Avenue family, but they make the best of it, and the mouse-son, Stuart, becomes a very interesting person.   9–11

The Trumpet of the Swan, ill. by Edward Frascino, Harper, 1970. Many complications ensue when Louis' father decides that he will steal a trumpet so that his son, who is mute, can lead a normal swan's life.
                                                    9–12

WIESNER, WILLIAM, *The Magic Slippers*, ill. by author, Norton, 1967. A story by Wilhelm Hauff provided the

inspiration for this humorous picture book. It recounts the adventures of Hassan and his magic slippers in the service of the Caliph of Bagdad.   6–9

WILDE, OSCAR, *The Complete Fairy Tales of Oscar Wilde*, ill. by Charles Mozley, Watts, 1960. Nine original fairy stories by a noted nineteenth-century poet and author. They now seem somewhat dated but are nevertheless worth introducing to the better readers.
                                                    9–11

WILLIAMS, JAY, and RAYMOND ABRASHKIN, *Danny Dunn, Invisible Boy*, ill. by Paul Sagsoorian, McGraw, 1974. One of a series of Danny Dunn books, this is about an Invisibility Simulator via which Danny can sit in a laboratory yet be projected elsewhere.
                                                    9–11

WILLIAMS, URSULA MORAY, *Island MacKenzie*, ill. by Edward Ardizzone, Morrow, 1960. The two survivors from a shipwrecked pleasure cruiser find themselves on the same island. MacKenzie, the captain's cat, loves humans; Miss Pettifer, the other survivor, loathes cats. A fine mixture of humor, fantasy, and suspense in which MacKenzie remains true to his cat nature.
                                                    9–11

The Moonball, ill. by Jane Paton, Meredith, 1967. A group of resourceful English children appoint themselves protectors of the moonball—a weird, silky-haired, grapefruit-size, living object—which a professor wishes to subject to scientific investigation.
                                                    7–9

WINTERFELD, HENRY, *Castaways in Lilliput*, tr. by Kyrill Schabert, ill. by William Hutchinson, Harcourt, 1960. After being adrift on a rubber raft, three Australian children are cast ashore on fully modernized Lilliput. A good introduction to the Swift story.
                                                    9–13

Star Girl, tr. by Kyrill Schabert, ill. by Fritz Wegner, Harcourt, 1957. Three children, gathering mushrooms in the woods, accept the explanation of a strange child that she is from the planet Asra (Venus). When they take her home with them, the adults refuse to believe her story and many complications ensue.   8–11

WRIGHTSON, PATRICIA, *Down to Earth*, ill. by Margaret Horder, Harcourt, 1965.   10–12

The Nargun and the Stars, Atheneum, 1974. An Australian boy discovers ancient creatures in the remote outback and learns that his elderly cousins have seen them too.   10–12

The Ice Is Coming, Atheneum, 1977. In a memorable Australian fantasy, a young Aborigine, Wirrun, goes on a quest to prevent the ancient ice people from taking over the land. In the sequels, *The Dark Bright Water* (1979) and *Journey Behind the Wind* (1981) Wirrun again confronts some of the strange and wonderful spirit people and, in the end, is turned to stone.
                                                    11–14

YAMAGUCHI, TOHR, *Two Crabs and the Moonlight*, ill. by Marianne Yamaguchi, Holt, 1965. A tale of unselfish and fearless loyalty in the face of near hopelessness.   6–10

YOLEN, JANE, *Greyling; A Picture Story from the Islands of Shetland*, ill. by William Stobbs, World, 1968. Based on the Scottish legend of the seal-boy.   8–10

ZEMACH, HARVE, *The Tricks of Master Dabble*, ill. by Margot Zemach, Holt, 1965. The clever Master Dabble takes in everyone with his tricks except the servant boy, Andrew, who unmasks him as an impostor.   5–8

ZINDEL, PAUL, *Let Me Hear You Whisper,* ill. by Stephen Gammell, Harper, 1974. An elderly cleaning woman can, by her kindness, get a laboratory dolphin to talk while the scientists fail.   12–up

ZOLOTOW, CHARLOTTE, *Mr. Rabbit and the Lovely Present,* ill. by Maurice Sendak, Harper, 1962. A small girl gravely consults a distinguished rabbit regarding a present for her mother. The beautiful illustrations are in perfect harmony with the gentle story.   5–7

Adult References: Modern Fantasy[5]

ATTERBERY, BRIAN, *The Fantasy Tradition in American Literature: From Irving to Le Guin,* Indiana University Press, 1980. A history of the literary fantasy in the United States, with emphasis on its relation to folklore.

CAMERON, ELEANOR, *The Green and Burning Tree,* Little, 1969, Part 1, "Fantasy."

CARROLL, LEWIS, *Alice's Adventures Under Ground,* Dover, 1965 (paperback), McGraw, 1966 (clothbound). Facsimile of the author's manuscript book with additional material from the facsimile edition of 1886 and with a new introduction by Martin Gardner. This also contains a facsimile of Carroll's "Easter Greeting" and "Christmas Greetings," as published in the 1886 edition. Another facsimile of the manuscript was published by University Microfilms in 1964.

The Annotated Alice: Alice's Adventures in Wonderland and *Through the Looking Glass,* ill. by John Tenniel. With an introduction and notes by Martin Gardner, Potter, 1960. Gardner's notes in the margins of the pages clarify many allusions that are likely to mystify the modern reader.

Claremont Reading Conference: Thirtieth Yearbook, ed. by Malcolm P. Douglass, Claremont Graduate School Curriculum Laboratory, 1966. A compilation of the addresses and discussions of the conference which had as its theme, "Beyond Literacy." The articles by Frank G. Jennings, Augusta Baker, and Mark Taylor deal with the profound need of children for literature which takes them beyond the confines of the here and now and gives wings to their imagination.

Essays Presented to Charles Williams, Eerdmans (paperback). A group of distinguished British authors who were friends of Charles Williams contributed to this memorial volume. Among the essays, those by C. S. Lewis and J. R. R. Tolkien are valuable for the reader who seeks understanding of the importance of the fairy tale.

HIGGINS, JAMES, *Beyond Words: Mystical Fancy in Children's Literature,* Teachers College Pr., 1970.

TOLKIEN, J. R. R., *Tree and Leaf,* Houghton, 1965. The first part of this slender volume provides a definition of fairy stories and discusses their origin and use. The remainder of the book is devoted to a short story, "Leaf by Niggle," which demonstrates the author's ability to imbue fantasy with the very texture of reality.

[5]In addition to the books listed here, many of the entries in "General References" (p. 880) include discussions specifically concerned with modern fantasy. See especially the Sutherland and Arbuthnot, Chukovsky, Duff, Fisher, Frye, Hazard, and Morton titles.

TOWNSEND, JOHN ROWE, *Written for Children,* Lothrop, 1967, Chapter 13, "Fantasy Between the Wars."

WAGGONER, DIANA, *The Hills of Faraway: A Guide to Fantasy,* Atheneum, 1978. A study and a bibliography of major modern fantasy novels.

YOLEN, JANE, *Touch Magic: Fantasy, Faerie and Folklore in the Literature of Childhood,* Philomel, 1981. A collection of essays that stress the importance of fantasy and discuss the functions of folk and fairy tales in children's intellectual and emotional growth.

Realistic Stories
Animal Stories

ANDERSON, C. W., *Billy and Blaze,* ill. by author, Macmillan, 1936.   4–8
Blaze and the Forest Fire, ill. by author, Macmillan, 1938.   4–8
High Courage, ill. by author, Macmillan, 1941.   10–14
Salute, ill. by author, Macmillan, 1940.   7–12
These are excellent horse stories for children, and the drawings that illustrate them are superb.

AVERILL, ESTHER, *Fire Cat,* ill. by author, Harper, 1960. An easy-to-read story about an adventurous cat who wasn't content to be a mere house pet.   6–8

BAUDOUY, MICHEL-AIMÉ, *Old One-Toe,* tr. by Marie Ponshot, ill. by Johannes Troyer, Harcourt, 1959. A French version of the hunted and the hunters with both fox and human characters warmly portrayed.   10–12

BROWN, MARCIA, *How Hippo!* ill. by author, Scribner's, 1969. Baby Hippo learns to roar most convincingly in this humorous little tale illustrated with striking woodcuts.   4–7

BUFF, MARY and CONRAD, *Dash and Dart, A Story of Two Fawns,* ill. by authors, Viking, 1942. The first year in the life of twin fawns is beautifully told and illustrated. The cadenced prose reads aloud well and the pictures in sepia and full color are exquisite.   5–8

BULLA, CLYDE R., *Star of Wild Horse Canyon,* ill. by Grace Paull, T. Crowell, 1953. An easy-to-read western story.   7–9

BURNFORD, SHEILA, *The Incredible Journey,* ill. by Carl Burger, Little, 1961.   10–14

BYARS, BETSY, *The Midnight Fox,* ill. by Ann Grifalconi, Viking, 1968.   9–11

CALHOUN, MARY, *Houn' Dog,* ill. by Roger Duvoisin, Morrow, 1959. A warm and humorous tale that will be enjoyed by many young readers.   7–9

DE JONG, MEINDERT, *Along Came a Dog,* ill. by Maurice Sendak, Harper, 1958.   10–13
The Easter Cat, ill. by Lillian Hoban, Harper, 1971. Millicent is torn between love for the stray kitten she finds on Easter morning and concern for her mother's allergic reaction.   8–10
The Little Cow and the Turtle, ill. by Maurice Sendak, Harper, 1955. Humorous, read-aloud story about a frisky cow and her adventures.   8–12
Smoke Above the Lane, Harper, 1951. Here is told an amusing and touching story of a strange friendship.   6–10

DELAFIELD, CLELIA, *Mrs. Mallard's Ducklings,* ill. by Leonard Weisgard, Lothrop, 1946. A beautiful picture book with interesting text of the seasonal cycle of ducks from egg to winter flight.   6–8

DILLON, EILÍS, *A Family of Foxes,* ill. by Vic Donahue, Funk, 1965. When four boys find two black foxes washed ashore on the Irish isle of Inishowan they know they must hide them from the adults who hate foxes.   10–12

DOTY, JEAN SLAUGHTER, *Winter Pony,* ill. by Ted Lewin, Macmillan, 1975. Two girls have the exciting experience of training a pony to pull an old-fashioned sleigh.   8–10

FLACK, MARJORIE, *Angus and the Ducks,* ill. by author, Doubleday, 1930. *Story About Ping,* ill. by Kurt Wiese, Viking, 1933. Each story is unique, each has a well-defined plot, delightful style, and just enough suspense or surprise to keep children interested.   5–8

GAGE, WILSON, *Mike's Toads,* ill. by Glen Rounds, World, 1970. Mike's offer to take care of a neighbor's toads turns into a full-time project.   8–10

GATES, DORIS, *A Morgan for Melinda,* Viking, 1980. Reversing the usual pattern of girls' horse stories, this describes a girl who learns to ride and love her horse only after her father has insisted on buying one.   9–11

GEORGE, JEAN, *The Cry of the Crow,* Harper, 1980. Set in the Florida Everglades, the story of a girl who trains and protects the pet crow her brothers would like to shoot.   10–12

GEORGE, JOHN L., and JEAN GEORGE, *Masked Prowler: The Story of a Raccoon,* ill. by Jean George, Dutton, 1950. This is a story about Procyon, a young raccoon, and the dangers and joys he encounters in growing up.   11–15
Vulpes the Red Fox, ill. by Jean George, Dutton, 1948. The fascinating biography of a red fox and the skills he possesses to outwit the hunters.   10–14

GIPSON, FRED, *Old Yeller,* ill. by Carl Burger, Harper, 1956. *Savage Sam,* ill. by Carl Burger, Harper, 1962. Two excellent stories of the importance of hound dogs in the lives of the frontier settlers. For mature readers.   12–16

GRIFFITHS, HELEN, *Just a Dog,* ill. by Victor Ambrus, Holiday, 1975. An unsentimental but touching story about a stray.   10–12

HALL, LYNN, *A Horse Called Dragon,* ill. by Joseph Cellini, Follett, 1971. Fictional framework for a sympathetic story of a real horse, a Mexican mustang.   10–12
Danza! Scribner's, 1981. A Puerto Rican boy, Paulo, travels with his grandfather's horse when Danza is borrowed by a Louisiana trainer.   10–12

HENRY, MARGUERITE, *Album of Horses,* ill. by Wesley Dennis, Rand, 1951.
Brighty of the Grand Canyon, ill. by Wesley Dennis, Rand, 1953.   9–12
Justin Morgan Had a Horse, ill. by Wesley Dennis, Rand, 1954.   9–12
King of the Wind, ill. by Wesley Dennis, Rand, 1948. Newbery Medal.   8–14
Misty of Chincoteague, ill. by Wesley Dennis, Rand, 1947.   8–12
White Stallion of Lippiza, ill. by Wesley Dennis, Rand, 1964.   8–12

Horse stories by this author are invariably dramatic and exciting but never sensational, and they are written with fidelity to the animal's nature. Most children, having read one, will read them all.

HOFF, SYD, *Julius,* ill. by author, Harper, 1959. The humorous account of a gorilla who makes friends with a small boy. A beginning-reading book.   6–7

JAMES, WILL, *Smoky, the Cowhorse,* ill. by author, Scribner's, 1926. One of the great animal stories for children, this poignant story is told in cowboy vernacular. Newbery Medal.   11–16

KELLOGG, STEVEN, *A Rose for Pinkerton,* ill. by author, Dial, 1981. An affectionate Great Dane puppy welcomes the kitten who's added to the household but it takes an act of canine heroism before the kitten will accept Pinkerton.   4–7

KJELGAARD, JIM, *Big Red,* ill. by Bob Kuhn, Holiday, 1956.   12–14
Kalak of the Ice, ill. by Bob Kuhn, Holiday, 1949.   10–14
These justly popular stories are well written, with plenty of action, and both human characters and animals are well drawn. Big Red is an Irish setter, the constant companion of Danny Pickett. Their adventures together climax in tracking down a huge outlaw bear. Kalak, known to the Eskimos as the "mist bear," is a heroic figure in her struggle to protect her cubs and survive.

KNIGHT, ERIC, *Lassie Come Home,* ill. by Marguerite Kirmse, Holt, 1940. A popular story of a collie's faithfulness to her master and her ability to track her way home over a great distance.   10–16

LATHROP, DOROTHY, *Who Goes There?* ill. by author, Macmillan, 1935. Exquisitely illustrated story about a winter picnic for birds and animals of the forest.   7–9

LIERS, EMIL, *A Beaver's Story,* ill. by Ray Sherin, Viking, 1958.
A Black Bear's Story, ill. by Ray Sherin, Viking, 1962.
An Otter's Story, ill. by Tony Palazzo, Viking, 1953. Three excellent animal biographies which depict the dangers facing each species from man as well as other animals. Exciting natural history.   9–12

LIPKIND, WILLIAM, and NICOLAS MORDVINOFF, *The Two Reds,* Harcourt, 1950. The two Reds, boy and cat, both city dwellers, were enemies because they both yearned for the same goldfish, but for different reasons.   4–8

LIPPINCOTT, JOSEPH WHARTON, *Gray Squirrel,* ill. by George F. Mason, Lippincott, 1954.
The Wahoo Bobcat, ill. by Paul Bransom, Lippincott, 1950.   12–15
Mr. Lippincott's tales of the wilderness life of hunted creatures are scientifically accurate, and in the process of reading them children develop understanding and sympathy for wild animals.

MC CLOSKEY, ROBERT, *Make Way for Ducklings,* ill. by author, Viking, 1941. Since this episode really happens in Boston each year, it is largely realistic with a few thoughts and words permitted the sagacious Mrs. Duck. Caldecott Medal.   4–8

MC CLUNG, ROBERT M., *Spike, the Story of a Whitetail Deer,* ill. by author, Morrow, 1952. A clear, factual story of the first year in the life of a whitetail deer.   5–10
Stripe, the Story of a Chipmunk, ill. by author, Mor-

row, 1951. These easy-to-read animal stories by a scientist and artist are well told, interesting to read to five-year-olds, and good reading for slow readers of nine and ten.   5–10

MILES, MISKA, *Fox and the Fire,* ill. by John Schoenherr, Little, 1966. A suspenseful portrayal of the plight of a young fox fleeing a forest fire.   7–11
Nobody's Cat, ill. by John Schoenherr, Little, 1969. An unforgettable portrait of a rough, tough alley cat.
5–9

MONTGOMERY, RUTHERFORD, *Kildee House,* ill. by Barbara Cooney, Doubleday, 1949. A raccoon and some skunks enliven the home planned as a solitary refuge.
10–12

MOREY, WALT, *Kävik, the Wolf Dog,* ill. by Peter Parnall, Dutton, 1968. A dog makes his way back from Seattle to the Alaskan home where he had first found love and kindness from a boy.   11–14
Runaway Stallion, Dutton, 1973. A runaway stallion and a lonely boy help each other adjust.   10–13

NAKATANI, CHIYOKO, *The Day Chiro Was Lost,* ill. by author, World, 1969. The busy city of Tokyo as seen from a dog's eye.   4–7

NEWBERRY, CLARE TURLAY, *April's Kittens,* ill. by author, Harper, 1940.
Mittens, ill. by author, Harper, 1936.
Clare Newberry's drawings of cats are so entrancing that the slight stories do not matter.   5–8

O'HARA, MARY, *Green Grass of Wyoming,* Lippincott, 1946.   12–adult
My Friend Flicka, Lippincott, 1941.   10–14
Thunderhead, Lippincott, 1943.   10–14
These books are a trilogy about the McLaughlin's horse ranch, where the problems are complicated by a bad wild-horse strain. Exciting reading.

PHIPSON, JOAN, *Birkin,* Harcourt, 1965. This is a story about a young calf, Birkin, who grows up into a monstrous steer. He and his owners lead an eventful life, and Birkin almost ends up as steak and roast beef.
10–12

PIATTI, CELESTINO, *The Happy Owls,* ill. by author, Atheneum, 1964. In a stunningly illustrated book, the owls try to explain to the quarreling barnyard animals the secret of being happy, but their wisdom is rejected.   6–8

RAWLINGS, MARJORIE KINNAN, *The Yearling,* ill. by N. C. Wyeth, Scribner's, 1939. This is a poignant story of growing up, when the boy Jody learns to accept the tragic necessity of disposing of his pet deer which has become a menace to the family's livelihood.
10–adult

ROUNDS, GLEN, *The Blind Colt,* ill. by author, Holiday, 1960. A wild colt, blind from birth, is patiently trained by a boy of ten.   9–11
Stolen Pony, ill. by author, Holiday, 1948. A moving story of a pony stolen by horse thieves and abandoned when it was found that he was blind. A faithful dog guides the pony home.   8–12

SEREDY, KATE, *Gypsy,* ill. by author, Viking, 1951. Children of any age and all cat-loving adults will enjoy Miss Seredy's magnificent pictures and simple account of a growing kitten.   4–up

STONG, PHIL, *Honk: the Moose,* ill. by Kurt Wiese, Dodd, 1935. This is undoubtedly one of the most amusing animal tales we have. A hard winter drives a hungry moose into the cozy confines of a livery stable, and the

problem is to get rid of him.   9–12

WARD, LYND, *The Biggest Bear,* ill. by author, Houghton, 1952. The Orchard family said, "Better a bear in the orchard than an Orchard in a bear." But Johnny was bound to get a bear and he did. A prize tale with wonderful pictures.   4–8

Life in the United States

ALIKI, *The Two of Them,* ill. by author, Greenwillow, 1979. A quiet and touching story about the love between an old man and his small grandchild and about her poignant longing when he dies.   5–8

ANGELL, JUDIE, *Dear Lola: or How to Build Your Own Family,* Bradbury, 1980. Eighteen-year-old Lola and five other orphans run away to live as a family; Lola writes an advice column under that name, but is a male—a loving father figure to the others.   9–11

BABBITT, NATALIE, *Goody Hall,* ill. by author. Farrar, 1971. A mystery-adventure story, both Gothic and humorous.   9–11

BECKMAN, DELORES, *My Own Private Sky,* Dutton, 1980. Shy, terrified by the swimming lessons on which his mother insists, Arthur is given courage by the example of an elderly friend's courage when she adjusts to having a leg amputated.   9–11

BLUME, JUDY, *Are You There, God? It's Me, Margaret,* Bradbury, 1970. Eleven, Margaret is perturbed about religion (she has one Jewish parent) and about physical evidence of maturing. A warm, humorous story.
10–12
Blubber, Bradbury, 1974. Jill discovers what it's like to be a taunted outsider, and gains compassion.   9–11
Tales of a Fourth Grade Nothing, ill. by Roy Doty, Dutton, 1972. A very funny story about the troubles Peter has with an obstreperous two-year-old brother.
8–9
Superfudge, Dutton, 1980. Peter, in fifth grade, feels it's bad enough to have a precocious younger brother, Superfudge, but do his parents have to have another child? A very funny, lighthearted family story.
8–10

BONHAM, FRANK, *Durango Street,* Dutton, 1965. Rufus Henry has two choices: to become involved with a street gang and face being sent back to a home for delinquents or to get himself killed because he lacks gang protection. A realistic portrait of life in the Los Angeles slums.   12–15

BRADBURY, BIANCA, *Andy's Mountain Top,* ill. by Robert MacLean, Houghton, 1969. A story of a family, grandparents and two children, whose family solidarity is broken by eviction from their property. 10–13

BRINK, CAROL RYRIE, *Family Grandstand,* ill. by Jean M. Porter, Viking, 1952.
Family Sabbatical, ill. by Susan Foster, Viking, 1956. These delightful stories tell of the activities of a professor's family in a Midwestern college town and during a year's trip to France.   9–12

BULLA, CLYDE, *A Ranch for Danny,* ill. by Grace Paull, T. Crowell, 1951.
Surprise for a Cowboy, ill. by Grace Paull, T. Crowell, 1950. Two stories of a city boy's adventures on his uncle's ranch where he learns how to be a cowboy.
7–10

BURCH, ROBERT, *Queenie Peavy,* ill. by Jerry Lazare, Viking, 1966.   10–14
Skinny, ill. by Don Sibley, Viking, 1964. An eleven-year-old works in a hotel while waiting for admission to an orphanage.   9–11
Tyler, Wilkin, and Skee, ill. by Don Sibley, Viking, 1963. The three brothers in the title have grand times together; their relationships with each other and their parents are warmly portrayed, sometimes with humor, sometimes with poignancy.   8–12
Ida Early Comes Over the Mountain, Viking, 1980. In a story set in rural Georgia during the Depression Era, Ida Early endears herself to the four Sutton children who have recently lost their mother.   9–11
BYARS, BETSY, *Go and Hush the Baby,* ill. by Emily McCully, Viking, 1971. Will is asked to pacify a baby brother, and does so by telling an original fairy tale.   2–5
The House of Wings, ill. by Daniel Schwartz, Viking, 1972. Sammy learns to love both his grandfather and the animals that have free rein in his home.   9–11
The Summer of the Swans, ill. by Ted CoConis, Viking, 1970. The climax of an unsatisfying summer for fourteen-year-old Sara is the disappearance of her retarded younger brother. A humorous and poignant story. Newbery Medal.   12–15
The Cybil War, ill. by Gail Owens, Viking, 1981. Simon and Tony are both smitten by their fourth-grade classmate, Cybil, in a story that has warmth, wit, and spontaneity.   8–10
The Night Swimmers, ill. by Troy Howell, Delacorte, 1980. A wonderfully perceptive story about a girl who reluctantly gives up the mother's role in caring for her younger brothers.   10–12
CAMERON, ELEANOR, *A Room Made of Windows,* ill. by Trina Schart Hyman, Atlantic, 1971. A selfish adolescent girl gains in her understanding of the problems of others.   10–13
CAUDILL, REBECCA, *A Certain Small Shepherd,* ill. by William Pène DuBois, Holt, 1965. At six, Jamie still cannot speak. Then, on Christmas Eve, his father befriends a man and woman, and the mysterious power of love of one's fellow man goes to work and Jamie can talk. Moving without being overly sentimental.   5–8
Did You Carry the Flag Today, Charley? ill. by Nancy Grossman, Holt, 1966.   5–7
A Pocketful of Cricket, ill. by Evaline Ness, Holt, 1964. A tender story of a young boy who takes his pet cricket to school.   5–8
CLARK, MARGERY, *The Poppy Seed Cakes,* ill. by Maud and Miska Petersham, Doubleday, 1924. A book of realistic, gay, and funny tales, told in a Russian atmosphere.   7–11
CLEARY, BEVERLY, *Ellen Tebbits,* ill. by Louis Darling, Morrow, 1951.   8–10
Henry and Beezus, ill. by Louis Darling, Morrow, 1952.
Henry and Ribsy, ill. by Louis Darling, Morrow, 1954.
Henry Huggins, ill. by Louis Darling, Morrow, 1950. Three of the many fine stories about one of the most believable young boys in all of fiction. Fun to read aloud to almost any age group, and nine- or ten-year-olds can read these books for themselves.   8–12
Mitch and Amy, ill. by George Porter, Morrow, 1967. Although they battle each other, the fourth-grade twins present a united front against a bully.   9–11
Ramona the Brave, ill. by Alan Tiegreen is a sequel to *Ramona the Pest,* ill. by Louis Darling (Morrow, 1975, 1968) and the hilarious stories of a kindergarten dropout who becomes a brave seven-year-old.   8–10
Ramona Quimby, Age 8, ill. by Alan Tiegreen, Morrow, 1981. The indomitable Ramona battles her way through each day in this very funny and endearing story, the fifth story about a memorable child.   7–9
CLEAVER, VERA and BILL, *Ellen Grae,* ill. by Ellen Raskin, Lippincott, 1967.   9–11
Grover, ill. by Frederic Marvin, Lippincott, 1970. A penetrating look at Grover and his adjustment to life after his mother's suicide.   9–12
Where the Lilies Bloom, ill. by Jim Spanfeller, Lippincott, 1969. The indomitable Mary Call Luther, fourteen, holds the family together when they are orphaned. A moving story set in Appalachia.   11–14
CLYMER, ELEANOR, *My Brother Stevie,* Holt, 1967. Stevie is a problem to his older sister Annie. How Annie turns Stevie's energies from delinquent activities to constructive uses is a sensitively told, understated story.   9–12
COHEN, MIRIAM, *First Grade Takes a Test,* ill. by Lillian Hoban, Greenwillow, 1980. After taking a multiple-choice test, some first-grade children squabble in a funny, pithy story that realistically reflects the ebullience and diversity in a multiethnic classroom.   6–7
CONFORD, ELLEN, *The Luck of Pokey Bloom,* ill. by Bernice Loewenstein, Little, 1975. Amusing incidents about an incorrigible contest-entrant; a good family story.   9–11
CORCORAN, BARBARA, *The Winds of Time,* ill. by Gail Owens, Atheneum, 1974. Running away from an uncle she dislikes, Gail stumbles into an odd household where she is given both freedom and concealment from authorities.   10–12
CORMIER, ROBERT, *The Chocolate War,* Pantheon, 1974. A strong indictment of power-hungry students and teachers in a boys' high school.   12–up
CRAYDER, DOROTHY, *She, the Adventuress,* ill. by Velma Ilsley, Atheneum, 1973. Going alone from Iowa to Italy, Maggie proves resourceful during an exciting adventure.   9–11
CREDLE, ELLIS, *Down Down the Mountain,* ill. by author, Nelson, 1934. This story of two southern mountain children who yearn to own a pair of squeaky shoes has action and good humor.   7–8
DANZIGER, PAULA, *There's a Bat in Bunk Five,* Delacorte, 1980. A yeasty camp story about Marcy's first experience as a junior counselor, written with vigor, perception, and humor.   11–13
ECKERT, ALLAN, *Incident at Hawk's Hill,* ill. by John Schoenherr, Little, 1971. A child of six wanders off and is adopted by a badger. Touching, dramatic.   12–up
ENRIGHT, ELIZABETH, *The Four-Story Mistake,* ill. by author, Holt, 1942.
The Saturdays, ill. by author, Holt, 1941.
Then There Were Five, ill. by author, Holt, 1938. One of the trilogy about the Melendy family, *The Saturdays* is set in New York City, where the children evolve a scheme for taking turns in spending their allowances; the other titles are set in the country.   8–12

Thimble Summer, ill. by author, Holt, 1938. A delightful story of the adventures of a little girl on a Wisconsin farm. Newbery Medal.   8–12

ESTES, ELEANOR, *The Middle Moffat,* ill. by Louis Slobodkin, Harcourt, 1942.

The Moffats, ill. by Louis Slobodkin, Harcourt, 1941.

Rufus M., ill. by Louis Slobodkin, Harcourt, 1943. The Moffat family is fatherless and bordering on real poverty, but the spirit is one of good humor and warm relationships.   9–12

Ginger Pye, ill. by author, Harcourt, 1951. The author's Newbery Medal book centers around the theft of a dog and the children's attempts to find the thief.   9–12

The Hundred Dresses, ill. by Louis Slobodkin, Harcourt, 1944. Children are not likely to forget Wanda, who was rejected by the group, nor the culprits who taunted her.   9–11

ETS, MARIE HALL, *Bad Boy, Good Boy,* ill. by author, T. Crowell, 1967. A sensitive, honest portrayal of a newly arrived Mexican family striving to adjust to life in a California town.   6–8

Play with Me, ill. by author, Viking, 1955. This is a charming picture-story of a little girl and all the little wild things she meets on a walk.   2–5

FENTON, EDWARD, *Duffy's Rocks,* Dutton, 1974. Tim Brennan goes from the dreary suburb of Duffy's Rocks to try finding his long-absent father.   11–13

FITZGERALD, JOHN, *The Great Brain Does It Again,* ill. by Mercer Mayer, Dial, 1975. Amusing episodes about an older brother who is a wheeler-dealer are told by a boy.   9–11

FITZHUGH, LOUISE, *Harriet the Spy,* ill. by author, Harper, 1964.   9–12

FLACK, MARJORIE, *Wait for William,* Houghton, 1935. This amusing circus story turns upon the most natural conflict in the world—a four-year-old's trouble with his shoelace and the older children's impatience with his slowness.   5–8

FOX, PAULA, *Portrait of Ivan,* ill. by Saul Lambert, Bradbury, 1969. When his photographer father decides to have his son's portrait painted, the lonely withdrawn boy begins to make new friends and become more sure of himself.   10–12

The Stone-Faced Boy, ill. by Donald McKay, Bradbury, 1968. A perceptive account of a timid middle child in a noisy, outgoing family.   8–12

GAGE, WILSON, *Dan and the Miranda,* ill. by Glenn Rounds, World, 1962. Humorous story of Dan's half-hearted attempts to do a project for the fifth-grade science fair.   8–11

GATES, DORIS, *Blue Willow,* ill. by Paul Lantz, Viking, 1940. The story of Janey Larkin, daughter of migrant workers, who longed for a real home.   9–12

GEORGE, JEAN, *Gull Number 737,* ill. by author, T. Crowell, 1964. When birds cause a fatal plane crash, Dr. Rivers and his son Luke are called upon to help drive the birds from the runways. A natural science detective story with important human values.   12–14

My Side of the Mountain, ill. by author, Dutton, 1959.   11–14

Who Really Killed Cock Robin? Dutton, 1971. An ecology-minded small town learns that there are dire and complicated results to pollutants.   10–12

GREENE, CONSTANCE, *A Girl Called Al,* ill. by Byron Barton, Viking, 1969. A moving story of two girls growing in sensitivity and self-confidence as they cultivate a friendship with their apartment superintendent.   11–13

The Unmaking of Rabbit, Viking, 1972. Friendship brings courage to a shy boy who doesn't want to be called "Rabbit."   9–11

Ask Anybody, Viking, 1983. Schuyler and her friends are baffled but intrigued by the new girl, Nell, who knows all about everything ("Ask anybody," she sneers) and is a marvelously amoral and pathetic misfit.   10–12

Dotty's Suitcase, Viking, 1980. The empty suitcase Dotty has found proves to be a passport to a dangerous but exciting adventure.   10–12

GREENWALD, SHEILA, *Give Us a Great Big Smile, Rosy Cole,* ill. by author, Little, Brown, 1981. Her uncle wants to do a book about her, as he's done with her sisters (one's a dancer, the other an equestrienne) but poor Rosy knows she's an abominable violinist and fights back.   8–10

GUILFOILE, ELIZABETH, *Nobody Listens to Andrew,* ill. by Mary Stevens, Follett, 1957. A humorous sustained story for beginning readers. The title describes the grownups' reaction when Andrew tells them there is a bear in his bed.   6–7

HALL, LYNN, *Sticks and Stones,* Follett, 1972. A mature story about an adolescent who becomes the subject of malicious gossip due to an innocent friendship with another male.   12–15

HAYWOOD, CAROLYN, *"B" Is for Betsy,* ill. by author, Harcourt, 1939.

Eddie's Valuable Property, ill. by author, Morrow, 1975.

Little Eddie, ill. by author, Morrow, 1947.

Penny and Peter, ill. by author, Harcourt, 1946. Carolyn Haywood has written over two dozen books about the mild adventures of suburban children at home, at school, or in the community. Eddie has more humor in his life than the others.   5–9

HILDICK, EDMUND W., *Manhattan Is Missing,* ill. by Jan Palmer, Doubleday, 1969. English children vacationing in New York with their parents are involved in an exciting chase as they attempt to solve the mystery of a disappearing Siamese cat.   9–12

HODGES, MARGARET, *The Making of Joshua Cobb,* ill. by W. T. Mars, Farrar, 1971. An only child adjusts to preparatory school.   9–11

HUNT, IRENE, *Up a Road Slowly,* Follett, 1967. Julie Trelling, left motherless at age seven, is sent to live with her Aunt Cordelia and Uncle Haskell, who, between them, provide her with insight into the qualities necessary to become a mature, happy individual. Newbery Medal.   12–16

HURWITZ, JOANNA, *Baseball Fever,* ill. by Ray Cruz, Morrow, 1981. Ezra's scholarly father tries to understand his son's passion for baseball in this witty and amusing story.   8–10

ISH-KISHOR, SULAMITH, *Our Eddie,* Pantheon, 1969. A penetrating study of the influence of a self-centered fanatical Jewish father on his son and other members of the family.   12–up

JACKSON, JACQUELINE, *The Taste of Spruce Gum,* ill. by Lillian Obligado, Little, 1966. A well-told story of eleven-year-old Libby and her adjustment to life in a lumber camp and her new father.   10–13

KERR, M. E., *Dinky Hocker Shoots Smack,* Harper, 1972.

Dinky doesn't do it, but she paints that sentence on walls to make her parents realize that she has problems as well as the addicts they're helping. Perceptive writing.   12–15

Little Little, Harper, 1981. Kerr makes fun of social pretensions and snobbery and show biz, but never of her protagonists, a dwarf and a midget, in a brisk and witty love story.   12–14

KINGMAN, LEE, *The Peter Pan Bag,* Houghton, 1970. A girl of seventeen discovers more pathos than fun in urban communal living.   12–15

The Year of the Raccoon, Houghton, 1966. A perceptively written story of Joey, a boy struggling for identity and self-worth in the shadow of two gifted brothers and a dynamic father.   11–13

KONIGSBURG, E. L., *About the B'nai Bagels,* ill. by author, Atheneum, 1969. Mark thinks his troubles are unique: his mother is manager of his Little League team, his big brother is coach, and with all that he has to get ready for his Bar Mitzvah.   9–11

Altogether, One at a Time, ill. by Gail Haley et al., Atheneum, 1971. Four witty, perceptive short tales.   9–11

From the Mixed-up Files of Mrs. Basil E. Frankweiler, ill. by author, Atheneum, 1967. Newbery Medal.   10–12

Jennifer, Hecate, Macbeth, William McKinley, and Me, Elizabeth, ill. by author, Atheneum, 1967. The adventures of Elizabeth as apprentice witch under the tutelage of Jennifer, a self-declared witch, are perceptively told and give us a memorable portrait of the friendship which develops between two ten-year-old girls.   8–10

Journey to an 800 Number, Atheneum, 1982. A snobbish boy learns to make allowances for people when he travels with his father on the fair and convention circuit.   10–13

KRUMGOLD, JOSEPH, *Henry 3,* ill. by Alvin Smith, Atheneum, 1967.

Krumgold's ... *and now Miguel* is listed under Minority Groups in the United States since Miguel's Spanish-American heritage is central to the story.

Onion John, ill. by Symeon Shimin, T. Crowell, 1959. Andy Rusch, Jr., is a typical American boy growing up in a small town, devoted to his father who is his hero, but fascinated by Onion John, an eccentric town character. There is a father-son conflict which is more happily resolved than Onion John's problems when the town tries to civilize him. Amusing, and skillfully told. Newbery Medal.   10–14

LENSKI, LOIS, *Cotton in My Sack,* ill. by author, Lippincott, 1949. A story of sharecropping in Arizona.   8–10

Cowboy Small, ill. by author, Walck, 1949.   3–7
Strawberry Girl, ill. by author, Lippincott, 1945. Set in rural Florida. Newbery Medal.   8–10
The Little Airplane, ill. by author, Walck, 1938.
The Little Train, ill. by author, Walck, 1940.
Papa Small, ill. by author, Walck, 1951.
It is hard to overestimate the appeal of Lenski's "little" books. Indeed, the Small Family has become a tradition for untold numbers of small children.   3–7

LOWRY, LOIS, *Anastasia Krupnik,* Houghton, 1979. Wry and sophisticated, this is a laugh-aloud novel about the engaging ten-year-old child in an academic family.

The sequels, *Anastasia Again!* (1981) and *Anastasia at Your Service* (1982) are just as lively and funny.   9–11

Autumn Street, Houghton, 1980. A poignant and candid story about an interracial friendship and a child's adjustment to death.   10–12

Taking Care of Terrific, Houghton, 1983. "Terrific" is the name that Enid's four-year-old charge has taken in a hilarious story with serious undertones, in which a group of oddly assorted characters steals a ride on a Boston swan boat at midnight.   10–12

MC CLOSKEY, ROBERT, *Blueberries for Sal,* ill. by author, Viking, 1948. A picture story about Sal and her mother, who tangle with a bear and her cub.   3–7

Homer Price, ill. by author, Viking, 1943, 1963.   9–11

Lentil, ill. by author, Viking, 1940. Amusing story of a boy living in a small Midwestern town who saves the day with his harmonica.   6–9

Time of Wonder, ill. by author, Viking, 1957. In full color, McCloskey captures both the fun of a vacation in Maine and the power of a hurricane. Caldecott Medal.   6–9

MILES, BETTY, *Maudie and Me and the Dirty Book,* Knopf, 1980. Maudie and Kate never dream, when they read *Birthday Dog* to a first-grade class, that they'll precipitate a community controversy about the freedom to read.   11–13

MOSER, DON, *A Heart to the Hawks,* Atheneum, 1975. Fourteen and an ardent naturalist, Mike tries to save the woodland near his Cleveland home. The characterization is as strong as the message of conservation.   11–14

NEUFELD, JOHN, *Edgar Allan,* ill. by Loren Dunlap, Phillips, 1968. The reaction of townspeople, congregation, and family to the adoption of a black child by the minister and his wife is described by their elder son.   10–13

NEVILLE, EMILY, *Berries Goodman,* Harper, 1965. Sharply written story of the effects of anti-Semitism on the friendship of two suburban boys.   10–14

It's Like This, Cat, ill. by Emil Weiss, Harper, 1963. Dave Mitchell is an average fourteen-year-old trying to come to grips with himself and his family. This Newbery Medal book has depth and subtlety, humor and realism.   9–13

NORDSTROM, URSULA, *The Secret Language,* ill. by Mary Chalmers, Harper, 1960.   7–9

PECK, RICHARD, *Don't Look and It Won't Hurt,* Holt, 1972. A tender picture of a girl who assumes a protective role when her younger sister gets in trouble.   11–14

Representing Super Doll, Viking, 1974. A sensible girl chaperones a friend who wins a beauty contest.   11–13

PECK, ROBERT, *A Day No Pigs Would Die,* Knopf, 1972. A strong family story about a Shaker boy on a Vermont farm who must adjust to the death of a father.   12–up

PEVSNER, STELLA, *A Smart Kid Like You,* Seabury, 1975. Discerning treatment of a girl's adjustment to her father's remarriage.   10–12

PFEFFER, SUSAN BETH, *Marly the Kid,* Doubleday, 1975. A plump, plain adolescent finds more security with her father and stepmother than she had with her mother. Sensitive and witty.   11–14

Courage, Dana, ill. by Jenny Rutherford, Delacorte, 1983. Ashamed of her timidity, Dana acts with spontaneous courage to save a small boy's life and learns that courage can also mean making a choice between right and wrong.   9–12

REDFORD, POLLY, *The Christmas Bower,* ill. by Edward Gorey, Dutton, 1967. A department store family puts on a Christmas display of live birds. Result: riot.   10–12

ROBERTSON, KEITH, *Henry Reed, Inc.,* ill. by Robert McCloskey, Viking, 1958.
Henry Reed's Baby-Sitting Service, ill. by Robert McCloskey, Viking, 1966.
Henry Reed's Journey, ill. by Robert McCloskey, Viking, 1963.
Three very funny stories about a literal-minded boy who provides laughter for everyone but himself.   10–12
In Search of a Sandhill Crane, ill. by Richard Cuffari, Viking, 1973. From an elderly aunt and her Indian friend, a bored boy learns to appreciate wildlife.   10–13

SACHS, MARILYN, *The Bears' House,* ill. by Louis Glanzman, Doubleday, 1971. The dollhouse with a bear family is Fran Ellen's escape from an intolerable home situation.   9–11
Veronica Ganz and *Peter and Veronica,* ill. by Louis Glanzman, Doubleday, 1968 and 1969. Two stories in which Veronica, long the bully of her class, meets her match in undersized Peter and a painful friendship begins.   10–14
Bus Ride, ill. by Amy Rowen, Dutton, 1980. A growing friendship between two high school students is told almost entirely in dialogue, and is eminently suitable for slow as well as average readers.   11–14

SCHAEFER, JACK, *Old Ramon,* ill. by Harold West, Houghton, 1960. A convincing character study of an old shepherd who is wise not only in the ways of sheep but also in the ways of young boys. An effective read-aloud story.   10–14

SHARMAT, MARJORIE WEINMAN, *Gladys Told Me to Meet Her Here,* ill. by Edward Frascino, Harper, 1970.
I'm Not Oscar's Friend Anymore, ill. by Tony DeLuna, Dutton, 1975.
Two funny, touching stories of misunderstanding.   5–8

SHULEVITZ, URI, *Dawn,* ill. by author, Farrar, 1974. A truly beautiful book about two campers' dawn.   5–7

SLEPIAN, JAN, *The Alfred Summer,* Macmillan, 1980. The intricacies of love and courage are perceptively depicted in a tender yet funny story about two handicapped boys who become friends.   10–12
Lester's Turn, Macmillan, 1981. The sequel brings the death of gentle, retarded Alfred, in a story told by Lester, who has cerebral palsy.   10–12

SLOTE, ALFRED, *Matt Gargan's Boy,* Lippincott, 1975. Danny learns that wishing isn't going to bring his divorced father back or keep a girl off the baseball team.   9–11
My Father, the Coach, Lippincott, 1972. Good baseball, a strong father-son relationship.   9–11

SMITH, DORIS BUCHANAN, *A Taste of Blackberries,* ill. by Charles Robinson, T. Crowell, 1973. A most moving story about a child's adjustment to his friend's death.   9–11

SNYDER, ZILPHA KEATLEY, *The Egypt Game,* ill. by Alton Raible, Atheneum, 1967.   9–12
The Velvet Room, ill. by Alton Raible, Atheneum, 1965. Mystery adds suspense to a story of migrant workers.   10–12
The Birds of Summer, Atheneum, 1983. Summer strives to protect her little sister and find her own niche when her shiftless mother is arrested.   11–14
A Fabulous Creature, Atheneum, 1981. Smitten by a flirt while on a mountain vacation, James is disappointed when she doesn't share his protective love for a beautiful stag—but is it the stag or the younger child who shares his concern that is the fabulous creature?   11–14

SORENSEN, VIRGINIA, *Miracles on Maple Hill,* ill. by Beth and Joe Krush, Harcourt, 1956. A warm story of a family's experiencing the wonder of woods and fields at all seasons. Newbery Medal.   9–12

SPYKMAN, E. C., *A Lemon and a Star,* Harcourt, 1955. The amusing adventures of four motherless Cares youngsters. For superior readers.   11–14

STOLZ, MARY, *The Bully of Barkham Street,* ill. by Leonard Shortall, Harper, 1963. An unusual companion volume to the title cited below, giving the same story from another view.
A Dog on Barkham Street, ill. by Leonard Shortall, Harper, 1960.   9–12
Noonday Friends, ill. by Louis S. Glanzman, Harper, 1965. Being poor, wearing old clothes, and having a free lunch pass given to needy children nags at eleven-year-old Franny Davis. An inspiring book—sometimes funny, always perceptive in its sensitivity.   9–12

TRESSELT, ALVIN, *Follow the Wind,* ill. by Roger Duvoisin, Lothrop, 1950.
I Saw the Sea Come In, ill. by Roger Duvoisin, Lothrop, 1954.
These picture-stories are little dramas of weather and seasonal changes.   4–6

TUNIS, JOHN R., *All-American,* Harcourt, 1942. No one writes better sports stories than John R. Tunis. In addition to sports, his books center on adolescent problems resulting from religious and racial prejudices.   12–14

TWAIN, MARK (pseud. for Samuel Clemens), *The Adventures of Huckleberry Finn.*   11–up
The Adventures of Tom Sawyer.   12–up
Both classics are available in many editions.

UDRY, JANICE, *The Moon Jumpers,* ill. by Maurice Sendak, Harper, 1959. The delight of playing in the moonlight out-of-doors is caught in the artist's luminous drawings. A rare book.   4–7

VOIGT, CYNTHIA, *Dicey's Song,* Atheneum, 1982. A sequel to *Homecoming* (1981) in which four children come to live with their grandmother, this is a rich and perceptive story in which the children adjust to their new life. Newbery Medal.   10–13

YASHIMA, TARO (pseud. for Jun Iwanatsu), *Umbrella,* ill. by author, Viking, 1958. Day after day small Momo waited and hoped for rain so that she might use her bright red boots and new umbrella. Stunning illustrations.   5–8

ZOLOTOW, CHARLOTTE, *My Grandson Lew,* ill. by William Pène Du Bois, Harper, 1974. A boy and his mother fondly remember a loving grandfather.   3–7
William's Doll, ill. by William Pène Du Bois, Harper,

1972. Grandmother is the only one who understands that boys as well as girls can love dolls.   4–8

Minority Groups

ANGELO, VALENTI, *The Bells of Bleecker Street*, ill. by author, Viking, 1949.
Hill of Little Miracles, ill. by author, Viking, 1942.
In *The Bells of Bleecker Street* twelve-year-old Joey finds himself the accidental possessor of a toe from the statue of St. John. His struggles to return the toe, his adventures with his gang, and his father's return from the war make an amusing story and bring this Italian neighborhood vividly to life. *Hill of Little Miracles* shows Ricco, who was born with one leg too short, starting on the road to normalcy.   10–14

ARMER, LAURA ADAMS, *Waterless Mountain*, ill. by Sidney and Laura Adams Armer, McKay, 1931. A poetic story of Navaho life containing little action and much mysticism. For the special reader.   12–14

ARMSTRONG, WILLIAM H., *Sounder*, ill. by James Barkley, Harper, 1969. A somber moving novel of a black sharecropper's family who surmount injustice with dignity. Newbery Medal.   11–up

ASSOCIATION FOR CHILDHOOD EDUCATION, *Told Under Spacious Skies*, ill. by William Moyers, Macmillan, 1952.
Told Under the Stars and Stripes, ill. by Nedda Walker, Macmillan, 1945.
The first book is made up of regional stories; the second book is an anthology of short stories about various minority groups in our cities throughout the country.   8–12

BAKER, BETTY, *And One Was a Wooden Indian*, Macmillan, 1970. A young Apache learns that he has the true vision of the shaman.   11–15
Little Runner of the Longhouse, ill. by Arnold Lobel, Harper, 1962. Easy-to-read story of an Iroquois boy and his New Year celebration.   6–7
The Shaman's Last Raid, ill. by Leonard Shortall, Harper, 1963. Very funny account of what happens when Great-Grandfather, who rode with Geronimo, tries to teach the old ways to modern Indian children.   8–12

BEIM, LORRAINE and JERROLD, *Two Is a Team*, ill. by Ernest Crichlow, Harcourt, 1945. Two little boys find that they get more done as a team than singly. That they are of two different races makes no difference; it's the team that is important.   5–8

BONHAM, FRANK, *Viva Chicano*, Dutton, 1970. A young Chicano on parole gets a second chance.   12–15

BUFF, MARY, *Dancing Cloud, the Navajo Boy*, rev. ed., ill. by Conrad Buff, Viking, 1957.   9–10
Hah-Nee of the Cliff Dwellers, ill. by Conrad Buff, Houghton, 1956.   8–10
Magic Maize, ill. by Conrad Buff, Houghton, 1953.   9–12
Three fine Indian stories.

BULLA, CLYDE, *Eagle Feather*, ill. by Tom Two Arrows, T. Crowell, 1953.
Indian Hill, ill. by James J. Spanfeller, T. Crowell, 1963.
Bulla has a special touch which makes his easy reading books especially appealing to reluctant readers.   7–10

BUTTERWORTH, WILLIAM, *LeRoy and the Old Man*, Four Winds, 1980. Because he's witnessed a crime and his mother is fearful of retribution, LeRoy is sent to Mississippi to stay with his grandfather, in a story in which the integrity and dignity of an old man change a cocky adolescent.   12–14

CHILDRESS, ALICE, *A Hero Ain't Nothin' but a Sandwich*, Coward, 1973. The story of a young drug addict, brilliantly told from his own and others' viewpoints, is candid and touching, with superb characterization.   11–14

CLARK, ANN NOLAN, *Blue Canyon Horse*, ill. by Allan Houser, Viking, 1954. A beautiful story of a young Indian boy and his horse.   8–10
In My Mother's House, ill. by Velino Herrera, Viking, 1941. This is a fine story written with simplicity and beauty about the Tewa Indian children.   8–12
Little Navaho Bluebird, ill. by Velino Herrera, Viking, 1943. The story of a little Navaho girl who loves her home and the old ways of life, but who learns to accept going to the white man's school.   8–12

CLYMER, ELEANOR, *The Spider, the Cave, and the Pottery Bowl*, ill. by Ingrid Fetz, Atheneum, 1971. Each summer Kate returns to the Indian village where her grandmother lives.   8–10

DAVIS, RUSSELL G., and BRENT K. ASHABRANNER, *The Choctaw Code*, McGraw, 1961. The Choctaws granted a year of freedom to a man under the death sentence. This moving story recounts how youthful Tom Baxter learned to accept the inevitability of his friend's death.   10–14

DE ANGELI, MARGUERITE, *Henner's Lydia*, ill. by author, Doubleday, 1936.
Skippack School, ill. by author, Doubleday, 1939.
Two stories of life in a Mennonite community in Pennsylvania.   8–10
Yonie Wondernose, ill. by author, Doubleday, 1944. A favorite, especially when his "wondering" pays off and he proves his courage as well. There could hardly be a more appealing introduction to the Pennsylvania Dutch than Yonie.   6–9

ERWIN, BETTY K., *Behind the Magic Line*, ill. by Julia Iltis, Little, 1969. A well-told story of a close-knit black family in a midwest ghetto and their move to the northwest to begin a new life.   10–12

FAULKNER, GEORGENE, and JOHN BECKER, *Melindy's Medal*, ill. by C. E. Fox, Messner, 1945. A humorous and tender story of a little girl's achievement.   8–11

FIFE, DALE, *Who's in Charge of Lincoln?* and its sequels, *What's New, Lincoln?*, *What's the Prize, Lincoln?* and *Who Goes There, Lincoln?* ill. by Paul Galdone, Coward, 1965, 1970, 1971, and 1975. Lively, humorous stories about an imaginative black boy.   7–10

FITZHUGH, LOUISE, *Nobody's Family Is Going to Change*, Farrar, 1974. Emma's black and brilliant, but her father scoffs at her wanting to become a lawyer.   10–12

FOX, PAULA, *How Many Miles to Babylon?* ill. by Paul Giovanopoulos. White, 1967.   9–11

GREENE, BETTE, *Philip Hall Likes Me, I Reckon Maybe*, ill. by Charles Lilly, Dial, 1974. Funny, breezy story of a smitten black girl of eleven, Beth, whose mother knows she's bright about everything except That Boy.   9–11
Get On Out of Here, Philip Hall, Dial, 1981. A second

story about redoubtable Beth and her ambivalent feelings about the boy who's her best friend and worst rival.   9–11

GREENFIELD, ELOISE, *She Come Bringing Me That Little Baby Girl*, ill. by John Steptoe, Lippincott, 1974. Kevin's jealousy is assuaged by Mama's wise approach.   3–5

HAMILTON, VIRGINIA, *The House of Dies Drear*, ill. by Eros Keith, Macmillan, 1968.   9–12
M. C. Higgins the Great, Macmillan, 1974. The oldest boy in a mountain family, M. C. dreams of a better life for them all. Rich in setting and characterization, written with distinction. Newbery Medal.   11–13
The Time Ago Tales of Jahdu, ill. by Nonny Hogrogian, Macmillan, 1969. A small black inhabitant of Harlem is held in wonder by Mama Luka's tales of Jahdu.   6–9
Zeely, ill. by Symeon Shimin, Macmillan, 1967. A perceptive and sensitively written story with focus upon the problems of a young girl beginning to grow up.   9–11

HURMENCE, BELINDA, *Tough Tiffany*, Doubleday, 1980. The youngest child in a black family, Tiffany is sensitive and curious, tough only in her resilience. 10–12

HUNTER, KRISTIN, *Guests in the Promised Land*, Scribner's, 1973.   11–14
The Soul Brothers and Sister Lou, Scribner's, 1968. A memorable story of Louretta Hawkins and her singing group who take the tragic events which surround them in the ghetto and turn them into soul music.   12–15

JACKSON, JESSE, *Call Me Charley*, ill. by Doris Spiegal, Harper, 1945. The story of the ups and downs in a young black boy's friendship with a white boy in a white community.   9–12

JONES, WEYMAN, *The Edge of Two Worlds*, ill. by J. C. Kocsis, Dial, 1968. The story of an encounter between an aged, very ill Cherokee Indian and a white boy stranded in the wilderness and their gradual acceptance of the fact of their interdependence.   10–14

JORDAN, JUNE, *New Life: New Room*, ill. by Ray Cruz, T. Crowell, 1975. Three children in a black family resent having to share a room because another child is to be born, but find it's fun planning and rearranging.   5–8

KEATS, EZRA JACK, *Peter's Chair*, ill. by author, Harper, 1967.
The Snowy Day, ill. by author, Viking, 1964. Caldecott Medal.
Whistle for Willie, ill. by author, Viking, 1964.
Three beautifully illustrated stories about a little boy's adventures in the first snow; how, when he is a little older, he learns to whistle for his dog; and his final acceptance of his new little sister.   4–7

KINGMAN, LEE, *The Best Christmas*, ill. by Barbara Cooney, Doubleday, 1949. A simple, moving story of a Finnish-American family's Christmas.   8–11

KRASILOVSKY, PHYLLIS, *Benny's Flag*, ill. by W. T. Mars, World, 1960. The true story of how an Indian boy's entry in a flag contest came to be chosen as the official flag of Alaska. Striking illustrations of Alaska.   7–9

KRUMGOLD, JOSEPH, *. . . and now Miguel*, ill. by Jean Charlot, T. Crowell, 1953. The story of twelve-year-old Miguel, who wishes to be accepted as a man, is told with humor and tenderness. Fine picture of sheepherding in New Mexico. Newbery Medal.   10–14

LAURITZEN, JONREED, *The Ordeal of the Young Hunter*, ill. by Hoke Denetsosie, Little, 1954. A distinguished story of a twelve-year-old Navaho boy who grows to appreciate what is good in the cultures of the white man and the Indian.   11–14

LEXAU, JOAN, *Benjie on His Own*, ill. by Don Bolognese, Dial, 1970. When his grandmother fails to pick him up after school, Benjie tries to find his own way. When he arrives home and finds her very ill, he must use even more initiative to get help.   5–7

MATHIS, SHARON BELL, *The Hundred Penny Box*, ill. by Leo and Diane Dillon, Viking, 1975. Soft pictures of a wrinkled old black face and an eager young one echo the love that is the theme of this tender story.   8–10

MEANS, FLORENCE CRANNELL, *Great Day in the Morning*, Houghton, 1946. In this book a lovable black girl experiences the bitterness of racial prejudice but has the courage to go on. At Tuskegee she comes to know Dr. Carver and decides to become a nurse.   12–14

MILES, MISKA, *Annie and the Old One*, ill. by Peter Parnall, Atlantic, 1971. A Navajo grandmother helps little Annie understand that death is an inevitable part of life.   8–10

MILHOUS, KATHERINE, *The Egg Tree*, ill. by author, Scribner's, 1950. This beautifully illustrated book of an Easter egg tree in rural Pennsylvania has started egg trees blooming all over the country. Caldecott Medal.   6–8

MOHR, NICHOLASA, *Nilda*, ill. by author, Harper, 1973. A somber but candid picture of life in Spanish Harlem.   11–14

MONTGOMERY, JEAN, *The Wrath of Coyote*, ill. by Anne Siberell, Morrow, 1968. A story which depicts the impact of the white man's civilization upon the Miwok Indians of Northern California.   11–14

MURRAY, MICHELE, *Nellie Cameron*, ill. by Leonora Prince, Seabury, 1971. Set in Washington, D.C., the story of a black child who overcomes a reading problem also presents a warm picture of family life.   9–11

MYERS, WALTER, *Won't Know Till I Get There*, Viking, 1982. Stephen, age fourteen, adjusts to having a foster brother and participates, with the other black adolescents of *The Young Landlords* (1979) in a project that gains some independence for the residents of an old people's home.   11–14

NEWELL, HOPE, *A Cap for Mary Ellis*, Harper, 1953. Two young nursing students enter as the first black trainees in a New York State hospital. Their story is told with warmth and humor.   11–14

OAKES, VANYA, *Willy Wong: American*, ill. by Weda Yap, Messner, 1951. Here is the old struggle of a little Chinese boy to be accepted as a one hundred percent American. A good family story.   10–up

PALMER, CANDIDA, *Snow Storm Before Christmas*, ill. by H. Tom Hall, Lippincott, 1965. Two children in a middle-class black family go Christmas shopping.   8–10

POLITI, LEO, *A Boat for Peppe*, ill. by author, Scribner's, 1950.
Juanita, ill. by author, Scribner's, 1948.
Little Leo, ill. by author, Scribner's, 1951.
Mieko, ill. by author, Golden Gate, 1969.
Moy Moy, ill. by author, Scribner's, 1960.
Pedro, the Angel of Olvera Street, ill. by author, Scribner's, 1946.

Song of the Swallows, ill. by author, Scribner's, 1949. Caldecott Medal.

These appealing picture-stories have slight plots but a tender beauty that is unique. Pedro and Juanita show the Christmas and Easter customs of the Mexican colony on Olvera Street in Los Angeles. The swallows are the famous birds of San Capistrano Mission. Peppe takes part in the blessing of the fishing boats at Monterey, but Little Leo journeys to Italy and converts a whole village of children to the charms of playing Indian. Moy Moy, the little sister of three brothers in Chinatown, finds the New Year's festivities wonderful, and Mieko yearns to be queen of Nisei Week in Los Angeles. 5–8

ROSENBERG, SONDRA, *Will There Never Be a Prince?* ill. by Mircea Vasiliu, St. Martin's, 1970. A very amusing tale of a Jewish girl's adolescence, told partly in diary form. 11–14

SANDOZ, MARI, *The Horsecatcher,* Westminster, 1957. Compelling story of Young Elk, a Cheyenne, who faces disapproval because he would rather capture horses than kill men. 11–14

SEBESTYEN, OUIDA, *Words by Heart,* Atlantic/Little, Brown, 1979. A percipient story of a black family's adherence to nonviolence in the face of cruel provocation. 10–12

SHOTWELL, LOUISA, *Magdalena,* ill. by Lilian Obligado, Viking, 1971. Grandmother has old-fashioned Puerto Rican ideas, Magdalena feels, but they reach agreement. 10–12
Roosevelt Grady, ill. by Peter Burchard, World, 1963. 9–11

SONNEBORN, RUTH, *Friday Night Is Papa Night,* ill. by Emily McCully, Viking, 1970. Working at two jobs, Papa came home only on Fridays, so to Pedro it was the best time of the week. 5–7

STEPTOE, JOHN, *Stevie,* ill. by author, Harper, 1969. A vivid portrayal of the feelings of a young boy who resents the child his mother cares for during the week. 5–8

STERLING, DOROTHY, *Mary Jane,* ill. by Ernest Crichlow, Doubleday, 1959. A young black girl enrolls in a newly integrated junior high school where she is lonely and has problems to solve in winning friendship. 12–14

TALBOT, CHARLENE, *Tomás Takes Charge,* ill. by Reisie Lonette, Lothrop, 1966. Tomás and Fernanda, alone in New York, take refuge in an abandoned building rather than let the welfare authorities find them. 9–12

TAYLOR, SYDNEY, *All-of-a-Kind Family,* Follett, 1951. This is a heart-warming story of an affectionate Jewish family, living in the early 1900's. 9–12
More All-of-a-Kind Family, ill. by Mary Stevens, Follett, 1954. 9–12
All-of-a-Kind Family Downtown, ill. by Beth and Joe Krush, Follett, 1972. Another cozy story. 9–12

THOMAS, DAWN, *Mira! Mira!* ill. by Harold James, Lippincott, 1970. Ramon, newly arrived from Puerto Rico, is enchanted by his first snow. 5–7

UCHIDA, YOSHIKO, *The Promised Year,* ill. by William M. Hutchinson, Harcourt, 1959. A little Japanese girl and her cat learn to adjust to their new home and friends in California. 8–12
A Jar of Dreams, Atheneum, 1981. A visitor from Japan gives new confidence to a Japanese-American family in coping with financial problems and racial bias. 8–10

UDRY, JANICE MAY, *Mary Jo's Grandmother,* ill. by Eleanor Mill, Whitman, 1970. A small black girl copes resourcefully when the grandmother she's visiting has an accident. 5–8

YEP, LAURENCE, *Sea Glass,* Harper, 1979. Craig, who has come to live with cousins who feel he's more Chinese than American, learns that time brings perspective and the clarity that smooths sea glass. 11–14

Life in Other Lands

England, Ireland, Scotland

ARDIZZONE, EDWARD, *Little Tim and the Brave Sea Captain,* ill. by author, Walck, 1936. A picture-story book about life at sea with five-year-old Tim as the hero. 6–8
Tim All Alone, ill. by author, Walck, 1957. This is a story about a young seafaring lad who is the personification of achievement. 6–8

BAWDEN, NINA, *The Runaway Summer,* Lippincott, 1969. A finely drawn portrait of lonely Mary as she slowly adjusts to life after her parents' divorce. 9–11
Squib, Lippincott, 1971. An older girl loves an orphaned waif of seven who reminds her of the small brother who had died. Set in England. 10–11
Kept in the Dark, Lothrop, 1982. In a dramatic story with good pace and suspense, a household is menaced by a cruel and amoral bully. 10–12
The Robbers, Lothrop, 1979. It is his grandmother's understanding sympathy when nine-year-old Philip champions the cause of an interracial family that makes him decide to stay with her rather than with his cold, domineering father. 9–11

BREINBURG, PETRONELLA, *Doctor Shawn* and *Shawn Goes to School,* ill. by Errol Lloyd, T. Crowell, 1975 and 1974. A small English boy plays doctor, and has his first day at nursery school; these are among the few British books with black characters. 3–5

BROWN, ROY, *The Day of the Pigeons,* Macmillan, 1969. As a reform school runaway searches London for his father he is drawn into the affairs of a group of children intent upon a search of their own. 10–12
Flight of Sparrows, Macmillan, 1973. Gang life in a squalid London neighborhood, tough but touching.
The White Sparrow, Seabury, 1975. Two of the characters from the first book go off on their own, and one finds a home with an understanding family. 12–14

CRESSWELL, HELEN, *Ordinary Jack: Being the First Part of the Bagthorpe Saga,* Macmillan, 1977. Sometimes slapstick, but usually witty, this is the first of a series of stories about a charming but rather daft family. Others in the series are *Absolute Zero* (1978), *Bagthorpes Unlimited,* (1978) and *Bagthorpes v. the World* (1979), all equally uproarious. 10–12

DICKINSON, PETER, *Emma Tupper's Diary,* ill. by David Omar White, Atlantic, 1971. Planned as a quiet Highlands vacation, Emma's visit provides high drama. 11–14

DILLON, EILÍS, *The Coriander,* ill. by Vic Donahue, Funk, 1964. Set on the Irish island of Inishgillan, this story of a kidnaped doctor who reluctantly is pressed into service offers more than just an exciting plot. 11–14

GARDAM, JANE, *The Summer After the Funeral,* Macmillan, 1973. A wheedling mother arranges summer plans for her three children. Witty and perceptive.
11–14

Bridget and William, ill. by Janet Rawlins, Watts, 1981. Bridget's father relents about the cost of a pony when it enables her to get to the village and fetch the doctor to deliver a baby brother.
7–9

The Hollow Land, ill. by Janet Rawlins, Greenwillow, 1981. A series of interwoven stories about a lifelong friendship.
10–12

GARNER, ALAN, *The Stone Book,* ill. by Michael Foreman, Collins/World, 1978. The first of a quartet of beautifully written short novels that link several generations of a family in rural Cheshire. Others are *Granny Reardun* (1978), *Tom Fobble's Day* (1979) and *The Aimer Gate* (1979).
9–11

GODDEN, RUMER, *The Kitchen Madonna,* ill. by Caro Barker, Viking, 1967. A tender little novel of two London children and their painstaking effort to create an acceptable Madonna for their homesick Polish-Ukrainian maid.
8–12

The Rocking-Horse Secret, ill. by Juliet Smith, Viking, 1978. A lonely child threatened with the loss of her home and a lost will that solves all problems believably are the dramatic material for a smoothly told story.
9–11

HILDICK, E. W., *Louie's Snowstorm,* ill. by Iris Schweitzer, Doubleday, 1974. One of a series of books about a British milkman and the boys who help him; here a plucky American girl helps during a Christmas snowstorm.
10–12

HUNTER, MOLLIE, *The Third Eye,* Harper, 1979. A Scottish story has a deft weaving of plot threads as it gives a vivid picture of a community.
11–14

LINGARD, JOAN, *Across the Barricades,* Nelson, 1973. One of a trilogy, this describes the tragic tension between Protestant and Catholic children in Ireland.
11–14

MACKEN, WALTER, *The Flight of the Doves,* Macmillan, 1968. An exciting chase results when Finn Dove and his younger sister flee to relatives in Ireland to escape a vicious stepfather.
9–12

MC NEILL, JANET, *The Battle of Saint George Without,* ill. by Mary Russon, Little, 1968. A lively and believable story of some English children who conspire to save a derelict church from the wrecking crew.
9–12

Goodbye, Dove Square, ill. by Mary Russon, Little, 1969. In this sequel to the story listed above we see the same children two years later as they adjust to new homes in council housing and cope with the problems of adolescence.
11–14

MAC PHERSON, MARGARET M., *The Shinty Boys,* ill. by Shirley Hughes, Harcourt, 1963. Earning money on the Isle of Skye is not easy, and the boys must earn fifty pounds over the summer if they are to keep their shinty team.
10–12

MAGORIAN, MICHELLE, *Good Night, Mr. Tom,* Harper, 1982. A small, frightened boy is sent to stay with a crusty old man during the London blitz, and a deep love grows between them, in a touching but not saccharine story.
11–14

MARK, JAN, *Thunder and Lightnings,* Crowell, 1979. Winner of the 1976 Carnegie Medal, this describes the friendship that makes one boy tolerant of another's passionate interest in aircraft.
11–14

MAYNE, WILLIAM, *Royal Harry,* Dutton, 1972. Told with fluent grace, a mystery story in which a girl of twelve inherits a house and a mountain.
10–12

PEARCE, PHILIPPA, *What the Neighbors Did and Other Stories,* ill. by Faith Jacques, Crowell, 1973. A fluent style and strong characterization make eight stories about children in a Cambridgeshire village a delight.
9–11

PEYTON, K. M., *Pennington's Last Term,* ill. by author, T. Crowell, 1971. The first of several books about a tough adolescent who becomes a concert pianist.
11–14

RANSOME, ARTHUR, *Swallows and Amazons,* ill. by Helene Carter, Lippincott, 1931. This is the only title in a seven-volume series which is still in print. It is the story of a summer vacation spent on an island by a group of children. They are far enough from home to feel independent, but close enough to feel secure. A satisfying book for special readers.
10–12

ROBINSON, VERONICA, *David in Silence,* ill. by Victor G. Ambrus, Lippincott, 1968. A memorable story, set in England, about a deaf boy and his attempts to join in the activities of normal children.
10–12

TOWNSEND, JOHN ROWE, *Good-Bye to the Jungle,* Lippincott, 1967. This fine novel about English slums is a sometimes amusing, sometimes sad, story of what happens to six people when they move into a new neighborhood.
12–15

The Intruder, ill. by Joseph A. Phelan, Lippincott, 1970. An account of a psychopathic stranger's attempt to usurp the name and rights of a foundling lad in a British coastal village.
12–up

Pirate's Island, Lippincott, 1968. Two children in a decaying neighborhood, a neglected girl and a fat over-indulged boy, manage to resolve their personal problems and find friendship and adventure.
9–12

Trouble in the Jungle, ill. by W. T. Mars, Lippincott, 1969.
10–14

TURNER, PHILIP, *Colonel Sheperton's Clock,* ill. by Philip Gough, World, 1966.

The Grange at High Force, ill. by W. T. Mars, World, 1967.

Although both books contain a slight element of mystery, it is the relationships among the three boys and between the boys and the adults which lend flavor to these pictures of small village English life.
12–14

VAN STOCKUM, HILDA, *The Cottage at Bantry Bay,* ill. by author, Viking, 1938. The escapades of the O'Sullivan children—Michael, Brigid, and the twins Francie and Liam—make a lively tale.
10–12

WESTALL, ROBERT, *The Machine Gunners,* Greenwillow, 1976. Winner of the Carnegie Medal, this vividly recreates the drama and tension of a small town strafed daily by German planes, the action focused on a group of children who find and hide a machine gun from a German plane.
10–14

France

BEMELMANS, LUDWIG, *Madeline,* ill. by author, Simon, 1939. Madeline inhabits a French boarding school with "twelve little girls in two straight lines" doing everything in two straight lines, except the appendix that only Madeline had to have removed. The other *Madeline* books are equally as much fun as this one.
5–8

BERNA, PAUL, *The Horse Without a Head,* tr. from the French by John Buchanan-Brown, ill. by Richard Kennedy, Pantheon, 1958. The right combination of an exciting mystery and the French *joie de vivre* in a picture of lower-class children in France.   9–12

BISHOP, CLAIRE HUCHET, *Twenty and Ten,* ill. by William Pène DuBois, Viking, 1952. During the Nazi occupation of France, nineteen French children with their teacher were asked to feed and hide ten Jewish children. How these fifth-graders shared their food and managed with their teacher held in jail is a moving and satisfying story.   9–12

CARLSON, NATALIE SAVAGE, *The Family Under the Bridge,* ill. by Garth Williams. Harper, 1958.   8–10
The Happy Orpheline, ill. by Garth Williams, Harper, 1957. An imaginative and amusing story of twenty orphans, happy in their home outside of Paris, afraid only of being adopted.   8–10
A Brother for the Orphelines, ill. by Garth Williams, Harper, 1959. A delightful sequel to *The Happy Orpheline,* this tells of the efforts of the orphans to keep a baby boy foundling left on their doorstep.   8–10
A Grandmother for the Orphelines, ill. by David White, Harper, 1980. In another story about the orphans of the old castle, the children search for a grandmother-figure and find one who comes with a bonus —a grandfather for them.   8–10

Holland

DE JONG, MEINDERT, *Far Out the Long Canal,* ill. by Nancy Grossman, Harper, 1964. At nine, Moona alone among his classmates cannot skate and his only dream is to learn.   10–12
Journey from Peppermint Street, ill. by Emily A. McCully, Harper, 1968. Siebren experiences three days filled with excitement and adventure on his first journey away from home. The author skillfully portrays the inner thoughts and feelings of the young boy. National Book Award.   8–10
The Wheel on the School, ill. by Maurice Sendak, Harper, 1954. A tenderly told, warmly humorous story of how a Dutch fishing village brings back the storks to settle there again. Newbery Medal.   9–12

DODGE, MARY MAPES, *Hans Brinker; or the Silver Skates,* ill. by Hilda Van Stockum, World, 1946. Although still considered a classic, this lengthy story of Hans should not be a first choice for books about Holland.   10–12

KRASILOVSKY, PHYLLIS, *The Cow Who Fell in the Canal,* ill. by Peter Spier, Doubleday, 1957. Stunning picture book which combines humor with an accurate look at Dutch life.   5–8

Italy

ANGELO, VALENTI, *The Honey Boat,* ill. by author, Viking, 1959. Friendly picture of an Italian family at work and play.   10–12

BETTINA (pseud. for Bettina Ehrlich), *Pantaloni,* ill. by author, Harper, 1957. This author-artist has never created more beautiful pictures than those for this appealing picture-story of an Italian boy's search for his dog.   5–9

Mexico and South America

BEHN, HARRY, *The Two Uncles of Pablo,* ill. by Mel Silverman, Harcourt, 1959. The contrast between Pablo's two uncles creates a real problem for him. How he reunites the family is sensitively told. Fine reading aloud.   9–12

CLARK, ANN NOLAN, *Secret of the Andes,* ill. by Jean Charlot, Viking, 1952. In this Newbery Medal book, Cusi lives among the great peaks of the Andes Mountains, guarding a hidden herd of royal llamas and learning from old Chuto the sacred traditions of his Incan ancestors.   10–14

ETS, MARIE HALL, and AURORA LA BASTIDA, *Nine Days to Christmas,* ill. by Marie Hall Ets, Viking, 1959. Small Ceci enjoys her first posada in this Caldecott Medal book of present-day Mexico.   5–8

KALNAY, FRANCIS, *Chúcaro: Wild Pony of the Pampa,* ill. by Julian de Miskey, Harcourt, 1957. Excellent depiction of life on the Argentine pampas with a story that leaves the reader with much to think about.   9–12

O'DELL, SCOTT, *The Black Pearl,* ill. by Milton Johnson, Houghton, 1967. An unforgettable tale of Ramon Salazar, a pearl diver and his fortunes after he brings up to the surface a great black pearl.   11–14

SOMMERFELT, AIMÉE, *My Name Is Pablo,* ill. by Hans Norman Dahl, Criterion, 1965. Portrait of modern Mexico's poverty problem as seen through the eyes of Pablo, who is befriended by a Norwegian family.   10–12

STOLZ, MARY, *The Dragons of the Queen,* ill. by Edward Franscino, Harper, 1969. Two Americans meet a queenly old Mexican woman and are charmed by her.   10–12
Juan, ill. by Louis S. Glanzman, Harper, 1970. A poignant story of Juan who refuses to accept the fact that he is an orphan.   8–11

The Orient[6]

AYER, JACQUELINE, *NuDang and His Kite,* ill. by author, Harcourt, 1959.
A Wish for Little Sister, ill. by author, Harcourt, 1960. Colorful picture-stories of Thailand.   5–8

BUCK, PEARL, *The Big Wave,* prints by Hiroshige and Hokusai, Day, 1948. Significant story built around the theme that "life is stronger than death." Two Japanese boys adventure together, survive a terrible catastrophe, and begin life anew.   9–12

DE JONG, MEINDERT, *The House of Sixty Fathers,* ill. by Maurice Sendak, Harper, 1956. Set in China during World War II, this is the story of how Tien Pao and his pig, Glory of the Republic, were finally able to rejoin Tien Pao's family.   10–12

HANDFORTH, THOMAS, *Mei Li,* ill. by author, Doubleday, 1938. The pleasant adventures of a little Chinese girl at the fair. Caldecott Medal.   5–8

LATTIMORE, ELEANOR FRANCES, *Little Pear,* ill. by author, Harcourt, 1931.   6–9

---

[6]Included in this section are stories of China, India, Japan, Thailand, Tibet, etc.

Little Pear and His Friends, ill. by author, Harcourt, 1939.   6–9
Little Pear and the Rabbits, ill. by author, Morrow, 1956.   6–9
Three adventure stories of a likable little Chinese boy.
LEWIS, ELIZABETH FOREMAN, *Young Fu of the Upper Yangtze,* ill. by Kurt Wiese, Holt, 1932. This Newbery Medal book gives us a graphic picture of the inner strife and conflict in the life of a young Chinese boy. The details are Chinese, but Fu is any boy of any country trying to make his way in the world.   10–14
MARTIN, PATRICIA MILES, *The Pointed Brush,* ill. by Roger Duvoisin, Lothrop, 1959. Story of Chung Wee, small sixth son of the House of Chung, who goes to school only because he is least needed in the rice fields, and who convinces his family that "the man who knows the written word has strength."   6–8
MERRILL, JEAN, *The Superlative Horse,* ill. by Ronnie Solbert, W. R. Scott, 1961. When Po Lo, Chief Groom in Duke Mu's court, grows too old to retain his position, he recommends Han Kan, son of a fuel hawker, as his successor. Han Kan's test is to select one horse for the Duke's stable of already magnificent horses.   8–11
SAY, ALLEN, *The Ink-Keeper's Apprentice,* Harper, 1979. Set in Tokyo after World War II, this is the story of a boy so talented that he is taken as an apprentice by Japan's greatest cartoonist.   12–14
SOMMERFELT, AIMÉE, *The Road to Agra,* ill. by Ulf Aas, Phillips, 1961. Thirteen-year-old Lalu's younger sister Maya is going blind, and he decides to take her to the UNICEF hospital in Agra. The trip is long and hazardous, and events depict the poverty of India's small villages and its effects upon people.   9–12
UCHIDA, YOSHIKO, *Sumi and the Goat and the Tokyo Express,* ill. by Kazue Mizumura, Scribner's, 1969. It is a most unusual day for Sumi and her classmates as Mr. Odo's goat stops the crack train to Kyoto.   6–9
Takao and Grandfather's Sword, ill. by William M. Hutchinson, Harcourt, 1958. One of a number of good stories by this author which depicts both modern Japan and its rich heritage.   8–10
WIESE, KURT, *Fish in the Air,* ill. by author, Viking, 1948. An amusing account of what happens to a small Chinese boy when he buys the largest kite in the market. Lovely, bright pictures.   6–8
YASHIMA, TARO (pseud. for Jun Iwanatsu), *Crow Boy,* ill. by author, Viking, 1955. This story of a small outcast Japanese boy has unusual social values as well as great pictorial beauty.   6–8
YASHIMA, TARO, and HATOJU MUKU, *The Golden Footprints,* ill. by author, World, 1960. A beautiful story of the devotion of two foxes to their captured cub and how it affects a young Japanese boy. Excellent reading aloud.   8–11

Pacific Islands

CLARK, MAVIS T., *Blue Above the Trees,* ill. by Genevieve Melrose, Meredith, 1969. A memorable account of the Whitburn family's struggle to build a new life on a farm located in the rain forest of Australia.   11–13
The Min-Min, Macmillan, 1969. A troubled teen-ager and her younger brother leave home on a quest for the guidance and security not offered them at home.   11–15
COWLEY, JOY, *The Silent One,* ill. by Hermann Greissle, Knopf, 1981. In a primitive island community of the South Pacific, a deaf-mute boy fights in vain against the superstitious fear that makes him an outcast.   9–11
OTTLEY, REGINALD, *Boy Alone,* ill. by Clyde Pearson, Harcourt, 1966.   10–12
Rain Comes to Yamboorah, ill. by Robert Hales, Harcourt, 1968. The final book of the trilogy which began with *Boy Alone.*   10–13
Roan Colt, ill. by Clyde Pearson, Harcourt, 1967. A very fine sequel to *Boy Alone.*   10–13
PHIPSON, JOAN, *The Boundary Riders,* ill. by Margaret Horder, Harcourt, 1963.
The Family Conspiracy, ill. by Margaret Horder, Harcourt, 1964.
Threat to the Barkers, ill. by Margaret Horder, Harcourt, 1965.
These three fine stories are set in the back country of Australia and show how rugged life is in the wilds.   10–12
SOUTHALL, IVAN, *Ash Road,* ill. by Clem Seale, St. Martin's, 1965.
Hill's End, ill. by Clem Seale, St. Martin's, 1963. Two unforgettable stories from Australia about people under pressure from a disastrous fire and a flood. High drama at its best.   10–14
Josh, Macmillan, 1972. A city boy adjusts to rural life in Australia.   10–14
SPERRY, ARMSTRONG, *Call It Courage,* ill. by author, Macmillan, 1940. This Newbery Medal book is an exciting adventure story and also the tale of one boy's conquest of fear. Beautifully illustrated and poetic text.   10–12
WRIGHTSON, PATRICIA, *A Racecourse for Andy,* ill. by Margaret Horder, Harcourt, 1968. A poignant story of a retarded boy, his loyal friends, and the events which follow his supposed purchase of a racetrack.   9–12

Scandinavian Countries

ANCKARSVÄRD, KARIN, *The Mysterious Schoolmaster,* tr. from the Swedish by Annabelle Macmillan, ill. by Paul Galdone, Harcourt, 1959. A coastal village in Sweden provides the background for this captivating tale of two children who outwit an international spy.   10–12
Robber Ghost, tr. from the Swedish by Annabelle Macmillan, ill. by Paul Galdone, Harcourt, 1961. A sequel to the above, with numerous escapades.   10–12
BESKOW, ELSA, *Pelle's New Suit,* ill. by author, Harper, 1929. This beautifully illustrated picture book of how Pelle works for his new suit has acquired the status of a classic.   4–7
FRIIS-BAASTAD, BABBIS, *Don't Take Teddy,* tr. by Lise Sømme McKinnon, Scribner's, 1967. A retarded boy of fifteen is protected by a younger brother.   10–13
GRIPE, MARIA, *Hugo and Josephine,* ill. by Harald Gripe, Delacorte, 1969. A prize-winning story from Sweden of the mishaps and adventures of two children at home and school.   8–10

The Night Daddy, tr. by Gerry Bothmer, ill. by Harald Gripe, Delacorte, 1971. A young writer becomes a father figure to a child whose mother, a nurse, is on night duty.   9–11

Elvis and His Friends and *Elvis and His Secret,* both ill. by Harald Gripe, tr. by Sheila La Frage, Delacorte, 1976. Two wry and poignant stories about a small boy who finds emotional security in friendships that he cannot get from his flighty, carping mother.   9–11

JANSSON, TOVE, *The Summer Book,* tr. by Thomas Teal, Pantheon, 1975. A lovely, lyric story about a child and her grandmother.   10–12

LINDGREN, ASTRID, *Rasmus and the Vagabond,* tr. from the Swedish by Gerry Bothmer, ill. by Eric Palmquist, Viking, 1960. Nine-year-old Rasmus runs away from the Swedish orphanage and meets Paradise Oscar, a lovable tramp. How he finds a home and happiness is well told in this touching tale.   10–12

I Want a Brother or a Sister, ill. by Ilon Wiklund, tr. by Barbara Lucas, Harcourt, 1981. Peter gets over his dethronement problems and his jealousy of little sister Lena when a third child comes along and he finds Lena is now an ally.   5–7

VESTLY, ANNE-CATH, *Hello, Aurora,* ill. by Leonard Kessler, tr. by Eileen Amos, Crowell, 1974. A bouncy story of a Norwegian family in which Mother works and Father, a doctoral candidate, keeps house. In the sequel, *Aurora and Socrates* (1977), Vestly deals with peer jealousy and separation anxiety with a light touch.   7–9

Switzerland

CHÖNZ, SELINA, *A Bell for Ursli,* ill. by Alois Carigiet, Walck, 1950. One of the most beautiful picture stories to come out of Europe, this is also an exciting adventure story of a small Swiss boy's determination to have the largest bell to ring in the spring processional.   5–7

SPYRI, JOHANNA, *Heidi.* Any edition.   9–11

ULLMAN, JAMES RAMSEY, *Banner in the Sky,* Lippincott, 1954. A dramatic and exciting story of young Rudi's determination to become a mountain climber and one day conquer the Citadel. Captures, as no other book does, the fascination of mountain climbing.   12–16

VAN DER LOEFF-BASENAU, ANNA RUTGERS, *Avalanche!* ill. by Gustav Schrotter, Morrow, 1958.   11–13

Eskimo Stories

FREUCHEN, PIPALUK, *Eskimo Boy,* ill. by Ingrid Vang Nyman, Lothrop, 1951. This epic tale, translated from the Danish, is the grimmest, most terrifying picture of Eskimo life we have had. It is the story of a boy's fight to save his family from starvation. The realistic details make it unsuitable for young children, but the heroism of the boy and his deeds are good for older children to read about.   10–12

GEORGE, JEAN CRAIGHEAD, *Julie of the Wolves,* ill. by John Schoenherr, Harper, 1972. A young Eskimo girl survives in the Arctic by living with a wolf pack after learning to communicate with the wolves. Newbery Medal.   10–13

GRIESE, ARNOLD, *At the Mouth of the Luckiest River,* ill. by Glo Coalson, T. Crowell, 1973. An Athabascan boy of the past creates a bond between his people and an Eskimo tribe they had feared.   9–11

HOUSTON, JAMES A., *Akavak, An Eskimo Journey,* ill. by author, Harcourt, 1968. A revealing portrait of Eskimo life is presented in this story of the struggle of a boy and his grandfather to reach their destination.   9–12

LIPKIND, WILLIAM, *Boy with a Harpoon,* ill. by Nicolas Mordvinoff, Harcourt, 1952. This, like Freuchen's book, should banish forever the igloo stereotype of Arctic life. An absorbing story of a boy's attempts to rid himself of a derogatory nickname and win a respected place in the community of men.   7–10

Other Countries

ALMEDINGEN, E. M., *Young Mark: The Story of a Venture,* ill. by Victor G. Ambrus, Farrar, 1968. The author tells of her great-great-grandfather's trek from the Ukraine to St. Petersburg through Czarist Russia.   11–15

BENARY-ISBERT, MARGOT, *The Ark,* Harcourt, 1953.   12–14

Castle on the Border, tr. from the German by Richard and Clara Winston, Harcourt, 1956.   12–15
Two stories of life in postwar Germany and the problems encountered in rebuilding a normal life out of the ruins of World War II.

BESS, CLAYTON, *Story for a Dark Night,* Houghton, 1982. A touching story, set in Liberia, of the communal support given to a family stricken by illness.   10–13

BLOCH, MARIE H., *Aunt America,* ill. by Joan Berg, Atheneum, 1963. Without moralizing, Bloch makes clear the meaning of freedom by depicting the lives of those who live in the Communist-dominated Ukraine.   9–12

DONNELLY, ELFIE, *So Long, Grandpa,* tr. by Anthea Bell, Crown, 1981. In a moving story, a German child is the narrator, describing his reactions when a beloved grandparent sickens and dies.   9–11

FEELINGS, MURIEL L., *Zamani Goes to Market,* ill. by Tom Feelings, Seabury, 1970. The story of a young Ugandan boy's first trip to market with his father and older brothers is well told and conveys the atmosphere of village life in Africa.   7–10

FROLOV, VADIM, *What It's All About,* tr. by Joseph Barnes, Doubleday, 1968. Contemporary life for Russian adolescents shows common concerns.   12–15

GEBHARDT, HERTHA VON, *The Girl from Nowhere,* tr. from the German by James Kirkup, ill. by Helen Brun, Phillips, 1959. An absorbing story of Magdalene, a nine-year-old from nowhere, who arouses wonder and suspicion among the children of a small German town. When she leaves, they find they are lost without her.   10–12

HÁMORI, LÁSZLÓ, *Dangerous Journey,* tr. from the Swedish by Annabelle Macmillan, ill. by W. T. Mars, Harcourt, 1962. The dramatic, but believable, story of two Hungarian boys who make their escape to freedom in Vienna.   10–12

HOLM, ANNE S., *North to Freedom*, tr. from the Danish by L. W. Kingsland, Harcourt, 1965. A tremendously moving story of young David's trip from a concentration camp to Denmark and freedom. Contrasts between the camp and life in the free world are excellently drawn and David's experiences arouse in the reader a new appreciation of a way of life we often take for granted. A unique book. 10–14

JONES, TOECKEY, *Go Well, Stay Well*, Harper, 1980. The story of her friendship with a Zulu girl is told by adolescent Candy, a member of the British community in Johannesburg. 12–14

KASSIL, LEV, *Once in a Lifetime*, tr. by Anne Terry White, Doubleday, 1970. A Moscow girl of thirteen has a movie role, then decides to go back to school. 11–14

KINGMAN, LEE, *The Meeting Post; A Story of Lapland*, ill. by Des Asmussen, T. Crowell, 1972. A Lapp child, sent to a Finnish boarding school, adjusts to his new life. 8–10

KORINETZ, YURI, *There, Far Beyond the River*, tr. by Anthea Bell, ill. by George Armstrong, O'Hara, 1973. A Russian boy remembers the vitality and affection of a boisterous uncle. 10–12

LITTLE, JEAN, *From Anna*, ill. by Joan Sandin, Harper, 1972. 9–11
Kate, Harper, 1971, and *Look Through My Window*, ill. by Joan Sandin, Harper, 1970, to which it is a sequel, are about the friendship between two Canadian girls and the problems of one (Kate) who has one Jewish parent. 9–12

MIRSKY, REBA P., *Seven Grandmothers*, ill. by W. T. Mars, Follett, 1955.
Thirty-one Brothers and Sisters, ill. by W. T. Mars, Follett, 1952.
Two stories of Nomusa, a young Zulu girl. Warmly drawn picture of life in a Zulu kraal. 8–10

NAGENDA, JOHN, *Mukasa*, ill. by Charles Lilly, Macmillan, 1973. A good family story based on the author's childhood in Uganda. 9–11

OFEK, URIEL, *Smoke Over Golan*, ill. by Lloyd Bloom, tr. by Israel Taslitt, Harper, 1979. Alone at home when the attack on the Golan Heights came, a boy helps capture an enemy officer. 11–13

SEREDY, KATE, *Chestry Oak*, ill. by author, Viking, 1948. An involved and difficult story with a deeply significant theme—the fall of an ancient house and its rebirth in a new land. The boy Michael and his great horse Midnight are the central figures in the tale. 10–14
The Good Master, ill. by author, Viking, 1955. 10–12

SERRAILLIER, IAN, *The Silver Sword*, ill. by C. Walter Hodges, Phillips, 1959. An inspiring narrative of four courageous children of Warsaw after World War II. The three who have been separated from their parents set off to find them and are joined by a fourth child. Their journey covers three hard years, but their spirit never falters. 10–14

SHANNON, MONICA, *Dobry*, ill. by Atanas Katchamakoff, Viking, 1934. Beautifully written and rich in unique characters, this slow-moving story of a Bulgarian peasant boy may be more appealing to children if read aloud. Newbery Medal. 11–14

SLOBODKIN, FLORENCE, *Sarah Somebody*, ill. by Louis Slobodkin, Vanguard, 1970. A small girl delights in going to school in a Polish village at the turn of the century. A warm Jewish family story. 8–10

STINETORF, LOUISE A., *Musa, the Shoemaker*, ill. by Harper Johnson, Lippincott, 1959. A lame Algerian boy, apprenticed to a shoemaker, grows up in a village of acrobats but achieves success with another skill. 9–11

STORR, CATHERINE, *Kate and the Island*, ill. by Gareth Floyd, Faber, 1978. Although Kate is teased because she insists on digging for treasure while visiting a Greek island, she does make a valuable find. 9–11

TAYLOR, THEODORE, *The Cay*, Doubleday, 1969. After a ship is torpedoed in World War II, the survivors, a blinded white boy and a highly competent old black sailor, are stranded on a barren island in the Caribbean. 11–14

WUORIO, EVA-LIS, *Save Alice!* Holt, 1968. Set in Spain, a lively and humorous mystery story involves British and American children in saving a white cockatoo. 10–12
Detour to Danger, Delacorte, 1981. There's suspense and action in the story of a Spanish adolescent who unravels the mystery of what seems to be a neo-Nazi plot. 11–15

Historical Fiction

American

ALCOTT, LOUISA MAY, *Little Women*, ill. by Jessie Willcox Smith, Little, 1934 (1868). Although this forerunner of modern realism for children and young people is chiefly a story of family life, it is also a story of life in Civil War times. There are numerous attractive editions available. 10–14

BACON, MARTHA, *Sophia Scrooby Preserved*, ill. by David C. White, Little, 1968. A rather romantic tale of a Zulu chieftain's daughter sold into slavery who triumphs over hardships to achieve success as a singer in London. 10–13

BAKER, BETTY, *Walk the World's Rim*, Harper, 1965. Chakoh, a young Indian, went to Mexico City with four Spanish survivors of a force of six hundred which had set out to search for gold in the sixteenth-century land of America. 10–12
The Great Desert Race, Macmillan, 1980. Two girls of sixteen participate in a race for steam-powered automobiles, set in 1908. 11–13

BEATTY, PATRICIA, *Lacy Makes a Match*, Morrow, 1979. A lively girl of 13 looks for wives for her older brothers, in a story set in California in 1893. 10–12

BENCHLEY, NATHANIEL, *Small Wolf*, ill. by Joan Sandin, Harper, 1972. The eviction of native Americans from Manhattan Island. 6–8
George the Drummer Boy, ill. by Don Bolognese, Harper, 1977. Humor and information are nicely blended in this story about the start of the American Revolution as seen from the viewpoint of a young British soldier. 6–8

BLOS, JOAN, *A Gathering of Days: A New England Girl's Journal, 1830–32,* Scribner's, 1980. Set in New Hampshire, a narrative in journal form, Newbery Medal.
10–12

BROOKS, JEROME, *Make Me a Hero,* Dutton, 1980. A boy of twelve yearns to be important—just like the three brothers who are serving in the armed forces.
11–14

BULLA, CLYDE ROBERT, *Down the Mississippi,* ill. by Peter Burchard, T. Crowell, 1954.   8–10

BURCHARD, PETER, *Bimby,* ill. by author, Coward, 1968. One day in the life of a young slave boy as he tries to decide whether to make a break for freedom.
9–12

Jed, The Story of a Yankee Soldier and a Southern Boy, ill. by author, Coward, 1960.   10–12

CAUDILL, REBECCA, *Tree of Freedom,* ill. by Dorothy B. Morse, Viking, 1949. An outstanding pioneer story which gives a detailed picture of life in 1770, near Louisville, Kentucky. The story involves some stormy family relationships and appealing characters.
12–14

CLAPP, PATRICIA, *Constance; A Story of Early Plymouth,* Lothrop, 1968.   12–15

Witches' Children: A Story of Salem, Lothrop, 1982. A first-person account gives immediacy to a story of the mass hysteria of the Salem witch hunt.   11–14

COATSWORTH, ELIZABETH, *Away Goes Sally,* ill. by Helen Sewell, Macmillan, 1934. The first of a series of historical stories about Sally, this one has to do with the migration of her whole family of aunts and uncles from Massachusetts to Maine after the American Revolution.
10–12

Five Bushel Farm, ill. by Helen Sewell, Macmillan, 1939. This book sees Sally's family established on their new farm and introduces Andy to her circle of friends.
8–10

COBLENTZ, CATHERINE CATE, *Martin and Abraham Lincoln,* ill. by Trientja, Childrens Pr., 1947.   7–10

COLLIER, JAMES LINCOLN and CHRISTOPHER, *My Brother Sam Is Dead,* Four Winds, 1974. A poignant story of a Connecticut family during the Revolutionary War.   11–14

War Comes to Willy Freeman, Delacorte, 1983. Black and free, Willy poses as a boy in the story of the Revolutionary War test case heard in a Connecticut court.
11–14

DALGLIESH, ALICE, *Adam and the Golden Cock,* ill. by Leonard Weisgard, Scribner's, 1959. A small boy faces a personal problem of divided loyalty when General Rochambeau's army comes to his Connecticut town during the Revolution.   7–9

The Bears on Hemlock Mountain, ill. by Helen Sewell, Scribner's, 1952. This adventure story is based on a historical episode. There weren't supposed to be any bears on Hemlock Mountain, but there *were,* as poor Jonathan proved. Jonathan's ingenuity in hiding from the bears will delight every young reader.   7–9

EDMONDS, WALTER D., *The Matchlock Gun,* ill. by Paul Lantz, Dodd, 1941. A thrilling story of young Edward's courage in defending his home while his father is away fighting the Indians during the French and Indian wars. Stunning illustrations capture the drama. Newbery Medal.   8–10

FIELD, RACHEL, *Calico Bush,* ill. by Allen Lewis, Macmillan, 1931.   12–14

FORBES, ESTHER, *Johnny Tremain,* ill. by Lynd Ward, Houghton, 1943. Newbery Medal.   11–14

FOX, PAULA, *The Slave Dancer,* ill. by Eros Keith, Bradbury, 1973. A white boy of 1840 is impressed into work on a slave ship. Newbery Medal.   11–14

FRITZ, JEAN, *And Then What Happened, Paul Revere?* ill. by Margot Tomes, Coward, 1973.
Can't You Make Them Behave, King George? ill. by Tomie dePaola, Coward, 1977. Gives a good view of the resolutely moral monarch who deplored his unruly colonial subjects.   8–10

Brady, ill. by Lynd Ward, Coward, 1960. The Underground Railroad station in a small Pennsylvania town is endangered because Brady can't keep his mouth shut. A fine story of how a boy becomes a man when he learns that there are more important things in the world than his own well-being.   10–12

The Cabin Faced West, ill. by Feodor Rojankovsky, Coward, 1958. Appealing story of frontier life and of a little girl who learns to like being a pioneer. 9–12

Early Thunder, ill. by Lynd Ward, Coward, 1967. An outstanding novel set in pre-Revolutionary War days with both British and Colonial views presented objectively. Teen-age Daniel considers both sides but when the issues become clear to him he takes a stand.
11–14

GOBLE, PAUL and DOROTHY, *Red Hawk's Account of Custer's Last Battle,* ill. by authors, Pantheon, 1970. Seen from the viewpoint of a young Sioux, a brilliantly illustrated, dramatic story.   10–12

GREENE, BETTE, *Summer of My German Soldier,* Dial, 1973. A Jewish girl in a small southern town, unhappy at home, finds solace in helping a German war prisoner.   11–14

GRIFFIN, JUDITH, *Phoebe and the General,* ill. by Margot Tomes, Coward, 1977. Serving as housekeeper for George Washington in his New York presidential headquarters, thirteen-year-old Phoebe catches a spy and saves Washington's life.   8–10

HALL, DONALD, *Ox-Cart Man,* ill. by Barbara Cooney, Viking, 1979. The bucolic pictures illustrate the year's work cycle for a self-sufficient farm family in the early nineteenth century. Caldecott Medal.   5–8

HODGES, C. WALTER, *Columbus Sailed,* ill. by author, Coward, 1939. Fiction, but based on facts, and tremendously moving. This is a popular book.   12–14

HUNT, IRENE, *Across Five Aprils,* Follett, 1964. Jethro is nine when the Civil War begins and he sees it in terms of parades and dashing soldiers marching in bright uniforms. When the war is over, Jethro knows better.
12–14

JOHNSON, ANNABEL and EDGAR, *Torrie,* Harper, 1960. Fourteen-year-old Torrie Anders travels by covered wagon from St. Louis to California in 1846. In the excitement of the adventure, she gains a new understanding of and admiration for her family.   12–16

Wilderness Bride, Harper, 1962. A realistic picture of the persecution of the Mormons, built around a moving love story.   12–16

KEITH, HAROLD, *Rifles for Watie,* T. Crowell, 1957. Jeff Bussey, Union volunteer at sixteen, gains insight into and sympathy for the problems and ideals of both the North and the South in this powerful Civil War story. Newbery Medal.   12–16

MC MEEKIN, ISABEL, *Journey Cake,* ill. by Nicholas Panesis, Messner, 1942. Six motherless children, in the care of an intrepid old free black woman, journey through the wilderness to join their father in Boone's Kentucky.   10–12

MEANS, FLORENCE CRANNELL, *A Candle in the Mist*, ill. by Marguerite de Angeli, Houghton, 1931. Pioneer life in a Minnesota settlement in the 1870's is difficult, but fifteen-year-old Janey faces it with high courage.   12–14

MEIGS, CORNELIA, *Covered Bridge*, ill. by Marguerite de Angeli, Macmillan, 1936.

Willow Whistle, ill. by E. B. Smith, Macmillan, 1931. These well-written stories of other days and ways are not easy reading, but they are rewarding books for the able child. Action and theme carry the interest.   10–14

MELTZER, MILTON, *Underground Man*, Bradbury, 1973. Based on the antislavery activities of Joshua Bowen, an exciting story set in 1835.   12–up

MOERI, LOUISE, *Save Queen of Sheba*, Dutton, 1981. The boy, King David, protects and encourages his six-year-old sister, Queen of Sheba, when a Sioux attack parts them from their wagon train.   9–11

MONJO, F. N., *The Drinking Gourd*, ill. by Fred Brenner, Harper, 1970. An easy-to-read story of Tommy and his chance involvement in the activities of the Underground Railroad.   6–9

The Secret of the Sachem's Tree, ill. by Margot Tomes, Coward, 1972. Hallowe'en in colonial times.   7–9

MURRAY, MICHELE, *The Crystal Nights*, Seabury, 1973. Elly's father brings Jewish kin from Germany, during World War II, and she is baffled by their ingratitude.   12–15

O'DELL, SCOTT, *Island of the Blue Dolphins*, Houghton, 1960. An Indian girl shows remarkable courage and resourcefulness in living alone on an island off the coast of Southern California for eighteen years. An outstanding historical episode. Newbery Medal.   10–14

The King's Fifth, Houghton, 1966. A remarkable story of the power of gold to corrupt men. It is basically the story of young Esteban, who accompanies the Spanish in their search for the golden cities of Cibola.   12–16

Sing Down the Moon, Houghton, 1970.   11–14

Sarah Bishop, Houghton, 1980. Her father and brother killed fighting on opposite sides in the Revolutionary War, Sarah goes to a cave to live, embittered by the fighting and by having been accused of witchery.   11–14

SNOW, RICHARD, *Freelon Starbird*, ill. by Ben Stahl, Houghton, 1976. Tart and funny, candid about the war, this gives a vivid picture of a soldier's life during the Revolutionary War.   12–14

SPEARE, ELIZABETH, *The Sign of the Beaver*, Houghton, 1983. Alone in the Maine wilderness, Matt is befriended by some Indians who teach him not only survival techniques but also the dignity and beauty of their way of life.   10–14

TALBOT, CHARLENE, *The Sodbuster Venture*, Atheneum, 1982. Two young women, both alone in the world, face the rigors of the Kansas prairie together in 1870.   10–12

UCHIDA, YOSHIKO, *Journey to Topaz*, ill. by Donald Carrick, Scribner's, 1971. A moving story of a Japanese-American family's evacuation and relocation during World War II.   10–12

Journey Home, ill. by Charles Robinson, Atheneum, 1978. A sequel, equally touching, set just after the war, when the family returns to California.   10–12

Samurai of Gold Hill, ill. by Ati Forberg, Scribner's, 1972.   10–13

WIBBERLEY, LEONARD, *Peter Treegate's War*, Farrar, 1960. American Revolutionary days are vividly recreated as the background for the hero, a high-spirited sixteen-year-old boy, who attempts to resolve conflicting loyalties between his real and foster fathers. (Sequel to *John Treegate's Musket*, Farrar, 1959; followed by *Treegate's Raiders*, Farrar, 1962.) 11–14

WILDER, LAURA INGALLS, *By the Shores of Silver Lake*, ill. by Garth Williams, Harper, 1953.

Farmer Boy, ill. by Garth Williams, Harper, 1953.

Little House in the Big Woods, ill. by Garth Williams, Harper, 1953.

Little House on the Prairie, ill. by Garth Williams, Harper, 1953.

The Long Winter, ill. by Garth Williams, Harper, 1953.

On the Banks of Plum Creek, ill. by Garth Williams, Harper, 1953.

These Happy Golden Years, ill. by Garth Williams, Harper, 1953.

Originally published in the 1930's and reissued with completely new illustrations in 1953, these seven books cover the saga of a pioneer family and the childhood of the author to the time of her marriage. This is the family invincible, able to stand up to misfortunes and tragedies because it is strong in love and in loyalty. For most children the books are a totally satisfying reading experience.   9–12

YOLEN, JANE, *The Gift of Sarah Barker*, Viking, 1981. A perceptive and candid story of a Shaker community in the mid-19th century.   11–14

European

AVERY, GILLIAN, *Ellen and the Queen*, ill. by Krystyna Turska, Nelson, 1975. A nine-year-old country girl has an unexpected meeting with Queen Victoria. 8–10

BAER, EDITH, *A Frost in the Night*, Pantheon, 1980. Not like the olden days, Grandfather said, when Jews were persecuted, but Eva finds that Nazi oppression reaches even their small German town.   11–14

BAWDEN, NINA, *The Peppermint Pig*, Lippincott, 1975. A turn-of-the-century family story, written with grace.   9–11

BEATTY, JOHN and PATRICIA, *Master Rosalind*, Morrow, 1974.   12–14

BUFF, MARY, *Apple and the Arrow*, ill. by Conrad Buff, Houghton, 1951. The stirring story of William Tell and his son Walter, with many dramatic illustrations by Swiss-born Conrad Buff.   8–11

BURTON, HESTER, *Beyond the Weir Bridge*, ill. by Victor Ambrus, T. Crowell, 1970. A compelling story of 17th-century Quakers in England.   12–15

Time of Trial, ill. by Victor Ambrus, World, 1964. A novel on the theme of freedom of speech is set in London in 1801. Carnegie Medal.   12–15

CHUTE, MARCHETTE, *The Innocent Wayfaring*, ill. by author, Dutton, 1955. Fourteenth-century England brought vividly and authentically to life.   11–14

COOPER, SUSAN, *Dawn of Fear,* ill. by Margery Gill, Harcourt, 1970. A World War II story, perceptive in depicting the effect of war on children. 9–11

DE ANGELI, MARGUERITE, *Door in the Wall,* ill. by author, Doubleday, 1949. When Robin is stricken with an illness that leaves his legs paralyzed and his back bent, it is brother Luke who helps him to find a "door in the wall" and nurses him back to strength and courage. A valuable addition to children's literature of the medieval period which should bring courage to handicapped children. Newbery Medal. 8–10

FECHER, CONSTANCE, *The Leopard Dagger,* Farrar, 1973. A foundling boy who works at the Globe theater finds his mother. 11–13

FENTON, EDWARD, *The Refugee Summer,* Delacorte, 1982. Five children living in an Athenian suburb in 1942 become involved as partisans in the war against Turkish Anatolia. 11–13

GARDAM, JANE, *A Long Way from Verona,* Macmillan, 1972. A lively, funny story about a would-be writer of 13. 11–13

GARFIELD, LEON, *The Sound of Coaches,* ill. by John Lawrence, Viking, 1974. A picaresque romance of 18th-century England has colorful period details. 12–up

Footsteps, Delacorte, 1980. A deliberately exaggerated adventure story is set in eighteenth-century London. 10–13

The Confidence Man, Viking, 1979. A band of German emigrants follows a scamp of a leader to London and then to America. 11–14

GARRIGUE, SHEILA, *All the Children Were Sent Away,* Bradbury, 1976. A girl of eight travels to Canada and across the country to Vancouver as an evacuee during the bombing of England. 8–10

GRAY, ELIZABETH JANET, *Adam of the Road,* ill. by Robert Lawson, Viking, 1942. When Adam, by mischance, loses both his father and his dog, he seeks them on the highways and byways of thirteenth-century England. Newbery Medal. 10–14

HARNETT, CYNTHIA, *Caxton's Challenge,* ill. by author, World, 1960. The scriveners of England saw the printing press as a manner of depriving them of a living, and they fought by fair means and foul to keep William Caxton from successfully operating his business. Exciting storytelling, excellent history. 11–14

HAUGAARD, ERIK CHRISTIAN, *The Little Fishes,* ill. by Morton Johnson, Houghton, 1967. The hapless condition of homeless children in World War II is shown as three children straggle northward from Naples to Cassino, Italy. 10–14

Chase Me, Catch Nobody! Houghton, 1980. A Danish boy, visiting Germany in 1937, becomes involved in working against the Nazi movement. 11–14

HUNTER, MOLLIE, *The Ghosts of Glencoe,* Funk, 1969. An absorbing story set against the massacre of Glencoe in 1692. 11–13

KELLY, ERIC P., *The Trumpeter of Krakow,* ill. by Janina Domanska, Macmillan, new ed., 1966. Medieval Poland comes vividly alive in this tale of the youthful trumpeter who finishes the Heynal and prevents tragedy. Newbery Medal. 11–14

KONIGSBURG, ELAINE, *The Second Mrs. Giaconda,* Atheneum, 1975. A fictional approach to Leonardo da Vinci's relationship with his pert young apprentice Salai and members of the d'Este family. 11–14

KULLMAN, HARRY, *The Battle Horse,* tr. by George Blecher and Lore Thygesen-Blecher, Bradbury, 1981. A vivid picture of social strata in Stockholm fifty years ago, in a taut, dramatic story. 11–12

LASKY, KATHRYN, *The Night Journey,* ill. by Trina Schart Hyman, Warne, 1981. Although this has a contemporary frame, it is really the story of the escape of a Jewish family from Tsarist Russia. 9–11

LEVITIN, SONIA, *Journey to America,* ill. by Charles Robinson, Atheneum, 1970. The story of a Jewish family's escape from Nazi Germany as told by one of the daughters. 10–13

LINGARD, JOAN, *The File on Fraulein Berg,* Elsevier/Nelson, 1980. Set in Belfast, this story of three schoolgirls who decide their German teacher is a spy ends on a poignant note: they learn she is a Jewish refugee, the only member of her family still alive. 11–14

NAMIOKA, LENSEY, *Village of the Vampire Cat,* Delacorte, 1981. Two young samurai solve a mystery in a story set in medieval Japan. 11–14

O'DELL, SCOTT, *The Captive,* Houghton, 1979. In the first of a trilogy set in the sixteenth century, a young Spanish seminarian comes to the New World and, by a quirk of fate, is taken for the god Kukulcan by the Mayan Indians. Most of the two sequels, *The Feathered Serpent* (1981) and *The Amethyst Ring* (1983) focus on the subjugation of the Maya by Spanish conquistadores. 11–14

PATERSON, KATHERINE, *The Master Puppeteer,* ill. by Haru Wells, Crowell, 1976. Into the world of the puppet theater in feudal Japan, a note of mystery intrudes: Who is the mysterious bandit who takes from the rich to help the poor? 11–14

PELGROM, ELS, *The Winter When Time Was Frozen,* tr. by Maryka and Rafael Rudnik, Morrow, 1980. Two Dutch children help a Jewish family who are hiding in a cave, spy on the Germans, and help welcome any refugee who comes to their farm near Amsterdam. 9–11

PEYTON, K. M., *Flambards* and *The Edge of the Cloud,* ill. by Victor G. Ambrus, World, 1968 and 1969. Two exciting novels which carry the same characters through the early days of flying in England during World War I. 11–14

PICARD, BARBARA L., *Ransom for a Knight,* ill. by C. Walter Hodges, Walck, 1956. After the English loss to the Scots at Bannockburn, young Alys sets forth to try and ransom her father and brother. Excellent picture of the times, combined with a fast-moving plot. 12–15

PYLE, HOWARD, *Men of Iron,* ill. by author, Harper, 1891. The training of knights, the clash of battle, and all the glamor of feudal England under Henry IV. 12–14

Otto of the Silver Hand, ill. by author, Scribner's, 1888. The appealing story of a boy whose father, a German robber baron, places him in a medieval monastery to assure his safety. 10–12

REISS, JOHANNA, *The Upstairs Room,* T. Crowell, 1972. Based on the author's life, this is the taut, touching story of Jewish sisters who were hidden by a Dutch family during the Nazi occupation. 9–12

SUTCLIFF, ROSEMARY, *Eagle of the Ninth,* ill. by C. Walter Hodges, Walck, 1954. 12–15

Lantern Bearers, ill. by Charles Keeping, Walck, 1959. 12–15

Silver Branch, ill. by Charles Keeping, Walck, 1957.
                                                    12–15
Three magnificent novels about the Roman impact upon England, and the influence of England upon the conquerors.
Warrior Scarlet, Walck, 1958. This is a story about a young handicapped boy's long, painful struggle to become a great warrior, told in heroic language that captures the harshness and discipline needed to survive as a Bronze Age inhabitant of England.   12–15
SYMONS, GERALDINE, *Miss Rivers and Miss Bridges,* ill. by Alexy Pendle, Macmillan, 1972. Two lively girls join the suffragette cause in pre-World War I London.
                                                    11–13
VIVIER, COLETTE, *The House of Four Winds,* tr. and ed. by Miriam Morton, Doubleday, 1969. The story of a young boy's service in the resistance movement of Nazi-occupied Paris.   10–12
WALSH, JILL P., *Fireweed,* Farrar, 1970. A tender and sensitively written novel of two teen-agers adrift in London during the Blitz.   12–16
YEP, LAURENCE, *Dragonwings,* Harper, 1975. A Chinese boy comes to San Francisco just before the earthquake.   10–12
ZEI, ALKI, *Petros' War,* trans. by Edward Fenton, Dutton, 1972.   10–12
Wildcat Under Glass, tr. by Edward Fenton, Holt, 1968. The story of a Greek family whose home life is torn by the Fascists' rise to power in 1936. The author shows both the hidden and overt methods used by a totalitarian government to enforce conformity.
                                                    10–13

Ancient Times

BEHN, HARRY, *Faraway Lurs,* World, 1963. A tenderly told story of tragic yet inspiring dimensions, of a girl of the Forest People who made the mistake of falling in love with a boy of the Sun People.   12–14
BENCHLEY, NATHANIEL, *Beyond the Mists,* Harper, 1975. A vivid tale of a young Viking's New World travels.   11–13
Snorri and the Strangers, ill. by Don Bolognese, Harper, 1976. A child in a Norwegian settlement in North America a thousand years ago encounters his first Native Americans.   6–7
CLARKE, PAULINE, *Torolv the Fatherless,* ill. by Cecil Leslie, Faber, 1978. A Viking waif is stranded in Saxon England and becomes a beloved foster child. 11–13
DICKINSON, PETER, *The Dancing Bear,* ill. by David Smee, Atlantic, 1973. A slave boy and his pet bear escape when the Huns sack Byzantium.   10–13
HAUGAARD, ERIK CHRISTIAN, *The Rider and His Horse,* ill. by Leo and Diane Dillon, Houghton, 1968. A story narrated by the main character, David Ben Joseph, tells of his struggle to find meaning for life in a country devastated by the Romans.   12–14
HUNTER, MOLLIE, *The Stronghold,* Harper, 1974. An evocative story of the struggle for power between a local chieftain, a Druid leader, and the Romans, set in ancient Scotland.   11–15
KING, CLIVE, *Ninny's Boat,* Macmillan, 1981. A young slave in fifth-century Britain searches for his roots in a lively story.   10–13
KIRTLAND, G. B., *One Day in Ancient Rome,* ill. by

Jerome Snyder, Harcourt, 1961. Latin words are used in a context that makes them perfectly clear in this witty book about a day in the life of a Roman family.
                                                    10–14
LINEVSKI, A., *An Old Tale Carved Out of Stone,* tr. by Maria Polushkin, Crown, 1973. An archeologist writes with fluency of a Stone Age tribe in Siberia.   12–15
MC GRAW, ELOISE JARVIS, *Mara, Daughter of the Nile,* Coward, 1953. Mara, a slave of the Egyptians, is promised every luxury and eventual freedom if she will spy for the Queen, the Pharaoh, Hatshepsut.   13–17
MORRISON, LUCILE, *The Lost Queen of Egypt,* ill. by Franz Geritz, Lippincott, 1937. This story of ancient Egypt solves the mystery of the disappearance of the young queen when her husband Tutankhamen, king of Egypt, dies.   12–14
SUTCLIFF, ROSEMARY, *The Capricorn Bracelet,* ill. by Richard Cuffari, Walck, 1973.   11–14
Heather, Oak, and Olive, ill. by Victor Ambrus, Dutton, 1972. Three superbly written stories of ancient times, one set in ancient England, one in Britain during the Roman occupation, the third in Greece.
                                                    10–13
Blood Feud, Dutton, 1977. Jestyn, an Englishman, reminisces about being a Viking slave and later serving the Constantine Emperor in the Varangian Guard.
                                                    12–14
TREASE, GEOFFREY, *Message to Hadrian,* Vanguard, 1955. Young Paul must journey from England to Rome with a message for Emperor Hadrian if his friend Severus is to stay alive. Paul's trip is one headlong dash, reading like a modern spy thriller for all its historical accuracy.   11–14
WALSH, GILLIAN PATON, *Children of the Fox,* ill. by Robin Eaton, Farrar, 1978. Three young people tell about their adventures, their stories linked by their association with the Athenian hero Themistocles.
                                                    10–13
WINTERFELD, HENRY, *Mystery of the Roman Ransome,* ill. by Fritz Biermann, tr. by Edith McCormick, Harcourt, 1971. The boys who turned sleuths in *Detectives in Togas* again become involved in an adventure.
                                                    10–13

Biography

ADAMS, SAMUEL (1722–1803)
Alderman, Clifford L., *Samuel Adams, Son of Liberty,* Holt, 1961. A vivid re-creation of prerevolutionary Boston and Adams' role in the Sons of Liberty.
                                                    11–14
ADDAMS, JANE (1860–1935)
Meigs, Cornelia Lynde, *Jane Addams, Pioneer for Social Justice,* ill. with photos, Little, 1970. The major emphasis in this work is upon Miss Addams' forty years at Hull House and her numerous crusades for reform and social justice.   12–16
AGASSIZ, LOUIS (1807–1873)
Tharp, Louise Hall, *Louis Agassiz, Adventurous Scientist,* ill. by Rafaello Busoni, Little, 1961. This Swiss-born immigrant raised natural science to an honored position in the United States.   10–12
ALCOTT, LOUISA MAY (1832–1888)
Fisher, Aileen, and Olive Rabe, *We Alcotts,* ill. by Ellen Raskin, Atheneum, 1968.   11–14

Meigs, Cornelia, *Invincible Louisa*, ill. with photos, Little, 1933. The life of the author of *Little Women*. Newbery Medal.   12–15

Peare, Catherine Owens, *Louisa May Alcott: Her Life*, ill. by Margaret Ayer, Holt, 1954. An easier-to-read version of the life of America's most popular nineteenth-century lady author.   8–10

ALEXANDER THE GREAT (353–323 B.C.)
Krensky, Stephen, *Conqueror and Hero: The Search for Alexander*, ill. by Alexander Farquharson, McDougal, 1981. The focus here is on the thirteen years during which Alexander built his empire, and the text concludes with a brief description of the events that followed Alexander's death.   10–14

ALLEN, ETHAN (1738–1789)
Holbrook, Stewart H., *America's Ethan Allen*, ill. by Lynd Ward, Houghton, 1949. Spirited illustrations add to the dramatic story of the "Green Mountain Boys" and their fighting leader.   10–14

ANDERSEN, HANS CHRISTIAN (1805–1875)
Collin, Hedvig, *Young Hans Christian Andersen*, ill. by author, Viking, 1955. Sensitively told story of the Danish writer from his unhappy childhood years to his first literary recognition.   10–13

ANDERSON, MARIAN (1902–   )
Tobias, Tobi, *Marian Anderson*, ill. by Symeon Shimin, T. Crowell, 1972. Softly drawn pictures add to the warmth of a simply written biography.   7–9

ARCHIMEDES (287?–212? B.C.)
Bendick, Jeanne, *Archimedes and the Door of Science*, ill. by author, Watts, 1962. A usable history of the life and achievements of the Greek physicist and mathematician.   11–14

ARMSTRONG, LOUIS (1900–1971)
Eaton, Jeanette, *Trumpeter's Tale: The Story of Young Louis Armstrong*, ill. by Elton C. Fax, Morrow, 1955. From New Orleans slums to king of the trumpeters is the stirring story of "Louis the Lip."   12–16

ARNOLD, BENEDICT (1741–1801)
Fritz, Jean, *Traitor: The Case of Benedict Arnold*, Putnam, 1981. An objective and astute picture of the egotistical and ambitious soldier.   11–14

AUDUBON, JOHN JAMES (1785–1851)
Brenner, Barbara, *On the Frontier with Mr. Audubon*, Coward, 1977. A thirteen-year-old assistant describes his travels on the Mississippi with the artist, in a fictional novel based on fact.   10–13

BALBOA, VASCO NUÑEZ DE (1475?–1519)
Mirsky, Jeannette, *Balboa, Discoverer of the Pacific*, ed. by Walter Lord, ill. by Hans Guggenheim, Harper, 1964. An interesting, sympathetically written account of Balboa's work from 1510–1519.   10–13

BANNEKER, BENJAMIN (1731–1806)
Lewis, Claude, *Benjamin Banneker: The Man Who Saved Washington*, ill. by Ernest T. Crichlow, McGraw, 1970. Story of the Afro-American scientist who helped survey and plan Washington, D.C.
                                                    11–14

BEETHOVEN, LUDWIG VAN (1770–1827)
Goss, Madeline B., *Beethoven: Master Musician*, ill. by Carl Schultheiss, Holt, 1946. A sensitive and thwarted genius portrayed with rare sympathy.   12–14

BELL, ALEXANDER GRAHAM (1847–1922)
Shippen, Katherine, *Mr. Bell Invents the Telephone*, ill. by Richard Floethe, Random, 1952. Alexander

Graham Bell's achievement is doubly satisfying because of the disheartening failure that preceded his successful invention.   10–13

BERNSTEIN, LEONARD (1918–   )
Cone, Molly, *Leonard Bernstein*, ill. by Robert Galster, T. Crowell, 1970. An interesting short biography of one of America's most popular composers and conductors.   7–11

BETHUNE, MARY MC LEOD (1875–1955)
Peare, Catherine Owens, *Mary McLeod Bethune*, Vanguard, 1951.   12–14
Sterne, Emma Gelders, *Mary McLeod Bethune*, ill. by Raymond Lufkin, Knopf, 1957.   12–16
Two fine biographies of a great black educator who dedicated her life to her people.

BLACKWELL, ELIZABETH (1821–1910)
Clapp, Patricia, *Dr. Elizabeth: The Story of the First Woman Doctor*, Lothrop, 1974. A first-person fictionalization of the life of the woman who broke the barriers to a profession that was considered appropriate for men only.   11–14

BOONE, DANIEL (1734–1820)
Meadowcroft, Enid, *Holding the Fort with Daniel Boone*, ill. by Lloyd Coe, T. Crowell, 1958.
An easy-to-read book which emphasizes the pioneers' struggles rather than details about Boone.   8–11

BRAILLE, LOUIS (1809–1852)
Neimark, Anne E., *Touch of Light, The Story of Louis Braille*, ill. by Robert Parker, Harcourt, 1970. A somewhat fictionalized account of the life of an extraordinary man who succeeded in doing something worthwhile for other blind people.   8–12

BRONTË, CHARLOTTE (1816–1855)
Kyle, Elisabeth, *Girl with a Pen, Charlotte Brontë*, Holt, 1964. Fine biography of the author of *Jane Eyre*, from the age of seventeen through thirty-one.
                                                    12–15

BROWNING, ELIZABETH BARRETT (1806–1861)
Waite, Helen, *How Do I Love Thee?* Macrae, 1953. An absorbing story of the Victorian poetess, climaxed by her romance with Robert Browning.   12–16

BUDDHA (Gautama Siddhartha) (563?–483? B.C.)
Kelen, Betty, *Gautama Buddha in Life and Legend*, Lothrop, 1967. A carefully written story which discriminates between fact and legend surrounding this religious leader.   12–up

BUNCHE, RALPH J. (1904–1971)
Kugelmass, J. Alvin, *Ralph J. Bunche: Fighter for Peace*, rev. ed., ill. by Elton Fox, Messner, 1962. Reared in Detroit's slums, Bunche was one of America's most honored citizens and a winner of the Nobel Peace Prize.   12–16

CABOT, JOHN (1450–1498)
Hill, Kay, *And Tomorrow the Stars*, ill. by Laszlo Kubinyi, Dodd, 1968. Carefully researched, dramatic, and written with vitality, this biography of the Venetian explorer received the Canadian children's book award.   12–up

CARNEGIE, ANDREW (1835–1919)
Judson, Clara Ingram, *Andrew Carnegie*, ill. by Steele Savage, Follett, 1964. The excellent story of America's great philanthropist who used his fortune that all people might live better lives.   10–13

CARSON, CHRISTOPHER (1809–1868)
Bell, Margaret, *Kit Carson, Mountain Man*, ill. by

Harry Daugherty, Morrow, 1952. A short, dramatic biography with large print and lively illustrations.
8–11

CARSON, RACHEL (1907–1964)
Sterling, Philip, *Sea and Earth: The Life of Rachel Carson,* ill. with photos, T. Crowell, 1970. A well-documented account of the life of the conscientious civil servant who was one of the first to raise her voice against the despoiling of our planet.   13–up

CARTIER, JACQUES (1491–1557)
Averill, Esther, *Cartier Sails the St. Lawrence,* ill. by Feodor Rojankovsky, Harper, 1956. A fascinating and factual account of Cartier's three voyages to the New World.   10–14

CARVER, GEORGE WASHINGTON (1864?–1943)
Means, Florence Crannell, *Carver's George,* ill. by Harve Stein, Houghton, 1952. A moving account of the great black scientist from his tragic infancy to his triumphant old age, honored and beloved by the world.   10–14

CASSATT, MARY (1845–1926)
Wilson, Ellen, *American Painter in Paris; A Life of Mary Cassatt,* Farrar, 1971. A discerning portrait of the artist and the trends that influenced her work.
11–14

CATHER, WILLA (1876–1947)
Franchere, Ruth, *Willa: The Story of Willa Cather's Growing Up,* decorations by Leonard Weisgard, T. Crowell, 1958. A flowing narrative relates Willa Cather's early experiences in Nebraska and the influences which produced her adult novels.

CHAVEZ, CESAR (1928–   )
Franchere, Ruth, *Cesar Chavez,* ill. by Earl Thollander, T. Crowell, 1970. A story for younger readers of biography with focus upon the early struggles and self-sacrifice of this resolute leader.   7–11

CHIEF JOSEPH (1840?–1904)
Davis, Russell, and Brent Ashabranner, *Chief Joseph —War Chief of the Nez Percé,* McGraw, 1962. The tragic story of a peace-loving chief forced into war as his people opposed the westward movement. 12–16

CHILD, LYDIA MARIA (1802–1880)
Meltzer, Milton, *Tongue of Flame,* T. Crowell, 1965. The life story of the first American to write a book attacking slavery.   12–17

CHURCHILL, WINSTON (1875–1965)
Wibberley, Leonard, *The Complete Life of Winston Churchill,* rev. ed., Farrar, 1968. An account of the life of one of England's greatest notables, told with humor and dignity.   12–16

CLARK, WILLIAM (1770–1838) (See Lewis, Meriwether.)
CLEMENS, SAMUEL LANGHORNE (See Twain, Mark.)
COCHISE (?–1874)
Wyatt, Edgar, *Cochise: Apache Warrior and Statesman,* ill. by Allan Houser, McGraw, 1953. Few readers will be unmoved by the betrayal of Cochise by the whites. Most readers will find themselves rooting for Cochise to win despite their knowledge of his defeat.
10–14

CODY, WILLIAM (1846–1917)
D'Aulaire, Ingri and Edgar Parin, *Buffalo Bill,* ill. by authors, Doubleday, 1952. Colorful pictures highlight the enthralling story of a man who was a legend in his own time.   5–9

COLUMBUS, CHRISTOPHER (1446?–1506)

Sperry, Armstrong, *The Voyages of Christopher Columbus,* ill. by author, Random, 1950. A historically accurate account of the four important voyages undertaken by Columbus.   9–11
Fritz, Jean, *Where Do You Think You're Going, Christopher Columbus?* ill. by Margot Tomes, Putnam, 1980. A candid account of the man who ended his life, wealthy and avaricious, unaware that the American continents existed.   8–10

COOK, JAMES (1728–1779)
Latham, Jean Lee, *Far Voyager: The Story of James Cook,* maps by Karl Stuecklen, Harper, 1970. An engrossing narrative of the rise of a poor boy to officership in the British Navy and great achievement as explorer and scientist.   12–up

COPLEY, JOHN SINGLETON (1738–1815)
Ripley, Elizabeth, *Copley: A Biography,* Lippincott, 1967. Presents the life of the artist in alternating pages of text and pictures.   12–14

COURT, MARGARET (1942–   )
Sullivan, George, *Queens of the Court,* ill. with photos, Dodd, 1974. Brisk, informative sketches of Margaret Court, Billie Jean King, and other tennis stars.
11–15

CRAZY HORSE (1844?–1877)
Garst, Doris Shannon, *Crazy Horse, Great Warrior of the Sioux,* ill. by William Meyers, Houghton, 1950.
12–14

CROCKETT, DAVY (1786–1836)
LeSueur, Meridel, *Chanticleer of Wilderness Road: A Story of Davy Crockett,* ill. by Aldren A. Watson, Knopf, 1951. Legends, tall tales, and facts are humorously woven together to produce a delightful book.
10–14

DARROW, CLARENCE (1857–1938)
Gurko, Miriam, *Clarence Darrow,* T. Crowell, 1965. America's most famous trial lawyer's life is also the story of America's coming of age in many areas of social concern.   13–16

DICKENS, CHARLES (1812–1870)
Kyle, Elizabeth, *Great Ambitions: A Story of the Early Years of Charles Dickens,* Holt, 1968. This fictional biography covers Dickens' life from age twelve to twenty-seven and offers a valuable introduction to the author's books.   12–14

DICKINSON, EMILY (1830–1886)
Fisher, Aileen, and Olive Rabe, *We Dickinsons,* decorations by Ellen Raskin, Atheneum, 1965. An emotionally appealing book. The technique of having Emily's brother Austin tell the story is an interesting one for young people.   12–16

DOUGLASS, FREDERICK (1817–1895)
Bontemps, Arna, *Frederick Douglass,* ill. by Harper Johnson, Knopf, 1959. A vivid picture of the life of one of the most influential black leaders of the abolition movement.   10–14
Davis, Ossie, *Escape to Freedom: A Play About Young Frederick Douglass,* Viking, 1978. A dramatization of Douglass' life by a noted black actor and playwright.
11–14

DRAKE, FRANCIS (1540?–1596)
Syme, Ronald, *Francis Drake, Sailor of the Unknown Seas,* ill. by William Stobbs, Morrow, 1961. A highly abbreviated account of Drake's career from boyhood through the defeat of the Spanish Armada.   9–11

DREW, CHARLES (1904–1950)
Bertol, Roland, *Charles Drew*, ill. by Jo Polseno, T. Crowell, 1970. A story for younger readers about the pioneer blood researcher. 7–11

DU BOIS, WILLIAM EDWARD BURGHARDT (1868–1963)
Hamilton, Virginia, *W.E.B. Du Bois*, T. Crowell, 1972. A carefully researched and well-written biography of the eminent teacher, writer, and political leader. 12–15

DUNBAR, PAUL (1872–1906)
Gould, Jean, *That Dunbar Boy*, Dodd, 1958. A sympathetic biography of a great poet who showed the world that black people could write poetry. 12–16

EDISON, THOMAS ALVA (1847–1931)
North, Sterling, *Young Thomas Edison*, ill. with photos, decorations, diagrams, and maps by William Barss, Houghton, 1958. Warm biography of the scientific wizard. 10–14

EINSTEIN, ALBERT (1879–1955)
Levinger, Elma Ehrlich, *Albert Einstein*, Messner, 1949. A worthwhile account of the achievements and life of a great scientist despite the author's use of invented dialogue. 12–15

ELEANOR OF AQUITAINE, QUEEN OF ENGLAND (1122?–1204)
Konigsburg, Elaine, *A Proud Taste for Scarlet and Miniver*, ill. by author, Atheneum, 1973. This is highly and superbly fictionalized, it has elements of fantasy (most of the discussion takes place in Heaven), yet it is above all a delightful biography of the indomitable wife of Henry II. 11–up

FARFAN, TATO (1970–)
Krementz, Jill, *A Very Young Circus Flyer*, with photographs by the author, Knopf, 1979. Nine-year-old Tato, youngest in a family of aerial performers, describes his training and the circus milieu. 9–11

FORTEN, CHARLOTTE (1837–1914)
Longsworth, Polly, *I, Charlotte Forten, Black and Free*, T. Crowell, 1970. The daughter of a prominent black Philadelphia family describes her life during the Civil War period and Reconstruction. 11–14

FORTEN, JAMES (1766–1842)
Douty, Esther M., *Forten the Sailmaker, Pioneer Champion of Negro Rights*, ill. with photos, Rand, 1968. The life story of a man who battled for civil rights and freedom for his people. 11–14

FORTUNE, AMOS (1709?–1801)
Yates, Elizabeth, *Amos Fortune: Free Man*, ill. by Nora S. Unwin, Dutton, 1950. Moving story of a colonial Negro who spent his life buying freedom for other slaves, and eventually bought his own and died a free man. Newbery Medal. 11–14

FOSTER, STEPHEN (1826–1864)
Purdy, Claire Lee, *He Heard America Sing: The Story of Stephen Foster*, ill. by Dorothea Cooke, Messner, 1940. A sympathetic picture of America's first popular composer. 11–14

FRANCIS OF ASSISI (1182–1226)
Bulla, Clyde, *Song of St. Francis*, ill. by Valenti Angelo, T. Crowell, 1952. The appealing story of St. Francis presented in simple fashion for the youngest readers. 7–10

FRANKLIN, BENJAMIN (1706–1790)
D'Aulaire, Ingri and Edgar, *Benjamin Franklin*, ill. by authors, Doubleday, 1950. 8–10
Daugherty, James, *Poor Richard*, ill. by author, Vi-

king, 1941. A beautifully written and illustrated book which emphasizes Franklin's patriotic achievements. 12–16

FREEMAN, ELIZABETH (?–1829)
Felton, Harold W., *Mumbet: The Story of Elizabeth Freeman*, ill. by Donn Albright, Dodd, 1970. The story of the first American black woman to win her human rights by court action. 9–12

FRITZ, JEAN (1915–)
Fritz, Jean, *Homesick: My Own Story*, ill. by Margot Tomes, Putnam, 1982. The noted author describes the last two years of her childhood in China and her arrival in the homeland she'd never seen. 11–14

FULLER, BUCKMINSTER (1895–1983)
Rosen, Sidney, *Wizard of the Dome: R. Buckminster Fuller, Designer for the Future*, Little, 1969. Candid and vigorous, an interesting book about the inventor-architect. 12–up

GALILEI, GALILEO (1564–1642)
Cobb, Vicki, *Truth on Trial: The Story of Galileo Galilei*, ill. by George Ulrich, Coward, 1979. Although Cobb gives all relevant facts about Galileo's personal life, the focus here is on his scientific theories and discoveries. 9–10

GANDHI, MOHANDAS (1869–1948)
Coolidge, Olivia, *Gandhi*, Houghton, 1971. Forthright and objective. 12–up
Eaton, Jeanette, *Gandhi: Fighter Without a Sword*, ill. by Ralph Ray, Morrow, 1950. A fine biography of the Hindu nationalist who worked for the political independence of his people. 12–15

GARIBALDI, GIUSEPPE (1807–1882)
Syme, Ronald, *Garibaldi*, ill. by William Stobbs, Morrow, 1967. A competent, easy-to-read story of the brilliant man who succeeded in freeing and uniting Italy. 9–12

GARRISON, WILLIAM LLOYD (1805–1879)
Faber, Doris, *I Will Be Heard*, ill. with portraits, Lothrop, 1970. A well-written account of Garrison's life with much attention to his work in the abolitionist movement. 10–14

GERONIMO (1829–1909)
Wyatt, Edgar, *Geronimo: The Last Apache War Chief*, ill. by Allan Houser, McGraw, 1952. Unlike most Indian chiefs, Geronimo lived a long and peaceful life after being defeated by the whites. 10–14

GERSHWIN, GEORGE (1898–1937)
Ewen, David, *Story of George Gershwin*, ill. by Graham Bernbach, Holt, 1943. Memories of an American composer of popular music by a personal friend. 12–15

GOODALL, JANE (1934–)
Fox, Mary Virginia, *Jane Goodall: Living Chimp Style*, ill. by Nona Hengen, Dillon, 1981. A biography that gives minimal coverage to the subject's personal life, this emphasizes her work in Africa observing the behavior of chimpanzees. 8–9

GORGAS, WILLIAM CRAWFORD (1854–1920)
Judson, Clara Ingram, *Soldier Doctor: The Story of William Gorgas*, ill. by Robert Doremus, Scribner's, 1942. A lively account of the man whose work against yellow fever made possible the building of the Panama Canal. 9–12

GRANT, ULYSSES S. (1822–1885)
Kantor, MacKinlay, *Lee and Grant at Appomattox*, ill. by Donald McKay, Random, 1950. Excellent portraits

of two very different men, focusing upon the last weeks of the war and the surrender.   10–14

GRIEG, EDVARD HAGERUP (1843–1907)
Kyle, Elizabeth, *Song of the Waterfall*, Holt, 1969. The story of the composer and his wife and their musical world.   12–15

HAMILTON, ALEXANDER (1755–1804)
Lomask, Milton, *Odd Destiny: A Life of Alexander Hamilton*, Farrar, 1969. A vivid portrayal of Hamilton and his relationships with Washington, Jefferson, and Burr.   12–14

HAMMARSKJÖLD, DAG HJALMER (1905–1961)
Simon, Charlie May, *Dag Hammarskjöld*, Dutton, 1969. A book which offers a personalized view of the statesman through use of excerpts from his diary and speeches.   12–14

HANDY, WILLIAM CHRISTOPHER (1873–1958)
Montgomery, Elizabeth Rider, *William C. Handy; Father of the Blues*, ill. by David Hodges, Garrard, 1968. A simply written biography of the Negro composer and music publisher.   8–11

HAUTZIG, ESTHER (1930–   )
Hautzig, Esther, *The Endless Steppe: Growing Up in Siberia*, T. Crowell, 1968. A Polish-Jewish family is sent to Siberia in 1941, when Russian troops took over Vilna. Stark, gripping, and touching.   11–14

HENRY, PATRICK (1736–1799)
Campion, Nardi Reeder, *Patrick Henry: Firebrand of the Revolution*, ill. by Victor Mays, Little, 1961. A fascinating and well-documented biography that never glosses over the weaknesses of its hero.   12–up
Daugherty, Sonia, *Ten Brave Men*, Lippincott, 1951.   10–12

HOLMES, OLIVER WENDELL (1841–1935)
Judson, Clara Ingram, *Mr. Justice Holmes*, ill. by Robert Todd, Follett, 1956. A wonderfully exciting book about a great Supreme Court judge whose legal opinions were always tempered with a sense of humanity.   12–16
Meyer, Edith Patterson, *That Remarkable Man, Justice Oliver Wendell Holmes*, ill. with portraits, Little, 1967. A well-written, objective account of the life of America's great champion of freedom of expression.   13–up

HUGHES, LANGSTON (1902–1967)
Walker, Alice, *Langston Hughes, American Poet*, ill. by Don Miller, T. Crowell, 1974. A candid and sympathetic biography for younger readers.   7–9

HYMAN, TRINA SCHART (1939–   )
Hyman, Trina, *Self-Portrait: Trina Schart Hyman*, ill. by author, Addison, 1981. A brief, candid, informal, and humorous account of the artist's life and work.   10–14

ISHI (1861?–1916)
Kroeber, Theodora, *Ishi; Last of His Tribe*, ill. by Ruth Robbins, Parnassus, 1964. The touching story of the last surviving member of the Yahi tribe.   12–up

JACKSON, ANDREW (1767–1845)
Foster, Genevieve, *Andrew Jackson: An Initial Biography*, ill. by author, Scribner's, 1951. This excellent biography provides insight into the character of Jackson.   8–10

JACKSON, MAHALIA (1911–1972)
Jackson, Jesse, *Make a Joyful Noise Unto the Lord!* ill. with photos, T. Crowell, 1974. A biography that really captures the vitality and dedication of the beloved gospel singer.   11–14

JEFFERSON, THOMAS (1743–1826)
Judson, Clara Ingram, *Thomas Jefferson, Champion of the People*, ill. by Robert Frankenberg, Follett, 1952.   10–14
Lisitzky, Gene, *Thomas Jefferson*, ill. by Harrie Wood, Viking, 1933.   12–16
Both titles capture the essence of this brilliant and great American.

JOAN OF ARC (1412–1431)
Fisher, Aileen, *Jeanne d'Arc*, ill. by Ati Forberg, T. Crowell, 1970. A short, beautifully illustrated and accurate account of the life of the young saint.   8–10
Paine, Albert B., *Girl in the White Armor*, Macmillan, 1964. A historically accurate yet passionate portrait of the Maid of France.   11–14

JONES, JOHN PAUL (1747–1792)
Syme, Ronald, *Captain John Paul Jones, America's Fighting Seaman*, ill. by William Stobbs, Morrow, 1968. A balanced history of the naval hero's life.   9–11

JUÁREZ, BENITO (1806–1872)
Syme, Ronald, *Juárez; The Founder of Modern Mexico*, ill. by Richard Cuffari, Morrow, 1972. Not only a good biography, this is also an excellent history of Mexico in the nineteenth century.   10–13

KELLER, HELEN ADAMS (1880–1968)
Bigland, Eileen, *Helen Keller*, ill. by Lili Cassel-Wronker, Phillips, 1967. A fine treatment of the subject's life from early childhood to old age.   12–14
Peare, Catherine Owens, *The Helen Keller Story*, T. Crowell, 1959.   11–14

KING, MARTIN LUTHER, JR. (1929–1968)
Preston, Edward, *Martin Luther King: Fighter for Freedom*, Doubleday, 1968. A simply written narrative of King's life with emphasis upon the period from 1954 until his death in 1968.   9–12

LA FLESCHE, SUSETTE (1854–1903)
Crary, Margaret, *Susette La Flesche; Voice of the Omaha Indians*, Hawthorn, 1973. As an Indian woman of her time, Susette La Flesche had no legal rights, but she fought all her life for reform and justice.   10–14

LEE, ROBERT E. (1807–1870)
Commager, Henry Steele, *America's Robert E. Lee*, ill. by Lynd Ward, Houghton, 1951. Lee is a hero all America should be proud of, and this biography shows why.   11–15

LEEUWENHOEK, ANTON VAN (1632–1723)
Payne, Alma S., *Discoverer of the Unseen World: A Biography of Antoni van Leeuwenhoek*, ill. by Donn Albright, World, 1966. Solidly researched, readable biography of the self-educated Dutchman whose work with the microscope opened up new vistas for other scientists.   11–14

LEWIS, MERIWETHER (1774–1809)
Daugherty, James, *Of Courage Undaunted*, ill. by author, Viking, 1951. One of the most exciting books in any library, this account, with its subtitle, "Across the Continent with Lewis and Clark," makes clear the courage and resourcefulness demanded of the men who explore the unknown.   10–14

LINCOLN, ABRAHAM (1809–1865)
D' Aulaire, Ingri and Edgar Parin, *Abraham Lincoln*, ill. by authors, rev. ed., Doubleday, 1957.   5–9

Foster, Genevieve, *Abraham Lincoln,* ill. by author, Scribner's, 1950.   8–11

Meadowcroft, Enid, *Abraham Lincoln,* ill. by Kurt Wiese, T. Crowell, 1959.   9–12

Sandburg, Carl, *Abraham Lincoln Grows Up,* ill. by James Daugherty, Harcourt, 1928.   11–14

Each of these books has its own approach to Lincoln, and the range of reading difficulty offers something for almost everyone.

LIND, JENNY (1820–1887)

Benét, Laura, *Enchanting Jenny Lind,* ill. by George G. Whitney, Dodd, 1939. The romantic and appealing story of the "Swedish Nightingale," who won the hearts of the world in the nineteenth century.

12–14

LITTLE, MALCOLM (1925–1965)

Adoff, Arnold, *Malcolm X,* ill. by John Wilson, T. Crowell, 1970. An easy-to-read account which sketches the events which influenced Malcolm X from childhood on and plainly sets forth his importance as a black leader.   8–10

Curtis, Richard, *The Life of Malcolm X,* Macrae, 1971.

11–14

LONGFELLOW, HENRY WADSWORTH (1807–1882)

Peare, Catherine Owens, *Henry Wadsworth Longfellow: His Life,* ill. by Margaret Ayer, Holt, 1953. The life of the poet who immortalized both the village blacksmith and Paul Revere.   9–12

LUTHER, MARTIN (1483–1546)

McNeer, May, and Lynd Ward, *Martin Luther,* ill. by Lynd Ward, Abingdon, 1953. Luther's fighting spirit makes his complex life both difficult and thrilling.

12–14

MARSHALL, THURGOOD (1908–   )

Fenderson, Lewis H., *Thurgood Marshall: Fighter for Justice,* ill. by Dave Hodges, McGraw, 1969. A lively narrative of Marshall's private and public life from childhood until his appointment to the Supreme Court.   8–10

MARTÍN DE PORRES, SAINT (1579–1639)

Bishop, Claire Huchet, *Martín de Porres, Hero,* ill. by Jean Charlot, Houghton, 1954. Moving story of the Peruvian mulatto boy who, despite poverty and the racial taunts of other children, grew up to be filled with love for his fellow men.   9–12

MENDEL, GREGOR (1822–1884)

Sootin, Harry, *Gregor Mendel: Father of the Science of Genetics,* Vanguard, 1958. A straightforward biography of the scientist who explained the laws of heredity.   12–16

MICHELANGELO (1475–1564)

Ripley, Elizabeth, *Michelangelo, A Biography,* ill. by Michelangelo, Walck, 1953. One of more than a dozen biographies of famous artists by this author. All are illustrated by the artist's work and represent landmarks in the artist's life or his artistic development.

12–14

MOSES (c. 1200 B.C.?)

Shippen, Katherine B., *Moses,* Harper, 1949. The story of a great leader's sense of dedication to his people and to God.   12–16

MOZART, WOLFGANG AMADEUS (1756–1791)

Komroff, Manuel, *Mozart,* ill. by Warren Chappell and by photos, Knopf, 1956.   10–14

Mirsky, Reba Paeff, *Mozart,* ill. by W. T. Mars, Follett, 1960.   9–12

Komroff's book is an outstanding example of the best in musical biography. Mirsky, while basically accurate, is more fictionalized and is for a younger audience.

MUIR, JOHN (1838–1914)

Swift, Hildegarde Hoyt, *From the Eagle's Wing: A Biography of John Muir,* ill. by Lynd Ward, Morrow, 1962. Very readable biography of the Scotch immigrant whose writings on nature helped the United States recognize the need to conserve its natural resources.   12–15

NEHRU, JAWAHARLAL (1889–1964)

Lengyel, Emil, *Jawaharlal Nehru; The Brahman from Kashmir,* Watts, 1968. A careful examination of Nehru's life from childhood to old age. Good explanations of Indian culture and customs.   12–15

NEWTON, ISAAC (1642–1727)

Tannenbaum, Beulah, and Myra Stillman, *Isaac Newton: Pioneer of Space Mathematics,* McGraw, 1959. Newton's personal life and his contributions to scientific knowledge are well combined in this science biography.

NIGHTINGALE, FLORENCE (1820–1910)

Nolan, Jeannette Covert, *Florence Nightingale,* ill. by George Avison, Messner, 1947. This warm, readable biography of the "Lady with the Lamp" stresses her work rather than her personal life.   11–14

PAINE, THOMAS (1737–1809)

Coolidge, Olivia E., *Tom Paine, Revolutionary,* Scribner's, 1969. The life and significant writings of the famous revolutionary are objectively presented in this work.   13–up

Gurko, Leo, *Tom Paine: Freedom's Apostle,* ill. by Fritz Kredel, T. Crowell, 1957. Exciting portrait of the man whose writings helped prove the power of the pen.   12–16

PANKHURST, EMMELINE (1858–1928)

Noble, Iris, *Emmeline and Her Daughters; The Pankhurst Suffragettes,* Messner, 1971.   11–15

PARACELSUS, PHILIPPUS (1493?–1541)

Rosen, Sidney, *Doctor Paracelsus,* ill. by Rafaello Busoni, Little, 1959. Excellent biography of the sixteenth-century Swiss-German physician and alchemist who challenged the medical superstitions of his time.   12–16

PARKS, ROSA (1913–   )

Greenfield, Eloise, *Rosa Parks,* ill. by Eric Marlow, T. Crowell, 1973. A competent book about the quiet woman whose sense of justice precipitated the Montgomery bus strike.   7–9

PASTEUR, LOUIS (1822–1895)

Wood, Laura Newbold, *Louis Pasteur,* ill. with photos, Messner, 1948. The story of one of the world's great scientists whose experiments and research made tremendous contributions to modern medicine.   12–14

PENN, WILLIAM (1644–1718)

Gray, Elizabeth Janet, *Penn,* ill. by George Whitney, Viking, 1938.   11–14

PICASSO, PABLO (1881–1973)

Greenfeld, Howard, *Pablo Picasso,* Follett, 1971. Illustrated with examples of the artist's work, this is as perceptive in revealing the man as it is knowledgeable about his role in art history.   7–10

POCAHONTAS (1595?–1617)
Aulaire, Ingri and Edgar Parin d', *Pocahontas,* ill. by authors, Doubleday, 1949. Large, colorful pictures make this story of the Indian maid who saved John Smith's life useful for reading aloud to young children.
5–9

POTTER, BEATRIX (1866–1943)
Aldis, Dorothy, *Nothing Is Impossible, the Story of Beatrix Potter,* ill. by Richard Cuffari, Atheneum, 1969. Depicts the events in the author's life and the atmosphere of her family in an excellent way.
8–12

REVERE, PAUL (1735–1818)
Forbes, Esther, *America's Paul Revere,* ill. by Lynd Ward, Houghton, 1946.   8–11

ROBESON, PAUL (1898–1976)
Hamilton, Virginia, *Paul Robeson; The Life and Times of a Free Black Man,* ill. with photos, Harper, 1974. A perceptive, detailed biography that also gives a good picture of the period and of the struggles of the black performer.   12–up

ROBINSON, JACK (1919–1972)
Rudeen, Kenneth, *Jackie Robinson,* ill. by Richard Cuffari, T. Crowell, 1971. A balanced treatment of Robinson's baseball career is brisk and candid.
7–9

ROOSEVELT, ANNA ELEANOR (1884–1962)
Goodsell, Jane, *Eleanor Roosevelt,* ill. by Wendel Minor, T. Crowell, 1970. An easy-to-read story of the courageous humanitarian woman who became a legend in her own lifetime.   7–11

ROOSEVELT, FRANKLIN D. (1882–1945)
Johnson, Gerald White, *Franklin Delano Roosevelt: Portrait of a Great Man,* ill. by Leonard E. Fisher, Morrow, 1967. An objective view of Roosevelt and his role in domestic and world affairs.   11–14
Peare, Catherine Owens, *The FDR Story,* T. Crowell, 1962. A remarkably perceptive biography of Roosevelt as an individual and as a political figure. 12–15

ROOSEVELT, THEODORE (1858–1919)
Foster, Genevieve, *Theodore Roosevelt,* ill. by author, Scribner's, 1954. Simply written story of the weakling who grew up to lead his country in its early days as a world force.   8–12
Monjo, Ferdinand, *The One Bad Thing About Father,* ill. by Rocco Negri, Harper, 1970.   7–8

ROSS, DIANA (1944–   )
Haskins, James, *I'm Gonna Make You Love Me: The Story of Diana Ross,* Dial, 1980. Candid about the ups and downs of the singer's career, this is written with restrained admiration.   12–15

SALOMON, HAYM (1740?–1785)
Fast, Howard, *Haym Salomon: Son of Liberty,* ill. by Eric M. Simon, Messner, 1941. A moving story of the Polish immigrant who helped finance the American Revolution, using his own fortune and cajoling others into giving more money than they wanted to.
12–16

SAMPSON, DEBORAH (1760–1827)
McGovern, Ann, *The Secret Soldier: The Story of Deborah Sampson,* ill. by Ann Grifalconi, Four Winds, 1975. The exiting story of the woman who posed as a man so that she could serve in the Continental Army during the Revolutionary War.   8–10

SCHWEITZER, ALBERT (1875–1965)
Manton, Jo, *The Story of Albert Schweitzer,* ill. by Astrid Walfard, Abelard, 1955. Fine biography of the man who gave up a comfortable life to work as a missionary in Africa.   12–16

SCOTT, SIR WALTER (1771–1832)
Gray, Elizabeth Janet, *Young Walter Scott,* Viking, 1935. Even readers who are bored by Scott's novels will enjoy this portrait of the author.   12–15

SHACKLETON, ERNEST HENRY (1874–1922)
Bixby, William, *The Impossible Journey of Sir Ernest Shackleton,* Little, 1960. A dramatic and informative account of Shackleton's trans-Antarctic expedition, 1914–1917.   11–13

SHELLEY, MARY WOLLSTONECRAFT (1797–1851)
Harris, Janet, *The Woman Who Created Frankenstein: A Portrait of Mary Shelley,* Harper, 1979. Candid about Mary Shelley's personal life, this focuses on her book as a pioneer volume of science fiction. 12–15

SINGER, ISAAC BASHEVIS (1904–   )
Singer, Isaac Bashevis, *A Day of Pleasure: Stories of a Boy Growing Up in Warsaw,* ill. with photos, Farrar, 1969. Intimate glimpses of the author's boyhood in the Warsaw ghetto before the first World War. National Book Award.   11–15

SMITH, ELISABETH (1898–1937)
Moore, Carman, *Somebody's Angel Child; The Story of Bessie Smith,* T. Crowell, 1970. The sad and dramatic life of the great blues singer is told with skill and candor.   11–14

SQUANTO (?–1622)
Bulla, Clyde R., *Squanto, Friend of the Pilgrims,* ill. by Peter Burchard, T. Crowell, 1954. Easy-to-read story of the Wampanoag Indian who gave aid to the Plymouth colonists.   8–10

STEVENSON, ROBERT LOUIS (1850–1894)
Proudfit, Isabel, *Treasure Hunter: The Story of Robert Louis Stevenson,* ill. by Hardie Gramatky, Messner, 1939. A full-length biography of a favorite children's author.   12–16

STRATTON, CHARLES (1838–1883)
Cross, Helen, *The Real Tom Thumb,* ill. by Stephen Gammell, Four Winds, 1980. A carefully researched account of the midget known as "Tom Thumb" who gained international fame through the publicity efforts of Phineas Barnum.   9–11

SUN YAT-SEN (1866–1925)
Spencer, Cornelia, *Sun Yat-sen: Founder of the Chinese Republic,* ill. with photos, Day, 1967. A well-documented telling of the sources of the Chinese revolutionary movement and Sun's role within it.   12–14

TALLCHIEF, MARIA (1925–   )
Tobias, Tobi, *Maria Tallchief,* ill. by Michael Hampshire, T. Crowell, 1970. Of Osage and Scots-Irish heritage, Maria Tallchief became one of our country's outstanding prima ballerinas.   7–9

TERESHKOVA, VALENTINA (1937–   )
Sharpe, Mitchell, *"It Is I, Sea Gull," Valentina Tereshkova, First Woman in Space,* ill. with photos, T. Crowell, 1975. Despite weaknesses of style, this is a fascinating account of the first woman cosmonaut.
11–15

THOREAU, HENRY DAVID (1817–1862)
North, Sterling, *Thoreau of Walden Pond,* ill. by

Harve Stein, Houghton, 1959. A biography which begins with the boyhood of the great independent thinker and ends with his death.   12–15

TOUSSAINT L'OUVERTURE (1743–1803)
Syme, Ronald, *Toussaint the Black Liberator*, ill. by William Stobbs, Morrow, 1971. An interesting biography that is candid and authoritative.   10–13

TRUMAN, HARRY S. (1884–1972)
Hayman, LeRoy, *Harry S. Truman; A Biography*, ill. with photos, T. Crowell, 1969. A history of Truman's life, personal and public, from childhood until the end of his presidency.   10–14

TRUTH, SOJOURNER (1797?–1883)
Barnard, Jacqueline, *Journey Toward Freedom*, ill. with photos and engravings, Norton, 1967. Though born in slavery, Sojourner Truth earned her freedom and went on to champion the rights of labor, women, and blacks.   12–16

TUBMAN, HARRIET ROSS (1821?–1913)
Epstein, Samuel and Beryl, *Harriet Tubman, Guide to Freedom*, ill. by Paul Frame, Garrard, 1968. An easy-to-read episodic story of the life of the dauntless woman who guided hundreds of her fellow slaves to freedom.   8–10
Petry, Ann, *Harriet Tubman, Conductor on the Underground Railroad*, T. Crowell, 1955.   12–16

TURNER, NAT (1800–1831)
Griffin, Judith Berry, *Nat Turner*, ill. by Leo Carty, Coward, 1970. A brief but dignified biography of the slave who led a rebellion.   8–10

TWAIN, MARK (1835–1910)
Eaton, Jeannette, *America's Own Mark Twain*, ill. by Leonard Everett Fisher, Morrow, 1958.   10–13

VERNE, JULES (1828–1905)
Freedman, Russell, *Jules Verne*, ill. with old photos and drawings, Holiday, 1965. Well-written account of the first genuine science-fiction author.   12–16

VINCI, LEONARDO DA (1452–1519)
Hahn, Emily, *Leonardo da Vinci*, ill. by Mimi Korach, Random, 1956.   10–13
Ripley, Elizabeth, *Leonardo da Vinci, A Biography*, ill. by Leonardo, Walck, 1952.   12–14
These two books taken together make a beginning at capturing the genius of Leonardo. Ripley's has more art criticism than the other.

WALD, LILLIAN (1867–1940)
Block, Irvin, *Neighbor to the World; The Story of Lillian Wald*, ill. with photos, T. Crowell, 1969. An account of the remarkable woman who introduced the concept of public nursing.   10–14

WASHINGTON, GEORGE (1732–1799)
D'Aulaire, Ingri and Edgar Parin, *George Washington*, ill. by authors, Doubleday, 1936.   5–9
Judson, Clara Ingram, *George Washington, Leader of the People*, ill. by Robert Frankenberg, Follett, 1951. The nation's first President emerges as very human in these excellent books.   10–12

WHITMAN, NARCISSA (1808–1847)
Eaton, Jeanette, *Narcissa Whitman: Pioneer of Oregon*, ill. by Woodi Ishmael, Harcourt, 1941. Inspiring story of a great pioneer woman, based on early letters and memoirs.   12–15

WHITMAN, WALT (1819–1892)
Stoutenberg, Adrien, and Laura N. Baker, *Listen America*, Scribner's, 1968. An objective view of the life of one of America's greatest poets. Many of his poems are included.   13–16

WILDER, LAURA INGALLS (1867–1957)
Wilder, Laura Ingalls, *West from Home; Letters of Laura Ingalls Wilder, San Francisco, 1915*, ed. by Roger Lea Macbride, Harper, 1974. A vivid evocation of place and period as well as a delightfully intimate picture of the author.   11–up

WILLIAM THE CONQUEROR (1027–1087)
Costain, Thomas B., *William the Conqueror*, ill. by Jack Coggins, Random, 1959. An excellent appraisal of William and of the events which preceded and followed his conquest of Britain.   12–15

WILLIAMS, ROGER (1603?–1683)
Eaton, Jeanette, *Lone Journey*, ill. by Woodi Ishmael, Harcourt, 1944. Williams' fight for religious freedom remains one of the stirring moments in early American history.   12–15

WILSON, WOODROW (1856–1924)
Peare, Catherine Owens, *The Woodrow Wilson Story: An Idealist in Politics*, Crowell, 1963. Objective but sympathetic biography of the college president who made good in politics.   12–16

WREN, SIR CHRISTOPHER (1632–1723)
Weir, Rosemary, *The Man Who Built a City; A Life of Sir Christopher Wren*, Farrar, 1971. Well-researched, solidly written, and informative.   11–14

WRIGHT, WILBUR (1867–1912) and ORVILLE (1871–1948)
Glines, Carroll V., *The Wright Brothers, Pioneers of Power Flight*, Watts, 1968. A factual recounting of the Wrights' experiments and the reaction of the public to their work.   11–14

ZENGER, PETER (1697–1746)
Galt, Tom, *Peter Zenger: Fighter for Freedom*, ill. by Ralph Ray, Crowell, 1951. Freedom of the press in America begins with Peter Zenger, who was a hero almost by accident.   11–14

Informational Books

ADLER, DAVID, *Redwoods Are the Tallest Trees in the World*, ill. by Kazue Mizumura, Crowell, 1978. Size, longevity, and growth patterns are described in a simply written book.   7–8

ADLER, IRVING, *The Sun and Its Family*, rev. ed., ill. by Ruth Adler, Day, 1969. A clear presentation of the history of astronomical knowledge. A few chapters contain new scientific knowledge gained in the ten years since the first publication.   10–13
Time in Your Life, rev. ed., ill. by Ruth Adler, Day, 1969. A clear and accurate explanation of the development of clocks, watches, and calendars, with some discussion of nature's rhythms.   10–14

ALIKI, *Fossils Tell of Long Ago*, ill. by author, Crowell, 1972. Discusses formation of fossils and how to find them.   7–8
Corn Is Maize: The Gift of the Indians, ill. by author, Crowell, 1976. Discusses the origin of the plant, its care and harvesting, and its uses.   7–9
Digging Up Dinosaurs, ill. by author, Crowell, 1981. The procedures of excavating, preserving, packing, and reassembling fossil remains is lucidly described.   7–9

ANDERSON, NORMAN, and WALTER BROWN, *Halley's Comet*, Dodd, 1981. Stressing the difference between fact and theory, this describes the work of earlier astronomers and the research that led Halley to discover the comet that was named in his honor.   10–14

ANDREWS, ROY CHAPMAN, *Exploring with Andrews*, Putnam, 1938. Thirteen selections for young readers drawn from three of the great explorer's adult books: *On the Trail of Ancient Man, Ends of the Earth,* and *This Business of Exploring.*   12–up
In the Days of the Dinosaurs, ill. by Jean Zallinger, Random, 1959. The author, former director of the American Museum of Natural History, discusses authoritatively and simply the types of dinosaurs and their world and tells about a fossil hunt he led in Asia.   8–10

ANNO, MITSUMASA, *Anno's Britain,* ill. by author, Philomel, 1982. A superbly illustrated wordless book that shows a range of settings as a traveller moves across the British Isles.   All ages
Anno's Journey, ill. by author, Collins-World, 1978. The art and architecture of northern Europe are beautifully displayed in a wordless book that pictures a journey from coastal village to city.   All ages

ASIMOV, ISAAC, *ABC's of the Earth,* Walker, 1971. Photographs and text are nicely integrated in an alphabetical arrangement of brief topics.   8–10
Building Blocks of the Universe, Abelard, 1957. In his usual entertaining, readable style, the author discusses the chemical elements out of which the universe is built—their discovery and naming, their uses, their place in the periodic table.   12–16
Great Ideas of Science, ill. by Lee Ames, Houghton, 1969.   11–14
How Did We Find Out About Oil? ill. by David Wool, Walker, 1980. A clear discussion of how oil forms, how its uses were discovered, and how it is used today.   9–11

BAKER, BETTY, *Settlers and Strangers: Native Americans of the Desert Southwest and History as They Saw It,* Macmillan, 1977. With full historical background, this presents the Native American view of Indian-white relations and concludes with problems faced by Native Americans today.   9–13

BAKER, LAURA NELSON, *A Tree Called Moses,* ill. by Penelope Naylor, Atheneum, 1966. The Moses tree is an actual tree, estimated to be 2500 years old, growing near Sequoia National Forest in California. A vivid recounting of all its struggles to live.   9–12

BAKER, LIVA, *World Faiths, A Story of Religion,* ill. with photos and art reproductions, Abelard, 1966. A highly interesting work which treats major world religions covering their beliefs, sacraments, holidays, history, scriptures, and artistic expressions.   12–16

BARR, GEORGE, *Fun and Tricks for Young Scientists,* ill. by Mildred Waltrip, McGraw, 1968. Clear instructions for performing a variety of safe tricks based on scientific principles. Included are riddles, puzzles, and jokes. Readily available materials.   9–12

BAUMANN, HANS, *The Caves of the Great Hunters,* tr. by Isabel and Florence McHugh, ill., Pantheon, 1954. Four boys and their dog discover the Lascaux cave paintings and are informed by Abbé Breuil, a famous archaeologist, of the historical significance of their discovery. Many of the illustrations are reproductions of the cave paintings.   9–11

BEALER, ALEX, *Only the Names Remain; The Cherokees and the Trail of Tears,* ill. by William Bock, Little, 1972. Interesting, accurate, and poignant.   9–11

BEELER, NELSON F., *Experiments in Sound,* ill. by George Giusti, T. Crowell, 1961. This study of sound approaches its subject in a scientific manner by providing numerous simple experiments to accompany the informal, readable text.   8–12

BENDICK, JEANNE, *Why Can't I?* ill. by author, McGraw, 1969. Children learn about the reasons why they cannot do some of the things animals can do.   5–7
The Wind, ill. by author, Rand, 1964. Offers a simple explanation of the nature and measurement of wind, windstorms, and the influence of wind upon weather. Also includes superstitions, myths, and sayings about the wind.   7–10

BERGAUST, ERIK, and WILLIAM O. FOSS, *Oceanographers in Action,* ill., Putnam, 1968. A brief survey of research and study projects and an outline of requisites for a career in oceanography.   10–14

BERGER, GILDA, *The Coral Reef: What Lives There,* ill. by Murray Tinkelman, Coward, 1977. Although repetitive, this is a good introduction to understanding the formation of a coral reef and to the ecological balance of the reef community.   7–9

BERNSTEIN, JOANNE, and STEPHEN GULLO, *When People Die,* Dutton, 1977. A sensible and sensitive answer to questions most small children ask about death.   5–8

BIERHORST, JOHN, *A Cry from the Earth: Music of the North American Indians,* Four Winds, 1979. Simple and authoritative, this describes the kinds of songs and the rites with which they are associated, as well as the instruments used.   10–up

BLEEKER, SONIA, *The Pygmies: Africans of the Congo Forest,* ill. by Edith G. Singer, Morrow, 1968. A sympathetic account of the tribal culture and society of the Pygmies. This author has written a series of books about American Indian and African tribes.   9–12

BLOUGH, GLENN, *Discovering Insects,* ill. by Jeanne Bendick, McGraw, 1967. Good basic introduction to insects, well illustrated. Suggests many ways young readers can study and collect insects themselves.   6–9

BLUMBERG, RHODA, *The First Travel Guide to the Moon: What to Pack, How to Go, and What to See When You Get There,* ill. by Roy Doty, Four Winds, 1980. A straight-faced spoof is funny, brisk, and informative about space flight and lunar conditions.   9–12

BLUMENTHAL, SHIRLEY, *Coming to America: Immigrants from Eastern Europe,* Delacorte, 1981. Based on careful research and smoothly written, this can help readers understand the reasons immigrants left their homes to face an arduous journey and the uncertainty of the future in a new land.   11–14

BONTEMPS, ARNA, *Story of the Negro,* rev. ed., ill. by Raymond Lufkin, Knopf, 1960. This very readably written history tells the story of the earliest tribes in Africa, the crossing of slave ships to the new world, the early struggles for freedom and those of the post–Civil War period up to the emergence of Martin Luther King in Montgomery.   10–13

BRADFORD, WILLIAM, and EDWARD WINSLOW, *Pilgrim Courage,* adapted and ed. by E. Brooks Smith and

Robert Meredith, ill. by Leonard Everett Fisher, Little, 1962. William Bradford's history, for which he used his own journal and that of Edward Winslow, has been edited to a dramatic, colorful, and often humorous account of the Pilgrims' difficulties and adventures. 10–up

BRANDHORST, CARL T., and ROBERT SYLVESTER, *The Tale of Whitefoot*, ill. by Grambs Miller, Simon, 1968. Nature's unending cycle of life, death, and renewed life is presented in this story of a whitefooted mouse. A fine blend of sensitive writing and scientific observation. 8–12

BRANLEY, FRANKLYN M., *Eclipse: Darkness in Daytime*, ill. by Donald Crews, T. Crowell, 1973. Explains lucidly the phenomenon of the total solar eclipse. 7–9

Experiments in Sky Watching, ill. by Helmut K. Wimmer, T. Crowell, 1959. The author provides clear directions for constructing some simple pieces of apparatus and then gives directions for using them to locate and study heavenly bodies. 12–14

The Mystery of Stonehenge, ill. by Victor G. Ambrus, T. Crowell, 1969. "Its mysteries may be locked forever within the silent stones" is the concluding sentence in this description of the efforts of anthropologists, engineers, historians, and astronomers to solve the mystery that, thus far, is still unsolved. Illustrations provide beauty as well as information. 10–12

Age of Aquarius: You and Astrology, ill. by Leonard Kessler, Crowell, 1979. Although he points out the fallacies of astrological beliefs, Branley gives good coverage to the history of astrology, explains the signs, and shows how to cast a horoscope. 9–11

BRENNER, BARBARA, *A Snake-Lover's Diary*, ill., Young Scott, 1970. A great deal of scientific information is woven into this account of a young boy and his reptile collection. 8–12

BRIDGES, WILLIAM, *The Bronx Zoo Book of Wild Animals, A Guide to Mammals, Birds, Reptiles and Amphibians of the World*, ill. with photos, Golden Pr., 1968. Begun as a guidebook of the Bronx Zoo, this book became a reference book on 2000 mammals, birds, reptiles, and amphibians. Illustrations are photographs, in black and white as well as color. Excellent index. 10–14

BRONOWSKI, J., and MILLICENT E. SELSAM, *Biography of an Atom*, ill. by Weimar Pursell and with photos, Harper, 1965. The life of a carbon atom is described from its explosive birth in a star, billions of years ago, until it becomes part of the earth and finally part of a human being. 8–12

BROWN, LLOYD ARNOLD, *Map Making: The Art That Became a Science*, ill. by Aldren A. Watson, Little, 1960. The art by which ancient people mapped discoveries or conjectures about the world and the advances in map making over the centuries. 12–16

BUEHR, WALTER, *Automobiles, Past and Present*, ill. by author, Morrow, 1968. Covers the history of the automobile in the United States, basic mechanical principles, assembly line production, and the importance of experimental autos. 9–12

Strange Craft, ill. by author, Norton, 1962. Unusual ships designed over the centuries. 8–12

BUELL, HAL, *The World of Red China*, ill. with photos, Dodd, 1967. A description of life in mainland China today with a brief overview of Chinese history. 9–12

BUFF, MARY and CONRAD, *The Colorado: River of Mystery*, ill. by Conrad Buff, Ritchie, 1968. The geological and human history of the Colorado River with a description of Powell's exploration. 8–10

Elf Owl, ill. by Conrad Buff, Viking, 1958. Drama of desert life as seen by an elf owl who lives in a saguaro cactus. The illustrations and text give the story a poetic quality. 6–8

BULLA, CLYDE ROBERT, *Flowerpot Gardens*, ill. by Henry Evans, T. Crowell, 1967. Easy instructions for starting and growing twenty common plants indoors. 8–10

BURTON, VIRGINIA LEE, *Life Story*, ill. by author, Houghton, 1962. The evolution of the earth is presented in lucid text and unusual format. Excellent for reading aloud. 8–10

CARSON, RACHEL, *The Sea Around Us*, adapted by Anne Terry White, Golden Pr., 1958. This young reader's edition lacks some of the beauty of the original work but retains the fascinating aspects of the story of the sea. 12–16

CHARLIP, REMY, MARY BETH, and GEORGE ANCONA, *Handtalk; An ABC of Finger Spelling & Sign Language*, Parents, 1974. Superb photographs and a minimum of text show the signs for words and letters; an adventure for the child who hears, a necessity for the child who doesn't. 8–up

CHASE, ALICE ELIZABETH, *Famous Paintings: An Introduction to Art*, rev. ed., ill., Platt, 1962. Almost 200 pictures, some in full color, of all periods and styles provide an introduction to art appreciation. The author discusses all the examples and, although the text is brief, gives information on techniques, historical periods and styles, and the artists themselves. 8–up

Looking at Art, ill., T. Crowell, 1966. How artists throughout the centuries have looked at the world around them and pictured it. The author takes several aspects of the artist's craft, such as perspective, and shows how each has been used in different times and cultures. 10–14

CHERRY, MIKE, *Steel Beams and Iron Men*, Four Winds, 1980. A lively and colorful account of the various kinds of jobs done by ironworkers. 11–15

CLARK, ANN NOLAN, *Along Sandy Trails*, photos by Alfred A. Cohn, Viking, 1969. A small Indian girl walks across the desert as this author's poetic prose and Alfred Cohn's incomparable color photographs inform the reader of desert life. A glossary identifies the eleven desert plants pictured. 7–9

CLARKE, ARTHUR C., *The Challenge of the Sea*, ill. by Alex Schomburg, Holt, 1960. An exciting book about resources of the sea, their exploration, and their possible future uses as mineral and food sources. 12–up

CLARKE, CLORINDA, *The American Revolution 1775–83, a British View*, ill. by H. Toothill and H. S. Whithorne, McGraw, 1967. 10–14

CLEMONS, ELIZABETH, *Shells Are Where You Find Them*, ill. by Joe Gault, Knopf, 1960. A simple identification book of the commonest shells on our ocean beaches gives the areas where the shells can be found and the scientific names as well as the common ones. Advice on how to clean, catalog, and mount them. 8–11

Waves, Tides and Currents, ill., Knopf, 1967. The author acknowledges much expert help on this explanation of the causes, characteristics, and uses of waves, tides, and currents. Photographs, diagrams, charts, glossary, bibliography, and index facilitate use as a reference book.   9–11

CLYMER, ELEANOR, *The Second Greatest Invention: Search for the First Farmers*, ill. by Lili Réthi, Holt, 1969. This account of archaeologists' search for the first farmers is distinguished for both its writing and its illustration. Concluding chapters discuss today's food production problems.   10–13

COBB, VICKI, *The Secret Life of School Supplies*, ill. by Bill Morrison, Lippincott, 1981. Descriptions of how ink, paper, and other materials are made is augmented by explanations of the scientific principles that make each substance appropriate for its use.   9–12

COHEN, ROBERT, *The Color of Man*, ill. with photos by Ken Heyman, Random, 1968. A survey of the facts known about skin color and the development of prejudice. The need for racial understanding is stressed. Magnificent photos.   10–12

COLE, JOANNA, *A Chick Hatches*, ill. by Jerome Wexler, Morrow, 1976. The development from egg to embryo to chick is simply and clearly explained and is illustrated by excellent color photographs.   5–8

COLMAN, HILA, *Making Movies; Student Films to Features*, ill. by George Guzzi, World, 1969. Career-oriented, this gives a broad picture of opportunities in the field.   12–15

CONKLIN, GLADYS, *The Bug Club Book: A Handbook for Young Bug Collectors*, ill. by Girard Goodenow, Holiday, 1966. In a chatty, informal style the author gives general information and activities which are appropriate for the solitary collector as well as for groups. Tells how to organize a bug club.   8–12

COOLIDGE, OLIVIA, *The Golden Days of Greece*, ill. by Enrico Arno, T. Crowell, 1968. An authority on the Egyptian, Greek, and Roman worlds, this author has written here a simplified version of her earlier *Men of Athens*. In the simplifying, however, she has not sacrificed accuracy, nor does she write down to the reader.   9–11

COOMBS, CHARLES, *Be a Winner in Baseball*, Morrow, 1973. Lively style, good coverage, sensible advice.   10–12

Spacetrack, Watchdog of the Skies, ill. with photos and diagrams, Morrow, 1969. Since humans are cluttering space with an average of six objects a week put into orbit, *Spacetrack* tells the story of attempts to keep track of this debris.   11–14

COOPER, ELIZABETH, *Science in Your Own Back Yard*, ill. by author, Harcourt, 1958. No one could resist becoming a "scientist" after reading this book.   4–6

COSGRAVE, JOHN O'HARA, *America Sails the Seas*, ill., Houghton, 1962. American ships from the Indian canoe to the Polaris submarine are described; over 200 ships are pictured; and well-labeled diagrams help explain the parts and construction of ships.   9–13

COSGROVE, MARGARET, *A Is for Anatomy*, ill. by author, Dodd, 1965. Focus is upon the human body as a "machine" perfectly adapted for the tasks it must perform.   10–up

Bone for Bone, ill. by author, Dodd, 1968. This well-illustrated introduction to comparative anatomy explores relationships in three ways: comparison of

today's vertebrates, study of fossils of yesterday, and study of embryos.   10–14

COY, HAROLD, *The Americans*, ill. by William Moyers, Little, 1958. A breezily written history of the United States telling about the beginnings of "democracy, ice cream, free schools, railroads, skyscrapers, bathrooms, automobiles, movies, airplanes, social security, penicillin, and atomic energy." A bibliography for each chapter and an extensive index make this a handy reference book.   11–14

CZAJA, PAUL, *Writing with Light; A Simple Workshop in Basic Photography*, Chatham/Viking, 1973. There's information about a camera, instructions for making pictures without one, and an encouragement of observation and imagination.   11–up

DALGLIESH, ALICE, *The Thanksgiving Story*, ill. by Helen Sewell, Scribner's, 1954. A simple telling for young readers of the founding of Plymouth and the celebration of the first Thanksgiving.   6–8

DARLING, LOUIS, *The Gull's Way*, ill. with photos, Morrow, 1965. The author gives a sensitive report on a summer's observations of herring gulls on a Maine island.   9–12

Kangaroos and Other Animals with Pockets, ill., Morrow, 1958. The evolution of the unusual marsupial mammals and their isolation in Australia are explained.   8–10

DARWIN, CHARLES, *The Voyage of the Beagle*, abr. by Millicent E. Selsam, ill. by Anthony Ravielli, Harper, 1959. Each chapter of this excellent abridgement has an introduction that clarifies the following material and that helps tie together the text preceding and following. Included are biographical information and suggestions for further reading.   12–up

DAUGHERTY, JAMES, *Of Courage Undaunted: Across the Continent with Lewis and Clark*, ill. by author, Viking, 1951. A spirited account of the Lewis and Clark expedition that is excellent for reading aloud.   11–13

DAY, BETH, and DR. MARGARET LILEY, *The Secret World of the Baby*, ill. with photos, Random, 1968. Factual, simple, effective account of the baby's growth from conception through about the first year.   10–12

DE BORHEGYI, SUZANNE, *Ships, Shoals and Amphoras; the Story of Underwater Archaeology*, ill. by Alex Schomburg, Holt, 1961. The preparations for an underwater exploration are described, as are famous underwater archaeological finds around the world.   12–16

DENNY, NORMAN, and JOSEPHINE FILMER-SANKEY, *The Bayeux Tapestry; the Story of the Norman Conquest: 1066*, ill., Atheneum, 1966. A great art masterpiece, in color, section by section, with a brief text that tells what is happening in each. Explanation, speculation, and commentary in smaller print accompany each picture and give a good notion of the process of historical interpretation.   10–13

DIETZ, BETTY W., and MICHAEL B. OLATUNJI, *Musical Instruments of Africa: Their Nature, Use, and Place in the Life of a Deeply Musical People*, ill. by Richard M. Powers and with photos, Day, 1965. The vital significance of music in African life is emphasized in this book about the musical instruments, how they are made and how they are played. Includes music of African songs and a record of examples of music.   10–12

D'IGNAZIO, FRED, *Working Robots,* Elsevier/Nelson, 1982. A computer analyst surveys types of robots and their uses in medicine, the classroom, industry, etc. and concludes with a look at the future of robotics.
11–up

DOWDEN, ANNE, *State Flowers,* ill. by author, Crowell, 1978. Precise botanical drawings are accompanied by information about state statutes that are pertinent.
11–up

DOWNER, MARION, *Roofs over America,* ill. with photos, Lothrop, 1967. Two or three paragraphs on each page, accompanied by full-page photographs, introduce thirty-two roofs: saddle, gambrel, overhang, gabled, dormer, paperfold, etc. No other technical vocabulary is used in this unified treatment of American architecture from the Plymouth Colony to the present.
10–14

The Story of Design, ill. with photos, Lothrop, 1963. The instinct of design has dominated human life since primitive time. Sensitive text and numerous fine photographs illustrate the use of design.
10–14

DUGGAN, ALFRED, *Growing Up in 13th Century England,* ill. by C. Walter Hodges, Pantheon, 1962. A very readable account of what it was like in thirteenth-century England as the child of an earl, of a country knight, of a peasant, of a rich merchant, and of a craftsman.
11–14

EARLE, OLIVE, *Praying Mantis,* ill. by author, Morrow, 1969. The life cycle of the praying mantis is described in detail carefully delineated by words and illustration. Anecdotes about the author's own pet mantis add interest to this careful scientific description.
6–10

The Strangler Fig and Other Strange Plants, ill. by author, Morrow, 1967. A simply written discussion of such parasites, epiphytes, and saprophytes as Spanish moss, orchids, mistletoe, and mushrooms. Excellent drawings and large print make this volume attractive for younger readers.
9–11

ERDOES, RICHARD, *The Sun Dance People,* ill. by author, Knopf, 1972. A sympathetic overview of the Plains Indians, their history and way of life.
11–up

ESKENAZI, GERALD, *Hockey,* ill. by photos, Grosset, 1973. Despite the lack of index, this is a survey superior to most, comprehensive but informally written.
11–14

EVANS, EVA KNOX, *People Are Important,* ill. by Vana Earle, Capitol, 1951. The differences among the people of the world are described in simple text that shows how a person is related to one's culture.
5–8

FENNER, CAROL, *Gorilla Gorilla,* ill. by Symeon Shimin, Random, 1973. Accurate and straightforward, a description of a gorilla in the wild and in captivity.
8–10

FISHER, AILEEN, *Valley of the Smallest; the Life Story of a Shrew,* ill. by Jean Zallinger, T. Crowell, 1966. A dramatic, beautifully illustrated story of this tiny creature. We learn about some of the other animals that inhabit its world and how all contribute to a larger natural plan.
10–13

FISHER, LEONARD EVERETT, *The Potters,* ill. by author, Watts, 1969 (Author's Colonial American Craftsmen series). A brief history of pottery making in colonial times, along with the author's unique combination of text and simply detailed illustration to describe the potters' craft. Includes index and listing of colonial American potters and potteries of the seventeenth and eighteenth centuries.
9–11

The Newspapers, ill. by author, Holiday, 1981. In a series of books about nineteenth-century America, the author links descriptive material to the matrix of the society in which the newspapers existed.
10–12

The Sports, ill. by author, Holiday, 1980. In the same series, Fisher describes the emergence of many new sports as well as the ways in which competitive and noncompetitive sports were played.
10–12

FLANAGAN, GERALDINE LUX, *Window into an Egg,* ill. with photos, Young Scott, 1969. A clearly written, detailed account of the development of a chicken within its egg from fertilization to the twenty-first day when it breaks out.
10–13

FOSTER, GENEVIEVE, *Birthdays of Freedom: America's Heritage from the Ancient World,* 2 vols., ill. by author, Scribner's, 1952 and 1957. Great historical events in man's struggle for freedom, from prehistoric times to July 4, 1776.
12–15

George Washington's World, ill. by author. Scribner's, 1941.
10–13

The World of Columbus and Sons, ill. by author, Scribner's, 1965. The world of Columbus is portrayed in a series of episodes that give a broad picture of the important people and events of that time. Very informative. The author has written a book for younger readers, *Year of Columbus: 1492* (1969).
12–15

FREEMAN, MAE BLACKER, *Finding Out About the Past,* ill. with photos, Random, 1967. An excellent introduction to archaeology which shows how this study is conducted and how it helps us learn about the people of the past.
7–10

FROMAN, ROBERT, *The Many Human Senses,* ill. by Feodor Rimsky, Little, 1966. Basic information, clearly written, on the traditional five senses and other obscure senses, such as ESP. Up-to-date scientific research in different areas is discussed.
10–14

GALLANT, ROY A., *Exploring the Universe,* rev. ed., ill. by Lowell Hess, Doubleday, 1968. One of the best introductions to astronomy, this book explains what scientists believe were the origins of the stars, the sun, and the planets, provides a brief history of the development of astronomy, and discusses many astronomical terms and phenomena. Helpful illustrations.
10–14

Man Must Speak; The Story of Language and How We Use It, ill., Random, 1969. Beginning with a discussion of what has been learned about animal language, the author goes on to describe theories about the origin and development of human language and the later development of writing.
12–up

GANS, ROMA, *When Birds Change Their Feathers,* ill. by Felicia Bond, Crowell, 1980. Describing first the way that many animals shed their outer coverings, Gans discusses the ways in which various species of birds molt.
7–8

GARVER, SUSAN, and PAULA MC GUIRE, *Coming to North America: From Mexico, Cuba, and Puerto Rico,* Delacorte, 1981. With emphasis on Mexican immigrants, this discusses problems of adjustment in their new homes as well as the reasons for migration.
11–14

GEKIERE, MADELEINE, *Who Gave Us . . . Peacocks? Planes? & Ferris Wheels?* ill. by author, Pantheon, 1953. International interdependence is introduced in this original picture book.
5–8

GEORGE, JEAN CRAIGHEAD, *Spring Comes to the Ocean,* ill. by John Wilson, T. Crowell, 1965. Spring comes as emphatically to the ocean as it does to the land, and this book poetically describes the changes that come to the animal and plant life.   12–15

GERSTEN, IRENE, and BETSY BLISS, *Ecidujerp/Prejudice: Either Way It Doesn't Make Sense,* ill. by Richard Rosenblum, Watts, 1974. Direct language and an objective tone add to the effectiveness of a discussion of what prejudice is, and how to recognize and combat it.   9–11

GIBLIN, JAMES, *The Skyscraper Book,* Crowell, 1981. A good survey of the development and proliferation of an architectural phenomenon.   10–14

GILBERT, SARA, *How to Live with a Single Parent,* Lothrop, 1982. Sensible, moderate, broad in scope, and nonjudgmental, this gives impartial advice on parent-child relations.   11–14

GLUBOK, SHIRLEY, *The Art of India,* ill. with photos, Macmillan, 1969. The three major religions of India, illuminated through a study of art throughout the years, helps us understand the present. See, also, other books in this author's series: *The Art of Africa,* Harper, 1965; *The Art of Ancient Greece,* Atheneum, 1963; *The Art of Ancient Peru,* Harper, 1966; *The Art of America in the Early Twentieth Century,* Macmillan, 1974.   11–14

GLUBOK, SHIRLEY, ed., *Home and Child Life in Colonial Days,* abr. from *Home Life in Colonial Days* (1898) and *Child Life in Colonial Days* (1899) by Alice Morse Earle, photos by Alfred Tamarin, Macmillan, 1969. Browsing in the index reveals the fascinating content of this meticulously written and illustrated book on the colonial period: Bathing, infrequency of; Betty lamps; Corncobs, uses of; Diseases among children; Girls, importance of erect bearing; Names for children; Rattlewatch; Stone bee; Voider; and Whispering sticks. Excellent reference source.   11–up

GORDON, ESTHER and BERNARD GORDON, *There Really Was a Dodo,* ill. by Lawrence DiFiori, Walck, 1974. An interesting account of the evolutionary background of the now-extinct bird that lived on the island of Mauritius.   8–9

GORODETZKY, CHARLES, and SAMUEL CHRISTIAN, *What You Should Know about Drugs,* Harcourt, 1970. Simply written but dignified enough for adults, this is objective in tone and comprehensive in coverage.   10–up

GOUDEY, ALICE E., *Butterfly Time,* ill. by Adrienne Adams, Scribner's, 1964. The simple text and detailed illustrations make this an excellent introduction to butterflies for the youngest.   4–7

Here Come the Dolphins! ill. by Garry MacKenzie, Scribner's, 1961.   7–9

Houses from the Sea, ill. by Adrienne Adams, Scribner's, 1959. In a context young children can identify with, information about shells with careful labeling of each is presented. Illustrations supply information beyond textual content. Good to read aloud to prereaders.   4–7

GUILCHER, JEAN MICHEL, and ROBERT HENRY NOAILLES, *A Fruit Is Born,* ill., Sterling, 1960. The simple text and superb photographs explain the development of different kinds of fruits.   9–11

GUSTAFSON, ANITA, *Burrowing Birds,* ill. by Joel Schick, Lothrop, 1981. An overview of avian species that nest underground has soft, realistically detailed illustrations.   9–11

HADER, BERTA and ELMER, *The Big Snow,* ill. by authors, Macmillan, 1948, 1962. How the small animals on a country hillside survive a heavy snow storm. Caldecott Medal.   4–7

HALACY, DANIEL, *The Energy Trap,* Four Winds, 1975. A competent assessment of the complex problems of energy needs and population pressures.   12–15

HALL, LYNN, *Kids and Dog Shows,* ill. by photos, Follett, 1975. Facts on grooming, training, judging, and all the small details of canines in the ring.   10–14

HAMBLIN, DORA, *Pots and Robbers,* Simon, 1970. True stories about some of the more dramatic aspects of archaeology are written with wit and vigor.   12–up

HARDENDORFF, JEANNE, *Libraries and How to Use Them,* Watts, 1979. An explicit and well-organized text on the organization and use of library materials.   9–11

HARRIS, JANET, *The Long Freedom Road; The Civil Rights Story.* McGraw, 1967.   11–15

HARRIS, JANET, and JULIUS W. HOBSON, *Black Pride, a People's Struggle,* ill., McGraw, 1969. From Dred Scott to Eldridge Cleaver this account of activist blacks tells the story of the long struggle for freedom from the point of view of opponents on nonviolence.   12–14

HARRIS, LOUISE and NORMAN, *Flash: The Life Story of a Firefly,* ill. by Henry B. Kane, Little, 1966. Interesting and accurate scientific observation in this story of Flash, who is born a glowworm and turns into a firefly.   8–10

HARTMAN, GERTRUDE, *Medieval Days and Ways,* ill., Macmillan, 1937. A wide and varied picture of many facets of life in the Middle Ages. The author goes beyond the description to discuss our heritage from that period.   10–15

HERZIG, ALISON, and JANE MALI, *Oh, Boy! Babies!,* Little, Brown, 1980. A photodocumentary about an elective course in a boys' school, this is amusing, touching, and informative, as the boys learn techniques of baby care by practicing on real babies.   9–11

HILTON, SUZANNE, *The Way It Was—1876,* Westminster, 1975. Comprehensive and witty, with a touch of nostalgia, this describes and pictures aspects of daily life.   11–up

HIRSCH, S. CARL, *The Globe for the Space Age,* ill. by Burt Silverman, Viking, 1963. A well-written history of globe-making—from the first crude model made in 150 B.C. to the accurately detailed globes in the U.S. space program—with much interesting related information.   10–14

Meter Means Measure; The Story of the Metric System, Viking, 1973. Historical background prefaces an appreciative description of the advantages of the system.   11–15

This Is Automation, ill. by Anthony Ravielli, Viking, 1964. A book which deals with the social aspects of automation. There is a brief explanation of binary mathematics but no attempt to explain how computers work.   9–14

HOBAN, TANA, *Look Again!* Macmillan, 1971.   2–4
Shapes and Things, Macmillan, 1970.   2–5
The first book uses photographs and cutout portions of the page, the second uses pictures made without a camera to show new ways of looking at familiar objects.

Take Another Look, Greenwillow, 1981. Hoban uses cutout pages in her photographs of objects, lending a game element to a book that can encourage observation skills.   3–5

HODGES, C. WALTER, *The Spanish Armada; the Story of Britain*, ill. by author, Coward, 1967. Well-illustrated and well-written book that takes account of the Spanish viewpoint in the battles between the English and the Spanish Armada in 1588.   10–13

HODGMAN, ANN, and RUDY DJABBAROFF, *Skystars: The History of Women in Aviation,* Atheneum, 1981. All major figures and many minor ones are included, from the women balloonists of the eighteenth century to the contemporary fliers who are candidates for space shuttle pilots.   12–up

HOGBEN, LANCELOT, *The Wonderful World of Energy,* rev. ed., ill., Doubleday, 1968. A dramatic history of people's efforts to harness power from the prehistoric use of fire to the development of today's atomic power. An illustrated glossary is included.   10–13

HOLLING, HOLLING C., *Paddle-to-the-Sea*, ill. by author, Houghton, 1941. An Indian boy carves a toy canoe and sets it afloat in a stream in Canada. Its travels through the Great Lakes and down the St. Lawrence to the sea are an opportunity to tell much about the geography, the industry, and the history of the areas with full-page illustration and text.   10–12

HOLME, BRYAN, *Drawings to Live With*, ill. with reproductions, Viking, 1966. Each chapter of this book offers a different aspect of drawing. By the end of the book the reader will have learned about drawings, art techniques, art history, and artists, too.   10–14

HOWE, JAMES, *The Hospital Book*, Crown, 1981. Clear photographs extend the text of a book that introduces hospital procedures candidly and fully.   7–9

HUGHES, LANGSTON, *The First Book of Rhythms*, ill. by Robin King, Watts, 1954. A beautifully written book showing how rhythms are to be found in all aspects of life. An excellent introduction for young readers to an awareness of the harmonies around them.   10–14

HUTCHINS, ROSS E., *The Amazing Seeds*, photos by author, Dodd, 1965. Superb close-up photographs and lively text tell the story about seeds plus some unusual facts about them.   9–12

Travels of Monarch X, ill. by J. P. Connolly, Rand, 1966. A true story of the migration of a tagged Monarch butterfly from Canada to Mexico. Well documented, handsomely illustrated, overall pleasingly designed.   8–10

HYDE, MARGARET O., *Animal Clocks and Compasses*, ill. by P. A. Hutchinson, Whittlesey, 1960. The fascinating natural rhythms by which animals live and travel are explored. A section of science projects is included.   9–12

JANSON, H. W., and DORA JANE JANSON, *The Story of Painting for Young People; from Cave Painting to Modern Times*, ill. with reproductions, Abrams, 1952. The history of how painting began and how it developed through the ages, with 245 reproductions. The authors convey successfully how artists have chosen to express themselves differently in different periods.   12–16

JENNESS, AYLETTE, *Dwellers of the Tundra: Life in an Alaskan Eskimo Village*, photos by Jonathan Jenness, Crowell-Collier, 1970. A sympathetic account of the lives of 150 Eskimos who live in Makumiut on the Bering Sea by an author and photographer who lived with them for more than a year.   12–16

JOHNSON, ERIC, *Love and Sex in Plain Language*, rev. ed., ill. by Edward C. Smith, Lippincott, 1977. Outstanding for its dignity, informality, and candor.   12–15

JOHNSON, GERALD W., *America, a History for Peter*, 3 vols., ill. by Leonard Everett Fisher, Morrow, 1959–1960. A readable, easily understood history which makes clear the issues and underlying causes of the events chronicled. (The Peter of the title is the author's grandson.)   12–14

The Congress, ill. by Leonard Everett Fisher, Morrow, 1963. In this and two companion volumes (*The Presidency*, 1962, and *The Supreme Court*, 1962), the author presents authoritative, informative overviews of the three branches of the federal government. A related volume is *The Cabinet*, 1966.   11–13

KAVALER, LUCY, *Dangerous Air*, ill. by Carl Smith, Day, 1967. A succinct discussion of the causes of air pollution beginning with the discovery of fire and what government, industry, and individuals must do to eliminate this danger.   12–up

KIRK, RUTH, *The Oldest Man in America: An Adventure in Archeology*, photos by Ruth and Louis Kirk, Harcourt, 1970. Fascinating description of the findings at a dig in the state of Washington.   10–14

KUMIN, MAXINE, *The Beach Before Breakfast*, ill. by Leonard Weisgard, Putnam, 1964. A grownup and a child dig clams on a beach at sunup. Text, meant for a young child, uses a style somewhat awkward for reading aloud but ideal for talking about the full-page illustrations that invite looking and relooking.   6–8

KURELEK, WILLIAM, *A Prairie Boy's Summer*, ill. by author, Houghton, 1975, and *A Prairie Boy's Winter*, Houghton, 1973. A Canadian painter describes in text and handsome pictures his childhood on a Manitoba dairy farm.   8–10

LAFFIN, JOHN, *Codes and Ciphers: Secret Writing Through the Ages*, ill. by C. de la Nougerede, Abelard, 1964. A history of codes and ciphers from ancient to modern times makes fascinating and exciting reading. At the end of the book are cipher messages that the reader should be able to break.   11–15

LASKY, KATHRYN, *Dollmaker: The Eyelight and the Shadow*, Scribner's, 1981. Photographs of fine quality illustrate the textual description of the work of a professional dollmaker as she constructs an amazingly lifelike doll modeled on her son.   11–up

LATHROP, DOROTHY P., *Let Them Live*, ill. by author, Macmillan, 1951. The disasters that can occur when people interfere with the balance of nature are forcefully presented in a group of essays.   8–12

LAUBER, PATRICIA, *Bats; Wings in the Night*, ill. with photos, Random, 1968. Up-to-date, extensive study of types of bats and their eating and living habits. Excellent photographs.   8–12

What's Hatching Out of That Egg? Crown, 1979. Observation and deduction are encouraged by the clues that precede each disclosure of the identity of each newly hatched creature.   7–9

LAWSON, ROBERT, *They Were Strong and Good*, ill. by author, Viking, 1940. The author's own ancestors provide the opportunity to move from the present to long ago in a simple, personal approach to "history" for younger children. Caldecott Medal.   7–10

Watchwords of Liberty: A Pageant of American Quotations, rev. ed., ill. by author, Little, 1957. A collection which highlights important occasions in American history. Background and circumstances surrounding each quotation are explained.   8–12

LEHR, PAUL E., *Storms: Their Origins and Effects; Forecasting and Weather Lore,* ill. by Harry McNaught and Nino Carbe and with photos, Golden Pr., 1966. The author, a meteorologist with the U.S. Weather Bureau, describes all kinds of storms, storm patterns, and frontal storms. Included is a discussion of famous winds of the world and of weather lore.   9–12

LERNER, CAROL, *Flowers of a Woodland Spring,* ill. by author, Morrow, 1979. Delicate color drawings, meticulously detailed, illustrate a text that describes the ephemeral flowers of early spring.   8–10

LESTER, JULIUS, *To Be a Slave,* ill. by Tom Feelings, Dial, 1968. A collection of published and unpublished reminiscences by ex-slaves weaves a moving history of black Americans from their abduction from Africa through slavery, the Civil War, and its aftermath.   12–16

LIFTON, BETTY JEAN, *Return to Hiroshima,* photos by Eikoh Hosoe, Atheneum, 1970. This picture book records Hiroshima as it is 25 years after the atomic bomb blast—the survivors, the Peace Museum, and so many chilling reminders of the past.   10–15

LIPSYTE, ROBERT, *Assignment: Sports,* Harper, 1970. A compilation of colorful articles about diverse sports.   10–up

LUBELL, WINIFRED and CECIL, *Green Is for Growing,* ill., Rand, 1964. Without attempting to be comprehensive, this beautiful book discusses the plant kingdom and the classification of groups, giving some examples. The importance of plant life to humankind is made clear.   8–12

MACAULAY, DAVID, *Cathedral; The Story of Its Construction,* ill. by author, Houghton, 1973. Superbly illustrated, this describes—step by step—the building of a Gothic cathedral.   11–up
City; A Story of Roman Planning and Construction, ill. by author, Houghton, 1974. An engrossing and detailed account of the planning and building of a Roman city.   11–up
Unbuilding, ill. by author, Houghton, 1980. Although this is humorous and has a fictional framework (Arabian money buys the Empire State building to dismantle and reconstruct in the desert), it shows, in the stripping process, every detail of the structure of a landmark skyscraper.   10–up

MARCUS, REBECCA B., *Prehistoric Cave Paintings,* ill., Watts, 1968. The discovery and subsequent study of Cro-Magnon cave art in France and Spain. The author includes discussion of various theories about the purposes of the paintings.   10–13

MARRIOTT, ALICE LEE, *Indians on Horseback,* rev. ed., ill. by Margaret Lefranc, T. Crowell, 1968. The author describes how the first Indian tribes settled along the edges of the Great Plains and later, with the coming of horses, moved into that area to live and hunt. These people came to be called Plains Indians and this book provides a very thorough history of their customs, government, arts, and religion.   10–14

MATTHEWS, WILLIAM H., III, *The Story of the Earth,* ill. by John E. Alexander, Harvey, 1968. An introductory book on geology, straightforward, simple. Includes glossary of geological terms.   9–12

MAY, JULIAN, *Why the Earth Quakes,* ill. by Leonard Everett Fisher, Holiday, 1969. The clear drawings and simple text clarify the causes of earthquakes.   7–10
Before the Indians, ill. by Symeon Shimin, Holiday, 1969. This picture book with only a few lines of text per page is not as simple as it appears. It presents an excellent picture of the work of archaeologists who, in this case, are piecing together the story of pre-Indian inhabitants of the Americas.   8–10

MC CLUNG, ROBERT M., *Black Jack, Last of the Big Alligators,* ill. by Lloyd Sanford, Morrow, 1967. A realistic narrative, illustrated with many accurate drawings, of the life cycle of an alligator in the Okefenokee Swamp.   9–11

MC COY, J. J., *The Hunt for the Whooping Cranes; A Natural History Detective Story,* maps and drawings by Ray Abruzzi, Lothrop, 1966. A suspense story about the eleven-year search by naturalists and conservationists for the Canadian nesting grounds of the whooping cranes, a search which was undertaken to save them from extinction.   12–16

MC NEER, MAY, *The American Indian Story,* ill. by Lynd Ward, Ariel, 1963. The life and history of the American Indians are told in a series of dramatic anecdotes and vigorous pictures.   10–14

MEAD, MARGARET, *People and Places,* ill. by W. T. Mars and Jan Fairservis and with photos, World, 1959. An extensive and exciting picture of the anthropologist's profession.   12–16

MELTZER, MILTON, *Brother, Can You Spare a Dime. The Great Depression 1929–1933,* ill. with contemporary prints and photos, Knopf, 1969. "How it started and why and what it felt like . . ." is what this book tells about "the human side" of the Great Depression as it affected auto workers, wheat farmers, clerks, secretaries, miners, teachers, sharecroppers, and doctors. Much documentation is from newspaper headlines, articles, cartoons, and pictures from periodicals; also from art, literature, and songs of this period.   12–14
Remember the Days; A Short History of the Jewish American, ill. by Harvey Dinnerstein, Doubleday, 1974. Broad in coverage, serious and well-researched.   12–up
All Times, All Peoples: A History of Slavery, ill. by Leonard Everett Fisher, Harper, 1980. Handsome scratchboard illustrations add drama to a comprehensive account that covers all times and all countries but stresses black slavery in America.   10–12

MELTZER, MILTON, ed., *In Their Own Words: A History of the American Negro,* 3 vols., ill. with facsimiles and portraits, T. Crowell, 1964, 1965, 1967. A unique history told through excerpts from documents, journals, letters, diaries, and speeches. Background information and sources are given for each item.   12–up

MELTZER, MILTON, and AUGUST MEIER, *Time of Trial, Time of Hope; The Negro in America, 1919–1941,* ill. by Moneta Barnett, Doubleday, 1966. One of a series commissioned to present historically the contribution made by minority groups to the development of the United States. The print size, illustration, and writing style invite the average or below average adolescent reader of any race to understand and appreciate the black during the heights of the 1920's and the depths of the 1930's.   12–16

MOORE, JANET GAYLORD, *The Many Ways of Seeing; An Introduction to the Pleasures of Art,* ill. with reproductions and photos, World, 1968. In the first half of this book the author discusses how artists see things in different ways and suggests ways of sharpening one's perception in art. Following a collage of pictures and quotations, the author suggests simple exercises to investigate some of the ideas and terms used earlier. A simple, personal, and enthusiastic presentation. 12–16

MORISON, SAMUEL ELIOT, *The Story of the "Old Colony" of New Plymouth,* ill. by Charles H. Overly, Knopf, 1956. Thoroughly familiar with his subject, this writer, well known for his historical works for adults, continues the story of the Pilgrims beyond Plymouth Rock and the first Thanksgiving. He writes authentically and with humor about the everyday lives of these people, as well as about the more conventional historical events. 12–16

MORRISON, SEAN, *Armor,* ill. by author, T. Crowell, 1963. In a lively style the author describes the armor of the ancient and feudal worlds and the men who wore it. Detailed and careful illustrations. 12–16

MORRISON, VELMA, *Going on a Dig,* Dodd, 1981. Following an introduction to the science of archeology, Morrison describes a dig in which junior and senior high school students participated. 10–12

MURPHY, E. JEFFERSON, *Understanding Africa,* ill. by Louise E. Jefferson, T. Crowell, 1969. The author dispels stereotypes about Africa and its people. A general overview of the geography, people, and history, mainly of that part of Africa south of the Sahara Desert. 12–14

MURPHY, ROBERT, *A Heritage Restored; America's Wildlife Refuges,* ill. with photos and maps, Dutton, 1969. An introduction to America's wildlife and its unfortunate past history. The author describes representative refuges in the national system of refuges. 12–up

NANCE, JOHN, *Lobo of the Tasaday,* Pantheon, 1982. Text and photographs focus on Lobo, a boy of ten, to describe the life-style of a primitive society on a Philippine island. 9–11

NICKEL, HELMUT, *Arms and Armor in Africa,* Atheneum, 1971. Objects described by the Curator of Arms and Armor at the Metropolitan Museum are related to tribal cultures. 10–14

OXFORD SCIENTIFIC FILMS, *Harvest Mouse,* Putnam, 1982. Fine color photographs illustrate a brisk, direct text that describes the harvest mouse and deplores the farm machines that are depleting the species. 8–10
The Stickleback Cycle, Putnam, 1979. Dramatic pictures, often magnified, illustrate a crisp and authoritative text about the three-spine stickleback. 8–10

PACE, MILDRED, *Wrapped for Eternity; The Story of the Egyptian Mummy,* ill. by Tom Huffman, McGraw, 1974. 10–14

PAIGE, DAVID, *Behind the Scenes at the Aquarium,* Whitman, 1979. Good color photographs show the beauty of exhibits and expand textual descriptions of the work members of an aquarium staff. 9–11

PAINE, ROBERTA M., *Looking at Sculpture,* ill. with photos, Lothrop, 1968. Nearly a hundred works of sculpture, ancient to modern, are shown and discussed. Biographical information on the artists is included along with a glossary and suggested reading list. 12–16

PATON, ALAN, *The Land and People of South Africa,* rev. ed., ill. with photos, Lippincott, 1964. The author makes very clear his views of South Africa's racial problems but also states fairly the opposite point of view. A thought-provoking study of the geography and the various racial groups. 12–16

PERKINS, CAROL MORSE, and MARLIN PERKINS, *"I Saw You from Afar": A Visit to the Bushmen of the Kalahari Desert,* ill. with photos, Atheneum, 1965. The daily life of the bushmen in photographs and simple text. The treatment is sympathetic and dignified. 8–11

PETERSON, ROGER TORY, and the Editors of *Time-Life* Books, *The Birds,* ill. with photos and drawings, Time Inc., 1967 (Young Readers Edition). An outstanding book with beautiful color photos. *The Mammals* (1967) is another excellent book in this series of Young Readers Editions of *Life Nature Library.* 10–16

PETTIT, FLORENCE, *How to Make Whirligigs and Whimmy Diddles; and Other American Folkcraft Objects,* ill. by Laura Louise Foster, T. Crowell, 1972. Useful for the hobbyist, entertaining for the general reader. 12–up

POLGREEN, JOHN and CATHLEEN, *The Stars Tonight,* ill. with photos, Harper, 1967. Descriptions of constellations and their legends, galaxies, and nebulae are all accompanied by charts to help locate them in the sky. 10–14

PORTAL, COLETTE, *The Beauty of Birth,* ill. by author, ad. by Guy Daniels, Knopf, 1971. A French artist's lovely watercolors and her reverent text show the development of a newborn from insemination. 8–11

PRICE, CHRISTINE, *Made in the Middle Ages,* ill. by author, Dutton, 1961. This is a book about the craftsmen and their products in a period that produced so many splendid objects. See, also, *Made in the Renaissance,* 1963, and *Made in Egypt,* 1970. 12–16

PRINGLE, LAURENCE, *Dinosaurs and Their World,* ill., Harcourt, 1968. One of the best books on dinosaurs with explanatory illustrations. Readable text includes descriptions of field work and museum study methods. 7–10

RAVIELLI, ANTHONY, *From Fins to Hands: An Adventure in Evolution,* ill. by author, Viking, 1968. A well-illustrated account of the human hand through the stages of fin, paw, and claw with emphasis upon the period from early primates to humans. 8–12
Wonders of the Human Body, ill. by author, Viking, 1954. An attractive, clear study of anatomy which portrays the body as a perfect machine. Simple analogies describe parts of the body and their functions. 8–12

REED, W. MAXWELL, *Patterns in the Sky: The Story of the Constellations,* ill. by D. F. Levett Bradley, Morrow, 1951. The constellations are located in the sky with the help of charts, and the origins of their names are explained. 8–12

REED, W. MAXWELL, and WILFRID S. BRONSON, *The Sea for Sam,* rev. ed. edited by Paul F. Brandwein, Harcourt, 1960. Originally written in the 1930's for the nephew of W. Maxwell Reed, astronomy professor at Harvard, this edition has been revised and checked by authorities. Most photographs are new and the whole book has been redesigned. See, also, *The Earth for Sam* and *The Stars for Sam,* both similarly updated by Paul F. Brandwein. 11–14

REISS, JOHN, *Colors,* Bradbury, 1969. Identifying captions are the only text for Reiss' stunning pictures. An excellent first book for small children. See also *Numbers,* 1971, and *Shapes,* 1974. 2–6

RIPPER, CHARLES L., *Bats,* ill., Morrow, 1954. Clear text and drawings tell the life cycle and habits of bats the world over. Corrects some misconceptions. 10–12

ROCKWELL, ANNE, *Temple on a Hill; the Building of the Parthenon,* ill. with line drawings, Atheneum, 1969. A good deal of history is included with the account of the building of the Parthenon. 10–14
The Toolbox, ill. by Harlow Rockwell, Macmillan, 1971. A simple text and clear, spacious pictures show basic tools and their uses. 5–7

ROOSEVELT, ELEANOR, and HELEN FERRIS, *Partners: United Nations and Youth,* ill. with photos, Doubleday, 1950. The story of United Nations agencies' efforts to help children and young people around the world, made more dramatic by numerous true anecdotes. 12–14

ROSEN, ELLSWORTH, *Spiders Are Spinners,* ill. by Teco Slagboom, Houghton, 1968. Accurate information about spiders and their habits is presented in sprightly verse and attractive illustrations. 4–8

ROSS, FRANK, JR., *Transportation of Tomorrow,* ill. with drawings by the author and photos, Lothrop, 1968. Different modes of future transportation, some of almost science-fiction sort, are discussed, but the author is very conscious of the social usefulness and reality of what he describes. 10–14

RUCHLIS, HY, *Bathtub Physics,* ill. by Ray Skibinski, Harcourt, 1967. This book shows how some everyday laws of physics can be discovered in the bathtub. Each chapter includes brain teasers and investigations for the reader to pursue for oneself. 10–14

SASEK, MIROSLAV, *This Is the United Nations,* ill. by author, Macmillan, 1968. An excellent, bright picture book that brings the U.N. vividly to life. Other books in this author's series about the great cities of the world include *This Is London,* 1959; *This Is Paris,* 1959; *This Is Rome,* 1960. 8–10

SAVAGE, KATHERINE, *The Story of Marxism and Communism,* ill. with photos and maps, Walck, 1968. The author traces the philosophical origins of communist thought, describes the creation of a communist state in Russia, and provides vivid portraits of the men who shaped it. She also describes the other Eastern European communist states and communist China's divergent path. 12–16

SCHALLER, GEORGE B., and MILLICENT E. SELSAM, *The Tiger: Its Life in the Wild,* ill. with photos and drawings, Harper, 1969. The author's firsthand experiences give excitement to this complete account of a great deal that is known about tigers. Myths about these animals are also recounted. 9–14

SCHECHTER, BETTY, *The Peaceable Revolution,* ill. with photos, Houghton, 1963. The nonviolent way of solving human problems is traced through the perspective of history: Thoreau, Gandhi, and into today's civil rights movement. 12–16

SCHEELE, WILLIAM E., *Prehistoric Animals,* ill., World, 1954. A well-written account of animal life during the first five million years of life on the earth. The locations of fossil finds and museums in which fossil remains may be found are included. 9–14

SCHEFFER, VICTOR, *Little Calf,* ill. by Leonard Everett Fisher, Scribner's, 1970. Adapted beautifully by Scheffer from his adult title, *The Year of the Whale,* this is as accurate as it is imaginative. 12–up

SCHELL, ORVILLE, and JOSEPH ESHERICK, *Modern China; The Story of a Revolution,* Knopf, 1972. Lucid and objective, a thoughtful analysis of China today. 11–up

SCHNEIDER, HERMAN and NINA, *How Big Is Big? From Stars to Atoms,* ill. by Symeon Shimin, W. R. Scott, 1946. Relativity of size is treated in this picture book with its pleasant illustrations and easy text. Included is a list of the approximate measurements of the things compared in the text. 6–9
How Your Body Works, ill. by Barbara Ivins, W. R. Scott, 1949. The parts of the body and their different functions, the nervous system, the senses are all described. 8–12
You Among the Stars, ill. by Symeon Shimin, W. R. Scott, 1951. A clever approach introduces the young child to the wonders of astronomy. 8–10
Your Telephone and How It Works, 3rd ed., ill. by Jeanne Bendick, Whittlesey, 1965. An easily understood explanation of the workings of the telephone with helpful diagrams. 10–13

SCHWARTZ, ALVIN, *The City and Its People,* photos by Sy Katzoff, Dutton, 1967. Amply illustrated with photographs, this book describes a real modern city, Trenton, New Jersey, with its urban renewal, poverty, city court, garbage removal, traffic, etc. 11–14
The Night Workers, ill. by Ulli Steltzer, Dutton, 1966. Each hour from 6 P.M. to 6 A.M. is represented by a night worker whose work is often unknown to day people: newspaper pressman, night-school teacher, produce-market workers, disc jockey, jazz musicians, and many others—all are shown at work in photographs taken in a big city setting. 8–11

SCOTT, JACK DENTON, *That Wonderful Pelican,* photos by Ozzie Sweet, Putnam, 1975. A photo-essay, detailed and authoritative, on every aspect of pelican life. 10–up

SEEGER, ELIZABETH, *The Pageant of Chinese History,* McKay, 1934, rev. ed., 1962. This social, cultural, and political history from 3000 B.C. to the present time appears formidably thick and detailed, but with the help of its excellent index, can be an accurate and readable resource on the Chinese people. 12–14

SELSAM, MILLICENT E., *All Kinds of Babies,* ill. by Symeon Shimin, Four Winds, 1969. Very brief text with beautiful illustrations gives this picture book special appeal for young children. Develops two concepts very clearly, related to both familiar and less familiar animals: every living thing makes more of its own kind and babies look like their parents. 5–8
Benny's Animals; And How He Put Them in Order, ill. by Arnold Lobel, Harper, 1966. 6–8
Birth of an Island, ill. by Winifred Lubell, Harper, 1959. The evolution of a volcanic island is described in simple, lucid language from the initial eruption to the time when a variety of plant and animal life occupy it. 7–9.
See also, *Birth of a Forest,* 1964. 8–10
How Animals Tell Time, ill. by John Kaufmann, Morrow, 1967. With her usual clarity and directness, the author discusses the biological clocks that seem to be a part of all animal life. In conclusion she mentions some of the experiments going on that may answer many remaining questions. 8–12

See Through the Forest, ill. by Winifred Lubell, Harper, 1956. Plant and animal life at various levels of the forest, from the ground to the treetops, is described in this author's usual simple and accurate style. See, also, *See Through the Sea,* 1955; *See Through the Jungle,* 1957; *See Through the Lake,* 1958.   7–10

SELSAM, MILLICENT, and JOYCE HUNT, *A First Look at Sharks,* ill. by Harriett Springer, Walker, 1979. Designed, as are other books in this "first look" series, to teach younger children the principles of classification, this shows not only what a shark is like, but how it differs from other fish.   7–8

A First Look at Spiders, ill. by Harriett Springer, Walker, 1983. Detailed drawings show the distinguishing characteristics by which spiders of various kinds can be recognized.   7–8

SHIPPEN, KATHERINE B., *The Great Heritage,* ill. by C. B. Falls, Viking, 1947; rev. ed., 1962. One by one this author looks at the natural resources—fur, timber, iron, gold, wheat, corn, etc.—that constitute the heritage for which the people of the U.S. are responsible.   12–16

Men, Microscopes, and Living Things, ill. by Anthony Ravielli, Viking, 1955. At least twenty pioneers in biology are discussed in this outstanding account of how our understanding of living things has changed over the centuries. The scientists' own writings are woven into the text.   12–16

SHIPPEN, KATHERINE BINNEY, and ANCA SEIDLOVA, *The Heritage of Music,* ill. by Otto van Eersel, Viking, 1963. This history of the development of Western music concentrates upon major composers and their contributions. A helpful glossary of musical terms is included.   12–16

SHOWERS, PAUL, *Use Your Brain,* ill. by Rosalind Fry, T. Crowell, 1971. A fine introduction, clear and simple. *Where Does the Garbage Go?* ill. by Loretta Lustig, T. Crowell, 1974. Conservation and recycling are seen from the child's point of view.   7–8

SHUTTLESWORTH, DOROTHY, *All Kinds of Bees,* ill. by Su Zan N. Swain, Random, 1967. In this simply written, clearly illustrated book, the author describes the different families of bees and the ways they live.   8–10

Clean Air—Sparkling Water: The Fight Against Pollution, ill., Doubleday, 1968. The author describes the growth of a fictional city to explain the steady increase in water and air pollution. She goes on to describe worldwide problems and control efforts.   8–10

SILVERBERG, ROBERT, *The Auk, the Dodo, and the Oryx: Vanished and Vanishing Creatures,* ill. by Jacques Hnizdovsky, T. Crowell, 1967. A well-written plea for conservation is included in this book which uses eyewitness accounts from persons who saw the animals described in this volume.   11–13

Vanishing Giants; the Story of the Sequoias, ill. with photos, Simon, 1969. This story of the redwoods concludes with an account of the numerous efforts to save the trees through the establishment of national parks.   10–14

SILVERSTEIN, ALVIN, and VIRGINIA B. SILVERSTEIN, *A Star in the Sea,* ill. by Symeon Shimin, Warne, 1969. The dramatic telling of the life cycle of a starfish named Stella, from her hatching in a tidal pool through such dangers as storms and attacks by gulls to her laying her eggs and the beginning of the cycle anew.   6–10

Unusual Partners: Symbiosis in the Living World, ill. by Mel Hunter, McGraw, 1968. An excellent study of a variety of symbiotic relationships which can be related to the study of ecology.   8–10

SIMON, HILDA, *Insect Masquerades,* ill. by author, Viking, 1968. The unusual and wonderful shapes and colors that camouflage some insects are described. The book concludes with a chapter "Nightmare Insects" for which no explanation of natural selection seems adequate.   10–14

Snakes; The Facts and the Folklore, ill. by author, Viking, 1973. Meticulously detailed drawings add to the usefulness of an excellent text.   10–14

SIMON, MINA LEWITON, *Is Anyone Here?* ill. by Howard Simon, Atheneum, 1967. Creative language and excellent illustration are combined with accurate scientific observation of the seaside environment in this picture book for young readers.   5–9

SIMON, SEYMOUR, *The Paper Airplane Book,* ill. by Byron Barton, Viking, 1971. A book that describes the principles of flight as well as giving instructions for making paper airplanes.   8–11

The Rock-Hound's Book, ill. by Tony Chen, Viking, 1973. A fine book for the beginning collector.   9–11

SKURZYNSKI, GLORIA, *Bionic Parts for People: The Real Story of Artificial Organs and Replacement Parts,* ill. by Frank Schwartz, Four Winds, 1978. A thriving medical frontier is explored in a clearly written survey that describes advances and continuing research.   11–up

SOULE, GARDNER, *Mystery Monsters of the Deep,* Watts, 1981. New machines and new technology have disclosed unusual creatures in the ocean community.   11–up

SPENCER, CORNELIA, *Made in Japan,* ill. by Richard M. Powers and with photos, Knopf, 1963. A very readable book about the architecture, the crafts, the visual arts, literature, and music of this country. Includes a section of photographs. See also, *Made in Mexico,* 1952; . . . *Italy,* 1957; . . . *Thailand,* 1964.   12–16

STERLING, DOROTHY, *Caterpillars,* ill. by Winifred Lubell, Doubleday, 1961. A zestful, well-written book about caterpillars—the life cycles of many species, the differences between moths and butterflies, and instructions for keeping caterpillars.   8–10

Forever Free; The Story of the Emancipation Proclamation, ill. by Ernest Crichlow, Doubleday, 1963. A comprehensive, well-written history of slavery in the United States with information on famous as well as little-known fighters for freedom.   12–16

Tear Down the Walls! A History of the American Civil Rights Movement, ill., Doubleday, 1968. Moving episodes from the black's struggle in America for equality. Explores some of the causes of today's anger.   12–up

STEVENS, CARLA, *The Birth of Sunset's Kittens,* photos by Leonard Stevens, W. R. Scott, 1969. Clear photographs show each step of the ever miraculous birth process.   5–8

STEVENS, LEONARD, *The Town That Launders Its Water,* Coward, 1971. An engrossing report on a California town that learned to reclaim sewage-laden water.   11–up

STONE, A. HARRIS, *The Chemistry of a Lemon,* ill. by Peter P. Plasencia, Prentice, 1966. A group of simple experiments leads the young reader to apply methods of scientific research and thinking to discover certain chemical principles for oneself.   8–11

STONE, A. HARRIS, and IRVING LESKOWITZ, *Microbes Are Something Else,* ill. by Peter P. Plasencia, Prentice, 1969. An excellent book of meaningful activities to be conducted with a microscope which will lead one to discover some fascinating facts about microbes.   8–12

SUTTON, ANN and MYRON, *Animals on the Move,* ill. by Paula A. Hutchison, Rand, 1965. Animal migration has always been a fascinating mystery and this book discusses the superstitions, guesses, and scientific information on the subject.   8–10

SWIFT, HILDEGARDE, *North Star Shining,* ill. by Lynd Ward, Morrow, 1947. One of the earlier accounts of black contributions to United States history.   10–14

TAYLOR, THEODORE, *Air Raid—Pearl Harbor! The Story of December 7, 1941,* ill. by W. T. Mars, Crowell, 1971. Well-documented, a vivid account of the events that led up to Pearl Harbor is told from both the Japanese and the American viewpoint.   11–14

TREASE, GEOFFREY, *This Is Your Century,* ill., with photos, maps, and drawings, Harcourt, 1965. Beginning with Queen Victoria's death in 1901 and going through 1964, this fascinating history introduces young people to the events and people who have shaped today's world.   12–16

TRELEASE, ALLEN, *Reconstruction; The Great Experiment,* Harper, 1971. Objective in tone but dramatic in treatment, an outstanding book about the post-Civil War years in the United States.   11–14

TRESSELT, ALVIN, *The Beaver Pond,* ill. by Roger Duvoisin, Lothrop, 1970. The story of the cycle of a beaver colony also gives an introduction to a balanced ecology. Beautiful.   5–8

Hide and Seek Fog, ill. by Roger Duvoisin, Lothrop, 1965.   5–8

White Snow, Bright Snow, ill. by Roger Duvoisin, Lothrop, 1947. The simple and quiet text evokes the feeling of the first snowfall and the landscape, describes people's activities, and concludes with the return of spring. Caldecott Medal.   5–7

TUNIS, EDWIN, *Chipmunks on the Doorstep,* ill. by author, Crowell, 1971. The author's experiences taming chipmunks.   10–up

Colonial Craftsmen and the Beginnings of American Industry, ill. by author, World, 1965. The comprehensive, lucid text and the excellent illustrations make this a very useful book for the study of crafts and industries in the New World.   10–13

Colonial Living, ill. by author, World, 1957. This first-rate reference book provides a detailed look at life in the United States in the seventeenth and eighteenth centuries. See also, *Frontier Living,* 1961.   8–12

Shaw's Fortune: The Picture Story of a Colonial Plantation, ill. by author, World, 1966. Almost everything you read in the text of this book you can find illustrated by the full-page facing picture or the small, well-labeled drawings filling margins and unused portions of the page. An excellent example of a picture book appropriate for all age groups, it covers over 100 years of the Shaw family's living, up to 1752.   9–12

The Young United States, 1783 to 1830, ill. by author, World, 1969. A superb book that captures an overall feeling of these early years, the diversity of views, activities, and people.   10–13

TURNBULL, COLIN M., *The Peoples of Africa,* ill. by Richard M. Powers, World, 1962. An informative survey of the basic tribal cultures of Africa by the Curator of African Ethnology at the American Museum of Natural History.   12–16

Tradition and Change in African Tribal Life, World, 1966. An anthropologist looks at the institutions of tribal life in an effort to see how they meet the needs of people. The survey includes the fishers, desert hunters, forest hunters, and mountain farmers of various parts of Africa.   12–up

UDEN, GRANT, *A Dictionary of Chivalry,* ill. by Pauline Baynes, T. Crowell, 1968. More than a thousand entries, many with detailed illustrations, provide a very thorough picture of the world of knighthood and chivalry.   11–up

UNGERER, TOMI, *Snail, Where Are You?* ill. by author, Harper, 1962. Not a word of text is needed to make the simple point that spiral shape and form are everywhere around us.   5–8

USHINSKY, K., *How a Shirt Grew in the Field,* adapted from the Russian by Marguerita Rudolph, ill. by Yaroslava, McGraw, 1967. When originally written over a hundred years ago, this account of a Russian peasant boy's watching his shirt "grow" from seeds to finished product was an authentic picture of living in the Ukraine before modern machinery and factory-produced textiles. Both adapter and illustrator have Ukrainian connections and have designed this book with loving care for authenticity as well as beauty.   5–7

VALENS, EVANS G., *Wingfin and Topple,* ill. by Clement Hurd, World, 1962. A good read-aloud picture book with lovely illustrations describes the adventures of a flying fish.   4–7

Me and Frumpet: An Adventure with Size and Science, ill. with photos, Dutton, 1958. A boy's play with his model railroad and a pipecleaner man is the vehicle for familiarizing the reader with the kind of reasoning in such scientific concepts as relativity.   7–9

VAN LOON, HENDRIK WILLEM, *The Story of Mankind,* ill. by author, Boni & Liveright, 1926. Newbery Medal.   12–15

VARNER, VELMA, *The Animal Frolic,* ill. by Toba Sojo, Putnam, 1954. A twelfth-century Japanese scroll, showing small animals, can be studied section by section in a modern picture book.   8–12

VLAHOS, OLIVIA, *African Beginnings,* ill. by George Ford, Viking, 1967. Anthropological and archaeological discoveries of Africa's past bring the reader to understand some of the differences between today's Africa and Western society. The author gives a very complete account of the many African tribes and kingdoms that arose before much contact with the West.   12–16

VON HAGEN, VICTOR W., *The Incas; People of the Sun,* ill. by Alberto Beltrán, World, 1961. The story of the Inca Empire is told through the eyes of a fictional young boy, Huamán. The authenticity and vigor of the text and illustrations make this a distinguished book.   12–16

South American Zoo, ill. by Francis Lee Jacques, Messner, 1946. Scientific information supplemented by illustration tells about animal life in different geographic areas of South America. 8–12

VON WARTBURG, URSULA, *The Workshop Book of Knitting*, Atheneum, 1973. Clear directions and a progression of projects from simple to difficult are provided, as well as advice on materials. 10–up

WARREN, RUTH, *The Nile: The Story of Pharaohs, Farmers, and Explorers*, ill. by Victor Lazzaro, McGraw, 1968. A well-written overview of the history and geography of the Nile region from the time of the Pharaohs to the Aswan High Dam. 10–14

WATERS, BARBARA and JOHN, *Salt-Water Aquariums*, ill. by Robert Candy, Holiday, 1967. Detailed guide to setting up a salt-water aquarium, ranging from the simplest type to the very complex. Advice is included on handling small marine animals and performing harmless but instructive experiments with them. 6–up

WATSON, JANE, *Deserts of the World: Future Threat or Promise?* Philomel, 1981. Deserts shift, spreading over more fertile land; Watson discusses the methods scientists propose to alleviate this. 11–14

WEISS, HARVEY, *Pencil, Pen, and Brush*, ill. by author, W. R. Scott, 1961. Instructions in basic drawing techniques combine with illustrative examples from the masters. See also, *Sticks, Spools, and Feathers*, 1962; *Ceramics: from Clay to Kiln*, 1964; *Paint, Brush, and Palette*, 1966; and *Collage and Construction*, 1970. 10–up

Sailing Small Boats, ill. by Peter Barlow, Young Scott, 1967. Brief history of sailing, description of various types of boats, and instructions for building a sailboat. Includes definitions of nautical terms. 10–15

WHITE, ANNE TERRY, *Lost Worlds: Adventures in Archaeology*, Random, 1941. A description of the discovery of four ancient civilizations: Troy and Crete, Egypt, Assyria, and the Mayan Indian of Central America. 13–16

Prehistoric America, ill. by Aldren Watson, Random, 1951. A simple account of prehistoric times told through the discoveries of bones, fossils, and other remains. 9–11

WILLIAMS, GURNEY, *True Escape and Survival Stories*, ill. by Michael Deas, Watts, 1977. The drama of real-life danger makes a series of factual accounts exciting. 10–12

WILLIAMS, SELMA, *Kings, Commoners, and Colonists; Puritan Politics in Old and New England, 1603–1660*, Atheneum, 1974. A fine analysis of Massachusetts politics and England's reaction. 12–up

WINN, MARIE, *The Fisherman Who Needed a Knife*, ill. by John Johnson, Simon & Schuster, 1970. An introduction for young children to the idea of the use of money as a medium of exchange, the concept ramified by a narrative about the cumbersome practice, in early civilization, of swapping. 5–7

WOLF, BERNARD, *Don't Feel Sorry for Paul*, photos by author, Lippincott, 1974. A sympathetic documentary about a severely handicapped child. 8–11

ZIM, HERBERT S., *Blood*, ill. by René Martin, Morrow, 1968. A clear explanation of the composition of the blood and the processes by which the body makes and uses it. Also discussed are blood groups and the uses of vaccines and antitoxins. 8–12

ZIM, HERBERT S., and SONIA BLEEKER, *Life and Death*, ill. by René Martin, Morrow, 1970. A dispassionate survey of aging, death, and funeral practices of other times and places as well as our own. 9–12

ZIM, HERBERT S., and JAMES R. SKELLY, *Hoists, Cranes and Derricks*, ill. by Gary Ruse, Morrow, 1969. In simple language the authors describe these three machines and the work they do. 8–10

ZOLOTOW, CHARLOTTE, *The Storm Book*, ill. by Margaret Bloy Graham, Harper, 1952. The effect of a summer storm on the country, the city, the ocean, and the mountains is shown without being frightening. 4–7

Children's Book Awards

The awards and prizes given in the children's book field by organizations, schools, publishers, and newspapers, in the United States and other countries, have grown to a sizable number. The Newbery and Caldecott Medals and National Book Award for Children's Literature, all given annually, are the best-known United States awards, and the Hans Christian Andersen Medal, given biennially, the best-known international award. The International Reading Association Children's Book Award is the only award that singles out new authors. The National Council of Teachers of English Award for Excellence in Poetry for Children is the first children's book award given solely for poetry. The Laura Ingalls Wilder Award is given every three years in honor of Wilder. The Carnegie and Kate Greenaway Medals are major British awards for children's books, and the Canadian Library Awards are the most significant given in Canada. In most cases, the awards are given for books published during the preceding year. Following are brief histories of these awards and listings of the winners and runners-up.

The Newbery Medal

Frederic G. Melcher, editor of *Publisher's Weekly Magazine*, donated and named this award as a tribute to John Newbery (1713–1767), the first English publisher of books for children. Beginning in 1922 and every year since, the Newbery Medal has been given by an awards committee of the Children's Services Division of the American Library Association to the author of the most distinguished contribution to literature for children published in the United States during the preceding year. The author must be a citizen or resident of the United States.

1922 *The Story of Mankind* by Hendrik Willem van Loon, Liveright
Honor Books: *The Great Quest* by Charles Hawes, Little; *Cedric the Forester* by Bernard Marshall, Appleton; *The Old Tobacco Shop* by William Bowen, Macmillan; *The Golden Fleece and the Heroes Who Lived Before Achilles* by Padraic Colum, Macmillan; *Windy Hill* by Cornelia Meigs, Macmillan

1923 *The Voyages of Doctor Dolittle* by Hugh Lofting, Lippincott
Honor Books: No record

1924 *The Dark Frigate* by Charles Hawes, Atlantic/ Little
Honor Books: No record

1925 *Tales from Silver Lands* by Charles Finger, Doubleday
Honor Books: *Nicholas* by Anne Carroll Moore, Putnam; *Dream Coach* by Anne Parrish, Macmillan

1926 *Shen of the Sea* by Arthur Bowie Chrisman, Dutton
Honor Book: *Voyagers* by Padraic Colum, Macmillan

1927 *Smoky, The Cowhorse* by Will James, Scribner's
Honor Books: No record

1928 *Gayneck, The Story of a Pigeon* by Dhan Gopal Mukerji, Dutton
Honor Books: *The Wonder Smith and His Son* by Ella Young, Longmans; *Downright Dencey* by Caroline Snedeker, Doubleday

1929 *The Trumpeter of Krakow* by Eric P. Kelly, Macmillan
Honor Books: *Pigtail of Ah Lee Ben Loo* by John Bennett, Longmans; *Millions of Cats* by Wanda Gág, Coward; *The Boy Who Was* by Grace Hallock, Dutton; *Clearing Weather* by Cornelia Meigs, Little; *Runaway Papoose* by Grace Moon, Doubleday; *Tod of the Fens* by Elinor Whitney, Macmillan

1930 *Hitty, Her First Hundred Years* by Rachel Field, Macmillan
Honor Books: *Daughter of the Seine* by Jeanette Eaton, Harper; *Pran of Albania* by Elizabeth Miller, Doubleday; *Jumping-Off Place* by Marian Hurd McNeely, Longmans; *Tangle-Coated Horse and Other Tales* by Ella Young, Longmans; *Vaino* by Julia Davis Adams, Dutton; *Little Blacknose* by Hildegarde Swift, Harcourt

1931 *The Cat Who Went to Heaven* by Elizabeth Coatsworth, Macmillan
Honor Books: *Floating Island* by Anne Parrish, Harper; *The Dark Star of Itza* by Alida Malkus, Harcourt; *Queer Person* by Ralph Hubbard, Doubleday; *Mountains are Free* by Julia Davis Adams, Dutton; *Spice and the Devil's Cave* by Agnes Hewes, Knopf; *Meggy Macintosh* by Elizabeth Janet Gray, Doubleday; *Garram the Hunter* by Herbert Best, Doubleday; *Ood-Le-Uk the Wanderer* by Alice Lide and Margaret Johansen, Little

1932 *Waterless Mountain* by Laura Adams Armer, Longmans
Honor Books: *The Fairy Circus* by Dorothy P. Lathrop, Macmillan; *Calico Bush* by Rachel Field, Macmillan; *Boy of the South Seas* by Eunice Tietjens, Coward; *Out of the Flame* by Eloise Lownsbery, Longmans; *Jane's Island* by Marjorie Allee, Houghton; *Truce of the Wolf and Other Tales of Old Italy* by Mary Gould Davis, Harcourt

1933 *Young Fu of the Upper Yangtze* by Elizabeth Foreman Lewis, Winston
Honor Books: *Swift Rivers* by Cornelia Meigs, Little; *The Railroad to Freedom* by Hildegarde Swift, Harcourt; *Children of the Soil* by Nora Burglon, Doubleday

1934 *Invincible Louisa* by Cornelia Meigs, Little
Honor Books: *The Forgotten Daughter* by Caroline Snedeker, Doubleday; *Swords of Steel* by Elsie Singmaster, Houghton; *ABC Bunny* by Wanda Gág, Coward; *Winged Girl of Knossos* by Erik Berry, Appleton; *New Land* by Sarah Schmidt, McBride; *Big Tree of Bunlahy* by Padraic Colum, Macmillan; *Glory of the Seas* by Agnes Hewes, Knopf; *Apprentice of Florence* by Anne Kyle, Houghton

1935 *Dobry* by Monica Shannon, Viking
Honor Books: *Pageant of Chinese History* by Elizabeth Seeger, Longmans; *Davy Crockett* by Constance Rourke, Harcourt; *Day on Skates* by Hilda Van Stockum, Harper

1936 *Caddie Woodlawn* by Carol Brink, Macmillan
Honor Books: *Honk, The Moose* by Phil Stong, Dodd; *The Good Master* by Kate Seredy, Viking; *Young Walter Scott* by Elizabeth Janet Gray, Viking; *All Sail Set* by Armstrong Sperry, Winston

1937 *Roller Skates* by Ruth Sawyer, Viking
Honor Books: *Phebe Fairchild: Her Book* by Lois Lenski, Stokes; *Whistler's Van* by Idwal Jones, Viking; *Golden Basket* by Ludwig Bemelmans, Viking; *Winterbound* by Margery Bianco, Viking; *Audubon* by Constance Rourke, Harcourt; *The Codfish Musket* by Agnes Hewes, Doubleday

1938 *The White Stag* by Kate Seredy, Viking
Honor Books: *Pecos Bill* by James Cloyd Bowman, Little; *Bright Island* by Mabel Robinson, Random; *On the Banks of Plum Creek* by Laura Ingalls Wilder, Harper

1939 *Thimble Summer* by Elizabeth Enright, Rinehart
Honor Books: *Nino* by Valenti Angelo, Viking; *Mr. Popper's Penguins* by Richard and Florence Atwater, Little; *"Hello the Boat!"* by Phyllis Crawford, Holt; *Leader by Destiny: George Washington, Man and Patriot* by Jeanette Eaton, Harcourt; *Penn* by Elizabeth Janet Gray, Viking

1940 *Daniel Boone* by James Daugherty, Viking
Honor Books: *The Singing Tree* by Kate Seredy, Viking; *Runner of the Mountain Tops* by Mabel Robinson, Random; *By the Shores of Silver Lake* by Laura Ingalls Wilder, Harper; *Boy with a Pack* by Stephen W. Meader, Harcourt

1941 *Call It Courage* by Armstrong Sperry, Macmillan
Honor Books: *Blue Willow* by Doris Gates, Viking; *Young Mac of Fort Vancouver* by Mary Jane Carr, T. Crowell; *The Long Winter* by Laura Ingalls Wilder, Harper; *Nansen* by Anna Gertrude Hall, Viking

1942 *The Matchlock Gun* by Walter D. Edmonds, Dodd

Honor Books: *Little Town on the Prairie* by Laura Ingalls Wilder, Harper; *George Washington's World* by Genevieve Foster, Scribner's; *Indian Captive: The Story of Mary Jemison* by Lois Lenski, Lippincott; *Down Ryton Water* by Eva Roe Gaggin, Viking

1943 *Adam of the Road* by Elizabeth Janet Gray, Viking
Honor Books: *The Middle Moffat* by Eleanor Estes, Harcourt; *Have You Seen Tom Thumb?* by Mabel Leigh Hunt, Lippincott

1944 *Johnny Tremain* by Esther Forbes, Houghton
Honor Books: *These Happy Golden Years* by Laura Ingalls Wilder, Harper; *Fog Magic* by Julia Sauer, Viking; *Rufus M.* by Eleanor Estes, Harcourt; *Mountain Born* by Elizabeth Yates, Coward

1945 *Rabbit Hill* by Robert Lawson, Viking
Honor Books: *The Hundred Dresses* by Eleanor Estes, Harcourt; *The Silver Pencil* by Alice Dalgliesh, Scribner's; *Abraham Lincoln's World* by Genevieve Foster, Scribner's; *Lone Journey: The Life of Roger Williams* by Jeanette Eaton, Harcourt

1946 *Strawberry Girl* by Lois Lenski, Lippincott
Honor Books: *Justin Morgan Had a Horse* by Marguerite Henry, Rand; *The Moved-Outers* by Florence Crannell Means, Houghton; *Bhimsa, The Dancing Bear* by Christine Weston, Scribner's; *New Found World* by Katherine Shippen, Viking

1947 *Miss Hickory* by Carolyn Sherwin Bailey, Viking
Honor Books: *Wonderful Year* by Nancy Barnes, Messner; *Big Tree* by Mary and Conrad Buff, Viking; *The Heavenly Tenants* by William Maxwell, Harper; *The Avion My Uncle Flew* by Cyrus Fisher, Appleton; *The Hidden Treasure of Glaston* by Eleanore Jewett, Viking

1948 *The Twenty-one Balloons* by William Pène du Bois, Viking
Honor Books: *Pancakes-Paris* by Claire Huchet Bishop, Viking; *Li Lun, Lad of Courage* by Carolyn Treffinger, Abingdon; *The Quaint and Curious Quest of Johnny Longfoot* by Catherine Besterman, Bobbs; *The Cow-Tail Switch, and Other West African Stories* by Harold Courlander, Holt; *Misty of Chincoteague* by Marguerite Henry, Rand

1949 *King of the Wind* by Marguerite Henry, Rand
Honor Books: *Seabird* by Holling C. Holling, Houghton; *Daughter of the Mountains* by Louise Rankin, Viking; *My Father's Dragon* by Ruth S. Gannett, Random; *Story of the Negro* by Arna Bontemps, Knopf

1950 *The Door in the Wall* by Marguerite de Angeli, Doubleday
Honor Books: *Tree of Freedom* by Rebecca Caudill, Viking; *The Blue Cat of Castle Town* by Catherine Coblentz, Longmans; *Kildee House* by Rutherford Montgomery, Doubleday; *George Washington* by Genevieve Foster, Scribner's; *Song of the Pines* by Walter and Marion Havighurst, Winston

1951 *Amos Fortune, Free Man* by Elizabeth Yates, Aladdin
Honor Books: *Better Known as Johnny Ap-*

pleseed by Mabel Leigh Hunt, Lippincott; *Gandhi, Fighter Without a Sword* by Jeanette Eaton, Morrow; *Abraham Lincoln, Friend of the People* by Clara Ingram Judson, Follett; *The Story of Appleby Capple* by Anne Parrish, Harper

1952 *Ginger Pye* by Eleanor Estes, Harcourt
Honor Books: *Americans Before Columbus* by Elizabeth Baity, Viking; *Minn of the Mississippi* by Holling C. Holling, Houghton; *The Defender* by Nicholas Kalashnikoff, Scribner's; *The Light at Tern Rock* by Julia Sauer, Viking; *The Apple and the Arrow* by Mary and Conrad Buff, Houghton

1953 *Secret of the Andes* by Ann Nolan Clark, Viking
Honor Books: *Charlotte's Web* by E. B. White, Harper; *Moccasin Trail* by Eloise McGraw, Coward; *Red Sails to Capri* by Ann Weil, Viking; *The Bears on Hemlock Mountain* by Alice Dalgliesh, Scribner's; *Birthdays of Freedom*, Vol. 1 by Genevieve Foster, Scribner's

1954 *. . . and now Miguel* by Joseph Krumgold, T. Crowell
Honor Books: *All Alone* by Claire Huchet Bishop, Viking; *Shadrach* by Meindert DeJong, Harper; *Hurry Home Candy* by Meindert DeJong, Harper; *Theodore Roosevelt, Fighting Patriot* by Clara Ingram Judson, Follett; *Magic Maize* by Mary and Conrad Buff, Houghton

1955 *The Wheel on the School* by Meindert DeJong, Harper
Honor Books: *The Courage of Sarah Noble* by Alice Dalgliesh, Scribner's; *Banner in the Sky* by James Ullman, Lippincott

1956 *Carry on, Mr. Bowditch* by Jean Lee Latham, Houghton
Honor Books: *The Secret River* by Marjorie Kinnan Rawlings, Scribner's; *The Golden Name Day* by Jennie Lindquist, Harper; *Men, Microscopes, and Living Things* by Katherine Shippen, Viking

1957 *Miracles on Maple Hill* by Virginia Sorensen, Harcourt
Honor Books: *Old Yeller* by Fred Gipson, Harper; *The House of Sixty Fathers* by Meindert DeJong, Harper; *Mr. Justice Holmes* by Clara Ingram Judson, Follett; *The Corn Grows Ripe* by Dorothy Rhoads, Viking; *Black Fox of Lorne* by Marguerite de Angeli, Doubleday

1958 *Rifles for Watie* by Harold Keith, T. Crowell
Honor Books: *The Horsecatcher* by Mari Sandoz, Westminster; *Gone-Away Lake* by Elizabeth Enright, Harcourt; *The Great Wheel* by Robert Lawson, Viking; *Tom Paine, Freedom's Apostle* by Leo Gurko, T. Crowell

1959 *The Witch of Blackbird Pond* by Elizabeth George Speare, Houghton
Honor Books: *The Family Under the Bridge* by Natalie S. Carlson, Harper; *Along Came a Dog* by Meindert DeJong, Harper; *Chucaro: Wild Pony of the Pampa* by Francis Kalnay, Harcourt; *The Perilous Road* by William O. Steele, Harcourt

1960 *Onion John* by Joseph Krumgold, T. Crowell
Honor Books: *My Side of the Mountain* by Jean George, Dutton; *America Is Born* by Gerald W. Johnson, Morrow; *The Gammage Cup* by Carol

Kendall, Harcourt

1961 *Island of the Blue Dolphins* by Scott O'Dell, Houghton
Honor Books: *America Moves Forward* by Gerald W. Johnson, Morrow; *Old Ramon* by Jack Schaefer, Houghton; *The Cricket in Times Square* by George Selden, Farrar

1962 *The Bronze Bow* by Elizabeth George Speare, Houghton
Honor Books: *Frontier Living* by Edwin Tunis, World; *The Golden Goblet* by Eloise McGraw, Coward; *Belling the Tiger* by Mary Stolz, Harper

1963 *A Wrinkle in Time* by Madeleine L'Engle, Farrar
Honor Books: *Thistle and Thyme* by Sorche Nic Leodhas, Holt; *Men of Athens* by Olivia Coolidge, Houghton

1964 *It's Like This, Cat* by Emily Cheney Neville, Harper
Honor Books: *Rascal* by Sterling North, Dutton; *The Loner* by Ester Wier, McKay

1965 *Shadow of a Bull* by Maia Wojciechowska, Atheneum
Honor Book: *Across Five Aprils* by Irene Hunt, Follett

1966 *I, Juan de Pareja* by Elizabeth Borten de Trevino, Farrar
Honor Books: *The Black Cauldron* by Lloyd Alexander, Holt; *The Animal Family* by Randall Jarrell, Pantheon; *The Noonday Friends* by Mary Stolz, Harper

1967 *Up a Road Slowly* by Irene Hunt, Follett
Honor Books: *The King's Fifth* by Scott O'Dell, Houghton; *Zlateh the Goat and Other Stories* by Isaac Bashevis Singer, Harper; *The Jazz Man* by Mary H. Weik, Atheneum

1968 *From the Mixed-Up Files of Mrs. Basil E. Frankweiler* by E. L. Konigsburg, Atheneum
Honor Books: *Jennifer, Hecate, Macbeth, William McKinley, and Me, Elizabeth* by E. L. Konigsburg, Atheneum; *The Black Pearl* by Scott O'Dell, Houghton; *The Fearsome Inn* by Isaac Bashevis Singer, Scribner's; *The Egypt Game* by Zilpha Keatley Snyder, Atheneum

1969 *The High King* by Lloyd Alexander, Holt
Honor Books: *To Be a Slave* by Julius Lester, Dial; *When Shlemiel Went to Warsaw and Other Stories* by Isaac Bashevis Singer, Farrar

1970 *Sounder* by William H. Armstrong, Harper
Honor Books: *Our Eddie* by Sulamith Ish-Kishor, Pantheon; *The Many Ways of Seeing: An Introduction to the Pleasures of Art* by Janet Gaylord Moore, World; *Journey Outside* by Mary Q. Steele, Viking

1971 *Summer of the Swans* by Betsy Byars, Viking
Honor Books: *Kneeknock Rise* by Natalie Babbitt, Farrar; *Enchantress from the Stars* by Sylvia Louise Engdahl, Atheneum; *Sing Down the Moon* by Scott O'Dell, Houghton

1972 *Mrs. Frisby and the Rats of NIMH* by Robert C. O'Brien, Atheneum
Honor Books: *Incident at Hawk's Hill* by Allan W. Eckert, Little; *The Planet of Junior Brown* by Virginia Hamilton, Macmillan; *The Tombs of Atuan* by Ursula K. Le Guin, Atheneum; *Annie and the Old One* by Miska Miles, Atlantic/Little; *The Headless Cupid* by Zilpha Keatley Snyder, Atheneum

1973 *Julie of the Wolves* by Jean George, Harper
Honor Books: *Frog and Toad Together* by Arnold Lobel, Harper; *The Upstairs Room* by Johanna Reiss, Crowell; *The Witches of Worm* by Zilpha Keatley Snyder, Atheneum

1974 *The Slave Dancer* by Paula Fox, Bradbury
Honor Book: *The Dark Is Rising* by Susan Cooper, Atheneum/McElderry

1975 *M. C. Higgins, the Great* by Virginia Hamilton, Macmillan
Honor Books: *Figgs & Phantoms* by Ellen Raskin, Dutton; *My Brother Sam Is Dead* by James Lincoln Collier & Christopher Collier, Four Winds; *The Perilous Gard* by Elizabeth Marie Pope, Houghton; *Philip Hall Likes Me. I Reckon Maybe* by Bette Greene, Dial

1976 *The Grey King* by Susan Cooper, Atheneum/McElderry
Honor Books: *The Hundred Penny Box* by Sharon Bell Mathis, Viking; *Dragonwings* by Lawrence Yep, Harper

1977 *Roll of Thunder, Hear My Cry* by Mildred D. Taylor, Dial
Honor Books: *Abel's Island* by William Steig, Farrar; *A String in the Harp* by Nancy Bond, McElderry/Atheneum

1978 *Bridge to Terabithia* by Katherine Paterson, Crowell
Honor Books: *Anpao: An American Indian Odyssey* by Jamake Highwater, Lippincott; *Ramona and Her Father* by Beverly Cleary, Morrow

1979 *The Westing Game* by Ellen Raskin, Dutton
Honor Book: *The Great Gilly Hopkins* by Katherine Paterson, Crowell

1980 *A Gathering of Days: A New England Girl's Journal, 1830–32* by Joan Blos, Scribner's
Honor Book: *The Road from Home: The Story of an Armenian Girl* by David Kherdian, Greenwillow

1981 *Jacob Have I Loved* by Katherine Paterson, Crowell
Honor Books: *The Fledgling* by Jane Langton, Harper; *A Ring of Endless Light* by Madeleine L'Engle, Farrar

1982 *A Visit to William Blake's Inn: Poems for Innocent and Experienced Travelers* by Nancy Willard, Harcourt
Honor Books: *Ramona Quimby, Age 8* by Beverly Cleary, Morrow; *Upon the Head of a Goat* by Aranka Siegel, Farrar

1983 *Dicey's Song* by Cynthia Voight, Atheneum
Honor Books: *The Blue Sword* by Robin McKinley, Greenwillow; *Dr. De Soto* by William Steig, Farrar; *Graven Images* by Paul Fleischman, ill. by Andrew Glass, Harper; *Homesick: My Own Story* by Jean Fritz, ill. by Margot Tomes, Putnam; *Sweet Whispers, Brother Rush* by Virginia Hamilton, Philomel

The Caldecott Medal

This award is named in honor of Randolph Caldecott (1846–1886), the English illustrator whose pictures still delight children. In 1937, Frederic G. Melcher, the

American editor and publisher who had conceived the idea of the Newbery Medal some years earlier, proposed the establishment of a similar award for picture books, and since 1938 the Caldecott Medal has been awarded annually by an awards committee of the American Library Association's Children's Services Division to the illustrator of the most distinguished picture book for children published in the United States during the preceding year. The award is limited to residents or citizens of the United States.

In cases where only one name is given, the book was written and illustrated by the same person.

1938　*Animals of the Bible* by Helen Dean Fish, ill. by Dorothy P. Lathrop, Lippincott
　　　Honor Books: *Seven Simeons* by Boris Artzybasheff, Viking; *Four and Twenty Blackbirds* by Helen Dean Fish, ill. by Robert Lawson, Stokes

1939　*Mei Li* by Thomas Handforth, Doubleday
　　　Honor Books: *The Forest Pool* by Laura Adams Armer, Longmans; *Wee Gillis* by Munro Leaf, ill. by Robert Lawson, Viking; *Snow White and the Seven Dwarfs* by Wanda Gág, Coward; *Barkis* by Clare Newberry, Harper; *Andy and the Lion* by James Daugherty, Viking

1940　*Abraham Lincoln* by Ingri and Edgar Parin D'Aulaire, Doubleday
　　　Honor Books: *Cock-A-Doodle Doo . . .* by Berta and Elmer Hader, Macmillan; *Madeline* by Ludwig Bemelmans, Viking; *The Ageless Story*, ill. by Lauren Ford, Dodd

1941　*They Were Strong and Good* by Robert Lawson, Viking
　　　Honor Book: *April's Kittens* by Clare Newberry, Harper

1942　*Make Way for Ducklings* by Robert McCloskey, Viking
　　　Honor Books: *An American ABC* by Maud and Miska Petersham, Macmillan; *In My Mother's House* by Ann Nolan Clark, ill. by Velino Herrera, Viking; *Paddle-to-the-Sea* by Holling C. Holling, Houghton; *Nothing at All* by Wanda Gág, Coward

1943　*The Little House* by Virginia Lee Burton, Houghton
　　　Honor Books: *Dash and Dart* by Mary and Conrad Buff, Viking; *Marshmallow* by Clare Newberry, Harper

1944　*Many Moons* by James Thurber, ill. by Louis Slobodkin, Harcourt
　　　Honor Books: *Small Rain: Verses from the Bible* selected by Jessie Orton Jones, ill. by Elizabeth Orton Jones. Viking; *Pierre Pigeon* by Lee Kingman, ill. by Arnold E. Bare, Houghton; *The Mighty Hunter* by Berta and Elmer Hader, Macmillan; *A Child's Good Night Book* by Margaret Wise Brown, ill. by Jean Charlot, W. R. Scott; *Good Luck Horse* by Chih-Yi Chan, ill. by Plao Chan, Whittlesey

1945　*Prayer for a Child* by Rachel Field, ill. by Elizabeth Orton Jones, Macmillan
　　　Honor Books: *Mother Goose* ill. by Tasha Tudor, Walck; *In the Forest* by Marie Hall Ets, Viking; *Yonie Wondernose* by Marguerite de Angeli, Doubleday; *The Christmas Anna Angel* by Ruth Sawyer, ill. by Kate Seredy, Viking

1946　*The Rooster Crows . . .* (traditional Mother Goose) ill. by Maud and Miska Petersham, Macmillan
　　　Honor Books: *Little Lost Lamb* by Golden MacDonald, ill. by Leonard Weisgard, Doubleday; *Sing Mother Goose* by Opal Wheeler, ill. by Marjorie Torrey, Dutton; *My Mother Is the Most Beautiful Woman in the World* by Becky Reyher, ill. by Ruth Gannett, Lothrop; *You Can Write Chinese* by Kurt Wiese, Viking

1947　*The Little Island* by Golden MacDonald, ill. by Leonard Weisgard, Doubleday
　　　Honor Books: *Rain Drop Splash* by Alvin Tresselt, ill. by Leonard Weisgard, Lothrop; *Boats on the River* by Marjorie Flack, ill. by Jay Hyde Barnum, Viking; *Timothy Turtle* by Al Graham, ill. by Tony Palazzo, Viking; *Pedro, the Angel of Olvera Street* by Leo Politi, Scribner's; *Sing in Praise: A Collection of the Best Loved Hymns* by Opal Wheeler, ill. by Marjorie Torrey, Dutton

1948　*White Snow, Bright Snow* by Alvin Tresselt, ill. by Roger Duvoisin, Lothrop
　　　Honor Books: *Stone Soup* by Marcia Brown, Scribner's; *McElligot's Pool* by Dr. Seuss, Random; *Bambino the Clown* by George Schreiber, Viking; *Roger and the Fox* by Lavinia Davis, ill. by Hildegard Woodward, Doubleday; *Song of Robin Hood* ed. by Anne Malcolmson, ill. by Virginia Lee Burton, Houghton

1949　*The Big Snow* by Berta and Elmer Hader, Macmillan
　　　Honor Books: *Blueberries for Sal* by Robert McCloskey, Viking; *All Around the Town* by Phyllis McGinley, ill. by Helen Stone, Lippincott; *Juanita* by Leo Politi, Scribner's; *Fish in the Air* by Kurt Wiese, Viking

1950　*Song of the Swallows* by Leo Politi, Scribner's
　　　Honor Books: *America's Ethan Allen* by Stewart Holbrook, ill. by Lynd Ward, Houghton; *The Wild Birthday Cake* by Lavinia Davis, ill. by Hildegard Woodward, Doubleday; *The Happy Day* by Ruth Krauss, ill. by Marc Simont, Harper; *Bartholomew and the Oobleck* by Dr. Seuss, Random; *Henry Fisherman* by Marcia Brown, Scribner's

1951　*The Egg Tree* by Katherine Milhous, Scribner's
　　　Honor Books: *Dick Whittington and His Cat* by Marcia Brown, Scribner's; *The Two Reds* by William Lipkind, ill. by Nicholas Mordvinoff, Harcourt; *If I Ran the Zoo* by Dr. Seuss, Random; *The Most Wonderful Doll in the World* by Phyllis McGinley, ill. by Helen Stone, Lippincott; *T-Bone, the Baby Sitter* by Clare Newberry, Harper

1952　*Finders Keepers* by William Lipkind, ill. by Nicholas Mordvinoff, Harcourt
　　　Honor Books: *Mr. T. W. Anthony Woo* by Marie Hall Ets, Viking; *Skipper John's Cook* by Marcia Brown, Scribner's; *All Falling Down* by Gene Zion, ill. by Margaret Bloy Graham, Harper; *Bear Party* by William Pène du Bois, Viking; *Feather Mountain* by Elizabeth Olds, Houghton

1953　*The Biggest Bear* by Lynd Ward, Houghton
　　　Honor Books: *Puss in Boots* by Charles Perrault, ill. and tr. by Marcia Brown, Scribner's; *One Morning in Maine* by Robert McCloskey, Viking; *Ape in a Cape* by Fritz Eichenberg, Harcourt; *The Storm Book* by Charlotte Zolotow, ill. by

Margaret Bloy Graham, Harper; *Five Little Monkeys* by Juliet Kepes, Houghton

1954 *Madeline's Rescue* by Ludwig Bemelmans, Viking
Honor Books: *Journey Cake, Ho!* by Ruth Sawyer, ill. by Robert McCloskey, Viking; *When Will the World Be Mine?* by Miriam Schlein, ill. by Jean Charlot, W. R. Scott; *The Steadfast Tin Solider* by Hans Christian Andersen, ill. by Marcia Brown, Scribner's; *A Very Special House* by Ruth Krauss, ill. by Maurice Sendak, Harper; *Green Eyes* by A. Birnbaum, Capitol

1955 *Cinderella, or the Little Glass Slipper* by Charles Perrault, tr. and ill. by Marcia Brown, Scribner's
Honor Books: *Book of Nursery and Mother Goose Rhymes,* ill. by Marguerite de Angeli, Doubleday; *Wheel on the Chimney* by Margaret Wise Brown, ill. by Tibor Gergely, Lippincott; *The Thanksgiving Story* by Alice Dalgliesh, ill. by Helen Sewell, Scribner's

1956 *Frog Went A-Courtin'* ed. by John Langstaff, ill. by Feodor Rojankovsky, Harcourt
Honor Books: *Play with Me* by Marie Hall Ets, Viking; *Crow Boy* by Taro Yashima, Viking

1957 *A Tree Is Nice* by Janice May Udry, ill. by Marc Simont, Harper
Honor Books: *Mr. Penny's Race Horse* by Marie Hall Ets, Viking; *1 Is One* by Tasha Tudor, Walck; *Anatole* by Eve Titus, ill. by Paul Galdone, McGraw; *Gillespie and the Guards* by Benjamin Elkin, ill. by James Daugherty, Viking; *Lion* by William Pène du Bois, Viking

1958 *Time of Wonder* by Robert McCloskey, Viking
Honor Books: *Fly High, Fly Low* by Don Freeman, Viking; *Anatole and the Cat* by Eve Titus, ill. by Paul Galdone, McGraw

1959 *Chanticleer and the Fox* adapted from Chaucer and ill. by Barbara Cooney, T. Crowell
Honor Books: *The House That Jack Built* by Antonio Frasconi, Harcourt; *What Do You Say, Dear?* by Sesyle Joslin, ill. by Maurice Sendak, W. R. Scott; *Umbrella* by Taro Yashima, Viking

1960 *Nine Days to Christmas* by Marie Hall Ets and Aurora Labastida, ill. by Marie Hall Ets, Viking
Honor Books: *Houses from the Sea* by Alice E. Goudey, ill. by Adrienne Adams, Scribner's; *The Moon Jumpers* by Janice May Udry, ill. by Maurice Sendak, Harper

1961 *Baboushka and the Three Kings* by Ruth Robbins, ill. by Nicolas Sidjakov, Parnassus
Honor Book: *Inch by Inch* by Leo Lionni, Obolensky

1962 *Once a Mouse . . .* by Marcia Brown, Scribner's
Honor Books: *The Fox Went Out on a Chilly Night* by Peter Spier, Doubleday; *Little Bear's Visit* by Else Holmelund Minarik, ill. by Maurice Sendak, Harper; *The Day We Saw the Sun Come Up* by Alice E. Goudey, ill. by Adrienne Adams, Scribner's

1963 *The Snowy Day* by Ezra Jack Keats, Viking
Honor Books: *The Sun Is a Golden Earring* by Natalia M. Belting, ill. by Bernarda Bryson, Holt; *Mr. Rabbit and the Lovely Present* by Charlotte Zolotow, ill. by Maurice Sendak, Harper

1964 *Where the Wild Things Are* by Maurice Sendak, Harper
Honor Books: *Swimmy* by Leo Lionni, Pantheon; *All in the Morning Early* by Sorche Nic Leodhas, ill. by Evaline Ness, Holt; *Mother Goose and Nursery Rhymes,* ill. by Philip Reed, Atheneum

1965 *May I Bring a Friend?* by Beatrice Schenk de Regniers, ill. by Beni Montresor, Atheneum
Honor Books: *Rain Makes Applesauce* by Julian Scheer, ill. by Marvin Bileck, Holiday; *The Wave* by Margaret Hodges, ill. by Blair Lent, Houghton; *A Pocketful of Cricket* by Rebecca Caudill, ill. by Evaline Ness, Holt

1966 *Always Room for One More* by Sorche Nic Leodhas, ill. by Nonny Hogrogian, Holt
Honor Books: *Hide and Seek Fog* by Alvin Tresselt, ill. by Roger Duvoisin, Lothrop; *Just Me* by Marie Hall Ets, Viking; *Tom Tit Tot* by Evaline Ness, Scribner's

1967 *Sam, Bangs & Moonshine* by Evaline Ness, Holt
Honor Book: *One Wide River to Cross* by Barbara Emberley, ill. by Ed Emberley, Prentice

1968 *Drummer Hoff* by Barbara Emberley, ill. by Ed Emberley, Prentice
Honor Books: *Frederick* by Leo Lionni, Pantheon; *Seashore Story* by Taro Yashima, Viking; *The Emperor and the Kite* by Jane Yolen, ill. by Ed Young, World

1969 *The Fool of the World and the Flying Ship* by Arthur Ransome, ill. by Uri Shulevitz, Farrar
Honor Book: *Why the Sun and the Moon Live in the Sky* by Elphinstone Dayrell, ill. by Blair Lent, Houghton

1970 *Sylvester and the Magic Pebble* by William Steig, Windmill
Honor Books: *Goggles!* by Ezra Jack Keats, Macmillan; *Alexander and the Wind-Up Mouse* by Leo Lionni, Pantheon; *Pop Corn & Ma Goodness* by Edna Mitchell Preston, ill. by Robert Andrew Parker, Viking; *Thy Friend, Obadiah* by Brinton Turkle, Viking; *The Judge* by Harve Zemach, ill. by Margot Zemach, Farrar

1971 *A Story—A Story* by Gail E. Haley, Atheneum
Honor Books: *The Angry Moon* by William Sleator, ill. by Blair Lent, Atlantic/Little; *Frog and Toad Are Friends* by Arnold Lobel, Harper; *In the Night Kitchen* by Maurice Sendak, Harper

1972 *One Fine Day* by Nonny Hogrogian, Macmillan
Honor Books: *If All the Seas Were One Sea* by Janina Domanska, Macmillan; *Moja Means One: Swahili Counting Book* by Muriel Feelings, ill. by Tom Feelings, Dial; *Hildilid's Night* by Cheli Duran Ryan, ill. by Arnold Lobel, Macmillan

1973 *The Funny Little Woman* retold by Arlene Mosel, ill. by Blair Lent, Dutton
Honor Books: *Anansi the Spider* adapted and ill. by Gerald McDermott, Holt; *Hosie's Alphabet* by Hosea, Tobias and Lisa Baskin, ill. by Leonard Baskin, Viking; *Snow-White and the Seven Dwarfs* translated by Randall Jarrell, ill. by Nancy Ekholm Burkert, Farrar; *When Clay Sings* by Byrd Baylor, ill. by Tom Bahti, Scribner's

1974 *Duffy and the Devil* by Harve Zemach, ill. by Margot Zemach, Farrar
Honor Books: *Three Jovial Huntsmen* by Susan Jeffers, Bradbury; *Cathedral: The Story of Its Construction* by David Macaulay, Houghton

1975 *Arrow to the Sun* adapted and ill. by Gerald

McDermott, Viking
Honor Book: *Jambo Means Hello* by Muriel Feelings, ill. by Tom Feelings, Dial

1976   *Why Mosquitoes Buzz in People's Ears* retold by Verna Aardema, ill. by Leo and Diane Dillon, Dial
Honor Books: *The Desert Is Theirs* by Byrd Baylor, ill. by Peter Parnall, Scribner's; *Strega Nona* retold and ill. by Tomie de Paola, Prentice

1977   *Ashanti to Zulu: African Traditions* by Margaret Musgrove, ill. by Leo and Diane Dillon, Dial
Honor Books: *The Amazing Bone* by William Steig, Farrar; *The Contest* retold & ill. by Nonny Hogrogian, Greenwillow; *Fish for Supper* by M. B. Goffstein, Dial; *The Golem* by Beverly Brodsky McDermott, Lippincott; *Hawk, I'm Your Brother* by Byrd Baylor, ill. by Peter Parnall, Scribner's

1978   *Noah's Ark* ill. by Peter Spier, Doubleday
Honor Books: *Castle* by David Macaulay, Houghton; *It Could Always Be Worse* retold & ill. by Margot Zemach, Farrar

1979   *The Girl Who Loved Wild Horses* by Paul Goble, Bradbury
Honor Books: *Freight Train* by Donald Crews, Greenwillow; *The Way to Start a Day* by Byrd Baylor, ill. by Peter Parnal, Scribner's

1980   *Ox-Cart Man* by Donald Hall, ill. by Barbara Cooney, Viking
Honor Books: *Ben's Trumpet* by Rachel Isadora, Greenwillow; *The Garden of Abdul Gasazi* by Chris Van Allsburg, Houghton

1981   *Fables* by Arnold Lobel, Harper
Honor Books: *The Bremen-Town Musicians* by Ilse Plume, Doubleday; *The Grey Lady and the Strawberry Snatcher* by Molly Bang, Four Winds; *Mice Twice* by Joseph Low, McElderry/Atheneum; *Truck* by Donald Crews, Greenwillow

1982   *Jumanji* by Chris Van Allsburg, Houghton
Honor Books: *Where the Buffaloes Begin* by Olaf Baker, ill. by Stephen Gammell, Warne; *On Market Street* by Arnold Lobel, ill. by Anita Lobel, Greenwillow; *Outside Over There* by Maurice Sendak, Harper; *A Visit to William Blake's Inn* by Nancy Willard, Harcourt

1983   *Shadow* by Blaise Cendrars, trans. and ill. by Marcia Brown, Scribner's
Honor Books: *When I Was Young in the Mountains* by Cynthia Rylant, ill. by Diane Goode, Dutton; *A Chair for My Mother* by Vera B. Williams, Greenwillow

The Laura Ingalls Wilder Award

This prize, administered by the Association for Library Service to Children, was first awarded in 1954. Since 1960 it has been given every five years to an author or illustrator whose books, published in the United States, have made a substantial and lasting contribution to children's literature. It is now given every three years.

1954   Laura Ingalls Wilder
1960   Clara Ingram Judson
1965   Ruth Sawyer
1970   E. B. White
1975   Beverly Cleary
1980   Theodor Geisel (Dr. Seuss)
1983   Maurice Sendak

The National Book Award

In March 1969, the National Book Awards included for the first time in its twenty-year history a prize for Children's Literature. The $1000 prize, contributed by the Children's Book Council and administered by the National Book Committee, is presented annually to a juvenile title that a panel of judges considers the most distinguished written by an American citizen and published in the United States in the preceding year.

1969   *Journey from Peppermint Street* by Meindert DeJong, Harper
1970   *A Day of Pleasure: Stories of a Boy Growing Up in Warsaw* by Isaac Bashevis Singer, Farrar
1971   *The Marvelous Misadventures of Sebastian* by Lloyd Alexander, Dutton
1972   *The Slightly Irregular Fire Engine* by Donald Barthelme, Farrar
1973   *The Farthest Shore* by Ursula K. Le Guin, Atheneum
1974   *The Court of the Stone Children* by Eleanor Cameron, Dutton
1975   *M. C. Higgins, The Great* by Virginia Hamilton, Macmillan
1976   *Bert Breen's Barn* by Walter D. Edmonds, Little
1977   *The Master Puppeteer* by Katherine Paterson, Crowell
1978   *The View from the Oak* by Judith and Herbert Kohl, Sierra Club/Scribner's
1979   *The Great Gilly Hopkins* by Katherine Paterson, Crowell

(This award was discontinued in 1979 and replaced by the American Book Award)

The American Book Award

1980   Hardcover: *A Gathering of Days: A New England Girl's Journal, 1830–32* by Joan W. Blos, Scribner's
Paperback: *A Swiftly Tilting Planet* by Madeleine L'Engle, Dell

1981   Fiction:
Hardcover: *The Night Swimmers* by Betsy Byars, Delacorte
Paperback: *Ramona and Her Mother* by Beverly Cleary, Dell
Nonfiction: *Oh, Boy! Babies!* by Alison Cragin Herzig and Jane Lawrence Mali, Little

1982   Fiction:
Hardcover: *Westmark* by Lloyd Alexander, Dutton
Paperback: *Words by Heart* by Ouida Sebestyen, Bantam
Nonfiction: *A Penguin Year* by Susan Bonners, Delacorte
Picture Books:
Hardcover: *Outside Over There* by Maurice Sendak, Harper
Paperback: *Noah's Ark* by Peter Spier, Zephyr Books/Doubleday

International Reading Association Children's Book Award

Given for the first time in 1975, this award is presented annually for a book, published in the preceding year, written by an author "who shows unusual promise in the children's book field." Sponsored by the Institute for Reading Research, the award is administered by the International Reading Association.

1975 *Transport 7-41-R* by T. Degens, Viking
1976 *Dragonwings* by Laurence Yep, Harper
1977 *A String in the Harp* by Nancy Bond, McElderry/Atheneum
1978 *A Summer to Die* by Lois Lowry, Houghton
1979 *Reserved for Mark Anthony Crowder* by Alison Smith, Dutton
1980 *Words by Heart* by Ouida Sebestyen, Atlantic/Little
1981 *My Own Private Sky* by Delores Beckman, Dutton
1982 *Good Night, Mr. Tom* by Michelle Magorian, Kestrel/Penguin (Great Britain); Harper (U.S.A.)

National Council of Teachers of English Award for Excellence in Poetry for Children

First presented in the fall of 1977 by the National Council of Teachers of English, the award is given to a living American poet in recognition of his or her aggregate work.

1977 David McCord
1978 Aileen Fisher
1979 Karla Kuskin
1980 Myra Cohn Livingston
1981 Eve Merriam
1982 John Ciardi

The Carnegie Medal

The Carnegie Medal, established in 1937, is awarded annually by the British Library Association to an outstanding children's book written in English and first published in the United Kingdom.

1936 *Pigeon Post* by Arthur Ransome, Cape
1937 *The Family from One End Street* by Eve Garnett, Muller
1938 *The Circus Is Coming* by Noel Streatfeild, Dent
1939 *Radium Woman* by Eleanor Doorly, Heinemann
1940 *Visitors from London* by Kitty Barne, Dent
1941 *We Couldn't Leave Dinah* by Mary Treadgold, Penguin
1942 *The Little Grey Men,* by B. B., Eyre & Spottiswoode
1943 No Award
1944 *The Wind on the Moon* by Eric Linklater, Macmillan
1945 No Award
1946 *The Little White Horse* by Elizabeth Goudge, Brockhampton Press

1947 *Collected Stories for Children* by Walter de la Mare, Faber
1948 *Sea Change* by Richard Armstrong, Dent
1949 *The Story of Your Home* by Agnes Allen, Transatlantic
1950 *The Lark on the Wing* by Elfrida Vipont Foulds, Oxford
1951 *The Wool-Pack* by Cynthia Harnett, Methuen
1952 *The Borrowers* by Mary Norton, Dent
1953 *A Valley Grows Up* by Edward Osmond, Oxford
1954 *Knight Crusader* by Ronald Welch, Oxford
1955 *The Little Bookroom* by Eleanor Farjeon, Oxford
1956 *The Last Battle* by C. S. Lewis, Bodley Head
1957 *A Grass Rope* by William Mayne, Oxford
1958 *Tom's Midnight Garden* by Philippa Pearce, Oxford
1959 *The Lantern Bearers* by Rosemary Sutcliff, Oxford
1960 *The Making of Man* by I. W. Cornwall, Phoenix
1961 *A Stranger at Green Knowe* by Lucy Boston, Faber
1962 *The Twelve and the Genii* by Pauline Clarke, Faber
1963 *Time of Trial* by Hester Burton, Oxford
1964 *Nordy Banks* by Sheena Porter, Oxford
1965 *The Grange at High Force* by Philip Turner, Oxford
1966 No Award
1967 *The Owl Service* by Alan Garner, Collins
1968 *The Moon in the Cloud* by Rosemary Harris, Faber
1969 *The Edge of the Cloud* by K. M. Peyton, Oxford
1970 *The God Beneath the Sea* by Leon Garfield and Edward Blishen, Kestrel
1971 *Josh* by Ivan Southall, Angus & Robertson
1972 *Watership Down* by Richard Adams, Rex Collings
1973 *The Ghost of Thomas Kempe* by Penelope Lively, Heinemann
1974 *The Stronghold* by Mollie Hunter, Hamilton
1975 *The Machine-Gunners* by Robert Westall, Macmillan
1976 *Thunder and Lightnings* by Jan Mark, Kestrel
1977 *The Turbulent Term of Tyke Tiler* by Gene Kemp, Faber
1978 *The Exeter Blitz* by David Rees, Hamish Hamilton
1979 *Tulku* by Peter Dickinson, Gollancz
1980 *City of Gold* by Peter Dickinson, Gollancz
1981 *The Scarecrows* by Robert Westall, Chatto & Windus

The Kate Greenaway Medal

This medal is awarded each year by the British Library Association for the most distinguished work in illustration of a children's book first published in the United Kingdom during the preceding year.

In cases where only one name is given, the book was written and illustrated by the same person.

1956 *Tim All Alone* by Edward Ardizzone, Oxford
1957 *Mrs. Easter and the Storks* by V. H. Drummond, Faber
1958 No Award

1959 *Kashtanka and a Bundle of Ballads* by William Stobbs, Oxford
1960 *Old Winkle and the Seagulls* by Elizabeth Rose, ill. by Gerald Rose, Faber
1961 *Mrs. Cockle's Cat* by Philippa Pearce, ill. by Antony Maitland, Kestrel
1962 *Brian Wildsmith's ABC* by Brian Wildsmith, Oxford
1963 *Borka* by John Burningham, Cape
1964 *Shakespeare's Theatre* by C. W. Hodges, Oxford
1965 *Three Poor Tailors* by Victor Ambrus, Hamilton
1966 *Mother Goose Treasury* by Raymond Briggs, Hamilton
1967 *Charlie, Charlotte & the Golden Canary* by Charles Keeping, Oxford
1968 *Dictionary of Chivalry* by Grant Uden, ill. by Pauline Baynes, Kestrel
1969 *The Quangle-Wangle's Hat* by Edward Lear, ill. by Helen Oxenbury, Heinemann; *Dragon of an Ordinary Family* by Margaret May Mahy, ill. by Helen Oxenbury, Heinemann
1970 *Mr. Gumpy's Outing* by John Burningham, Cape
1971 *The Kingdom Under the Sea* by Jan Pienkowski, Cape
1972 *The Woodcutter's Duck* by Krystyna Turska, Hamilton
1973 *Father Christmas* by Raymond Briggs, Hamilton
1974 *The Wind Blew* by Pat Hutchins, Bodley Head
1975 *Horses in Battle* by Victor Ambrus, Oxford; *Mishka* by Victor Ambrus, Oxford
1976 *The Post Office Cat* by Gail E. Haley, Bodley Head
1977 *Dogger* by Shirley Hughes, Bodley Head
1978 *Each Peach Pear Plum* by Janet and Allan Ahlberg, Kestrel
1979 *The Haunted House* by Jan Piénkowski, Heinemann
1980 *Mr. Magnolia* by Quentin Blake, Cape
1981 *The Highwayman* by Charles Keeping, Oxford

The Canadian Library Awards

This award, first presented in June 1947, was established by the Canadian Library Association. It is given annually to a children's book of outstanding literary merit, written by a Canadian citizen. Since 1954 a similar medal has also been awarded yearly to an outstanding children's book published in French.

1947 *Starbuck Valley Winter* by Roderick Haig-Brown, Collins
1948 *Kristli's Trees* by Mabel Dunham, Hale
1949 No Award
1950 *Franklin of the Arctic* by Richard S. Lambert, McClelland & Stewart
1951 No Award
1952 *The Sun Horse* by Catherine Anthony Clark, Macmillan of Canada
1953 No Award
1954 No English Award *Mgr. de Laval* by Emile S. J. Gervais, Comité des Fondateurs de l'Eglise Canadienne
1955 No Awards
1956 *Train for Tiger Lily* by Louise Riley, Macmillan of Canada

No French Award
1957 *Glooskap's Country* by Cyrus MacMillan, Oxford
No French Award
1958 *Lost in the Barrens* by Farley Mowat, Little *Le Chevalier du Roi* by Béatrice Clément, Les Editions de l'Atelier
1959 *The Dangerous Cove* by John F. Hayes, Copp Clark *Un Drôle de Petit Cheval* by Hélène Flamme, Editions Lémèac
1960 *The Golden Phoenix* by Marius Barbeau and Michael Hornyansky, Walck *L'Eté Enchanté* by Paule Daveluy, Les Editions de l'Atelier
1961 *The St. Lawrence* by William Toye, Oxford *Plantes Vagabondes* by Marcelle Gauvreau, Centre de Psychologie et de Pédagogie
1962 No English Award *Les Iles du Roi Maha Maha II* by Claude Aubry, Les Editions du Pélican
1963 *The Incredible Journey* by Sheila Burnford, Little *Drôle d'Automne* by Paule Daveluy, Les Editions du Pélican
1964 *The Whale People* by Roderick Haig-Brown, William Collins of Canada *Feerie* by Cécile Chabot, Librairie Beauchemin Ltée.
1965 *Tales of Nanabozho* by Dorothy Reid, Oxford *Le Loup de Noël* by Claude Aubry, Centre de Psychologie de Montréal
1966 *Tikta'Liktak* by James Houston, Kestrel *Le Chêne des Tempêtes* by Andrée Maillet-Hobden, Fides *The Double Knights* by James McNeal, Walck *Le Wapiti* by Monique Corriveau, Jeunesse
1967 *Raven's Cry* by Christie Harris, McClelland & Stewart
No French Award
1968 *The White Archer* by James Houston, Kestrel *Légendes Indiennes du Canada* by Claude Mélancon, Editions du Jour
1969 *And Tomorrow the Stars* by Kay Hill, Dodd
No French Award
1970 *Sally Go Round the Sun* by Edith Fowke, McClelland & Stewart *Le Merveilleuse Histoire de la Naissance* by Lionel Gendron, Les Editions de l'Homme
1971 *Cartier Discovers the St. Lawrence* by William Toye, Oxford University *La Surprise de Dame Chenille* by Henriette Major, Centre de Psychologie de Montréal
1972 *Mary of Mile 18* by Ann Blades, Tundra
No French Award
1973 *The Marrow of the World* by Ruth Nichols, Macmillan of Canada *Le Petit Sapin Qui A Poussé Sur Une Étoile* by Simone Bussières, Presses Laurentiennes
1974 *The Miraculous Hind* by Elizabeth Cleaver, Holt of Canada
No French Award
1975 *Alligator Pie* by Dennis Lee, Macmillan of Canada
No French Award
1976 *Jacob Two-Two Meets the Hooded Fang* by Mordecai Richler, Knopf

1977 *Mouse Woman and the Vanished Princesses* by
    Christie Harris, McClelland & Stewart
    No French Award
1978 *Garbage Delight* by Dennis Lee, Macmillan
    No French Award
1979 *Hold Fast* by Kevin Major, Clarke, Irwin
    No French Award
1980 *River Runners* by James Houston, McClelland &
    Stewart
1981 *The Violin Maker's Gift* by Donn Kushner, Mac-
    millan of Canada
1982 *The Root Cellar* by Janet Lunn, Lester & Orpen
    Dennys

No French Award

The Canadian Library Association has awarded the
Amelia Frances Howard-Gibbon Medal annually since
1971 for outstanding illustrations in a children's book
published in Canada. The illustrator must be a native or
resident of Canada.

1971 *The Wind Has Wings,* ed. by Mary Alice Downie
    and Barbara Robertson, ill. by Elizabeth Cleaver,
    Oxford
1972 *A Child in Prison Camp* by Shizuye Takashima,
    Tundra
1973 *Au Dela du Soleil/Beyond the Sun* by Jacques de
    Roussan, Tundra
1974 *A Prairie Boy's Winter* by William Kurelek, Tun-
    dra
1975 *The Sleighs of My Childhood/Les Traineaux de
    Mon Enfance* by Carlos Italiano, Tundra
1976 *A Prairie Boy's Summer* by William Kurelek,
    Tundra
1977 *Down by Jim Long's Stage: Rhymes for Children
    and Young Fish* by Al Pittman, ill. by Pam Hall,
    Breakwater
1978 *The Loon's Necklace* by William Toye, ill. by
    Elizabeth Cleaver, Oxford
1979 *A Salmon for Simon* by Betty Waterton, ill. by
    Ann Blades, Douglas & McIntyre
1980 *The Twelve Dancing Princesses,* retold by Janet
    Lunn, ill. by Laszlo Gal, Methuen

1981 *The Trouble with Princesses* by Douglas Tait,
    McClelland & Stewart
1982 *Ytek and the Arctic Orchid: An Inuit Legend* by
    Heather Woodall, Vanguard

The Hans Christian Andersen Award

This award was established in 1956 by the International
Board on Books for Young People and is given every two
years to one living author who, by his or her complete
work, has made an important international contribution
to children's literature. Since 1966 an artist's medal has
also been given. Each national section of the International Board proposes one author and one illustrator as
nominees and the final choice is made by a committee
of five, each from a different country.

1956 Eleanor Farjeon (Great Britain)
1958 Astrid Lindgren (Sweden)
1960 Erich Kästner (Germany)
1962 Meindert DeJong (U.S.A.)
1964 René Guillot (France)
1966 Author: Tove Jansson (Finland)
    Illustrator: Alois Carigiet (Switzerland)
1968 Authors: James Krüss (Germany) Jose Maria
    Sanchez-Silva (Spain)
    Illustrator: Jiri Trnka (Czechoslovakia)
1970 Author: Gianni Rodari (Italy)
    Illustrator: Maurice Sendak (U.S.A.)
1972 Author: Scott O'Dell (U.S.A.)
    Illustrator: Ib Spang Olsen (Denmark)
1974 Author: Maria Gripe (Sweden)
    Illustrator: Farshid Mesghali (Iran)
1976 Author: Cecil Bødker (Denmark)
    Illustrator: Tatjana Mawrina (U.S.S.R.)
1978 Author: Paula Fox (U.S.A.)
    Illustrator: Otto S. Svend (Denmark)
1980 Author: Bohumil Riha (Czechoslovakia)
    Illustrator: Suekichi Akaba (Japan)
1982 Author: Lygia Bojunga Nunes (Brazil)
    Illustrator: Zbigniew Rychlicki (Poland)

Publishers and Publishers' Addresses

ABELARD. Abelard-Schuman, Ltd. See Harper & Row,
    Publishers, Inc.
ABINGDON. Abingdon Press, 201 Eighth Ave. S., Nash-
    ville, TN 37202
ABRAMS. Harry N. Abrams, Inc., 110 E. 59th St., New
    York, NY 10022
ADDISON. Addison-Wesley Pub. Co., Inc., Reading, MA
    01867
ALA. American Library Association Pub. Dept., 50 E.
    Huron St., Chicago, IL 60611

ALDINE. Aldine Pub. Co., 200 Saw Mill River Rd., Haw-
    thorne, NY 10532
AM. ASSOC. FOR THE ADVANCEMENT OF SCIENCE. 1515
    Massachusetts Ave., NW, Washington, DC 20005
AM. COUNCIL ON EDUCATION. One Dupont Circle, NW,
    Washington, DC 20036
APPLETON. Appleton-Century-Crofts, 25 Van Zant St.,
    East Norwalk, CT 06855
ARIEL. Ariel Books. See Simon & Schuster
ATHENEUM. Atheneum Pubs., 597 Fifth Ave., New York,

NY 10017

ATHERTON. Lieber-Atherton, Inc., 1841 Broadway, New York, NY 10023

ATLANTIC. Atlantic Monthly Press. See Little, Brown & Co.

BALLANTINE. Ballantine Books, Inc., 201 E. 50th St., New York, NY 10022

BARNES. Barnes & Noble Books, 10 E. 53rd St., New York, NY 10022

BASIC. Basic Books, Inc., 10 E. 53rd St., New York, NY 10022

BEHRMAN. Behrman House, Inc., 1261 Broadway, New York, NY 10001

BOBBS. Bobbs-Merrill Co., Inc., 4300 W. 62nd St., Indianapolis, IN 46206

BOWKER. R. R. Bowker & Co., 1180 Avenue of the Americas, New York, NY 10036

BRADBURY. Bradbury Press, Inc., 2 Overhill Rd., Scarsdale, NY 10583

BRODART. Brodart, Inc., 500 Arch St., Williamsport, PA 17705

BROWN. William C Brown Group, 2460 Kerper Blvd., Dubuque, IA 52001

BURGESS. Burgess Pub. Co., 7108 Ohms Lane, Minneapolis, MN 55435

CBS Educational Publishing, 383 Madison Ave., New York, NY 10007

CAMBRIDGE UNIV. PRESS, 32 E. 57th St., New York, NY 10022

CAPE. Jonathan Cape, 99 Main St., Salem, NH 03079

CAXTON. The Caxton Printers, Ltd., Box 700, Caldwell, ID 83605

CELESTIAL. Celestial Arts, 231 Adrian Rd., Millbrae, CA 94030

CHATHAM/VIKING. See Viking Press.

CHELSEA. Chelsea House Pubs., 133 Christopher St., New York, NY 10014

CHILDREN'S BOOK COUNCIL, Inc., 67 Irving Pl., New York, NY 10003

CHILDRENS PRESS. Childrens Press, Inc., 1224 W. Van Buren, Chicago, IL 60607

CHILTON. Chilton Book Co., Chilton Way, Radnor, PA 19089

COLLIER. Collier-Macmillan, Inc., 866 Third Ave., New York, NY 10022

COLLINS. See Philomel Books

COPP CLARK. Copp Clark Pitman, 517 Wellington St. W., Toronto, Ont. M5V IGI, Canada

COWARD. Coward, McCann & Geoghegan. See G. P. Putnam's Sons

CRITERION. Criterion Books Inc., 10 E. 53rd St., New York, NY 10022

CROWELL. Thomas Y. Crowell Co. See Harper & Row

CROWN. Crown Pub., Inc., One Park Ave., New York, NY 10016

DAWNE-LEIGH. See Celestial Arts

DAY. The John Day Co. See Harper & Row

DELACORTE. Delacorte Press. See Dell

DELL. Dell Pub. Co., Inc., One Dag Hammarskjold Plaza, New York, NY 10017

DEVIN. Devin-Adair Co., Inc., 143 Sound Beach Ave., Old Greenwich, CT 06870

DIAL. The Dial Press, Inc. See E. P. Dutton, Inc.

DILLON. Dillon Press, Inc., 500 S. Third St., Minneapolis, MN 55415

DODD. Dodd, Mead & Co., 79 Madison Ave., New York, NY 10016

DOUBLEDAY. Doubleday & Co., Inc., Garden City, NY 11530

DOVER. Dover Pubns., Inc., 180 Varick St., New York, NY 10014

DUELL. Duell, Sloan & Pearce. See Hawthorn

DUFOUR. Dufour Editions, Inc., Chester Springs, PA 19425

DUTTON. E. P. Dutton, Inc., 2 Park Ave., New York, NY 10016

EDUCATIONAL FILM LIBRARY ASSOC., 43 W. 61st St., New York, NY 10023

EERDMANS. William B. Eerdmans Pub. Co., 225 Jefferson Ave., SE, Grand Rapids, MI 49503

ELSEVIER. Elsevier Science Pub. Co., Inc., 52 Vanderbilt Ave., New York, NY 10017

EVANS. M. Evans & Co., Inc., 216 E. 49th St., New York, NY 10017

FARRAR. Farrar, Straus & Giroux, Inc., 19 Union Square West, New York, NY 10003

FAXON. F. W. Faxon Co., Inc., 15 Southwest Park, Westwood, MA 02090

FERNHILL. Fernhill House, Ltd. See Humanities Press, Inc.

FILM NEWS, 250 W. 57th St., New York, NY 10019

FOLLETT. Follett Pub. Co., 1010 W. Washington Blvd., Chicago, IL 60607

FOUR WINDS. Four Winds Press, 730 Broadway, New York, NY 10003.

FUNK. Funk & Wagnalls, Inc., 53 E. 77th St., New York, NY 10021

GALE. Gale Research Co., Penobscot Bldg., Detroit, MI 48226

GARRARD. Garrard Pub. Co., 1607 N. Market St., Champaign, IL 61820

GOLDEN GATE. Golden Gate Junior Books. See Childrens Press

GOLDEN BOOKS. See Western Publishing Co.

GREENWILLOW. Greenwillow Books. See William Morrow

GROSSET. Grosset & Dunlap, Inc., 51 Madison Ave., New York, NY 10010

HALL. G. K. Hall & Co., 70 Lincoln St., Boston, MA 02111

HARCOURT. Harcourt Brace Jovanovich, Inc., 757 Third Avenue, New York, NY 10017

HARLIN QUIST. See Dell Publishing Co.

HARPER. Harper & Row, Pub., 10 E. 53rd St., New York, NY 10022

HARVEY. Harvey House Pubs., 20 Waterside Plaza, New

York, NY 10010

HASTINGS. Hastings House Pub., Inc., 10 E. 40th St., New York, NY 10016

HAWTHORN. Hawthorn/Dutton. See E. P. Dutton, Inc.

HILL. Lawrence Hill and Co., Pubs., Inc., 520 Riverside Ave., Westport, CT 06880

HILL & WANG. See Farrar, Straus & Giroux

HOLIDAY. Holiday House, Inc., 18 E. 53rd St., New York, NY 10022

HOLT. Holt, Rinehart & Winston, Inc., 521 Fifth Ave., New York, NY 10175

HORN BOOK. The Horn Book, Inc., 31 St. James Ave., Boston, MA 02116

HOUGHTON. Houghton Mifflin Co., 2 Park Street, Boston, MA 02108

HUMANITIES. Humanities Press, Inc., 171 First Ave., Atlantic Highlands, NJ 07716

IND. UNIV. PRESS, Tenth and Morton Sts., Bloomington, IN 47401

KNOPF. Alfred A. Knopf, Inc., 201 E. 50th St., New York, NY 10022

LANDERS FILM ASSOC., Box 69760, Los Angeles, CA 90069

LAWRENCE. Seymour Lawrence, Inc., 61 Beacon St., Boston, MA 02108

LERNER. Lerner Pubns. Co., 241 First Ave. N., Minneapolis, MN 55401

LIBRARY OF CONGRESS, Supt. of Documents, U.S. Government Printing Office, Washington, DC 20402

LIPPINCOTT. J. B. Lippincott Co., East Washington Sq., Philadelphia, PA 19105

LITTLE. Little, Brown & Co., 34 Beacon St., Boston, MA 02106

LONGMAN. Longman, Inc., 19 W. 44th St., New York, NY 10036

LOTHROP. Lothrop, Lee & Shepard Co. See William Morrow

MC DOUGAL. McDougal, Littell & Co., P.O. Box 1667, Evanston, IL 60204

MC GRAW. McGraw-Hill Inc., 1221 Avenue of the Americas, New York, NY 10020

MC KAY. David McKay Co., Inc., 2 Park Avenue, New York, NY 10016

MACMILLAN. Macmillan Pub. Co., Inc., 866 Third Ave., New York, NY 10022

MESSNER. Julian Messner. See Simon & Schuster

METHUEN. Methuen, Inc., 733 Third Ave., New York, NY 10017

MORROW. William Morrow & Co., Inc., 105 Madison Ave., New York, NY 10016

NAT. COUNCIL FOR THE SOCIAL STUDIES, 3501 Newark St., NW, Washington, DC 20016

NAT. COUNCIL OF TEACHERS OF ENGLISH, 1111 Kenyon Rd., Urbana, IL 61801

NATURAL HISTORY PRESS, American Museum of Natural History, Central Park W. at 79th St., New York, NY 10024

NELSON. Thomas Nelson, Inc., Nelson Pl. at Elm Hill Pike, Nashville, TN 37214

NEW AMERICAN LIB. New American Library, Inc., 1633 Broadway, New York, NY 10019

NEW YORK PUBLIC LIBRARY, Fifth Ave. and 42nd St., New York, NY 10018

NOBLE. Bowmar/Noble Pubs., 4563 Colorado Blvd., Los Angeles, CA 90039

NORTON. W. W. Norton & Co., Inc., 500 Fifth Ave., New York, NY 10010

OXFORD. Oxford Univ. Press Inc., 200 Madison Ave., New York, NY 10016

PANTHEON. Pantheon Books, 201 E. 50th St., New York, NY 10022

PARENTS. Parents Magazine Press, 685 Third Ave., New York, NY 10017

PARNASSUS. Parnassus Press. See Houghton Mifflin Co.

PHILLIPS. S. G. Phillips, Inc., P.O. Box 83, Chatham, NY 12037

PHILOMEL. Philomel Books, 51 Madison Ave., New York, NY 10010

PLATT. Platt & Munk, Inc., 51 Madison Ave., New York, NY 10010

POTTER. Clarkson N. Potter, Inc. See Crown Pubs., Inc.

PRENTICE. Prentice-Hall, Inc., Englewood Cliffs, NJ 07632

PRINCETON. Princeton Univ. Press, 41 Williams St., Princeton, NJ 08540

PUTNAM. The Putnam Publishing Group, Children's Book Div., 51 Madison Ave., New York, NY 10010

RAND. Rand, McNally & Co., 8255 Central Park Ave., Skokie, IL 60076

RANDOM. Random House, Inc., 201 E. 50th St., New York, NY 10022

REGNERY. Regnery Gateway, Inc., 360 W. Superior St., Chicago, IL 60610

ROW. See Harper & Row

ST. MARTIN'S. St. Martin's Press, Inc., 175 Fifth Ave., New York, NY 10010

SCARECROW. The Scarecrow Press, 52 Liberty St., Metuchen, NJ 08820

SCHOLASTIC. Scholastic, Inc., 730 Broadway, New York, NY 10003

SCOTT. Scott Publishers. See Harper & Row

SCOTT, FORESMAN. Scott, Foresman and Co., 1900 East Lake Ave., Glenview, IL 60025

SCRIBNER'S. The Scribner Book Companies, Inc., 597 Fifth Ave., New York, NY 10017

SEABURY. The Seabury Press, Inc., 815 Second Ave., New York, NY 10017

SIMON. Simon & Schuster, Inc., 1230 Avenue of the Americas, New York, NY 10020

SMITHSONIAN INST. PRESS, 900 Washington Dr. SW, Washington, DC 20560

STANFORD. Stanford Univ. Press, Stanford, CA 94305

STERLING. Sterling Pub. Co., Inc., 2 Park Avenue, New York, NY 10016

TAPLINGER. Taplinger Pub. Co., Inc., 132 W. 22nd St., New York, NY 10011

TEACHERS. Teachers College Press, Columbia Univ., 1234 Amsterdam Ave., New York, NY 10027

TIME INC. Time-Life Books, Inc. Alexandria, VA 22314

TOWER. Tower Pubns., Inc., 2 Park Avenue, New York, NY 10016

TROLL. Troll Associates, 320 Rte. 17, Mahwah, NJ 07430

TUTTLE. Charles E. Tuttle Co., Inc., 28 S. Main St., Rutland, VT 05701

UNIV. OF CALIF. PRESS, 2223 Fulton St., Berkeley, CA 94720

UNIV. OF CHICAGO PRESS, 5801 S. Ellis Ave., Chicago, IL 60637

UNIV. OF PA. PRESS, 3933 Walnut St., Philadelphia, PA 19104

VANGUARD. Vanguard Press, Inc., 424 Madison Ave., New York, NY 10017

VAN NOSTRAND. Van Nostrand Reinhold Co., 135 W. 50th St., New York, NY 10020

VIKING. The Viking Press, 40 W. 23rd St., New York, NY 10010

WALCK. Henry Z. Walck, Inc. See David McKay

WALKER. Walker & Co., 720 Fifth Ave., New York, NY 10019

WARNE. Frederick Warne & Co., Inc., 2 Park Avenue, New York, NY 10016

WATTS. Franklin Watts, Inc., 387 Park Ave. S., New York, NY 10016

WESTERN. Western Pub. Co., Inc., 1220 Mound Ave., Racine, WI 53404

WESTERN RESERVE PR., 3530 Warrensville Ctr. Rd., Cleveland, OH 44122

WESTMINSTER. The Westminster Press, 925 Chestnut St., Philadelphia, PA 19107

WEYBRIGHT. Weybright & Talley, Inc. See David McKay

WHITE. David White, Inc., One Pleasant Ave., Port Washington, NY 11050

WHITMAN. Albert Whitman & Co., 5747 W. Howard St., Niles, IL 60648

WHITTLESEY. Whittlesey House. See McGraw-Hill, Inc.

WILSON. H. W. Wilson Co., 950 University Ave., Bronx, NY 10452

WINDMILL. Windmill Books, Inc., 1230 Avenue of the Americas, New York, NY 10020

YALE UNIV. PRESS, 302 Temple St., New Haven, CT 06520

Pronunciation Guide

The following list contains foreign words and phrases and the names of authors, places, and story characters selected from Parts One, Two, Three, and Four. Words that can be found in a standard college dictionary are not included.

Symbols used in the pronunciation are as follows: a as in *hat;* ā as in *age;* ä as in *care;* ä as in *father;* e as in *let;* ē as in *see;* ėr as in *term;* i as in *pin;* ī as in *five;* o as in *hot;* ō as in *go;* ô as in *order, all;* oi as in *oil;* ou as in *house;* th as in *thin;* ŧh as in *then;* u as in *cup;* ù as in *full;* ü as in *rule;* ū as in *use;* zh as in *measure;* ə as in the unaccented syllables of *about, taken, pencil, lemon, circus;* H as in the German *ach;* N as in the French *bon* (not pronounced, but shows that the vowel before it is nasal); œ as in the French *peu* and the German *könig* (pronounced by speaking ā with the lips rounded as for ō); Y as in the French *du* (pronounced by speaking ē with the lips rounded as for ü). All other symbols represent the consonant sounds that they commonly stand for in English spelling.

ABUELITA (ä bwä lē′tə)

ABUELO (ä bwä′lō)

ACHILLES (ə kil′ēz)

ACHREN (äk′ren)

ADJAI (at′də zhä)

AEETES (ē ē′tēz)

AENEAS (ē nē′əs)

AESIR (ē′sėr)

AFANASIEV (ä fä nä′syif)

AGAMEMNON (ag a mem′non)

AICHINGER (ī′kin jėr)

AIX (eks)

AK SHEHIR (äk she hēr′)

ALDIS (ôl′dis)

ALEIAN (ä′lä an)

ANANSI (ə nan′sē)

ANDROMACHE (an drom′ə kē)

ANNUVIN (ä nü′vin)

ANSEIS (äN sä ēs′)

ANTEA (an tē′ə)

ANTIGONE (an ti′gō nē)

APENNINES (a′pü nīnz)

APRAKSIYA (ə prä′ksē ə)

ARACHNE (a rak′nē)

ARAWN (ä ron′)

ARDIZZONE (är di zō′ni)

ARHA (är′hä)

ARIADNE (ar i ad′nē)

ARMAND (är mäN′)

ARRA (ar′ə)

ARRIETTY (är′i e tē)

ARTEMIS (är′te mis)

ARTZYBASHEFF (är tsi ba′shif)

ASBJÖRNSEN (äs′byėrn sen)

ASGARD (as′gärd)

ASTARTE (as tär′te)

ATALANTA   (at ə lan′tə)
AUDE   (ōd)
AUDHUMLA   (ou t̸hum′lä)
AULNOY, D'   (dō nwä′ or dōl nwä′)

BALDER   (bôl′dėr)
BALLAGHADEREEN   (bä lä hä′də rēn)
BARBEAU, MARIUS   (bär bō′, ma′rē Ys)
BARGI   (bär′gē)
BÄRLI   (bär′lē)
BARTEL   (bär′tel)
BASHO   (bä shō)
BASILE, GIAMBATTISTA   (bä zē′lā, jäm′bät tēs′tä)
BEAUMONT, DE   (də bō môN′)
BEEREEUN   (bā rä ün′)
BEHN   (bān)
BELLEROPHON   (bə ler′ō fon)
BELLOC, HILAIRE   (bel′ok, hi lār′)
BENÉT   (be nā′)
BERTHE   (bert)
BEWICK   (bū′ik)
BIALKA   (byäl′kä)
BIDPAI   (bid′pī)
BINGAWINGUL   (bing′ə wing′əl)
BLASS   (bläs)
BLEGVAD   (bleg′vad)
BOBADIL   (bob′ə dil)
BOGATIR   (bō gä tēr′)
BOONDI   (bün′dē)
BORSKI, LUCIA MERECKA   (bōr′skē, lü′syä mə res′kä)
BOULANGER   (bü läN zhä′)
BOUQUI   (bü kē′)
BRAGI   (brä′gē)
BREIDABLIK   (brī′də blik)
BREMEN   (brem′ən or brā′mən)
BUDULINEK   (bə dü′lə nek)
BULLAI BULLAI   (bul′ī bul′ī)

CABALLO   (ka bä′yō)
CAER DATHYL   (kī̇ėr dä thil′)
CAMILLE   (ca mēl′)
CARABAS   (ka′rə bas)
CARIGIET, ALOIS   (kä rē zhē ā′, al wä′)
CAUDILL   (kô′dl)
CELEUS   (sē′lē əs)
CENDRARS, BLAISE   (sen drärs, blez)
CERES   (sir′ēz or sē′rēz)
CHIMAERA   (kī mē′rə or ki mē′rə)
CHUKOVSKY, KORNEI   (chu kôf′skē, kôr nā′)
CHUTE, MARCHETTE   (chüt, mär shet′)
CIARDI   (chär′dē)
COLLOP   (käl′əp)
COLUM, PADRAIC   (kol′um, pôd′rig)
COMENIUS   (kə mē′ni us)
CONTES DE MA MERE L'OYE   (kôNt də mä mär lwä)
COOLABAH   (kü′lə bä)

CUCULLIN   (kü kü′lin)
CYANE   (sī′ə nē)

DAEDALUS   (ded′ə lus)
DAEN   (dä′ə n)
DASENT   (dā′sənt)
DE ANGELI   (də an′jel ē)
DEENYI   (dēn′yē)
DE GASZTOLD, CARMEN BERNOS   (də gaz′tōl, bėr′nōs)
DEIPHOBUS   (dē if′ō bus)
DE LA MARE   (de la mär′)
DELPHI   (del′fī)
DÈMI   (dem′ē)
DE REGNIERS   (də rān′yä)
DEUTSCH, BABETTE   (doich, bab et′)
DINKY   (ding′kē)
DIOMEDES   (dī′ō mē′dēz)
DOOLOOMAI   (dü′lü mī′)
DOON-GARA   (dün′gä rä)
DOOWI   (dü′wē)
DORJE   (där′jē)
DRAUPNER   (droup′nėr)
DU BOIS, PÈNE   (dœ bwä′, pen)
DUIRMUID   (dir′mid)
DURRI   (dur′ē)
DUVOISIN   (dœ vwä zaN′)

ECRETTE   (e kret′)
EE   (ä)
EEHU   (ē′hü)
EER-DHER   (ēr′t̸her)
EICHENBERG   (ī′ken bėrg)
EJE   (ā′yə)
ELYSIAN   (ē lizh′ən)
ENCELADUS   (en sel′ə dəs)
ENGELIER   (oN je′lē ā)
ENKIDU   (en′kə dü)
ERIS   (ē′ris)
ERYX   (er′iks)
ESU   (ä′sü)
EUMÊLUS   (yü mē′ləs)
EVERINGEN   (ā′ver in gən)
EVOE   (u̇′ō ā)

FALADA   (fä lä′dä)
FARJEON   (fär′jun)
FELLAHIN   (fel′ə hēn)
FENRIS   (fen′ris)
FIONN   (fin)
FREY   (frā)
FREYA   (frā′ə)
FUNJI   (fün′jē)
FYLEMAN   (fīl′man)

GACHUI   (gä′chwē)
GÁG   (gäg)

GAGNON (ga nyōN′)

GALLAND, ANTOINE (gə läN′, äN twon′)

GANELON (gan′ə lən)

GATLESS (gat′lis or gôt′lis)

GERIN (zhā raN′)

GIBICH (gi′biH)

GIDYA (gid′yä)

GILGUY HOLE (gil′gī hōl)

GINNUNGAGAP (gin′nöng ä gäp)

GIUFA (jü′fə)

GIUSEPPE (jü zep′pē)

GLEED (glēd)

GLEIPNIR (glāp′nēr)

GOO-GOOR-GAGA (gü′gür gä′gä)

GOOLA-GOOL (gü′lä gül′)

GOOLAY-YALI (gü′lā yä′lē)

GOOMBEELGA (güm bēl′gä)

GOOWEERA (gü wē′rä)

GOUDEY (gou′dē)

GRAINNE (grôn′yə)

GRANDMERE (gräN mär′)

GUINEDA (gē nā′də)

GUITERMAN (git′ėr mən)

GURAGE (gü′rä gā′)

GURGI (gœ r′jē)

GUSLA (gü′slə)

GWYDION (gwi′dē on)

HAGEN (hä′gən)

HAILU (hī′lü)

HAPTOM HASEI (hap′təm hä sē′)

HAZARD, PAUL (a zar′, pōl)

HEIDI (hī′dē)

HEIMDALL (hām′däl)

HELHEIM (hel′hām)

HELLE (hel′ē)

HERMES (hėr′mēz)

HERMOD (her′müd or her məd)

HIISI (hī′si)

HIITOLA (hī′tō lä)

HIPPOMENES (hi pom′ə nēz)

HIROSHIMA NO PIKA (hir ə shē′mə or hə rō′shə mə nō pē kə)

HOCH (hōch)

HODER (hō′dėr)

HODJA (hō′jə)

HOLLE (hôl′lə)

HOMILY (hom′i lē)

HORUS (hō′rus)

HUNG VUONG (hun vwun)

HYRIEUS (hī ri′ē us)

HYRROKEN (hī′rō kin)

ICARUS (ik′ə rus)

IDUNA (ē dün′ä)

IJOMAH (ē′jō mə)

INJERA (in jā′rä)

IOBATES (ī ob′ə tēz)

IONESCO (yō nes′kō)

ISIS (ī′sis)

ISKWAO (isk wā′ō)

ISS (is)

JAGENDORF (yä′gen dôrf)

JANCSI (yan′sē)

JANNA (yä′nə)

JATAKA (jä′tə kə)

JEAN LEBLANC (zhäN lə bläN′)

JOAQUIN (wä kēn′)

JŌSŌ (jō′sō)

JOTUNHEIM (yō′tùn häm)

JUNO (jü′no)

KAKAPO (kä′kə pō)

KALASHNIKOFF (kä läsh′ni kôf)

KAMBO (käm′bō)

KIBOKO (ki bō′kō)

KITINGARA (kē tēn gä′rä)

KJELGAARD (kel′gärd)

KLAPHEK (kläp′hek)

KNOWE (nou or nō)

KOBI (kō′bē)

KOICHI (kō′i chi)

KONIGSBURG (kō′nigs bėrg)

KRAKEN (krā′ken)

KRYLOV (kril ôf′)

KUBLA KHAN (kü′blə kän′)

KWAKU ANANSI (kwa′kü ə nan′sē)

KYORAI (kyô ra ī)

LAIVA (lī′vä)

LAOCOON (lā ok′ō on)

LEDOUX (lə dü′)

LE GALLIENNE (lə gal′yən)

LENSKI (len′skē)

LING BROOM (ling brüm)

LIONNI (lē ō′nē)

LOKI (lō′kē)

LÖNNROT, ELIAS (lėrn′rôt, ə lī′əs)

MACHREE (mə krē′)

MAEVE (māv)

MAKAH (mä kää)

MALI (mä′lē)

MALICE (mä′lēs′)

MANACHAR (ma′nə kôr)

MÄRCHEN (mär Hən)

MARMOT (mar mō′)

MAZO (mä′zō)

MEDIO POLLITO (mä′dē ō pō lyē′tō)

MELYNGAR (me′lin′gär)

MENELAUS (men ə lā′us)

METANIRA (met ə nī′rə)
MICHEL MILOCHE (mē shel′mā lôsh′)
MIDAS (mī′dəs)
MIDGARD (mid′gärd)
MIKOLAYCAK (mīk ô lā′chək)
MILNE (miln)
MINERVA (mi nėr′və)
MINOTAUR (min′ō tôr)
MIZUMURA, KAZUE (mi′zä mü rä, kä zü′ä)
MJOLNER (myôl′nėr)
MOE, JÖRGEN (mōə, yer′gən)
MOERI (mô′rē)
MONTRESOR, BENI (mōN trə sôr, bā′nē)
MUHINDI (mü hēn′dē)
MUNACHAR (mü′nə kôr)
MUNARI, BRUNO (mü nä′rē, brü′nō)
MUNGU (mün′gü)
MUSPELHEIM (mùs′pel hām)
MUSTAPHA (müs′tä fä)
MUTUNYEUSI (mü tün yeü′sē)
MUZUNGU (mü zün′gü)
MY CHAU (mē jou)
MZURI (əm zür′ē)

NAGY (nod′yə or noj)
NANNA (nä′nä)
NASR-ED-DIN (näs′red din′)
NEPHTHYTIS (nef′thĭd əs)
NEUGEBAUER (noi′gə bour)
NICHET (nē shā′)
NIC LEODHAS, SORCHE (nik lē ō′dəs, sôr′ä)
NIFELHEIM (niv′l hām)
NIKOLAI (nē kō lī′)
NINA-CUX (ni ña-cux)
NISSE (ni′sə)
NNEKEH (nek′e)
NOORTJE (nôr′chə)
NUNKU (nun′kü)
NUNNOOS (nun′üs)

ODALA (ō dä′lä)
ODIN (ō′din)
O'FAOLAIN (ō fwā′lôn)
OGIER (ō′ji ėr)
OJIISAN (ō jē sän)
OKEI (ō kē′)
ONITSURA (ō nē tsėr′ä)
OONAGH (ō′nä)
ORGEL (ôr′gel)
ORION (ō rī′ən)
OSIRIS (ō sī′ris)

PADRE PORKO (pä ŧhre pôr′kō)
PALAMEDES (pal ə mē′dēz)
PALLAS ATHENA (pal′əs ə thē′nə)
PANCHATANTRA (pän chə tän′trə)

PARRA, NICANOR (pä′rä, nē′kä nôr)
PAVEL (pä′vel)
PEGASUS (peg′ə sus)
PELEUS (pē′lūs or pē′lē us)
PENTAMERONE (pen tä mä rō′nā)
PERRAULT, CHARLES (pe rō′, sharl)
PETROS (pe′trōs)
PHRIXOS (frik′sus)
PIACEVOLI NOTTI, LE (lā pyä chā′vô lē nôt′tē)
PICARD (pē kar′)
PIES (pyesh)
PIMA (pē′mə)
PIRENE (pī rē′nē)
POLYIDUS (pol′ē ī′dəs)
POSEIDON (pō sī′dən)
PRELUTSKY (pre lut′skē)
PRIAM (prī′əm)
PROETUS (prô ē′təs)
PROSERPINE (prō sėr′pi nə)
PRYDAIN (pri dān′)
PTOLEMY (täl′ə mē)

QUERIDA (kā rē′ŧhə)

RA (rä)
RAGNAROK (rä′nyä rùk′)
RECUERDO (rā kwâr′ŧhō)
RIEU (rü)
RINTARO (rin tä′rō)
ROETHKE (ret′kē)
ROJANKOVSKY (rō jan kôf′skē)
ROSLIE (rōs′lē)
RUTHVEN (ri′vən)

SAINT-EXUPERY, ANTOINE DE (san tāg zœ pā rē, än twän′də)
SALVE (säl′wā)
SCHWANLI (shwän′lē)
SEANACHIE (shän′ə hē)
SÊCHE (sesh)
SEMAMINGI (sā mä min′gē)
SEREDY (shär′ə dē)
SERRAILLIER (sə räl′yä)
SHIKI (shē kē)
SHMELKA (shmel′kä)
SHMELKICHA (shmel′ki chä)
SHULEVITZ, URI (shü lə vitz, ü′rē)
SLEIPNER (slāp′nir)
SLOOGEH (slü′gə)
SMOLICHEK (smol′i chek)
SOLEAE (sō′le ī)
SONAM (sō′näm)
SON TIEN (shun tin)
SOTIRIS (sō ti′ris)
SPIEWNA (shpyev′nä)
SPYRI, JOHANNA (shpē′rē, yō hä′nä)

STOLZ (stōlts)
STRAPAROLA (strä pä rō′lä)

TAILLEFER (tä′yə fär′)
TANUKI (tä nü′kē)
TARAN (ta′ran)
TASHJIAN (täs jun)
TENNIEL (ten′yel)
THESEUS (thē′sē us)
THETIS (thē′tis)
THOK (thôk)
THOR (thôr)
THORNE-THOMSEN, GUDRUN (tôrn tom′sen, gü′drun)
THOTH (thoth or tōt)
THRYM (thrim or trēm)
THRYMHEIM (thrim′hām)
THUY TIEN (tù′ē tin)
TIMO (ti mō)
TOIVO (toi′vō)
TOLKIEN (tôl′ken)
TSIGANE (tsē gán′)
TUNIS (tū′nis)
TUPA (tù′pä)
TYR (tir)

UCHIDA, YOSHIKO (ü chē dä, yō shē kō)
ULI (ū′lē)
ULYSSES (ū lis′ēz)
URASHIMA, TARO (ü rä shē mä, tä rō)
URUK (ü′ruk)

VALE (wä′lä)
VALHALLA (val hal′ə)
VALKYRIES (val kir′ēz)

VAN DER LOEFF (van′dèr ləf)
VANIR (vä′nir)
VASSILISSA (va syē′le sa)
VE (vä)
VELUWE (vä′lüėvù)
VENDLA (vend′lä)
VENUS (vē′nus)
VILI (vē′lē)
VILLENEUVE (vēl nœ v′)
VLEI (flä)

WAKAI (wä′kā)
WEEDAH (wē′dä)
WIRINUN (wir′ē nun)
WOLTHUIS (vōlt′hous)
WOMBA (wom′bä)

XANADU (za′nə dü)

YASHIMA, TARO (yä′shi ma, tä′rō)
YEVTUSHENKO, YEVGENY (yiv tù shen′kō, yiv gā′nyē)
YGGDRASILL (ig′drä sil)
YHI (yē)
YMIR (ē′mir)
YSTRAD (ə sträd′)
YVE (ēv)
YVOIRE (ē vwär′)

ZEMACH (zē′mak)
ZEUS (züs)
ZHENYA (zhā nyə)

Subject Matter Index

This Subject Matter Index has been developed to meet the needs of potential users of the *Scott, Foresman Anthology*. It reflects, within reason, the content of the majority of entries in the *Anthology*.

A major goal of the Index is to bring together the different literary genres about the same subject. Thus, under CATS, for example, are found poems, fairy tales, and modern fiction. Not all headings will reflect a similar range of material, but many do.

The majority of headings are those found in most library tools. However, there are deviations, and the user is encouraged to browse through the Index for ideas not usually reflected in traditional indexes. One example of this is the heading CINDERELLA THEME. A teacher who wants to help children understand how different cultures develop a similar theme should find the heading helpful.

A beginning has been made toward developing headings that treat concepts as well as specifics. *Snow-White and the Seven Dwarfs* is listed under PRIDE AND VANITY since the Queen's motivation to kill Snow-White stems from these personal characteristics.

The headings used for the excerpts from complete books refer to the selection within the *Anthology* and not to the entire book. For instance, *Harriet the Spy* is not basically about DANCES AND DANCING, but the selection included here is.

Finally, the Index is not definitive, but it should provide a starting point for users interested in interrelating the literary genres within this *Anthology*.

ABC BOOKS, 816

AFRICA
Anansi's Hat-Shaking Dance, 313 • *The Fire on the Mountain*, 303 • *The Great Tug-of-War*, 306 • *Men of Different Colors*, 305 • *The Sloogeh Dog and the Stolen Aroma*, 317 • *The Stepchild and the Fruit Trees*, 319 • *Unanana and the Elephant*, 314 • *Why Frog and Snake Never Play Together*, 310

AIRPLANES. *See also* FLYING, ROCKETS, TRAVEL
George Washington's World, 807

ALLIGATORS
Mr. 'Gator, 78

AMERICA. *See also* UNITED STATES
I Hear America Singing, 94

AMERICAN FOLK POETRY
Buffalo Girls, 97 • *Clementine*, 121 • *Go Tell Aunt Rhody*, 72 • *I Ride an Old Paint*, 45 • *John Henry*, 28 • *Mississippi Sounding Calls*, 98 • *Skip to My Lou*, 97 • *The Streets of Laredo*, 23 • *The Tree in the Wood*, 137 • *Yankee Doodle*, 141

AMERICAN FOLK TALES, 352, 358, 363, 375. *See also* SOUTH AMERICAN FOLK TALES
The Boomer Fireman's Faster Sooner Hound, 368 • *In Arkansas Stick to Bears; Don't Mess with Swampland Skeeters*, 372 • *Jack and the Robbers*, 358 • *The Knee-High Man*, 375 • *Master James' Nightmare*, 378 • *Mike Fink*, 364 • *Mike Hooter and the Smart Bears in Mississippi*, 370 • *Mr. Yowder and the Train Robbers*, 373 • *Pecos Bill and His Bouncing Bride*, 365 • *Why the Waves Have Whitecaps*,

376 • *The Wonderful Tar-Baby Story*, 377 • *Young Melvin*, 361

AMERICAN INDIANS
Far, far will I go, 44 • *Gray Moss on Green Trees*, 387 • *The great sea*, 131 • *House Blessing*, 35 • *How Summer Came to Canada*, 469 • *How the Little Owl's Name Was Changed*, 390 • *Little Burnt-Face*, 388 • *My great corn plants*, 83 • *Nicely while it is raining*, 92 • *Save Queen of Sheba*, 696 • *Small Star and the Mud Pony*, 383 • *Song of Creation*, 131 • *Wind Song*, 134

AMERICAN REVOLUTIONARY WAR
Johnny Tremain, 712 • *Phoebe and the General*, 692

ANIMALS, 63–70. *See also* BIRDS, CATS, DOGS, FARM ANIMALS, SMALL CREATURES, ZOO ANIMALS, and Names of individual animals
Alice's Adventures in Wonderland, 522 • *Basil and the Pygmy Cats*, 491 • *The Bremen Town Musicians*, 188 • *Camel Gets His Own Back*, 344 • *Charlotte's Web*, 485 • *The Great Tug-of-War*, 306 • *The Hare That Ran Away*, 341 • *The Hare with Many Friends*, 409 • *The Incredible Journey*, 684 • *Jack and the Robbers*, 358 • *Just So Stories*, 487 • *Lambikin*, 343 • *The Three Billy-Goats Gruff*, 227 • *The Tiger, the Brahman, and the Jackal*, 341 • *Why Frog and Snake Never Play Together*, 310 • *The Wonderful Tar-Baby Story*, 377

ANTS. *See also* INSECTS
The Ant and the Grasshopper, 409 • *The Cricket and the Ant*, 417 • *The Grasshopper and the Ant*, 417

APRIL FOOLS' DAY
Oh! Have You Heard, 141

ARABIA
Aladdin and the Wonderful Lamp, 295 • *The Owls and the Crows*, 414

ARMENIA
The Clever Thieves, 279 • *The Foolish Man*, 277 • *Master and Man*, 279

ART. *See* ILLUSTRATIONS

AUSTRALIA
Beereeun the Miragemaker, 345

AUTOMOBILES. *See* CARS

AUTUMN. *See* SEASONS

BABIES
Oh, Boy! Babies! 767

BALLADS, 4. *See also* NARRATIVE POEMS
The Ballad of Newington Green, 121 • *The Ballad of the Harp-Weaver*, 106 • *The Pied Piper of Hamelin*, 107 • *Sir Patrick Spence*, 133

BASEBALL
Baseball Fever, 594 • *The Base Stealer*, 91 • *Night Game*, 88

BASKETBALL
Forms of Praise, 90

BATS
The Bat, 49, 821

BEARS
East o' the Sun and West o' the Moon, 236, 812 • *Grizzly Bear*, 64 • *Mike Hooter and the Smart Bears in Mississippi*, 370 • *Paddington Abroad*, 480 •

Index of Titles, Authors, and Illustrators